Public Law

Third edition

PROFESSOR MARK ELLIOTT
University of Cambridge

PROFESSOR ROBERT THOMAS
University of Manchester

OXFORD

OXFORD
UNIVERSITY PRESS

Great Clarendon Street, Oxford, OX2 6DP,
United Kingdom

Oxford University Press is a department of the University of Oxford.
It furthers the University's objective of excellence in research, scholarship,
and education by publishing worldwide. Oxford is a registered trade mark of
Oxford University Press in the UK and in certain other countries

First edition 2011
Second edition 2014

Impression: 1

Published in the United States of America by Oxford University Press
198 Madison Avenue, New York, NY 10016, United States of America

British Library Cataloguing-in-Publication Data

Data available

Library of Congress Control Number: 2017933153

ISBN 978-0-19-876589-9

Printed in Italy by
L.E.G.O. S.p.A.

About the Online Resource Centre

Public Law is accompanied by an Online Resource Centre that provides a range of additional features and resources for students and lecturers. These resources are ready to use, free of charge, and designed to complement and enhance the textbook.

www.oxfordtextbooks.co.uk/orc/elliott_thomas3e/

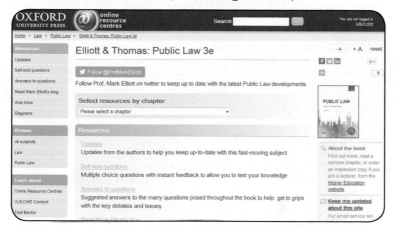

Updates

Updates are an indispensable resource that help keep you up to date with any significant changes in the law that have occurred since publication of the book. New updates are regularly added to the site and are organised by chapter to enable you to easily identify any material that has been superseded or supplemented.

Multiple-choice questions

A selection of questions with instant feedback that enables you to test your understanding as you work through each chapter of the book.

Annotated web links

A selection of annotated web links chosen by the authors offers a head start when it comes to research. The additional annotation will help you to identify which links are most relevant to your areas of study.

Diagrams

All of the 103 diagrams from the book are provided electronically for you to download. Each one has been carefully designed to help you visualise and understand some of the more complex topics and concepts essential to the study of public law.

Brief Contents

Detailed Contents   vii

Expert Commentaries   xiii

Preface   xv

Update on the Supreme Court's Judgment in the Miller *Case*   xix

Table of Cases   xxv

Table of UK Legislation   xxxvii

Table of European and International Legislation   xlvi

Part I Introduction to Public Law

1 Constitutions and Constitutional Law   3

2 Themes, Sources, and Principles   36

Part II The Constitution—Institutions and Principles

3 Separation of Powers—An Introduction   87

4 UK Central Government   104

5 The UK Parliament   166

6 The Judiciary   257

7 Devolution and the Territorial Constitution   297

8 The European Union and Brexit   336

Part III Good Governance—Scrutiny, Accountability, and Transparency

9 Good Governance—An Introduction   381

10 Parliamentary Scrutiny of Central Government   401

Part IV Judicial Review

11 Judicial Review—An Introduction   475

12 The Grounds of Judicial Review   497

13 Judicial Review—Scope, Procedures, and Remedies   556

14 The Effectiveness and Impact of Judicial Review   589

Part V Administrative Justice

15 Ombudsmen and Complaints   633

16 Tribunals   682

17 Inquiries   728

Part VI Human Rights

18 Human Rights and the UK Constitution   759

19 Freedom of Expression   816

20 Freedom of Assembly   859

21 Policing—Powers, Accountability, and Governance   891

Index   917

Detailed Contents

Expert Commentaries   xiii

Preface   xv

Update on the Supreme Court's Judgment in the Miller *Case*   xix

Table of Cases   xxv

Table of UK Legislation   xxxvii

Table of European and International Legislation   xlvi

Part I Introduction to Public Law

1 Constitutions and Constitutional Law   3

    1. Introduction   3

    2. Constitutions   4

    3. Case studies   14

    4. Conclusions   32

    Expert commentary   33

    Further reading   35

2 Themes, Sources, and Principles   36

    1. Introduction   36

    2. Three key themes   37

    3. Sources of the constitution   42

    4. Constitutional principles   62

    5. Legality and the rule of law   65

    6. Codification and the constitution   77

    7. Concluding remarks   81

    Expert commentary   81

    Further reading   84

Part II The Constitution—Institutions and Principles

3 Separation of Powers—An Introduction   87

    1. The three branches of government   87

    2. The basic idea of the separation of powers   89

    3. Why embrace the separation of powers?   91

    4. Different conceptions of the separation of powers 93

5. The separation of powers in the UK 97
6. Conclusions 99
Expert commentary 100
Further reading 102

4 UK Central Government 104
1. Introduction 104
2. The modern executive and its constitutional position 105
3. Central government 116
4. The powers of the executive 138
5. Conclusions 162
Expert commentary 163
Further reading 165
Useful websites 165

5 The UK Parliament 166
1. Introduction 166
2. Parliament: an overview 167
3. Parliament and democracy 168
4. Parliamentary privilege 200
5. Parliament and the legislative process 211
6. Parliament's powers 228
7. Concluding remarks 253
Expert commentary 253
Further reading 255
Useful websites 256

6 The Judiciary 257
1. Introduction 257
2. The structure of the judicial system 258
3. The role of the judiciary 264
4. The characteristics of the judiciary 271
5. Concluding remarks 293
Expert commentary 293
Further reading 295
Useful websites 296

7 Devolution and the Territorial Constitution 297
1. Introduction 297
2. Devolution in Northern Ireland, Scotland, and Wales 298
3. England 308

4. The nature and development of the territorial constitution   323

5. Conclusions   331

Expert commentary   332

Further reading   334

Useful websites   335

8 The European Union and Brexit   336

1. Introduction   336

2. The EU in context   340

3. EU law and national law   347

4. The supremacy of EU law and UK parliamentary sovereignty   359

5. Conclusions   374

Expert commentary   375

Further reading   377

Useful websites   377

Part III Good Governance—Scrutiny, Accountability, and Transparency

9 Good Governance—An Introduction   381

1. Introduction   381

2. What is good governance?   382

3. Accountability   387

4. Pulling it together   394

5. Conclusion   396

Expert commentary   396

Further reading   400

10 Parliamentary Scrutiny of Central Government   401

1. Introduction   401

2. Parliamentary control and government   402

3. Parliament and government   404

4. Ministerial responsibility   409

5. The mechanics of parliamentary scrutiny of government   424

6. Scrutinising how government spends public money   444

7. Freedom of information   452

8. Accountability and oversight of the security and intelligence services   460

9. Conclusion   467

Expert commentary   468

Further reading   470

Useful websites   471

Part IV Judicial Review

11 Judicial Review—An Introduction   475

   1. An example   475
   2. What judicial review is and is not about   476
   3. Judicial review and administrative law   478
   4. Judicial review and our three key themes   479
   5. The constitutional basis of judicial review   485
   6. Concluding remarks   494
   Expert commentary   494
   Further reading   496

12 The Grounds of Judicial Review   497

   1. Introduction   497
   2. Interpreting and applying the statute   499
   3. Acting fairly   506
   4. Exercise of discretion   526
   5. Review of the outcome of the decision-making process   539
   6. Concluding remarks   551
   Expert commentary   553
   Further reading   554

13 Judicial Review—Scope, Procedures, and Remedies   556

   1. Introduction   556
   2. What decisions can be judicially reviewed?   557
   3. Procedure   567
   4. Remedies   578
   5. Conclusions   586
   Expert commentary   586
   Further reading   588

14 The Effectiveness and Impact of Judicial Review   589

   1. Judicial review and government   589
   2. Judicial review litigation   592
   3. Judicial competence and capacity   605
   4. Judicial impact and administrative reaction   611
   5. Conclusion   627
   Expert commentary   627
   Further reading   629

Part V Administrative Justice

15 **Ombudsmen and Complaints**   633

    1. What is administrative justice?   633

    2. The wider complaint-handling system   634

    3. Ombudsmen: an example—the 'debt of honour' case   640

    4. Public sector ombudsmen in the UK   642

    5. The role of public sector ombudsmen   645

    6. Investigations   652

    7. Compliance   666

    8. Concluding remarks   676

    Expert commentary   678

    Further reading   680

    Useful websites   681

16 **Tribunals**   682

    1. Tribunals—an introduction   682

    2. Tribunals—their place in the UK's public law system   686

    3. The reorganisation of tribunals   692

    4. Tribunal procedures   700

    5. Judicial oversight of tribunal decision-making   717

    6. Conclusions   723

    Expert commentary   724

    Further reading   727

    Useful websites   727

17 **Inquiries**   728

    1. Introduction   728

    2. Inquiries—nature, function, and legal framework   728

    3. The inquiry process   735

    4. The effectiveness of inquiries and the alternatives   746

    5. Conclusion   751

    Expert commentary   751

    Further reading   755

    Useful websites   755

Part VI Human Rights

18 **Human Rights and the UK Constitution**   759

    1. Introduction   759

    2. Human rights   760

3. Human rights in the UK   765
4. The future   806
5. Conclusions   812
Expert commentary   813
Further reading   814
Useful websites   815

19 **Freedom of Expression**   816
1. Why freedom of expression matters   816
2. Article 10 of the European Convention on Human Rights   820
3. Media freedom   822
4. Defamation   835
5. Criminal offences   841
6. Privacy   845
7. Official secrecy   852
8. Conclusions   855
Expert commentary   856
Further reading   858

20 **Freedom of Assembly**   859
1. Introduction   859
2. Domestic law   864
3. Prohibition of certain types of behaviour   865
4. Statutory powers to regulate protests   870
5. Common law powers to regulate protests   877
6. Conclusions   887
Expert commentary   888
Further reading   890

21 **Policing—Powers, Accountability, and Governance**   891
1. Introduction   891
2. Police powers   895
3. Governance, accountability, and remedies   905
4. Conclusion   914
Further reading   915
Useful websites   916

Index   917

Expert Commentaries

You will find an expert commentary at the end of almost all the chapters in the book. They are written by leading scholars in the field and are designed to give you an additional perspective on the topics covered in order to demonstrate the contested nature of public law as a subject.

1. Constitutions and Constitutional Law
Aileen McHarg, Professor of Public Law, University of Strathclyde

2. Themes, Sources, and Principles
Dawn Oliver, Emeritus Professor of Constitutional Law, University College London

3. Separation of Powers—An Introduction
Nick Barber, Associate Professor, University of Oxford

4. UK Central Government
Alan Page, Professor of Public Law, University of Dundee

5. The UK Parliament
Sir Jeffrey Jowell, Emeritus Professor of Public Law, University College London

6. The Judiciary
Graham Gee, Professor of Public Law, University of Sheffield

7. Devolution and the Territorial Constitution
Stephen Tierney, Professor of Constitutional Theory, University of Edinburgh

8. The European Union and Brexit
TRS Allan, Professor of Jurisprudence and Public Law, University of Cambridge

9. Good Governance—An Introduction
Jeff King, Professor of Law, University College London

10. Parliamentary Scrutiny of Central Government
Tony Wright, Professorial Fellow, Department of Politics, Birkbeck, University of London

11. Judicial Review—An Introduction
Christopher Forsyth, Emeritus Sir David Williams Professor of Public Law, University of Cambridge

12. The Grounds of Judicial Review
Liz Fisher, Professor of Environmental Law, University of Oxford

13. Judicial Review—Scope, Procedures, and Remedies
Paul Daly, Senior Lecturer in Public Law, University of Cambridge

14. The Effectiveness and Impact of Judicial Review
Simon Halliday, Professor of Socio-Legal Studies, University of York

15. **Ombudsmen and Complaints**

Richard Kirkham, Senior Lecturer in Law, University of Sheffield

16. **Tribunals**

Michael Adler, Emeritus Professor of Socio-Legal Studies, University of Edinburgh

17. **Inquiries**

Trevor Buck, Emeritus Professor of Socio-Legal Studies, De Montfort University

18. **Human Rights and the UK Constitution**

David Feldman, Rouse Ball Professor of English Law, University of Cambridge

19. **Freedom of Expression**

Jacob Rowbottom, Tutorial Fellow and CUF Lecturer in Law, University College, Oxford

20. **Freedom of Assembly**

David Mead, Professor of UK Human Rights Law, University of East Anglia

Preface

To say that public law in the United Kingdom is a fast-moving subject would be an understatement. We were putting the finishing touches to the first edition of this book as the coalition government, which was in office from 2010 to 2015, was formed—a development that had significant constitutional implications, some of which, perhaps most notably the Fixed-term Parliaments Act 2011, are still being felt. At its inception, the coalition government endorsed a substantial programme of constitutional reform, although key elements of it—including the possibility of changing the voting system for UK general elections, investigating the replacement of the Human Rights Act 1998 with a 'Bill of Rights', and the replacement of the current House of Lords with a wholly or mainly elected second chamber—ultimately did not come to fruition.

The second edition of *Public Law* was published in 2014, shortly before the referendum on Scottish independence that took place in September of that year. Although the referendum delivered a majority against independence, the political and constitutional significance of the referendum—thanks not least to how close the 'Yes' campaign came to securing a majority in favour of independence—would be difficult to exaggerate. As the referendum approached and the break-up of the country appeared to be in prospect, the leaders of the major political parties made a 'vow' to the people of Scotland promising greater autonomy within the UK if independence was averted. That promise was subsequently reflected in the devolution of additional powers to Scotland via the Scotland Act 2016, and forms part of the backdrop to the Wales Act 2017.

We have been writing this, the third edition of the book, in the immediate aftermath of the referendum held on 23 June 2016 concerning the UK's membership of the European Union (EU). The result of that referendum, in which just over half of those who voted favoured the UK's departure from the EU, sent political and economic shockwaves across the globe, and is an event of historic significance. The implications of 'Brexit' will extend far beyond its consequences for the UK's constitutional arrangements. But its impact upon those arrangements will nevertheless be profound, as the possibility of a second Scottish independence referendum shows. We explore the likely constitutional significance of Brexit in detail in Chapter 8. However, reference is also made in many other parts of the book to the possible consequences of Brexit.

To the student attempting to get to grips with UK public law, the speed and frequency with which substantial elements of the constitution change may seem bewildering and disorientating, and such phenomena can certainly be an obstacle to understanding. In writing this new edition, we have attempted to guard against that risk. In doing so, we have not sought to disguise the significance or complexity of the changes that the UK's constitutional arrangements have undergone in recent years and will undergo in the years to come. However, we have attempted to examine such developments in a way that is grounded in a clear exposition of the fundamental, and more enduring, elements of the constitutional order. As in past editions, therefore, we place the three fundamental principles of the UK constitution—the rule of law, the separation of powers, and the sovereignty of Parliament—front and centre, using them as anchor points by reference to which the changing nature of the constitution falls to be understood, calibrated, and evaluated. For similar reasons, we have also retained our three key themes—the importance of accountability, the relationship between legal and political constitutionalism, and the multilayered nature of the constitution. Those themes are used as vehicles for exploring and making sense of the modern UK constitution, and form a means by which the often disparate parts of the subject can be understood in a more cohesive way.

New to this edition

Every chapter in this edition has been thoroughly updated, and many parts of the text have been fundamentally rewritten. As explained above, we have attempted to reflect the richness and diversity of the constitutional developments that have taken place since the previous edition was written, while placing those developments in context by reference to the constitution's fundamental principles and the book's key themes. The new material and developments found in this edition are far too numerous to list exhaustively, but the following are worth emphasising.

- Chapter 7 has been rewritten and its focus has been reoriented, as the new title—'Devolution and the Territorial Constitution'—indicates. The chapter fully reflects recent changes to the UK's territorial constitution, including those reflected in the Scotland Act 2016, the Wales Act 2017 and the Cities and Local Government Devolution Act 2016.

- Chapter 8—on 'The European Union and Brexit'—has been extensively rewritten in the light of the outcome of the referendum on the UK's membership of the EU. The chapter continues to examine the implications of EU membership, not least because the UK remains a member of the EU for the time being, the referendum outcome notwithstanding. However, the orientation of the chapter has been changed, with the focus now being on understanding the implications of EU membership in order that the constitutional significance and impact of Brexit can properly be understood.

- The chapters on judicial review have been thoroughly updated, and the discussion of substantive judicial review in Chapter 11 has been rewritten in order to take account of recent key UK Supreme Court decisions including *Pham v Secretary of State for the Home Department*[1] and *Keyu v Secretary of State for Foreign and Commonwealth Affairs*.[2] The chapters have also been updated to take account of important statutory changes to judicial review introduced by the Criminal Justice and Courts Act 2015.

- The chapters on administrative justice have been thoroughly updated. For instance, the discussion of ombudsmen in Chapter 15 has been revised to include important developments, such as the UK government's proposals to create a

---

[1] [2015] UKSC 19, [2015] 1 WLR 1591.   [2] [2015] UKSC 69, [2015] 3 WLR 1665.

Public Service Ombudsman, which will encompass the existing jurisdictions of the Parliamentary and Health Service Ombudsman and the Local Government Ombudsman. Similarly, Chapter 17 on inquiries has been updated to include key developments such as the publication of the Iraq Inquiry and the establishment of the Independent Inquiry into Child Sexual Abuse.

- The chapters on human rights have been extensively updated in order to reflect recent developments in that area. For instance, Chapter 18, on the UK's human rights framework, contains an expanded discussion of the notion of common law constitutional rights following UK Supreme Court judgments such as *R (Osborn) v Parole Board*[3] and *Kennedy v Charity Commission*.[4] Chapter 19, on freedom of expression, takes account of recent developments in relation to such matters as media regulation—including the creation of the Press Recognition Panel and the Independent Press Standards Organisation, as well as the abolition of the BBC Trust—and the Law Commission's recommendations in relation to contempt of court. Chapter 19 also reflects recent Supreme Court judgments such as *PJS v News Group Newspapers Ltd*[5] and *Re JR38*.[6] Chapter 20, on freedom of assembly, examines the implications for the right to protest of Public Spaces Protection Orders, introduced by the Anti-social Behaviour, Crime and Policing Act 2014, while Chapter 21, on police powers, governance, and accountability, examines changes to the police complaints system under the Policing and Crime Act 2017.

In addition to the new material and developments reflected in this edition, two other changes are worth highlighting. First, we have increased the amount of material presented in this edition in the form of tables, figures, and diagrams. We have drawn extensively from sources of empirical and statistical data in order to provide an additional perspective on the practical workings of the constitution and to deepen readers' understanding. Our intention is that this will enable appropriate information to be conveyed in ways that are both economical and visually stimulating. Second, we added 'expert commentaries' to some chapters in the second edition. Such commentaries are now to be found at the end of nearly every chapter. They are intended to add a further dimension to the book by exposing readers to a particular point of view or way of looking at a topic that adds to what is said in the chapter itself. In this way, we seek to demonstrate to students—and to encourage readers to reflect upon—the contestable and contested nature of public law as a subject.

Our work on the manuscript of this edition was completed in November 2016. Other than making very minor changes at the proofs stage, it has not been possible to accommodate developments since then. One such development is the decision of the Supreme Court in *R (Miller) v Secretary of State for Exiting the European Union*,[7] in which it was held that the process for withdrawing from the European Union could be initiated only by the enactment of parliamentary legislation. As a result, Parliament

---

[3] [2013] UKSC 61, [2014] AC 1115.   [4] [2014] UKSC 20, [2015] AC 455.
[5] [2016] UKSC 26, [2016] 2 WLR 1253.   [6] [2015] UKSC 42, [2015] 3 WLR 155.
[7] [2017] UKSC 5.

enacted the European Union (Notification of Withdrawal) Act 2017. Although it has not been possible to include discussion of the *Miller* judgment in the main text of this edition, an account of the case and of its implications for key issues examined in the book has been added; it can be found immediately after this preface.

Acknowledgements

We wish to thank the following friends and colleagues who have contributed expert commentaries to this edition: Michael Adler, Trevor Allan, Nick Barber, Trevor Buck, Paul Daly, David Feldman, Liz Fisher, Christopher Forsyth, Graham Gee, Simon Halliday, Jeffrey Jowell, Jeff King, Richard Kirkham, Aileen McHarg, David Mead, Dawn Oliver, Alan Page, Jake Rowbottom, Stephen Tierney, and Tony Wright. We are also grateful to all who have been involved in the commissioning, editing, and production of the book. In particular, we record our thanks to Carol Barber, Liliane Johnston, and Tom Young at Oxford University Press, and to Philip Moore for his work on the proofs. Finally, and most importantly, we are immensely grateful to our respective families—in Mark's case, to his wife, Vicky, and their daughter Maisie; and in Robert's case, to his wife, Nicola, and their children, Penelope, Rosamund, Constanza, Edward, and Gwendolyn—for their love and support.

Mark Elliott, Cambridge
Robert Thomas, Manchester
March 2017

Update on the Supreme Court's Judgment in the *Miller* Case

After the main text of this book had been finalised, the Divisional Court gave its judgment in the case of *R (Miller) v Secretary of State for Exiting the European Union*.[1] Bypassing the Court of Appeal, the case then went directly to the Supreme Court, which gave judgment in January 2017.[2] The production process for the book did not enable the main text to be amended in order to take account of the *Miller* case. However, it has been possible to add the following discussion of the case. While not integrated into the main text, the following identifies how the various issues raised by *Miller* relate to matters considered in the book. In writing this analysis of the *Miller* case, we inevitably anticipate matters that are addressed later in this book. Readers may therefore wish to refer back to this discussion of *Miller* at relevant points—in particular after having read about the royal prerogative (in Chapter 4), parliamentary sovereignty (in Chapter 5), devolution and the territorial constitution (in Chapter 7), and EU law and Brexit (in Chapter 8).

The issues in *Miller*

Those who participated in the referendum that was held on 23 June 2016 voted by a margin of 52 to 48 per cent in favour of the United Kingdom leaving the European Union. Following the referendum, the government assumed that it could initiate the formal process whereby the UK would withdraw from the EU by using its prerogative powers to conduct foreign relations. Its thinking was that exit from the EU would involve the UK ceasing to be a party to the EU Treaties, and that the process of withdrawal from those treaties could therefore be begun by using the foreign relations prerogative, which is regularly used, among other things, in relation to entry into and withdrawal from international treaties. The government thus planned to use its prerogative power to notify the European Council of the UK's intention to withdraw, thereby starting the exit process under Art 50 of the Treaty on European Union. Once that process is triggered, the Member State leaves the EU two years later, unless a withdrawal agreement is reached sooner or all the Member States agree to an extension of the two-year period.

However, in *Miller*, it was argued that the government could not trigger the Art 50 withdrawal mechanism using prerogative power. The argument on this issue—we will call it the 'prerogative issue'—went like this:

- Individuals in the UK had acquired rights through EU law.
- EU law was given effect in the UK by an Act of Parliament (the European Communities Act 1972 (ECA)).

---

[1] [2016] EWHC 2768 (Admin).   [2] [2017] UKSC 5.

- Triggering Art 50 would have the effect of removing rights granted by statute, because once the Art 50 'trigger' was pulled, the rights would (all other things being equal) terminate two years later.
- Rights provided for by statute could not be taken away via the prerogative, because the prerogative cannot be used in opposition to an Act of Parliament.
- The prerogative could therefore not be used to trigger Art 50: only Parliament could trigger Art 50 or authorise the government to do so.

The Divisional Court accepted this line of argument, holding that the prerogative was unavailable to the government in these circumstances and that (implicitly) an Act of Parliament was therefore required.

When the case reached the Supreme Court, a further issue—the 'devolution issue'—arose. Some aspects of it had already been canvassed before the High Court in Northern Ireland,[3] but a broader set of such arguments was raised in the Supreme Court proceedings, in which the devolved administrations were given permission to intervene. For present purposes, one of the key devolution-related issues that arose was whether triggering Art 50 would engage the Sewel Convention, thereby requiring the consent of the devolved legislatures. The Convention applies when (among other things) UK legislation adjusts the scope of devolved competence—an effect that Brexit will have, because it will remove EU law-related limitations on devolved bodies' powers. Since the Convention is understood to apply only when the UK Parliament is legislating, it would have been difficult to sustain the argument if legislation was not needed to trigger Art 50. But if, as the Divisional Court had held, legislation triggering Brexit was required, would the Sewel Convention require the devolved legislatures' consent to its enactment? And, given that the Convention is now acknowledged in legislation, did that mean that the devolved nations had a *legal* means of opposing Brexit?

The judgment and its aftermath

Miller was heard by an unprecedented 11-Justice panel of the Supreme Court. On the devolution issue, the Justices were unanimous: the Sewel Convention was not a matter for the Court, and the Court gave short shrift to the argument that the devolved legislatures' consent was legally required. On the prerogative issue, the Justices ruled by an 8–3 majority against the government, explicitly holding that Art 50 could not be triggered without an Act of Parliament. Three Justices dissented. Lord Reed gave a substantial minority judgment with which Lords Carnwath and Hughes agreed; they also gave their own separate, shorter dissenting judgments.

A matter of days after the judgment was delivered, the government introduced a two-clause Bill into the House of Commons. Although the Bill attracted substantial opposition in the House of Lords, the Upper House ultimately yielded to the will of the House of Commons and the government, and the Bill was enacted

---

[3] *Re McCord, Judicial Review* [2016] NIQB 85.

without amendment. The European Union (Notification of Withdrawal) Act 2017 thus received royal assent on 16 March 2017, authorising the Prime Minister to initiate the Brexit process by notifying the European Council of the UK's intention to withdraw under Art 50. The Prime Minister exercised that power on 29 March 2017, making it highly likely that, by the end of March 2019, the UK will have left the EU.

The Supreme Court's decision in *Miller* raises a number of issues that are highly relevant to the matters considered in this book. Here, we briefly draw attention to three key aspects of the decision. The first two, taken in combination, concern the treatment of the prerogative issue. The third relates to the devolution issue.

The extent of prerogative power

First, and most obviously, *Miller* addresses the extent of the government's prerogative powers (on which see further Chapter 4). However, while arguments about the extent of those powers—and how they interact with legislation—were central to the case, in the end both the majority and dissenting judges largely affirmed existing principles. As to the principles themselves, the majority confirmed that the prerogative 'will be displaced in a field which becomes occupied by a corresponding power conferred or regulated by statute', that it 'does not enable ministers to change statute law or common law', and that 'ministers cannot [use the prerogative to] frustrate the purpose of a statute or a statutory provision' by (for example) 'emptying it of content or preventing its effectual operation'. These propositions reflect the principle of parliamentary sovereignty (on which see Chapter 5). They were derived from existing case law and did not break new ground. It was their application to the particular circumstances of this case that caused the disagreement between the majority and dissenting judges, largely because they disagreed about the status of EU law within the UK—a point that we examine below.

The only arguably novel point regarding the prerogative that is made by the majority relates to an argument of 'scale': 'It would be inconsistent with long-standing and fundamental principle', said the majority, 'for such a far-reaching change to the UK constitutional arrangements to be brought about by ministerial decision or ministerial action alone.' However, it is far from clear that, in saying this, the majority intended to articulate a new or distinct restraint upon the use of the prerogative whereby it cannot be used to effect 'far-reaching' constitutional changes—both because the 'scale' point is not absolutely central to the majority's analysis and because it is hard to see how such an imprecise criterion could be serviceable as a principled restriction on the prerogative.

The status of EU law in the UK

In Chapter 5 of this book we explore the idea of parliamentary sovereignty, according to which there are no legal restrictions on the UK Parliament's legislative authority. We go on, in Chapter 8, to note that the requirements of EU membership are not obviously compatible with parliamentary sovereignty, given that—at least according to the Court of Justice of the European Union—EU law is supreme. That means, among other things, that it takes effect in spite of incompatible domestic law in member states like the UK, and that incompatible national law must therefore yield to EU law. Whether, and if so how, the competing claims of primacy made by EU law and by UK legislation can be resolved is a matter of considerable debate, as we explain in Chapter 8.

That debate turns in part upon how we understand the place—and so the status—of EU law within the UK's domestic legal and constitutional system. In *Miller*, the majority's analysis of this point was central to its conclusion that the royal prerogative could not be used to trigger Art 50. As far as the place of EU law within the domestic system is concerned, the majority held that EU law had become an 'independent' and 'overriding' source of UK law. In the light of that, it held that triggering Art 50—and thereby bringing about the removal of EU law from the UK legal system—would result in getting rid of law that had become national law. Once EU law was seen in this way—as something that had become part and parcel of *domestic* law—it stood to reason that the *foreign* relations prerogative could not be used to remove it. Moreover, said the majority, the scheme of the ECA was that EU law should become part of domestic law, and allowing the prerogative to be used to trigger EU law's excision from (the rest of) UK law would be incompatible with the arrangements Parliament had laid down in 1972.

Lord Reed, with whom the other dissenting judges agreed, saw the ECA very differently. On Lord Reed's analysis, the Act 'imposes no requirement, and manifests no intention, in respect of the UK's membership of the EU'. In other words, Parliament, when enacting the ECA, was neutral as to whether the UK should be and remain a member of the EU. The Act, on this view, is nothing more than a 'scheme under which the effect given to EU law in domestic law reflects the UK's international obligations under the Treaties, whatever they may be'. Lord Reed bases this analysis in part upon the fact that s 2(1) of the ECA provides for the domestic legal effect only of such rights as are provided for by the Treaties 'from time to time'. Hence: 'Withdrawal under article 50 alters the application of the 1972 Act, but is not inconsistent with it.' For Lord Reed, then, the ECA simply facilitates access at UK level to whatever rights and so on the UK is required by its Treaty obligations to facilitate access to. Moreover, on this view, EU law is not a source of domestic law: rather, it remains a distinct body of law given effect domestically by the ECA. Using the foreign relations prerogative to trigger Art 50 would therefore not involve the removal of a source of domestic law, and nor would it frustrate the purpose or scheme of the ECA—which, on this view, was only ever intended to give domestic effect to EU law to the extent required by any Treaty obligations.

To the extent that *Miller* hinges upon these competing analyses of the ECA, its significance might seem limited. After all, it is likely that the ECA will be repealed as soon as the UK leaves the EU, rendering debate about the Act of historical interest only. However, to jump to that conclusion would be to miss a larger point that will likely be of more enduring relevance. In holding that EU law became an 'independent' and 'overriding' source of domestic law, the majority reveals something of the malleability of the doctrine of parliamentary sovereignty. It tells us that (at least according to this view) Parliament is capable, by enacting legislation like the ECA, to alter the legal order in a quite fundamental way, by introducing a new source of law that is not only independent of the statute that opened the door to it but which acquires overriding force. The majority view is certainly not without difficulty. For instance, it is light on detail when it comes to explaining precisely how and why EU law came to occupy this unusual status. But the mere fact that it did acquire such a status is significant, not least because it suggests that Parliament can put in place arrangements that—at least while they remain in place—sit in tension with its own sovereignty.

Devolution and the territorial constitution

We have seen so far that *Miller* both affirms parliamentary sovereignty (by insisting that the prerogative cannot be used to unpick arrangements put in place by Parliament) and challenges it (by characterising EU law as something which is independent of and can override Acts of Parliament). The arguments raised in *Miller* about devolution and the territorial constitution raise a further set of questions about parliamentary sovereignty in particular, and the nature of the modern UK constitution more generally. We note in Chapter 7 that devolution is understood to be compatible with parliamentary sovereignty because it involves a non-exclusive *sharing* of power rather than a *transfer* of power. On this view, devolved legislatures are free to legislate on matters over which the UK Parliament has given them power: but the devolved legislatures' authority does not diminish the UK Parliament's authority. Being sovereign, the UK Parliament cannot have limited its own power by creating the devolution settlement.

Taken at face value, this analysis of devolution—which places the sovereignty of the UK Parliament front and centre—risks undermining the very spirit of devolution. It implies that the UK Parliament can interfere in devolved matters whenever it wishes, including by undoing or changing devolved legislation with which it disagrees. The Sewel Convention was a response to the concerns raised by these possibilities. It amounts to a political understanding according to which the UK Parliament will not normally legislate on devolved matters unless the relevant devolved legislature consents. Over time, the category of devolved matters for this purpose has come to encompass both legislation on matters over which devolved bodies have power as well as legislation affecting the scope of devolved bodies' powers. As noted above, Brexit will change those powers by freeing devolved institutions from any obligation to abide by EU law. This raises the question whether legislation providing for the triggering of Art 50—and hence Brexit—engages the Sewel Convention.

Such questions about constitutional conventions are usually understood to be political questions. On that view, any disagreement about whether the Sewel Convention applied would fall to be resolved through political channels, such as negotiation between UK and devolved institutions. However, in *Miller*, it was argued that the Supreme Court could—and should—rule on the Sewel Convention in the light of recent legislation. Section 28(7) of the Scotland Act 1998 says that although that Act authorises the Scottish Parliament to legislate, that 'does not affect the power of the Parliament of the United Kingdom to make laws for Scotland'. However, s 28(8), inserted by the Scotland Act 2016, now goes on to say—in language that closely tracks the Sewel Convention itself—that 'it is recognised that the Parliament of the United Kingdom will not normally legislate with regard to devolved matters without the consent of the Scottish Parliament'.

Did this mean that the Scottish Parliament's consent would be needed to any UK legislation authorising the triggering of Art 50? The Supreme Court held not. It said that judges 'are neither the parents nor the guardians of political conventions; they are merely observers'. This meant that while courts 'can recognise the operation of a political convention in the context of deciding a legal question . . . they cannot give legal rulings on its operation or scope, because those matters are determined within the political world'. And the Court rejected the argument that legislation had converted the Sewel Convention into a legal rule: rather, the legislation was merely 'recognising the convention for what it is, namely a political convention'. The Court was careful not to say that the Convention was inapplicable (or that it was applicable) in the circumstances of the case. Rather, the Court declined to rule on that question because of the political nature of the Convention.

The Court's position on the Sewel Convention is relevant to two matters that we address in the book. First, it casts doubt on the argument (considered in Chapter 7) that the UK's constitution is becoming a 'federal' constitution in which power is formally divided. It may very well be that the Sewel Convention makes it politically difficult for the UK Parliament to legislate on certain matters without devolved consent. But *Miller* makes it clear that there are no *legal* guarantees here. Indeed, in the absence of such guarantees, the UK Parliament went on to enact the European Union (Notification of Withdrawal) Act 2017 *without* securing the consent of the devolved legislatures. The UK government, in its Explanatory Notes to what was then the Bill, baldly asserted that it 'does not contain any provision which gives rise to the need for a legislative consent motion in the Scottish Parliament, the National Assembly for Wales or the Northern Ireland Assembly'.

Second, *Miller* draws a particularly sharp distinction between the political and legal aspects of the constitution (the relationship between which forms one of our key themes). The Court views the Convention as part of the 'political world', whereas judges are concerned only with the legal realm. Given the delicate constitutional issues raised by *Miller*, it is perhaps unsurprising that the Court took a cautious approach to this matter. However—as we note in Chapter 2, and as the Supreme Court acknowledged in *Miller*—courts can certainly take account of constitutional conventions in determining how legal rules apply. They have also, on occasions, gone further: the Upper Tribunal's judgment in *Evans* evidencing close judicial analysis of the content and reach of certain conventions.[4] Whether *Miller*—given the Supreme Court's view that courts should not rule on the 'scope' of conventions—will leave *Evans* marooned at the high-water mark of judicial engagement with constitutional conventions remains to be seen.

---

[4] *Evans v Information Commission* [2012] UKUT 313 (AAC).

Table of Cases

A v B plc [2002] EWCA Civ 337, [2003] QB 195 . . . 849

A v Secretary of State for the Home Department [2004] UKHL 56, [2005] 2 AC 6 . . . 817–19, 31, 32, 33, 546–7, 792

A v UK (2002) 36 EHRR 917 . . . 207

Abrams v US (1919) 250 US 616 . . . 818

Adam v Ward [1917] AC 309 . . . 838

AH (Sudan) v Secretary of State for the Home Department [2007] UKHL 49, [2008] 1 AC 678 . . . 653–8, 720

Ahmed v HM Treasury [2010] UKSC 2, [2010] 2 WLR 378 . . . 244–5, 580

Ahnee v Director of Public Prosecutions [1999] 2 AC 294 . . . 828

Airedale NHS Trust v Bland [1993] AC 789 . . . 268

Al-Jedda v United Kingdom (2011) 53 EHRR 789 . . . 814

Al-Skeini v United Kingdom (2011) 53 EHRR 589 . . . 814

Albert and Le Compte v Belgium (1983) 5 EHRR 533 . . . 517

Ali v Birmingham City Council [2010] UKSC 8, [2010] 2 WLR 471 . . . 516–17

Ambrose v Harris [2011] UKSC 43, [2011] 1 WLR 2435 . . . 904

American Cyanamid Co v Ethicon Ltd [1975] AC 396 . . . 583

Amministrazione delle Finanze dello Stato v Simmenthal SpA, Case 106/77 [1978] ECR 629 . . . 361

Animal Defenders International v United Kingdom (2013) 34 BHRC 137 . . . 187

Anisminic Ltd v Foreign Compensation Commission [1969] 2 AC 147 . . . 74, 245–6, 248, 491, 493, 501–2, 558–9, 587–8, 592, 613, 621, 768, 770

Appleby v UK (2003) 37 EHRR 38 . . . 857

Application by JR55 for Judicial Review (Northern Ireland), Re an [2016] UKSC 22 . . . 679

Argyll and Bute Council v SPSO [2007] CSOH 168 . . . 678

Ashby v Minister of Immigration [1981] 1 NZLR 222 . . . 536

Ashworth Hospital Authority v MGN Ltd [2002] UKHL 29, [2002] 1 WLR 2033 . . . 834

Associated Provincial Picture Houses Ltd v Wednesbury Corporation [1948] 1 KB 223 . . . 539, 541–2, 549–51, 554, 580, 587, 591, 608, 776, 805

Aston Cantlow and Wilmcote with Billesley Parochial Church Council v Wallbank [2003] UKHL 37, [2004] 1 AC 546 . . . 796–7

Attorney-General ex rel Tilley v Wandsworth London Borough Council [1981] 1 WLR 854 . . . 530

Attorney-General for New South Wales v Trethowan [1932] AC 526 . . . 241

Attorney-General of Hong Kong v Ng Yuen Shiu [1983] 2 AC 629 . . . 534

Attorney-General v Beard [2013] EWHC 2317 (Admin) . . . 833

Attorney-General v De Keyser's Royal Hotel Ltd [1920] AC 508 . . . 560

Attorney-General v English [1983] 1 AC 116 . . . 829–32

Attorney-General v Jonathan Cape Ltd [1976] QB 752 . . . 60

Attorney-General v Mulholland [1963] 2 QB 477 . . . 833

Attorney-General v National Assembly for Wales Commission [2012] UKSC 53, [2013] 1 AC 792 . . . 327

Attorney-General v News Group Newspapers plc [1987] QB 1 . . . 829

Attorney-General v News Group Newspapers plc [1989] QB 110 . . . 832

Attorney-General v Observer Ltd [1990] 1 AC 109 . . . 847–8, 852–3

Austin v Commissioner of Police of the Metropolis [2007] EWCA Civ 989, [2008] QB 660 . . . 879, 881, 884–7

AXA General Insurance Ltd, Re [2010] CSOH 2 . . . 301

AXA General Insurance Ltd v Lord Advocate [2011] UKSC 46, [2012] 1 AC 868 . . . 249–50, 301, 574, 577

Bank Mellat v HM Treasury (No 2) [2013] UKSC 39 . . . 147, 155

Barnard v National Dock Labour Board [1953] 2 QB 18 . . . 525, 527

Bates v Lord Hailsham of St Marylebone [1972] 1 WLR 1373 . . . 147

Beatty v Gillbanks (1881–82) LR 9 QBD 308 . . . 878

Belfast City Council v Miss Behavin' Ltd [2007] UKHL 19, [2007] 1 WLR 1420 . . . 544

Belize Bank Ltd v Attorney General of Belize [2011] UKPC 36 . . . 512

Bellinger v Bellinger [2003] UKHL 21, [2003] 2 AC 467 . . . 783

Belmarsh case *see* A v Secretary of State for the
    Home Department
Benkharbouche v Embassy of the Republic
    of Sudan [2015] EWCA Civ 33, [2016] QB
    347 . . . 362
Bibby v Chief Constable of Essex (2000) 164 JP
    297 . . . 879, 887
Blackburn v Attorney-General [1971] 1 WLR
    1037 . . . 242
Blackpool Corporation v Locker [1948] 1 KB
    349 . . . 146
Boddington v British Transport Police [1999] 2
    AC 143 . . . 572, 580–1, 587
Bose Corp v Consumers Union (1984) 466 US
    485 . . . 817
Bowman v UK (1998) 26 EHRR 1 . . . 821
Bradlaugh v Gosset (1884) 12 QBD 271 . . . 202
Braganza v BP Shipping Ltd [2015] UKSC 17,
    [2015] 1 WLR 1661 . . . 566
Brandenburg v Ohio (1969) 395 US 444 . . . 819
Branson v Bower (No 2) [2002] QB 737 . . . 837
Brasserie du Pêcheur SA v Federal Republic
    of Germany; R v Secretary of State for
    Transport, *ex p* Factortame (No 4), Joined
    Cases C-46/93 and C-48/93 [1996] QB
    404 . . . 355–6
Bribery Commission v Ranasinghe [1965] AC
    172 . . . 241
British Oxygen Co Ltd v Minister of Technology
    [1971] AC 610 . . . 530
British Railways Board v Pickin [1974] AC
    765 . . . 202, 232
Bromley London Borough Council v Greater
    London Council [1983] AC 768 . . . 606, 626
Brutus v Cozens [1973] AC 854 . . . 865
Bryan v United Kingdom (1996) 21 EHRR
    342 . . . 517
Buckley v Valeo (1976) 424 US 1 . . . 185
Burmah Oil Ltd v Lord Advocate [1965] AC
    75 . . . 623
Bushell v Secretary of State for the Environment
    [1981] AC 75 . . . 528
Byrne v Dean [1937] 1 KB 818 . . . 836

Cadder v HM Advocate [2010] UKSC 43, [2010]
    1 WLR 2601 . . . 904
Campaign for Nuclear Disarmament v Prime
    Minister of the United Kingdom [2002]
    EWHC 2777 . . . 606
Campbell v Mirror Group Newspapers
    Ltd [2004] UKHL 22, [2004] 2 AC
    457 . . . 802–4, 847–51
Canada (House of Commons) v Vaid [2005] 1
    SCR 667 . . . 204
Carltona Ltd v Commissioners of Works [1943]
    2 All ER 560 . . . 140, 527–9
Case of Proclamations (1611) 2 Co Rep
    74 . . . 560

Castle v DPP [2014] EWHC 587, [2014] 1 WLR
    4279 . . . 528–9
Chambers v Director of Public Prosecutions
    [2012] EWHC 2157 (QB), [2013] 1 WLR
    1833 . . . 827
Chandler v Director of Public Prosecutions
    [1964] AC 763 . . . 561, 853
Cheng v Tse Wai Chun [2000] HKCFA 35,
    [2000] 3 HKLRD 418 . . . 838
Chief Constable of North Wales Police v Evans
    [1982] 1 WLR 1155 . . . 522
Chokolingo v Attorney-General of Trinidad and
    Tobago [1981] 1 WLR 106 . . . 828
Chorherr v Austria (1994) 17 EHRR
    358 . . . 863
Christian Institute v The Lord Advocate [2016]
    UKSC 51, 2016 SLT 805 . . . 327
CIA Security SA v Signalson SA, Case C-194/94
    [1996] ECR I-2201 . . . 354
City of London Corporation v Samede [2012]
    EWCA Civ 160, [2012] PTSR 1624 . . . 873
Clark v University of Lincolnshire and
    Humberside [2000] 1 WLR 1988 . . . 572
Clarke v Norton [1910] VLR 494 . . . 837
Coco v AN Clark (Engineers) Ltd [1969] RPC
    41 . . . 847
Commission v Italy, Case 39/72 [1973] ECR
    101 . . . 349
Congreve v Home Office [1976] QB 629 . . . 538
Cooke v MGN Ltd [2014] EWHC 2831 (QB),
    [2015] 1 WLR 895 . . . 835
Cooke v Secretary of State for Social Security
    [2002] 3 All ER 279 . . . 720
Cooper v Attorney General [2010] EWCA Civ
    464 . . . 355
Cooperativa Agricola Zootecnica S Antonio v
    Amministrazione delle Finanze dello Stato,
    Joined Cases C-246/94 to C-249/94 [1997] 1
    CMLR 1112 . . . 349
Costa v Enel, Case 6/64 [1964] CMLR 425,
    [1964] ECR 585 . . . 360–1
Couderc and Hachette Filipacchi Associés v
    France, Application 40454/07 [2015] ECHR
    992 . . . 849
Council of Civil Service Unions v Minister for
    the Civil Service [1985] AC 374, [1984] AC
    374 . . . 57, 497, 532, 539, 553, 560, 592, 606
CREEDNZ v Governor-General of New
    Zealand [1981] 1 NZLR 172 . . . 537
Crocket v Tantallon Golf Club 2005 SLT
    663 . . . 567
CTB v News Group Newspapers Ltd [2011]
    EWHC 1326 . . . 849

Da Silva Mouta v Portugal (2001) 31
    EHRR 4 . . . 779
Davidson v Scottish Ministers (No 2) [2004]
    UKHL 34, 2005 1 SC (HL) 7 . . . 512

Denkavit International BV v Bundesamt für Finanzen, Case C-283/94 [1996] ECR I-5063 . . . 355

Derbyshire County Council v Times Newspapers Ltd [1993] AC 534 . . . 836

Dimes v The Proprietors of the Grand Junction Canal (1852) 3 HLC 759 . . . 509

DM v Secretary of State for the Home Department [2014] CSIH 29, 2014 SC 635 . . . 533

Dominguez (Maribel) v Centre informatique du Centre Ouest Atlantique and Préfet de la région Centre, Case C-282/10, ECLI:EU:C:2012:33 . . . 356–7

Donoghue v Poplar Housing and Regeneration Community Association Ltd [2001] EWCA Civ 595, [2002] QB 48 . . . 607

Douglas v Hello! Ltd (No 3) [2005] EWCA Civ 595, [2006] QB 125, [2007] UKHL 21, [2008] 1 AC 1 . . . 847, 850

DPP v Blum [2006] EWHC 3209 (Admin) . . . 875

DPP v Haw [2007] EWHC 1931 (Admin), [2008] 1 WLR 379 . . . 528

DPP v Hawkins [1988] 1 WLR 1166 . . . 901

DPP v Jones [1999] 2 AC 240 . . . 872–3, 887

DPP v Selvanayagam, The Times, 23 June 1999 . . . 869

DPP v Whyte [1972] AC 849 . . . 845

Dr Bonham's Case (1610) Co Rep 113 . . . 235

Du Plessis v De Klerk 1996 (3) SA 850 . . . 802

Dudgeon v United Kingdom (1982) 4 EHRR 149 . . . 543–4, 845

Duke of Brunswick v Harmer (1849) 14 QB 185 . . . 840

Duncan v Jones [1936] 1 KB 218 . . . 863, 878–9

Duport Steels Ltd v Sirs [1980] 1 WLR 142 . . . 97, 269

Dyson v Attorney-General [1911] 1 KB 410 . . . 482

E v Secretary of State for the Home Department [2004] EWCA Civ 49, [2004] QB 1044 . . . 719

EB v France (2008) 47 EHRR 21 . . . 779

Eba v Advocate General for Scotland [2011] UKSC 29, [2011] 3 WLR 149 . . . 502

Ellen Street Estates Ltd v Minister of Health [1934] 1 KB 590 . . . 234, 240

Entick v Carrington (1765) 19 St Tr 1030 . . . 72, 75, 898

Evans v Information Commissioner [2012] UKUT 313 (AAC) . . . xxiv, 59, 250, 458–9

Ezeh v United Kingdom (2004) 39 EHRR 1 . . . 516

Faccini Dori v Recreb Srl, Case C-91/92 [1995] 1 CMLR 665 . . . 351

FCC v Pacifica Foundation, 438 US 726 (1978) . . . 824

Ferrazzini v Italy (2002) 34 EHRR 45 . . . 516

Fleet Street Casuals see R v Inland Revenue Commissioners, ex p National Federation of Self-Employed and Small Businesses Ltd

Flood v Times Newspapers Ltd [2012] UKSC 11, [2012] 2 AC 273 . . . 840

Foster v British Gas plc, Case C-188/89 [1991] 1 QB 405 . . . 352

Foster v British Gas plc [1991] 2 AC 306 . . . 352

FP (Iran) v Secretary of State for the Home Department [2007] EWCA Civ 13 . . . 619, 710

Francovich v Italy, Joined Cases C-6/90 and C-9/90 [1991] ECR I-5357 . . . 354, 356

Franz Grad v Finanzamt Traustein [1970] ECR 825 . . . 349

Garland v British Rail Engineering Ltd [1983] 2 AC 751 . . . 49

Gaunt v Ofcom [2011] EWCA Civ 692, [2011] 1 WLR 2355 . . . 824

Gay News Ltd and Lemon v United Kingdom (1983) 5 EHRR 123 . . . 843

GCHQ case see Attorney-General v Jonathan Cape Ltd; Council of Civil Service Unions v Minister for the Civil Service

Gertz v Robert Welch Inc (1974) 418 US 323 . . . 818

Ghaidan v Godin-Mendoza [2004] UKHL 30, [2004] 2 AC 557 . . . 778–82, 784, 787, 799

Gibbs v Rea [1998] AC 786 . . . 914

Gillan v UK (2010) 50 EHRR 45 . . . 897

Gillick v West Norfolk and Wisbech Area Health Authority [1986] AC 112 . . . 584

Gillies v Secretary of State for Work and Pensions [2006] UKHL 2, [2006] 1 WLR 781 . . . 512, 693

Glynn v Keele University [1971] 1 WLR 487 . . . 578

Golden Chemical Products Ltd, Re [1976] Ch 300 . . . 527–8

Goodwin v News Group Newspapers Ltd [2011] EWHC 1437 (QB), [2011] EMLR 27 . . . 848

Goodwin v UK (1996) 22 EHRR 123 . . . 834

Griffin v South West Water Services Ltd [1995] IRLR 15 . . . 352

Gundem v Turkey (2001) 31 EHRR 49 . . . 857

Guzzardi v Italy (1981) 3 EHRR 333 . . . 885

Hadjianastassiou v Greece (1993) 16 EHRR 219 . . . 525

Hall v Mayor of London [2010] EWCA Civ 817, [2011] 1 WLR 504 . . . 870

Hammond v DPP [2004] EWHC 69 (Admin) . . . 866

Handyside v UK (1979–80) 1 EHRR 737 . . . 845, 868

Hanks v Minister of Housing and Local Government [1963] 1 QB 999 . . . 536

Harris v Minister of the Interior 1952 (2) SA
    428 . . . 241
Harrison v Duke of Rutland [1893] 1 QB
    142 . . . 872
Hatton v United Kingdom (2003) 37 EHRR
    28 . . . 481, 483
Hayes v Chief Constable of Merseyside Police
    [2011] EWCA Civ 911, [2012] 1 WLR
    517 . . . 900
Hazell v Hammersmith London Borough
    Council [1992] 2 AC 1 . . . 607
Helle v Finland (1997) 26 EHRR 159 . . . 525
High v Billings (1903) 89 LT 550 . . . 527
Hill v Chief Constable of West Yorkshire [1989]
    AC 53 . . . 914
Hinds v The Queen [1977] AC 195 . . . 97
Hirst v UK (No 2) (2006) 42 EHRR
    41 . . . 174, 794
HM Advocate v Beggs (No 2) 2002 SLT
    139 . . . 831
Hoare v UK [1997] EHRLR 678 . . . 21, 843
Huang v Secretary of State for the Home
    Department [2007] UKHL 11, [2007] 2 AC
    167 . . . 543, 546

İletmiş v Turkey (ECtHR, Application 29871/96,
    judgment 6 December 2005) . . . 845
Inquiry under the Companies Securities
    (Insider Dealing) Act 1985, Re an [1988] AC
    660 . . . 834
International Transport Roth GmbH v
    Secretary of State for the Home Department
    [2002] EWCA Civ 158, [2003] QB 728 . . . 546
Internationale Handelsgesellschaft mbH v
    Einfuhr- und Vorratsstelle für Getreide
    und Futtermittel, Case 11/70 [1970] ECR
    1125 . . . 361
IO v Entry Clearance Officer, Lagos ('Points in
    Issue') Nigeria [2004] UKIAT 00179 . . . 713
IS v The Director of Legal Aid Casework [2015]
    EWHC 1965 (Admin) . . . 707

Jennings v Buchanan [2004] UKPC 36, [2005]
    1 AC 11 . . . 507
Jersild v Denmark (1995) 19 EHRR 1 . . . 821
John v Express Newspapers [2000] 1 WLR
    1931 . . . 834
John v Rees [1970] Ch 345 . . . 507
Johnston v Chief Constable of the Royal
    Ulster Constabulary, Case 222/84 [1987] QB
    129 . . . 352
Jones v First-tier Tribunal and Criminal Injuries
    Compensation Authority [2013] UKSC 19,
    [2013] 2 WLR 1012 . . . 503, 716, 720–21
Jordan v United Kingdom (2001) 37 EHRR
    52 . . . 736
JR38 [2015] UKSC 42, [2015] 3 WLR 155,
    Re . . . xvii, 848, 851

Kanda v Government of Malaysia [1962] AC
    322 . . . 523
Kay v Commissioner of Police of the
    Metropolis [2008] UKHL 69, [2008] 1
    WLR 2723 . . . 876
Kaye v Robertson [1991] FSR 62 . . . 846–7
Kennedy v Charity Commission [2014] UKSC
    20, [2015] AC 455 . . . xvii, 769
Kerr v Department for Social Development
    [2004] UKHL 23 . . . 706
Keyu v Secretary of State for Foreign and
    Commonwealth Affairs [2015] UKSC 69,
    [2015] 3 WLR 1665 . . . xvi, 549–50
Khawaja v Secretary of State for the Home
    Department [1984] AC 74 . . . 505
Knuller (Publishing, Printing and Promotions
    Ltd) v DPP [1973] AC 435 . . . 845
Köbler v Austria, Case C-224/01 [2003] ECR
    I-10239 . . . 356
König v Federal Republic of Germany (1979–80)
    2 EHRR 170 . . . 516
Kücükdeveci v Swedex, Case C-555/07 [2010]
    ECR I-365 . . . 356
Kurt v Turkey (1999) 27 EHRR 373 . . . 804
Kuznetsov v Russia, Application 10877/04
    [2008] ECHR 1170 . . . 860

Lachaux v Independent Print Ltd [2015] EWHC
    2242 (QB), [2016] QB 402 . . . 835
Lavender and Sons Ltd v Minister of Housing
    and Local Government [1970] 1 WLR
    1231 . . . 527
Lawal v Northern Spirit Ltd [2003] UKHL 35,
    [2004] 1 All ER 187 . . . 512
Leech v Deputy Governor of Parkhurst Prison
    [1988] AC 533 . . . 569
Lesage v Mauritius Commercial Bank Ltd
    [2012] UKPC 41 . . . 513
Lewis v Attorney General of Jamaica [2001]
    2 AC 50 . . . 562
Lewis v Chief Constable of South Wales [1991]
    1 All ER 206 . . . 901
Lingens v Austria (1986) 8 EHRR 407 . . . 837
Lloyd v McMahon [1987] AC 625 . . . 520–1, 587
Locabail (UK) Ltd v Bayfield Properties Ltd
    [2000] QB 451 . . . 508–10
Lochner v New York (1905) 198 US 45 . . . 608
Loutchansky v Times Newspapers Ltd (No 2)
    [2001] EWCA Civ 1805, [2002] QB 783 . . . 840

M, Re [1994] 1 AC 377 . . . 75, 582–4
Maaouia v France (2001) 33 EHRR 42 . . . 516
Macarthys Ltd v Smith [1979] 3 All ER
    325 . . . 367
McCann v United Kingdom (1995) 21 EHRR
    97 . . . 736
McCord, Re [2016] NIQB 85 . . . xx
McGowan v Langmuir 1931 JC 10 . . . 845

McInnes v Onslow-Fane [1978] 1 WLR 1520 . . . 520

McKennitt v Ash [2006] EWCA Civ 1714, [2008] QB 73 . . . 848

Madzimbamuto v Lardner-Burke [1969] 1 AC 645 . . . 59

Malone v Metropolitan Police Commissioner [1979] Ch 344 . . . 72, 160

Malone v United Kingdom (1985) 7 EHRR 14 . . . 160, 463

Mandalia v Secretary of State for the Home Department [2015] UKSC 59, [2015] 1 WLR 4546 . . . 74, 533

Mangold v Helm, Case C-144/04 [2005] ECR I-9981 . . . 356-7

Marbury v Madison, 5 US 137 (1803) . . . 247

Marshall v Deputy Governor of Bermuda [2010] UKPC 9 . . . 608-9

Marshall v Southampton and South West Hampshire Area Health Authority, Case 152/84 [1986] ECR 723 . . . 351

Marshall v Southampton and South West Hampshire Area Health Authority (No 2) [1994] 1 AC 530 . . . 352

Matadeen v Pointu [1999] 1 AC 98 . . . 550

Mathieu-Mohin v Belgium (1988) 10 EHRR 1 . . . 174

Maxwell v Department of Trade and Industry [1974] QB 523 . . . 745

Mayor of London v Hall [2010] EWCA Civ 817 . . . 875

Medicaments and Related Classes of Goods, Re (No 2) [2001] 1 WLR 700 . . . 511-13

Merricks v Nott-Bower [1965] 1 QB 57 . . . 838

MGN v Attorney-General [1997] EMLR 284 . . . 830

MK (duty to give reasons) Pakistan [2013] UKUT 00641 (IAC) . . . 711

Mongan v Department of Social Development [2005] NICA 16 . . . 706

Moohan v Lord Advocate [2014] UKSC 67, [2015] AC 901 . . . 493

Morgan v Odhams Press Ltd [1971] 1 WLR 1239 . . . 835

Morris v Crown Office [1970] 2 QB 114 . . . 33

Mosley v News Group Newspapers Ltd [2008] EWHC 1777 (QB), [2008] EMLR 20 . . . 849

Mosley v United Kingdom (2011) 53 EHRR 30 . . . 850

Moss v McLachlin [1985] IRLR 76 . . . 880-1

Municipal Council of Sydney v Campbell [1925] AC 339 . . . 73, 538

National Union of Teachers v Governing Body of St Mary's Church of England (Aided) Junior School [1997] 3 CMLR 630 . . . 352

Nold Kohlen- und Baustoffgrosshandlung v Commission of the European Communities, Case 4/73 [1975] ECR 985 . . . 362

Norris v Ireland (1991) 13 EHRR 186 . . . 805

Norwood v DPP [2003] EWHC 1564 (Admin) . . . 866

Nottinghamshire County Council v Secretary of State for the Environment [1986] AC 240 . . . 484, 540, 607

Nzolameso v Westminster City Council [2015] UKSC 22, [2015] PTSR 549 . . . 531

Odelola v Secretary of State for the Home Department [2009] UKHL 25, [2009] 1 WLR 1230 . . . 145

Office of Government Commerce v Information Commissioner [2008] EWHC Admin 737, [2010] QB 98 . . . 206

Öllinger v Austria (2008) 46 EHRR 38 . . . 857, 863-4

O'Reilly v Mackman [1983] 2 AC 237 . . . 567, 570-2, 623

Osman v UK (2000) 29 EHRR 245 . . . 914

Padfield v Minister of Agriculture, Fisheries and Food [1968] AC 997 . . . 536-7, 582, 592, 612

Palacios de la Villa v Cortefiel Servicios SA, Case C-411/05 [2007] ECR I-8531 . . . 356

Paponette v Attorney General of Trinidad and Tobago [2010] UKPC 32, [2012] 1 AC 1 . . . 535

Parliament case (1609) 13 Co Rep 63 . . . 204

Pearlman v Keepers and Governors of Harrow School [1979] QB 56 . . . 501, 503

Peck v UK (2003) 36 EHRR 41 . . . 851

Pepper v Hart [1993] AC 593 . . . 201, 206-7

Percy v Director of Public Prosecutions [1995] 1 WLR 1382 . . . 878

Pergamon Press, Re [1971] Ch 388 . . . 745

Pergau Dam case see R v Secretary of State for Foreign and Commonwealth Affairs, ex p World Development Movement Ltd

Persey v Secretary of State for Environment, Food and Rural Affairs [2002] EWHC 371 (Admin), [2003] QB 794 . . . 736

Pfeiffer v Deutsches Rotes Kreuz, Kreisverband Waldshut Ev, Case C-397/01 [2005] 1 CMLR 44 . . . 353

Pham v Secretary of State for the Home Department [2015] UKSC 19, [2015] 1 WLR 1591 . . . xvi, 550

Pickin v British Railways Board [1974] AC 765 . . . 203

Pinochet No 1 see R v Bow Street Metropolitan Stipendiary Magistrate, ex p Pinochet Ugarte

PJS v News Group Newspapers Ltd [2016] UKSC 26, [2016] 2 WLR 1253 . . . xvii, 821-2, 847-8

Plattform 'Ärzte für das Leben' v Austria (1991) 13 EHRR 204 . . . 862-3, 879

Porter v Magill [2001] UKHL 67, [2002] 2 AC 357 . . . 511-12

Portgás v Ministério da Agricultura, do Mar, do Ambiente e do Ordenamento do Território Case, C-425/12 [2014] 2 CMLR 30 . . . 352

Poyser and Mills' Arbitration, Re [1964] 2 QB 467 . . . 525, 711

Practice Statement (Judicial Precedent) [1966] 1 WLR 1234 . . . 82

Pubblico Ministero v Ratti, Case 148/78 [1979] ECR 1629 . . . 351

Pullman v Walter Hill and Co Ltd [1891] 1 QB 524 . . . 835

R (A) v Croydon London Borough Council [2009] UKSC 8, [2009] 1 WLR 2557 . . . 505

R (Abbasi) v Secretary of State for Foreign and Commonwealth Affairs [2002] EWCA Civ 1598, [2003] UKHRR 76 . . . 562

R (Al Rawi) v Secretary of State for Foreign and Commonwealth Affairs [2006] EWCA Civ 1279, [2008] QB 289 . . . 563

R (Alconbury Developments Ltd) v Secretary of State for the Environment, Transport and the Regions [2001] UKHL 23, [2003] 2 AC 295 . . . 263, 516–17

R (Ali) v Secretary of State for the Home Department [2003] EWHC 899 (Admin) . . . 612

R (Amin) v Secretary of State for the Home Department [2003] UKHL 51, [2004] 1 AC 653 . . . 735

R (Anderson) v Secretary of State for the Home Department [2002] UKHL 46, [2003] 1 AC 83 . . . 515, 781–3, 785

R (Anufrijeva) v Secretary of State for the Home Department [2003] UKHL 36, [2004] 1 AC 604 . . . 73, 145–6

R (Association of British Civilian Internees: Far East Region) v Secretary of State for Defence [2003] EWCA Civ 473, [2003] QB 1397 . . . 549, 641

R (Bancoult) v Secretary of State for Foreign and Commonwealth Affairs (No 2) [2008] UKHL 61, [2009] 1 AC 453 . . . 157, 489, 561, 789

R (BAPIO Action Ltd) v Secretary of State for the Home Department [2008] UKHL 27, [2008] 1 AC 1003 . . . 109, 147

R (Barda) v Mayor of London [2015] EWHC 3584 (Admin), [2016] 4 WLR 20 . . . 875

R (Behre) v London Borough of Hillingdon [2003] EWHC 2075 (Admin), [2004] 1 FLR 439 . . . 616

R (Ben Hoare Bell Solicitors) v Lord Chancellor [2015] EWHC 523 (Admin) . . . 599

R (Bhudia) v Secretary of State for the Home Department [2016] UKUT 00025 (IAC) . . . 603

R (Bibi) v Newham London Borough Council [2001] EWCA Civ 607, [2002] 1 WLR . . . 534

R (Bourgass) v Secretary of State for Justice [2015] UKSC 54, [2016] AC 384 . . . 24, 140, 523, 529

R (Bradley) v Secretary of State for Work and Pensions [2007] EWHC 242 (Admin), [2008] EWCA Civ 36, [2009] QB 114 . . . 658, 672–5

R (Brooke) v Parole Board [2008] EWCA Civ 29, [2008] 1 WLR 1950 . . . 608

R (Burke) v General Medical Council [2005] EWCA Civ 1003, [2006] QB 273 . . . 585

R (Carroll) v Secretary of State for the Home Department [2005] UKHL 13, [2005] 1 WLR 688 . . . 512

R (Cart) v Upper Tribunal [2011] UKSC 28, [2012] 1 AC 663 . . . 250, 503, 559, 722–3

R (Casey) v Restormel Borough Council [2007] EWHC Admin 2554 . . . 600

R (Castle) v Commissioner of Police of the Metropolis [2011] EWHC 2317 (Admin) . . . 814

R (Catt) v Commissioner of Police for the Metropolis [2015] UKSC 9 . . . 889

R (Cavanagh) v Health Service Commissioner for England [2005] EWCA Civ 1578, [2006] 1 WLR 1229 . . . 664

R (Condron) v National Assembly for Wales [2006] EWCA Civ 1573, [2007] 2 P & CR 4 . . . 514

R (Corner House Research) v Director of the Serious Fraud Office [2008] UKHL 60, [2009] 1 AC 756 . . . 123

R (Cowl) v Plymouth City Council [2001] EWCA Civ 1935, [2002] 1 WLR 803 . . . 569, 604

R (Daly) v Secretary of State for the Home Department [2001] UKHL 26, [2001] 2 AC 532 . . . 74–5, 541–2, 545, 550–1, 592, 608, 620, 769

R (Davies) v Revenue and Customs Commissioners [2011] UKSC 47, [2011] 1 WLR 2625 . . . 532

R (Equitable Members Action Group) v HM Treasury [2009] EWHC 2495 (Admin) . . . 673–4

R (Evans) v Attorney General [2015] UKSC 21, [2015] AC 1787 . . . 251, 453, 458

R (F) v Secretary of State for the Home Department [2010] UKSC 17, [2011] 1 AC 331 . . . 808, 812

R (G and H) v Secretary of State for the Home Department [2016] EWHC 239 (Admin) . . . 723

R (Gallagher) v Basildon District Council [2010] EWHC Admin 2824 . . . 675–6

R (GC) v Commissioner of Police of the
Metropolis [2011] UKSC 21, [2011] 1 WLR
1230 . . . 781

R (Gudanaviciene) v Director of Legal Aid
Casework and Lord Chancellor [2014] EWCA
Civ 1622 . . . 707

R (Hasan) v Secretary of State for Trade and
Industry [2007] EWHC 2630 (Admin) . . . 524

R (Haw) v Secretary of State for the Home
Department [2006] EWCA Civ 532, [2006]
QB 780 . . . 875

R (Hicks) v Commissioner of Police for the
Metropolis [2017] UKSC 9, [2017] 2 WLR
824 . . . 888

R (Hooper) v Secretary of State for Work and
Pensions [2003] EWCA Civ 813, [2003] 1
WLR 2623 . . . 565

R (HS2 Action Alliance Ltd) v Secretary of State
for Transport [2014] UKSC 3, [2014] 1 WLR
324 . . . 46, 372–4, 376

R (Iran) v Secretary of State for the Home
Department [2005] EWCA Civ 982, [2005]
INLR 633 . . . 718

R (Island Farm Development Ltd) v Brigend
County Borough Council [2006] EWHC 2189
(Admin), [2007] BLGR 60 . . . 514

R (Jackson) v Attorney General [2005] UKHL
56, [2006] 1 AC 262 . . . 13, 72, 238, 241, 248–50,
254, 329, 368–9, 493

R (Javed) v Secretary of State for the Home
Department [2002] QB 129 . . . 155

R (JL) v Secretary of State for the Home
Department [2007] EWCA Civ 767, [2008] 1
WLR 158 . . . 735

R (Jones) v First-tier Tribunal [2013] UKSC 19,
[2013] 2 WLR 1012 . . . 559

R (K) v Camden and Islington Heath Authority
[2001] 3 WLR 553 . . . 108

R (Karas and Miladinovic) v Secretary of State
for the Home Department [2006] EWHC 747
(Admin) . . . 609

R (Khatun) v Newham London Borough Council
[2004] EWCA Civ 55, [2005] QB 37 . . . 520

R (L) v West London Mental Health NHS
Trust [2014] EWCA Civ 47, [2014] 1 WLR
3103 . . . 519

R (Laporte) v Chief Constable of
Gloucestershire Constabulary [2006] UKHL
55, [2007] 2 AC 105 . . . 879–83, 885, 887

R (Lim) v Secretary of State for the Home
Department [2007] EWCA Civ 773, [2008]
INLR 60 . . . 569

R (Limbuela) v Secretary of State for the Home
Department [2006] 1 AC 396 . . . 597

R (Litvinenko) v Secretary of State for the
Home Department [2014] EWHC 194
(Admin) . . . 736

R (London Borough of Hillingdon) v Secretary
of State for Education and Skills [2007]
EWHC 514 (Admin) . . . 616

R (Lumba) v Secretary of State for the Home
Department [2011] UKSC 12, [2012] 1 AC
245 . . . 74, 533, 914

R (M) v The School Organisation Committee,
Oxfordshire County Council [2001] EWHC
Admin 245 . . . 569

R (McKenzie) v Waltham Forest London Borough
Council [2009] EWHC 1097 (Admin) . . . 585

R (Mahmood) v Secretary of State for the Home
Department [2001] 1 WLR 840 . . . 545

R (Mengesha) v Commissioner of Police
for the Metropolis [2013] EWHC 1695
(Admin) . . . 890

R (Miller) v Secretary of State for Exiting
the European Union [2016] EWHC 2768
(Admin) . . . xix, 34

R (Miller) v Secretary of State for Exiting the
European Union [2017] UKSC 5 . . . xvii

R (Mohamed) v Secretary of State for Foreign
and Commonwealth Affairs (No 1) [2008]
EWHC 2048 (Admin), [2009] 1 WLR
2579 . . . 462

R (Mohamed) v Secretary of State for Foreign
and Commonwealth Affairs [2010] EWCA
Civ 65 . . . 462

R (Mohamed) v Secretary of State for Foreign
and Commonwealth Affairs [2010] EWCA
Civ 158 . . . 462

R (Moos) v Commissioner of Police of the
Metropolis [2012] EWCA Civ 12 . . . 880

R (Munir) v Secretary of State for the Home
Department [2012] UKSC 32, [2012] 1 WLR
2192 . . . 560

R (Munjaz) v Mersey Care NHS Trust [2005]
UKHL 58, [2006] 2 AC 148 . . . 145

R (Murray) v Parliamentary Commissioner
for Administration [2002] EWCA Civ
1472 . . . 663

R (New London College) v Secretary of State
for the Home Department [2013] UKSC
51 . . . 160

R (Nicklinson) v Ministry of Justice
[2014] UKSC 38, [2015] AC 657 . . . 547,
785–6, 791–3

R (NS) v Secretary of State for the Home
Department, Joined Cases C-411/10 and
C-493/10 [2013] QB 102 . . . 362

R (Osborn) v Parole Board [2013] UKSC 61
[2014] AC 1115 . . . xvii, 521, 613–14

R (Patel) v General Medical Council [2013]
EWCA Civ 327, [2013] 1 WLR 2801 . . . 532,
536, 769

R (ProLife Alliance) v BBC [2003] UKHL 23,
[2004] 1 AC 185 . . . 856, 866, 868

R (Quark Fishing Ltd) v Secretary of State for
    Foreign and Commonwealth Affairs [2002]
    EWCA Civ 1409 . . . 609
R (Reilly and Wilson) v Secretary of State
    for Work and Pensions [2013] EWCA Civ
    66 . . . 72, 623
R (Roberts) v Commissioner of Police of the
    Metropolis [2015] UKSC 79, [2016] 1 WLR
    210 . . . 897
R (Rotherham Metropolitan Borough Council)
    v Secretary of State for Business, Innovation
    and Skills [2015] UKSC 6, [2015] PTSR
    322 . . . 550
R (Runa Begum) v Tower Hamlets Borough
    Council [2003] UKHL 5, [2003] 2 AC
    430 . . . 516, 606
R (Rusbridger) v Attorney General [2003]
    UKHL 38, [2004] 1 AC 357 . . . 585, 806
R (S) v Secretary of State for the Home
    Department [2006] EWHC 1111 (Admin),
    [2006] EWCA Civ 1157 . . . 551, 609, 624,
    716–17, 807
R (Sandiford) v Secretary of State for Foreign
    and Commonwealth Affairs [2014] UKSC 44,
    [2014] 1 WLR 2697 . . . 562
R (Shoesmith) v Ofsted [2011] EWCA Civ 642,
    [2011] PTSR 1459 . . . 569
R (Smith) v Parole Board [2005] UKHL 1, [2005]
    1 WLR 350 . . . 521, 710
R (UK Uncut Legal Action Ltd) v
    Commissioners of HM Revenue and Customs
    [2012] EWHC 2017 (Admin) . . . 575
R (Weaver) v London and Quadrant Housing
    Trust [2009] EWCA Civ 587, [2010] 1 WLR
    363 . . . 798
R (Wheeler) v Prime Minister [2008] EWHC
    1409 (Admin) . . . 561
R (Wooder) v Feggetter [2002] EWCA Civ 554,
    [2003] QB 219 . . . 525
R (Yogathas and Thangarasa) v Secretary of
    State for the Home Department [2003] 1 AC
    920 . . . 623
R (Youssef) v Secretary of State for Foreign
    and Commonwealth Affairs [2016] UKSC 3,
    [2016] 2 WLR 509 . . . 549
R v A (No 2) [2001] UKHL 25, [2002] 1 AC
    45 . . . 781
R v Board of Visitors of HM Prison, The Maze,
    ex p Hone [1988] AC 379 . . . 521
R v Bow Street Metropolitan Stipendiary
    Magistrate, ex p Pinochet Ugarte (No
    1) [2000] 1 AC 61 . . . 278, 510
R v Bow Street Metropolitan Stipendiary
    Magistrate, ex p Pinochet Ugarte (No
    2) [2000] 1 AC 119 . . . 509–10
R v British Broadcasting Corporation, ex p
    ProLife Alliance [2003] UKHL 23, [2004]
    1 AC 185 . . . 606, 790–1, 793

R v Cambridge Health Authority, ex p B [1995] 2
    All ER 129, (1995) 25 BMLR 5 . . . 610–11
R v Chaytor [2010] UKSC 52, [2011] 1 AC
    684 . . . 203–5
R v Chief Constable of Devon and Cornwall,
    ex p Central Electricity Generating Board
    [1982] QB 458 . . . 878
R v Chief Constable of the Merseyside Police,
    ex p Calveley [1986] QB 424 . . . 569
R v Chief Rabbi of the United Hebrew
    Congregations of Great Britain and the
    Commonwealth, ex p Wachmann [1992]
    1 WLR 1036 . . . 565
R v City of London Corporation, ex p Matson
    [1997] 1 WLR 765 . . . 525
R v Commissioner for Local Administration,
    ex p Croydon London Borough Council
    [1989] 1 All ER 1033 . . . 652, 664
R v Commissioner of Police of the Metropolis,
    ex p Blackburn [1968] 2 QB 118 . . . 894
R v Cooke [1995] 1 Cr App R 318 . . . 913
R v Criminal Injuries Compensation Board,
    ex p Lain [1967] 2 QB 864 . . . 159, 560, 566
R v Dairy Produce Quota Tribunal for England
    and Wales, ex p Caswell [1990] 2 AC 738 . . . 569
R v Department of Education and Employment,
    ex p Begbie [2000] 1 WLR 1115 . . . 532–3
R v Director of Public Prosecutions, ex p
    Kebilene [2000] 2 AC 326 . . . 546
R v Disciplinary Committee of the Jockey Club,
    ex p Aga Khan [1993] 1 WLR 909 . . . 565–6
R v Duffy, ex p Nash [1960] 2 QB 188 . . . 833
R v Fulling [1987] QB 426 . . . 912
R v Gibson [1990] 2 QB 619 . . . 845
R v Gloucestershire County Council, ex p Barry
    [1997] AC 584 . . . 537
R v Gough [1993] AC 646 . . . 511
R v Graham-Campbell, ex p Herbert [1935]
    1 KB 594 . . . 202
R v Harwood [2012] EW Misc 27 (CC) . . . 831
R v Higher Education Funding Council, ex p
    Institute of Dental Surgery [1994] 1 WLR
    242 . . . 524
R v Hillingdon London Borough Council, ex p
    Puhlhofer [1986] AC 484 . . . 503, 627
R v HM Inspectorate of Pollution, ex p
    Greenpeace (No 2) [1994] 4 All ER
    329 . . . 576
R v HM Treasury, ex p Smedley [1985] QB
    657 . . . 203
R v Howell [1982] QB 416 . . . 878
R v Inland Revenue Commissioners, ex p MFK
    Underwriting Agencies Ltd [1990] 1 WLR
    1545 . . . 532
R v Inland Revenue Commissioners, ex p
    National Federation of Self-employed and
    Small Businesses Ltd [1982] AC 617 . . . 575–6,
    587, 592

R v Inland Revenue Commissioners, *ex p* Preston [1985] AC 835 . . . 568

R v Inner West London Coroner, *ex p* Dallaglio [1994] 4 All ER 139 . . . 511

R v Lancashire County Council, *ex p* Huddleston [1986] 2 All ER 941 . . . 608

R v Lemon [1979] QB 10, [1979] AC 617 . . . 608, 842

R v Liverpool Corporation, *ex p* Liverpool Taxi Fleet Operators' Association [1972] 2 QB 299 . . . 581

R v Local Commissioner for Administration for the South, the West Midlands, Leicestershire, Lincolnshire and Cambridgeshire, *ex p* Eastleigh Borough Council [1988] QB 855 . . . 674–5

R v London Borough of Ealing, *ex p* Times Newspapers [1987] IRLR 129 . . . 856

R v Looseley [2001] UKHL 53, [2001] 1 WLR 2060 . . . 913

R v Lord Chancellor, *ex p* Witham [1998] QB 575 . . . 72, 74, 154, 491, 768–9

R v Lord President of the Privy Council, *ex p* Page [1993] AC 682 . . . 502–3

R v McGovern (1991) 92 Cr App R 228 . . . 912

R v Medical Appeal Tribunal, *ex p* Gilmore [1957] 1 QB 574 . . . 717

R v Ministry of Agriculture, Fisheries and Food, *ex p* Hedley Lomas (Ireland) Ltd, Case C-5/94 [1997] QB 139 . . . 355

R v Ministry of Defence, *ex p* Murray [1998] COD 134 . . . 525

R v Ministry of Defence, *ex p* Smith [1996] QB 517 . . . 541, 554

R v Monopolies and Mergers Commission, *ex p* South Yorkshire Transport [1993] 1 WLR 23 . . . 503

R v North and East Devon Health Authority, *ex p* Coughlan [2001] QB 213 . . . 531–2, 534–5, 540, 586–7, 592, 622

R v North West Leicestershire District Council, *ex p* Moses [2000] Env LR 443 . . . 570

R v Panel on Takeovers and Mergers, *ex p* Datafin plc [1987] QB 815 . . . 159, 564–5, 594

R v Paris (1993) 97 Cr App R 99 . . . 912

R v Parliamentary Commissioner for Administration, *ex p* Balchin (No 1) [1997] JPL 917 . . . 658, 664

R v Parliamentary Commissioner for Administration, *ex p* Balchin (No 2) [2000] 79 P & CR 157 . . . 664–5

R v Parliamentary Commissioner for Administration, *ex p* Balchin (No 3) [2002] EWHC 1876 (Admin) . . . 665

R v Parliamentary Commissioner for Administration, *ex p* Dyer [1994] 1 WLR 621 . . . 663–4

R v Parliamentary Commissioner for Standards, *ex p* Fayed [1998] 1 WLR 669 . . . 202, 522

R v Port of London Authority, *ex p* Kynoch Ltd [1919] 1 KB 176 . . . 30

R v Rochdale Metropolitan Borough Council, *ex p* Cromer Ring Mill Ltd [1982] 3 All ER 761 . . . 569

R v Secretary of State for Defence, *ex p* Association of British Civilian Internees [2003] EWCA Civ 473, [2003] QB 1397 . . . 641

R v Secretary of State for the Home Department, *ex p* Carlile [2014] UKSC 60, [2015] AC 945 . . . 548

R v Secretary of State for Foreign and Commonwealth Affairs, *ex p* World Development Movement Ltd [1995] 1 WLR 386 . . . 538, 576–7, 592

R v Secretary of State for Health, *ex p* Wagstaff [2001] 1 WLR 292 . . . 741

R v Secretary of State for Social Security, *ex p* Joint Council for the Welfare of Immigrants [1997] 1 WLR 275 . . . 154, 623

R v Secretary of State for Social Services, *ex p* Sherwin (1996) 32 BMLR 1 . . . 528–9

R v Secretary of State for the Environment, *ex p* Hammersmith and Fulham London Borough Council [1991] 1 AC 521 . . . 607

R v Secretary of State for the Environment, *ex p* Kirkstall Valley Campaign Ltd [1996] 3 All ER 304 . . . 513–14

R v Secretary of State for the Home Department, *ex p* Adan, Subraskran and Aitsegeur [1999] 4 All ER 774, [2001] 2 AC 477, HL . . . 623

R v Secretary of State for the Home Department, *ex p* Anderson [2002] UKHL 46, [2003] 1 AC 837 . . . 608

R v Secretary of State for the Home Department, *ex p* Bentley [1994] QB 349 . . . 562

R v Secretary of State for the Home Department, *ex p* Brind [1991] 1 AC 696 . . . 49, 206, 545, 776

R v Secretary of State for the Home Department, *ex p* Doody [1994] 1 AC 531 . . . 490, 522, 524, 587, 608

R v Secretary of State for the Home Department, *ex p* Fayed [1997] 1 All ER 228, [1998] 1 WLR 763 . . . 522

R v Secretary of State for the Home Department, *ex p* Fire Brigades Union [1995] 2 AC 513 . . . 98–9, 105, 159, 482, 485, 613

R v Secretary of State for the Home Department, *ex p* Hargreaves [1997] 1 WLR 906 . . . 535

R v Secretary of State for the Home Department, *ex p* Khawaja [1984] AC 74 . . . 505, 913

R v Secretary of State for the Home Department, *ex p* Muboyayi [1992] QB 244 . . . 913

R v Secretary of State for the Home Department, *ex p* Oladehinde [1991] 1 AC 254 . . . 528

R v Secretary of State for the Home Department, *ex p* P [1995] 1 All ER 870 . . . 609

R v Secretary of State for the Home Department, *ex p* Pierson [1998] AC 539 . . . 73, 244, 491, 768

R v Secretary of State for the Home Department, *ex p* Salem [1999] 1 AC 450 . . . 585, 603

R v Secretary of State for the Home Department, *ex p* Simms [2000] 2 AC 115 . . . 74, 768–9, 819

R v Secretary of State for the Home Department, *ex p* Tarrant [1985] QB 251 . . . 520–1

R v Secretary of State for the Home Department, *ex p* Venables and Thompson [1998] AC 407 . . . 65, 537, 553

R v Secretary of State for Transport, *ex p* Factortame Ltd, Case C-213/89 [1990] ECR I-2433 . . . 364

R v Secretary of State for Transport, *ex p* Factortame Ltd, Case C-221/89 [1992] QB 680 . . . 364

R v Secretary of State for Transport, *ex p* Factortame Ltd (No 1) [1990] 2 AC 85 . . . 376

R v Secretary of State for Transport, *ex p* Factortame Ltd (No 2) [1991] 1 AC 603 . . . 365–6, 368, 374, 376, 484, 582, 613

R v Servite Houses, *ex p* Goldsmith (2001) 33 HLR 369 . . . 566

R v Shannon [2001] 1 WLR 51 . . . 913

R v Shayler [2002] UKHL 11, [2003] 1 AC 247 . . . 855

R v Sheer Metalcraft Ltd [1954] 1 QB 586 . . . 147

R v Somerset County Council, *ex p* Dixon [1998] Env LR 111 . . . 574

R v Somerset County Council, *ex p* Fewings [1995] 1 All ER 513, [1995] 1 WLR 1037 . . . 159, 476, 538

R v Sussex Justices, *ex p* McCarthy [1924] 1 KB 256 . . . 508, 511

R v Warwickshire County Council, *ex p* Collymore [1995] ELR 217 . . . 530

R v Wicks [1998] AC 92 . . . 581

Racal Communications Ltd, Re [1981] AC 374 . . . 503

Rassemblement Jurassien et Unite Jurassienne v Switzerland, Application 8191/78 (1979) 17 DR 93 . . . 859

RAV v City of St Paul, Minnesota (1992) 505 US 377 . . . 841

Raymond v Honey [1983] 1 AC 1 . . . 24

Redmond-Bate v Director of Public Prosecutions [2000] HRLR 249 . . . 879, 887

Reilly v Secretary of State for Work and Pensions [2016] EWCA Civ 413 . . . 623

Resolution to amend the Constitution, Re [1981] 1 SCR 753 . . . 53, 59

Reynolds v Times Newspapers Ltd [2001] 2 AC 127 . . . 838–9

RG (Ethiopia) v Secretary of State for the Home Department [2006] EWCA Civ 339 . . . 711

Ridge v Baldwin [1964] AC 40 . . . 74, 519, 592

Ringeisen v Austria (No 1) (1979–80) 1 EHRR 455 . . . 515

Robson v Hallett [1967] 2 QB 939 . . . 898

Rocknroll v News Group Newspapers Ltd [2013] EWHC 24 (Ch) . . . 850

Roe v Wade 273 410 US 113 (1973) . . . 232

Rowland v Environment Agency [2002] EWCA Civ 1885, [2005] Ch 1 . . . 536

Roy v Kensington and Chelsea and Westminster Family Practitioner Committee [1992] 1 AC 624 . . . 572, 587

Royal Aquarium and Summer and Winter Garden Society Ltd v Parkinson [1892] 1 QB 431 . . . 837

Royal College of Nursing v Department of Health and Social Security [1981] AC 800 . . . 584–5

Russell v Smith [2003] EWHC 2060 (Admin), (2003) 147 SJLB 1118 . . . 145

S (Minors), Re (Care Order: Implementation of Care Plan) [2001] EWCA Civ 757, [2001] 2 FLR 582, [2002] UKHL 10, [2002] 2 AC 291 . . . 783

S v Secretary of State for the Home Department [2006] EWCA Civ 1157 . . . 625

Saadi v UK (2008) 47 EHRR 427 . . . 886

Salduz v Turkey (2009) 49 EHRR 19 . . . 904

Saleem v Home Secretary [2000] Imm AR 529 . . . 683

Salih v Secretary of State for the Home Department [2003] EWHC 2273 (Admin) . . . 146

Saltman Engineering Co Ltd v Campbell Engineering Co Ltd (1948) 65 RPC 203 . . . 847

Salvesen v Riddell [2013] UKSC 22 . . . 301, 327, 790

Sanchez v Spain (2012) 54 EHRR 24 . . . 857

Sanoma Uitgevers BV v Netherlands (2010) 51 EHRR 31 . . . 834

Save Britain's Heritage v Secretary of State for the Environment [1991] 1 WLR 153 . . . 711

Scoppola v Italy (No 3) (2013) 56 EHRR 19 . . . 794

Secretary of State for Defence v Guardian Newspapers Ltd [1985] AC 339 . . . 834

Secretary of State for Education and Science v Tameside Metropolitan Borough Council [1977] AC 1014 . . . 484

Secretary of State for the Home Department v AF (No 3) [2009] UKHL 28, [2009] 3 WLR 74 . . . 507

Secretary of State for the Home Department v Pankina [2010] EWCA Civ 719 . . . 145

Secretary of State for the Home Department v Rehman [2001] UKHL 47, [2003] 1 AC 153 . . . 547

Sharma v Brown-Antoine [2006] UKPC 57, [2007] 1 WLR 780 . . . 568

Shizad v Secretary of State for the Home Department (sufficiency of reasons: set aside) [2013] UKUT 85 (IAC) . . . 711

Short v Poole Corporation [1926] Ch 66 . . . 539

Shrewsbury and Atcham Borough Council v Secretary of State for Communities and Local Government [2008] EWCA Civ 148 . . . 72, 160

Sirros v Moore [1975] QB 118 . . . 281–2

Smith v Scott [2007] CSIH 9 . . . 794

Smith v United Kingdom (2000) 29 EHRR 493 . . . 543–5

Smith and Grady v United Kingdom (2000) 29 EHRR 493 . . . 619–20

South Buckinghamshire District Council v Porter [2004] UKHL 33, [2004] 1 WLR 1953 . . . 525, 711

South East Asia Fire Bricks Sdn Bhd v Non-Metallic Mineral Products Manufacturing Employees Union [1981] AC 363 . . . 501

Sporrong v Sweden (1983) 5 EHRR 35 . . . 516

Spycatcher case see Attorney-General v Observer Ltd

Steel v UK (1999) 28 EHRR 603 . . . 878, 883

Stefan v General Medical Council [1999] 1 WLR 1293 . . . 525

Stephens v Avery [1988] Ch 449 . . . 847

Stockdale v Hansard (1839) 9 Ad & E 1, (1839) 112 ER 1112 . . . 202, 204–5, 209,

Stoll v Switzerland (2008) 47 EHRR 59 . . . 827

Storck v Germany (2006) 43 EHRR 6 . . . 845

Sullivan v The New York Times (1964) 376 US 254 . . . 838–9

Sunday Times v UK (1979–80) 2 EHRR 245 . . . 829, 832

Sunday Times v UK (No 2) (1992) 14 EHRR 229 . . . 834

Taylor v Lawrence [2002] EWCA Civ 90, [2003] QB 528 . . . 513

Theakston v MGN Ltd [2002] EWHC 137, [2002] EMLR 22 . . . 849

Thoburn v Sunderland City Council [2002] EWHC 195 (Admin), [2003] QB 151 . . . 46, 240, 368–9, 372–5

Thornton v Telegraph Media Group Ltd [2010] EWHC 1414 (QB), [2011] 1 WLR 1985 . . . 835

Times Newspapers v UK [2009] EMLR 14 . . . 840

Town Investments Ltd v Department of the Environment [1978] AC 359 . . . 107, 109

Traghetti del Mediterraneo SpA v Italy, Case C-173/03 [2006] ECR I-5177 . . . 355

Transportes Urbanos v Administracion del Estado, Case C-118/08 [2010] 2 CMLR 39 . . . 355

Trim v North Dorset District Council [2011] EWCA Civ 1446, [2011] 1 WLR 1901 . . . 570

Trustees of the Dennis Rye Pension Fund v Sheffield City Council [1998] 1 WLR 840 . . . 570

United Kingdom v Council, Case C-84/94 [1996] ECR I-5755, [1996] 3 CMLR 671 . . . 348

Uppal v United Kingdom (1981) 3 EHRR 391 . . . 516

Uprichard v Scottish Ministers [2013] UKSC 21, 2013 SC (UKSC) 219 . . . 526

V v United Kingdom (2000) 30 EHRR 121 . . . 515

Van Duyn v Home Office (No 2), Case 41/74 [1974] ECR 1337 . . . 350

Van Gend En Loos, Case 26/62 [1963] ECR 1 . . . 348–9

Vauxhall Estates Ltd v Liverpool Corporation [1932] 1 KB 733 . . . 240

Vidal-Hall v Google Inc [2015] EWCA Civ 311, [2015] 3 WLR 409 . . . 847

Von Colson v Land Nordrhein-Westfalen, Case 14/83 [1984] ECR 1891 . . . 353

Von Hannover v Germany (2005) 40 EHRR 1 . . . 849, 851–2

W v United Kingdom (1988) 10 EHRR 29 . . . 516

Wainwright v Home Office [2003] UKHL 53, [2004] 2 AC 406 . . . 803–4

Walton v The Scottish Ministers [2012] UKSC 44, [2013] PTSR 51 . . . 577

Wandsworth London Borough Council v Winder [1985] AC 461 . . . 572

Wason, ex p (1868–69) LR 4 QB 573 . . . 207

Watt v Longsdon [1930] 1 KB 130 . . . 838

Watt v Lord Advocate, 1979 SC 120 . . . 502

Wennhak v Morgan (1888) LR 20 QBD 635 . . . 835

West v Secretary of State for Scotland, 1992 SC 385 . . . 567

Wheeler v Leicester City Council [1985] AC 1054 . . . 765

Wilson v First Country Trust Ltd (No 2) [2003] UKHL 40, [2004] 1 AC 816 . . . 207

Wingrove v United Kingdom (1997) 24
    EHRR 1 . . . 843

X Ltd v Morgan Grampian (Publishers) Ltd
    [1991] 1 AC 1 . . . 834

YL v Birmingham City Council [2007] UKHL
    27, [2008] 1 AC 95 . . . 47, 797–9

Z v UK (2002) 34 EHRR 3 . . . 914
Zumtobel v Austria (1993) 17 EHRR 116 . . . 517

Table of UK Legislation

Primary legislation

Academies Act 2010
  Sch 2, para 10 . . . 455
Access to Medical Records Act 1988 . . . 452
Access to Personal Files Act 1987 . . . 452
Acquisition of Land Act 1919, s 7(1) . . . 240
Acquisition of Land Act 1981
  s 23 . . . 559
  s 25 . . . 559
Act of Settlement 1700, s 3 . . . 173
Administration of Justice Act 1960, s 1 . . . 262
Administration of Justice Act 1969, Pt II . . . 262
Anti-social Behaviour, Crime and Policing Act
  2014 . . . 873, 888
  s 35 . . . 888
  s 59(2) . . . 873
  s 59(3) . . . 873
  s 59(4) . . . 873
  s 59(5) . . . 874
  s 60 . . . 873
  s 62 . . . 874
  s 66 . . . 874
  s 67 . . . 873
  s 67(3) . . . 874
  s 72(1) . . . 874
Anti-terrorism, Crime and Security Act
  2001 . . . 14, 16–19, 196, 225, 230, 792, 821
  Pt 4 . . . 15, 18–19
Asylum and Immigration (Treatment of
  Claimants, etc.) Act 2004 . . . 622
Asylum and Immigration Act 1996 . . . 623

Bill of Rights 1689, Art IX . . . 45, 201, 203, 206,
  208, 210, 372, 838
British North America Act 1867 . . . 52
Broadcasting Act 1990 . . . 823
  s 166 . . . 835
Broadcasting Act 1996, s 107 . . . 23

Canada Act 1982 . . . 59
Channel Tunnel Act 1987 . . . 213
Charities Act 2006, s 6 . . . 135
Children Act 1989 . . . 616, 783
  s 20(1) . . . 505
  s 105(1) . . . 505
Cities and Local Government Devolution Act
  2016 . . . 45, 322
  s 2 . . . 321

s 8 . . . 321
s 15 . . . 321
Sch 3 . . . 321
Civil Contingencies Act 2004 . . . 143–4, 146
  Pt 2 . . . 139
  s 19(1) . . . 144
  s 20(2) . . . 144
  s 22(1) . . . 144
  s 22(3) . . . 144
  s 22(3)(c) . . . 144
  s 22(3)(d)–(e) . . . 44
  s 22(3)(g) . . . 144
  s 22(3)(j) . . . 144
Claim of Right Act 1689 . . . 201
Communications Act 2003
  s 127 . . . 827
  ss 319–320 . . . 187
  ss 319–326 . . . 823
  s 321 . . . 187
  ss 325–326 . . . 823
  s 333 . . . 187
Companies Act 2006, ss 942–965 . . . 564
Constitutional Reform Act 2005 . . . 11, 28–9,
  45, 122–3, 272, 279, 294
  s 1 . . . 65
  s 2 . . . 123, 281
  s 3 . . . 624, 693
  s 3(1) . . . 281
  s 5(1) . . . 281
  s 7(1) . . . 280, 281
  s 24 . . . 274
  s 25 . . . 273
  s 26(3) . . . 274
  s 26(5) . . . 274
  s 27(1B) . . . 74
  s 27(1C) . . . 275
  s 27(5A) . . . 291
  s 33 . . . 282
  s 34(4) . . . 282
  s 36 . . . 282
  s 40 . . . 262
  s 40(4)(b) . . . 263
  s 62 . . . 274
  s 63 . . . 273
  s 63(2) . . . 290
  s 63(4) . . . 291
  s 64(1) . . . 290
  s 68 . . . 274
  s 69 . . . 274

s 73 . . . 274
s 75E . . . 274
s 82 . . . 274
ss 85–93 . . . 699
s 90 . . . 274
s 137A . . . 291
Sch 8 . . . 273
Sch 9 . . . 263
    Pt 2 . . . 327
Sch 13 . . . 274
Sch 14 . . . 699
Constitutional Reform and Governance
    Act 2010
    Pt 1 . . . 157, 397
    Pt 2 . . . 155, 157, 561
    s 5 . . . 164
    s 7(2) . . . 124
    s 7(4) . . . 131, 134
    s 7(5) . . . 133
    s 8(1) . . . 134
    s 8(5) . . . 135
    s 8(6) . . . 135
    s 10 . . . 164
    s 15 . . . 134
    Sch 7, para 3 . . . 55
Contempt of Court Act 1981 . . . 13, 829, 833
    s 1 . . . 829
    s 2(2) . . . 830, 833
    s 2(3) . . . 831
    s 3 . . . 831
    s 4(1) . . . 830
    s 5 . . . 832
    s 6(c) . . . 732
    s 10 . . . 834
    Sch 1, paras 4–5 . . . 31
Coroners and Justice Act 2009, s 62 . . . 843
Counter-Terrorism and Security Act
    2015 . . . 889
County Courts Act 1984, ss 40–42 . . . 262
Courts Act 1971, s 17(4) . . . 283
Courts Reform (Scotland) Act 2014, s 89 . . . 568, 569
Crime (Sentences) Act 1997, s 29 . . . 515, 782
Crime and Courts Act 2013 . . . 275, 291
    s 1(11) . . . 893
    ss 1–16 . . . 893
    s 22 . . . 593, 721
    s 33 . . . 828
    ss 34–42 . . . 826
    s 41(1) . . . 828
    s 41(1)(a) . . . 828
    s 57 . . . 868
    Sch 13, Pt 4 . . . 274
    Sch 15 . . . 828
        para 8 . . . 828
        para 8(4) . . . 828
Criminal Appeal Act 1968
    Pt I . . . 262
    s 33 . . . 262

Criminal Justice Act 1988, s 171(1) . . . 98–9
Criminal Justice and Courts Act 2015 . . . 600, 621
    s 71 . . . 833
    s 84 . . . 579
Criminal Justice and Immigration Act 2008
    s 79(1) . . . 842
    ss 130–137 . . . 625
Criminal Justice and Public Order Act 1994
    s 4 . . . 905
    s 34(2A) . . . 905
Criminal Justice (Terrorism and Conspiracy)
    Act 1998 . . . 225
Criminal Law Act 1967, s 3 . . . 914

Data Protection Act 1984 . . . 452
Data Protection Act 1988, s 6 . . . 685
Data Protection Act 1998 . . . 452, 846
Defamation Act 1996, s 14 . . . 837
Defamation Act 2013 . . . 840
    s 1(1) . . . 835
    s 2(1) . . . 836
    s 3 . . . 837
    s 3(2) . . . 837
    s 3(3) . . . 837
    s 3(4) . . . 837
    s 3(5) . . . 837
    s 4 . . . 839–40
    s 4(1) . . . 839
    s 4(4) . . . 839
    s 5(2) . . . 840
    s 8 . . . 840
    s 14 . . . 837
Dentists Act 1878 . . . 46

Education (Schools) Act 1997 . . . 532
Education Act 1976 . . . 317
Education Act 2002, s 52 . . . 700
Electoral Administration Act 2006,
    ss 17–18 . . . 173
Electoral Registration and Administration
    Act 2013, s 6 . . . 177
Enterprise Act 2002, s 58(2A)–(2B) . . . 827
Enterprise and Regulatory Reform Act 2013,
    s 96 . . . 826
Equality Act 2010 . . . 359, 768, 772
    Sch 17 . . . 620
Equitable Life (Payments) Act 2010 . . . 671,
    674, 676
European Communities Act 1972 . . . 45, 49,
    237, 242, 365, 370, 372–4, 376
    s 2(1) . . . 358–9
    s 2(4) . . . 375–6
European Union Act 2011 . . . 239, 358–9,
    s 2(1) . . . 358–9, 363–4
    s 2(4) . . . 364, 367
    s 18 . . . 363, 366
European Union (Notification of Withdrawal)
    Act 2017 . . . xxi, xxiv

Exchequer and Audit Departments Act
  1866 . . . 446
Export Controls Act 2002 . . . 746

Financial Services (Banking Reform) Act
  2013 . . . 142–3
Fixed-term Parliaments Act 2011 . . . 45, 120,
  172–3, 390
  s 2 . . . 408
Foreign Compensation Act 1950 . . . 501
  s 4(4) . . . 245, 557–8
Freedom of Information Act 2000 . . . 59, 60,
  146, 384, 431, 452–60, 524, 667
  s 1 . . . 454, 524
  s 1(1) . . . 454
  s 2(2)(b) . . . 455
  s 2(3) . . . 455
  s 3 . . . 454
  s 10 . . . 456
  s 12 . . . 455
  s 13 . . . 455
  s 14 . . . 455
  s 19 . . . 454
  s 22 . . . 455
  s 23 . . . 455
  s 24 . . . 455
  s 26 . . . 455
  s 27 . . . 455
  s 29 . . . 455
  s 32 . . . 455
  s 34 . . . 455
  s 35 . . . 455
  s 35(1) . . . 58
  s 36 . . . 55
  s 41 . . . 455
  s 44 . . . 455
  s 50 . . . 456
  s 52 . . . 456
  s 53 . . . 250–1, 456, 458
  s 53(2) . . . 458
  ss 57–59 . . . 456
  s 84 . . . 524
  Sch 1 . . . 454
Freedom of Information (Scotland) Act
  2002 . . . 452

Government of Wales Act 2006 . . . 45
  s A1 . . . 304, 327
  s 1 . . . 305
  ss 37–40 . . . 10
  s 42 . . . 201
  s 45 . . . 305
  ss 46–48 . . . 305
  Sch 9 . . . 327
Greater London Authority Act 1999,
  s 385 . . . 875

Health and Social Care Act 2008, s 145 . . . 799
Health and Social Care Bill 2011 . . . 223

Health Service Commissioners Act 1993 . . . 643
  ss 2–2B . . . 653
  s 3(1) . . . 655, 657–8
  s 3(4)–(6) . . . 655
  s 3(7) . . . 655
  s 4(1) . . . 651–52
  s 18ZA . . . 644
Higher Education Act 2004 . . . 635
Highways Act 1980, s 137 . . . 873
House of Commons Disqualification Act
  1975 . . . 45
  s 1 . . . 173
  s 2(1) . . . 121, 425
House of Lords Act 1999 . . . 27, 45
  s 1 . . . 173
  s 3 . . . 173
Housing Act 1925 . . . 240
Housing Act 1996 . . . 643
  s 204 . . . 690
Human Rights Act 1998 . . . 11, 17, 30–1, 40,
  45, 49, 74, 76–7, 100–2, 113–14, 206, 219, 246,
  252, 263, 266–9, 276, 284, 301, 385–6, 394,
  459, 545, 549–50, 515, 552, 566–7, 574, 597,
  613, 623, 759–60, 765, 767–9, 770, 771–2,
  783–4, 787–8, 790–1, 792, 800–14, 820, 822–3,
  846, 861, 864, 866, 869, 877, 883, 887
  s 1 . . . 76, 813–14
  s 1(1) . . . 771
  s 2(1) . . . 263, 814
  s 3 . . . 76, 585, 775–8, 780–9, 792, 795, 800,
    805–6, 811, 855
  s 3(1) . . . 245, 787
  s 4 . . . 77, 775–8, 785–7, 790, 795,
    811, 897
  s 4(2) . . . 785
  s 4(5) . . . 785
  s 4(6)(a) . . . 786
  s 6 . . . 76, 775, 791, 795–6, 799, 801, 803, 805,
    874, 882, 911, 913
  s 6(1) . . . 47, 795, 799, 801, 804, 813
  s 6(2) . . . 795
  s 6(3) . . . 207, 796, 801
  s 6(3)(b) . . . 796
  s 6(5) . . . 796
  s 7 . . . 805
  s 7(1) . . . 804
  s 7(7) . . . 804
  s 10 . . . 775, 786–7
  s 12(3) . . . 850
  s 19 . . . 774–5, 791
  s 21(1) . . . 788, 790, 813–14
Human Tissue Act 2004 . . . 746
Hunting Act 2004 . . . 238

Immigration Act 1971, s 3(5) . . . 139
Immigration Act 2014 . . . 687
  s 15 . . . 691
  s 63 . . . 691

Immigration and Asylum Act 1999
  s 11(1) . . . 623
  s 60(9)(a) . . . 529
Inquiries Act 2005 . . . 138, 734–5, 737, 739–40,
  742, 745, 747
  s 1(1) . . . 735
  s 2(1) . . . 737
  s 5 . . . 737
  s 6 . . . 737
  s 8 . . . 740
  s 9 . . . 740
  s 11 . . . 739–40
  s 13 . . . 735
  s 14 . . . 735
  s 17(1) . . . 742
  s 17(3) . . . 743
  s 18 . . . 737, 742
  s 19 . . . 737
  s 19(2)(b) . . . 754
  s 19(4) . . . 742
  s 24(1) . . . 745
  s 24(3) . . . 745
  s 25(1)–(2) . . . 745
  s 25(4)–(5) . . . 745
  s 26 . . . 746
  s 38 . . . 743
Insolvency Act 1986, s 426A . . . 173
Instrument of Government 1653 . . . 11
Intellectual Property Act 2014,
  s 20 . . . 455
Intelligence Services Act 1994 . . . 463, 465
  s 1 . . . 463
  s 1(2) . . . 463
  s 3(1) . . . 463
  s 3(2) . . . 463
  s 5 . . . 463
  s 10(3) . . . 466
Interception of Communications Act
  1985 . . . 463
Investigatory Powers Act 2016, s 3 . . . 846

Jobseekers Act 1995 . . . 623
Jobseekers (Back to Work Schemes) Act
  2013 . . . 226, 623
Juries Act 1974, s 20A . . . 833
Justice and Security Act 2013 . . . 452, 462,
  465, 467
  s 1 . . . 465–6
  s 2 . . . 465
  s 2(3) . . . 466
  s 3 . . . 466
  s 3(4) . . . 467
  s 5 . . . 464

Law in Wales Act 1535 . . . 299
Law of Property Act 1925, s 84 . . . 694
Law Reform (Miscellaneous Provisions)
  (Scotland) Act 1990

s 35 . . . 273
Sch 4 . . . 273
Legal Aid, Sentencing and Punishment of
  Offenders Act 2012 . . . 707
  s 10 . . . 707
Licensing Act 2003
  s 1 . . . 822
  Sch 1 . . . 822
Life Peerages Act 1958 . . . 190
Limitation Act 1980, ss 2 and 5 . . . 569
Local Audit and Accountability Act
  2014 . . . 319
Local Democracy, Economic Development and
  Construction Act 2009 . . . 320, 322
  s 107A . . . 321
  Sch 5A
    para 1 . . . 321
    para 3 . . . 321
Local Government Act 1972 . . . 45
Local Government Act 1974 . . . 643
  s 25 . . . 653
  s 26(1) . . . 655
  s 26A(1) . . . 657–8
  s 26(6) . . . 651–2
  s 26(8) . . . 654
  s 26A(1) . . . 657
  s 33ZA . . . 644
  s 34(3) . . . 655
Local Government Act 1985 . . . 316
Local Government Act 1988, s 28 . . . 317
Local Government Act 1999
  s 3(1) . . . 318
  s 15(6)(a) . . . 318
Local Government Act 2000 . . . 45
Local Government (Access to Information) Act
  1985 . . . 452
Local Government and Public Involvement in
  Health Act 2007 . . . 45
Local Government Finance Act 1988, Sch
  11 . . . 685
Local Government Finance Act 1992
  ss 52A–52Y . . . 317
  ss 52ZA–52ZY . . . 317
Localism Act 2011 . . . 45, 317
  s 1 . . . 318
  s 2 . . . 318
  s 5 . . . 318
  s 25 . . . 514
  s 46 . . . 302
London Olympic Games and Paralympic Games
  Act 2006, s 19 . . . 146

Magistrates' Courts Act 1980
  s 1 . . . 900
  s 108 . . . 261
  s 111 . . . 262
Magna Carta (1297) . . . 45
  Ch 29 . . . 600

Mental Capacity Act 2005 . . . 572
Mental Health Act 1983
  Pt 5 . . . 686
  s 118(1) . . . 145
Mental Health Act 1988, s 118(1) . . . 146
Mental Health Act 2007 . . . 686
Merchant Shipping Act 1988 . . . 364–5,
  367–8, 376
Ministers of the Crown Act 1975 . . . 108
  s 8(1) . . . 121

National Assistance Act 1948 . . . 797–9
National Audit Act 1983
  s 1(2) . . . 446
  s 6(2) . . . 446
  s 8 . . . 446
National Health Service Act 1977, ss 2 and
  84 . . . 734
Nationality, Immigration and Asylum Act 2002,
  s 55 . . . 154
Northern Ireland Act 1998 . . . 45
  s 1 . . . 300
  ss 5–8 . . . 301
  s 6(2)(b) . . . 301
  s 6(2)(c)–(d) . . . 301
  s 7 . . . 301
  s 16A . . . 305
  s 18 . . . 305
  ss 44–45 . . . 210
  s 50 . . . 201
  Sch 2 . . . 301
  Sch 10 . . . 327

Obscene Publications Act 1959
  s 1(1)–(2) . . . 844
  s 2(1) . . . 844
  s 4(1) . . . 844
Official Secrets Act 1911, s 1 . . . 852
Official Secrets Act 1989 . . . 465, 667, 852, 855
  s 1 . . . 465
  ss 1–4 . . . 853, 855
  s 7 . . . 853

Parliament Acts 1911–49 . . . 45, 152, 191–3, 216,
  224–5, 236, 238, 241–2
Parliament Act 1911 . . . 58, 193
  preamble . . . 27
  s 1 . . . 192
  s 1(1) . . . 192, 238
  s 2(1) . . . 192, 238
Parliamentary Commissioner Act 1967 . . . 643,
  645–7, 667, 672–3
  s 4(1) . . . 653
  s 4(2) . . . 653
  s 5(1) . . . 648, 655
  s 5(1)(a) . . . 655–6, 658
  s 5(1A) . . . 648, 655
  s 5(1B) . . . 655

s 5 (1C) . . . 655
s 5(2) . . . 652
s 5(3) . . . 654
s 7(1) . . . 666
s 7(2) . . . 667
s 8(1) . . . 666
s 8(2) . . . 666
s 8(3) . . . 667
s 8(4) . . . 667
s 10(1)–(2) . . . 667
s 10(3) . . . 647, 650, 669, 671
s 10(4) . . . 647, 667
s 11(2)(b) . . . 667
s 11ZAA . . . 644
s 12(3) . . . 655
Sch 2 . . . 653, 655
Sch 3 . . . 654
  para 9 . . . 654
Parliamentary Constituencies Act 1986
  s 1 . . . 174
  Sch 2
    para 1 . . . 177
    para 2 . . . 177
Parliamentary Papers Act 1840 . . . 211
  s 1 . . . 202, 838
  s 2 . . . 202
  s 3 . . . 202
Parliamentary Standards Act 2009 . . . 428, 456
Parliamentary Voting System and
  Constituencies Act 2011 . . . 177
Police (Northern Ireland) Act 2000
  s 1 . . . 893
  s 33 . . . 893
Police Act 1996 . . . 734
  s 1 . . . 893
  s 2 . . . 893
  s 5A . . . 893
  s 6 . . . 909
  s 49 . . . 734
  s 88 . . . 914
  s 89(2) . . . 882
  Sch 1, para 1 . . . 893
Police and Criminal Evidence Act 1984 . . . 895,
  899, 903
  Pt V . . . 903
  s 1 . . . 895–6
  s 1(2) . . . 895
  s 1(3) . . . 895
  s 1(7) . . . 895
  s 8 . . . 898
  s 8(1) . . . 898
  s 8(1A) . . . 899
  s 8(1C) . . . 899
  s 8(2) . . . 899
  s 8(3) . . . 898
  s 10 . . . 898
  s 11 . . . 898
  s 14 . . . 898

s 17 . . . 899
s 17(1) . . . 899
s 17(2)(a) . . . 899
s 17(5) and (6) . . . 899
s 18 . . . 899
s 18(1) . . . 899
s 18(2) . . . 899
s 18(4) . . . 899
s 24 . . . 900
s 24(5) . . . 900
s 24A . . . 900
s 28 . . . 901
s 30(1A) . . . 901
s 32(2)(b) . . . 899
s 32(6) . . . 899
s 39 . . . 903
s 40 . . . 902
s 41 . . . 901
s 42 . . . 901–2
s 43 . . . 901–2
s 44 . . . 901–2
s 54 . . . 903
s 54A . . . 903
s 55 . . . 903
s 56(1) . . . 903
s 58 . . . 904
s 60 . . . 897
s 60(1) . . . 903
s 60A . . . 903
s 61 . . . 904
s 62 . . . 904
s 76 . . . 912
s 76(2) . . . 912
s 76(8) . . . 912
s 78 . . . 912–13
s 82(1) . . . 912
s 88 . . . 914
s 117 . . . 914
Police and Fire Reform (Scotland) Act 2012,
    s 6 . . . 893
Police Reform Act 2002 . . . 635
    Pt 2A . . . 908
    s 10 . . . 906
    Sch 3
        para 4A . . . 906
        para 13A . . . 906
        para 14CA . . . 906
        para 15(4A)–(4C) . . . 907
        para 23 . . . 908
Police Reform and Social Responsibility Act
    2011 . . . 909–10
    s 1 . . . 909
    s 2 . . . 893
    s 2(3) . . . 910
    s 3 . . . 909
    s 4 . . . 893
    ss 5–8 . . . 909

s 5(6) . . . 910
s 8(2) . . . 909
ss 21–25 . . . 909
s 26 . . . 909
s 28 . . . 910
s 29 . . . 910
s 30 . . . 910
ss 32–33 . . . 910
s 38 . . . 909
s 79 . . . 910
s 141(1) . . . 875
ss 142–148 . . . 875
Sch 5 . . . 909
    para 4 . . . 910
Sch 6 . . . 910
Sch 8
    Pt 1 . . . 910
    Pt 2 . . . 910
Policing and Crime Act 2017 . . . 638, 905
Political Parties, Elections and Referendums
    Act 2000
    s 3 . . . 177
    s 5 . . . 187
    s 6 . . . 188
    s 12 . . . 186
    s 13 . . . 188
    s 14 . . . 188
    s 54 . . . 185
    s 62 . . . 185
    s 71M . . . 185
    s 79 . . . 187
    s 145 . . . 187
    Sch 3 . . . 187
Prison Act 1952 . . . 20–1
Protection from Harassment Act 1997 . . . 868
    s 1(1) . . . 869
    s 1(1A) . . . 869
    s 1(3) . . . 869
    s 2(1) . . . 869
    s 3 . . . 868
    s 3A . . . 868
    s 4(1) . . . 868–9
    s 4(2) . . . 869
    s 7(2) . . . 869
    ss 8–11 . . . 868
Protection of Children Act 1978, s 1 . . . 843
Protection of Children Act 1999, s 9 . . . 686
Protection of Freedoms Act 2012, s 103 . . . 455
Public Bodies Act 2011 . . . 137–8, 437
Public Order Act 1936, s 5 . . . 865
Public Order Act 1986 . . . 842–3, 869, 873–4,
    877, 883
    Pt I . . . 865
    ss 1–3 . . . 865
    s 4 . . . 865–8
    s 4A . . . 865–8
    s 5 . . . 865–8, 889

ss 11–13 . . . 876
ss 11–14C . . . 884
s 11(1) . . . 876
s 11(7) . . . 876
s 12 . . . 876, 888
s 13(1) . . . 876
s 13(2)–(4) . . . 876
s 13(7)–(8) . . . 876
s 14 . . . 870–1, 876
s 14(1) . . . 871
s 14(2) . . . 870
s 14(4) . . . 871
s 14(5) . . . 871
s 14A . . . 871–2
s 14A(1) . . . 871–2
s 14A(2)–(4) . . . 872
s 14A(5) . . . 872
s 14A(9) . . . 871
s 14B(1)–(2) . . . 872
s 16 . . . 870
s 17 . . . 841
ss 18–23 . . . 841
s 29A . . . 842
ss 29AB–29F . . . 43
ss 29B–29F . . . 842
s 29J . . . 842
Public Order and Criminal Justice Act 1994,
    s 60 . . . 896
Public Records Act 1958 . . . 452
Public Services Ombudsman Act (Northern
    Ireland) 2016 . . . 642
    s 5 . . . 648
    s 5(1) . . . 657
    s 21 . . . 651
    ss 20–22 . . . 654
    s 23 . . . 655
    s 23(3)(a) . . . 652
    s 46 . . . 647
    s 46(2) . . . 647
    ss 52–53 . . . 672
    ss 54–55 . . . 672
    Sch 3 . . . 653
    Sch 5 . . . 654
Public Services Ombudsman (Wales) Act
    2005 . . . 642
    s 4 . . . 648
    s 4(1) . . . 657–8
    s 7(1) . . . 655
    s 9(1) . . . 651
    s 9(2) . . . 652
    s 10 . . . 654
    s 11(1) . . . 655
    s 11(2) . . . 655
    s 24 . . . 647
    s 31 . . . 645
    Sch 1, para 14 . . . 647
    Sch 3 . . . 653

Public Services Reform (Scotland) Act 2010,
    s 119 . . . 681

Racial and Religious Hatred Act
    2006 . . . 842
Railways and Transport Safety Act 2003,
    Pt 3 . . . 893
Regulation of Investigatory Powers Act
    2000 . . . 72, 463
    Pt 1 . . . 160
    s 57 . . . 118, 464
    s 59 . . . 118, 464
    s 59A . . . 464
    s 65 . . . 464
Rent Act 1977 . . . 778–82, 799
    Sch 1, para 2 . . . 778
Representation of the People Act 1918 . . . 174
Representation of the People Act
    1983 . . . 45, 173
    s 1 . . . 173
    s 3 . . . 73
    s 3(1) . . . 794
    s 3A . . . 173
    s 75 . . . 187
    s 76 . . . 186
    s 90ZA . . . 186
    s 91 . . . 186
    s 113 . . . 188
    s 120 . . . 188
    s 121 . . . 188
    s 122 . . . 188
    s 144 . . . 188
    s 160 . . . 173
    Sch 4A . . . 186
Revenue and Customs Act 2005
    s 8 . . . 136
    s 11 . . . 136
Road Traffic Act 1991, s 73 . . . 686
Road Traffic Act 1998, s 38(7) . . . 145
Road Traffic Regulation Act 1984 . . . 141

School Standards and Framework Act 1998,
    s 94 . . . 686
Scotland Act 1998 . . . 45
    ss 23–26 . . . 210
    s 28(7) . . . 327
    s 28(8) . . . 58, 61, 327
    ss 28–30 . . . 301
    s 29(2)(b) . . . 301
    s 29(2)(c) . . . 301
    s 29(2)(d) . . . 301
    s 41 . . . 201
    ss 45–46 . . . 304
    s 47 . . . 304
    s 52 . . . 304
    s 53 . . . 304
    s 63A . . . 304

s 63A(1) . . . 328
s 63A(2) . . . 328
s 63A(3) . . . 329
s 95(6)–(10) . . . 282
Sch 4 . . . 301
Sch 5 . . . 301
Sch 6 . . . 327
Scotland Act 2012, Pt 3 . . . 302
Scotland Act 2016 . . . 80, 302, 303, 329, 333
s 1 . . . 35, 301, 328–9
s 2 . . . 58, 61, 327
Scottish Public Services Ombudsman Act
2002 . . . 642
s 5(3) . . . 657–8
s 7(1) . . . 655
s 7(2) . . . 655
s 7(8) . . . 651–2
s 8 . . . 654
s 9 . . . 648
s 15 . . . 647
s 16 . . . 647
Sch 2 . . . 653
Security Service Act 1989 . . . 463
s 1 . . . 463
s 1(2) . . . 463
s 3 . . . 463
Senior Courts Act 1981 . . . 45, 261, 575
s 2 . . . 291
s 4 . . . 291
s 5 . . . 263
s 5(A) . . . 580
s 10(3)(a) . . . 273
s 10(3)(b) . . . 273
s 11(3) . . . 282
s 11(8) . . . 282
s 12(3) . . . 282
s 16(1) . . . 262
s 28 . . . 261
s 31 . . . 567, 592
s 31(1) . . . 580
s 31(2A) . . . 579
s 31(2B) . . . 579
s 31(3) . . . 573
s 31(3A)–(3D) . . . 579
s 31(5)(a) . . . 580
s 31(5)(b) . . . 580
s 31(5A) . . . 580
s 31(6) . . . 569–70
s 31A(3) . . . 721
Septennial Act 1715 . . . 45, 171
Serious Organised Crime and Police Act 2005,
ss 132–138 . . . 875
Social Security Act 1998 . . . 727
Pt 1 . . . 686
Statutory Instruments Act 1946
s 2(1) . . . 146
s 3(2) . . . 147

Suicide Act 1961 . . . 547

Terrorism Act 2000 . . . 896–7, 902
s 41 . . . 902–3
s 41(3) . . . 903
s 44(3) . . . 897
s 47A(1) . . . 98
Sch 8 . . . 902
para 7 . . . 904
para 8 . . . 903, 904
para 38 . . . 902
Terrorism Act 2006 . . . 216
Terrorist Asset-freezing (Temporary Provisions)
Act 2010 . . . 245
Town and Country Planning Act 1990,
s 76A . . . 139
Transport (London) Act 1969, s 1 . . . 606
Treason Felony Act 1848 . . . 585
Tribunals, Courts and Enforcement Act
2007 . . . 45, 399, 682–4, 692–4, 699, 704, 717,
720–1, 726
s 1 . . . 693
s 2 . . . 698
s 2(3) . . . 698
s 3 . . . 694
s 3(4) . . . 698
s 3(5) . . . 694
ss 9–10 . . . 718
s 11 . . . 694, 717
s 11(5) . . . 718
s 12 . . . 718
s 13 . . . 719
s 13(6) . . . 720
s 14 . . . 719
s 15 . . . 721
s 15(1) . . . 722
s 16 . . . 722
s 22(1) . . . 704
s 22(4) . . . 705
s 23 . . . 705
s 37 . . . 696
s 39(1) . . . 694
s 43 . . . 698
s 50 . . . 699
Sch 2, paras 3–4 . . . 283
Sch 3, paras 3–4 . . . 283
Sch 7 . . . 726
para 13(4) . . . 699
Tribunals and Inquiries Act 1958 . . . 684
Tribunals and Inquiries Act 1992
s 1 . . . 699
s 10 . . . 524
s 11 . . . 717
Tribunals of Inquiry (Evidence) Act 1921 . . . 734
s 1(1) . . . 734, 742
Tribunals (Scotland) Act 2014 . . . 696

Union with Ireland Act 1800 . . . 45, 299
Union with Scotland Act 1706 . . . 45–6, 299
United Nations Act 1946, s 1(1) . . . 244–5

Wales Act 2014 . . . 303
Wales Act 2017 . . . 303, 304, 328, 333
  s 1 . . . 304, 327
War Damage Act 1965 . . . 623
Welfare Reform Act 2012 . . . 699
  s 102 . . . 699

Secondary legislation

A5 Trunk Road (Llangollen, Denbighshire)
  (Temporary 40 mph Speed Limit)
  Order 2016, SI 2016/567 . . . 141
Access to Justice Act 1999 (Destination of
  Appeals) Order 2000, SI 2000/1071
  art 3(1) . . . 262
  art 4 . . . 262
Act of Sederunt (Rules of the Court of Session
  1994) 1994, SI 1994/1443
  ch 58 . . . 567, 572
  r 58(3) . . . 568
Al-Qaida and Taliban (United Nations
  Measures) Order 2006, SI 2006/
  2952 . . . 244
Appeals from the Upper Tribunal to the
  Court of Appeal Order 2008, SI 2008/2834,
  para 2 . . . 720
Asylum and Immigration Tribunal (Procedure)
  (Amendment) Rules 2007, SI 2007/835,
  r 2 . . . 619

Civil Enforcement of Parking Contraventions
  (England) General Regulations 2007,
  SI 2007/3483 . . . 686
Civil Procedure Rules 1998, SI 1998/3132
  Pt 3, r 1(2) . . . 569
  Pt 21 . . . 572
  Pt 30, r 3 . . . 262
  Pt 54 . . . 592, 688
  r 4 . . . 568
  r 5(1)(a) . . . 569
  r 5(1)(b) . . . 569
  r 5(5)–(6) . . . 569
  r 17 . . . 577
  r 20 . . . 572, 577
Civil Procedure (Amendment No 4) Rules 2013,
  SI 2013/1412 . . . 600

Civil Service (Amendment) Order in Council
  1997 . . . 135
Civil Service (Amendment) (No 2) Order in
  Council 2007 . . . 135

Defamation (Operators of Websites)
  Regulations 2013, SI 2013/3028 . . . 840

Environmental Information Regulations 1992,
  SI 1992/3240 . . . 452

Freedom of Information (Designation as Public
  Authorities) Order 2011, SI 2011/2598 . . . 455
Freedom of Information (Designation as Public
  Authorities) Order 2015, SI 2015/851 . . . 455
Freedom of Information and Data Protection
  (Appropriate Limit and Fees) Regulations
  2004, SI 2004/3244 . . . 455

High Court and County Courts Jurisdiction
  Order 1991, SI 1991/724 . . . 262

Inquiry Rules 2006, SI 2006/1838
  rr 10–11 . . . 742
  r 13 . . . 744
  r 17 . . . 745

Police and Criminal Evidence Act 1984 (Codes
  of Practice) (Code E) Order 2003, SI 2003/
  705 . . . 903
Policing Protocol Order 2011, SI 2011/
  2744 . . . 910
Prison Rules 1999, SI 1999/728 . . . 21

Rules of the Supreme Court (Amendment No 3)
  1977, SI 1977/1955, Order 53 . . . 592

Statutory Instruments Regulations 1947,
  SI 1948/1 . . . 146
Supreme Court (Judicial Appointments)
  Regulations 2013, SI 2013/2193
  r 18 . . . 275
  r 20 . . . 275

Terrorism (United Nations Measures) Order
  2006, SI 2006/2657 . . . 244
Transfer of Functions (Immigration Appeals)
  Order 1987, SI 1987/465 . . . 693
Tribunal Procedure (First-tier Tribunal) (Social
  Entitlement Chamber) Rules 2008, SI 2008/
  2685, rr 33–34 . . . 710

Table of European and International Legislation

Australian Parliamentary Privileges Act 1987, s 7(1) . . . 210

Basic Law for the Federal Republic of Germany (1949), Art 33 . . . 397

Canadian Constitution . . . 52
Convention on the Rights of the Child . . . 813
Council Directive 2006/112/EC . . . 342

Directive 2001/95/EC . . . 342
Directive 2003/87/EC . . . 342
Directive 2003/88/EC . . . 342
Directive 2006/54/EC . . . 342

EU Charter of Fundamental Rights . . . 362
    Art 31(2) . . . 357
European Convention on Human Rights
    (ECHR) . . . 14–15, 31, 49, 76–7, 164, 174, 207,
    219, 286, 300, 515, 585, 608, 771, 775–6, 778,
    780–1, 783–4, 789, 790–7, 799, 800–4, 805,
    807–14, 829, 855, 864, 868, 875, 879, 882–3,
    887, 913
    Art 1 . . . 771, 793, 814
    Arts 2–12 . . . 771
    Art 2 . . . 735–6, 772
    Art 3 . . . 624, 685, 717, 772, 806–7, 912
    Art 4 . . . 772
    Art 5 . . . 209, 685, 772, 792, 804, 884–7
    Art 5(1) . . . 901
    Art 5(1)(a) . . . 901
    Art 5(2) . . . 901
    Art 5(3) . . . 901
    Art 6 . . . 209–10, 276, 525, 707, 772, 782, 829,
        904, 914
    Art 6(1) . . . 515–17
    Art 7 . . . 773
    Art 8 . . . 160, 463, 543, 685, 773, 779, 783,
        798, 800, 803, 822, 845–6, 850–1, 869, 897
    Art 8(1) . . . 773, 801
    Art 8(2) . . . 543–4, 801, 846, 850, 897
    Art 9 . . . 773
    Art 10 . . . 101, 773, 813, 820–1, 823–4, 828,
        834–5, 840–1, 843, 845–6, 850, 853, 855,
        862, 869, 874, 884
    Art 10(1) . . . 820–2
    Art 10(2) . . . 820–1, 823, 843, 846, 856, 866
    Art 11 . . . 773, 861–4, 869, 871, 874, 876, 884
    Art 11(1) . . . 861

Art 11(2) . . . 861–2, 866
Art 12 . . . 773
Art 14 . . . 771–2, 774, 779, 806
Art 19 . . . 771
Art 33 . . . 771
Art 34 . . . 771, 804
Art 41 . . . 771
Art 46 . . . 63, 793
Art 46(1) . . . 771, 814
Protocol 1 . . . 771–2, 813
    Art 1 . . . 771–2, 774, 898
    Art 2 . . . 771–2, 774
    Art 3 . . . 771–2, 774
Protocol 4, Art 2 . . . 885
Protocol 12 . . . 772
Protocol 13 . . . 772, 813
Art 1 . . . 774
European Social Charter . . . 813

French Declaration of the Rights of Man and
    Citizen 1789, Art 6 . . . 397

International Covenant on Civil and Political
    Rights . . . 813

Regulation (EC) No 1/2003 . . . 342
Regulation (EC) No 261/2004 . . . 342

South African Constitution . . . 8

Treaty of Lisbon . . . 341–2, 346
Treaty of Paris . . . 340–1
Treaty of Rome . . . 341, 363
Treaty on European Union (TEU) . . . 341
    Art 3 . . . 339
    Art 4(3) . . . 353
    Art 5 . . . 348
    Art 5(3) . . . 346
    Art 6(1) . . . 362
    Art 6(2) . . . 771
    Art 6(3) . . . 771
    Art 11(4) . . . 346
    Art 15 . . . 344
    Art 16(1) . . . 343
    Art 16(2) . . . 343
    Art 16(4) . . . 345
    Art 16(6) . . . 343
    Art 16(9) . . . 344
    Art 17(4) . . . 343

Art 18(3) . . . 344
Art 50 . . . 371
Protocol on the Principles of Subsidiarity and
    Proportionality, Arts 6–7 . . . 346
Protocol on the Role of National Parliaments
    in the EU . . . 346
Treaty on the Functioning of the European
    Union (TFEU) . . . 341
    Art 4(3) . . . 342
    Art 4(4) . . . 342
    Art 18 . . . 342
    Art 30 . . . 347, 349
    Art 49 . . . 364
    Art 145 . . . 349

Arts 191–192 . . . 347
Art 254 . . . 347
Art 258 . . . 343
Art 263 . . . 343
Art 267 . . . 348
Art 288 . . . 349–51, 356
Arts 289–294 . . . 343
Art 294 . . . 343–4

UN Security Council Resolution 1373,
    para 1(c) . . . 244
United States Constitution . . . 9–10, 92, 94,
    230–2, 247, 324, 819
    Art 5 . . . 10, 324

PART I

Introduction
to Public Law

1

Constitutions and Constitutional Law

1. Introduction	3
2. Constitutions	4
3. Case studies	14
4. Conclusions	32
Expert commentary	33
Further reading	35

1. Introduction

People often say that the United Kingdom does not have a constitution. They are wrong. It may not have a *written* constitution, in the sense of a single document entitled 'The Constitution'. Nonetheless, the UK undoubtedly has a constitution. What, though, is a constitution? And what are constitutions for?

No organisation can work effectively without ground rules setting out who is responsible for doing particular things, how they should do them, and what should happen if things go wrong. This is true of companies, schools, and universities, and even of sporting clubs and debating societies. Does the head teacher have the authority to compel science teachers to teach creationism? (And, if she has no such authority, but tries to do so anyway, what can be done?) Who gets a say in appointing the head of a university? Can the chair of the debating society be removed if she tries to stifle open discussion and, if so, how? In the absence of rules providing for eventualities such as these, a number of risks arise. Without an effective mechanism for bringing him into line or getting rid of him, a dictatorial leader may be able to carry on unchecked. Chaos might reign if there is no accepted way of deciding who should be in charge and what should be done if that person misbehaves. People might end up being treated in ways that are widely considered to be unacceptable if the authority of those in power is not subject to appropriate and effective limits.

Such circumstances are undesirable in most walks of life, but they are particularly undesirable when it comes to the running of a country. If someone dislikes how his company or club or university is governed, there are at least the options—albeit ones that might be practically difficult to take—of walking away or of joining another organisation. But, short of emigration, people do not have that option if the country is governed badly or corruptly.

For that reason (and, as we will see, many others), it is especially important that transparent, widely accepted rules exist concerning the arrangements for governing the country and for changing how it is run—and by whom—if a particular government, or an aspect of the system of government, is felt to be deficient. How is the Prime Minister chosen? How often must elections be held? If no political party wins a clear majority in an election, how do we decide who should form the next government? Can the government sack the judges if the courts give Ministers a hard time? To what extent can the government intervene in people's lives, including by restricting their fundamental rights, in order to promote what it considers to be the common good? For example, can the government put people in prison because it thinks that they are at risk of committing serious criminal offences, or torture people to extract confessions, or are people entitled not to be treated in such ways?

Questions like these raise issues relating to how the country is run, the powers of those in government, and the rights of those of us who are governed. These issues are fundamental. They are the concern of public law. And they are the sort of questions with which we will engage in this book.

2. Constitutions

In most countries, many of the ground rules concerning how governments are formed, what their powers are, and what rights citizens have are found in written constitutions. In the absence of that type of constitution, the position is different in the UK. But the ground rules nevertheless exist—and so too, therefore, does a constitution (of sorts). Among the key purposes of this book are explaining what those ground rules are in the UK and subjecting them to critical assessment. First, however, we must consider what constitutions are *for*.

At a very basic level, a constitution serves the same purpose as any other set of rules. It anticipates issues that may arise—the resignation of a Prime Minister, an attempt by the government to suppress freedom of speech, a row between central and devolved governments about who is responsible for doing what—and says what should happen when they do, or at least provides mechanisms by which such matters might be resolved. However, constitutions also serve a number of specific functions and possess a number of particular characteristics that distinguish them from ordinary rules and laws.[1] In sections 2.1–2.4, we examine these functions and characteristics in *general* terms by considering how constitutions typically work. Later in the

---

[1] See, eg Feldman, 'None, One or Several? Perspectives on the UK's Constitution(s)' [2005] CLJ 329.

chapter, our focus shifts to the *specific* features of the UK constitution. By proceeding in this way, we can begin to appreciate what is distinctive about the UK's constitutional arrangements.

2.1 **Power allocation**

Many legal rules are concerned with regulating the conduct of *private parties*: individuals, companies, and so on. For example, the criminal law stipulates that certain things—such as intentionally killing someone—may generally not be lawfully done, and specifies what punishment may be applied to offenders. And the law of tort says that people must take reasonable care to avoid causing foreseeable harm to those liable to be affected by their actions, otherwise they may have to pay compensation. In contrast, the pre-eminent function of a constitution is to allocate *state* power—that is, the power to do things such as make laws (such as legislation), exercise governmental power (such as administer government programmes), and determine disputes between people (through the judicial process). These are things that ordinary people cannot do, either for practical reasons (if you were to say that you had made a 'law', everyone would ignore it) or because it would be unlawful if they did (if you were to lock someone in your cellar because they had stolen from you, you would be acting unlawfully). In contrast, the state has both the legal power (because it is given such power by the constitution) and the practical wherewithal to do such things. If the state body responsible for making law says that something is illegal and, if committed, is punishable by several years' imprisonment, most people will sit up and take notice.

One of the functions of a constitution, then, is to allocate state power. From this general point, three more specific points arise.

First, constitutions generally do not simply allocate power to 'the government': they *divide powers among different institutions of government*. These divisions are usually along functional lines. In most systems, there is a legislative branch that is authorised to make law, an executive branch that is empowered to implement the law, and a judicial branch that is responsible for determining disputes about the interpretation and application of the law. It is, as we will see, the function of the constitution to determine precisely where these dividing lines should be situated, how rigidly they should be enforced, and what should happen if they are crossed.

Second, along with these 'vertical' dividing lines (so-called for reasons that Figure 1.1 makes apparent),[2] constitutions generally also *divide power horizontally*— that is, they allocate power to different tiers of government. For example, in the UK, government power is shared (at least for now) between the European Union (EU), the UK government, the governments of the devolved nations, and local authorities.

Third, a key function of most constitutions is to lay down not only the internal divisions of power within government, but also to determine *where government power*

---

[2] Vertical dividing lines are shown in Figure 1.1 only in respect of central government. Although some such dividing lines exist in relation to other levels of government, they tend to be drawn in rather different ways, as we explain in Chapters 7 and 8, in which we deal with the European Union, devolution, and local government.

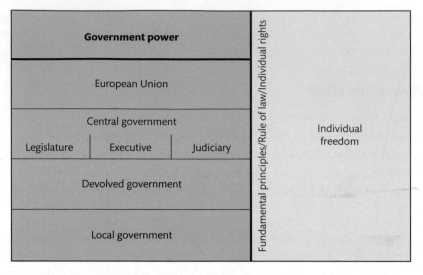

Figure 1.1 Government power and individual freedom

stops and individual freedom begins. There are a number of ways of thinking about this matter.

We might say that what government can do is limited by *fundamental constitutional principles* (or what are sometimes referred to as the principles of 'the rule of law'). An example will help to illustrate this point. Assume that, on 1 February 2017, a blogger publishes a post that is strongly critical of government policy. On 1 March 2017, a new government is elected and immediately enacts a law that, *with retrospective effect*, makes criticism of government policy a criminal offence. This means that people, like the blogger in our example, who engaged in criticism *before* the new law was enacted will still be guilty of the new criminal offence, even though it did not exist when the relevant conduct occurred.

This type of law, known as 'retroactive criminal legislation', is unconstitutional in many countries—that is, the legislature is not constitutionally authorised to enact such legislation. Why? Because it offends against the fundamental principle of legal certainty, which says that people should have the opportunity to know what the law is so that they can make informed choices about whether to conform to it and thus avoid legal liability.

In many countries, denying people that sort of choice is regarded as so unfair that the constitution prohibits the enactment of legislation that would have such an effect. There are many other principles that might, and in many countries do, similarly limit government power. What those principles are is presently unimportant;[3] the point, for now, is simply that constitutions often restrict what the state can do by denying government the power to infringe such principles.

---

[3] We discuss such principles in Chapter 2.

Alternatively, or additionally, the constitutional limits of government authority may be characterised in terms of *individuals' rights*. In many legal systems, the constitution confers fundamental human rights on people and provides that the government must not interfere with those rights. For example, the constitution might give people a right to free speech—the corollary of which will be that the government is denied constitutional authority to make laws (or do other things) criminalising (or otherwise limiting) free speech.[4] Viewed in this way, our imaginary law criminalising criticism of the government would be unconstitutional because it strikes at the very heart of freedom of expression. Thus the fundamental rights of the individual can, and in many countries do, limit the scope of government power: they determine the position of the line dividing areas in which the government has the constitutional power to act and those in which individuals are free to do as they please.

2.2 Accountability

It has been said that 'Power tends to corrupt, and absolute power corrupts absolutely'.[5] There is more than a grain of truth in this. If someone is given extensive power to do as he wishes, he might exercise it wisely and selflessly. But he might—because he is incompetent, badly advised, or downright corrupt—make imprudent or self-serving decisions. An employer fearful of such conduct on the part of employees will seek to guard against it by carefully vetting people before appointing them. But the employer could also monitor the performance of her employees by requiring them to account for how they are spending their time and checking to see whether their work is of an acceptable standard.

Politicians in charge of a government go through a very public form of vetting procedure in the form of elections. Their jobs are not secure—they must submit themselves to re-election periodically. However, the sheer amount of power wielded by government, and the importance of the tasks with which it is entrusted, mean that it would be extremely unwise to leave politicians to their own devices for the periods of several years that normally elapses between elections. A government might, for instance, use its armed forces to invade another country in breach of international law.[6] Alternatively, a government might introduce a new benefits system with a flawed design which results in incorrect payments running to several billions of pounds.[7] In such circumstances, most people would consider it desirable, if not imperative, to have systems in place enabling those responsible to be identified, making them explain themselves, requiring them to put things right (where possible), enabling them to learn lessons for the future, and providing redress in the event of unlawful, as opposed to merely unwise, government action. All of these enterprises fall under the broad heading of *accountability*. A key purpose of a democratic constitution is

[4] Of course, this depends on what is contained within the right to free speech and whether it is subject to any limits—see Chapter 19.

[5] Acton, Letter to Bishop Mandell Creighton, 3 April 1887.

[6] As has been said to be the case in respect of the invasion of Iraq in 2003.

[7] As in the case of the tax credits system: see House of Commons Public Accounts Committee, *HM Revenue and Customs: Tax Credits and Income Tax* (HC 311 2008–09).

to ensure that those entrusted with power exercise it responsibly and are called to account when they do not.

2.3 Legitimacy and consensus

The fact that a country has a constitution and is governed in accordance with it does not necessarily guarantee *good* government. A constitution might, for example, ascribe very broad powers to the government, and accord very few rights to individuals, making the state capable of lawfully doing things that most people in the country concerned would consider unacceptable. There are many such constitutions to be found around the world. Within the democratic tradition, however, the purpose of a constitution is not only to allocate power; it is also to allocate power *in a manner that is regarded as morally acceptable.*

This view of the purpose of constitutions conceals a number of important value judgements. Key amongst them, however, is that people are not objects to be governed by those in power. Instead, each individual is to be recognised as an autonomous, morally valuable being, whose views are worthy of respect (or at least of being heard). Respecting individual autonomy does not, however, mean that everyone can do as they wish. People's desires inevitably conflict—one person may like to play very loud music at 2.00 am; her neighbour may like a good night's sleep—and so law is used as a means of ensuring that the exercise of a given person's autonomy does not unreasonably impact on others. Such laws are legitimate not because everyone necessarily agrees with them, but because those responsible for making, implementing, and adjudicating on such laws have been authorised to do so via a democratic process.[8]

One of the main purposes of a constitution is to put in place a set of arrangements that enjoys popular legitimacy, which enables the people of a given country to be governed in a way that they regard as acceptable, and which thereby renders legitimate the exercise of power by the institutions of government. There are a number of practical ways in which a constitution may be imbued with this sort of legitimacy.

The most obvious and transparent way is to have a genuinely inclusive national debate about what the constitution should say and then to secure popular approval of the new constitution through a referendum or some other democratic process. Such an approach was followed in South Africa in the 1990s as it emerged from the shadow of apartheid.[9] Constitutions thus derive legitimacy from the fact that they reflect some sort of consensus about how the country should be governed, and about where the line should be drawn between the powers of the government and the autonomy of the individual.

But is it really possible to achieve such a consensus in practice? Within most societies, there will be sharp divisions of opinion about what the government should do and how it should do it. Should the state provide health care that is funded from general taxation and free at the point of access, or should people pay for their own

---

[8] Democracy itself is a complex and contested notion. We explore its different possible meanings in Chapter 5.

[9] The new constitution was endorsed not in a referendum but by the South African Parliament.

health insurance? Should the main purpose of the criminal justice system be deterring criminality through harsh punishment or rehabilitating offenders by helping them to rebuild their lives?

Democratic politics is premised on the assumption that disagreements like these exist, and on the resulting need to make provision for choosing between competing visions of how the country should be governed. If consensus is generally so hard to achieve, how is it attained in relation to constitutions (in which context, we have noted, consensus is all-important)? Here, two crucial features of constitutions need to be considered: their *generality* and their *fundamentality*. We address each in turn.

First, constitutions tend to be drafted in general, lofty, unspecific terms, *raising* difficult questions without *answering* them. For example, a constitution may say that 'everyone has the right to life'. But does this mean that people have a right to choose when and how their life should be ended, meaning that the government is not allowed to enact laws criminalising euthanasia? If, as is often the case, constitutions themselves dodge such hard questions, they ought at least to make provision for them to be answered in some way.

This, in turn, raises a very thorny issue: if the constitution is unclear and its meaning disputed, who should be responsible for deciding what it means? In particular, should courts have the last word (constitutions are legal texts, so judges are surely best placed to interpret them) or does democracy require that this should be left to politicians (it being arguable that elected representatives have a more legitimate claim to decide upon controversial social issues)?

Many constitutions fail even to address this question. Although the former position applies in the USA (where courts can strike down unconstitutional laws), its Constitution does not explicitly address this point. It fell to the US Supreme Court, shortly after the adoption of the US Constitution at the turn of the nineteenth century, to assert a strike-down power—an assertion that proved controversial, given the absence of any express constitutional basis for it.[10]

Second, constitutions often secure consensus by focusing on fundamental matters on which a *natural* consensus exists. Many of the matters with which constitutions deal are genuinely uncontroversial because they reflect views that are both deeply and widely held. For example, few people would dissent from the propositions that criminal liability and punishment should not be imposed upon someone unless he has received a fair trial before an independent court. Similarly, it is universally accepted that, in a democracy, a government only holds office for a limited period, after which it must submit itself to an election.

This is not to deny that difficult questions arise even in relation to the most fundamental matters. (Is the constitutional requirement of a fair trial met if the government, citing national security concerns, refuses to let the defendant adduce potentially helpful evidence? Must the government be dissolved and an election held on the constitutionally appointed date even if large swathes of the country are ravaged by a natural disaster the week before, such that many people would be unable to exercise

---

[10] *Marbury v Madison* 5 US 137 (1803).

their right to vote?) Nevertheless, some principles—even though they may have to be applied in unforeseen circumstances that raise hard questions—are regarded as sufficiently fundamental to be the subject of genuine consensus and, as such, they find a natural home in the constitution.

2.4 **Permanency**

This leads on to a final, closely related point. If constitutional principles are in this sense fundamental, then they are also, in a sense, timeless. Many of the laws that the legislature enacts remain on the statute book for only a few years, to be replaced by a new set of laws enacted by different—or even the same—legislators, convinced that they have found a better, cheaper, or more palatable solution to a given problem.

However, if constitutions are repositories of fundamental principles, should they be capable of being amended with the same ease as regular law? Few, if any, people would argue that constitutions should be wholly incapable of amendment, such that societies should be made to live in thrall to the past, enslaved by the values of earlier, perhaps less enlightened, generations. However, most constitution-drafters across the world have taken the view that constitutions should not be *easy* to amend. If their purpose is to reflect genuinely fundamental principles that represent a deep-seated consensus that limits the power of the government and protects the rights of the individual, constitutions should not be capable of being amended casually and thoughtlessly as a knee-jerk reaction to some passing fashion or crisis.

Constitutions therefore often prescribe an amendment process that demands a consensus that is so broad as to make alteration difficult. For example, to change the US Constitution, an amendment must be proposed by a two-thirds' majority of both chambers of the national legislature and then approved by three-quarters of the individual states' legislatures.[11]

If constitutions are *too easy* to change, they lose their value as guarantees of what is considered fundamental. But there are risks in making constitutions *too difficult* to amend. However hard constitution-drafters try to include only fundamental principles, it is inevitable that a constitution will, to some extent, reflect the views, attitudes, and circumstances that prevailed when the constitution was adopted. If the constitution is very difficult to amend, then courts may have to be relied upon to reinterpret provisions that are regarded as out of date.[12] This, in turn, places immense powers in judicial hands. For instance, the US Constitution includes a 'right to bear arms'. That provision was included in the Constitution long ago, when the USA lacked professional military and police forces. But unless the Supreme Court is willing to

---

[11] US Constitution, art 5. (There is an alternative process that is even harder to comply with, but which has never been successfully used.)

[12] Not everyone agrees that such reinterpretation is legitimate. While some courts and commentators take the view that constitutional texts are 'living instruments' to be interpreted according to contemporary circumstances, the school of thought known as 'originalism' holds that courts are simply required to ascertain and implement the original intention of those who drafted the constitution, however long ago that was. See generally Goldsworthy (ed), *Interpreting Constitutions: A Comparative Study* (Oxford 2006).

interpret it much more narrowly than it has done to date, it will continue to gravely restrict the extent to which legislators can tackle the pressing issue of gun control.

The easier it is to amend a constitution, the less point there is in having it in the first place. If a constitution can be amended or overridden with ease, its very status as a genuine constitution is called into question. But if a constitution is very hard to amend, the risk arises that, unless judges can be persuaded to reinterpret the constitution, lawmakers may find that their hands are tied by principles that were adopted centuries earlier in radically different social circumstances and which are arguably inappropriate today. Getting that balance right is one of the hardest tasks faced by those who have to draft constitutions.

2.5 **What about the UK?**

Our concern so far has been with the functions and characteristics that constitutions *generally* have. But what about the UK *specifically*? There are a number of respects in which the UK constitution is consistent with what has been said of constitutions so far. Power is divided vertically (albeit, as we will see, in a rather incomplete fashion) between three branches of the state (legislature, executive, and judiciary). Power is also divided horizontally between several tiers of government (European, UK, devolved nations, and local). Provision is made for holding the government to account both politically and legally. People are said to possess constitutional and human rights, and fundamental constitutional principles are recognised.

At least most of these arrangements enjoy a form of consensus-based legitimacy. Some of the UK's arrangements have received popular endorsement through referendums (eg the UK's decision to leave the European Union in 2016 and the devolution of power to Scotland, Wales, and Northern Ireland in the late 1990s). Some constitutional arrangements have been put in place by the UK's democratically elected Parliament and could therefore only be changed by Parliament (eg the Human Rights Act 1998 and the guarantee of judicial independence under the Constitutional Reform Act 2005). Furthermore, while many constitutional arrangements have not been enacted by Parliament (eg the constitutional convention by which government Ministers are accountable to Parliament), such arrangements could in future be altered by Parliament, and could therefore be said to have a form of indirect democratic legitimacy.

Whatever the similarities, however, there are important differences between the constitution of the UK and the constitutions of most other countries. That the UK's constitution is not 'written' is the most obvious difference[13]—but it is not the *crucial* difference. The key point of distinction is that the UK's constitutional arrangements have *no special legal status*.[14] It is the possession of such status—rather than the mere

---

[13] During the English Civil War, the monarchy was overthrown in 1649 and an English republic was briefly established. Under the terms of the Instrument of Government (1653)—England's first and only written constitution—executive power passed to an elected Lord Protector (Oliver Cromwell). However, upon restoration of the monarchy in 1660, the Instrument of Government was discarded.

[14] We note in Chapter 5 a suggestion that courts should only be willing to accept that Parliament has interfered with certain pieces of constitutionally important legislation if it specifically says that this is its

fact of being 'written'—to which many of the typical characteristics of constitutions considered earlier in this chapter are attributable.

When such status is given to constitutional law, several things are likely to follow. First, the constitution will enjoy a degree of *permanence*—that is, it will be capable of amendment only if the appropriate constitutional process is fulfilled. Second, other law will exist *in the shadow of the constitution*—that is, it will be valid only if it is consistent with the constitution. Third, as a result, *fundamental constitutional values*[15] will constitute an absolute brake on government—that is, it will be unauthorised to act contrary to them, even through the medium of democratically enacted legislation, and, if it tries to do so, the courts will be able to intervene.

In the UK, none of these things is true. First, because there is no legally distinct (and superior) category of constitutional law, *the law dealing with constitutional matters has the same status as all other law*. This means that any aspect of the constitution can be changed as easily as any regular law can be changed. Second, it follows that *'regular' law does not exist in the shadow of 'constitutional' law*—because no such distinction exists. The validity of any given law therefore cannot be called into question on the ground that it is inconsistent with the constitution. Third, as a result, *fundamental constitutional values and human rights cannot exist in the UK in the sense that they exist in many legal systems*. Specifically, they cannot operate as an absolute brake on government power because there is no body of constitutional law or principle that is hierarchically superior to ordinary law. The government can therefore, by causing legislation to be passed, do anything—even if that involves contradicting long-established constitutional principles or rights that people regard as fundamental.

The discussion so far provides only a brief sketch of the UK's constitutional arrangements. All of the issues just mentioned are addressed in detail in subsequent chapters. It is, however, necessary to enter three qualifications, not because they contradict what has been said, but because it is necessary to give a rather fuller picture. Despite the UK's unusual constitutional arrangements, fundamental principles and rights are generally respected.

First, the fact that important principles in the UK are not written into laws that have special, higher constitutional status *does not mean that there are no such principles*. In many countries, lawmakers respect fundamental rights and principles because they are legally impotent to do otherwise: retroactive criminal laws (which would offend legal certainty) and laws criminalising criticism of the government (which would contradict free speech) remain unenacted because the constitution denies the legislature any power to make such laws. In the UK, such rights and principles are also regarded as important. Criticising the government has not been made into a criminal offence. Further, criminal law does not normally have retroactive effect. The difference is that in the UK lawmakers are legally *capable* of enacting legislation that conflicts with fundamental principles and rights—yet they generally *choose* not to. There are several

intention. However, even if this suggestion were to come to be widely accepted, it would result in constitutional law enjoying a superior status to regular law only in a very limited sense.

[15] Or 'rule of law principles', or 'fundamental human rights'—the terminology is, for the time being, unimportant.

reasons for this, including (hopefully) legislators' own sense of morality and, in any event, fear of adverse consequences at the next election.

> **Q** Is it acceptable that, in the UK, basic rights and fundamental constitutional principles rely, for their ongoing existence, upon lawmakers choosing not to interfere with them, rather than being legally incapable of doing so?

Second, the fact that lawmakers can, if they are determined to do so, enact laws that conflict with fundamental constitutional principles *does not mean that such principles are without any legal significance*. When, in this chapter, we refer to 'lawmakers' and 'legislation', we mean the UK Parliament and the laws that it enacts. Acts of the UK Parliament are the highest form of law within the UK constitution and, as such, cannot be struck down by courts if they conflict with fundamental constitutional principles. However, *other lawmakers*, such as the legislatures of the devolved nations, and *other parts of the government*, such as Ministers and local authorities, do not wield the sort of power that the UK Parliament possesses.

We will see that, in relation to such lawmakers and parts of the government, it often *is* possible for the courts to police their conduct—overturning things that they have done, where appropriate—in order to ensure compliance with fundamental constitutional principles. In this sense, then, such principles *do* have legal significance: they are enforceable against a broad range of legislators and parts of the government, albeit that the UK Parliament itself can, if it is determined to do so, lawfully act contrary to such principles.

Third, *the orthodox view of the UK constitution presented here is not a universally accepted one*. While the view that constitutional principles do not have a special, higher legal status in the UK remains the dominant one, that view is increasingly being questioned. Indeed, three very senior judges indicated in 2005 that if laws were enacted that offended against the most fundamental constitutional principles, the courts might consider themselves capable of striking down, or refusing to apply, such laws.[16]

Whether such statements are anything more than empty threats is a question that is beyond the scope of this introductory chapter. Neither Parliament nor the government have endorsed the view. However, we note that, if the UK courts were to adopt such a position, it would imply that the UK *does* have a body of constitutional principles that is superior to all other law. Furthermore, this would remove the principal factor that distinguishes the UK's constitutional arrangements from those that apply in many comparable countries, namely the doctrine of parliamentary sovereignty under which Parliament has the *absolute* right to make or unmake *any* law at all.

---

[16] See the speeches of Lord Hope, Lord Steyn, and Baroness Hale in *R (Jackson) v Attorney General* [2005] UKHL 56, [2006] 1 AC 262.

3. Case studies

One of the difficulties involved in studying public law is that its many different aspects are interconnected. It is hard to grasp any given topic without knowing something about other parts of the subject. We therefore conclude this introductory chapter with three case studies that aim to provide a sense of how the different topics to be considered in this book relate to one another. The case studies convey a flavour of the type—and importance—of the issues with which public law is concerned.

3.1 Terrorism and public law

When Al-Qaeda terrorists killed around 3,000 people by flying aircraft into prominent landmarks in the USA—most notably the World Trade Center in New York—on 11 September 2001 ('9/11'), the geopolitical consequences were immeasurable. The most obvious such consequence was the decision of the US and UK governments, only weeks after the 9/11 attacks, to invade Afghanistan, Al-Qaeda's main stronghold, and to overthrow its Taliban-led government, which was supportive of Al-Qaeda. Domestically, the US and UK governments took other drastic steps. Most notoriously, the US government established an enormously controversial detention camp at a US military base at Guantánamo Bay, Cuba, where 'enemy combatants' were held. Most were never charged with or convicted of any criminal offence, and received no recognisable form of due process. A form of torture known as 'waterboarding', involving simulated drowning, was practised there.

The UK's domestic response was different from that of the USA, but was, at least in some respects, no less draconian. The centrepiece of that response was the Anti-terrorism, Crime and Security Act 2001. The Act dealt with a wide range of matters,[17] but we are concerned with one particular aspect. In the wake of 9/11, the government perceived that a major threat to the security of the UK was posed by foreign Islamic extremists.[18] Ordinarily, that perceived threat could have been dealt with in one of two ways: by instituting criminal proceedings or by deporting the suspects to their countries of origin.

However, the government was unable or unwilling to adopt either of those courses of action. On the one hand, criminal proceedings (eg for conspiracy) could not be brought because, it was asserted, securing convictions would involve revealing to the court evidence that would compromise national security. On the other hand, physically removing such people from the UK by deporting them to their home countries was not legally possible. This is because the European Convention on Human Rights (ECHR)—which, as a matter of international law, is binding upon the UK[19]—prohibits deportation if there is a real risk that the person concerned will be tortured

---

[17] For a concise, critical overview, see Tomkins, 'Legislating against Terror: The Anti-terrorism, Crime and Security Act 2001' [2002] PL 205.

[18] We note in passing that the terrorist attacks on the London transport network on 7 July 2005 were carried out by British citizens.

[19] Because the UK chose to become bound by it.

or otherwise ill-treated on return to his home country. Many of the people about whom the UK government was concerned came from countries in which precisely that risk would arise. Taking the view that neither deportation nor criminal proceedings were viable, the government instead invited Parliament to pass the 2001 Act.

As Figure 1.2 shows, the effect of Pt 4 of the Act was to allow the government to imprison (notwithstanding the absence of any criminal charge or trial) suspected foreign terrorists who could not be deported. This involved depriving relevant suspects of their liberty on the say-so not of an independent court, but of the executive government, and not on the basis of criminal charges proven beyond reasonable doubt, but on the basis of suspicion—reasonable belief—that the person concerned was a threat to national security and involved in terrorism. Although detainees could appeal to a judicial tribunal (the Special Immigration Appeals Commission), they could not, for national security reasons, know the case against them or the evidence on which the decision to detain them was made; they could, however, be represented by a security-cleared lawyer (a Special Advocate).

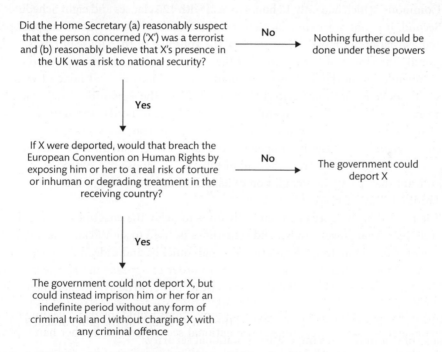

Figure 1.2 Part 4 of the Anti-terrorism, Crime and Security Act 2001

This regime proved to be highly controversial, opinion being divided between those who supported the government's attempts to contain the perceived threat posed by the individuals concerned and those who deplored such a flagrant breach of basic rights and due process. This episode tells us a great deal about the UK constitution. In the remainder of this section, we focus on three key aspects of the story: the relative ease with which the legislation could be enacted, the involvement of the courts and the use of human rights law to challenge the legislation, and the aftermath of the legal process.

3.1.1 The enactment of the legislation

How and why was the government able to get Parliament to confer these extraordinary powers upon it? The answer lies in three interlocking features of the UK constitution.

First, in the UK, the political party with a majority of seats in the *House of Commons* is asked by the Queen to form the government.[20] (The House of Commons is one of the two chambers of the UK Parliament, the other being the House of Lords.) The government's majority means that it is almost always assured of getting its proposals for new legislation through the Commons: members of each political party usually vote as instructed by the party's leadership. However, the House of Commons was even more supine than usual when it came to passing the 2001 Act. In a climate of genuine fear created by the 9/11 attacks in the USA, politicians were falling over themselves to be seen as tough on terrorism. Many opposition, as well as government, Members of Parliament (MPs) were therefore willing to support the legislation, and it received almost no genuine scrutiny. Indeed, a parliamentary committee later observed that 'many important elements of the [legislation] were not considered at all in the House of Commons, which had only 16 hours to deal with 126 clauses and eight Schedules'.[21]

Second, it is not normally sufficient for the House of Commons to support proposed legislation: in most circumstances, the approval of the *House of Lords* is also required. The House of Lords—most of the members of which are appointed on the recommendation of the leaders of the main political parties, and none of whom is elected—looked much more critically and carefully at the legislation. Grave concerns were expressed by some of its members, but the House of Lords eventually approved the legislation. In part, this reflects the House of Lords' consciousness that if it asserts itself too vigorously, it lays itself open to the charge that it is an undemocratic institution with no right to frustrate the will of the elected House of Commons. It is also significant that, partly in recognition of its lack of democratic legitimacy, the House of Lords has limited powers.

The most that the Lords can normally do is to delay the enactment of legislation for one year. That power can be, and sometimes is, used to significant effect if a government is desperate to get legislation through quickly, and indeed the government did agree to some significant amendments in order to appease the House of Lords. Ultimately, however, the Lords did not exercise its power to delay the enactment of the legislation, no doubt accepting that it would have been inappropriate to block measures regarded by the elected branches of the constitution—ie the government and the House of Commons—as imperative to national security.

So far, we have seen that the executive branch of government is in a strong position to get legislation through Parliament, because of its effective control of the House of Commons and the subservient position of the House of Lords. However, a third, crucially important, point must be noted: as we have already seen, *the UK constitution imposes no absolute limits upon the authority of lawmakers.* There is no body of constitutional law or principle that has a special, higher legal status and therefore

---

[20] 'Seats' in the House of Commons refers to the number of Members of Parliaments (MPs).
[21] Joint Committee on Human Rights, *Anti-terrorism, Crime and Security Bill: Further Report* (HL 51 HC 420 2001–02), [2].

even fundamental principles—such as the liberty of the individual—can be abolished or limited provided that the government can persuade Parliament to enact legislation having such an effect. This means that the executive branch of government is in effective control of a legislature that has unlimited constitutional authority to make law. It would be a gross oversimplification to say that this means the government can do whatever it wants. However, the 9/11 experience shows that, at least in some circumstances, the government is in an extraordinarily powerful position.

3.1.2 The *Belmarsh* case

What, then, of the courts? Courts in the UK cannot strike down an Act of Parliament, even if it impinges upon fundamental constitutional values. This follows from the constitutional doctrine of parliamentary sovereignty. There are, however, two things that they *can* do when faced with law that appears to conflict with such values.

First, the courts adopt as their starting point the assumption that lawmakers do not wish to enact legislation that offends basic constitutional principles or cuts across human rights. The courts therefore generally attempt to interpret the law in a way that is consistent with such rights and principles. But this approach can work—in the sense of yielding an outcome that is consistent with constitutional principles—only if it is possible to interpret the legislation in such a way. If lawmakers have made their intention to override basic rights sufficiently clear—as they doubtless did when, in passing the Anti-terrorism Act, they authorised the government to deprive people of their liberty without charge or trial—then this approach cannot bear fruit. If the law clearly affronts fundamental constitutional values, the courts must nevertheless apply the law as enacted by Parliament.[22]

However, the courts have a second string to their bow. In 1998, Parliament enacted the Human Rights Act 1998 (HRA). This Act authorises the courts, in appropriate cases, to consider whether legislation is compatible with certain human rights. If not, the courts can issue a 'declaration of incompatibility'. This does not deprive the legislation of legal force, but it does amount to a formal statement from the court that the legislation breaches human rights standards. Precisely such a declaration was issued in respect of the Anti-terrorism Act.

In 2004, in the *Belmarsh* case[23]—so-called because the people detained under the Act were held in Belmarsh high-security prison—a number of detainees asked the court to rule on whether the Anti-terrorism Act breached their right to liberty, which is one of the rights protected by the HRA. The answer to that question might seem obvious. The detainees were clearly being deprived of their liberty, and none of the circumstances in which the right to liberty can validly be restricted—such as detention following conviction and sentencing by a criminal court—applied. However, there was a complication. Under the HRA, it is possible to suspend certain rights—including the right to liberty—if, and to the extent that, a war or a public emergency threatening the life of the nation makes it necessary to do so.

---

[22] This is the orthodox view. It is not universally shared, as we explain in Chapter 5.
[23] *A v Secretary of State for the Home Department* [2004] UKHL 56, [2005] 2 AC 68.

The court therefore had to decide whether those conditions were satisfied. If they were, it would not be possible (as the detainees wished the court to do) to declare that the Anti-terrorism Act was incompatible with the detainees' right to liberty—because their right to liberty would have been lawfully suspended. If, however, those conditions were not met, the court would be able to issue such a declaration, because the right to liberty would remain in force.

The court held that the conditions were *not* satisfied. Although most of the judges refused to overrule the government's view that, following 9/11, the risk posed by terrorism constituted a public emergency threatening the life of the nation, the majority held that the government had not shown that it was necessary to detain foreign suspects without charge or trial. They noted that the government had not taken any steps to detain *British* suspects, and said that 'if it is not necessary to lock up the nationals it cannot be necessary to lock up the foreigners'.[24] The right to liberty had therefore not been validly suspended, and the court declared that the relevant provisions of the Anti-terrorism Act were incompatible with it.

3.1.3 The aftermath

What use was a mere declaration which, as a matter of law, Parliament was free to ignore? This question throws into sharp relief a fundamental aspect of the UK constitution that we have so far only addressed in passing—that is, that while there are no *legal* limits that confine lawmakers' powers, there are considerable *political* limits upon the exercise of such powers. We mentioned in section 2.5 that, the absence of legal limits notwithstanding, there are several reasons explaining why UK legislators are unlikely to enact oppressive laws. One of the most important such reasons is that, even if they are tempted to do so, elected legislators will be sensitive to public opinion: there may be public protests or hostile media comment in response to oppressive laws, and MPs may fear losing their seats in the House of Commons at the next election if they vote in favour of legislation that is considered unacceptable to a sufficient number of people. Thus, in practice, the political process provides a brake on the exercise of lawmaking power.

Against this background, a declaration issued by the highest court in the land that an Act of Parliament is inconsistent with basic human rights has a great deal of significance. It does not, for reasons that we have already mentioned, amount to the court striking down the legislation. As one of the *Belmarsh* judges put it, the impact of a declaration of incompatibility 'is political not legal'.[25] But that political significance should not be underestimated: a declaration will be grist to the mill of those inside and outside Parliament who wish to see the legislation repealed.

The declaration issued in the *Belmarsh* case had precisely that effect: the government found itself under irresistible pressure to repeal Pt 4 of the Anti-terrorism Act. The then Home Secretary told the House of Commons that he 'accept[ed] the [court's] declaration of incompatibility' and its 'judgment that new legislative measures must

---

[24] *A* at [231], *per* Baroness Hale.   [25] *A* at [142].

apply equally to nationals as well as to non-nationals'.[26] He later stated, when seeking Parliament's approval of fresh legislation, that it had been 'designed to meet the [court's] criticism that the previous legislation was both disproportionate and discriminatory'.[27]

What we see here, then, is an example of the *legal* process, which resulted in a declaration that the Anti-terrorism Act was incompatible with fundamental constitutional principles, triggering a *political* process that resulted in those principles being upheld. In turn, this phenomenon raises the ideas of *legal constitutionalism* and *political constitutionalism*.

We address these matters in Chapter 2. Indeed, we argue that the relationship between them is key to understanding how the UK constitution works. For now, however, we simply say that they reflect two different views of how fundamental constitutional values should be upheld. The former puts its faith in the courts; the latter relies on the political process. Quite sensibly, few countries put all of their eggs in one basket—but, as we explain in more detail in Chapter 2, the absence in the UK of a body of constitutional law that ties the hands of lawmakers means that unusually heavy reliance has to be placed upon the safeguards afforded by the political process. Whether those safeguards are adequate is another matter—and one that we explore throughout this book.

3.1.4 Conclusions

What, then, does this episode tell us about the UK constitution? Without rehearsing all that has been said so far, three points should be emphasised.

First, the episode underlines *the pivotal position occupied by the government*. It wields enormous power because of its capacity to get legislation enacted—a capacity that is attributable to its control of the House of Commons and the constitutionally inferior position of the House of Lords.

Second, the power of the executive is strengthened by the fact that Parliament is *not subject to any absolute constitutional limits*. There is no hierarchically superior body of constitutional law in the UK. Parliament is legally free to do as it wishes—a constitutional feature that, perhaps paradoxically, augments the *government's* power once account is taken of the fact that the government, by virtue of its majority in the House of Commons, exerts a high degree of control over Parliament.

Third, however, we have seen that this does not mean that *fundamental constitutional principles* are irrelevant. The principle at stake in the *Belmarsh* case, concerning the liberty of the individual, was ultimately upheld through the combined effect of the legal and political processes. While lacking the power to strike down the offending provisions of the Anti-terrorism Act, the court's declaration that it conflicted with the right to liberty proved to be of enormous political significance, prompting the executive government to ask Parliament to repeal Pt 4 of the Act. As we embark on our study of public law, this episode therefore serves as a reminder of the importance of examining public *law* within its wider *political* context.

---

[26] HC Deb, vol 430, col 306 (26 January 2005).
[27] HC Deb, vol 431, col 151 (22 February 2005).

3.2 **Prisons**

At first glance, it might be assumed that the prisons system has more to do with criminal law and justice than with public law, but that is not so. The prisons system comprises a large administrative apparatus that is run, managed, and financed by the government. It is the means by which key policy goals are pursued: the punishment and rehabilitation of offenders, the protection of the public, and the reduction of future reoffending. The prisons system is also a large-scale area of government. There are approximately 140 prisons in England and Wales, housing roughly 85,000 inmates. Some 26,000 prison officers work within HM Prison Service, the government agency that manages and runs the prisons system. In 2014–15, the Ministry of Justice spent nearly £3 billion on the prisons system. There is also a government Minister who is answerable to Parliament on matters concerning prisons.

The government needs extensive legal powers to run the prisons system. These are provided by the Prison Act 1952, which gives the power to the government to confine and treat prisoners. However, while this Act provides the legal basis for the prisons system, for two reasons it is only the tip of the legislative iceberg. First, over the years, *new legislation* has been introduced as government policy and the challenges of running prisons have changed. For example, the 1952 Act said nothing about testing prisoners for drugs, provision for which is made by subsequent Acts of Parliament. Second, many of the detailed rules governing the regulation and management of prisons are set down not in primary legislation (ie Acts of Parliament) but in *secondary legislation*. Secondary legislation, which is commonplace, is enacted by the government under powers conferred by an Act of Parliament. For instance, the 1952 Act authorises the government to make rules concerning the regulation and management of prisons. These rules—the Prison Rules—govern matters such as prisoners' physical welfare and work, their communications with people outside prison, and the ability of prison officers to search prisoners' property. These are the detailed rules that are administered by prison officers on a daily basis.

3.2.1 Public administration and administrative law

The prisons system illustrates three important points that will be relevant to our study of public law. First, the prisons context demonstrates that 'the constitution' is inhabited not only by Parliament, government Ministers, and the courts. Much of the frontline work of government is actually carried out by other public bodies, such as *government departments* and other *administrative agencies*. Thus it is HM Prison Service that is responsible for the running of the prisons system. Similarly, Highways England is responsible for operating, maintaining, and improving the strategic road network in England; HM Revenue and Customs collects the taxes that fund public services; and the Environment Agency is charged with addressing climate change, and improving air and water quality. These are only a few examples of the many government agencies that form part of the larger governmental machine. As we shall see, such administrative agencies are accompanied by a whole host of other bodies, such as regulators, tribunals, and ombudsmen.

Why do we have such bodies? In the UK, as in many other countries, the 'state' aspires to do a great deal of things. But if government policy is to be turned from aspiration into reality, it must be implemented in practice. So, for instance, if the government's criminal justice policy requires tens of thousands of people to be behind bars at any given point in time, the government must put this into practice. And when it seeks to turn policy into reality in this way, government usually acts through the medium of an administrative agency. In the case of prisons, it is HM Prison Service that manages and governs prisons, and this agency is staffed by permanent officials who are appointed and not elected.

Indeed, elected politicians personally perform very few, if any, of the basic operational tasks of government; this is the responsibility of public officials and civil servants who work in administrative agencies. While the Prime Minister is the head of the UK government, she does not personally deliver public services. The task of the Prime Minister and other government Ministers is to oversee and direct the work of government agencies rather than to perform governmental functions themselves. In the context of prisons, it is prison governors and officers, not Ministers, who actually run and manage prisons.

The development and growth of administrative agencies has gone hand in hand with the development of a particular type of law. Take the Prison Act 1952. This is what might be labelled *administrative legislation*—that is, legislation that does not impose duties upon or confer rights on private individuals, but which lays down the legal rules as to how a particular part of government is to operate and be organised. Such legislation will typically confer legal powers and obligations on administrative agencies, which are needed so that they can perform their public functions.

Indeed, *most* legislation is of this character. As long ago as 1901, it was noted that 'the substantial business of Parliament as a legislature is to keep the machinery of the state in working order'—and that the net result of Parliament's legislative activity 'has been the building up piecemeal of an administrative machine of great complexity, which stands in constant need of repair, renewal, reconstruction, and adaptation to new requirements'.[28] Parliament keeps the governmental machine—the administrative state—in working order by enacting administrative legislation. In order to manage the myriad policy programmes for which government is now responsible—managing the economy, policing, taxation, social security, planning, immigration, transport, environment, climate change, and so on—it is necessary to have legislation setting out the legal powers, duties, and organisation of government agencies and bodies.

While much of this legislation is detailed and complex, it is often only a *partial statement of the law*. As we have noted, the Prison Act 1952 is supplemented by delegated legislation in the form of the Prison Rules. Today, the volume of such delegated legislation far outstrips that of primary legislation. In 2014, Parliament enacted 30 Acts of Parliament, while there were over 3,000 'statutory instruments'—pieces of secondary legislation—made by the UK government. As a parliamentary select

---

[28] Ilbert, *Legislative Methods and Forms* (Oxford 1901), pp 210, 212, and 213.

committee has noted, 'secondary legislation makes up the majority of the law of this country. When implemented it affects every sphere of activity'.[29] The reason for this is simple: the scale and complexity of modern government far outstrips the legislative capacity of Parliament, and so the executive itself must shoulder a large part of the lawmaking burden.

These points are not unique to the prisons context. Rather, that context illustrates the broader truth that modern government is a very large and complex organisation. And the business of government—or 'administration'—can be carried on in a lawful and coherent manner only if there is a suitable legal framework—a body of 'administrative law' that sets out the powers of the government and its many agencies. Administrative law is thus a crucial component of modern public law, without which the modern state could not function. Viewed from that perspective, administrative law *facilitates* government by enabling it to do things. But that is only one side of the coin. The other concerns the *control* of government by providing redress if the government exceeds its powers. It is against that background that we turn—again with reference to the prisons context—to consider the notion of accountability.

3.2.2 Government accountability

In 2006, it emerged that over 1,000 foreign national prisoners had been released from prison by HM Prison Service without first being considered for deportation to their country of origin by the Immigration and Nationality Directorate, as should have happened. Both HM Prison Service and the Immigration and Nationality Directorate were administrative agencies within the same parent government department, the Home Office. The release of the prisoners was a major failure within government to coordinate the activities of these two agencies and to protect the public. As a consequence, the Home Secretary was dismissed by the Prime Minister.

The following year, there was an important reorganisation within government—a 'machinery of government' change, which is a structural reorganisation of the responsibilities of different government agencies. To enable the Home Office to focus on its core mission of protecting the public, it was stripped of responsibility for prisons by transferring HM Prison Service to a new government department, the Ministry of Justice. This was a major change in the organisation of executive government, and the decision had various ramifications as regards the funding of government and the relationship between the executive and the judiciary. This decision was, however, simply announced by the Prime Minister to Parliament not by way of an oral statement to the House of Commons, but through a written ministerial statement. MPs in the House of Commons regretted that there had been no opportunity for detailed parliamentary scrutiny of this significant change to the architecture of government.

These two episodes each raise a number of questions. Why was the Home Secretary dismissed when the failure had been that of the two agencies within his government department to coordinate their activities? Who is responsible for the overall

---

[29] House of Lords Merits of Statutory Instruments Committee, *What Happened Next? A Study of Post-Implementation Reviews of Secondary Legislation* (HL 180 2008–09), [1].

organisation of the executive government? What role is there for Parliament to scrutinise the government, whether in relation to specific issues such as the failure to consider deporting foreign prisoners or big-picture questions such as changes in the organisation of central government? All of these questions are, at root, about accountability. In any area of government activity, it is imperative that there should be systems for ensuring that power is being exercised responsibly, that decisions are being taken conscientiously and fairly, and that corrective action can be taken if these standards are not met. Taking the prisons system as an example, how should, and how can, those responsible for its operation be held to account?

First, given the importance of the functions performed by the prisons system, it is important that Parliament is able to *scrutinise* policy and administration in this area of government. This can be done by asking questions of relevant Ministers in Parliament or by holding parliamentary debates on policy issues pertaining to the prisons system. Moreover, in the UK, each government department is overseen by a parliamentary select committee made up of MPs. Since the prisons system falls within the remit of the Ministry of Justice, it is overseen by the House of Commons Justice Committee, which conducts inquiries and publishes reports into the prisons system.

Second, the prisons system is funded by government—meaning that it is paid for by taxpayers. An essential attribute of a good government is that it does not waste public money, but spends it wisely. Given the cost of the prisons system, it is important that there are effective mechanisms for overseeing how money is spent within it and whether such money could be spent more efficiently. The public needs to know that government is delivering value for money—and so it is necessary to have *financial accountability*. This raises issues that are peculiar to government. If a given company is inefficient, customers will flock to better, cheaper providers, but if people do not think that government is providing value for money, they cannot go elsewhere. In the absence of the sort of discipline normally supplied by market economics, distinctive audit bodies are needed to oversee how government spends public money. In the UK, the principal audit body is the National Audit Office; it reviews government agencies to assess whether or not they are delivering value for money and then reports its findings to Parliament.

Third, decisions are made within the prisons system that profoundly affect people's lives and rights. For instance, within certain parameters, prison officials can decide on the leniency or strictness of the regime to which a given prisoner is subject—up to and including holding a prisoner in solitary confinement. It is important that such decisions are open to *challenge*, and public law provides a variety of different mechanisms by which this can be done. One such mechanism is for the individual concerned to take the government agency concerned to a court in order to test the lawfulness of its decision. This court process is known as 'judicial review' and it is the principal mechanism by which individuals can challenge the legality of public decisions.

Indeed, legal challenges against prison decisions are a major area of judicial review. The courts have recognised that 'under English law, a convicted prisoner, in spite of his imprisonment, retains all civil rights which are not taken away expressly or by necessary implication'.[30] Consequently, if a decision by the prison authorities infringes the rights of a prisoner, then the prisoner is able to take the prison authorities to court in order to protect her rights.

For example, in the case of *Bourgass*,[31] two prisoners had been held in solitary confinement for unbroken periods of several months. They sought judicial review, arguing that the prison authorities had acted unlawfully by keeping them in solitary confinement for prolonged periods without referring the matter to the Home Office. The Supreme Court agreed, holding that the relevant legislation required the involvement of the Home Office in such matters in order to ensure that decisions about something as serious as prolonged solitary confinement could be taken only with the involvement of officials who were external to, and independent of, the management of the particular prison concerned. In this way, judicial review served to ensure that individual prisoners received the benefit of an important safeguard.

While important, judicial review is not the only way of challenging decisions by government bodies. There are a range of non-court processes that, together, comprise the administrative justice system. We can illustrate here two such mechanisms that operate in the general context of prisons and criminal justice.

First, there are mechanisms for investigating complaints that individuals make against government bodies. Such complaints may be investigated by an 'ombudsman' or another specialist complaint-handling body. For example, the Prisons and Probation Ombudsman investigates complaints from prisoners about their treatment by prisons. Such a complaint mechanism is an important safeguard against the abuse of power by prison officers.[32]

Second, tribunals enable individuals who have received a negative decision from a government body to appeal against that decision. For example, the UK government has a long-established policy of providing money (compensation) to people who have been physically or mentally injured because they were the blameless victim of a violent crime. This policy is administered by a government body, the Criminal Injuries Compensation Authority. If someone thinks that her application has been wrongly refused by the Authority, she can appeal against the Authority's decision to an independent judicial tribunal.[33] It adjudicates upon such disputes and can substitute its own decision for that of the Criminal Injuries Compensation Authority.[34]

3.2.3 Conclusions

The prisons context illustrates a number of matters that are important as we develop our understanding of public law. It demonstrates that government is sprawling and diverse; that the modern administrative state extends well beyond 'the government' in the sense of the Prime Minister, other Ministers, and the great departments of state; and that a complex body of law—administrative law—both enables the government

---

[30] *Raymond v Honey* [1983] 1 AC 1, 10.
[31] *R (Bourgass) v Secretary of State for Justice* [2015] UKSC 54, [2016] AC 384.
[32] We examine ombudsmen in detail in Chapter 15.
[33] Known as the 'First-tier Tribunal (Criminal Injuries Compensation)'.
[34] We examine tribunals in detail in Chapter 16.

and other public bodies to operate and sets limits, enforceable through judicial review, upon governmental power.

The prisons context also illustrates that just as government is diverse and complicated, so the arrangements for holding government to account are many and varied. Any given department or agency needs to be scrutinised by reference to a range of standards—including political, administrative, legal, and financial—and a network of accountability institutions capable of undertaking those forms of scrutiny is therefore required. This serves as a useful reminder, as we embark upon our study of public law, that government is a large and complicated enterprise, and that the different accountability processes that oversee government operations do not work in isolation from each other, but together comprise a wide-ranging system for holding government to account. Whether or not those institutions, individually or collectively, provide wholly adequate scrutiny is an important question—but one that we can tackle only in subsequent chapters, as we look at each area in detail.

3.3 **Post-1997 constitutional reforms**

The Labour governments of 1997–2010 implemented a far-reaching set of constitutional reforms.[35] They include 'devolution' (ie the creation of new governments and legislatures in Northern Ireland, Scotland, and Wales); the introduction of new voting arrangements for elections to the devolved legislatures; the creation of a city-wide system of government in, and an elected mayor for, London; significant changes to local government; the enactment of freedom of information and human rights legislation; the removal from the House of Lords of most members who inherited their seats; the near-abolition of the ancient office of Lord Chancellor; the abolition of the judicial functions of the House of Lords; the creation of the UK Supreme Court; and the creation of a statutory body responsible for dealing with MPs' pay and allowances.

By any measure, this is a significant set of changes to the country's constitutional arrangements. But the coalition government that took office in 2010 did not by any means consider its predecessor's constitutional reforms to be the last word: it promised, or at least contemplated, a range of significant changes, including to the House of Lords, the voting system, the electoral cycle, the powers of devolved institutions, and human rights law—albeit that many of those policies foundered on the rocks of coalition realpolitik. It is not our purpose here to address the individual or collective significance of these changes and proposals, actual or proposed (although many are examined in detail in subsequent chapters); rather, our present concern is with the way in which constitutional reform is undertaken in the UK.[36]

In most countries, constitutional reform is a big deal. Changing constitutions is usually hard: a wide consensus is normally needed in order to secure compliance with the constitutionally prescribed amendment process. Politicians (who are usually the

---

[35] See generally Bogdanor, 'Our New Constitution' (2004) 120 LQR 242; Bogdanor, *The New British Constitution* (Oxford 2009).

[36] See generally Baker, 'Our Unwritten Constitution' (2010) 167 Proceedings of the British Academy 91; Beatson, 'Reforming an Unwritten Constitution' (2010) 126 LQR 48.

initiative-takers in such matters) therefore do not casually seek the amendment of constitutions. The possibility is only mooted if the matter is of pressing importance, and, even then, only if it is felt that the proposed change would withstand the intense scrutiny that it would be likely to attract and stand a good chance of commanding the necessary support. We noted in section 2.4 that there are good reasons for making constitutions difficult to amend: they are supposed to represent a brake on government power, a guarantee of individuals' rights, and a repository of fundamental principles that should not be allowed to yield just because a government can muster a bare majority in the legislature.

Unusually, the UK constitution is capable of being amended in precisely such circumstances. Constitutional law having no higher legal status, everything is up for grabs provided that the government can persuade Parliament to enact the necessary legislation.

This simple fact of constitutional life in the UK has profound implications for the process of constitutional reform. It means the difficulties, formality, and momentousness that usually attend attempts to change and reform constitutions elsewhere are normally absent in the UK. It is often relatively easy for the government to reform the UK constitution; perhaps too easy. One risk is that a government might adopt a casual approach to constitutional reform, which produces piecemeal or ill-thought-through reforms. These are not mere possibilities. The post-1997 constitutional reforms were practically influenced in a number of ways—several of which we highlight in sections 3.3.1–3.3.3—by the relative ease with which they could be accomplished.

3.3.1 Piecemeal reform

Human nature is such that, generally speaking, the harder something is to do, the less keen people will be to do it. If you live a long walk from the nearest water source, you will take the biggest container you can carry and fill it up before returning home, rather than making several daily trips to fill 500ml bottles. Likewise, if constitutions are hard to amend, governments (or anyone else putting forward proposals) will be inclined to think long and hard before suggesting changes: repeatedly going through a protracted constitutional amendment process is likely to be unattractive. Attaching a degree of difficulty to constitutional amendment is therefore a disincentive to the presentation of ill-thought-through, disjointed, piecemeal proposals. Since the converse is also true, it is unsurprising that the post-1997 constitutional changes cannot be said to amount to a *programme* of reform in the sense of being a coherent package. The myriad Acts of Parliament that effected the reforms were introduced over a period of several years; the first reforms were thus drafted and implemented many years before not only the shape of later reforms was known, but before such reforms had even been contemplated. As a result, difficult questions were simply brushed aside or postponed (perhaps indefinitely). Reviewing the general approach to constitutional reform in the UK, a parliamentary committee noted in 2009 that ' "unfinished business" has been the enduring motif of many of the strands of constitutional renewal'.[37]

---

[37] House of Commons Justice Committee, *Constitutional Reform and Renewal* (HC 923 2008–09), [1].

As we will see in Chapter 7, shortly after it was elected in 1997, the Blair government introduced devolution in Scotland, Wales, and Northern Ireland.[38] It did so, however, without any clearly worked-out plan in relation to England, which, in the absence of devolution, continues to be governed and legislated for by the UK executive and Parliament. One of the strangest results of this is the so-called West Lothian question,[39] which, briefly, asks why it is legitimate for MPs representing the devolved nations to be allowed to vote on laws affecting only England, now that English MPs cannot vote on laws affecting only the devolved nations (because the latter are enacted by devolved legislatures in which English MPs do not sit). Lord Irvine, the Cabinet Minister responsible for driving through many of the post-1997 reforms, famously said: 'Now that we have devolution up and running, I think the best thing to do about the West Lothian question is to stop asking it.'[40] Indeed, it was not until 2015 that a serious attempt to address this issue was made, when a so-called 'English votes for English laws' procedure was introduced in the House of Commons. Whether the introduction of that procedure is a good thing is a question for a later chapter;[41] for now, the point is simply that the government that introduced devolution in the late 1990s clearly felt no obligation to present a cohesive package of proposals that addressed the West Lothian question.

The piecemeal nature of constitutional reform in the UK is a phenomenon that is not confined to the post-1997 changes. We will see in Chapter 5 that the democratic credentials of the House of Commons are a fairly recent innovation: it is less than 100 years since all adult men and women were given the right to vote in elections to the Commons. As the democratisation of the Commons proceeded, the view developed, unsurprisingly, that it was anomalous to have a wholly unelected House of Lords. In 1909–11, in circumstances that we relate later in the book, legislation was enacted to curtail the powers of the Lords, eliminating its involvement in financial legislation and giving it a power only to delay, rather than block, other legislation. The preamble to the Parliament Act 1911—the Act that imposed those limits on the House of Lords—explicitly stated that it was a temporary measure, pending the replacement of the House of Lords with 'a Second Chamber constituted on a popular instead of hereditary basis'. More than a century later, that has not yet happened.

However, one of the first elements of the post-1997 reforms to be implemented was the removal from the House of Lords of 'hereditary peers'—that is, those who had inherited the right to sit in the upper chamber.[42] This change was introduced before a Royal Commission established by the government had made its recommendations about full reform of the House of Lords, and was intended to be a stopgap measure pending large-scale reform. But no such reform has (yet) occurred.

---

[38] The position in Northern Ireland was complicated by its unusual political circumstances and the need to broker a deal that would facilitate an end to terrorist violence; as such, it was something of a special case. See further Chapter 7.

[39] Named after Tam Dalyell, who, when MP for West Lothian, drew public attention to this issue.

[40] HL Deb, vol 602, col 1201 (25 June 1999).   [41] See Chapter 7.   [42] House of Lords Act 1999.

3.3.2 **Constitutional reform on the hoof**

A second feature of constitutional reform in the UK is that it can be undertaken in a relatively informal way that is unaccompanied by the sort of consultation and fore-thought that is likely to be exhibited in systems in which reform is a more difficult business. As the House of Lords Constitution Committee has noted: 'The constitution is the foundation upon which law and government are built. Yet the United Kingdom has no agreed process for constitutional change.'[43] There is no clearer example of the extemporaneous and impromptu nature of constitutional reform in the UK than the aptly titled Constitutional Reform Act 2005.

On 12 June 2003, a government press release was issued stating the following:

- the office of Lord Chancellor (who was head of the judiciary, a senior government Minister, and speaker[44] of the House of Lords) was to be abolished;

- a new post (and a new government department to go along with it) of Secretary of State for Constitutional Affairs was to be created;

- a new way of appointing judges in England and Wales was to be established; and

- the Appellate Committee of the House of Lords, which had served as the court of final appeal for most matters in the UK, was to be abolished, and a new Supreme Court created.[45]

These announcements concerned constitutional changes of momentous significance, going to the heart of the legal system, the principle of judicial independence, and the relationship between the courts and the government. Yet they were announced without any consultation. Even the senior judiciary, including those directly affected by the proposals, knew nothing of them until the day on which they were announced.

And all of this happened in the middle of a Cabinet reshuffle in which the then Lord Chancellor, Lord Irvine, left the government, giving rise to strong suspicions that these major changes were as much about personality as about constitutional reform. One commentator has said that 'it is difficult to resist the conclusion that the reforms were the product of policy making on the hoof', not least because they directly contradicted things that the government had said shortly before the announcements were made.[46] Thus the new Supreme Court has been characterised as one 'born of secret ministerial cabal and a press release'.[47]

Lord Irvine—the then Lord Chancellor—subsequently disclosed that he only learned of the proposals a week before they were announced.[48] At the time Lord Irvine asked the then Prime Minister, Tony Blair,

> how a decision of this magnitude could be made without prior consultation with me, with . . . my Permanent Secretary [ie the most senior civil servant in his department],

---

[43] House of Lords Constitution Committee, *The Process of Constitutional Change* (HL 177 2010–11), [5].

[44] ie the presiding officer.

[45] Le Sueur, 'The Conception of the UK's New Supreme Court', in Le Sueur (ed), *Building the UK's New Supreme Court* (Oxford 2004), p 4.

[46] Le Sueur, p 4.   [47] Le Sueur, p 5.

[48] House of Lords Constitution Committee, *The Cabinet Office and the Centre of Government* (HL 30 2009–10), Ev 81–4.

within government, with the judiciary, with the authorities of the House of Lords which
would lose its Speaker and with [Buckingham] Palace.

Blair, according to Irvine, 'appeared mystified and said that these machinery of government changes always had to be carried into effect in a way that precluded discussion because of the risk of leaks'.

Taken at face value, this is an extraordinary view that treats fundamental changes
to the architecture of the constitution as akin to such commonplace phenomena
as the rebranding of government departments and the transfer of responsibilities
between them. So poorly thought-through were the government's initial proposals
that those involved appeared ignorant of the fact that the 700-year-old office of Lord
Chancellor—to which there were over 5,000 statutory references—could be abolished only through the enactment of complex primary legislation. In fact, as we
relate in Chapter 6, the office of Lord Chancellor still remains today, albeit that the
Constitutional Reform Act 2005 radically reshaped it. The purpose of this discussion
is not to consider the substantive merits of the reforms introduced by that Act. There
were, as we will see later in the book, strong—perhaps even compelling—arguments
for many or all of the changes that it ushered in. But even those who support the
effects of the Act have expressed concern about the *process* (or rather lack of process)
that preceded it. Indeed, Blair himself concedes that the process was 'bumpy' and
'messy', and that questions of detail were only addressed at the 'last minute'—but,
he maintains, 'the outcome was right', the implication being that this is what really
matters.[49]

Nonetheless, it is highly likely that the process of constitutional reform will remain
ad hoc and haphazard. In 2011, the House of Lords Constitution Committee criticised the absence of any clearly defined (and especially rigorous) process for effecting constitutional changes, arguing that such a process should be established.[50] In
response, the government made clear its unwillingness to become locked into a particular procedure for constitutional reform: 'It is intrinsic in the United Kingdom's
constitutional arrangements that we do not have special procedures for dealing with
constitutional reform.'[51]

3.3.3 Constitutional reform as an ongoing process

The third and (for the purposes of this discussion) final implication of the ease with
which the UK constitution can be changed is that it allows constitutional reform to be,
in effect, a rolling process that lacks finality. This has important implications. Some
might be regarded as advantages. Treating the constitution as a perpetual 'work in
progress' makes it possible to keep it under review, and to react quickly when it is felt
that things are not working well or that established arrangements need to be updated.
For example, the systems of devolution introduced in Scotland and Wales have been

---

[49] House of Lords Constitution Committee, HL 30, Ev 86–7.
[50] House of Lords Constitution Committee, *The Process of Constitutional Change* (HL 177 2010–11).
[51] Deputy Prime Minister, *The Government Response to the House of Lords Constitution Committee
Report 'The Process of Constitutional Change'* (Cm 8181 2011), [27].

reviewed and significantly altered since their introduction in 1999—including by significantly extending the powers of the Scottish Government and Parliament in the
aftermath of the close-fought 2014 referendum on Scottish independence. Meanwhile,
notwithstanding the extensive nature of the post-1997 reforms, the Brown government, in 2009—responding, it seems, to public disaffection with politics and government following a scandal concerning MPs' expenses—mooted the possibility of a new
swathe of changes, perhaps even including a written constitution.[52] And today, the
UK stands on the brink of what might prove to be profound and far-reaching constitutional changes as a result of its departure from the European Union.

The way in which the UK's constitutional arrangements evolve might be said to
showcase their greatest strength—namely, the high degree of flexibility that enables
them to adapt to changing needs and circumstances. There is certainly something to
be said for this, and indeed it is hard to argue against the proposition that it should
not be unduly difficult to improve constitutional arrangements that prove to be
defective or outmoded.

However, it is important, in thinking about this matter, to make sure that two
conceptually distinct matters are not confused with one another. The fact that *some
issues, such as detailed, technical arrangements*, should be capable of being amended
with relative ease does not mean that *all constitutional arrangements, including those
pertaining to fundamental principles*, should be amenable to equally casual amendment. After all, one of the main points of enshrining such principles in constitutional
law is to ensure that they cannot be discarded whenever they prove inconvenient to
the government of the day.

This distinction is one that is, or at least can be, well served by legal systems with
hard-to-amend written constitutions. Fundamental matters can be reflected in the
constitutional text itself, while matters of detail can be dealt with in regular law, which
(subject to the limits imposed by the constitution) can be amended with relative ease
as circumstances change and experience develops. The difficulty is that, in the UK,
this distinction does not exist in formal terms. It is possible to say that arrangement
'X' is fundamental and should not be interfered with readily, but that matter 'Y' is a
mere point of detail that should be more readily capable of amendment. However,
no such distinction is reflected in *law*. The result is that even constitutional arrangements concerning indisputably fundamental principles remain exposed to the chill
winds of party politics. A good illustration of this is the way in which the HRA has
been kicked around by the main parties as if it were a political football.

The effect of the HRA is considered in outline in Chapter 2 and in detail in
Chapter 18. For now, it suffices to say that it gives effect in UK law to certain fundamental human rights, such as the right not to be tortured, the right to a fair trial,
and the right to free speech. In many countries, such rights enjoy constitutional
status—that is, they are recognised by the written constitutional text and thus limit
the powers of the executive government and the legislature. Within such a system,
constitutional rights can be removed or otherwise interfered with only by amending
the constitution itself—which, as we know, is likely to be difficult.

---

[52] Prime Minister's Office, *Building Britain's Future* (Cm 7654 2009), ch 1.

The position is different in the UK. Lacking such a higher body of constitutional law, the UK could not adopt that sort of approach to the legal protection of human rights and so the HRA was enacted. Being an ordinary Act of Parliament (there being no other type), the HRA is capable of being amended or even repealed, just like any other such law. This fact has not evaded the notice of politicians from both of the main parties. One of the great ironies of the Act is that the very government that caused it to be enacted subsequently complained bitterly when judges applied it (quite properly) in ways that stopped government Ministers from doing things that they wanted to do. We saw in section 3.1.3 that, to its credit, the Blair government accepted the historic ruling in the *Belmarsh* case, but the courts' judgments in human rights cases have not always been so meekly received by government.

For instance, in the wake of the terrorist attacks on the London transport network in July 2005, Tony Blair said that he would consider seeking the amendment of the HRA if it were to turn out that it would stop the government from effectively fighting the so-called 'war on terror'.[53] And in 2009, responding, it would seem, to the view expressed strongly in certain sections of the media that the HRA gives undue weight to the interests of criminals and asylum seekers at the expense of the so-called law-abiding majority, the Brown government proposed replacing or supplementing the Act with a 'Bill of Rights and Responsibilities'.[54]

Meanwhile, the Conservative Party undertook, in its 2010 and 2015 election manifestos, to repeal the HRA, replacing it with a 'British Bill of Rights'. Those promises have so far gone unfulfilled, but senior Conservative politicians continued to vent their fury at decisions taken under the HRA and the ECHR to which it gives effect. A decision concerning prisoners' right to vote made David Cameron, who served as Prime Minister from 2010 to 2016, feel 'physically sick',[55] while another, which appeared to obstruct the deportation of a terror suspect, made his 'blood boil'.[56] Theresa May, the current Prime Minister, has advocated not only repeal of the HRA but also withdrawal from the ECHR itself, albeit that this does not appear to be a policy she intends to pursue for the time being.[57]

We consider the merits or otherwise of the HRA and of possible reforms in Chapter 18. For the moment, our point is simply that the fact that the HRA—the closest thing that the UK has to a constitutional Bill of Rights—is perceived as fair game by politicians tells us something important about the UK constitution. Ultimately, very little is sacrosanct in the UK constitution.

To some extent, the normal principles of constitutionalism are turned on their head. In other countries, the constitution is hierarchically at the top of the system of law and government: everything else has to fit around it. In the UK, the constitution, such as it is, is malleable. If existing constitutional arrangements prove to be an

---

[53] Downing Street press conference, 5 August 2005.

[54] Ministry of Justice, *Rights and Responsibilities: Developing Our Constitutional Framework* (Cm 7577 2009). The proposal was tentative and the relationship of the proposed Bill of Rights and Responsibilities with the HRA was unclear.

[55] HC Deb, vol 517, col 921 (3 November 2010).

[56] 'Deported Qatada faces terror charge', *London Evening Standard*, 7 July 2013.

[57] 'Theresa May's speech on Brexit', *ConservativeHome*, 25 April 2016.

obstacle to what the government regards as the efficient processing of asylum seekers, the effective prosecution of the 'war on terror', or the avoidance of critical comment in the tabloid press, then such arrangements can, if the political will can be mustered, be changed or done away with.

> **Q** Is this a good or a bad thing? Might it be argued that the British approach is democratic, in the sense that politicians are able to do whatever the people want? What might be the disadvantages of such a system? In particular, why might the British approach serve the interests of minorities—especially of unpopular minorities, such as asylum seekers and suspected terrorists—poorly?

4. Conclusions

This chapter has looked at the sort of things that constitutions generally do and (in a necessarily introductory fashion) at whether, and if so how, the UK's constitution does those things. We have seen that the main factor that distinguishes the UK's arrangements is that none of them is laid down in a body of law that has a status higher than regular law. The net results of this idiosyncrasy of the UK system are twofold.

First, those laws that deal with constitutional matters can, in principle, be *amended as easily as any other law*. This means that the UK constitution does not legally restrict the powers of government to the same extent as constitutions that do have a higher legal status and which can be changed only by going through a hard-to-comply-with amendment process.

Second, it follows that, if arbitrary government is to be avoided in the UK, greater faith must be placed in the capacity of the *political process* to guard against the misuse of public power and the enactment of oppressive legislation. Public opinion is a powerful deterrent against such conduct. However, we will see later in the book that, although courts cannot ultimately strike down legislation enacted by the UK Parliament that conflicts with fundamental rights and principles, the constitution nevertheless supplies a wealth of mechanisms that seek to guard against, and correct, abuses of power by those in authority.

Some of those mechanisms—such as judicial review, as was undertaken in the *Belmarsh* case—are legal in nature. And that highlights a further important point. Although it is sometimes said that, for the reasons set out in the last paragraph, the UK has a 'political constitution' rather than a 'legal constitution', it is clear that today there is *far more constitutional law* in the UK than ever before—thanks not least to the post-1997 reforms. As a result, people have a wider array of legal rights that they can enforce against the government: rights of access to information under freedom-of-information legislation; and fundamental civil and political rights—to free speech, to respect for private life, to freedom of religion, and so on—under human rights law. In this sense, the UK now has a 'legal constitution' to a greater extent than it ever has done.

This does not detract from the fact that the UK's constitution is still a political one in the sense that it is politics and not law that is the ultimate safeguard against abuse of power. On any traditional analysis, if the political process were to fail to deter such a step from being taken, Parliament could take away any of the legal rights that people currently enjoy and the courts ultimately would be powerless to do anything about it.[58]

However, what must not be overlooked is the way in which the legal and the political dimensions of the constitution interact with one another. Once legal arrangements concerning fundamental constitutional matters are put in place—for example, entitling the people of Scotland, Wales, and Northern Ireland to run their own affairs, or giving people enforceable human rights—it may not be easy for politicians, at a stroke of the legislative pen, to get rid of or override them, even though, in theory, they have the power to do so. (Think back to the *Belmarsh* case: the court lacked power to strike down the offending law, but the government felt obliged to ask Parliament to repeal it once the judges had said that it infringed human rights standards.) Once the genie is out of the bottle, it is hard to get it back in. In this way, the legal aspects of the constitution, while not technically immutable, may well shape the political landscape—and those aspects of the constitution that are highly valued by people generally may become so ingrained as to become, in practice, constitutional limits as real as any laid down in a written constitution.

The UK constitution is idiosyncratic and messy. It has strengths and weaknesses. Certainly, no one sitting down with a blank sheet of paper would design such a constitution. However, constitutions that are designed from scratch are not perfect either: they have their own difficulties and complications. We should keep this in mind as we embark, in the following chapters, upon a detailed exploration of the UK's constitutional arrangements and as we try to work out whether they are merely eccentric or genuinely inadequate.

Expert commentary
Constitutional change in the United Kingdom
Aileen McHarg, Professor of Public Law, University of Strathclyde

As this chapter points out, one of the defining features of the UK's constitution is its flexibility: the relative ease (in formal terms at least) with which change even to fundamental aspects of the constitution can be secured. For many, this is the constitution's greatest strength; for others, it potentially creates problems (some of which are discussed in the chapter).

However, it is important to realise that just because everything *can* be changed, this does not mean that things necessarily *do* change. On the contrary, the UK constitution is marked by a high degree of historical continuity. Key institutions, such as the monarchy or the UK Parliament have very deep historical roots. They survive because they have managed to adapt to changing expectations, and to retain their popular legitimacy. Thus the role of the Monarch has evolved from the absolutist institution of the Middle Ages wielding comprehensive governmental power, to the constitutionally limited, politically neutral, and largely ceremonial Head of State that exists

---

[58] We noted that this traditional analysis is increasingly contested. We assess criticisms of it in Chapter 5.

today. Conversely, the UK Parliament has evolved from its medieval roots as a body of advisers to the Monarch, summonsed and dissolved at will, to become the central source of legal and political authority within the state. It has adapted to, and drawn legitimacy from, the advent of mass democracy, and has developed from a body essentially concerned with granting supply (money) to the government and occasionally passing legislation, to one charged with overseeing and legitimising the vast machinery of the modern state.

In other respects, though, the survival of constitutional institutions and doctrines may be indicative, not of successful adaptation, but rather of resistance to change. For one thing, as in any constitution, the existence of vested interests and/or conflicting reform objectives may make it difficult to secure political agreement for change. The House of Lords is a case in point, where, as the chapter notes, constitutional reformers have tried for over a century, and so far failed, to replace it with a democratically elected second chamber.

But more fundamentally—and paradoxically—it may be argued that resistance to change is in fact a structural feature of the UK's constitution which goes hand in hand with its flexibility. The chapter describes the piecemeal and sometimes casual approach to constitutional reform that flexibility permits, or even encourages. Such an approach has an inherently conservative quality which tends to limit the impact of reforms.

One problem is that reforms that are introduced too quickly and without broad political support may fail to take root and be vulnerable to reversal by supporters of the traditional constitutional order. One example discussed in the chapter is the Human Rights Act, which gives judges a stronger role in upholding individual rights—a role that continues to be seen by many as incompatible with the British tradition of relying on Parliament rather than the courts to delimit what rights people should enjoy.

A second problem is that reforms may be introduced without a clear understanding of how they relate to, or qualify, existing constitutional arrangements. A good example is the increasing use of referendums to determine controversial constitutional issues. Referendums were unknown to the British constitution until the 1970s, and were often argued to be incompatible with our system of parliamentary democracy. Since then, referendums have been used on a number of occasions, but on an essentially ad hoc basis, and without any attempt to clarify their constitutional status. This issue came to a head with the 2016 EU referendum, in which a narrow majority voted to leave the EU—a result which Leave voters might reasonably have expected to be decisive. Nevertheless, in *R (Miller) v Secretary of State for Exiting the European Union*,[59] the referendum result was described as merely advisory—its significance was political rather than legal—and therefore insufficient to entitle the government to notify the EU of Britain's intention to withdraw; to do so required a further vote in Parliament to confirm (or—potentially—override) the referendum result.

A third problem is that reform is often undertaken in the most minimal form necessary, sometimes without even changing the law. For instance, in order to protect the newly created devolved legislatures against encroachment by the UK Parliament—which as a consequence of the doctrine of parliamentary sovereignty may continue to legislate on devolved matters— the then Labour government simply announced that it expected a constitutional convention to develop whereby the UK Parliament would not legislate on devolved matters without the consent of the relevant devolved legislature (the 'Sewel Convention'). As a constitutional convention, however, this is not legally enforceable, and so the UK Parliament can ignore the consent requirement if it chooses.

---

[59] [2016] EWHC 2768 (Admin).

In fact, parliamentary sovereignty is itself an obstacle to fundamental constitutional reform. This is partly because politicians are unwilling to agree to changes that curtail the flexibility that parliamentary sovereignty allows them, but also because the rule that Parliament may make or unmake any law it likes prevents a Parliament from binding its successors: any subsequent Parliament may simply repeal a rule it dislikes, even if it is expressed to be permanent or fundamental. For example, the enactment of s 1 of the Scotland Act 2016, which declared the devolved Scottish Parliament and Scottish Government to be permanent parts of the constitution, subject to abolition only following a referendum in Scotland, was hedged about with statements from Ministers that this was a symbolic declaration only that would not be legally binding. Admittedly, as the chapter acknowledges, not all judges accept that parliamentary sovereignty is unlimited, and so a statutory provision of this nature could turn out to have legal consequences. However, it is hard for constitutional reformers to predict how judges will react to attempts to constrain the UK Parliament. Thus the effect of parliamentary sovereignty, while giving strong constitutional recognition to the principle of democracy as manifested in the UK Parliament, is to make it difficult to accord fundamental constitutional status to any other institutions or principles, no matter how important they may be.

Further reading

BOGDANOR, *The New British Constitution* (Oxford 2009)
An examination of the constitutional reforms of recent years and of their cumulative effect.

FELDMAN, 'None, One or Several? Perspectives on the UK's Constitution(s)' [2005] CLJ 329
Critical reflection on the nature of the UK's constitutional settlement.

KING, *The British Constitution* (Oxford 2007)
A useful overview of the subject.

LOUGHLIN, *The British Constitution: A Very Short Introduction* (Oxford 2013)
A useful overview.

2

Themes, Sources, and Principles

1. Introduction	36
2. Three key themes	37
3. Sources of the constitution	42
4. Constitutional principles	62
5. Legality and the rule of law	65
6. Codification and the constitution	77
7. Concluding remarks	81
Expert commentary	81
Further reading	84

1. Introduction

We saw in Chapter 1 that constitutions tend to perform a number of different functions and to have certain characteristics. We also looked briefly, against that background, at the United Kingdom's constitutional arrangements. In this chapter, our focus switches more fully to those arrangements. In particular, we consider four important matters concerning the UK constitution of which it is necessary to be aware at the outset. First, we set out the *three key themes* that, in our view, emerge from the study of contemporary UK public law. These themes reflect the dominant characteristics of and challenges faced by public law in the UK today. Being aware of them right at the beginning of our study of the subject is important. It will help us to understand their significance as we examine different topics during the course of the book. It will also, we hope, help to illustrate that while public law, like any branch of the law, consists of a good deal of technical, detailed material, it is also an area in which big ideas and broad narratives are to be found. Public law is also a subject that invites debate and disagreement—much of which, as we will see, centres upon the themes around which this book is based.

Second, we examine the *sources of the UK constitution*. We have already said that the UK does not have a 'written constitution', in the sense of a constitutional text with superior legal status. Where, then, do we look if we wish to ascertain the constitutional arrangements applicable in the UK? As we will see, the UK's constitution is to be found in a range of sources—written and unwritten, legal and political.

Third, we address a number of *principles that occupy a central role in UK public law*. Many of these principles are considered in greater detail in subsequent chapters. But it is necessary to be aware of them, at least in outline, at the outset, because of their pervasive relevance to the matters considered in this book.

Fourth, we consider whether the UK should adopt a *written, or 'codified',* *constitution*.

2. Three key themes

2.1 The role of the executive and the importance of accountability

Our first theme concerns *the central role occupied in the UK constitution by the executive branch of government*, and the fundamental importance of *ensuring that the executive is effectively held to account*. We saw in Chapter 1 that Parliament is all-powerful, in that it can enact any law that it wishes, but it is nevertheless the executive branch of central government—the Prime Minister, other Ministers, their government departments, and civil servants—that is in the driving seat. It is, for instance, the executive branch that formulates a programme for government and then seeks to implement it, including by getting Parliament to enact legislation. The executive government is in a strong position in this regard, bearing in mind that it will almost inevitably have a majority in the House of Commons and that the House of Lords ultimately lacks the power to block legislation. It follows that, because the courts are subservient to Parliament (in that they cannot strike down the laws that it enacts) and because Parliament is, in a sense, subservient to the executive (for the reasons just given), the executive finds itself in a very powerful position. This, in turn, means that one of the central challenges that arises in relation to the UK constitution is to make sure that the executive is properly held to account for its actions and decisions, and its policies and their implementation.

We explore the concept of accountability in detail in Chapter 10. For now, it suffices to say that holding the government to account involves requiring it to explain and justify what it is doing and why, particularly when things have gone wrong—and, where appropriate, providing the means by which corrective or punitive action may be taken against those guilty of wrongdoing or bad judgement. Holding government to account in these ways goes hand in hand with the notion of democracy. After all, in a democracy, government is supposed to act as the servant, as opposed to the master, of the people. To perform the many tasks deemed necessary in modern society, the people collectively delegate their power to government so that it can act on their behalf. However, human nature being what it is, there is always the risk that government may exceed the limits of its powers, betray the trust of the people, or be incompetent. It is therefore necessary for the people to be able to call the government to account.

General elections are the ultimate form of accountability. But they are a blunt instrument. They enable the electorate to render a single judgement on the government's overall performance—but given the enormous amount and diversity of the tasks undertaken by governments, there is a clear need for a more granular form of scrutiny and oversight. Elections therefore have to be supplemented by other accountability processes, such as parliamentary and judicial scrutiny. Their effectiveness is one of the main issues that falls to be examined in this book.

2.2 Legal and political constitutionalism

The second of our key themes, concerning the *shift from a more political to a more legal form of constitutionalism* in the UK, is closely connected to our first theme. Holding government to account involves ensuring that it behaves constitutionally— that is, in accordance with the requirements and values of the constitution—and taking appropriate action when it does not. But how is this to be achieved? It is in relation to this question that the distinction between legal and political constitutionalism emerges: each is a theory—a set of views—concerning how, in practice, constitutional behaviour should be promoted and unconstitutional conduct dealt with.

Advocates of *political constitutionalism* put their faith in the political process. Simply put, political constitutionalists hold two core views. First, the constitution is a product of a set of political relationships between the different institutions of the state—Parliament, government, and the courts. As such political relationships develop and change, so too do constitutional rules and practices. The basic point is that the practices governing the exercise and distribution of government power are determined not by *legal rules*, but by a set of *political understandings*.

Second, political constitutionalists argue that, in a democracy, the political process is the most legitimate means of guarding against unconstitutional behaviour by those in authority. The role of the courts in scrutinising government ought to be fairly limited because judges lack any democratic legitimacy. For political constitutionalists, then, it is the political process that deters politicians from doing unconstitutional things (because Parliament or the people might think badly of this and might therefore refuse to support the government in a vote in the Commons or at a general election) and provides a corrective if such things are done (because the people can vote for a different party, which might govern in a more constitutionally acceptable manner). This is not to suggest that political constitutionalists think that regular elections are sufficient to secure accountability. However, for political constitutionalists, more nuanced accountability devices—such as public inquiries and investigations by parliamentary committees—are ultimately oriented towards equipping parliamentarians and the public in the best possible position to judge whether the government is behaving acceptably. The ultimate focus, therefore, remains on the ballot box.

Unsurprisingly, the emphasis of those who advocate *legal constitutionalism* is rather different. They prefer to put their faith in the judicial, not the political, system. Both philosophical and pragmatic arguments underpin this view. In philosophical terms, it is said that there are certain moral principles—principles of 'natural law' or 'higher law'—that are so fundamental as to be immutable. A 'law' that contradicts such principles cannot be a genuine law at all and should not be enforced by courts—a view that means that, in practice, courts have the task of ensuring that politicians do not overstep the mark. There are also practical reasons why it might be thought that courts should have such a role in the UK. The most obvious is that the executive's influence over Parliament means that there is, in effect, a fusion of power between the legislature and executive—a phenomenon that leads some to argue that there must be a *separate* body, such as the judiciary, capable of ensuring that the political branches of government act constitutionally.[1] For reasons that we explain in Chapter 3, confidence in the ability of the political branches to regulate themselves and each other has declined in recent years, adding impetus to the view that courts should be able to step in when things go wrong.

A further argument advanced in favour of legal constitutionalism is that while reliance on the political process is likely to result in the interests of the majority being adequately looked after, the same might not be true of minorities of various sorts. The majority, acting through political institutions such as Parliament, might be inclined to do things—such as locking up suspected foreign terrorists without charge or trial[2]—that serve their own interests at the expense of unpopular, marginalised groups. In order to prevent this from happening, it is necessary to empower judges— whose independence allows them to be uninfluenced by public opinion—to protect the constitutional rights of *everyone*, even if that means curbing the self-serving instincts of the majority.

To this suggestion, political constitutionalists retort that giving judges such power overlooks the fact that 'law is not and cannot be a substitute for politics'.[3] Thus Waldron, a leading critic of US judges' capacity to strike down unconstitutional legislation, argues that giving courts such powers 'disenfranchises ordinary citizens and brushes aside cherished principles of representation and political equality in the final resolution of issues about rights'.[4] The argument against giving judges extensive powers of this nature may be thought to be stronger still in the UK, given that no popularly endorsed text lays down what the fundamental principles of the constitution are. Giving judges such powers, it has been said, 'would arguably be tantamount to the abdication of democracy in favour of a system of democracy layered with aristocracy (the decisions of the elite)'.[5]

Although it is helpful to be aware of the broad distinctions between legal and political constitutionalism, neither is a monolithic concept—there are many different views about precisely what each concept should mean. And, in any event, it is simplistic to suppose that a given constitutional system must opt for one or other of those two models. The UK constitution, like all developed constitutions, relies upon

---

[1] This argument is put forward by several commentators in different ways and with different emphases. For leading examples, see Allan, *Constitutional Justice* (Oxford 2001); Woolf, '*Droit Public*: English Style' [1995] PL 57; Laws, 'Law and Democracy' [1995] PL 72.

[2] See Chapter 1, section 3.1.   [3] Griffith, 'The Political Constitution' (1979) 42 MLR 1, 16.

[4] Waldron, 'The Core of the Case against Judicial Review' (2006) 115 Yale LJ 1346, 1353.

[5] Poole, 'Dogmatic Liberalism? TRS Allan and the Common Law Constitution' (2002) 65 MLR 463, 475. See further Poole, 'Questioning Common Law Constitutionalism' (2002) 25 LS 142.

both legal and political processes for the purpose of encouraging and enforcing compliance with constitutional principles. The question, therefore, is not whether we should put our faith in the legal *or* political process, but the *balance* that should be struck between those two means of securing constitutional governance.

In recent years, that balance has shifted in the UK in favour of legal forms of control. Legislation such as the Human Rights Act 1998 (HRA) has been a major driver of this trend, by authorising and requiring courts to scrutinise both government decisions and legislation on human rights grounds. Thus the second of our three key themes is that the direction of constitutional travel in the UK is towards a more legal form of constitutionalism. We will see several examples of this phenomenon throughout the book; as we encounter them, we will need to think critically about whether it is wise to place growing reliance on the legal system in this regard. One prominent critic of this trend, for example, has argued that, to the extent that such reliance is motivated by dissatisfaction with the political process, strengthening that process would be preferable to leaving it to courts to step in.[6]

Q Which of the two schools of thought outlined above—'legal constitutionalism' and 'political constitutionalism'—do you find more appealing? Do you agree that each has strengths and weaknesses, and, if so, can you think of ways in which the best features of the two systems might be combined?

2.3 The multilayered nature of the modern UK constitution

The UK has traditionally been a highly centralised state. Executive and legislative power was, until comparatively recently, largely concentrated at the centre: the UK executive government was responsible for the running of the whole country, while the UK Parliament made law for the whole of the UK. Local government has long existed alongside central government, and it fulfils many important functions, but it only has the powers given to it via law made by the UK Parliament. Over recent decades, central government has tended to restrict and confine local government, which, in turn, has often come to be seen, to some extent, as an offshoot of central government—an implementer of the latter's policies—rather than a constitutionally separate branch of government with its own independent area of authority.[7]

However, this picture—of a system in which central government has a monopoly of real power—has changed markedly in recent years. There has been a clear shift from a system in which power is concentrated almost wholly in central government to one in which power is shared by a number of different levels of government.

This shift to a system of *multilayered governance* is the third of our three key themes. The drivers of this change are threefold: the UK's membership of the European Union (EU), which, for the time being, persists; the devolution of power to Scotland, Wales,

---

[6] Tomkins, *Our Republican Constitution* (Oxford 2005), ch 4.   [7] See further Chapter 7.

and Northern Ireland; and, most recently, what has been branded, perhaps a little optimistically, 'devolution' to English regions.[8] The result is that power is dispersed to an unprecedented extent. The picture will change again—in ways that cannot yet be confidently predicted—when the UK leaves the EU, as powers that had been conceded to European institutions flow back to the UK. However, some—perhaps many—of those powers may end up in the hands of devolved governments and legislatures, rather than being exercised by UK institutions on a UK-wide basis. While Brexit will therefore change the complexion of multilayered governance, it certainly will not be is death knell.

The emergence of multilayered governance forces us to confront questions that previously simply did not arise and to reassess established ways of thinking. For example, once power is shared between different levels of government, questions of demarcation must be confronted:

- Does a given function fall to be performed at the local, devolved, national, or (for as long as the UK remains a member of the EU) European level?

- What are the powers of the different governments in relation to one another?

- Who has the last word in the event of a disagreement?

- What should be the role of the courts in attempting to resolve such disputes?

Once we start to think about issues of this nature, we are also forced to consider whether certain long-established constitutional principles remain relevant. For example, as we saw in Chapter 1, the traditional principle is that the UK Parliament can make any law that it wishes. But can this orthodoxy withstand devolution? In particular, is the UK Parliament free to make laws that cut across the powers of devolved institutions—by, for example, repealing a Scottish law with which it disagrees? We consider the answer to that question—and other challenges to orthodoxy raised by devolution—later in the book. However, it is important from the outset to bear in mind that the multilayered nature of the modern constitution forces us to think afresh about long-held principles such as parliamentary sovereignty.

2.4 **Conclusion**

It would be misleading to suggest that the whole of the subject matter of this book could be organised meaningfully around these three key themes. But that is not the point of identifying those themes. Rather, the point is that they reflect three of the major characteristics of, and issues faced by, UK public law today. It is in relation to our three key themes—the need to hold the executive to account, the balance between legal and political forms of constitutionalism, and the implications of distributing power among several tiers of government—that many of the most important, difficult, and pressing questions in modern UK public law arise.

---

[8] See Chapters 8 and 7 respectively.

3. Sources of the constitution

3.1 Introduction

No constitution is to be found in a single document; even 'written constitutions' are only a starting point. For reasons considered in Chapter 1, such documents are likely to contain only a statement of the most fundamental principles—which might well be expressed in vague language that leaves many questions unanswered. In systems based on written constitutions, such texts must therefore be supplemented and fleshed out. This is likely to happen in three ways.

First, *ordinary legislation* will make detailed provision in relation to matters referred to in the constitution. For example, the constitutional text might say that free and fair elections to the national legislature must be held at reasonable intervals, while leaving the detailed arrangements—exactly how regularly must elections be held, who is entitled to vote, and so on—to be set out in a statute.

Second, it will often be necessary for courts to *interpret* the constitutional text; in this way, a body of judicial precedent will develop that itself can properly be regarded as a source of constitutional law. For example, if the constitution says that elections must be held 'at reasonable intervals', and the legislature passes a law providing for elections every ten years, a court might well be called upon to decide whether such relatively infrequent elections meet the constitutional requirement that they be held at reasonable intervals.

Third, there may be certain matters in relation to which no provision is made, either in the constitutional text itself or in ordinary legislation. When issues arise that have not been anticipated by any law, one possibility is that those involved might arrive at an informal resolution. If it proves satisfactory, and the relevant parties appear willing to adhere to it, it might be felt that there is no need to enshrine it in law; rather, a political precedent or *constitutional convention* with which future parties will be expected to comply will arise. Several examples of such conventions are given in Table 2.1.[9]

Except for the absence of a written constitution, the position in the UK is essentially the same as that which is set out in the preceding paragraphs. The sources of the UK's constitutional arrangements are therefore to be found in a combination of ordinary law (including legislation, international treaties, and common law), judicial precedent (eg concerning the interpretation of legislation), and political precedent.

3.2 Legislation

A great deal of constitutional legislation—that is, legislation dealing with constitutional matters—exists in the UK. Indeed, there is so much legislation that it could be argued that it is misleading to say that the UK lacks a *written* constitution. A large proportion of its constitutional arrangements *are* in fact written down in statutes; it

---

[9] See also section 3.5.2.

Table 2.1 Constitutional conventions

Convention	Precedent	Evidence that relevant parties feel bound	Constitutional reason
Legally, a Bill approved by Parliament can become law only if the monarch assents to it, and the monarch is under no legal duty to do so. However, by convention, the monarch always assents.	No monarch has withheld royal assent to a Bill for over three hundred years.	It is highly unlikely that every monarch since the early 1700s has agreed with every Bill. This strongly suggests that monarchs feel obliged to grant assent whatever their personal views.	Today, Parliament is a democratic institution. It would be fundamentally undemocratic for an unelected monarch to thwart the wishes of the elected legislature.
On being appointed, judges sever any ties they have had with political parties.	Appointees who are affiliated to political parties habitually end such affiliations upon appointment.	The Judges' Council, the judges' representative body, accepts and stipulates that political ties must be severed.	The law must be applied by independent and impartial judges without reference (or the appearance of reference) to extrinsic factors such as party politics.
The Prime Minister and other Ministers regularly appear in Parliament to answer questions from MPs or peers (depending on which chamber they belong to).	The Prime Minister and Ministers habitually do this.	There are often occasions (eg when a Minister is embroiled in personal or political controversy) when it may be advantageous to the Minister not to appear in Parliament; but Ministers do appear even in such circumstances.	It is important that the government is held to account for its policies and their implementation; this is a way of doing so.
The monarch retains certain 'prerogative' powers (eg to declare war and to sign international treaties) but only, and always, exercises them on the advice of the government.	There are no modern examples of monarchs exercising these powers of their own accord, or of refusing to exercise them when advised to do so by the government.	Consistent compliance with the convention implies that monarchs accept that their only role in this area is to do as the government advises.	In a democracy, it would be inappropriate for major policy decisions to be taken by an unelected head of state.

(Continued)

Table 2.1 (*Continued*)

Convention	Precedent	Evidence that relevant parties feel bound	Constitutional reason
Although senior Ministers can be members of the House of Lords, the Queen will only appoint as Prime Minister someone who is a member of the House of Commons.	It is more than 100 years since a Prime Minister served without being or becoming a member of the House of Commons.	When Alexander Douglas-Home was appointed Prime Minister in 1963, he renounced his peerage and became a member of the House of Commons by winning a by-election.	As the most senior member of the government, it would be undemocratic for the Prime Minister not to be a member of and directly accountable to the elected chamber.
Under the 'Sewel Convention', the UK Parliament will not normally legislate for parts of the country with devolved governments on matters within the competence of the latter without the prior consent of the relevant devolved legislature.	This convention has been respected since devolution; but since devolution only began in 1999, there is not a long precedent.	The UK government has publicly stated that it accepts this convention.	Underlying devolution is acceptance of the principle that certain parts of the country should, within certain limits, be able to govern themselves. Unwanted interference by the UK legislature would contravene that principle.

is just that those arrangements (or at least the fundamental principles underpinning them) have not been codified into a single text called 'The Constitution'.[10]

But because statutory constitutional law is to be found in regular legislation rather than in a separate constitutional text, there is no straightforward, formal way of identifying such legislation. In other words, constitutional law is not contained in statutes that are labelled 'constitutional'. Instead, we can only say that a statute deals with constitutional law if it seems that, in substance, the statute concerns constitutional matters.[11] It is helpful, in this regard, to distinguish between the two principal types of such matters.

[10] See, eg Bogdanor, *The New British Constitution* (Oxford 2009), pp 8–9. But this point should not be overstated. However much constitutional legislation there is in the UK, it is still only legislation: it is not constitutional law that has a higher legal status in the sense discussed in Chapter 1.

[11] See further House of Commons Political and Constitutional Reform Committee, *Ensuring Standards in the Quality of Legislation* (HC 85 2013–14), [43]–[45].

First, constitutional law is concerned with the *organisation of, and the allocation of power to, the institutions of government*. A good deal of legislation deals with such matters.[12] Prominent examples include the legislation that provides for the devolution of executive and lawmaking power to the Scottish, Welsh, and Northern Irish governments and legislatures.[13] Similarly, legislation was enacted when the UK joined the EU in order to make provision for (among other things) EU law to take effect in the UK and to be enforceable by national courts.[14] A great deal of legislation exists concerning the role and functions of local government and its relationship with central government.[15] Meanwhile, important issues concerning the UK Parliament itself—including the limitation of the powers of the House of Lords,[16] eligibility for membership of Parliament,[17] elections to the House of Commons,[18] and the frequency of elections[19]—are dealt with by legislation. There is also legislation concerning the judicial system:[20] the UK Supreme Court was, for example, created by an Act of Parliament.[21] Indeed, the creation of the United Kingdom itself is attributable in part to legislation, the joining of England and Wales with Scotland and Ireland having been effected by statute.[22]

Second, there is a good deal of legislation concerning the other main aspect of constitutional law: *the regulation of the relationship between the individual and the state*. Formal statements setting out important rights and interests to be respected by the state are not a modern innovation. Consider, for example, Magna Carta 1215, which (among other things) made provision concerning the liberty of the individual and the right to trial by jury. Also noteworthy is the Bill of Rights 1689, parts of which remain in force today: art 9, for example, lays down the principle of parliamentary privilege, whereby things said in Parliament cannot be the subject of legal proceedings (eg for defamation), thus ensuring that parliamentarians are free to express their views uninhibited by the threat of litigation. Today, the most significant legislation concerning the rights of the individual vis-à-vis the state is the HRA.[23]

Legislation dealing with fundamental constitutional matters is, ultimately, still only regular legislation; it can therefore be amended or even repealed simply by enacting a further piece of such legislation. This absence of hierarchy in UK statutory law—the notion that all laws are equal—was vividly captured by the Victorian scholar

---

[12] The examples of such legislation discussed in this section are considered in more detail in the relevant chapters of this book.

[13] Scotland Act 1998, Government of Wales Act 2006, Northern Ireland Act 1998.

[14] European Communities Act 1972.

[15] See in particular Local Government Act 1972, Local Government Act 2000, Local Government and Public Involvement in Health Act 2007, Localism Act 2011, Cities and Local Government Devolution Act 2016.

[16] Parliament Acts 1911–49.

[17] House of Lords Act 1999, House of Commons Disqualification Act 1975.

[18] eg Representation of the People Act 1983.

[19] Fixed-term Parliaments Act 2011; Septennial Act 1715.

[20] eg Senior Courts Act 1981; Tribunals, Courts and Enforcement Act 2007; Constitutional Reform Act 2005.

[21] Constitutional Reform Act 2005.

[22] Union with Scotland Act 1706; Union with Ireland Act 1800.   [23] See section 5.11.

Dicey, who remarked that 'neither the Act of Union with Scotland nor the Dentists Act 1878 has more claim than the other to be considered a supreme law'.[24]

However, this view has been questioned in recent times. In *Thoburn v Sunderland City Council*, it was suggested by Laws LJ that '[w]e should recognise a hierarchy of Acts of Parliament: as it were "ordinary" statutes and "constitutional" statutes'.[25] The latter category, he said, included legislation that 'conditions the legal relationship between citizen and state in some general, overarching manner' or that affects individuals' fundamental rights.[26] Importantly, Laws LJ's argument was that this distinction should be one to which legal significance attaches. The general principle, as we will see in Chapter 5, is that whenever two pieces of legislation conflict, the courts will prioritise the more recent one: even if the later Act does not explicitly say that it is overriding the earlier one, it will have that effect. However, in *Thoburn*, Laws LJ said that this doctrine of 'implied repeal' should not apply to *constitutional* statutes. On this view, legislation dealing with constitutional matters can still be repealed or amended simply by Parliament enacting another piece of legislation—but only if, in that legislation, Parliament specifically says that it intends to override an earlier piece of constitutional legislation.

Laws LJ's analysis in *Thoburn* received some support from the Supreme Court in the *HS2* case.[27] However, even if constitutional statutes are legally acknowledged in this way, the upshot is relatively modest. Technically, it means that there is now a special category of *harder*-to-amend constitutional legislation in the UK. But such legislation is still not particularly *hard* to amend: all that is needed is express words of repeal. It therefore remains the case that the UK lacks a hierarchy of statutory law that invests fundamental constitutional arrangements with any great degree of legal permanence.

> **Q** Do you agree that constitutional law should be more difficult to amend than other forms of law? If so, how difficult? If not, why not?

3.3 Judge-made law and common law

The principal role of courts is to decide disputes between litigants by resolving disagreements about the facts and then applying the law to the facts. It may be thought that this is a mechanical process whereby the court simply decides whether the facts fit whatever test is laid down in the statute. The reality, however, is more complex, and in many situations, courts end up *making* law—and, in cases with a constitutional dimension to them, making *public law*. It follows that judicial precedent—that is, the

---

[24] Dicey, *An Introduction to the Study of the Law of the Constitution* (London 1959), p 145.

[25] *Thoburn v Sunderland City Council* [2002] EWHC 195 (Admin), [2003] QB 151, [62].

[26] *Thoburn* at [62]. Much, or even all, of the legislation mentioned earlier would fall into the category of 'constitutional legislation'.

[27] *R (HS2 Action Alliance Ltd) v Secretary of State for Transport* [2014] UKSC 3, [2014] 1 WLR 324.

body of decisions made by courts when deciding cases—itself constitutes an important source of public law. This is so in three senses.

The first is concerned with the *interpretation of constitutional legislation*. Such legislation may be—and indeed often is—unclear or unspecific, capable of being interpreted in different ways, each of which would produce a different practical outcome for the parties. In this sense, courts augment legislation by interpreting it: they put flesh on the bones by giving it the more precise meaning that it turns out to require once it falls to be applied in real cases.

For example, the HRA obliges 'public authorities' to respect the rights protected by the Act.[28] But this term is highly imprecise. Indeed, in a leading case on this point, one of the judges candidly admitted that the relevant words are 'so imprecise in their meaning' that the court has to try to work out the policy underlying them. Thus the statute has to be interpreted by reference to extrinsic considerations about what the judge thinks Parliament was trying to achieve[29]—yet the judge went on to admit that the 'identification of the policy is almost inevitably governed, at least to some extent, by one's notions of what the policy should be'.[30] There are therefore clearly occasions on which, in interpreting legislation dealing with constitutional matters, courts make law by filling gaps in the statute or giving precise meaning to statutory language that is, taken in isolation, so vague as to be almost meaningless. Furthermore, the views of the courts as to what the law actually is will, to some degree, be inevitably influenced by their views as to what the law ought to be.

Second, the principal hallmark of a *common law* system is that the lawmaking role of courts extends beyond the interpretation of legislation. The common law is a body of law that is unambiguously judge-made. Large areas of private law, such as much of the law of tort, are based on common law—that is, on legal principles articulated and refined by judges on a case-by-case basis. Important parts of public law, too, consist of judge-made common law rules. For example, public bodies, such as government Ministers, frequently exercise discretionary powers—such as in deciding whether someone should be granted asylum or British citizenship. When exercising such powers, public bodies must act in accordance with certain legal principles of 'good administration'. This means, among other things, that the decision must be made in a procedurally fair manner and that the decision must not be irrational or unreasonable. These public law principles have been developed by the courts, in accordance with the common law method, in much the same way as the law of tort has been developed.

Third, judge-made law is a source of public law to the extent that courts have articulated *common law constitutional principles*. These principles are distinct from straightforward common law rules. If the latter are breached, the person concerned may sue the perpetrator. This is true in private law (if X acts negligently and causes foreseeable harm to you, you can sue him) and in public law (if Minister Y decides to deport you without first giving you a fair hearing, you can take legal action against her). The legal relevance of common

---

[28] Section 6(1).

[29] *YL v Birmingham City Council* [2007] UKHL 27, [2008] 1 AC 95, [128], *per* Lord Neuberger.

[30] *YL* at [128].

law constitutional principles, on the other hand, is more subtle: such *principles* influence how courts interpret and apply existing legal *rules*.

We explore these issues in section 5. For the time being, a brief example will suffice. In Chapter 1, we noted that the principle of legal certainty is recognised in many countries, including the UK, as a fundamentally important one. The principle means, among other things, that people should be able to know what the law is in order that they can (if they wish) regulate their conduct so as to stay on the right side of it. In the UK, this principle is regarded as a common law constitutional principle. It is not recorded in a written constitution—and it is, thanks to parliamentary sovereignty, possible for the UK Parliament to override it. But this does not rob it of any practical significance.

For instance, fundamental constitutional principles have a *political* relevance: a government that wishes to do something that flies in the face of such a principle is likely to face considerable opposition. The existence of fundamental constitutional principles thus helps to shape public debate, and to determine what it is politically possible for governments to do. In addition, and perhaps more concretely, courts will strive to interpret legislation and to develop the common law in ways that respect common law constitutional principles. Thus, for example, if the wording of a statute were unclear, such that it could be interpreted as either creating or not creating criminal liability in respect of acts committed before its enactment, the court would adopt the latter interpretation, so as to render the legislation compatible with the principle of legal certainty.

An important question that this raises is just how far courts can go: if the statute is crystal clear, do they have to enforce it even if it fundamentally conflicts with an important constitutional principle? The traditional answer to this question is that, because Parliament is sovereign, the court would have to apply the legislation however repugnant it was to such a principle—but, as we explain in Chapter 5, this view is not universally shared.

Finally in this section, mention should be made of the *royal prerogative*. This is considered in more detail in Chapter 4. For now, it is sufficient to say that the prerogative is generally regarded as part of the common law that, among other things, authorises (in practice) the executive branch of government to do certain things such as declaring war and granting honours. The prerogative is an historical anachronism that reflects the fact that government used to be carried on by or under the direction of the monarch exercising the 'royal prerogative'. Most vestiges of the prerogative have by now been swept away by legislation, upon which the vast majority of executive authority depends, but pockets of prerogative power remain. Although formally belonging to the monarch, such powers are generally exercised on her behalf by government Ministers.

3.4 International law

International law is an important influence upon, and in some senses a source of, UK constitutional law. This is so in two main ways.[31]

---

[31] See further Crawford, *Brownlie's Principles of Public International Law* (Oxford 2012), ch 3.

First, when the UK becomes party to a treaty—that is, an agreement with one or more other states that is binding in international law—it is often given effect in national law through the enactment of legislation. For example, the treaties concerning the EU are, for the time being, given domestic legal effect by the European Communities Act 1972, while a separate treaty, the European Convention on Human Rights (ECHR), is given effect by the HRA. The EU treaties (via the 1972 Act) have had, and the ECHR (via the HRA) will continue to have, significant implications for the UK's constitutional arrangements.

Second, even if legislation is not enacted so as to give domestic effect to a treaty, there is a well-established principle that national law should be interpreted, where possible, in conformity with treaties to which the UK is a party.[32] Thus, for example, prior to the enactment of the HRA, the ECHR was not ignored by UK courts; rather, it was, at the very least, used as an aid to interpretation when the meaning of national law was unclear.[33]

3.5 **Conventions and political practice**

3.5.1 **Introduction**

Law is an important source of constitutional rules, but many aspects of the constitution are not regulated by strict rules of law.[34] There are many crucial constitutional matters for which no relevant law exists. Assume, for example, that there is a Conservative government, that a general election is held, and that the Labour Party wins a majority of the seats in the House of Commons. The convention is that a government or Prime Minister who cannot command the confidence of the House of Commons is required to resign. So, if a general election results in a clear majority for a different political party, then the Queen must invite the leader of that party to form a new government. Applying this convention to our scenario, we would expect the Conservative Prime Minister to resign, and the Queen to invite the leader of the Labour Party to become Prime Minister and to form a new government. It would be extremely surprising if these things did not happen. But no law requires that they take place. No legal wrong would be committed by a Prime Minister who refused to resign after his party lost its majority at a general election, and no legal wrong would be committed if the Queen were to invite the leader of a party other than that which had secured a majority to form a government.

But the fact that the *law* does not regulate such matters does not mean that the relevant people are, in practice, free to do as they please. This is because, in relation to many constitutional matters, *legal freedom* is constrained by *political precedent*. For example, while the Queen is *legally* free to ask someone other than the leader of the

---

[32] *Garland v British Rail Engineering Ltd* [1983] 2 AC 751, 771.

[33] *R v Secretary of State for the Home Department, ex p Brind* [1991] 1 AC 696. See further Hunt, *Using Human Rights Law in English Courts* (Oxford 1997).

[34] See generally Brazier, *Constitutional Practice* (Oxford 1994) and Marshall, *Constitutional Conventions* (Oxford 1984), for discussion of a range of constitutional matters governed largely by political practice as distinct from legal rules.

majority party to form a government, there is a long-standing *political* precedent—
or 'constitutional convention'—to the effect that she will ask that person to become
Prime Minister. Such political rules are not found uniquely in systems, such as that of
the UK, that lack a written constitution, but they do assume a particular prominence
in such systems.

Traditionally, conventions have existed as the 'unwritten rules of the game' by
which all parties implicitly agreed to abide. However, there is now a trend towards
the codification of conventions. This does not mean that they are being converted
into laws but, rather, that it is increasingly common for them to be recorded in an
official, and so relatively authoritative, form. Take, for instance, the standards of
conduct for government Ministers. These used to be entirely unwritten. It was simply
assumed that Ministers would both know and adhere to accepted standards of propriety appropriate to their position in public life. It was also an unwritten assumption that government Ministers would be accountable to Parliament for the policies,
decisions, and actions of their departments and agencies. However, unwritten conventions are likely to be both vague and ambiguous, which renders them liable to
exploitation and manipulation by the unscrupulous. Following notable lapses of
ministerial probity in the 1990s, successive Prime Ministers have published a formal
code—the Ministerial Code—that sets out the principles and standards expected of
Ministers.[35] In this way, unwritten conventions have transmuted into a formal—but
still non-legal—code.

A further, and particularly wide-ranging, example of this trend is supplied by *The
Cabinet Manual*, the origins of which lie in the period immediately prior to the 2010
election. At that time, the Cabinet Secretary, the most senior civil servant in the UK
government, published draft guidance on the applicable conventions in the event of a
hung Parliament (ie, a Parliament in which no single party controls a majority of the
seats).[36] When the 2010 election produced precisely such a situation, the draft guidance provided certainty as to the constitutional position. The coalition government
was thus formed in the light of a clear understanding of the relevant constitutional
position—that is, that any coalition would, collectively, have to be able to command
a majority in the House of Commons to have the authority to govern. That guidance
concerning government formation now forms just one part of the *Cabinet Manual*,
the first edition of which was published in 2011.[37] Its primary purpose is to be a 'guide
for those working in government, recording the current position rather than driving
change'.[38]

However, whilst important, there are limits to the significance of such formal statements of conventions. First, such statements can amount to no more than a snapshot
of how the convention is perceived at the time. Whereas a legislative text is the *source*
of a legal rule, a written statement of a convention can be no more than an attempt to

---

[35] Cabinet Office, 'Ministerial Code' (London 2016).

[36] This guidance was presented by the Cabinet Secretary to the House of Commons Justice Committee.
See House of Commons Justice Committee, *Constitutional Processes Following a General Election* (HC 296
2009–10).

[37] Cabinet Office, *The Cabinet Manual* (London 2011).   [38] *Cabinet Manual*, p iv.

record, as accurately as possible, a political rule. It is possible, then, for such a written statement to be—or, as conditions and attitudes evolve, to become—inaccurate in a way that is not true of a legislative text. Second, even when formally written down, constitutional conventions remain binding only in a political sense. The distinction between those areas of the constitution that are regulated by conventions—whether codified or not—and those areas to which legal regulation applies is therefore relevant to the difference, considered earlier in this chapter, between legal and political constitutionalism. Those areas that are governed by convention fall within the realm of the political constitution: to the extent that people are obliged to respect (or in any event actually respect) the norms underlying constitutional conventions, they do so for reasons unconnected with legal coercion. Conventions are (at least on a traditional view) legally unenforceable; their enforceability, such as it is, derives from the political process.

3.5.2 **What counts as a convention—and does it matter?**

There is no shortage of definitions of constitutional conventions.[39] Dicey said that they form the 'morality' of the constitution, defining them as 'understandings, habits, or practices' that 'regulate the conduct of the several members of the sovereign power, of the Ministry, or of other officials'.[40] Other writers have characterised conventions as the 'flesh which clothes the dry bones of the law'[41] and as 'rules of constitutional behaviour which are considered to be binding by and upon those who operate the constitution'.[42] From these various definitions, or descriptions of the role, of conventions, we can deduce the following:

- Constitutional conventions are concerned, unsurprisingly, with *constitutional matters*; they are therefore different, in that sense at least, from mere social conventions (eg that people generally hold the door open for the person immediately behind them rather than allowing it to slam in their face).

- Conventions operate in a manner that is *supplementary to law*: as we have already seen, convention may operate so as to constrain the exercise of a legal power or freedom—a constitutional actor who is legally free to do something may be constrained from doing so by convention.

- Those at whom conventions are directed regard themselves as *bound* by them—that is, they feel obligated in some sense (albeit not a legal one) to do as the convention says.

- Dicey's reference to 'habits' and 'practices' implies that there must be some sort of track record of—or *precedent* for—doing things in the way concerned. This suggests that conventions are not created, but rather that they crystallise over a period of time.

---

[39] See generally Jaconelli, 'The Nature of Constitutional Convention' (1999) 19 LS 24.
[40] Dicey, *An Introduction to the Study of the Law of the Constitution* (London 1959), p 24.
[41] Jennings, *The Law and the Constitution* (London 1959), p 81.
[42] Marshall and Moodie, *Some Problems of the Constitution* (London 1967), p 26.

- If conventions represent the 'morality' of the constitution, they must have some sort of basis in *fundamental constitutional principles*. For example, the convention that requires the Queen to invite the party best able to command a majority in the House of Commons to form a government is underpinned by a fundamental constitutional principle—that is, democracy. In the absence of any law determining how the government is appointed, it ensures that the wishes of the people are reflected when a government is formed.

Many of these ideas are reflected in the so-called Jennings test, according to which '[w]e have to ask ourselves three questions' in order to determine whether a given practice amounts to a convention:[43]

- What *precedent*, if any, is there for the practice?
- Do those adhering to the precedent believe that they are *bound* to do so, as if by a rule?
- Is there a *reason* for the rule?

Applying these criteria, it is easy to see why many accepted constitutional conventions are so regarded. Table 2.1 lists a number of prominent conventions, indicating how the Jennings criteria apply to them.

For a more detailed example of the Jennings test in action, it is helpful to turn to events that occurred in Canada several decades ago. Once part of the British Empire, Canada was, by the mid-twentieth century, to most intents and purposes a separate country wholly independent of the UK. However, one vestige of its colonial past remained: the Canadian constitution was based on a piece of UK legislation—the British North America Act 1867. A number of steps had been taken over the years to transfer to Canada greater control over its own affairs, but certain matters were still governed by the 1867 Act, meaning that when Canada wanted to make changes in respect of such matters, it had to ask the UK government to procure UK legislation amending the 1867 Act. By 1980, the Canadian government felt that this arrangement was no longer appropriate, and took steps to 'patriate' the Canadian constitution— that is, it asked the UK government to get the UK Parliament to pass legislation severing the legal connection between the UK and Canada once and for all, giving Canada full control over its own constitutional arrangements.

However, the Canadian government's proposals were not uniformly welcomed within Canada. The system of government in Canada was (and is) a federal one: the constitution divides power between a national (federal) government and regional (provincial) governments. The provincial governments were concerned that the federal government's proposals would affect the balance of power in a manner adverse to the provinces. Only two of the ten provinces supported the proposal. The other provinces argued that the federal government, by pressing on in spite of their opposition, was acting in breach of a constitutional convention that stipulated that UK legislation amending the Canadian constitution should be sought only with the support of the majority of the provinces. They therefore took the unusual step of seeking

---

[43] Jennings, p 136.

an injunction—a legal remedy prohibiting the federal government from asking the UK to enact the necessary legislation.[44] This required the Canadian Supreme Court to decide whether the convention asserted by the provinces existed. The Court concluded that it did—and came to that view by applying the Jennings test.[45]

First, the court asked whether there was a *precedent*. Historically, had the assent of the provinces been sought and obtained by the federal government before it asked the UK to enact constitutional changes? It certainly had. The majority observed that 'no amendment changing provincial legislative powers has been made . . . when agreement of a province whose legislative powers would have been changed was withheld. There are no exceptions'.[46] Moreover, the judges noted that when, in 1951, a proposal that would have affected the provinces' powers did not meet with the approval of certain provinces, it was dropped.[47]

Second, the court asked whether the federal government felt *bound* to seek the provinces' consent. The Court held that the government did consider itself so bound. In fact, the federal government had said as much: in an official document—which, the Court noted, was a 'carefully drafted document', not a 'casual utterance'—it had accepted that 'the Canadian Parliament will not request an amendment directly affecting federal–provincial relationships without prior consultation and agreement with the provinces'.[48]

Third, the Court considered whether there was a constitutional *reason* for the rule. It concluded that there clearly was. As we explain in Chapter 7, the essence of a federal system of government is that there is a carefully defined balance of power between the central and regional levels of government. Such a system demands that neither tier of government can unilaterally change the balance of power to the other's disadvantage. It follows that allowing the Canadian federal government, acting without provincial consent, to get the UK to amend the constitution in ways that were detrimental to the provinces' powers would have been directly contrary to the federal principle.

So, having applied the Jennings test, the Canadian Supreme Court came to the conclusion that there was, as the provinces asserted, a clear constitutional convention— to which, by asking the UK to change the constitution without the provinces' support, the federal government was acting contrary. But if (as we will see when we return to this case in section 3.5.4) the general position is that breaches of convention do not give rise to any form of *legal* liability, an obvious question arises. Why does it matter whether something passes the Jennings test (such that it counts as a convention) or fails it (such that it counts not as a convention, but merely as something falling short of that status—a 'tradition', say)?

Figure 2.1 may help us to think about this question. The solid vertical line represents the distinction between legal and non-legal constitutional rules. If the former are enforceable by courts, but the latter are not, this dividing line is a significant

---

[44] *Re Resolution to amend the Constitution* [1981] 1 SCR 753.
[45] *Re Resolution to amend the Constitution* at 888.
[46] *Re Resolution to amend the Constitution* at 893.
[47] *Re Resolution to amend the Constitution* at 893.
[48] *Re Resolution to amend the Constitution* at 899–900.

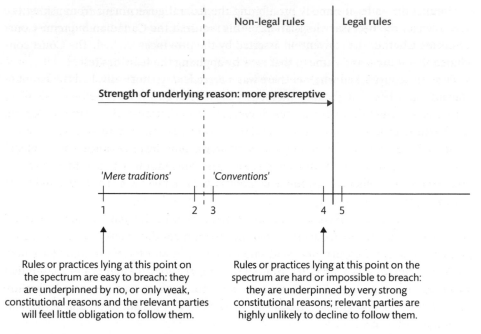

Figure 2.1 Law, convention, and tradition

one: knowing on which side of it a given rule falls is important, because that determines whether it can be legally enforced. The Jennings test implies that it makes sense to draw a *further* distinction, represented in the figure by the broken vertical line, between non-legal rules that qualify as conventions and non-legal rules that do not. Yet if all of these non-legal rules are legally unenforceable, why bother with this further distinction?

On one view, the further distinction postulated by the Jennings test *does* matter: categorising a rule as a convention may confer rhetorical force upon it, making those to whom it is addressed feel a greater sense of compulsion to follow it.[49] However, a different view is to be preferred. In reality, the convention/tradition line is largely irrelevant and, once we accept this, we can appreciate that the Jennings test asks the wrong questions—or, more precisely, that it asks the right questions in the wrong way.[50] The key issues are not *whether* there is a precedent, *whether* the actors feel bound, and *whether* there is a reason for the rule. The more pertinent questions are *how strong* is the precedent, *to what extent* do the actors feel bound by it, and *how good* is the reason for it? Once it is recognised that the real questions are ones of degree, their purpose can better be appreciated: while the *side of the tradition/convention line* on which a given rule falls is unimportant, *where the rule lies on the non-legal part of the spectrum* is much more significant. So while it is relatively unimportant whether a given rule occupies position 2 or position 3 in Figure 2.1, more turns on

---

[49] See Jaconelli, 'The Nature of Constitutional Convention' (1999) 19 LS 24, 27.
[50] Munro, *Studies in Constitutional Law* (London 1999), pp 86–7.

whether it occupies position 1 (barely scraping into the category of mere tradition) or position 4 (a rule that, although a convention, lies close to the boundary between conventional and political rules).

The reason for this lies in the underlying factors that, in the first place, determine where on the spectrum a given rule lies. What, then, are those factors? We have already said that they consist of the matters identified in the Jennings test, albeit posed as questions of degree, but some further consideration of this matter is needed. The three Jennings criteria—precedent, sense of obligation, and reason—are not co-equal. The second of those criteria is of principal practical relevance—how obliged the actors feel will determine how seriously the convention is taken, how easy it is to breach it, and whether anyone will care if it is breached—while the first and third criteria determine or reflect, in the first place, the extent to which a sense of obligation exists. The stronger the precedent, the greater will be the expectation that the relevant actors will continue to behave in accordance with the rule: in this, as in most contexts, long-established practices are harder to deviate from than those that have only existed for a very short time. Jennings conceded that the absence of a long-standing precedent is not necessarily of decisive importance.[51] The main determinant of the practical importance of a given non-legal rule is therefore the strength of the reason underlying it: the stronger the constitutional reason for the rule, the greater will be the extent to which those to whom it is addressed feel obliged to abide by it—and the more dire the likely consequences if they do not.

Some examples will help to illustrate these points. Since 1961, it has been the practice of the Prime Minister personally to answer questions in the House of Commons. The practice of successive Prime Ministers was to spend 15 minutes in the House of Commons on Tuesdays and Thursdays answering MPs' questions. However, when he became Prime Minister in 1997, Tony Blair changed the arrangements for Prime Minister's questions, attending one weekly 30-minute session every Wednesday. While there were mutterings in some quarters that Blair was guilty of a breach of convention, he clearly felt, and in fact was, perfectly free to make this change. The reason, it would appear, is that the original practice, involving twice-weekly questions, was not an important convention—it was a practice occupying a position nearer to position 1 than to position 4 in Figure 2.1—because no strong constitutional reason required the Prime Minister to answer questions *on Tuesdays and Thursdays*. The absence of any such reason presumably accounts for why Blair felt free to dispense with that practice—and for why there was no great outcry when he did so.

Q Would the position be different if a Prime Minister were to decide not to attend the House of Commons to answer questions *at all* (rather than simply, as Blair did, to change the detailed arrangements for such attendance)? (When thinking about this question, consider what constitutional reason underlies the practice whereby the Prime Minister periodically attends the House of Commons to answer MPs' questions.)

[51] Jennings, *The Law and the Constitution* (London 1959), p 136.

This may be contrasted with the conventions set out in Table 2.1. All of these are important conventions—that is, they are not mere traditions that can be flouted with ease; rather, they are rules that are taken with the utmost seriousness and which, in many cases, no one would dare to breach. Because the political reasons underlying them are so strong, it is highly unlikely that such conventions will be broken. If, for example, the Queen were to withhold royal assent from a Bill because she personally disagreed with it, she would be undermining the democratic nature of governance in the UK. We develop this point in section 3.5.3, but for now we will confine ourselves to saying that it stands to reason that, even if legal sanctions are unavailable, people are less likely to disrespect rules that are underpinned by a strong reason.

This accounts for Jennings's view that lack of precedent need not be decisive. A given rule might thus constitute a strong convention—one that lies near the law/convention borderline and that is taken very seriously by those to whom it is addressed—notwithstanding the absence of much, if anything, by way of precedent. A good example is provided by the 'Sewel Convention', which holds that the UK Parliament will not normally legislate on devolved matters without the prior consent of the relevant devolved legislature. Unlike most conventions, which *emerge* over a period of time and which thus have a degree of precedent behind them by the time they are acknowledged to be conventions, the Sewel Convention was, in effect, *created*. The UK government accepted, when devolution was instituted, that unwanted interference by the UK Parliament in devolved affairs would be improper, and entered into a political agreement with the devolved administrations undertaking that it would respect this principle.

The initial lack of precedent notwithstanding, it was (and still is) widely accepted that a convention to this effect exists. The absence of precedent was more than compensated for by the fact that a strong constitutional principle—namely, that relevant parts of the UK should enjoy a degree of self-government—underlies the Sewel Convention.[52] This is not to say that precedent is unimportant, since the longer the period during which the convention (and thus the underlying constitutional principle) is respected, the more difficult in practice it will become to act contrary to it. It would, however, be a mistake to think that a centuries-long track record of compliance is a condition precedent to the existence of a convention.

3.5.3 Why are conventions obeyed—and what if they are not?

If—as traditional theory would have us believe—conventions are unenforceable by courts, how, if at all, are they enforceable? One way of thinking about this question is to ask why rules that *are* legally enforceable are respected. Clearly, one reason for obeying legal rules is to avoid legal liability: a person might desist from deliberately killing another person because she fears that she may be caught and punished for the crime of murder. There are, however, undoubtedly other reasons why most people try to stay on the right side of the law. They might do so because the law in question (eg the law of homicide) coincides with their personal sense of morality (that killing people is wrong). But even if a given law (eg a law prohibiting the taking of certain

---

[52] This convention is considered in more detail in Chapter 7.

drugs) does not coincide with a person's own sense of morality (eg because they think consenting adults should be allowed to take whatever drugs they like in private), they might obey it because they respect society's right to make a collective judgement about the bounds of acceptable conduct. In addition, considerations of self-interest might enter into play: not only in relation to the avoidance of punishment, but also in relation to the avoidance of being stigmatised as someone who has failed to accept the socially accepted rules.

Against this background, we can better understand why constitutional actors might obey conventions even though they are not legally enforceable:

- As practical applications of underlying fundamental constitutional principles, conventions will (it is to be hoped) generally reflect individual constitutional actors' *personal sense of constitutional* morality. Most judges, for example, would personally agree that it is wholly improper for people to retain political affiliations following appointment to judicial office.

- Even if a given constitutional actor does not personally *agree* with the principle underlying a given convention, they may nevertheless respect it because they recognise that it reflects a *widely shared sense of constitutional morality*, and that there is a moral obligation to act accordingly.

- Someone might go along with a convention for *self-serving reasons*. Even though legal liability need not result from breaching a convention, plenty of other unpleasant consequences might. For example, a hypothetical monarch might personally think that democracy is hugely overrated, that he knows best, and that he should be able to withhold royal assent from Bills as he sees fit. Yet he might go along with the convention that says monarchs should grant assent as a matter of course, recognising that any other approach would be so undemocratic as to jeopardise the monarchy itself. A variant of this argument from self-serving reasons is that politicians in government might choose to play by the conventional rules for fear that failing to do so might incline opposition politicians— when they are in government at some point in the future—to do likewise.[53]

It follows from all of this that, their legal unenforceability notwithstanding, constitutional conventions (or at least those that are underpinned by strong constitutional reasons) are not merely *descriptive*. By that, we mean that they do not simply distil current and historical practice in a morally neutral way. Rather, conventions can be *prescriptive*, in the sense of directing how things *should* be done. That obligatory dimension of conventions derives not from legal enforceability, but from the combined effect of the other matters already considered.

However, in spite of what has been said, conventions are not *always* respected (just as laws are not). When conventions are not respected, one of three situations is likely to arise. First, in some circumstances a convention may be breached *without any significant consequences*. If this happens, it suggests either that the convention was an unimportant one (that can be, and now has been, safely disregarded) or that it admits

---

[53] See further Jaconelli, 'Do Constitutional Conventions Bind?' [2005] CLJ 149.

of a hitherto unacknowledged exception. (Think back to the example concerning the change in practice in 1997 regarding Prime Minister's questions.)

Second, and conversely, a breach of convention may produce *substantial practical effects*. For instance, if an individual government Minister were to refuse to abide by an important convention, his colleagues, or the public, might expect him to resign, and his position might become untenable. And if a whole government were to be tainted with unconstitutional behaviour—by virtue, for example, of collective ministerial action in breach of key conventions—it might face dire consequences at the following general election.

Third, even though conventions are not themselves generally regarded as legally enforceable, there is always the possibility that they may be *turned into laws* through the enactment of legislation. Taking such a step should be necessary only rarely: if the underlying principle is so important as to warrant legal protection, breaches of the convention in question should be extremely unlikely in the first place. However, in some circumstances, it may be practically desirable—or politically expedient—to place a given convention on a legal footing. A prominent example arises from the constitutional crisis of 1909–11, in which the House of Lords (which was dominated by Conservative peers) refused to pass a finance Bill that had been endorsed by the House of Commons, thus preventing the Liberal government from implementing key aspects of its programme. So grave was the situation, and so serious were its consequences, that legislation was subsequently enacted that denied the House of Lords any real role in the enactment of financial legislation.[54] It might equally be argued that the Sewel Convention, concerning UK legislation on devolved matters, has been given legal effect. Recently enacted legislation provides that while the UK Parliament can legislate on devolved matters, it is 'recognised' that it 'will not normally' do so 'without the consent of the Scottish Parliament'.[55] However, the better view is that rather than making the convention into a law, this provision merely signals Parliament's acknowledgement of (what remains) a convention.

Q When do you think it is appropriate to legislate so as to turn conventions into laws? Should all conventions be made into laws in this way?

3.5.4 Are conventions legally irrelevant?

The general view, as we have noted, is that conventions are legally unenforceable. This view has been advanced by commentators[56] and has often been endorsed by courts. The case concerning the patriation of the Canadian constitution, considered

---

[54] Parliament Act 1911. See further Chapter 5.

[55] Scotland Act 1998, s 28(8), inserted by Scotland Act 2016, s 2.

[56] See, eg Dicey, *An Introduction to the Study of the Law of the Constitution* (London 1959), p cxlv; Marshall and Moodie, *Some Problems of the Constitution* (London 1967), pp 12–17. However, not all commentators share this view: Allan, *Law, Liberty, and Justice* (Oxford 1993), ch 10, and Jennings, *The Law of the Constitution* (London 1967), disavow any rigid distinction between law and convention.

in section 3.5.2, is a good example. The Canadian Supreme Court held that the federal government, if it proceeded in spite of most provinces' objections, would be acting 'unconstitutional[ly] in the conventional sense'.[57] But the Court went on to conclude that no *law* prevented the government from proceeding with its attempt to reform the constitution against the provinces' wishes. The Court was therefore unable to grant any remedy against the federal government.[58]

UK courts have also been unreceptive to the argument that conventions can be legally enforced. For example, in *Madzimbamuto v Lardner-Burke*,[59] it was argued that the UK Parliament had acted improperly by enacting legislation in circumstances that breached a clear convention. This argument, however, was given short shrift. Even if it was 'unconstitutional' for Parliament to legislate thus—for example, if people would have thought there to be 'moral', 'political', or 'other reasons', making it 'highly improper' for Parliament to act as it had done—the court, 'in declaring the law', was 'not concerned with these matters'.[60] It must be borne in mind, however, that this case concerned a challenge to the constitutionality of an Act of Parliament: the fact that the court was unwilling to entertain such a challenge is unsurprising, given that Parliament is said to have unlimited lawmaking power.

While there is no clear authority supporting the proposition that conventions are *straightforwardly enforceable*, certain case law does suggest that conventions are *not wholly legally irrelevant*. In considering this matter further, it is helpful to distinguish between two forms of significance that conventions might have, concerning, respectively, the *application of the law to the facts*, and the *content of the law itself*.

First, it is hard to deny that convention can influence, and on occasion has influenced, the application of the law to the facts of cases. Consider, for example, *Evans v Information Commissioner*,[61] which involved a challenge to the government's refusal to disclose 'advocacy' letters to Ministers in which Prince Charles sought to advance the interests of his charities or promote his own views. Under the Freedom of Information Act 2000, as it stood at the relevant time,[62] the central question for the Upper Tribunal was whether disclosure would be in the public interest. In arguing that it would not, the government relied upon the so-called 'education convention', according to which 'the heir to the throne is entitled and bound to be instructed in and about the business of government',[63] and contended that that convention extended to *all* of Charles's correspondence with government. The Tribunal, however, concluded that while the convention attached to correspondence about such matters

---

[57] *Re Resolution to amend the Constitution* at 909.

[58] However, as noted, the UK took the view that it did not have to accede to a request made by the Canadian federal government in breach of constitutional convention. As a result, the Canadian government changed the proposals, casting them in terms more palatable to the provinces. They were later enacted in that revised form: see Canada Act 1982 (UK).

[59] [1969] 1 AC 645.

[60] *Madzimbamuto* at 723, *per* Lord Reid, speaking for the majority of the Judicial Committee of the Privy Council. On the nature and role of that body, see Chapter 6.

[61] [2012] UKUT 313 (AAC).

[62] It has since been amended to provide fuller protection against disclosure in relation to members of the royal family.

[63] *Evans* at [67].

as the functioning of government, it did not cover advocacy correspondence. In turn, this shaped the Tribunal's conclusion that the public interest favoured the disclosure of the letters.[64] Thus while the Tribunal did not 'enforce' the convention, its analysis of the convention played a major part when it came to deciding whether the relevant legal test—that is, whether disclosure was in the public interest—was satisfied.

A second way in which conventions may influence the application of the law to the facts of a case is through the doctrine of legitimate expectation. This legal principle is considered in detail in Chapter 12; for now, we need only say that it allows claimants, in certain circumstances, to obtain a remedy if a public body fails to do that which it has led the claimant to expect, whether through an express promise or through consistent past practice. In the *GCHQ* case, the relevant Minister had habitually consulted trade unions before changing employment conditions at the government's communications headquarters.[65] The court in *GCHQ* accepted that this established practice—which, it has been suggested, amounted to a convention[66]—had given rise to a legitimate expectation. The court would therefore have been willing to strike down the Minister's decision to change important employment conditions *without* consultation had it not been for other considerations[67] that need not for now be rehearsed.

3.5.5 Some conclusions—and the distinction between legal and political constitutionalism

For reasons already considered, conventions are not legally irrelevant. But can they be enforced themselves, rather than merely informing the application of the law? Full enforceability would dissolve the distinction between convention and law, given that that distinction consists pre-eminently in legal enforceability of law but not of convention. After all, the very idea of convention is of a body of *political* practice that supplements the legal rules of the constitution; conferring full legal enforceability upon conventions would rob them of their distinctive character. Is distinctiveness worth preserving?

A possible argument against preserving the unenforceability—and hence distinctiveness—of conventions might be that their unenforceability renders them futile. But that argument can summarily be dismissed since, as we have seen, conventions exert real influence over constitutional actors even if they cannot ultimately be enforced by courts. Meanwhile, a positive argument in favour of legal unenforceability can be made. The enforcement of constitutional rules by courts is undoubtedly important—but it is not a panacea. A healthy constitution will, alongside appropriate judicial oversight of government, incorporate a political system whereby those in positions of authority can be held to account for what they do. Many constitutional conventions deal with the sort of political matters that, for reasons we explore in Chapter 13, are generally unsuitable for adjudication by courts. If, for instance, a Minister

---

[64] In fact, they were not released, because the government exercised its 'override' power under the 2000 Act. That power is considered in Chapter 10, section 7.3.2.

[65] [1976] QB 752.   [66] See, eg Allan, *Law, Liberty, and Justice* (Oxford 1993), p 242.

[67] ie the national security implications of the case.

refuses to submit to being questioned by MPs in the House of Commons, it is far from obvious that such a matter ought to be dealt with by a court. Viewed in this way, the existence of a body of political constitutional norms, in the form of conventions, is entirely appropriate, because some matters are more properly dealt with by the political process.

This argument ultimately reduces to the proposition that legal and political forms of constitutionalism are mutually complementary, and that the constitution's recognition of a distinction between legal and conventional rules is therefore apt. However, there is a danger inherent in this analysis. While it is important to recognise the distinction between, and the appropriate spheres of operation of, legal and political forms of constitutionalism, that distinction should not be overstated. In particular, it should not be permitted to obscure the fact that, in this area, both legal and political rules are underpinned by constitutional principles—and that any given principle might be upheld by a combination of convention and law.[68] It follows that even if it is inappropriate for courts straightforwardly to enforce conventions, this does not mean that they should close their eyes to them when developing or seeking to ascertain the meaning of the law.

An example will help to illustrate the argument. Consider the Sewel Convention, which holds that the UK Parliament should not normally legislate on devolved matters without the consent of the relevant devolved legislature. This rule of political practice, being a convention, cannot be directly enforced by the courts. It would, for example, be impossible to obtain an injunction preventing the enforcement of legislation enacted in breach of the Sewel Convention.[69] This does not, however, mean that courts, in appropriate cases, should ignore the principle underlying it. The relevant principle is that the constitutional right of the devolved nations to govern themselves (within the confines of the devolution settlements) should be respected. If a court were to be faced with a piece of UK legislation that appeared to have been enacted in breach of the Sewel Convention, it would be perfectly entitled—taking account of the principle underlying the convention, just as courts take account of other important constitutional principles—to attempt to interpret the legislation in a way that confined its operation to England, or to those devolved nations the legislatures of which had consented to its enactment. This is not the same as saying that conventions are, or should be, enforceable by courts; it simply recognises that a single body of principle underlies legal and conventional systems of constitutional rules, and that just because a given principle is primarily upheld by one of those systems does not render it irrelevant to the operation of the other.

Q Would it be appropriate to go further? Should courts directly enforce conventions?

---

[68] See generally Allan, ch 10.

[69] This remains the case even though the existence of the convention is now 'recognised' by the Scotland Act 1998, s 28(8) (inserted by the Scotland Act 2016, s 2). Statutory acknowledgement of the convention's existence does not deprive it of its essential character as a convention.

One final point needs to be made about conventions. It is apparent from what has been said so far that anyone who knew only about UK constitutional law and nothing about conventions would have a very inaccurate picture of the contemporary UK constitution. She would, among other things, expect there to be a monarch with absolute power to veto legislation and capable of exercising significant legal powers without reference to the democratic parts of government, and a government free to continue in office after losing a general election. That this impression is hopelessly inaccurate demonstrates that, in order to understand how the UK system really works, constitutional law has to be overlaid with convention; once this is done, the picture changes markedly. Powers and freedoms that exist as a matter of law turn out to be little more than mirages, because convention prevents them from being exercised, or prescribes how they are to be exercised. In this way, it is often left to convention to ensure that the constitution operates in accordance with contemporary principles such as democracy.

We might say, then, that convention bridges the gap between a legal constitution that is, in some respects, outdated—few people today would think it appropriate to allow the monarch to veto Bills—and a 'real' constitution within which anachronistic laws are neutralised or otherwise rendered acceptable through the operation of convention. To the traditional British mindset, this facilitates a pleasing form of double-think. Contemporary principles of constitutionalism can be embraced, but beneath a dignified veneer of historical continuity. Thus we encounter phenomena such as an all-powerful monarch who turns out to be largely powerless.

Is this approach satisfactory? Why not get rid of outdated legal arrangements, rather than simply, in effect, agree to overlook them? The greater the gap between the legal and real constitutions, the greater the traction of this sort of argument—on the grounds of promoting public understanding of the constitution, if nothing else.

4. Constitutional principles

4.1 The role of constitutional principles

By constitutional principles, we mean fundamentally important values that concern the constitution and which serve at least one (and often all) of several functions.

First, constitutional principles may perform an *explanatory function*. Such principles help us to make sense of the constitution as it is: they enable us to understand why certain arrangements obtain, why certain rules, whether legal or conventional, exist, and how the constitution operates.

Second, constitutional principles have a *practical impact*. On a political level, they are given effect via conventions that influence how constitutional actors behave. On the legal plane, they shape the interpretation and development of the law. Courts habitually attempt to interpret and apply the law in a way that makes it consistent with fundamental values. Such values also exert influence over legislators: a government seeking to procure the enactment of legislation that conflicts with very basic constitutional principles is likely to face considerable opposition, both within Parliament and from the wider public.

Third, constitutional principles perform an *evaluative role* that has both political and legal dimensions. The political dimension is an extension of the immediately preceding point. Whether or not a given form of conduct—whether the enactment of a particular piece of legislation, a government policy, or decision taken by a Minister—is legitimate and acceptable falls to be judged (by the public, MPs, and so on) by reference to a number of factors, prominent among which will be the fundamental principles of the constitution. In turn, the extent to which a government has complied with such principles will inform people's assessments of it, and may influence how they vote at the following election. For example, the Blair government's decision to invade Iraq in circumstances involving (in the view of many leading authorities) a breach of international law arguably showed disregard for the fundamental constitutional principle of 'legality', or the 'rule of law'. The political legacy is arguably still being felt today. The evaluative function of constitutional principles also possesses a *legal dimension*: subject to one important exception, legislative and government action taken in breach of relevant constitutional principles can be struck down by courts as unlawful.

4.2 **Democracy and parliamentary sovereignty**

The exception mentioned in the last sentence of section 4.1 relates to the first key constitutional principle, to which we now turn. The principle in question is often said to be *parliamentary sovereignty*, although in truth that concept is merely one way of implementing a deeper underlying principle—*democracy*. At a basic level, the notion of democracy is straightforward, being based on the idea that people should be allowed to shape how they are governed. However, there are different views both as to what exactly constitutes the principle of democracy and how that principle should be implemented in practical terms. In the UK, democracy is ultimately understood as meaning that the wishes of the majority should prevail—a view that is given concrete effect through the principle of parliamentary sovereignty.

The exact meaning of that principle, like that of the underlying notion of democracy, is the subject of some disagreement. In essence, however, it means that an Act of the UK Parliament is the highest form of law in the UK. From that, it follows that no court can refuse to apply Acts of Parliament and that other law (eg judge-made common law and legislation enacted by other bodies) is invalid if inconsistent with parliamentary legislation.

We consider parliamentary sovereignty in detail in Chapter 5. For the time being, we simply note that its influence is substantial. Indeed, it shapes the UK constitution at a fundamental level. In particular, it accounts for the key characteristic, considered in Chapter 1, whereby no special category of constitutional law exists. If Parliament is sovereign, such that it can make, amend, or repeal any law, this removes the possibility of there being any higher body of constitutional law that is binding upon legislators. It follows that all other constitutional principles exist in the shadow of parliamentary sovereignty: as a matter of strict law, they exist only to the extent that Parliament chooses not to disturb them. On this orthodox view, Parliament is in ultimate legal

control of the constitution, such that the UK constitution is, and will remain, a significantly political one.

4.3 **Responsible government and the separation of powers**

A second key constitutional principle is that of the *separation of powers*. Like parliamentary sovereignty, separation of powers is really just a particular way of securing
an underlying objective—in this case, *responsible government*. Human nature being
what it is, there is a real possibility—one that is realised on a grand scale and on a
daily basis in many countries—that those in authority will exercise their power in
arbitrary, abusive, unwise, or corrupt ways. Such conduct is the antithesis of responsible government—a paradigm within which authority is used fairly and wisely to
advance the public good. Many practical measures can be taken to minimise the
chances of abuse of government power. The separation of powers is such a measure,
and one that operates at a fundamental—architectural—level.

In systems that embrace a strict doctrine of separation of powers, the three
principal functions of government are allocated to three wholly distinct bodies,
as Table 2.2 shows.

Table 2.2 Government functions under the separation of powers

Legislature	Courts	Executive
Making the law by enacting and amending legislation	Resolving disputes about the meaning and application of the law	Carrying out the administration of the country, eg by developing policy and implementing government programmes

We consider these matters in Chapter 3, and will see that, in the UK, while there
are three largely distinct branches of government performing three largely distinct
functions, the separation of powers is not rigorously adhered to. It nevertheless
serves several of the functions, mentioned in section 4.1, which are associated with
constitutional principles. For example, until 2009, an appellate committee of the
House of Lords acted as the UK's court of final appeal on many matters. The decision to transfer that role to a newly created Supreme Court, wholly separate from
the other branches of government, was plainly influenced by the fact that such an
arrangement would better comply with the separation of powers principle. Moreover,
we will see that the principle is an important influence on the courts. For example,
legislation used to allow Ministers to decide on the length of sentences to be served
by convicted murderers. This involved a breach of the separation of powers in that it
entailed members of the executive branch exercising a classically judicial function.
Since the sovereign Parliament had decreed that this should be so, the courts could
not remove that function from Ministers—but they did insist that if Ministers were
to exercise a judicial function, they had to act as if they were judges. This meant
that Ministers had to make decisions based purely on relevant matters, such as the

seriousness and circumstances of the offending, while ignoring extrinsic factors such as public opinion.[70]

Our first two constitutional principles, then, are the sovereignty of Parliament and the separation of powers. They will be considered further in separate chapters. We turn now to our third constitutional principle, which warrants a section of this chapter in its own right given that this is our primary discussion of it.

5. Legality and the rule of law

5.1 Introduction

The *rule of law* is, in many senses, the most elusive of the main constitutional principles. Indeed, it is not really a principle at all; rather, it is best thought of as an envelope that contains a set of more specific principles.[71] One of the many oddities of the rule of law is that most people agree that it is a good thing while disagreeing sharply about what it means.[72] In order to understand the importance of the rule of law as it relates to the UK constitution, it is necessary to address two distinct, but related, issues:

- What does the rule of law *mean*? What are the specific principles that we find when we peer into the 'rule of law' envelope?

- What does the rule of law *do*? What, in other words, is the practical relevance, if any, of the rule of law?

These questions cannot be considered in isolation from one another.

The horizontal axis of the diagram in Figure 2.2 sets out three views ascribing different—and, as we progress along the axis, increasingly practically important— roles to the rule of law. At one extreme, it is simply a political philosophy: a set of opinions about what the characteristics of the law ought to be. Understood in this way, the rule of law is little more than a rhetorical device: someone might seek to add gravitas to their support for or criticism of a given legal provision by saying that it does or does not comply with the rule of law, but that is as far as it goes. When the *role* of the rule of law is conceived of in such a limited way, its *content* is relatively unimportant: if we disagree about it, then that might be philosophically interesting, but it will be practically insignificant. At the other extreme, some people argue that the rule of law determines the *validity* of law: that laws that conflict with the principles of the rule of law are invalid. If this is so, then the content of the rule of law is dramatically more important—it is something that is really worth arguing about—because

---

[70] *R v Secretary of State for the Home Department, ex p Venables* [1998] AC 407.

[71] For example, Bingham, 'The Rule of Law' [2007] CLJ 67, argues that the rule of law consists of eight 'sub-rules'.

[72] Section 1 of the Constitutional Reform Act 2005 explicitly recognises the 'constitutional principle of the rule of law', but says nothing about its meaning.

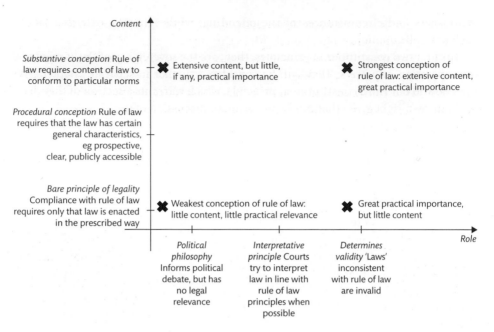

Figure 2.2 The contested content and role of the rule of law

it constrains lawmakers' power. Courts, within this model, are entitled to refuse to enforce 'laws' that conflict with the rule of law, because such measures are not, in the first place, truly entitled to be treated as law.

What, then, is the position in the UK? The rule of law is certainly treated as an important political principle in the sense that it informs political discourse. Proposals for new laws might, for example, be criticised on the ground that they affront this or that aspect of the rule of law. However, when used in this way, the term 'rule of law' proves to be a highly elastic one that becomes nothing more than 'one of those self-congratulatory rhetorical devices that grace the public utterances of Anglo-American politicians'.[73] However, as it is understood in relation to the UK's constitution, the rule of law is more than a political philosophy: it is also a legal principle of more precise meaning.[74] For instance, it produces legal effects by influencing the interpretation of legislation: courts will construe legislation in line with the rule of law where possible. Meanwhile, it determines the validity of government action and legislation enacted by most lawmaking bodies[75] (eg local authorities and devolved legislatures). Such legislation can be struck down by a court if is incompatible with the rule of law. The UK Parliament, however, is sovereign (at least in orthodox theory), in which case it must be capable of making laws that affront rule of law principles. Whether that

[73] Shklar, 'Political Theory and the Rule of Law', in Hutchinson and Monahan (eds), *The Rule of Law: Ideal or Ideology* (Toronto 1987), p 1.

[74] We examine what that meaning is in sections 5.6–5.9.

[75] Unless such a body has been specifically authorised by an Act of the UK Parliament to pass legislation in contravention of rule of law principles.

view is a desirable or even an accurate one today is a question we return to briefly at the end of this section and in more depth in Chapter 5.

These preliminary conclusions help to focus the terms of our inquiry. If there is a set of principles collectively known as the rule of law upon which courts will rely in the ways described, we need to know what those principles are. But in order to place in context discussion of what the rule of law *actually means* in UK law, it is necessary first to say something about the range of views that exist about what the rule of law *ought to mean*.[76]

5.2 Legality

The vertical axis of the diagram in Figure 2.2 sets out three (increasingly extensive) views concerning the latter point. The most modest way in which the rule of law can be conceived is as a *bare principle of legality*. This simply holds that if something is to be regarded as a law, it must be enacted in whatever way the relevant legal system prescribes. For example, in UK law, something will count as an Act of Parliament if it is approved by both Houses of Parliament and by the Queen. A measure that has not been approved by the House of Commons or the Queen cannot be regarded as a law because there will have been a failure to adhere to the required process.[77] The principle of legality thus ensures that only constitutionally authorised institutions are able to make law—and only if they play by whatever are the established rules for doing so.

This very limited conception of the rule of law is uncontroversial. It is also imperative if law is to exist as an identifiable body of rules. If anyone could make law in any way, then law would quickly cease to exist in any meaningful sense. The key point, however, is that the bare principle of legality is morally neutral: *any* law, whatever its content, will pass muster provided that it is enacted by the appropriate institution in the prescribed way. If the rule of law is coextensive with the bare principle of legality, then heinous laws providing for such things as racial segregation, slavery, and the like would be fully compliant with the rule of law, as long as they were enacted in the right way.

Q Do you think that the rule of law should be defined as narrowly as this? If not, before reading on, consider what additional principles you would wish to see as part of the rule of law.

5.3 Formal conceptions of the rule of law

Many writers argue that the bare principle of legality is only one component of the rule of law, and that, properly understood, the rule of law goes further. On this view, enactment by the authorised body in the required way is a necessary, but not sufficient,

---

[76] This debate is normally conducted on the assumption that the rule of law determines the validity of law, in that laws that breach rule of law principles are invalid and can be struck down by courts.

[77] In limited circumstances, an Act of Parliament can be passed without the approval of the House of Lords: see Chapter 5.

condition for a measure to comply with the rule of law. What, then, are the additional requirements laid down by the rule of law? Here, we encounter a sharp division of opinion between those who favour *formal* and *substantive* conceptions of the rule of law.[78] The nature of that distinction—where, precisely, it lies—is contested.

However, the essential point is that adherents to the formal view contend that the rule of law should stipulate that legal rules must possess certain general characteristics that are agnostic as to the content of the law. As Allan puts it, on this view, 'Like a sharp knife, the rule of law is morally neutral—[law is therefore] an efficient instrument for good purposes, or wicked'.[79] In contrast, those who favour a substantive conception of the rule of law argue that it lays down requirements as to law's content; thus the rule of law amounts to the rule of *good* law.

The distinction between the formal and substantive views of the rule of law can best be appreciated by reference to some practical examples—which will also show how hard it is to draw the distinction clearly. One of the leading proponents of the formal conception of the rule of law is Raz.[80] He argues that the primary function of the rule of law is to ensure that 'the law should conform to standards designed to enable it effectively to guide action'.[81] This means, among other things, that the law:

- should be publicly and clearly stated;
- should not have retroactive effect;[82] and
- should not change too often.[83]

If the law has these characteristics, people will be able to know where they stand: they will be able to plan their lives and make informed choices about their actions in full knowledge of the constraints imposed by the law.

Raz goes on to argue that there must be practical arrangements capable of ensuring that these principles are actually observed. In particular, people must have access to courts the independence of which equips them to resolve disputes objectively in accordance with legal principles. If this task were entrusted to other bodies that might make decisions by reference to considerations other than law, then the potential of clear, public, non-retroactive legal rules to bring about certainty would remain unrealised: decisions in particular cases might be made for all sorts of reasons— political, moral, social, financial—and people would be unable to rely on the predictable application of the law.[84]

A related point is that if the law gives the authorities very wide discretionary powers (eg 'the Home Secretary may detain anyone whom she believes to be a terrorist'), this may undermine the rule of law by introducing a degree of unpredictability that makes it hard for people to plan their lives.[85] Thus Dicey famously said that 'government based on the exercise by persons in authority of wide, arbitrary, or

---

[78] See, eg Craig, 'Formal and Substantive Conceptions of the Rule of Law: An Analytical Framework' [1997] PL 467.
[79] Allan, *Law, Liberty, and Justice* (Oxford 1993), p 23.
[80] Raz, *The Authority of Law* (Oxford 1979), ch 11.   [81] Raz, p 218.
[82] See Chapter 1, section 2.1 on the meaning of this concept.   [83] Raz, pp 214–15.
[84] Raz, pp 216–18.   [85] Raz, p 216.

discretionary powers of constraint' would be contrary to the rule of law.[86] However, as Raz correctly points out, the existence of such government powers—which is commonplace today, including in the UK—is not per se problematic provided that there is an adequate framework of law governing how such powers are to be exercised.[87]

5.4 **Should the rule of law be confined to formal matters?**

Writers like Raz argue for a formal—and *only* a formal—conception of the rule of law for two reasons. The first argument is a *positive one*. It is that the law must have such characteristics as facilitate legal certainty, so that people can know where they stand. This argument is morally neutral in the sense that it does not seek to bring moral considerations into play in the sense of denying lawmakers the capacity to pursue particular policies: Raz concedes that a legal system based on the denial of human rights or on racial, gender, or religious discrimination could still conform to his version of the rule of law.[88]

Yet Raz's argument is not actually a morally neutral one. The importance that he attaches to legal certainty is itself based on his underlying conviction that 'human dignity' should be respected—which means 'treating human beings as persons capable of planning and plotting their future'.[89] If the system allows people to be caught out by, and punished pursuant to, laws about which they could never reasonably have known—retroactive criminal laws being the prime example of such measures—there is a basic failure to respect their dignity and autonomy as individuals.

The second argument is a *negative one*: it holds that, while the moral principles underlying the formal conception of the rule of law are modest and uncontentious, taking the rule of law further would transform it into nothing more than a contestable political theory. Raz cites a 1959 report of the International Committee of Jurists that adopted a substantive view of the rule of law, according to which the principle encompasses 'civil and political rights' and requires 'social, educational and cultural conditions which are essential to the full development of [each person's] personality'. Raz retorts that, 'If the rule of law is the rule of the good law then to explain its nature is to propound a complete social philosophy'.[90]

There is, however, an obvious difficulty with this argument. As we have already noted, the formal conception of the rule of law is not itself morally neutral; rather, it is premised on the importance of respecting the autonomy and dignity of the individual. Requiring legal certainty via the principles advocated by Raz is *one* way of securing such respect. But if we accept that respect for individual autonomy and dignity is our starting point, do not other conclusions follow from this—for example, that it would be improper for the state to enact laws (however clear and prospective) making provision for torture, which on any view must be incompatible with respecting victims' dignity? Should we, then, not embrace a fully substantive account of the rule of law?

---

[86] Dicey, *An Introduction to the Study of the Law of the Constitution* (London 1959), p 188.
[87] Raz, *The Authority of Law* (Oxford 1979), p 216.   [88] Raz, p 211.   [89] Raz, p 221.
[90] Raz, p 211.

There is no shortage of such accounts in the literature,[91] and they differ from one another in important respects, but they often place under the rule of law rubric such matters as respect for freedom of expression and principles of equality (such as non-discrimination on racial, religious, and gender grounds).[92] Even a view of the rule of law as extensive as this can be traced back to foundational concerns about the autonomy and dignity of the individual, which considerations suggest that people should be free to express themselves and that it is improper (because it is a denial of dignity) to treat people less favourably because of their gender, race, or religion.

Two points should be made in conclusion to this part of our discussion. First, although it is, as we have just seen, difficult to draw a fully principled distinction between formal and substantive conceptions of the rule of law, this does not mean that there is no difference. What is clear is that as we move further along the continuum from procedural to substantive principles, the scope for disagreement increases. Few people would dispute that it is improper to punish someone for breaching a retroactive law that did not exist at the time the conduct in question occurred. The scope for disagreement is comparatively great in relation to (for example) the proposition that everyone should have a right to strike or a right to a high standard of living. There is certainly an argument for restricting the rule of law to that body of principles which, within a given society, are regarded as sufficiently fundamental as to be relatively uncontroversial. Whether the dividing line thereby entailed coincides with that which separates the formal and substantive conceptions of the rule of law is another matter.

Second, it does not follow that those who are sceptical about conceiving of the rule of law in broad, substantive terms are in favour of such things as arbitrary discrimination and the illiberal suppression of freedoms. They are not arguing that such things are unobjectionable. Rather, they are challenging the contention that the 'rule of law' is the right, or a useful, benchmark by which to determine the wrongness of such things.

5.5 The rule of law, legitimacy, and the unwritten constitution

We said at the beginning of section 5 that questions about the *content* of the rule of law cannot be divorced from questions about its *role*, and it is time that we reminded ourselves of that fact. The more extensive—the more *substantive*—the operative conception of the rule of law, the more likely people are to disagree about it, and the less comfortable they are likely to be with ascribing a decisive practical role to it (such as determining the validity of legislation). But all of this begs a question that we have

---

[91] For examples, see Allan, *Constitutional Justice* (Oxford 2001); Laws, 'The Constitution: Morals and Rights' [1996] PL 622; Bingham, 'The Rule of Law' [2007] CLJ 67.

[92] This form of equality is to be distinguished from the much more modest argument advanced by Dicey that the rule of law requires 'equality before the law'. By this, he meant that no one—and here he specifically had in mind government officials—should be above the law. This fits with a substantive conception of the rule of law (because he was arguing that the *content* of the law should not provide special exemption for officials), but it is a more limited proposition than one that holds that the rule of law demands substantive equality on gender etc grounds.

not so far explicitly addressed. If the rule of law is to have practical, legal force, as opposed simply to being a point of philosophical discussion, *who ultimately decides what it means?*

As a preface to answering this question, it is important to note that, in many legal systems, some or all of the matters considered so far in this chapter would be dealt with in a written constitution. Constitutions typically flesh out the principle of legality by determining which bodies are allowed to legislate and pursuant to what procedures. Written constitutions generally also lay down what constraints—whether formal or substantive—the legislature is under. Many constitutions, for example, enshrine certain human rights, such as free speech and non-discrimination, explicitly depriving legislators of any authority to make laws inconsistent with such rights. This does not mean that the rule of law is irrelevant in such systems, since underlying principles of the type that might fall within the rule of law rubric will often have to be relied upon when making sense of vague constitutional provisions. Nevertheless, it is undeniable that the rule of law assumes greater importance in a system such as that of the UK. Without a written constitution to serve as a starting point in identifying fundamental constitutional values, there is a greater need to engage directly with the rule of law if we are seeking to work out what those values are.

So who decides what the rule of law means? The answer is 'the judges'. As we will see shortly, the main vehicle through which the principles comprising the rule of law are articulated in the UK is judicial interpretation of legislation and judicial evaluation of the legality of government action. This is the anvil on which the rule of law has been refined in the UK as a legal concept, and it necessarily follows that it is the courts that have been responsible for undertaking that task. Judges have generally recognised that formal and procedural principles have what Laws has called 'a settled, overarching quality'.[93] They are more likely to be the subject of the sort of consensus referred to than are more substantive principles. This, in turn, has meant that judges have felt themselves to be on safer ground—in terms of the perceived legitimacy of their articulation of the rule of law—in relation to more formal principles.

5.6 The rule of law as a constitutional principle in the UK

Against this background, we turn to consider what the rule of law means as a constitutional principle in the UK. In doing so, it is helpful—subject to the already entered health warning that clear dividing lines are hard to draw—to distinguish between the three senses of the rule of law shown in Figure 2.2.

5.7 The bare principle of legality

The most modest aspect of the rule of law—*the bare principle of legality*—is undoubtedly recognised in UK law. This is exemplified by the *Jackson* case, in which it was argued that an Act of Parliament was invalid because it had not been enacted in

---

[93] 'The Limitations of Human Rights' [1998] PL 254, 260.

conformity with the relevant procedure.[94] As we have seen, the principle of parliamentary sovereignty means that courts cannot (at least on a traditional reading of that principle) refuse to apply Acts of Parliament. However, the question in *Jackson* was whether, in the first place, the measure in question was truly such an Act. Although, in the end, the court held that it was, the fact that the question was asked indicates that the principle of legality was applied: the court accepted that the measure concerned would only count as a law if, when it was enacted, the relevant requirements for making an Act of Parliament had been complied with.

The same principle is at stake when courts strike down legislation enacted by bodies other than Parliament. For example, in *Witham*, a government Minister had been given a limited power to make certain rules.[95] The claimant (to whom the application of the rules would have caused hardship) argued that the Minister had exceeded his power—that he had, in effect, made rules that he had not been authorised by Parliament to make. The court agreed, striking down the rule and upholding the principle of legality in doing so. The Minister could only make rules that were within the parameters stipulated by Parliament; by exceeding those parameters, he had acted without lawful authority and so in breach of the principle of legality.

Finally, on this point, note the celebrated case of *Entick v Carrington*.[96] A government Minister issued a warrant that purported to authorise state agents to break into the claimant's house and seize his papers, in clear breach of the claimant's property rights. Since the Minister could point to no law enabling him to issue such warrants, the warrant was ineffective and the agents had acted unlawfully. This decision was animated by the principle of legality: the state could not lawfully override individuals' property rights unless, in the first place, the law authorised the state to do so. However, the limits of this principle were demonstrated in the *Malone* case, in which it was held that the government had not acted unlawfully by listening in to the claimant's telephone conversations.[97] At the time that the case was decided, no right to privacy was recognised in English law, no law prevented the interception of telephone calls, and no physical trespass (in breach of recognised property rights) had been committed.[98] This case shows that the principle of legality does not require positive legal authorisation for government action when such action will not affect others' recognised legal rights.[99]

5.8 A formal conception of the rule of law

There is also plenty of evidence showing judicial recognition of a *formal conception of the rule of law*.

---

[94] *R (Jackson) v Attorney General* [2005] UKHL 56, [2006] 1 AC 262. This case is discussed in more detail in Chapter 5.

[95] *R v Lord Chancellor, ex p Witham* [1998] QB 575.   [96] (1765) 19 St Tr 1030.

[97] *Malone v Metropolitan Police Commissioner* [1979] Ch 344.

[98] The position is now different: the Regulation of Investigatory Powers Act 2000 regulates the interception of communications and a (limited) common law right to privacy is recognised (on which, see Chapter 19).

[99] See further *Shrewsbury and Atcham Borough Council v Secretary of State for Communities and Local Government* [2008] EWCA Civ 148, [44], *per* Carnwath LJ.

We saw in section 5.2 that a key component of that view of the concept is the principle of legal certainty—which means, among other things, that people should be able to know where they stand. This principle was strongly endorsed in *Anufrijeva*.[100] The claimant was an asylum seeker whose benefit payments were stopped. Under the relevant legislation, her entitlement to such payments ceased when her claim had been 'determined'—a condition that the government said had been fulfilled because it had decided that her asylum claim should be turned down. Crucially, however, the claimant was not told of this—and the House of Lords agreed with her that until she was told, her entitlement to benefits continued. In reaching this conclusion, Lord Steyn explicitly invoked the rule of law, saying that it

> requires that a constitutional state must accord to individuals the right to know of a decision before their rights can be adversely affected. The antithesis of such a state was described by Kafka:[101] a state where the rights of individuals are overridden by hole in the corner decisions or knocks on doors in the early hours. That is not our system.[102]

A related aspect of the principle of legal certainty is that laws should not have retroactive effect—an axiom that is clearly regarded as an aspect of the rule of law in the UK. This is illustrated by *Pierson*,[103] in which the Home Secretary, under a misapprehension as to the circumstances in which the claimant had committed a double murder, decided that he should spend at least 20 years in prison.[104] However, on established principles and a correct understanding of the circumstances, 15 years' detention would have been the norm. The Home Secretary later accepted that he had been under a misapprehension, but confirmed his decision that the claimant should serve at least 20 years. By doing so, the Home Secretary had, in effect, subjected the claimant to a harsher punishment than that which would have been imposed had the original decision been taken on a correct basis. This, said the court, was unlawful: it was contrary to 'the fundamental principle that a sentence lawfully passed should not retrospectively be increased'.[105]

We saw in section 5.3 that, for writers such as Raz, a formal conception of the rule of law does not rule out conferring broad discretionary powers on (for example) government Ministers. But we also saw that it demands a legal framework that constrains such discretion, rendering its use predictable enough to meet the requirements of legal certainty. Such a framework undoubtedly exists in English law. For example, if legislation permits Ministers to exercise a given power for a given purpose, the courts will not permit Minsters to use that power for other purposes that could not have been deduced from the wording of the legislation.[106] Equally, if the government announces that it will exercise a given power in accordance with a stated policy—for example, that it will

---

[100] *R (Anufrijeva) v Secretary of State for the Home Department* [2003] UKHL 36, [2004] 1 AC 604.

[101] In Franz Kafka's dystopian novel *The Trial* (1925), the protagonist is accused of and punished for a crime, the nature of which is never disclosed to him.

[102] *Anufrijeva* at [28].

[103] *R v Secretary of State for the Home Department, ex p Pierson* [1998] AC 539.

[104] Neither the Home Secretary nor any other government Minister is today involved in making decisions of this nature. However, the principle illustrated by this case remains relevant.

[105] *Pierson* at 591, *per* Lord Steyn.   [106] *Municipal Council of Sydney v Campbell* [1925] AC 339.

not deport asylum seekers in stated circumstances—the courts will generally hold that it is unlawful for the government to refuse to honour such pledges unless it has good reason not to do so.[107] In these ways, the exercise of discretionary powers is rendered more predictable—and so the existence of such powers is reconciled with the principle of legal certainty.

Finally, recall that (for the reasons considered in section 5.3) a formal conception of the rule of law requires that people must be able (if they so wish) to have legal disputes resolved by independent courts. The principle of access to courts is a well-established one in UK law. In the *Witham* case, mentioned in section 5.7,[108] the rules in question had the effect of substantially increasing the fees to be paid by people wishing to initiate litigation. The claimant successfully argued that the rules contravened the principle of access to court by, in effect, preventing people on low incomes from making legal claims. In light of this, the court held that the rules were unlawful.

More dramatically, in *Anisminic*, when faced with legislation stipulating that no decisions taken by a body established by the government could 'be called in question in any court of law', the House of Lords[109] refused to accept that Parliament had meant entirely to preclude judicial review of such decisions.[110] In this way, access to court—by way of judicial review—was preserved.

5.9 A substantive conception of the rule of law?

There is, then, no doubt that a formal conception of the rule of law is recognised. But does the law go further? It certainly recognises some rule of law principles that cannot easily be characterised as merely formal. For example, many of the principles of judicial review—that is, the principles that courts use to determine whether government action is lawful—reflect a substantive conception of the rule of law. Thus courts will strive to read legislation compatibly with, and will strike down executive action that conflicts with, such principles as the right to a fair hearing,[111] the right to freedom of expression,[112] and the right to confidential legal advice.[113] The courts' willingness and capacity to uphold such principles is now augmented by the HRA, but it is clear[114] that such principles are recognised by English law independently of that Act.

For example, in *Daly*, a government policy was held to be unlawful because it conflicted with the right to communicate confidentially with one's lawyer. Although the 1998 Act was in force when the case was decided, Lord Bingham emphasised that he had reached his decision through 'orthodox application of common law principles'.[115]

---

[107] *R (Lumba) v Secretary of State for the Home Department* [2011] UKSC 12, [2012] 1 AC 245; *Mandalia v Secretary of State for the Home Department* [2015] UKSC 59, [2015] 1 WLR 4546.

[108] *R v Lord Chancellor, ex p Witham* [1998] QB 575.

[109] Acting in its now-abolished judicial capacity.

[110] *Anisminic Ltd v Foreign Compensation Commission* [1969] 2 AC 147.

[111] *Ridge v Baldwin* [1964] AC 40.

[112] *R v Secretary of State for the Home Department, ex p Simms* [2000] 2 AC 115.

[113] *R (Daly) v Secretary of State for the Home Department* [2001] UKHL 26, [2001] 2 AC 532.

[114] Including from the cases cited in *Ridge* and *Daly*, which were decided before the Act came into force.

[115] *Daly* at [23].

Furthermore, Lord Cooke said that 'some rights [such as the one at stake in *Daly*] are inherent and fundamental to democratic civilised society. Conventions, constitutions, bills of rights and the like respond by recognising rather than creating them'.[116]

It is also clear that the courts recognise the principle of equality as an aspect of the rule of law. Here, too, the picture is complicated by the existence of legislation: statute provides extensive protection against discrimination on grounds such as gender, race, and sexual orientation—but the fundamental principle of equality is recognised, independently of such legislation, as an aspect of the rule of law. *Entick v Carrington*, considered in section 5.7, illustrates this point. It would have been unlawful for an ordinary individual to break into someone's house and steal his papers—and, absent any statutory authority, it was just as unlawful for a government Minister or his agents to do so. The latter were therefore to be treated no more favourably than a regular citizen.

This point is underlined by *Re M*,[117] in which, in clear breach of a court order, the Home Secretary instructed that an asylum seeker should be deported. If an ordinary individual breaches a court order, she may be convicted of the criminal offence of contempt of court and punished by fine or imprisonment. Despite the Home Secretary's protestations to the contrary, it was held that the same rule applied to government Ministers. Lord Templeman noted that the Home Secretary's argument 'would, if upheld, establish the proposition that the executive obey the law as a matter of grace and not as a matter of necessity, a proposition which would reverse the result of the Civil War'.[118]

5.10 Some conclusions on the rule of law

We end this discussion of the rule of law with the point with which it began—that the *meaning* of the concept cannot be addressed without reference to its *practical effect*. In the UK, the main practical effects of the rule of law are threefold:

- Courts will strike down government action that is inconsistent with the rule of law.

- Courts try, whenever possible, to give legislation a meaning that is compatible with the rule of law.

- Courts will generally hold legislation (other than Acts of Parliament) to be invalid if it cannot be interpreted compatibly with the rule of law.

All of this is subject to the longstop that, in orthodox theory at least, the UK Parliament is sovereign. It can therefore legislate contrary to the rule of law—including by authorising others, such as government Ministers, to breach the rule of law—if it so desires. Hence Parliament can, for instance, reverse the effect of a judicial decision by enacting legislation with retroactive effect.[119] The upshot is that while the rule of law—and hence the meaning of that concept—is important, it is not decisively important: for as

---

[116] *Daly* at [30].   [117] [1994] 1 AC 377.   [118] *M* at 395.
[119] But not legislation enacted by the UK Parliament.

long as Parliament is sovereign, legislation enacted by it can trump rule of law principles. In this sense, politics can ultimately overrule law.

However, not everyone takes that view. There is a growing school of thought that holds that certain fundamental principles are so important that they should be (and, some argue, *are*) beyond interference even by Parliament. This introductory chapter is not the appropriate point at which to consider these views in any detail. (We do that in Chapter 5.) We mention those views here simply to indicate that there is disagreement about the very fundamentals of the UK constitution, and that the meaning and status of the rule of law are central to that disagreement.

5.11 **The Human Rights Act 1998**

We indicated in sections 5.4 and 5.5 that there is an overlap between the concepts of the rule of law and human rights, particularly if the former is conceived of in more than purely formal terms. Detailed consideration of human rights matters, including the HRA, can be found in the final part of this book.[120] The relevance and influence of human rights and the HRA is pervasive. Relevant aspects of the HRA will need to be considered at various points in subsequent chapters, and so we provide in this introductory chapter an overview of the main features of the Act. The purpose of what follows is not to explain those features in detail; rather, it is to highlight points that will need to be considered in context in later parts of the book. With that in mind, six key points should be noted.

First, the HRA gives effect in UK law to the ECHR, an international treaty that, irrespective of the existence of the HRA, is binding upon the UK as a matter of international law. The purpose of the HRA is to enable people to enforce their ECHR rights in UK courts, rather than being able to do so only, or at least mainly, in the European Court of Human Rights (ECtHR) in Strasbourg.

Second, although UK law itself recognises—and through the medium of the rule of law confers some protection on—some human rights, the HRA clarifies and expands the range of rights that can be protected by UK courts. The rights that can be protected under the HRA—the 'Convention rights'[121]—are set out in Table 18.2.[122]

Third, the HRA authorises courts to strike down decisions and rules made by public bodies if they are incompatible with any of the Convention rights.[123] As we explain in Chapter 12, this has resulted in UK courts scrutinising government action more rigorously than in the past, which, in turn, raises questions about the balance of power, under the separation of powers doctrine, between the courts and the executive.

Fourth, the HRA places courts under a duty to interpret legislation, including Acts of Parliament, compatibly with the Convention rights if it is possible to do so.[124] We will see in Chapter 18 that this gives the courts extensive powers to mould legislation so as to render it consistent with the ECHR.

Fifth, the HRA does not empower courts to strike down Acts of Parliament. The HRA is therefore, at least formally, consistent with the doctrine of parliamentary

---

[120] See Chapters 18–21.   [121] HRA, s 1.   [122] See Chapter 18, section 3.3.1.
[123] HRA, s 6.   [124] HRA, s 3.

sovereignty. However, the HRA does authorise courts to declare that an Act of Parliament is incompatible with Convention rights.[125] Such a declaration of incompatibility does not affect the validity of the legislation; rather, it is left to the executive and Parliament to decide whether, and if so how, to reform the law so as to render it consistent with the ECHR.

Sixth, the discussion of the rule of law earlier must be read in the light of the HRA's implications. The HRA certainly does not make the rule of law irrelevant: the Convention rights and the principles upheld under the banner of the rule of law may overlap, but the two categories are not precisely coterminous. Moreover, the HRA, being a mere Act of Parliament, is not necessarily a permanent feature of the constitution: like any other Act, it can be repealed. However, the HRA and the rule of law do work in tandem. To the extent that the Convention rights coincide with rule of law principles, the HRA endorses, and lends a form of democratic legitimacy to, the courts' pre-existing tendency to attempt to interpret legislation compatibly with such principles. Moreover, the fact that the courts now have at their disposal the option of issuing a declaration of incompatibility removes some of the heat from the debate about whether courts should be able to strike down provisions in Acts of Parliament that conflict with the rule of law. When a court declares an Act to be incompatible with human rights law, it is neither striking down the Act nor holding it to be unconstitutional. Nonetheless, a declaration of incompatibility is (as we explain in Chapter 18) a very significant power, and one that makes a formal strike-down power less practically important.

6. Codification and the constitution

Over recent years, the UK's constitutional arrangements have become more formalised. Important conventions have been codified, and much constitutional legislation—on issues such as human rights and devolution—has been enacted. As we shall see throughout this book, one consequence of this has been a shift from a political to a more legal form of constitutionalism. Two questions arise from this. First, why has the constitution taken the form it has? Second, should the UK now take the next step and adopt a fully codified constitution?

6.1 Why no codified constitution?

The explanations for the absence in the UK of a single document called 'The Constitution' are partly historical. Codified constitutions tend to come about after there has been a severe rupture in the political system of the country concerned—as a result of, for example, revolution, civil war, the ending of dominance by another country,[126] or a fundamental reordering of society.[127] In such circumstances, a new constitution facilitates and underlines the country's 'fresh start'.

---

[125] HRA, s 4.
[126] For example, the grant of independence to a colony or the end of Soviet domination of eastern European countries in the early 1990s.
[127] For example, the ending of apartheid in South Africa in the early 1990s.

But the UK has not—at least not since the English civil war in the seventeenth century—experienced any of these cataclysmic events. There has never been a 'constitutional moment' at which the fundamental rules required clarification and laying down in a single document; instead, there has been an unusual degree of continuity in the governing institutions. Over the centuries, those institutions have changed beyond all recognition—no one now believes in the divine right of kings, and the powers of the Crown are no longer personally exercised by the monarch—but the changes have been gradual. Partly as a result of this, the central concept of parliamentary sovereignty has endured, serving on a conceptual level to preclude the adoption of any constitutional text that can assert priority over ordinary legislation.

The lack of a codified constitution can also be explained by reference to a lack of public appetite. Indeed, the British people have sometimes assumed—whether rightly or not—that the distinctive nature of their unwritten constitution has provided them with superior protection of their rights and liberties, and that 'paper rights' count for little. Furthermore, it has long been thought that an uncodified constitution provides a degree of flexibility in constitutional arrangements that is preferable to the rigidity of a codified constitution—although we saw in Chapter 1 that a highly flexible constitution is arguably a contradiction in terms, given that constitutions are generally regarded as repositories of fundamental, enduring values.

Several consequences flow from the uncodified nature of the UK constitution. First, that constitution is not the product of a conscious and deliberate design. No group of people ever sat down together to design the UK constitution; rather, it has simply evolved over time. This in turn suggests a particular approach toward constitutional issues: one that eschews a rationalistic, comprehensive approach that would seek to settle all important issues at the outset. Instead, the approach in the UK has always been an incremental, ad hoc one, whereby the constitution develops piecemeal over time. As we saw in Chapter 1, this approach was evident in the fact that the major constitutional reforms undertaken since 1997 have taken the form of a rolling, sometimes disjointed, programme rather than a coherent package.

Second, what the constitution actually is or means may be unclear. Constitutional debate and disagreement often arise because, as we have already noted, constitutional lawyers hold different views as to what the constitution ought to be. Given the nature of the UK constitution, it can often be difficult to separate out description of the constitution and its evaluation. As noted, such debates are an inherent feature of most constitutions, but in an uncodified constitution they may become more prominent.

Third, although an uncodified constitution need not necessarily be an unentrenched one—that is, one that lacks special legal status and is therefore harder than normal law to amend—the latter characteristic, in practice, tends to follow from the former. So it is in the UK—with the result, as we saw in Chapter 1, that nothing in the constitution (except the principle of parliamentary sovereignty) is fixed.[128]

---

[128] This presupposes that Parliament is, in the first place, sovereign. Criticism of this view is considered in Chapter 5.

6.2 **To codify or not to codify?**

Arguments in favour of codification tend to be based on one (or both) of two underlying concerns. It is argued by some that codification would provide for a clearer, more accessible set of constitutional arrangements. This is an ultimately *formal* argument that emphasises the potentially educative effect of codification: collecting together the fundamental constitutional rules in a single place might make it easier for people to understand the constitution.[129] However, advocacy of codification often forms part of a broader argument in favour of *substantive* change.[130] Codification, on this view, represents an unprecedented opportunity for major reform that might (among other things) address concerns about the scale of executive power, the adequacy of arrangements for holding the executive to account, the unelected nature of the House of Lords, the electoral system, and the lack of entrenched protection for human rights. The adoption of a written constitution would both provide an occasion on which to think in a joined-up way about these (and other) issues, and would be imperative if some of these issues (such as placing human rights beyond legislative interference) were to be realised.

However, codification would create risks as well as opportunities. First, it is far from universally accepted that codification is *necessary or desirable*. As we saw in Chapter 1, when change is considered necessary, reform can be undertaken in individual areas rather than via wholesale codification. Indeed, it is arguable that problems are more likely to be successfully resolved by way of smaller-scale constitutional reform projects focusing upon particular issues. It would be naive to assume that a codified constitution would be some universal cure for all constitutional problems[131]—although to the extent that those problems arise because of a lack of joined-up thinking, it might at least help.

Second, adopting a codified constitution would require *hard questions* to be confronted. How detailed would the constitution be? Would it be a relatively short document containing a statement of general principles, values, and aspirations, or a long, detailed document setting out all of the respective legal powers of the legislature, executive, and judiciary? Would conventions be included? Would they be made legally enforceable? And which conventions would be included? Would the constitution make detailed provision about such matters as the voting system for the House of Commons and whether the second chamber should be wholly or mainly elected? Would it entrench the constitutional position of local government? Would the constitution have entrenched protection for human rights with a constitutional court to review the constitutionality of legislation? Would the constitution itself be entrenched and, if so, would it seek to extinguish parliamentary sovereignty? Can that be done? And, if so, how?

---

[129] For one attempt to draft a codified constitution without substantive constitutional reform, see Bogdanor, Khaitan, and Vogenauer, 'Should Britain Have a Written Constitution?' (2007) 78 Political Quarterly 499, 506–17.

[130] For examples of draft constitutions, see Institute for Public Policy Research, *The Constitution for the United Kingdom* (London 1991); Gordon, *Repairing British Politics: A Blueprint for Constitutional Change* (Oxford 2010).

[131] Barber, 'Against a Written Constitution' [2008] PL 11.

Third, the fact that such questions would have to be confronted suggests that producing a codified constitution would require the adoption of a *complex* process that would be lengthy and potentially costly. It would be foolhardy to attempt to codify the constitution by way of an ordinary statute enacted by Parliament in the usual way. To effect such a major change, the whole enterprise would need to follow a special, distinctive procedure capable of generating consensus and thereby conferring legitimacy on the resulting constitutional document. The enterprise would be daunting in scale and complexity, and there could be no guarantee that it would succeed.[132]

None of this is to suggest that the adoption of a codified constitution would necessarily be a bad thing or that it should not be attempted. But it is certainly not a task that could be undertaken lightly.

6.3 The future

The UK adopts a highly pragmatic approach to its constitutional arrangements. Of all the reasons that help to explain why the UK has never adopted a codified constitution, the most significant is that a compelling need to do so has never been felt by sufficient people. That may remain the case for decades to come. But one does not need a crystal ball to foresee at least the possibility that things might change radically and quickly. At the time of writing, the UK stands poised to embark upon the process—which may well be a very protracted one—of withdrawing from and fundamentally changing the terms of its relationship with the European Union. That is a major constitutional change for reasons that we explore in Chapter 7.

It certainly cannot be assumed that Brexit will prompt serious and widespread calls for a written constitution. But it is perfectly conceivable that it may set in train a series of events that will, at the very least, raise questions about the durability of the UK's present constitutional arrangements. For instance, if and when powers—including lawmaking powers—that are presently exercised by the EU are returned to the UK, questions will arise about where those powers should be situated. It should not be taken for granted that all such powers will be returned to the UK government and Parliament; some, perhaps many, might be invested in devolved bodies, resulting in a significant deepening of devolution.

It is also possible that Brexit might—even if not in the very short term—make a second referendum on Scottish independence more likely. If Scotland were to leave the UK, Wales and Northern Ireland might wish to secure their own constitutional positions by dividing power between London, Belfast, and Cardiff in ways that are more formal and permanent than the present devolution model allows—and in ways that perhaps only an entrenched, codified constitution would permit. Indeed, even if such dramatic events as Scotland's departure from the UK were not to come to pass, it is plain that the UK—by, for instance, declaring the 'permanence' of the Scottish Government and Parliament, as the Scotland Act 2016 does—is headed in a direction

---

[132] HM Government, *The Governance of Britain* (Cm 7170 2007), [213].

that might in time require the powers of UK institutions to be limited by means of a written constitution.

> **Q** In your opinion, should the UK have a fully codified constitution? If so, then how might it be possible to overcome the obstacles mentioned in this section?

7. Concluding remarks

In the absence of a 'written constitution', the UK's constitution is to be found in a number of places. Having examined the range of sources from which the UK constitution is drawn, it can be said that they are of three main types. First, there are *rules that are straightforwardly legal in nature*. Such rules are either set down in legislation or are the result of judicial development of the common law. Second, there are *principles that find expression principally as constitutional conventions*. As we have seen, such conventions (or at least a subset of sufficiently important ones) are binding in a political sense, but are of limited legal relevance; they are generally thought not to be directly enforceable by courts. Third, there are *the fundamental principles of the constitution*. The relevance of such principles is both legal and political. Principles such as parliamentary sovereignty, the separation of powers, and the rule of law are of undoubted legal significance: courts apply Acts of Parliament as the law because the doctrine of parliamentary sovereignty ascribes lawmaking power to Parliament; and courts are prepared to strike down administrative action and to adopt particular interpretations of legislation in order to uphold such principles. Such principles also have a broader, political significance: they form benchmarks against the legitimacy of government action and proposals for legislation fall to be evaluated.

It therefore becomes apparent that the UK constitution is both a political and a legal constitution: both law and politics supply the norms that determine how the constitution works, how those in charge are judged, and how they are held to account. As we explained at the beginning of the chapter, the relationship between legal and political approaches to constitutionalism is one of the key themes of this book, the others being the power of the executive branch and the importance of holding it to account, and the growing diffusion of government power as the UK shifts to a multi-layered form of constitutionalism. Those three themes will be to the fore as we commence, in Chapter 3, our study of the three main branches of government.

Expert commentary
Accountability, sovereignty, democracy, and rights: some fundamental questions
Dawn Oliver, Emeritus Professor of Constitutional Law,
University College London

The chapter provides a very clear, well organised, and authoritative introduction to some of the most important aspects of the British constitution, and lays the ground well for more detailed discussion in later chapters. In what follows I indicate some of the fascinating issues that, to me, the topics open up; issues not normally discussed in law books but which can cast light on some of the 'mysteries' (Mark Elliott's term[133]) of the British constitution.

First, *what is accountability, one of the three big themes of this book, supposed to achieve?* We can work this out by asking the following question: what would be wrong if, for instance, MPs, Ministers, civil servants, the police, or the army, were strongly accountable to a church or other religious body or to trade associations or a foreign country? The answer must be that the right sorts of accountability are supposed to ensure that public bodies use their powers to promote the shared and general interests of the country and to prevent them from indulging in self-serving or partisan actions. Wrong kinds of accountability are inconsistent with these principles. In other words the ultimate objectives of accountability arrangements should be (and the British public expects this) to promote the public or general interest and public service principles. The phrase 'widely shared sense of constitutional morality' puts this neatly.[134] These principles, in my view, are *foundational* to the good working of any liberal democratic system—even more important than what we often call *fundamental* principles. If a government did not consider itself bound to the public or general interest and to public service, to this sense of constitutional morality, then democratic government, the rule of law, and protection of civil liberties and human rights could not function effectively. Can you think of a liberal democracy for which this is not true?

Second, *what justifications are there for parliamentary sovereignty in our uncodified, unentrenched constitution?*[135] A lot is written about what is wrong with it, and not much positive. The 'democratic' argument in favour boils down to (i) assumptions not borne out by election statistics that the party or parties which form a government won a majority of the votes cast: this has not been true for decades; and (ii) equating democracy with majoritarianism, which leaves room for discrimination against minorities (or even against the majority of the population, women). This is surely not what democracy is about. So is there a persuasive justification for parliamentary sovereignty?

It is sometimes suggested that the Supreme Court ought to take it upon itself to refuse to give effect to provisions in Acts of Parliament which are contrary to what the Court considers to be the rule of law or fundamental constitutional principles such as access to the courts, judicial review, and so on: to challenge parliamentary sovereignty. A major problem if, one day, the Supreme Court so held, is that this would rupture one of the unspoken bulwarks of our constitutional arrangements: mutual respect and comity between the three main organs of state. If the government, Parliament, and the press criticised the Court's decision as antidemocratic, wrong-headed, etc, the Court might find that the respondent governmental body refused to obey its orders and that it could not enforce them coercively; it might have to rely on the 1966 Practice Statement,[136] change its mind, and decide that the courts have no power, after all, to strike down a statutory provision. The need for such a U-turn would not be good for the reputation or status of the courts or the rule of law generally. In sum, parliamentary sovereignty is in my view justified on practical and pragmatic grounds: for a court to reverse the doctrine would not work. If the UK had an entrenched, written constitution with provision for strike-down powers, the Court's decision would have legitimacy, which it could not have under present arrangements. But that is not where we are.

---

[133] See 'Interpretative Bills of Rights and the Mystery of the Unwritten Constitution' [2011] NZ L Rev 591.
[134] See section 3.5.3.   [135] See section 4.2.
[136] In which the Supreme Court's predecessor, the Appellate Committee of the House of Lords, said that it would depart from the precedent established by its own earlier decisions when it appeared 'right to do so': [1966] 1 WLR 1234.

Third, *is democracy really about the public delegating powers to govern to those they elect?*[137] Another way of looking at it is that over many centuries the public have been willing to *tolerate* the exercise of executive and legislative powers *only on changing conditions*—the transfer of substantive legislative powers from the monarch to Parliament, ministerial responsibility to Parliament, requirements for free elections and thus possible changes in government, devolution where there is a demand for it, and so on.[138]

Fourth, *why has the protection of civil liberties and human rights become so important in the UK as in many liberal democracies and in international law in the last 60 years or so, when it was not so central before?* Here I am aware that I am moving into complex, and very controversial territory; but why not?

It is commonly taken for granted that 'out there' in the ether, or perhaps as a matter of pure, 'out there' reason, advanced civilised states and educated individuals will respect human rights, that they are right to do so, and that they are entitled to require other countries to do the same. While I too expect the human rights of all individuals to be respected and protected by law, I do not accept that either reason, or something 'out there' in the ether, provides convincing justification for human rights laws. There must be other explanations.

One of the explanations for the human rights movement is obvious: *practical* lessons were learned by many countries and individuals which experienced or observed the disastrous political, economic, and personal consequences of conflicts which manifested themselves in breaches of human rights by fascist regimes before and during the two world wars, and indeed elsewhere. This led to the International Covenant on Civil and Political Rights, the European Convention on Human Rights, even to the formation of the European Communities; free trade being a way to avoid conflict between nation states and with it breaches of human rights.

Another, connected, obvious explanation for the rise of the human rights movement is that people all round the world were deeply shocked and upset when they learned about the horrors of concentration and extermination camps and other mistreatment of civilians and others during the wars of the twentieth century. This latter point about public reaction to these horrors tells us something important about human nature: *humans empathise with others with whom they identify* (eg as members of a group to which they too belong, whether family, tribe, local community, class, or nationality). Empathy leads people to want to provide strong protections against violations of the dignity, autonomy, or respect of group members. This is a matter of innate human psychology.

But not everyone considers all other humans to 'belong' to their group and to deserve such protections: that was obvious in Nazi Germany, where some were regarded as 'subhuman', and it is obvious today in many countries where civil conflicts rage. The problem is that humans are predisposed to distinguish between those who belong to their groups and those who do not. Often generating negative stereotypes about 'others' serves to increase in-group solidarity when the group feels insecure, and is to that small and rather nasty extent 'rational'. However, many millions of people consider that *all* other humans deserve their empathy, that all humans belong to one group when it comes to rights. This, I suggest, is part of the explanation for why human rights movements have grown strong round the world as modern communications bring us all increasingly into contact with 'others' and their misfortunes, whom we come to accept as 'us'. It is to do with what is 'in here' in human minds, rather than something 'out there', either in the ether or in the realm of reason.

---

[137] See section 2.1.　　　[138] See, eg Wicks, *The Evolution of a Constitution* (Oxford 2006).

Further reading

BARBER, 'Laws and Constitutional Conventions' (2009) 125 LQR 294
An examination of the relationship between the respective roles of law and convention.

BINGHAM, 'The rule of law' [2007] CLJ 67
A concise and highly influential analysis of what the rule of law means in the context of the UK's constitution.

CABINET OFFICE, *The Cabinet Manual* (London 2011) (**https://www.gov.uk/government/ uploads/system/uploads/attachment_data/file/60641/cabinet-manual.pdf**)
An authoritative document published by the UK government setting out a range of matters— including numerous constitutional conventions—relating to the functioning of government.

CRAIG, 'Formal and Substantive Conceptions of the Rule of Law: An Analytical Framework' [1997] PL 467
An examination of the differences and relationships between formal and substantive conceptions of the rule of law.

FELDMAN, 'Constitutional Conventions' in Qvortrup (ed), *The British Constitution: Continuity and Change* (Oxford 2013)
A detailed analysis of the nature of constitutional conventions and of their role in the UK constitution.

HOUSE OF COMMONS POLITICAL AND CONSTITUTIONAL REFORM COMMITTEE, *A New Magna Carta?* (**http://www.publications.parliament.uk/pa/cm201415/cmselect/cmpolcon/ 463/463.pdf**)
A major piece of work examining the possibility of a codified constitution for the UK.

PART II

The Constitution— Institutions and Principles

3

Separation of Powers– An Introduction

1.	The three branches of government	87
2.	The basic idea of the separation of powers	89
3.	Why embrace the separation of powers?	91
4.	Different conceptions of the separation of powers	93
5.	The separation of powers in the UK	97
6.	Conclusions	99
	Expert commentary	100
	Further reading	102

1. The three branches of government

This part of the book is concerned with the main institutions that, together, comprise the UK constitution: the executive, the legislature, and the judiciary. We will consider the responsibilities of these institutions—that is, what they do. We will also consider how these institutions fit into the constitutional system and how they relate to one another.

The constitutions of most countries share and distribute public power among the following three principal branches of government:

- The *legislative branch*. The principal role of the legislature is to represent the views of the people and to make legislation. In the UK, the principal legislative body is the UK Parliament (often known simply as 'Westminster'), but there are other legislatures, such as the Scottish Parliament, the Welsh Assembly, and the Northern Ireland Assembly. Parliament also seeks to hold the executive to account.

- The *judicial branch*—that is, the system of courts and tribunals that interpret the law and adjudicate upon legal disputes. In the UK, the court system contains many different types of court and tribunal, with the Supreme Court at its apex.

- The *executive* or *administrative branch* (often referred to colloquially simply as 'the government'). The executive is responsible for making and implementing public policy. In the UK, there is the central UK government. There are also the devolved governments in Scotland, Wales, and Northern Ireland.

Figure 3.1 presents the key features and aspects of these branches of government in the context of the UK constitution. This may seem unfamiliar or confusing at first, and it may be useful to refer back to this figure.

Another complicating factor is that these branches of the state—the legislature, the executive, and the judiciary—are no longer confined solely to the UK level. They also exist both above and below the UK level. Above the UK level of government, there is, for as long as the UK remains a member, the European Union (EU). Below the UK level, there are the governments in Scotland, Wales, and Northern Ireland. There is also local government. This is what we call the 'multilayered constitution'. Table 3.1 presents these institutions and their place within the three branches of government.

Legislature/Parliament	Executive/government	Judiciary/the courts
Elected representatives	An elected government	Appointed judges
Members of Parliament	Ministers and civil servants located in government departments	The UK Supreme Court and other courts
Democracy	The governing party(-ies)	Judicial independence: courts are non-political
Adversarial party politics	Policy and administration	The rule of law
Political debate	The right of initiative	Adjudication: courts decide disputes according to law
Sustaining and supporting the elected government	Making and implementing public policy	Protecting individuals' legal and human rights
Scrutinising the government and holding it to account: through parliamentary questions and select committees	Raising and spending public money	Reviewing the legality of government decisions
Legislation	Ministerial responsibility	Common law principles
The customs and practices of Parliament	Accounting to Parliament	Legal precedents
Parliamentary privilege: parliamentary debates cannot be questioned in any court	Protecting public safety and delivering public services	Statutory interpretation
The constitutional doctrine of parliamentary sovereignty	Legislation, rules, policies, and administrative decisions	Judges are 'lions under the throne' (Francis Bacon, 1625)
But, in practice, dominated by the government's Commons majority	Constitutional conventions	'[T]he weakest of the three departments of power', the judiciary 'has no influence over either the sword or the purse . . . neither FORCE nor WILL, but merely judgment' (Federalist No 78, 1788)
	The government's dominance of Parliament: an 'elective dictatorship' or the necessary basis of its constitutional legitimacy?	

Figure 3.1 Key features of the legislature, executive, and judiciary in the UK

Table 3.1 Legislative, executive, and judicial institutions in the multilayered constitution

Constitutional theme	Layer of government	Legislature	Executive	Judiciary
The UK's European constitution	European Union	European Parliament	European Commission Council of Ministers	Court of Justice of the European Union
	European Human Rights	–	–	European Court of Human Rights
The UK's core constitution	UK central institutions	UK Parliament	UK government	Courts
The UK's territorial constitution	Scotland	Scottish Parliament	Scottish Government	Courts
	Wales	Welsh Assembly	Welsh Government	Courts
	Northern Ireland	Northern Ireland Assembly	Northern Ireland Executive	Courts
	England	UK Parliament is de facto English legislature— English Votes for English Laws	Local authorities and Combined Authorities	Courts

2. The basic idea of the separation of powers

We begin our examination of the institutions of government by thinking about how they relate to one another—and also how these institutions *ought* to relate to each other. We will spend much of this part of the book considering the former matter in relation to the UK. However, at the outset, it is important to consider the latter point. How should a system of government be designed? What should be the respective powers and functions of the different branches? And should they be independent of or interconnected with one another?

There are no straightforward answers to these questions. Any answers will necessarily depend on what one is trying to achieve. A dictator would plainly design a system of government in such a way as to enable him to do as he wished without interference from others; he would not, for example, want to be troubled by an independent judiciary liable to tell him that the law prevented him from doing certain things. He might therefore (if he had to tolerate the existence of a judiciary at all) design the system so that he could appoint tame judges who would be unlikely to challenge him, and dismiss them if they did.

Thankfully, most systems of government are not designed in such a way. Instead, there is a broad consensus that government should be organised according to the separation of powers doctrine. The tripartite system of government briefly described in this section reflects the separation of powers doctrine, in that it distinguishes between judicial, executive, and legislative branches. That doctrine has been described as one of the two 'great pillar[s] of Western political thought' that underpin the notion of 'constitutional' government (the other being representative democracy).[1] That there should be three branches, and that they should be distinct from one another, is the central tenet of the separation of powers doctrine, at least according to its classical definition.[2]

However, beyond this very rudimentary outline, there is no uniform view as to what the precise relationships between the legislative, executive, and judicial branches should be. A strict formulation of the doctrine would require that no branch should be capable of exercising power *over* another branch, that none should be able to exercise the powers *of* another, and that no individual person should be a *member* of more than one branch. This is not the only interpretation of the doctrine, although we will use it, for the time being, as our working definition. However, as we will see later, this view of the doctrine may be regarded, as one commentator put it, as an 'extreme' formulation.[3] There are other, arguably better, interpretations.

What, then, is the separation of powers doctrine—and what is it not? It is, ultimately, merely an idea—a model, or template, that sets out how some people think the system and institutions of government ought to be organised. It is not the only way in which government *may be* organised, it is not the only way in which government *is* organised, and it is not—at least in the strict form set out in the previous paragraph—the way in which government is organised *in the UK*. This is not to suggest that the separation of powers is unimportant. It is an influential idea with a long historical pedigree.[4]

Down the ages, the doctrine of the separation of powers has been regarded by many constitutional writers as representing the ideal governmental structure, and it is reflected in the constitutions of many countries—including, to a limited extent, the UK. Indeed, Montesquieu, one of the writers most closely associated with the separation of powers doctrine, based his elaboration of it on his perceptions of the constitution of eighteenth-century England (although it is generally thought that Montesquieu misunderstood the English constitution).[5]

In any event, the view that government should be organised in line with the separation of powers doctrine is not one that is universally held, and the failure of a country fully to implement the doctrine is not *necessarily* a bad thing. Whether one thinks that such failure is *actually* a bad thing depends on whether one agrees with the assumptions that underlie the separation of powers doctrine.

We therefore need critically to examine those assumptions. Why is the separation of powers thought to be a *good* thing? Is this correct?

---

[1] Vile, *Constitutionalism and the Separation of Powers* (Oxford 1967), p 2.
[2] Montesquieu, *The Spirit of the Laws* [1748] (Cambridge 1989), Book XI, ch 6.   [3] Vile, p 13.
[4] Vile, ch 2; Munro, *Studies in Constitutional Law* (London 1999), pp 295–302.
[5] Montesquieu.

3. Why embrace the separation of powers?

One way of addressing this question is to consider what might happen in a constitutional system *without* any recognisable separation of powers. Let us imagine what
such a system might look like. Even if there were not a separate legislature, executive,
and judiciary, many of the functions that would, in most countries, be carried out by
those three institutions would still somehow have to be performed. Laws would have
to be made, implemented, and adjudicated upon.[6] In the absence of distinct institutions, therefore, it would presumably fall to a single institution—let us call it simply
the 'government'—to perform all such functions.

> **Q** Against that background, consider the following hypothetical scenario.
>
> In a system with no separation of powers, the government decides that it wants to be
> able to expel from its territory foreign nationals who are likely to pose a security threat.
> The government therefore drafts and enacts legislation that gives government Ministers
> the power to expel from its territory 'any foreign national who, in the opinion of any
> Minister, may pose a threat to national security'. Government Ministers subsequently
> expel certain persons who are critical of the government, but who, most right-thinking
> people believe, pose no threat to national security. Those persons appeal to Ministers ask-
> ing them to reverse their decisions, but Ministers refuse to do so.
>
> Why might the scenario described be regarded as an example of abuse of power? What
> forms does that abuse take? To what extent does the absence of a separation of powers
> enable (or make easier) such abuse? Would the existence of a separation of powers neces-
> sarily mean that such abuse would not occur?

It is highly unlikely that the situation described could come about in a constitutional
system based upon the separation of powers doctrine. In such a system, if Ministers—
that is, members of the executive branch—were to desire legal powers to do certain
things, then they would, in general, have to ask the legislature to confer such powers
upon them. The legislature, as a separate and independent institution, might agree to
the request—but it might decline the request outright, or it might agree to provide the
requested powers, but only on terms different from those proposed by the executive.
For example, if the executive were to request (as in the example) a power to expel 'any
foreign national who, in the opinion of any Minister, may pose a threat to national
security', the legislature might take the view that while it is appropriate for the executive to have powers to exclude or expel dangerous individuals, it should not have a
power to expel anyone who Ministers *think* is or *may be* dangerous. The legislature
may therefore respond by granting Ministers a power to expel any foreign national
who is *reasonably* believed by a Minister to pose a *serious* threat to national security—
a much narrower power than the one desired by Ministers. Moreover, the existence, in
a system that embraces the separation of powers, of an independent judiciary would
provide a forum in which Ministers' exercises of the power could be challenged.

---

[6] This assumes (which, for present purposes, we do) that the country concerned is governed in a way
that is based on some form of law, rather than, say, on brute force.

Excluded individuals could, for example, ask courts to overturn Ministers' decisions if Ministers were unable to identify objective grounds demonstrating the reasonableness of their belief, or if the evidence did not establish a serious—as opposed to a fanciful—risk to national security.

It should be apparent from the scenario sketched that, within a constitutional system without any vestige of the separation of powers, there is a very serious risk—if not an inevitability—of the *abuse of power*. Lord Acton's famous statement that 'Power tends to corrupt and absolute power corrupts absolutely' is obviously a generalisation, but it certainly contains a kernel of truth.[7] Acton went on to explain his view by saying that '[g]reat men'—he was writing at a time when only men tended to be great in the sense of wielding power and when government Ministers were all men—'are almost always bad men'.[8]

This is perhaps going too far, but it is clearly important to guard against the abuse of power by ensuring that the bad—as well as the merely well-intentioned, but incompetent or misguided—cannot do precisely as they please. That is precisely what the separation of powers doctrine seeks to do: it provides a model of government in which the risks of the abuse of power are reduced.

The separation of powers does not necessarily always guard against the abuse of power. For instance, all three branches might be prepared to collude in the abuse of public power. However, the separation of powers doctrine makes the abuse of power far less likely. As James Madison—the fourth US President and a key architect of its Constitution—put it: 'The accumulation of all powers, legislative, executive, and judiciary, in the same hands, whether of one, a few, or many, and whether hereditary, self-appointed, or elective, may justly be pronounced the very definition of tyranny.'[9] Similarly, Montesquieu feared the use of power in a 'tyrannical manner' if it was not divided among legislative, executive, and judicial branches.[10]

> **Q** Why is abuse of power less likely in a system of government characterised by the separation of powers? If separation of powers cannot guarantee that power will not be abused, what other safeguards might be necessary?

Organising a system of government according to the separation of powers is then undertaken in order to limit and prevent abuse of power by providing checks and balances. Placing the prevention of abuse of power centre stage implies a set of assumptions—in particular, preserving the liberty of the individual against inappropriate governmental interference.[11] Those who place greater faith in the capacity of government, through the pursuit of collectivist policies, to secure the public good might approach the matter differently. In particular, they would be inclined to characterise the primary purpose of the separation of powers not as preventing the government from doing bad things, but as helping it to do beneficial things, such as

---

[7] Letter to Bishop Mandell Creighton, 3 April 1887.   [8] Letter to Bishop Mandell Creighton.
[9] Hamilton, Madison, and Jay, *The Federalist* [1787–88] (Washington DC 1992), no 47.
[10] Montesquieu, *The Spirit of the Laws.*   [11] Vile, p 14.

securing the liberty of the individual and of the community as a whole, by ensuring that any given function is allocated to the institution best capable of discharging it.[12]

These two objectives—the prevention of tyranny and the facilitation of socially useful conduct by government—are not mutually exclusive. It might, for example, be desirable to strike a balance between a government so powerful as to be liable to act tyrannically and one so weak as to be unable to do anything useful. In any event, both views fit our notion of the separation of powers as a means to an end. Viewed thus, the separation of powers is a methodology. It is a way of organising things so as to secure or prevent particular outcomes.

The separation of powers doctrine and democracy are often found together. Indeed, the two ideas might be said to be mutually reinforcing. Democracy is likely to assist with attaining goals (such as preventing abuse of power) that are the objective of separation of powers, the prospect of having to submit to re-election being a powerful—but not necessarily sufficient[13]—incentive against such abuse. The separation of powers is likely to bolster democracy. By requiring the legislative function to be performed by the legislature, the separation of powers helps to ensure that the most significant changes to law and policy can be made only with the approval of the branch that is the most representative of the people.

4. Different conceptions of the separation of powers

That the doctrine of the separation of powers is not an end in itself is an important insight. It helps us to think more carefully about how systems of government should be designed and to evaluate critically existing constitutional arrangements, including those of the UK. In particular, conceiving of the separation of powers in this way should caution us against thinking of the doctrine as laying down a set of prescriptive rules any infraction of which is necessarily a bad thing.

Q Consider each of the following provisions of an imaginary constitution. Before reading further, think about any senses in which they disclose a breach of the separation of powers doctrine. To the extent that the following situations disclose such breaches, are they necessarily problematic?

  (i)   Senior members of the executive may dismiss judges at will.
  (ii) The executive can enact any legislation that it chooses without needing to obtain the consent of the legislature.
  (iii) Judges may strike down legislation that is inconsistent with a constitutional Bill of Rights.
  (iv) The president may veto legislation passed by the legislature (unless the legislature overrides the president by a two-thirds majority).

---

[12] See, eg Barber, 'Prelude to the Separation of Powers' [2001] CLJ 59.

[13] Thomas Jefferson, the third US President, thought democracy without separation of powers to be far from ideal. It risked 'elective despotism' in that the government, once elected, was free to do as it wished due to an overconcentration of power in its hands. See 'Notes on the State of Virginia', quoted in *The Federalist*, no 48.

All of the situations described in the box involve one branch of government being capable of interfering with, or undertaking, the business of another. If the separation of powers were conceived of as an end in itself, any breach—and hence all of those set out—would be problematic. That view of the doctrine has been referred to as the *pure version* of the separation of powers because it is conceived in absolute terms: the dividing lines between the legislature, executive, and judiciary must be crystal clear, and must not be crossed in any circumstances.[14]

This may be contrasted with the *partial version* of the separation of powers doctrine.[15] On this view, arrangements that would be regarded as breaches of the pure version are not regarded as either inherently problematic or illegitimate; rather, the acceptability of any such 'breach' depends on whether, and if so to what extent, it compromises achievement of the ultimate objective that the separation of powers doctrine pursues. Indeed, we can go further than this by observing that a paradox lies at the heart of the separation of powers doctrine. On the one hand, its ultimate objective is (for many commentators) to guard against the abuse of power; yet, on the other hand, the achievement of that objective is likely to be fundamentally compromised by the sort of literal implementation of the doctrine envisaged under the pure version. If each branch of government is truly independent and free from any sort of control, interference, or oversight by the others, then the abuse of power by each branch remains a distinct possibility.

This was a major influence on the framers of the US Constitution, who thought that it would be unwise simply to lay down in a constitutional text the boundaries of the three branches' powers and to 'trust [such] parchment barriers against the encroaching spirit of power'.[16] Thus, they said, it was necessary to design 'the interior structure of government [such] that its several constituent parts may, by their mutual relations, be the means of keeping each other in their proper places'.[17] This meant striking a balance between, on the one hand, keeping the three branches as distinct as possible in order to avoid the risk of tyranny created by overconcentration of power, and, on the other hand, enabling the institutions of government to regulate one another and to keep one another in check.

It follows that within this partial, or 'checks and balances', conception of the separation of powers, the ability of one branch to involve itself in matters that are the primary concern of another branch is not necessarily a bad thing—and may indeed be regarded as entirely positive. It is therefore necessary, once this more nuanced view of the separation of powers is embraced, to distinguish between constructive 'breaches' (ie situations in which one branch is somewhat involved in the work of another) and destructive breaches.

- *Constructive breaches* are to be welcomed, because they contribute to the attainment of the overall goal of preventing tyranny. The example given of a presidential power of legislative override subject to the possibility of reversal by a

---

[14] Vile, *Constitutionalism and the Separation of Powers* (Oxford 1967), ch 1.
[15] Vile, ch 1; Barendt, 'Separation of Powers and Constitutional Government' [1995] PL 599.
[16] *The Federalist*, no 48.   [17] *The Federalist*, no 51.

legislative super-majority may be regarded as a constructive breach of the separation of powers: it creates a balance of power between the executive and legislative branches, making it harder, but not impossible, for the legislature to do something to which the executive is opposed, while preserving the supremacy of the former in matters of lawmaking.

- *Destructive breaches* are to be deplored, because they make the attainment of the goal of preventing tyranny less likely. Consider, for instance, executive powers to dismiss judges at will or to enact legislation without the consent of the legislature. Such powers could be regarded as problematic breaches of separation of powers: they effectively make the executive dominant over the other two branches and serve to create not a balance of power, but an overconcentration of power in executive hands. Such arrangements do not contribute to the important task of the various branches keeping one another in their 'proper places'.

Q Look again at situation (iii) in the previous question box. Under a partial conception of the separation of powers, would a judicial power to strike down legislation as unconstitutional be regarded in positive or negative terms?

This view of the separation of powers also fits better with the reality of modern government.[18] Over the last 200 years, many countries with constitutions based upon the separation of powers have witnessed the development of administrative agencies that undertake many of the day-to-day tasks of government. However, these agencies cannot comfortably be slotted into only one of the three traditional categories (ie legislative, executive, or judicial). It has been noted that it is commonplace in the USA for administrative agencies to 'engage in [lawmaking], to formulate and apply policies, and to take individual decisions, often after a formal hearing'.[19] Such agencies constitute a 'one-stop shop' that deals with many aspects—legislative, executive, and judicial—of a particular subject matter. The US Food and Drug Administration, which exists, among other things, to ensure the safety of medicines and food, is an example of such a body.

The UK also has such large-scale government departments and administrative bodies. Some are headed by government Ministers; others are not. Such bodies cannot be neatly characterised as performing only executive, legislative, or judicial functions. A pure conception of separation of powers would demand that such bodies did not exist: the blurring of the lines between the three branches would be unacceptable. In contrast, the partial version of the separation of powers doctrine holds that such

---

[18] Vile, p 319, goes further by arguing that it is simply impossible to draw clean distinctions (such as would allow their allocation to different institutions) between 'rule-making, rule-application and rule-adjudication': '[M]ost operations of government are much too complex, requiring a whole stream of decisions to be taken, such that it is impossible to divide them up' in this way.

[19] Barendt, 'Separation of Powers and Constitutional Government' [1995] PL 599, 607.

agencies are not per se objectionable; rather, the question is whether they threaten the objective(s) that the doctrine exists to serve.

Barendt, for example, argues that the existence of administrative agencies that span the three branches of government is unobjectionable provided that they can be held adequately to account for their actions (eg via political accountability to the legislature and through the possibility of judicial review).[20] Barber goes as far as to suggest that the traditional 'tripartite vision of the state' is a distraction. The existence of the type of agencies described here and of multilayered governance arrangements means that it is no longer—if it ever was—the case that the state consists of 'three great monoliths': a legislature, an executive, and a judiciary.[21] He therefore concludes that the proper concern of the separation of powers cannot be the preservation of clear dividing lines between (what are, for him at least) chimerical institutions, but rather the allocation of power in the way most likely to realise the objective underlying the separation of powers.[22] Of course, this might well still entail that a given agency should be unable to wield overweening power and marginalise other institutions of government—but, for Barber, there is no particular need to carve up government along rigid lines demarcating legislative, executive, and judicial functions.

Consider the matter in this way. Given the inherent imprecision that attaches to labels such as 'legislative', 'executive', and 'judicial', it is often impossible in practice to agree in advance a distribution of *functions* between different *institutions*. According to a strict understanding of the separation of powers we would expect the legislature, Parliament, to legislate. However, in practice, the legislative agenda is highly influenced—even dictated—by the government. Government also makes the vast body of secondary legislation.

Similar complications arise when we consider the role of the courts. According to a strict separation of powers approach, the courts and only the courts adjudicate disputes. Furthermore, the courts would have no role as regards legislative and executive functions. Looking at what happens in practice, it can certainly be said that adjudication is the core task of the courts. Yet, when the courts adjudicate public law disputes, their judgments often have important policy and administrative consequences for government. Similarly, whenever the courts interpret legislation, they are undertaking a role closely akin to a legislative function.

The upshot is that the dividing lines between the exercise of legislative, administrative, and judicial functions are often vanishingly thin. The separation of powers is an intuitively appealing abstract ideal, but is often illusory in practice. As Cane has noted, 'unless we adopt the circular approach of defining the legislative function as what the legislature does, the executive function as what the executive does, and the judicial function as what the judiciary does, a realistic assessment will lead us to the conclusion that all three branches of government effectively perform all three functions'.[23]

---

[20] Barendt at 607.   [21] Barber, 'Prelude to the Separation of Powers' [2001] CLJ 59, 70–1.

[22] For Barber, the principal objective of the separation of powers is the protection of liberty. His argument, however, is equally relevant if the main purpose of the doctrine is regarded as the prevention of tyranny.

[23] Cane, *Administrative Law* (5th edn, Oxford 2011), p 49.

Few countries stick rigidly to a pure version of the separation of powers doctrine, but most constitutional systems embody a recognisable partial separation of powers in which a genuine attempt is made to demarcate legislative, executive, and judicial functions, allocating them to institutionally distinct branches of government. This is combined with the insertion of appropriate checks and balances to ensure that each branch is subject to oversight, or is counterbalanced, by another. At the same time, not every government body or constitutional actor can neatly be assigned to one of the three standard categories. Whether or not that is a problem from a separation of powers standpoint depends on whether such bodies threaten the underlying purposes of the doctrine and whether adequate arrangements exist for minimising the possibility of their doing so.

5. The separation of powers in the UK

Does the UK constitution embody the separation of powers doctrine? There is no consensus as to whether the doctrine either is or should be a fundamental feature of the UK constitution. There are even different views as to whether the doctrine exists in any meaningful form in the UK constitution.

Lord Diplock, a senior judge, once noted that 'the basic concept of separation of legislative, executive and judicial power . . . had been developed in the unwritten constitution of the United Kingdom'.[24] For Diplock, the UK constitution was 'firmly based upon the separation of powers'.[25] By contrast, the nineteenth-century constitutional writer and journalist Bagehot noted that the 'efficient secret of the English Constitution may be described by the close union, the nearly complete fusion, of the executive and legislative powers'.[26] In other words, in the UK, there is a substantial overlap between the executive and Parliament, with the executive exerting a powerful influence over the work of Parliament.

We will see in later chapters that there are certainly important respects in which the UK constitution fails to adhere to a pure conception of the separation of powers. Indeed, some writers have contended that the UK constitution does not adhere to the separation of powers *at all*. The doctrine has been described as a 'myth',[27] and as 'an irrelevant distraction'.[28] These views were made some time ago and the UK constitution has changed significantly in the meantime. That point aside, however, such views—based as they are on examples of technical breaches of the separation of powers doctrine[29]—rather miss the point. Indeed, to suppose that a constitution must either exhibit *separation* of powers or, as Bagehot put it, *fusion* of powers[30] is to postulate a false dichotomy.[31]

---

[24] *Hinds v The Queen* [1977] AC 195, 212.   [25] *Duport Steels Ltd v Sirs* [1980] 1 WLR 142, 157.
[26] Bagehot, *The English Constitution* (London 1867), p 12.
[27] Hood Phillips, 'A Constitutional Myth: Separation of Powers' (1977) 93 LQR 11.
[28] De Smith, 'The Separation of Powers in New Dress' (1966–67) 12 McGill Law Journal 491.
[29] Hood Phillips, 12.   [30] Bagehot, p 12.
[31] Vile, *Constitutionalism and the Separation of Powers* (Oxford 1967), pp 213–14.

The pure version of the doctrine is unrealistic (few, if any, countries adhere to it) and even undesirable (because it precludes measures, such as checks and balances, which are likely to promote the overall objective of preventing tyranny). The important question, therefore, is not whether the UK adheres to a pure conception of the separation of powers (it manifestly does not), but whether its institutions of government are organised in such a way as to guard satisfactorily against the abuse of power. This is a complex issue that we investigate throughout this book. We will encounter instances in which one institution has so much power over another branch as to create precisely the sort of overconcentration of power that enhances the risk of its abuse; the extent to which the executive branch is able to dominate and control proceedings in Parliament is perhaps the most obvious example of such a phenomenon.[32] On the other hand, we will find many situations in which a strict separation of powers *is* adhered to, the independence of the judiciary being a clear example of such a situation.[33] And we will confront situations in which the absence of strict separation actually serves to guard against abuse of power, an example being the courts' power to review the legality of executive action and to strike down any such action that is unlawful.[34]

Critically assessing the UK constitution from a separation of powers standpoint is not straightforward. First, it is too simplistic merely to ask whether the UK constitution either does or does not adhere to the doctrine. Rather, the question is one of degree. To what extent does the UK constitution adhere to the separation of powers? Whatever the answer to that question might be, it is clear at the outset that the British constitution should not be condemned as faulty merely because it does not embody the sort of rigid distinctions inherent in the pure conception of the separation of powers.[35]

This leads on to a second difficulty. The partial conception of the separation of powers necessarily calls for the striking of a balance between, on the one hand, the separateness of government institutions (so as to avoid overconcentration of power) and, on the other hand, the existence of relationships between them (in order that they may keep one another in their 'proper places'). There is little agreement as to what constitutes the 'right' balance.

To illustrate, we will consider the *Fire Brigades Union* case.[36] In this case, the Home Secretary had refused to exercise his power under s 171(1) of the Criminal Justice Act 1988 to bring into force a new scheme (contained elsewhere in the statute) for compensating victims of crime. The Home Secretary had also indicated that he had no intention of bringing the statutory scheme into force. This was tantamount to repeal of the relevant parts of the 1988 Act. The case therefore raised important questions as to whether, under the separation of powers, it was appropriate for a government Minister to be allowed, in effect, to repeal an Act of Parliament—something that, it might be thought, should be done only by Parliament itself—and, if not, whether it was appropriate for the court to intervene.

---

[32] See Chapters 4 and 5.   [33] See Chapter 6.   [34] See Chapters 11–14.

[35] See further Munro, *Studies in Constitutional Law* (London 1999), ch 9, and Munro, 'The Separation of Powers: Not Such a Myth' [1981] PL 19.

[36] *R v Secretary of State for the Home Department, ex p Fire Brigades Union* [1995] 2 AC 513.

By a three–two majority, the House of Lords held that the Home Secretary had exceeded his powers. Yet, all five judges justified their conclusions by reference to the separation of powers doctrine, even though they arrived at completely different conclusions. The majority concluded that the Home Secretary had acted unlawfully by breaching the duty to keep under active consideration the implementation of the statutory compensation scheme that was held to be implicit in the s 171(1) discretion. The majority was therefore willing to intervene in order to prevent executive usurpation of a legislative function. The dissenting judges, however, considered it inappropriate for the court to intervene in such a matter because it concerned legislation that was not yet fully in force, thereby making the issue a political one, which should have been resolved by Parliament and the executive. They were concerned that judicial intervention would entail the *courts* contravening the separation of powers by interfering in a matter outside their area of constitutional responsibility.

This case illustrates how views can differ about how to strike the balance between the separateness of government institutions and the pursuit of relationships between them, within which checks and balances may be provided. The minority considered the separateness of the judiciary—in the sense of remaining outside the political arena—to be of overriding importance. In contrast, the majority emphasised the importance of checks and balances; judicial intervention was necessary to ensure that the executive could not arrogate to itself powers of repealing legislation that should belong exclusively to the legislature.

> **Q** Which of the two views adopted in *Fire Brigades Union* do you find more persuasive? Why?

6. Conclusions

The separation of powers doctrine is capable of being stated in relatively simple terms. However, the doctrine is far from straightforward. Once we recognise that distinguishing between legislative, executive, and judicial functions, and allocating each to a different institution, is merely a means to an end, the extent to which any constitutional system precisely adheres to the doctrine, thus stated, becomes insignificant. The more important matter is whether the system is designed so as to be capable of adequately guarding against the misuse of power. This is likely to involve striking a balance between, on the one hand, the need to avoid an overconcentration of power by allocating different functions to different institutions and, on the other hand, the need to ensure that the various branches relate to one another in constructive ways that allow for sufficient checks and balances.

The separation of powers doctrine is closely related to—indeed, is a way of pursuing—the concept of accountability, ensuring that those who exercise public power are held to account. Accountability, like the separation of powers, is ultimately a means to an end, rather than an end in itself. Both concepts may assist in ensuring that governmental power is used responsibly, for the public good, rather than abused.

Expert commentary
The separation of powers is a tricky principle
Nick Barber, Associate Professor, University of Oxford

Unlike its close cousin, the rule of law, doubts have been expressed about the attractions of the separation of powers at several levels of abstraction. At the most general, some have challenged the utility of the separation of powers, arguing that whatever work it does could better be done by other constitutional arguments. As Geoffrey Marshall put it, perhaps the separation of powers is 'a jumbled portmanteau of arguments for policies which ought to be supported or rejected on other grounds.'[37] Sir Ivor Jennings went so far as to contend that the principle rested on a mistake: there was no material distinction to be drawn between legislative, judicial, and executive powers.[38] More cautiously, other writers have been prepared to accept that the principle characterises some constitutions, but challenge its applicability to parliamentary systems, such as that of the UK. Perhaps the separation of powers is a characteristic of *presidential* systems, in which the executive branch has a constitutionally protected area of power and its own, discrete, source of electoral legitimacy, and does not characterise *parliamentary* systems in which the executive is dependent upon the legislature.[39]

Despite these doubts, the principle of separation of powers has grown in popularity in recent years, a rise that parallels a broader resurgence of interest in institutional design and competence.[40] And both developments have gone hand in hand with the expanding role of the judges in our constitution. With devolution, the Human Rights Act 1998, the growth of administrative law, and, for now at least, European law, judges are being asked to answer questions that raise broad political issues. Some of the renewed interest in the separation of powers is spurred by a concern that the institutional structure of the court limits the capacity of the judges to answer these questions satisfactorily. Accordingly, analysing this growth in judicial power—whether we decide to defend or critique it—requires us to locate the courts within a broader constitutional structure.

The first question that might be asked of the separation of powers is what, precisely, the principle requires of those creating and maintaining the constitution. There are numerous versions of the separation of powers. The most popular understanding of the principle presents the three branches of state—the legislature, the courts, and the executive—each of which is then divided into three features. The three divisions are between institutions, between powers, and between officials in those institutions. We can imagine a table with three rows and three columns: the columns being the three branches of state, with the rows being the three types of division between those branches.

---

[37] Marshall, *Constitutional Theory* (Oxford 1971), p 124.
[38] Jennings, *Law and the Constitution* (5th edn, London 1959), pp 281–2 and 303.
[39] Bagehot, *The English Constitution* [1867] (London 1964), ch 1.
[40] For a pioneering reassessment, see Munro, 'The Separation of Powers: Not Such a Myth' [1981] PL 19; Allan, *Law, Liberty, and Justice* (Oxford 1993), ch 3; and, more recently, Barber, 'Prelude to the Separation of Powers' (2001) 60 CLJ 59.

Many accounts of the separation of powers focus on the importance of dividing the elements found in the different rows—ordinarily, for instance, the courts should not legislate. However, an equally important feature is the unity found in the columns. For example, the principle requires that the legislature should be staffed by legislators, and act through legislation; the separation of powers demands that structure, skill, and power be drawn together. Some writers have embraced a 'liberty model' of the separation of powers—a version of the principle that sees it as requiring the division of powers between state institutions in order to make oppression of individuals more difficult; power is divided, state action is made harder, and liberty is protected. But such models fall short in this respect: they can explain the divisions, but they cannot explain the unity.

A convincing account of the separation of powers rests upon a convincing account of the state. Such an account cannot be provided here. But if we assume that the state exists to allow the people to govern themselves effectively, it is possible to see the outlines of a justification for the standard account of the separation of powers. To allow self-government, there is a need for a legislature—an institution which contains a large number of people—who are elected, and who act through the issuing of statutes, laws that set out the broad policy objectives of the state. There is also a need for an executive branch, divided into task-focused departments. These offices are staffed by members of two distinct groups: government Ministers, who set the policy direction of government, and unelected officials who possess the technical skills to make decisions about the application (and the implications) of the law. And there is a need for a body that can authoritatively resolve disputes over the law—a legally skilled set of officials, ie judges—who focus on the issues raised in particular cases.

Some of the so-called 'pure' theories of the separation of powers suggest that these different branches of the state should—and could—avoid interacting with each other. This is a fantasy. Part of the task of the separation of powers is to explain how these bodies *should* relate to each other. The older liberty-focused models of separation of powers presented this interaction as characterised by friction: the institutions of the constitution were set in tension and, by means of this tension, the state's capacity to harm the individual was reduced. Newer accounts of the separation of powers are grounded not in restricting the state, but in facilitating effective state action. Such accounts see comity, rather than friction, as the primary mode of interaction. Normally—though not invariably—interaction between these bodies should be characterised by comity: the branches of state should support and respect each other, and the constitution should be designed to encourage and support such a relationship.

The Human Rights Act 1998 (HRA) illustrates the implications of the separation of powers. It is interesting to reflect on what the principle might have to say about this statute. There is, as always, a temptation to rush to extremes. On the one hand, sceptics of the HRA warn that the statute pushes judges into making political decisions that second-guess Parliament. For instance, Art 10 of the European Convention on Human Rights (ECHR) protects freedom of expression, but such protection is qualified; it is lawful to limit freedom of speech in various circumstances. Reflecting on this, John Griffith famously warned that Art 10 ECHR was simply a statement of a political conflict pretending to be a resolution of it.[41] On this view, the HRA flouts the separation of powers by shifting political questions out of the elected legislature into the unelected courts. On the other hand, fans of the HRA celebrate the move, claiming

---

[41] Griffith, 'The Political Constitution' (1979) 42 MLR 1, 13–14.

that questions of people's rights are, paradigmatically, questions for judges and should not be dependent on the whims of the majority in the electorate. On this view, the separation of powers requires the courts to make decisions about the implications of human rights, and uphold these rights against the executive and legislature. If anything, the HRA does not go far enough: the courts should be given the power to strike down statutes that run contrary to human rights.

So does the principle of the separation of powers oppose the Human Rights Act or demand it be strengthened? Perhaps neither view is correct.[42] The metaphor of 'dialogue' invoked by some writers on the Human Rights Act is problematic, but the essential idea that the metaphor seeks to convey is a powerful one.[43] Dialogue models argue that both the legislature and the courts (and, indeed, the executive, too) have a role to play in protecting rights. The normal demands of the separation of powers—that institutions undertake tasks that they are well suited to execute and that they support and respect other constitutional institutions—makes a compatible claim. Ideally, the various institutions of the constitution will examine a single action, or potential action, of the state in a number of different contexts: the legislature assesses its broad impact on the public good, the executive examines its technical impact on the groups it affects, and the court sees its impact on particular individuals. The separation of powers requires that these different strengths are combined to ensure that the totality of the impact of the action is assessed. The protection of rights and the assessment of what rights entail may be a task that all of the branches of the state play a part in, a part conditioned by their complementary institutional strengths.

A final point should be made about the significance of the separation of powers. As we have seen, the principle speaks to the creation of state institutions and to their interaction. However, it does not follow from this that the separation of powers is a legal principle to be applied by the courts. The separation of powers speaks to the powers of the judges as much as to the powers of the executive and legislative branches. If the judges were to assert an unconstrained right to police the division of powers in the constitution—applying their conception of the separation of powers over the decisions of Parliament found in statutes—this might, in itself, run against the principle. Perhaps surprisingly, the separation of powers might itself require that the judges did not apply the principle directly. Whilst the separation of powers should certainly inform judicial decision-making, it may also require the judges to abide by the understandings of that principle found in the decisions of other branches of the state—even when, sometimes, the judges think those other constitutional actors have got it wrong.

Further reading

BARENDT, 'Separation of Powers and Constitutional Government' [1995] PL 599
    This article analyses the separation of powers as an essential principle of liberal constitutionalism and its place within the UK constitution.

---

[42] On this, see Barber, 'Self-Defence for Institutions' (2013) 72 CLJ 558, 572–7; Kavanagh, 'The Constitutional Separation of Powers' in Dyzenhaus and Thorburn, *Philosophical Foundations of Constitutional Law* (Oxford 2015).
[43] Young, *Democratic Dialogue and the Constitution* (Oxford 2017).

HAMILTON, MADISON, and JAY, *The Federalist*, nos 47–51 (**http://thomas.loc.gov/home/histdox/fedpapers.html**)

 Described as 'the best analysis of the fundamental principles of a liberal constitution ever written in the English language' (Barendt), *The Federalist* Papers were written in 1787–88 during the ratification of the US Constitution.

VILE, *Constitutionalism and the Separation of Powers* (Oxford 1967)

 This book provides a conceptual and historical survey of the idea of the separation of powers.

4

UK Central Government

1. Introduction   104
2. The modern executive and its constitutional position   105
3. Central government   116
4. The powers of the executive   138
5. Conclusions   162
   Expert commentary   163
   Further reading   165
   Useful websites   165

1. Introduction

The executive (or the 'government', or 'administration') is the governing body of the state. This chapter is concerned with the UK central government. It is not the only executive institution in the UK. We will see in Chapter 7 that, with devolution, Scotland, Northern Ireland, and Wales each has their own institutions that perform executive functions within those policy areas that have been devolved to them. Local government also has important executive responsibilities. Nonetheless, the UK central government is, by far, the UK's most powerful executive institution. It exists by virtue of its majority in the Commons and there are no legal limits upon Parliament's lawmaking powers.

This chapter explores the following issues: what the executive is, and what it does; how it relates to other branches of government—with particular reference to its relationship with Parliament; how it is held to account, both politically and legally;[1] the institutions and constitutional actors that make up the modern UK executive; and the considerable powers that it has at its disposal. An appreciation of the executive is therefore central to any understanding of the contemporary UK constitution.

---

[1] See also Chapters 9–17.

2. The modern executive and its constitutional position

2.1 **What is the executive?**

The basic purpose of the executive is to make and implement public policy across the range of areas for which it is responsible. The executive is that branch of the state responsible for executing and administering laws enacted by the legislature. The legislature debates and enacts legislation. It also scrutinises the executive. By contrast, the purpose of the judiciary is primarily to adjudicate upon and resolve legal disputes. The executive and the legislature are then the most political branches of the state. Their actions are directly guided by political factors, whereas the judiciary is non-political.

As a starting point, the executive's role is distinctive in two senses. First, the executive is responsible for *running the country*.[2] This is a very imprecise notion, but it reflects the idea that it is the executive that is responsible for doing things as diverse as managing the National Health Service (NHS), detaining certain convicted criminals in prison, controlling immigration, making sure that the country's energy needs are met, conducting relations with other states and with international bodies such as the European Union (EU), ensuring that the UK meets its obligations under international treaties in areas ranging from human rights to climate change, collecting taxes, distributing welfare payments, regulating myriad forms of activity such as the conduct of financial institutions and utility companies, fighting wars, and so on.

Second, the executive is the only branch of government that can fairly be described as an *initiative-taker*. The role of the courts is limited by their modus operandi: they make decisions in whatever cases come before them. Judicial decisions can sometimes have far-reaching implications, but the courts only decide cases if litigants bring their disputes before them. Similarly, Parliament is not generally in a position to take the initiative. Its role is usually limited to scrutinising and enacting the government's legislative agenda. Parliamentary approval is required before a Bill can become law, but law is made, in the sense of being 'formulated in a coherent form', by the executive.[3] By contrast, the executive is 'the dominant institution to which the other two institutions react'.[4]

It therefore falls to the executive branch, in two ways, to take the initiative. First, it is the executive that develops and designs planned changes in public policy. Important changes such as the creation of the NHS or the conferral of independence upon the Bank of England occurred because the executive thought of them, designed them, and implemented them. Second, it is also the executive, as initiative-taker, to which the task of reacting to sudden, unforeseeable (or at least unforeseen) events falls.

The policy areas for which government is responsible are neither fixed nor static. Instead, the scope of executive action is constantly changing and often a contentious

---

[2] See, eg *R v Secretary of State for the Home Department, ex p Fire Brigades Union* [1995] 2 AC 513, 567–8.
[3] Norton, 'Parliament and Legislative Scrutiny: An Overview of Issues in the Legislative Process', in Brazier (ed), *Parliament, Politics and Law Making: Issues and Developments in the Legislative Process* (London 2004), p 5.
[4] Griffith, 'The Common Law and the Political Constitution' (2001) 117 LQR 42, 49.

area of political debate. In earlier centuries, the executive had comparatively few areas of responsibility. In medieval times, government was under the personal influence of the monarch of the day, the Crown, and possessed very little responsibility other than for the defence of the realm. If the country were being invaded or if the monarch were to wish to conquer other countries, then the monarch could personally decide whether or not to go to war. During the nineteenth century, however, with the Industrial Revolution, government began to assume new functions, such as maintaining law and order, and the regulation of trade and industry. Government was still limited—the pervasive ethos was that of laissez-faire: state intervention was relatively slight—but its role was growing.

Now let us compare that with modern government. Today, government assumes responsibility for a bewildering variety and seemingly endless number of public tasks, such as managing the economy; protecting the public from terrorism; administering the welfare state; regulating the media and financial services; maintaining immigration control; delivering public services, such as education, health care, policing, and transport; protecting the environment; securing energy supplies; promoting the arts and culture; regulating food production; and promoting (among other things) sex and race equality. The daily influence of government on all of our lives is so pervasive that often we do not even realise it. In terms of its size and complexity, modern government is without precedent and dwarfs anything attempted by the largest global corporations. The basic point is that modern government is an enormous and highly complex organisation that exerts influence over many aspects of our lives.

The growth of government has been driven by a number of factors, including the increasing complexity and interconnectedness of modern life (simple, primitive societies generally require less regulation), and people's changing expectations of government. Today, when citizens want something done—whether it is reducing childhood obesity or carbon emissions, building new roads and transport infrastructure, ensuring animal health and welfare, guarding against terrorism, regulating the banking system, or ensuring food is safe to eat—it is the executive to which they look. When a major catastrophe looms or occurs it is the executive branch that has to respond. For instance, in 2007–08, the government committed hundreds of billions of pounds of public money to shore up the banking system during the global financial crisis. This action was essential to maintain the financial and banking system. Given that the executive now has responsibility for so many different public functions, it is unsurprising that it has been transformed over the last century. While globalisation has, to some extent, limited the abilities of national governments to deal with worldwide problems (think, for example, of the concerted international action needed to combat climate change or third-world debt), at the national level, the executive is the most powerful institution of the state. In summary, politics is essentially about managing and implementing change in society. In the UK, the central government assumes primary responsibility for deciding upon and implementing such change. This is a highly political issue. Accordingly, the principal forces that motivate government are political, as are many of the forces that constraint it.

2.2 **The modern executive in the UK**

UK central government is a large institution. It is peopled by government Ministers and civil servants and headed up by the Prime Minister. The machinery of government is organised into several departments each with its own areas of responsibility. These central government departments—such as the Department for Education, the Department of Health, the Foreign and Commonwealth Office, and the Ministry of Justice—are known collectively as 'Whitehall', after that area of central London in which they are located. Each central government department is headed by a Minister—known as the Secretary of State. However, government departments are populated by many civil servants—the administrators who undertake much of the day-to-day work of government. Civil servants are politically neutral and provide impartial advice to Ministers in addition to carrying out much of the routine work of government. In considering the constitutional position of the executive, we will need to examine the nature of the relationships between Ministers and civil servants. Furthermore, Ministers are nowadays also assisted by special advisers, who provide assistance from a perspective that is more political than that which civil servants can properly adopt. In addition to government departments, there are also many other public bodies that deliver public services but operate at 'arm's length' from Ministers; for example, HM Prison Service, Highways England, and the Environment Agency.

Put simply, the twenty-first-century executive is a large and highly complex set of organisations. It comprises the government Ministers who act as our political leaders, and the many civil servants who implement and administer policy. It is the executive that, for the most part, makes the decisions by which society is governed. To this end, the executive has a number of different tools at its disposal, including, as we will see, the use of coercive powers, and the collection and distribution of wealth and resources.

2.3 **The executive and public law**

What is the constitutional and legal status of the UK executive in public law? In formal terms, the executive is not recognised by public law. The term 'the executive' is 'barely known to the law'.[5] As Maitland noted, in the UK, the executive is not a legal organisation. This does not mean that the executive is an illegal organisation, but that it is an 'extra-legal organisation; the law does not condemn it; but it does not recognise it—knows nothing about it'.[6]

In strict legal terms, it is only the constituent parts of the executive that exist. It follows, for example, that when Parliament wishes to grant powers to the executive branch, it actually confers them not upon the executive as a whole, but upon specific Ministers (and thus, in practice, upon the government departments which they lead). There is no Act of Parliament setting out the legal status of the UK government. The term 'the executive' is merely convenient shorthand for the collection of Ministers

---

[5] *Town Investments Ltd v Department of the Environment* [1978] AC 359, 398, *per* Lord Simon.
[6] Maitland, *The Constitutional History of England* (Cambridge 1908), p 387.

and government departments that *are* recognised in legal terms. UK public law's failure to recognise the executive as a legal entity is of a piece with its failure to recognise any concept of the 'state': like the executive, '[t]he state is not an entity recognised by English public law in its present stage of development'.[7]

At first sight, the lack of recognition given by public law to the vast entity of the modern executive or the state might seem bizarre. How can public law achieve one of its principal purposes—that of holding the executive to account—if it does not even formally recognise the existence of either the executive or the state? This curious problem arises for mainly historical reasons. By virtue of the historical development of their constitution and its unwritten nature, the British people have continued to use the concept of 'the Crown' to signify an executive, rather than recognising a separate concept of the executive or the state.

Another part of the explanation is that long-established practice largely obviates the difficulties that failing to recognise the executive might be expected to create. As noted in this section, the functions and powers of modern government are conferred not on the executive as a whole, because in legal terms it does not exist, but on individual Ministers, public officers, and public authorities. When public power is delegated by Parliament to the executive, it is habitually conferred on 'the Secretary of State', meaning a senior government Minister. The office of the Secretary of State is supposed to be a single, unitary office, but in fact there are many Secretaries of State and it is possible for powers conferred on one Secretary of State to be transferred to another under the Ministers of the Crown Act 1975. Furthermore, the exercise of most powers allocated to the Secretary of State will (unless the relevant legislation provides otherwise) often be delegated to civil servants who make decisions in the name of the Secretary of State. For example, the Home Secretary has responsibility for administering immigration control and has a statutory power to allow foreign nationals to enter the UK. In practical terms, it would be impossible for one individual to make the very many decisions required; the vast majority of decisions are therefore made not by the Home Secretary personally, but by officials acting on her behalf.

> **Q** The executive clearly exists, even though it is not legally recognised as such. Why, in this, as in so many other areas, does the formal, legal constitution of the UK fail fully to reflect political reality? Should this phenomenon be regarded as a weakness of UK current constitutional arrangements and, if so, how might it be remedied?

2.4 The Crown

Consider the following phrases of British constitutionalism: the 'Crown in Parliament', 'Her Majesty's government', 'Ministers of the Crown', the 'Royal Courts of Justice', the 'royal prerogative', and 'royal assent'.

---

[7] *R (K) v Camden and Islington Heath Authority* [2001] 3 WLR 553, 586, *per* Sedley LJ.

These pervasive references to the Crown might appear to indicate that it is the Queen personally who runs the country rather than her government. In formal, constitutional terms, the Queen does indeed possess executive powers to appoint Ministers, to dissolve Parliament, and to grant royal assent to legislation. However, in practice, such powers are exercised not by the monarch personally, but by elected politicians. Again, legal theory does not correspond with political reality.

What then does the concept of the Crown actually mean? In one sense, the Crown is merely 'an object of jewelled headgear under guard at the Tower of London'.[8] In another sense, the Crown is an important symbol of continuity and change in the British constitution. As a symbol of royal authority, the Crown was used in pre-modern, medieval times to refer to the monarch when doing acts of government as opposed to acts undertaken by the monarch in his or her personal capacity. To preserve continuity with the past, the concept of the Crown has been retained, although in practice governmental power is now exercised by both elected politicians and their administrators in the name of the Crown rather than by the monarch personally.

In other words, the language of public law has not kept pace with the evolution of modern executive power in democratic times. As Maitland put it, the concept of the Crown is a 'convenient cover for ignorance'.[9] Executive power is not exercised by the Crown through its inherent powers of government. Instead, real executive power resides with the government of the day. As Lord Diplock noted, it would be better, instead of speaking of the Crown, to speak of the 'government'—'a term appropriate to embrace both collectively and individually all the ministers of the Crown and parliamentary secretaries under whose direction the administrative work of government is carried on by the civil servants employed in the various government departments'.[10] For (almost) all practical purposes, 'the Crown' now simply means 'the government'. Thus, as Lord Rodger has noted, the 'executive power of the Crown is, in practice, exercised by a single body of ministers, making up Her Majesty's government'.[11]

2.5 **Executive–legislative relations: an 'elective dictatorship'?**

The relationship between the executive and the Crown is not the only relationship that we must consider to appreciate the constitutional position of the executive in the UK. What of the relationships between the UK government and Parliament, and between the government and the judiciary? These relationships are central to how the constitution seeks to promote and sustain effective, accountable, and lawful executive action. Much of this book is concerned with considering these particular and complex relationships in more detail. For the moment, though, we only need to consider the basic aspects of those relationships.

---

[8] *Town Investments* at 397.

[9] Maitland, p 418. See generally Sunkin and Payne (eds), *The Nature of the Crown: A Legal and Political Analysis* (Oxford 1999).

[10] *Town Investments* at 381.

[11] *R (BAPIO Action Ltd) v Secretary of State for the Home Department* [2008] UKHL 27, [2008] 1 AC 1003, [33].

First, let us consider the relationship between the executive (the government) and the legislature (Parliament). Central to this relationship is the fact that, in the UK, the composition of Parliament determines the political complexion of the executive. As we explain in more detail in Chapter 5,[12] general elections in the UK are *directly* concerned only with membership of the House of Commons. The executive is only *indirectly* elected, in the sense that, following an election, the Queen asks the leader of the political party most likely to able to command the confidence of the House of Commons—that is, to secure a majority in it—to form a government.[13] Normally, this will be the leader of the party with an overall majority (ie over half of the MPs).[14] Very occasionally, an election produces no party with such a majority. For example, in 2010, the Conservative Party won more seats than any other, but fewer than half of the total; the leader of that party, David Cameron, was nevertheless asked to form a government when it became clear that he was best placed to command the confidence of the Commons by entering into a coalition arrangement with another party, the Liberal Democrats.

Whether the government consists of a single party or a coalition, it is Parliament's function to hold the government to account. Most of the important government Ministers will be MPs drawn from the party or parties that form the government, while some Ministers will be members of the unelected chamber, the House of Lords. The government's majority of MPs in the House of Commons sustains the government in power by enabling it to have the votes to support its policies and legislation. At the same time, it is Parliament's task to hold the government to account, to criticise and oppose it. Parliament's function in providing the government of the day with the authority to govern is complemented by its role in holding the government to account and scrutinising its actions. In summary, Parliament serves a dual purpose with regard to the government: sustaining the government in power, while at the same time scrutinising what it does whilst in power.

To understand what all of this means in practice, consider the process, sketched in Figure 4.1, whereby an idea for a new policy or a change to existing policy may take practical effect. Assume, for example, that, in the interests of fairness (as it perceives it), the executive wishes to abolish the policy that health care should be free at the point of access, replacing it with a sliding scale of charges such that the unemployed

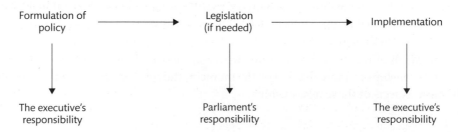

Figure 4.1 How policy changes are effected

and those on low incomes would pay nothing, while those earning at higher levels would pay for treatment (the fees to be paid by any given individual being related to his income).

If the government wants to see such measures implemented, then its first task is to *formulate the policy* in terms that are specific enough to be capable of being turned into legislation. (At what income level would charges begin to be levied? Would people on higher incomes ever be exempt from charges—for example, if they were to have a very serious or chronic illness? How high should the charges be? Should the charges be prescribed centrally, or should hospitals be allowed to set their own charges, thus introducing competition?)

The *enactment of the legislation* would then be a matter for Parliament. The government would put its proposals to Parliament in the form of a Bill, but it would be for Parliament to decide whether to enact it as proposed, to insist upon amendments, or to refuse to enact it at all.[15] If enacted, the *implementation* of the new legislation would be a matter for the government. For example, it would be for the government to put in place whatever practical arrangements the legislation stipulated for setting and collecting fees, determining the fee level applicable to individual patients, deciding whether a given patient qualified for exemption from the requirement to pay fees, and so on. (In practice, however, the government—in the interests of efficient administration—sometimes pre-empts Parliament by undertaking preparatory implementation work in anticipation of Parliament enacting a Bill.[16])

This scheme implies an important division of labour. The initiative rests with the government. It gets the ball rolling by devising policy proposals, and is ultimately responsible for implementing them. However, the process is punctuated by the involvement of Parliament at the legislative stage. On the face of it, therefore, the government's ability to get its own way is constrained by the need to obtain parliamentary approval. It is one thing for the executive to propose that legislation along the lines described in the health care scenario is enacted. Whether Parliament agrees and is prepared to do as the executive wishes is (it might be thought) a different matter entirely. Parliament might, for example, disagree fundamentally with the executive's suggestion, preferring to retain the principle that health care should be provided free of charge at the point of access; or it might agree with the general policy, but prefer to make everyone pay something, rather than providing free health care for certain people; or it might be willing to enact the government's proposals provided that there are safeguards exempting people with chronic illnesses. Nonetheless, the government will have its parliamentary majority.

The important point is that where the executive needs parliamentary legislation to be enacted so that its policy may be implemented, Parliament's involvement means that the executive cannot automatically always have its way. It has to convince Parliament that its ideas make sense, and it may have to negotiate and make certain compromises to persuade Parliament to enact the proposals in some form.

---

[15] For detailed discussion of how Bills are enacted, see Chapter 5, section 5.

[16] House of Lords Constitution Committee, *The Pre-emption of Parliament* (HL 165 2012–13).

So much for the theory; the reality is rather different. The British system of parliamentary government means that the executive and legislative branches are, to a significant extent, intertwined in such a way as to place the former in a very powerful position—so powerful that Lord Hailsham, a former Lord Chancellor, argued that the UK's constitutional arrangements reduce to an 'elective dictatorship'.[17] Three interlocking points, all of which we explore more fully in subsequent chapters, are particularly important in terms of understanding why the executive finds itself in such a powerful position.

The first point is that, as noted, the executive is not directly elected; rather, by convention, the monarch invites the party leader best able to command the confidence of the House of Commons to become (or remain) Prime Minister and form a government. The composition of the *executive* is therefore determined by the outcome of elections to the *legislature*.[18]

Second, the party from which the executive is drawn will normally account for more than half of the MPs in the Commons. In the event of a coalition, the governing parties between them will normally have more than half of the MPs.

Third, the government's numerical dominance in the Commons means that most of the time the government can rely upon its MPs for support. This does not always happen. For example, government MPs may be willing to rebel if the executive attempts to push through legislation that is especially controversial and that attempts to do things that are felt to be so objectionable as to override MPs' sense of loyalty (self-serving or otherwise). Moreover, the extent to which the government can be certain of getting its own way is heavily dependent upon the size of its majority in the Commons. Figure 4.2 shows the size of government majorities in the Commons between 1945 and 2015.

As can be seen, the size of government majorities has varied considerably. Both the Thatcher and Blair governments had very large majorities and therefore an almost free hand. Conversely, other governments were much more constrained by their smaller majority in the Commons. The Conservative government that assumed office after the 2015 election has only 51 per cent of the seats. With a small majority, it takes only a small number of 'rebel' MPs to side with the opposition parties for a government Bill to be placed in jeopardy. The picture is further complicated if the government takes the form of a coalition between two (or more) parties. Furthermore, Parliament has arguably developed a new assertiveness over recent decades.[19]

> **Q** Do you regard the nature of the relationship, as described in section 2.5, between the executive and legislative branches as either a strength or a weakness of the UK constitution? Why?

[17] Lord Hailsham, *The Dilemma of Democracy* (London 1978), ch 20.
[18] See Chapter 5, section 3.2 on elections.
[19] Norton, 'Parliament: A New Assertiveness?' in Jowell, Oliver, and O'Cinneide, *The Changing Constitution* (8th edn, Oxford 2015), p 171.

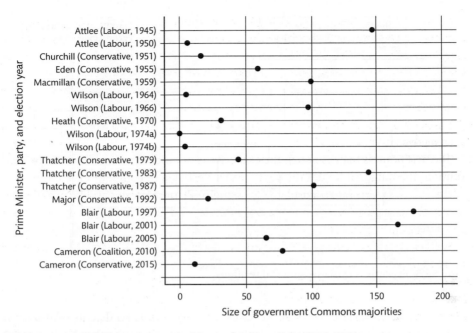

Figure 4.2 Size of government majorities in the Commons, 1945–2015

Source/Note: House of Commons Library Briefing Paper, *UK Election Statistics 1918–2015* (CBP7529 2016), p 10. Government majority is calculated as the number of seats held by the governing parties minus the number of seats held by all other parties or independent MPs.

2.6 **Executive–judicial relations**

What is the relationship between the government and the judiciary? By contrast with the overlap between the government and Parliament, there is a strict separation between both the government and Parliament on the one hand and the judiciary on the other. To maintain the integrity of the administration of justice and public confidence in the judiciary, the judiciary must be wholly independent of the government.

While it is the task of the government to govern, it is the role of the judiciary to adjudicate on legal disputes and to provide legally authoritative rulings. Sometimes, these rulings will concern challenges (eg under the Human Rights Act 1998) to the legality of government decisions. The government is expected to respect the judiciary's rulings and in this way to ensure that government acts in compliance with the rule of law. The courts are themselves bound by the doctrine of parliamentary sovereignty to respect primary legislation. Accordingly, their role is one of interpreting and giving effect to legislation. As the government tends to exert much influence over the content of legislation, it will also exert a degree of influence over how the courts interpret it. So while the government must respect judicial interpretations of legislation, it is always possible for the government to bring forward new proposals to amend legislation to reverse a particular judicial decision.[20] Although the judiciary is independent of the government, and although the government must comply with

---

[20] We are assuming, for the time being, that Parliament is sovereign in the orthodox sense. For further discussion, see Chapter 5, section 6.

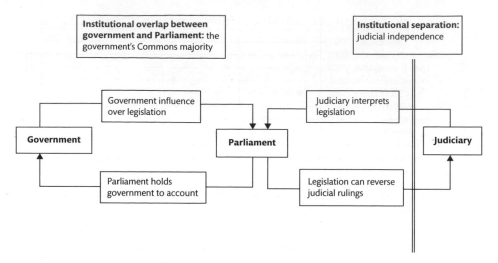

Figure 4.3 Executive–legislative–judicial relations

court rulings, the government's influence over the *legislature* renders its relationship with the *judiciary* more subtle and more complex than it might otherwise be. Figure 4.3 draws together the preceding discussion.

2.7 The executive in a political constitution

To appreciate the constitutional position of the executive, we need to understand the nature of its relationships with the other branches of government. We also need to recognise the political realities that exist underneath constitutional principles such as parliamentary sovereignty and the rule of law. From the executive's perspective, its constitutional role is not necessarily governed by constitutional or legal principles, but by the political imperative to run and manage the country in accordance with the wishes of the electorate. On this approach, at the heart of the constitution lies the recognition that the government of the day may take any action necessary for the furtherance of the public interest subject to the following caveats.[21] First, the government may not infringe the legal rights of others unless expressly legally authorised to do so. Second, if the government should wish to change the law, whether by adding to its existing legal powers or otherwise, then it must attain the assent of Parliament. Third, any governmental action must comply with applicable EU law and the Human Rights Act 1998.

This is an unorthodox way of viewing the constitution. Instead of focusing upon parliamentary sovereignty, the separation of powers, and the rule of law, it places the political power of the executive at the centre of the British constitution. Given the centrality

---

[21] Griffith, 'The Political Constitution' (1979) 42 MLR 1, 15. See also Foley, *The Politics of the British Constitution* (Manchester 1999).

of the executive's role and place within the constitution, this approach might be said to offer a more realistic perspective as to what really happens within the constitution.

Furthermore, we need to note a fundamental difference of approach in how the nature of the British constitution is both understood and conceptualised. Is the nature of the constitution fundamentally based on law or politics? Is it a legal or a political constitution? This is a question that often divides constitutional scholars. There is no single 'correct' answer. Some people argue that the constitution is firmly based on legal principles, whereas others argue that it is pre-eminently based on politics and the political relationships between different institutions and actors in the constitution. For the moment, we can note that those who emphasise the role of the courts and Parliament as the pre-eminent actors within the constitution often argue that the constitution is fundamentally based upon legal principles such as the rule of law and parliamentary sovereignty. By contrast, those who emphasise the role of the executive tend to emphasise that the British constitution is, above all, a political constitution—one that is shaped and reshaped by changing political circumstances, and therefore continually on the move.

2.8 **Political and legal accountability of the executive**

Whatever approach is preferred, the centrality of the executive within the constitution, and the power that it possesses, highlights one of the key themes of this book—that is, the importance of holding the executive to account. Governmental effectiveness in making and implementing policy—essentially, getting things done— is, of course, important. But, at the same time, government must be accountable for the exercise of its powers.

Broadly speaking, there are two ways in which the executive can be held to account: legally, by the courts; and politically, by Parliament. The former means that individual claimants may, by issuing judicial review proceedings against government departments, require Ministers to justify their policies, decisions, and actions by reference to the principles of law that courts have developed for the purpose of ensuring good standards of governance. Meanwhile, political accountability might, for example, involve Ministers, including the Prime Minister, being required to submit to questioning by MPs, justify their actions, explain why problems have arisen, and set out how past mistakes will be learned from rather than repeated.

However, the notion that Ministers are accountable for their actions to Parliament raises an obvious paradox. We have already seen that the executive is, at least to a considerable extent, in control of the legislature (or at least of the House of Commons) by virtue of its numerical dominance and the general willingness of government MPs to comply with the wishes of the leaders of the governing party or parties. The precise nature of the difficulties that arise as a result fall to be considered elsewhere,[22] but even leaving the details to one side for now, it is clear that Parliament's capacity to hold the executive to account is necessarily compromised by the dominance of the latter.

[22] See Chapter 10.

This, in turn, raises another of our key themes—that is, the relationship and balance between legal and political notions of constitutionalism.[23] While few people would argue that the executive should be held to account solely by legal, or solely by political, means, there is considerable debate about the extent to which each of these mechanisms should be relied upon. There has been a tendency in recent decades to look increasingly to the courts, the thinking being that legal accountability may plug the gap that arises as a result of Parliament's limited ability to enforce political accountability. This implies a drift towards a more court-centred approach—something that is not universally welcomed as a positive development. As we explain in Chapter 11, it is relatively uncontroversial that it is appropriate for courts to rule on obviously legal questions such as whether Ministers have contravened the terms of the legislation under which they purport to be acting. However, it is not immediately apparent that judges are the right people to decide whether the government is correct to prefer one policy option over another. Unelected and (therefore) independent judges are well placed to make decisions about the propriety of government conduct where there is an objective yardstick by which to measure it. At the same time, it is ultimately for elected politicians to evaluate the wisdom of what the government is doing where this essentially reduces to making value judgements about the merits of one approach over another. This suggests that political and legal mechanisms for holding the executive to account complement one another, such that both are required within a healthy system of governance.

We explore all of these issues in depth in Chapters 9–17. For the time being, the important points to bear in mind are that the existence of effective ways of holding the executive to account is imperative, not least because of the uniquely powerful position that it occupies within the UK's constitutional arrangements. The government is subject to both legal and political accountability. Thus two of our key themes—the importance of holding the executive to account, and the relationship between legal and political notions of constitutionalism—intersect in this area; exploring the nature and implications of their interaction is something to which we will have to return in a number of contexts.

3. Central government

We now examine in more detail the component parts of the executive. An important theme here concerns the nature of the constitutional rules governing the relationships between the different office-holders. In this respect, much has traditionally been governed by constitutional conventions rather than by legal rules laid down in legislation. In considering the constitutional aspects of the different parts of the executive, we therefore need to recognise that the executive largely inhabits the world of the political constitution, the rules governing the operation of the executive and its

---

[23] See generally Chapter 2.

relationship with other branches being principally shaped and reshaped by political understandings.[24] For example, the office of Prime Minister is virtually nowhere recognised by legislation. It is almost entirely a creature of convention. So, too, is the Cabinet, the collection of the principal government Ministers.

However, the fact that the relationships are a product of the political constitution does not mean that conventions are necessarily unwritten or readily dispensable. Indeed, over recent years, it has become increasingly common for conventions to be set down in codes—some of which will be considered later[25]—that are produced and published by the government itself. Furthermore, conventions can only be understood against the political context in which they develop and operate; there can be no better illustration of this than the convention governing the exercise of the monarch's prerogatives.

3.1 **The monarch's personal prerogatives**

We have already considered the significance of the concept of the Crown, noting that most of the monarch's prerogative powers are actually exercised by, or on the advice of, the executive. But what of the monarch's so-called personal prerogatives? In formal, constitutional terms, the Queen has a number of important constitutional powers that are exercised under the prerogative. The sovereign may appoint anyone to be her Prime Minister, and may appoint and dismiss government Ministers.[26] To what extent does the Queen personally exercise such powers? The relationship between the Queen and her government, and the exercise of these powers, is governed by the convention that the Queen does not personally command her Ministers. Instead, the Queen acts on ministerial advice. In this way, the exercise of such powers supports the symbolism of the monarchy while at the same time ensuring that political power, and with it, responsibility for the exercise of such power, resides with the government.

Consider, for example, the principles concerning the formation of governments. Bearing in mind the possibility (that eventuated) of a 'hung Parliament' in which no party had an overall majority, there was particular focus in the run-up to the 2010 general election on the monarch's role in appointing a Prime Minister. As a result, the conventions in this area were published by the Cabinet Secretary—the most senior civil servant in the country.[27] According to this guidance: 'If the Prime Minister resigns on behalf of the Government, the Sovereign will invite the person who appears most likely to be able to command the confidence of the House to serve as Prime Minister and to form a government.'[28] It is also emphasised that, in the event of a hung Parliament, 'the expectation is that discussions will take place between political parties on who should form the next Government', but that '[t]he Monarch

---

[24] On conventions, see generally Chapter 2, section 3.5.

[25] See section 3.4 (the 'Ministerial Code'), section 3.7 (the 'Civil Service Code'), and section 3.8 (the 'Code of Conduct for Special Advisers').

[26] The monarch has also traditionally been legally free to dissolve Parliament, although this power has now been removed by the Fixed-term Parliaments Act 2011.

[27] Cabinet Office, *The Cabinet Manual* (London 2011).   [28] *Cabinet Manual*, p 14.

would not expect to become involved in such discussions'.[29] The value of these conventions lies in ensuring both that government is democratically elected and accountable to Parliament, and that the Queen does not exercise, or even appear to exercise, any political influence. Similarly, the appointment and dismissal of government Ministers is, in practice, a matter purely for the Prime Minister.[30] To adopt Bagehot's famous analysis, the constitution may be divided into two general parts: those dignified parts 'which excite and preserve the reverence of the population'; and the efficient parts—'those by which it, in fact, works and rules'.[31] If so, then the sovereign belongs to the dignified parts, whereas the Prime Minister clearly belongs to its efficient parts.

It is because the conventions or political understandings have been accepted by all concerned that this system of governance has operated so smoothly.[32] If, however, the parties concerned were to decide that they no longer wished to adhere to the conventions—for example, suppose that the Queen did not decide to appoint as Prime Minister the leader of the political party best able to command the confidence of the House of Commons—then the relationships would break down. Constitutional crisis would ensue, firmer and clearer constitutional rules would be demanded, and there might even be calls for reform of the monarchy itself.

> **Q** Do you regard it as acceptable for the monarch to retain legal powers such as those described in this section? Is the fact that she only exercises them in line with constitutional convention an adequate response to the charge that it is undemocratic for the Queen to be legally empowered to influence such matters as the identity of the Prime Minister?

3.2 **The Prime Minister**

The Prime Minister, as the leader of the government of the day, is the most important politician in the UK. By convention, the Prime Minister is also a member of the House of Commons and the person best able to command the confidence of that House. As the head of the UK government, the Prime Minister is ultimately responsible for its policies and decisions. The Prime Minister oversees the operation of the Civil Service and government agencies, appoints members of the government, and is the principal government figure in the House of Commons. The Prime Minister also chairs the Cabinet, selects and dismisses Ministers, and is responsible for the overall organisation of the executive. The office of Prime Minister is almost solely one of convention and political practice. The Prime Minister has few formal legal powers and is only occasionally mentioned specifically in legislation.[33] However, for the most part, the power exercised by the Prime Minister results not from legislation, but from the

---

[29] *Cabinet Manual*, p 15.   [30] *Cabinet Manual*, p 21.

[31] Bagehot, *The English Constitution* [1867] (Fontana 1993), p 63.

[32] See Bogdanor, *The Monarchy and the Constitution* (Oxford 1995).

[33] For a rare example, see Regulation of Investigatory Powers Act 2000, ss 57 and 59, which authorises the Prime Minister to appoint the Interception of Communications and Intelligence Services Commissioners.

political influence that the office-holder is able to exert. In other words, the power of the Prime Minister is usually in terms of directing and influencing other Ministers to make decisions and policies in accordance with his wishes. As HH Asquith (Prime Minister, 1908–16) noted, 'The office of Prime Minister is what its holder chooses to make it'.[34]

The roles and powers of the Prime Minister are not precisely defined in legislation or elsewhere. The post is indeed often what the particular individual who holds it makes of it. Unsurprisingly, being Prime Minister is an exceptionally demanding job. Some previous Prime Ministers, such as Margaret Thatcher (1979–90) and Tony Blair (1997–2007), gained reputations for being strong, dominant Prime Ministers, for not welcoming or accepting dissension from their own views, and for not paying due regard to discussions over policy within the Cabinet. The personal style of individual Prime Ministers has prompted debate over the extent to which 'prime ministerial' government has taken over, or even the extent to which there has been a move towards a British presidency, but without the necessary checks and balances to constrain such power.[35] Those concerned about such matters will not have taken comfort from the presidential-style televised debates between the main party leaders that took place, for the first time in the UK, during the 2010 general election campaign. On the other hand, other Prime Ministers have gained a reputation for operating in a more consensual way and for taking more account of Cabinet discussions.

To a large extent, the style adopted by any individual Prime Minister is influenced not only by the personality of the individual officer-holder, but also by the political authority of the Prime Minister.[36] This is largely dependent upon the size of the government's majority in the House of Commons. The larger the government's Commons majority is, and the more disciplined it is, then the greater the authority of the Prime Minister. Conversely, the smaller the government's Commons majority, then the greater may be the need for the Prime Minister to adopt a more consensual style of governing. This point applies more acutely and obviously when the government consists of a coalition between two or more parties. For example, the Conservative–Liberal Democrat coalition formed after the 2010 general election adopted a formal protocol under which the Prime Minister's powers were, in practice, more limited than usual; for example, the appointment of Ministers was the shared responsibility of the Conservative Prime Minister and the Liberal Democrat Deputy Prime Minster.[37]

In one sense, the debate over the role and power of the Prime Minister is central to our constitutional arrangements. The Prime Minister has enormous political power to influence policy, public appointments, the management of the Civil Service, and

[34] Asquith, *Fifty Years of Government* (1928), vol II, p 185.
[35] Foley, *The British Presidency* (Manchester 2000); Allen, *The Last Prime Minister: Being Honest About the UK Presidency* (Thorverton 2003). See also Blick and Jones, *Premiership: The Development, Nature and Power of the Office of the British Prime Minister* (Exeter 2010).
[36] See this event, 'From Gladstone and Disraeli to Blair and Cameron: how prime ministers lead' (2013), http://www.instituteforgovernment.org.uk/events/gladstone-and-disraeli-blair-and-cameronhow-prime-ministers-lead.
[37] HM Government, *Coalition Agreement for Stability and Reform* (London 2010).

so on. Should the Prime Minister be able to exert so much power? If the office of Prime Minister has developed into a de facto presidency, then there should be appropriate checks and balances. At the same time, the nature of governing has changed radically over the last hundred years; new challenges have arisen from the complexity of governmental action in the modern age and the pressure on governments to deliver public services. The basic deal upon which our system of government is based is that the public elects MPs to the House of Commons, thereby determining who is the Prime Minister, and which party (or parties) forms the government. The Prime Minister is then able to exercise considerable power for up to five years, albeit that, for two reasons, she is not invulnerable. First, a Prime Minister may fall for internal party reasons. For example, in 2007, Tony Blair stood down as Prime Minister against the background of internal divisions within the Labour Party, and was succeeded by Gordon Brown. More recently, in 2016, David Cameron resigned in the immediate aftermath of the EU referendum, having led the unsuccessful Remain campaign. Second, there is a long-standing convention that if the government loses a vote of confidence in the Commons, the Prime Minister should resign and a general election should be held. The Fixed-term Parliaments Act 2011 has modified this position somewhat: an election is now triggered only if a new government capable of commanding the confidence of the House of Commons cannot be formed within fourteen days of a vote of no confidence in the previous administration.[38]

The Prime Minister is accountable to the public through general elections and constant media scrutiny and to Parliament through the weekly Prime Minister's questions in the House of Commons; since 2002, the House of Commons Liaison Committee (comprising the chairs of the House's select committees) has regularly heard evidence from the Prime Minister on matters of public policy. Furthermore, while the Prime Minister appoints Cabinet members, it is clear that, on occasion, the Cabinet may hold in check a Prime Minister. However, the effectiveness of some of these methods for holding the Prime Minister to account politically might readily be questioned. The relative infrequency of general elections means that accountability must also attach to the actions of the Prime Minister *during* his term of office. While, in formal terms, Prime Minister's questions in the House of Commons is an exercise in holding the Prime Minister to account, in practice, it has often been described as a 'Punch and Judy' show in which the opposition leaders and other MPs attack the Prime Minister, prompting her to retaliate with the support of her MPs. Furthermore, while the Prime Minister attends meetings of the Liaison Committee, this only occurs on a comparatively infrequent basis.

3.3 **Ministers**

'Minister of the Crown' means 'the holder of any office in Her Majesty's government in the United Kingdom, and includes the Treasury ... and Defence

---

[38] The Act also provides that (irrespective of any vote of no confidence) an earlier-than-usual election would also be triggered if two-thirds of MPs were to support a motion to that effect. See further Chapter 5, section 3.2.2.

Council'.[39] Ministers of the Crown are members of the governing political party who have been appointed to a political office in the government.

While, formally, Ministers are appointed by the Crown on the advice of the Prime Minister, in practice the Prime Minister has the ultimate say on who is appointed as a Minister. A strong Prime Minister may be able to decide unilaterally on ministerial appointments, while a weak Prime Minister may have to appease factions within his own party; one who leads a coalition, as noted, will have to operate collaboratively with the leader of the other party or parties involved when making appointments.

By convention, Ministers are members of either House of Parliament; most are members of the Commons. This is a feature of ministerial responsibility to Parliament; Ministers exercise public power and constitutional convention demands that they are accountable to Parliament for the exercise of such power. By statute, there can be no more than 95 holders of ministerial office in the House of Commons; this rule is designed to prevent the executive from unduly dominating the House of Commons.[40] In practice, governments have got around this statutory limit by appointing MPs to *unpaid* government posts, such as Parliamentary Private Secretaries. In 2012, there were 95 MPs in paid government positions, and 43 MPs acting as unpaid Parliamentary Private Secretaries. A total of 138 MPs—21 per cent of all MPs—therefore formed part of the government.[41]

There is a clear hierarchy of governmental positions. Ministers are graded in terms of their importance and areas of responsibility. Each of the principal *Secretaries of State* heads up a government department, sits in the Cabinet, and also in Cabinet committees. Figure 4.4 lists the Secretaries of State who comprise the Cabinet. The Minister in charge of a department is accountable to Parliament for the exercise of the powers on which the administration of that department depends. For example, the Secretary of State for Health is the senior Minister responsible for health policy. In practice, though, no individual Minister could ever assume sole responsibility for managing and running a large organisation such as a central government department. The basic task of the Secretary of State is to provide political leadership to his department and to be responsible to Parliament and the public for its policy and performance. According to the Ministerial Code, it is desirable that Ministers in charge should devolve to their junior Ministers responsibility for a defined range of departmental work, particularly in relation to Parliament.[42] The legal powers of the Secretary of State are then often delegated to a Minister of State, a Parliamentary Under Secretary, or, as happens far more often, to civil servants. So, for example, the Home Secretary is responsible for the overall work of the Home Office, but there are also three Ministers of State (respectively responsible for security, immigration, and

---

[39] Ministers of the Crown Act 1975, s 8(1). See generally Brazier, *Ministers of the Crown* (Oxford 1997).

[40] House of Commons Disqualification Act 1975, s 2(1).

[41] See also Chapter 10, Figures 10.1 and 10.2. Data taken from **http://www.theguardian.com/news/ datablog/2012/oct/12/size-government-uk**

[42] Cabinet Office, 'Ministerial Code' (London 2016), [4.6], **https://www.gov.uk/government/uploads/ system/uploads/attachment_data/file/579752/ministerial_code_december_2016.pdf**

The UK government Cabinet (as of July 2016)
Cabinet Ministers
Prime Minister, First Lord of the Treasury, Minister for the Civil Service
Chancellor of the Exchequer
Secretary of State for the Home Department
Secretary of State for Foreign and Commonwealth Affairs
Lord Chancellor and Secretary of State for Justice
Secretary of State for Defence
Secretary of State for Exiting the European Union
Secretary of State for Work and Pensions
Secretary of State for Health
Secretary of State for Business, Energy and Industrial Strategy
Leader of the House of Commons
Secretary of State for International Development
Secretary of State for Education
Leader of the House of Lords
Secretary of State for Transport
Secretary of State for International Trade
Secretary of State for Northern Ireland
Secretary of State for Environment, Food, and Rural Affairs
Secretary of State for Communities and Local Government
Secretary of State for Wales
Chancellor of the Duchy of Lancaster
Secretary of State for Culture, Media, and Sport
Secretary of State for Scotland

Figure 4.4 UK government Cabinet (July 2016)

policing) and a Parliamentary Under Secretary of State (responsible for equalities). In practice, most governmental powers are exercised by civil servants.

In some governments, there is also a *Deputy Prime Minister*. There is no legal or constitutional requirement for such a post, but its existence is sometimes politically expedient.

Next, we turn to the *whips*. Their role is to ensure, wherever possible, that the government wins votes in the Commons and the Lords. They do this by 'encouraging' MPs and peers who are members of the governing party or parties to vote with the government. If a parliamentary vote is subject to a 'three-line whip', then backbench MPs must vote with the government or else risk expulsion from the governing political party or parties.

Special mention might be made of the constitutional position of the *Lord Chancellor*. For centuries, the office of the Lord Chancellor occupied a unique place in the constitution. The Lord Chancellor was a member of the government and in charge of the Lord Chancellor's Department, speaker of the House of Lords, and head of the judiciary. The Lord Chancellor could also sit as a member of the Appellate Committee of the House of Lords and give opinions as a Law Lord. By convention, it was assumed that the post was not to be occupied by a 'career politician' in search of political advancement, but by an individual with a legal background who would know how to balance the several different roles of an office that, in formal terms, appeared to offend the principle of the separation of powers. However, in the Constitutional Reform Act

2005, Parliament legislated to change this position to establish a clearer separation of powers.[43] The Lord Chancellor is no longer the head of the judiciary and can no longer sit as a judge. Unusually for appointment as a Minister, there is, under s 2 of the 2005 Act, a statutory qualification for appointment to the office of Lord Chancellor. However, this provision is drafted so broadly as to be virtually meaningless, and in practice the post has now become a regular Cabinet portfolio: a development underlined by the appointment in 2012 of Chris Grayling, a non-lawyer, to the post. The principal role of the Lord Chancellor is now heading up the Ministry of Justice, which he does in his capacity as Secretary of State for Justice. These changes have prompted some concern as to whether the Lord Chancellor can continue to act as an effective constitutional guardian. In 2014, the Lords Constitution Committee noted that it has become more difficult for post-reform Lord Chancellors with their wider policy responsibilities, more overtly political positions as Secretaries of State for Justice, and their reduced role in relation to the judiciary to carry out this duty in relation to the rule of law—a position not endorsed by the government.[44]

The role of the *Attorney-General* should also be noted. The Attorney-General has three main functions: as the government's chief legal adviser; as the Minister responsible for the criminal justice system, superintending the Crown Prosecution Service and Serious Fraud Office; and as the guardian of the public interest. As regards the provision of legal advice, the Law Officers (the Attorney-General and the Solicitor-General) must be consulted in good time before the government is committed to critical decisions involving legal considerations.[45] At the same time, the Attorney-General is a member of the government who takes the party whip and attends, but is not a member of, the Cabinet. The office therefore combines both legal and political responsibilities, which can sometimes conflict. For example, recent controversies have concerned the Attorney-General's legal advice to the government as to the legality of the invasion of Iraq (was the Attorney-General placed under political pressure to produce legal advice favourable to the government's intention of invading Iraq?) and the Attorney-General's decision to halt a criminal investigation by the Serious Fraud Office into whether Saudi officials were bribed to win an order for British arms (did the Attorney-General drop the investigation because of political pressure from the Prime Minister? If so, then what of the rule of law?).[46] Controversies such as these have raised concerns as to political bias and lack of independence, and prompted calls for reform of the office by, for example, dividing up responsibility for the Attorney-General's various functions.[47]

---

[43] See further Lord Windlesham, 'The Constitutional Reform Act 2005: Ministers, Judges and Constitutional Change' [2005] PL 806 and 'The Constitutional Reform Act 2005: The Politics of Constitutional Reform' [2006] PL 35.

[44] House of Lords Constitution Committee, *The Office of Lord Chancellor* (HL 75 2014–15).

[45] 'Ministerial Code', [2.10].

[46] The latter decision was unsuccessfully challenged by way of judicial review: *R (Corner House Research) v Director of the Serious Fraud Office* [2008] UKHL 60, [2009] 1 AC 756.

[47] House of Commons Constitutional Affairs Committee, *Constitutional Role of the Attorney-General* (HC 306 2006–07).

3.4 **Ministerial standards**

Ministers find themselves in positions of great power and influence. It stands to reason that those in such positions should be required to adhere to certain standards of probity to ensure that the business of government is conducted in a way that is transparently fair and in the public interest. Such standards are contained in the Ministerial Code issued by the Prime Minister. Since 1997, the Code has been updated regularly, the current version having been issued following the 2015 election.[48] The Code is intended as a helpful guide to the principles and practices underpinning the way in which Ministers should discharge their duties. The Code is not therefore a set of legally binding rules possessing the force of law. Nevertheless, Ministers are clearly expected to follow the Code fully. The Code is a governmental, rather than a parliamentary, document and is therefore capable of subsequent amendment by the government. At the same time, some aspects of the Code—particularly those parts of it concerning ministerial accountability to Parliament—have been approved by a resolution of Parliament.

According to the Ministerial Code, Ministers are expected to behave in a way that upholds the highest standards of propriety. The Code is to be read against the background of the overarching duty on Ministers to comply with the law, including international law, and to uphold the administration of justice and to protect the integrity of public life. Ministers are expected to observe the seven principles of public life: selflessness, integrity, objectivity, accountability, openness, honesty, and leadership.

The most important principles of ministerial conduct to which the Code requires adherence relate to the doctrine of ministerial responsibility to Parliament.[49] Earlier in this chapter, we explained the meaning of this concept in outline, and we examine it in detail in Chapter 10. However, the Ministerial Code also specifies other standards. Ministers must ensure that no conflict arises, or appears to arise, between their public duties and their private interests. They should not accept any gift or hospitality that might, or might reasonably appear to, compromise their judgement or place them under an improper obligation. Ministers in the House of Commons must keep separate their roles as Minister and constituency member. Ministers must not use government resources for party political purposes. Ministers must also uphold the political impartiality of the Civil Service and not ask civil servants to act in any way that would conflict with the Civil Service Code.[50] In more detailed provisions, the Code elaborates on these general principles.

One particular issue as to the operation of the Ministerial Code concerns the question of investigating alleged breaches of the Code by Ministers and of its enforcement—both of which are ultimately matters for the Prime Minister. But if the public is to have confidence that Ministers adhere to the standards of propriety contained in the Code, then should there not also be a mechanism for investigating

---

[48] 'Ministerial Code'.   [49] *Collective* responsibility is discussed in section 3.5.

[50] And that Code must itself require civil servants to act in a politically neutral manner: Constitutional Reform and Governance Act 2010, s 7(2).

alleged infringements of the Code that is itself manifestly independent of the government? On the other hand, it is said that the Prime Minister must be the ultimate judge of the standards of behaviour expected of Ministers and the appropriate consequences of a breach of those standards: Ministers only remain in office for as long as they retain the confidence of the Prime Minister. Furthermore, the Prime Minister is ultimately accountable to Parliament. To introduce an independent investigatory mechanism to determine breaches of the Code and any sanction would weaken this core principle. It would also constrain the Prime Minister's ability to make what are ultimately political judgements about the conduct of Ministers by introducing a quasi-judicial element into what are essentially matters of political practice. Nevertheless, if there is no independent investigatory mechanism, the risk is that the news media, with its voracious appetite for stories of political impropriety, may replace ordinary due process and place Ministers against whom allegations have been made, but not proved, either under pressure to resign or make their discharge of their governmental duties acutely difficult.

Such arguments culminated in the recognition that a mechanism was needed whereby complaints could be independently investigated, to promote public confidence, but without undermining the Prime Minister's right to decide whether a Minister has breached the Code.[51] In 2006, the Independent Adviser on Ministers' Interests was appointed to provide an independent check and source of advice to government Ministers on the handling of their private interests, to avoid conflict between those interests and their ministerial responsibilities; and to investigate—when the Prime Minister, advised by the Cabinet Secretary, so decides—allegations that individual Ministers may have breached the Code. Whilst being welcomed as a positive step forward, the post also has some limitations. The Independent Adviser cannot instigate his own investigations, but can only act if invited to do so by the Prime Minister. Findings of investigations will not necessarily be published. Furthermore, as the Independent Adviser is appointed by the Prime Minister and dependent on the government for staff and assistance, the post cannot be described as being fully independent.[52] This concern was reiterated by the House of Commons Public Administration Select Committee, criticising the appointment in 2011—via a non-transparent process—of a career civil servant.[53]

> **Q** Is it appropriate for the standards that Ministers are expected to observe to be set by the Prime Minister? Should there be a fully independent office to investigate alleged breaches of the Ministerial Code?

[51] House of Commons Public Administration Select Committee, *The Ministerial Code: The Case for Independent Investigation* (HC 1457 2005–06).

[52] House of Commons Public Administration Select Committee, *Investigating the Conduct of Ministers* (HC 381 2007–08).

[53] House of Commons Public Administration Select Committee, *The Prime Minister's Adviser on Ministers' Interests: Independent or Not?* (HC 1761 2010–12).

3.5 **The Cabinet**

The Cabinet is the supreme directing authority of British government. It works by integrating what would otherwise be 'a heterogeneous collection of ministers, officers and authorities exercising a mass of apparently unrelated miscellaneous functions'.[54] In other words, in a plural executive consisting of various different departments, the Cabinet, as the supreme decision-making body, is a force for ensuring unity within government. Cabinet members are also parliamentarians. As Bagehot noted, the Cabinet is 'a combining committee—a *hyphen* which joins, a *buckle* which fastens, the legislative part of the State to the executive part of the State'.[55]

Like the executive, the Cabinet is unknown to the law and is extra-constitutional. It is, again, a creature of convention. The Cabinet itself does not possess any legal powers: they are held by Secretaries of State. However, a key doctrine or constitutional norm is that members of the Cabinet have collective responsibility to Parliament, so all members are bound to support Cabinet decisions.

The Cabinet normally meets once a week and is chaired by the Prime Minister. The principal business of the Cabinet consists of resolving questions that significantly engage the collective responsibility of the government, because they raise major issues of policy or because they are of critical importance to the public, and questions on which there is an unresolved argument between government departments.[56] Matters wholly within the responsibility of a single Minister and which do not significantly engage collective responsibility need not be brought before the Cabinet or to a ministerial Committee unless the Minister wishes to inform his colleagues or to have their advice.[57] The role of the Cabinet is, then, to make the most important policy decisions and to resolve differences within government. The whole premise of the Cabinet system is that of collective responsibility. This means that while Ministers are able to discuss policy options in the Cabinet, once a decision has been made, all Ministers must then agree to that decision and defend it irrespective of their personal views. As the Ministerial Code explains, collective responsibility, when it applies

> requires that Ministers should be able to express their views frankly in the expectation that they can argue freely in private while maintaining a united front when decisions have been reached. This in turn requires that the privacy of opinions expressed in Cabinet and ministerial Committees, including correspondence, should be maintained.[58]

If a Minister is unable to agree to a decision made by the Cabinet, then he should resign from the government. For example, when the Blair government decided to invade Iraq in 2003, Robin Cook, then leader of the House of Commons, decided to resign from the government because he did not agree with this policy.[59] Alternatively, Ministers may simply hold their tongue and leak their disagreement to the media, ensuring that it is anonymously reported.

Like all conventions, collective responsibility is flexible rather than rigid. It can be suspended in relation to specific issues. For instance, during the EU referendum

---

[54] Jennings, *Cabinet Government* (Cambridge 1959), p 90.   [55] Bagehot, p 70.
[56] 'Ministerial Code', [2.2].   [57] 'Ministerial Code', [2.4].   [58] 'Ministerial Code', [2.1].
[59] Cook, *The Point of Departure* (London 2003).

campaign of 2016, Cabinet Ministers were permitted to campaign to remain or leave the EU. Similarly, the Conservative–Liberal Democrat coalition agreement left it open for Ministers of both parties to adopt different public positions on electoral reform.[60] Such 'agreements to disagree' illustrate the flexibility of constitutional conventions, which operate, and can only really be understood, against the backdrop of politics.

Whether the Cabinet really does possess the decision-making power that is normally attributed to it has been widely questioned. With the growth in prime ministerial power, concerns have commonly been expressed that Cabinet may often operate as a 'rubber stamp' to approve important decisions already made elsewhere. For example, during the Blair government, Cabinet meetings were brief and took few real decisions, because the Prime Minister's practice had been to take important decisions beforehand that were then announced to the Cabinet.[61] This has been criticised as 'sofa government'.[62] In effect, the role of the Cabinet is inseparable from the style adopted by the Prime Minister. It follows that if the Prime Minister is weak (eg due to a small majority) or if there is a coalition government (which demands a more collaborative approach), the Cabinet is likely to assume a more prominent role.

However, there are other reasons for the declining importance of Cabinet. One is the development of ministerial committees and subcommittees. Given the mass of decisions for which government is responsible, it is simply not practicable to expect a single Cabinet to make all policy decisions. In practice, it is necessary to have a number of other bodies that have responsibility for particular policy areas. There are currently 31 ministerial committees and subcommittees.[63]

3.6 Government departments

In one sense, the executive does not exist as a single legal entity. There are also many practical senses in which it does not function as a single organisation. It is arguably best thought of as a federation of central government departments, each of which has its particular responsibilities.[64] In other words, the executive is plural rather than unitary. Far from being monolithic, the executive comprises a number of large organisations—government departments—each administering their own areas of policy. As Mount has observed: '[T]he loose-baronial nature of the system is not something accidental or fleeting; it is inherent. This is the reality of day-to-day executive power.'[65]

There are currently 25 ministerial central government departments, 22 non-ministerial departments, and 374 government agencies and other public bodies.[66] In short,

---

[60] HM Government, *The Coalition: Our Programme for Government* (London 2010), p 27.

[61] See Foster, 'Cabinet Government in the Twentieth Century' (2004) 67 MLR 753, 766.

[62] See, eg *Review of Intelligence on Weapons of Mass Destruction* (HC 898 2003–04), p 148, criticising 'the informality and circumscribed character of the Government's procedures which we saw in the context of policy-making towards Iraq'.

[63] Cabinet Office, *Cabinet Committees System* (London 2016).

[64] Sir William Armstrong quoted in Hennessy, *Whitehall* (London 2001), p 380.

[65] Mount, *The British Constitution Now* (London 1992), p 156.

[66] See https://www.gov.uk/government/organisations

British government consists of a complex and changing Byzantine structure through which few can pick their way with any certainty. The arcane and pragmatic nature of the governmental system is illustrated by the fact that there is no legal definition of the term 'government department'. Government departments owe their establishment, organisation, and powers to two principal sources of law: legislation and the prerogative. There is no overarching constitutional framework for government departments. In constitutional terms, government departments do not generally seem to exist as distinct entities in their own right because statutory and prerogative powers are usually conferred upon the Secretary of State rather than the department itself. Instead, departments have developed on an ad hoc basis over time. The upshot is that there is no coherent pattern of government departments. Instead, the constitutional and legal position of government departments is characterised by pragmatic arrangements rather than consistent principle.[67] For instance, following the referendum vote in June 2016 for Brexit, two new government departments were established: the Department for International Trade (DIT) and the Department for Exiting the European Union (DExEU). The latter department is responsible for overseeing negotiations to leave the EU and establishing the future relationship between the UK and EU.

It is appropriate to highlight a more general point. Most government departments perform tasks that are absolutely essential to the continued existence and preservation of modern society. For instance, the country simply could not continue to exist without internal law and order (the basic responsibility of the Home Office), protection against external threats (Ministry of Defence, the Home Office, and the security services), or finance and taxation (HM Treasury, HM Revenue and Customs). It is no exaggeration at all to describe government departments as 'immortal' institutions. In all its scale, government is an essential prerequisite of a civilised society.

Government departments headed up by Cabinet Ministers may be classified in a number of different ways.[68] First, there are what might be termed 'central' government departments (central not in the sense that they are part of central as opposed to local government, but in the sense that they affect all government action in one way or another). Key among these is HM Treasury, which is responsible for formulating and implementing the government's financial and economic policy. As such, it determines matters such as taxation, public borrowing, and public spending, and is thus the most powerful government department. The Treasury is primarily responsible for maintaining financial order and regularity across government and therefore exerts a powerful influence over other departments. As a former Prime Minister, Harold Wilson, once noted: 'Whichever party is in office, the Treasury is in power.'[69] Why? Because virtually all governmental action requires resources, which the Treasury controls. The Minister responsible for the Treasury, the Chancellor of the Exchequer, is second in importance only to the Prime Minister.

The other principal central department is the Cabinet Office, which, with the Treasury, constitutes the 'head office' of government. The Cabinet Office was created

---

[67] See Jordan, *The British Administrative System: Principles Versus Practice* (London 1994).
[68] Hennessy, p 381.   [69] Quoted in Sampson, *The Changing Anatomy of Britain* (London 1982).

in 1916 to record Cabinet proceedings and to transmit decisions to relevant government departments. However, given the pressure on modern governments and the complexity of public business, the Cabinet Office now sits at the centre of government in the middle of an extensive and intricate web of other government agencies.[70] The Cabinet Office supports the Prime Minister to ensure effective development, coordination, and implementation of policy.[71]

Second, there are those departments that deal with policy concerning overseas and defence matters: the Foreign and Commonwealth Office, the Department for International Development, the Ministry of Defence, and the Department for Exiting the EU. Third, other departments concern social policy—the Departments for Work and Pensions; Health; Communities and Local Government; Education; Culture, Media and Sport; and the Government Equalities Office. Fourth, there are departments for economic policy—the Department for Business, Energy and Industrial Strategy; the Department for International Trade; the Department for Transport; and the Department for Environment, Food and Rural Affairs. Fifth, there are the territorial departments: the Northern Ireland Office, the Scotland Office, and the Wales Office. Finally, the Home Office, the Ministry of Justice, and the Attorney-General's Office have responsibility for internal affairs, the legal system, and the administration of justice.

There is another point to make here concerning the impact of devolution upon UK central government. We shall see in Chapter 7 that various functions have been devolved to the Scottish, Welsh, and Northern Irish governments. This has had profound implications for UK central government. For instance, the Departments of Health and Education formally remain *UK* government departments, but they are now de facto *English* government departments because those policy areas have largely been devolved. By contrast, the Ministry of Defence and the Foreign & Commonwealth Office are part of the UK government both in form and substance because their functions are retained at the UK level.

While Ministers head up government departments, the actual management of the department is entrusted to its Permanent Secretary, the most senior civil servant in the department. Ministers decide on policies, and set strategic objectives and priorities, while the Permanent Secretary chairs the department's board to ensure that the department delivers those objectives. The Permanent Secretary is, as the department's accounting officer, accountable to Ministers for the department's performance, organisation, and delivery; and to Parliament for the effectiveness, efficiency, and propriety of spending by the department.[72] Below the level of Permanent Secretary, various grades of civil servant undertake the vast majority of the work within a government department.

Ensuring the effective government of a country is, to put it mildly, a highly problematic enterprise. In the UK, one particular challenge has always been to ensure that

[70] See House of Lords Constitution Committee, *The Cabinet Office and the Centre of Government* (HL 30 2009–10).
[71] https://www.gov.uk/government/organisations/cabinet-office
[72] HM Treasury, *Managing Public Money* (London 2007), ch 3.

different government departments work together effectively. However, the cultures of different government departments are deeply engrained and this can sometimes lead to difficulties when the government needs to deal with policy issues that cut across several departments' areas of responsibility: individual departments may not necessarily agree on how that issue should be handled or which department should bear the cost of dealing with it. Indeed, it is not unknown for different units within the *same* government departments to fail to cooperate with each other; as an example, consider the failure of the Home Office to deport foreign national prisoners in 2006. This major operational failure arose because of a lack of coordination between two Home Office agencies—one responsible for immigration and the other for prisons— and led to the resignation of the then Home Secretary.[73] This episode illustrates an important aspect of how government actually operates. It has become customary, from one perspective, to view the executive and the office of the Prime Minister as a bastion of enormous executive power. However, from another perspective, one of the major challenges for the Prime Minister, and the government as a whole, is to ensure that government departments work together to ensure that policy is implemented effectively. In short, while government should be held to account for its actions, it is important not to lose sight of the fact that effective governance is, at the best of times, a highly elusive endeavour.

3.7 **The Civil Service**

The Civil Service comprises the permanent officials—civil servants—who work in government; without them, it would be impossible for government to operate. The prevalent model in the UK has been that of a permanent and politically impartial Civil Service, which exists to serve the government of the day while also being prepared to serve future governments. The Civil Service has three principal roles. First, around 70 per cent of civil servants are involved in the direct operational delivery of policies, such as paying benefits, running employment services, staffing prisons, and issuing driving licences. Second, a small number of civil servants provide policy advice and support to Ministers. Third, civil servants are responsible for implementing programmes and projects, such as large-scale infrastructure projects (eg highspeed rail) or system-changing projects (eg the introduction of Universal Credit into the benefits system). There are different grades of civil servant. The most senior civil servants are the Cabinet Secretary and the Head of the Civil Service. Each government department has a Permanent Secretary—a senior civil servant responsible for its management. Beneath them, there are many grades of civil servant going down to the 'front-line' officials. There are currently some 405,573 civil servants—a decline of 27 per cent since 2005.[74] There are currently 25 recognised professions in the Civil Service. In addition, there are also many other public sector workers, such as teachers and nurses.

---

[73] House of Commons Home Affairs Committee, *Immigration Control* (HC 775 2005–06).
[74] Office for National Statistics, *Civil Service Statistics: 2015* (Newport 2015).

Constitutionally, civil servants are servants of the Crown, that is, the government of the day. This means that the core function of the Civil Service is implementing the policies of the government. As the Civil Service Code explains:

> The Civil Service is an integral and key part of the government of the United Kingdom. It supports the government of the day in developing and implementing its policies, and in delivering public services. Civil servants are accountable to Ministers, who in turn are accountable to Parliament.[75]

The Civil Service is a largely permanent service in which civil servants are expected to serve whichever political party forms the government of the day. The tradition of a permanent, independent, and politically neutral Civil Service in which appointments are made on merit rather than as political patronage dates back to the Northcote Trevelyan Report on the Civil Service published in 1854.[76]

Since its inception, the Civil Service has been managed by the government under the royal prerogative—despite the original recommendation of the Northcote Trevelyan Report in 1854 that the Civil Service should have a statutory basis, not least so that its core principles and values may be enshrined in law. This has now finally been done.[77] The Constitutional Reform and Governance Act 2010 placed the Civil Service on a statutory footing. Among other things, the legislation requires the Civil Service Code to be laid before Parliament.[78] This Code prescribes the core values of the Civil Service. These are integrity (putting the obligations of public service above personal interests), honesty (being truthful and open), objectivity (basing advice and decisions on rigorous analysis of the evidence), and impartiality (acting solely according to the merits of the case and serving equally well governments of different political persuasions).

It is questionable whether the role of civil servants is really limited to merely advising Ministers and implementing their wishes. On the one hand, the traditional role of the Civil Service is that of 'speaking truth unto power'—that is, telling Ministers what can and cannot be delivered. On the other hand, in reality, the Civil Service may often possess considerable power both to make and implement policy. For example, a former Home Secretary, David Blunkett, observed that senior civil servants frequently told Ministers that 'Department policy is this' rather than 'Department policy is what Ministers, on behalf of the government, say it is so long as it is in line with legislation, the stated government policy and/or the party manifesto'.[79] Furthermore, the reality is that civil servants, even middle-ranking ones, are heavily involved in policy-making over which there may be little, if any, ministerial supervision. Therefore, the chain linking Parliament, Ministers, and civil servants, upon which the doctrine of ministerial responsibility is based, may often be rather weak. The reality behind the

---

[75] Civil Service, 'Civil Service Code' (London 2015), [2].

[76] *Report on the Organisation of the Permanent Civil Service* (1854).

[77] For background, see Ministry of Justice, *The Governance of Britain* (Cm 7170 2007), [40]–[48].

[78] Constitutional Reform and Governance Act 2010, s 7(4).

[79] House of Commons Public Administration Select Committee, *Politics and Administration: Ministers and Civil Servants* (HC 122 2006–07), [36].

fiction is that civil servants do make policy over which there may be little ministerial supervision and for which Ministers may not be held responsible in Parliament.

From one perspective, government Ministers may be said to form the 'temporary' government—they come and go; by contrast, the Civil Service is part of the 'permanent' government. It is not therefore surprising that civil servants often possess some degree of power in both making and implementing policy. In practice, no Minister ever exercises full control over every aspect of work going on within a governmental department—government is just too large and too complex. The Minister's role is then normally to provide political leadership—to define the general course of action, while the civil servants consider the most appropriate and effective means of giving effect to policy. For example, it has been argued that civil servants work under the twin principles of 'improvised expertise' and 'invited authority'.[80] Improvised expertise means that, in a generalist Civil Service, in which officials often change to different types of work, officials are usually good at acquiring quickly an expertise in the particular policy area to which they have been moved. Meanwhile, invited authority implies that Ministers usually have little time to think through how to turn desirable, although vague, goals into concrete administrative programmes; civil servants inevitably have to do much policy work in giving effect to the wishes of politicians.

This is not to imply that the Civil Service is always effective. Over recent years, there have been various concerns that the Civil Service's performance has not been consistently high. The concerns are that operational delivery failures have sometimes occurred, that the quality of policy advice to Ministers has sometimes been wanting, and that the management and implementation of large-scale programmes and projects has sometimes been inadequate, with projects not being delivered on time and to budget. The wider concern is that the Civil Service has, on occasions, lacked the skills and abilities necessary to deliver and implement policy effectively. Consider the experience of the immigration agency. In 2006, the agency failed to consider foreign national prisoners for deportation and was branded as not 'fit for purpose' by the then Home Secretary. A new UK Border Agency was created in 2008. Yet, in 2013 this agency was disbanded with the Home Secretary telling Parliament that the agency's performance was still not good enough and that it had created a closed, secret, and defensive culture. There have been many instances of government failure over recent years.[81] The wider concern has been that, like all institutions, the Civil Service needs to move with the times and to change to provide a better quality of public service. This is especially important given the challenge of delivering improved public services during a period of reduced public spending.

In 2012, the coalition government published its Civil Service reform plan[82] setting out a number of action points for reform, such as improving the Civil Service's policymaking capability, changing the Civil Service's culture to a more flexible and

---

[80] Page and Jenkins, *Policy Bureaucracy: Government with a Cast of Thousands* (Oxford 2005).

[81] See Bacon and Hope, *Conundrum: Why Every Government Gets Things Wrong—And What We Can Do About It* (London 2013); King and Crewe, *The Blunders of Our Governments* (London 2013).

[82] HM Government, *The Civil Service Reform Plan* (London 2012).

outcome-focused culture, better policy implementation and accountability of the Civil Service, and a Civil Service with enhanced capabilities. Government departments have been implementing this reform plan.[83] Particular controversy has arisen in relation to the involvement of Ministers in the appointment of the most senior civil servants—Permanent Secretaries—who manage government departments. Given Ministers' direct accountability to Parliament for the performance of their departments, the government had wanted Ministers to have greater influence over such appointments. On the other hand, concerns have been raised that ministerial involvement should be limited so as to avoid the politicisation of the Civil Service. In 2012, the Civil Service Commission published new guidance. This enhances ministerial involvement in appointments, but does not give Ministers a choice in the appointment of Permanent Secretaries.

However, the Commons Public Administration Select Committee argued that the Civil Service reform plan is not based on any comprehensive analysis of the fundamental problems and challenges facing the Civil Service.[84] It does not constitute a comprehensive programme for changing or transforming the Civil Service and is therefore unlikely to succeed. There are, the Committee stated, important issues that need to be addressed, such as the capabilities of the Civil Service; the relationship between Ministers and the Civil Service; and whether the traditional doctrine of ministerial accountability remains appropriate for the modern age, and how it could be updated. The Committee therefore recommended that a Parliamentary Commission into the Civil Service be established, but this has not happened.

3.8 **Special advisers**

Special advisers are employed to help Ministers on matters in relation to which the work of government and the work of the governing party or parties overlap—an area in which it would be inappropriate for permanent civil servants to become involved. The Code of Conduct for special advisers explains that the rationale for such advisers is that they provide an additional source of advice for the Minister, from a standpoint that is more politically committed and politically aware than that which a civil servant could provide.[85] Special advisers provide assistance to Ministers on the development of government policy and its presentation.[86] They are also able to represent Ministers' views on government policy to the media with a degree of political commitment that would not be possible for the permanent Civil Service.[87] In recognition of their political allegiance to the governing party or parties, special advisers are exempt from the normal requirements to behave impartially and objectively.[88]

---

[83] See https://www.gov.uk/government/organisations/civil-service-reform
[84] House of Commons Public Administration Select Committee, *Truth to Power: How Civil Service Reform Can Succeed* (HC 74 2013–14).
[85] Cabinet Office, 'Code of Conduct for Special Advisers' (London 2010), [2].
[86] 'Code of Conduct for Special Advisers', [13].
[87] 'Code of Conduct for Special Advisers', [16].
[88] Constitutional Reform and Governance Act 2010, s 7(5).

Under the Ministerial Code, with the exception of the Prime Minister,[89] Cabinet Ministers may each appoint up to two special advisers. The Prime Minister may also authorise the appointment of one special adviser by Ministers who are not Cabinet Ministers as such, but who regularly attend Cabinet meetings.[90] Legally, special advisers may now only be appointed with the prior written approval of the Prime Minister.[91] Their appointment ends when the Minister who appointed them ceases to hold the ministerial office to which the appointment related or, if earlier, the day after the first general election following the appointment.[92]

In 2000, the Committee on Standards in Public Life concluded that special advisers perform a valuable function within government, but that they should be required to observe a code of conduct drafted to reflect their special position.[93] The Public Administration Committee also concluded that special advisers can make a positive contribution to good government by broadening the range of policy advice upon which Ministers can draw, but that they should be subject to a code of conduct.[94] In 2001, the government published a Code of Conduct for Special Advisers that governs their behaviour and which was last updated in 2015.[95] The existence of such a code is now statutorily required.[96] Because special advisers are civil servants, they are bound by the normal obligation to act with honesty and integrity.[97] In addition, special advisers should not deceive or know-ingly mislead Parliament or the public; neither should they misuse their official position or information acquired in the course of their official duties to further their private interests or the private interests of others.[98] Under the Ministerial Code, Ministers are responsible for the management and conduct of their special advisers, who act in their name, yet 'experience suggests that this responsibility is more theoretical than actual'. It has been noted that 'special advisers have on occasion seemed to be made accountable themselves for the lack of supervision and guidance they should be entitled to expect. To cynics, it might seem that spe-cial advisers have sometimes been an insurance policy, available to be cashed in to save ministerial careers'.[99]

Two controversial issues as to the role of special advisers should be noted. The first concerns their function in the presentation and media management of governmental policy. During the Blair government (1997–2007), special advisers gained a reputation

---

[89] Who in 2015 had 31 special advisers: Cabinet Office, *Special Adviser Data Releases: Numbers and Costs* (2015).

[90] 'Ministerial Code', [3.2].   [91] Constitutional Reform and Governance Act 2010, s 15.

[92] Constitutional Reform and Governance Act 2010, s 15.

[93] Committee on Standards in Public Life, *Sixth Report: Reinforcing Standards* (Cm 4557 2000), [6.26].

[94] House of Commons Public Administration Committee, *Special Advisers: Boon or Bane?* (HC 293 2000–01), [81].

[95] Cabinet Office, 'Code of Conduct for Special Advisers' (London 2016), **https://www.gov.uk/ government/uploads/system/uploads/attachment_data/file/579768/code-of-conduct-special-advisers-dec-2016.pdf**

[96] Constitutional Reform and Governance Act 2010, s 8(1).

[97] Constitutional Reform and Governance Act 2010, s 7(4).

[98] 'Code of Conduct for Special Advisers'.

[99] House of Commons Public Administration Select Committee, *Special Advisers in the Thick of It* (HC 1340 2012–13), [91].

for their involvement in 'spin'—that is, the presentation of information and of stories in the media to show the government in its best light. The most notorious episode occurred when, shortly following the terrorist attacks in the USA on 11 September 2001 ('9/11'), the special adviser to the Transport Secretary sent an email noting that it was 'a very good day to get out anything we want to bury'. In other words, because the world's attention was focused upon the terrorist attacks, the government could make use of the opportunity to disclose adverse information (such as statistics concerning train delays). The special adviser subsequently resigned.

Under the Code of Conduct, special advisers may represent to the media the views (including party political views) of their Minister, provided that they have been authorised by the Minister to do so. All contacts with the news media should be authorised by the appointing Minister and be conducted in accordance with government guidelines on communications. However, special advisers must 'observe discretion and express comment with moderation, avoiding personal attacks'.[100]

Second, some unease has been expressed that the proliferation of special advisers could undermine the neutrality of the Civil Service. The concern is that because special advisers are essentially political advisers to Ministers, their role may at times undermine the non-political and impartial advice given by civil servants. In 1997, Tony Blair authorised his three special advisers to issue instructions to civil servants.[101] However, this authorisation was removed when Gordon Brown became Prime Minister in 2007,[102] and primary legislation now states that special advisers may not exercise 'any power in relation to the management of any part of the civil service' except in relation to other special advisers.[103]

3.9 Other public agencies

We now need to consider a final part of the executive: those public bodies and agencies that operate at 'arm's length' from Ministers and government departments. These agencies fall into three categories: non-ministerial departments, non-departmental public bodies (NDPBs), and executive agencies. Such agencies and public bodies proliferate because of the range of tasks undertaken by government and the need for such functions to be performed at one level removed from Ministers at the centre of the government machine.

First, non-ministerial departments are those departments created, often by statute, to discharge a particular public function. They exercise their functions on behalf of the Crown, and their separation from central government and Ministers is normally introduced to confer a degree of independence upon them. For example, the Charity Commission is the independent regulator of charitable activity and is not subject to the direction or control of any Minister of the Crown or other government department.[104] Having said that, Ministers may have the power to appoint members

---

[100] 'Code of Conduct for Special Advisers', [11].
[101] The Civil Service (Amendment) Order in Council 1997.
[102] The Civil Service (Amendment) (No 2) Order in Council 2007.
[103] Constitutional Reform and Governance Act 2010, s 8(5) and (6).
[104] Charities Act 2006, s 6.

of such departments and to provide oversight. For example, HM Revenue and Customs (HMRC)—the government department responsible for taxation—is a non-ministerial department in order to reduce the risk of direct political interference in tax matters. Yet, the Commissioners of the HMRC are to be treated as if they were Ministers of the Crown and must comply with any directions of a general nature given to them by the Treasury.[105]

Second, there are NDPBs. These are bodies that have a role in the processes of national government, but are not government departments or part of one, and which accordingly operate to a greater or lesser extent at arm's length from Ministers.[106] They fall into three categories:

(i) Bodies with executive powers (eg the Environment Agency).

(ii) Advisory bodies that are set up by Ministers to advise them and their departments on matters within their area of responsibility (eg the Social Security Advisory Committee provides advice to the Department for Work and Pensions).

(iii) Independent monitoring boards (eg the independent monitoring boards of prisons act as independent 'watchdogs' for overseeing prisons, their administration, and treatment of prisoners).

That such functions are conferred on NDPBs means that there is recognition that they have a degree of independence from Ministers in carrying out those functions. At the same time, Ministers are accountable to Parliament for such bodies, their usefulness as an instrument of government policy, and their overall effectiveness and efficiency. NDPBs have recently fallen out of favour with central government, not least on the ground that they are perceived to be expensive.

Third, there are executive agencies. In 1988, the Thatcher government established executive agencies as a means of securing better managed and more efficient public services. The essential idea was that the executive and operational functions of government would be carried out by agencies operating at 'arms-length' from Ministers.[107] Many aspects of the work of government departments were then 'hived off' to executive agencies. Each executive agency is headed not by a Minister who is directly accountable to Parliament, but by an official—a chief executive. The relationship between executive agencies and their 'parent' government departments are formally set out in framework agreements. The executive agency works to performance targets set down by the parent department and is also funded by it. For example, the Driver and Vehicle Licensing Agency, the parent department of which is the Department for Transport, issues driving and vehicle licences; meanwhile, the National Offender Management Service, an executive agency of the Ministry of Justice, is responsible for adult offender management services and the delivery of prison services.

The establishment of executive agencies provides another example of how the executive in the UK is able to reorganise itself without the need for any recourse

---

[105] Commissioners for Revenue and Customs Act 2005, ss 8 and 11.

[106] Cabinet Office, *Public Bodies 2009* (London 2009), p 5.

[107] Jenkins, *Politicians and Public Services: Implementing Change in a Clash of Cultures* (Cheltenham 2008).

to legislation. Executive agencies have been established without any parliamentary approval or oversight because none was required. Framework agreements governing the relationship between parent departments and executive agencies are not formally, legally binding. It is, though, government policy to review periodically the work and status of executive agencies.

For the most part, executive agencies operate to deliver public services more efficiently and effectively. However, problems can arise in relation to the accountability of such agencies. We can see that the responsibility chain has become lengthened—the Minister is responsible to Parliament, but the executive agency is responsible to the Minister—so can Parliament effectively hold the executive agency to account? In practical terms, parliamentary select committees can hear evidence from the chief executives of executive agencies, meaning that chief executives are increasingly responsible for operational matters while Ministers remain responsible for policy matters. But what is the precise difference between policy and operations?

The classic example of how difficult it is to draw that distinction, and of how Ministers might be tempted deliberately to manipulate this ambiguity to evade accountability, is provided by the 'Howard–Lewis' affair that occurred in 1995. Michael Howard was the Home Secretary and Derek Lewis was the chief executive of the Prison Service. Following a number of prison escapes, Howard demanded Lewis's resignation because of operational failures; by contrast, Lewis argued that the Home Secretary had interfered in operational matters, while simultaneously wishing to escape responsibility for a failure for which he was ultimately accountable to Parliament.[108] The obvious concern is that the principle of ministerial responsibility has been weakened or even manipulated to the benefit of Ministers and the detriment of officials. As Drewry has argued more generally, the largely fictional character of ministerial responsibility in an era of large-scale government and huge public bureaucracies has been increasingly apparent since the latter part of the nineteenth century—even though much of the fiction has been preserved, largely for the convenience of Ministers who are happy to accept the credit for successful initiatives, but quick to pass the buck to their officials when things go wrong.[109]

A final point is that concerns have often sometimes been expressed at the number of 'unaccountable' government agencies and 'quangos';[110] in response, it is often argued that such bodies perform many useful public roles. When the coalition government came to power in 2010, it promised to shrink the 'quango state' as part of the drive to reduce public spending and to bring some functions back into ministerial departments, thereby enhancing parliamentary scrutiny. The Public Bodies Act 2011 enables Ministers to abolish and merge public bodies through secondary legislation

---

[108] Barker, 'Political Responsibility for UK Prison Security: Ministers Escape Again' (1998) 76 Public Administration 1.

[109] Drewry, 'The Executive: Towards Accountable Government and Effective Governance?', in Jowell and Oliver (eds), *The Changing Constitution* (Oxford 2011), p 211. These issues are explored more fully in Chapter 10.

[110] 'Quango' stands for 'quasi-autonomous non-governmental organisation', and is used as a catch-all term to refer to a range of public bodies.

that must be made pursuant to an enhanced parliamentary scrutiny process.[111] This Act has to date been used to abolish some public bodies, but not as many as the government initially envisaged.

4. The powers of the executive

We now consider the powers of the executive. How does the executive actually govern? By what legal (and other) means does it get things done and, more generally, project influence?

4.1 Statutory powers generally

Most obviously, the executive has at its disposal a vast array of statutory powers given to it by Parliament. Why does Parliament delegate statutory powers to Ministers (and others)?[112] The most obvious answer to this is: to get things done! Parliament does not itself govern the country. It could never legislate for every eventuality or decision to be taken. The work of government is far too extensive for this to happen. Furthermore, on many issues, Parliament is not competent to undertake the detailed decision-making required; rather, its role is limited to resolving general policy questions.

Consider, for example, the Inquiries Act 2005, which makes provision for the holding of inquiries into matters of public concern.[113] In theory, every time an event occurs that caused such concern, it would be possible for Parliament to legislate to establish an inquiry, set out the matters that should be investigated, appoint people to carry out the inquiry, and so on. But this would not be a sensible use of Parliament's time. For that reason, the Inquiries Act 2005 confers statutory powers upon Ministers to set up inquiries, decide who should chair them, determine their terms of reference, and so on. Of course, the legislation only authorises Ministers to act within certain parameters; for example, they cannot appoint people to run inquiries who appear to have vested interests, and they must inform Parliament that an inquiry is being established. In this way, the Inquiries Act, like all Acts that grant statutory powers to Ministers, reflects a division of labour between executive and legislature. The latter lays down the ground rules and general principles, while the more detailed decision-making required by the administration of policy is left to the former.

However, leaving certain matters for ministerial decision is not simply a necessary evil that must be endured because Parliament cannot do everything. There are also a number of positive reasons for leaving certain matters to the executive branch. It is generally appropriate for decisions concerning particular individuals or sensitive issues, or requiring detailed consideration of specific facts, to be taken otherwise

---

[111] House of Lords Secondary Legislation Scrutiny Committee, *Special Report—Public Bodies Act 2011: One Year On* (HL 90 2012–13).

[112] For example, non-departmental public bodies, local authorities, and so on. Our focus here, however, is on the powers of central government ministerial departments.

[113] See further Chapter 17.

than by Parliament. Government departments may have greater expertise. Ministers receive advice from civil servants. Government can also adopt a more appropriate style of decision-making: it may, for example, be necessary or desirable to take detailed evidence from individuals liable to be affected by the decision, perhaps even affording certain such individuals some form of fair hearing. It is abundantly clear that Parliament is not institutionally well placed to carry out such tasks. It is equally clear that the executive branch may need to be authorised in certain contexts to take urgent decisions, bearing in mind that it is far better equipped than Parliament to respond quickly to events.[114] For reasons such as these, it is the executive, rather than Parliament, that can, among other things, decide that a foreign national should be deported on the ground that his presence in the UK is not conducive to the public good,[115] decide whether the go-ahead should be given to major infrastructure projects of regional or national importance,[116] and introduce emergency measures when this is necessary to deal with matters that threaten serious damage to human welfare, the environment, or national security.[117]

> **Q** What general principles would you wish to see applied by Parliament when determining whether a particular matter should be left to the executive branch to decide under statutory powers or determined by Parliament itself by means of primary legislation?

The amount of statutory power conferred upon government by Parliament increased dramatically during the last century. This is hardly surprising. Over that period, the government took on a much broader range of responsibilities—and therefore needed the powers necessary to discharge them. As Wade and Forsyth note, if the state is to 'care for its citizens from the cradle to the grave'—providing education, training, health care, social security, and so on—then 'it needs a huge administrative apparatus'.[118] This throws into especially sharp relief questions about the accountability of the executive in its use of statutory powers. The existence of adequate mechanisms for ensuring the accountable use of such power is self-evidently important, but all the more so given the sheer scale of the powers at the disposal of today's executive branch. In this sphere, we therefore encounter a clear example of the phenomenon mentioned at the beginning of this chapter—that is, the intersection of our two key themes of holding the executive to account, and the relationship between legal and political forms of constitutionalism. It might be thought that the task of ensuring the responsible use of statutory power ought to fall to the institution—Parliament—that confers it in the first place.

However, for reasons that we outlined at the outset of this chapter, and which we explore in more depth in Chapter 5, Parliament is, in fact, poorly situated to discharge this function. As a result, the extent to which the executive is politically accountable to the legislature for the exercise of statutory powers is today

---

[114] Not least because Parliament is in 'recess'—ie does not sit—for a substantial proportion of each year.
[115] Immigration Act 1971, s 3(5).   [116] Town and Country Planning Act 1990, s 76A.
[117] Civil Contingencies Act 2004, Pt 2.   [118] *Administrative Law* (Oxford 2014), p 4.

eclipsed in some respects by the former's legal accountability to the courts, which have assumed primary responsibility for ensuring that the government does not misuse its legal powers. We consider the means—known as 'judicial review'—by which the courts discharge this responsibility in Chapters 11–14.

It is also worth bearing in mind the implications for the present context of the matters considered earlier in this chapter concerning the nature of the relationship between the legislature and the executive. The executive only has the statutory powers that Parliament gives to it; and those statutory powers that it does have are granted on whatever terms, and subject to whatever restrictions, Parliament chooses to impose. It might therefore be anticipated that Parliament would normally frame statutory powers in relatively narrow terms, to ensure that those permitted to exercise them may do so only for the specific purposes and in the particular way intended by Parliament. In practice, however, statutory powers are often granted in very broad terms, thus affording the executive a wide degree of latitude vis-à-vis the uses to which such powers may be put and the manner of their exercise.[119] It is not hard to work out why this tends to happen. We explained at the beginning of the chapter that the reality of Parliament's relationship with the executive is that the latter is in a strong position to secure the enactment of legislation by the former. It follows that although, in strictly technical terms, it is for Parliament to decide which powers to confer on the executive, and on what terms, the actual position is that the executive is strongly placed to get Parliament to confer upon it the powers that it wants on the terms that it wants them.

When Parliament delegates statutory powers to the government, it confers those powers upon either 'the Secretary of State' or the holder of an independent statutory office (eg Immigration Officers or Prison Governors). Powers conferred upon the Secretary of State can be—and more often than not are—exercised by civil servants under the '*Carltona* doctrine'.[120] For instance, the Department for Work & Pensions takes millions of decisions each year as to whether claimants qualify for social security benefits. No such scheme could operate if only the Minister personally took such decisions. That is not what happens. In practice, such decisions are taken by thousands of civil servants under the authority of the Minister. Under the *Carltona* doctrine, civil servants can exercise these ministerial powers on the understanding that the Minister remains constitutionally responsible to Parliament for the exercise of such powers.[121]

4.2 Statutory powers to make delegated legislation

The sort of statutory powers thus far considered concern the making of decisions in individual cases within the framework of rules laid down by Parliament in the relevant statute. However, it is very common for Parliament to authorise the executive not

---

[119] Without prejudice to this point, it is important not to overstate the degree of the executive's freedom in this regard; not least because, as we explain in Chapter 12, if the exercise of statutory powers is challenged legally, courts are often prepared to read restrictions into broadly worded legislation.

[120] *Carltona Ltd v Commissioners of Works* [1943] 2 All ER 560. See Chapter 12, section 4.1.

[121] *R (Bourgass) v Secretary of State for Justice* [2015] UKSC 54.

only to make decisions of that nature, but also to make some of the legal rules itself. Such rules are known as *delegated legislation* and *Statutory Instruments* (SIs).[122]

4.2.1 The use of delegated legislation

We noted earlier that government exerts considerable influence over primary legislation. Government itself also makes an enormous volume of delegated legislation. Figure 4.5 shows the number of SIs enacted during the period 1950–2015. The figure reminds us that delegated lawmaking also extends to the devolved administrations, the Scottish Government and the Northern Ireland Assembly.[123] The figure also includes the number of Acts of the UK Parliament. Clearly, the volume of delegated legislation far exceeds that of primary legislation. An alternative way of measuring legislation is to compare the length—the number of pages—of SIs with Acts of Parliament (see Figure 4.6). Again, there is a substantial difference.

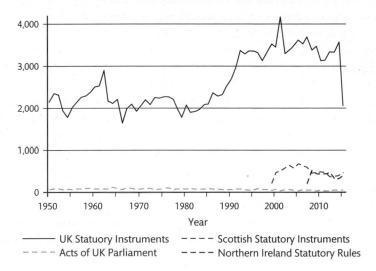

Figure 4.5 The volume of Statutory Instruments, 1950–2015

Source: House of Commons Library Briefing Paper, *Acts and Statutory Instruments: The Volume of UK legislation 1950 to 2015* (CBP7438 2015).

In considering these figures, it is important to bear in mind the following points. First, SIs vary tremendously in terms of their scope and length: some are substantial pieces of legislation in their own right. However, many SIs—such as road orders—are overwhelmingly routine and non-controversial.[124] Second, most primary legislation is nowadays essentially 'framework' or 'enabling legislation'; the detail is reserved for

---

[122] The terms 'secondary', 'subordinate', 'executive', and 'administrative' legislation are also used.

[123] The number of SIs made by the Welsh Assembly since 1999 are included in the UK totals.

[124] See, for instance, the A5 Trunk Road (Llangollen, Denbighshire) (Temporary 40 mph Speed Limit) Order 2016, SI 567/2016 made under the Road Traffic Regulation Act 1984. In 2015, Highways England was created and given the authority to make road orders without these being SIs. This dramatically reduced the number of SIs made in relation to Road Traffic regulations and accounts for the decline in the number of SIs since 2015 in Figure 4.5.

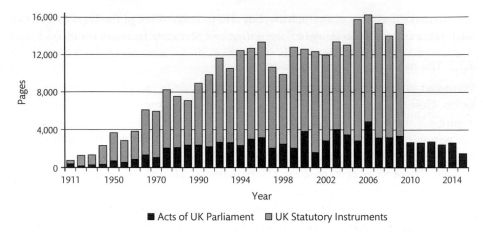

Figure 4.6 Pages of Acts and Statutory Instruments, 1990–2015

Note: Data for the number of pages for SIs are available only up to 2009.

delegated legislation. Legislation—primary and secondary—is largely a function of the governmental process of making and implementing policy.[125]

The reasons for allowing the use of delegated legislation are similar to those that militate in favour of permitting the executive to use statutory powers generally. The sheer volume of legislation that is felt to be necessary today means that Parliament does not have the capacity to enact all of it. In effect, therefore, Parliament has to contract out to the executive branch the enactment of a good deal of legislation. This may seem inconsistent with the separation of powers, but extensive governmental rule-making is simply a fact of life and an inevitable consequence of the scale and complexity of governmental responsibilities: 'Parliament and Government would grind to a halt if there were not built into our constitution an adequate system of Executive legislation.'[126]

The focus of concern in this area is not whether the executive should have legislative powers—that is now accepted. The focus is whether those powers are subject to adequate controls and safeguards, and whether the extent of the modern executive's lawmaking powers is appropriate. For example, it has been argued that there is 'too great a readiness in Parliament to delegate wide legislative powers to Ministers, and no lack of enthusiasm on their part to take such powers', resulting in 'an excessive volume of delegated legislation'.[127] The issue of whether or not to use primary or secondary legislation can sometimes pose a difficult question for government and Parliament. For instance, the Financial Services (Banking Reform) Act 2013 is an

---

[125] On primary legislation, see Chapter 5, section 5.

[126] Joint Committee on Statutory Instruments, *First Special Report* (HC 169 1977–78), [37]. See also Taggart, 'From "Parliamentary Powers" to Privatization: The Chequered History of Delegated Legislation in the Twentieth Century' (2005) 55 UTLJ 575.

[127] House of Commons Select Committee on Procedure (HC 152 1995–96), [14]. These comments were endorsed more recently by the same select committee: see House of Commons Select Committee on Procedure, *Delegated Legislation* (HC 48 1999–2000), [26].

enabling Act that delegates substantial legislative rule-making powers to the government: this enables government to respond quickly to financial innovations over time; also, putting all the detail in primary legislation would result in a very large Bill. However, the lack of detail in a Bill reduces parliamentary scrutiny and there may be a need for clear parliamentary approval for some policies.[128]

4.2.2 Henry VIII powers

There are different *types of lawmaking power* that the executive can exercise. Most straightforwardly, the executive may be allowed to fill in the details of a statutory scheme. As mentioned in section 4.2.1, the powers conferred by the Financial Services Act include powers of this type.

However, it has been observed that there is 'an increasing tendency for governments to use delegated legislation as a means of dealing with matters of principle and policy rather than [just] with detail'.[129] Particular concerns have been expressed in relation to 'Henry VIII powers',[130] which, as Figure 4.7 shows, authorise Ministers to make secondary legislation amending or even repealing Acts of Parliament. In some instances, Henry VIII powers are relatively modest: they may, for instance, permit the amendment or repeal only of specific statutory provisions, or of a specific class of such provisions. However, the Civil Contingencies Act 2004 illustrates just how broad executive powers to legislate can be. It allows certain Ministers to make 'emergency regulations' if it is considered that it is urgently necessary to do so to make provision to prevent, control, or mitigate an aspect or effect of an emergency that has

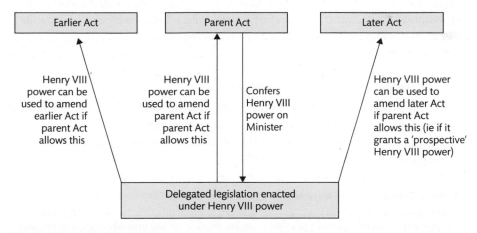

Figure 4.7 Henry VIII powers

---

[128] Parliamentary Commission on Banking Standards, *Banking Standards* (HL 98 HC 848 2012–13), [117]–[125].

[129] Page, *Governing by Numbers* (Oxford 2001), p 25.

[130] So-called because of King Henry VIII's arrogation to himself of powers to enact measures having the same force as statutes. See further Barber and Young, 'The Rise of Prospective Henry VIII Clauses and Their Implications for Sovereignty' [2003] PL 112, 113.

occurred, is occurring, or is about to occur, and if the urgency of the situation is such that more cumbersome legislative procedures cannot practically be used.[131]

The breadth of what can be accomplished under these powers is immense: emergency regulations can, among other things, 'provide for . . . the destruction of property, animal life or plant life (with or without compensation)',[132] 'prohibit . . . travel at specified times', and 'prohibit'[133] or 'require . . . movement to or from a specified place'.[134] Moreover, the Act makes clear that emergency regulations 'may make provision of any kind that could be made by Act of Parliament',[135] including the disapplication and modification of primary legislation.[136] The power to make emergency regulations is therefore a particularly broad form of Henry VIII power, since it can potentially be used in relation to any Act of Parliament for any of a very wide range of purposes.[137] Barber and Young argue that Henry VIII clauses of this type, which can be used in relation to all primary legislation whether enacted before or after the Act conferring the power, are objectionable in constitutional terms. The essence of their argument is that when Parliament confers a 'prospective' Henry VIII power—that is, one that can be used in relation to legislation not yet on the statute book—it cannot fully appreciate the uses to which it might be put, because those uses include the amendment or repeal of primary legislation not yet enacted. They point out that this creates 'the risk that as yet unthought of statutes will be overturned through the exercise of delegated power', such that 'Parliament must put its trust entirely in the body to whom power is delegated'.[138]

> **Q** According to Lord Judge, a former Lord Chief Justice, 'unless strictly incidental to primary legislation, every Henry VIII clause, every vague skeleton bill, is a blow to the sovereignty of Parliament. And each one is a self-inflicted blow, each one boosting the power of the executive.'[139] Do you agree?

4.2.3 The legal effect of delegated legislation

In many instances, the legal effect of delegated legislation is clear. For example, it is commonplace for primary legislation to specify that contravention of regulations made thereunder is a criminal offence. This establishes that the regulations form part of the criminal law.

---

[131] Civil Contingencies Act 2004, s 20(2). By s 19(1):

An 'emergency' is, for these purposes, an event or situation which threatens serious damage to human welfare in the United Kingdom or in a Part or region; an event or situation which threatens serious damage to the environment of the United Kingdom or of a Part or region; or war, or terrorism, which threatens serious damage to the security of the United Kingdom.

[132] Civil Contingencies Act 2004, s 22(3)(c).   [133] Civil Contingencies Act 2004, s 22(3)(g).

[134] Civil Contingencies Act 2004, s 22(3)(d) and (e).

[135] Civil Contingencies Act 2004, s 22(3).   [136] Civil Contingencies Act 2004, s 22(3)(j).

[137] Provided that they are considered by the Minister to be necessary for preventing, controlling, or mitigating an aspect or effect of the emergency in question: Civil Contingencies Act 2004, s 22(1).

[138] Barber and Young, 114.

[139] Lord Judge, 'Ceding Power to the Executive; the Resurrection of Henry VIII' (12 April 2016), http://www.kcl.ac.uk/law/newsevents/newsrecords/2015-16/Ceding-Power-to-the-Executive---Lord-Judge---130416.pdf

However, the position is not always as simple. Particular difficulties arise where the executive is authorised by statute—or takes it upon itself—to issue guidance, rules, regulations, and suchlike, the legal status of which is not made clear by the parent Act or otherwise. For example, s 38(7) of the Road Traffic Act 1998 stipulates that while breach of the Highway Code is not in itself a criminal offence, such a breach may be relied upon in criminal or civil proceedings 'as tending to establish or negative any liability which is in question in those proceedings'. So while a breach of the Highway Code is not actionable in itself, its contravention by a defendant may help the claimant establish liability for negligence.[140] Similarly, under s 118(1) of the Mental Health Act 1983, the Secretary of State is required to issue a 'code of practice' concerning, among other things, the treatment of patients suffering from mental disorders. The House of Lords concluded in the *Munjaz* case that such a code of practice could not be regarded as having the binding force of law.[141] It followed that when the defendant hospital departed from it, by operating a regime for supervising patients confined to their rooms that was less rigorous than that required under the code, this was not unlawful per se. However, their Lordships did hold that the code of practice—and the fact that the hospital had departed from it—was relevant to determining whether the hospital had acted lawfully according to the normal principles governing the use of statutory powers. What this meant, in effect, was that the hospital had to show that its refusal to apply the code was not unreasonable—a burden that it discharged by virtue of the fact that it cared for an unusually high number of unusually dangerous patients.

It is therefore appropriate to think of the various sorts of measure that the executive enacts as existing on a spectrum, as shown in Figure 4.8. At one end, we find such things as the regulations made under s 19 of the Olympics Act: those regulations can self-evidently be regarded as 'law', in the sense that they are directly legally enforceable, and here the term 'delegated legislation' is manifestly appropriate. However, as we move along the spectrum, we enter the realm of so-called 'soft law', or quasi-legislation—measures that may have some, less direct legal relevance, but which cannot straightforwardly be regarded as laws in the sense of being directly enforceable in legal proceedings.[142]

4.2.4 Publication

The idea that law should be published is central to the notion of the rule of law. Individuals can only plan their lives and choose to behave in a way that is lawful if they can know what the law is; that, in turn, is possible only if all legal rules are publicly available. As Lord Steyn pointed out in *Anufrijeva*, speaking in an analogous context, a situation in which 'the rights of individuals are overridden by hole in the corner decisions or knocks on doors in the early hours' is antithetical to the British

---

[140] *Russell v Smith* [2003] EWHC 2060 (Admin), (2003) 147 SJLB 1118. See further *Odelola v Secretary of State for the Home Department* [2009] UKHL 25, [2009] 1 WLR 1230 and *Secretary of State for the Home Department v Pankina* [2010] EWCA Civ 719 for discussion of the legal status of the Immigration Rules.

[141] *R (Munjaz) v Mersey Care NHS Trust* [2005] UKHL 58, [2006] 2 AC 148.

[142] See further Ganz, *Quasi-Legislation: Recent Developments in Secondary Legislation* (London 1987).

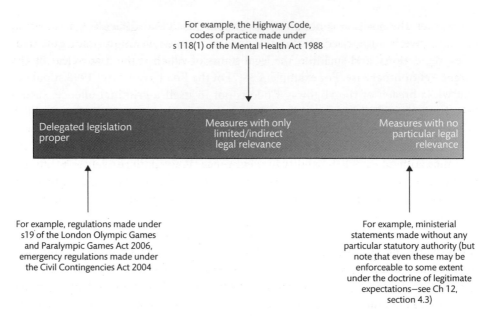

Figure 4.8 Delegated legislation and 'soft law'

tradition of the rule of law. He continued: 'That is not our system. . . . In our system of law surprise is regarded as the enemy of justice.'[143] It is therefore unsurprising that the Statutory Instruments Act 1946, s 2(1), provides that 'statutory instruments' must be published.[144] However, two issues arise.

First, delegated legislation only constitutes a statutory instrument if the parent Act, in conferring the power to make delegated legislation, stipulates that it must be made in the form of statutory instrument. Where that is not the case, the publication requirement in the 1946 Act does not apply. In such circumstances, as Scott LJ pointed out in *Blackpool Corporation v Locker*, individuals may remain 'in complete ignorance' of the law, meaning that, '[f]or practical purposes, the rule of law, of which the nation is so justly proud, breaks down'.[145] However, some other publication requirement may apply; for example, the Act conferring the power to enact the delegated legislation in question may insist upon publication[146] or the Freedom of Information Act 2000[147] may require publication.

Second, in light of the importance—from a rule of law perspective—of publication, it might be thought that failure to publish delegated legislation (where this is legally required) should result in its invalidity (or at least unenforceability pending publication). However, it appears that this is not so, and that delegated legislation

---

[143] *R (Anufrijeva) v Secretary of State for the Home Department* [2003] UKHL 36, [2004] 1 AC 604, [28]–[30].

[144] For certain exceptions to this requirement, see the Statutory Instruments Regulations 1947, SI 1948/1.

[145] *Blackpool Corporation v Locker* [1948] 1 KB 349, 362.

[146] Indeed, courts may be willing to read an implied obligation to that effect into the parent Act. See (in an analogous context) *Salih v Secretary of State for the Home Department* [2003] EWHC 2273 (Admin).

[147] See Chapter 10, section 7.

remains valid and enforceable even if it is not published[148]—although it is, subject to certain exceptions, a defence to a *criminal* charge of contravening a statutory instrument to prove that the legislation had not been published at the date of the alleged contravention.[149]

4.2.5 Consultation

We will see in Chapter 12 that when the executive branch makes decisions under statutory powers of the type considered in section 4.2.4, it is generally required to act fairly. An important aspect of acting fairly in this sense is allowing those likely to be affected by the decision to have their say *before* any decision is made. There are many different ways in which this can be done; such practices, depending on the context, may be referred to as providing a fair hearing or consulting interested parties. When the executive enacts delegated legislation (as opposed simply to making decisions) under statutory powers, the relevant legislation may require consultation; when it does not, there is generally no common law duty to consult or otherwise to treat fairly those liable to be affected.[150] More recently, however, in the *BAPIO* case, Sedley LJ said that 'the common law could recognise a general duty of consultation in relation to proposed measures which are going adversely to affect an identifiable interest group or sector of society', but went on to conclude that it would often be inappropriate, in the absence of a statutory duty to consult, for the courts to impose one: doing so, he said, may require the court to adopt the position of a legislator.[151] Meanwhile, Maurice Kay LJ, with whom Rimer LJ agreed, pointed out that if (as is often the case, as we will explain) the parent Act were to make Parliament responsible for scrutinising the executive legislation in question, it would be inappropriate for the court to superimpose a common law duty to consult.[152] The Supreme Court has, however, held that the formal categorisation of a measure as 'legislative' is not determinative of a duty to consult. Such a duty was therefore held to have arisen when a measure—notwithstanding that it took the form of a statutory instrument—was 'targeted against identifiable individuals'.[153] For some commentators, the general absence of any requirement to consult prior to enacting secondary legislation is a source of concern: Page calls executive lawmaking 'the politics of seclusion', the (pejorative) implication being that it is an activity that takes place in a way that lacks adequate transparency.[154]

While there is no general legal duty for the executive to consult on delegated legislation, this does not, of course, preclude such consultation. It should not be assumed that the executive is generally unwilling to consult. On the contrary, the government

---

[148] *R v Sheer Metalcraft Ltd* [1954] 1 QB 586, 590, *per* Streatfield J.
[149] Statutory Instruments Act 1946, s 3(2).
[150] *Bates v Lord Hailsham of St Marylebone* [1972] 1 WLR 1373.
[151] *R (BAPIO Action Ltd) v Secretary of State for the Home Department* [2007] EWCA Civ 1139, [47] (decided on other grounds by the House of Lords: [2008] UKHL 27, [2008] 1 AC 1003). Sedley LJ had in mind the fact that the court would have to make a series of detailed decisions about the nature of the required consultation exercise.
[152] *BAPIO Action Ltd*, [58].
[153] *Bank Mellat v HM Treasury (No 2)* [2013] UKSC 39, [46], per Lord Sumption.
[154] Page, *Governing by Numbers* (Oxford 2001), ch 1.

has published a general policy on consultation—the Consultation Principles—which recognises that ongoing dialogue between government and stakeholders is an important part of policymaking.[155]

4.2.6 The role of Parliament

There is something paradoxical in addressing Parliament's role in relation to delegated legislation. After all, an important part of the purpose behind granting to the executive powers to make such legislation is Parliament's inability to cope with the volume of lawmaking that is deemed necessary today. However, it is inevitable that Parliament must, in the first place, be involved in *conferring powers* on the executive to enact delegated legislation—and it is desirable that Parliament should be involved in *overseeing the exercise of such powers*.

As to the former, it is clearly for Parliament to decide whether it wishes to confer upon the executive powers to enact legislation in relation to any given matter—and, if it does, on what terms. However, here, we encounter the familiar point that all is not as it seems as regards the relationship between the executive and the legislature. The reality, as we now know, is that the former is well situated to get the latter to do as it wishes. It is therefore unsurprising that both the amount and scope of the contemporary executive's lawmaking powers are very considerable indeed. Having said that, it is worth noting that systematic scrutiny of the appropriateness of granting legislative powers to the executive is provided by the House of Lords Select Committee on Delegated Powers and Regulatory Reform, which, among other things, scrutinises Bills for unduly wide or otherwise inappropriate executive powers.[156] One of the factors that the Committee takes into account is whether the grant of executive powers is accompanied in the Bill by provision for adequate parliamentary oversight of their exercise. The conferral of legislative powers on the executive is not necessarily inappropriate—provided that they 'are exercised with the knowledge of Parliament, and in direct subjection to its control'.[157]

Parliamentary scrutiny of delegated legislation takes two main forms. *Technical scrutiny* is provided by the Joint Committee on Statutory Instruments.[158] It is concerned with matters such as whether proposed delegated legislation is poorly drafted and whether it relates to matters that may be outside the powers under which it is being made. In a sense, the work of the Committee anticipates the sort of issues that might otherwise be the subject of litigation—and, perhaps for that reason, the executive tends to acquiesce when the Committee is of the view that proposed legislation needs to be changed before being finalised.[159]

---

[155] Cabinet Office, 'Consultation Principles' (London 2012). See also House of Lords Secondary Legislation Scrutiny Committee, *The Government's New Approach to Consultation—'Work in Progress'* (HL 100 2012–13).

[156] See House of Lords Delegated Powers and Regulatory Reform Committee, *Special Report: Strengthened Statutory Procedures for the Scrutiny of Delegated Powers* (HL 19 2012–13).

[157] Todd, *Parliamentary Government in England* (London 1892), vol 2, p 170.

[158] See generally Wallington and Hayhurst, 'The Parliamentary Scrutiny of Delegated Legislation' [1988] PL 547.

[159] See further Page, pp 161–8.

Complete delegation	Negative Instruments	Affirmative Instruments	SIs with added scrutiny
Minister can make law on her own authority. eg closing a road, commencement orders	Minister must lay before Parliament for 40 days—can be rejected by a prayer motion.	Laid as draft. Cannot come into effect until both Houses have debated and approved it.	Laid as SIs but with specific scrutiny procedure set out in Act. eg Legislative Reform Orders and Public Body Orders
Approx 2,200 a year	Approx 800 a year	Approx 200–250 a year	Fewer than 10 a year
Can only be amended by another instrument			*Limited change possible*

Figure 4.9 Secondary legislation: levels of delegation

Source: This figure is taken from the House of Lords Delegated and Regulatory Reform Committee, *Special Report: Response to the Strathclyde Review* (HL 119 2015–16), appendix C.

Meanwhile, *policy scrutiny* of delegated legislation is patchy at best. It is clear that Parliament cannot debate at length every governmental proposal for such legislation: such an approach would be self-defeating, given that the executive is, in the first place, authorised to make law due to limited parliamentary time. SIs are subject to one of four types of Parliamentary scrutiny, as summarised in Figure 4.9:

(i)   no Parliamentary scrutiny at all; the SI is made and comes into force; there is no requirement to lay the SI before Parliament;

(ii) the negative resolution procedure (annulment), which applies to 'negative instruments' that take effect unless Parliament takes steps to disapprove it within a 40-day period;

(iii) the positive resolution procedure, which applies to 'affirmative instruments' that must be approved by Parliament within 40 days before taking effect; and

(iv) the 'super-affirmative' resolution procedure. Under this procedure, during a 60-day period, the SI will be scrutinised and subject to representations, a resolution of either House, or a report of a scrutiny committee of either House. The Minister must then have regard to any such representations.

How does this work in practice? Affirmative instruments receive some policy scrutiny as a matter of course, since they must be debated in committee, but negative instruments are only rarely debated. Prima facie, this system represents a sensible use of scarce parliamentary time and resources: some delegated legislation—presumably that which is the most important or contentious—is subject to debate, whereas the

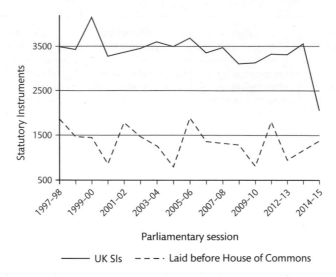

Figure 4.10 SIs made and laid before the House of Commons, 1997–2015

Source: House of Commons Library Briefing Paper, *Acts and Statutory Instruments: The Volume of UK legislation 1950–2015* (CBP7438 2015).

rest is not. The difficulty, however, is that the distinction between affirmative and negative instruments is often not aligned with the distinction between delegated legislation that is worthy of debate and that which it is appropriate to subject to less (or no) scrutiny. As a result, it was suggested that Parliament should create a system of triage—a 'sifting committee'—to identify at an early stage which pieces of delegated legislation need close scrutiny and which do not.[160] The suggestion that a joint committee of both Houses should be formed for this purpose was rejected by the government,[161] but the House of Lords has now created its own sifting committee—the House of Lords Secondary Legislation Scrutiny Committee—which identifies which SIs should be the subject of closer scrutiny by the upper House.[162]

We can now explore the number of SIs scrutinised by Parliament in more detail. Figure 4.10 shows the number of SIs made and then laid before the House of Commons. What is notable here is that a considerable number of SIs are not even laid before Parliament. Many, though not all, of these SIs are road traffic regulations or commencement orders. In short, many SIs are not even laid before Parliament, let alone debated or approved.

Both Houses have similar procedures for debating SIs: a debate in Committee and a debate in the Chamber. Figure 4.11 shows the number of SIs considered in both the

---

[160] See House of Commons Select Committee on Procedure, *Delegated Legislation* (HC 152 1995–96) and *Delegated Legislation: Proposals for a Sifting Committee* (HC 501 2002–03); Royal Commission on the Reform of the House of Lords, *A House for the Future* (Cm 4534 2000), p 74.

[161] House of Commons Select Committee on Procedure, *Delegated Legislation: Proposals for a Sifting Committee: The Government's Response to the Committee's First Report* (HC 684 2002–03).

[162] This Committee was formerly known as the House of Lords Merits Committee. See House of Lords Select Committee on the Merits of Statutory Instruments, *Special Report: Inquiry into Methods of Working* (HL 18 2003–04).

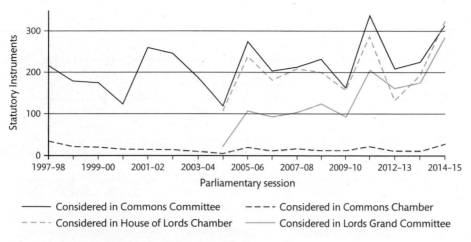

Figure 4.11 SIs debated in Parliament, 1997–2015

Source: House of Commons Library Briefing Paper and House of Lords Constitution Committee, *Delegated Legislation and Parliament: A Response to the Strathclyde Review* (HL 116 2015–16). Data for the House of Lords is only available from the 2004–05 Parliamentary session.

chambers and committees of the Commons and Lords. Three points should be noted. First, Commons Committees debate more SIs than any other forum. Second, far more SIs are debated in the Lords Chamber than the Commons Chamber. Third, the number of SIs debated by the Lords Grand Committee has been increasing. Overall, the Lords debates more SIs than the Commons—and this suggests that the Lords is a more effective scrutiniser of secondary legislation than the Commons.

Another way to compare the work of the two Houses is to consider the amount of time spent in the chambers of both Houses debating SIs. Figure 4.12 shows the hours spent in both the Commons and Lords Chambers and the Lords Grand Committee debating SIs. Again, three points arise. First, the Lords Grand Committee has spent the most—and an increasing—amount of time debating SIs, suggesting that it provides more in-depth scrutiny. Second, the Lords Chamber has spent more time debating SIs than the Commons Chamber. Third, the amount of time spent debating SIs in the Commons Chamber has declined.

Both Houses have the same blunt mechanism for scrutinising delegated legislation: a vote to annul. Neither House can amend delegated legislation. As the elected chamber, the House of Commons has an unlimited *constitutional* power to veto delegated legislation, but its *political* power to do so is almost entirely conditioned by the dominance of the government. Accordingly, very few SIs are rejected by the Commons: 'The last time the Commons rejected an instrument was in 1979, and it appears that that may have been a mistake.'[163]

Should the Commons do more? The answer might seem to be 'yes, of course'. At the same time, some political realism is needed. The government always has a majority.

---

[163] House of Lords Scrutiny of Secondary Legislation Committee, *Response to the Strathclyde Review: Effective Parliamentary Scrutiny of Secondary Legislation* (HL 128 2015–16), [46].

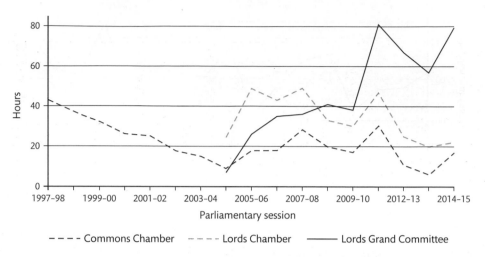

Figure 4.12 Parliamentary time spent debating SIs, 1997–2015

Source: House of Commons Library Briefing Paper and House of Lords Constitution Committee, *Delegated Legislation and Parliament: A Response to the Strathclyde Review* (HL 116 2015–16), appendix 1. Data for the House of Lords is only available from the 2004–05 Parliamentary session. Data for the length of time spent debating SIs by Commons Committees are unavailable. However, according to Fox and Blackwell, *The Devil is in the Detail: Parliament and Delegated Legislation* (2014), in the 2013–14 session, the average length of a Commons Committee SI debate was 26 minutes; the shortest debate was 22 seconds.

Further, MPs have many demands placed upon them in addition to their own personal political ambitions and outside interests. Scrutinising secondary legislation is a politically unrewarding activity. To suppose that MPs will willingly devote more time to this is, at best, a triumph of hope over experience.

As regards the House of Lords, it is clear that the Lords can reject an SI. The Parliament Acts do not apply to delegated legislation.[164] Delegated legislation rejected by the Lords cannot have effect even if approved by the Commons. However, under a much-debated and contentious convention, the unelected chamber only exercises this power in exceptional circumstances. In practice, the Lords has rejected secondary legislation more frequently than the Commons. Since 1968, the House of Lords has defeated the government on six motions relating to five SIs. Figure 4.13 shows the number of SIs subject to divisions (votes) on fatal motions in the House of Lords 1997–2016. Add this to the higher number of SIs considered in the Lords Chamber and the Lords Grand Committee (Figure 4.11), and there is a widely held view that the Lords scrutinises secondary legislation more effectively than the Commons.

The number of SIs rejected by the Lords hardly represents a massive constraint upon government. Nonetheless, such is the intense sensitivity of the issue that even a single rejection of secondary legislation by the House of Lords can instigate major constitutional stress. The government's instinctive mode of thought is always that it—and it alone—must govern, subject to parliamentary *approval*. Parliamentary

---

[164] On the Parliament Acts, see Chapter 5, section 3.3.3.

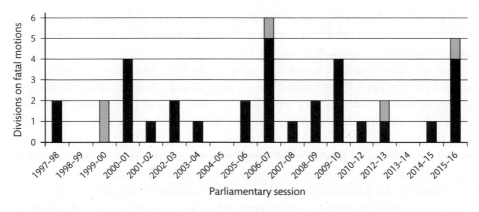

Figure 4.13 SIs subject to divisions on fatal motions in the House of Lords, 1997–2016

Source: House of Lords Constitution Committee, *Delegated Legislation and Parliament: A Response to the Strathclyde Review* (HL 116 2015–16), appendix 1.

disapproval is rarely envisaged by the government, let alone welcomed. Consequently, interference by unelected peers is perceived as either misguided amateurism or illegitimate interference.

In October 2015, the relatively obscure issue of the Lords' role in scrutinising secondary legislation was suddenly propelled into the political limelight. The government had introduced an SI to reduce significantly the amount of money received through tax credits by people on low incomes—a major policy change that would have reduced public spending by a few billion pounds and hit poor families hard. The government had argued that this concerned financial privilege and was therefore a matter exclusively for the Commons. Nonetheless, the Lords voted down the SI. This forced the government into a policy U-turn. The government also established the Strathclyde Review to review the power of the Lords. This concluded that the Lords convention on secondary legislation had been stretched to breaking point by the Lords' vote. Strathclyde advanced three options. Option 1 would remove the Lords from secondary legislation procedure altogether; option 2 would entail the reframing of the convention governing the exercise of the power of the Lords so that the 'veto is left unused'; and, option 3—the preferred option—would create a new statutory procedure which would remove the power of the Lords to reject an instrument but would allow the Lords to invite the Commons to 'think again' in an unspecified way.[165] The proposal was criticised on the ground that it was a hasty overreaction that missed the wider issue of inadequate Parliamentary scrutiny of delegated legislation. Further, 'given that the House of Commons is controlled by the Government, the effect of the three Strathclyde options would be to tilt power away from Parliament towards Government.'[166] In November 2016, the government announced that it would not

---

[165] *Strathclyde Review: Secondary Legislation and the Primacy of the House of Commons* (Cm 9177 2015).

[166] House of Lords Delegated and Regulatory Reform Committee, *Special Report: Response to the Strathclyde Review* (HL 119 2015–16), p 3. See also House of Lords Scrutiny of Secondary Legislation

proceed with changes proposed by the Strathclyde Review. However, the government noted that it could rethink its position if the Lords 'misused' its power to block secondary legislation, especially in light of Brexit.

The episode exemplifies a wider paradox of the UK constitution: to what extent should we rely upon the unelected chamber to remedy insufficient scrutiny by the government-dominated elected chamber? To counter the government-dominated Commons, scrutiny must be undertaken by the Lords, but this House is unelected and therefore vulnerable to criticism. What is the answer? An idealistic solution would be to advocate fundamental constitutional reform—for instance, an elected second chamber. But, the power to achieve such reform rests almost entirely with the government, which has a huge vested interest in maintaining the status quo.

Constitutional reform only tends to occur when it serves the interests of the governing party. Accordingly, 'proposals for constitutional reform are often the poetry of the politically impotent'; many such proposals lose their allure when power is gained.[167] The upshot is that the normal state of affairs of the core UK constitution is an ongoing constitutional paralysis in which concessions have to be wrenched reluctantly from the government through a political struggle, unless the reforms in question are ones that the government is willingly prepared to undertake.

4.2.7 Judicial review

The courts are able to intervene (provided that a litigant pursues the matter) if executive lawmakers exceed the powers granted to them by Parliament. Most obviously, courts can step in if the executive, when making secondary legislation, fails to do things that Parliament has indicated must be done if the legislation is to be valid (or at least enforceable). Courts are also willing to go beyond the plain words of the parent Act by reading implied restrictions into provisions conferring lawmaking powers upon the executive. For example, when the Home Secretary attempted to use a statutory power to make delegated legislation precluding subsistence payments to certain categories of asylum seeker, it was held that he had exceeded his powers: Simon Brown LJ, in the *JCWI* case, said that the secondary legislation in question, if it were allowed to stand, would reduce the asylum seekers to whom it applied to 'a life so destitute that to my mind no civilised nation can tolerate it'.[168] Parliament, said his Lordship, must be assumed not to have intended to authorise Ministers to make secondary legislation that would bring about such a state of affairs.[169]

Judicial review of delegated legislation often involves a balance between wider policy considerations, respect for Parliament, and legality. On the one hand, Lord Sumption

---

Committee, *Response to the Strathclyde Review: Effective Parliamentary Scrutiny of Secondary Legislation* (HL 128 2015–16); House of Lords Constitution Committee, *Delegated Legislation and Parliament: A Response to the Strathclyde Review* (HL 116 2015–16).

[167] Mount, p 2.

[168] *R v Secretary of State for Social Security, ex p Joint Council for the Welfare of Immigrants* [1997] 1 WLR 275, 292. In fact, this decision was, to a substantial effect, reversed by Parliament: see Nationality, Immigration and Asylum Act 2002, s 55.

[169] See also *R v Lord Chancellor, ex p Witham* [1998] QB 575.

has noted that 'when a statutory instrument has been reviewed by Parliament, respect for Parliament's constitutional function calls for considerable caution before the courts will hold it to be unlawful on some ground (such as irrationality) which is within the ambit of Parliament's review'.[170] This point applies especially to SIs founded on considerations of general policy. On the other hand, delegated legislation does not attract the same immunity from challenge in the courts that Acts of Parliament enjoy. This is because an SI is made by a Minister (or other decision-maker) who is given limited power by the enabling Act to make it. Furthermore, the courts possess the jurisdiction to determine the legality of an SI even if it has been approved by both Houses of Parliament under the affirmative resolution procedure.[171] The courts can then strike down delegated legislation, but this does not occur frequently.

4.3 Prerogative powers

So far, we have been concerned with general statutory powers and statutory powers to enact delegated legislation. However, certain important executive powers take the form of prerogative—or common law—rather than statutory powers. At one time, the prerogative was the principal legal means by which government was carried on. However, whenever Parliament enacts a statute conferring power on the executive, any prerogative power with which it overlaps is supplanted.[172] Gradually, the metaphorical ocean of prerogative power shrank as islands and later larger land masses of statutory power grew up;[173] today, the vast array of statutory powers that exist means that the prerogative remains only in the form of isolated pockets of power. But those remaining pockets are important. Among the things that Parliament has never authorised the executive to do—and which therefore remain the preserve of prerogative power—are the declaration of war, the disposition of the armed forces, the signing of treaties,[174] the granting of mercy and of honours, the issuing of passports, and the conduct of international relations. For public lawyers, the fact that such matters remain the subject of prerogative—rather than of statutory—power is of interest for two reasons.

First, the exercise of prerogative powers, unlike the exercise of statutory powers, was traditionally not subject to judicial review. This was regarded, at least by some writers, as strong grounds for objecting to the existence of the prerogative. However, as we explain in Chapter 13, the position has now changed, and the exercise of most prerogative powers can generally be examined by the courts in much the same way as the use of statutory powers.

Second, notwithstanding that their use is now amenable to judicial scrutiny, prerogative powers may be regarded as objectionable at a more fundamental level. In

---

[170] *Bank Mellat v HM Treasury (No 2)* [2013] UKSC 39 [44].

[171] *R (Javed) v Secretary of State for the Home Department* [2002] QB 129, 153, *per* Lord Phillips MR.

[172] See further Chapter 13, section 2.2.2.

[173] Nolan and Sedley, *The Making and Remaking of the British Constitution* (London 1997), p 15.

[174] Although still founded in the prerogative, this power is now subject to statutory regulation that gives Parliament the right to veto the UK's entering into treaty obligations: Constitutional Reform and Governance Act 2010, Pt 2.

considering these matters further, it is helpful to distinguish between two rather different forms of prerogative power. We have already considered the *monarch's personal prerogatives* concerning such matters as the appointment of Prime Ministers and the conferral of royal assent upon Bills (without which they cannot become law). In these matters, the monarch is directly—personally—involved. Viewed in such baldly legal terms, the monarch appears to enjoy considerable powers and to occupy a role that is at odds with democratic principle. However, we saw earlier in this chapter that the exercise of these prerogatives is heavily regulated by convention. In this way, political practice supplements the legal constitution, producing a 'real' constitution that is markedly less anachronistic than the purely legal position implies.

> **Q** Would it be better if the monarch were stripped of these powers, so as to remove any impression that she has a say in relation to such questions as who should lead the government? If so, how should the answers to such questions be determined instead?

Alongside the monarch's personal prerogatives, we find a wider set of *executive prerogative powers*. Into this category fall the powers mentioned at the beginning of this section, including the declaration of war and the signing of treaties. As noted, the prerogative is effectively a residual power: to the extent that it exists today, it is what remains of the power that monarchs used in earlier times to govern the country. However, it is not only the width of the prerogative that has changed over the centuries as statute has gradually encroached. Save in relation to her personal prerogatives, the general position is that, as Markesinis has observed, what we used to call the *royal* prerogative is today 'to all intents and purposes [a] government or even prime ministerial prerogative'.[175] In other words, while prerogative power belongs, in constitutional theory, to the monarch, who has been said to have the rights 'to be consulted', 'to encourage', and 'to warn',[176] the exercise of executive prerogative powers is essentially a matter for the government of the day. This raises the question whether it is acceptable in a twenty-first-century liberal democracy for that branch of government to be endowed with common law powers that have not been conferred by, and which have therefore not been the subject of debate in or restriction by, Parliament. Such a situation might be thought to be profoundly undemocratic.[177] For instance, following the Brexit referendum vote in 2016, the UK government has proposed to use its prerogative powers to trigger the process of leaving the European Union without direct Parliamentary approval. This has caused great controversy. Many MPs, including some who campaigned to leave the European Union, have argued that the House of Commons must be able to debate and approve the process by which the UK leaves the European Union and that it should not be left entirely to the government.

---

[175] Markesinis, 'The Royal Prerogative Revisited' [1973] CLJ 287, 288.

[176] Bagehot, *The English Constitution* (London 1968), p 111.

[177] For critical views of the prerogative, see Institute of Public Policy Research, *The Constitution of the United Kingdom* (London 1991); Styrett, 'Prerogative Powers: New Labour's Forgotten Constitutional Reforms?' [1998] Denning Law Journal 111.

The basic problem here is that it is extremely difficult for Parliament to hold Ministers to account for decisions taken under the prerogative—according to former Prime Minister John Major, it is 'for individual Ministers to decide on a particular occasion whether and how to report to Parliament on the exercise of prerogative powers'.[178] It is also felt by some to be objectionable that the scope of the prerogative is unclear: Ministers have said that it would be impossible to produce a precise list of prerogative powers.[179] We note (in passing for now, although we return to this point in Chapter 13) that this lack of transparency is also problematic in terms of judicial review of decisions taken under the prerogative: in a recent case, the House of Lords divided three–two on whether a power to expel an indigenous population from a British colony *existed*.[180]

An obvious response to criticism of the prerogative is that Parliament could, if it wished, abolish any prerogative powers it regarded as objectionable, replacing them, if it desired, with more limited statutory powers. The fact that certain prerogatives remain may, on this view, be taken to imply that Parliament is content with such a state of affairs. However, the view that at least some prerogatives should be replaced with statutory powers is now gaining ground—including within Parliament. In an influential report in 2004, the Public Administration Select Committee recommended that the government should compile a comprehensive list of prerogative powers and that legislation should then be enacted putting certain powers, where appropriate, on a statutory footing.[181] It appears that three policy considerations lay behind these recommendations. First, the Committee thought it objectionable that—as Brazier puts it—the government should possess 'imprecise powers'; instead, Ministers should be able to identify the 'nature and extent of their powers'.[182] Second, transparency was felt to be important not only as an end in itself, but also as a means by which to make possible the effective parliamentary supervision of executive action. The Committee pointed out that 'because Parliament does not know what Ministers are empowered to do until they have done it, Parliament cannot properly hold government to account'.[183] Third, the Committee wished to see limitations placed on certain prerogative powers—for example, it felt strongly that decisions to engage in armed conflict should not be made without the consent of Parliament.[184]

Ministers were persuaded by at least the general thrust of some of these arguments. In 2007, the government said that 'in general the prerogative powers should be put onto a statutory basis and brought under stronger parliamentary scrutiny and control'.[185] As a result, legislation has recently been enacted placing the organisation of the Civil Service on a statutory footing and introducing statutory regulation of the government's treaty-making powers.[186]

---

[178] HC Deb, vol 220, col 19W (1 March 1993).

[179] House of Commons Public Administration Select Committee, *Taming the Prerogative: Strengthening Ministerial Accountability to Parliament* (HC 422 2003–04).

[180] *R (Bancoult) v Secretary of State for Foreign and Commonwealth Affairs* [2008] UKHL 61, [2009] 1 AC 453.

[181] *Taming the Prerogative*.

[182] *Taming the Prerogative*, p 24.

[183] *Taming the Prerogative*, p 17.   [184] *Taming the Prerogative*, p 16.

[185] Ministry of Justice, *The Governance of Britain* (Cm 7170 2007), pp 15–17.

[186] Constitutional Reform and Governance Act 2010, Pts 1 and 2.

One particular issue concerns whether the prerogative power to deploy the armed forces in conflict ought to be put on a statutory basis. Calls for such a law have grown after military interventions in Iraq, Afghanistan, and Libya. In 2011, the government acknowledged that 'a convention has developed in the House [of Commons] that before troops are committed, the House should have an opportunity to debate the matter'.[187] This convention would be observed except in an emergency. The coalition government had stated that it was minded to put this prerogative power on a statutory basis. However, in 2016, the government announced a change of mind: the prerogative power to commit armed forces in conflict would not be put into statute—nor would the convention of a prior Commons debate be codified or put into a resolution of the House. The government's rationale was the need to retain the ability of the government and the armed forces to protect the security and interests of the UK in circumstances that cannot be predicted, and to avoid such decisions becoming subject to legal action.[188]

> **Q** Would abolishing or converting all prerogative powers into statutory powers be a good idea? What would be the advantages and disadvantages of doing so?

4.4 'Third source powers'

Legal scholars disagree about the precise definition of the prerogative.[189] Dicey argued that '[e]very act which the executive government can lawfully do without the authority of an Act of Parliament is done in virtue of . . . [the] prerogative',[190] whereas Blackstone thought the prerogative to be 'singular and eccentrical', comprising only 'those rights and capacities which the King enjoys alone, in contradistinction to others, and not . . . those which he enjoys in common with any of his subjects'.[191] The subject of this disagreement is therefore the sort of things that ordinary people can do (eg enter into contracts). Do such acts—when committed by the executive—fall under the prerogative? And, if not, how do we account for the fact that the executive can do such things? The disagreement between Blackstone and Dicey relates principally to the first of these questions. For Dicey, anything done by the government not under statutory power—including things that individuals can do—must be done under the prerogative; Blackstone confined the prerogative to those things that only the executive can do, such as sign treaties. What, then, of situations in which the government wishes to commit acts that an individual could lawfully commit, but in which it does not have statutory power to do so?

---

[187] HC Deb, vol 524, col 1066 (10 March 2011) (Leader of the House of Commons, Sir George Young MP).
[188] HC Deb, vol 608, col 11WS (18 April 2016) (Michael Fallon MP, Secretary of State for Defence).
[189] See generally Harris, 'The "Third Source" of Authority for Government Action' (1992) 108 LQR 626 and 'The "Third Source" of Authority for Government Action Revisited' (2007) 123 LQR 225.
[190] *An Introduction to the Study of the Law of the Constitution* (London 1964), p 425.
[191] *Commentaries on the Laws of England* (Oxford 1765), vol 1, p 239.

It may be that if the government is unable to point to a specific statutory or prerogative power, it is simply not able lawfully to act. But this view is strongly counter-intuitive. It is clearly impossible for the government to point to a specific power in relation to *everything* it does—ordering paper clips being the standard example—and yet it would be ridiculous to suggest that, in the absence of a specific power, the government may not lawfully do such things.

It might therefore be preferable to accept that Dicey was right all along: the prerogative should be construed widely, as including not only special governmental powers such as to declare war, but also as authorising the government to do that which everyone else can do. The courts have, on the whole, tended to prefer—or at least to assume the correctness of—Dicey's definition. For example, on more than one occasion, it has been judicially taken for granted that government schemes (not established under statute) to compensate victims of crime must have been set up under the prerogative, notwithstanding that any sufficiently wealthy individual could establish such a scheme.[192] Yet this view is problematic. As Wade has pointed out, there is nothing 'prerogative' about the government doing such things: it can do them 'because any one and every one can do them, and it has no need of "singular and eccentrical" power for the purpose'.[193] The better view, therefore, is that, as Lloyd LJ put it, 'the term "prerogative" should be confined to those powers which are unique to the Crown'.[194]

How, then, are we to account for the fact that the government does many things for which it has no specific statutory authorisation and no prerogative power (unless we are prepared to accept Dicey's overly broad definition of the prerogative)? Our response to this question depends on which of the two rival views of the government's legal and constitutional position is to be preferred.

The first view, set out by Laws J in the *Fewings* case, is that whereas individuals 'may do anything . . . which the law does not prohibit', the 'opposite' rule applies to public bodies: anything that they do 'must be justified by positive law'.[195] The principal argument in favour of this view is that considerations of transparency and legal certainty require that the government's powers should be enumerated, and that it should have no capacity to do anything not permitted by its enumerated powers. However, two difficulties arise. It would, in practice, be impossible to anticipate everything that the government might wish to do, and there would therefore need to be a conferral of a very general power upon the government that would hardly advance the interests of legal certainty and transparency. Moreover, Laws J's view that a special rule (requiring positive authorisation for everything) applies to 'public bodies' introduces practical difficulties: UK constitutional law is not predicated on a clear conception of the state, and it is therefore unclear to whom Laws J's special rule would apply.

---

[192] *R v Criminal Injuries Compensation Board, ex p Lain* [1967] 2 QB 864; *R v Secretary of State for the Home Department, ex p Fire Brigades Union* [1995] 2 AC 513.

[193] 'Procedure and Prerogative in Public Law' (1985) 101 LQR 180, 191.

[194] *R v Panel on Takeovers and Mergers, ex p Datafin plc* [1987] QB 815, 848.

[195] *R v Somerset County Council, ex p Fewings* [1995] 1 All ER 513, 524. See also the comments of Sir Thomas Bingham MR in the same case in the Court of Appeal: [1995] 1 WLR 1037, 1042.

The alternative view—and, it is submitted, the better one—is that everyone (including the government) may do anything that is not unlawful. This position was endorsed by Carnwath LJ in *Shrewsbury and Atcham Borough Council v Secretary of State for Communities and Local Government*,[196] when he said that executive powers 'are not confined to those conferred by statute or prerogative, but extend, subject to any relevant statutory or public law constraints, and to the competing rights of other parties, to anything which could be done by a natural person'. The government's freedom to do anything that is not unlawful constitutes what Harris calls the 'third source' of government power, alongside statutory and prerogative powers.[197] As Lord Sumption has noted: 'It has long been recognised that the Crown possesses some general administrative powers to carry on the ordinary business of government which are not exercises of the royal prerogative and do not require statutory authority'.[198]

The extent of such 'third source' powers and their precise juridical basis are controversial. One aspect of such 'third source' powers is the so-called 'Ram doctrine', which has been interpreted as enabling Ministers, as representatives of the Crown, to do anything that a natural person may do except if prohibited by statute.[199] However, it has been argued that this approach misinterprets the Ram memorandum, in which the doctrine was set out, and embodies a legal fallacy. The Lords Constitution Committee has noted that the Ram memorandum is not an accurate reflection of the law today. In addition to statutory restraints, Ministers' ability to exercise common law powers is constrained by the public law limitations on government action as enforced through judicial review, human rights law, and the pre-existing rights and significant interests of private persons. For the Committee, the description of the common law powers of the Crown encapsulated by the phrase 'the Ram doctrine' is inaccurate, and should no longer be used.[200]

The main objection to the existence of a 'third source' of governmental power is that it appears to concede wide, almost infinite, powers to the government. For example, it was held in *Malone* that the government could lawfully listen into telephone conversations because no law prevented this.[201] However, properly understood, the difficulty highlighted by *Malone* is not with the idea of third source powers, but simply that, when it was decided, English law did not make it unlawful to invade people's privacy. Had there been such a law, the government, lacking specific legal powers to tap telephones, would have been acting unlawfully in doing so. The position, therefore, is that the government may do anything that is not unlawful. What that means in effect is that anything that it does must either (i) not be prohibited by the general

---

[196] [2008] EWCA Civ 148, [44].

[197] See 'The "Third Source" of Authority for Government Action' and 'The "Third Source" of Authority for Government Action Revisited'. See also *Malone v Metropolitan Police Commissioner* [1979] Ch 344, 367.

[198] *R (New London College) v Secretary of State for the Home Department* [2013] UKSC 51, [28].

[199] The Ram memorandum, 2 November 1945. See also Lester and Weait, 'The Use of Ministerial Powers Without Parliamentary Authority: The Ram Doctrine' [2003] PL 415.

[200] House of Lords Constitution Committee, *The Pre-emption of Parliament* (HL 165 2012–13), [50]–[65].

[201] *Malone v Metropolitan Police Commissioner*; cf *Malone v United Kingdom* (1985) 7 EHRR 14, in which the European Court of Human Rights found that there had been a breach of Art 8 of the European Convention on Human Rights. See now Pt 1 of the Regulation of Investigatory Powers Act 2000.

law applicable to individuals; or (ii) if it is contrary to the general law, be permitted by reference to specific statutory or prerogative powers. For example, agents of the state may only lawfully enter onto private property to carry out a search in relation to a criminal investigation provided that there is positive authority in law to justify such conduct (which would otherwise constitute trespass to land). Similarly, the government can only imprison certain convicted criminals and deport certain foreign nationals because statute law allows it to do these things (that would otherwise constitute, among other things, trespass to the person).

4.5 **Contractual power**

Finally, we should mention the role that contractual power occupies in relation to the executive. It is important to begin by noting that such power is functionally different from statutory and prerogative powers. As Figure 4.14 shows, Acts of Parliament and the prerogative have the effect of *empowering* the executive to do certain things. This notion of empowerment may be resolved into two component elements.

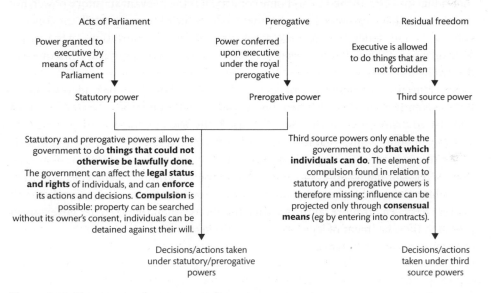

Figure 4.14 Three types of governmental power

First, Acts of Parliament and the prerogative constitute a *source of authority*, in that they make it possible for the government lawfully to do things that could not otherwise be lawfully done. For example, it is generally unlawful to erect buildings without planning permission. Such permission—the effect of which is to render lawful construction that would otherwise be unlawful—cannot be granted except by those governmental bodies that are statutorily authorised to do so. The relevant legislation therefore empowers such bodies to do that which they could not otherwise do—that is, to grant planning permission.

Second, statutory and prerogative powers constitute a *means by which the government may get things done, project influence, and implement policy*. This follows because its decision whether (and, if so, how) to exercise its statutory and prerogative powers will produce legal consequences—which may, in turn, produce practical consequences. For example, if the government decides that planning permission for a particular project should be granted subject to certain conditions (eg as to the height of the building) that the developer goes on to flout, the latter will thereby act unlawfully; enforcement action may be taken that might culminate in the punishment (eg the imposition of fines) upon those responsible for carrying on the unauthorised building work. The fact that such consequences may ensue incentivises compliance with the terms of the original decision, thus underlining the capacity of decisions taken under statutory (or prerogative) powers to project influence, further the government's policy objectives (eg of not allowing tall buildings in architecturally sensitive areas), and so on.

Contractual power exists only in the latter, not the former, sense—that is, it does not constitute a source of authority; it is merely a means by which the government may seek to secure objectives and implement policies that it is already allowed to pursue. For example, to implement a statutorily authorised decision to deport a failed asylum seeker, the government may enter into a contract with an airline so that the individual may be returned to his home country. It is the relevant statutory power, not the contract, that *empowers* the government to have the person deported; the contract with the airline merely *facilitates* the statutorily authorised deportation—it is a means of ensuring that the decision taken under statute produces the practical consequences desired by the government.

Nevertheless, the importance of contractual power should not be underestimated. It is frequently used by government bodies today, and is an important tool by which modern government is carried out.[202] Indeed, the use of contracts by government as a way of doing things that it is required or permitted to do is now commonplace. It has always been necessary—as in the example given of the deportation of an asylum seeker—for public bodies to enter into contracts to fulfil certain aspects of their legal obligations and execute certain decisions. However, the contracting out of such matters has been far more common since the 1980s, when the Thatcher government procured the enactment of legislation *requiring* local authorities to put the provision of many services out to tender.

5. Conclusions

The executive occupies a pivotal role in the UK constitution. The absence of any absolute separation of powers between the legislative and executive branches places the latter in a strong position. The executive has considerable powers at its disposal and is strongly situated to obtain, via the enactment of primary legislation, further legal powers on favourable terms. There are, in effect, three possible responses to this state of affairs. First, we might not regard it as problematic: we might think that the fact that the government has to submit to elections every five years provides an adequate safeguard against, or corrective

---

[202] See generally Harden, *The Contracting State* (Buckingham 1992).

in the event of, misuse of power. Second, we might advocate radical constitutional change, perhaps arguing that the UK should embrace a more full-blooded version of the separation of powers doctrine, such that the executive and the legislature are rendered more distinct. Under such arrangements, the executive might be less capable of getting Parliament to confer powers on it (or at least on the terms that it desires) and Parliament might be better able to hold the executive to account. Third, we might opt to steer a middle course, recognising that, in practice, such radical change is unlikely, instead seeking to rely upon—and where necessary improve—existing systems such that the executive is held to account in a more rigorous fashion. If such an approach is to be pursued, then Parliament must play a central role. It is to Parliament that we turn in Chapter 5.

Expert commentary
Why constitutional lawyers should be interested in the executive
Alan Page, Professor of Public Law, University of Dundee

The executive is a surprisingly neglected area of constitutional law scholarship. The concentration is much more on Parliament and the courts than on the executive. A number of reasons may be suggested for this, including the excessive secrecy which was for a long time the hallmark of British government. Another reason, when it comes to the inner workings of the executive, is the apparent absence of 'real' law. For lawyers who are only interested in the law as laid down by Parliament or the courts, there is on the face of it relatively little to be discussed.

And yet, as the chapter emphasises, the executive is the central actor in our constitutional arrangements. It is through the executive that the actual business of government is carried on. It is to the executive we look to control immigration, to tackle failing hospitals, to rescue banks, and to get us out of recession. If we are to arrive at a proper understanding of our constitutional arrangements therefore it seems unlikely that we can do so without an understanding of the executive and where it fits into those arrangements. Without that understanding we are always likely to labour under an incomplete picture.

There is a further reason for constitutional lawyers to be interested in the executive and that is the recognition that the parliamentary and judicial controls that are our stock-in-trade depend, for their effectiveness, on the executive's ability to control itself. That it does indeed possess that ability we tend to take for granted, but without it the strictures of Parliament and the courts would be unlikely to have much impact.

In *The Executive in the Constitution*,[203] Terence Daintith and I set out to explore the controls the executive applies to itself and the relationship between those controls and the parliamentary and judicial controls more familiar to the constitutional lawyer. The starting point was an article intriguingly titled 'Can Government Regulate Itself?'[204] in which, after reviewing a catalogue of government failures, two American political scientists suggested that it might be easier for public agencies to change the behaviour of private actors than that of other public agencies.

There is no question that the control by government of itself is an enterprise that is fraught with difficulty. As the third section of the chapter illustrates, we are not talking about a single, unified organisation but a multiplicity of organisations—departments, executive agencies, non-departmental public bodies, or quangos, not to mention those organisations or bodies outside government to which functions may be entrusted.

---

[203] (Oxford 1999).   [204] Wilson and Rachal (1977) 46 The Public Interest 3.

The most important of these bodies, the basic building block of the executive branch, is the ministerial department. It is in the department, or rather the ministerial head of the department, normally the Secretary of State, rather than the government as a whole, that the functions of government are normally vested; it is to departments that budgets are allocated; it is departments that account to Parliament for the use of public money; it is departments that are subject of judicial review proceedings.

Properly analysed, the problem thus becomes one of the coordination and control of a number of departments of equal authority. A feature of the departmental system is that no department has the power to give directions to another—whose political heads are members of the executive's supreme decision-making body, the Cabinet, and thus well placed to resist attempts to interfere with those matters for which (so traditional constitutional doctrine tells us) they and they alone are accountable to Parliament.

The 'solution' that has been devised has been to treat 'compliance' as an essentially cooperative endeavour, as a matter first and foremost for departments, but subject to the overall coordination and control of the 'centre' either in the shape of the Cabinet Office or more commonly the Treasury. The strength of this system is that it places responsibility for compliance firmly on the shoulders of departments; their sense of responsibility is not diminished as a result of responsibility being seen to lie elsewhere. Its weakness is that it is vulnerable to non-compliance, which is why trust within government has never been total but has been buttressed by various forms of oversight such as that exercised over Civil Service recruitment by the Civil Service Commission or over the use of public money by the former Exchequer and Audit Department and now the National Audit Office.

In terms of the agenda of internal coordination and control, two matters in particular have always been prominent—expenditure and staffing; the former in the exercise of the Treasury's 'ancient authority' over financial resources, the latter originally as part of the same system of control but since the 1960s as a separate system of control in its own right. The Civil Service has recently been put on a statutory basis by the Constitutional Reform and Governance Act 2010, but the core Civil Service values remain unchanged—selection on merit on the basis of fair and open competition, loyalty, integrity and honesty, objectivity and impartiality.[205]

What, however, of legality and democratic accountability, which are likely to rank more highly among the day-to-day concerns of constitutional lawyers? Here we are faced with an interesting contrast. Traditionally, government ran its legal services rather like those of a very loosely structured conglomerate in which each subsidiary had its own firm of solicitors who might—or might not—consult head office lawyers when things got difficult. That is changing as a result of European law and the European Convention on Human Rights, and the rise of judicial review. The basic structure remains decentralised, but legal advice has become much more coordinated and integrated into policymaking over the last 30 years.

Democratic accountability by contrast remains largely uncoordinated. With the principal exception of accountability for the use of public money, it is treated essentially as a matter for departments. As a result the priority attached to parliamentary demands may vary from department to department. That the executive does not always speak and act with one voice is a persistent source of confusion and frustration for parliamentarians, but it is a reflection of the executive's dominance of the legislature and the lower priority attached as a consequence to parliamentary demands.

---

[205] Constitutional Reform and Governance Act 2010, ss 5 and 10.

Further reading

DAINTITH and PAGE, *The Executive in the Constitution* (Oxford 1999)
This book is the leading analysis of the constitutional position of the UK government.

FOSTER, 'Cabinet Government in the Twentieth Century' (2004) 67 MLR 753
This paper analyses developments in the position and role of the Cabinet.

McHARG, 'Reforming the United Kingdom Constitution: Law, Convention, Soft Law' (2008) 71 MLR 853
This interesting paper examines constitutional conventions.

Useful websites

https://www.gov.uk/
The website of the UK government

https://www.gov.uk/government/organisations/prime-ministers-office-10-downing-street
The website of 10 Downing Street

https://www.gov.uk/government/organisations/cabinet-office
The Cabinet Office website

http://www.civilservice.gov.uk
The Civil Service website

https://www.gov.uk/government/uploads/system/uploads/attachment_data/file/579752/ministerial_code_december_2016.pdf
The Ministerial Code

5

The UK Parliament

1.	Introduction	166
2.	Parliament: an overview	167
3.	Parliament and democracy	168
4.	Parliamentary privilege	200
5.	Parliament and the legislative process	211
6.	Parliament's powers	228
7.	Concluding remarks	253
	Expert commentary	253
	Further reading	255
	Useful websites	256

1. Introduction

This chapter concerns Parliament—that is, the UK Parliament, which meets in the Palace of Westminster in London.[1] We focus on four principal issues.

First, the *democratic credentials* of Parliament. It is trite to state that Parliament is a democratic institution, but what exactly does this mean? Who sits in Parliament? How do they get there? And is the form of democracy that the UK Parliament can lay claim to a satisfactory one? Second, *parliamentary privilege*, that is, the rights and immunities that Parliament needs to function effectively. What rights and immunities does Parliament have and what is their constitutional significance? Third, *Parliament's legislative role*. What is the contribution of Parliament to the making of legislation and what does this tell us about the relationship between Parliament and the executive government? Fourth, we examine *Parliament's powers*. In constitutional theory at least, Parliament is 'sovereign', meaning its legal powers are unlimited. We consider why this is, whether it is acceptable, and whether the notion of parliamentary sovereignty remains accurate today.

---

[1] The Scottish Parliament and the Northern Ireland and Welsh Assemblies are considered in Chapter 7.

In this chapter, we encounter two of our key themes. First, there is *Parliament's role in holding the executive government to account*. We look at the accountability of the executive to Parliament in Chapter 10, but Parliament's lawmaking function itself raises questions about Parliament's capacity to hold the executive to account. Second, there are questions concerning *the relationship between legal and political forms of constitutionalism*. We will see that, for all that the legal constitution allocates unlimited lawmaking power to Parliament, the political constitution imposes real limits upon Parliament's authority. We will ask whether it is right to leave that task to the political process, or whether the legal constitution should—or in fact already does—play a part in controlling Parliament's freedom to make law.

2. Parliament: an overview

Parliament is an institution that has evolved and developed over many centuries. Its evolution since the thirteenth century 'in the maelstrom of royal demands, baronial complaints, and feudal grievances had no single moment of conception'.[2] This chapter does not provide a parliamentary history.[3] But it is helpful to start with a brief overview of the present composition of Parliament (what is it made up of?) and its functions (what is Parliament for?). This is essential in order to understand how this institution works. Figure 5.1 sets out the composition of Parliament.

This figure contains many important and interesting features. First, we can see that Parliament comprises two Houses: the Commons and Lords. Second, the political membership of each House is divided between the governing party and opposition parties (in the Lords there are also crossbenchers, who are not affiliated to any political party). Third, we can see that the UK government is deeply embedded within Parliament. Fourth, both the governing party and opposition parties are divided between frontbenchers and backbenchers. The frontbenchers include both government and shadow Ministers (in the governing party and opposition parties respectively). There are also backbenchers in both the governing party and opposition parties: those Members of Parliament (MPs) in the Commons and members or peers

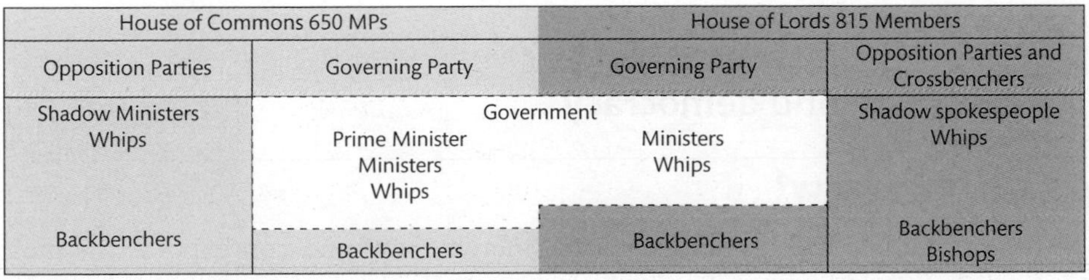

House of Commons 650 MPs		House of Lords 815 Members	
Opposition Parties	Governing Party	Governing Party	Opposition Parties and Crossbenchers
Shadow Ministers Whips	Government		Shadow spokespeople Whips
	Prime Minister Ministers Whips	Ministers Whips	
Backbenchers	Backbenchers	Backbenchers	Backbenchers Bishops

Figure 5.1 The UK Parliament

[2] Bryant, *Parliament* (London 2014), p 33.
[3] For an entertaining and accessible history, see Bryant.

House of Commons	House of Lords
• The elected chamber	• The second—unelected—chamber
• Comprised of 650 elected and salaried MPs (around 140 MPs are members of the government)	• Comprised of 815 appointed and unsalaried members (88 remaining hereditary peers, 701 life peers, and 26 bishops). Around 26 peers are in paid government posts
• UK government formed from a Commons majority	• Has no role in the formation of a government
• Overwhelming party political culture	• The culture of the Lords is less party political than the Commons; crossbenchers are non-party political
• Scrutiny: checks and challenges the work of the government through parliamentary questions, debates, and select committees	• Scrutiny: checks and scrutinises the work of the government through parliamentary questions, debates, and select committees
• Legislation: makes and changes laws, but in practice the government exerts considerable influence over legislation	• Legislation: the Lords acts as a revising chamber and can ask the Commons to think again. It can delay the passage of legislation
• Debates important issues, but much of the time MPs' behaviours in the Commons are ritualistic, pointscoring, and unproductive in terms of achieving policy improvements	• Debates important issues
• Financial privilege: the Commons checks and approves government spending	• Has very limited role as regards finance

Figure 5.2 The House of Commons and the House of Lords

in the Lords who are neither government Ministers nor shadow Ministers, but whose votes are relied upon by their respective frontbenches.

What is Parliament for? It has a number of different roles. Parliament is a democratic and representative institution. It gives the government political legitimacy through its majority in the Commons. It scrutinises government policy and administration. It is a forum for the perpetual election campaign between the parties. It holds debates and legislates. It enables the government to raise taxes and spend money. And MPs represent the interests and concerns of their constituents in the House of Commons and enable the redress of their grievances. Figure 5.2 compares aspects and roles of the Commons with those of the Lords.

It may help to refer back to these figures as we progress. We now turn to Parliament's democratic credentials.

3. Parliament and democracy

3.1 Why democracy?

The word 'democracy' is used in many different ways and contexts.[4] At its most basic, it describes a system in which the people have a decisive say over how and

---

[4] See Morison, 'Models of Democracy: From Representation to Participation?', in Jowell and Oliver (eds), *The Changing Constitution* (Oxford 2007).

by whom they are governed. This is most obviously so where the government is elected by the people. Democratic countries embrace the notion that no individual or group has any inherent right to govern, and that, instead, the people have the right to be governed as they wish. The antithesis of democratic government is dictatorship: a system in which a particular individual or group obtains or retains power without in any formal way securing public assent. All government, whether democratic or undemocratic, is ultimately about the exercise of power. The key difference between democracy and dictatorship is that the latter involves the naked exercise of power by those with the means and audacity to seize it and who rule by brute force rather than consent. By contrast, power in democracies is clothed in legitimacy through the existence of accepted systems for determining by whom, and on what terms, power should be wielded.

> **Q** Is dictatorship 'wrong'? Can you identify principled arguments (as opposed to relying on an instinctive reaction) to justify your answer?

It is possible to divide the main attractions of—and hence reasons for embracing—democratic government into two broad categories.

The first consists in deductions drawn from *a particular normative view of the human condition*, which holds that every individual should be recognised as autonomous and that all people are equally valuable in moral terms. Various consequences flow from this, one of which is that everyone should, in general, be allowed to make their own decisions about how they live their lives. At an individual level, this philosophy is institutionalised in many countries in human rights laws guaranteeing freedom of speech, religion, movement, and so on. But it would be impossible for everyone to do what they wanted (since people's wishes would conflict). Therefore, a system of government is required to provide a framework within which the autonomy of individuals can be reconciled with the existence of an ordered civil society in which people are able peacefully to coexist.

Nonetheless, recognition of the autonomy and dignity of individuals means that the system of government must enable people to have some say in how they are governed. When questions arise about whether one person's freedom (eg to protest by lying in the middle of a road) should be restricted for the benefit of another person (eg who wishes to drive down the road), democracy requires that they are resolved in a manner recognised as legitimate by the people collectively. In this way, the autonomy of the individual is translated into the autonomy of the people: the people collectively are free to order society in the way in which they see fit; they are also treated as equals.

The nineteenth-century English philosopher Mill argued that a person's interests 'are only secure from being disregarded' when he is 'able and habitually disposed to stand up for them'. The interests of the 'excluded'—that is, those who play no role in or have no influence over government—are, at the very least, 'always in danger of being overlooked'.[5] Accordingly, giving everyone a voice in the democratic process is the best way of ensuring people's interests are not overlooked and thereby recognising the equality of individuals.

Second, there are *practical reasons for preferring democratic government*. Giving people a 'voice in their own destiny' promotes the flourishing of individuals: it encourages intellectual endeavour and the development of 'moral capacities' by incentivising participation in the business of, and debate about, government.[6] Such participation in turn makes it likely that the society will be better governed. Harnessing the wisdom, insight, and experience of many people is more likely to produce good results than relying on the views of a few people.

> **Q** Not everyone shares this view. The philosopher Plato wrote that 'when a man is ill, whether he be rich or poor, to the physician he must go, and he who wants to be governed, to him who is able to govern'.[7] Although his argument was complex, its essence was that governing is a complicated business, that few people are qualified to do it, and that the masses might well be ill-equipped to identify such people. Do these arguments constitute a convincing case against democratic government?

Democracy can be implemented in different ways. Two can be noted. First, *representative democracy* involves selecting, through elections, people who will represent them and make decisions on their behalf and in the public interest. The benefit of representative democracy is that it enables people to vote for their representatives who reflect their views. However, the downside is that it reduces democracy to crossing a ballot paper once every five years or so.

Second, there is *participative democracy*. This entails forms of public participation in the governmental process beyond voting in elections. For instance, 'direct democracy' involves referendums on the more important changes in public policy and law before they take effect. More modest forms of participative democracy seek to ensure an ongoing dialogue—rather than one that exists only when elections loom—between the people and the government. For example, this could involve government supplying extensive information to the public before decisions are made, and obliging the government to consult the public and take its views into account.

In reality, many systems of government built on the representative notion of democracy also embrace aspects of participative democracy. In the UK, the election of MPs to Parliament is the most high-profile manifestation of democracy. Yet, the public is occasionally asked to vote on important constitutional changes in referendums, and more routinely informed about and consulted upon the development of public policy.[8]

---

[5] Mill, *Considerations on Representative Government* (New York 1862), ch 3.   [6] Mill, ch 3.

[7] *Republic*, ch VI.

[8] See further Ministry of Justice, *A National Framework for Greater Citizen Engagement* (London 2008).

Once we recognise that democracy exists in a range of different forms, it becomes apparent that the distinction drawn in this chapter between democracies and dictatorships is an ultimately arid one. Even an unelected government may exhibit vestiges of participative democracy by consulting people on certain matters or informally taking account of public sentiment. Such a system of government could not, however, reasonably claim to be democratic in a conventional sense. The more meaningful inquiry is not *whether* a country is democratic (yes/no), but rather what *degree* of democracy it possesses.

How democratic, then, is the UK?

3.2 Elections to the House of Commons

3.2.1 The point of general elections

The UK's most basic claim to be a democracy is that people can vote for MPs, who sit in the House of Commons in Parliament.[9] The UK is, then, a parliamentary democracy. Parliament is bicameral: it consists of two chambers. For the time being, we are concerned only with the House of Commons. The other chamber, the House of Lords, is considered in section 3.3.

General elections in the UK serve two functions. First, they determine membership of the House of Commons. Second, general elections determine which political party forms the government. Government Ministers are drawn from the party (or from a coalition of parties) with more than half of the seats in the Commons. General elections therefore determine the make-up of both the House of Commons and the government—the two are indissolubly linked. It is also crucial to note that political parties dominate UK politics. While electors vote for an independent candidate to be their MP, votes are cast on party lines. Traditionally, the two big parties—Conservatives and Labour—have dominated. However, over recent years, the political system is becoming more fragmented following devolution and the growth of smaller parties, as shown in Figure 5.3.

3.2.2 Calling a general election

General elections must be held every five years.[10] However, within that period, Prime Ministers were, until 2011, able to call an election whenever they wanted.[11] The absence of fixed-term Parliaments proved a double-edged sword for governments. It enabled them to hold an election at a time of their choosing, but also reflected the fact that government required the ongoing confidence of the House of Commons. The convention was that (on a simple majority) a vote of 'no confidence' in the government triggered the dissolution of Parliament and so a general election.

---

[9] And also, in Scotland, Members of the Scottish Parliament, Assembly Members for the Welsh Assembly, and Members of the Legislative Assembly for the Northern Ireland Assembly.

[10] Septennial Act 1715.

[11] See Marshall, *Constitutional Conventions* (Oxford 1987), ch 3; Blackburn, 'The Prerogative Power of Dissolution of Parliament: Law, Practice and Reform' [2009] PL 766.

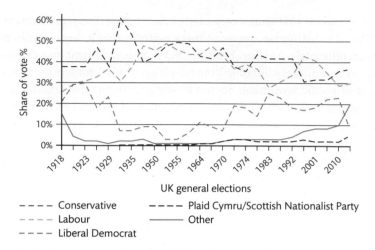

Figure 5.3 Share of the vote by party: UK General Elections, 1918–2015
Source: House of Commons Library Briefing Paper, *UK Election Statistics 1918–2015* (CBP7529 2016).

The 2010 election produced no overall majority for any party. A coalition government was then formed. Against this background, five-year fixed-term Parliaments were introduced. The Prime Minister lost the discretion to decide when to call an election. In principle, this is a good idea. There is no valid reason why the Prime Minister should have the power to determine the date of an election. But fixed-term Parliaments may raise practical difficulties. A government may lose the confidence of the Commons (whether through the break-up of a coalition or internal dissension within a single governing party) part-way through a Parliament. This suggests the need for an escape clause whereby an early election can be triggered to avoid the prospect of a 'lame duck' government unable to get its Bills enacted. On the other hand, retaining the traditional rule—whereby a simple majority on a no-confidence vote leads to dissolution—undermines the notion of fixed-term Parliaments. This is because a governing party or coalition, provided that it controlled more than half the seats in the Commons, would be able to engineer a vote of no confidence to trigger an election.[12] Similarly, a coalition partner could withdraw at any time and join with opposition parties to vote against the government, again triggering an election.

These issues were recognised during the passage of the Fixed-term Parliaments Act 2011. This Act provides that elections will normally happen at five-yearly intervals. An early election can be held in only one of two circumstances: if two-thirds of MPs support such a proposal or if the government loses (on a simple majority) a confidence vote and a new government—for example, through the formation of a (new) coalition—cannot be formed within 14 days. Under these arrangements, a government (unless it

---

[12] This issue has arisen elsewhere. See, eg Apel et al, 'The Decision of the German Federal Constitutional Court of 25 August 2005 Regarding the Dissolution of the National Parliament' (2005) 6 German Law Journal 1243.

had a substantial—ie two-thirds—majority) cannot directly trigger an early election. Although there is the option of engineering a vote of no confidence, an election would not automatically follow—other parties would first have the option of trying to work together to form a new government.

The move to fixed-term Parliaments has largely been welcomed. It is an important reduction of prime ministerial power that provides a platform of greater certainty for legislative, strategic, and financial planning by both Parliament and government.[13]

3.2.3 Voting and standing in elections

Genuine democracy calls for the widest possible involvement of the public. This requires that the widest possible range of people should be entitled to *stand for election* and to *vote in elections*. As regards standing for elections, UK citizens, citizens of the Republic of Ireland, and certain Commonwealth citizens may stand for election to the House of Commons provided they are over the age of 18 when nominated.[14] Certain people are expressly disqualified from membership of the House of Commons. They include many judges, civil servants, members of the armed forces and the police, and many public office-holders.[15] Members of the House of Lords are also disqualified from membership of the Commons,[16] as are bankrupts[17] and those convicted of corrupt or illegal practices committed in relation to an election.[18]

The entitlement to vote in parliamentary elections extends, subject to certain exceptions, to all UK and Irish and to certain Commonwealth citizens who are over the age of 18 and who have complied with the necessary formalities concerning registration.[19] The exceptions concern convicted criminals serving custodial sentences,[20] certain people who are detained for mental health reasons,[21] and those convicted of corrupt or illegal practices as mentioned in the previous paragraph.[22]

In general, these eligibility rules enable a wide range of people to participate in elections (both in terms of voting and standing for election). To the extent that the rules disbar certain categories of person from standing or voting, it is generally possible to identify rational justifications based on age, mental capacity, and so on.

Two points, however, should be highlighted. First, the width of participation provided for by the current rules is a relatively recent phenomenon. Historically, the right to vote in elections was tied to the ownership of land: the majority of people—bearing in mind that home ownership has only recently become commonplace—were

---

[13] House of Commons Political and Constitutional Reform Committee, *The Role and Powers of the Prime Minister: The Impact of the Fixed-term Parliaments Act 2011 on Government* (HC 440 2013–14).

[14] Act of Settlement 1700, s 3; Electoral Administration Act 2006, ss 17–18.

[15] House of Commons Disqualification Act 1975, s 1.

[16] However, hereditary peers who are barred from membership of the House of Lords by s 1 of the House of Lords Act 1999 are not (by operation of s 3 of the 1999 Act) disqualified from membership of the Commons. On hereditary peers and the 1999 Act, see section 3.3.1.

[17] Insolvency Act 1986, s 426A.   [18] Representation of the People Act 1983, s 160.

[19] Representation of the People Act 1983, s 1.   [20] Representation of the People Act 1983, s 3.

[21] Representation of the People Act 1983, s 3A.

[22] Representation of the People Act 1983. The position concerning members of the House of Lords is the same as for eligibility to stand for election: they may not do so, subject to the proviso in s 1 of the House of Lords Act 1999.

therefore disenfranchised. It was not until the enactment of the Representation of the People Act 1918 that the modern system based on one vote per person was introduced. Women have only been allowed to vote since 1918.

Second, the blanket and automatic ban on prisoner voting was held by the European Court of Human Rights (ECtHR) in 2006 to constitute an indiscriminate violation of the right to vote in, and stand for, elections to national legislatures.[23] The Court required the UK government to bring forward legislative proposals to comply with the European Convention on Human Rights (ECHR). Prisoner voting is a highly politically contentious issue—former Prime Minister David Cameron once said the idea made him feel physically ill.[24] Successive governments have delayed implementing the ruling.

3.2.4 The voting system

The type of voting system adopted is crucially important. Elections to the House of Commons are held under the 'first-past-the-post' (FPTP) voting system. The UK is divided into 650 geographical areas—'constituencies'—each of which sends an MP to the House of Commons.[25] In a general election, the votes in each constituency are counted up and the candidate with the most votes becomes the MP for that constituency. This means that it is possible—indeed, extremely likely—for the winning candidate to have fewer than 50 per cent of the votes cast in the constituency. Figure 5.4 shows the current state of the political parties in the House of Commons. Figure 5.5 shows the longer-term trends.

FPTP raises three issues. First, democracy is partly underpinned by the concept of equality: everyone should be allowed to vote, and *everyone's vote should count equally*. It is doubtful that FPTP meets this requirement. Everyone gets one vote—but, in practice, people's votes do not count equally. For example, in the 2010 general election in the constituency of East Ham, the Labour candidate got 70 per cent of the vote; the Conservative candidate got only 15 per cent. In such constituencies, the outcome is, in practice, a foregone conclusion, and it is unsurprising that voters in such areas feel that their vote is unlikely to make a real difference. As a result, the focus of campaigning is always in marginal constituencies in which two or more candidates have a real chance of winning. Consider, for example, the constituency of Bolton West: in 2010, the winning Labour candidate got 18,327 votes, while her Conservative rival got 18,235.

Second, *the only thing votes count for under FPTP is determining which candidate has the most votes in the constituency in question.* Whether a candidate wins with a majority of 27,826, as in East Ham, or 92, as in Bolton West is irrelevant. Votes for losing candidates have no effect on the national picture. A Conservative voter in East Ham cannot comfort himself by thinking that, although his vote did not succeed in getting a Conservative MP elected for that constituency, it might help the

---

[23] Protocol 1, Art 3, as interpreted in *Mathieu-Mohin v Belgium* (1988) 10 EHRR 1, [46]–[51]; *Hirst v UK (No 2)* (2006) 42 EHRR 41.

[24] HC Deb, vol 517, col 921 (3 November 2010).

[25] Parliamentary Constituencies Act 1986, s 1.

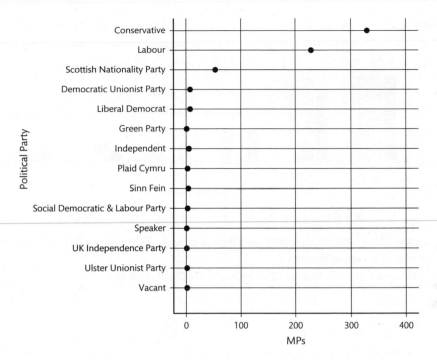

Figure 5.4 The current state of the political parties in the House of Commons, 2016
Source: **http://www.parliament.uk/mps-lords-and-offices/mps/current-state-of-the-parties/**

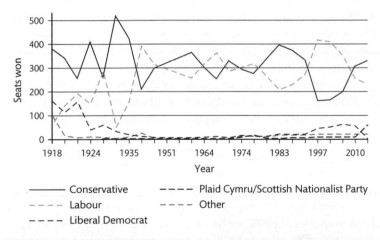

Figure 5.5 Seats won in the House of Commons by political party, 1918–2015
Source: House of Commons Library Briefing Paper, *UK Election Statistics 1918–2015* (CBP7529 2016).

Conservatives to win power nationally. Once the winner in a given constituency has been decided, that is the end of the matter. This is why this system is sometimes dubbed 'winner takes all'. FPTP may therefore produce a House of Commons that does not closely reflect how people voted.

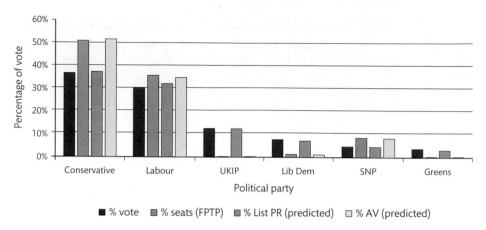

Figure 5.6 UK general election 2015: distribution of votes, seats under FPTP, and predicted seats under other voting systems

Source: Electoral Reform Society, *The 2015 General Election* (London 2015).

This is clear from Figure 5.6. This shows the relationship between the percentage of votes cast for each party and the percentage of constituencies won by each party in 2015. Compare the differences between the proportions of votes for each party with the proportions of Commons seats gained under FPTP. Some parties got more seats than votes; some fewer.

FPTP has been subject to much criticism. It is disproportionate because the number of seats does not accurately reflect the number of votes cast. Looking at Figure 5.6, it is clear Conservative, Labour, and the SNP all won more seats than they actually deserved. By contrast, smaller parties (UKIP, Liberal Democrats, and the Greens) lost out. UKIP secured 3.8 million votes giving it the third-largest vote share nationally (12.6 per cent), overtaking the Liberal Democrats. However, this result delivered just one UKIP MP. By contrast, the Conservative party received 331 times as many MPs on the basis of 11.4 million votes—only three times as many votes. Under FPTP, not all votes are of equal weight.

Furthermore, the two largest parties—Conservative and Labour—attained 67 per cent of the vote and nearly 87 per cent of the seats. Neither party has achieved anything close to 50 per cent of the vote since the 1960s. Yet, the governing party has alternated between Conservative and Labour during this period.

Indeed, the iniquities of FPTP are becoming more acute over time. FPTP is suited to a two-party system of politics, but UK politics is moving toward multi-party politics. The 2015 election was the most disproportionate result in election history.[26] A further dimension is the increasingly territorialised nature of UK politics. The SNP won 50 per cent of the Scottish vote share, but won 95 per cent of Scottish seats. This leaves

---

[26] Electoral Reform Society, *The 2015 General Election* (London 2015).

three MPs (5 per cent) to represent Scottish unionist support at Westminster—a body of opinion that received 55.3 per cent of votes in the 2014 Scottish independence referendum. The FPTP system exacerbates the regional polarisation of the electorate.

Third, *the way in which constituency boundaries are drawn is very important*— at least in relation to marginal constituencies. Where, say, the Labour Party has a small majority in a mainly urban constituency, a small boundary change could make all the difference: if a Conservative-supporting suburban area were to be brought within the constituency, that might tip the balance at the next election. The practice of manipulating boundaries so as to influence election results is known as 'gerrymandering', after Elbridge Gerry, a US state governor, who caused the redrawing of electoral districts—the shape of one of which was said to resemble a salamander—to the benefit of his party. UK law attempts to ensure that this does not happen. The Parliamentary Constituencies Act 1986 provides for the independent determination of the boundaries of parliamentary constituencies. The bodies responsible are the Boundary Commissions for England, Northern Ireland, Scotland, and Wales. Each of the Boundary Commissions is chaired by an Electoral Commissioner. The latter are appointed by the Queen on the recommendation of the House of Commons, and each must be an independent person in the sense of not being a member of or a current or recent employee of a registered political party.[27] They are required to review, every 8 to 12 years, the boundaries of parliamentary constituencies, applying the rules laid down in the Act. Those rules, among other things, prescribe the total number of constituencies,[28] and that, in general, all constituencies should contain roughly equal numbers of voters[29]—although in practice there can be significant variations between constituencies, not least because the present approach aims to align parliamentary constituencies with local authority boundaries.

Under the Parliamentary Voting System and Constituencies Act 2011, the number of constituencies is to be reduced from 650 to 600 and in the process end up with more equal-sized constituencies.[30] The government has also been keen to cut the cost of politics. A proposed review by the Boundary Commissions stalled in 2013 because of disagreement within the coalition government. In 2012, the Liberal Democrat party withdrew its support for the boundary review after the Conservative Party withdrew its support for House of Lords reform.[31] Another review was announced in 2016 and must be completed by September 2018.[32]

---

[27] Political Parties, Elections and Referendums Act 2000, s 3.

[28] Parliamentary Constituencies Act 1986, Sch 2, para 1 prescribes 600 constituencies. However, for the reason explained in the remainder of this paragraph, there will remain 650 constituencies until reviews of constituency boundaries report in 2018.

[29] Parliamentary Constituencies Act 1986, Sch 2, para 2.

[30] At present, Parliamentary constituencies range in size from 22,000 to 108,000 electors. One aim of the review is to ensure that every new constituency has roughly the same number of electors; no fewer than 71,031 and no more than 78,507.

[31] On the House of Lords, see section 3.3.

[32] Electoral Registration and Administration Act 2013, s 6.

3.2.5 **Reform**

There is intense concern that the health of UK democracy is not what it should be. The evidence demonstrates public disaffection with politicians and the political process.[33] Public participation in politics has declined over the last half century. Politicians are mistrusted and the system is seen as being unrepresentative and irrelevant.[34] Membership of the two main parties has plummeted dramatically over the last 50 years.[35] People's identification with political parties has declined and is particularly low amongst young people. Voter turnout at recent general elections has also declined (Figure 5.7). At the same time, new forms of participation—for example, online activism—have emerged. This may become increasingly important, especially for younger people.

The reasons for disaffection with politics are contested and complex. They may be partly mundane. For example, turnout could be improved by holding elections at weekends and allowing voting via the Internet rather than in person.[36] Nonetheless, it has been persuasively argued that the voting system is an important factor.[37]

FPTP may discourage people from voting if they feel that their vote will not really count because they support a party that is unlikely to win in their particular constituency, or which stands no realistic chance of getting enough seats to secure a majority in the House of Commons.[38] Alternatively, people resort to tactical voting. For example,

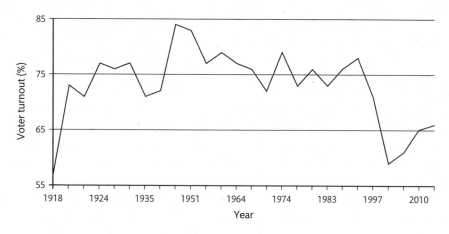

Figure 5.7 Turnout at UK general elections, 1918–2015

Source/Note: House of Commons Library Briefing Paper, *UK Election Statistics 1918–2015* (CBP7529 2016). Turnout at the 1918 General Election was partly due to a low service vote and a large number of uncontested seats (107 out of a total of 707 seats).

---

[33] House of Commons Library Briefing Paper, *Political Disengagement in the UK: Who is Disengaged?* (CBP7501 2016), **http://researchbriefings.files.parliament.uk/documents/CBP-7501/CBP-7501.pdf**

[34] House of Commons Parliamentary Office of Science and Technology, *Trends in Political Participation* (2015), **http://researchbriefings.files.parliament.uk/documents/POST-PN-0498/POST-PN-0498.pdf**

[35] House of Commons Library Briefing Paper, *Membership of UK Political Parties* (SN05125 2015), **http://researchbriefings.files.parliament.uk/documents/SN05125/SN05125.pdf**

[36] See, eg Ministry of Justice, *Election Day: Weekend Voting* (London 2008).

[37] See, eg The Power Inquiry, *Power to the People: An Independent Inquiry into Britain's Democracy* (London 2006).

[38] *Power to the People*, p 182.

in a constituency in which the Conservatives stand no chance, a Conservative supporter might vote Liberal Democrat in an attempt to defeat the Labour candidate.

There are arguments in favour of FPTP. Its great strength is always said to be that it delivers a clear majority for one party, resulting in stable government. This is not always the case—witness the result of the 2010 election. But FPTP is simpler than the alternatives and easy for people to comprehend.

Against this background, reform of the voting system has, for many years, been debated. There are different kinds of electoral system.[39] The one that most obviously contrasts with FPTP is the *party list* system, often referred to simply as *proportional representation* (PR), under which people are asked to vote for a party rather than an individual candidate. Seats in the legislature are then shared out in direct proportion to the votes cast: if a given party were to obtain 32 per cent of the national vote, it would be given 32 per cent of the seats in the legislature. The individual party members who are allocated the seats are determined by reference to the party list: each party has a rank order of candidates; it works down that list until all of the seats that it has won have been allocated. All votes therefore count equally, and the legislature precisely reflects each party's share of the vote. Figure 5.6 shows the Electoral Reform Society's predictions of how many seats each party would have got in 2015 under a party list PR voting system.

There are, however, significant disadvantages with such a voting system. There is no link between MPs and constituencies because there are no constituencies. A profusion of small parties is encouraged, possibly resulting in fragile coalition governments, which frequently collapse.[40] A version of the party list system is used for elections in the UK to the European Parliament. However, there is little prospect of its being adopted for elections to the House of Commons.

In 1997, Prime Minister Tony Blair created the Jenkins Commission to review the voting system. In doing so, it was made plain that a party list system would be unacceptable, requiring the Commission to design a system that would maintain 'a link between MPs and geographical constituencies'.[41] In reaching its conclusions, the Commission was impressed by two voting systems.

The first is *alternative vote* (AV). It can best be explained through an example. Assume that, as in Table 5.1, there are three candidates—A, B, and C—standing for election in a given constituency. Voters can rank the candidates in order of preference. For example, if a voter were to want to see candidate A elected, the voter would put a '1' next to that candidate's name, and would put a '2' next to C's name if he were to prefer C to B. When the votes are initially counted, only the 'first preference votes'—that is, the '1's—are taken into account. If a candidate gets more than half of such votes, she wins outright. But if (as in our example) no such candidate emerges, then there is a second round of counting. In it, the candidate with the fewest first-preference votes—C in our example—is eliminated, and the second-preference votes

---

[39] See generally http://www.electoral-reform.org.uk

[40] This problem can be alleviated by requiring a party to cross a minimum threshold before becoming eligible for legislative seats.

[41] Home Office, *The Report of the Independent Commission on the Voting System* (Cm 4090 1998), [1].

Table 5.1 Alternative vote

Candidate	Count 1 (taking into account only first preference votes)	Count 2 (taking into account second preference votes of voters who put C first)
A	45	45 + 12 = 57 (wins with more than half of the votes)
B	35	35 + 8 = 43
C	20 (of whom 12 put A as second preference and 8 put B as second preference)	n/a

of voters who put that candidate first are allocated to the remaining candidates. In the example, of the 20 people who put '1's next to C's name, 12 put '2's next to A's name, and 8 put '2's next to B's name. In the second round of counting, therefore, A is given 12 and B is given 8 additional votes. This gives A 57—more than half of the total 100 votes—and so A is the winner. If, after a given round, no one emerges with more than half the votes, the most unpopular remaining candidate is eliminated and his votes reallocated, the process being repeated until someone gets a majority.

The Jenkins Commission noted AV's 'very considerable advantage of ensuring that every constituency member gains majority acquiescence' and its capacity to free voters from their present dilemma of voting ideologically (for the candidate whom they really like) or practically (for the candidate whom they like best out of the two or three with a realistic chance of winning).[42] However, Jenkins recognised that this is not a system of proportional representation. Like FPTP, it is based on constituencies. AV is unlikely to produce a legislature the political composition of which precisely mirrors the various parties' national shares of the vote. AV might increase the number of seats obtained by third parties such as the Liberal Democrats. It is also likely—particularly where the winning party is very popular, as with Labour in 1997—to give the main opposition party an even smaller—more disproportionate—number of seats than FPTP.[43]

Figure 5.6 shows the Electoral Reform Society's predictions of how many seats each party would have got in 2015 under AV.[44] It can be seen that the alternative vote system would not have affected the outcome. Indeed, the Conservatives would have gained slightly more seats. However, AV may help reduce the inequities of FPTP. For instance, by requiring MPs to have more than 50 per cent of their voters' support, AV ensures a much broader base in the constituency. However, AV is not a proportional system and can produce more disproportionate outcomes than FPTP.

The Jenkins Commission therefore looked at other systems—in particular, the *additional member* system. This applies in elections to the Scottish Parliament and Welsh Assembly, and is described in Chapter 7. For now, it suffices to say that it

---

[42] Cm 4090, [46] and ch 9.

[43] Cm 4090, [82]; Baston, *A Better Alternative? What AV Would Mean for Westminster* (London 2008).

[44] See http://www.electoral-reform.org.uk

combines a constituency-based system (like FPTP or alternative vote) with the party list system: people cast two votes—for an individual to represent their constituency, and for a party. Some seats in the legislature are occupied by constituency representatives, with the remainder being filled by candidates on party lists. The idea is that the party list seats can be used to adjust the political make-up of the legislature to render it more proportionate than it would otherwise be.

In the end, the Jenkins Commission recommended that 80–85 per cent of seats in the House of Commons should be filled by constituency MPs selected using the alternative vote system, and that the balance should be filled by candidates chosen through the party list system. This, the Commission felt, would harness the strength of the alternative vote system while offsetting the risk that it might otherwise lead to serious under-representation in the Commons of the main opposition party.[45] These recommendations found little favour with the government and the matter rested there.

However, a referendum on electoral reform was held in 2011 as part of the coalition government agreement between the Conservatives and the Liberal Democrats. The referendum question put was whether to adopt the AV system. Over 19 million electors voted (a turnout of 42.2 per cent): 13 million (67.9 per cent) voted No and 6 million (32.1 per cent) voted Yes.[46] The outcome was a decisive vote to retain FPTP.

The AV referendum was only the second UK-wide referendum ever to be held.[47] It is unlikely that the voting system could now be changed except through a further referendum, and there is little prospect of such a referendum being held in the foreseeable future.

> **Q** Which voting system do you prefer, and why? Which system do you think would best be capable of reinvigorating democracy in the UK and enhancing public trust in politicians and the political process?

A further issue concerns whether voters can 'recall' their MP, that is, to force a local by-election because of the sitting MP's corrupt or unethical behaviour, so making it possible to sack the MP *between* general elections. This idea rose to prominence following the 2009 MPs' expenses scandal. In an attempt to restore faith in the political process, the coalition government proposed a process by which an MP could lose his or her seat in the House of Commons if the MP is guilty of serious wrongdoing and if 10 per cent of voters in the constituency sign a petition.[48] This would trigger a by-election in which the ousted MP can stand as a candidate.

---

[45] Cm 4090, ch 9.

[46] Electoral Commission, *Referendum on the Voting System for UK Parliamentary Elections: Report on the May 2011 Referendum* (London 2011).

[47] The first UK referendum in 1975 concerned UK membership of what was then the European Economic Community. The third was the EU referendum in 2016.

[48] HM Government, *Recall of MPs Draft Bill* (Cm 8241 2011).

There are three alternative conditions for the opening of a recall petition: the MP is convicted of an offence and receives a custodial sentence; following a report from the Committee on Standards, the MP is suspended from the Commons for at least ten sitting days; or the MP is convicted of providing false or misleading information for allowances claims. This was criticised for being too restrictive—constituents themselves would not be able to initiate a recall petition—and therefore unlikely to increase public confidence in politics.[49] Moreover, existing democratic and legal processes have worked well by removing MPs guilty of serious wrongdoing during the expenses scandal. Nonetheless, the recall mechanism—described by the government as 'a modest innovation to fill a gap in the regulatory oversight of MPs who have demonstrably committed wrongdoing' but who ignore public pressure and remain as MPs[50]—was subsequently enacted.[51] To date, no MP has been subject to recall.

3.2.6 The social background of MPs

Another way of analysing membership of the Commons is to consider the social backgrounds of MPs.[52] For many years, there have been concerns over the narrow social composition of Parliament. A familiar criticism is that the Commons is dominated by white men from relatively privileged backgrounds.[53] So what are the social backgrounds of MPs?

Following the 2015 general election, there were 191 women MPs (29 per cent)—the highest ever number.[54] However, as women make up 51 per cent of the UK population, they remain significantly under-represented.[55] In relation to ethnicity, the first non-white MPs—four MPs—were elected in 1987. In 2015, there were 41 non-white MPs (6 per cent). This compares with 13 per cent of the UK population from a non-white background: again, there is significant under-representation.

As regards the occupations of MPs, the number of manual workers who have become MPs has declined from 16 per cent of all MPs in 1979 to 3 per cent in 2015. MPs from the traditional professions (eg law, medicine, Civil Service, and education) have declined from 45 per cent in 1979 to 31 per cent in 2015. By contrast, those MPs who worked previously as a politician/political organiser has increased from 3.4 per cent in 1979 to 17 per cent in 2015. In 2015, 31 per cent of MPs previously worked in business.

[49] House of Commons Political and Constitutional Reform Committee, *Recall of MPs* (HC 373 2012–13). See also Judge, 'Recall of MPs in the UK: "If I Were You I Wouldn't Start from Here"' (2013) 66 Parliamentary Affairs 732.

[50] Deputy Prime Minister, *Government Response to the Report of the Political and Constitutional Reform Committee on the Draft Recall of MPs Bill* (Cm 8640 2013), [4].

[51] Recall of MPs Act 2015.

[52] The data in this section is drawn from House of Commons Library Briefing Paper, *Social background of MPs 1979–2015* (CBP7483 2016).

[53] See Cairney, Keating, and Wilson, 'Solving the Problem of Social Background in the UK "Political Class": Do Parties do Things Differently in Westminster, Devolved and European Elections?' (2012) 11 British Politics 142.

[54] This puts the Commons above the European average of 24.3 per cent, but below the UK's other legislatures: National Assembly for Wales—41.7 per cent; Scottish Parliament—34.9 per cent; and Northern Ireland Assembly—27.8 per cent. See also Women in National Parliaments, http://www.ipu.org/wmn-e/world.htm

[55] This puts the UK behind many of its European counterparts (Germany, France, and Sweden), and well behind other countries such as Rwanda, Cuba, and Kazakhstan.

One third of MPs elected in 2015 had attended fee-paying schools (Labour 16 per cent, Liberal Democrat 13 per cent, Conservatives 50 per cent, and SNP 7 per cent). By comparison, independent (fee-paying) schools account for 7 per cent of pupils in UK schools. Three-quarters of MPs elected in 2015 were university graduates. The proportion of MPs who studied at non-Oxbridge universities has increased. In 1979, 36 per cent of MPs from the three main parties had studied at Oxford or Cambridge; in 2015, it was 23 per cent.

The social background of MPs matters. Overall, there are still concerns whether MPs are—in social terms—representative of the public as a whole. Political parties have experimented with ways of widening the backgrounds of parliamentary candidates, such as quotas and all-women shortlists.[56] The 2015 Parliament may be the most diverse ever. However, 'to put the progress made in perspective, the UK would need to elect 130 more women and double the current number of black and ethnic minority MPs to make its Parliament descriptively representative of the population it serves—and the political parties are still not offering enough candidates from these groups in the right places to make that happen.'[57]

3.2.7 Political parties

Political parties play a particularly important role in politics. Most politicians tend to behave tribally, expressing views and voting in ways that tow the party line. The House of Commons does not consist of 650 independent representatives who speak their own mind. In practice, it consists of two opposing sides—the government and the opposition parties. This is even reflected in the architecture of the House of Commons: government MPs sit on one side; opposition MPs on the other.

Much of British political life is dominated by what amounts, in practice, to a perpetual election campaign between the main political parties. Parties structure the policy choices presented to voters. They select the candidates who become MPs and the leaders who become either Prime Ministers or leaders of the opposition. They also exert an enormous influence over how the government is both run and held to account. Within this system, people are unlikely to get anywhere in politics unless they ally themselves with a party. Independent candidates do occasionally succeed, but they are very much the exception.[58]

This is unsurprising. Political parties are both inevitable and desirable. It is in the nature of like-minded people to gravitate together. Such behaviour is both instinctive and purposeful, in that it enables such people to achieve more collectively than they could achieve individually. It is for precisely such reasons that political parties are

---

[56] The Sex Discrimination (Election Candidates) Act 2002 allows political parties to draw up all-women shortlists of candidates for elections.

[57] Hudson and Campbell, 'UK elects most diverse parliament ever but it's still not representative', *Constitution Unit* blog, 14 May 2015, **https://constitution-unit.com/2015/05/14/uk-elects-most-diverse-parliament-ever-but-its-still-not-representative/**

[58] As is conventional, the Speaker of the House of Commons stood, and was elected, as an independent candidate, but this is not a true exception: the Speaker had been a Conservative MP, and (again as is conventional) the main parties do not stand against the Speaker.

formed. Political parties are also desirable because, at least in parliamentary democracies, they provide voters with a meaningful way of influencing membership of the government.

If people simply voted for independent MPs, then the nature of politics could very well be rendered largely unpredictable and ineffectual.[59] It is only through organised political parties that the public can be reassured that the democratic mandate given to politicians at an election will in fact be put into practice by carrying into law the policies that the public voted for. In a sense, then, the party system simply short-circuits, and makes rather more transparent, the sort of process that would have to precede the formation of a government: inevitably, each party is a reasonably 'broad church', encompassing people with a range of views, but before an election is held, each party, through its own internal processes, must decide on what its central policies and priorities will be.

This system is undoubtedly imperfect. Political parties may not be straightforward with voters. They might, for example, try to conceal, or downplay, potentially unpalatable policies (eg tax rises or public spending cuts). Furthermore, if, as in 2010, an election yields no overall majority for any party, a degree of horse-trading must necessarily occur. This can mean backroom deals as potential coalition parties have to compromise in an attempt to forge a stable government.

3.2.8 Funding, spending, and fair play

It is in the nature of politics that politicians—and the parties into which they organise themselves—will attempt to persuade others of the correctness of their views. In this way, they seek to win power in order that they may put those views into practice. While this process of debate and persuasion is an ongoing one, it assumes particular prominence in the weeks immediately before a general election. Election campaigns are expensive: parties will inevitably want to spread their message as widely and as effectively as possible. This raises questions concerning the *funding of political parties* and the *rules on campaign spending.*[60]

Party finance has been the subject of controversy and debate. Tony Blair was almost brought down six months into his first administration by allegations (which he denied) that a donation to the Labour Party of £1 million had influenced a subsequent government decision to exempt Formula One motor sport from a ban on tobacco advertising. More recently, a police investigation was held into allegations that certain individuals had been offered life peerages in return for making loans to the Labour Party.[61] And it was alleged that large accountancy firms gave hundreds of thousands of pounds' worth of resources to the Conservative Party before the 2010 election, hoping that they would retain and win new government contracts in the event of a Conservative government.[62] More recently still, the 'cash for access' scandal

---

[59] For debate on this issue, see Tomkins, *Our Republican Constitution* (Oxford 2005), pp 136–9; Nicol, 'Professor Tomkins' House of Mavericks' [2006] PL 467.

[60] See generally Rowbottom, *Democracy Distorted* (Cambridge 2010).

[61] On life peerage, see section 3.3.1.

[62] 'Windfall for Tories as firms eye £4bn contracts', *The Independent*, 29 July 2009.

arose in 2012. Accusations were made that businesses and lobbyists could gain access to Conservative Ministers in return for making party donations.[63]

The suspicion—whether or not justified—is that it is possible to purchase influence. Few people can be naive enough to think that politicians make decisions without thinking about what is in it for them in terms of popularity, electoral success, and so on. But most people would also agree that the naked use of money to buy influence is improper. It may be regarded as a form of corruption and certainly undercuts the principle of political equality by benefiting those who can afford to buy influence.[64] Debate has therefore focused on whether there should be changes to the way in which political parties are funded in order to remove or reduce the risk of such practices occurring. There are three main positions that one might adopt in this debate.

First, it might be argued that *people should be free to make whatever donations they wish* to political parties. Donating to political parties, it might be argued, is a form of participation in the political process that it would be improper to restrict. It is even said that any limitation on donations would restrict parties' capacity to communicate their messages and would thus represent a restriction upon freedom of expression.[65] It is not inconsistent with this position to accept that the identity of those making donations should be a matter of public record; the point of such transparency being that it allows people to judge whether money really is buying influence: although cause and effect might be hard to determine, the electorate is at least in a position to attempt to form a judgement if donations are public knowledge. For precisely that reason, UK law requires registered political parties regularly to report to the Electoral Commission on the size and source of any donation of more than £7,500.[66] Following the 'loans for peerages' allegations mentioned, equivalent arrangements now apply to loans over £7,500.[67] The Electoral Commission maintains and publishes registers detailing all such donations and loans.

Second, there might instead be *a limit on the amount that any individual or organisation can donate* in a given year. Rowbottom explains that this form of regulation is motivated by concerns about equality—that is, that 'donation limits aim to restrict the activity of wealthy individuals to enhance the relative voice of others'.[68] A cap on donations thus has the potential to reduce the capacity of the rich to exert disproportionate influence—although that potential is unlikely to be fully realised unless the cap is set low enough to be within the reach of everyone, which would

---

[63] 'Tory treasurer's cash-for-access boast unacceptable, says David Cameron', *The Guardian*, 25 March 2012.

[64] See further Rowbottom, 'Political Donations and the Democratic Process: Rationales for Reform' [2002] PL 758.

[65] The closely related argument that limits on campaign spending may be an unlawful restriction on free speech have been accepted by the ECtHR and the US Supreme Court in *Bowman v UK* (1998) 26 EHRR 1 and *Buckley v Valeo* 424 US 1 (1976).

[66] Political Parties, Elections and Referendums Act 2000, s 62. There are also restrictions on who may make donations to registered political parties, eg individual donors must be registered to vote and resident for tax purposes in the UK (2000 Act, s 54).

[67] Political Parties, Elections and Referendums Act 2000, s 71M.   [68] Rowbottom, p 776.

be likely to drastically reduce the amount of funding available to political parties.[69] In the wake of the 'loans for peerages' allegations, an independent review of the funding of political parties was established under former senior civil servant Sir Hayden Phillips. It recommended new limits on election spending,[70] which would reduce the need for large donations, and a cap on donations of perhaps £50,000.[71] The review urged that any changes should be implemented on a consensual basis, but to date no consensus has emerged. A major sticking point has been the fact that the cap would drastically reduce the support available to major parties, which presently depend to a considerable degree on large donations from institutions and wealthy individuals.

Third, *state funding* might be made available to political parties in order to reduce reliance on donations. In fact, there is already limited state support in the UK: for example, election candidates get free postage so that they can send a mailing to voters in their constituency,[72] major parties get free airtime to make election broadcasts,[73] public money is given to the main opposition parties to support their parliamentary (but not campaigning) activities, and 'policy development grants' can be made to parties with more than one MP in the House of Commons.[74] The Electoral Commission has argued that state support should be increased modestly, partly through tax relief on individual donations,[75] and Phillips went much further, suggesting that public money should become a major source of income for political parties.[76] Phillips's main recommendations were not, however, implemented, and we explain in this section why this issue remains unfinished business.

> **Q** Which of the three positions outlined in relation to funding do you prefer? Why?

The way in which parties spend money—how much they are allowed to spend and on what—is also controlled. The purpose of such regulation is to attempt to create a level playing field by preventing a very well-resourced party or candidate from being able to buy victory through sheer spending power (eg on advertising). Four points arise.

First, there have, for a long time, been *constituency-level spending limits*. It is unlawful for any given candidate to spend more than approximately £10,500 on 'election expenses'[77]—which includes such things as advertising, transport, and administration.[78] It is also unlawful for others to spend more than £500 'with a view to promoting or

---

[69] Rowbottom, pp 776–7.   [70] Spending limits are addressed later in this section.

[71] Phillips, *Strengthening Democracy: Fair and Sustainable Funding of Political Parties* (London 2007).

[72] Representation of the People Act 1983, s 91.

[73] Election broadcasts are dealt with later in this section.

[74] Political Parties, Elections and Referendums Act 2000, s 12.

[75] *The Funding of Political Parties* (London 2004); for comment, see Rowbottom, 'The Electoral Commission's Proposals on the Funding of Political Parties' [2005] PL 468.

[76] Phillips, pp 17–20.

[77] Representation of the People Act 1983, s 76. The precise figure depends on the number of people on the electoral register in the relevant constituency.

[78] Representation of the People Act 1983, s 90ZA and Sch 4A.

procuring the election of a candidate'.[79] The sum used to be £5, but was raised after the ECtHR held—following the prosecution in the UK of an anti-abortion campaign group, which had exceeded the statutory spending limit—that such a severe restriction constituted an improper constraint upon freedom of speech.[80] This serves as a useful reminder of the tension between, on the one hand, permitting free and open debate, and, on the other hand, maintaining a playing field that is sufficiently level to enable a wide range of contributors to play an effective part in such debate.

Second, *national spending limits* were introduced in 2000. The amount that a party is allowed to spend (over and above the sums mentioned in the previous paragraph) depends on how many constituencies it is contesting.[81] If a party were to contest every seat in the UK, it would be allowed to spend £19.5 million. In the 2015 election, the Conservatives spent £15.6 million, Labour £12 million, the Liberal Democrats £3.6 million, UKIP £2.8m, and the SNP £1.4m.[82]

Third, there are ways of levelling the playing field other than imposing quantitative caps on spending. For example, there may be *legal regulation of the way in which parties are allowed to campaign.* In the UK, strict impartiality requirements apply to television and radio programmes,[83] and there is an absolute ban on paid-for advertising by political parties on broadcast media.[84] The ban was upheld in 2013 by the Grand Chamber of the ECtHR. It accepted that permitting such advertising might distort political discourse and held that the ban was a justified restriction on freedom of expression.[85] However, certain broadcasters are required, free of charge, to make airtime available to major political parties for party political broadcasts.[86] The relevant rules provide that the major parties will normally be offered a series of broadcasts before each election.[87] This system ensures that access to television and radio—which, notwithstanding the growth of the Internet, remain the most powerful advertising media—does not directly depend on the parties' resources.

Fourth, if elections are to be conducted in an even-handed and fair manner, it is clear that *the rules described must be conscientiously enforced,* and that the fairness of elections must be ensured more generally in order to guard against fraud and other forms of improper behaviour that would pollute the democratic process. The Electoral Commission is responsible for, among other things, monitoring compliance with the rules concerning donations to, and spending by, political parties and candidates;[88] maintaining the register of political parties; monitoring and reporting on the conduct of elections;[89] keeping under review certain political and electoral matters, such as the regulation of income

[79] Representation of the People Act 1983, s 75.   [80] *Bowman v UK* (1998) 26 EHRR 1.
[81] Political Parties, Elections and Referendums Act 2000, s 79 and Sch 3.
[82] See **http://www.electoralcommission.org.uk/find-information-by-subject/political-parties-campaigning-and-donations/political-party-spending-at-elections/details-of-party-spending-at-previous-elections**
[83] Communications Act 2003, ss 319–20, and Ofcom Broadcasting Code, ss 5 and 6. The BBC is subject to separate, but similar, rules under the terms of the agreement accompanying the BBC Charter.
[84] Communications Act 2003, s 321.
[85] *Animal Defenders International v United Kingdom* (2013) 34 BHRC 137.
[86] Communications Act 2003, s 333, and Ofcom Rules on Party Political and Referendum Broadcasts. The BBC is subject to separate, but similar, rules under the terms of the agreement accompanying the BBC Charter.
[87] Ofcom Rules, r 10. See also **http://www.broadcastersliaisongroup.org.uk**
[88] Political Parties, Elections and Referendums Act 2000, s 145.
[89] Political Parties, Elections and Referendums Act 2000, s 5.

and expenditure by political parties, and political advertising;[90] reviewing constituency boundaries;[91] and promoting public understanding of the electoral systems in the UK.[92]

The courts also play a significant role in two respects. First, there may be *criminal prosecutions* in respect of certain sorts of irregularity. Breach of many of the rules set out concerning donations and election spending constitute criminal offences. The criminal law also deals with more direct attempts to subvert the democratic process: it is, for example, an offence for a candidate to bribe voters to vote for him.[93] Second, a constituency result can be questioned through an *election petition*.[94] Such petitions may be presented by (among others) candidates and those entitled to vote[95] within 21 days of the result.[96] The courts have the power to determine that the election in the given constituency was void because of some relevant impropriety—for example, that spending limits were exceeded or that the candidate was not qualified to be a member of the House of Commons.[97]

Party finance and spending remains unfinished business. The concern has been to remove large donations to parties while also ensuring that they receive sufficient funding to perform their essential role in the democratic process—but it has proven difficult for the parties to reach an agreement on the matter. In 2011, the Committee on Standards in Public Life reported on party financing and made four recommendations.[98] First, the Committee stated that to remove big money from party funding, an annual cap, set at £10,000, should apply to donations from any individual or organisation to any political party. Second, this cap should apply to donations from all individuals and organisations, including trade unions. But it would be possible to regard trade union affiliation fees as a collection of individual payments to which the cap applied individually. Third, the existing limits on campaign spending in the period before an election should be cut by 15 per cent. But, fourth, even allowing for this, an inevitable consequence of the cap would be increased state funding for political parties, which would depend on the number of votes secured in the previous election.

Despite the importance of the issue to the health of the UK's democracy, the parties have yet to reach agreement, though there have been talks between them. A year after the Committee's report—during which there had not been any progress—its chair, Christopher Kelly, noted: 'the main parties need to look beyond their narrow party interests and act in the national interest to deal with this thorny issue. If not, we will continue to see damaging scandals which tarnish UK politics and erode confidence in standards in public life'.[99]

A final issue concerns the regulation of lobbying, that is, advocacy to politicians on behalf of organisations such as business, charities, and trade unions. Before becoming

---

[90] Political Parties, Elections and Referendums Act 2000, s 6.
[91] Political Parties, Elections and Referendums Act 2000, s 14.
[92] Political Parties, Elections and Referendums Act 2000, s 13.
[93] Representation of the People Act 1983, s 113.
[94] Representation of the People Act 1983, s 120.
[95] Representation of the People Act 1983, s 121.
[96] Representation of the People Act 1983, s 122.
[97] Representation of the People Act 1983, s 144.
[98] Committee on Standards in Public Life, *Political Party Finance: Ending the Big Donor Culture* (Cm 8208 2011).
[99] Committee on Standards in Public Life, Press Notice, 'Political Party Funding—Sir Christopher Kelly Urges Parties to Act', 22 November 2012.

Prime Minister in 2010, David Cameron described lobbying as the 'next big scandal waiting to happen'.[100] There have subsequently been instances that have caused considerable embarrassment in which parliamentarians have offered to lobby on behalf of businesses in return for payments.[101] Beyond these instances, it is apparent that many businesses and other organisations seek to influence the policy and lawmaking process through lobbying politicians. From one perspective, lobbying is an essential aspect of the way in which Parliament does its job: it helps inform policy decisions. However, while many lobbyists and parliamentarians may behave well, there is always the risk that some will engage in sustained, concealed efforts to peddle improper political influence.[102] In order to restore trust and confidence in the political system, Parliament in 2014 introduced a register of consultant lobbyists.[103] The purpose is to enhance transparency by requiring lobbyists to disclose the names of their clients on a publicly available register and to update those details regularly. The register complements an existing transparency regime under which government Ministers and senior civil servants proactively disclose information about who they meet on a quarterly basis.

3.3 The House of Lords

3.3.1 An anachronism?

The House of Lords is the unelected House. There are three categories of 'peer' (members of the House of Lords). Figure 5.8 shows the current membership of the Lords by party/group and type of peerage.

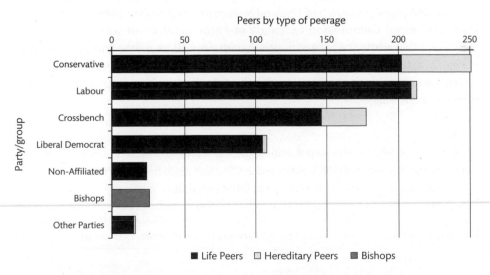

Figure 5.8 Composition of the House of Lords by party/group and type of peerage

Source: House of Lords Library Note, *Statistical Profile of Membership* (LLN 2016/0017).

---

[100] Speech by David Cameron, 'Rebuilding Trust in Politics', 8 February 2010.

[101] See **http://www.theguardian.com/politics/lobbying**

[102] House of Commons Public Administration Select Committee, *Lobbying: Access and Influence in Whitehall* (HC 36 2008–09).

[103] Transparency of Lobbying, Non-Party Campaigning and Trade Union Administration Act 2014.

First, there are 701 *life peers* (84 per cent of all peers). Life peerages are conferred by the Queen under the Life Peerages Act 1958, on the recommendation of the Prime Minister. There is no cap on the number of members of the House of Lords, and the number of life peers created each year varies.

Most life peers are *political peers*—that is, peers with a party affiliation whose names have been put forward to the Prime Minister by the leaders of each of the major parties. The Prime Minister decides how many new peers there should be from each party in any given year. The exercise of these powers of patronage has often been criticised. Through prime ministerial appointments, the government can manipulate Lords membership and offer peerages in return for political loyalty and favours (in tabloid language, the institution becomes a 'House of cronies').[104] Further, the size of the Lords keeps escalating.[105] A minority (roughly a quarter) of life peers are so-called *crossbenchers*. They have no party political affiliation and are now, in practice, appointed by the independent House of Lords Appointments Commission.[106]

Second, there are 88 *hereditary peers* (11 per cent of all peers). Such peerages are, as the name suggests, inherited. The death of a hereditary peer resulted in the peerage passing to his or her eldest son. Hereditary peers used to account for the majority of members of the House of Lords. There were over 700 such members by 1999. A second chamber dominated by hereditary (and largely Conservative) members was undeniably out of place in a supposedly meritocratic and democratic country. Accordingly, the House of Lords Act 1999, in effect, ejected the hereditary peers.[107] However, as a token of its intention to undertake more thoroughgoing reform, the Labour government accepted that 90 hereditary peers should be allowed to remain pending such reform.[108]

Third, there are 26 Church of England *bishops and archbishops*. This has been criticised. The Royal Commission on House of Lords Reform—of which more later—concluded that while the inclusion of religious, as well as moral and philosophical, views in a second chamber may be valuable, such representation should not be restricted to a single denomination or faith given the religious diversity that characterises the UK today.[109]

Q Is it acceptable for the Prime Minister to wield power to appoint life peers to the Lords? What difficulties might this pose in terms of the separation of powers doctrine?

Three other points about composition of the House of Lords. First, both women and black and minority ethnic (BME) people are under-represented. There are 217 female

[104] McKinstry 'The House of Lords is full of sycophants, failed MPs, and political donors. Sack them all', *The Daily Telegraph*, 27 August 2015.

[105] Russell and Semlyen, *Enough is Enough: Regulating Prime Ministerial Appointments to the Lords* (London 2015), https://www.ucl.ac.uk/constitution-unit/research/parliament/house-of-lords/enoughisenough

[106] See further http://lordsappointments.independent.gov.uk/. The role of crossbenchers is considered in section 3.3.4.

[107] House of Lords Act 1999, s 1.   [108] House of Lords Act 1999, s 2.

[109] Commission on Reform of the House of Lords, *A House for the Future* (Cm 4534 2000), ch 15.

peers (26 per cent).[110] There are only 44 BME peers (5.4 per cent).[111] Second, membership is distinctly slanted towards those who are more advanced in years.

Third, there is the issue of regional representation in the Lords. It is not the purpose of peers, unlike MPs, to represent particular geographical areas. Nonetheless, there are arguments that as legislators, the composition of the Lords should reflect different regions of the UK. Many peers are based in London and South East England.[112] By contrast, North West England, Yorkshire and the Humber, the East Midlands, and the North East are under-represented. In comparison, representation of Scotland, Wales, and Northern Ireland seems relatively good, given their population sizes. Regional representation is another part of the debate as to what a reformed Lords should look like.

3.3.2 Reform—framing the debate

Reform of the House of Lords has been on the political agenda for a very long time. Legislation enacted in 1911 limiting the Lords' legal powers was said, in its Preamble, to be a temporary measure pending the 'substitut[ion] for the House of Lords as it at present exists [with] a Second Chamber constituted on a popular instead of hereditary basis'.[113] Such a development is still awaited.

The focus of the debate has always been on how people should get into the second chamber—in particular, whether they should be elected. That is clearly an important question, but it is not the only one; and it is not the question with which we should start. Rather, we must begin with two other (closely related) questions—what should the House of Lords do, and what powers should it have?

If the House of Lords were a co-equal partner with the House of Commons in the legislative process, with the power to veto Bills that the Commons had approved, then that would fundamentally influence the debate about the composition of the Lords. In such circumstances, it would be very difficult to have anything other than a fully elected second chamber. However, that is not the current position, and nor is it how many of those who have contributed to the debate envisage a reformed House of Lords. The Royal Commission on House of Lords reform, which reported in 2000, took the view that the second chamber should complement, rather than replicate, the House of Commons—that it should be 'distinctively different'.[114]

In many regards, the Royal Commission, like many others who have contributed to the debate, considered that a reformed second chamber should serve a broadly equivalent function to that which the present House of Lords fulfils: a revising chamber capable of providing thoughtful scrutiny of legislation and executive action in a manner that is, and from a range of perspectives that are, different from those found in the

---

[110] Data taken from House of Lords Library Note, *Statistical Profile of Membership* (LLN 2016/0017). Under the Lords Spiritual (Women) Act 2015, eligible women Bishops are now given preference for 21 out of the 26 seats for Bishops up until 2025.

[111] House of Commons Library, *Ethnic Minorities in Politics, Government and Public Life* (SN/SG/1156 2013), p 7.

[112] House of Lords Library Note, *Regional Representation in the House of Lords* (LLN 2014/005 2014).

[113] See section 3.3.3 on the Parliament Acts 1911–49.

[114] Royal Commission on Reform of the House of Lords, *A House for the Future* (Cm 4534 2000), p 3.

Commons. The job of the House of Lords, said that Royal Commission, was to make 'the House of Commons think again': 'The second chamber should engender second thoughts.'[115] A second chamber along these lines raises three particular matters.

3.3.3 Powers

First, what *powers* should the second chamber have? At the moment, the House of Lords is less powerful than the House of Commons in two respects.

Under the Salisbury convention, the House of Lords should not reject a government Bill that implements a manifesto pledge and for which the government therefore has an electoral mandate.[116] This convention recognises that it would be undemocratic for the Lords, lacking a democratic mandate, to block such legislation.

There is also a *legal restriction* on the Lords' powers in the form of the Parliament Acts 1911–49. In 1909, the Liberal government failed to secure the enactment of legislation imposing new taxes on landowners because the Conservative-dominated Lords refused to approve the Bill. Amid great controversy, which included the holding of two general elections in 1910, the government proposed legislation limiting the power of the Lords, and obtained the King's agreement that if the Lords were to refuse to approve such legislation, he would flood the second chamber with enough Liberal peers to outvote the Conservatives on the matter. Faced with that prospect, the Lords agreed to the enactment of the Parliament Act 1911.

That Act (as amended by the Parliament Act 1949) limits the Lords' powers in two ways. The first concerns *money Bills*—that is, Bills that the speaker of the House of Commons has certified as dealing with such matters as taxation and government spending. If such a Bill, having been passed by the Commons, is not passed without amendment by the Lords within a month of having been sent to the Lords, it can be enacted anyway.[117] The upshot is that, in respect of money Bills, the House of Lords has only a *one-month delaying power*. The second limitation concerns *non-money Bills*. If, in two successive sessions (ie parliamentary years), the Lords rejects a non-money Bill that has been approved by the Commons, the Bill may be enacted nevertheless.[118] Thus, in relation to legislation other than money Bills, the Lords has, in effect, a *one-year delaying power*.

There is one—and only one—exception to what may be done by the Commons, without the Lords' consent, under the Parliament Act. The Act explicitly states that it cannot be used in respect of 'a Bill containing any provision to extend the maximum duration of Parliament beyond five years'.[119] It was suggested in *Jackson* that it would be open to the Commons—using the 1911 Act, without the Lords' consent—to enact two Bills. Act I would delete the exception regarding extending the life of Parliament.[120] Once that Bill were enacted, it would be possible for the Commons to use its 1911 Act powers to enact Act II—again without the Lords' consent—to extend

---

[115] Cm 4534, p 3.

[116] See further the report of the Joint Committee on Conventions (HL 265 HC 1212 2005–06).

[117] Parliament Act 1911, s 1.   [118] Parliament Act 1911, s 2.

[119] Parliament Act 1911, s 2(1).

[120] *R (Jackson) v Attorney General* [2005] UKHL 56, [2006] 1 AC 262.

the life of Parliament. This would make it possible for a government to extend its time in office by postponing a general election. All but one of the judges in *Jackson* rejected this analysis. The majority held that there was an implied prohibition in the 1911 Act on using it to pass anything resembling Act I: the Commons could not therefore unilaterally remove the exception regarding extending Parliament's life, and could not therefore pass Act II (an Act extending the life of Parliament) under the 1911 Act; such legislation would be possible only with the consent of the House of Lords.

Although welcome, this conclusion—that the Commons cannot unilaterally post-pone general elections—is a modest one. *Anything* else, said the court in *Jackson*, could be done by the Commons under the 1911 Act, including the enactment of major constitutional changes. Some of the judges acknowledged that, viewed thus, the effect of the Parliament Acts had been to 'erode the checks and balances inherent in the British constitution' by making it easier for the executive-dominated House of Commons to legislate without hindrance by the Lords.[121] This is an important point, but one that should not be overstated, bearing in mind that the Lords' power to delay legislation for a year is not insignificant: such delays can wreck the government's legislative programme, and it will often prefer to reach a compromise with the Lords rather than wait a year to push the Bill through without the Lords' consent. This does, however, underscore the fact that control of the government-dominated Commons is ultimately political rather than legal.

How does the Lords exercise its powers in practice? Government defeats in the Lords are relatively common (Figure 5.9).[122] During the coalition government (2010–15), there were 99 government defeats in the Lords. Various groupings in the Lords contribute to such defeats: rebels in the governing party, opposition parties, independent crossbenchers, and Bishops. The chamber has a reputation for being independent and non-partisan. Further, such defeats are not routinely overturned in the Commons: they often result in significant policy change.

There is another angle on this, closely related to Lords membership and the politics of Lords reform. The House of Lords Act 1999, which removed most hereditary peers, was a watershed moment. Before 1999, Labour governments had been defeated more frequently than Conservative governments in the Lords (most hereditary peers were Conservative and this gave the Conservatives an in-built majority in the Lords). Compare the number of Labour government defeats (1974–79) with the number of Conservative government defeats (1979–97).

Unsurprisingly, the Labour government in 1999 had a political party reason for removing hereditary peers. Since then, no party has had a majority in the Lords. Removing most hereditaries gave the Lords more confidence and a greater perception of its own legitimacy. This is reflected in the overall higher number of government defeats—Labour, Coalition, and Conservative governments—after 1999. According to Russell, the 1999 changes have strengthened the Lords against the government

---

[121] *Jackson*, [41], *per* Lord Bingham.
[122] See also the higher number of Statutory Instruments annulled by the Lords than by the Commons: Chapter 4, section 4.2.6.

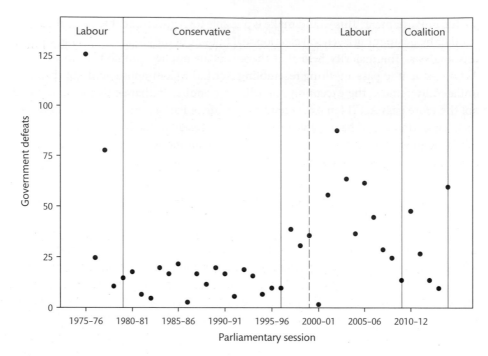

Figure 5.9 Government defeats in the House of Lords

Source/Note: **http://www.parliament.uk/about/faqs/house-of-lords-faqs/lords-govtdefeats/**. For more detail, see **https://www.ucl.ac.uk/constitution-unit/research/parliament/house-of-lords/lords-defeats**. Vertical solid lines mark a change of Government and the vertical dashed line marks the removal of most hereditary peers in 1999.

and, in doing so, strengthened Parliament as a whole.[123] Nonetheless, the wider debate over Lords reform remains.

3.3.4 Complementarity

If, as suggested, the role of a second chamber is to 'engender second thoughts', then it should *complement*, rather than *replicate*, the first chamber. Whatever its shortcomings, this is a criterion that the House of Lords presently fulfils, at least to some extent, in three ways.

First, whereas the Commons is a highly political chamber, the House of Lords is not. No political party has an *overall majority*, making it impossible for a single-party government unilaterally to get legislation through the Lords. Nor does the Conservative government formed in 2015 have a majority in the Lords. Moreover, just over a fifth of the Lords' members—crossbenchers—have *no party political affiliation*. This reduces the importance of party politics in the Lords. It is also said to encourage a more independent, objective, thoughtful way of conducting business. Even those members of the Lords affiliated to a political party are

---

[123] Russell, 'A Stronger Second Chamber? Assessing the Impact of House of Lords Reform in 1999 and the Lessons for Bicameralism' (2010) 58 Political Studies 866.

more likely to be independent-minded. Promises of promotion to the frontbenches are likely to be less appealing in the Lords, giving the parties less of a hold over the second chamber.

Second, the Lords is regarded as complementing the Commons in that it is able to bring *particular expertise* to the discharge of its functions. This reflects the fact that membership of the Lords is, at least in one sense, more diverse than that of the Commons. It is increasingly the case that the latter is dominated by career politicians who have spent most of their working lives in politics. Although there is no shortage of former MPs in the Lords—there are currently about 180—there is a substantial number of people who have been made members of the Lords because they have achieved distinction or prominence in some other field of activity, such as business, science, or the arts. In this sense, the House of Lords is able to scrutinise Bills and government activity with the benefit of a particular breadth of experience and depth of expertise.

Third, we have already noted that the FPTP voting system means that large political parties dominate in the Commons; *small parties, and groups seeking to highlight a particular issue*, are unlikely to win enough votes in any given constituency to secure even a single seat in the Commons. The House of Lords is arguably capable of giving a voice to issues and groups unlikely to be well served by a first chamber the members of which are eager to appeal to the majority whose interests naturally dominate in the Commons.

3.3.5 Composition

What, then, should happen with the House of Lords? There are, broadly speaking, three options: a wholly appointed second chamber; a wholly elected one; or a hybrid system, with some members elected and some appointed.

There are arguments for a wholly appointed second chamber. Such a system could ensure that political parties do not dominate, that a wide range of views and interests are represented, and that a wider range of people than those likely to stand for election is brought into the political process. But this overlooks one crucial point: that, in a democratic system, a legislature must be regarded as legitimate.[124] This is not an unanswerable argument against an appointed second chamber, particularly if, like the present House of Lords, it is less powerful than the first chamber. It was also argued by the then Lord Chancellor in 2003 that legitimacy may be conferred other than by the ballot box: judges, for example, are not elected, their legitimacy deriving instead from their independence and expertise. But, as Phillipson has argued, the second chamber 'exercises direct political power . . . the legitimacy for [which] can flow only from election'.[125]

---

[124] See, eg Public Administration Select Committee, *The Second Chamber: Continuing the Reform* (HC 494-I 2001–02), [68].

[125] Phillipson, '"The Greatest Quango of Them All", "A Rival Chamber" or "A Hybrid Nonsense"? Solving the Second Chamber Paradox' [2004] PL 352, 366.

Q This argument begins with the fact that the House of Lords has legislative authority (albeit limited) and concludes that it must therefore have democratic legitimacy. Bingham[126] advances the opposite argument: that the second chamber should be stripped of its legislative power entirely and constituted as an advisory body consisting (like the current House of Lords) of a broad range of people who can bring experience and expertise to the scrutiny of legislation. Bingham argues that, thus constituted, the second chamber would not need democratic legitimacy. Do you agree?

Recent debate has focused on whether the Lords should be wholly or only partly elected. The Royal Commission recommended a mainly appointed House, but with a 'significant minority' of members elected to represent and 'provide a voice for the nations and regions of the United Kingdom'.[127] This position was endorsed by the then government in 2002, which argued that a mainly elected second chamber would suffer from several 'practical disadvantages', including loss of independence and dominance of political parties.[128]

Yet, in 2007, the government announced that it would attempt to build consensus around the view that the second chamber should be half appointed and half elected.[129] And by 2008, the government had decided that a reformed second chamber should be mainly elected, but that, in order to preserve an independent element, perhaps 20 per cent of members should be appointees independent of any political party.[130]

Phillipson agrees that there should be an appointed element, but doubts whether 20 per cent would be sufficient.[131] Referring to the enactment of the Anti-terrorism, Crime and Security Act 2001—one of the case studies with which we opened this book—he argues that the architecture of the British constitution means that the 'composition of its second chamber must guarantee the presence of members who will instil a particularly strong culture of mature, objective, and long-termist scrutiny of the wisdom and necessity' of proposed legislation.[132] This persuasive argument raises a conundrum. In the absence of a written constitution limiting the power of Parliament and of a thoroughgoing separation of powers between the executive and the Commons, the existence of the Lords as an internal check upon the executive-dominated Commons is imperative. However, its effectiveness as a real counterweight to the power of the executive and the Commons is dependent upon its capacity for independent-minded scrutiny that is not stifled by the sort of party politics likely to be engendered by elections. The capacity of a small unelected element goes some way towards addressing this problem, but whether it goes far enough is debatable.

Lords reform has been widely discussed for a long time and many proposals have been advanced. The debate has so often resulted in deadlock. Why? Clearly, current

---

[126] 'The House of Lords: Its Future?' [2010] PL 261.
[127] Commission on Reform of the House of Lords, *A House for the Future* (Cm 4534 2000), p 114.
[128] HM Government, *The House of Lords: Completing the Reform* (Cm 5291 2002), [36]–[40].
[129] HM Government, *The House of Lords: Reform* (Cm 7027 2007), p 5.
[130] Ministry of Justice, *An Elected Second Chamber: Further Reform of the House of Lords* (Cm 7438 2008).
[131] Phillipson, 379.   [132] Phillipson, 371.

members of the Lords have much to lose from reform, but the principal concern relates to the balance of power between the two Houses and the government. An elected Lords would seek to assert its own legitimacy, thereby challenging the Commons' supremacy. This would either weaken the government's position or simply turn the chamber into a replica House of Commons. Apart from this, there are so many different reform proposals that no single proposal commands sufficient support to provide a clear way ahead.

The last serious attempt at Lords reform occurred during the coalition government (2010–15). Lords reform was part of the coalition government's 2010 agreement: the intention was a wholly or mainly elected second chamber, with elections on the basis of proportional representation.[133] For the junior partner in the coalition—the Liberal Democrats—an elected Lords is a long-cherished goal, but not so for the rank and file of the Conservative party. The Liberal Democrats won Lords reform as part of the coalition agreement deal. A draft Bill proposed a smaller second chamber of 450 members—either 80 per cent or wholly elected—who would sit for a single non-renewable term of three normal election cycles, which, given five-year fixed term Parliaments, would be 15 years. Elections would be made under the *single transferable vote* system.[134] There would be no change at all to the Lords' functions or powers.

These proposals were critically examined,[135] but were ultimately abandoned because of opposition within the Conservative Party. In return for withdrawing from this part of the coalition agreement, Nick Clegg, then Deputy Prime Minister, withdrew Liberal Democrat support for proposals to reduce the size of the Commons from 650 to 600 MPs and redraw parliamentary boundaries (which it is thought is likely to favour the Conservatives). Now that the Conservative Party has a majority, it is again pursuing the reduction in the size of the Commons, but, given Brexit, there is no appetite for returning to Lords reform at present.

There have, though, been minor reforms concerning the resignation, expulsion, and exclusion of peers from the House. Previously, peers could only leave the House through death or the House's voluntary retirement scheme. Peers can now leave the House in the following circumstances: death, resignation, non-attendance for an entire session (subject to certain exceptions), conviction of a serious offence resulting in a custodial sentence of a year or more, and expulsion from the House for a breach of its code of conduct.[136]

Lords reform remains as intractable as ever. Constitutional reform is inherently politicised and politics often results in an ongoing stalemate simply because the issues are so difficult and exasperating. As far as parliamentary reform is concerned, the political constitution remains firmly in place.

---

[133] HM Government, *The Coalition: Our Programme for Government* (London 2010), p 27.

[134] HM Government, *House of Lords Reform Draft Bill* (Cm 8077 2011).

[135] Joint Committee on the Draft House of Lords Reform Bill, *Draft House of Lords Reform Bill* (HC 1313 HL 284 2010–12).

[136] House of Lords Reform Act 2014; House of Lords (Expulsion and Suspension) Act 2015.

Q Do you agree that a hybrid second chamber with a majority of elected members is the best way forward for the House of Lords? Why, or why not?

3.4 The UK: a democracy or an oligarchy?

So far, we have considered democracy in the UK from a traditional constitutional law perspective. However, our discussion has necessarily been limited and imperfect. Why so? Because a successful democracy is not merely a matter of having a perfect institutional structure. It also depends inescapably on 'actual behaviour patterns and the working of social and political interactions.'[137] Institutional form matters, but so does how politics actually works in practice.

In this respect, there has, for some years, been a growing concern in the UK about the practical workings of politics and government. The principal anxiety is that power has become increasingly concentrated in the hands of an oligarchy—a small group of powerful and largely unelected people. This concern is not held just by those on the fringes of mainstream politics. It is also widely espoused by commentators from across the political spectrum. According to Marquand, the UK's 'democratic forms conceal an increasingly oligarchic substance'.[138] Similarly, Mount has argued that 'power and wealth have, slowly, but unmistakably, begun to migrate into the hands of a relatively small elite'—a migration that shows no sign of abating.[139] There is a strong perception that the UK government works largely for the benefit of the corporate and financial sectors rather than the benefit of ordinary people. In theory, everyone has an equal say in the political process, but in practice, some people—and corporations— have a much greater say.

The many different features of this phenomenon are not to be found in formal constitutional rules, but in the behaviour of politicians and the informal social and political networks between politicians and business. There are, for instance, the close connections between senior politicians, media moguls, and the corporate elite. Other aspects include the dependence of political parties upon corporate funding, increased influence of the corporate sector over government through lobbying and its active leverage over policy across all areas of public life, tax evasion by large companies, and the informal influence of business upon government.

Another feature is the 'revolving door' between government and business. This has two dimensions. First, there is the ability of former politicians and civil servants to take up lucrative employment in businesses and consultancy roles. For instance, upon leaving office, Tony Blair took up a position with a finance bank for (reportedly) £500,000 per year; his consultancy firm makes £13 million per year by using contacts gained during Blair's term in office. Second, there is the increasing reliance of government upon members of the business community to make policy decisions.

---

[137] Sen, *The Idea of Justice* (London 2010), p 354.
[138] Marquand, *Mammon's Kingdom: An Essay on Britain, Now* (London 2014), p 170.
[139] Mount, *The New Few: Or a Very British Oligarchy* (London 2012), p 2.

For instance, the introduction of higher student tuition fees followed a review by Lord Browne, the then chief executive officer of BP. In 2010, Stephen Byers MP—a former government Minister—was caught on camera claiming that he was able to influence government decisions and describing himself as 'a bit of a cab for hire'.[140] The businessman Sir Philip Green, who avoided paying tax through an offshore tax avoidance scheme, subsequently undertook a review of public spending for the UK government.[141] There are many more such examples.[142]

All of these connections and linkages and both public and private influence strongly suggest that Britain is governed by a small oligarchy of politicians, businessmen, and corporate leaders. As Beetham has explained, the concept of the 'power elite' denotes 'a group identified by the *power* they exercise in one domain of activity, which can be transferred or parlayed to another'.[143] Beetham concludes that the development of a commanding power elite reveals a gaping democratic deficit: '[I]nstead of popular control we have subordination to an oligarchy of the wealthy and economically powerful. Instead of everyone counting for one, we have the easy purchase of political influence and the well-oiled revolving door between government and the corporate sector'.[144]

It is not possible here to do justice to the breadth of the wider discussion concerning the state of British democracy and society. There are also related developments, such as increasing social inequality and decreasing social mobility. However, the following points can be made.

First, it is abundantly clear that the powerful corporate and finance sectors exert far more influence upon government and politics than ordinary people. As Peston has noted, 'the voices of the super-wealthy are heard by politicians well above the babble of the crowd'.[145] Second, there has been a noticeable trend towards anti-politics, a kind of politics that is against 'the system'. There are many different strands to this trend from both the traditional left and right wings, and also environmentalist, anti-globalisation, and anti-corporate groups. The growth in support for the UK Independence Party is another manifestation. This movement extends far beyond the UK. A related issue concerns the nature of the UK's social and economic divisions as highlighted by the 2016 Brexit vote. Third, there is an extremely wide-ranging debate as to how British democracy could be improved. Marquand, for instance, has argued for a new public philosophy grounded upon the reinvigoration of the public realm, the development of open, tolerant, and accountable elites imbued with an ethic of civic duty and public services, and a conception of democracy as public reasoning.[146] There are many other contributions to this broader debate.[147] Finally, it should never

---

[140] http://news.bbc.co.uk/1/hi/uk_politics/8579348.stm

[141] Green was severely criticised in 2016 for extracting hundreds of millions of pounds of pension money from British Home Stores, an episode described as 'the unacceptable face of capitalism': House of Commons Work and Pensions and Business, Innovation and Skills Committees, *BHS* (HC 54 2016–17).

[142] See Mount and Peston.

[143] Beetham, *Unelected Oligarchy: Corporate and Financial Dominance in Britain's Democracy* (Liverpool 2012), p 11, https://democraticaudituk.files.wordpress.com/2013/06/oligarchy.pdf

[144] Beetham, p 21.   [145] Peston, *Who Runs Britain?* (London 2008), p 346.   [146] Marquand.

[147] For a very small sample of a wide literature, see Crewe and King, *The Blunders of Our Governments* (London 2013); Hutton, *How Good We Can Be* (London 2015); Lucas, *Honourable Friends? Parliament and the Fight for Change* (London 2015).

be forgotten that democracy has both formal and substantive dimensions; the formal structures of constitutional law can only be understood against the backdrop of day-to-day politics and how politics works in practice.

Overall, the UK's democracy is imperfect. Nonetheless, as Winston Churchill once noted, 'Democracy is the worst form of government, except for all those other forms that have been tried from time to time.' Democracy is immensely important and it needs to be valued, improved, and enhanced.

4. **Parliamentary privilege**

Parliamentary privilege is an integral aspect of the UK's constitutional arrangements. It is of ancient origin and an often overlooked and little understood part of the constitution.[148] It is also of vital importance to the constitutional status of Parliament, the nature of parliamentary democracy, and the relationship between Parliament and the courts. Parliamentary privilege protects those rights and immunities that Parliament needs in order to operate effectively and independently, and it does so by overriding ordinary legal rights as enforced by the courts. It also raises one of our themes: *the relationship between political and legal forms of constitutionalism*. If Parliament possesses certain rights and immunities, then which institution—Parliament or the courts—should make and interpret the law concerning the ambit and scope of those rights and immunities? What is the acceptable boundary between Parliament's rights and immunities on the one hand and the rule of law and individual rights on the other?

These questions fall to be addressed against the backdrop of the wider tension between political and legal modes of constitutionalism. If representative democracy as a value is prioritised, then this goes hand in hand with an emphasis upon political constitutionalism and an expansive conception of parliamentary privilege at the expense of judicially protected legal rights. Conversely, if the rule of law and judicial protection of legal rights are to be predominant, then this leads to an attenuated conception of parliamentary privilege. This tension underlies the operation and development of parliamentary privilege, but first it is necessary to define and examine it.

4.1 **What is parliamentary privilege?**

Parliament performs a number of important constitutional roles: debating public affairs, legislating, raising taxes, calling government to account, and airing grievances. To perform these functions effectively, Parliament must be able to act freely and independently without interference from the government, the courts, or any other body. Parliamentarians must be free to speak their minds in debates and MPs must be able to represent their constituents' views without fear or favour. Parliament

---

[148] Part of the difficulty may be that parliamentary *privilege* carries a connotation of benefit or advantage—for instance, that parliamentarians are above the law—unrelated to public need or duty. This is misleading. It is more appropriate to understand parliamentary privilege as comprising the rights and immunities that Parliament needs to perform its roles.

possesses certain rights and immunities which are an expression of its unique authority and which are known collectively as parliamentary privilege. These rights and privileges belong to Parliament as an institution.

There are two key components of parliamentary privilege: freedom of speech *in Parliament* and *exclusive cognisance*. Freedom of speech in Parliament is protected by Art IX of the Bill of Rights 1689, 'one of the pillars of the United Kingdom constitution'[149] and 'a provision of the highest constitutional importance'.[150] Article IX states that 'the freedome of speech and debates or proceedings in Parlyament ought not to be impeached or questioned in any court or place out of Parlyament'.[151]

Some historical background is helpful here. Since the Middle Ages, Parliament, and in particular the House of Commons, had sought to assert its right to debate and proceed without royal interference. During the seventeenth century, the Stuart kings thought that they could rule without parliamentary approval and also intimidate MPs by, for instance, arresting those who criticised the Crown. From one perspective, the English civil war can be seen as an assertion of Commons privilege against the Crown. After the restoration of the monarchy in 1688, the Bill of Rights 1689 was enacted by Parliament to vindicate and assert its ancient rights and liberties. The preamble to the Bill of Rights notes that King James II had sought to subvert the liberties of the realm 'by Prosecutions in the Court of King's Bench for Matters and Causes cognizable only in Parliament'. Article IX enables MPs to discuss what they, rather than the Crown or the courts, chose to.

Article IX affords legal immunity to parliamentarians for what they say or do in proceedings in Parliament, and that immunity extends to any court or place outside Parliament. Suppose that an MP in the House of Commons makes a statement that someone outside Parliament considers defamatory. Under the ordinary law, the person concerned could sue and seek damages, but Art IX provides a comprehensive and absolute immunity for statements made within Parliament.[152] This is because the possibility of subsequent judicial scrutiny of parliamentary speech could deter the free exchange of political views and the fearless pursuit of the national interest. The public interest in free political debate and guaranteeing Parliament's independence and autonomy outweighs ordinary legal rights.

The second key aspect of parliamentary privilege is known, somewhat archaically, as *exclusive cognisance*. Parliament has the right to determine its own rules and the procedures it uses to legislate, and to regulate its own internal affairs.[153] Parliament also possesses certain disciplinary and penal powers. Conduct, whether of a member

---

[149] Joint Committee on Parliamentary Privilege, *Parliamentary Privilege* (HL 43 HC 214 1998–99), [7] (hereinafter JCPP 1999).

[150] *Pepper v Hart* [1993] AC 593, 638, *per* Lord Browne-Wilkinson.

[151] The Bill of Rights was passed by the English Parliament. In Scotland, a separate but similar Act, the Claim of Right Act 1689, protects freedom of speech.

[152] Statute provides an absolute immunity against defamation concerning proceedings in the Scottish Parliament, the National Assembly for Wales, and the Northern Ireland Assembly. See Scotland Act 1998, s 41; Government of Wales Act 2006, s 42; Northern Ireland Act 1998, s 50.

[153] Sir William Blackstone, *Commentaries on the Laws of England* (Oxford 1765), pp 58–9, famously noted that the maxim underlying the law and custom of Parliament is that 'whatever matter arises concerning

or non-member, which improperly obstructs or interferes with Parliament, or the performance by members or officers of their duties, is a contempt of Parliament.

There are several instances of judicial recognition of Parliament's exclusive cognisance. *Bradlaugh v Gosset* concerned an elected MP, who, being an atheist, refused to swear the parliamentary oath to God as required under statute law.[154] Bradlaugh then commenced legal action against the Sergeant-at-Arms of the House of Commons for excluding him. Dismissing Bradlaugh's case, the court noted that 'what is said or done within the walls of Parliament cannot be inquired into in a court of law' and that the 'House of Commons is not subject to the control of Her Majesty's courts in its administration of that part of the statute law which has relation to its own internal proceedings'.[155]

The courts will refuse to question the proceedings by which an Act was passed to establish whether Parliament, in passing it, was misled by fraud or otherwise.[156] The courts also have no jurisdiction to suspend a parliamentarian as a member of either House. Parliament has its own procedures concerning the conduct of its members.[157] Furthermore, the courts will not entertain judicial review of the Parliamentary Commissioner for Standards (the parliamentary officer who investigates complaints as to the alleged impropriety of an MP's behaviour).[158]

Two other aspects of parliamentary privilege should be noted. First, *reports of parliamentary proceedings are protected*. This is because parliamentary free speech would be of little value if parliamentary debates and proceedings could not be freely communicated outside Parliament. In *Stockdale v Hansard*, the court held that parliamentary privilege protected papers printed by Parliament for use by its own members, but not papers made available outside Parliament to the public.[159] The Parliamentary Papers Act 1840 reversed this judgment by conferring absolute immunity upon parliamentary publications, such as Hansard (the official reports of parliamentary debates) and other parliamentary papers (eg reports of select committees).[160] The Act also confers qualified privilege upon extracts or abstracts from Hansard or other parliamentary papers, which will be protected if published '*bonâ fide* and without malice'.[161]

Second, privilege extends to *the application of the statute law to Parliament*. In the *Herbert* case, it was, the court held, outside its jurisdiction to hear a case as to whether it is necessary to possess a licence to sell alcohol in Parliament.[162] This ruling has generated uncertainty as to the application of statute law to Parliament. One view is that

either house of parliament, ought to be examined, discussed, and adjudged in that house to which it relates, and not elsewhere'.

[154] *Bradlaugh v Gossett* (1884) 12 QBD 271.

[155] *Bradlaugh v Gossett*, 275, *per* Lord Coleridge CJ, and 278, *per* Stephen J.

[156] *British Railways Board v Pickin* [1974] AC 765, 799, *per* Lord Simon of Glaisdale.

[157] The Parliamentary Commissioner for Standards considers complaints about MPs and is overseen by the Commons Standards Committee.

[158] *R v Parliamentary Commissioner for Standards, ex p Fayed* [1998] 1 WLR 669.

[159] *Stockdale v Hansard* (1839) 9 Ad & E 1, (1839) 112 ER 1112.

[160] Parliamentary Papers Act 1840, ss 1 and 2. See Stockdale, 'The Unnecessary Crisis: The Background to the Parliamentary Papers Act 1840' [1990] PL 30.

[161] Parliamentary Papers Act 1840, s 3.   [162] *R v Graham-Campbell, ex p Herbert* [1935] 1 KB 594.

statute does not apply to Parliament unless it says so explicitly; the alternative view is statute applies to Parliament unless it interferes with Parliament's internal affairs. This uncertainty has been criticised. After all, it seems odd that Parliament is not required to comply with its own laws on matters such as health and safety, employment, or the sale of alcohol. It has been recommended that Parliament adopt resolutions that it will in future be expressly bound by legislation creating individual rights which could impinge on parliamentary activities.[163]

4.2 Determining the scope of parliamentary privilege

Parliamentary privilege overrides ordinary legal rights, as enforced by the courts. It therefore raises wider questions concerning the relationship between Parliament and the courts. This relationship is governed by the principle of comity. In a spirit of mutual respect, Parliament and the courts recognise their respective constitutional roles and do not intrude into the spheres reserved to each other.[164] The courts protect ordinary legal rights and protect freedom of speech and Parliament's recognised rights and immunities, but they do not control how Parliament conducts its business. Parliament enacts legislation, the courts interpret and apply it. The enactment of legislation, and the process by which legislation is enacted, are matters for Parliament, not the courts. Parliament, for its part, must not interfere with how courts decide cases.

Inevitably, from time to time, boundary disputes arise concerning the precise dividing line between those areas in which the ordinary law prevails and the no-go areas in which the courts should pull back and not interfere with Parliament. For instance, which activities are covered by the phrase 'proceedings in Parliament' in Art IX? It clearly applies to words spoken in the course of a Parliamentary debate, but it may be uncertain whether it applies to briefings or correspondence that is preparatory to that debate. Not only must questions of this nature be answered: it is also necessary to determine who, in the first place—Parliament or the courts—gets to supply the answer.

Consider the Supreme Court case of *Chaytor*.[165] This case was heard amidst much public concern following the MPs' expenses scandal. In 2009, it was disclosed that many MPs had been exploiting the system of parliamentary expenses for their own personal benefit. The prosecuting authorities sought to prosecute three MPs and one peer for false accounting. In response, the four parliamentarians invoked parliamentary privilege, arguing that the prosecution would contravene free speech under Art IX and that the system of parliamentary expenses fell within Parliament's exclusive cognisance.

---

[163] Joint Committee on Parliamentary Privilege, *Parliamentary Privilege* (HL 30 HC 100 2013–14), [226] (hereinafter JCPP 2013).

[164] See *Pickin v British Railways Board* [1974] AC 765, 799, *per* Lord Simon of Glaisdale; *R v HM Treasury, ex p Smedley* [1985] QB 657, 666, *per* Lord Donaldson of Lymington.

[165] *R v Chaytor* [2010] UKSC 52, [2011] 1 AC 684.

The first question concerned *the appropriate division of responsibility between Parliament and the courts for determining the scope of parliamentary privilege*. Which institution decides? During the seventeenth and eighteenth centuries, there were various controversies between Parliament and the courts as to which institution was the final arbiter of matters concerning parliamentary privilege.[166] This was finally resolved in the courts' favour. In *Stockdale v Hansard*, while accepting that 'whatever be done within the walls of either [House] must pass without question in any other place', the court rejected the proposition that the House of Commons, in its guise as a court, had sole jurisdiction over the *extent* of its own privileges.[167] The courts determine the scope of parliamentary privilege, but once the subject matter falls within parliamentary privilege, the courts cannot question it.[168] This was confirmed by the Supreme Court in *Chaytor*: '[T]he extent of parliamentary privilege is ultimately a matter for the court'.[169]

The second issue in *Chaytor* concerned *the test for determining the scope of parliamentary privilege*. The applicable test is known as the necessity or functionality principle: parliamentary privilege displaces the normal application of the law only when this is necessary to safeguard the effective functioning of Parliament.[170] According to Lord Phillips: 'In considering whether actions outside the Houses and committees fall within parliamentary proceedings because of their connection to them, it is necessary to consider the nature of that connection and whether, if such actions do not enjoy privilege, this is likely to impact adversely on the core or essential business of Parliament.'[171]

Applying this test, the Supreme Court unanimously held that parliamentary privilege did not preclude judicial scrutiny of MPs' use of parliamentary expenses through the criminal justice process. Such scrutiny by the courts would neither adversely affect Parliament's core business nor inhibit parliamentary debate or freedom of speech.[172] Also, it would not interfere with Parliament's exclusive cognisance. Parliament has never challenged, in general, the application of criminal law within its precincts, but has accepted the jurisdiction of the criminal courts.[173] The prosecution was therefore able to proceed and the four parliamentarians were convicted.

Three points arise. First, as noted earlier, *the relationship between Parliament and the courts is based upon the long-standing principle of comity*. Each takes care not to intrude onto, or to undermine, the other's territory. Parliamentary privilege ensures that Parliament does not have its proceedings questioned by the courts. Yet, the scope of parliamentary privilege is determined by the courts. This affords the courts a certain degree of interpretive power to determine what is and is not covered by privilege.

---

[166] eg in the seventeenth century, each House of Parliament claimed the right to be the sole exclusive judge of its own privileges and the extent of that privilege. See *Parliament case* (1609) 13 Co Rep 63.

[167] *Stockdale v Hansard*, [114].   [168] *Stockdale v Hansard*, [147]–[148].

[169] *Chaytor*, [16].

[170] JCPP 1999, [4]; JCPP 2013, [20]–[28]; Jack, 'Parliamentary Privilege: A Dignified or Efficient Part of the Constitution?', The Seventeenth Policy & Politics Annual Lecture, University of Bristol, 29 March 2012, p 2, **http://www.policypress.co.uk/PDFs/General/Malcolm%20Jack%20Lecture%20NEW.pdf**

[171] *Chaytor*, [47]. See also *Canada (House of Commons) v Vaid* [2005] 1 SCR 667, [4].

[172] *Chaytor*, [48].   [173] *Chaytor*, [79]–[83].

As always, however, if Parliament takes exception to the courts' interpretation of the law, it can legislate. Subject to the provisos that Parliament's legislative freedom is constrained by EU law and by the UK's obligations under the ECHR, it could, for instance, make new or more precise rules concerning parliamentary privilege, which would then fall to be interpreted by the courts.

Second, *it is insufficient for Parliament to assert its privileges through mere resolutions of the House* (as distinct from legislation). During the long-running lawsuit of *Stockdale v Hansard*, the Commons passed various resolutions asserting the extent of its privileges, but this was rejected as 'abhorrent to the first principles of the constitution'.[174] It was necessary for Parliament to enact legislation to clarify the law. Unlike Acts of Parliament, resolutions of the House of Commons do not benefit from the doctrine of legislative supremacy.

Third, *the ambiguous extent of parliamentary privilege can be viewed in either positive or negative terms.* It enables parliamentary privilege to evolve and change over time, which may be a good thing. However, with such flexibility comes a degree of uncertainty, at least at the edges, as to precisely which activities are covered by parliamentary privilege. As *Chaytor* shows, particular difficulty arises in relation to ancillary matters—that is, things said or done outside parliamentary proceedings themselves, but which are somehow connected to those proceedings. Whether or not codification is the best response to such difficulties is a matter we consider in section 4.4.

> **Q** Why is parliamentary privilege of constitutional importance? Who do you think should determine the scope of parliamentary privilege—Parliament or the courts?

4.3 Contemporary issues and challenges

As we have explained, parliamentary privilege developed because of the need to protect Parliament against high-handed monarchs who wanted to interfere with it and intimidate members of Parliament—a historical context that obviously no longer applies. However, parliamentary privilege is 'not static or immutable'.[175] It is 'a living concept, and still serves to protect Parliament, each House, their committees, and all those involved in proceedings'.[176] Free speech in parliamentary proceedings remains fundamentally important, but the contemporary threats to Parliament's ability to discharge its functions differ from those that account for the development of privilege several centuries ago. What, then, are the current issues and challenges?

4.3.1 Judicial questioning of proceedings in Parliament

The courts used to be reluctant to make any reference to parliamentary proceedings. They still are reluctant to do so. But, over recent years, the courts accepted that judicial reference to parliamentary debates is, in some instances, permissible. This is not

---

[174] *Stockdale v Hansard*, [108].   [175] JCPP 1999, [17].   [176] JCPP 2013, [13].

necessarily problematic—provided that the courts do not, contrary to Art IX, either 'impeach or question' parliamentary proceedings in a way that would inhibit the core business of Parliament.

Consider the following situations. First, a court has to interpret ambiguous legislation. Can it use Hansard as an aid to the interpretation of the statute? Second, a litigant before a court seeks to rely upon a report of a parliamentary select committee. Is the court entitled to take account of that litigant's reliance upon a select committee report (bearing in mind that the other party may take issue with it)?

The first scenario is covered by the rule in *Pepper v Hart*.[177] In this case, the House of Lords recognised an exception to the exclusionary rule against using Hansard in statutory interpretation: the courts may rely upon clear statements made by a Minister or the MP promoting a Bill in Parliament as an aid when interpreting ambiguous legislation. Reference to Hansard would not infringe the prohibition in Art IX against judicial questioning of parliamentary debate. Lord Browne-Wilkinson explained that '[f]ar from questioning the independence of Parliament and its debates, the courts are giving effect to what is said and done there'.[178] This ruling has been controversial and its application has subsequently been carefully confined.[179]

Compare this with the second scenario in which a court relies upon a parliamentary select committee report in support of its decision. The courts have held this to be impermissible.[180]

This difference of approach turns upon whether or not the court is either merely *referring to* parliamentary proceedings or *questioning* them. When a court refers to Hansard when interpreting ambiguous legislation, it is not questioning what was said in Parliament, but relying upon it as an aid to construction. However, in the second scenario, the court is questioning the views of a select committee and also potentially the process by which it reached them. If an individual relies upon a select committee report in the context of an adversarial judicial system, then the other party will seek to question it. The court would then have to either approve or reject the select committee's report, which would contravene Art IX and blur the separate constitutional roles of Parliament and the judiciary.

The Lord Chief Justice has accepted that instances of this practice have been inadvertent mistakes by the courts.[181] According to the Joint Committee on Parliamentary Privilege, judicial reliance upon select committee reports is 'not only constitutionally inappropriate, but risks having a chilling effect upon parliamentary debate'.[182]

There are other areas in which the courts will more readily refer to debates within Parliament. In judicial review proceedings, the courts have adopted the practice of referring to ministerial statements made to Parliament to demonstrate what government policy is.[183] Also, when, under the Human Rights Act 1998 (HRA), questions

---

[177] [1993] AC 593.   [178] *Pepper v Hart*, 638, *per* Lord Browne-Wilkinson.

[179] Steyn, '*Pepper v Hart*: A Re-examination' (2001) 21 OJLS 59; Kavanagh, '*Pepper v Hart* and Matters of Constitutional Principle' (2005) 121 LQR 98.

[180] *Office of Government Commerce v Information Commissioner* [2008] EWHC 737 (Admin), [2010] QB 98, [59].

[181] JCPP 2013, [129].   [182] JCPP 2013, [136].

[183] *R v Secretary of State for the Home Department, ex p Brind* [1991] 1 AC 696.

arise about the compatibility of an Act of Parliament with the ECHR, the courts may rely upon ministerial statements to Parliament as background information.[184]

Different views have been expressed as to whether or not such developments threaten parliamentary privilege. The government's view is that these apparent exceptions to freedom of speech do not involve the questioning of parliamentary proceedings by courts. Instead, such uses of parliamentary materials by the courts are widely accepted by Parliament, government, and the courts as 'representing sensible, pragmatic positions'.[185] By contrast, Joseph has argued that such gradual judicial incursions cumulatively weaken free speech in Parliament, compromise Parliament's ability to function independently, and created uncertainty and confusion as to the scope of free speech in Parliament.[186]

The concern is that judicial reference to parliamentary proceedings exerts an unintended chilling effect that inhibits debate and deters Ministers from presenting policies and decisions clearly and honestly before Parliament for fear of judicial review. Indeed, Lord Browne-Wilkinson in *Pepper v Hart* accepted that reference to parliamentary debates 'by the courts might affect what is said in Parliament'.[187] Parliamentary anxiety is itself less severe, but nonetheless present. In 2013, the Joint Committee on Parliamentary Privilege noted that it did not 'at this stage believe that the problem of judicial questioning is sufficiently acute to justify . . . legislation prohibiting use of privileged material by the courts', but warned that Parliament should be prepared to legislate if necessary to protect freedom of speech in Parliament from judicial questioning.[188]

4.3.2 **Parliamentary criticism of non-members**

Under parliamentary privilege, parliamentarians can say whatever they think fit in a parliamentary debate. MPs should exercise this privilege responsibly, but what happens if an MP speaks offensively of another person so that his reputation is adversely affected or if a select committee criticises someone unfairly?

Parliamentary privilege provides absolute immunity against defamation proceedings so there can be no recourse to UK courts.[189] However, matters may be less clear-cut with regard to other courts, especially if human rights law is invoked. The HRA does not apply to parliamentary proceedings,[190] but the ECHR itself contains no analogous qualification—meaning that an individual can pursue a challenge before the ECtHR.

This occurred in *A v UK*.[191] An MP had been highly critical of one of his constituents, describing her as a 'neighbour from hell'. The constituent claimed that the MP's comments infringed her Convention rights, in particular, her rights to a fair trial

---

[184] *Wilson v First Country Trust Ltd (No 2)* [2003] UKHL 40, [2004] 1 AC 816, [51]–[67].

[185] HM Government, *Parliamentary Privilege* (Cm 8318 2012), [85].

[186] Joseph, 'Parliament's Attenuated Privilege of Freedom of Speech' (2010) 126 LQR 568.

[187] *Pepper v Hart*, 639, *per* Lord Browne-Wilkinson. [188] JCPP 2013, [136].

[189] *Ex p Wason* (1868–69) LR 4 QB 573, 576. Statements made outside Parliament, even if they amount to a repetition of statements made during the course of parliamentary debates on matters of public interest do not attract absolute immunity: *Jennings v Buchanan* [2004] UKPC 36, [2005] 1 AC 115.

[190] HRA, s 6(3).   [191] (2002) 36 EHRR 917.

and to a private life.[192] Under Art IX, the MP's speech was immune from any judicial questioning before a domestic court, but the ECtHR considered itself to be under no equivalent inhibition. The court held that the use of parliamentary privilege was not a disproportionate interference with the claimant's human rights. Nonetheless, the court's President expressed some reservations as to the absolute nature of privilege and suggested that that hitherto unyielding principle might need to be tempered by a recognition of human rights.

The challenge failed, but the case suggests that there is a potential clash between parliamentary privilege and the need to safeguard the rights and interests of other individuals. At present, an individual who considers herself to have been the subject of offending remarks by an MP is not entirely without recourse. The person may petition the Commons through any MP with a view to securing a retraction. In extreme cases, deliberately misleading statements by an MP may be censured or even punished by Parliament as a contempt. However, the effectiveness of such mechanisms is questionable.

One possible solution would be to enable individuals who might potentially be criticised in Parliament to be put on notice of this and/or to introduce a right for the offended party to make representations, which could be subsequently considered by the Committee of Privileges.[193] However, in 1999, the Joint Committee on Parliamentary Privilege recommended against a right to reply. Such a scheme would raise expectations that it could not fulfil: it would not establish the truth or falsity of the criticism, no financial redress would be forthcoming, and a statement published in Hansard would not necessarily attract publicity matching the original comments.[194]

4.3.3 The powers of select committees

Questions about the contemporary scope and nature of parliamentary privilege also arise in relation to the powers of parliamentary select committees. Select committees, which we examine in more detail in Chapter 10, have become increasingly important, and now constitute the most widely recognised means by which Parliament scrutinises government. The increasing prominence of committees has raised questions concerning their powers. Select committees can call for persons, papers, and records, but what if an individual refuses to attend a committee hearing or does attend but gives false and misleading evidence?

Such incidents are rare, but in 2012 the Commons Liaison Committee noted that 'long-standing uncertainties about the extent and enforceability of select committees' powers' had recently been brought to the fore.[195] For instance, in 2011, the Chief Executive Officer of Kraft Foods refused to appear before a Commons select

---

[192] See Chapter 18.

[193] See House of Lords Committee for Privileges and Conduct, *Mr Trevor Phillips: Allegation of Contempt* (HL 15 2010–12); House of Lords Procedure Committee, *Criticism of Individuals in House of Lords Select Committee Reports* (HL 127 2010–12).

[194] JCPP 1999, [217]–[223].

[195] House of Commons Liaison Committee, *Select Committee Effectiveness, Resources and Powers* (HC 697 2012–13), [129].

committee inquiring into the takeover of Cadbury.[196] Also, during the phone-hacking scandal, Rupert Murdoch, proprietor of News International, was summoned to a select committee, prompting discussion as to what would happen if he had refused. In the event, Murdoch attended, but the select committee found that the behaviour of News International and certain witnesses had demonstrated contempt for the select committee system in the most blatant fashion.[197]

Scrutiny by select committees is most effective when there is cooperation—rather than confrontation—between committees and witnesses, but this cannot always be guaranteed. In theory, Parliament can fine and imprison to punish an individual who obstructs parliamentary business, but has been reluctant to exercise its penal powers for fear of appearing to be oppressive. In 1978, Parliament resolved that such powers should be exercised as sparingly as possible and only when necessary to prevent a substantial interference with its functions.[198]

There are also considerable doubts whether such powers are still enforceable. The Commons last issued a fine in 1666. While there is judicial authority for the power of the Commons to imprison,[199] there would be real objections to the exercise of this power and a challenge against Parliament under the ECHR would carry a substantial reputational risk.[200] The other option, calling an individual to the Bar of the House to be admonished by the Speaker before the entire Commons, would be distinctly out of place in the age of televised parliamentary proceedings—'a theatre of the absurd'[201]—and could backfire. Yet, doing nothing would be unacceptable.[202] Committees may occasionally need coercive powers to deal with serious failures. The lack of practically exercisable coercive powers poses a threat to the legitimacy and effectiveness of select committees.[203] Their integrity and effectiveness depends upon witnesses presenting truthful evidence.

There are other options.[204] Parliament could legislate to *criminalise a failure to attend or give evidence*. Such a process would have to contain sufficient procedural safeguards to comply with the right to a fair trial under Art 6 ECHR. It has been argued that reconciliation of the imperatives here—the need for stronger coercive select committees with adequate legal protection for witnesses—may require legislation.[205] Indeed, the devolved Parliament and Assemblies have statutory powers to summon witnesses, who can be prosecuted if they either fail to attend or answer

---

[196] House of Commons Business, Innovation and Skills Committee, *Is Kraft Working for Cadbury?* (HC 871 2010–12), [7]–[17].

[197] House of Commons Culture, Media and Sport Committee, *News International and Phone Hacking* (HC 903 2010–12), [279].

[198] Resolution of the House of Commons, 6 February 1978.   [199] *Stockdale v Hansard*, [114].

[200] The relevant Convention rights would be the right to liberty (Art 5) and the right to a fair trial (Art 6). See further Chapter 18.

[201] JCPP 2013, vol II, Ev 119 (Michael Jack, former Clerk of the House of Commons).

[202] House of Commons Liaison Committee, [134]; JCPP 2013, [61].

[203] Gordon and Street, *Select Committees and Coercive Powers—Clarity or Confusion* (London 2012), p 21.

[204] See the written evidence submitted by the Clerk of the House of Commons, Robert Rogers, on the powers of select committees (2012): http://www.publications.parliament.uk/pa/cm201213/cmselect/cmliaisn/697/697we36.htm

[205] Gordon and Jack, *Parliamentary Privilege: Evolution or Codification?* (London 2013), [113]–[123].

questions.[206] Such powers have enhanced the independence and status of the committees of the devolved Parliament and Assemblies.

However, Westminster select committees have been reluctant to recommend legislation. This might lead to judicial challenges in individual cases, possibly entail a radical transfer of powers from Parliament to the courts, and risk transforming select committee proceedings.[207] In other words, if the stakes were to be raised by criminalising failure to cooperate with select committees, this would inevitably lead to judicial examination of proceedings before select committees—including, perhaps, judicial scrutiny of the procedural fairness and adequacy of such proceedings. It is for precisely this reason—greater judicial involvement in the work of select committees— that select committees themselves have resisted this option.

A third option would be for Parliament to reassert its existing powers and to enumerate formally those kinds of behaviour likely to constitute contempt.[208] Such reassertion could be effected if Parliament amended its Standing Orders, handled such instances through the Committee of Privileges, and adopted a process that treated recalcitrant witnesses fairly. If such a process complied with the right to a fair trial (Art 6 ECHR), then parliamentary admonishment of a miscreant witness could have considerable reputational (and in some cases, financial) impact. This option, however, is not without legal risk, not least because penal proceedings would attract challenges under the ECHR.

> **Q** What powers do you think select committees should have?

4.4 Should parliamentary privilege be codified?

Parliamentary privilege is little understood. The relevant law is scattered amongst various sources and is obscure. Is it time for wholesale codification? Codification could increase clarity and transparency and allow for the law to be updated. On the other hand, it could inhibit the ability of the law to develop incrementally and flexibly to accommodate new and unforeseen developments. It may also have unintended consequences.

The 1999 Joint Committee on Parliamentary Privilege recommended a Parliamentary Privileges Act to codify parliamentary privilege.[209] Codification would provide a coherent framework in which Parliament could exercise its legitimate privilege openly. It would also increase clarity and transparency. For instance, ambiguous phrases in Art IX of the Bill of Rights, such as 'proceedings in parliament', could be clearly defined.

---

[206] Scotland Act 1998, ss 23–6; Northern Ireland Act 1998, ss 44–5; Government of Wales Act 2006, ss 37–40. The Australian Parliamentary Privileges Act 1987, s 7(1) gives the Australian House of Representatives the power to imprison for up to six months.

[207] House of Commons Liaison Committee, [133]; JCPP 2013, [63]–[75].

[208] JCPP 2013, [76]–[100].

[209] JCPP 1999, [376]–[385]. See also Gordon and Jack, *Parliamentary Privilege: Evolution or Codification?* (London 2013).

The existing law could also be updated. For example, the Parliamentary Papers Act 1840, which is expressed in an impenetrable early Victorian style, could be replaced with a modern statute. As we have noted, it has also been argued that if select committees need clearer and coercive powers, then legislation is the best option. For these reasons, codification has been advanced.

There are arguments against codification. One is the need for flexibility; Parliament's working practices change and privilege should not be immutable, but should be free to adapt and evolve. It would be undesirable to identify and specify every aspect of parliamentary privilege. Further, a codifying statute—however precisely drafted— could have unintended consequences. It could lead to uncertainty as to how it might be interpreted by the courts in the context of new circumstances unforeseen when the statute was enacted. It could also possibly lead to judicial interference in parliamentary matters, upset the constitutional balance between Parliament and the judiciary, and diminish parliamentary privilege.

For these reasons, the 2013 Joint Committee on Parliamentary Privilege recommended against statutory codification, a view endorsed by the government.[210] Legislation should be used very much as a last resort and carries the risk that statute law, and the judicial interpretation of it will, over time, ossify privilege, taking away the possibility of evolution and adaptation to changing circumstances.

The Committee did, though, recognise that specific legislation might be needed, albeit only when absolutely necessary, to resolve uncertainty or in the unlikely event of Parliament's exclusive cognisance being materially diminished by the courts.[211] For instance, the Committee recommended the long overdue replacement of the Parliamentary Papers Act 1840—'an updating of archaic legislation rather than the creation of new legislation'.[212]

> **Q** The 2013 Joint Committee on Parliamentary Privilege stated that parliamentary privilege 'has proved its ability to evolve and adapt to new circumstances. Codification would severely curtail such evolution'.[213] Do you agree?

5. Parliament and the legislative process

Most of the rules that regulate our daily lives—whether by requiring or forbidding us to do certain things—originate either from legislation or from the numerous rules and regulations made under such legislation. It is the single most important source of law in our society. The volume of legislation enacted today is enormous—though quantity does not necessarily mean quality. Legislation is used to achieve a variety of different and important public purposes. It creates new criminal offences, increases taxes, distributes welfare, enables government to make appropriations of public

---

[210] HM Government, *Parliamentary Privilege* (Cm 8318 2012), [37]; Leader of the House of Commons, *Government Response to the Joint Committee on Parliamentary Privilege* (CM 8771 2013).
[211] JCPP 2013, [41]–[47].   [212] JCPP 2013, [280].   [213] JCPP 2013, [276].

money, and authorises the use of such resources. Legislation is a vital resource of public policy.[214] Legislation is closely intertwined with the broader political process. Acts of Parliament are the product of political debate. In a democracy, we would expect the legislative process to be as open as possible and for the legislature to scrutinise effectively all proposed legislation—'Bills'—before they became law. However, the degree to which Parliament does engage in effective scrutiny is open to question. This relates to one of our principal themes—ensuring the responsible exercise of executive power. Parliament's role in the legislative process is centred not upon making legislation itself, but upon scrutinising the legislation that the government would like to be enacted. The purpose here is to examine the effectiveness of Parliament as a scrutiniser of legislation.

5.1 The legislative process—Parliament and government

5.1.1 Types of legislation

Let us start by considering the number of Acts of Parliament enacted each year. Figure 5.10 shows the number of statutes enacted since 1950 throughout the UK. The following points arise. First, the spikes in the number of Acts of Parliament tend to coincide with the first year of a new government. Second, there has been a downward trend in the number of Acts of Parliament enacted since the mid-1970s. Third, while the UK Parliament had, for many years, a total monopoly of primary

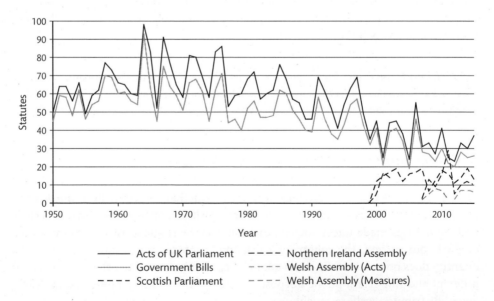

Figure 5.10 Primary legislation enacted throughout the UK, 1950–2015

Source: House of Commons Library Briefing Paper, *Acts and Statutory Instruments: The Volume of UK Legislation 1950–2015* (CBP7438 2015). Data on government Acts is up to 2012.

---

[214] Rose, 'Law as a Resource of Public Policy' (1986) 39 Parliamentary Affairs 297.

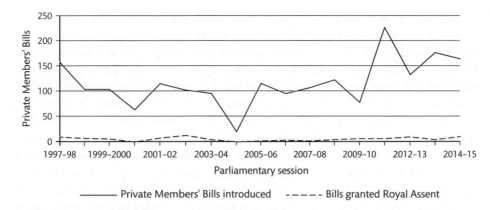

Figure 5.11 Private Members' Bills 1997–2015

Source: House of Commons Library Briefing Paper, *Number of Public Bills Introduced and Gaining Royal Assent Since 1997* (SN02283 2015).

legislative power, that is clearly no longer the case as evidenced by legislation enacted by the Scottish Parliament and the Welsh and Northern Ireland Assemblies.

As Figure 5.10 shows, public or government Bills comprise the overwhelming majority of statutes enacted each year. There are also *Private Members' Bills*, which are introduced by individual MPs and peers. Most Private Members' Bills stand little, if any, chance of being enacted, unless they have government support, but they may raise the political profile of an issue.[215] Look at Figure 5.11 and compare the number of Private Members' Bills introduced with those Bills granted Royal Assent (ie those enacted).

Other types of Bills include *private Bills*, which are usually promoted by organisations, such as local authorities or private companies, and *hybrid Bills*, which mix the characteristics of public and private Bills, because they affect the general public, but also have a significant impact for specific individuals or groups.[216] We will concentrate largely upon the legislative process as regards public or government Bills, the predominant type of legislation.

5.1.2 Roles—Parliament, Ministers, and government departments

The legislative process is dominated by the government: 'Parliament is not, and never has been, a legislature, in the sense of a body specially and primarily empowered to make laws'.[217] Parliament debates, scrutinises, and enacts the government's legislation rather than making its own. Parliament is thus not a lawmaking, but a *law-effecting*, institution.[218]

---

[215] Marsh and Marsh, 'Tories in the Killing Fields? The Fate of Private Members' Bills in the 1997–2001 Parliament' (2002) 8 Journal of Legislative Studies 91; House of Commons Procedure Committee, Private Members' Bills (HC 684 2015–16).

[216] The Channel Tunnel Act 1987, for example, was a hybrid Bill.

[217] Amery, *Thoughts on the Constitution* (Oxford 1953), pp 11–12.

[218] Norton, 'Parliament and Legislative Scrutiny: An Overview of Issues in the Legislative Process', in Brazier (ed), *Parliament, Politics and Law Making: Issues and Developments in the Legislative Process* (London 2004), p 5.

The executive is, then, in the driving seat. Ministers are certainly involved, but their involvement is largely at a strategic level. The Cabinet Committee on Parliamentary Business and Legislation manages the government's current legislative programme, advises the Cabinet on strategic management of the forthcoming programme, and ensures that the government's legislative programme reflects the government's overall priorities and that the passage of each of those Bills through Parliament is as smooth as possible.[219] The detailed work of turning policy proposals into Bills is undertaken by civil servants, who are organised into Bill teams. Such teams operate under the general direction of Ministers, but work with a substantial degree of autonomy in developing legislative policy. In turn, Bill teams' instructions are turned into draft legislation by the Office of Parliamentary Counsel, a specialised team of lawyers with expertise in legislative drafting, based in Whitehall. 'The idea that the politician is the author of legislation confuses constitutional formality with empirical reality.'[220]

Government departments will themselves play a substantial role in the legislative process. 'A Bill is first and foremost the legal expression of a policy developed within a particular Government department.'[221] This is not a recent development. As Low noted in 1904, 'the Ministry is the real law-making organ and . . . it can count on the support of its Parliamentary majority for any legislative project, so long as the majority holds together'.[222]

5.2 Parliamentary scrutiny

5.2.1 Introduction

Parliament spends more of its time scrutinising legislation than on any other activity (though, as we shall see, the amount of time spent has been declining), and its assent is required for a Bill to become law. Without robust and rigorous parliamentary scrutiny, the risk is that poor-quality legislation may be enacted. Such legislation may not achieve its goals, may impose undue burdens upon individuals or businesses, may have undesirable or unintended side effects, may violate human rights standards, or may be counterproductive. Effective parliamentary scrutiny is therefore essential and can perform a number of important functions.

Parliament can examine the policy justifications underpinning a Bill to ensure that the measure is desirable in principle. It can examine whether the means devised to accomplish policy goals are adequate and fit for purpose. Parliament can also scrutinise the technical quality of legislation. On the whole, better scrutiny tends to produce better legislation. Finally, Parliament provides the vital representative link between the government and the people who will be governed by legislation, and the process of parliamentary scrutiny has the advantage that it is structured, transparent, and

---

[219] Cabinet Office, *Guide to Making Legislation* (London 2013).

[220] Page, 'The Civil Servant as Legislator: Law Making in British Administration' (2003) 81 Public Administration 651, 674.

[221] Goldsmith, 'Parliament for Lawyers: An Overview of the Legislative Process' (2002) 4 European Journal of Law Reform 511, 513.

[222] Low, *The Governance of England* (London 1904), p 65.

public. More generally, parliamentary scrutiny is one aspect of Parliament's broader function of holding government to account.

Nevertheless, despite the significance of parliamentary scrutiny of legislation, it has been widely recognised for many years that Parliament is often unable effectively to scrutinise legislation.[223] The complaint has often been that governments have forced important—and sometimes poorly thought through—laws through a complaisant and submissive Parliament in which they receive little, if any, effective scrutiny. In 1953, Amery described Parliament as 'an overworked legislation factory'.[224] More recently, Tony Wright, former chair of the House of Commons Public Administration Committee, has noted that the ineffectiveness of parliamentary accountability is most apparent in its scrutiny of legislation:

> In outward form legislation is carefully scrutinized through an elaborate series of parliamentary stages, including detailed consideration in committee. The reality is that the whole process is firmly controlled by the government, serious scrutiny by government members is actively discouraged, any concession or amendment is viewed as a sign of weakness, and the opposition plays a game of delay. The result is that much legislation is defective, vast quantities of amendments have to be introduced by the government at the House of Lords stage, and the government's control of the parliamentary timetable means that many of these amendments are then simply voted through by the Commons without any scrutiny at all. It is all deeply unsatisfactory, and felt to be so by almost everyone involved in it.[225]

This portrayal may conjure up a rather jaundiced image of MPs as lobby fodder who are simply told how to vote by their 'party whips' (ie those MPs or peers appointed by a political party to maintain parliamentary discipline among its members so as to ensure attendance and voting). This is an oversimplification: not all MPs and peers are willing to do precisely what they are told. Some rebel. The government responds to the anticipated reaction of Parliament through concessions. Nonetheless, there is more than a grain of truth in this general depiction of parliamentary scrutiny. There are several reasons why the effectiveness of parliamentary scrutiny of legislation is limited.

5.2.2 Adversarial party politics and government dominance of the House of Commons

The first, and perhaps the principal, constraint upon the effectiveness of parliamentary scrutiny arises from two defining and interlocking features of the UK's parliamentary system: the dominance of the government of the day over the House of Commons, and the pervasive adversarial culture of Westminster party politics. We have already noted that virtually every aspect of Parliament's work is dominated by party politics; the same applies to the legislative process. The overriding assumption is that MPs support or oppose a Bill according to their party loyalties. And because the government (whether composed of a single party or a coalition of parties) will normally have

---

[223] Rippon, *Making the Law: The Report of the Hansard Society on the Legislative Process* (London 1992).
[224] Amery, *Thoughts on the Constitution* (Oxford 1953), p 41.
[225] Wright, *British Politics: A Very Short Introduction* (Oxford 2003), p 89.

more than half of the MPs, this means that the government can generally be confident of getting its Bills through the House of Commons.[226] The degree to which backbench government MPs refuse to support government Bills is normally seen as a test of the government's strength. Most MPs are loyal to their party or else placed under pressure by the government's whips to support the government's legislative programme; if the government whips declare that a particular vote will be subject to a 'three-line whip', then rebellious MPs risk being expelled from the governing party or parties.

This does not mean that the whips are always successful in maintaining party discipline. The government may offer concessions in order to prevent a rebellion, but this is the exception rather than the norm, because the government will usually have a sufficient number of MPs to prevent a defeat.[227] For example, the Labour government elected in 1997 experienced its first defeat in the House of Commons only in 2005 when backbench Labour MPs refused to approve the government's proposal to allow the pre-charge detention of terrorist suspects for up to 90 days.[228] By contrast with government backbench MPs, opposition parties will often oppose government Bills, but will, by definition, lack the necessary support with which to defeat the government.

Parliament can, of course, offer criticism and advice, and can subject legislation to public scrutiny, but the legislative process is primarily a political process in which the governing party—the government—holds the upper hand. Consequently, rather than being primarily focused upon the scrutiny of legislation, Parliament's role in the legislative process is often that of providing a forum in which the political parties engage in a continuous electoral campaign by seeking to score political points off one another.

5.2.3 Parliament's limited competence

A second constraint upon parliamentary scrutiny of legislation concerns the competence of Parliament. In the nineteenth century, Mill concluded that 'a numerous assembly is . . . little fitted for the direct business of legislation': the 'detailed and skilled work of legislation' should be left to those 'with the requisite skill', with the legislature's role being limited to 'either approving or disapproving the results'.[229]

The complexity of public policy and legislation has increased exponentially since Mill made these comments. In the context of the contemporary legislative process, the competence of parliamentarians to perform even this scrutiny function has often been questioned. There is a 'contemporary shortage in the House of Commons itself of the kind of experience and skills demanded by the task' of scrutinising legislation.[230] So, what do MPs themselves think of their own ability to scrutinise the mass of complex

---

[226] For reasons considered earlier in this chapter, the position in the House of Lords is different, but the likelihood of the government facing insuperable obstacles in the Lords is reduced by virtue of the Salisbury convention and the Parliament Acts.

[227] See Cowley, *The Rebels: How Blair Mislaid His Majority* (London 2005).

[228] Terrorism Act 2006.

[229] Mill, *Considerations on Representative Government* (New York 1862), pp 277–9.

[230] Johnson, *Reshaping the British Constitution: Essays in Political Interpretation* (Basingstoke 2004), p 109.

legislation put before them? According to a study of the legislative process (which drew upon interviews with MPs and peers):

> Parliamentarians were often open in admitting that coping with the reality of massive amounts of complicated legislation severely compromised their effectiveness, and that they often do not understand the subject matter of the Bills they are scrutinizing . . . a number of parliamentarians explained . . . that the content of anywhere from a quarter to a half of all legislation they voted on was effectively a mystery to them . . . MPs and Peers tend to focus on bits they understand but often do not understand the larger picture.[231]

Perhaps this is understandable: MPs are generalists and can only develop an expertise in a handful of areas of public policy. After all, Parliament is a relatively small institution when compared with the scale and complexity of the largest organisation in the UK: the government. It is worth reminding ourselves, then, of one of the arguments against a fully elected House of Lords: that an appointed element makes room for people who, not being career politicians, may bring other forms of expertise and experience to the scrutiny process.

5.2.4 The government's dominance of the legislative procedure

A third constraint arises from parliamentary procedure and, in particular, the government's influence over the procedure by which legislation is scrutinised by Parliament. Most Bills are introduced by the government and the government has the ability to specify precisely how much time is to be allocated to parliamentary discussion of Bills. This is known as *programming*—that is, the government's imposition of a timetable for the passage of a Bill after its second reading (the first substantive and general debate that a Bill receives). Although there is a legitimate public interest in arranging matters such that the government is able to have Bills enacted in reasonable time, the risk (and often the reality) is that government programming prevents a Bill from being scrutinised in adequate depth; it is sometimes even the case that some parts of a Bill receive no scrutiny at all because time runs out.[232]

5.2.5 Assessing the legislative process—different perspectives

Whether the current situation is satisfactory very much depends on the perspective adopted.

From the governmental perspective, the legislative process is a tool by which the governing party can get its policies enacted into law. Governments are elected and have an electoral mandate to implement their manifesto; this often requires legislation and there is a strong desire in the executive to ensure that its legislative programme can be implemented as easily and efficiently as possible. From this perspective,

---

[231] Brazier, Kalitowski, and Rosenblatt, with Korris, *Law in the Making: Influence and Change in the Legislative Process* (London 2008), p 194.

[232] House of Commons Modernisation Committee, *Programming of Bills* (HC 1222 2002–03); House of Commons Procedure Committee, *Programming of Legislation* (HC 325 2003–04); Brazier, 'Programming of Legislation: From Consensus to Controversy', in Brazier (ed), *Parliament, Politics and Law Making: Issues and Developments in the Legislative Process* (London 2004), p 130.

parliamentary scrutiny should not prevent the government from carrying out the work that it was elected to do. Indeed, from this perspective, the present system is generally seen to work quite well.

From an entirely different (antithetical) standpoint—the non-executive parliamentarian perspective—the legislative process currently functions quite badly. The whole process is almost entirely executive-driven: Parliament often functions as a rubber-stamp mechanism approving laws that have been written elsewhere; and parliamentarians lack the necessary time and resources to subject legislation to robust scrutiny. From this perspective, urgent reform of the whole process is required so as to enable fuller debate of legislation. Parliamentary scrutiny of legislation needs to be strengthened considerably and executive domination needs to be ended.

Debate over the legislative process in the UK tends to be characterised by a constant tension between these two perspectives. The governmental perspective is generally predominant, although there have been some recent concessions to the non-executive parliamentarian perspective.

Given the dominance of the executive, what then are the purposes of parliamentary scrutiny in the legislative process? Parliamentary scrutiny can serve three principal purposes.[233] First, Parliament can act as an *inhibitor* of the government. Even though a government will normally have a majority, the fact that it must justify its proposals will itself inhibit it from advancing proposals that would expose it to political embarrassment. Second, Parliament can act as a *collaborator* with government in the legislative process to make better law. Third, and more cynically, parliamentary scrutiny may serve a *theatrical* function in that it provides for a ritual public affirmation of policy decisions already taken by the government.

Q What role do you think Parliament should play in the legislative process?

5.3 Parliamentary scrutiny and the legislative process

We now consider the different stages of the legislative process. We also consider three related topics: legislative standards, fast-track legislation, and post-legislative scrutiny.

5.3.1 The pre-legislative process

The government's legislative programme is announced in the Queen's Speech at the start of the parliamentary year, though it may be trailed in the media. The Queen's Speech is a ritual symbolising the involvement of the sovereign as a constituent part of the legislature. But beneath the pomp and pageantry of the state opening of Parliament lies a barely concealed and efficient aspect of the constitution at work. As legislation is essential to a government's ability to get on with the job of running the country and its political fortunes, the Queen's Speech is prepared by the

---

[233] Oliver et al, 'Parliament's Role and the Modernisation Agenda', in Giddings (ed), *The Future of Parliament: Issues for a New Century* (London 2005), pp 118–19.

Legislation Secretariat of the Cabinet Office on behalf of the Parliamentary Business and Legislation Committee.[234] There are other important aspects of the pre-legislative stage. These include internal legal scrutiny to ensure compliance with matters such as (for the time being) EU law and the ECHR.[235] Furthermore, Bills are nowadays accompanied by various ancillary documents, to which members of the public and parliamentarians may turn to make sense of them, such as the explanatory notes and impact assessments.

5.3.2 **Pre-legislative scrutiny**

Most Bills are introduced directly into Parliament, but some may first be subject to pre-legislative scrutiny. This is a comparatively recent feature of the legislative process and involves the publication of a draft Bill by the government and its scrutiny by a parliamentary committee, usually in the parliamentary session preceding that in which the Bill is formally introduced to Parliament. The aim is to produce better law by enabling Parliament and the public to have a real input into the making of legislation before the minds of Ministers are set. Pre-legislative scrutiny is 'one of the best ways of improving legislation and ensuring that it meets the quality standards that Parliament and the public are entitled to expect'.[236] It should be an integral and mandatory part of the process of consideration for every public Bill; the only exceptions should be cases in which there is an accepted and pressing need for immediate legislation.[237] The number of draft Bills published by the government for pre-legislative scrutiny has fluctuated over time, but is significantly lower than the total number of government Bills (Figure 5.12).

Pre-legislative scrutiny has been welcomed for its ability to improve the quality of legislation, smooth the passage of legislation during the subsequent legislative process, and to achieve cross-party consensus.[238] Nonetheless, its role and effectiveness is dependent upon the government's willingness to engage. The Commons Liaison Committee has stated that 'there is scope to go further . . . the benefits of pre-legislative scrutiny in terms of improving the quality of legislation which reaches the statute book and in easing the passage of controversial, technical and complex Bills through their parliamentary stages warrant the inevitable increase in resources required if committees are to scrutinise more draft legislation'.[239]

---

[234] Cabinet Office, *Guide to Making Legislation* (London 2013), ch 2. In 2007, the Labour government introduced a new process, the Draft Legislative Programme, by which the government set out its proposals in advance for consultation to enhance transparency. However, the coalition government reverted back to normal practice.

[235] The UK Parliament remains free to legislate contrary to the HRA and the schemes concerning devolution, but, as we explain in Chapters 7 and 18, it generally tries to avoid doing so.

[236] House of Commons Political and Constitutional Reform Committee, *Ensuring Standards in the Quality of Legislation* (HC 85 2013–14), [115].

[237] House of Commons Political and Constitutional Reform Committee, *Revisiting Rebuilding the House: The Impact of the Wright Reforms* (HC 82 2013–14), [35].

[238] See Kennon, 'Pre-Legislative Scrutiny of Draft Bills' [2004] PL 477; House of Commons Modernisation Committee, *The Legislative Process* (HC 1097 2005–06), [12]–[29]; Smookler, 'Making a Difference? The Effectiveness of Pre-Legislative Scrutiny' (2006) 3 Parliamentary Affairs 522.

[239] House of Commons Liaison Committee, *Legacy Report* (HC 954 2014–15), [66].

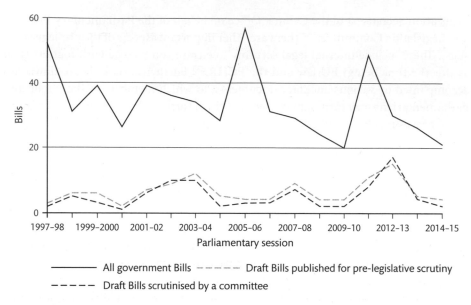

Figure 5.12 Draft Bills, 1997–2015

Source: House of Commons Library Briefing Note, *Pre-Legislative Scrutiny under the Coalition Government 2010–15* (SN05859 2015).

5.3.3 Legislative scrutiny

While pre-legislative scrutiny only applies to a relatively small number of Bills, the main process of legislative scrutiny applies to all of them. However, a general word of warning before proceeding further: parliamentary procedure is arcane and complex; this section merely provides an overview. The key point is that underpinning the details of parliamentary procedure for scrutinising legislation is a basic tension, reflecting the different perspectives on the legislative process. From the non-executive parliamentarian standpoint, the rules of parliamentary procedure ought to facilitate effective scrutiny of legislation by Parliament; from the governmental perspective, it has been argued that parliamentary procedure is best understood as a political instrument largely designed to enable the governing party to legislate.[240]

At the same time, over recent years, there has been an initiative to modernise parliamentary procedures and to enhance parliamentary scrutiny of legislation.[241] The rules of parliamentary procedure are, then, in a sense, the product of the tension between two different and competing pressures: the government's desire to get its legislation through Parliament and the desire of Parliament to scrutinise that legislation.

What, then, is the procedure for passing Bills through Parliament? This procedure is broadly similar in both Houses of Parliament and consists of a number of stages, as Table 5.2 shows. Bills can be introduced into either House. Whether a Bill is introduced into the Lords or the Commons will often depend upon the nature of

[240] Walkland, *The Legislative Process in Great Britain* (London 1968), p 68.
[241] House of Commons Modernisation Committee, *The Legislative Process* (HC 190 1997–98).

Table 5.2 The legislative process

Prior to introduction into Parliament	Parliament	Royal assent
Initial steps • Bill may be foreshadowed in governing party's (or parties') *manifesto(s)* • Issues to be addressed in Bill may be the subject of a *consultation exercise* **Draft Bill** • Draft Bill will be *scrutinised within government* for (among other things) compliance with human rights and devolution implications • Draft Bill may be published and examined by a *parliamentary committee* **Preparation of accompanying documentation** • *Explanatory notes* (to help the reader to understand what a Bill does, how it does it, and to provide helpful background) • *Impact Assessment* (explains the costs and benefits of the Bill) • *Equality Impact Assessment* (must, by law, be published; sets out race, gender, and disability implications of legislation) • *Delegated Powers Memorandum* (for the House of Lords Delegated Powers and Regulatory Reform Committee: identifies every provision conferring powers to enact delegated legislation, explaining why the matter has been left to delegated legislation rather than included in the Bill, and the form of parliamentary scrutiny to which the enactment of delegated legislation will be subject)	**House of Commons** • *First reading* (formal introduction of Bill without debate) • *Public reading* (pilot scheme allowing public to comment via Internet) • *Second reading* (general debate on the policy of Bill) *Committee stage* (detailed examination, debate, and amendments; in the House of Commons this stage takes place in a Public Bill Committee) • *Report stage* (opportunity for further amendments) • *Third reading* (final chance for debate; amendments are possible in the Lords) **House of Lords** • Bill, in its amended state, goes to the House of Lords, where it is put through a similar process. **Ping pong** • Unless the Lords approves the Bill in precisely the form it left the Commons, the Bill, as amended by the Lords, must go back to the Commons. • The Bill bounces back and forth between the two Houses until they both agree on the text. NB: a Bill can commence its passage in the Lords, in which case the process set out above is reversed.	• The Bill becomes an Act, and thus a law, when it is granted *royal assent* by the monarch. • This may not, however, result in the entirety of the Act entering into force: it may provide that certain parts of it are only to enter into force *when a Minister decides* that this should happen. This allows practical arrangements to be made for the entry into force of the new law.

the Bill itself and parliamentary timetabling. It has been customary for politically high-profile Bills to be introduced in the Commons. By contrast, non-controversial Bills conventionally start off in the Lords thereby making efficient use of limited parliamentary time.

The first reading of a Bill is a mere formality by which the Bill is presented to Parliament. At second reading, there will be a debate on the Bill's general policy. The Bill will then be voted upon and, if it is a government Bill, it will almost always survive this stage. While the ostensible purpose of the second reading is to scrutinise a Bill by means of a general debate, its real purpose is to enable the political parties to state their respective positions.

Next comes the committee stage. Here, the Bill will be discussed in detail—line by line—by a committee of MPs reflecting the political composition of the Commons. Amendments can be tabled, debated, and voted upon. That is the theory; informed insiders tell a very different tale. According to one MP, the committee stage has become a dead letter.[242] The whips ensure that the government MPs on the committee, who are always in the majority, say absolutely nothing. A government MP who goes on a committee with the genuine intention of scrutinising legislation may risk their career. However, the whips do their best to ensure that anyone who knows or cares about the legislation does not get on a committee in the first place. Instead, many MPs use the time to work through their correspondence; the upshot is that poorly prepared Bills are not properly scrutinised.[243]

In 2007, the committees were reformatted as Public Bill Committees, which can take oral and written evidence, and question Ministers. Since 2010, a new 'public reading stage' has been introduced whereby the public can comment on Bills. Following its use on a pilot basis, the public reading stage was used for the first time in relation to the Children and Families Bill in 2013.[244] It has been recognised that these committees have added slightly to Parliament's scrutiny of legislation.[245] Oral evidence sessions have changed the scrutiny behaviour of MPs, acting as a vehicle for the formulation of substantive changes to government bills and as an additional opposition scrutiny and debating tool, thereby increasing the capacity of committees and MPs to make an impact on government bills.[246]

Nevertheless, the degree of scrutiny that committees offer is often constrained because the government is still able to influence their composition and to ensure that the committees are made up of a majority of backbench MPs who will vote for the government. For example, Dr Sarah Wollaston, a Conservative MP and a former doctor—and therefore someone with considerable experience of the NHS—had

---

[242] Abbott, 'The dead hand of the whips', *The Guardian*, 15 February 2011, **http://www.theguardian.com/commentisfree/2011/feb/15/whips-legislation-mps-government**. See also HC Deb, vol 442, cols 1073–4 (9 February 2006) (Tony Wright MP).

[243] House of Commons Modernisation Committee, *The Legislative Process* (HC 1097 2005–06), [50].

[244] See further House of Commons Library Note, *Public Reading Stage of Bills* (SN06406 2012).

[245] Levy, 'Public Bill Committees: An Assessment Scrutiny Sought; Scrutiny Gained' (2010) 63 Parliamentary Affairs 534.

[246] Thompson, 'Evidence Taking under the Microscope: How Has Oral Evidence Affected the Scrutiny of Legislation in House of Commons Committees?' (2014) 9 British Politics 385.

wanted to sit on the Public Bill Committee considering the Health and Social Care Bill 2011, the most significant legislative change ever to the NHS. However, when Dr Wollaston suggested to the government whips that she would like to table some amendments, they made certain that she would not be a member of the committee. By contrast, those MPs who did sit on the committee had no experience or even recorded interest in health or social care; their role was merely to turn up on time, say nothing and vote with the government.[247]

As Graham Allen MP, has noted: 'It is unacceptable that Government Bills are scrutinised by Committees appointed by Government appointees. . . . The legislative scrutiny process in Bill Committees is so unchallenging and so irredeemable that some of us actually helped to invent pre-legislative scrutiny to try to bring some order and some sense to it.'[248] Part of the solution must be to ensure that the membership of Public Bill Committees becomes more transparent and legitimate and determined by the House of Commons, not the government.[249] Another suggestion is that Bill Committees be reformed to inject greater permanence and specialisation among both members and staff.[250]

After the committee stage, the Bill (as amended) will then return to the main chamber for its report stage; at this point, there will be further debate, and more amendments may be tabled. In particular, the government may, at this stage, table various new amendments to a Bill. If this is done, then such amendments will not necessarily receive detailed scrutiny, as the Bill will not return to the committee stage; rather, it will be for the other House (typically the Lords) to undertake the detailed line-by-line scrutiny. Immediately following the report stage, a Bill will receive its third reading. The Bill will be considered again as a whole in a short debate and, if approved, sent to the other House. Again, the opportunity provided by third reading debates is normally limited.[251]

If a Bill is amended by one House, then these amendments will need to be considered by the other House. If there is a difference between the two Houses, then this will need to be reconciled. The process by which this happens is potentially the most complex part of the legislative process. For example, if a Bill has completed its passage through the Commons but is then amended by the Lords, it will have to return to the Commons to be considered again. If the amendments are accepted, then the Bill will then proceed to royal assent; if they are rejected, the Bill will be sent back to the Lords for further consideration. Both Houses must agree on the final text and there may be several rounds of exchanges between the two Houses until agreement is reached on every word of the Bill. This process is known as 'ping pong' because the Bill may bounce back and forth between the two Houses until agreement has been reached.

---

[247] Wollaston, 'Creeping patronage, new politics and the payroll vote', *The Guardian*, 11 February 2011, http://www.theguardian.com/commentisfree/2011/feb/10/creeping-patronage-house-commons-mps-whips

[248] HC Deb, vol 566, col 1337 (18 July 2013).

[249] House of Commons Political and Constitutional Reform Committee, *Revisiting Rebuilding the House: The Impact of the Wright Reforms* (HC 82 2013–14), [36].

[250] Russell, Morris, and Larkin, *Fitting the Bill* (London 2013), http://www.ucl.ac.uk/constitution-unit/research/parliament/legislative-committees/tabs/Fitting_the_Bill_complete_pdf.pdf

[251] House of Commons Modernisation Committee, *The Legislative Process* (HC 1097 2005–06), [94].

If no agreement can be reached, then the House of Commons (or rather the government) may decide to use the procedure under the Parliament Acts.[252]

Once agreement has been reached between the two Houses or the Parliament Acts have been invoked, the Bill will then proceed to the next stage—that of royal assent, when the Queen will give formal approval to the Bill. As with the Queen's Speech at the start of the parliamentary session, royal assent is merely a ritualistic formality. Once a Bill has received royal assent, it will become an Act of Parliament and can be brought into force.

The effectiveness of parliamentary scrutiny is also conditioned by the nature and type of legislation. Many statutes are enabling Acts: they provide a broad framework in which Ministers and other public agencies will subsequently supply the detail through delegated legislation. This enables government to respond flexibly and make detailed technical rules. Yet, excessive reliance upon secondary legislation limits parliamentary scrutiny.[253]

Another input into the quality of legislative scrutiny is the amount of parliamentary time devoted to debating legislation. All things being equal, we might assume that the greater the amount of time devoted to scrutinising legislation, then the deeper and more thorough the scrutiny. The number of hours spent in the House of Commons Chamber debating government Bills between 1997 and 2015 is provided in Figure 5.13. Looking at this figure, it can be seen that the Commons spent more time debating legislation in the first year following a general election in order to debate legislation introduced by the government.

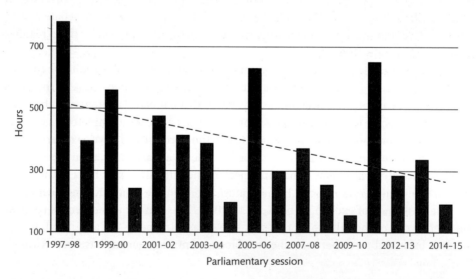

Figure 5.13 Hours spent in the House of Commons Chamber debating government Bills, 1997–2015

---

[252] See section 3.3.3.

[253] Parliamentary Commission on Banking Standards, *First Report* (HC 848 HL 98 2012–13); House of Commons Energy and Climate Change Committee, *Draft Energy Bill: Pre-Legislative Scrutiny* (HC 275 2012–13), [26].

5.3.4 **Assessing parliamentary scrutiny**

To what extent does Parliament exert influence over the legislative process? The orthodox view is that the government dominates and Parliament acts as an elaborate rubber stamp, but there never was a 'golden age' in which Parliament subjected all legislation to detailed scrutiny. At the same time, it would be incorrect to assume that Parliament has no influence at all. Indeed, the research literature has identified various reasons for doubting the orthodox view.[254]

First, the hundreds of successful government amendments to Bills during their passage overstates government success because most of these amendments have little substance. Further, most substantive government amendments respond to Parliamentary pressure and therefore represent parliamentary influence over the legislative process. Second, the high number of unsuccessful amendments to Bills by non-government MPs and peers tends to overstate non-government failure. This is so for two reasons. There may be several non-government amendments on the same issue. Further, many non-government amendments do not aim to change the Bill; they are often 'probing' amendments designed to highlight a particular matter and which are understood at Westminster as not intended to be put to a vote.

Third, Parliament influences policy before the formal legislative process commences. Parliament exerts 'preventive' influence in conditioning what the government can and cannot propose. By anticipating the likely reaction of Parliament, the government seeks to avoid alienating its own backbenchers and defeat in the Lords. 'Where ministers depend on parliament for their survival, it should be no surprise that they seek to implement parliamentarians' policy wishes, and refrain from proposing policies that parliament will not accept.'[255]

Finally, Parliament can influence policy following the completion of the legislative process: select committees oversee the implementation of policy and have opportunities to influence how legislation is put into practice. Instead of seeing the government's Commons majority as a means of executive domination, the relationship between government and Parliament should be viewed as a fluid and dynamic one in which there is continuous discussion and debate (both publicly and behind the scenes). 'Parliament's greatest power is one of "anticipated reactions."'[256]

5.3.5 **Fast-track legislation**

Should legislation be fast-tracked through Parliament? Normally, the legislative process can take several months, but occasionally, a pressing issue arises and government uses an accelerated procedure that might take only weeks or even days.[257] For instance, the Anti-terrorism, Crime and Security Act 2001 was fast-tracked through Parliament following 9/11 to give the Home Secretary draconian powers to detain indefinitely foreign nationals suspected of involvement in terrorism. More recently,

---

[254] Russell, Gover, and Wollter, 'Does the Executive Dominate the Westminster Legislative Process? Six Reasons for Doubt' (2016) 69 Parliamentary Affairs 286.

[255] Russell et al, 305.   [256] Russell et al, 305.

[257] eg the Criminal Justice (Terrorism and Conspiracy) Act 1998, introduced after the Omagh bombing in Northern Ireland in 1998, went through Parliament in two days.

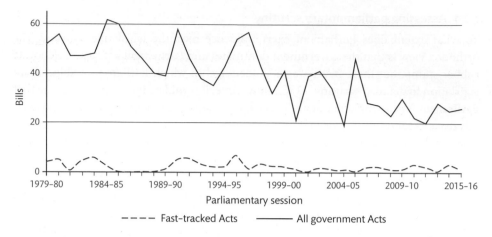

Figure 5.14 Fast-tracked Acts and government Acts

Source: House of Commons Library Briefing Paper, *Expedited Legislation: Government Bills receiving their Second and Third Reading on the same day in the House of Commons* (SN04974 2015), **http://researchbriefings.parliament.uk/ResearchBriefing/Summary/SN04974**

the Jobseekers (Back to Work Schemes) Act 2013—which reversed a ruling by the Court of Appeal—was introduced in the House of Commons on 14 March 2013 and completed its passage through the House of Lords on 25 March 2013. The Lords Constitution Committee concluded that the government had not advanced a good rationale for the Bill to be fast-tracked.[258] The concern was that the government was rushing through legislation to avoid detailed scrutiny.

The number of fast-tracked Bills is significant, but when compared with the total number of government Bills, the number of fast-tracked Bills is not so high as to suggest that the government regularly abuses this procedure (Figure 5.14).[259]

The concern with fast-track legislation is obvious. For 'fast-tracked' read 'poorly scrutinised' legislation: 'Legislate in haste; repent at leisure.' Should fast-track legislation attract additional safeguards? The Lords Constitution Committee certainly thinks so.[260] Government needs to justify fast-track procedures. Such legislation should be subject to a sunset clause—that is, the legislation expires after a certain date, unless renewed. Furthermore, there should be early post-legislative scrutiny of fast-track legislation. The government accepted the basic thrust of these recommendations, but has continued to make use of fast-track legislation—to the consternation of some parliamentary committees, fuelling concerns that this undermines effective legislative scrutiny.[261] The Joint Committee on Human Rights has been unable to scrutinise properly the human rights implications of emergency legislation.[262]

---

[258] House of Lords Constitution Committee, *Jobseekers (Back to Work Schemes) Bill* (HL 155 2012–13), [11].

[259] On fast-tracked legislation generally, see further House of Lords Constitution Committee, *Fast-Track Legislation: Constitutional Implications and Safeguards* (HL 116 2008–09).

[260] Ibid.

[261] *Jobseekers (Back to Work Schemes) Bill*, [7].

[262] Joint Committee on Human Rights, *Legislative Scrutiny Update* (HC 1077 HL 157 2012–13), [25].

5.3.7 Post-legislative scrutiny

Once enacted, legislation must be implemented. This might involve, for instance, new criminal offences being enforced by the police and the criminal courts. As most legislation is concerned with governmental policy, its implementation depends upon the relevant government departments. There is no guarantee that legislation is always effective in securing its objectives. Legislation can have positive, negative, or unintended consequences, or may be of no consequence at all. It might stand the test of time, or it might quickly be repealed or amended. In many policy areas, such as criminal justice, immigration, and social security, government has repeatedly resorted to new legislation in attempts to correct problems with previous legislation, but in many instances has only succeeded in increasing the complexity of the law without resolving the underlying policy and administrative issues.

Such difficulties are not necessarily an indication of failure, but more a reflection of the deep policy challenges facing government. They do, though, raise the question as to whether or not Parliament should be involved in post-legislative scrutiny—the examination of how legislation is implemented—to determine whether or not a given piece of legislation has been successful and, if not, what lessons can be learnt.

It is always open for Parliament or the government to subject legislation to post-legislative review, but in practice this has happened rarely. The lack of effective post-legislative scrutiny has been widely acknowledged to be a major gap. In 2008, the government introduced a more systematic process of post-legislative scrutiny.[263] Three to five years after legislation has been enacted, the relevant government department will—for most Acts—publish and submit to the relevant parliamentary select committee a post-legislative memorandum providing an assessment of how the relevant statute has worked in practice. The committee can then decide whether a fuller review is necessary at that point. The purpose of this process is to identify those legislative contexts in which things need to be put right, as well as those in which things have gone well (and which might therefore serve as examples for the future).

Post-legislative scrutiny 'has the potential to make a valuable difference to the scrutiny of legislation'.[264] But how well does it operate in practice? One issue is that post-legislative scrutiny takes time—and the resources of select committees are finite. There has so far been a low uptake of post-legislative scrutiny by select committees.[265]

Of the 58 government post-legislative scrutiny memoranda published up to 2013, only three had been subject to dedicated reports by committees, though committees do incorporate them as part of a wider inquiry into government policy. If only a handful of memoranda are followed up, then a more targeted approach based on

---

[263] Office of the Leader of the House of Commons, *Post-Legislative Scrutiny: The Government's Approach* (Cm 7320 2008). See also House of Lords Constitution Committee, *Parliament and the Legislative Process* (HL 173 2003–04), [165]–[193]; Law Commission, *Post-Legislative Scrutiny* (Cm 6945 2006).

[264] House of Commons Liaison Committee, *The Work of Committees 2007–08* (HC 291 2008–09), [69].

[265] House of Commons Political and Constitutional Reform Committee, *Ensuring Standards in the Quality of Legislation* (HC 85 2012–13), [116]–[121].

discussions between departments and committees may be a more efficient use of resources.[266] Another challenge is simply the pace of legislative change: 'In many of the areas where legislation is controversial—health, social security, taxation, criminal justice, and asylum and immigration, for example—the statute book rarely stays static long enough to be put under the microscope.'[267]

5.4 Conclusion

Given the UK's basic constitutional set-up—the executive's political control of the legislature—the legislative process is largely, but not wholly, an extension of the governmental process. Is this acceptable? After all, there is much disquiet concerning the quality of much legislation and there is no reason to assume that the government must always have its way or that its policies are always preferable. The problem extends beyond government Bills. The process by which Private Members' Bills are considered 'is in danger of appearing broken and discredited', thereby damaging Parliament's reputation.[268]

The government could relax its grip. It could, in some instances, transfer the primary responsibility for Bills to Parliament, perhaps to a committee. The committee could hold evidence sessions, be assisted by civil servants, and consult widely. This might change the legislative process from a government-driven and adversarial party political process to a deliberative one that builds and develops a cross-party consensus on difficult and complex issues of public policy. It just might—who knows?—improve the quality of legislation and its implementation. It might also produce longer-lasting legislative solutions to complex issues rather than the recurrent cycle of 'legislate quickly, amend, repeal, legislate quickly'.

Unfortunately, to those schooled in the UK's government-dominated legislative process, the radical suggestion that Parliament might actually be given a wider legislative role is likely to be disdainfully rejected as outlandish and perplexing. Instead, constitutional reformers have advanced much more modest proposals: better preparation of Bills in the first place, more pre-legislative scrutiny, elected Public Bill Committees with relevant experience, and limited use of fast-track legislation. Just attaining these smaller reforms would be welcome.

6. Parliament's powers

This section considers the *powers* that Parliament enjoys. What, exactly, can Parliament (or, taking account of our discussion so far, the *government* through Parliament) do? The orthodox view is that Parliament is legally 'sovereign'. It can make and unmake

---

[266] House of Commons Liaison Committee, *Select Committee Effectiveness, Resources and Powers: Responses to the Committee's Second Report of Session 2012–13* (HC 911 2012–13), p 12.

[267] Oliver et al, 'Parliament's Role and the Modernisation Agenda', in Giddings (ed), *The Future of Parliament: Issues for a New Century* (London 2005), p 123.

[268] House of Commons Procedure Committee, *Private Members' Bills* (HC 684 2015–16), [1].

any law. There is no legal restriction on the laws that it may enact.[269] Further, no other body can invalidate legislation.

In this section, we ask three principal questions: *should* Parliament be sovereign? If it is sovereign, *what exactly does that mean*? And is the conventional wisdom holding that Parliament is sovereign *correct*?

6.1 Should Parliament be sovereign?

6.1.1 Political and legal constitutionalism

To say that a legislature can enact *any* law—that there is *nothing* that it is legally incapable of doing—is, on the face of it, an extravagant claim. Stephen famously pointed out that '[i]f a [sovereign] legislature decided that all blue-eyed babies should be murdered, the preservation of blue-eyed babies would be illegal'.[270] This prompts several questions, the answers to most of which are—to anyone with a conventional moral compass—obvious. Should such a law be enacted? No. Should legislators be free to enact such a law if they so wish? No. What should stop them from doing so? Here, the answer is perhaps less obvious—and it is here that we encounter a fissure between the traditions of legal and political constitutionalism, the distinction between which is one of the key themes running throughout this book.

Political constitutionalism holds that non-legal factors will prevent the enactment of laws such as that described. Legislators' own sense of morality means, it is to be hoped, that they would never be tempted to enact such a law. And even if they were, self-interest would ensure that they did not: public opinion would not stand for it. Any politician who voted in favour of such a law would be almost certain to lose his or her parliamentary seat at the following election, and it is highly likely that, in such an extreme case, there would be widespread civil and official disobedience, with individuals refusing to obey, and organisations such as the police refusing to enforce such a law.

The essential point is that political constitutionalism puts its faith in the political process—legislators will do the right thing because that is what public opinion will require of them—making legal restrictions upon their powers unnecessary. There must be some division between law and politics. The doctrine of parliamentary sovereignty means that politics can always trump law.

It is hard to dispute this analysis in relation to truly extreme laws: it is impossible to imagine circumstances in which the political process would yield a law such as that referred to by Stephen. But what about a law that denied members of one gender the right to vote? Or that required racial segregation on public transport? Or that denied to suspected terrorists the right to liberty and to a fair trial in an attempt to enhance the safety of everyone else?

These are not far-fetched examples: they are all things that have been done in the last hundred years in Western countries. Indeed, as we saw in Chapter 1, a law along

---

[269] Dicey, *An Introduction to the Study of the Law of the Constitution* (London 1959), p 10.
[270] Stephen, *The Science of Ethics* (London 1882), p 137.

the lines of the last example was enacted in the UK in 2001.[271] The political process may not—and indeed has not—been sufficient to prevent the enactment of laws such as these.[272] That is precisely why, legal constitutionalists argue, we should not put all of our faith in politics.

Legislators, left to their own devices, may do the wrong thing—and while, in a democracy, they must generally be allowed to do as they think best, we must look to the law to remove unacceptable choices from them in the first place. Legal constitutionalism therefore has no truck with legislative sovereignty. Instead, it holds that legislators should be given only limited powers and that courts should have the authority to strike down legislation enacted without such powers. The best-known example of such a system is the USA. The US Constitution confers only limited powers upon Congress—the American equivalent of Parliament—and authorises the courts to set aside unconstitutional legislation (ie laws that transgress the constitutional limits on Congress's power).

6.1.2 Democracy

The foregoing discussion implicitly suggests that legal constitutionalism's central thesis is that *legislators* cannot be trusted to do the right thing. But the position is actually more subtle. Legislators' desire to be re-elected will generally ensure that they do only popular things, making it unlikely that they would enact a law that they anticipate would displease most people. Viewed thus, it seems that legal constitutionalism's thesis is really that *people generally*—or at least *the majority*—cannot be trusted to do the right thing. They might—indeed they may be quite likely—to act in a self-interested way that prioritises their own interests over those of others. The majority might therefore wish laws to be enacted that benefit themselves at the expense of the minority—wishes to which legislators, wanting to be re-elected, might accede. Legislation such as that which was enacted in the UK in the wake of the 9/11 attacks incarcerating suspected foreign terrorists—an unpopular minority if ever there was one—is a prime example of such behaviour.

If, then, legal constitutionalism's mission (or part of it) is to protect minorities against the tyranny of a self-interested majority, does this not make it profoundly undemocratic? On a so-called *majoritarian* view of democracy, it certainly does. That view holds that democracy simply means giving effect to the wishes of the majority of people: if they wish to organise society in a way that advantages them at the expense of smaller, weaker groups, then so be it. Of course, in enlightened societies, majorities may not behave thus: they might, for example, recognise a moral code that embraces concern for the dignity and equality of individuals, and that precludes the exploitation of those who are insufficiently powerful to safeguard their own interests through the political process. The key point, however, is that, on a majoritarian

---

[271] Anti-terrorism, Crime and Security Act 2001.

[272] This might either be because a majority of people are happy to see such laws enacted or because politicians take it upon themselves to do things that are out of step with public opinion. The former point raises questions about democracy that we address in section 6.1.2; the latter point, meanwhile, underlines the fact that if political constitutionalism is to be embraced, the political process must be of a sufficient quality to justify the faith thereby placed in it. See generally Tomkins, *Our Republican Constitution* (Oxford 2005).

view of democracy, whether the majority behaves self-interestedly or altruistically is a matter of choice—for the majority. Legislative sovereignty, on this view, is therefore wholly justified; indeed it is imperative—it would be undemocratic to constrain the legislature from doing whatever it is that the majority wants it to do.[273]

But this is not the only—and may not be the best—view of democracy. The opposing view, known as *countermajoritarianism*, holds that true democracy requires society to be governed in a way that takes due account of everyone's interests, not only those of 50.1 per cent of the people. James Madison, who played a leading role in the drafting of the US Constitution, warned against making laws 'not according to the rules of justice and the rights of the minor party, but by the superior force of an interested and overbearing majority'.[274]

There are a number of ways in which this objective might be realised. Some are political: the voting system may be designed so as to make it unlikely that two big parties will dominate the legislature,[275] some or all votes in the legislature may be capable of being carried only with support in excess of a bare majority,[276] opposing parties might even be forced to work together in order to instil a consensual approach.[277] Instead, or as well, the power of the legislature might be legally limited in order to ensure that particular values, including minority interests, cannot be overridden.

This is generally how systems based on written constitutions work. Paradoxically, the adoption and maintenance of a constitution denying the legislature the legal capacity to subjugate minority interests requires, in the first place, that the majority is prepared to go along with such arrangements, assuming that the constitution is adopted pursuant to and/or can be amended by a popular vote. In this sense, the sort of legal constitutionalism engendered by such arrangements *is* democratically endorsed, even if, once such arrangements are in place, they result in specific instances of courts setting aside as unconstitutional legislation that the majority would like to see enacted.

Since it is usually possible to amend a written constitution—typically through a process that includes asking the people to vote—it is normally possible in systems based on written constitutions for the people to remove some constitutional inhibition that would otherwise prevent the enactment of a law that they wished to see passed. However, most written constitutions require something more than a simple majority—and the greater the size of the majority required for constitutional amendment, the harder it is for the majority to shift the ground rules in their favour and to the disadvantage of smaller interest groups.

6.1.3 Constitutional interpretation and judicial politics

In many systems based on written constitutions, the constitution is difficult to amend. In such circumstances, the meaning of the existing text becomes all-important.[278] This, in turn, gives considerable power to the judiciary, the job of which it ultimately is

---

[273] See generally Bickel, *The Least Dangerous Branch* (New Haven 1986).

[274] *The Federalist*, no 10.

[275] See discussion of proportional representation in section 3.2.5.

[276] eg a two-thirds majority might be required.   [277] As in Northern Ireland: see Chapter 7.

[278] See further Chapter 1, section 2.4.

in most countries to interpret the constitution. For example, in the famous case of *Roe v Wade*, the US Supreme Court was asked to determine whether the US Constitution meant that a Texan law prohibiting abortion except in very limited circumstances was unconstitutional.[279] Although the US Constitution did not explicitly address this question, the Supreme Court held that it contained an implied right to privacy that included a right to abort pregnancies in a much wider range of circumstances than those permitted by the Texan law. This is a good example of the way in which a system based on legal constitutionalism that incorporates legal restrictions on legislative power can result in certain matters being taken out of the hands of legislators and placed in the hands of judges.

Once the Court determined that abortion was a matter that engaged the US Constitution, it was for the Court to determine whether and in what circumstances women should be permitted to terminate pregnancies. This is not an argument clearly in favour of or against legally limiting the powers of the legislature; rather, it is merely an implication of doing so.

6.1.4 Conclusion

This discussion does not lead to a definitive conclusion about whether it is right that the UK Parliament *should* be sovereign. There is no objectively correct answer to that question. It is ultimately a matter of opinion.

The division of opinion between those who support and oppose a legally untrammelled legislature is not, in reality, between those who do and do not think that a law should be enacted to the effect that all blue-eyed babies should be killed. Rather, the disagreement is about what it is that should prevent the enactment of unacceptable laws—and about how the limits of acceptability should be determined in the first place.

> **Q** Reflecting on the discussion so far, what is *your* view? Should courts in the UK have the power to strike down unacceptable laws? Or should we continue to rely on the self-restraint of legislators, and the controlling effect of public opinion and the electoral process?

6.2 What does 'parliamentary sovereignty' mean?

Orthodox constitutional doctrine says,[280] and the courts generally appear to accept,[281] that Parliament is sovereign. There is no legal limit to the laws that it may enact: any restraint that Parliament exercises therefore flows from the political, not the legal, system. Dicey observed that the flip side of this coin is that no one can lawfully override, derogate from, or set aside an Act of Parliament.[282]

---

[279] *Roe v Wade* 410 US 113 (1973).
[280] See generally Goldsworthy, *The Sovereignty of Parliament* (Oxford 1999).
[281] See, eg *British Railways Board v Pickin* [1974] AC 765, 782, *per* Lord Reid.
[282] Dicey, *An Introduction to the Study of the Law of the Constitution* (London 1959), p 38.

On this view, then, UK courts cannot strike down or refuse to apply Acts of Parliament because there are no *external constraints* upon what Parliament can do. In the absence of constitutional restrictions on its authority, orthodox theory says that there are no benchmarks against which courts can test the constitutionality of legislation. The notion of an unconstitutional Act of Parliament is therefore an oxymoron. Parliament is incapable of acting unconstitutionally because it is constitutionally unrestrained.

This orthodox position is open to question on a number of grounds. But if we accept the orthodox position for the moment, then a separate question arises. Even if the constitution imposes no *external constraints* upon Parliament, are *self-imposed constraints* a possibility? Could Parliament limit its own powers?

This question raises a paradox. If Parliament can do literally *anything*, then that must include the competence to limit its own powers—but if Parliament were so to exercise its powers, surely it would no longer be sovereign? We need to examine this matter more closely. This question is not merely of philosophical interest. It is also of practical significance. It raises fundamental questions about the nature and source of the principle of parliamentary sovereignty.

The question is, in essence, whether Parliament is capable of *entrenching* legislation. In other words, could it enact legislation and stipulate either that it could not be repealed or amended *at all*, or alternatively that it could not be repealed or amended *in the absence of compliance with some special condition* (such as securing a majority bigger than the bare majority that is normally needed)? For example, could Parliament enact a Bill of Rights stipulating that all future Parliaments were required to respect the Bill of Rights and that any Bills enacted in breach of it would be invalid?

6.3 Model I—parliamentary sovereignty as a constitutional fixture

6.3.1 No entrenchment

For some writers, the answer to that question is straightforwardly 'no'. In an influential article published in 1955, Wade argued that it is impossible for Parliament to entrench legislation because the courts are constitutionally required to give effect to the most recent expression of parliamentary intention whenever two Acts conflict.[283] The implications of this are twofold.

First, it is always possible for Parliament to state in a later Act that some or all of an earlier Act is repealed. When Parliament lays down a new set of laws in a given Act, it often adds to that Act a schedule listing the older Acts (or provisions in older Acts) that are repealed. This is known as *express repeal*.

But, second, if Parliament enacts new legislation that is at odds with an earlier statute and fails explicitly to address this matter, it is still the courts' constitutional duty to enforce the new law and, therefore, to disregard the older law to the extent of any inconsistency between the two.

[283] 'The Basis of Legal Sovereignty' [1955] CLJ 172.

This is known as *implied repeal*: in the absence of express words of repeal in the later Act, the earlier Act is nevertheless treated as impliedly repealed to the extent that the two Acts are incompatible with one another. The doctrine of implied repeal was endorsed in *Ellen Street Estates Ltd v Minister of Health*.[284]

The doctrines of express and implied repeal are merely manifestations of the underlying principle that the courts are constitutionally obliged to give effect to the most recent expression of parliamentary intention, preferring more recent legislation over earlier legislation when the two conflict. Crucially for the purposes of our inquiry about entrenchment, Wade argued that this principle admits of no exceptions: there is no way in which the doctrines of express and implied repeal can be displaced. If this is true, two conclusions follow; they are best explained through examples.

First, assume that Parliament enacts legislation on a given matter, and that the Act contains a section that says: 'This Act may not be repealed.' On Wade's view, that section would be without legal effect. It would still be the courts' job to give effect to the most recent expression of Parliament's will in the event of a conflict between two Acts, meaning that any subsequent legislation that contained either express words of repeal or a provision impliedly incompatible with the earlier Act would result in the repeal of the latter. *Absolute entrenchment*—that is, placing an Act wholly beyond repeal—is, then, impossible.

Second, assume that the original Act says not that it cannot be repealed *at all*, but that it cannot be repealed unless some condition is first fulfilled—for example, a two-thirds (as opposed to a simple) majority in the House of Commons. What would then happen if Parliament were subsequently to legislate expressly to repeal, or impliedly legislate inconsistently with, the earlier Act without fulfilling the condition? On Wade's view, the latter Act would succeed in repealing the earlier Act whether or not the condition stipulated in the latter had been fulfilled. Again, this follows from the fundamental principle that the courts' duty is to implement the most recent expression of parliamentary intention. It follows that *contingent entrenchment*, like absolute entrenchment, is impossible. This, in turn, means that all Acts of Parliament are legally equal: none can be made harder or impossible to repeal.

Two questions arise.

6.3.2 Continuing and self-embracing sovereignty

First, how is it possible for Wade simultaneously to assert (i) that Parliament is sovereign, but (ii) that there is something—that is, entrenching legislation—that it cannot do? This apparent paradox is resolved by recognising that when we say that Parliament is 'sovereign', we must mean one of two things.

One possibility is that Parliament has a *self-embracing sovereignty*, meaning that its power extends to destroying its own sovereignty. It could, on this view, pass a law entrenching legislation, and the entrenchment would be effective: Parliament would subsequently be incapable of amending or repealing the law in question, and so would no longer be sovereign.

---

[284] [1934] 1 KB 590.

The other possibility is that Parliament has a *continuing sovereignty*—one that cannot be destroyed, and which therefore means that the one thing that it cannot do is entrench legislation (because that would detract from the authority of future Parliaments to do whatever they like). Wade says that the UK Parliament has the second kind of sovereignty, which explains why he thinks that it cannot entrench legislation.

6.3.3 Why continuing sovereignty?

Yet this just raises a second question: *why* does Wade think that Parliament has a continuing, rather than a self-embracing, sovereignty? To answer this question, we need to consider what it is that gives Parliament the authority to make law in the first place. In most developed countries, the legislature is authorised to make law by a constitutional text. That text will prescribe the limits of the legislature's authority and will set out a process whereby the constitution can be amended so as to increase or reduce the legislature's powers. In such systems, legislative authority can be traced to a *legal source* in the form of the written constitution.

But of course the UK does not have a written constitution—so what is it that authorises Parliament to make the law? The answer (at least as far as Wade is concerned) lies in an event known as the Glorious Revolution. Seventeenth-century England witnessed considerable tumult that included a civil war and a period of republican government. An important factor underlying those events was a running tension between the monarchy and Parliament. The two were, in effect, vying for constitutional primacy; successive monarchs asserted powers to dispense with—that is, to disregard—Acts of Parliament. In 1688, when a new king took to the throne, it was agreed that the monarchy would no longer lay any claim to constitutional primacy in the sense of having any power to dispense with Acts of Parliament. And the courts, which at the beginning of the seventeenth century had suggested that *they* could dispense with Acts of Parliament by setting them aside if they offended basic principles of justice,[285] accepted, along with the monarch, that duly enacted parliamentary legislation had to be recognised as the law of the land.

The basis of Parliament's authority to make law is therefore said to consist in this *political agreement* between the monarchy, Parliament, and the courts. That agreement gave rise to a constitutional rule to the effect that Parliament can enact any law and that the courts will recognise parliamentary enactments as valid laws.

But Wade argues that this rule is not a *legal* rule in any recognisable sense—Parliament did not legislate its own sovereignty into existence; how could it?—but is, rather, 'the ultimate *political* fact upon which the whole system of legislation hangs'.[286]

This rule, or political fact, is what Hart refers to as a 'rule of recognition'—that is, the rule that tells everyone, including courts, what to recognise as law.[287] Hart goes on to explain that '[i]n the day-to-day life of a legal system its rule of recognition

---

[285] See, eg *Dr Bonham's Case* (1610) Co Rep 113.

[286] Wade, 'The Basis of Legal Sovereignty' [1955] CLJ 172, 188.

[287] Hart, *The Concept of Law* (Oxford 1961), ch 6.

is very seldom expressly formulated'; rather, 'its existence is *shown*'—and its content deduced—'in the way in which particular rules are identified'.[288] Subject to that caveat, it seems likely that the rule of recognition in the UK provides that something will constitute a valid and enforceable Act of Parliament if it

(i)   has been approved by the House of Commons, and

(ii) has been approved by the House of Lords (unless the Parliament Acts apply),[289] and

(iii) has been granted royal assent by the monarch, but

(iv) only to the extent that it is not inconsistent with any provision in a subsequently enacted Act of Parliament.

Element (iv) of the rule of recognition can be deduced from the fact that courts give effect to later Acts of Parliament when they are inconsistent with earlier ones. If courts were to behave differently—that is, if they were to be required to give effect to certain legislation, such as a Bill of Rights, even if it were inconsistent with a later Act—it stands to reason that the rule of recognition would have to be altered. Specifically, element (iv) of the rule of recognition would need to be made subject to a proviso, so that it read:

(iv) only to the extent that it is not inconsistent with any provision in a subsequently enacted Act of Parliament *except that the Bill of Rights shall take priority over all other inconsistent legislation, whether enacted before or after the Bill of Rights.*

Wade says that changing the rule of recognition—and hence entrenching legislation— is the one thing that Parliament cannot do. Why? Because whereas, in most countries, that rule is to be found in some shape or form in a written constitution—and can therefore be amended through whatever legal means the constitution prescribes—in the UK, it exists only in the form of Wade's 'political fact' that emerged because of the Glorious Revolution.

It follows that although Parliament is sovereign in the sense of being able to make and change any *law*, this does not mean that it can change the rule of recognition, because the rule of recognition is *not* a law. It exists only in the political realm, and changing it is therefore beyond Parliament's legislative reach. Wade therefore argued that the rule of recognition could only alter—precipitating a change in the powers enjoyed by Parliament—if the political agreement underpinning the rule of recognition were to collapse.

The most obvious way in which this might happen would be if the courts were to refuse to recognise an Act of Parliament as a valid law. This, said Wade, would be a 'revolution', in that it would entail the courts acting unconstitutionally by disregarding the agreement reached at the end of the seventeenth century: if parliamentary sovereignty is ultimately sustained only by that political compact, it can only in practice exist for as long as the parties to it continue to agree to it.

---

[288] Hart, p 98.

[289] The complications raised by the Parliament Acts are considered in detail in section 6.3.4.

6.3.4 **Evaluation**

Although highly influential, Wade's analysis has been criticised on three principal grounds. The first is that it provides *an exclusively historical explanation* for the sovereignty of Parliament and takes no account of what principled justification might exist for ascribing lawmaking power to Parliament today. The most obvious such justification, as we have noted,[290] is that Parliament[291] is now (unlike in 1688) a democratic institution. Some writers argue that this raises questions about the contemporary appropriateness of Wade's analysis. Some, for example, argue that if democracy justifies Parliament's exercising lawmaking power today, that same principle must limit its authority, meaning that it would be unconstitutional and unlawful for Parliament to attempt to enact legislation at odds with basic principles of democracy.

Second, Wade's theory is *arguably incoherent judged even on its own terms*. Even if we accept Wade's premise that the rule ascribing lawmaking authority to Parliament was generated through non-legal means, it does not necessarily follow that that rule cannot be legislatively manipulated. The fact that the original source of the rule is political does not conclusively determine whether the rule permits Parliament to (for example) limit its own powers: that question can be determined only by reference to the *content* of the rule.[292]

Third, in the absence of any constitutional text setting out the extent and nature of parliamentary authority, the content of the rule has to be deduced from what actually happens—*which is arguably at odds with what Wade's theory says should happen.* The central tenet of that theory is that the sovereignty of Parliament is an absolute fixture that cannot be changed through any legal or constitutional means;[293] in particular, Parliament cannot, by enacting legislation, impose limits upon itself. Yet there are two situations in which Parliament appears to have succeeded in doing precisely that.

The first concerns the European Communities Act 1972, which gives effect in the UK to laws enacted by the EU, and will continue to do so until the UK formally exits the EU. The nature of the EU and the way in which the 1972 Act works are considered in detail in Chapter 8. For the time being, we simply note that, in the 1972 Act, Parliament provided that EU law should take priority over UK law, including over Acts of Parliament, thereby effectively restricting its own powers. Although Wade suggested that this development could be reconciled with his theory by characterising it as a revolution,[294] we suggest in Chapter 8 that this is not a convincing explanation, bearing in mind that it was *Parliament*—which is supposed to be incapable of legislating away its sovereignty—that was responsible for bringing about this new state of affairs.

---

[290] In section 6.1.2.   [291] Or at least the House of Commons.

[292] Bradley, 'The Sovereignty of Parliament: Form or Substance?', in Jowell and Oliver (eds), *The Changing Constitution* (Oxford 2011), pp 48–52; Gordon, 'The Conceptual Foundations of Parliamentary Sovereignty: Reconsidering Jennings and Wade' [2009] PL 519, 531–4.

[293] Albeit that it would, in practice, collapse if the courts were to act unconstitutionally by refusing to recognise Acts of Parliament as valid laws.

[294] 'Sovereignty: Revolution or Evolution?' (1996) 112 LQR 568.

Second, there are the Parliament Acts 1911–49. The background to, and effect of, those Acts we have already considered.[295] However, the way in which they work on a technical level calls into question Wade's theory. If the rule of recognition is as stated in section 6.3.3, how is it possible for a Bill to 'become an Act of Parliament', as ss 1(1) and 2(1) of the 1911 Act put it, without the Lords' approval? Wade argued that legislation enacted under the Parliament Acts is not *really* an Act of Parliament; rather, he said, Parliament in 1911 in effect created a separate body—an inferior legislature—consisting of the monarch and the Commons. Measures enacted by it were therefore delegated legislation, not Acts of Parliament proper. While enabling Wade to reconcile the 1911 Act with his theory, this analysis compelled him to argue that the 1949 Act—and all legislation passed thereunder—is invalid, because it would have been impossible for the inferior legislature to extend its own powers: only Parliament proper could delegate further powers to the inferior body.[296]

Precisely this argument was advanced before the Appellate Committee of the House of Lords in the *Jackson* case, in which it was contended that the Hunting Act 2004 was invalid, having been enacted by the monarch and the Commons under the 1911 Act, as amended by the 1949 Act.[297] It was argued that the 1949 Act was (for the reasons given by Wade) invalid and that the 2004 Act was therefore invalid too. However, the Appellate Committee rejected this argument and the analysis on which it was based. It held that, by enacting the 1911 Act, Parliament had created not a subordinate legislature capable only of enacting delegated legislation, but a parallel route whereby full Acts of Parliament could be enacted. In other words, it had amended the rule of recognition by inserting into it a proviso whereby the House of Lords' assent is needed *unless the Parliament Acts apply.*

This suggests that Parliament in 1911 did the very thing that Wade said was impossible. It manipulated the rule of recognition. But this does not quite answer the question with which we started this section—that is, whether Parliament can *entrench* legislation. The Parliament Acts make it *easier* for legislation to be passed by creating a second mechanism for enactment alongside that which requires the assent of monarch, Lords, and Commons.

Does this mean that, by the same logic, Parliament could make it *harder* to enact legislation by, for example, stipulating that a given Act cannot be repealed or amended unless special conditions are met?

6.4 Model II—Parliament capable of controlling certain aspects of legislative process

6.4.1 The 'new view'

Proponents of the *new view* of parliamentary sovereignty—or the *manner and form theory* as it is sometimes called—have argued that the answer to the question at the

---

[295] In section 3.3.3.   [296] Wade, 'The Basis of Legal Sovereignty' [1955] CLJ 172, 193–4.
[297] *R (Jackson) v Attorney-General* [2005] UKHL 56, [2006] 1 AC 262.

end of the preceding section is 'yes'.[298] Their central contention is that Parliament is, and should be, capable of laying down binding conditions concerning *how and in what form* legislation is to be enacted, but that it is not, and should not be, capable of tying future legislators' hands as to *what* legislation they may enact. This boils down to the propositions that (i) Parliament can and should be able to make it *harder than usual* for a given statute to be amended or repealed, but that (ii) it cannot and should not be able to make it *impossible* for any law to be amended or repealed. Let us unpack each of these propositions.

As to the former, adherents to the new view agree with Model I in that they too think that *absolute entrenchment*—that is, placing an Act wholly beyond repeal—is, and should be, impossible. This is entirely sensible. Allowing absolute entrenchment would enable a given Parliament—controlled by a given government—to enshrine its views in legislation that could never be altered. This would be both undemocratic (what if people in the future were to decide that they do not like those policies?) and impractical (what if circumstances were to change such that those policies become inappropriate?). Even countries with written constitutions make provision for the constitution to be amended; constitution drafters might deliberately make amendment difficult, but it is widely recognised that no group of people can be so prescient as to be capable of laying down rules that will be appropriate for the rest of time.

But the new view does allow for *contingent entrenchment* of legislation. Assume that Parliament enacts legislation that stipulates that it can only be repealed by subsequent legislation that meets certain conditions—for example, that it is supported by a two-thirds (as opposed to a simple) majority in the House of Commons. If Parliament were subsequently to seek to repeal that Act by means of legislation not supported by the requisite majority, the earlier Act would (according to the new view) remain in force.

Supporters of the new view argue that permitting Parliament to entrench legislation in this way is a good thing because it steers a desirable middle course between two undesirable extremes. The first such extreme—permitting absolute entrenchment—we have already encountered; the second extreme is permitting no entrenchment whatsoever. This, say proponents of the new view, is also undesirable. If Parliament cannot make it harder than usual to repeal or amend certain laws, this means that, in effect, all laws are equal: all can be repealed or amended with the same ease—it takes only a bare majority in Parliament.

This, in turn, means that there can be no hierarchy of laws—no set of laws (such as laws dealing with important constitutional matters) that are marked out as especially significant, and with which interference is made commensurately difficult. For example, the European Union Act 2011 creates a 'referendum lock', whereby a treaty transferring additional powers to the EU could be entered into by the UK only if approved in a referendum. This undertaking is legally worthless unless the new view obtains, since legislation providing for a referendum lock could be overridden simply by passing a further Act of Parliament and without holding the stipulated referendum.

---

[298] See Heuston, *Essays in Constitutional Law* (London 1964), ch 1; Jennings, *The Law and the Constitution* (London 1959), ch 4.

Proponents of the new view argue that it is consistent with the notion of parliamentary sovereignty because, they contend, saying that Parliament is sovereign merely means that it is capable of enacting, amending, or repealing any law—and it continues to be capable of all of those things even if certain laws can only be enacted, amended, or repealed if certain conditions are first fulfilled.[299]

> **Q** Do you agree that the new view strikes the right balance between the two extreme positions mentioned? Do you think that the distinction between (prohibited) substantive and (permissible) formal modes of entrenchment can be clearly drawn? For example, on which side of the line would you put a condition in an Act stipulating that it could be repealed or amended only by a unanimous vote in both Houses of Parliament?

6.4.2 Is the new view correct as a matter of UK law?

Those who support the new view do not merely argue that it is a good idea; they also contend that it accurately describes the position currently adopted by UK law. But certain cases suggest that this is not so. The most direct judicial consideration of this point is to be found in two 1930s cases concerning the relationship between the Acquisition of Land Act 1919 and the Housing Act 1925.[300] The former set out a scheme for assessing the compensation that should be awarded to landowners whose property was compulsorily purchased by the state—and s 7(1) said that other legislation 'shall, in relation to the matters dealt with in this Act, have effect subject to this Act, and so far as inconsistent with this Act those provisions shall cease to have or shall not have effect'. It was argued that the 1919 Act was contingently entrenched—that it could only be repealed or departed from by subsequent legislation that used express words of repeal or derogation. And, it was said, since the 1925 Act did not explicitly depart from the 1919 Act, the 1919 Act should take priority over the later legislation. This suggestion was roundly rejected by the courts. Maugham LJ said that Parliament 'cannot . . . bind itself as to the form of subsequent legislation';[301] similar views were expressed by other judges.[302]

Much more recently, Laws LJ said in *Thoburn v Sunderland City Council*[303] that 'Parliament cannot bind its successors by stipulating against repeal' and 'cannot stipulate against implied repeal any more than it can stipulate against express repeal': 'Being sovereign, it cannot abandon its sovereignty.'

---

[299] Heuston, p 9.

[300] *Vauxhall Estates Ltd v Liverpool Corporation* [1932] 1 KB 733; *Ellen Street Estates Ltd v Minister of Health* [1934] 1 KB 590.

[301] *Ellen Street Estates*, 597.

[302] *Ellen Street Estates*, 595–6, *per* Scrutton LJ; *Vauxhall Estates*, 743, *per* Avory J, and 746, *per* Humphrys J.

[303] [2002] EWHC 195 (Admin), [2003] QB 151, [59]. Of course, proponents of the new view would say that the imposition of formal restrictions on future Parliaments does not constitute the abandonment of sovereignty, because future Parliaments would remain free to pass any laws that they wished provided that they complied with the conditions laid down in the earlier Act.

Until recently, the principal judicial authorities that were said to support the new view were cases concerning legislatures other than the UK Parliament, but which proponents of the new view said were analogically relevant.[304] For example, in *Ranasinghe*,[305] legislation enacted under the royal prerogative established a constitution for what was then the British colony of Ceylon[306] and provided, among other things, that the Ceylon legislature could legislate contrary to the constitution only if such legislation were supported by a two-thirds (rather than the usual bare) majority of legislators. When the Ceylon legislature purported to enact a Bill that departed from the constitution, but which had not been passed with a two-thirds majority, it was judicially held that the Bill was invalid. Although supporters of the new view say this proves the correctness of their argument, it does nothing of the sort.

It is entirely unsurprising that a legislature that derives its power from a constitutional text must abide by whatever *conditions the constitutional text lays down*. But this says nothing about whether a sovereign legislature that is not governed by any constitutional text can be subject to *binding conditions imposed by itself at an earlier point in time*.[307]

However, in *Jackson*, there was some *obiter* support for the new view. Some of the judges paid at least lip service to Wade's orthodoxy: Lord Hope, for example, reiterated that 'no Parliament can bind its successors'.[308] But others accepted that if (as in relation to the Parliament Acts) Parliament could legislate to make it easier to enact laws, it could also make it harder by imposing binding conditions on future Parliaments. As Baroness Hale put it, if Parliament—as in the Parliament Acts—can 'redefine itself downwards', by subtracting requirements (such as the Lords' consent) from the rule of recognition, then 'it may very well be that it can redefine itself upwards, [for example] to require a particular parliamentary majority'.[309] Lord Steyn was even more certain about this: he unequivocally said that 'Parliament could for specific purposes provide for a two-thirds majority in the House of Commons and the House of Lords', and went on to cite with approval the work of writers associated with the new view.[310]

So while it remains the case that no UK judgment has unequivocally held that the Westminster Parliament can formally entrench legislation—all discussion of this in *Jackson* being *obiter*—some of the speeches in *Jackson* at least give succour to that view; and the decision itself in *Jackson* is certainly at odds with Wade's view that the rule of recognition is immune from any attempt by Parliament to mould it through the enactment of legislation.

---

[304] *Attorney-General for New South Wales v Trethowan* [1932] AC 526; *Harris v Minister of the Interior* 1952 (2) SA 428; *Bribery Commission v Ranasinghe* [1965] AC 172.

[305] *Bribery Commission v Ranasinghe* [1965] AC 172.

[306] Now the independent state of Sri Lanka.

[307] This distinction was, without explanation, dismissed by Lord Steyn in *R (Jackson) v Attorney-General* [2005] UKHL 56, [2006] 1 AC 262, [85].

[308] *Jackson*, [113].   [309] *Jackson*, [163].   [310] *Jackson*, [81].

6.5 Is Parliament really sovereign?

6.5.1 The story so far—and a final question

So far, our inquiry has focused on whether Parliament is capable of imposing any sort of limits on itself. We have seen that Wade's continuing theory answers this question firmly in the negative, but that its veracity is open to question in the light of both the Parliament Acts and the European Communities Act. We have also seen that the new view holds that although Parliament cannot absolutely entrench legislation, it can impose conditions that must be fulfilled before legislation can be repealed or departed from.

But while the continuing theory and the new view differ on whether a given Parliament can ever be subject to *intended constraints*—that is, constraints that exist because of the intention of earlier Parliaments—they agree on one thing: that Parliament is sovereign in the sense that it can make any law.[311] It is therefore said that Parliament is free from *unintended constraints*—that is, constraints that do not derive from conditions imposed by Parliament itself at an earlier point in time. Our final question is whether that supposition is correct.

6.5.2 Model III—unintended constraints on parliamentary authority

We already know from our discussion in section 6.1 that not everyone thinks that Parliament *should* be free from unintended constraints: legal constitutionalists argue that legislative power should be subject to legal restrictions that can, if necessary, be enforced by the courts. But our question now is a different one: is the UK Parliament *actually* subject to such constraints? In order to answer this question, we need to distinguish between two sorts of such constraint.

It is obvious that there are *practical constraints* upon what Parliament may accomplish. Even if it has the legal power to enact any law, a law directing that the sun should never set over the UK again would accomplish nothing in practice. This reduces to the issue of enforceability: Parliament, if it is sovereign, can make any legal provision that it wishes, but whether it can secure real-world compliance with stipulations set down in legislation is another matter entirely. For example, it has been observed that if Parliament enacts 'that smoking in the streets of Paris is an offence, then it *is* an offence' as a matter of *UK* law— the *French* police and courts would take no notice of that law.[312]

Similarly, if Parliament is sovereign, then it can undo anything that it has previously done. It has therefore been noted that, as a matter of law, Parliament could repeal legislation conferring independence on countries that used to form part of the British Empire such that, as a matter of UK law, Parliament's authority to legislate for such countries would resume. But Lord Denning pointed out that 'Freedom once given cannot be taken away. Legal theory must give way to practical politics'.[313]

---

[311] Even if, on the new view, Parliament might have to comply with certain conditions when doing so.

[312] Jennings, *The Law and the Constitution* (London 1959), pp 170–1 (original emphasis).

[313] *Blackburn v Attorney-General* [1971] 1 WLR 1037, 1040.

The fact that there are things such as those mentioned that Parliament cannot practically accomplish is not inconsistent with asserting that it is legally sovereign, since that concept simply means that Parliament can enact any laws that it wishes (whether or not they are sensible or practically enforceable). But are there also *legal constraints* on what Parliament can do? Are there some laws that it is not constitutionally competent to enact—and which, even if *practically* enforceable, would not be *legally* enforced by the courts?

The answer to this question, in the absence of a written constitution in the UK, might seem obvious. How can there be legal constraints on Parliament's power if no written constitution prescribes any such constraints? But some writers—and now some judges—argue that the *unwritten* constitution may contain fundamental principles that are so important as to be immovable by Parliament.

There are a number of ways in which this argument has been expressed. Allan, one of its leading proponents, argues that Wade was wrong to suppose that parliamentary sovereignty simply has to be accepted as a matter of historical fact;[314] rather, Allan contends, the authority of a legislature to make law must derive from some recognised and accepted principle. And whatever the position might have been in 1688, the principle that today underpins Parliament's authority is democracy. He goes on to argue that because democracy constitutes the moral *foundation* of Parliament's lawmaking authority, it also traces the *extent* of that authority. It follows, says Allan, that if Parliament were to enact a law the 'effect [of which] would be the destruction of any recognizable form of democracy'—such as 'a measure purporting to deprive a substantial section of the electorate of the vote on the grounds of their hostility to government policies'—the courts should not enforce it.[315]

Other writers have expressed their arguments in different terms, but agree with Allan that Parliament is subject to constraints imposed by the unwritten constitution. Writing extrajudicially, Sir John Laws said that basic rights, such as freedom of expression, form part of a 'higher-order law'—that is, they constitute a set of principles that 'cannot be abrogated as other laws can'.[316]

This analysis situates Parliament not (as traditional sovereignty theory would have it) *at the apex* of the constitutional order, unconstrained by anything or anyone, but *beneath* a set of fundamental constitutional principles that bind Parliament and with which it is therefore impotent to interfere. This point was captured by Lord Woolf when he asserted that 'both Parliament and the courts derive their authority from the rule of law' and that both are therefore bound by it. It follows, he said, that 'there are . . . limits on the sovereignty of Parliament which it is the courts' inalienable responsibility to identify and uphold'.[317] More recently, Lord Phillips, then President of the UK Supreme Court, said that 'if Parliament did the inconceivable [by legislating contrary to a fundamental constitutional principle], we [the judges] might do

---

[314] *Law, Liberty, and Justice* (Oxford 1993), ch 11. [315] Allan, p 282.
[316] 'Law and Democracy' [1995] PL 72, 84. [317] *'Droit Public*: English Style' [1995] PL 57, 68–9.

the inconceivable as well'.[318] These are radical assertions that depart markedly from orthodox thinking about parliamentary sovereignty. Would the courts really take such a drastic step?

6.5.3 Constitutional values and the interpretation of legislation

The short answer is that we simply do not know for sure—but there are several clues in the case law and related developments that allow for informed speculation. Courts do not approach legislation from a position of constitutional neutrality. When presented with legislation in a particular case, courts interpret and apply legislation against background constitutional principles such as those falling under the rubric of the 'rule of law'.[319] This is often rationalised by the courts through reliance on a presumption about what Parliament intends when it enacts Bills. As Lord Steyn said: 'Parliament does not legislate in a vacuum. Parliament legislates for a European liberal democracy founded on the principles and traditions of the common law. And the courts may approach legislation on this initial presumption.'[320]

In many situations, this technique can readily be applied—for example, by reading a generally worded statutory provision as being subject to implied restrictions. *Ahmed v HM Treasury*[321] is a case in point. Following the 9/11 attacks in the USA in 2001, the United Nations Security Council required states to freeze the assets of 'persons who commit, or attempt to commit, terrorist acts or participate in or facilitate the commission of terrorist acts' and of specific individuals connected with Al-Qaeda and the Taliban.[322] In response, the UK enacted two pieces of secondary legislation under s 1(1) of the United Nations Act 1946, which authorises the enactment of Orders in Council (a form of delegated legislation) when this is 'necessary or expedient' for the purpose of giving effect to UN Security Council directions.[323] The claimants in *Ahmed* contended that the Orders in Council were unlawful on the ground that, properly construed, s 1(1) of the 1946 Act did not authorise them. These arguments rested on two main premises: that one of the Orders, by permitting the government to freeze the assets of anyone *reasonably suspected* by it of terrorist involvement, went beyond what the UN direction required;[324] and that the other Order undermined the right of access to courts by permitting the UK government to freeze the assets of people designated as suspected terrorists by the UN without affording them any opportunity to mount a judicial challenge to the UN's decisions so to designate them.[325]

These arguments succeeded in the Supreme Court. Lord Hope noted that the effect of freezing someone's assets 'can be devastating', not least because 'their freedom of movement is severely restricted without access to funds or other economic resources', which 'strike[s] at the very heart of the individual's basic right to live his own life as

---

[318] *Today*, BBC Radio 4, 2 August 2010.   [319] On the rule of law, see Chapter 2, section 5.

[320] *R v Secretary of State for the Home Department, ex p Pierson* [1998] AC 539, 587.

[321] [2010] UKSC 2, [2010] 2 WLR 378.   [322] UN Security Council Resolution 1373, para 1(c).

[323] On secondary legislation, see generally Chapter 4, section 4.2.

[324] Terrorism (United Nations Measures) Order 2006, SI 2006/2657.

[325] Al-Qaida and Taliban (United Nations Measures) Order 2006.

he chooses'.[326] The Supreme Court concluded that, as Lord Hope put it, 'by introducing the reasonable suspicion test . . ., the Treasury exceeded [its] powers under section 1(1) of the 1946 Act'. This, he said, was 'a clear example of an attempt to adversely affect the basic rights of the citizen without the clear authority of Parliament'.[327]

Similarly, the attempt to subject people to asset-freezing on the basis of their designation by the UN was unlawful: if Parliament were to have intended s 1(1) of the 1946 Act to authorise the enactment of Orders fundamentally at odds with the right of access to courts, it would have said so in clear language. As Lord Mance put it: 'The words of section 1(1) are general, but for that very reason susceptible to the presumption, in the absence of express language or necessary implication to the contrary, that they were intended to be subject to the basic rights of the individual.'[328]

This approach to interpretation—whereby legislation is, where possible, interpreted consistently with basic constitutional principles and rights—has a long pedigree in English law. But it is worth noting at this point that it is now bolstered by the HRA, s 3(1) of which requires courts to interpret legislation compatibly with certain fundamental rights when it is possible to do so.[329]

While cases like *Ahmed* demonstrate a willingness on the courts' part to do their best to give Acts of Parliament a meaning that is consistent with fundamental constitutional values, they do not provide evidence that—in line with the views of writers such as Allan, Laws, and Woolf that we have already considered—the UK constitution contains 'higher order' principles contravention of which renders legislation unlawful and ineffective. (Indeed, the immediate response of the UK government to *Ahmed* was to procure the enactment of primary legislation conferring validity on the secondary legislation impugned by the Supreme Court.[330])

However, Allan argues that the distinction between *interpreting* a provision in an Act and *refusing to apply* it is an elusive and, ultimately, unhelpful one.[331] In essence, his contention is that if a court were to adopt an interpretation of a statute that was so radical as to change its meaning entirely, that would be tantamount to a refusal to apply it whether or not the court openly admitted that it was doing so. It has been suggested by some commentators that that is precisely what happened in the *Anisminic* case.[332]

The case concerned a provision contained in an Act of Parliament that provided that decisions made by a particular public body known as the Foreign Compensation Commission 'shall not be called in question in any court of law'.[333] The meaning of such so-called *ouster clauses* seems perfectly clear: Parliament surely intends to displace (to oust) the power of judicial review—that is, the power to adjudicate on the legality of decisions—that courts would normally exercise in relation to public bodies.[334] The difficulty, of course, is that interpreting the Act in that way would wholly prevent the courts

---

[326] [2010] UKSC 2, [2010] 2 WLR 378, [60].   [327] *Ahmed*, [61].   [328] *Ahmed*, [249].

[329] See further Chapter 18, section 3.4.

[330] Terrorist Asset-freezing (Temporary Provisions) Act 2010. As its name implies, this Act was a stop-gap measure, pending more detailed legislative reform.

[331] 'Parliamentary Sovereignty: Law, Politics, and Revolution' (1997) 113 LQR 443, 447.

[332] *Anisminic Ltd v Foreign Compensation Commission* [1969] 2 AC 147.

[333] Foreign Compensation Act 1950, s 4(4).   [334] On judicial review, see Chapters 11–14.

from upholding the law and would result in the existence of a public body entirely free from any form of legal control.

Such a situation would fundamentally threaten the rule of law. It is hardly surprising, then, that in *Anisminic* the Appellate Committee of the House of Lords attempted to find an interpretation of the ouster clause that would preserve judicial review; what *is* surprising, given the clarity with which the clause was drafted, is that the majority succeeded—or at least claimed to have done so. It was held that when Parliament had said that the Commission's determinations could not be questioned in any court, it had *meant* that no *lawful* determination could be questioned.

This interpretation left intact the courts' normal powers to overrule public bodies' unlawful decisions, and the Law Lords claimed that this result had been achieved simply by construing the ouster clause in a proper way: Lord Wilberforce, for example, said that the Appellate Committee was merely 'carrying out the intention of the legislature'.[335]

Some writers are unconvinced: if a particular provision is interpreted in a way that runs wholly counter to its natural meaning, this inevitably begs the question whether the Court was really just engaging in interpretation or was, in effect, refusing to apply the provision at all. Wade argued that the ruling in *Anisminic* 'is tantamount to saying that judicial review [of government and public bodies' decisions] is a constitutional fundamental which even the sovereign Parliament cannot abolish'.[336]

6.5.4 Beyond interpretation?

But why is there no unequivocal evidence of courts refusing—and openly acknowledging that they are refusing—to apply Acts of Parliament? The first, and most obvious, possibility is that courts are simply *not prepared to* refuse to apply duly enacted primary legislation. On this view, writers such as Allan, Laws, and Woolf, who contend that Parliament's lawmaking authority is limited and subject to judicial control, are plainly wrong.

The second possibility is that, although courts *are prepared* to refuse to apply 'unconstitutional' legislation, they have never yet been faced with an Act of Parliament that is so repugnant to fundamental principles as to justify a refusal to apply it. It is also important to bear in mind that, as we explained in Chapter 1, for as long as the HRA is in force, the courts, because they are only empowered by that Act to declare legislation to be incompatible with fundamental rights, are not presented with a stark choice between applying or refusing to apply legislation that offends such rights.[337] There is, however, a third possibility: that the courts wish to characterise—perhaps even *disguise*—their endeavours as the interpretation of, rather than as a refusal to apply, legislation. In relation to this third possibility, three points should be considered.

First, why might courts want to avoid explicitly refusing to apply legislation? Everyone accepts that it is the courts' job to interpret and apply laws enacted by Parliament. It follows that while a very bold interpretation may (by giving the

---

[335] [1969] 2 AC 147, 208.   [336] Wade and Forsyth, *Administrative Law* (Oxford 2008), p 616.
[337] See further Chapter 18.

legislation a meaning radically different from that which was intended by Parliament) have a similar effect to refusing to apply it at all, such an approach is less likely to attract the criticism that judges are overstepping the mark.

Even in countries with written constitutions, judicial powers to strike down unconstitutional legislation remain controversial. For example, the US Constitution does not explicitly confer such powers on the courts. When, in the seminal case of *Marbury v Madison*,[338] the US Supreme Court held that such powers were *implicit* in the Constitution—why would the framers have limited the powers of government if they had not intended the courts to be able to enforce such limits?—this conclusion was not universally welcomed: the Court was criticised in some quarters for assuming powers that had not clearly been allocated to it by the Constitution.

Second, UK courts would find themselves in a particularly exposed position if they were to assert such powers. In the USA, there was no doubt that the *Constitution imposed limits* on (among other things) the legislative authority of Congress, albeit that there was some room for disagreement about *whether the Constitution assigned to the courts the task of policing those limits*. In the UK, in contrast, there is no written constitution to which judges can point in the first place to establish that Parliament's authority *is limited*—and even if we are prepared to accept that it is, there is no written constitution telling us (or the judges) *what those limits are*.

If the UK courts were to assert US-style powers to strike down Acts of Parliament, they would not only be *assuming an enforcement function* not explicitly assigned to them by the constitution, but would also be determining, without any evidence in the form of a written constitution, that *there are constitutional limits to Parliament's lawmaking authority* and *what those limits are*. As Griffith—a prominent critic of extensive judicial power—remarks, the 'trouble' with the argument that there are 'higher-order' laws restricting Parliament's authority and enforceable by courts is that they 'must be given substance, be interpreted, and be applied'. This, he says, leads to judges claiming 'superiority over democratically elected institutions'.[339]

It is perhaps for precisely these reasons that those who argue in favour of UK judges possessing a power to disregard unconstitutional legislation suggest that it arises only in *extreme* circumstances. Woolf, for example, said that he envisaged limits upon Parliament's lawmaking authority only 'of the most modest dimensions which I believe any democrat would accept'.[340]

> **Q** In section 6.1.2, we considered the 'majoritarian' objection to courts having powers to strike down legislation enacted by democratically elected legislatures. In the absence of a written constitution imposing limits on the legislature, do you regard those objections as unanswerable?

---

[338] 5 US 137 (1803).   [339] 'The Brave New World of Sir John Laws' (2000) 63 MLR 159, 165.
[340] Lord Woolf, 69.

Third, however, it seems that it is not only the courts that are, for the reasons explored in this chapter, keen to avoid the sort of confrontation that would bring out into the open the question of whether there are legally enforceable constitutional limits upon Parliament's lawmaking power. In 2003 the government sought to oust judicial review of immigration and asylum decisions.[341] This would have displaced what we have seen is regarded as the fundamental constitutional right of access to courts; indeed, the clause had been specifically drafted with a view to precluding the sort of interpretation accorded to the ouster clause in *Anisminic*.

A furore ensued and parliamentary select committees opposed the clause. The then Lord Chief Justice, Lord Woolf, said that if the clause were enacted, 'it would be so inconsistent with the spirit of mutual respect between the different arms of government that it could be the catalyst for a campaign for a written constitution'.[342] In the face of such opposition, the clause was withdrawn by the government.

There is, therefore, something of a stand-off. The courts, for the reasons discussed, are reluctant to assert a power to strike down Acts of Parliament that offend fundamental constitutional principles. Parliament and the executive are also reluctant to put the courts in a situation in which they are forced to nail their colours to the mast by choosing between, on the one hand, the application of an Act that is incontrovertibly contrary to fundamental principles and, on the other hand, enforcing such principles notwithstanding the existence of such legislation. But we cannot clearly say what would happen if such a situation were to arise.

Judicial opinion is divided. The President of the Supreme Court, Lord Neuberger, has noted that the courts must be vigilant to protect individuals against any abuses by an increasingly powerful executive, but they cannot go against Parliament's will as expressed in statute.[343] The courts *could* acquire the power to take such a step—but only as part of a fundamental reordering of the constitution, such as a written constitution, which had public backing.

However, other judges have expressed scepticism about the absolute conception of parliamentary sovereignty. Following the controversy over the ouster clause in 2004, in the *Jackson* case, Lord Steyn said that Dicey's 'pure and absolute' conception of parliamentary sovereignty was 'out of place' in modern Britain. He went on to argue that the supremacy of Parliament depends on judicial recognition of it, and that, if Parliament were to assert an extravagant power by, for example, seeking to remove judicial review, the courts 'may have to consider whether this is a constitutional fundamental which even a sovereign Parliament . . . cannot abolish'.[344] Lord Hope expressed similar views, opining that 'parliamentary sovereignty is no longer, if it ever was, absolute',[345] and that 'the rule of law enforced by the courts is the ultimate

---

[341] See Thomas, 'After the Ouster: Review and Reconsideration in a Single-Tier Tribunal' [2006] PL 674.

[342] 'The Rule of Law and a Change in the Constitution' [2004] CLJ 317, 329.

[343] Neuberger, 'Who Are the Masters Now?', Second Lord Alexander of Weedon Lecture, 6 April 2011, [72]–[73]. Similarly, Lord Bingham, *The Rule of Law* (London 2010), p 167 noted that parliamentary sovereignty is the fundamental principle: the judges did not establish the principle and they cannot, by themselves, change it.

[344] *R (Jackson) v Attorney-General* [2005] UKHL 56, [2006] 1 AC 262, [102].

[345] *Jackson*, [104].

controlling factor on which our constitution is based'.[346] Baroness Hale thought it possible that the courts may reject an attempt by Parliament to 'subvert the rule of law by removing governmental action affecting the rights of the individual from all judicial scrutiny'.[347]

More recently, in *AXA* Lord Hope noted that it was not entirely unthinkable that a government with a parliamentary majority might use its power to abolish judicial review or to diminish the role of the courts. Lord Hope continued: 'The rule of law requires that the judges must retain the power to insist that legislation of that extreme kind is not law which the courts will recognise.'[348] In 2015, the government responded to this by noting that it should govern in accordance with constitutional principles and recognise the importance of the rule of law. However, the government explicitly rejected Lord Hope's view that the judges possess some power to strike down legislation enacted by Parliament.[349] It should also be noted that Parliament itself has not even debated the issue let alone formulated a collective view on the matter.

There is no precedent at all for the courts striking down legislation as being contrary to the common law. The episode of the ouster clause was perhaps the nearest we have come in recent years. That clause was never enacted and the whole episode will serve as a glaring warning to any future government contemplating a similar proposal. Nevertheless, it is theoretically possible that circumstances might, in the future, arise in which the courts decide to take UK constitutional law into unchartered territory by acknowledging substantive limits upon parliamentary sovereignty.

6.5.5 Why no explicit constitutional review?

Even if the courts did assume a power to strike down legislation, it would probably only ever come into play in extreme cases, such as an attempt by the government to abolish judicial review. Absent some large-scale public and political debate as to whether or not the courts should be able to have such a power and also an agreed constitutional statement of the values against which the courts would assess the constitutionality of legislation, it is unlikely that legislation would be struck down—unless it offended absolutely fundamental principles, such as the rule of law. Such a wide-ranging public debate has not taken place.

In the absence of such debate, this issue is shrouded in ambiguity. But that may be no accident. According to Foley's theory of constitutional silences, 'the habitual willingness to defer indefinitely consideration of deep constitutional anomalies, for the sake of preserving the constitution from the type of conflict that would arise from attempts to remove them, represents the core of a constitutional culture.'[350] In other words, there are often tacit agreements—silences—between different constitutional players to keep difficult and unresolved constitutional issues in a state of genuine

---

[346] *Jackson*, [107]. [347] *Jackson*, [159].

[348] *AXA General Insurance Limited v Lord Advocate* [2011] UKSC 46, [51]. Lord Hope's comments were made in relation to Acts of the Scottish Parliament, but they apply by implication to the UK Parliament.

[349] Letter from the then Lord Chancellor, Chris Grayling MP, to Lord Lang, Chair of the House of Lords Constitution Committee, dated 26 February 2015, **http://www.parliament.uk/documents/lords-committees/constitution/GovernmentResponse/CC56GovtresponseOLC260215.pdf**

[350] Foley, *The Silence of Constitutions* (London 1989), p 10.

ambiguity because of a desire continually to postpone discussion of such anomalies that could lead to conflict. Such silences arise because resolving the matter directly would be intensely problematic, and potentially entail disproportionate inconvenience or damage to the system as it currently stands. Moreover, the constitutional ambiguities that arise from such silences can often be a source of strength rather than weakness.

Let us think this through. Just suppose that the courts struck down an Act of Parliament as being unconstitutional. This would intensely annoy those politicians who resent unelected judges interfering with their powers. It could prompt a revenge package by the executive and legislature against the courts. It could also increase demands for greater accountability of judges through, for example, pre-appointment hearings before Parliament to investigate the moral and political views of individual judges—something that the judges fear and would do anything to avoid.

Similarly, the government also has an interest in not provoking the judiciary into constitutional review. Many would view such an unprecedented step by the judiciary as evidence that the government and Parliament had stepped far over the line, that the government was not acting for benevolent motives but for authoritarian reasons. This could be accompanied by demands for a written constitution to control and limit both the government and Parliament—something that any government would much prefer to avoid. For government Ministers, constitutional issues are abstruse and spurious side-issues that distract attention from the really important and practical business of governing. In other words, entering into constitutional review of legislation could well prompt an unprecedented and undesirable constitutional struggle the outcome of which would be very far from certain and from which much could be lost for little gain. Opening Pandora's box would create the type of severe conflict that both sides—the government and the judiciary—have a mutual interest in avoiding, unless absolutely necessary.

The best solution all round is then mutual respect between the three branches.[351] In other words, the mere possibility of judges pursuing the sort of approach hinted at in *Jackson* and *AXA* should itself be a particularly compelling factor that invites political restraint by the government and Parliament. The willingness to defer the whole issue and to leave it ambiguous may not be a weakness of the constitution, but a strength.

The perpetuation of such ambiguity is illustrated by the *Evans* litigation. We noted in Chapter 2 that in *Evans v Information Commissioner*[352] the Upper Tribunal ordered the government to disclose Prince Charles's 'advocacy correspondence' under the Freedom of Information Act 2000. In response, the government invoked its 'veto power' under s 53 of the Act, in effect overriding the judgment of the Upper Tribunal—a superior court of record. The government's exercise of the veto was then

---

[351] In this respect, note the comments of Lord Phillips in *R (Cart) v Upper Tribunal* [2011] UKSC 28, [89]: 'The administration of justice and upholding of the rule of law involves a partnership between Parliament and the judges. . . . Parliament has not sought to oust or fetter the common law powers of judicial review of the judges of the High Court and I hope that Parliament will never do so.'

[352] [2012] UKUT 313 (AAC).

challenged by way of judicial review, a nine-member panel of the Supreme Court concluding by a majority that the government had acted unlawfully.[353] The veto was quashed and the correspondence was released.

In the light of our discussion above, this episode is instructive for two reasons. First, three of the five judges in the majority took the view that the veto power was highly constitutionally dubious. According to Lord Neuberger—with whom Lords Kerr and Reed agreed—a power enabling the executive to override a judicial decision with which it disagreed would be 'unique in the laws of the United Kingdom'. It would 'cut across two constitutional principles which are also fundamental components of the rule of law'—namely, that judicial decisions 'cannot be ignored by anyone', 'least of all . . . the executive', and that executive action, 'subject to jealously guarded statutory exceptions', must be subject to judicial scrutiny. Lord Neuberger's view was that broad override powers would 'flout . . . the first principle' and 'stand . . . the second principle on its head'.[354] In the light of this, he concluded that the veto power should be read very narrowly indeed, so as to be exercisable in only highly limited circumstances. The dissenting judges took a dim view of this. For Lord Hughes, Lord Neuberger's analysis contradicted Parliament's 'plainly shown' intention,[355] while Lord Wilson said that the judgment of the Court of Appeal—which, like Lord Neuberger, had adopted a very narrow view of the veto power—'did not . . . interpret' s 53 of the Act but rather 're-wrote' it.[356]

The government was far from happy about the Supreme Court's judgment. It responded by establishing a review of the Freedom of Information Act[357] and by raising the prospect of, in effect, the reversal of the judgment by amending s 53 so as to make clear the intended width of the veto power.[358] In the end, however, the government decided not to press ahead with that proposal, choosing to accept the Court's judgment rather than seeking to have it legislatively undone.

This sequence of events tells us two significant things with reference to Foley's theory of constitutional silence. First, it shows that while the courts may have no appetite for outright confrontation with Parliament (and, by implication, the government), the courts—or at least some senior judges—are willing to press statutory interpretation so far as to ensure that fundamental constitutional values can be overcome only by the clearest statutory language. Second, and correspondingly, it demonstrates that Parliament—and so, in reality, the government—must be prepared to invest considerable political capital in overturning such judgments: political capital that the government was not prepared to invest on this occasion. In this way, an uneasy silence takes hold, in which each side explores, without definitively testing, the limits of the other's constitutional authority.

---

[353] *R (Evans) v Attorney General* [2015] UKSC 21, [2015] AC 1787.
[354] *R (Evans) v Attorney General* [2015] UKSC 21, [2015] AC 1787, [51]–[52].
[355] *R (Evans) v Attorney General* [2015] UKSC 21, [2015] AC 1787, [154].
[356] *R (Evans) v Attorney General* [2015] UKSC 21, [2015] AC 1787, [168].
[357] Independent Commission on Freedom of Information, *Report* (London 2016).
[358] 'Cameron concedes defeat over publication of Prince Charles's letters', *The Guardian*, 26 March 2015.

6.6 **Summary**

We have examined three models of parliamentary authority. Model I holds that Parliament is fully sovereign and that sovereignty is fixed (or 'continuing'); it is therefore (paradoxically) impossible for Parliament to do anything that would limit its own powers. Model II agrees that Parliament is sovereign, in that it is always possible for it to make, amend, or repeal any law, but says that it is possible for Parliament to lay down binding conditions as to the process that must be followed if (for example) a given Act were to be repealed or amended. Model III says that Parliament is not sovereign: it lacks the power to make laws that violate fundamental constitutional principles.

The debate that underlies these three competing views ultimately turns on two questions: (i) can Parliament subject itself to any sort of limitations ('intended limitations'), and (ii) is Parliament subject to limitations that derive otherwise than from earlier Acts of Parliament ('unintended limitations')? We have seen that while there are no clear answers to either of these questions, there is at least circumstantial evidence that provides a basis for informed speculation.

The answer to question (i) is that while there is no unequivocal example of courts accepting that the UK Parliament can impose restrictions upon its successors, the reasoning, together with certain dicta, in the *Jackson* case provides some support for the view that Parliament *can* adapt the ground rules governing the enactment of legislation; thus allowing, for example, for legislation to be accorded limited entrenchment by precluding its amendment or repeal in the absence of express language or a super-majority.[359]

As far as question (ii) is concerned, we have seen that the courts—and indeed politicians—prefer, if possible, to avoid it. In particular, the courts seek to secure basic constitutional values by interpreting legislation consistently with them rather than by asserting a power to disregard Acts of Parliament that violate such values. And we know that the political process itself is likely to guard against most such legislation, but not necessarily all. However, we have also seen that some judges have asserted that if the unthinkable were to happen, they would be willing to consider refusing to apply such legislation.

Some of the heat has been removed from this debate by the fact that, as we saw in Chapter 1, the courts can, under the HRA, declare legislation to be incompatible with fundamental rights.[360] But that Act, at least in its present form, may not remain on the statute book forever; in any event, the underlying question—whether there are any enforceable limits on Parliament's lawmaking authority—remains an important one that goes to the heart of the nature of the British constitution.

We know that there are many things that Parliament is, in reality, extremely unlikely to do. What we do not know is whether, if the political process were to fail to prevent such legislative conduct, the courts would step in and provide legal redress by striking down the relevant Act. Ultimately, therefore, this question is about the extent

---

[359] eg a two-thirds majority—something greater than the bare majority that is normally required.

[360] See further Chapter 18.

to which the British tradition of political constitutionalism is supplemented—or has been replaced—by a legal form of constitutionalism that supplies clear lines that may not lawfully be crossed by legislators. And it is, as we have seen, a question that both judges and politicians seem anxious should never be allowed to arise.

7. Concluding remarks

This chapter has explored three principal issues relating to Parliament's role: its democratic credentials, its role in scrutinising legislation, and its legal powers. In addressing these matters, we have encountered two of the key themes that run throughout this book.

First, because of the UK constitution's idiosyncratic implementation of the separation of powers doctrine, Parliament is, in practice, dominated by the executive branch. As a result, its capacity to scrutinise effectively government Bills is limited, and Parliament as a lawmaker can, without exaggeration, be regarded as, in some senses, an offshoot of the executive. This engages our theme concerning the *importance of holding the government to account*. If Parliament is, in effect, part of the government rather than an independent scrutiniser of it and of its Bills, then this raises questions about the need for effective scrutiny *of Parliament*—whether internally (through the relationship between the two chambers) or externally (eg via judicial review of legislation).

Second, the debate concerning the extent of Parliament's powers goes to the heart of the wider debate about *the balance in the UK between political and legal forms of constitutionalism*. Although we were unable definitively to determine whether Parliament *is* truly sovereign, we *do* know for sure that whether we think that Parliament *should* be sovereign will depend on the faith that we are willing to put in politicians and in judges respectively.

Expert commentary
Parliamentary sovereignty: the new constitutional hypothesis
Sir Jeffrey Jowell, Emeritus Professor of Public Law, University College London

Should parliamentary sovereignty seriously be considered the 'ultimate' principle governing our constitutional settlement in the twenty-first century? Is it right that our courts lack the authority to strike down a statute under virtually any circumstance?

The country should, of course, be governed by those who represent the will of the people. And we should be deeply aware of our constitutional history, where the former tyrannical powers of the monarchs were progressively limited by the countervailing power of an increasingly representative Parliament. But, as the chapter reminds us, we should also remember the traumas of the twentieth century where it was shown in Germany, the Soviet Union, and elsewhere that governments clearly representing the will of the majority could act in a way just as contemptuous of human dignity, equality, and the rule of law as some of the monarchs of old. The historical shift of authority from the king to Parliament should, therefore, not be seen simply as the reallocation of sovereignty from one locus of power to another. It also entailed a revision of the very notion of sovereignty which, under the monarchs, meant the possession of unrestrained and uncontrolled power.

That transfer therefore involved the development of a new constitutional hypothesis,[361] containing two valid objectives. The first objective is that public policy should be determined in a manner which best permits those who make it to represent the public will. The second objective is that power should not be absolute, but constrained by principles that secure equal respect for human dignity. We tend to call the first of these the 'democratic' objective and the second the 'rights' objective; both are necessary in a modern constitutional democracy.

There will, of course, be tensions between the two objectives. Popular opinion will, from time to time, seek policies that offend rights. It is then for an independent judiciary to adjudicate upon whether rights or popular opinion ought to prevail. In such circumstances, it is not for Parliament to judge in its own cause. In so doing, the judiciary must have a sophisticated sense of which matters lie in the realm of policy (and therefore lie within the province of Parliament to decide) and which matters lie in the realm of fundamental rights and democratic principle (and therefore lie within the province of the courts). In the United Kingdom, our courts have not yet been so bold as to challenge Parliament's authority by striking down a law that fundamentally offends the new constitutional hypothesis (at least outside EU law, where Parliament itself conferred such authority on the courts). But are there any issues that might provoke the judiciary, in a country without a codified constitution, to assert such authority against an 'unconstitutional' law?

Let us discount the fanciful examples of laws against blue-eyed babies and laws to prevent smoking in the streets of Paris. What about the actual threat of a law to prevent judicial review of immigration decisions? As the chapter recounts, public lawyers eagerly engaged in a debate as to whether such a law was open to a judicial strike-down to protect a fundamental right of a minority. Later, one of our most senior judges, Lord Hope, advanced the tantalising proposition that Parliament should not be able to pass legislation which is 'absurd' or would not be acceptable to 'the populace at large.'[362] Take, for instance, a statute which outlawed elections for a period or which created a one-party state. Could any judge really uphold such a law without conniving in the undermining of the basic structure of constitutional democracy from which our modern Parliament derives its legitimacy?

Legitimacy is one reason, therefore, why the courts should be in a position to strike down legislation. The legitimacy of parliamentary sovereignty itself rests on Parliament's representative features. Laws which degrade those features negate the basis of that legitimacy and undermine the very condition upon which Parliament's supremacy rests. Similarly, a law that withdrew the right to criticise government would impair Parliament's accountability—which is another basic feature of a properly democratic society.[363]

Parliament may never come to pass such laws. The rule of law and the contemporary culture of human rights both carry heavy moral weight, even without the need for judicial intervention. If Parliament were to do so, and if our courts responded by striking down the law, a constitutional crisis would ensue. But the courts would at least have done their duty by declaring a hypothesis of democracy which should no longer be regarded as synonymous with majority rule and unfettered official power. To maintain that the courts today always lack the authority to invalidate any law overlooks both their authority and duty in a common law system. It also ignores the fundamental principles that justified our journey from tyranny to constitutional democracy.

---

[361] *Jackson v Attorney General* [2005] UKHL 56, [2006] 1 AC 262, [102], *per* Lord Steyn.
[362] *Jackson*, [120].   [363] *Jackson*, [159], *per* Baroness Hale.

Further reading

General

LANSLEY, 'The Legislature and the Executive', UK Parliament Open Lecture, 24 April 2013 (**http://www.parliament.uk/get-involved/outreach-and-training/resources-for-universities/open-lectures/the-legislature-and-the-executive/**)
This is a lecture by a former Leader of the House of Commons.

NORTON, *Parliament in British Politics* (Basingstoke 2005)
This book provides a detailed overview of Parliament.

OLIVER, 'Reforming the United Kingdom Parliament', in Jowell and Oliver (ed), *The Changing Constitution* (Oxford 2011)
This chapter provides an analysis of Parliamentary reform.

Parliament and democracy

ELECTORAL REFORM SOCIETY, *The 2015 General Election: A Voting System in Crisis* (2015) (**http://electoral-reform.org.uk/sites/default/files/files/publication/2015%20 General%20Election%20Report%20web.pdf**)
This report provides a detailed critical analysis of the 2015 general election.

HAYMAN, 'Reform in the House of Lords—Ending the Deadlock', UK Parliament Open Lecture, 25 January 2013 (**http://www.parliament.uk/get-involved/outreach-and-training/ resources-for-universities/open-lectures/reform-in-the-house-of-lords--ending-the-deadlock/**)
This lecture discusses House of Lords reform.

Parliamentary privilege

HM GOVERNMENT, *Parliamentary Privilege* (Cm 8318 2012)
This is a government white paper on parliamentary privilege.

JOINT COMMITTEE ON PARLIAMENTARY PRIVILEGE, *Parliamentary Privilege* (HL 30 HC 100 2013–14)
This select committee report provides a detailed overview of parliamentary privilege with recommendations.

Parliament and the legislative process

KORRIS, 'Standing Up for Scrutiny: How and Why Parliament Should Make Better Law' (2011) 64 Parliamentary Affairs 564
This paper considers the adequacy of parliamentary scrutiny of legislation.

NATZLER, 'The Passage of Legislation', UK Parliament Open Lecture, 10 May 2013 (**http:// www.parliament.uk/get-involved/education-programmes/universities-programme/ university-teaching-resources/the-passage-of-legislation/**)
This lecture by a Commons official provides an overview of the passage of legislation through Parliament.

PUTTNAM, 'The Role and Importance of Pre-Legislative Scrutiny in Parliamentary Life', UK Parliament Open Lecture, 12 December 2012 (**http://www.parliament.uk/get-involved/ education-programmes/universities-programme/university-teaching-resources/ the-role-and-importance-of-pre-legislative-scrutiny-in-parliamentary-life/**)
This lecture considers pre-legislative scrutiny.

Parliament's powers

GOLDSWORTHY, *The Sovereignty of Parliament* (Oxford 1999)
  This books provides a detailed analysis and defence of parliamentary sovereignty.

LAWS, 'Law and Democracy' [1995] PL 72
  This article by a former Lord Justice of Appeal argues that parliamentary sovereignty is ultimately
  subject to judicial controls.

Useful websites

General

http://www.parliament.uk
The website of the UK Parliament

Parliament and democracy

http://www.electoralcommission.org.uk
The website of the Electoral Commission

http://www.electoral-reform.org.uk
The website of the Electoral Reform Society

http://lordsappointments.independent.gov.uk
The website of the House of Lords Appointments Commission

Parliament and the legislative process

https://www.gov.uk/government/publications/guide-to-making-legislation
The Cabinet Office's Guide to Making Legislation

http://www.legislation.gov.uk
An online UK legislation service

6

The Judiciary

1. Introduction   257
2. The structure of the judicial system   258
3. The role of the judiciary   264
4. The characteristics of the judiciary   271
5. Concluding remarks   293
Expert commentary   293
Further reading   295
Useful websites   296

1. Introduction

This chapter focuses specifically on the judiciary—and on two issues in particular.

First, *what are courts and judges for*? The answer may seem obvious: to decide disputes, interpret legislation, and develop the common law. However, engaging with this question will enable us to appreciate both the function that the courts fulfil in upholding key constitutional principles such as the separation of powers and the rule of law, and the way in which such principles, in turn, inform the proper conception of the judicial role.

Second, *what characteristics do—and should—courts have* in order that they may effectively play their proper constitutional role? We will pay particular attention to the notion of judicial independence. This is the idea that judges should be free to interpret and apply the law in an objective way, free from political interference, and free from any need to worry about public opinion. While judicial independence is undoubtedly important, we will also ask whether this orthodoxy should be accepted unquestioningly. In particular, as judges acquire greater powers to pronounce on controversial matters—as a result of, among other things, the growth of judicial review of governmental action and the increasing prominence of human rights law—we will consider whether it is realistic to suppose that the business of judging is an activity wholly distinct and separate from the broader political process. We will also, in this regard, consider what characteristics, other than judicial independence, the judiciary should possess. How important, for example, is it that judges are representative—in gender, ethnic, social, and other terms—of the population at large?

2. The structure of the judicial system

Before addressing these matters, it is necessary first to outline the structure of the judicial system in the UK. It is beyond the scope of this book to examine in any detail the way in which the system of courts is organised and the exact scope of the respective jurisdictions of the courts that form that system. It is, however, necessary to consider the general shape of the system.

It can be seen from Figure 6.1 that *the judicial structure is a hierarchical one.* Different courts undertaking different tasks are located at different levels of the hierarchy. Broadly speaking, there are three main levels of this hierarchy. The bottom tier is made up of lower courts and tribunals, such as magistrates' courts, the county court, and the First-tier Tribunal. As first-instance courts whose role is to hear cases for the first time, they are normally involved in fact-finding—by hearing witnesses and considering evidence—and then applying the relevant law to those facts to reach a decision. Table 6.1 summarises the role of different types of judges within the system.

Above first-instance courts are courts of higher standing, such as the High Court and the Court of Appeal. Such courts may have a first-instance or appellate jurisdiction (or both). For example, the High Court is a first-instance court in some types of litigation, such as judicial review. By contrast, the Court of Appeal is an appellate

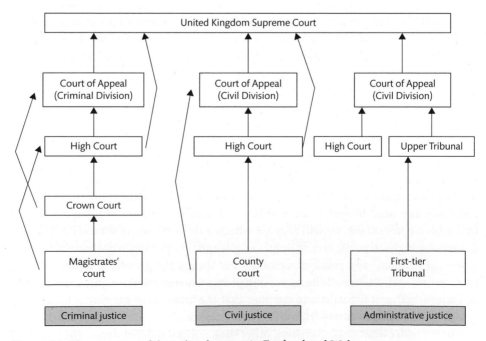

Figure 6.1 The structure of the judicial system in England and Wales

Table 6.1 The role of judges within the judicial system

Type of judge	Role
Supreme Court Justices	The most senior judges in the UK. The Supreme Court is the UK's final court of appeal and develops law in the most important cases. It replaced the Appellate Committee of the House of Lords in 2009.
Heads of Division	There are five Heads of Division: the Lord Chief Justice of England and Wales, the Master of the Rolls, the President of the Queen's Bench Division, the President of the Family Division, and the Chancellor of the High Court.
Lord Justices of Appeal	Senior judges with lengthy judicial experience who sit in the Court of Appeal (Civil Division) and (Criminal Division).
High Court judges	Senior judges who deal with the more complex and difficult cases. High Court judges are assigned to one of the three divisions of the High Court: the Queen's Bench Division, the Family Division, and the Chancery Division. High Court judges assigned to the Administrative Court undertake judicial review work.
Judge Advocates, Deputy Judge Advocates	Judges who deal with criminal trials of service men and women in the Royal Navy, the Army, and the Royal Air Force for serious offences.
Masters and Deputy Masters	Procedural judges who at first instance deal with all aspects of an action, from its issue until it is ready for trial by a trial judge—usually a High Court judge. After the trial the master resumes responsibility for the case.
Circuit judges	Some circuit judges deal specifically with criminal or civil cases, while some are authorised to hear public and/or private law family cases. Circuit judges are appointed to one of seven regions of England and Wales and sit in the Crown and County Courts within their particular region.
Recorders	Recorders may sit in both Crown and County Courts, but most start by sitting in the Crown Court. Their jurisdiction is broadly similar to that of a circuit judge, but they will generally handle less complex or serious matters coming before the court.
District judges and deputy district judges	District judges handle a wide spectrum of civil and family law cases such as claims for damages and injunctions, possession proceedings against mortgage borrowers and property tenants, divorces, child proceedings, domestic violence injunctions, and insolvency proceedings.
Upper Tribunal judges	Upper Tribunal judges are specialist judges that sit in one of the Upper Tribunal's chambers. They review and decide appeals against First–tier Tribunal decisions. Upper Tribunal judges also decide certain judicial review cases.
First-tier Tribunal judges	First-tier Tribunal judges hear and determine first-instance appeals, such as social security and immigration appeals. They sometimes sit with specialist non-legal members.

court: it only ever deals with cases that are appeals against decisions of a lower court or tribunal. Likewise, the Upper Tribunal, which has an equivalent status to the High Court, determines appeals on a point of law from the First-tier Tribunal. It also handles certain judicial review cases. Courts at this middle level are almost always concerned primarily with deciding points of law rather than making findings of fact.

At the apex of the hierarchy is the Supreme Court. It is only ever concerned with determining the most important legal issues. Its task is to concentrate on cases of the greatest public and constitutional importance, and to maintain and develop the role of the highest court in the UK as a leader in the common law world.[1]

It is useful to have some idea of the size of the judiciary. Figure 6.2 shows the number of court judges in England and Wales and Figure 6.3 shows the number of tribunal judges.

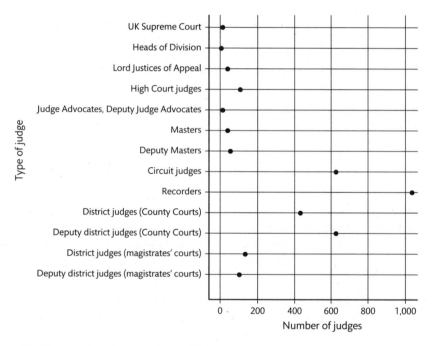

Figure 6.2 The number of court judges, 2016

Source: Judiciary of England and Wales, *Judicial Diversity Statistics 2016*, **https://www.judiciary.gov.uk/ publications/judicial-statistics-2016/**

Three points can be made here. First, there are relatively few judges at the top of the judicial hierarchy, for instance, in the Supreme Court. Most judges are located towards the lower end of the hierarchy. Second, while most court judges occupy full-time positions, this is not so for the tribunals judiciary. Over 90 per cent of the nearly 4,000 First-tier Tribunal judges are fee-paid, that is, they work part-time. Third, in addition to legally qualified judges, the judicial system relies heavily upon non-legally qualified individuals to make judicial decisions. There are some 17,000 lay magistrates or Justices of the Peace who hear less serious criminal cases in magistrates'

---

[1] **http://www.supremecourt.gov.uk/about/role-of-the-supreme-court.html**

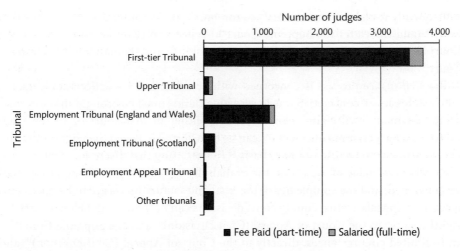

Figure 6.3 The number of tribunal judges, 2016

courts. Also, tribunals often have non-legally qualified members who sit alongside a legally qualified chairperson.

Going back to the judicial structure (Figure 6.1), this is actually more complex than so far indicated: Figure 6.1 is concerned only with the structure of the judicial system in *England and Wales*.[2] This is the largest legal system in the UK, but there are two other legal systems in the UK: the legal systems of *Northern Ireland* and of *Scotland*. These two legal systems are distinct, but very similar. Northern Ireland has its own Court of Appeal, High Court, and lower courts; appeals lying ultimately (as in England and Wales) to the Supreme Court.[3] Similarly, Scotland has its own equivalents to the High Court and Court of Appeal—the Inner and Outer Houses of the Court of Session—and its own lower courts, the Sheriff Courts. Again, the Supreme Court is the final court of appeal in respect of all non-criminal matters.[4]

As well as being organised hierarchically, the judicial structure is also *organised according to the subject matter and type of dispute being resolved*. Generally speaking, the legal system can be subdivided into three main categories: criminal justice, civil justice, and administrative justice.

The *criminal justice* process is concerned with the criminal prosecution of alleged offenders. Nearly all criminal cases begin in the magistrates' court. Cases concerning less serious offences are heard in that court, while more serious cases (eg murder) are heard before a Crown Court. A key difference is that while cases in the magistrates' court are heard by a panel of lay justices or a single judge, Crown Court cases involve trial by jury. Appeals from decisions of the magistrates' court can be made to the Crown Court[5] (and thereafter, on a point of law only, to the High Court,[6] and

---

[2] Note that there is an ongoing debate over whether Wales post-devolution should have its own distinct legal jurisdiction.

[3] See **https://www.courtsni.gov.uk/en-GB/Pages/default.aspx**

[4] See **http://www.scotland-judiciary.org.uk/1/0/Home**

[5] Magistrates' Courts Act 1980, s 108.   [6] Senior Courts Act 1981, s 28.

subsequently to the Supreme Court[7]) or (on points of law only) directly to the High Court[8] (and thereafter the Supreme Court[9]). Appeals in cases heard by the Crown Court lie to the Court of Appeal (Criminal Division)[10] and thereafter to the Supreme Court.[11]

The *civil justice* process is concerned with civil liability (eg actions for personal injury or breach of contract). Some lower-value claims must be brought in the county court, but many civil claims can be brought either in that court or in the High Court.[12] In such circumstances, cases can be transferred between the High Court and the county court on a discretionary basis.[13] In exercising that discretion, factors such as the financial value of the claim, the availability of judges specialising in the matter concerned, and the complexity of the legal and factual issues are to be taken into account.[14] Appeals against county court decisions can be made to the High Court[15]— and thereafter to the Court of Appeal (Civil Division)[16] and the Supreme Court[17]— or, in limited circumstances, directly to the Court of Appeal (Civil Division)[18] and thereafter to the Supreme Court.[19] Appeals against High Court decisions can be made to the Court of Appeal (Civil Division)[20] and thereafter to the Supreme Court;[21] in limited circumstances, an appeal can be made directly to the Supreme Court.[22]

The *administrative justice* process, or the public law system, is concerned with legal challenges against public or governmental decisions. Such challenges fall into two general categories. First, there are judicial review challenges against the legality of public decisions, which are determined by the Administrative Court (part of the High Court) and the Upper Tribunal. Part IV of this book is devoted to judicial review. Second, there are appeals against administrative decisions made by public bodies (such as welfare and immigration decisions). These appeals are determined by the First-tier and Upper Tribunals. Tribunals handle an enormous volume of cases each year.[23] We consider tribunals in Chapter 16. The administrative justice system also includes non-judicial mechanisms such as ombudsmen.[24]

Three additional points should be noted. First, the *legal jurisdictions* of the different courts and tribunals vary. Many courts have a statutory jurisdiction. By contrast, other courts have an inherent, non-statutory jurisdiction. For example, the High Court has an inherent common law jurisdiction: it is not conferred by

---

[7] Administration of Justice Act 1960, s 1.   [8] Magistrates' Courts Act 1980, s 111.

[9] Administration of Justice Act 1960, s 1.

[10] Criminal Appeal Act 1968, Pt I. In relation to certain other matters with which the Crown Court deals, appeals can be made to the High Court.

[11] Criminal Appeal Act 1968, s 33.

[12] High Court and County Courts Jurisdiction Order 1991, SI 1991/724.

[13] County Courts Act 1984, ss 40–2.   [14] Civil Procedure Rules, Pt 30, r 3.

[15] Access to Justice Act 1999 (Destination of Appeals) Order 2000, SI 2000/1071, art 3(1).

[16] Senior Courts Act 1981, s 16(1).   [17] Constitutional Reform Act 2005, s 40.

[18] Access to Justice Act 1999 (Destination of Appeals) Order 2000, art 4.

[19] Constitutional Reform Act 2005, s 40.   [20] Senior Courts Act 1981, s 16(1).

[21] Constitutional Reform Act 2005, s 40.   [22] Administration of Justice Act 1969, Pt II.

[23] Figure 6.1 shows only the tribunals that comprise the new tribunals system introduced in 2008. We explain in Chapter 16 that other tribunals exist outside that system.

[24] See Chapter 15.

legislation—and, at least on one view, cannot be excluded by legislation.[25] There are three 'divisions' of the High Court: the Family Division, the Chancery Division, and the Queen's Bench Division.[26] The last, as well as dealing with many commercial and other private law matters, also encompasses the Administrative Court, which handles judicial review cases.

Second, mention should be made of the *Judicial Committee of the Privy Council*. It acts as the court of final appeal for Jersey, Guernsey, the Isle of Man, UK overseas territories, and certain Commonwealth countries. The Judicial Committee also used to have jurisdiction over devolution issues within the UK, but that function is now undertaken by the Supreme Court.[27] When it hears cases, the Committee normally comprises five judges drawn from the Supreme Court.[28]

Third, an overview of the UK's judicial systems would be incomplete without mention of two international courts. First, there is the *Court of Justice of the European Union* (CJEU), which deals with matters concerning European Union (EU) law and sits in Luxembourg. Second, there is the *European Court of Human Rights* (ECtHR), which is concerned with the interpretation and application of the European Convention on Human Rights (ECHR) and sits in Strasbourg. Neither court can straightforwardly be said to form an integral part of the UK's judicial systems, but both nevertheless play a crucial role. As we explain in Chapter 8, UK courts can, and sometimes must, refer to the CJEU contested questions of EU law, the CJEU's role being to render an authoritative interpretation of the provision in question. The CJEU will continue to exercise jurisdiction in respect of the UK until the UK formally exits the EU.

Meanwhile, the ECtHR's influence is felt in two particular respects. First, UK courts, when deciding cases under the Human Rights Act 1998 (HRA), are statutorily required to take into account the ECtHR's case law[29] and have indicated that they will 'follow any clear and constant jurisprudence' of that Court unless special circumstances apply.[30] Second, the ECtHR's judgments are binding upon the UK as a matter of international law.[31]

This brief summary of the judicial structure may seem complicated, but the variety and number of cases that the judicial system is required to handle makes such complexity unavoidable. The system is necessarily large and intricate. In practice, the judicial system operates on a pyramid basis. At the base of the pyramid are the lower courts and tribunals, which deal with hundreds of thousands of cases per year. The vast majority of cases are resolved at this level. Most, though not all, such cases do not turn on issues of law, but on issues of fact. By contrast, in the top half of the pyramid are the higher courts (eg the High Court and the Court of Appeal) with the UK Supreme Court at the apex. These courts deal with fewer cases per year (though they are often overloaded with cases). The higher courts decide those cases that turn

---

[25] See Chapter 5, section 6.5.3.   [26] Senior Courts Act 1981, s 5.

[27] Constitutional Reform Act 2005, s 40(4)(b) and Sch 9.

[28] For more detailed information, see **http://www.jcpc.uk**

[29] Human Rights Act 1998, s 2(1).

[30] *R (Alconbury Developments Ltd) v Secretary of State for the Environment, Transport and the Regions* [2001] UKHL 23, [2003] 2 AC 295, [26], *per* Lord Slynn. This dictum has been endorsed in several subsequent cases.

[31] ECHR, Art 46.

largely on issues of law. The Supreme Court deals with a relatively low number of cases—fewer than a 100 per year—but it only decides those cases that raise points of law of general public importance.

3. The role of the judiciary

3.1 General matters

At root, the function of the judicial system is straightforward. It adjudicates disputes between two parties (litigants) according to the law. Whatever the context—whether it is a criminal trial, a civil matter, or a judicial review case—first-instance courts undertake three principal tasks: (i) they find the relevant facts, (ii) they determine the relevant law, and (iii) they apply the law to the facts as found.

First, then, the court must *ascertain what the relevant facts are*. For example, in a criminal case, the prosecution may contend that the defendant was present when the alleged offence was committed, whereas the defendant may claim that he has an alibi that establishes that he was elsewhere. As we have noted, courts and tribunals at the lower level of the judicial hierarchy—magistrates' courts and the First-tier Tribunal, for example—are primarily fact-finding bodies. By contrast, in some other types of litigation, there will be no dispute over the facts between the parties. For example, in judicial review proceedings, the parties normally agree on the facts; their dispute will centre upon whether or not a public decision is lawful. Fact-finding is then a fundamental task of the judicial process. The vast majority of cases decided by courts and tribunals turn on issues of fact rather than law.

Second, the court must *determine what the relevant legal rules or principles are*. In some instances, this may be quite straightforward; in others, the court might have to wrestle with points of law that are unclear or complicated. The court might even end up making law, by clarifying, developing, or supplementing existing principles or articulating new ones. While lower courts and tribunals are largely concerned with fact-finding, the role of higher appellate courts, such as the Court of Appeal, is to resolve points of law. Cases that raise difficult points of law of broader importance might proceed to the Supreme Court, the decision of which will be binding on all lower courts.

Third, the court must *apply the law to the facts*: it must decide whether the facts satisfy the relevant legal test. In a murder trial, for example, the court has to determine whether the evidence establishes that the defendant unlawfully caused the death of the victim and, in doing so, intended that the victim should either die or should suffer really serious harm. In a judicial review case, the High Court may have to decide whether a decision or policy announced by a government department constitutes a disproportionate interference with an individual's human rights.

Courts and tribunals are not, of course, uniquely capable of carrying out functions such as these. Other bodies can and do resolve disputes. For example, a contract might stipulate that disputes arising under it are to be resolved by an arbitrator rather than by a court, and that the parties are to accept the arbitrator's ruling. People may also resolve disputes through alternative dispute resolution (ADR) procedures such as mediation. However, the fact that courts are not the only bodies capable of resolving disputes does not mean that they are unnecessary. They are, in fact, essential in any civilised society. This is so for three main reasons.

First, *courts operate as a longstop*. It is, as we have already indicated, possible in some situations for people to arrange to resolve disputes otherwise than by recourse to the courts. In many instances, however, no such provision will or could have been made. This is most obviously the case when there is no pre-existing relationship between the parties. If X is injured by the carelessness of Y, a stranger, no arrangement will exist between X and Y as to how it should be decided whether, and if so to what extent, Y should compensate X. It would, of course, be possible for X and Y to reach a negotiated settlement—but, in contrast to a situation in which a contract provides for binding arbitration, neither party is locked into any extrajudicial process for the resolution of the dispute. This means that one of the parties might simply refuse to participate in an informal dispute resolution process, or that the parties might reach an impasse that cannot be resolved except by involving an independent third party capable of authoritatively determining the disputed point. It is unsurprising, therefore, that in many situations such as this the parties end up in court. Although unnecessary recourse to litigation should be discouraged—indeed there is a growing emphasis on the desirability of resolving disputes in other, cheaper ways—it is essential that courts exist as a longstop. In the absence of such an arrangement, some people would inevitably resort to less civilised means by which to resolve disputes. The risk would arise that the stronger party—whether in physical, social, or financial terms—would be likely to prevail. Such a system would be antithetical to justice and equality. In short, an effective and independent judicial system is necessary to the preservation of social order.

Second, *courts can exercise the coercive powers of the state*. Often, one party will not wish to participate in a dispute resolution process (particularly if she thinks that she will lose). And even if the parties do participate in such a process, the 'losing' party may, on reflection, be unwilling to do whatever was undertaken (eg pay compensation). One of the main differences between courts and other dispute resolution mechanisms, then, is that the courts have coercive powers. If one party validly issues legal proceedings against another, the latter cannot choose whether to allow the court to rule on the matter: submission to the court's jurisdiction will be compulsory, not a matter of election. Similarly, if the court issues a remedy—for example, if it requires the wrongdoer to pay compensation to the injured party or, in a criminal case, to pay a fine—it has a range of coercive powers that can be used to secure compliance. Ultimately, if someone refuses to do as a court lawfully instructs, they can be imprisoned for contempt of court. Furthermore, while courts exercise the coercive powers of the state, they are also able to exercise those powers against government itself. For example, if a court, through judicial review proceedings, determines that a government decision is unlawful, then the court can issue a remedy striking down that decision and the government must comply with the court's ruling in order to uphold the rule of law.

Third, that point leads on to a broader one: the courts' role is not confined to deciding disputes between individuals; rather, they are also *a necessary part of a balanced machinery of government under the separation of powers doctrine*. In this sense, they form a crucial part of the network of checks and balances that are needed if the powers of the other branches of government are to be adequately controlled. This aspect of the courts' role is of particular importance to the subject matter of this book. In section 3.2, therefore, we explore three particular issues that concern the courts' place within, and responsibility for upholding the principles of, the constitution.

3.2 The courts and the constitution

3.2.1 Courts as referees in public law cases

Just as courts act as referees in private disputes between individuals in civil litigation, they also adjudicate upon disputes with a public dimension to them. Some such cases involve disputes between two public bodies, but most concern situations in which a governmental body has made a decision that adversely affects the rights or interests of an individual who wishes to challenge the legality of that decision before the courts. In such 'judicial review' cases, as in other contexts, the court's ultimate responsibility is to determine the dispute by reference to the relevant facts, and in accordance with the relevant legal rules and principles. However, in cases involving government bodies, an additional layer of issues is in play.

When the court is adjudicating upon a dispute between an individual and a public body, it will be concerned to see that the latter has respected the special legal standards to which government is required to adhere. As we explain elsewhere, those standards include the principles of good decision-making enforceable through judicial review proceedings,[32] relevant aspects of the rule of law,[33] and the rights protected by the HRA.[34] The fact that public bodies are bound by these special standards implicitly acknowledges that the relationship between the individual and the state is an unequal one, with the state having the upper hand, and that this calls for particular safeguards to be enforced. It also recognises that public bodies are fundamentally different from private bodies (such as companies) and individuals. This is because public bodies exist in order to advance the broader public interest; for example, the Environment Agency exists in order to protect the environment while the role of the Home Office is to protect the public against crime and terrorism and to regulate immigration. However, in order to promote the broader public interest, a public body may often need to make decisions that adversely affect the rights and interests of an individual or business; for example, the Environment Agency will seek to protect the environment by fining a polluting business, while the immigration authorities will seek to enforce immigration control by deporting a foreign national who has unlawfully entered the UK. It is inevitable that tensions will arise between individuals' rights and interests, and public bodies' pursuit of the public interest. For precisely this reason, the state, in its various emanations, is subject to a set of distinctive

---

[32] See Chapter 12.   [33] See Chapter 2, section 5.   [34] See Chapter 18.

public law principles that seek to maintain an appropriate balance between providing adequate protection for the rights and interests of individuals, on the one hand, and enabling public bodies to make decisions in pursuit of their policy goals, on the other. This aspect of the courts' role has grown substantially in recent decades, partly but not exclusively as a result of the HRA. This reflects one of the key themes of this book and constitutes part of another: the growing prominence of the courts' role as a constitutional watchdog is born, at least in part, of concern about the peculiarly powerful position of the executive branch in the UK[35]—and the way in which the courts' role has expanded in this area is a key driver of the shift from a more political to a more legal form of constitutionalism.

In addition, disputes between one public body and another—as well as some disputes between individuals and public bodies—will raise demarcation-of-powers issues. For example, questions may arise about whether it is lawful for a given action to be undertaken by a particular body, such as the executive, or whether the matter concerned properly falls within the constitutional province of another institution, such as the legislature.

3.2.2 Beyond dispute resolution

The courts' dispute resolution function is a vitally important component of a democratic society. Is it—and should it be—their only function?

Resolving disputes is a retrospective business that involves looking back at what has already happened. However, the law—and the courts—can also operate in a more prospective, forward-looking manner. For example, under the doctrine of precedent, higher courts, such as the Supreme Court, make decisions that bind the lower courts in future cases and which also guide the future conduct of people. If, for example, a court interprets a piece of legislation so as to establish (contrary to previous understandings) that a given form of conduct is unlawful, then people may, in the future, choose to modify their behaviour in order to take account of the new interpretation of the statute. Similarly, the principles of public law articulated by the courts have the potential to influence the future behaviour of public bodies anxious to ensure that they behave in a lawful manner. This is illustrated by a government publication, entitled *The Judge Over Your Shoulder*, which aims to convey to public servants the legal principles with which their actions must comply if they are to survive scrutiny by the courts.[36] In this sense, the body of public law created and applied by the courts through decisions in individual cases has come to constitute a template of best practice that can, and often does, inform the way in which public administration is undertaken.

However, the sense in which the courts' function transcends one of dispute resolution is not confined to the fact that they (inevitably) set out legal principles that shape responsible parties' subsequent conduct. In some (albeit limited) circumstances, courts are prepared to involve themselves in situations that do not disclose any live

---

[35] On which, see generally Chapter 4.

[36] The most recent edition was published by the Treasury Solicitor's Office and the Government Legal Service in 2006.

dispute. The form that such involvement is most likely to take is the issuing of an 'advisory declaration', which states whether a given action (or omission) would, if it were to arise, be lawful. When courts do this, the relevant parties are not left (as in the situation described in the previous paragraph) to deduce from already-articulated principles whether a given course of conduct would be lawful; rather, the court indicates in specific terms how those principles apply to the situation in question, notwithstanding that the situation has not arisen (or at least is not in issue in the proceedings). For example, in the case of *Airedale NHS Trust v Bland*,[37] the House of Lords issued a declaration to the effect that if a hospital were to end the life support of a patient in a persistent vegetative state, then this would not amount to unlawful homicide. In this way, claimants are able to establish in advance whether or not a particular course of action would be lawful. And courts, meanwhile, expand their role from one that is concerned only with resolving disputes to one that encompasses expository justice—that is, the provision of guidance outside the confines of live disputes.[38]

The extent to which courts are prepared to provide such guidance is considered in more detail elsewhere in this book.[39] For the time being, we simply note that this sort of anticipatory intervention by courts is arguably especially appropriate in relation to matters of public law. Sir John Laws observes (as we did earlier) that there is a crucial difference between public bodies and private actors (such as individuals and companies). Whereas the latter can, and often do, act in a purely self-interested manner, public bodies cannot lawfully do so: having no interests of their own, the public official must act 'in the perceived interests of . . . his constituency, whether the public as a whole or a defined section of it'.[40] There is, says Laws, 'a clear distinction between a case where the claimant seeks in effect the court's advice only so that he can further his own private interests, and one where he seeks judicial guidance for the fulfilment of [public] duties which he owes or . . . are actually or putatively owed to him'.[41] On this view, courts should not be wedded, in the public law realm, to their traditional dispute resolution function; rather, there is a strong public interest in courts readily issuing advisory declarations in order to articulate or clarify the legal framework within which those who owe duties to the public are required to operate. In this way, the judicial role becomes a more forward-looking one that aims to ensure that public administration is conducted in a lawful manner in the first place.

Q Do you agree with Laws' argument? He goes on to suggest that if the government were contemplating the enactment of secondary legislation,[42] it should be possible for an advisory declaration to be obtained as to the legality of the draft legislation. This is not something that courts are currently willing to do—but should they be?

---

[37] [1993] AC 789.

[38] See further Miles, 'Standing under the Human Rights Act 1998: Theories of Rights Enforcement and the Nature of Public Law Adjudication' [2000] CLJ 133.

[39] See Chapter 13, section 4.5.

[40] Laws, 'Judicial Remedies and the Constitution' (1994) 57 MLR 213, 215–16.   [41] Laws, 217.

[42] On which, see generally Chapter 4.

3.2.3 Judicial lawmaking and the separation of powers

The adage that 'Parliament makes the laws, the judiciary interpret them'[43] is technically correct, but is misleading to the extent that it implies that *only* Parliament makes law. For example, we have already seen that government departments have wide lawmaking powers. Further, even though primary legislation is formally enacted by Parliament, the reality is that Parliament often just debates and approves the government's legislative proposals. Furthermore, it is undeniable that the courts, as well as applying the laws enacted by the other branches of government, themselves contribute to the lawmaking enterprise. This is so in two senses.

When courts *interpret legislation*, they can be said to be making law. It might be retorted that this is not the case, and that there is a difference between interpreting and making law. However, a debate conducted on that basis would be an ultimately arid one, for the distinction that it postulates, if it exists at all, is one of degree. There are, of course, situations in which a legislative rule is crystal clear, and in which the task of applying it to the established facts is a relatively mechanical one. However, surprisingly often, the precise meaning of legislation may be unclear and may be disputed between two parties. As the legal philosopher HLA Hart explained, legal rules are inherently 'open textured': a legislative rule might possess a core of settled meaning, but it will also contain a penumbra of uncertainty in which the meaning of the rule may be unclear and indeterminate.[44] The meaning of the rule in such instances will depend upon how it is interpreted.

The classic example is the meaning of a rule to the effect that 'no vehicles may be taken into the park': this would clearly prohibit the driving of a car or a bus through the park, but what of a child's toy car, a pram, or a wheelchair? The general point is that it is very often the case that a legislative text will be unclear or that it does not precisely answer the question raised by the factual matrix before the court. In such circumstances, the judge will be forced to choose between competing interpretations of the statute, and in doing so, will refine its meaning.

In other situations of statutory interpretation, the scale of the courts' role may be greater still. For example, we saw earlier that courts will often strain to interpret legislation compatibly with fundamental constitutional principles.[45] We will see later on that similar considerations may arise when a court is faced with legislation that, if accorded its natural meaning, would be incompatible with EU law[46] or with the rights protected by the HRA.[47] In such situations, the courts' role goes well beyond ascertaining the dictionary definition of the statutory text and applying it to the facts of the case; rather, the courts are called upon to find an interpretation of the legislation that can most comfortably be accommodated within the pre-existing legal and constitutional framework. Whether we call this 'interpretation' or 'lawmaking' is an ultimately semantic question; the reality is that, in interpreting legislation, judges are themselves, in a sense, often acting as lawmakers.

---

[43] *Duport Steels Ltd v Sirs* [1980] 1 WLR 142, 157, *per* Lord Diplock.
[44] *The Concept of Law* (Oxford 1994), p 128.   [45] See Chapter 2, section 5.
[46] See Chapter 8.   [47] See Chapter 18, section 3.4.

More obviously still, judges make law when they *develop the common law*. Although (as a consequence of the doctrine of parliamentary sovereignty) legislation displaces common law when the two overlap, certain areas of the law are either devoid of legislation or are only peripherally affected by it. For example, large swathes of private law—such as contract, tort, and restitution—are centrally based upon common law, albeit that certain aspects of those areas have been supplemented or modified by statute. By contrast, the overwhelming proportion of public law is governed by primary and secondary legislation that lays down the powers, duties, and policies of governmental bodies and the administrative rules that they apply. At the same time, however, when public authorities exercise their statutory powers and discharge duties placed upon them by legislation, they act lawfully only if they comply with the principles of judicial review that have been developed by the courts. For example, the well-known principle of judicial review that a public body cannot make a decision that is irrational because it outrageously defies logic or accepted moral standards does not derive from any Act of Parliament; rather, it has been created and developed by the courts in the same way as (for example) the common law rules of tort and contract.

Is judicial lawmaking, in either of these senses, inconsistent with the separation of powers doctrine? This largely depends on what we mean by the separation of powers. The concept is a malleable one: it can bear a variety of meanings, although a broad distinction between two schools of thought may be drawn. If we adopt what was referred to in Chapter 3 as a 'pure' conception of the separation of powers, then it follows that any form of judicial lawmaking is improper. On that view, the three principal functions of government would have to be performed by wholly separate institutions; it would therefore be unacceptable for the judicial branch to be involved in lawmaking as well as adjudication. However, we saw in Chapter 3 that this model of the separation of powers is both impossible to implement in practice and arguably unnecessary in principle. The fundamental purpose of the separation of powers doctrine is to guard against the abuse of power. It seeks to realise this objective by prescribing an institutional architecture that prevents any branch of government both from possessing too much power, and from wielding its power in a way that cannot adequately be checked and controlled by the other branches. On this—the better—view, the exercise by one branch of functions lying within the core responsibility of another is not objectionable per se. Rather, the question is whether, by allowing such a situation to obtain, the fundamental objective—of guarding against abuse of power—is compromised.

In addressing that question vis-à-vis the courts' lawmaking powers, it is significant, therefore, that those powers are limited. Although it was argued earlier that courts make law by interpreting legislation, the extent of such lawmaking is evidently constrained by the text concerned. Courts may (and do) make choices about the meaning of the legislation, but the range of choices open to the court is in the first place determined by the statutory text. Similarly, the lawmaking function performed by courts when they develop the common law is also constrained. First, common law can exist only to the extent that the relevant matter has not been dealt with by means of legislation. Second, when developing common law rules, courts typically act in an incremental fashion—moving slowly, one step at a time; courts are generally limited by precedent and they follow previous case law.

Third, Parliament can reverse a judicial decision through legislation if it wishes. The doctrine of parliamentary sovereignty means that legislation can replace or modify common law rules and reverse judicial decisions. In practice, however, this occurs relatively infrequently. The possibility of legislative retaliation can cut two ways. The prospect of legislative reversal might have the effect of making judges think twice before doing something that might be subject to such reversal. However, particularly where fundamental constitutional values or rights are in play, a court might in fact be emboldened by the possibility of reversal because that possibility helps to insulate judges from the allegation that they are undemocratically insisting on having the final word on the matter.

3.2.4 Reasons for judicial restraint—democratic and institutional considerations

From all of this, it follows that the courts' lawmaking function is subject to real and significant limits, the existence of which mean that judicial lawmaking is not usually problematic in separation of powers terms. This is largely because courts rightly recognise that their lawmaking role should be a limited one. For example, unlike legislatures and governments, courts are neither elected nor politically accountable. Unlike government, courts are unable to consult more broadly about possible changes to the law. Courts are reactive in the sense that they can act only in the cases that come before them. By contrast, government and Parliament can take the initiative to introduce new laws. Furthermore, courts are generalists in the sense that they are expected to deal with a dispute from any area of law; by contrast, government can draw upon the views of expert and specialist administrators and professionals when designing possible changes to the law. For these reasons, courts generally recognise that while they possess some lawmaking capacity, it must be exercised cautiously so as to ensure that courts do not overreach themselves. As Lord Phillips, the first President of the Supreme Court, put it when speaking for the judiciary as a whole: 'We recognise the boundaries of our role and the need to accord proper respect to the respective roles of the other two branches of the state . . . and we hope and expect that they will do the same in respect of our role'.[48]

> **Q** It might be argued that the considerations highlighted in the previous paragraph point towards the conclusion that judges should not have any involvement in lawmaking. Would you agree with such an argument?

4. The characteristics of the judiciary

What characteristics should the judiciary possess? And what steps are taken to ensure that the judiciary actually possesses those characteristics? These questions need to be asked both in relation to individual judges and the system as a whole. In this section

---

[48] *The Lord Chief Justice's Review of the Administration of Justice in the Courts* (HC 448 2007–08), [1.4].

we consider three issues: judicial appointments, judicial independence, and judicial diversity.

4.1 Judicial appointments

For two reasons, the process by which judges are appointed is of fundamental importance. First, that process is a key way in which steps can be taken to ensure that members of the judiciary possess the qualities necessary to be a good judge. According to the Judicial Appointments Commission, the body responsible for selecting judges for appointment in England and Wales, those qualities include a high level of expertise in the relevant area of the law, integrity, independence of mind, objectivity, an ability to deal with people fairly and courteously, efficiency, authority, and good communication skills.[49] Second, it is imperative not only that the appointments process actually results in the appointment of appropriate individuals, but also that the process is of such a nature as to lead people to trust that the system is staffed by people who have the necessary integrity and skills. If trust in the judicial system breaks down, the risk arises that people will seek to resolve their differences in other, less civilised, ways. It follows that the appointments process must be one that is not only rigorous and fair, but is also perceived as such.

The way in which judges are appointed has changed dramatically in recent years. Until recently, most judges were appointed by the monarch on the advice of the Lord Chancellor or the Prime Minister (who, in practice, relied on the Lord Chancellor's advice).[50] Although there have long been (and remain) concerns about the diversity of the judiciary,[51] there was a general consensus that, in practice, this system delivered a high-quality judiciary. There were, though, two major difficulties. First, although, in recent times, Lord Chancellors appeared to act in an even-handed fashion by appointing candidates on merit,[52] the system was not, and could not be perceived to be, independent of the government. Given that courts are involved in scrutinising the government, it was highly anomalous for a Minister to be centrally involved in the appointments process. Second, the process was not transparent. It was widely known as a 'tap on the shoulder' system. Vacancies at senior levels were not even advertised; rather, people were invited to apply on the basis of informal, confidential soundings. While the Lord Chancellor formally made appointments, his decisions were in practice based closely on information supplied by current judges.

In 2003, the government published proposals for radical reform of the appointments process.[53] This culminated in the Constitutional Reform Act 2005. Reflecting reforms that had already taken place in Scotland and Northern Ireland, that Act established a new body, the Judicial Appointments Commission (JAC), which is responsible for

---

[49] See **http://jac.judiciary.gov.uk/**

[50] See further Department for Constitutional Affairs, *Constitutional Reform: A New Way of Appointing Judges* (London 2003), ch 1.

[51] On which, see section 4.6.

[52] Not that this has always been the case: see Stevens, 'Reform in Haste and Repent at Leisure' (2004) 24 LS 1, 10–13.

[53] *Constitutional Reform: A New Way of Appointing Judges* (London 2003).

making judicial appointments in England and Wales. In this area, as in other parts of the UK constitution, we can detect a manifestation of a wider trend: areas of public power previously based upon informality and trust have been legalised and codified, that is, put upon a formal legal basis. Four points should be noted in this regard.

First, the JAC is *independent of the government*.[54] It consists of a chairman and 14 other commissioners, and must include lay, judicial, and professional members; the chairperson must be a lay member. Although commissioners are appointed on the recommendation of the Lord Chancellor, he does not have a free hand in making such recommendations; rather, he is only permitted to recommend the appointment of individuals who are nominated by the Judges' Council or by a panel that includes the Lord Chief Justice. Second, when deciding which candidate it should recommend in respect of a given vacancy, the JAC is *required by law to apply certain criteria*. There is, for example, an experience requirement, as Table 6.2 shows.[55] The JAC is also required to make appointments solely on merit and to select someone only if satisfied that she is of good character.[56] Third, the process is much more transparent than it used to be. Vacancies are advertised, and the JAC publishes extensive information about the criteria and processes used in selection.[57] The system also provides opportunities

Table 6.2 Eligibility for appointment to senior judicial offices

Judicial office	Requirement	Source
Justice of the Supreme Court	High judicial office (ie High Court or above) for two years, or qualified lawyer or holder of other relevant qualification for 15 years	Constitutional Reform Act 2005, s 25
Lord Chief Justice, Master of the Rolls, President of the Queen's Bench Division, President of the Family Division, Chancellor of the High Court	Already a Court of Appeal judge or eligible for appointment to the Court of Appeal	Senior Courts Act 1981, s10(3)(a)
Court of Appeal judge	Qualified lawyer or holder of other relevant qualification for seven years, or already a High Court judge	Senior Courts Act 1981, s 10(3)(b)
High Court judge	Qualified lawyer or holder of other relevant qualification for seven years, or two years' experience as a circuit judge	Senior Courts Act 1981, s 10(3)(a)

[54] The composition etc, of the Commission is prescribed in the Constitutional Reform Act 2005, Sch 8.
[55] Although Table 6.2 mentions Justices of the Supreme Court (JSCs), the JAC has no involvement in their selection; the arrangements for appointing JSCs are set out later. For the position regarding eligibility for senior judicial offices in Scotland, see Law Reform (Miscellaneous Provisions) (Scotland) Act 1990, s 35 and Sch 4.
[56] Constitutional Reform Act 2005, s 63.   [57] See **http://jac.judiciary.gov.uk/index.htm**

to challenge the decision-making process: the Judicial Appointments and Conduct Ombudsman investigates complaints about the judicial appointments process.[58]

Fourth, *the role of the government* in the selection of judges is now very limited. While the Lord Chancellor retains a role under the new system, it is much more modest than his former role. When a vacancy arises, the Lord Chancellor may (and in some circumstances must) seek to fill it.[59] He does this by asking the JAC to select a candidate. When such a request is made, this triggers a process that culminates in a JAC selection panel selecting one person. That name is then put to the Lord Chancellor. He does not have to accept it: he can either reject it outright or can ask the JAC to reconsider the matter.[60] If the Lord Chancellor rejects a given candidate, the JAC cannot select that person again, meaning that the Lord Chancellor has a right of veto. However, the Lord Chancellor cannot keep rejecting candidates until the JAC comes up with a name that he likes. In any given selection process, he may exercise his power to reject only once, and his power to require reconsideration only once. At most, then, the process will have three stages; at the final stage, the Lord Chancellor is statutorily required to accept either the name put to him at that stage or a name not rejected by him earlier in the process. Furthermore, as a matter of constitutional practice, the JAC makes efforts to avoid a situation in which the Lord Chancellor either rejects or requests reconsideration of its recommendations. Consequently, while, in formal terms it is correct to say that the Lord Chancellor has a veto over judicial appointments, this implies a greater degree of oversight than occurs in practice.

The Lord Chancellor's role has been further limited by the Crime and Courts Act 2013. The Lord Chancellor retains the theoretical power to decide upon appointment selections by the JAC in relation to the High Court and above. However, he now has no role at all in relation to other parts of the system. Appointments to courts below the High Court and to the First-tier and Upper Tribunals are now in the hands of the Lord Chief Justice and the Senior President of Tribunals respectively.[61]

There is an important exception to the arrangements set out in this section: the JAC has no involvement in appointments to the Supreme Court. The initial Justices of the Supreme Court were the judges in post as Law Lords immediately before the Supreme Court began to operate.[62] Vacancies are filled by the Queen on the recommendation of the Prime Minister. The Prime Minister has no discretion in this matter. The name that he passes to the Queen must be the one notified to him by the Lord Chancellor.[63] And, in turn, the Lord Chancellor has only very limited discretion. When a vacancy arises, the Lord Chancellor must convene a selection commission[64] comprising of at least one serving judge of the UK Supreme Court, one non-legally-qualified member, a member of the JAC, and one member from each of the equivalent bodies in Scotland and Northern Ireland.[65] The selection commission must consult other senior judges,

---

[58] Constitutional Reform Act 2005 s 62 and Sch 13. See also **https://www.gov.uk/government/ organisations/judicial-appointments-and-conduct-ombudsman**

[59] Constitutional Reform Act 2005, ss 68 and 69.

[60] Constitutional Reform Act 2005, ss 73, 75E, 82, and 90.

[61] Crime and Courts Act 2013, Sch 13, Pt 4.   [62] Constitutional Reform Act 2005, s 24.

[63] Constitutional Reform Act 2005, s 26(3).   [64] Constitutional Reform Act 2005, s 26(5).

[65] Constitutional Reform Act 2005, s 27(1B) (as amended by the Crime and Courts Act 2013).

the Lord Chancellor, the First Ministers of Scotland and Wales, and the Northern Ireland Judicial Appointments Commission.[66] The Lord Chancellor must either reject or confirm the selection commission's recommendation.[67]

The appointment of the judiciary is a matter of significant constitutional importance and legitimate public interest. It is widely accepted that the system of judicial appointments should be based upon the principles of judicial independence, appointment on merit, accountability, and the promotion of diversity—and that adequately reconciling these considerations is vital for maintaining public confidence in the judiciary and the legal system as a whole.[68]

Nonetheless, there remain considerable differences of view concerning the entire process of judicial appointments. Who should appoint judges? What is the appropriate role for the executive, legislature, and the judiciary itself in making judicial appointments? How should judges be appointed? These questions have few easy or simple answers.

The changes to the appointment system described so far imply a clear view that politicians should play no significant role in judicial appointments—the thinking being that their involvement may politicise the appointments process and undermine judicial independence. And so, as executive involvement in appointing judges has reduced, the involvement of the judiciary itself has increased. The central rationale for giving the judiciary a predominant role in judicial appointments is the need to protect judicial independence in the context of the separation of powers. However, while judges may have a legitimate role to play in judicial appointments, giving them the pivotal role that they enjoy under present arrangements carries the risk of 'judicial capture'; judges may establish a self-perpetuating clique by, subconsciously or otherwise, appointing others in their own image.[69] This could result in a judiciary that is neither sufficiently representative of society nor diverse.

There have been some recent improvements to the process of judicial appointments. For instance, the Constitutional Reform Act 2005 has been amended so that an outgoing President of the Supreme Court is no longer a member of the selection commission for his or her successor.[70] Nonetheless, the general point remains that the judiciary has the predominant role in appointing judges. It has been argued that 'the extent of the judicial involvement in the current system of appointments is problematic in a mature democracy' because it lacks any form of democratic input or accountability.[71] On this view, democratic legitimacy requires a meaningful degree of involvement by elected officials in the appointment of those adjudicating on the laws passed by elected officials. This suggests that the process for appointing judges should

---

[66] The Supreme Court (Judicial Appointments) Regulations 2013, SI 2013/2193, r 18.

[67] The Supreme Court (Judicial Appointments) Regulations 2013, r 20.

[68] House of Lords Constitution Committee, *Judicial Appointments* (HL 272 2010–12), [20].

[69] eg Sumption, 'Home Truths about Judicial Diversity', Bar Council Law Reform Lecture, 15 November 2012, has noted that while judges are not out 'to clone themselves . . . it would be foolish to pretend that they were not occasionally influenced by unconscious stereotyping and by perceptions of ability moulded by their own personal experience.'

[70] Constitutional Reform Act 2005, s 27(1C) (as amended by the Crime and Courts Act 2013).

[71] Paterson and Paterson, 'Guarding the Guardians? Towards an Independent, Accountable and Diverse Senior Judiciary' (Glasgow 2012), p 32.

be inclusive of *all* branches of government in a way and to an extent that the present system is not.

One option would be to require, as part of the process for selecting senior judges, pre- or post-appointment hearings before a parliamentary committee. The judiciary has traditionally been highly sceptical of such a proposal on the grounds that appointment hearings might politicise the process and undermine judicial independence. There is also a suspicion that politicians would try to ask questions relating to specific issues that could come before the courts or on candidates' individual political positions. Yet, on the other hand, such hearings could be beneficial. They would address the concern, noted earlier, about the democratic legitimacy of the appointment process and might aid mutual understanding and dialogue between the judiciary and legislature, enabling Parliament to explore the increasingly complex role of the senior judiciary and consider candidates' competing judicial philosophies. Such hearings could also increase both judicial accountability and legitimacy by enabling the judges to base their mandate on Parliament itself.[72]

The basic point is this: despite the reforms of recent years, there remain considerable differences of opinion concerning the nature and process of judicial appointments. Given the increasing and developing role of the judiciary in modern society, such issues are unlikely to disappear.

> **Q** What do you think is the optimal role of the executive, legislature, and the judiciary in the process of judicial appointments? Should judges attend pre- or post-appointment hearings before a parliamentary committee?

4.2 Independence—an introduction

It is of fundamental importance that courts are not only independent but are also perceived to be so. People should have confidence in both the integrity and fairness of the system. If they do not have such confidence, then there is the risk that people will resort to less desirable forms of dispute resolution. The requirement of judicial independence arises both in relation to individual judges and the system more generally.[73] Indeed, the right to have legal proceedings dealt with in a manner that is both actually and apparently unbiased is a fundamental right, and as such is enshrined in ECHR, Art 6, to which the HRA gives effect in UK law.

As far as individual judges are concerned, it stands to reason that if they have, or are perceived to have, an interest in the outcome of the case, this will constitute grounds for doubting the integrity of the process and the fairness of the outcome. In the light of that, judges are disqualified from sitting in cases in which they are (or are in a position equivalent to that of) a party, in that they have a financial interest, or in which they have some other interest that would lead a fair-minded and informed

---

[72] Paterson and Paterson, pp 69–71; House of Lords Constitution Committee, *Judicial Appointments* (HL 272 2010–12), [39]–[48].

[73] When applied to individual judges, the term 'impartiality', rather than 'independence', is normally used.

observer to entertain a reasonable suspicion of bias. These matters are considered in detail in Chapter 12, and therefore need not be expanded upon for the time being. Instead, our present focus is on the importance of, and the steps that are taken to secure, the independence of the judicial system itself.

4.3 Independence—the institutional situation of the courts

If the judiciary is to be—and is to be seen to be—independent, then it must be separate from, and immune from undue influence that might otherwise be exerted by, the other branches of government. The doctrine of the separation of powers in the UK does not apply in a rigorous fashion in the context of the relationship between the executive and legislature. However, the doctrine has long been taken with much greater seriousness in relation to the judiciary. Even here, of course, segregation is not complete. For example, judges exercise lawmaking functions. The key question, however, is whether the judiciary, in discharging its core adjudicatory function, is (and is perceived to be) able to get on with this task independently—in particular, without meddling or undue influence by politicians.

We consider this question at the level of individual judges later in this chapter.[74] We begin, however, at the institutional level. Is the judiciary, as an institution, sufficiently separate from the other branches of government?

Such separation is important both because its absence may increase the practical scope for political interference in judicial matters, and because, even if such interference does not actually occur, the absence of clear dividing lines may lead people to perceive that the judiciary is not truly independent. It is significant, then, that steps have been taken in recent years in order to enhance the level of separation between the judiciary and the other branches of government. In many respects, these steps were taken not to put an end to interference that was occurring. Generally speaking—and so far as it was possible to tell—such improper interference did not occur. However, the changes were introduced to make it clear to the world at large that there is a real institutional separation between the courts and the other parts of the government. Three examples should be noted.

4.3.1 The UK Supreme Court

The most visible manifestation of the trend referred to is the creation of the UK Supreme Court.[75] Until October 2009, the UK's highest court was, for most purposes, the Appellate Committee of the House of Lords. It acted as the court of final appeal in all civil and criminal matters in the UK, with the exceptions of Scottish criminal matters and 'devolution issues'.[76] On the face of it, this situation constituted a bizarre and flagrant breach of the separation of powers doctrine: the

---

[74] See section 4.4.

[75] For the leading study, see Paterson, *Final Judgment: The Last Law Lords and the Supreme Court* (Oxford 2013).

[76] ie questions whether given matters lie within the competence of devolved bodies. See further Chapter 7, section 2.4.

inappropriateness of allowing a committee of one of the legislative chambers to act as a court—let alone as the highest court in the land—is so obvious that it need not be spelled out. Yet in this context, as in many other matters of UK public law, not all was as it appeared to be. The Appellate Committee's members were the Lords of Appeal in Ordinary, or the 'Law Lords'—senior judges who were typically promoted from the Court of Appeal in England and Wales (or the equivalent courts in Scotland and Northern Ireland). The Law Lords decided cases in the same way as other judges, by reference to relevant facts and legal principles. Further, members of the House of Lords in its legislative capacity by convention did not participate in debates or votes concerning politically contentious matters. In most practical senses, the Appellate Committee, while technically a parliamentary committee, functioned as an independent court of law.

To those who understood how the system worked, there was little scope for doubting this. However, that is not the point (or at least, is not the whole point). As noted, public trust, and so perception, is crucial in this area. The physical location of the UK's highest court in the Palace of Westminster (hearings were held in a House of Lords committee room; judgments were delivered in the chamber) gave the strong impression that the apex of the constitutional system was characterised not by a separation, but by a fusion, of power. This difficulty was exacerbated by the facts that people (for good reason, as we saw in Chapters 4 and 5) do not always clearly distinguish between the executive and the legislature, and that the Appellate Committee was increasingly concerned with judicial review and human rights cases involving the political branches. As Steyn has noted:

> When judgments were delivered in *Pinochet No. 1*[77] [in which the Appellate Committee decided that Augusto Pinochet, the former Chilean head of state, could be extradited to stand trial for crimes against humanity] the crowded benches of the chamber apparently led foreign television viewers to believe that Lady Thatcher [who was present in the chamber whilst judgment was being delivered] was part of the dissenting minority who opposed the extradition of General Pinochet![78]

Because Thatcher was a former UK Prime Minister who had opposed the extradition of Pinochet, the perception that could reasonably arise was that the Appellate Committee of the House of Lords was not sufficiently independent.

In such circumstances, the case in favour of abolishing the Appellate Committee and replacing it with a *transparently* independent body was a strong one—although it did not convince everyone. Most of the Law Lords who were in post in 2003, when the proposal for a Supreme Court was consulted upon, argued that the established arrangements worked well and that there was no need for change.[79] However, the contrary view, advanced by a minority of the Law Lords in 2003, prevailed. They said that 'the functional separation of the judiciary at all levels from the legislature and the executive [is] a cardinal feature of a modern, liberal, democratic state governed by the

---

[77] [2000] 1 AC 61.   [78] 'The Case for a Supreme Court' (2002) 118 LQR 382, 382.

[79] *The Law Lords' Response to the Government's Consultation Paper on Constitutional Reform: A Supreme Court for the United Kingdom* (London 2003), p 1.

rule of law',[80] and that this should be reflected by creating an institutionally separate court of final appeal.

The legal basis for the UK Supreme Court is the Constitutional Reform Act 2005. The Supreme Court is, in many respects, identical to the Appellate Committee. The *jurisdiction* of the former is the same as the latter, save that the Supreme Court also decides devolution issues.[81] The Supreme Court, like the Appellate Committee before it, does not, however, deal with Scottish criminal appeals.[82] Meanwhile, the Supreme Court has the same *powers* as those that the Appellate Committee had. Despite being called the *Supreme* Court, the Court cannot strike down Acts of the *sovereign* Parliament. And the *role* of the Supreme Court is the same as that of the Appellate Committee.

It is apparent, then, that the changes wrought by the creation of the new Court were largely cosmetic. This might be perceived as a damning criticism—as evidence that the whole project was nothing more than an expensive rebranding exercise. But this would miss the crucial point that, in this sphere, appearance matters. The old system worked: a mixture of law, tradition, and convention ensured that the Appellate Committee functioned, in practice, as an independent court.

The new system differs in two ways. First, the independence of the Court is provided for not by unwritten convention, but by legislation: the Supreme Court is constituted by law as an institution that is separate from the other branches of government. Second, the Supreme Court is visibly independent of both Parliament and the government. This is most obviously apparent in physical terms. Whereas the Appellate Committee conducted its business within the precincts of the Palace of Westminster, the new Court occupies separate premises. Further, the Justices of the Supreme Court, unlike the Law Lords, do not have a legislative, as well as a judicial, role. As noted, the latter were full members of the House of Lords in its legislative capacity.[83] Justices appointed directly to the Supreme Court (as distinct from those who transferred to it from the Appellate Committee) do not, by virtue of such appointment, become members of the House of Lords.

> **Q** It follows from what has just been said that the link between active membership of the House of Lords and the UK's highest court has been broken. Is this to be welcomed? Might it, for example, be convincingly argued that the legislative process will be poorer because senior serving judges are now unable to participate in the business of the House of Lords?

4.3.2 The Lord Chancellor

The developments considered in this chapter cannot be fully understood without mention of the Lord Chancellor. We explained in Chapter 4 that, until recently, the

---

[80] *The Law Lords' Response to the Government's Consultation Paper on Constitutional Reform*, p 1.
[81] Previously, such matters were dealt with by the Judicial Committee of the Privy Council.
[82] The High Court of Justiciary is the final court of appeal in relation to such matters.
[83] Albeit that, by convention, they did not involve themselves in politically contentious matters.

Lord Chancellor held senior positions in all three branches of government. Of particular concern to the present discussion is the fact that the Lord Chancellor was both a Cabinet Minister—and so a senior member of the executive government—and the head of the judiciary. Not only did this mean that as a senior Minister he was (as we saw in section 4.1) responsible for appointing judges, but the Lord Chancellor was also entitled to—and did—sit as a member of the Appellate Committee of the House of Lords.

The obvious separation-of-powers difficulty inherent in this arrangement was, to some extent, assuaged by practice: Lord Chancellors did not sit in cases directly involving the government, and generally delegated their functions in terms of the management of the Appellate Committee's judicial business to the senior Law Lord. Nevertheless, the position remained that, in the person of the Lord Chancellor, there existed a fundamental breach of the separation of powers doctrine right at the apex of the judicial system. The defence, such as it was, of the Lord Chancellor's judicial role was (in the words of a Minister in 2001) that 'through it the judiciary has a representative in the Cabinet and the Cabinet has a representative in the judiciary. As such, . . . the Lord Chancellor is well placed mutually to represent the views of each branch of our constitution to the other'.[84]

However, in a devastating critique of the office of Lord Chancellor as it then existed, Lord Steyn—then a sitting Law Lord—said in 2002 that this argument was extremely misleading. He argued that the judiciary could speak for itself, and did not require a spokesperson in Cabinet. Meanwhile, the notion of a government representative in the judiciary was fundamentally misconceived, because it 'openly asserts that it is proper for the Lord Chancellor in his political function to inform the judiciary of the wishes of the Government of the day'.[85] Under the separation of powers, informing the judiciary of such matters is, of course, as unnecessary as it is improper.

Reform of the office of Lord Chancellor and the creation of a Supreme Court necessarily went hand in hand.[86] After initially announcing that the office of Lord Chancellor was to be abolished, the government eventually accepted that the office should remain, but that it should be substantially reformed. In particular, the Lord Chancellor ceased to be head of the judiciary, this function being taken over by the Lord Chief Justice;[87] lost (as we saw in section 4.1) much of his involvement in judicial appointments; and ceased to be a judge.[88]

In practice, then, the Lord Chancellor is now simply a government Minister with responsibility for, as opposed to direct involvement in, the judicial system. It is important to note here that the Lord Chancellor has responsibility for the judicial system in a wider sense, one that includes not just courts, but also areas such as prisons,

---

[84] Michael Wills MP, HC Deb, vol 376, col 155 (4 December 2001).

[85] 'The Case for a Supreme Court' (2002) 118 LQR 382, 392.

[86] Although it is unclear whether the real reason for proceeding with either reform was driven by constitutional principle or base politics. We noted in Chapter 1 that the proposals appeared to be rushed out in the context of a botched Cabinet reshuffle.

[87] Constitutional Reform Act 2005, s 7(1).

[88] The other main reform involved stripping the Lord Chancellor of his role as speaker of the House of Lords.

rehabilitation of offenders, and legal aid. This is now reflected in the fact that the Lord Chancellor is also styled Secretary of State for Justice, in which capacity he is in charge of the Ministry of Justice—the government department responsible for, among other things, courts, tribunals, prisons, and probation. These reforms constituted a major change in the relationship between the executive and judicial branches. The new division of responsibility between the Ministry of Justice and the judiciary was laid down in an agreement, or 'concordat',[89] made by the then Lord Chancellor and the then Lord Chief Justice in 2004, key elements of which were then incorporated in the Constitutional Reform Act 2005. Since the Lord Chancellor no longer sits as a judge, there is no expectation that he be legally qualified.[90]

Like all other Ministers, the Lord Chancellor is under a statutory obligation to uphold the independence of the judiciary.[91] The Constitutional Reform Act 2005 also makes provision for the Lord Chief Justice of England and Wales[92] to make written representations to Parliament 'on matters that appear to him to be matters of importance relating to the judiciary'.[93]

4.4 Independence–judicial seclusion

In section 4.3, we saw that judicial independence must be confronted at an institutional level—and that several recent developments in the UK have enhanced that sense of independence. However, institutional independence is merely a necessary, not a sufficient, condition for an adequately independent judicial system. The ultimate goal is that the judges responsible for making decisions in particular cases are, and are perceived to be, capable of doing so free from the influence of improper extrinsic factors. While considerations of institutional architecture such as those addressed so far are important in this regard, it is also necessary to examine the position of individual judges. The key question is: how can a situation of judicial seclusion— in the sense of freedom from undue incentives to take account of legally irrelevant matters—be brought about? In this section, we consider three potential forms of pressure that might lead judges to decide cases otherwise than on their legal merits.

4.4.1 Litigation

Lord Denning MR once remarked that each judge 'should be able to do his work in complete independence and free from fear. He should not have to turn the pages of his books with trembling fingers, asking himself: "If I do this, shall I be liable in damages?"'[94] It follows that, 'So long as he does his work in the honest belief that it is

---

[89] See **https://www.publications.parliament.uk/pa/ld200304/ldselect/ldcref/125/12514.htm**

[90] The Prime Minister must be satisfied that a person is 'qualified by experience' before appointing him or her to the office of Lord Chancellor, but experience other than as a lawyer can be taken into account: Constitutional Reform Act 2005, s 2. This requirement is so undemanding as to be largely meaningless.

[91] Constitutional Reform Act 2005, s 3(1).

[92] And, in the respective cases of Scotland and Northern Ireland, the Lord President of the Court of Session and the Lord Chief Justice of Northern Ireland.

[93] Section 5(1).   [94] *Sirros v Moore* [1975] QB 118, 136.

within his jurisdiction, then he is not liable to [legal] action'—even if he is 'mistaken in fact' or 'ignorant in law'.[95]

> **Q** Is this acceptable? Circumstances might, for example, arise in which, during the time taken to correct on appeal an erroneous judgment rendered at first instance, real losses (financial or otherwise) are suffered by one of the parties. What are the public policy reasons that would justify the application of the principles set out by Lord Denning in such a situation?

4.4.2 Security of tenure

It stands to reason that judges may not act in a fearless and independent way if, by doing so, they risk personal disadvantage such as dismissal.[96] It is unsurprising, therefore, that one of the central planks of judicial independence is security of tenure. This point is of particular (but far from unique) importance in relation to adjudication on public law matters. Just as a self-serving government with influence over judicial appointments might seek to fill the courts with judges likely to allow Ministers to do as they please, so such a government might attempt to use dismissal, or the threat thereof, as a means of ensuring judicial complaisance.

The terms on which senior judges in the UK hold office make this sort of interference by the government impossible in practice. Judges of the senior courts in England and Wales—that is, the High Court and the Court of Appeal—normally hold office until retirement. They can only be dismissed in one of two circumstances. The Lord Chancellor can dismiss on medical grounds, but only with the concurrence of a relevant senior judge.[97] Otherwise, judges of the senior courts hold office 'during good behaviour, subject to a power of removal by Her Majesty on an address presented to Her by both Houses of Parliament'[98]—a nuclear option that could in practice be exercised only in the gravest of circumstances. Equivalent provisions apply in relation to the Justices of the Supreme Court.[99] Finally, in this regard, it is worth noting that pressure can be brought to bear on judges in ways more subtle than (threatened) dismissal—for example, by slashing the pay of judges who make life difficult for the government. For this reason, legislation provides that the salaries of senior judges are protected and cannot be reduced.[100]

---

[95] *Sirros*, 136, *per* Lord Denning MR.

[96] This is not to suggest that all judges would compromise their personal and professional integrity by yielding to the threat of dismissal. That possibility cannot be discounted—and, in any event, people would *perceive* that, in such circumstances, judges might be inclined to decide cases otherwise than on their legal merits.

[97] Senior Courts Act 1981, s 11(8). The judge or judges whose concurrence is required depends on the nature of the office held by the person being dismissed.

[98] Senior Courts Act 1981, s 11(3). Similar arrangements exist in relation to judges of the Court of Session: Scotland Act 1998, s 95(6)–(10).

[99] Constitutional Reform Act 2005, ss 33 and 36.

[100] Senior Courts Act 1981, s 12(3) (judges of the Senior Courts); Constitutional Reform Act 2005, s 34(4) (Justices of the Supreme Court).

> **Q** The protections afforded to less senior judges are less extensive. For example, circuit, district, and tribunal judges can be dismissed by the Lord Chancellor (with the Lord Chief Justice's agreement) on the ground of incapacity or misbehaviour.[101] How, if at all, can the different levels of protection offered to judges of differing seniority be justified?

4.4.3 Judges, politics, and public debate

Conventional wisdom holds that judges and politics do not, and should not, mix.[102] This follows, it is said, because if judges are to be, and are to be seen as, independent, they should be separate from—even above—the political maelstrom. In fact, the point is rather broader than this. If judges are to be (and perceived as) independent, objective appliers of the law, then they should arguably play no part in public debate generally, not just in relation to matters that have a party political dimension to them. These points, if accepted, cut two ways. On the one hand, judges should not involve themselves either in party politics or, more generally, in matters of public or political controversy. On the other hand, judges should be protected from others' attempts to draw them into such matters. We consider each of these issues in turn.

On the first issue, it is relatively obvious that judges should not be directly involved in party politics. So, although they are allowed to vote in elections, they are required, upon appointment, to 'forego any kind of political activity'.[103] This means that judges must 'sever all ties with political parties' and avoid attendance at events (such as political gatherings or fundraising events) and conduct (such as financially supporting political parties) that would give an appearance of continuing ties.[104] Outside the specifically party political sphere, the rules concerning judicial participation in public debate are less restrictive than they once were. Under the 'Kilmuir rules',[105] the general position was that judges should not give radio or television interviews; the thinking being that '[s]o long as a judge keeps silent his reputation for wisdom and impartiality remains unassailable'.[106] Things have moved on somewhat since that view was articulated in 1955. The current guidance issued to judges says that they are free to contribute to public debate (including via the broadcast media) 'provided the issue directly affects the operation of the courts, the independence of the judiciary or aspects of the administration of justice'.[107] However, this is subject to the caveats that a judge should not speak out in circumstances that would 'cause the public to

---

[101] Courts Act 1971, s 17(4) (circuit and district judges); Tribunals, Courts and Enforcement Act 2007, Sch 2, paras 3 and 4 (judges of the First-tier Tribunal), and Sch 3, paras 3 and 4 (judges of the Upper Tribunal). (The 2007 Act uses the word 'inability' rather than 'incapacity'. The roles of the First-tier and Upper Tribunals are explained in Chapter 16.)

[102] Whether we should accept that conventional wisdom is a matter to which we turn in section 4.5.

[103] Judges' Council, *Guide to Judicial Conduct* (London 2013), [3.3].

[104] *Guide to Judicial Conduct*, [3.3].

[105] So-called after the Lord Chancellor who articulated them in a letter to the then Director-General of the BBC. The letter was printed at [1986] PL 383, 384–86.

[106] [1986] PL 383, 385.   [107] *Guide to Judicial Conduct*, [8.2.1].

associate the judge with a particular organisation, group or cause',[108] and that the risk should be borne in mind of 'expressing views that will give rise to issues of bias or pre-judgment in cases that later come before the judge'.[109]

One further point should be noted in this regard. It is increasingly common for judges to be appointed by the government to chair inquiries into matters of public controversy. While this has obvious attractions—not least the perception that a judge will get to the heart of the matter by adopting an independent and objective approach—serious concerns have been voiced about this practice. In particular, the risk arises that involvement in inquiries into very controversial matters may taint the judge in a way that subsequently compromises her (perceived) independence. For example, Lord Hutton, a Law Lord who chaired an inquiry that raised highly charged issues concerning the Blair government's claims about the case for war against Iraq, was strongly criticised when he produced a report that was perceived in some quarters as unduly pro-government. This matter is considered in more detail in Chapter 17.

The other side of the coin concerns judges being involuntarily drawn into matters of public or political controversy in ways that may damage the dignity and independence of the judicial system. In constitutional terms, the problem is particularly acute when members of the legislature or executive criticise judicial decisions. Under the separation of powers, each branch of government ought to respect the others' decisions made within their respective constitutional provinces. On this view, it is unseemly (at best) and wholly inappropriate (at worst) for politicians publicly to berate judges who make decisions with which they disagree.

The growth of judicial review and the HRA have enhanced the scope for discord between courts and politicians: courts are now increasingly called upon to pronounce upon the lawfulness of government decisions and whether primary legislation is compatible with human rights law. Of course, a degree of tension between the courts and the other branches may be healthy. As Lord Woolf has remarked, it may demonstrate 'that the courts are performing their role of ensuring that the actions of the Government of the day are being taken in accordance with the law'. Such tension may therefore be 'a necessary consequence of maintaining the balance of power between the legislature, the executive and the judiciary upon which our constitution depends'.[110]

On occasions, however, a line has arguably been crossed between legitimate disagreement and inappropriate confrontation; some examples were given in Chapter 1.[111] The difficulty is that such episodes present the courts with an uncomfortable dilemma: either judges adhere to the normal convention whereby they do not speak publicly about individual cases, or they allow themselves to be dragged into a public row. The choice is thus between, on the one hand, allowing allegations of incompetence or wrongheadedness to stand and, on the other hand, compromising the independence and dignity of the judiciary by publicly locking horns with Ministers. In an attempt to find a way through these difficulties, the Judiciary of England and Wales

---

[108] *Guide to Judicial Conduct*, [8.2.2].   [109] *Guide to Judicial Conduct*, [8.2.4].
[110] 'Judicial Review: The Tensions between the Executive and the Judiciary' (1998) 114 LQR 579, 580.
[111] See Chapter 1, section 3.3.3.

now undertakes greater central coordination of media issues through the Judicial Communications Office. This affords an opportunity, where appropriate, for misconceptions and criticisms to be dealt with in a way that avoids the individual judge concerned being drawn into the fray. It would be naive to think that tension between the judicial and political branches can be avoided altogether; but the bigger point is that each side must exercise appropriate self-restraint. As Lord Neuberger has remarked, 'Mutual respect between the judges and the politicians is essential. But as the word "mutual" emphasises, it is a two-way process: each must respect the other's turf and not trespass on it.'[112]

4.5 Independence—concluding remarks

The appropriateness of the notion of judicial independence elaborated in section 4.4 rests on an important set of assumptions concerning the judicial role. That judges should be independent in the senses just considered is unarguable if their function is an essentially mechanical one of applying established rules to fact situations. In such circumstances, the technically most able people should be appointed as judges and their independence should be jealously guarded so that they can get on with the business of applying the law to the facts.

However, the greater the extent to which the role of judges extends into the making of law and policy choices, the less obvious it becomes that they need to—or even should—be independent in the traditional sense. Imagine, for example, if UK judges were given the task of interpreting and enforcing a constitutional Bill of Rights that prevailed over all other law: even Acts of Parliament that were inconsistent with the Bill of Rights would be vulnerable to being struck down by the courts. Imagine, too, if the Bill of Rights were drafted in general, lofty terms, conferring such entitlements as 'the right to life'. And imagine if the courts were then asked to strike down legislation legalising abortion on the ground that it interfered with foetuses' right to life. The judicial task in such a scenario would patently transcend the mechanical application of established law to the facts: in the absence of clear textual guidance from the Bill of Rights, judges would have to decide by reference to other factors the stage of pregnancy, if any, at which a foetus acquired a constitutional right to life. It is unlikely that judges would be able to carry out such a task without (even if only subconsciously) being influenced by their own attitudes and experience. In such circumstances, a judge's outlook and background would be highly pertinent to the way in which he would be likely to approach his task. It is unsurprising, therefore, that in legal systems in which judges are called upon to perform functions such as the one sketched in this example, a great deal of interest is taken, before candidates are appointed to judicial office, in their views on the sort of matters upon which they might subsequently be asked to adjudicate. In the USA, for example, appointments to the Supreme Court are one of the most *politically* significant functions performed by the President: if a given President can achieve a situation in which the balance of opinion on the Court is sympathetic to his general philosophy, this will reduce the likelihood that his agenda

---

[112] 'Where Angels Fear to Tread', Holdsworth Club 2012 Presidential Address, 2 March 2012.

will be thwarted by adverse judgments. As such, judicial appointments are regarded as a legitimate subject of political inquiry, debate, and influence.

Within such a framework, conventional notions of judicial independence are arguably inapposite for a combination of two reasons. On the one hand, in our example, the loose wording of the Bill of Rights—it does not say *who* has a right to life—leaves considerable scope for judicial choice. On the other hand, the consequences of that choice are substantial, bearing in mind the existence of a strike-down power that means that courts ultimately have the last word in the event of a disagreement with the other branches. There are two possible responses to this state of affairs. One is to say that the courts are still engaged in a classically judicial endeavour involving the construction of a legal text; the other is to acknowledge that, in such circumstances, judges are executing an essentially political task. The latter view, if adopted, invites the questions why extensive steps should be taken to render judges immune from public and political pressure, and why they should be appointed solely on the grounds of technical legal ability. If the distinction between the legal and political processes is less watertight than we thought, then arguably the justification for judicial independence—which is, to a large extent, concerned with separating judges from the world within which politicians operate—is substantially weakened.

Q Do you agree with the argument outlined in this section?

Of course, the scenario sketched at the beginning of this section does not reflect the situation currently obtaining in the UK, in which judges do not have the power to strike down Acts of Parliament. However, that does not make the foregoing discussion irrelevant to the UK. Judges have very considerable powers in both of the senses described. First, they are increasingly called upon to interpret legal texts—most obviously the ECHR—the vague language of which leaves considerable scope for the making of judicial policy choices. And, second, while (for as long as the UK Parliament is sovereign) the courts are ultimately unable to insist that their view should prevail, the practical effect of such choices is nevertheless considerable, particularly where the legislation at stake has been enacted by a body, such as one of the devolved legislatures, which is not sovereign. This is not to say that the existing concept of judicial independence should be torn up. It is, however, important to take account of the fact that that concept is, or ought to be, a function of the judiciary's role. As that role evolves, this needs to be reflected in the operative principles of judicial independence and the practical arrangements that flow from them. Two examples will be given by way of conclusion.

First, if the courts' task is just mechanically applying rules, then the identity of the judge(s) assigned to a particular case is irrelevant, save to the extent that some may be more technically proficient at ascertaining and applying the law, and so more likely to get it 'right'. If, however, the courts' role is more open-ended—for example, if it involves choosing between competing possible meanings of the law, or developing legal rules against a largely blank canvas—then the position is very different. Here, the judges who are assigned to the case may crucially affect the outcome. Against this background, it has been argued that it is unacceptable that the Supreme Court (like the Appellate Committee of the House of Lords before it) sits in panels (five of the twelve Justices typically sit on each case) and that judges are not assigned to cases in a transparent manner.[113]

Second, in many jurisdictions, the problem mentioned is avoided by the practice of top courts sitting *en banc*, meaning that all members of the court sit in all cases. Of course, this has resource implications. If the UK Supreme Court were to adopt this practice, then it would either have to reduce substantially the number of cases it decides or spend less time on each case. More fundamentally, however, such an approach merely shifts the difficult question to a different stage. If all of the judges sit in all of the cases, then the crucial question concerns the balance of opinion within the Court as a whole. Without the element of randomness that might arise as a result of panel selection, outcomes might well be influenced through appointments to the Court. For precisely this reason, appointments to the US Supreme Court (which sits *en banc*) are, as foreshadowed earlier, the subject of intense political interest, and the political (if not *party*-political) views of candidates on such matters as abortion and freedom of speech are probed in great depth as part of the process whereby the legislature can confirm or reject candidates put forward by the President. Whatever the other arguments for and against this system, it at least has the virtue of acknowledging that the work of the US Supreme Court has a strongly political dimension to it.

> **Q** As we saw at section 4.1, politicians have almost no involvement in the reformed judicial appointments process in the UK. It might be argued that this reform was wholly misconceived, bearing in mind that the role of UK judges is broader than it has ever been in the light of the growth of judicial review and the implementation of the HRA. Would you agree with such an argument?

4.6 Judicial diversity

Over recent years, increasing emphasis has been placed on the need for the judiciary to be more diverse, particularly in terms of gender, ethnicity, and socioeconomic background. For many years, there has been growing public concern that the judiciary is selected from a narrow and elite section of society. Traditionally, judges came primarily from the Bar, a profession itself dominated by white men from privileged social backgrounds.[114] Much of the debate has focused upon the composition of the higher courts. At present, all twelve of the Supreme Court Justices are white, and all but one of the twelve are men. Below this level, of the 3,197 court judges, 28 per cent are female and 6 per cent identify themselves as

---

[113] Buxton, 'Sitting *En Banc* in the New Supreme Court' (2009) 125 LQR 288.

[114] Only 6 per cent of Queen's Counsel—the most senior barristers—are black or minority ethnic, and only 13 per cent are women: **https://www.barstandardsboard.org.uk/media-centre/research-and-statistics/statistics/queen's-counsel-statistics/**

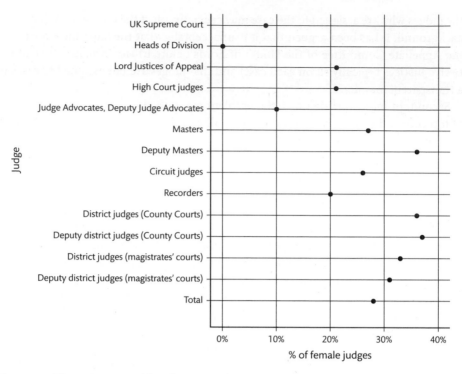

Figure 6.4 The percentage of female court judges, 2016

black or minority ethnic (BME).[115] This compares with the general population in which women represent 51 per cent and BME groups represent 12 per cent. Figures 6.4 and 6.5 show the detailed breakdown for the percentage of female and BME court judges.

There is some reason to think that this will improve over time. The higher proportion of younger female and BME judges (see Figure 6.6) suggests that the overall percentage of such judges will increase over time as these younger judges are promoted to higher judicial positions. Nonetheless, the relatively low proportion of BME judges suggests that there is still some distance to travel. Further, there are continuing concerns that the judiciary is drawn from a narrow socio-economic background.

By contrast, the tribunals judiciary is more diverse: of the 5,441 tribunal judges, 45 per cent are women and 12 per cent are from BME groups (Figure 6.7).[116]

Finally, there are Justices of the Peace, who sit in magistrates' courts. Of the 19,338 Justices of the Peace, there are 9,088 men (47 per cent) and 10,250 women (53 per cent). However, the magistracy is far less diverse when it comes to race and social class.[117]

Against this background, two questions arise. First, *does diversity matter*? Naturally, it matters if its absence (in this sphere as in any other) implies unlawful or otherwise

---

[115] The data is drawn from Judiciary of England and Wales, *Judicial Diversity Statistics 2016*, **https://www.judiciary.gov.uk/publications/judicial-statistics-2016/**

[116] On tribunals in general, see Chapter 16.

[117] See further House of Commons Justice Committee, *The Role of the Magistracy* (HC 165 2016–17).

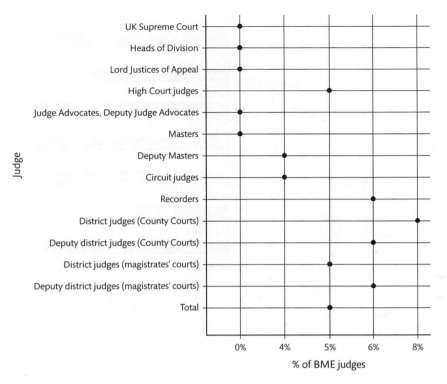

Figure 6.5 The percentage of BME court judges, 2016

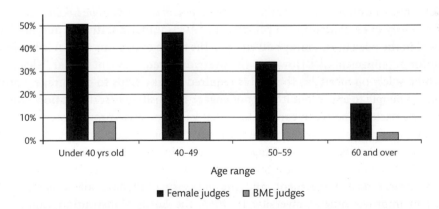

Figure 6.6 The percentage of female and BME court judges within each age range, 2016

unfair discrimination. Judicial diversity is also important for a number of other reasons too. A 'judiciary which is visibly more reflective of society will enhance public confidence'.[118] Also, a diverse judiciary allows for a wider range of perspectives to be reflected in judicial decision-making—a quality that is 'particularly important where

---

[118] *The Report of the Advisory Panel on Judicial Diversity 2010* (London 2010), [25].

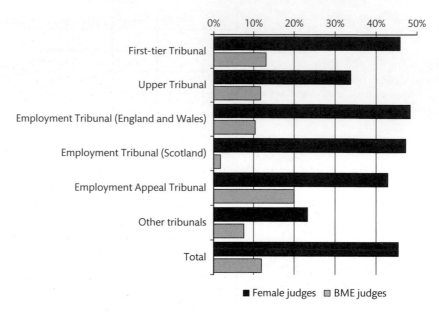

Figure 6.7 The percentage of female and BME tribunal judges, 2016

there is scope for the exercise of judicial discretion or where public interest considerations are a factor'.[119] If judicial positions are only open to a narrow proportion of the population, then, inevitably, the best and brightest candidates will not be appointed as judges.[120]

A second question therefore arises. *What steps can and should be taken to increase the diversity of the judiciary?* At present, the JAC is under a statutory duty to 'have regard to the need to encourage diversity in the range of persons available for selection for appointments'.[121] However, the overriding requirement is that '[s]election must be solely on merit'.[122] The JAC is required to take steps to encourage a broad range of people to apply, but it may not engage in 'positive discrimination' when it comes to deciding between candidates—that is, the positive promotion of an individual for a particular judicial office because of his or her gender or ethnicity. This is summed up in the JAC's 'guiding principle'—'diversity in the field, merit in the selection'.[123]

The government, Parliament, and the judiciary itself have all recognised the need to improve judicial diversity. In 2012, the Lords Constitution Committee noted that '[i]n order to increase public trust and confidence in the judiciary, there is a need to increase judicial diversity. We do not consider that sufficient steps

[119] *The Report of the Advisory Panel on Judicial Diversity 2010*, [26].

[120] See also Baroness Hale, 'Equality and the Judiciary: Why Should We Want More Women Judges?' [2001] PL 489 and 'Making a Difference? Why We Need a More Diverse Judiciary' (2005) 56 Northern Ireland Legal Quarterly 281.

[121] Constitutional Reform Act 2005, s 64(1).   [122] Constitutional Reform Act 2005, s 63(2).

[123] See **http://jac.judiciary.gov.uk/**

have yet been taken.'[124] In 2013, Lord Neuberger, President of the Supreme Court, acknowledged that

> [t]here is a diversity shortfall—especially at the top. . . . We have been making some progress. Gender diversity is improving. . . . A lot more work needs to be done in other respects: the ethnic minority representation among the senior judiciary is very low, and the socio-economic background of the senior judiciary is almost monolithic.[125]

Given that judges have security of tenure, part of the solution has been to reform the judicial appointments process so that the judiciary becomes more diverse and representative. The Crime and Courts Act 2013 introduced a number of measures to improve judicial diversity. First, the Act introduces the so-called 'tie-breaker' provision: when appointing judges, if there are two candidates of equal merit, then the requirement to select on merit does not prevent the JAC from preferring one candidate over another for the purpose of increasing judicial diversity.[126] In other words, the JAC cannot positively discriminate, but it can take account of the need to increase judicial diversity when making judicial appointments and there are two applicants of equal merit. Second, the JAC's duty to encourage judicial diversity has been extended to both the Lord Chancellor and Lord Chief Justice.[127] The purpose is to ensure that improving diversity is taken seriously as an aim within both government and the judiciary. Third, the Act allows flexible part-time working for judges,[128] the intention being that people with caring responsibilities—who are disproportionately female—can be accommodated within the judicial career structure.

Such measures represent an effort to enhance judicial diversity, but it remains to be seen how effective they will be in practice. For instance, the 'tie-breaker' provision may actually have little impact in practice because experience suggests that the JAC rarely finds two candidates to be of precisely equal merit.[129] Also, the tie-breaker provision is a negative permission rather than a positive obligation: the provision *does not prevent* the JAC from preferring one candidate over another, but nor is such a preference positively required.

How else might judicial diversity be enhanced? The first possibility relates to the *diversity of the legal profession* (from whose ranks judges are drawn). The Advisory Panel on Judicial Diversity argued that in order to stimulate applications from under-represented groups, it was necessary to address systemic issues that transcend the appointments process.[130] Thus it was necessary to encourage a greater diversity of entrants into the legal profession, and to encourage a greater diversity of members of the profession to apply for judicial posts. Achieving the latter objective, it was argued,

---

[124] House of Lords Constitution Committee, *Judicial Appointments* (HL 272 2010–12), [6].

[125] Neuberger, 'Judges and Policy: A Delicate Balance' (London 2013), [29]–[30]. See also: **http://www. instituteforgovernment.org.uk/events/judges-and-policy-delicate-balance**

[126] Constitutional Reform Act 2005, ss 27(5A) and 63(4) (as amended by the Crime and Courts Act 2013).

[127] Constitutional Reform Act 2005, s 137A (as amended by the Crime and Courts Act 2013).

[128] Senior Courts Act 1981, ss 2 and 4 (as amended by the Crime and Courts Act 2013).

[129] Paterson and Paterson, 'Guarding the Guardians? Towards an Independent, Accountable and Diverse Senior Judiciary' (Glasgow 2012), pp 47–48, **http://www.centreforum.org/assets/pubs/guarding-the-guardians.pdf**

[130] *The Report of the Advisory Panel on Judicial Diversity 2010*, [4].

would be aided by, among other things, dispelling myths about the nature of the judiciary (eg that, in order to be appointed, it is necessary to be 'part of the "club"').[131]

A second suggestion is that the criterion for judicial appointment—the concept of merit—should be recast in a way that takes account of candidates' 'awareness and understanding, acquired by relevant experience, of diversity of the communities which the courts serve'.[132] To date, the concept of merit has been interpreted narrowly to mean individualised merit. It has been argued that this narrow conception of merit is simply one culturally specific construction and one which tends to result in the appointment of white male barristers of 30 years' standing.[133] However, merit is not an objective concept; it involves subjective evaluation, and there is a risk that the concept of merit may subconsciously be interpreted in a manner that perpetuates the existing composition of the senior judiciary.[134] The answer, it has been argued, is to redefine merit in a way that relates to the needs of the judiciary as a collective institution, which include the need for a diverse judiciary. Diversity can therefore be understood as a key ingredient of merit. As Lord Bingham has explained, the concept of merit 'is not self-defining': it 'directs attention to proven professional achievement as a necessary condition, but also enables account to be taken of wider considerations, including the virtue of gender and ethnic diversity'.[135]

In 2012, the Lord Chief Justice launched the judiciary's diversity strategy.[136] This has three aspects. First, supporting existing judges who wish to progress to the more senior levels, encouraging suitable applicants from all backgrounds to consider applying for judicial office, and aimed at law students and others who may be considering a career in legal practice and have the potential to become the judges of the future. Second, is to remind all judicial officeholders of their responsibilities for promoting diversity, both within their courts and tribunals, and to the wider community. Third, the strategy seeks to inform the general public about the role of judges and the justice system so as to improve their understanding of and confidence in the rule of law. The judiciary has then been doing much to improve diversity, such as encouraging women and BME candidates to consider a judicial career, networking events, and judicial shadowing.[137]

A related area of debate concerns whether the achievement of a diverse judiciary requires positive discrimination or affirmative action. This is a complex issue on which senior judges have expressed different views. For Lord Sumption, seeking effective

[131] *The Report of the Advisory Panel on Judicial Diversity 2010*, [49].

[132] *The Report of the Advisory Panel on Judicial Diversity 2010*, [31].

[133] As Lord McNally, the Minister of State for Justice, has noted: '[T]he merit criterion is often deployed by people who, when you scratch the surface, are really talking about "chaps like us". That is the danger of merit. Who defines it?' (House of Lords Constitution Committee, *Judicial Appointments* (HL 272 2010–12), written evidence, p 425).

[134] Paterson and Paterson, pp 44–51.

[135] Bingham, 'The Law Lords: Who Has Served', in Blom-Cooper, Dickson, and Drewry (eds), *The Judicial House of Lords 1976–2009* (Oxford 2009), p 126. See also Rackley, *Women, Judging and the Judiciary: From Difference to Diversity* (London 2013).

[136] https://www.judiciary.gov.uk/about-the-judiciary/who-are-the-judiciary/diversity/message-from-lcj-judicial-diversity/

[137] See https://www.judiciary.gov.uk/about-the-judiciary/judges-career-paths/appointments-diversity/. See also 'Women Leaders' series: Legally Diverse? A conversation between Lady Justice Hallett and Richard Heaton' (2015), http://www.instituteforgovernment.org.uk/events/women-leaders%E2%80%99-series-legally-diverse-conversation-between-lady-justice-hallett-and-richard

and timely ways to increase judicial diversity presents us with a real dilemma: positive discrimination is the only measure that is likely to increase judicial diversity significantly, but it would dilute the quality of the bench and deter the best candidates from applying.[138] By contrast, Lady Hale's view is that just as the composition of the Supreme Court expressly includes the need for expertise in the law and practice in Scotland and Northern Ireland, it should be possible to take account of characteristics such as gender and race in the appointments process.[139]

The process of increasing judicial diversity is inevitably slow—possibly unacceptably slow. It has been variously estimated that it might take 30, 50, or even 100 years for the senior judiciary to become sufficiently diverse. In the meantime, there are growing concerns that an inadequately diverse judiciary lacks legitimacy. It would therefore not be surprising if the demands for greater judicial diversity were to become louder and more insistent.

Q Read the speeches by Lord Sumption and Lady Hale. Whose view do you prefer?

5. Concluding remarks

An independent judiciary is a prerequisite in any civilised society subject to the rule of law. Only through the existence of such an institution is it ultimately possible to ensure that disputes are generally settled in a way that is just and that does not simply result in the victory of the stronger party.[140] The courts also play a special role in constitutional terms. Under the separation of powers, the judiciary forms an essential element of the checks and balances system that is needed if the other branches of government are to be confined to their appropriate constitutional provinces and if fundamental constitutional principles are to be upheld. It follows that an independent judiciary is needed if the separation of powers is to be meaningfully enforced—but also that the separation of powers is necessary if there is, in the first place, to be a truly independent judiciary. The doctrine of the separation of powers finds its fullest and clearest expression in the principle of judicial independence.

Expert commentary
Judicial independence in a changing constitution
Graham Gee, Professor of Public Law, University of Sheffield

There is a widespread perception that the constitution is in transition, evolving away from the model of a 'political constitution' towards the model of a 'legal constitution'. The more

[138] Sumption, 'Home Truths about Judicial Diversity', Bar Council Law Reform Lecture, 15 November 2012, http://www.supremecourt.gov.uk/docs/speech-121115-lord-sumption.pdf
[139] Lady Hale, 'Equality in the Judiciary', Kuttan Menon Memorial Lecture, 21 February 2013, http://www.supremecourt.gov.uk/docs/speech-130221.pdf
[140] An independent judiciary is, of course, a necessary, but not a sufficient, condition in this respect: the law that falls to be applied by the courts must be consonant with outcomes that are just and fair.

that the UK embraces the legal model, the greater the attention paid to judicial independence. Although there is deep disagreement about the desirability of a legal constitution, there is broad agreement that judicial independence occupies an especially prominent position within it. There are two main levels at which connections might be mapped between judicial independence and the legal model.

First, at an intellectual level, judicial independence helps to rationalise the more expansive judicial role associated with the model of a legal constitution. Insofar as legal constitutionalists argue that judicial processes tend to be more reliable than political processes at realising constitutional goods, their argument relies in large part on the independence of judges. It is their independence from the rest of the governmental apparatus that is said to render judges especially well positioned to attach due weight to cherished constitutional goods, such as the rule of law and individual rights. Because they are both removed from the temptations and pressures of political life and do not have policy programmes to fulfil or political constituencies to placate, judges are well equipped to hold governmental actors to account for legal wrongs—most clearly by safeguarding an individual's rights against governmental abuse. Politicians, in contrast, because of their preoccupation with re-election, are said to be more susceptible to short-term pressures, and hence less likely to be swayed by constitutional considerations.

Second, judicial independence occupies a special place within a legal constitution at a more concrete level of institutional design. The more frequently judges are asked to review policy decisions, and possibly even to overturn the policy preferences of elected politicians, the greater the risk that they will be politically unpopular. In the face of ascendant judicial power, politicians might seek to undermine the constitutional position of the judiciary; for example, by lowering judicial pay, or threatening to withhold funding from the courts. Hence, it is unsurprising that the more closely judges review the policy decisions of elected politicians in the way envisaged by a legal constitution, the more attention is paid to checking whether adequate arrangements exist to regulate such matters as the tenure, appointment, pay, immunity, and discipline of judges, as well as the funding and management of the courts as a whole. More particularly, we should expect that greater attention will be paid within a legal constitution not only to the *individual* independence of this or that judge (ie the requirement that judges should be independent of the parties to the case at hand), but also the *collective* independence of the judiciary as a whole (ie the requirement that the judiciary should be institutionally independent from both the executive and the legislature within the wider system of government).

With this in mind, it is perhaps unsurprising that the Constitutional Reform Act 2005 is frequently cited as evidence of the constitution's embrace of the model of a legal constitution. More than a decade on, this Act has helped to modernise our understanding of how judicial independence should be secured in a changing constitution. Each of the Act's main reforms—the creation of the Supreme Court; new ways of selecting judges built around the Judicial Appointments Commission; and the emasculation of the office of Lord Chancellor, with many of its judiciary-related functions now exercisable by or jointly with the Lord Chief Justice—buttresses the collective independence of the judiciary. Yet, at the same time, it is important to appreciate the extent to which the Act remains consistent with the model of a political constitution. For a start, no change has been made to the overall appellate jurisdiction in the UK. The Lord Chancellor, whose role is now very clearly that of an ordinary Minister, retains the final say, at least formally, over senior judicial appointments. The statutory duty on the Lord Chancellor and other Ministers to uphold judicial independence is arguably declaratory only (ie not enforceable in the courts, but rather through ministerial responsibility to Parliament). The Lord Chief Justice's power to lay representations before Parliament about matters of concern to judges also recognises the role that Parliament plays in promoting and protecting judicial independence. Political accountability for the administration of justice is enhanced by the recognition that the office of Lord Chancellor is no longer reserved solely for lawyer peers: MPs can now be appointed to that role, and held to account in the Commons. Indeed, three of the six Lord Chancellors appointed since 2005 have been non-lawyers. All of this seems broadly consistent with the political model.

The important point here is not merely that reforms are seldom unambiguously premised on either the legal model or political model, although it is always helpful to be reminded of this. Rather, my point is that, in some respects, the more that the constitution evolves towards the *legal* model, the more important elements of the *political* constitution become in nurturing judicial independence. For judicial independence is, in an important and substantial sense, a product of the political system. It results from the willingness of most politicians to behave in ways that promote the independence of judges. It is true that some politicians will, from time to time, behave in ways that undermine that independence. But, for the most part, politicians recognise the indispensability of independent courts, and behave accordingly. They do not seek to influence judicial decisions, except by the force of arguments made in open court on their behalf by their lawyers. They refrain, for the most part, from criticising judges in intemperate terms where a court rules against them. They provide adequate resources for the judicial system as a whole, and do not interfere with the running of the courts.

Even in the age of austerity since the financial crisis of 2008, successive Lord Chancellors and their officials in the Ministry of Justice have done much to ensure that the courts are adequately funded, at least when compared with other parts of the public sector. In all of these ways and more, politicians—and Ministers in particular—give meaning to the 'independence' of judges. As the constitution evolves towards a legal model, the challenge for public lawyers is to think of new and fruitful ways of reminding the political class of the vital importance of judicial independence. This will require public lawyers to draw on the techniques, mechanisms, methodologies, and—ultimately—insights associated with a political constitution.

Further reading

LADY HALE, 'Equality in the Judiciary', Kuttan Menon Memorial Lecture, 21 February 2013 (**http://www.supremecourt.gov.uk/docs/speech-130221.pdf**)
A speech on judicial diversity.

NEUBERGER, 'Judges and Policy: A Delicate Balance' (London 2013) (**http://www.institute forgovernment.org.uk/events/judges-and-policy-delicate-balance**)
A speech giving an overview of the role of the judiciary.

PATERSON and PATERSON, 'Guarding the Guardians? Towards an Independent, Accountable and Diverse Senior Judiciary' (Glasgow 2012) (**http://www.centreforum.org/assets/pubs/ guarding-the-guardians.pdf**)
This paper discusses judicial diversity and makes suggestions for reform.

SUMPTION, 'Home Truths about Judicial Diversity', Bar Council Law Reform Lecture, 15 November 2012 (**http://www.supremecourt.gov.uk/docs/speech-121115-lord-sumption.pdf**)
A speech by Lord Sumption on judicial diversity.

LORD THOMAS OF CWMGIEDD, LORD CHIEF JUSTICE, 'The Judiciary, the Executive and Parliament: Relationships and the Rule of Law' (London 2014) (**http://www.instituteforgovernment. org.uk/events/judiciary-executive-and-parliament-relationships-and-rule-law**)
A keynote speech given by the Lord Chief Justice, Lord Thomas of Cwmgiedd, on relationships between the judiciary, the executive, Parliament, and the rule of law.

Useful websites

http://www.bailii.org
The website of the British and Irish Legal Information Institute

https://www.gov.uk/government/organisations/hm-courts-and-tribunals-service
The website of Her Majesty's Courts and Tribunals Service

http://jac.judiciary.gov.uk/
The website of the Judicial Appointments Commission

https://www.gov.uk/government/organisations/judicial-appointments-and-conduct-ombudsman
The website of the Judicial Appointments and Conduct Ombudsman

http://www.judiciary.gov.uk
The website of the Judiciary of England and Wales

https://www.gov.uk/government/organisations/ministry-of-justice
The website of the Ministry of Justice

http://www.courtsni.gov.uk
The website of the Northern Ireland Courts and Tribunals Service

http://www.scotland-judiciary.org.uk/1/0/Home
The website of the Scottish Courts

http://www.supremecourt.uk
The website of the Supreme Court

7

Devolution and the Territorial Constitution

1. Introduction	297
2. Devolution in Northern Ireland, Scotland, and Wales	298
3. England	308
4. The nature and development of the territorial constitution	323
5. Conclusions	331
Expert commentary	332
Further reading	334
Useful websites	335

1. Introduction

The United Kingdom used to be considered a highly centralised state, with legislative and executive power concentrated in London. Until quite recently, that picture of the UK was relatively accurate, albeit that there were important nuances. Scotland, for instance, has retained a distinct legal and judicial system ever since the union of England and Scotland over 300 years ago. Northern Ireland, meanwhile, had a high degree of autonomy from the rest of the UK for much of the twentieth century, with its own administration and lawmaking assembly. However, these caveats notwithstanding, the UK remained largely centralised until the turn of the millennium.

The territorial constitution of the UK—that is, the constitutional arrangements that regulate the powers of and the relationships between its component elements—has changed almost beyond recognition in the last 20 years. Those changes were triggered by the devolution of power to Northern Ireland, Scotland, and Wales. Those innovations occurred for varied and complex reasons. But an important part of the impetus was a desire to increase the elasticity of the territorial constitution, thereby enabling it to accommodate the diverse identities and interests of the UK's constituent nations. A more flexible Union, it was thought, would be capable of enduring in the face of demands for independence, particularly in Scotland. Devolution thus promised the best of both worlds: a *degree* of independence, but *within* the UK.

That strategy for preserving the territorial integrity of the UK came very close to abject failure in 2014, when the people of Scotland voted on the question: 'Should Scotland be an independent country?' As the date of the referendum approached, opinion polls indicated that the 'yes' campaign had taken a narrow lead. In the end, 55.3% of those who participated in the referendum voted 'no', while 44.7% voted 'yes'. But the strength of support for independence delivered a shock to the UK political system, and demonstrated that any assumption that devolution was necessarily an antidote to nationalist sentiment was as complacent as it was misplaced.

That the Union between Scotland and the rest of the UK will persist thus cannot be taken for granted—a point that is only underlined by the outcome of the referendum on the UK's membership of the European Union (EU). Although a narrow majority across the whole UK voted in favour of leaving the EU, Scotland voted decisively to remain. The same is true of Northern Ireland, albeit by a smaller majority. In contrast, England and Wales favoured leaving the EU. The EU referendum thus demonstrated the different constitutional destinies envisaged by the peoples of the UK's four nations. At the time of writing, that point is underlined by the growing likelihood of a second, Brexit-inspired referendum on Scottish independence.

That, then, is the backdrop against which we examine the territorial constitution in this chapter. That examination falls into three principal parts. We begin by considering why powers were devolved to Northern Ireland, Scotland, and Wales and how devolution operates in relation to those three nations. Then we examine the position of England, noting that the absence of devolution to England places it in an anomalous position. Finally, we evaluate how changing the territorial constitution affects the nature and prospects of the Union. In doing so, we note—with reference to one of our key themes—the ways in which the changing nature of the territorial constitution may form part of the engine that is driving the shift to a more legal approach to constitutionalism in the UK. Meanwhile, the whole of the chapter is, of course, relevant to another of our key themes, the remaking of the territorial constitution being central to the emergence of multilayered governance.

2. Devolution in Northern Ireland, Scotland, and Wales

2.1 Where should governmental power lie?

Devolution is an attempt to answer fundamental questions about where governmental power should reside. In a democracy, the answers to such questions must ultimately turn upon the sort of arrangements that are considered legitimate by the people. This helps to explain why there is great diversity of practice internationally. In states in which there is a strong sense of shared identity and destiny, it may be acceptable—even desirable—for there to be a highly centralised system of government; this is most likely to be the case where the population of a country is homogeneous in cultural, linguistic, ethnic, and economic terms. But where such bonds are weaker, the architecture of the state might be commensurately looser. People may be content to live under the umbrella of a single state—allowing it to deal with such high-level issues as defence, national security, and so on—while demanding regional governments to represent and serve their diverse interests and outlooks. Meanwhile, the peoples within a state may occasionally conclude that their interests are so distinct (or even conflicting) and affinities so lacking that they should go their separate ways entirely, leading to the break-up of the state—either peacefully or following civil war.

Why, then, does the UK's territorial constitution take the form it presently does? How did we arrive at the existing balance of power between the UK state level and the devolved level? As its name suggests, the UK was formed through the union of several nations. The history by which England and Wales were joined is complex, but a key milestone was reached in 1535 when, among other things, Welsh constituencies came to be represented in the English Parliament.[1] The United Kingdom of Great Britain, which was formed by the joining of England and Wales with Scotland in 1707,[2] later became the United Kingdom of Great Britain and Ireland in 1800.[3] Thereafter, all four of the 'home nations' were governed at a UK level; the laws applicable in them were enacted by the Westminster Parliament, and they were administered by the UK executive. That does not mean that the home nations were treated identically to one another—the UK Parliament frequently enacted legislation that applied only to Scotland, or only to England and Wales, while the UK executive established separate departments to deal with certain administrative matters in Northern Ireland, Scotland, and Wales. But there was no escaping the fact that the UK had one executive government and one legislature controlled by whichever political party secured a majority in the House of Commons.[4]

It followed that even if a particular part of the UK voted overwhelmingly for a given political party in a general election, it was possible for a different party to win control of the UK legislature and form the executive government. There is nothing unusual about the majority of voters in a *particular part of the country* favouring a party that nevertheless fails *nationally* to gain an overall majority in a general election. However, the position is complicated if the relevant part of the country identifies as a separate political unit within the UK—something that is more likely if, as is the case, for instance, in relation to Scotland, there exists a distinctive history and cultural identity. In the 2015 general election, the Scottish National Party won 56 of Scotland's 59 UK parliamentary constituencies—an outcome that might risk a sense of disenfranchisement given that the overall result of the election yielded a Conservative Government. Such difficulties, however, are today offset by the fact that in many respects Scotland is now governed by its own Parliament and Government, rather than by the UK institutions based in London.

---

[1] Law in Wales Act 1535.   [2] When the Acts of Union 1706 entered into force.

[3] Union with Ireland Act 1800.

[4] This statement needs to be qualified in that, for part of the twentieth century, devolved government existed in Northern Ireland. See section 2.2.

2.2 Demand and supply

In contrast to countries such as the USA, the UK's constitution was not designed as such: no one sat down with a blank sheet of paper and sketched the powers of, and relationships between, the different institutions and tiers of government. Rather, the constitution is the product of centuries of gradual change—of pragmatic responses to issues that have arisen from time to time. Devolution is of a piece with this tradition: it occurred *because* it was desired and *to the extent* that it was desired. In this sense, it has been governed by the laws of demand and supply.

Devolution is thus *asymmetrical*: different amounts and types of power have been devolved to different parts of the country. The scale of the appetite for change in Scotland—reflected by the 74 per cent support that devolution secured when put to a referendum—meant that the original devolution package (albeit that it has since been substantially augmented) was a relatively far-reaching one. In contrast, Wales was (at least at first) more ambivalent about devolution—only 50.3 per cent of those who voted in the referendum on Welsh devolution favoured it—and a more modest devolution package was thus introduced.

> **Q** What might be the practical limitations of this demand-and-supply model of constitutional reform? Why, for example, may it be difficult to establish precisely what the people of a particular nation or region want?

Northern Ireland is different again. There, the position was complicated by divisions—expressed through decades of terrorist atrocities that claimed over 3,000 lives—between Nationalists (who favoured Northern Ireland's cession from the UK) and Unionists (who did not). Devolution—which had existed in Northern Ireland for much of the twentieth century, but which ended in the early 1970s as violence escalated—was an obvious compromise, but one that risked pleasing no one. In this context, the law of demand and supply eventually delivered an unusual and highly bespoke form of devolution, including provision for Northern Ireland to leave the UK if such a step is supported in a referendum.[5] While no one's first choice, this scheme represented a compromise acceptable to both sides.[6]

England, meanwhile, has no system of devolved government—an oddity that underlines the fact that devolution in the UK is anything but neat and symmetrical. Indeed, to the casual observer ignorant of the underlying history and politics, the UK's contemporary territorial constitution must seem bizarre. The situation today is undoubtedly not one that would have eventuated had the constitution been designed from scratch—and in this sense the story of devolution is part of a much wider narrative. The UK's constitutional arrangements are informed by a raw pragmatism that

---

[5] Northern Ireland Act 1998, s 1. At present, the majority in Northern Ireland favours the union with Great Britain, but demographic trends suggest that this position may change over time.

[6] Of the 81.1 per cent who voted, 71.1 per cent were in favour of the devolution proposals.

accepts a certain roughness around the edges as the acceptable cost of accommodating diversity, history, and tradition. Nevertheless, there comes a point at which such relentless pragmatism—which has a 'reactive and piecemeal'[7] quality that overlooks the need for a 'coherent vision for the shape and structure of the United Kingdom'[8]— begins to create profound difficulties of its own. The way in which the eschewal of strategy and design resulted in the side-lining of England in this context has certainly caused problems, while more generally it has been argued that there has been a failure to take account of the 'cumulative effect' of devolution on the Union, creating the prospect of the former becoming an existential threat to the latter.[9]

2.3 Legislative power

The extent to which devolved governments possess legislative power is a key index of their ability to act independently. The UK's devolution schemes initially diverged radically on this front, but have subsequently begun to converge. This tells an interesting story about both the history of devolution to date, and about the dynamics that have arguably resulted in a 'levelling up' of powers across the relevant parts of the UK.

The Scottish Parliament and the Northern Ireland Assembly have, since their inception, possessed *general legislative competence*. This means that they are authorised to enact legislation on *any* issue, subject to certain exceptions.[10] Those exceptions relate both to specific legislation that the devolved legislatures are unable to alter, such as the Human Rights Act 1998 (HRA),[11] and particular subject areas, such as international relations and defence of the realm.[12] In addition, neither legislature can validly make law that conflicts (for now) with EU law or with certain provisions of the European Convention on Human Rights (ECHR),[13] or which infringes common law constitutional rights or rule-of-law standards.[14] Although broad, these legislative powers cannot be equated with the sovereign power that the Westminster Parliament enjoys (at least in orthodox theory).[15] It follows that if the Scottish Parliament or the Northern Ireland Assembly exceeds its legislative authority, the courts can intervene.[16]

This point notwithstanding, the Belfast and Edinburgh legislatures enjoy powers that are considerable judged by their *extent*. It is also important to note the *type* of powers they possess. Since the introduction of devolution, the Scottish Parliament and (whilst it has sat) the Northern Ireland Assembly have wielded primary lawmaking power: they are capable, within their legislative competence, of amending, repealing, and replacing Acts of the UK Parliament in so far as they apply to Scotland and

---

[7] House of Lords Constitution Committee, *The Union and Devolution* (HL Paper 149 2015–16), [3].

[8] House of Lords Constitution Committee, *Proposals for the Devolution of Further Powers to Scotland* (HL Paper 145 2014–15), [24].

[9] *The Union and Devolution*, [3].

[10] Northern Ireland Act 1998, ss 5–8; Scotland Act 1998, ss 28–30.

[11] Northern Ireland Act 1998, s 7; Scotland Act 1998, s 29(2)(c) and Sch 4.

[12] Northern Ireland Act 1998, s 6(2)(b) and Sch 2; Scotland Act 1998, s 29(2)(b) and Sch 5.

[13] Northern Ireland Act 1998, s 6(2)(c) and (d); Scotland Act 1998, s 29(2)(d).

[14] *AXA General Insurance Ltd v Lord Advocate* [2011] UKSC 46, [2012] 1 AC 868.

[15] *Re AXA General Insurance Ltd* [2010] CSOH 2.

[16] See, eg *Salvesen v Riddell* [2013] UKSC 22.

Northern Ireland respectively. This allows them, should they so wish, to pursue fundamentally different policy directions from other parts of the UK.

In contrast, the system originally adopted in Wales was merely one of *administrative* or *executive*—as opposed to *legislative*—devolution. The Welsh Assembly was only empowered to exercise in relation to Wales certain administrative powers that would otherwise have been exercised by UK Ministers. For example, where an Act of the UK Parliament gave Ministers discretionary power to make certain choices, they could be made, as far as they affected Wales, by the Welsh Assembly.[17] Equally, if UK legislation authorised Ministers to make secondary legislation,[18] this power could be exercised for Wales by the Assembly.[19] None of this, however, really enabled Wales to pursue a truly distinctive legislative agenda. This was a source of dissatisfaction: it was felt in some quarters that the Assembly lacked the power to be truly useful.[20] However, as we explain in the next section, the constitutional settlement just described was merely a starting point for Wales: significantly more was to come.

2.4 'A process not an event'

Ron Davies—who, as Secretary of State for Wales, was one of the architects of the Welsh devolution system—famously said that devolution is a 'process not an event'. The experience of the first two decades of devolution in the UK shows that statement to have been prescient. Indeed, in several respects, the devolution settlements introduced at the end of the 1990s have developed significantly—in ways that underline the susceptibility of devolution to the laws of demand and supply.

The first respect in which devolution has developed since its introduction concerns the range of powers held by the devolved institutions. For instance, powers relating to justice and policing matters—originally excluded from the devolution settlement as part of a compromise—were transferred to Belfast in 2010. Meanwhile, following the report of the Calman Commission,[21] which was charged with reviewing Scotland's devolution settlement, the powers of its Parliament were extended by the Scotland Act 2012. Most notably, the Act effected a significant devolution of competence in relation to financial matters, including certain aspects of taxation and borrowing.[22] However, the 2012 Act is eclipsed by the Scotland Act 2016, the roots of which lie in the independence referendum. In a last-ditch attempt to shore up support for the 'no' (to independence) campaign, leaders of the major UK political parties made a 'vow' to the people of Scotland promising the devolution of additional significant powers should Scotland remain within the UK. Against that background, the cross-party Smith Commission was established, and its report[23] formed the precursor to what

---

[17] Provided that the function in question had, in the first place, been transferred to the Welsh Assembly.

[18] See Chapter 4, section 4.2 on secondary legislation.

[19] Subject to the proviso discussed at Chapter 4, section 4.2.

[20] Commission on the Powers and Electoral Arrangements of the National Assembly for Wales, *Report of the Richard Commission* (Cardiff 2004), ch 3.

[21] Commission on Scottish Devolution, *Serving Scotland Better: Scotland and the United Kingdom in the 21st Century—Final Report* (Edinburgh 2009).

[22] Scotland Act 2012, Pt 3.

[23] The Smith Commission, *Report of the Smith Commission for Further Devolution of Powers to the Scottish Parliament* (Edinburgh 2014).

became the 2016 Act. Most significantly, the new Act provides for devolved control of a range of matters relating to taxation and welfare payments, making Scotland fiscally autonomous of the UK to an unprecedented degree.

The devolution settlement in Wales has also recently been substantially augmented. The Wales Act 2014 devolved relatively limited powers in relation to taxation, but also made provision for a referendum to be held on empowering the Welsh Assembly to change the rates of income tax payable by Welsh taxpayers. No such referendum was held, but the Wales Act 2017 removes the need for a referendum on this point and simply authorise the Welsh Assembly to begin exercising income tax varying powers. The Act also expands devolved competence in Wales in areas including energy, transport, equal opportunities and marine licensing.

It can be seen, then, that all three devolution settlements remain works in progress as far as the *scope* of devolved powers is concerned. However, devolution in Wales has developed over time in a second respect, concerning the *type* of powers possessed by the Assembly. We noted earlier that Wales's original devolution settlement differed from those in Northern Ireland and Scotland, both because the Welsh Assembly lacked the capacity to make primary legislation and because it had only those powers specifically conferred upon it (rather than a general legislative power subject to exceptions). The first of those discrepancies has already been removed. From 2007, the Assembly has been able to enact primary legislation, meaning that it can set Wales on a legislative course different from that of England. That system was introduced on a limited basis at first, which required the Assembly to obtain the UK government's blessing in relation to each piece of legislation—but, following endorsement of the new system in a referendum in 2011, the need to seek permission was dropped.

The other point of distinction between the Welsh and other devolution models—relating to the use in Wales of a conferred, rather than a reserved, powers model—has been removed by the Wales Act 2017. That Act abandons the conferred powers model in respect of Wales, opting instead for a reserved powers model that is in principle similar to that which has applied in Scotland from the outset. However, that will not make the Welsh Assembly and the Scottish Parliament equivalently powerful, given that there are substantially more reserved matters in respect of the Welsh Assembly than there are in respect of the Scottish Parliament. Nevertheless, the general direction of travel across the three nations with devolved governance arrangements is one of convergence, as those arrangements evolve in ways that erode at least some of the basic conceptual differences between the UK's various devolution models.

The devolution systems have, then, developed in terms of both the *degree* and *types* of power to which they relate. There is also a third important respect in which such evolution can be discerned. It relates to the *constitutional security* of the devolution arrangements. Until very recently, those arrangements were unaccompanied by any *legal* guarantees as to their permanence, the position being that devolution was established by, and could therefore be abolished by, the UK Parliament. That does not mean that it would have been politically straightforward for Westminster unilaterally to interfere with or abolish devolution. Nevertheless, it is noteworthy that legislation now recognises the 'permanence' of the Scottish Parliament and Government.[24] And the same position now applies in Wales as a result of the Wales Act 2017.[25] We examine just what (if anything) these statutory provisions legally amount to later, and the extent to which they contribute to a shift, in this context, from political to legal constitutionalism.[26] But, independently of the conclusions we reach on those points, the very fact that legislation now acknowledges the permanence of the Scottish and Welsh institutions is symbolic of the depth of the constitutional roots that devolution has acquired over the course of its first two decades of operation.

> **Q** Is it a good thing that devolution in the UK takes the form of (in effect) an ongoing work in progress? What are the advantages of such an approach? What might be the risks?

2.5 Executive power

All three of the UK's devolution schemes include the transfer of executive power to new devolved executive bodies—but, as with legislative authority, there are important differences between the schemes.

Following an election, members of the Scottish Parliament (MSPs) must nominate one of their number to be appointed First Minister by the Queen.[27] If one party secures an overall majority, its leader is highly likely to become First Minister; otherwise, a coalition is likely to be formed, with the leader of the biggest coalition party becoming First Minister. She then appoints the other Ministers drawn from MSPs who are members of her own party and any others with which it has formed a coalition.[28] This largely follows the UK model of a 'parliamentary government': an executive drawn from, and held to account by, the legislature. Like its Westminster counterpart, the Scottish Parliament can confer discretionary and delegated lawmaking powers on the Scottish Ministers,[29] who also exercise in relation to Scotland all powers relating to devolved matters that had been conferred on UK Ministers prior to devolution.[30] The upshot is that the Scottish Government now administers Scotland save in relation to those matters that remain the responsibility of the UK authorities. The role of UK Ministers in relation to Scotland is therefore relatively slight, given that the major domestic areas of governance—including the most politically high-profile issues of health and education—are largely devolved.

Originally, the position in Wales was very different: *only* executive power was transferred, and this vested in the Assembly itself, albeit that it could delegate such power.[31]

---

[24] Scotland Act 1998, s 63A (as inserted by Scotland Act 2016, s 1).
[25] Government of Wales Act 2006, s A1 (as inserted by Wales Act 2017, s 1).
[26] Section 4.3.   [27] Scotland Act 1998, ss 45–6.   [28] Scotland Act 1998, s 47.
[29] Scotland Act 1998, s 52.   [30] Scotland Act 1998, s 53.
[31] See Rawlings, *Delineating Wales* (Cardiff 2003), ch 3.

Today, however, the Assembly has primary lawmaking powers, and a formal legal distinction is made between the Assembly, as a legislative body, and the executive branch, known as the Welsh Government.[32] The Assembly's role is to enact legislation and hold the Government to account, while the latter now exercises the administrative powers in respect of devolved matters. A First Minister and other Welsh Ministers are appointed in broadly the same way as their Scottish counterparts; all must be Assembly Members, thus conforming to the familiar model of parliamentary government.[33]

Arrangements in Belfast also follow that pattern, with a separate Northern Ireland Executive drawn from the membership of the Assembly. However, the way in which the Executive is appointed and composed represents a highly bespoke solution to the specific problems faced by Northern Ireland. It was clear that, in a sharply divided community, devolved government would only be perceived as legitimate— and have any prospect of contributing to the ending of terrorist violence—if it enjoyed the support of both Nationalists and Unionists. This meant that it would be unacceptable to adopt a model that enabled a single party, or a coalition of like-thinking parties, to form the executive government. Instead, it was felt necessary to *require* parties representing *both* sections of the community to share power. So, following elections to the Assembly, the nomination for First Minister is made by the nominating officer of the largest political party of the largest political designation (currently the Unionists), while the nomination for Deputy First Minister is made by the nominating officer of the largest political party of the *second largest* political designation (currently the Nationalists). In practice, this means that the two senior ministerial offices are held by one Nationalist and one Unionist politician.[34] Detailed rules ensure that no political party[35] can monopolise the other ministerial portfolios.[36]

Northern Ireland is thus administered by a power-sharing executive, making coalition government the legally stipulated norm—a highly unusual approach that seeks to solve a set of very particular problems. There is no clearer illustration than this of the UK's approach to devolution, in which pragmatism is paramount: a 'differential approach to the arrangements for each country', reflecting their individual 'histories and contemporary circumstances'.[37] However, if the distinctiveness of the Northern Ireland model has been illustrative of how particular and different Northern Ireland's circumstances have been, one recent development is perhaps indicative of the fact that the political, and so constitutional, situation in Northern Ireland is (to some extent at least) normalising. Until 2016, there was no official opposition in the Assembly, and little by way of an unofficial opposition, given that most parties had ministerial members of the executive under the power-sharing arrangements. However, the Standing Orders—the internal rules—of the Assembly have now been amended to

---

[32] Government of Wales Act 2006, ss 1 and 45.   [33] Government of Wales Act 2006, ss 46–8.
[34] Northern Ireland Act 1998, s 16A.   [35] And, in practice, neither Nationalists nor Unionists.
[36] Northern Ireland Act 1998, s 18.
[37] Irvine, *Human Rights, Constitutional Law and the Development of the English Legal System* (Oxford 2003), p 90.

provide for one or more parties to form an official opposition.[38] Any party that was entitled to nominate one of its members for a ministerial post but which declined to do so can now choose to be recognised as part of the official opposition. The intention is that this will better equip the Assembly to perform its role of holding the Executive to account.

2.6 Democracy

As we saw earlier, one of the objectives underlying devolution is the enhancement of democracy by enabling people to be governed by institutions over which they feel they have real influence, and to which they therefore consider themselves genuinely connected. Devolution mainly pursues this goal by providing institutions that are more proximate—geographically, politically, and culturally—to the people. But it is, of course, also important that the *process* whereby representatives are elected to serve in the new devolved legislatures is a democratic one.

The system used for elections to the Scottish Parliament and Welsh Assembly differs from that used for elections to the House of Commons. Known as the *additional member system*, it involves dividing Scotland and Wales into both *constituencies* and larger *regions*. Voters cast ballots to select both constituency members and regional (or 'additional') members. The former are elected under the first-past-the-post (FPTP) system: the candidate with the greatest number of votes in each constituency becomes its representative in the legislature. This ensures the valuable link between constituents and their representatives. Meanwhile, additional members—of whom there are several for each region—are chosen by voters casting ballots for political parties rather than individuals. The regional seats are then allocated by applying a mathematical formula that seeks to ensure that a party's total number of seats in the legislature broadly reflects its overall share of the vote. This produces results that are more proportionate—particularly in respect of smaller parties—than the unadulterated FPTP system used for elections to the House of Commons. For instance, in the elections to the Scottish Parliament in 2016, the Liberal Democrats obtained 7 per cent of the votes cast and 4 per cent of the seats in the Scottish Parliament. In contrast, in the UK general election in 2015, the Liberal Democrats got 8 per cent of the votes cast but only 1 per cent of the seats in the House of Commons.

A system known as the *single transferable vote* is used for elections to the Northern Ireland Assembly; this is different from the model that applies in Scotland and Wales, but is also designed to ensure that the political make-up of the legislature closely reflects each party's share of the popular vote.[39] One important consequence of the additional member system and the single transferable vote is that they make it less likely that any one party will gain an overall majority, thus making minority or

---

[38] Standing Order 45A of the Northern Ireland Assembly.

[39] The single transferable vote is the system favoured by the Electoral Reform Society. For detailed information on how it works, see **http://www.electoral-reform.org.uk**

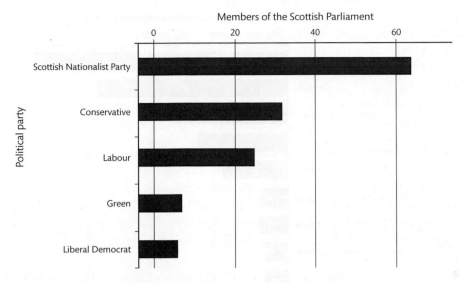

Figure 7.1 Elections to the Scottish Parliament, 2016

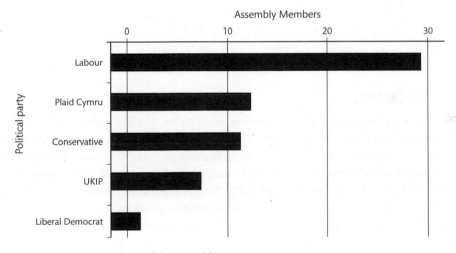

Figure 7.2 Elections to the Welsh Assembly, 2016

coalition government more probable in the devolved legislatures than it is in the UK Parliament.[40] Elections to all three of the devolved legislatures were held in 2016; the results are shown in Figures 7.1 to 7.3.

---

[40] Coalition is in any event a legal requirement in Northern Ireland: see section 2.5.

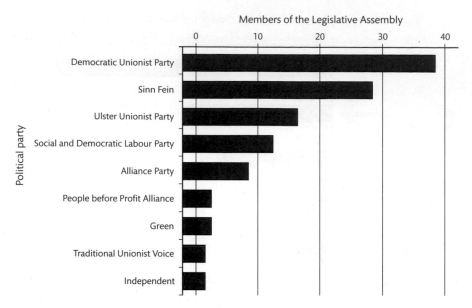

Figure 7.3 Elections to the Northern Ireland Assembly, 2016

3. England

3.1 Introduction

In relation to Northern Ireland, Scotland, and Wales, the UK government's role is residual: it does those things that the devolved institutions are not authorised to do. In England, however, there are no devolved institutions. The UK Parliament and the UK executive are therefore the de facto English legislature and government. This gives rise to what is sometimes called the 'English question', although it is in fact more accurate to think of two distinct—but related—questions.

First, should England *as a whole* be given a constitutional voice through, for instance, the creation of an English Parliament and an English Government? Second, should devolution (or something akin to it) apply to England *at a more granular level*? After all, if devolution is about taking power closer to the people, it is not obvious that devolving power to England as a whole would achieve very much: England accounts for roughly 53 million of the UK's 65 million-strong population. Power devolved to England's 53 million inhabitants would not therefore take it that much 'closer to the people'. This raises questions about whether regional government within England should be introduced, thus creating English political units of a size that would be comparable to those presently constituted by the devolved nations.

The position is made more complex by the fact that those questions interact with one another as well as with other issues. For instance, should it be a matter of choosing between the first and second approaches, or might they be combined? Should there be an all-England tier of government *and* regional governments within England, or just one of those (and, if only one, which one)? Questions also arise about how any of these arrangements might relate to the existing system of local government in England and how any such arrangements for England would fit into the bigger constitutional picture. Would it, for instance, require the adoption of a federal constitution?[41] In the following sections, we explore these issues, distinguishing—but also drawing connections—between all-England approaches and those based on regional government in England. We will see that, as things currently stand, England is in the process of adopting certain elements of each of the two approaches.

3.2 **England as a whole**

3.2.1 **A voice for England?**

As Oliver notes, no governmental institution exists that can provide a 'voice for England' by legitimately arguing its case 'as against Scotland, Wales, and Northern Ireland'.[42] Although the UK government acts de facto as England's government, Oliver argues that it cannot properly act as England's advocate—this 'would be seen as partisan, given that it is supposed to be promoting the interests of the UK as a whole'—thus giving rise to 'inequalities' within the UK that are not 'consistent with principles of good governance, transparency, and equality'.[43] While this point is difficult to refute, it is doubted by some whether England *needs* such an advocate. For example, Lord Falconer, when he was Lord Chancellor, argued that the 'essence of devolution is to protect the legitimate interests of Scotland and Wales'[44]—a requirement based on the fact that 'England and English MPs represent over 80 per cent of the population and over 80 per cent of MPs'.[45] England, on this view, is big enough to look after itself; only the smaller nations require the special voice afforded by devolution. Whether this is a satisfactory response depends on how we understand the purpose of devolution. If we understand its aim to be to take power closer to the people, Falconer's analysis cuts less ice.

The most immediately obvious solution is perhaps an English Parliament and an English Government. They would do for England the types of things that the Scottish Parliament and Government do for Scotland, while the UK institutions would deal with pan-UK matters such as defence, international relations, and certain aspects of taxation and spending. But for several reasons, there is no prospect of such an approach being followed. First, there is no obvious and strong public clamour for all-England institutions. Second, there is no clear appetite amongst the political class for the enormous upheaval that such a major constitutional innovation would entail. Third, it is far from clear that such a model would be viable. It has, for instance, been

---

[41] We consider the idea of federalism in section 4.

[42] Oliver, *Constitutional Reform in the UK* (Oxford 2003), p 290.   [43] Oliver, p 290.

[44] Northern Ireland was not mentioned, presumably because, when this speech was made, devolution there was suspended.

[45] Speech to ESRC Devolution and Constitutional Change Programme Final Conference, March 2006.

argued that English institutions—given England's size relative to the rest of the UK—would 'introduce a destabilising asymmetry of power to the Union'.[46]

3.2.2 The 'West Lothian question'

That an English-Parliament-and-Government model would not work has long been the received wisdom. As a result, proposals for reform in respect of England have tended to focus on the possibility of regional government within England. We examine that possibility later. However, even if the positive case for all-England institutions does not stack up (or at least lacks sufficient backing), that leaves in play a negative argument that concentrates on the perceived unfairness that England has suffered as a result of devolution.

That argument centres upon what has been called the *West Lothian question*.[47] It asks whether it is legitimate for MPs representing non-English constituencies to vote on Westminster legislation that (because it deals with matters that are devolved elsewhere) will affect only England. If the instinctive response to this question is 'no', two factors may help to explain this.[48] First, there is a lack of reciprocity in these arrangements: why, for example, should Scottish MPs vote in Westminster on education law, given that—education being a devolved matter in Scotland—English MPs have no influence over Scottish education law? Second, the fact that English law can be made by MPs unaccountable to the English electorate arguably raises problems of democratic legitimacy.[49]

These are difficult issues that go to the heart of the nature of the post-devolution territorial constitution. The only potentially viable defence of (what was, until very recently) England's situation was a pragmatic one—that although the position looked odd, it was acceptable because it did not, in practice, matter. However, experience indicates that this is not invariably so. For example, in 2003, a health Bill was put before Parliament concerning, among other things, National Health Service (NHS) reforms entailing the creation of so-called foundation hospitals. That part of the Bill pertained *only* to England—and as Table 7.1 shows, although a majority of *all* MPs supported the proposals, a majority of *English* MPs did not.

Table 7.1 MPs' votes on amendment to Health Bill, November 2003[50]

Nation	For foundation hospitals	Against foundation hospitals
England	234	251
Scotland	44	17
Wales	24	11
Northern Ireland	0	6
All	302	285

---

[46] House of Lords Constitution Committee, *The Union and Devolution* (HL Paper 149 2015–16), [376].

[47] So-called because, when devolution was considered in the late 1970s, this problem was most notably raised by the then MP for West Lothian in Scotland, Tam Dalyell, a staunch opponent of devolution.

[48] See Hadfield, 'Devolution, Westminster and the English Question' [2005] PL 286, 286–7.

[49] Hadfield, 286–7.

[50] See Constitution Unit, *Devolution and the Centre. Quarterly Report: November 2003* (London 2003), p 8.

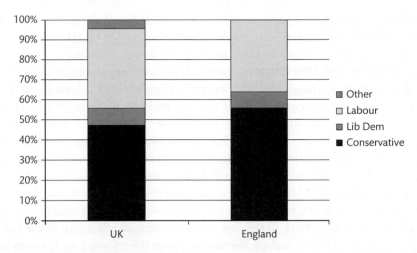

Figure 7.4 2010 general election results

Q Do you think that these voting figures imply some sort of unfairness? If so, can you pinpoint exactly what it is that gives rise to such unfairness?

Isolated examples like the Health Bill notwithstanding, the West Lothian question remained largely academic for some time. The Labour governments of 1997–2010 enjoyed comfortable—and usually very large—majorities, meaning that the implementation of their legislative programmes rarely depended on non-English votes. But the position was different during the 2010–15 Parliament. As Figure 7.4 shows, the outcome of the 2010 general election threw the West Lothian question into sharp relief: while the Conservative Party did not secure a majority of *all* seats in the UK Parliament, it secured a clear majority of *English* seats. England therefore found itself in the very position that triggered calls for Scottish devolution: a clear majority (at least expressed through the current voting system) expressed a preference for one party, yet voting patterns elsewhere meant that that party could not (on its own) form a government.

3.2.3 'English votes for English laws'

Following the 2010 election, the coalition government established the McKay Commission to consider the West Lothian question.[51] It concluded that any solution should be informed by the principle that '[d]ecisions at the United Kingdom level having a separate and distinct effect for a component part of the United Kingdom should normally be taken only with the consent of a majority of the elected representatives for that part of the United Kingdom'.[52] The Commission recommended that

---

[51] The McKay Commission, *Report of the Commission on the Consequences of Devolution for the House of Commons* (London 2013).
[52] McKay Commission, [109].

the principle be implemented by means of what it called a 'double-count' procedure. This would have involved making public not just the names of MPs who voted for and against a given Bill, but also the constituencies they represented—with a view to determining whether a Bill (or parts of it) likely to have a separate and distinct effect on England attracted the support of a majority of *English* MPs. Although no legal or procedural consequences would have ensued if a majority of the latter type were not secured, the Commission envisaged that a government that pressed on in the absence of the support of a majority of English MPs would likely have sustained 'severe political damage'.[53] The intention, therefore, was to *discourage* reliance upon MPs from unaffected parts of the country to push through legislation against the wishes of the majority of English MPs, whilst stopping short of *preventing* such a practice.

Although the McKay Commission's proposal was never implemented, this question came dramatically back to the fore in the immediate aftermath of the Scottish independence referendum. Indeed, the morning after the referendum, the then Prime Minister, David Cameron, said that we had 'heard the voice of Scotland', that 'the millions of voices of England must also be heard', and that a 'decisive answer' to the West Lothian question was required. Cameron thus sought to ensure that the promises of further devolution to Scotland made as panic set in towards the end of the referendum campaign were balanced against the perceived need to demonstrate to English voters that their position was being taken seriously. The government therefore undertook to introduce arrangements for 'English votes for English laws' (EVEL).

Such arrangements were implemented in 2015.[54] Perhaps surprisingly, this occurred not through the enactment of legislation, but by means of amending the Standing Orders—the internal rules—of the House of Commons. As a result, a set of very significant constitutional changes—which in some practical respects might be said to amount to the creation of a de facto English Parliament within the UK Parliament—were made in a notably informal way.[55]

A Bill—or a provision within a Bill—triggers the EVEL procedure if the Speaker of the House of Commons determines that the Bill or provision

- applies exclusively to England; and
- is a measure that, if it were to relate to one of the devolved nations, could be made by that nation's devolved legislature.

Whether a Bill or provision applies 'exclusively' to England is likely to prove a vexed question. For instance, the relevant rules provide that something can apply 'exclusively' to England even if it has 'minor or consequential effects' beyond England. But the boundary between effects on other parts of the country that are 'minor or consequential' in nature and those that are more substantial, and which therefore take the provision out of the EVEL regime, is liable to prove difficult to draw. Legislation that,

---

[53] McKay Commission, [219].

[54] These arrangements extend to legislation that applies exclusively to England and to legislation that applies exclusively to England and Wales. For reasons of concision, we explain how the EVEL rules apply to England-only legislation, although they apply equivalently to England-and-Wales-only legislation.

[55] The rules are set out in House of Commons Standing Orders 83J–83X.

on the face of it, seems to affect only England might well have a variety of 'consequential' effects. For instance, legislation that formally applies only to the NHS in England might have consequential effects in respect of Wales, given that some patients who live in Wales are referred to NHS hospitals in England.[56] Meanwhile, the Scottish Government has argued that legislation relating to England can affect levels of public expenditure in England. That, in turn, can affect the amount of funding received by Scotland because the arithmetical formula used to determine Scottish funding takes account of public expenditure in England.[57] It falls to the Speaker of the House of Commons to wrestle with these difficulties and ultimately determine whether the EVEL rules apply. Although fears have been voiced that the Speaker's determinations on these points might invite legal challenge, that is highly unlikely as a result of parliamentary privilege.[58]

Once it has been determined that a given Bill or provision falls within the EVEL rules, the core principle enshrined in those rules kicks in. That principle is that legislation to which the rules apply cannot be enacted unless it receives the support of a majority of *all* MPs *and* a majority of all MPs representing *English* constituencies.[59] This regime goes beyond that which was recommended by the McKay Commission, since it enables MPs representing English constituencies to block legislation, as opposed simply to registering an objection against it. It is therefore no longer possible for legislation relating exclusively to England to be 'imposed' upon *English* MPs simply because the legislation is supported by a majority of *all* MPs.

It will take some time for the full implications of the EVEL system to be appreciated. However, it is likely to provoke a variety of reactions. For some, EVEL raises concerns as to whether the Westminster Parliament can simultaneously function as the UK Parliament and as a de facto legislature for England. There is, for instance, a concern that two 'classes' of MPs have been created, given that English MPs now hold greater sway than other MPs in respect of England-only legislation. From a different perspective, however, there may be concerns that EVEL does not go far enough. It does not, for instance, allow English MPs to force through legislation that fails to secure the support of a majority of all MPs—it merely allows the enactment of England-only legislation to be resisted absent the majority support of English MPs. Nor does EVEL address larger questions concerning the relationship between the UK Parliament and a UK government that, in many respects, functions in practice as England's executive. No amount of finessing of the procedure whereby legislation is enacted can get around the possibility that elections to the UK Parliament may yield an executive that does not accurately reflect the wishes of voters in England (as refracted through Parliament as an electoral college). Indeed, the 2010 election is a case in point, in that the Conservative Party won an overall majority of English but not UK constituencies.

---

[56] House of Commons Procedure Committee, *Government Proposals for English Votes for English Laws Standing Orders: Interim Report* (HC 410 2015–16), [36].

[57] House of Commons Procedure Committee, [37].   [58] See Chapter 5, section 4.

[59] The majority must be of the relevant group of MPs who actually vote on the matter, rather than a majority of all MPs who belong to the relevant group.

3.3 Local and regional government in England

Viewed in one way, EVEL might be considered to be a form of devolution-lite for England: a mechanism whereby the UK Parliament is equipped to function as an English legislature, albeit only to a limited extent. However, the paradoxical question arises whether EVEL or some more thoroughgoing model involving the creation of distinct English institutions would truly amount to 'devolution' for England. The question arises because England is so large. Even if it had its own government and Parliament, those institutions would operate in respect of a population roughly ten times that of Scotland, and almost 30 times that of Northern Ireland. Could devolution really be delivered for England by creating all-England institutions, or would meaningful devolution require a more granular approach?

The latter view was taken by the Labour government in 2003. England was to be divided into eight regions,[60] each with its own elected regional assembly. However, the proposal disintegrated when it was resoundingly rejected in a referendum in North East England in 2004—not least because voters appreciated that the powers with which regional assemblies were to be invested were relatively modest. This raised the concern that a needless 'mezzanine' tier of government was being proposed at considerable cost but with few tangible benefits. In recent years, however, the notion of regional governance has re-emerged in a different form. We examine that matter in sections 3.3.5 and 3.3.6. We begin, however, with local government, which, as we will see, forms the foundation upon which the new model of English regional governance is being constructed.

3.3.1 Local government

Local government is important.[61] It employs hundreds of thousands of people, spends tens of billions of pounds annually, and plays a key role in the making of decisions, the formulation of policy, and the delivery of public services. That certain decisions should be made and tasks performed at a local level seems obvious on an instinctive level, but it is nevertheless worth reflecting on why we have local government—and why we have it in its current form.

A good starting point is the conclusions of the Widdicombe Committee, a body set up in the 1980s by central government to inquire into the conduct of local authority business.[62] It argued that the value of local government consists in three principal factors. First, it was said, local government is important for reasons of *pluralism*. Rather than having a single (central) seat of government, the existence of local authorities ensures that governmental power is, to some extent, diffused, thus avoiding the hegemony of central government. Second, local government facilitates *participation* in the business of governance—both by equipping citizens to shape local policy

---

[60] In addition to London, where a form of regional government—in the shape of the Greater London Authority—already exists.

[61] Lyons, *Place-Shaping: A Shared Ambition for the Future of Local Government* (London 2007), contains detailed discussion of the role of local government, past, present, and future.

[62] Committee of Inquiry into the Conduct of Local Authority Business, *The Conduct of Local Authority Business* (Cmnd 9797 1986).

through regular elections to councils and by virtue of the fact that individuals can more easily become directly involved in local, than in national, governance. The liberal writer John Stuart Mill considered these participative virtues of local government to be of great importance, arguing that they help to provide citizens with an education in democracy.[63] Third, the Widdicombe Committee emphasised the *responsiveness* of local government—that is, its capacity to make decisions and deliver services in ways that are appropriate to the particular needs of localities. Such responsiveness is facilitated by the proximity of local government to the electorate and the area concerned, equipping it with local knowledge and sensitivity to local mores. A more recent inquiry concluded that local government's key role is 'place-shaping', meaning 'the creative use of powers and influence to promote the general well-being of a community and its citizens'—an endeavour in which responsiveness is obviously imperative.[64]

3.3.2 Local and devolved government compared

A concern that has often been raised in relation to local government is that its capacity to realise the potential ascribed to it by the Widdicombe Committee is hobbled by central government's tendency to treat its local counterpart as a poor relation. Too often, it is argued by some, local government is regarded by central government as a service delivery mechanism: an implementer of central government policy without meaningful autonomy of its own. The dominance of central government vis-à-vis local government arises in part because of the latter's relatively weak constitutional position—a phenomenon that is observable when local government's position is contrasted with that of devolved governments.

As we saw earlier in this chapter, the devolved governments in Edinburgh, Cardiff, and Belfast were created by the UK Parliament. It is therefore possible, at least as a matter of constitutional theory, for the latter to interfere in the devolution settlements—for example, by curtailing the devolved governments' powers, making changes to how devolution works, or overriding laws passed by devolved legislatures. Local government is also a creation of the UK Parliament. Local authorities therefore possess only the powers given to them via Acts of the Westminster Parliament. And, just as that Parliament could, if it wished, fundamentally rewrite the devolution legislation, so it may interfere with local government, effecting major changes to its powers, structure, and so on.

It follows that, in *legal* terms, the UK level of government, via Acts of Parliament, has the capacity to intervene in the affairs of both devolved and local government. But does central government possess the *political* capacity to exploit such legal powers? We have already seen that it would be politically very difficult for central government to interfere in the devolution settlements without the consent of the devolved governments concerned. Now that devolution has allowed the genie of self-government out of the bottle, it would be nigh on politically impossible to put it back in. The same is not, however, true of local government. Although local, like devolved, government exists

---

[63] Mill, *Considerations on Representative Democracy* (New York 1862), pp 288–9.   [64] Lyons, p 60.

(among other things) to allow communities to order their own affairs in ways that best meet their peculiar needs and priorities, the institutions of local government—city councils, county councils, and so on—do not, in general, enjoy the same status or security as their devolved counterparts.

The political capacity of central government to intervene in other tiers of government within the UK is principally dependent upon citizens' perceptions of, and attitudes towards, the latter. People are most likely to entertain a sense of connection with—even the possession of a stake in—institutions with which they identify closely. National institutions, such as the devolved legislatures and administrations, enjoy a particular status deriving from the sense of shared identity and common destiny that nationhood inspires. This does not, of course, mean that people support everything that their devolved governments do—but the ties that bind together the citizens of the devolved nations are likely to lend a degree of popular legitimacy to, and support for the existence of, their national institutions. In contrast, senses of identification with institutions of local government may be less strong, bearing in mind that we live in an increasingly mobile society in which the membership of many communities is transient to a significant degree, and that such institutions may not, in the first place, necessarily be aligned with such senses of local identity as exist. Moreover, local government generally has rather a low profile. People often have only a rudimentary awareness of the role of local government; this inhibits the development of the sort of strong sense of connection with local authorities that might guard against central government interference.

> **Q** Does this lower level of identification with localities, as distinct from nations, *necessarily* follow? What factors might mean that in some areas—towns, cities, counties, regions—there is a stronger sense of local identity?

3.3.3 Intervention by the centre

The UK government frequently intervenes—on both the administrative and legislative planes—in matters pertaining to local government. Three points should be considered in this regard.

First, Parliament may intervene directly so as to alter the fundamental nature and structure of local government. The UK government, through its control of the House of Commons, is thus able to assert considerable influence over local government. The most dramatic example is perhaps the Thatcher administration's procurement of legislation to abolish the Greater London Council, which, under the control of the Labour Party, was highly and very publicly critical of central government policies in the 1980s.[65] The Thatcher government, informed by its ideological predilection for market economics, also made radical changes to how councils operated, resulting in the contracting out of many local authority core functions (eg housing management and refuse collection) and transforming councils in some spheres from service-providing to service-commissioning bodies.

---

[65] Local Government Act 1985.

Second, the governing UK party may choose to impose its own policy preferences on local government by requiring it to undertake or desist from undertaking certain actions. An example of the former is furnished by the attempts of Labour governments in the 1960s and 1970s to introduce a new system of secondary education. Legally, it was for local authorities to decide on the organisation of schools within their areas, but the government wished to institute the 'comprehensive' system on a national basis.[66] It attempted to do this by issuing administrative directions requiring local authorities to formulate plans for shifting to comprehensive education. When this met with opposition from some councils, legislation was introduced requiring local authorities to submit plans for the reorganisation of schools along the lines of the comprehensive model.[67] Meanwhile, the Thatcher administration secured the enactment of s 28 of the Local Government Act 1988, which banned local authorities from 'promot[ing] the teaching in any maintained school of the acceptability of homosexuality as a pretended family relationship'. This is a very clear example of the ability and willingness of central government to use primary legislation as a means of imposing its policy (including moral) preferences on local authorities, rather than allowing such issues to be debated and decided at a local level.[68]

Third, as well as using primary legislation directly to intervene in local affairs, the UK executive possesses numerous administrative powers[69] to intervene in, scrutinise, regulate, and even override the conduct of local government. An important element of this relates to financial affairs, in which local authorities lack any substantial measure of real autonomy. Although local authorities raise funds directly by levying the Council Tax, this accounts for a relatively small proportion of their total budget.[70] Councils depend for the remainder—that is, the vast majority—of their income on various types of grant from central government. This clearly gives the latter considerable influence, which is wielded by, among other things, attaching conditions to such grants and by 'ring-fencing' of local authority budgets, that is, specifying how resources are to be deployed by local authorities. Even in relation to Council Tax, however, councils do not enjoy complete autonomy. Until recently, the Secretary of State had the power to 'cap' Council Tax if he considered a local authority's budget to be 'excessive'. That remains the case in Wales,[71] but new arrangements have been introduced in England whereby a local referendum must be held if an 'excessive' increase in Council Tax is proposed.[72]

3.3.4 Localism

The replacement (in England) of ministerial capping powers with a requirement to hold a referendum forms part of a much larger 'localism' agenda, implemented through the Localism Act 2011, the aim of which was to shift power from the centre to local

---

[66] This system was intended to replace that under which pupils were sent to grammar or secondary modern schools depending on an assessment of their academic ability at age 11.

[67] Education Act 1976.   [68] Section 28 of the 1988 Act was repealed in 2003.

[69] Themselves conferred by primary legislation.

[70] Lyons, *Place-Shaping: A Shared Ambition for the Future of Local Government* (London 2007), p 223.

[71] Local Government Finance Act 1992, ss 52A–Y.

[72] Local Government Finance Act 1992, ss 52ZA–ZY, as inserted by the Localism Act 2011.

communities. However, old habits die hard. In relation to the referendum mechanism in respect of 'excessive' Council Tax increases, it is the Secretary of State who (subject to confirmation by the House of Commons) sets the principles that determine what counts as 'excessive'. Central government has not, therefore, relinquished all control over this aspect of local government finance.

The Localism Act 2011 also introduced a number of further reforms. One of the most significant concerns the legal powers of English local authorities. Traditionally, councils had only those powers conferred upon them by statute, making it necessary to identify a specific basis in law for anything a local authority wished to do. The coalition government considered that this risked stifling innovation, for fear of legal challenge. The Localism Act therefore gives English councils a 'general power of competence', meaning that they have 'the power to do anything that individuals generally may do'.[73] However, this power is subject to significant limitations. For instance, where councils have specific, restricted powers to do things, the general power cannot be used to circumvent such restrictions.[74] The Act allows the Secretary of State to make orders removing such restrictions, but also permits him to proscribe uses to which the general power may be put and to set conditions upon its exercise.[75]

The limits of the localism agenda can also be seen in relation to the longstop powers of central government to intervene where local government is deemed to be failing. For example, local government is legally required to 'make arrangements to secure continuous improvement in the way in which its functions are exercised, having regard to a combination of economy, efficiency and effectiveness'.[76] If satisfied that a local authority is failing to do this, the Secretary of State may direct 'that a specified function of the authority shall be exercised by the Secretary of State or a person nominated by him for a period specified in the direction or for so long as the Secretary of State considers appropriate'.[77] For instance, in the light of chronic failings at Doncaster Metropolitan Borough Council, this power was exercised, with certain functions falling under the direct control of the Secretary of State, and others under the control of commissioners appointed by him.[78] The Secretary of State subsequently announced that the council would be stripped of responsibility for children's services, with that role being taken over by an external provider.[79] Similar steps were taken in 2015 in the light of major failures at Rotherham Metropolitan Borough Council in relation to the tackling of child sexual exploitation.[80]

Where does this leave us? Is local government essentially a delivery mechanism—an 'executory agency for national policies'?[81] Or is local government truly autonomous:

---

[73] Localism Act 2011, s 1. See Bowes and Stanton, 'The Localism Act 2011 and the General Power of Competence' [2014] PL 392.

[74] Localism Act 2011, s 2.   [75] Localism Act 2011, s 5.

[76] Local Government Act 1999, s 3(1).   [77] Local Government Act 1999, s 15(6)(a).

[78] HC Deb, vol 512, col 44WS (30 June 2010).

[79] Letter from Education Secretary to Mayor of Doncaster, 26 September 2013.

[80] House of Commons Communities and Local Government Committee, *Government Interventions: The Use of Commissioners in Rotherham Metropolitan Borough Council and the London Borough of Tower Hamlets* (HC 42 2016–17).

[81] Loughlin, *Local Government in the Modern State* (London 1986), p 186, suggesting that some aspects of the work of local government could be described thus.

able to develop and implement its own policies in a way that is appropriate to the needs of individual communities, thus realising the potential that the Widdicombe Committee saw? Nothing that has been said so far should be taken to imply that local government is unimportant or lacking in power. It plays a fundamental role and exercises real power; local authorities are free, in many respects, to adopt their own policies and to develop distinctive solutions to local problems. It is also important to appreciate that the degree of central control of local government tends to ebb and flow; having reached a high-water mark in the 1990s and early 2000s, it is now beginning to recede somewhat. The Labour government stated in 2006 that 'we must have the courage at the centre to let go', in order to 'give local people and local communities more influence and power to improve their lives',[82] while, as we have seen, subsequent governments have also pursued a localism agenda. As well as enhancing the powers of local authorities, that agenda has extended to the abolition of Standards for England, the body which was responsible for upholding ethical standards in local government, and the abolition of the Audit Commission in favour of making councils responsible for appointing their own independent auditors.[83]

Nevertheless, it remains the case that local government is subject to a good deal of oversight and intervention by central government. For instance, an empirical study examining the impact of the 'localism' agenda during the 2010–15 Parliament concluded that 'a culture of centralism' persists, and that any future attempts at 'local democratic invigoration' would, if they were to succeed, have to 'cut away the centrally-set targets and objectives, remove the over-prescriptive supervision of local power and afford councils the freedom necessary to operate appropriately and effectively'.[84] Indeed, the localism agenda is itself telling: for all that it entails a shift of power from the central to the local level, it is a programme designed by central government itself. Paradoxically, the nature and extent of localism is a function of central government's preparedness to concede power to local authorities.

This goes to the heart of one of the main themes with which we are concerned in this book—that is, the extent to which governance in modern Britain is genuinely multilayered. The greater the extent to which central government intervenes in local government, the lower the degree of autonomy enjoyed by the latter, and the less it can lay claim to being a real counterweight to the power of the central bodies. If the diffusion of power—by means of constitutional arrangements under which authority and influence are shared rather than within the grasp of all-powerful central institutions—is the essence of multilayered governance, then local government clearly makes a contribution to this. But that contribution is constrained by the capacity and preparedness of central government to intervene in local government matters.

---

[82] Department for Communities and Local Government, *Strong and Prosperous Communities* (Cm 6939 2006), p 4. Ironically, however, the empowerment of *local people* involved the imposition of new policies on *local authorities* so as to guarantee individuals choice over such matters as childcare and housing. See Cm 6939, p 27.

[83] Local Audit and Accountability Act 2014.

[84] Stanton, 'Decentralisation and Empowerment under the Coalition Government: An Empirical Study of Local Councils in London' [2015] JPL 978, 991.

3.3.5 Regional governance: combined authorities

For all that the language of localism may not have matched the on-the-ground reality, it continues to exert a strong rhetorical pull on central government. However, the focus in recent years has begun to shift away from local authorities *per se* as the site of localism, and towards a regional tier of governance, albeit one that is built on local government. The foundations of this approach were put in place by the Local Democracy, Economic Development and Construction Act 2009, which makes provision for the creation of 'combined authorities'. Such authorities consist of two or more local authorities, the idea being that by working together enables issues that cross local authority boundaries to be addressed more effectively. A key plank of this policy is that combined authorities are able not only to work together in the exercise of existing local authority powers, but are able to exercise more extensive powers conferred upon—or 'devolved' to—them by central government.

Manchester has been in the vanguard in this area, the Greater Manchester Combined Authority (GMCA), which brings together ten local authorities, having been established in 2014. Under the 'deal' struck with central government, the GMCA was given (among other things) a devolved transport budget, strategic planning powers, control of a new £300m Housing Investment Fund, control of apprenticeship grants, and powers to reform further education provision across the GMCA area. More recently, Greater Manchester reached agreement with the UK government to 'devolve' £6bn of health and social care budgets.[85]

This process of devolving powers and budgets to combined authorities has recently been expanded by means of the Cities and Local Government Devolution Act 2016. Among other things, it provides for elected mayors for combined authority areas and extends the range of functions that can be conferred upon combined authorities. The Act also enables the Secretary of State to confer on elected mayors the functions of Police and Crime Commissioners for the combined authority area. Meanwhile, although the early focus was on devolution to 'city regions', non-urban local authorities are now actively joining the combined authorities programme. The net result, over time, will be a patchwork of combined authorities with elected mayors, supplying a mezzanine layer of government that sits between individual local authorities and central government.

3.3.6 Regional governance: analysis

It remains to be seen how things will progress in practice. However, there are several discordant notes and areas of concern. Four are particularly worth drawing attention to.

First, the rhetoric of localism notwithstanding, the making of devolution deals remains an essentially *top-down process*. The devolution deals and agreements must be negotiated with central government, and it is ultimately for the centre—in the form of the Treasury—to have the final say about the content of devolution deals. For

---

[85] HM Treasury and GMCA, *Further Devolution to the Greater Manchester Combined Authority and Directly-Elected Mayor* (London 2015).

instance, the UK government can—and in nearly all cases so far has—insisted that local authorities wishing to form combined authorities must accept an elected mayor as part of the deal.[86]

Second, there has been a notable *failure to engage with the public*, with 'devolution deals' instead being struck in private between central government and consortia of local authorities hoping to form combined authorities. The House of Commons Communities and Local Government Committee has flagged up 'a consistent very significant lack of public consultation, engagement and communication at all stages of the deal-making process', arguing that this sits in tension with the fact that '[f]or devolution to take root and fulfil its aims, it needs to involve and engage the people it is designed to benefit'.[87]

Third, the *new mayors* will be at the forefront of the new combined authorities. This raises two sets of issues. On the one hand, the government's keenness on mayors is not hard to fathom: it has been reluctant to cede powers and responsibilities without creating high-profile individuals who will have to carry the can when things go wrong. On the other hand, there are questions about whether mayors will be sufficiently locally accountable. Although mayors will be accountable to an overview and scrutiny committee within the new combined authorities, buried deep in the detail of the 2016 Act some limitations and centralising tendencies can be detected. For instance, overview and scrutiny committees only have the power to review and scrutinise decisions already taken—as opposed to future issues—while such committees can only recommend that a decision be reconsidered rather than block it altogether.[88] Central government also has influence over the committees, including in relation to membership, the chair, and what information must or must not be disclosed to the committees.[89] The Act also gives the Secretary of State a wide-ranging power to make provision about the governance arrangements of local authorities, including their constitution and membership.[90] The overall impression is that scrutiny may be impeded in practice and that combined authorities are not to be trusted to determine their own governance arrangements.

Fourth, the legal basis upon which regional devolution is being carried out is so *constitutionally fragile* as to call into question whether it really amounts to 'devolution'. In two key respects, the constitutional position in which combined authorities find themselves is unrecognisably different from that in which the national devolved institutions find themselves in Northern Ireland, Scotland, and Wales. In the first place, as we have already seen, the Scottish devolution legislation now includes provisions attesting to the permanence of the Scottish institutions. We have also seen that

[86] Section 107A of the Local Democracy, Economic Development and Construction Act 2009, as inserted by s 2 of the Cities and Local Government Devolution Act 2016, enables the Secretary of State to provide for there to be an elected mayor of a combined authority.

[87] House of Commons Communities and Local Government Committee, *Devolution: The Next Five Years and Beyond* (HC 369 2015–16), [53].

[88] Local Democracy, Economic Development and Construction Act 2009, Sch 5A, para 1, as inserted by the Cities and Local Government Devolution Act 2016, s 8 and Sch 3.

[89] Local Democracy, Economic Development and Construction Act 2009, Sch 5A, para 3.

[90] Cities and Local Government Devolution Act 2016, s 15.

the Welsh institutions now benefit from equivalent provisions. Although, as observed earlier in the chapter, these provisions may well not amount to cast-iron legal guarantees of the Scottish and Welsh institutions' permanence, their political-constitutional significance should not be underestimated. Combined authorities, of course, will not benefit from any statutory undertakings as to their permanence.

However, the extent of their constitutional fragility is not limited to that omission. The Cities and Local Government Devolution Act 2016[91] amounts to little more than enabling legislation that permits central government to make orders and statutory instruments creating bespoke arrangements for each combined authority. As a result, combined authorities' powers and governance arrangements are not actually set out in primary legislation, but only in secondary legislation—meaning that the government is able administratively to alter such authorities' governance structures and remove powers from them. This hardly provides combined authorities with a secure legal basis, and is once again testament to the centralising instincts of central government that yield a great reluctance to 'let go'.

3.4 England: taking stock

Whether a combination of 'English votes for English laws' in the UK Parliament and the creation of a mezzanine layer of government through the creation of combined authorities provides a satisfactory response to the English question (or questions) is a matter of perspective. Both solutions represent highly pragmatic responses that epitomise the approach to constitutional change adopted in the UK. EVEL seeks to address concerns about the representation of England within the wider UK by avoiding the undoubted difficulties and almost incalculable upheaval that would attend the creation of an English Parliament and Government. Instead, EVEL amounts to a typically makeshift type of constitutional reform that seeks to turn the UK Parliament into an institution that is also able to function, to a certain extent, as a de facto English legislature. And all of this is done by nothing more than amendments to the Standing Orders of the House of Commons. The making of what amounts to a very significant constitutional change in such a relatively informal and low-key way is a graphic illustration of the flexibility of the UK constitution.

The creation of combined authorities is a similarly pragmatic attempt to provide a measure of (what is at least termed) devolution within England. The irregular—one might say chaotic—governance landscape that will emerge from this process, as different combined authority areas acquire different amounts and types of power, is of a piece with the way in which devolution has been undertaken in respect of Northern Ireland, Scotland, and Wales. The result, in all its messiness, will be the very opposite of the sort of neatly designed constitution that is found in many other countries. Perhaps it is simply necessary to accept that this is the British way, and that any attempt to impose rigid and uniform governance structures would be doomed to failure. This does not, however, rule out the scope for legitimate concern. As the House of Lords

---

[91] Along with relevant parts of the Local Democracy, Economic Development and Construction Act 2009 that are inserted or amended by the 2016 Act.

Constitution Committee has noted, little consideration appears to have been given to how the envisaged multiplicity of 'devolution deals' will affect 'the overall governance of England in the longer-term'. Nor, it suggests, is there much evidence that the government has a clear 'vision of what it seeks to achieve with these reforms' or of where all of this will 'ultimately lead'.[92] As we will see in the next section, those concerns apply equally when consideration is given to the way in which the territorial constitution as a whole has been permitted to develop in recent years.

4. The nature and development of the territorial constitution

4.1 Introduction

We have seen so far in this chapter that the UK's territorial constitution has undergone highly significant changes over the last 20 or so years, thanks both to the introduction and development of devolution and, latterly, attempts to tackle the 'English question'. Our focus now shifts to the future prospects for the territorial constitution.

4.2 A federal UK?

Many constitutional systems around the world can fairly be described as federal in nature, and yet they differ in significant respects. Bearing that caveat in mind, we begin this section by taking the USA as an example of a federal system. The USA consists of 50 states, each with its own legislature and administration. Certain matters, however, are dealt with on a national level by the federal legislature—Congress—and the US administration headed by the President. On the basis of this brief description, federalism in the USA may seem similar to devolution in the UK. However, any similarity is only skin deep: there are three crucial differences.

First, the UK's system is, as we already know, *asymmetrical*: different parts of the UK have different amounts and types of devolved power. As a result, the UK Parliament and government's involvement differs across the country: they do far more in relation to England, for instance, than in respect of Scotland. In the USA, all states possess the same legal powers as one another. As a result, the federal government exercises the same degree of power in relation to all 50 states.

Second, the US federal system emerged from a *bottom-up* approach. The USA was formed by individual states deciding to join together in order that certain matters could be dealt with collectively by a federal government. Power thus originated at state level and was transmitted to the federal level only to a limited degree and along uniformly agreed lines, thus producing a symmetrical distribution of powers.[93] In contrast, devolution in the UK is a *top-down* system: the UK Parliament is legally sovereign, but has chosen to confer limited powers on the new devolved governments. And those

---

[92] House of Lords Constitution Committee, *The Union and Devolution* (HL Paper 149 2015–16), [406].

[93] An analogy may be drawn with the relationship between the EU and its member states: see Chapter 8.

conferrals of power were effected not on the basis of a single set of negotiated principles as to how the line should be drawn between central and devolved government, but in light of the differing histories, attitudes, and politics of the UK's constituent nations.

Third, UK devolution and US federalism enjoy different degrees of *constitutional security*. In the USA, the balance of power between federal and state levels is set by the Constitution—and the Constitution can be changed only by going through a procedure that requires (among other things) approval by 75 per cent of the states.[94] The balance of power therefore enjoys a high degree of security: changes are difficult to effect because they require a very wide consensus. In contrast, devolution in the UK was effected by passing Acts of Parliament—and it is always open to Parliament to amend its own enactments. The UK's devolution arrangements thus enjoy no legal security as a matter of strict law. However, this analysis is subject to two important qualifications. The first is that however much those arrangements might lack legal security, they benefit from considerable political security: it would be a brave, and extremely foolish, UK Parliament that attempted unilaterally to undermine or abolish devolution. The further qualification is that the UK Parliament has recently legislated so as to give some of the devolution arrangements at least the appearance of legal security.

We examine those matters in the next section. First, however, we make a final point about federalism. The UK's territorial arrangements do not currently conform to a federal model. The question arises, however, whether the UK is—or should be—moving in a federal direction. There might be advantages in doing so. For instance, a federalised UK constitution might better be able to accommodate constituent nations' desires for (at least) a high degree of autonomy within the UK through a more secure constitutional settlement. Such a constitution would also be neater, in the sense that all four nations would be in equivalent positions in respect of one another and in respect of the federal tier of government. Indeed, the cross-party Constitutional Reform Group has argued that the UK risks disintegration—especially following the Brexit vote—unless there is a new constitutional settlement guaranteeing the rights and autonomy of each constituent nation and region within a reformed UK under a new Act of Union.[95] On this view, to preserve and enhance the Union, the UK's governance arrangements must change radically, including by embracing federalism. The Group therefore proposes that each part of the UK would have full sovereignty over its own affairs. England, Scotland, Wales, and Northern Ireland would be separate units, free to deal with their own affairs to the extent that they desired, but also able to share functions they considered better discharged at a UK level. The Westminster Parliament would be reduced to 146 MPs, its role being to legislate in areas of pooled sovereignty such as common defence and security matters.

This would be a seismic change. And whatever its attractions might be, the neatness of a federal solution would itself come at a price. There are reasons why the present system is as messy as it is. And while some of those reasons might reduce to little more than historical happenstance, others are more deep-seated. In particular,

---

[94] US Constitution, Art 5.   [95] See **http://www.constitutionreformgroup.co.uk/**

confronting the prospect of a federal UK would require questions about England to be tackled head-on in a way that would go far beyond the steps that have been taken so far.[96] It would also require constitutional reform at the most fundamental level, not least because the doctrine of parliamentary sovereignty is flatly incompatible with a federal model in which power is held in balance as between federal and second-tier institutions, rather than emanating from a single, all-powerful national institution. Nor is it clear that a federal model can readily be applied to a state, one of whose territorial units—England—is so dominant in terms of population and economic power. Yet it would be naive entirely to rule out the possibility of a federal UK, both because of the pressures operating on the constitution that have been discussed in this chapter and as a result of the constitutional shock delivered to the UK by the outcome of the referendum on EU membership. The UK constitution finds itself today in a state whose fluidity is unusual, even for a constitution whose flexibility is its best-known characteristic. That said, however, the path to a fully federal UK would be far from simple, and it is certainly not something that appears to be immediately in prospect.

Q Do you favour a shift to a federal system in the UK? Would the sort of 'big bang' reform that the adoption of such a model would involve be preferable to the type of piecemeal, ongoing constitutional change to which the UK's constitutional arrangements are presently subject?

4.3 The territorial constitution: a legal or a political phenomenon?

4.3.1 Constitutional convention

The emergence and development of devolution is the paradigm example of the modern UK constitution's tiered character. In that sense, this chapter is concerned throughout with our key theme relating to the multilayered nature of the constitution. However, this intersects in important respects with another of our key themes— namely, the relationship between political and legal modes of constitutionalism, and the extent to which the direction of travel is towards the latter. We saw in the previous section that the UK's territorial constitution cannot currently be characterised as straightforwardly federal. But we also noted that federalism is a relatively broad concept, in that a range of constitutional arrangements fall under its umbrella. Whether a constitution is federal in nature is thus not a binary question, but a question of degree. And if one of the characteristics of federalism is that (what are in British vernacular) devolved institutions enjoy a degree of constitutional security, the extent to which the UK's constitution has become federalised turns on the extent of the constitutional security with which devolution is invested.

The degree of legal security enjoyed by the states in the USA is clearly high, and sits in contrast with the situation in which Scotland, Wales, and Northern Ireland have found themselves —at least until very recently—in the UK. However, the fact that, as a

---

[96] See section 3.

matter of strict law, the UK Parliament can unilaterally abolish or radically change the devolution settlements is only part of the story. Indeed, in the absence of exceptional circumstances, it would be nigh on impossible for it to do either. Here, then, we encounter a familiar characteristic of the UK constitution as a political constitution—that is, the disjunction between the positions prescribed by legal theory, on the one hand, and real-world politics, on the other. It is often the case that the gap between these two positions is bridged by constitutional convention, and devolution is no exception.

It was recognised in the early days of devolution that it would be wholly contrary to the spirit of the new constitutional arrangements if the UK Parliament were to interfere unilaterally in devolved matters. It thus quickly came to be accepted that the UK Parliament should not normally legislate on devolved matters *unless the relevant devolved legislature consents*. Thus a *political* agreement—a constitutional convention, known as the 'Sewel Convention'[97]—emerged, regulating the exercise of the Westminster Parliament's *legal* sovereignty and rendering its practice consistent with the spirit of devolution.

Indeed, convention is important not only as regards the relationship between Westminster and the devolved legislatures, but also in relation to how the various administrations relate to one another. Devolution has radically changed the UK system of government by creating new seats of political and administrative authority in Edinburgh, Cardiff, and Belfast, all of which must relate to the UK government and, to some extent, one another. It might therefore seem surprising that, as Rawlings has noted, 'almost nothing is said in the [devolution] legislation about the structures and processes of intergovernmental relations', thus creating a 'vast constitutional space'.[98] In the absence of law, that vacuum has been filled by 'concordats', which are best thought of as instant conventions: whereas conventions traditionally emerge implicitly through long practice, concordats are explicit, but legally non-binding, agreements entered into between political institutions.[99] A multilateral concordat known as the Memorandum of Understanding[100] sets out in general terms how the UK and devolved governments should relate to one another, while myriad bilateral concordats lay down the ground rules for relationships between particular central and devolved government departments. This heavy reliance on extra-legal agreements further illustrates the political dimension of the UK constitution generally, and its devolution settlement in particular.

4.3.2 Law

Although the UK's new territorial constitution has foundations that are, as explained in the previous section, significantly political in nature, that is not to deny that there

---

[97] So-called because it was first proposed by Lord Sewel: see HL Deb, vol 592, col 791 (21 July 1998). He made this suggestion during the committee stage of the Scotland Bill, but the UK government accepts that the same principle applies when Westminster contemplates legislating on matters over which *any* devolved legislature has competence: Cabinet Office, *Devolution: Memorandum of Understanding and Supplementary Agreements* (London 2013), [14].

[98] Rawlings, 'Concordats of the Constitution' (2000) 116 LQR 257, 258–9.

[99] Purists might argue that conventions, by definition, cannot be instantly created. For discussion, see Jaconelli, 'The Nature of Constitutional Convention' (1999) 19 LS 24.

[100] Office of the Deputy Prime Minister, Cm 5240.

is also a substantial legal dimension. Indeed, the devolution legislation amounts to a complex legal code setting out in often painstaking detail the powers—and the limits of the powers—of the devolved institutions. Moreover, the courts have a role in enforcing such limits. The devolution legislation makes special provision for judicial resolution of 'devolution issues'—that is, issues as to whether devolved bodies are acting or proposing to act beyond their legal competence—with final appeals on such matters ultimately lying to the Supreme Court.[101] Such questions may arise in the course of normal litigation,[102] can be the subject of judicial review challenges to the legality of devolved legislation,[103] or can be referred to the courts by the Attorney-General.[104]

Recently, however, the legal dimension of the territorial constitution has been augmented. Whereas it has always been the case that devolution settlements set out legal, judicially enforceable limits upon the powers of the devolved institutions, it has, at least until recently, been axiomatic that there are no corresponding limits upon the powers of the UK Parliament. In this respect, devolution is lopsided in a way that federalism is not, because the 'central legislature'—that is, the UK Parliament—has, as a matter of law, held all the cards. However, the Scotland Act 2016 changed—or at least appeared to change—this position in ways that we examine in the next two sections.[105]

4.3.3 Legislation on devolved matters

The Scotland Act 1998 already provided—and continues to provide—that the conferral of powers on the Scottish Parliament 'does not affect the power of the Parliament of the United Kingdom to make laws for Scotland'.[106] However, thanks to a provision inserted by the 2016 Act, the 1998 Act now goes on to say that 'it is recognised that the Parliament of the United Kingdom will not normally legislate with regard to devolved matters without the consent of the Scottish Parliament'.[107] This language, of course, reflects that of the Sewel Convention. However, to assume that this new legislation turns the Convention into a legal restraint on Westminster's would be rash.

For one thing, the legislation in fact refers only to part of the convention. Although the convention was originally understood—and continues in some places to be defined[108]—as applying only to Westminster legislation on matters that are within Scotland's devolved competence, a broader understanding of the convention has in fact emerged. On that understanding, the convention also applies to Westminster legislation that adjusts the scope of devolved competence. This limb of the convention

---

[101] See Scotland Act 1998, Sch 6; Government of Wales Act 2006, Sch 9; Northern Ireland Act 1998, Sch 10 (as amended by Constitutional Reform Act 2005, Sch 9, Pt 2).

[102] eg *Salvesen v Riddell* [2013] UKSC 22, 2013 SC (UKSC) 236.

[103] eg *The Christian Institute v The Lord Advocate* [2016] UKSC 51, 2016 SLT 805.

[104] eg *Attorney-General v National Assembly for Wales Commission* [2012] UKSC 53, [2013] 1 AC 792.

[105] Section A1 of the Government of Wales Act 2006, which was inserted by s 1 of the Wales Act 2017, now makes equivalent provision in respect of Wales. However, for purposes of concision, we refer only to Scotland in the text.

[106] Scotland Act 1998, s 28(7).

[107] Scotland Act 1998, s 28(8) (as inserted by Scotland Act 2016, s 2).

[108] See, eg Cabinet Office, *The Cabinet Manual* (London 2011), [8.5]; *Devolution: Memorandum of Understanding and Supplementary Agreements* (London 2013), [14].

would apply to devolution legislation enacted by Westminster in order to expand (or narrow) the scope of the powers of the Scottish Parliament or Government. However, while the UK government has accepted that the Sewel Convention now has this second limb,[109] it is not explicitly reflected in the legislation. At most, therefore, the legislation might be thought to give some form of legal effect to *part* of the convention.

However, it is far from clear that the legislation gives legal effect to *any* part of the convention. All that the Act says is that it is *recognised* that Westminster will not *normally* legislate on devolved matters without the Scottish Parliament's agreement. It follows, then, that even if it were possible for the UK Parliament to limit its own power, it has not unambiguously sought to do so. The legislation does not say that Westminster *cannot* or *will not* legislate on devolved matters absent Scottish consent. Nor does the legislation say that the Sewel Convention has *legal force*. Rather, the legislation amounts to a statement—albeit in a legal text—of the UK Parliament's acknowledgement of the existence of a conventional restraint upon its own power. However, the restraint remains just that: one that is based in convention, and which therefore has no legal force.

In the light of this, the better view is that—perhaps paradoxically—the significance of the 2016 Act's legislative acknowledgement of (part of) the Sewel Convention is political rather than legal. The legislation, by formally recognising the convention in legislation, explicitly makes the UK Parliament a party to the convention, in a way that likely exacerbates the political difficulties that would attend any attempt to legislate without consent. This does not mean that it would invariably be politically impossible to do so—after all, the convention and the Act say that Westminster will not *normally* do that—but the legislation undoubtedly makes it harder for the UK Parliament to legislate on devolved matters without the Scottish Parliament's agreement. In this way, the 2016 Act leverages the relationship between legal and political constitutionalism in a subtle but important way, in that *law*, in the form of legislation, is used to contribute to the augmentation of both the *political* restraints upon the UK Parliament and (hence) the *constitutional* security of the devolution settlements.

4.3.4 Continued existence of the devolved institutions

The 2016 Act inserts a new provision in the Scotland Act 1998 which provides that: 'The Scottish Parliament and the Scottish Government are a permanent part of the United Kingdom's constitutional arrangements.'[110] That rather bald statement is then qualified in two distinct ways. First, the new provision explains why the statement was made in the first place, saying that its purpose is 'to signify the commitment of the Parliament and Government of the United Kingdom to the Scottish Parliament and the Scottish Government'.[111] (That explanation is itself qualified, since it says that 'due regard' must be had to 'the other provisions' of the Scotland Act 1998—one of which, as we saw earlier, reasserts that the UK Parliament has renounced no legislative

---

[109] Department for Constitutional Affairs, *Devolution Guidance Note 10: Post-Devolution Primary Legislation Affecting Scotland* (DGN 10 2005), [4], [6].

[110] Scotland Act 1998, s 63A(1) (as inserted by Scotland Act 2016, s 1) The Wales Act 2017 makes equivalent provision.

[111] Scotland Act 1998, s 63A(2) (as inserted by Scotland Act 2016, s 1).

power.) Second, the 'commitment' as to permanence is accompanied by what is styled a 'declaration' to the effect that the Scottish institutions 'are not to be abolished except on the basis of a decision of the people of Scotland voting in a referendum'.[112] The obvious question raised by these provisions is whether they legally disable Westminster from abolishing the Scottish institutions absent the consent of the Scottish people expressed via a referendum. There are two reasons why we might be doubtful about this.

First, the 'permanence' provisions are framed in terms that do not unambiguously demonstrate that the UK Parliament intended to restrict its own legal powers. That follows partly because, we are told, the purpose of the provisions is merely to 'signify' the UK Parliament and government's 'commitment' to the Scottish institutions. Leaving to one side the difficulty of treating legislation enacted by *Parliament* as evidence of the *government's* position, it is plain from this wording that the provisions' purposes do not explicitly extend to disabling the UK Parliament from abolishing the Scottish institutions. It is also worth noting that nowhere in the 'permanence' provisions is it said that the UK Parliament *cannot* abolish the Scottish institutions absent support for such action in a referendum. Rather, it is merely 'declared' that they 'are not' to be abolished without such support. When it makes rules, Parliament does not normally 'declare' that something is or is not to happen; it usually simply states what the legal position is. This creates room for doubt about whether these provisions actually go so far as to seek to impose a legal restriction on the UK Parliament.

Second, even if that were the 'permanence' provisions' aim, that would raise the further question: can Parliament actually impose such limits upon itself? The 'permanence' provisions could be examined by reference to the 'manner and form' view that we considered in Chapter 5. On this analysis, we would understand support expressed through a referendum to be a condition precedent to the enactment of UK legislation abolishing the Scottish institutions. However, we saw in Chapter 5 that it is not certain whether such conditions, if Parliament seeks to impose them, will actually bind it. It is certainly not clearly established that such conditions, if unfulfilled, would invalidate legislation enacted in breach of them, although, as we noted in Chapter 5, there is some limited support for the imposition of such binding restrictions in the *Jackson* case.[113] Even so, the further question would arise whether the provisions setting out the referendum requirement could themselves be repealed without a referendum—a question to which the answer, again, is unclear.[114]

The upshot is that it cannot be said with confidence that the 'permanence' provisions legally change the position of the Scottish institutions by precluding their abolition absent support in a referendum. What, then, is the effect of the new provisions? It might be thought that—like the provisions concerning the Sewel Convention—they contribute to the political restraints that operate upon Westminster, by making

---

[112] Scotland Act 1998, s 63A(3) (as inserted by Scotland Act 2016, s 1).

[113] *R (Jackson) v Attorney-General* [2005] UKHL 56, [2006] 1 AC 262.

[114] There is nothing on the face of the 2016 Act provisions restricting the UK Parliament's power to repeal them. It might, however, be argued—in line with reasoning endorsed by most of the Law Lords in *Jackson*—that the express limitation (if that is what it is) in the 2016 Act provisions gives rise to some form of implied limitation on the repeal of the provision concerning the referendum requirement.

it more difficult, politically, for it to abolish the Scottish institutions without first securing the consent of the Scottish people. However, the prospect of Westminster attempting to do that is, in any event, vanishingly small. For the UK Parliament to abolish the Scottish Government and Parliament against the wishes of the people of Scotland would, in all presently conceivable circumstances, trigger the break-up of the UK. The political disincentive to unilateral abolition by Westminster of the Scottish institutions was therefore already so overwhelmingly strong that it is hard to see what the 'permanence' provisions could add in this respect.

Their contribution might therefore be best thought of as a symbolic token of good faith on the part of the UK Parliament. So characterising the 'permanence' provisions is not, however, to suggest that they are irrelevant. Symbolism can be important; and, in this context, it is. If nothing else, the 'permanence' provisions illuminate just how far the narrative has moved on from the idea that devolution amounts to nothing more than a revocable—and so potentially transitory—sharing by Westminster of part of its lawmaking power. That, in turn, serves to underline the fact that the political and constitutional reality of the modern territorial constitution is that power has been dispersed across the UK in ways that are, in all relevant practical senses, irreversible.

4.4 The viability and future of the Union

Ever since it got under way, nearly 20 years ago, devolution has driven the development of, and has fundamentally reshaped, the territorial constitution. During that time, a great deal of the focus in this area has been, perhaps understandably, on devolution itself—a tendency that has perhaps resulted in insufficient attention being paid to the Union: that is, to the aspects of the constitution that are concerned with the bonds between the UK's constituent nations, and with the UK tier of governance that coexists with the new devolved governments. One concern—at least from the perspective of those who wish the UK to continue as a single state—is that devolution might exert such strong centrifugal forces as to make the Union unviable, thus making inevitable its eventual disintegration. The question then becomes whether the UK's constitutional arrangements exert countervailing centripetal forces that are sufficient to hold the Union together. This is not to suggest that the Union and the devolved nations should be perceived as sitting in tension, or in competition, with one another. Rather, the question is about striking a balance between the different forces that are acting on the Union so as to enable the UK to remain a viable state whilst enabling its constituent nations to enjoy the benefits that flow from significant devolution of power.

These questions were addressed by the House of Lords Constitution Committee in a major report published in 2016.[115] The Committee argued that the Union, in terms of the ties that bind it together and the benefits it brings, can be grouped under five headings: 'economic', 'social', 'political', 'cultural', and 'security and defence'. It

---

[115] House of Lords Constitution Committee, *The Union and Devolution* (HL Paper 149 2015–16).

said, however, that the Union was 'under threat', that the UK government needed 'fundamentally to reassess how it approaches issues relating to devolution', and that successive UK governments have been guilty of an 'inattentive approach to the integrity of the Union'. A fundamental difficulty identified by the Committee was the tendency of power to be devolved to Northern Ireland, Scotland, and Wales in what it called 'an *ad hoc*, piecemeal fashion'. This, it said, showed that the UK government had 'taken the Union for granted' and had failed properly to consider the 'cumulative impact' of devolution on the integrity of the Union. In effect, the Committee concluded that there had been a fundamental failure to address the balance between the centrifugal and centripetal forces acting upon the Union, that the former were being allowed to predominate unchecked, and that this posed an existential risk to the UK as a State. The Committee said that a renewed focus should be placed on the Union itself, and that steps should be taken to identify the core functions that must remain at a UK level. The devolution of any additional powers, it concluded, should be viewed in the light of those considerations, with powers being devolved only to the extent that that would be compatible with the ongoing viability of the Union itself.

Whether the UK government will adopt a more Union-focused approach to devolution in the future remains to be seen. It is certainly the case that the closeness of the Scottish independence referendum in 2014 delivered a shock to the UK's political class, while the dominance of the Scottish National Party—which won nearly all of the Westminster seats in Scotland in the 2015 general election—has served to underline the fracturing of the UK political system. Against that background, the need to balance considerations of devolution and Union seems obvious, but the Constitution Committee's call for a more thoughtful, systematic, and holistic approach in this area may well go unheeded, not least because it is fundamentally at odds with the casual, disjointed way in which constitutional reform is typically undertaken in the UK.

5. Conclusions

Governance in the UK is significantly, and increasingly, multilayered. The idea of the UK as a unitary state governed from the centre is an increasingly inaccurate one. Although, as a matter of orthodox constitutional theory, most governmental power continues to emanate from, and can be recovered by, the UK Parliament, this sort of one-dimensional account of the constitution, founded on the doctrine of legislative supremacy, is becoming less and less sustainable. Our new constitutional reality is one in which the UK-tier authorities are part of a network of institutions of government, operating at local, regional, devolved, and state levels. And the assumption that the UK tier holds the trump card thanks to the sovereignty of the Westminster Parliament is increasingly misplaced as other seats of government become politically embedded aspects of our constitutional architecture. As the idea that governmental power is genuinely diffused among different institutions grows to be the new orthodoxy, so the notion of multilayered governance—of power shared by bodies with different roles and operating at different levels—takes root.

However, while it is important to recognise the changing dynamics within our constitution, they must not be exaggerated. The essence of truly multilayered governance is a situation in which all power does not reside at, or emanate from, the centre because other institutions exist that enjoy a legitimacy and a status that lend them a degree of permanence, thus giving rise to a genuinely pluralist constitution. The extent to which the different layers of governance in the UK have achieved such standing is debatable—and variable. For example, the strength of feeling in favour of devolution and public attachment to, and identification with, the devolved institutions in the devolved nations—perhaps most notably Scotland—makes them secure features of the UK constitution. And that makes them a true example of the constitution's multilayered nature—at least for as long as Scotland remains part of the Union. The constitutional (if not strict legal) security of devolution in Scotland and Wales is now further underlined by statutory provision as to the permanence of those nations' devolved institutions. In contrast, local government, including in its new, regional incarnation, generally finds itself in a more fragile position for reasons that we have explored.

The story of our multilayered constitution is therefore an uneven one, but it is also far from complete. The territorial constitution remains a work in progress. Indeed, constitutional change in this area is simply the norm. To the extent that that demonstrates the UK constitution's responsiveness to citizens' wishes, and to the heterogeneity of those wishes as they exist across and within the four constituent nations of the UK, such ongoing change might be considered a good thing. There is, however, a risk that the constant shifting of the pieces of the constitutional jigsaw obscure our view of the bigger picture, diverting attention from the overarching constitutional features that are necessary to hold the pieces together. At a time when the UK's constituent parts are perhaps more politically disparate than ever before, the importance of examining that bigger picture cannot be overstated.

Expert commentary
Devolution in historical and political context
Stephen Tierney, Professor of Constitutional Theory, University of Edinburgh

Devolution in the United Kingdom needs to be understood in light of two historical processes: the gradual formation of the state, and the more recent rise in sub-state nationalism. The UK as a state grew out of a series of unions. Indeed, we might think of the UK as a union state or a 'state of unions', with the four countries of the union retaining their own national culture (or 'cultures' in the case of Northern Ireland) within a larger UK nation. One consequence of this complexity is that we should not expect a constitutional 'settlement'. The territorial (or 'multilayered') constitution has been evolving since the latter part of the nineteenth century. It will continue to develop over time in response to the different constitutional aspirations of the UK's constituent peoples.

Since the 1960s, there has been a nationalist revival in Scotland and Wales. Notably the UK is not alone among Western democracies in experiencing pressure for self-government from its internal nations and regions. Similar assertions of 'nationhood' have been made by Quebec within Canada, Catalonia and the Basque Country within Spain, and Flanders within Belgium. Moves towards constitutional decentralisation have also been a feature of constitutional change in France and Italy. It is perhaps a paradox of the past half century that, just as European countries have been coming together through an integrating European Union, many of the EU's member states have also been decentralising through devolved government.

The UK experience in recent decades has been particularly complex for two main reasons. First, the very different histories of England, Wales, Scotland, and Northern Ireland have resulted in highly varied constitutional aspirations. England, the largest nation and hence the most influential, has until recently been content with a unitary United Kingdom. Wales, which is smaller than Scotland and enjoys a greater population flow with England, has tended to advance quite modest devolution aspirations. Scotland joined with England at a later date than Wales, and the maintenance of the civic institutions which were already in place by 1707 is one reason why Scottish nationalists have in recent times sought a stronger form of self-government. Northern Ireland is the most complicated case of all; the history of conflict there requiring a carefully tailored and very specific set of constitutional arrangements.

A second reason why UK devolution is so complex is that constitutional change to the territorial constitution since 1997 has taken place within the UK's uncodified or 'unwritten' constitution. Unlike most other countries, constitutional change in the UK can be effected simply by way of Act of Parliament. This has had three important consequences.

The first is constitutional flexibility. A series of devolution statutes in relation to Scotland, Wales, and Northern Ireland have each brought about significant constitutional change often quickly and with little national debate. A second consequence of the unwritten constitutional context is that it has helped create a picture of devolution as a never-ending process. In countries with a complicated amendment process, constitutional change is often a landmark event, occurring infrequently and only at high profile 'constitutional moments'. But in the UK, constitutional change is easily undertaken. The UK government and Parliament have frequently been tempted to respond to demands for further change, often for short-term political reasons. Much of this has been a consequence of vociferous Scottish nationalism. A knock-on consequence has been an attitude among Welsh nationalists that Wales should then get further powers in light of Scottish developments.

A third feature is that devolution was introduced (and subsequently developed) for each of Scotland, Wales, and Northern Ireland by way of separate processes and pieces of legislation. This has resulted in a system that is highly 'asymmetrical'. Although this has made the system very complex, overall it is a positive feature of devolution, reflecting societal and political differences across the UK. To take a recent example, although Welsh nationalists often look with envy at the Scottish model, and although one goal of the Wales Act 2017 is to give Wales a model of devolution similar to that of Scotland, substantial differences will still remain, reflecting the very different models of devolution created in 1998.

Although devolution has been responsive to demands, there are now significant concerns that the very ad hoc approach to constitutional change has left the territorial constitution incoherent, imbalanced, and potentially unmanageable. A key problem is the lack of principled or even strategic thinking. An example is the way in which the government reacted to the Scottish independence referendum of 2014. The extensive powers which were devolved in the Scotland Act 2016 were a consequence of a promise or 'vow' made just before the referendum in order to encourage voters to reject independence. This exemplifies a broader lack of direction. Further powers have been extended to the devolved territories without any attempt to coordinate the decentralisation of power in the interest of a stable, workable union. Far from stabilising the constitution, such radical change can unsettle our system of government.

Another deficit is that the trajectory of devolution has all been about hollowing power out of London to Edinburgh, Cardiff, and Belfast. What has been particularly lacking is any attempt to involve the devolved territories more closely in the running of the central state. Unlike a federal system, devolution has been about 'self-rule' for the regions, and not about 'shared rule' at the centre. Arguably, the latter aspect of the constitution should be developed to help foster closer bonds between the citizens of Scotland, Wales, and Northern Ireland and the UK state.

Another major lacuna has been the relative neglect of England in the whole process. The extension of more and more powers to Scotland and Wales has led to a growth in English nationalism and a growing disaffection within England towards the entire devolution project from which English citizens feel so excluded. It remains unclear whether constitutional solutions such as 'English votes for English laws' and the transfer of powers to English cities and regions will do anything to assuage these grievances.

The future is therefore unclear. A major factor now is the Brexit process. There are calls for the devolved territories to be closely involved in the negotiations, and inevitably there will be demands for many of the powers being recalled from Brussels to be devolved to Scotland, Wales, and Northern Ireland. There has even been the suggestion by the SNP Scottish Government of another Scottish independence referendum, depending upon the outcome of the Brexit process. It is difficult to make predictions about the nature of the territorial constitution, except to say that its further evolution is inevitable.

Further reading

BAILEY and ELLIOTT, 'Taking Local Government Seriously: Democracy, Autonomy and the Constitution' [2009] CLJ 436

An analysis of the constitutional position of local government.

BOGDANOR *The New British Constitution* (Oxford 2009), chs 4 and 10

These chapters examine devolution and localism as components of the contemporary UK constitution.

HOUSE OF LORDS CONSTITUTION COMMITTEE, *The Union and Devolution* (HL Paper 149 2015–16) (**http://www.publications.parliament.uk/pa/ld201516/ldselect/ldconst/149/149.pdf**)

A major report examining the implications of devolution in Scotland, Wales, and Northern Ireland, and of the introduction of regional government in England, for the viability of the UK as a single state.

JOWELL, OLIVER, and O'CINNEIDE (eds), *The Changing Constitution* (Oxford 2015), chs 9 (Dickson) and 10 (Leigh)

Discussion of devolution and local government.

MCKAY COMMISSION, *Report of the Commission on the Consequences of Devolution for the House of Commons* (**http://webarchive.nationalarchives.gov.uk/20130403030652/http://tmc.independent.gov.uk/wp-content/uploads/2013/03/The-McKay-Commission_Main-Report_25-March-20131.pdf**)

Proposals for tackling the West Lothian question; while these proposals were not precisely adopted when the 'English votes for English laws' arrangements were introduced in 2015, the McKay report contains a wealth of useful background material.

Useful websites

http://www.scottish.parliament.uk
http://www.gov.scot
Websites of the Scottish Parliament and the Scottish Executive

http://www.niassembly.gov.uk
http://www.northernireland.gov.uk
Websites of the Northern Ireland Assembly and the Northern Ireland Executive

http://www.assemblywales.org
http://www.wales.gov.uk
Websites of the Welsh Assembly and the Welsh Assembly Government

http://www.local.gov.uk
Website of the Local Government Association

8

The European Union and Brexit

1. Introduction	336
2. The EU in context	340
3. EU law and national law	347
4. The supremacy of EU law and UK parliamentary sovereignty	359
5. Conclusions	374
Expert commentary	375
Further reading	377
Useful websltes	377

1. Introduction

1.1 'Brexit'

The term 'Brexit'—an abbreviation of 'British exit'—refers to the UK's withdrawal from the European Union.[1] It is a term that had barely been coined when the last edition of this book was published in 2014. Today, however, Brexit dominates political discourse, and is likely to do so for many years to come.

On 1 January 1973, the United Kingdom became a member of the European Economic Community—what is now the European Union (EU). Just over 43 years later, on 23 June 2016, a slim but clear majority of those who participated in the referendum on EU membership voted that the UK should leave. Figure 8.1 shows the outcome of the referendum in the UK as a whole and its constituent parts. Table 8.1 shows the detailed referendum results while Figure 8.2 shows a map of the results.

The referendum campaign was both passionate and divisive, and the result, unexpected by many, sent political and economic shockwaves around the globe. It was

---

[1] The term is technically incorrect: the United Kingdom, rather than Britain, is the member state of the EU that will be leaving.

Table 8.1 Results of the UK's referendum on membership of the European Union, 23 June 2016

	Leave votes	Remain votes	Leave vote (%)	Remain Vote (%)	Turnout (%)
United Kingdom	17,410,742	16,141,241	51.9	48.1	72.2
England	15,188,406	13,266,996	53.4	46.6	73.0
Scotland	1,018,322	1,661,191	38.0	62.0	67.2
Wales	854,572	772,347	52.5	47.5	71.7
Northern Ireland	349,442	440,437	44.2	55.8	62.9

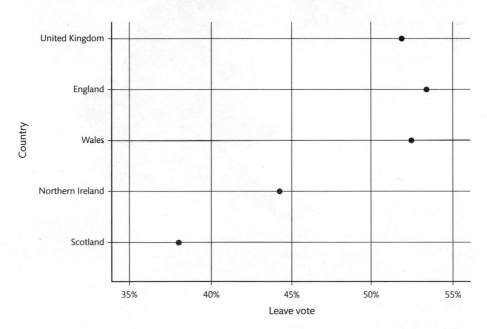

Figure 8.1 Outcome of the UK's referendum on membership of the European Union held on 23 June 2016

Note: Voter turnout was 72.2%. The remain vote won over 50% of the vote in three electoral regions: Scotland, Northern Ireland, and London.

a defining political event the implications of which will be felt for generations to come—most obviously in the UK, but also in the EU and beyond.

Just why a majority of people voted for Brexit is a complex and controversial issue,[2] but some key points should be noted:

[2] See 'Eight reasons Leave won the UK's referendum on the EU', *BBC News*, 24 June 2016, **http://www.bbc.co.uk/news/uk-politics-eu-referendum-36574526**

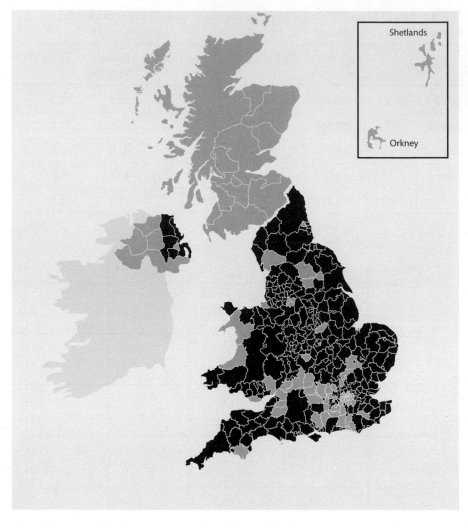

Key:
- ■ Majority leave
- ▨ Majority remain

Figure 8.2 Map of the results of the UK's referendum on membership of the European Union, 23 June 2016

- The UK's membership of the EU has long been a running sore in British politics. In particular, the Conservative Party has been split on the issue for many years. In holding a referendum, the then Prime Minister, David Cameron, sought to settle the issue—a strategy that spectacularly backfired.

- The referendum results revealed that different parts of the UK see their place in relation to Europe differently. Majorities in England and Wales voted Leave; majorities in Scotland and Northern Ireland voted Remain.

- Many voters were aware that, unlike ordinary general elections under the first-past-the post voting system, their votes would count directly and that everyone's votes would be of equal weight. This prompted an increase in voter registration and a high voter turnout.

- Some issues relevant to EU membership assumed great prominence during the referendum campaign—immigration in particular.

- The referendum highlighted deep divisions within British society.[3] The poorest households, with incomes of less than £20,000 per year, were much more likely to support leaving the EU than the wealthiest households—as were the unemployed and people in low-skilled and manual occupations. Those who have been 'left behind' by rapid economic change and feel cut adrift from the mainstream consensus were more likely to support Brexit. The referendum was thus not simply about the UK's relationship with the EU; it also concerned the very nature of, and divisions within, the UK itself.

At the time of writing, little is known about what 'Brexit' will look like. One possibility is 'hard Brexit', involving an end to the free movement of people, departure from the EU single market, and a drift away from cooperation with the rest of Europe. 'Soft Brexit' could involve the UK retaining its membership of the single market, maintaining the free movement of people and continued cooperation with Europe on security and terrorism issues. The precise nature of Brexit is likely to take some time to determine. Indeed, while the referendum resolved one question—whether the UK should leave the EU—it raised an enormous number of further questions about the form that 'Brexit' should take. Given these uncertainties, this chapter proceeds on the basis that the UK is still a member of the EU, and that EU law therefore continues to operate, and produce significant constitutional effects, in the UK. However, the likely constitutional implications of Brexit are taken into account throughout, and the constitutional legacy that EU membership will bequeath post-Brexit is assessed.

1.2 **The EU and the constitution**

The EU is an unusual—and in many ways unique—organisation. Its member states have each entered into agreements—Treaties—that bind them in international law to work together in the pursuit of a number of objectives. An illustrative selection of those objectives, drawn from Art 3 of the Treaty on European Union, are as follows.

---

[3] Joseph Rowntree Trust, *Brexit Vote Explained: Poverty, Low Skills and Lack of Opportunities* (2016), **https://www.jrf.org.uk/report/brexit-vote-explained-poverty-low-skills-and-lack-opportunities**

Eg

- The promotion of peace and well-being
- Sustainable development
- Economic growth
- Full employment
- Social progress
- Environmental protection
- Social justice
- Equality
- The safeguarding of Europe's cultural heritage
- Economic and monetary union, including a single currency
- In its relations with the rest of the world, free and fair trade, eradication of poverty, and protection of human rights

The Treaties also establish institutions—including a court, a legislature, and an executive branch—that in some respects make the EU look more like a state than an international organisation, and which ensure that the lofty aims spelt out in the Treaties can be pursued in meaningful, concrete ways.

The implications—for as long as they persist—of the UK's EU membership engage all three of the key themes of this book:

- EU membership has contributed to *the multilayered nature of the UK constitution*. By joining the EU, the UK transferred a significant amount of power, including considerable lawmaking power, to external institutions, giving rise to fundamental questions about how those institutions' powers relate to those of the UK Parliament and whether EU membership is compatible with parliamentary sovereignty.

- This feeds into our second key theme—*the shift from political to legal constitutionalism*—in that EU law's claim to primacy over domestic law introduced legal benchmarks against which even Acts of Parliament fell to be judged by the courts. That raises the further question of whether Brexit will involve a shift in the other direction, back towards a less legal, more political constitution.

- Our third theme—*the importance of effective accountability*—is relevant too. Indeed, while the causes of the Brexit vote in the UK were complex, it is fair to say that concerns about the EU's accountability and democratic responsiveness formed part of the story, epitomised by the Leave campaign's slogan: 'Vote Leave, take control.'

2. The EU in context

2.1 The development of the EU—four milestones

The roots of the EU can be traced to the Treaty of Paris, which was signed by Belgium, West Germany, France, Italy, Luxembourg, and the Netherlands in 1951. It created the *European Coal and Steel Community* (ECSC)—a common market in coal and steel. In the immediate aftermath of the Second World War, this was a radical and highly political step. As the French Foreign Minister Robert Schuman explained in 1950, solidarity in relation to the extraction and production of coal and steel—two ingredients crucial to the economy of the industrialised Europe of the mid-twentieth century—was intended to 'make it plain that any war between France and Germany becomes not merely unthinkable, but materially impossible'.[4] This was, however, a mere precursor to a more thoroughgoing project of European cooperation and integration—'the first concrete foundation of a European federation indispensable to the preservation of peace'.[5]

The second, and still the most significant, such foundation was laid in 1957 when the six ECSC members signed the Treaty establishing the *European Economic Community*.[6] Its Preamble records the member states' intentions to 'lay the foundations of an ever closer union among the peoples of Europe'. Key to the project are the 'four freedoms': the freedom of goods, persons, services, and capital to move between member states. Free movement of persons—whereby citizens of one member state have the right to live and work in any member state—and its implications for immigration control was one of the defining issues of the Brexit referendum campaign.

The third milestone in the development of the EU was the *Treaty on European Union* (TEU), signed in Maastricht in 1992. Among other things, it introduced a framework for member states to work together in new policy areas such as policing, justice, foreign affairs, and security, and provided for the introduction of a single European currency.

An important aspect of the EU's development not so far mentioned is its enlargement. Four main waves of growth saw additional western European countries—the UK, Denmark, and Ireland—join in 1973, followed by the southern countries of Greece, Spain, and Portugal in the 1980s; the northern states of Austria, Finland, and Sweden in 1995; and ten eastern European countries,[7] as well as Malta and Cyprus in 2004–07 and Croatia in 2013. There are now 28 member states with a combined population exceeding 500 million. The expansion of the EU led to our fourth milestone: the *Lisbon Treaty*, which entered into force in 2009. It was adopted in an attempt to enable a radically enlarged EU to function better, the thinking being that structures and processes suited to an original institution consisting of six member states needed to be overhauled and streamlined for a Union of 28. The Lisbon Treaty did not replace but amended two existing treaties. Thus the legal foundations of the EU are today found in the TEU, which sets out the EU's basic constitutional architecture, and the Treaty on the Functioning of the European Union (TFEU), which deals with more detailed matters such as the EU's specific legal powers.

2.2 The EU's areas of activity

Although many of the policies adopted and laws implemented by the EU relate directly to the single market, its influence goes much further than this. For example,

---

[4] Schuman Declaration, 9 May 1950.   [5] Schuman Declaration.

[6] Often referred to as the Treaty of Rome, after the city in which it was signed.

[7] ie Bulgaria, the Czech Republic, Estonia, Hungary, Latvia, Lithuania, Poland, Romania, Slovakia, and Slovenia.

it is authorised to undertake such activities as research, technological development, space exploration,[8] and the provision of humanitarian aid.[9] In practical terms, the impact of the EU is felt in three main ways.

First, it *makes law*. Indeed, a great deal of the law currently applicable in the UK, as in other member states, is either law enacted by the EU or domestic law enacted at its behest. The following example box gives some illustrative examples of laws made by the EU. The list is highly selective, and is intended merely to give an indication of the range of areas into which EU law reaches.

Eg

Limitation of working time and requirement of paid annual leave Directive 2003/88/EC

Equal pay for men and women Directive 2006/54/EC

European greenhouse gas emissions trading scheme Directive 2003/87/EC

Safety of consumer products Directive 2001/95/EC

Investigation and termination of anti-competitive practices Council Regulation (EC) No 1/2003

Minimum levels of value added tax Council Directive 2006/112/EC

Compensation for air passengers in the event of delays or cancellations Regulation (EC) No 261/2004

Second, the EU *redistributes wealth*. The money that is redistributed is acquired principally from national governments (and hence taxpayers), which generally pay into the EU in proportion to the size of their respective economies: at present, the EU's total income each year is approximately €155bn—just over 1 per cent of the combined gross national income of the member states.[10] For instance, the EU assists its economically poorer regions by providing funds for the improvement of infrastructure.

Third, the EU *facilitates cooperation between member states and the coordination of policy* other than simply by enacting EU-wide laws. Under its common foreign and security policy, the EU is an important player on the world stage, and its members increasingly project global influence by acting in concert rather than alone. The Lisbon Treaty sought to lend greater coherence to the EU's external relations by creating the post of High Representative (or 'Foreign Minister'),[11] supported by a new EU diplomatic corps known as the External Action Service.

Q Are there particular issues for which you think the EU should or should not be responsible? What principles would you wish to see employed in determining those matters for which member states remain responsible and those in relation to which the EU has authority to adopt a coordinated, pan-European approach?

---

[8] TFEU, Art 4(3).   [9] TFEU, Art 4(4).

[10] See further **http://ec.europa.eu/budget/index_en.cfm**   [11] TFEU, Art 18.

2.3 **The institutional architecture of the EU**

So much for *what* the EU seeks to do. *How* does it do it? In this section, we explain and evaluate the role of the EU's principal institutions.

2.3.1 **Separation of powers—the Commission, the Council, and the Parliament**

As Figure 8.3 shows, the EU does not adhere to an orthodox conception of the separation of powers.[12] In particular, *the Commission straddles the distinction between executive and legislative functions*. The Commission is comprised of one Commissioner from each of the member states, each of whom has responsibility for a particular portfolio (eg trade, external relations, competition) and who must act independently rather than as a representative of the government responsible for his or her appointment.[13]

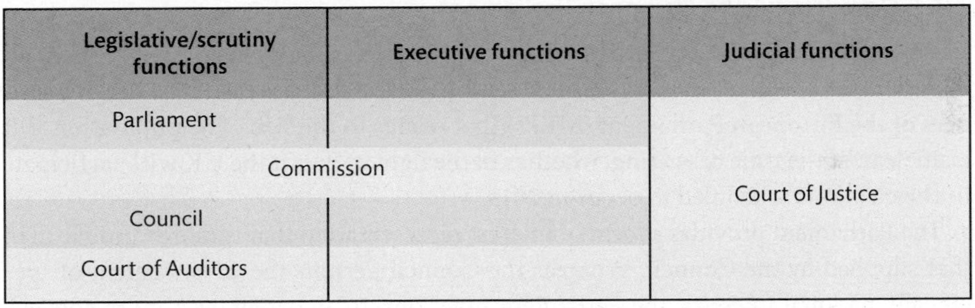

Legislative/scrutiny functions	Executive functions	Judicial functions
Parliament		
Commission		
Council		Court of Justice
Court of Auditors		

Figure 8.3 Institutional architecture

In its *executive* guise, the Commission is responsible for seeing that EU law is applied; for example, it can take legal action against member states[14] or other EU institutions[15] that it believes to be in breach of EU law. The Commission also has a pivotal *legislative* role: in general, a proposal from the Commission is required before the legislative process can commence.[16] However, the EU possesses *no single body that is identifiably the legislature*; rather, three institutions—the Commission, the Council, and the Parliament—are involved in the enactment of legislation. Once the Commission has initiated the process, its proposal is considered by the Parliament (considered later) and the Council.[17]

The Council of the EU is, in a sense, the hardest of the EU institutions to place within a traditional tripartite separation-of-powers model. It carries out 'policy-making and coordinating functions'[18] and plays a central role in the enactment of legislation. It consists of 'a representative of each Member State at ministerial level, who may commit the government of the Member State in question and cast its vote'.[19] In practice, the membership of the Council is fluid: the Minister nominated by a member state to attend a particular Council meeting depends on the subject matter of the meeting.[20] For example, if the Council is to discuss economic matters, it will be the Finance Ministers who attend; if it is to discuss agricultural policy, the Agriculture Ministers

---

[12] On the separation of powers generally, see Chapter 3.
[13] TEU, Art 17(4).   [14] TFEU, Art 258.   [15] TFEU, Art 263.   [16] TFEU, Arts 289–94.
[17] TFEU, Art 294.   [18] TEU, Art 16(1).   [19] TEU, Art 16(2).   [20] TEU, Art 16(6).

will attend. Countries take it in turn to hold the presidency of the Council[21] (except when it meets to discuss foreign policy, when the EU 'Foreign Minister' presides[22]). Although, in theory, holding the presidency affords each member state an opportunity to shape the direction of EU policy, scope for doing so is limited by the fact that the presidency rotates every six months.

The agenda-setting role of the *Council of the EU* is further reduced by the existence, post-Lisbon, of a separate institution, known as the *European Council*. This used to be the informal name given to (usually biannual) meetings of heads of EU governments. However, as a result of the Lisbon Treaty, the European Council now constitutes a separate entity under the leadership of a President who serves for a period of up to five years. Its role is to provide the 'necessary impetus for [the] development' of the EU and to 'define the general political directions and priorities thereof'.[23]

2.3.2 Democracy—the European Parliament

Elections to the European Parliament are held simultaneously every five years in all member states, with each member state sending to the Parliament a number of members of the European Parliament (MEPs) that relates to the size of its population.[24] It is unclear, at the time of writing, whether in the light of Brexit the UK will participate in the elections scheduled to occur in 2019.

The Parliament provides a form of interest representation that is more familiar than that supplied by the Council. Whereas the Council permits the advancement of specifically national interests, the Parliament functions, to an extent, as a more conventional legislature in which the dividing lines are political or philosophical rather than national. Although MEPs tend to be members of national political parties, many of those parties are affiliated to larger groupings within the Parliament. As a result, the sort of political dividing lines that are familiar within national discourse are also evident in the European Parliament.

Representing a citizenry approximately 500 million strong, the European Parliament is one of the world's largest democratic legislatures. It is therefore (at least prima facie) perverse that one of the most persistent criticisms levelled at the EU is that it suffers from a 'democratic deficit'. The reasons for this are several. But one important factor is that, until recently, a substantial amount of EU legislation could be enacted without the consent of the Parliament—meaning that the EU's most obviously democratic institution was effectively sidelined. The Lisbon Treaty sought to address this problem by substantially expanding the range of legislation that can be enacted only with the consent of the Parliament. It did so by increasing the number of subject areas in which the 'ordinary legislative procedure' has to be used.[25] As Figure 8.4 shows, under this procedure, a proposal cannot become law without the Parliament's approval.

---

[21] TEU, Art 16(9). However, the UK's scheduled presidency has been cancelled in anticipation of Brexit: Council Decision (EU) 2016/1316.

[22] TEU, Art 18(3).

[23] TEU, Art 15.   [24] eg Luxembourg has only 6 MEPs; Germany has 99.

[25] TFEU, Art 294.

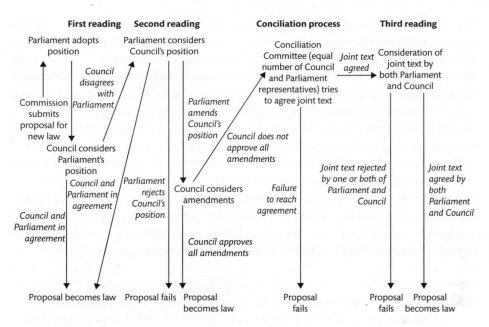

Figure 8.4 The ordinary legislative procedure

2.3.3 National interests and the legislative process—the Council of the EU

Although the EU undoubtedly represents an unparalleled example of nation states pooling resources and authority in order to further their common interests, it is inevitable that individual states' interests do not always coincide. This used to be reflected by the fact that Council decisions could be taken only unanimously, thus handing every member state a veto. However, as the EU expanded, unanimity became harder to secure. Member states therefore agreed—as a price that had to be paid if things were ever to be done—to give up their veto powers in many subject areas.

Today, roughly 80 per cent of EU legislation is enacted under arrangements known as *qualified majority voting* (QMV). This allows measures to be enacted—and thereafter to be applicable to *all* member states—even if some object. Under QMV, legislation can be approved by the Council only if a 'double majority' is secured. This means that both of the following conditions must be satisfied: [26]

- At least 55 per cent of member states (ie at least 16 out of 28) vote in favour of the legislation.

- Member states representing at least 65 per cent of the total EU population vote in favour.

The debate about the acceptability of QMV reflects a much deeper discourse about the nature of the EU itself. We noted in Chapter 7 that the willingness of people within a single country to submit to common sets of laws, notwithstanding that some such laws might benefit some areas more than others, turns on whether everyone feels that they

---

[26] TEU, Art 16(4).

belong to a single political unit. If a given geographical area identifies itself as a distinct political unit (as is the case, to some extent at least, in relation to Scotland within the UK), its population is less likely to be prepared to tolerate what might be perceived as the imposition of laws by a central legislature that may favour the interests of other areas (eg England). These issues arise in a more acute form in the EU. It is for precisely that reason that national interests are explicitly represented in the legislative process through the medium of the Council. However, the extent to which the Council facilitates the prosecution of such interests is clearly limited if QMV, rather than unanimity, applies.

The technicalities of QMV played no role in the Brexit debate in the UK. However, the fact that the UK (like all other member states) can be required to abide by EU laws to which it objected was certainly one of the concerns in play, and contributed to the notion that there had been a loss of 'control'. The referendum tested the hypothesis that people in the UK feel European enough to be prepared to tolerate the pooling of legislative autonomy implied by QMV. That hypothesis was disproven.

> **Q** Why do you think the issues referred to above may arise 'in a more acute form' in rela-tion to the EU than in relation to a single state such as the UK? What do you think might be the principal obstacles to member states' willingness to give up their national veto in particular policy areas?

2.3.4 Accountability—Parliament and the courts

In most constitutional systems, the Parliament is responsible not only for legislat-ing, but also for holding the executive to account. The view that the EU suffers from a democratic deficit reflects the perception held in some quarters that the EU is a distant and remote organisation over which individual citizens have little influence or control, and which is not sufficiently accountable for its use of public power and money. The Lisbon Treaty sought to address such concerns by (among other things) requiring national Parliaments to be consulted as part of the EU lawmaking process[27] and requiring the Commission to consider proposing legislation when requested to do so by at least 1 million EU citizens.[28] The general requirement of 'subsidiarity'—that the EU should act only if action at member state level would not be appropriate[29]—is also given some teeth by allowing national Parliaments to object to (but not to veto) legislative proposals on subsidiarity grounds.[30]

However, a deeper difficulty is that the levers of democratic control do not work in relation to the EU in the same way as they function in relation to, for example, the UK government. If the British public is dissatisfied with the latter, it can precipitate a change of government at the next election. No equivalent democratic mechanism is open to EU citizens who disapprove of how the EU is run. Citizens can vote in elections to the European Parliament, but membership of that Parliament has no effect upon the identity or political outlook of the Commissioners and Council Members who, as we

---

[27] Protocol on the Role of National Parliaments in the EU.   [28] TEU, Art 11(4).

[29] TEU, Art 5(3).

[30] Protocol on the Principles of Subsidiarity and Proportionality, Arts 6 and 7.

have seen, find themselves in the driving seat when it comes to initiating and push-ing through legislative changes. Citizens in a given state can, in theory, exert pressure on their national government with respect to who it nominates as its Commissioner and how its Ministers bargain at Council meetings. However, voters in one state have no way of influencing the behaviour of the other 27 Commissioners and the other 27 Council Members. Such concerns gained traction in the Brexit debate, many voters instinctively preferring the idea of siting power closer to home in domestic govern-ments and legislatures whose members can be 'voted out' if they fail to deliver.

What, then, of legal, as opposed to political, accountability? The Court of Justice of the European Union (CJEU) consists of judges drawn from across the EU who must be relevantly legally qualified persons 'whose independence is beyond doubt'.[31] The Court is responsible for ensuring that EU law is correctly interpreted and applied by and within the member states and that the EU institutions themselves act lawfully. Thus it is possible, under TFEU, Art 263, for proceedings to be initiated before the Court by individuals, member states, and certain EU institutions for judicial review of the legality of action taken by the Parliament, the Council, the Commission, and the European Central Bank (ECB).

3. EU law and national law

Having considered what the EU does, and the various institutions that comprise it, we now turn our attention to a more specific matter. If the EU is to achieve its objectives, it is often necessary for it to make law that applies throughout the 28 member states. But the European project would be unviable if those laws were ineffective. EU law must therefore be enforceable in member states' courts. And member states must not be allowed to pick and choose which EU laws operate within their national legal systems, since it is central to the purpose and ethos of the EU that common legal standards must (in relevant fields) apply throughout the Union. EU law must therefore take priority over any conflicting domestic law. These prerequisites for an effective EU legal system are reflected in the fundamental principles that EU law can have *direct effect* and has *supremacy* over domestic law. We address those principles later. First, however, it is necessary to say something about the different types of EU law that exist.

3.1 Types of EU law

Some EU law is contained in the Treaties themselves. For example, TFEU, Art 30 sets out a specific legal rule that prohibits customs duties on imports and exports between member states, thus helping to facilitate free movement of goods. However, as well as being a source of *law*, the Treaties are a source of *lawmaking authority*. For example, TFEU, Arts 191–2 authorise the enactment of legislation for the purpose of 'preserv-ing, protecting and improving the quality of the environment'. So, as Figure 8.5 indi-cates, the relationship between the Treaties and (other forms of) Union legislation is analogous to that which exists between a national constitution and legislation enacted thereunder, or between Acts of Parliament and secondary legislation.

---

[31] TFEU, Art 254.

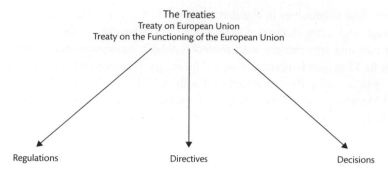

Figure 8.5 Types of EU law

The EU is allowed to do only those things that the Treaties authorise it to do: it has no 'inherent' or 'original' power.[32] Hence there is no question of the EU enjoying 'sovereign' lawmaking power in the way that the UK Parliament (at least on a traditional analysis) does. Rather, the EU's lawmaking authority is conferred and confined by the Treaties just as many national legislatures' powers are defined by constitutional texts. The EU's legislative acts are therefore vulnerable to judicial review if, for example, they are enacted in an unauthorised manner[33] or if they deal with subject areas with which the EU has not been authorised to deal.

3.2 Direct effect

3.2.1 The reasons for, and nature of, the principle

We have already seen that the CJEU plays an important role in seeing that EU law is respected. It also helps to ensure that EU law is consistently applied: national courts, under TFEU, Art 267, refer to the CJEU questions concerning the interpretation of Union law. However, it is clear that the CJEU could not in practice have sole responsibility for upholding EU law—the task is simply too large. Moreover, the very notion of the EU as a 'new legal order'[34] means that individuals should be able to enforce EU law in their own courts. For these reasons, the principle of direct effect signifies that those EU laws to which it applies are enforceable in ordinary legal proceedings before national courts without further ado, meaning that national courts must resolve legal disputes by applying both relevant domestic law and directly effective EU law. The latter is just as much a part of the applicable body of law as the former. It is therefore commonplace for individuals to take action in national courts against the government, companies, and other individuals in order to enforce rights derived from EU law just as they do in relation to rights granted by national law.

3.2.2 Regulations and treaty provisions

How do we know whether a given EU law is directly effective? The answer, as Table 8.2 indicates, is that it depends on the *type* of EU law concerned.

---

[32] TEU, Art 5.
[33] Case C-84/94 *United Kingdom v Council* [1996] ECR I-5755, [1996] 3 CMLR 671.
[34] Case 26/62 *Van Gend En Loos* [1963] ECR 1, 12.

Table 8.2 Direct effect

Type of EU law	Directly effective?
Regulations	Yes
Treaty provisions	Only if unconditional and sufficiently precise
Directives	Only against the state, and even then only if (a) the implementation date has passed; and (b) the provisions are unconditional and sufficiently precise

The position in relation to *regulations* is the most straightforward: all regulations have direct effect.[35] There is a clear basis for this in the Treaty—TFEU, Art 288 says that a regulation is 'binding in its entirety and directly applicable in all Member States'—and the CJEU therefore had little difficulty in arriving at the view that regulations are directly effective.[36]

In contrast, the Treaties do not explicitly say that *treaty provisions* themselves are directly effective. Nevertheless, the Court held in *Van Gend En Loos* that the doctrine of direct effect was in principle applicable to treaty provisions. However, whereas regulations are inevitably drafted with the intention of being enforceable—and therefore are, or at least should be, worded with the sort of precision that makes it possible for courts to make sense of them—that is not true of every part of the Treaties. Thus the CJEU has held that treaty provisions will only be enforceable in national courts if they meet certain conditions for direct effect. There are two such conditions, both of which must be satisfied:[37]

- The provision in question must be 'unconditional', meaning that it must set out 'an obligation which is not qualified by any condition, or subject, in its implementation or effects, to the taking of any measure either by the Community institutions or by the Member States'.

- The provision must be 'sufficiently precise', in the sense of being 'unequivocal'.

Ultimately, these conditions reduce to a test of justiciability: is the provision clear and complete enough to be capable of being applied as a legal rule? Certain treaty provisions, such as TFEU, Art 30—which, as noted earlier, lays down a clear rule banning customs duties on goods moving between member states—clearly meet these conditions and are therefore directly effective.[38] But many, such as TFEU, Art 145—which requires member states and the EU to 'work towards developing a coordinated strategy for employment'—are not.

---

[35] The same is true of decisions: see TFEU, Art 288; *Franz Grad v Finanzamt Traustein* [1970] ECR 825, [5].

[36] Case 39/72 *Commission v Italy* [1973] ECR 101, [17].

[37] Joined Cases C-246/94 to 249/94 *Cooperativa Agricola Zootecnica S Antonio v Amministrazione delle Finanze dello Stato* [1997] 1 CMLR 1112.

[38] *Van Gend En Loos.*

3.2.3 Directives

A directive is 'binding, as to the result to be achieved, upon each Member State to which it is addressed, but shall leave to the national authorities the choice of form and methods'.[39] Directives are not, then, intended to be enforceable by individuals; rather, they are directed to the states themselves, which are obliged to amend domestic law so as to conform to the directive. It follows, as Figure 8.6 illustrates, that directives and regulations[40] are fundamentally different: the latter puncture the distinction between European and national law by automatically becoming enforceable in domestic courts, whereas the former are only intended to stimulate the amendment by national legislative authorities of domestic law.

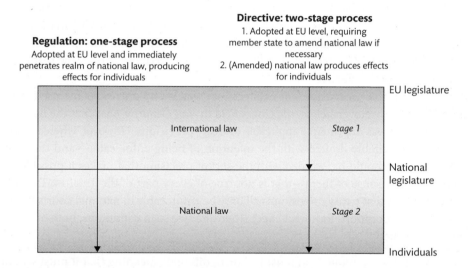

Figure 8.6 Direct effect—regulations and directives compared

What if a member state fails to implement a directive? Can it have direct effect, meaning that non-implementation does not really matter? Faced with this question, the CJEU has found itself walking something of a tightrope. Its general view that EU law should be enforceable (in order that the EU may take effect as a real legal order) suggests that directives should be directly effective, so as to ensure that, whether by accident or design, they cannot be rendered unenforceable by the failure of member states correctly to implement them. Yet TFEU, Art 288 seems to indicate that directives are not directly effective.

In an attempt to resolve the tension between these competing forces, the Court has held that unimplemented directives can produce domestic legal effects—but only if three conditions are satisfied:

- The conditions for direct effect must be met, so only those parts of directives that are clear and unconditional (in the senses set out earlier) can have direct effect.[41]

---

[39] TFEU, Art 288.   [40] And, as discussed earlier, certain Treaty provisions.
[41] Case 41/74 *Van Duyn v Home Office (No 2)* [1974] ECR 1337.

- The deadline for implementing the directive must have passed.[42]
- The situation is a 'vertical', as distinct from a 'horizontal', one.[43]

The first two conditions need no elaboration. The third refers to the distinction between those ('horizontal') situations in which someone wishes to enforce an unimplemented directive against a private party and those in which ('vertical') enforcement is sought against the state (or some manifestation of it). The principle is that unimplemented directives can be enforced vertically but not horizontally.

3.2.4 Why vertically, but not horizontally, effective?

It may seem arbitrary that directives can be enforced only against state bodies. However, the Court has identified a justification for permitting directives to have vertical, but not horizontal, effect. The *default position* must be, because of what is said in TFEU, Art 288, that directives do not have any direct effect—but it is legitimate to carve out an *exception* to that rule to the extent that it would, if applied, produce unconscionable results. If a member state's government itself was a defendant to legal proceedings in which someone was seeking to enforce rights contained in an unimplemented directive, it would be unconscionable to allow the government to win the case by relying on the failure to implement the directive. That would be to allow the government to prevail by virtue of its own breach of its EU law obligation to implement the directive. The doctrine of vertical effect prevents states from benefiting in such a way from their own unlawful inaction.[44]

However, the same point does not apply when the case is a horizontal one. If the defendant is a private party, there is nothing unconscionable in it relying on the state's failure to implement the directive. In doing so, it would not be benefiting from any unlawful conduct on its own part, because it was never its responsibility to enact a national law implementing the directive. In horizontal cases, then, there is no justification for departing from the general rule, as set down in TFEU, Art 288, that directives do not have direct effect. Indeed, as the Court has recognised, if directives were capable of horizontal as well as vertical effect, this would largely assimilate them with regulations. This, the Court maintains, would be unacceptable, because it would disregard the clear distinction drawn in the Treaty between regulations and directives.[45]

3.2.5 The scope of the vertical direct effect doctrine

How, then, is the line to be drawn between state bodies, which are susceptible to vertical effect, and non-state bodies, which are not? If the justification for vertical effect is to preclude state bodies benefiting (by escaping legal liability) from their

---

[42] Case 148/78 *Pubblico Ministero v Ratti* [1979] ECR 1629.

[43] Case 152/84 *Marshall v Southampton and South West Hampshire Area Health Authority* [1986] ECR 723; Case C-91/92 *Faccini Dori v Recreb Srl* [1995] 1 CMLR 665.

[44] *Faccini Dori*, [23].   [45] *Faccini Dori*, [24].

wrongful failure to take steps to implement directives, then surely the vertical effect doctrine should apply only to those state bodies responsible for taking such steps. This suggests that only a narrow range of public bodies—for example, central government departments responsible for seeing that EU law is implemented—should be subject to vertical effect. In this sphere, as in many others, the Court has felt the strong pull of its desire to see that EU law is as effective as possible.[46] It has therefore defined the state in much broader terms—thereby ensuring that unimplemented (or incorrectly implemented) directives are enforceable against a wide range of defendants—by reference to such factors as whether the defendant is responsible for providing a public service, has special powers, and is under government control.[47] These tests are applied in a relaxed fashion: they are merely 'indicia which point to the appropriateness of treating the body in question as an emanation of the state', and courts should therefore refer to them simply as guidelines rather than as absolute preconditions all of which must be met before the defendant can be characterised as a state body.[48] As well as central government departments, unimplemented directives can be enforced against the police,[49] publicly run hospitals,[50] nationalised utility companies,[51] privatised utility companies,[52] and even Church of England primary schools.[53] In most situations, it will be private parties that wish to enforce unimplemented directives against such bodies. But it has recently been held, somewhat paradoxically, that the state itself can enforce unimplemented directives against emanations of the state.[54]

Q Is it acceptable for the CJEU to have characterised public authorities so broadly? Has it managed satisfactorily to balance fidelity to the Treaties with its policy of ensuring the effectiveness of EU law?

While the scope of vertical effect is wide, it has its limits: by definition, it cannot assist those who want to enforce directives against defendants that fail to satisfy the (admittedly broad) definition of the 'state'. However, as Figure 8.7 shows, the Court has developed four ways of filling the gap in legal protection created by the absence of horizontal effect.

---

[46] See further Spink, 'Direct Effect: The Boundaries of the State' (1997) 113 LQR 524.

[47] Case C-188/89 *Foster v British Gas plc* [1991] 1 QB 405.

[48] *National Union of Teachers v Governing Body of St Mary's Church of England (Aided) Junior School* [1997] 3 CMLR 630.

[49] Case 222/84 *Johnston v Chief Constable of the Royal Ulster Constabulary* [1987] QB 129.

[50] *Marshall v Southampton and South West Hampshire Area Health Authority (No 2)* [1994] 1 AC 530.

[51] *Foster v British Gas plc* [1991] 2 AC 306.

[52] *Griffin v South West Water Services Ltd* [1995] IRLR 15.   [53] *St Mary's School.*

[54] Case C-425/12 *Portgás v Ministério da Agricultura, do Mar, do Ambiente e do Ordenamento do Território* [2014] 2 CMLR 30.

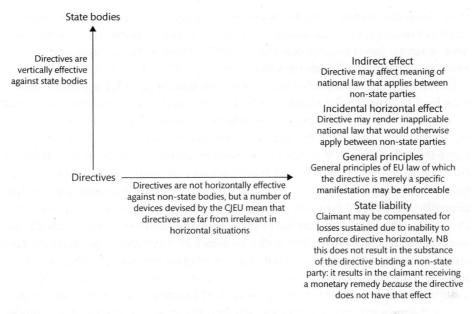

Figure 8.7 The legal effects of unimplemented directives

3.2.6 Indirect effect

TEU, Art 4(3) requires member states to 'take any appropriate measure' to fulfil their obligations under EU law. This obviously requires member states' legislatures to take the necessary steps to make sure that national law is drafted in a way that gives effect to the directive. However, the Court has held that (what is now) TEU, Art 4(3) also applies to national courts.[55] If, therefore, a given member state's legislature fails to take steps to implement a directive, its courts are nevertheless required to do 'whatever lies within [their] jurisdiction, having regard to the whole body of rules of national law, to ensure that [the directive is] fully effective'.[56] This is known as the principle of *indirect effect*. Under it, a claimant in a horizontal case might win because national law—once the court has sought to interpret it in line with the relevant directive—turns out to mean the same thing as the unimplemented directive. This is not, however, a panacea: it can produce results only if national law on the general matter already exists, and only if that law is amenable to being interpreted in a way that gives effect to the directive.

3.2.7 Incidental horizontal effect

A second way in which unimplemented (or incorrectly implemented) directives, although lacking horizontal direct effect, may nevertheless have some impact other

---

[55] Case 14/83 *Von Colson v Land Nordrhein-Westfalen* [1984] ECR 1891, [26].

[56] Case C-397/01 *Pfeiffer v Deutsches Rotes Kreuz, Kreisverband Waldshut Ev* [2005] 1 CMLR 44, [118]. This obligation of consistent interpretation is not restricted to directives: all domestic legislation must, whenever possible, be interpreted compatibly with all relevant forms of EU law.

than upon state bodies is via the doctrine of *incidental horizontal effect*. Whereas indirect effect results in the modification of the *meaning* of the relevant domestic law, incidental direct effect is concerned with the *enforceability* of domestic law. An example will help to illustrate the point.

In *CIA Security SA v Signalson SA*,[57] Signalson claimed that CIA was acting unlawfully by supplying burglar alarms that had not received official approval as required by Belgian law. CIA, said Signalson, should be required to withdraw its alarm system from the market until or unless such approval was obtained. In response, CIA pointed out that an EU directive required national authorities to notify the European Commission if they proposed to enact certain laws that restrict the free movement of goods between member states. CIA successfully argued that the law of which it was allegedly in breach fell into that category, and that the requisite notification had not been given. The CJEU held that the Belgian law in question was therefore unenforceable, that CIA was therefore not acting in breach of any enforceable domestic law, and that, as a result, it was free to continue to market its product notwithstanding the absence of official approval.

This illustrates the operation of the principle of incidental horizontal effect. In particular, it shows that when a directive is sufficiently clear and precise, it will render any conflicting domestic law unenforceable, including in legal proceedings between private parties. As a result, directives that have not been implemented (in the sense that national law does not fully comply with them) may nevertheless affect the legal position as between private parties; thus, in the case considered, the directive precluded Signalson from invoking Belgian law so as to stop CIA from marketing its product.[58]

3.2.8 State liability

All of the devices so far considered for ameliorating the impact of the absence of horizontal direct effect have one thing in common: they make it possible for cases to be decided in ways that are consistent with directives that have not been properly implemented in national law. The state liability principle, in contrast, may assist when cases *cannot* be decided in a way that is consistent with the directive.[59] That principle was developed by the CJEU in the case of *Francovich*.[60] The Court concluded that its policy of attempting to ensure the 'full effectiveness' of EU law would be thwarted 'if individuals were unable to obtain redress when their rights are infringed by a breach of [Union] law for which a Member State can be held responsible'.[61] It followed that

---

[57] Case C-194/94 *CIA Security SA v Signalson SA* [1996] ECR I-2201.

[58] While this may appear to be a substantial exception to the rule that directives do not have horizontal effect, it seems that its compass may be restricted to 'public' directives that are addressed principally to the exercise of member states' powers, as distinct from directives that predominantly concern legal relationships between individuals. See further Dashwood, 'From *Van Duyn* to *Mangold* via *Marshall*: Reducing Direct Effect to Absurdity?' (2007) 9 CYELS 81.

[59] This is not to imply that state liability is simply a substitute for direct effect. In appropriate fact situations, claimants may seek to enforce a right contained in a directive *and* obtain compensation, under the state liability principle, for past denials of the right.

[60] Joined Cases C-6/90 and C-9/90 *Francovich v Italy* [1991] ECR I-5357.

[61] *Francovich*, [33].

those who are denied their EU law rights by the unlawful action (or inaction) of a member state should be compensated by the state.

Three conditions must be met in order for compensation to be recoverable:[62]

- The directive was 'intended to confer rights on individuals'.
- The state's breach of EU law is 'sufficiently serious'.
- There is a 'direct causal link between the breach . . . and the damage sustained by the injured [party]'.

It is unnecessary to say much about the first and third conditions: the first will depend on the wording of the directive, while the third has to be determined by domestic courts applying national rules on causation.[63] The second condition requires more detailed explanation. Whether any given breach is sufficiently serious turns upon such matters as the clarity and precision of the EU law that has been breached, whether the breach and the damage thereby caused was intentional, and whether any legal error committed by the member state is excusable or inexcusable.[64] A government that has failed absolutely to implement a directive will almost inevitably be guilty of a sufficiently serious breach if it fails to legislate.[65] However, a member state may be able to escape liability where it has taken some steps to implement a directive, but, in doing so, turns out to have misunderstood what the directive requires such that national law is imperfectly aligned with the directive. When such circumstances arose in *Denkavit*, the CJEU held that the member state concerned was not liable to pay compensation because it, like several other states, had adopted a reasonable— albeit incorrect—interpretation of an ambiguous directive.[66]

As we have seen, state liability originally developed to compensate claimants unable to secure rights due to them under unimplemented (or incorrectly implemented) directives. However, the principle is now acknowledged to be much more widely applicable.[67] It is therefore possible, for example, to claim damages where the state has breached directly effective treaty provisions.[68] The Court has also made clear that the conduct of any branch of the state, including the legislature,[69] the executive,[70] and the judiciary,[71] can give rise to liability in damages. However, outside the context of straightforward obligations to implement directives, the CJEU recognises that liability must not be imposed so readily as to paralyse the exercise of legislative and judicial

---

[62] Joined Cases C-46/93 and C-48/93 *Brasserie du Pêcheur SA v Federal Republic of Germany; R v Secretary of State for Transport, ex p Factortame (No 4)* [1996] QB 404, [51].

[63] *Factortame (No 4)*, [65]. Other relevant national rules, eg as to procedure, can be applied to state liability claims, provided that they are not less favourable than those rules applicable to equivalent claims under domestic law: Case C-118/08 *Transportes Urbanos v Administracion del Estado* [2010] 2 CMLR 39.

[64] *Factortame (No 4)*, [56].

[65] Case C-5/94 *R v Ministry of Agriculture, Fisheries and Food, ex p Hedley Lomas (Ireland) Ltd* [1997] QB 139, [28].

[66] Case C-283/94 *Denkavit International BV v Bundesamt für Finanzen* [1996] ECR I-5063.

[67] *Factortame (No 4)*, [17]–[22].   [68] *Factortame (No 4)*.   [69] *Factortame (No 4)*.

[70] *Hedley Lomas*.

[71] Case C-173/03 *Traghetti del Mediterraneo SpA v Italy* [2006] ECR I-5177. See also *Cooper v Attorney General* [2010] EWCA Civ 464.

discretion by member states. As a result, the bar for establishing a sufficiently serious breach of EU law is higher in such circumstances, the test being 'whether the member state . . . manifestly and gravely disregarded the limits on its discretion'.[72]

3.2.9 Directives that reflect general principles of EU law

In *Mangold*,[73] the claimant sued his employer. He alleged that a term in his contract—which, if enforced, would be disadvantageous to him—was incompatible with a directive concerning equal treatment (specifically age discrimination) in employment. The claimant faced apparently insuperable difficulties: domestic law permitted the inclusion of the disadvantageous term; the directive was not horizontally enforceable against the employer, which was a non-state body; and the implementation date had not expired. Nonetheless, he succeeded. The CJEU held that the directive was merely a specific manifestation of a general principle of EU law that required equal treatment and therefore prohibited age discrimination. The principle (unlike the directive) was horizontally effective,[74] and the claimant could therefore make a claim against the employer for breaching the general principle itself.

This decision has been criticised, not least because it is said to risk entirely consuming the rule that says directives are not horizontally effective. A sufficiently bold Court would be capable of relating many, if not all, directives to some general principle of law. If pressed to its logical conclusion, the *Mangold* doctrine means that there is no 'real sense in which the no horizontal direct effect rule for directives can be said to survive'.[75] The alarm bell was sounded by Advocate-General Mazák,[76] who argued that the *Mangold* doctrine 'call[ed] into question the distribution of competence between the [Union] and the Member States' by enabling the imposition of EU law obligations upon individuals in a way that runs directly contrary to the way in which TFEU, Art 288 limits the effect of directives.[77] The precise status and scope of the *Mangold* doctrine remain unclear. It was applied by the CJEU in *Kücükdeveci*, which, like *Mangold*, concerned equality of treatment on grounds of age. However, in *Dominguez*, the question arose whether—in the absence of the adequate implementation of a directive concerning the right to paid annual leave—an individual could nevertheless enforce that right, *à la Mangold*, horizontally. The Court's answer was 'no': the claimant should pursue a *Francovich*-style claim for damages instead.

It is unclear from *Dominguez* why *Mangold* was not applied. *Mangold* may apply only to non-discrimination, but that would seem arbitrary. An alternative explanation

---

[72] *Factortame (No 4)*, [55]. The test in relation to the judicial branch is whether 'the court has manifestly infringed the applicable law': Case C-224/01 *Köbler v Austria* [2003] ECR I-10239.

[73] Case C-144/04 *Mangold v Helm* [2005] ECR I-9981.

[74] This in itself is controversial, as it had not previously been established that general principles of EU law were horizontally effective.

[75] Dashwood, p 88. Other commentators have presented *Mangold* as a less radical decision, suggesting that it is simply an application of the incidental horizontal effect principle: Jans, 'The Effect in National Legal Systems of the Prohibition of Discrimination on Grounds of Age as a General Principle of Community Law' (2007) 34 Legal Issues of Economic Integration 53.

[76] The role of advocates-general is advisory: they present reasoned opinions to the Court prior to judgment.

[77] Case C-411/05 *Palacios de la Villa v Cortefiel Servicios SA* [2007] ECR I-8531, [AG138].

is that the principle at stake in *Dominguez* was not considered sufficiently fundamental to be characterised as a 'general principle' of Union law, and therefore failed to trigger *Mangold*. However, this in turn creates a further conundrum, since the right to paid annual leave is included in the EU's Charter of Fundamental Rights.[78] This may suggest that only some of the rights included in the Charter are fundamental *enough* to attract the application of the *Mangold* doctrine—thus requiring the courts to draw a difficult distinction between categories of basic rights.[79].

3.3 EU law in a post-Brexit UK

EU law has had an enormous impact upon UK law. The EU Treaties and (in particular) the legislation enacted under them form a significant component of the body of law that applies in the UK today. One of the many pressing questions raised by the prospect of Brexit concerns what will happen to EU law in the UK following withdrawal. Some newspaper reports published shortly after the referendum naively assumed that all of EU law had already ceased to apply in the UK. This was incorrect. Until the UK leaves the EU, EU law remains applicable in the UK in full.

But the question arises: what will happen post-Brexit? That question can usefully be broken down into two more specific questions—one normative, and one technical. The normative question is whether EU law *should* simply be excised from the UK legal system upon withdrawal: would that be a good thing? Meanwhile, the technical question is about *how* the disentangling of EU and UK law will need to be managed. We examine those two questions in turn.

3.3.1 The normative question

From the perspective of the committed Leave voter, the correct answer to the normative question might instinctively appear to be 'yes'. That might even seem to be the right answer from a more detached perspective: if Brexit won majority support in the referendum, then surely that should mean (among other things) ridding UK law of the influence of EU law? However, the position is in fact more complex.

Even the most enthusiastic supporter of Brexit would find it difficult to argue that all laws made by the EU are bad laws. It would therefore be perverse to get rid of every last trace of EU law from the UK legal system simply because of those laws' EU origins. Indeed, following a thorough evaluation of the corpus of EU law, the conclusion might well be reached that some—and perhaps many—EU laws are perfectly good laws that it would be sensible to retain. The Brexit enthusiast might retort that this would not do, because the mere fact that EU legislation was made *by the EU* raises concerns about the democratic credentials of such legislation such as to warrant excising it from the UK legal system. But there are two responses to that position. On the one hand, the enormity of the Brexit process will undoubtedly mean that there is simply no time or capacity for indulging such concerns of ideological purity. On the other hand, if the UK government or Parliament were to undertake some form of

---

[78] Article 31(2). On the Charter, see section 4.2.
[79] See further de Mol, '*Dominguez*: A Deafening Silence' (2012) 8 Eur Const L Rev 280.

audit of EU law and conclude that some should be kept, then that would amount to a form of domestic democratic process that ought to address even the purist's concerns.

Ideological considerations will, in any event, have to take a back seat in the face of some very basic practical considerations. Whatever one's view of the EU, it is plain that EU law has become an integral part of the UK legal system over the last 40 or so years, and it is impossible to overstate the chaos that would ensue if EU law simply disappeared overnight. The assumption that EU law amounts to no more than a troublesome bolt-on to domestic law that brings nothing but over-regulation and red tape—such that getting rid of it would be straightforward and desirable—is based on a caricature. The reality is that if EU law is to be removed, much of it will need to be replaced with domestic law—a process that, as we suggest later, is likely to take some considerable time.

A related point must also be noted. Saying that EU law amounts to a substantial part of the body of law that applies in the UK might give the impression that EU law, for all that it is quantitatively significant, is somehow separate and distinct. If that were so, its separateness would perhaps—it might be thought—make its excision a relatively simple enterprise. However, the reality—like most aspects of Brexit—is far from simple. EU law is not a redundant limb that can easily be severed from the body of UK law. Rather, it amounts to a corpus of law that has become intimately interwoven into domestic law. UK law gives effect to EU law in myriad ways; many UK laws have been made specifically in order to give effect to, or in the light of, EU law; and UK law presupposes the existence of EU law. EU law's removal from the body of UK law will therefore be a delicate and very lengthy surgical procedure; rapid amputation is simply not an option.

3.3.2 The technical question

What then of the technical question, that is, how will EU law and UK law be disentangled? The government's plan is to enact a 'Great Repeal Bill' that will repeal the European Communities Act 1972 (ECA), but will, at least as a transitional measure, preserve the effect of EU law in the UK. How this will be technically accomplished will vary as between different types of EU law.

As far as EU directives are concerned, the position is relatively straightforward. We have already seen that directives do not have direct effect in the same way that other forms of EU law do; rather, directives fall to be implemented in member states through the enactment of national law. There is no reason why the substance of suitable directives could not be retained, at least on a temporary basis, by means of keeping in force the UK primary or secondary legislation that was enacted in order to give effect to them. That would then allow for more leisurely decisions about whether, in the longer term, such legislation should be preserved, amended, replaced, or simply repealed. For instance, to the extent that directives have been implemented under powers conferred by the ECA, the repeal of that legislation upon Brexit could provide that secondary legislation enacted under the ECA for the purpose of implementing directives is to continue to have effect.

The position concerning directly effective EU law is different. Such EU measures become effective in UK law upon enactment at the EU level. They do not need to be, and are not, enacted in national law. Rather, s 2(1) of the ECA gives effect in the UK to whatever directly effective EU measures the UK is required to give effect to at any given point in time under the EU Treaties. However, once the UK leaves the EU, it will not be required by the Treaties to give effect in domestic law to any EU laws. The upshot is that on Brexit day—whether or not the ECA is repealed—the default position will be that all directly effective EU law ceases to be applicable and enforceable in the UK. But for reasons already considered, this sort of radical and immediate break with EU law would be highly undesirable. One way around this difficulty would be to take a snapshot of the body of directly effective EU law that existed immediately prior to Brexit. That body of law, or at least selected parts of it, could then be kept in force in the UK on a temporary basis. That might, for instance, be accomplished by modifying the ECA so as to cause s 2(1) to bite upon the corpus of directly effective EU law to which the UK was required to give effect immediately before Brexit.

Just as excising the whole of EU law immediately upon Brexit would be problematic, it would not be sensible to preserve the whole of EU law, some parts of which would instantly cease to be appropriate or relevant post-Brexit. If, for instance, the UK ended up opting, or being forced to settle, for a form of 'hard Brexit' involving both departure from the single market and ending the free movement of people, it would make little sense to keep in force EU laws granting rights of free movement or making associated provision. On the other hand, it is presumably very unlikely that the UK Parliament would wish—immediately upon Brexit or at all—to get rid of legislation such as the Equality Act 2010, which was enacted in order to consolidate and extend predecessor legislation that had been adopted in part to give effect to the UK's EU obligations in relation to non-discrimination. What will therefore be necessary is a gradual approach, whereby EU law is assessed, decisions about its fate in a post-Brexit UK made, and appropriate legislative action taken.

Ultimately, UK legislation will need to be enacted on an industrial scale in order to manage the consequences of Brexit. In the light of that, there will be a great temptation for the government to get Parliament to give it extensive powers to enact secondary legislation relating to Brexit. It is highly unlikely that there will be sufficient parliamentary time to do everything through primary legislation. Government will naturally want as much flexibility as possible. But even if this is so, to think that this could all be accomplished by Brexit day—assuming that withdrawal is to be accomplished by the end of the present Parliament in 2020—would be delusional. Indeed, the disentanglement of EU law from UK law has much in common with the wider Brexit project of which that legislative process will form a part: both will be painstaking, time-consuming, highly technical, and enormously complex enterprises.

4. The supremacy of EU law and UK parliamentary sovereignty

4.1 Introduction

'Vote Leave, take control' became the mantra of the Leave campaign in the run-up to the referendum on the UK's membership of the EU. The idea that the UK was bound by EU rules on such matters as the free movement of people, meaning that it was not the master of its own destiny in relation to such things as immigration policy and numbers, featured heavily in the arguments of those advocating withdrawal and plainly struck a chord with the electorate. The conduct of the Brexit debate has been criticised as evidencing a slide into 'post-truth politics'. It is certainly the case that some of the claims made by both sides could not withstand even moderate scrutiny.

However, whether one considers the 'take control' argument to be a good or a bad one, the underlying premise was not one that could be consigned to the realm of fantasy. The notion of a 'loss' of control is implicitly pejorative, and the matter could be framed in more positive terms. For instance, it might be (and was) argued that EU membership involves the trading off of a degree of autonomy in order to secure the corresponding benefits that accrue to EU member states. But however one looks at the matter, it is evident that being a member of the EU involves sacrificing a degree of national independence.

That diminution of independence is evidenced in part by the QMV system that is now used when the vast majority of EU law is made. As already noted,[80] under QMV a given member state that votes against a new piece of EU legislation will nevertheless be bound by it if enough states—a 'qualifying majority'—vote in favour of its enactment. From a 'loss of control' perspective, similar concerns might be raised when the impact of EU law is examined over a period of time. For instance, a member state with a left-wing government might agree to a given EU law, but there might then be a substantial shift in public opinion in that state that triggers a change of government. A new right-wing government would not, however, straightforwardly be able to unpick the EU law to which its left-wing predecessor had agreed, since changing EU law—like making it from scratch—is not something that can be undertaken unilaterally by individual member states.

None of this would matter if the member states were at liberty to *ignore* EU law. If it were the case that member states could pick and choose which EU laws to abide by and which to put to one side, no relevant loss of 'control' would occur. On that approach, even under QMV, a member state that did not manage to stop an EU law from being enacted could be sanguine about such a failure, since it would be free simply to ignore the newly made legislation. But the EU—at least as it is presently conceived—simply could not function if member states were able to cast aside EU legislation with which it disagreed. This throws into sharp relief questions about the relative priority of domestic and EU law. If member states are to be disabled from disregarding EU laws that they dislike, it stands to reason that they must be denied the capacity to enact domestic legislation that overrides EU law. In other words, EU law must prevail over national law in order to prevent member states from legislating their way around EU law.

The CJEU thus affirmed in the *Costa* case that it is not legally possible for member states to derogate from EU law by enacting conflicting domestic provisions because 'the member-States, albeit within limited spheres, have restricted their sovereign rights and created a body of law applicable both to their nationals and to themselves'.[81] In this way, the CJEU laid the foundations for the principle of the supremacy

---

[80] See section 2.3.3.   [81] Case 6/64 *Costa v Enel* [1964] CMLR 425, 455.

of EU law—a principle that epitomises the tension between those who prize the independence of individual nation states and those who favour the sharing of authority in exchange for what follows from EU membership. That tension lay at the heart of the debate that took place in the UK prior to the referendum in 2016. The outcome demonstrated that the majority of those who voted considered the loss of 'control' or 'sovereignty' that is inherent in the EU system to be too great a price to pay for membership of the Union.

> **Q** Why must EU law take priority over conflicting domestic law? In what senses would the purposes of the EU be thwarted if such domestic law could prevail over Union law?

4.2 **The scope and implications of the supremacy principle**

Although *Costa* clearly established the principle of supremacy of EU law, questions remained about its precise scope and implications. Subsequent case law clarified two important points.

First, in *Simmenthal*, the CJEU addressed *the implications of the supremacy principle for national courts*.[82] The case arose from an Italian law requiring meat importers to pay for veterinarian checks at the national border. Although it was established that this was contrary to directly effective EU law concerning the free movement of goods, the Italian government argued that domestic courts could not order it to repay the fees until and unless the Italian Constitutional Court annulled the law in question. This view did not find favour with the CJEU, which took the opportunity to spell out the practical consequences of the supremacy doctrine for domestic courts faced with incompatible national laws. The CJEU said it was the task of national courts to protect the rights conferred upon individuals by EU law.[83] Domestic courts therefore had to 'apply [Union] law in its entirety', disregarding 'any provision of national law'—whenever enacted—'which may conflict with it', and ignoring any national rules that, if applied, would compromise domestic courts' capacity to do the foregoing things.[84]

Second, in *Internationale Handelsgesellschaft*, the CJEU held that the principles laid down in *Simmenthal* applied to *all* types of national law, including provisions of member states' constitutions, and including provisions in such constitutions concerning the protection of human rights.[85] It was therefore the duty of national courts to disapply national constitutional human rights guarantees to the extent that EU law was inconsistent with them. Unsurprisingly, this conclusion provoked a good deal of disquiet, but the Court was careful to say that such situations should arise rarely (if at all). This was because EU law itself recognised the fundamental rights common to the constitutional traditions of member states. As a result, the Union was bound by those rights and powerless to

---

[82] Case 106/77 *Amministrazione delle Finanze dello Stato v Simmenthal SpA* [1978] ECR 629.
[83] *Simmenthal*, [16].   [84] *Simmenthal*, [17]–[22].
[85] Case 11/70 *Internationale Handelsgesellschaft mbH v Einfuhr- und Vorratsstelle für Getreide und Futtermittel* [1970] ECR 1125.

legislate or otherwise act in breach of them.[86] It would therefore rarely, if ever, be the case that a national court was forced to choose between a national human rights law and a *valid* EU provision.

An obvious difficulty with this approach is that it fails to identify with any precision the body of human rights recognised by EU law (particularly now that the membership is so large and diverse).[87] For that reason (among others), the member states adopted a Charter of Fundamental Rights in 2000 that was made legally effective by the Lisbon Treaty.[88] Although the UK (along with Poland) has a so-called opt-out from the Charter,[89] the CJEU has held that its effect is merely to *explain* certain limitations that are written into the Charter itself, rather than to place the UK in a different position from other member states.[90] The UK, like other member states, is therefore required to respect the rights set out in the Charter when it is implementing EU law. This means, for instance, that when Parliament legislates in an area to which EU law relates, it is required, as a matter of EU law, to abide by the Charter.[91]

4.3 Parliamentary sovereignty and EU law

4.3.1 Introduction

The language of 'sovereignty' was often used in the Brexit debate, although it was generally used imprecisely, and the notions of the UK's sovereignty *as a state* and the UK Parliament's sovereignty *as an institution* were often conflated. Our concern here is with the extent to which EU membership—and so the principle of supremacy of EU law—is compatible with sovereignty in the latter, ie parliamentary, sense.

The orthodox doctrine of parliamentary sovereignty holds that Acts of Parliament are the highest form of law known in the UK, and that it is the first duty of UK courts to give effect to them. It is unclear whether—and, if so, how—that view can be reconciled with the EU supremacy principle. As we will see, various attempts have been made to square this circle; whether any of them are convincing is a different matter. However, before assessing judges' and commentators' attempts to explain *how* UK constitutional law may accommodate the supremacy principle, it is necessary to set out *what* the current position is.

That position will change once the UK's withdrawal from the EU has been completed. But it is important to set out the current position not least because it *is* the current position—and will remain so until the UK leaves the EU. There is, however, a deeper reason for continuing to grapple with questions about the relationship

---

[86] Case 4/73 *J Nold Kohlen- und Baustoffgrosshandlung v Commission of the European Communities* [1975] ECR 985. See further Tridimas, *General Principles of EU Law* (Oxford 2005), ch 7.

[87] Carruthers, 'Beware of Lawyers Bearing Gifts: A Critical Evaluation of the Proposals on Fundamental Rights in the EU Constitutional Treaty' [2004] EHRLR 424.

[88] TEU, Art 6(1).

[89] Protocol on the Application of the Charter of Fundamental Rights of the European Union to Poland and to the United Kingdom.

[90] Joined Cases C-411/10 and C-493/10 *R (NS) v Secretary of State for the Home Department* [2013] QB 102, [120].

[91] *Benkharbouche v Embassy of the Republic of Sudan* [2015] EWCA Civ 33, [2016] QB 347.

between the EU supremacy principle and parliamentary sovereignty, the UK's impending departure from the EU notwithstanding. As we will see in the remainder of this chapter, EU law's assertion of primacy over domestic law represented a fundamental challenge to orthodox perceptions of the UK constitutional order. That challenge presented UK courts and constitutional lawyers with a unique opportunity to re-examine that orthodoxy in order to determine whether and how it could accommodate EU law's ostensibly competing claims. The upshot is that the domestic impact of EU law triggered a debate that teaches important lessons about the UK constitution generally, and parliamentary sovereignty in particular—lessons that will remain relevant even *after* the EU membership that triggered it comes to an end.

4.3.2 Two contrasting perspectives

When we confront questions about the relationship between EU supremacy and parliamentary sovereignty, it is difficult to know what to choose as a starting point, because two quite different possibilities arise. From *the perspective of EU law*, the starting (and, for that matter, finishing) point is the supremacy principle itself. The CJEU's view is that EU law enjoys priority over national law *as a matter of EU law*.[92] The Court has said that the Treaty of Rome—the forerunner of today's Treaties—created 'its own legal system which, on the entry into force of the Treaty, became an integral part of the legal systems of the Member States and which their courts are bound to apply'.[93] On this view, national law cannot detract from the supremacy of EU law: such law is, and will be, supreme within all member states for as long as they remain members of the Union.

However, from *the perspective of British constitutional law*, this analysis is problematic. As a matter of domestic law, treaties to which the UK is a party only impinge upon national law to the extent that they are incorporated by means of an Act of Parliament. Indeed, this view is explicitly endorsed by s 18 of the European Union Act 2011, which says that EU law 'falls to be recognised and available in law in the United Kingdom only by virtue of' the European Communities Act 1972 (ECA). What, then, does the 1972 Act say? Section 2(1) of the ECA provides that

> All such rights, powers, liabilities, obligations and restrictions from time to time created or arising by or under the Treaties, and all such remedies and procedures from time to time provided for by or under the Treaties, as in accordance with the Treaties are without further enactment to be given legal effect or used in the United Kingdom shall be recognised and available in law, and be enforced, allowed and followed accordingly.

Section 2(1) is the domestic counterpart to the doctrine of direct effect, in that it provides that all EU provisions that have direct effect as a matter of Union law should be regarded as legally effective as a matter of UK law. In this way, s 2(1) can be thought of as the gateway through which EU law enters the domestic system.

---

[92] An argument of this nature was canvassed before the High Court of England and Wales, but ultimately rejected, in *Thoburn v Sunderland City Council* [2002] EWHC 195 (Admin), [2003] QB 151, [53]–[57].
[93] Case C-6/64 *Costa v Enel* [1964] ECR 585, 593–4.

Meanwhile, s 2(4) says that 'any enactment passed or to be passed . . . shall be construed and have effect subject to the foregoing provisions of this section'. What does this mean? One of the 'foregoing provisions of this section' is s 2(1)—which, as we have just seen, makes directly effective EU law domestically effective. Section 2(4) is, then, saying that any Act of Parliament, whether enacted before or after the entry into force of the ECA, 'shall be construed and have effect subject to' directly effective EU law. The phrase 'shall be construed' suggests that UK courts are merely required, where possible, to interpret domestic legislation consistently with EU law. On this view, s 2(4) amounts to no more than a *rule of interpretation*. But saying that UK legislation shall 'have effect subject to' EU law hints at something else altogether: it suggests that Acts of Parliament are only effective to the extent that they are consistent with EU law, and that they are ineffective, or unenforceable, to the extent that they are not. This implies that s 2(4) constitutes not only a rule of interpretation, but also a *rule of priority*—one which determines that, in the event of a conflict, EU law is to take precedence.

4.3.3 The *Factortame* decision

As the House of Lords' historic decision in *Factortame* demonstrates, it is the latter view that has prevailed in the UK.[94] The dispute centred upon (what is now) TFEU, Art 49, which entitles EU nationals to establish businesses in any EU state. Contrary to that right, the UK Parliament enacted the Merchant Shipping Act 1998 to protect the British fishing industry by preventing foreign nationals from exploiting British fish stocks. The CJEU eventually held that the nationality restrictions imposed by the Act were incompatible with Art 49.[95] However, it took several years to obtain this ruling, and in the meantime the claimants asked the British courts to suspend the operation of the Act.

As the House of Lords noted,[96] the doctrine of parliamentary sovereignty would appear to prevent the setting aside—whether permanently or merely temporarily—of primary legislation.[97] The CJEU, however, reminded the Law Lords that the supremacy principle requires national courts to apply EU law in preference to national law, and to ignore any national rule or principle—including the doctrine of parliamentary sovereignty—that would impede domestic courts in that endeavour.[98] The House of Lords therefore took the unprecedented step of issuing an injunction disapplying the relevant parts of the Merchant Shipping Act 1988 in order that the claimants could exercise their conflicting rights under the Treaty.[99]

How can this novel judicial power to set aside primary legislation be accounted for in terms of constitutional law and theory? *Factortame* itself is far from illuminating

---

[94] *R v Secretary of State for Transport, ex p Factortame Ltd (No 2)* [1991] 1 AC 603.

[95] Case C-221/89 *R v Secretary of State for Transport, ex p Factortame Ltd* [1992] QB 680.

[96] *R v Secretary of State for Transport, ex p Factortame Ltd (No 1)* [1990] 2 AC 85.

[97] As explained in Chapter 7, no such complications arise in relation to the devolved legislatures, since they are in no sense sovereign; the devolution legislation provides a clear and straightforward legal basis for courts to set aside devolved legislation that contradicts EU law.

[98] Case C-213/89 *R v Secretary of State for Transport, ex p Factortame Ltd* [1990] ECR I-2433.

[99] *Factortame (No 2).*

in this respect. Only one of the judges, Lord Bridge, considered the matter directly, and even his analysis was sparse. He observed that the supremacy of EU law was 'well established in the jurisprudence of the [CJEU] long before the United Kingdom joined the [Union]', such that 'whatever limitation of its sovereignty Parliament accepted when it enacted the European Communities Act 1972 was entirely voluntary'.[100] In the following sections, we evaluate the position arrived at in *Factortame* against the backdrop of the three interpretations of parliamentary sovereignty advanced in Chapter 5.

> **Q** Before reading on, review the three models of parliamentary sovereignty discussed in Chapter 5. How do you think proponents of each of the three models might attempt to explain the outcome of *Factortame*?

4.4 Parliamentary sovereignty: three perspectives

4.4.1 Parliamentary sovereignty as a constitutional fixture

Lord Bridge's assertion that Parliament had 'voluntarily' accepted limitations upon its sovereignty presupposes that it is *capable* of doing so. The difficulty with this analysis is that it is at odds with the premise underlying what is, or at least was, generally regarded as the dominant account of parliamentary sovereignty. As we saw in Chapter 5, the so-called *continuing theory* propounded by Wade holds that the constitutional rule that establishes the sovereignty of Parliament—by requiring courts to recognise all Acts of Parliament as valid laws and to prefer the most recent expression of parliamentary intention over any earlier conflicting intentions—is ultimately a political, not a legal, one. This, said Wade, means that it is 'a rule which is unique in being unchangeable by Parliament'.[101]

For Wade, therefore, there are two central truths about parliamentary sovereignty. First, as a matter of constitutional law, the sovereignty of Parliament is fixed: it is a given that cannot be changed by legislation or by any other legal means. It is therefore simply not open to Parliament to accept, voluntarily or otherwise, limitations upon its sovereignty. But, second, the authority of Parliament may be diminished through non-legal means. This would involve courts acting unconstitutionally in refusing to recognise an Act of Parliament as an enforceable law. They would thereby bring the old constitutional order (in which Parliament was sovereign) crashing down and, as a matter of practical politics, establish a new order (in which Parliament is not sovereign). Thus Wade says that the sovereignty of Parliament can be 'changed [only] by revolution not by legislation'.[102] This analysis forces Wade to characterise *Factortame* as a judicial revolution: the judges refused to do what the old constitutional order required of them (ie applying the Merchant Shipping Act 1988) and instead shifted

---

[100] *Factortame (No 2)*, 658–9.
[101] Wade, 'The Basis of Legal Sovereignty' [1955] CLJ 172, 188–9.
[102] Wade, 'The Basis of Legal Sovereignty', 189.

their allegiance to EU law as the highest form of law applicable in the UK.[103] For this reason, Wade sees this change as a permanent one, in the sense that it does not follow that Parliament can simply repeal the ECA and thus restore its 'ultimate' sovereignty.[104] The pre-1973 position could be restored only if a further revolution were to occur in which judges shifted their allegiance back to the Westminster Parliament as supreme lawmaker for the UK—something that is, self-evidently, not within *Parliament's* gift. The assertion in s 18 of the European Union Act 2011 that EU law has effect (including supremacy) only because (and so to the extent that) UK legislation allows is then, *on this view*, factually inaccurate. Parliament may have played a part in bringing about the new constitutional reality, but it is not within its gift to reverse what has happened. This means that, as far as Brexit is concerned, Parliament cannot unilaterally shrug off whatever limits upon its authority EU membership involved. Rather, sovereignty will be restored only if and when a further 'revolution' occurs, whereby judicial allegiance shifts back to the UK Parliament.

Wade's rationalisation of *Factortame* is consistent with his general theory of parliamentary sovereignty, but is problematic on two levels. First, it does not accord with Lord Bridge's (admittedly sparse) analysis in *Factortame* itself, in which he implied that legislation, not a judge-led 'revolution', was the cause of any modification of Parliament's authority. Second, Wade's attempt to accommodate *Factortame* within his theory of sovereignty highlights substantial problems with that theory. If Wade is to be believed, the authority to make laws applicable in the UK—whether by Parliament, the EU, or some other body—is a house of cards propped up by judicial acquiescence alone. On this view, any institution possesses lawmaking authority only to the extent to which, and for as long as, the judges are prepared to tolerate it. Equally, attempts to shift lawmaking authority—however strong the democratic pedigree of a given shift—will be successful only to the extent that it secures judicial approval.

Brexit is a case in point. On Wade's analysis, parliamentary legislation implementing the result of the referendum would not, as a matter of UK law, strip the EU of its lawmaking authority in respect of the UK. Rather, such legislation would succeed in recovering authority from the EU only if the judiciary were to go along with that enterprise. Judges are often called upon to make legal determinations whether legislation has this or that effect. But, crucially, within Wade's framework judges pronouncing on whether Brexit legislation restored full power to the Westminster Parliament would ultimately be making an extra-legal determination. That is so because they would be deciding not upon whether Parliament has the legal power to restore its authority (on Wade's view, it plainly does not). Rather, the judges would be deciding whether to recognise the occurrence of an extra-legal revolution signifying a break with the old legal order (in which EU law was supreme) and the establishment of a new legal order (in which Parliament was, once more, supreme).

These issues, as Goldsworthy points out, hint at an underlying difficulty with Wade's theory. It presupposes that just because Parliament could not logically have conferred sovereignty upon itself, the judges must have done so. Goldsworthy argues

---

[103] Wade, 'Sovereignty: Revolution or Evolution?' (1996) 112 LQR 568.
[104] Wade, 'Sovereignty: Revolution or Evolution?'

that, in reality, the authority of the legislature must depend upon and be sustained by something both broader and deeper than merely the courts' recognition of it. At the very least, there must be a consensus across the various branches of government—and, it might be added, in wider society—about where lawmaking power resides.[105] All branches of government were involved in the UK's becoming a member of the EU and in EU law becoming effective in the UK, and membership of the EU was supported by the public in a referendum. To suggest that the supremacy of EU law supplanted the sovereignty of Parliament merely because the judges said so fails to chime with that historical reality, and paints a one-dimensional picture of a constitution propped up by a judicial elite.

4.4.2 Parliament's capability to control certain aspects of legislative process

How else, then, might the contemporary status of EU law in the UK be explained? Wade's model sees sovereignty as absolutely fixed in a legal sense (albeit that judges, acting extra-constitutionally, might bring it crashing down). As we saw in Chapter 5, other writers take a more nuanced view by distinguishing between the substance of parliamentary sovereignty and the formal conditions according to which it may be exercised. Proponents of the so-called *new view* contend that while Parliament cannot do anything that would cut down its sovereignty in the substantive sense, it may require future Parliaments to comply with certain formal conditions when making law.

Can this analysis provide a convincing rationalisation of the status of EU law in the UK? It has been suggested that it can.[106] The ECA, the argument runs, can be read as laying down a formal requirement such that any Parliament wishing to legislate contrary to EU law would have to use express language indicating such an intention.[107] So when it enacted the Merchant Shipping Act 1988, Parliament, being substantively sovereign, could have succeeded in its attempt to deprive the Spanish fishermen of their EU law rights, but only if it exercised its sovereignty in the correct way—that is, by complying with the procedural requirement of express language supposedly laid down in the ECA. The absence of such language in the 1988 Act explains why Parliament failed to revoke the claimants' EU law rights.

There are, however, two difficulties with this analysis. First, it sits uncomfortably with the language of s 2(4) of the ECA, which says that UK law takes effect 'subject to' EU law. This suggests that Parliament was attempting to create a rule of priority, rather than simply to lay down a formal requirement about how Parliament should go about enacting legislation that is inconsistent with EU law. Second, it is based on an approach that is somewhat parochial. Lord Denning said that if Parliament were deliberately to attempt to act inconsistently with EU law and '[say] so in express terms then . . . it would be the duty of our courts to follow the statute of our Parliament'.[108]

---

[105] *The Sovereignty of Parliament* (Oxford 1999), pp 238–46.

[106] See, eg Laws, 'Law and Democracy' [1995] PL 72, 88–9.

[107] eg by stating that the relevant provisions of the Act were to take effect notwithstanding any inconsistency with EU law.

[108] *Macarthys Ltd v Smith* [1979] 3 All ER 325, 329.

But this presupposes that the matter can and should be analysed purely in terms of domestic law. This overlooks, or at least attaches no weight in domestic legal terms to, the fact that the use of express language would cut no ice whatever at the EU level. At that level, EU law is regarded as supreme. Member states are incapable of opting out of EU law by enacting inconsistent national legislation, however explicitly the intention to derogate might be stated. Characterising the EU-related limitations on Parliament's legislative freedom as purely formal ones may, in conjunction with the new view, provide a workable explanation of why the Merchant Shipping Act 1988 was disapplied in *Factortame*. However, by proceeding on the implicit premise that Parliament remained truly sovereign in the substantive sense, and could have overridden EU law if only it had used express language, this analysis is ultimately weakened by an air of unreality.

4.4.3 EU law as evidence of the legal malleability of parliamentary authority

The two models so far considered have arguably failed to supply a convincing account of how EU law has acquired its present status in the UK. A third possibility lies in rejecting the premise of the first model by characterising the sovereignty of Parliament as a *legal phenomenon* rather than a purely political one, such that it can be manipulated like other legal norms. This view shares some common ground with the third model of sovereignty considered in Chapter 5 and is perhaps the most radical one. By characterising the authority of Parliament as a legal phenomenon it requires lawyers to engage with difficult but important questions, and rules out seeking refuge in the notion that such questions belong exclusively to the realm of politics. We saw in Chapter 5 that the courts are increasingly—but tentatively at this stage—developing the idea that the authority of Parliament to make law is something that is subject to, and therefore controllable by, constitutional law: that there is a line that Parliament is not allowed to cross, albeit that the location of that line remains, for now, uncertain. This view presents the authority of Parliament as a dynamic, legal phenomenon: its scope is a function of the contemporary constitution as interpreted by the judges. On that view, EU law—while the UK remains a member of the EU—may well be regarded as forming part of the line delimiting the authority of Parliament to make law. Indeed, in *Jackson*, Lord Hope went as far as to say that 'the supremacy of [Union] law restricts the absolute authority of Parliament to legislate as it wants in this area'.[109]

If this is what has happened, then its significance transcends EU membership—and hence will persist post-Brexit. It suggests that the law is, or can come to be, a restriction upon the authority of Parliament, giving rise to a notion of bounded authority that is at odds with orthodox notions of sovereignty. Yet this view is not without difficulty. It is one thing to say that the width of Parliament's authority to make law is itself a function of law and may therefore be changed by legal means. However, precisely what are those legal means? In *Jackson*, Lord Hope said that the restriction on parliamentary sovereignty inherent in EU membership was a 'product of measures enacted by Parliament' itself—that, by enacting the ECA, Parliament had limited its future lawmaking power.[110] In contrast, Laws LJ in *Thoburn* suggested that the width

---

[109] *Jackson v Attorney-General* [2005] UKHL 56, [2006] 1 AC 262, [105].   [110] *Jackson*, [105].

of Parliament's lawmaking power is set not by Parliament, but by the constitution.[111] This presupposes that, as in a system with a written constitution, Parliament has only so much power as the constitution concedes to it; as the constitution evolves over time, the amount of power wielded by Parliament may alter. On this analysis, if Parliament is (while the UK remains in the EU) incapable of enacting enforceable legislation that is contrary to EU law, that is because the UK constitution, as presently interpreted, prevents it from doing so. The problem is that, in the absence of a written constitution, we have only the word of the judges that such is the position.

The truth probably lies somewhere between the positions adopted by Lord Hope in *Jackson* and Laws LJ in *Thoburn*. The emerging modern orthodoxy is that the capacity of Parliament to legislate is a legal, not a purely political, phenomenon. In other words, the width of Parliament's power is determined by constitutional law. It can be changed if, and only if, the relevant constitutional law changes. The key questions are: how can the constitutional law that determines the extent of Parliament's authority be changed? And who decides whether such change has occurred? For the reasons considered in Chapter 5, to suggest that this is a matter entirely within the hands of Parliament is unsatisfactory—not least because it would be dangerous to concede entirely to the legislature control over this matter. That Parliament is not master of its own destiny in this respect is reflected in the suggestions in *Jackson* that there might be some limits on Parliament's authority—for example, it might be impotent to abolish judicial review of executive action—that cannot be attributed to any intention evidenced in Acts of Parliament.

Q Why would it be dangerous to recognise in Parliament an unqualified power to impose substantive limits on its own and its successors' legislative authority?

However, it is equally unsatisfactory to suggest that this is a matter wholly in the hands of the judges such that neither Parliament's nor anyone else's view is relevant, since that way lies the risk of uncontrolled judicial supremacism. In any event, it does not chime with reality. It is self-evident that the judges did not simply take it on themselves to decide that EU law should take priority over domestic law, just as they did not unilaterally decide that it should be possible for legislation to be enacted without the involvement of the House of Lords.[112] Rather, they were clearly influenced by legislation in arriving at those conclusions.

Laws LJ's view that it is the unwritten constitution, as interpreted by the judges, that ultimately sets the terms on which Parliament wields power must therefore be supplemented by recognising that the judges' interpretation of the constitution will and should be influenced by Acts of Parliament. It follows that the constitutional terms on which Parliament holds legislative power are within the exclusive control of neither Parliament nor the courts. They are set by the constitution, the content of

---

[111] *Thoburn v Sunderland City Council* [2002] EWHC 195 (Admin), [2003] QB 151.
[112] See discussion of the Parliament Acts in Chapter 5, section 3.3.3.

which necessarily falls to be determined by judges, but which can be influenced by Acts of Parliament. This analysis addresses some of the difficulties discussed earlier in respect of Wade's approach. We saw then that Wade's approach can be criticised because it ascribes to the courts the extra-legal (and so legally unregulated) function of determining whether a 'revolution' has occurred. In contrast, the present view envisages a bounded judicial authority to articulate the conditions, if any, that apply to and constrain the exercise of Parliament's legislative power.

Viewed thus, judicial enforcement of any EU-related limits upon Parliament's law-making power can be understood as a judicial attempt to devise a legal theory of legislative authority that can be accommodated given other features of the constitutional order. EU membership was (and, for now, still is) a cardinal feature of that order, thanks in no small measure to the legislation enacted by Parliament itself in 1972. In those circumstances, and on the present analysis, the courts can be said to have acted properly in seeking to advance an understanding of parliamentary authority that accorded with EU membership. But it must equally follow that when the UK leaves the EU, the constitutional order will be remade in terms that would render it wholly improper for any judge to give effect to, let alone prioritise, EU law over an Act of Parliament. Crucially, however, on the present view (unlike on Wade's) the judicial response to Brexit will involve reconsideration of the position of Parliament in the light of legal changes to the constitutional framework within which Parliament sits. There is no need, on this approach, for recourse to the idea of a 'revolution', implying that judges have to fall back on extra-legal criteria when deciding what to do. Rather, if a court, post-Brexit, were to affirm that Acts of Parliament could no longer be challenged on the ground of incompatibility with EU law, it would simply be giving effect to changes to the legal environment wrought by Brexit. Those changes will (assuming that full Brexit occurs) include the removal of any EU obligations upon which the ECA can bite and, no doubt, the repeal of the ECA itself.

4.5 EU membership, Brexit, and broader constitutional considerations

There are many aspects to the constitutional implications of Brexit. In this section, we address two particularly significant aspects. The first is about the process whereby Brexit will be accomplished and, in particular, where responsibility lies in respect of the Brexit process. The second matter concerns the constitutional legacy that the UK's EU membership is likely to have once the withdrawal process is complete.

4.5.1 The Brexit process

Brexit will be a complicated business. It will present a legislative, diplomatic, and bureaucratic challenge unprecedented in both scale and complexity. No attempt will be made here to provide a comprehensive overview of what the process will involve. But two points—respectively concerning authority and accountability—are worth making about certain constitutional aspects of the process. To some extent, those issues form two sides of a single coin.

As to authority, almost as soon as the referendum result was announced, controversy arose about who had the authority to initiate the formal mechanism for withdrawing from the EU as set out in TEU, Art 50. In particular, questions arose about whether the executive government had legal authority, in the form of the royal prerogative, to trigger Art 50, or whether the withdrawal process could be initiated only by (or under authority conferred by) an Act of the UK Parliament.[113] Controversy also arose about whether the triggering of Art 50 was a matter exclusively for the UK tier of government (whether in its executive or legislative guise) or whether the territorial governments were entitled to have a say. The First Minister of Scotland, for instance, suggested shortly after the referendum that the Scottish Parliament might pose an obstacle to Brexit. Those questions about where authority lay to *initiate* withdrawal were subsequently joined by questions about where authority lay to *conduct* the withdrawal process. For instance, the House of Lords Constitution Committee, in a report published in 2016, argued that it was essential that the conduct of the process was not entrusted exclusively to the UK executive government, and that Parliament should play a significant role.[114] In these ways, Brexit has thrown into sharp relief questions about where constitutional authority—in respect of a matter that is of the most profound constitutional significance—does and ought to lie.

There are also important questions concerning the holding to account of those who will take the lead in negotiating the terms of Brexit. Such questions arise in part because of the unusually cross-cutting nature of the issues raised by Brexit. Very many areas of policy will be affected by Brexit in some way or other. The accountability picture was further complicated by the machinery of government changes made shortly after the referendum, including the creation of a Department for Exiting the European Union and a Department for International Trade. A fundamental difficulty that arises in this area, as the House of Lords EU Committee noted, is that some elements of the negotiations, such as those relating to trade, 'may have to be conducted confidentially'. Nevertheless, said the Committee, considerations of confidentiality will have to be balanced against those of transparency so as to achieve 'the overarching objective of holding the Government effectively to account'.[115] By contrast, David Davis, Secretary of State for Exiting the European Union, has told Parliament that 'Clearly there is a need for Parliament to be informed without giving away our negotiating position. I may not be able to tell you everything, even in private hearings'.[116] A fundamental tension thus arises, between government's desire to be in the driving seat and to pursue a negotiating position uncompromised by detailed and ongoing parliamentary scrutiny and, on the other hand, parliamentarians' desire to hold government to account for a negotiation process whose outcome will shape the UK's economic, social, and geopolitical prospects for several decades to come.

Striking the balance between accountability and transparency will be a major test for Parliament as the Art 50 process unfolds. Indeed, it would be ironic, to say the least, if a referendum that was intended to return power to the sovereign UK

---

[113] At the time of writing, this matter is the subject of litigation in which the Supreme Court is expected to give judgment in early 2017.

[114] *The Invoking of Article 50* (HL Paper 44 2016–17).

[115] *Scrutinising Brexit: The Role of Parliament* (HL Paper 33 2016–17), [22].

[116] Oral evidence of David Davis MP to the House of Lords European Union Select Committee, 12 September 2016.

Parliament were to result in an executive-dominated withdrawal process of which Parliament was nothing more than an impotent observer.

4.5.2 The constitutional legacy of the UK's EU membership

We have seen so far that the UK's membership of the EU has afforded opportunities for—and required—reflection upon the nature of the doctrine of parliamentary sovereignty. Brexit will remove the trigger that prompted those reflections, but the lessons that have been learned, in terms of how we think about sovereignty, will remain of value even after withdrawal. The implications of EU membership have also been the anvil upon which a different, and in some respects more refined, understanding of the broader constitution has been beaten out. In particular, it is in the context of attempting to come to terms with the nature and degree of EU law's impact that courts have had cause to reflect upon the inherent features of the common law constitution.

In this regard, two cases—*Thoburn*[117] and *HS2*[118]—stand out as being of particular importance. The former demonstrates how the primacy of EU law might be explained by reference to aspects of the common law constitution. Meanwhile, the latter, by showing how EU law's primacy might itself be qualified by the common law, shines new light upon the contours of the domestic constitutional order. Although these insights were stimulated by the interaction of UK and EU law, their significance, as we will see, transcends that context.

In *Thoburn*, a power conferred by the ECA 1972 to implement EU regulations was used to make UK secondary legislation that was at odds with an Act of Parliament enacted in 1985. The question was whether the regulation-making power in the 1972 Act could be used in such a way. The defendants contended that it could not, arguing that the 1985 Act must have narrowed the 1972 power such that the latter could not be used in a way that was incompatible with the former. That contention was rejected on the ground (among others) that the 1972 Act was a 'constitutional statute' and was, as such, immune from implied repeal or implied amendment. Since nothing in the 1985 Act explicitly sought to remove or narrow the powers conferred by the 1972 Act, those powers remained fully intact. Crucially, Laws LJ, giving the only reasoned judgment, said that the ECA enjoyed this special status because the *common law* recognised it as a constitutional statute.

This analysis helps to make sense of why the *Factortame* case was decided as it was. The Merchant Shipping Act 1988—an 'ordinary', as distinct from a 'constitutional' statute—did not explicitly attempt to stop the ECA from giving effect in UK law to the EU rights that the claimants in *Factortame* were seeking to exercise. In the absence of any such explicit attempt, the earlier constitutional statute—turning the doctrine of implied repeal on its head—prevailed over the later ordinary statute, and the ECA therefore continued to give effect, and assign priority, to the relevant EU rights.

However, while this innovative reading of the UK constitution's basic architecture might assist our understanding of how EU law could prevail over Acts of Parliament passed after the ECA was enacted, its significance is much broader than that. Among

---

[117] *Thoburn v Sunderland City Council* [2002] EWHC 195 (Admin), [2003] QB 151.
[118] *R (HS2 Action Alliance Ltd) v Secretary of State for Transport* [2014] UKSC 3, [2014] 1 WLR 324.

other things, it suggests that the conditions upon which Parliament exercises legislative authority are determined by the common law constitution, and that it is by recourse to that constitution that we discover the extent of—and any limits upon—Parliament's authority. *Thoburn* acknowledged only the very modest limit that Parliament is incapable of impliedly repealing constitutional legislation. But Laws LJ's judgment lays the conceptual foundation for the articulation of more substantial—and substantive—criteria that might in future demarcate the scope of Parliament's lawmaking power.

If *Thoburn* helped us—among other things—to understand how the common law constitution might secure a degree of priority for EU law over domestic legislation, *HS2* helped us to understand why that same common law constitution might at the same time place limits upon that priority's extent. It was argued that the parliamentary process whereby permission would be granted for the construction of the UK's new 'HS2' high-speed rail network fell foul of EU law. In the end, the Supreme Court held that the process complied with EU law. But was the adequacy of the parliamentary process something that the Court was entitled to consider in the first place?

That question arose because of what Lord Reed described as 'long-established constitutional principles governing the relationship between Parliament and the courts',[119] including the principle reflected in Art 9 of the Bill of Rights 1689. It provides that parliamentary proceedings 'ought not to be impeached or questioned in any court'. In the end, the Court held that it could carry out the requisite scrutiny of the parliamentary process without infringing that principle. But in proceeding along that line of analysis, the Court had to deal with what is, for present purposes, the crucial argument: that Art 9 of the Bill of Rights—one of Laws LJ's 'constitutional statutes' in *Thoburn*—and the principle it reflected had been swept away by EU law. On that view, the Court did not need to bother deciding whether the principle would be offended by carrying out the scrutiny of the parliamentary process that EU law required, since the principle had been eclipsed by EU law.

The Court rejected that argument. In doing so, it had to confront questions that had not arisen in *Thoburn* about the relationship between one constitutional statute (the ECA) and another constitutional statute (the Bill of Rights)—or, looking at the matter slightly differently, the relationship between a constitutional statute (the ECA) and a fundamental constitutional principle (concerning the relationship between the courts and Parliament) that was reflected in the text of a constitutional statute (ie Art 9 of the Bill of Rights). Lords Neuberger and Mance, whose judgment commanded the unanimous support of the Court, approached this conundrum by noting that it is 'certainly arguable' that there may be 'fundamental principles, whether contained in other constitutional instruments or recognised at common law, of which Parliament when it enacted the European Communities Act 1972 did not either contemplate or authorise the abrogation'.[120]

This suggests that there is a hierarchy of constitutional values—and hence of legislation that reflects or enshrines those values. On this view, not all such values or statutes are equally fundamental: some might be even more fundamental than others. This in turn means that the priority accorded by the ECA to EU law goes only

---

[119] *HS2*, [78].   [120] *HS2*, [207].

so far: the priority does not extend to overriding constitutional legislation or values whose fundamentality goes deeper than the ECA itself. In this way, it would have been possible for the Court to conclude—if it had thought that EU law and the Art 9 principle were in tension—that the latter principle prevailed because its fundamentality outstripped that of the ECA which gives effect to EU law.

It can be seen, then, from cases like *Thoburn* and *HS2* that the UK's membership of the EU has required the courts to confront questions of constitutional priority and that, in doing so, the courts have broken new ground. However, as Brexit beckons, it is important to note that these cases' significance is not confined to the EU context. Rather, they suggest that the UK constitution is layered, or hierarchical, in ways that had not previously been fully appreciated. The twin ideas for which *Thoburn* and *HS2* stand—that Parliament legislates under conditions set by a dynamic body of constitutional law, and that that body of law knows a hierarchy of fundamental principles—supply a vision of the UK constitution that is richer and more complex than traditional accounts allow. And while that vision of the constitution may have been sketched out on a canvas afforded by the questions raised by EU membership, it is a vision whose relevance will long survive Brexit.

5. Conclusions

Membership of the EU has profoundly affected the UK, its law, and its constitutional arrangements. Brexit will trigger equally profound changes. Nonetheless, the legal and constitutional legacy of the UK's EU membership will be enduring. The task of disentangling EU from UK law will be a complex and lengthy process, and even when complete, EU law will likely leave a lasting legal imprint. But for the purposes of this book, it is the constitutional legacy of EU membership that is most significant.

One way of assessing that legacy is by reference to two of this book's key themes that are directly implicated by EU membership: the relationship between legal and political forms of constitutionalism, and the multilayered nature of the constitution. EU membership has entailed legal, judicially enforceable limits on Parliament's freedom to make law, such as that revealed in *Factortame*. It has also contributed towards the wider shift, which we have already noted in several contexts, to a more legal form of constitutionalism. Indeed, it is only in relation to EU law that UK courts have to date asserted jurisdiction to disapply Acts of Parliament, judicial review of primary legislation being one of the clearest and most distinctive hallmarks of legal constitutionalism. Meanwhile, EU membership has supplied a paradigm aspect of the UK's increasingly multilayered form of constitutionalism—the essence of that model being the existence of multiple loci of power within the constitutional order.

Will Brexit simply reverse all of this? Will it herald a shift away from legal constitutionalism? How will Brexit affect the multilayered nature of the UK constitution? Answering these questions—like answering so many questions concerning Brexit—is made difficult by the presently amorphous nature of Brexit. Some tentative answers can nevertheless be ventured. Indeed, there is one thing that is abundantly clear: there can be no going back to the past. The UK constitution after Brexit will not revert to what it was like before 1973 when the UK joined what is now the EU. Much has happened in the last four decades that will not be simply undone by Brexit. The territorial constitution of the UK has, as charted in Chapter 7, been altered almost beyond recognition as a result of devolution. If the union between the four territories of the UK survives the existential threat that Brexit poses to it, then devolution will continue to be a crucial part of the glue that holds it together. But, more than that, Brexit may well hasten the deepening of the devolution settlements. Many powers repatriated from the EU may not necessarily be handed back to UK central government in London, but to devolved governments in Edinburgh, Cardiff, and Belfast.

Nor does Brexit necessarily signify a retreat from legal constitutionalism. The hard limits on parliamentary sovereignty implied by the EU supremacy principle have formed a component of that more legal approach, but that it is far from the only component. Moreover, part of the legacy that EU membership has bequeathed to the UK is a new appreciation of the legal hierarchy that we find within the domestic constitutional order, and which supplies a basis for the legal protection of constitutional values.

In a phrase ridiculed for its vacuity, the newly appointed Prime Minister Theresa May said shortly after taking office that 'Brexit means Brexit'. At the time of writing, what 'Brexit' means remains uncertain. But, from a constitutional perspective, we can at least be sure of two things. The constitutional implications of Brexit, like those of joining the EU, will be profound. But the constitution we are left with in the wake of Brexit—and, equally importantly, our understanding of that constitution—will be significantly different from the one we had before the UK joined the EU.

Expert commentary
Parliamentary sovereignty: an interpretative approach
TRS Allan, Professor of Jurisprudence and Public Law, University of Cambridge

In their analysis of the European Communities Act 1972 (ECA), s 2(4), the authors distinguish between divergent readings. While the phrase 'shall be construed ... subject to' EU law suggests a mere rule of interpretation, the adjacent phrase 'have effect subject to' suggests instead a rule of priority. A priority rule would require that in any conflict between domestic and European law, the latter must always take precedence. That interpretation is consistent with Laws LJ's analysis in *Thoburn*, which allows EU law to take priority over the conflicting provisions of an Act of Parliament unless that Act expressly provides otherwise. As a 'constitutional statute', the ECA is immunised against implied repeal: its requirements, as regards the faithful application of EU law, must be followed unless expressly overridden.[121]

It would be a mistake, however, to neglect the power of judicial interpretation along more traditional lines. While Laws LJ's judgment in *Thoburn* may be applauded for its admirable breadth and clarity, it arguably imposes too schematic a straitjacket on the common law constitution. We could avoid the problems of distinguishing between 'constitutional' and 'ordinary' statutes, which are not inconsiderable, by simply acknowledging that the correct application of any statute always depends on an interpretation of the law as a whole—all the

---

[121] *Thoburn v Sunderland City Council* [2002] EWHC 195 (Admin), [2003] QB 151.

relevant statutory and common law rules forming parts of a larger, integrated unity. Forging that unity, as far as necessary to resolve the immediate case, is the essence of common law adjudication.[122]

The Merchant Shipping Act 1988 was read subject to the primacy of EU law in *Factortame* because that made most sense of the law as a whole. The validity of the 1988 Act was not in doubt; it was simply 'disapplied' in the case of nationals of EU member states who would otherwise be deprived of rights that Parliament had recognized by passing the ECA. The scope of the 1988 Act, in other words, was limited by reference to the constitutional background, which included the supremacy of EU law—a supremacy not (at least explicitly) contradicted by the later statute. In *Factortame (No 1)*, Lord Bridge explained that the effect of ECA, s 2(4) was the same 'as if a section were incorporated in . . . the 1988 Act which in terms enacted that the provisions with respect to registration of fishing vessels were to be without prejudice to the directly enforceable [EU] rights of nationals of any member state'.[123]

So it was, at root, a question of interpretation after all. There was no question of implied repeal of the ECA, but only a question about its *effect* in the relevant circumstances; no special priority rule was therefore needed to preclude implied repeal. When, in *Factortame (No 2)*, Lord Bridge observed that 'whatever limitation of its sovereignty Parliament accepted when it enacted the European Communities Act 1972 was entirely voluntary', he was not expressing a novel constitutional theory.[124] He was, as the context shows, simply responding to criticism of the judiciary for bowing to the supremacy of the European Court of Justice. He was explaining the political circumstances in which the courts were now obliged to make sense of Parliament's various enactments.[125]

It is important to grasp the dependence of an Act's meaning—its consequences for the facts of particular cases—on the law regarded as a coherent whole. Statute and common law have to be integrated, all legal rules being ultimately subject to compatibility with fundamental principles—principles of legality and legitimacy that underpin our allegiance or loyalty to the legal and constitutional order.[126] The language of priority rules, like talk of absolute parliamentary sovereignty, lends only a spurious simplicity, imposing an unnecessary rigidity on legal analysis. As *HS2* shows,[127] the priority of EU law was never automatic but, instead, dependent on all relevant constitutional considerations being taken into account.

Legal interpretation, properly conducted, has no need of any 'rule of recognition' or fundamental political rule, somehow placed above and outside the law. Any such rule could only be a rough summary approximation of the relationship between the courts and Parliament: it is an external description of the sort made by a political scientist. Legal interpretation, by contrast, must be internal—invoking that balance of reasons for decision that appears to the interpreter (after careful analysis) to reflect the demands of constitutional principle in all the circumstances. Against the importance of respecting the primacy of EU law, in the present context, we must set the democratic imperative that Parliament at Westminster should be free to amend UK law: appropriate weight must be given to each principle according to the specific context.

Law students, like most legal commentators, crave clear rules defining the respective jurisdictions of courts and Parliament. They want an unwritten constitution to be more like a codified one. The common law constitution, however, proves resistant: it makes judgments in hard cases

---

[122] See generally Allan, *The Sovereignty of Law: Freedom, Constitution, and Common Law* (Oxford 2013).
[123] *R v Secretary of State for Transport, ex p Factortame Ltd (No 1)* [1990] 2 AC 85, 140.
[124] *R v Secretary of State for Transport, ex p Factortame Ltd (No 2)* [1991] 1 AC 603, 658.
[125] See further Allan, *Sovereignty of Law*, 149–50.   [126] See further Allan, especially ch 1.
[127] *R (HS2 Action Alliance Ltd) v Secretary of FState for Transport* [2014] UKSC 3, [2014] 1 WLR 324.

dependent on analysis of all the pertinent reasons applicable to the context in point. UK membership of the EU has demonstrated the constitution's flexibility—its capacity for embracing political change while ensuring stability by maintaining harmony between old and new.

We have seen that parliamentary sovereignty is more complex than is often understood, providing for an application of statute in particular cases that is fully responsive to all the relevant legal reasons. When we recognize that we can discover the implications of statute only by studying the reasons in favour of competing interpretations, and not simply by reading the text in isolation, we can see why legal analysis is more subtle than reliance on competing versions of any supposed 'rule of recognition', or ultimate legal rule, would allow. Neither joining nor leaving the EU involves any political 'revolution' of a kind that makes ordinary legal analysis inapt or redundant. The resources of the common law constitution are equal to both.

Further reading

CRAIG, 'Sovereignty of the United Kingdom Parliament after *Factortame*' (1991) 11 YB Eur L 221

Discussion of the constitutional implications of the *Factortame* judgment.

BOGDANOR, 'Imprisoned by a Doctrine: The Modern Defence of Parliamentary Sovereignty' (2012) 32 OJLS 179

An examination of the doctrine of parliamentary sovereignty viewed in its contemporary constitutional context.

DASHWOOD, 'From *Van Duyn* to *Mangold* via *Marshall*: Reducing Direct Effect to Absurdity?' (2007) 9 CYELS 81

Analysis and critique of the development of the CJEU's case law on the capacity of directives to produce direct effects.

DOUGAN, 'The Treaty of Lisbon 2007: Winning Minds, Not Hearts' (2008) 45 CML Rev 617

Detailed discussion of the Lisbon Treaty and its implications.

WADE, 'Sovereignty: Revolution or Evolution?' (1996) 112 LQR 568

Wade's examination of the *Factortame* case by reference to his previous writings on the nature of parliamentary sovereignty.

Useful websites

https://www.gov.uk/government/organisations/department-for-exiting-the-european-union
Website of the UK government's Department for Exiting the European Union

http://europa.eu/european-union/index_en
Website of the European Union

http://eur-lex.europa.eu/
Online access to the Treaty on European Union and the Treaty on the Functioning of the European Union

PART III

Good Governance– Scrutiny, Accountability, and Transparency

9

Good Governance—An Introduction

1.	Introduction	381
2.	What is good governance?	382
3.	Accountability	387
4.	Pulling it together	394
5.	Conclusion	396
	Expert commentary	396
	Further reading	400

1. Introduction

So far, we have considered the structures and institutions of government in the multilayered constitution of the UK. This part of the book focuses upon the practical arrangements by which government is held to account and the means by which government is required to adhere to the principles of good governance.

Good governance is essential if people are to accept, cooperate with, and recognise the legitimacy of the institutions of government—all of which are imperative to the existence of a peaceful, well-functioning, civilised, and productive society. Mechanisms must therefore exist that require, or at least encourage, those in power to adhere to the standards of good governance. The electoral process is clearly important in this regard, but is not by itself sufficient. Not all institutions of government are under the direct control of elected politicians. And even in relation to those that are, infrequent elections constitute a crude, insufficiently granular form of scrutiny. Voters can do little more than pass broad judgement on the performance of the government as a whole.

Good governance, then, is integral to the legitimacy of government. The desirability of good governance is beyond dispute, but it is more difficult to define *what it actually means and how to achieve it.* There is no definitive set of standards of good governance upon which everyone agrees. Nonetheless, it could be said that there is a set of core principles that, together, are widely regarded as comprising good governance, although their precise details may vary and change over time. The notion of good governance is inseparable from that of democracy. Good governance ultimately reduces to the idea of government being conducted in ways that are *acceptable to* the (majority of) people—hence our point that good governance is necessary for the *acceptance of* government by the people.

The principles of good governance derive from—indeed, are constituted by—values that are widely held within society. Some such values are reflected in the sort of constitutional principles that we encountered in earlier chapters. This is unsurprising. One of the purposes of a constitution is to capture and institutionalise values that are deep-seated and enduring within the relevant society. The average person may not readily adopt the language of 'separation of powers' or 'rule of law'. However, he or she would most likely subscribe to propositions inherent in those constitutional principles—for example, that politicians should not interfere in judicial proceedings. A government that sought to do this would have breached the standards of good governance.

The standards of good governance are not confined to ones reflected in fundamental constitutional principles. The concept encompasses a broader range of norms concerning how institutions of government should behave. They reflect expectations widely held by those subject to government. People expect the government, and the politicians running it, to act lawfully. But those in power should also behave in ways that are not necessarily, or not comprehensively, mandated by law. They should, for instance, act honestly, openly, straightforwardly, competently, with integrity, and selflessly. Lawful governance is necessary, but is not a sufficient condition for good governance. Further, the standards of good governance are upheld not only through legal, but also through political, means.

This raises a fundamental question: are the political mechanisms responsible for upholding standards of good governance adequate? And, if not, should legal control of government be expanded? In other words, what is the right balance in this context between legal and political modes of constitutionalism? These are questions for later chapters. We now focus upon what good governance means.

2. What is good governance?

Given the lack of a definitive or universally accepted list of standards of good governance, we have to look at a variety of sources in order to locate what can be regarded as the prevailing standards of good governance. According to *The Federalist* Papers (1787–88): 'A good government implies two things: first, fidelity to the object of government, which is the happiness of the people; secondly, a knowledge of the means by which that object can be best attained.'[1] More recently, in 2009, a parliamentary select committee identified five prerequisites for good government: good people, good process, good accountability, good performance, and good standards.[2] The following

---

[1] Hamilton, Madison, and Jay, *The Federalist* [1787–88] (Washington DC 1992), no 62.
[2] House of Commons Public Administration Select Committee, *Good Government* (HC 97 2008–09).

discussion divides the standards of good governance into different categories in order to aid explanation. However, in practice, many of the standards are interrelated.

2.1 Governing in the public interest

Governments have no legitimate interests of their own, and nor, when acting in their official capacities, do the individuals who lead and work in governments. In a democracy, citizens elect a government in order to protect, advance, and serve their interests. In normative terms, democratic governance presupposes that government acts as the servant—rather than the master—of the people. There are two dimensions to this notion that good governance means (among other things) governing in the public interest.

The positive dimension is that *government should make decisions that advance the public good*. The public good is a highly contestable notion. Concepts such as good governance and the public good do not supply objective yardsticks against which the legitimacy of governmental action can be determined. However, there must be mechanisms by which the wisdom of government policy and decisions can be measured and judgement pronounced. In a democracy, the ultimate question is not whether the government is acting in an objectively correct way (whatever that might mean); rather, it is whether it is governing in a manner that is regarded as broadly acceptable by the public. Elections are the pre-eminent means of doing this. The public can kick out the current government and elect a new one. But, elections are, taken on their own, insufficient. Government needs to be kept on a shorter leash than that supplied by the electoral process. There are a number of different ways that enable or require government to take account of the views and wishes of the people: the need to obtain parliamentary approval of legislative proposals; submission to scrutiny by Parliament, the media, courts, tribunals, and ombudsmen; and public participation in government decision-making (eg by consulting with the public).

To take one specific example, it is a relatively uncontentious proposition that, when using public resources—especially public money—government should, so far as possible, seek to attain value for money. Government is largely funded by the public through taxation. Accordingly, the public can, in turn, rightfully expect that government should not waste its money. Instead, government should use public money wisely so that the public receives value for its money. Just because government *ought* to behave in a certain way does not mean that this necessarily always happens in practice. There is therefore a real need for mechanisms that scrutinise government.

Governing in the public interest has a second, negative dimension. Government *must not act in a self-interested manner*. Governments do not have any *legitimate* interests of their own. Self-interested behaviour by governmental institutions is a breach of the standards of good governance. For instance, it would be improper for an elected public body—whether the UK central government, a devolved government, or a local authority—to elevate *political gain* above the public good.

The proscription against self-interested governance also means that those involved in government must not act for improper *personal gain*. If, in our example, the Minister were choosing between two potential sites for a new airport and the arguments were otherwise evenly balanced, it would be improper (and, again, unlawful) for her to choose one site over the other if she would stand to gain financially by that decision.[3] The impropriety of such behaviour is widely recognised.

The Committee on Standards in Public Life is the independent public body that advises the UK government on ethical standards across the whole of public life in the UK. It has drawn up a list of principles that encapsulate the standards expected of those involved in public life. Among these principles are the requirements that those involved in public life act with selflessness (acting in public, not private, interest), integrity (freedom from influence from outside interests), objectivity (making decisions on merit), and honesty.[4] These principles are not legally binding. They have, though, come to inform public life and other codes of conduct, such as the Ministerial Code and the Civil Service Code, which are respectively applicable to government Ministers and civil servants. Politicians and officials who fall short of these standards deserve to be held to account and criticised. A prime example of this was the public revulsion that followed the 2009 MPs' expenses scandal, when it transpired that some MPs had made expenses claims that were widely regarded as highly improper.

2.2 Governing transparently

It can be hard to distinguish the *content* of the principles of good governance from the *mechanisms* necessary to secure (or at least to incentivise) it. So it is with the requirement of transparency or openness—another of the principles articulated by the Committee on Standards in Public Life and upheld in a number of different ways, including via the Freedom of Information Act 2000. According to the Committee, openness requires that '[h]olders of public office should be as open as possible about all the decisions and actions that they take', 'should give reasons for their decisions', and should 'restrict information only when the wider public interest clearly demands'.

Transparency is arguably desirable in and of itself. It recognises that people are 'grown-ups'. They deserve to be told what is being decided and why. But transparency is also a means to another, important, end. A government that is both open and transparent is likely to avoid acting in a way that is otherwise improper, and which may undermine the trust that people place in it. As Brandeis observed: 'Sunlight is said to be the best form of disinfectant.'[5] Unsurprisingly, the regulatory body set up in response to the MPs' expenses scandal now publishes MPs' expenses claims as a matter of course.[6] Good governance therefore implies not merely that government pursues the public interest (and only the public interest), but also that it does so openly and transparently.

---

[3] eg if she owned land consisting of part of one of the potential sites, such that choosing that site would increase the value of that land.

[4] See **http://www.public-standards.gov.uk**. The other principles are accountability and transparency (which we address later) and leadership (meaning that '[h]olders of public office should promote and support [the other] principles by leadership and example').

[5] 'Other people's money', *Harper's Weekly*, 20 December 1913.

[6] Independent Parliamentary Standards Authority, *The MPs' Expenses Scheme* (London 2010).

2.3 Respecting the dignity, rights, and interests of individuals

Good governance also encompasses the standards of the rule of law. Government must act lawfully. It is, for example, a long-established legal principle that government is obliged to adopt a fair process when it goes about the task of making decisions that affect individuals. Government must give affected individuals an opportunity to be heard—to put their side of the story—rather than simply make decisions without knowledge of, or regard to, such individuals' circumstances and interests. The courts enforce this principle—known as *procedural fairness*—and other legal principles through the process known as judicial review. A related point is that, under the Human Rights Act 1998 (HRA), government must respect individuals' human rights.

2.4 Governing competently

Many of the requirements of good governance are underpinned by or related to a further, and very basic, requirement—that of competence. Government is not merely a collection of government Ministers, but a very much larger enterprise. It consists of departments and agencies that make and administer public policy. When members of the public interact with government, they rarely, if ever, do so by way of direct contact with the Prime Minister or government Ministers—they are much more likely to come into contact with front-line officials and public servants. Unlike government Ministers, these officials are neither directly elected nor accountable to Parliament; instead, they are appointed as full-time public employees on the basis of their knowledge and expertise.

The public rightfully expects that these officials and public agencies also operate in accordance with the standards discussed so far—that is, they seek to further the public interest, are open and transparent, obey the law, and do not infringe human rights. The public also expects these officials and public servants to be competent in what they do. They should follow the basic principles of good administration. These principles require, among other things, that governmental agencies advise individuals correctly and precisely on the detailed rules governing, for example, their tax liability or entitlement to welfare benefits, that they are customer focused, and that, when mistakes are made, these are acknowledged and corrected quickly and effectively.[7]

Furthermore, good governance often requires the potential for incompetence to be recognised and anticipated. This means that when an individual receives a negative decision from a government agency (eg when an individual's application for a welfare benefit has been refused), it is often appropriate that some form of redress is available via, for example, a complaints scheme, a tribunal, or an ombudsman. When a major issue of public concern has arisen because of some failing within government, the issue may need to be investigated independently. Institutions such as these—ombudsmen, tribunals, and inquiries—form the 'administrative justice' system. Finally, competent government requires that those in power are able and willing to learn lessons when things go wrong so as to prevent the recurrence of similar errors in the future.

---

[7] See, eg Parliamentary and Health Service Ombudsman, *Principles of Good Administration* (London 2009).

2.5 **Some preliminary conclusions**

The discussion so far is necessarily tentative. Much of the rest of this book is devoted to detailed examination of the principles of good governance and the mechanisms for their enforcement. Nevertheless, it is appropriate, at this stage, to make two points by way of preliminary conclusion.

First, there is no comprehensive and definitive list of standards that together comprise good governance—nor, perhaps, could there be. The standards that define good governance are likely to vary and change in response to changes within public life itself. For example, the Committee on Standards in Public Life was itself established, in 1994, in the context of much concern about propriety in public life following the 'cash for questions' affair in which it was disclosed that some MPs had been asking parliamentary questions in return for financial payments. While basic lapses of probity were not, before that episode, regarded as acceptable, it placed such concerns centre stage, resulting in a renewed emphasis upon them. Likewise, the precise nature of the legal controls over governmental action imposed by the courts have, over recent decades, intensified often as a result of changes in the courts' own perceptions as to the necessary demands of legality and of the (in)adequacy of alternative methods of scrutinising government. Furthermore, the recognition that openness and transparency within government are important standards that need to be secured was, after many years of persuasion, finally formally recognised by Parliament when it enacted the Freedom of Information Act 2000. The broader picture is, then, that the notion of good governance is dynamic, because it reflects contemporary and changing social, moral, and democratic mores.

Second, the nature of *modern* government makes good governance a more acute concern than ever before. While there are competing ideas about what government should and should not do, it has been said that there are four basic responsibilities that any legitimate government owes to its own citizens:[8] protecting its own citizens by preserving their freedom so that they can live safe and secure lives, promoting the welfare of its citizens, enforcing justice by punishing crimes and resolving disputes, and promoting truth and knowledge.

Exactly how government seeks to discharge these responsibilities varies over time and between different countries. Perhaps the most noticeable development over the last 200 years or so in Western countries has been the growth in the scale and complexity of governmental action deemed necessary to fulfil these basic responsibilities. Modern government is an agglomeration of a multitude of large and complex organisations. If the public desires some change or other in society— for example, a better transport system, better provision of public services such as education and health, more effective regulation of banks and financial institutions, or protection from worldwide flu pandemics—then it is usually government that is called upon to act. Government is often the only means by which the necessary resources can be collected, organised, and mobilised. Moreover, it is certainly plausible to assume that the scope and role of government is unlikely to diminish

---

[8] Mulgan, *Good and Bad Power: The Ideals and Betrayals of Government* (London 2006), pp 44–58.

significantly in the future. If, for example, countries are to attempt to confront some of the world's major challenges—global terrorism, climate change, maintaining the supply of energy, and managing the global economy—then governmental action is required.

People cannot lead their lives without some element of governmental influence. If citizens wish to pursue collective goals, then they must generally agree to confer power on government to achieve these goals for them. Accordingly, government itself becomes very powerful. Governmental power may be used for either good or ill. And the notion of good governance seeks to ensure that such powers are used only for good, and that there are adequate systems in place to provide correction and redress if they are used for ill. Good governance is then a necessary corollary to the very powerful systems of government found in many countries, including the UK, today. However, it is not enough that good governance exists merely as an abstract idea. There must be adequate systems in place to scrutinise whether government is acting in accordance with the standards of good governance. This leads us to the concept of accountability.

3. Accountability

3.1 **The concept of accountability**

In an ideal world, all governments and public office-holders would simply uphold the standards of good governance. And if those standards were considered to be either ambiguous or insufficiently precise, then government could be expected to determine what those standards required in any particular set of circumstances and then respect them. There would consequently be little, if any, need to have other bodies to oversee government in order to check for compliance with these standards.

However, there is a constant risk that government will fail to live up to these standards or that it may seek to misuse its powers. No particular government—or even system of government—can be perfect or infallible. Experience often demonstrates that those who hold public office sometimes fall short of the standards expected of them. Various accountability mechanisms are therefore required. The purpose of such mechanisms is to ensure that government is held to account, that it properly observes the standards of good governance, and that its activities are properly scrutinised. In this way, the standards of good governance are given real bite.

Over recent decades, the concept of accountability has increasingly come to prominence. Yet accountability is also an elusive concept. It has various meanings. We therefore need to take some care when considering it.

In essence, the concept of accountability represents the response of democracies to the need to oversee government. As Mulgan has noted, accountability—the obligation to be called to account—is

> a method of keeping the public informed and the powerful in check. It implies a world which is at once complex, where experts are needed to perform specialised tasks, but still

fundamentally democratic in aspiration, in which members of the public assert their right to question the experts and exercise ultimate control over them.[9]

Government may get things wrong—whether by deciding upon a bad policy, by using an inadequate means of implementing a good policy, by wasting public money, or by acting unlawfully. Part of the responsibility of a democratic constitution is to provide adequate and effective safeguards. The purpose of these safeguards is to uncover bad government, to lay blame and criticism where it is required on those in power, and in that way to seek to prevent bad governance while at the same time promoting good governance.

What then does accountability mean? At its most basic level, accountability can be understood as a relationship between an actor and an accountability forum.[10] To be held to account, an actor (eg the government or a government Minister) is obliged to explain and to justify his or her conduct. The relevant accountability forum (eg Parliament or the courts) can ask questions and pass judgement. The actor may then face consequences. The accountability forum can either reward or punish the actor on the basis of the conduct or explanation given.

The precise identity of both the actor and the accountability forum can, of course, vary. The actor will normally be someone or something that has the ability to exercise public power and so will often be a government Minister, a civil servant, a government department or agency, or the government as a whole. Likewise, the accountability forum will assume different guises. It may be the public, Parliament (whether an individual Member of Parliament, a parliamentary select committee, or Parliament as a whole), a court of law, an audit agency, an ombudsman, a public inquiry, or a tribunal.

Depending on who or what the actor is and what the accountability forum is, the relationship between the two will differ. For example, the process by which Parliament holds a government Minister to account is very different from that adopted by a court of law. In the former instance, politically aligned parliamentarians will ask questions of the Minister either in Parliament or in a committee hearing; in the latter, an individual will challenge the legality of the Minister's decision before an independent court. The nature of the actor and the forum will then influence both the operative procedure and the applicable standards of good governance.

3.2 Multiple accountability mechanisms

Government is held to account through a variety of different accountability mechanisms, each of which subjects government to a different type of scrutiny and accountability. Broadly speaking, there are three different types of accountability that recur over and over again.[11]

---

[9] Mulgan, *Holding Power to Account: Accountability in Modern Democracies* (London 2003), p 1.

[10] Bovens, 'Public Accountability', in Ferlie, Lynn, and Pollitt (eds), *The Oxford Handbook of Public Management* (Oxford 2005), pp 184–5.

[11] See Day and Klein, *Accountabilities: Five Public Services* (London 1987), pp 4–29; Flinders, *The Politics of Accountability in the Modern State* (Aldershot 2001); Mashaw, 'Accountability and Institutional Design: Some Thoughts on the Grammar of Governance', in Dowdle (ed), *Public Accountability: Designs, Dilemmas and Experiences* (Cambridge 2006), pp 120–2; Bovens, 'Analysing and Assessing Accountability: A Conceptual Framework' (2007) 13 Eur LJ 447, 462–4.

First, there is *political accountability*. This seeks to ensure that government is subject to democratic and popular control. This form of accountability is exercised by voters through elections and on their behalf by Parliament. Political accountability is primarily concerned with the policy choices facing government.

Second, there is the *legal accountability* of government. This ensures government according to law. This form of accountability is undertaken normally, although not exclusively, by the courts. The purpose is to guard against the abuse of power and to protect the rights and interests of individuals adversely affected by governmental action in order to maintain the rule of law. In addition to courts that review the legality of public decisions, tribunals also determine appeals against negative administrative decisions.

Third, there is *administrative accountability*. This type of accountability operates both within government itself and is also undertaken by independent audit agencies. This type of accountability is concerned with ensuring that government is both effective and efficient in administering and implementing public policy. Administrative accountability is concerned with neither the political desirability of government action, nor with its legality. Instead, administrative accountability is concerned with ensuring that government effectively implements the desired policy goals, that is, that government gets the job done.

3.3 Political accountability

In democracies, the most important type of accountability is political accountability. Government is politically accountable to both the public and the legislature that represents the views of the public, for its policies. The rationale for political accountability reflects the nature of public power in a democracy. In a democracy, power rests with the people. It is they who decide to delegate power to government to achieve common goals. Government is legitimate only if it acts in the name of the people via the power they have conferred upon it. Accordingly, the people have the right to call government to account. The people are thereby equipped to exercise a form of control over those in public office by expressing their own views as to what the public interest requires. Since, as we noted earlier, there is no objectively correct definition of what the public good requires, political accountability forms an imperative connection between the views of the public at any given time and those in power who are charged with pursuing the public good.

The most conspicuous form of political accountability is the election. Elected politicians are accountable to the electorate. By voting for elected representatives, the public delegates power to them. In the UK, the electorate votes, among other things, for MPs to be returned to the House of Commons and members to the devolved legislatures. This, in turn, determines who forms the government. If voters disapprove of the government's policies, then they can elect a different government at the next general election.

Virtually all Western democracies owe a huge intellectual debt to ancient Greece, which is where the concept of democracy originates.[12] According to Aristotle,

---

[12] Dunn, *Setting the People Free: The Story of Democracy* (London 2005).

democracy meant direct democracy in which all citizens were to rule and be ruled in turn.[13] However, while elections remain the basic foundation of any country's claim to be a democracy, they are, for a variety of reasons, by themselves usually less than fully effective mechanisms for holding government to account. Elections are infrequent. In the UK, general elections to Parliament are usually held every five years.[14] Consequently, the involvement of voters in the governmental process is not continuous, but intermittent. There are many decisions that government must take that are neither discussed during elections nor upon which the public has a direct say. Elections are then inherently constrained in the extent to which they enable government to be held to account. The function of elections is usually just to determine the composition of the political executive—which political party should form the government—and therefore the broad direction of government policy.

Elections must be supplemented by a more granular form of control by holding government to account, between elections, for its specific policies and decisions. In the UK, this is achieved, in part, by making government Ministers accountable to Parliament through the doctrine of ministerial responsibility. This doctrine requires Ministers to provide an account of their actions and conduct in a variety of different ways.[15] In Parliament, Ministers are asked questions, policies are queried and debated, and specialist parliamentary select committees scrutinise the work of government. Such committees regularly produce (sometimes highly critical) reports on aspects of government policy and administration. Meanwhile, public inquiries into matters of grave public concern[16]—such as extreme incompetence or highly questionable judgement on the part of government—provide an alternative, or supplement, to parliamentary mechanisms of accountability.[17]

The effectiveness of the sanctions that may flow from such forms of political accountability is not always clear. Parliament may criticise a particular government policy. Whether such criticism will prompt the government to think again will often depend not only upon the cogency of that criticism, but also upon whether sufficient MPs are prepared to vote against the government. In a parliamentary system such as that of the UK, there have long been concerns that the process of political accountability is not as effective as it should be. Parliament is rarely successful in overturning government decisions because it is dominated by the government of the day that exerts control over its own MPs. Equally, if a public inquiry contains excoriating criticism of government, there is no guarantee that anything in particular will happen as a result.

This is not to say, however, that the absence of coercive power robs inquiries and parliamentary forms of accountability of any teeth. Given the right political

[13] Aristotle, *The Politics* (Harmondsworth 1962).
[14] Fixed-term Parliaments Act 2011.   [15] For more detail, see Chapter 10.
[16] The decision to go to war in Iraq—which has been the subject of several public inquiries—being an obvious example.
[17] On inquiries, see Chapter 17.

circumstances,[18] government may, in effect, have no choice but to take whatever corrective action Parliament or an inquiry demands.

3.4 **Legal accountability**

Legal accountability is a central aspect of the rule of law. Government must follow the law. However, the nature of the legal relationship between government and individuals is of a completely different nature from that between one individual and another. Private law regulates those forms of activity that anyone can undertake (such as entering into contracts). By contrast, public law embodies distinctive rules and principles that regulate the activity of governing. The most fundamental principle is that of legality. Whereas individuals can do anything that is not unlawful, the general principle is that government can do only that which it is legally authorised to do. If government undertakes unauthorised tasks, or undertakes authorised tasks in an improper way, it acts unlawfully. Unlawful governmental acts are invalid (of no legal effect) and, as such, can be struck down by the courts via judicial review.[19]

The rationale behind legal accountability is that anyone whose rights or interests have been adversely affected by the actions of someone else has the right to hold that person to account to determine whether such actions are lawful. Government has extensive and coercive powers that can be used to the detriment of people. Special arrangements are therefore needed to protect individuals against excessive or abusive use of those powers. Legal accountability is primarily concerned with protecting the rights and interests of individuals against the government. The courts do this by examining whether decisions taken by government comply with general principles of public law. These principles are:

- *legality*: government can only act within the scope of its legal powers;
- *procedural fairness*: government must adopt a fair decision-making process;
- *rationality*: government decisions must be rational or reasonable; and
- *proportionality*: infringements of human rights must be proportionate to the desired end.

There are some inherent limitations as to how legal accountability by courts operates. First, the courts do not have a free-roaming mandate to rule upon the legality of any government decision. The jurisdiction of the courts is only engaged if they have been called to adjudicate upon a legal dispute in which an individual or other body wishes to challenge a government decision. Second, the courts can only determine whether a government decision is unlawful. They have no jurisdiction to consider whether a public decision is right or wrong, or to substitute it with a decision of their own. The

---

[18] eg if the report of an inquiry or parliamentary committee captures public attention and harnesses public anger, the government may find itself backed into a corner.

[19] Judicial review is considered in detail in Chapters 11–14.

courts therefore need to be careful when reviewing the legality of a public decision to ensure that they do not themselves lapse into error by telling the government whether or not a particular policy or decision is a good one. If the courts were to do this, then they would be intruding into the realm of political accountability.

While legal accountability is subject to these constraints, it does possess a particular strength: the effectiveness of its sanctions or remedies. Legal remedies against a government that has acted unlawfully are legally binding. Government has no choice whether or not to comply with a court judgment and can be compelled by the courts to do so.

While undoubtedly important, the courts are not the only mechanism of legal accountability. In many instances, an individual who has received a negative decision from a government agency (eg refusal of a welfare benefit) can appeal against that decision to an independent, judicial tribunal. Tribunals handle vastly more cases each year than the courts. They are also staffed by specialist judges who possess expertise in the particular area of law concerned. Furthermore, unlike courts, tribunals are specifically empowered to substitute their own decision for that produced by the government.[20]

3.5 Administrative accountability

Administrative accountability is concerned with ensuring that government 'gets the job done'—that it implements policy effectively and efficiently. It is concerned with the performance of government and its ability to deliver policy on the ground. It is one thing for a government to have a policy, but putting that policy into practice is a different matter entirely. Indeed, implementing policy is where most of the real challenges faced by government arise.[21] Administrative accountability therefore focuses upon the organisation and management of government. It is concerned with issues such as whether government agencies are well organised, staffed by competent and honest people, and able to perform and deliver public services effectively and efficiently.

On one level, administrative accountability operates internally within government. It is a means by which government exercises control over itself. Given the scale of modern government, the Prime Minister cannot hope to exert much effective control over the operations of the governmental machine. He therefore appoints Ministers who, in turn, are able to instruct their civil servants and officials as to how they ought to operate. The Civil Service itself is made up of different grades, and civil servants work within different government departments and agencies. To ensure coordination and control, higher-level officers are able to issue instructions to lower-level officers. Such instructions can take a number of different forms, such as rules, policies, and guidance that lower-level officials need to follow and apply. These factors—hierarchy of authority, specialisation, and a system of rules—are the basic characteristics of

---

[20] On tribunals, see Chapter 16.

[21] See, eg Bacon and Hope, *Conundrum: Why Every Government Gets Things Wrong—And What We Can Do About It* (London 2013).

public administration.[22] Given the essentially administrative nature of modern government, it is necessary to design mechanisms of administrative accountability to ensure that government departments and other administrative agencies work effectively and efficiently.

A noticeable form of administrative accountability over recent decades has been the setting out by government of the targets and actions that individual government agencies are tasked with achieving. By doing so, government can then monitor performance against these targets to determine how well they are doing in terms of implementing government policy. In this way, departments and agencies can be called to account for their activities. For instance, the Labour government (1997–2010) operated a system of public service agreements (PSAs). The Conservative–Liberal Democrat coalition government that was formed in 2010 replaced PSAs with a system of business plans. Under the current Conservative government, each government department has a plan setting out its objectives until 2020.[23]

As we noted earlier, officials and civil servants are not subject to direct political accountability in Parliament. They are accountable to Ministers, who are in turn accountable to Parliament and the public. Mechanisms such as targets and business plans seek to establish objective yardsticks by which the performance of departments and agencies, and the individuals within them, can be monitored.

Administrative accountability does not operate solely within the government machine itself. There are various other bodies that have been established in order to oversee government and to hold it to account. The National Audit Office (NAO) oversees how the UK government spends public money and whether it provides value for money in the delivery of public services.[24] The NAO is neither a judicial nor a legislative body. It is itself an administrative body established by Parliament. Its purpose is to inspect the government's accounts and to examine the economy, efficiency, and effectiveness with which government agencies use their resources when discharging their functions.

There are other public bodies that oversee government. For example, ombudsmen investigate complaints lodged by individuals complaining of maladministration—bad administrative practice—by government.[25] Ombudsmen investigate individuals' complaints against government. If they find that there has been 'maladministration' resulting in injustice, ombudsmen can make recommendations to government, for example, that it reorganise its processes and administrative systems in order to prevent similar injustices reoccurring. Ombudsmen can also recommend that government pays out compensation to individuals who have suffered some loss as a result of its maladministration. Unlike audit agencies such as the NAO, ombudsmen are not concerned with either auditing government accounts or promoting value for money; rather, they are concerned with promoting adherence to the principles of good administration by government in order to ensure a better quality of government.

A distinctive feature of bodies such as the NAO and ombudsmen is that they provide expert and non-political oversight of government. They are generally accepted

---

[22] Blau and Meyer, *Bureaucracy in Modern Society* (New York 1987).
[23] **https://www.gov.uk/government/collections/single-departmental-plans-for-2015-to-2020**
[24] See further Chapter 10.   [25] See further Chapter 15.

to be credible and trustworthy mechanisms for holding government to account, and their reports often become topics of political and public comment. At the same time, this type of accountability has its limitations. Unlike the courts, neither audit agencies nor ombudsmen can impose legally binding sanctions or remedies upon government. Nonetheless, their recommendations are, more often than not, accepted and acted upon by government.

It is also important to recognise that accountability systems do not exist in complete isolation from one another. Administrative accountability often feeds into political accountability. For example, reports by the NAO are often followed up by parliamentary select committees—in particular, the House of Commons Public Accounts Committee. Likewise, when the government refuses to comply with a recommendation of the Parliamentary Ombudsman, the House of Commons Public Administration and Constitutional Affairs Select Committee often conducts an inquiry to assess whether or not the government's refusal is justified—and, if it thinks not, this may put the government under additional pressure to comply. In this way, different accountability mechanisms—and, indeed, different forms of accountability—overlap with and complement one another.

4. **Pulling it together**

It is now appropriate to pull the preceding discussion together. Table 9.1, on the next page, presents the three accountability regimes and their various dimensions.

Figure 9.1 presents an overview of the structure of accountability of central government. It can be seen that at the core of the figure is the UK's central government. It is surrounded by the various accountability processes, which subject government to different types of accountability.

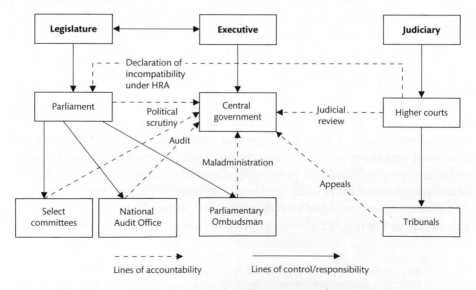

Figure 9.1 The accountability structure in the UK constitution for central government

Table 9.1 Accountability regimes for UK central government*

Accountability regime	Who is accountable?	To whom?	Accountability criteria	What are they accountable for?	Accountability processes	What effects?
Political accountability	Minsters Civil servants	Citizens Elected representatives	Political choices	Policy	Elections Parliamentary scrutiny	Criticism Resignation or dismissal from office
Legal accountability	Minsters Civil servants	Affected individuals	Legal rules and principles	Legality	Courts—judicial review Tribunals—appeals	Judicial remedies Appeals—allowed or dismissed
Administrative accountability	Ministers Departmental Accounting Officers Civil servants	National Audit Office (NAO) Commons Public Accounts Committee (PAC) Ombudsmen	Effectiveness Efficiency Value for money Maladministration	Policy implementation Performance and delivery	Internal monitoring within government Inquiries by NAO PAC hearings Ombudsmen investigations	Reforms within government Compensation

* This table draws upon and modifies Mashaw, p 128.

Figure 9.1 may seem complicated, but it is in fact a simplified presentation of the basic accountability processes. The figure only covers UK central government. It excludes other levels of government that exist in the multilayered constitution. The following chapters will examine these accountability processes in detail.

5. Conclusion

The public has a variety of different expectations as to how government should conduct itself. The standards of good governance are not fixed or static, but fluid and dynamic. These standards develop over time. They reflect some of the most basic standards of a polity. As a polity develops, so do the prevailing standards of good governance. At the most basic level, however, those standards require that government acts for the public good, that it acts lawfully, and that it is both effective and efficient in performing its assigned tasks. In order to ensure that government adheres to these broad standards, it is necessary that it is held to account by different bodies in different ways.

From one perspective, the imposition of extensive and complex webs of accountability upon government may present its own risks. Government may spend so much of its time being held to account that its capacity to govern effectively is undermined. Too much accountability may be just as problematic as insufficient or deficient accountability. As Bovens has noted, public institutions are frequently faced with the *'problem of many eyes*: they are accountable to a plethora of different forums, all of which apply a different set of criteria'.[26] Furthermore, there may often be tensions between different accountability processes. For instance, excessive political accountability may prompt Ministers to seek short-term political gains by interfering in administrative matters in a way that has disruptive longer-term consequences. Likewise, a high volume of legal challenges against government decisions may well make it more difficult for government to implement policy efficiently and speedily.

At the same time, accountability is necessary to fulfil the ideals of good governance. The crucial issue that arises is then the operation and effectiveness of particular types of accountability. Examining the operation of the different accountability mechanisms that function in the context of the UK is the task of the chapters that follow.

Expert commentary
Good Governance, Accountability, and the Constitution
Jeff King, Professor of Law, University College London

This chapter rightly shows that 'good government' is essential in a modern democracy. It also shows that accountability is multifaceted and integral to good government. Yet two concerns remain that are worthy of further exploration. First, is good, efficient, and expert administration in irresolvable tension with the forms of accountability that may interfere with it? Is the latter

---

[26] Bovens, 'Analysing and Assessing Accountability: A Conceptual Framework' (2007) 13 Eur LJ 447, 455. See also Bovens, Schillemans, and Hart, 'Does Public Accountability Work? An Assessment Tool' (2008) 86 Public Administration 225, 227–30.

corrosive of the former, in other words? Second, why ought we to think of this subject as a distinctly *constitutional* rather than merely public policy concern?

Let me begin with the second of these two general concerns. I agree with the tenor of this chapter and its position in this book that good governance has constitutional dimensions. The authors demonstrate that the principles of government include governing in the public interest rather than in self-interest, transparency, economic efficiency, impartial administration, and respecting the basic rights of individual citizens. Those values are also good public policy. But when we consider the institutions many countries have established to secure these values, their constitutional character becomes evident. Consider the Civil Service. The emergence of the modern Civil Service in Britain dates to the Northcote-Trevelyan Report of 1854, which recommended the creation of a unified civil service appointed by competitive examination, organised along clear hierarchical lines, and in which promotion is based on merit rather than patronage. Though the organisation of the Civil Service was left historically to management under the royal prerogative powers, its constitutional character has been recognised by convention and more formally of late in chapter 7 of the Cabinet Manual and in Part I of the Constitutional Reform and Governance Act 2010.

In France, the establishment of patronage appointments under *l'Ancien Regime* was a major source of aggravation prior to the revolution of 1789. It was one of the major motivations for Art 6 of the Declaration of the Rights of Man and Citizen 1789, part of which provides that 'all public positions and occupations' be open to citizens 'without distinction except that of their virtues and talents.' Similarly, Art 33 of the Basic Law of Germany (1949) requires constitutionally that laws relating to the public service show 'due regard [for] the traditional principles of the professional civil service.' Indeed, according to the website of the Constitute Project (a database of the world's written constitutions), 53 countries around the world address civil service recruitment in their written constitutions. This constitutional preoccupation with good administration extends beyond the civil service, however. Over 100 constitutions provide for some form of state auditing procedure, and over 80 refer to some form of ombudsman. Freedom of information and transparency will likely be the next big wave. In my view, the *fundamental* and *non-partisan* character of these concepts and institutions has made them apt objects for constitutional regulation, and hence for discussion in this book.

The second issue is the perennial concern that good and efficient administration is being obstructed rather than enhanced by accountability devices such as rules and oversight, sometimes with a sanction of some sort. Most students considering the issue afresh will soon come to the view that some combination of leeway and oversight is necessary. Otherwise we will have both abuse of power *and* wayward organisation leading to inefficiency, if not outright crisis. How can one run a complex organisation such as the National Health Service or army without a lot of rules and oversight? The wisdom of this truth has long been recognised.

Among Max Weber's many contributions to social thought was his distinction between three ways in which political authority was given legitimation in complex societies: charismatic authority (leading by dint of personality), traditional authority (relying on customs and institutions having longstanding acceptance), and rational legal authority (legitimacy based on rules, statute, and hierarchical bureaucratic organization).[27] Weber modelled the third

---

[27] Weber, 'Politics as Vocation', in Gerth and Wright Mills (translated and edited), *From Max Weber: Essays in Sociology* (New York 1946), pp 77–128 [originally published 1919]; Weber, *Economy and Society: An Outline of Interpretive Sociology*, eds Roth and Wittich (Berkeley, CA 1968), vol 1, Pt I, ch III; vol 2, ch XI [originally published 1922].

idea on the emergence of modern bureaucracy in Western, particularly European civilization. He also acknowledged the major role played by Roman law thinking. According to Weber, then, modern bureaucracy and law are joined together both conceptually and genealogically. The organisation of bureaucracy is loosely similar to the organisation of a legal system, with abstract rules setting out hierarchical relationships, and rational and clear allocation of duties and rights. Administering officials are appointed on merit and are conferred a degree of institutional independence from government to enable the dispassionate application of the rules and honest advice or counsel. This account describes the justice system nearly as well as it does the broader civil service, and this is no accident. Weber's account, which is dominant, illustrates a high degree of unity between the very ideas of modern bureaucracy and law rather than any tension between them.

This is not to deny that conflicts between administrative government and formal oversight are real and very important. I mentioned the NHS and army above as requiring rules and oversight, yet both are notoriously free (at least until recently) from deep intrusion by courts of law. And Weber's account is an ideal-type view of how bureaucracy functions. Writers on administrative justice have explored the relationship between administration and accountability in great depth. They distinguish, loosely, between internal and external forms of accountability.[28] The internal controls concern things such as internally administered audit, managerial control, internal review, and quality assessments, and so on. Jerry Mashaw's *Bureaucratic Justice*[29] is a masterful illustration of the comparative merits of internal oversight. External controls concern political accountability (local council, ministerial, or parliamentary), and legal accountability in courts and tribunals, and through administrative justice institutions such as ombudsmen. Getting the right mix of rules, discretion, and accountability is the holy grail of administrative justice. It requires constant experimentation and review, and varies over time and between communities. It is thus unfortunate that the UK government decided to abolish the Administrative Justice and Tribunals Council in 2013. Nonetheless, the following lessons have emerged from the post-war experience of administrative justice in the UK.

One relates to the role of 'rules' and policies in administrative decision-making. In America, Kenneth Culp Davis argued that administrative discretion is crucial but generates problems that judicial review alone can hardly control.[30] He advocated structuring discretion through open policies, plans, and processes. Others such as Robert Baldwin and Keith Hawkins, echoing earlier observations from the social policy scholar Richard Titmuss, countered that this idea of rule-governed administration and its attendant 'rights' would constrict the exercise of beneficial discretion, and become like the 'red-tape' we all know and fear. It is interesting to note in this connection, however, that an ever-increasing number of state functions are being outsourced to private companies. So, care for the elderly, the running of prisons, and even 'work capability assessments' determining eligibility for core social security benefits are now frequently outsourced. The argument that rules are unnecessary and that public-spirited discretion should guide is not tenable in such situations. Furthermore, the types of rule are themselves variable. In practice, government departments tend to issue statutory guidance for carrying out statutory functions. Such guidance is not legally binding, but it may be unreasonable (and hence unlawful) to depart from it without cogent justification. This illustrates the potential for guiding

---

[28] Adler, 'A Socio-Legal Approach to Administrative Justice' (2003) 25 Law and Policy 323.
[29] *Bureaucratic Justice: Managing Social Security Disability Claims* (New Haven, CT 1985).
[30] *Discretionary Justice: A Preliminary Inquiry* (Baton Rouge, LA 1969).

standards short of binding rules, and how even courts of law can give weight to such standards without adopting an attitude of strict enforcement.

Another site of discussion is the role for legal accountability in complex administration. The administrative justice landscape has been shaped in the UK by the historical perception that courts were for the wealthy and that judges were biased, emerging from an elitist Bar. As the welfare and regulatory state blossomed, so too did the idea that administrative tribunals could provide adjudication that is cheaper, more accessible, and staffed with lay members to counteract bias and provide subject matter expertise. And as administration grew to behemoth proportions, the need for ombudsmen to investigate and report on maladministration became undeniable. Ombudsmen are cheap, accessible for complainants, and investigate poor administration rather than patent illegality. But the perception that law courts were pro-capital and anti-poor, whereas the new non-judicial accountability substitutes were somehow non-legal, continued to perpetuate misguided belief that legality was inherently neoliberal or conservative and that tribunals and ombudsmen should resist any change that might be seen as 'juridification'.

In reality, the political complexion of the judiciary has changed enormously, and the political hostility to public law has shifted from left to right in organised politics. Indeed, the majority of judicial review is taken by marginalised groups or people resisting deportation in the immigration system. Bondy, Platt, and Sunkin estimate that, in their sample years taken prior to deep legal aid cuts in 2012, around 70 per cent of judicial review claims were funded through legal aid.[31] The legal nature of tribunal decision-making is clearer than ever after the reforms initiated under the Tribunal, Courts and Enforcement Act 2007, and the ombudsman role has in my view grown into a component of rather than alternative to the justice system. The danger here is that we risk letting the ghosts of the past rule the future of the constitution.

I would sum up these preceding views in the following way. Good government has important constitutional dimensions. Good bureaucracy operates on the application of rules, and requires a type of rationality, consistency, transparency, and responsibility that has legal-type characteristics. At the same time, its rules are mostly administered internally, and broad administrative discretion is an essential feature of good government. The rules and discretion of administration generate a demand for accountability. Accountability begins internally to the administration through hierarchical management, quality assessment, periodic reviews, and internal complaints procedures. External accountability arises where there is a special need for independence from the initial decision-maker, usually due to the potential for abuse of power, inertia, bias, or systemic incompetence. Where the conduct at issue is significant or at 'macro' level, political institutions will be well adapted to provide oversight. Where it concerns the breach of binding rules, fairness to individuals, or the basic rights of potentially marginalised groups, legal accountability is an attractive and often necessary option. The essence of legal accountability, in my contention, is the conferment upon individuals of a legal right to complain to an official body that is empowered to apply public standards and determine on the record in reasoned fashion whether such standards were breached.

Now, looking at the whole of this, we can say that some of these internal and external accountability features would be required to make any administration *fair*. But all of them are required to make any administration *good*.

---

[31] Bondy, Platt, and Sunkin, *The Value and Effectiveness of Judicial Review: The Nature of Claims, Their Outcomes, and Consequences* (London 2015), pp 8, 48.

Further reading

Bovens, 'Analysing and Assessing Accountability: A Conceptual Framework' (2007) 13 European Law Journal 447

This paper discusses a conceptual framework for understanding accountability.

Mulgan, *Holding Power to Account: Accountability in Modern Democracies* (London 2003)

This book provides an overview of the concept of accountability in modern democracies.

10

Parliamentary Scrutiny of Central Government

1. Introduction   401

2. Parliamentary control and government   402

3. Parliament and government   404

4. Ministerial responsibility   409

5. The mechanics of parliamentary scrutiny of government   424

6. Scrutinising how government spends public money   444

7. Freedom of information   452

8. Accountability and oversight of the security and intelligence services 460

9. Conclusion   467

Expert commentary   468

Further reading   470

Useful websites   471

1. Introduction

Government Ministers are responsible—collectively and individually—to Parliament. The government derives its authority, democratic legitimacy, and ability to govern from Parliament by virtue of its majority in the House of Commons. In turn, Parliament holds the government to account by scrutinising the policies, administration, and expenditure of government departments.

Political accountability takes two principal forms: electoral and non-electoral accountability. General elections determine the political composition of both Parliament and the government. They provide the democratic basis of the constitution, but they occur relatively infrequently.[1] In the meantime, political accountability is undertaken by Parliament. This chapter examines the constitutional relationship

[1] See further Chapter 5, section 3.2.

between government and Parliament, the mechanisms used by Parliament to scrutinise governmental action, the effectiveness of such mechanisms, and their possible reform.

Central to any consideration of the accountability of government to Parliament is the convention of ministerial responsibility—the obligation of Ministers to account to Parliament. At the same time, Parliament's role in scrutinising government is directly related to, and in some senses dependent upon, another major aspect of any constitution—the ability and power of the executive to govern. It is therefore necessary to consider the broader relationship between Parliament and government and the constitutional doctrine of ministerial responsibility in some detail. We explore these questions: what is Parliament's proper role in scrutinising government? What does the constitutional convention of ministerial responsibility mean? And how does it operate in practice?

Having examined parliamentary scrutiny of government and ministerial responsibility, the chapter then considers three related topics: financial scrutiny of government, freedom of information, and accountability of the security and intelligence services.

2. Parliamentary control and government

2.1 Political accountability

All democratic constitutions possess an inevitable and built-in tension between two major forces: governing and scrutinising. The first force reflects the essential need for a polity to be governed—that is, for a relatively small collection of people (the government) to decide how they are going to govern the country, which policies they will adopt, and how those policies are to be implemented. The basic responsibilities of government are to protect its people and to promote their welfare. No successful country has ever existed without an effective government.

The second force in a democratic constitution is the need to call to account those who do the governing. This involves scrutinising their actions; asking questions to determine whether their policies are, in fact, beneficial and well considered; and analysing whether such policies are being implemented effectively, fairly, and efficiently. In a democracy, government can only rule by consent, and such consent is meaningful only if government is open to scrutiny. The primal need for government is logically prior to the need for scrutiny—but effective scrutiny is a prerequisite of *legitimate* government.

Political accountability of government is fundamentally important. It enables *democratic control* over government. Much of the scrutinising has to be done by people—elected representatives, such as MPs—who are themselves representative of, and accountable to, the people. Political accountability requires government to *explain and justify* its actions and policies. In turn, this encourages better thought-out policy-making and implementation. It requires government to listen to, take account of, and respond to views different from its own. Finally, political accountability often involves the *making of judgements* as to the success or otherwise of governmental action. These judgements inform citizens' votes and so the formation of future governments.

Effective political accountability can be difficult to secure in practice. The two forces—governing and scrutinising—very often compete with one another. If too much emphasis is placed upon governing, then this may unduly restrict the scope for effective scrutiny of government and allow greater scope for the government to abuse its power. Conversely, if too much emphasis is placed upon scrutinising government, then its capacity to do its job will be impeded. The solution, then, is to find some appropriate balance between governing and scrutiny. This is easier said than done.

2.2 **Political accountability in the UK**

The general issue of the accountability of one branch of the state—the executive—to another—the legislature—raises a number of questions. How does the legislature seek to scrutinise the executive? What are the particular scrutiny mechanisms that Parliament uses? How effective are they? What are their limitations? How could they be improved? Such questions are of considerable constitutional significance in any democratic country, but, over recent years, these questions have assumed particular importance in the UK for various reasons.

First, there have long been *concerns about whether the UK Parliament can and does subject the government to effective scrutiny*. Public confidence in Parliament is perhaps the lowest it has been for decades, due in part to the fact that Parliament's agenda and composition are largely dominated by the government of the day. Consequently, Parliament possesses little, if any, ability to scrutinise government effectively.

This is known as the 'parliamentary decline thesis'. This became the predominant way of thinking about Parliament during the twentieth century amongst people in politics, universities, and the media.[2] The thesis goes like this: during the twentieth century, the government gradually became ascendant over Parliament. MPs became obedient members of the party machine rather than independent-minded, elected representatives. Accordingly, Parliament became increasingly sidelined and peripheral. The decline of Parliament was almost universally lamented as a decidedly bad thing—commentators harked back to the 'golden age' of the nineteenth century during which independent MPs powerfully scrutinised government.

In this chapter, we will ask whether this thesis stacks up. This thesis has provided the principal way of thinking about Parliament. But, the argument is a simple—some would say, way too simple—approach to understanding Parliamentary scrutiny of government.[3] Should the 'parliamentary decline thesis' be accepted uncritically or is the reality more nuanced and subtle?

A second reason for exploring parliamentary scrutiny is that Parliament—and in particular, the House of Commons—has come to be seen as *increasingly remote*

---

[2] Flinders and Kelso, 'Mind the Gap: Political Analysis, Public Expectations, and the Parliamentary Decline Thesis' (2011) 13 British Journal of Politics and International Relations 249, 254–60.

[3] See Flinders and Kelso.

from the concerns of the public. All too often, the public's perception of the House of Commons is that it is either the scene of 'Punch and Judy politics', in that the apparent role of MPs is to cheer for their own side and jeer at the other side, or else that the Commons chamber is almost entirely empty, with only a handful of MPs discussing a particular issue. These images contrast sharply with the ideal of a modern, professional legislature—one that closely scrutinises executive policies and decisions, and is able to extract information from the executive, point out wrongdoing, and prevent its reoccurrence.

Third, these specific institutional concerns over the scrutiny role of Parliament are connected to a broader political problem: *widespread public cynicism and even contempt for politicians.* In the UK, public confidence in Parliament received a battering when, in 2009, the MPs' expenses scandal erupted. Many, although not all, MPs had made expenses claims from which they were able to profit personally. While one upshot of this episode was changes to the law governing parliamentary standards, another was the establishment of the House of Commons Reform Committee—the Wright Committee—to improve parliamentary scrutiny of the government.

More generally, the wider problem is *public disengagement from politics.* Politics affects virtually every aspect of our lives, but—paradoxically—many people have little, if any, interest in it. This problem has various causes and is by no means confined to the UK. It is, though, credible to suppose that responsibility can partly be ascribed to the sort of concerns about Parliament and politicians considered so far. Furthermore, when the public have recently voted in high numbers—for instance, in the Brexit referendum in 2016—this has been interpreted, at least in part, as an expression of dissatisfaction with the existing system of political representation. The issues considered in this chapter possess a wider political and constitutional relevance in relation to the political process and the democratic system.

Parliamentary scrutiny is carried out via three main mechanisms: oral and written questions to Ministers, parliamentary debates, and inquiries by parliamentary select committees. To assess the effectiveness of these mechanisms we will need to consider each in turn. First, however, it is necessary to consider the general institutional setting within which they are deployed by considering the political relationship between government and Parliament and the constitutional doctrine of ministerial responsibility. It is important to consider both of these topics because, as we noted earlier, parliamentary scrutiny of government takes place within a context characterised by the tension between governing and scrutinising. To appreciate that context, we need to explore the nature of the power relationship between government and Parliament.

3. Parliament and government

3.1 Roles and responsibilities

The relationship between government and Parliament is complex and dynamic and has two defining aspects. First, it is wholly governed by political considerations. Second, governments dominate Parliament through their Commons majority. From one perspective, this domination gives rise to an undesirable 'elective dictatorship' by which the government is able to force through any measure—a classic parliamentary decline argument.[4] However, from a different perspective, the phrase 'elective dictatorship' is merely a simplistic cliché: the constitution actually requires the government to dominate Parliament. If it did not do so, then it would forfeit its right to govern. The government only acquires its authority from its majority in the House of Commons and the first obligation of government is to govern—that is, to make and implement public policy.

To understand Parliament's scrutiny function, it is then necessary to understand the respective roles of Parliament and government. The Victorian Prime Minister William Gladstone once said to the House of Commons: 'Your business is not to govern the country, but it is, if you see fit, to call to account those who govern it.'[5] In a similar vein, JS Mill wrote:

> Instead of the function of governing, for which it is radically unfit, the proper office of a representative assembly is to watch and control the government; to throw the light of publicity on its acts; to compel a full exposition and justification of all of them which any one considers questionable; to censure them if found condemnable, and, if the men who compose the government abuse their trust, or fulfil it in a manner which contradicts with the deliberate sense of the nation, to expel them from office, and either expressly or virtually appoint their successors.[6]

Parliament does not itself govern—it is not equipped to do so. Indeed, the British people have never had government *by* Parliament, simply because it has always been accepted that this would not work. What the British people do have, though, is government *through* Parliament. Parliament provides the government of the day with the authority to govern: the government can then get on with the job of governing, subject to the fact that Parliament also seeks to hold the government of the day to account.

To understand further Parliament's role, we can draw upon Polsby's distinction between 'transformative' and 'arena' legislatures. A 'transformative' legislature possesses its own 'independent capacity, frequently exercised, to mold and transform proposals from whatever source into laws'.[7] Such legislatures have an existence separate from that of the executive branch; the classic example is the US Congress. By contrast, 'arena' legislatures 'serve as formalized settings for the interplay of significant political forces in the life of a political system'.[8] Whereas transformative legislatures are able to exert significant influence over how a country is governed and hold government robustly to account, arena legislatures tend merely to provide a forum in which

---

[4] Hailsham, *The Dilemma of Democracy: Diagnosis and Prescription* (Glasgow 1978).

[5] HC Deb, Series 3, vol 136, col 1202 (29 January 1855).

[6] 'Considerations on Representative Government' [1861], in Mill, *On Liberty and Other Essays* (Oxford 1991), p 282.

[7] Polsby, 'Legislatures', in Greenstein and Polsby (eds), *Handbook of Political Science, Volume 5: Governmental Institutions and Processes* (Reading, MA 1975), p 277.

[8] Polsby, p 277.

the theatre of politics is conducted, and exercise little real power. The focus for arena legislatures is not upon governing, but upon debating what the government does.

The UK Parliament has long been held up as the archetypal arena legislature. As King explains, Parliament 'is simply not equipped to function as a transformative legislature'.[9] Parliament provides the forum in which competing political parties confront each other through the roles of government and opposition. Parliament is also a reactive legislature in the sense that much of its time is spent not in developing its own laws or policy proposals, but in responding to and scrutinising the government's proposals for new laws or policies. As Amery noted, 'Our system is one of democracy, but of democracy by consent and not by delegation, of government of the people, for the people, with, but not by, the people'.[10]

The initiative rests with the government of the day. At a mundane level, this means that the role of individual MPs is limited to the simple alternative of voting for or against a motion tabled in the House of Commons—usually, though not always, by the government—and which the government almost invariably wins.

Parliament is also reactive in the sense that all of the work of government—the delivery and administration of government policy—is undertaken outside Parliament by government departments and other public bodies. As Flinders has explained, the UK's constitutional framework is such that Parliament adopts 'a passive rather than active role in relation to the administration' by 'hold[ing] ministers responsible for the way in which they steer the ship of state'.[11] Parliament provides a forum in which political debate occurs, to enable different views within society to be represented, but real power remains with the government.

> **Q** What are the roles of Parliament in relation to the government? Why would changing the role of Parliament require a wider redesign of the UK's system of government?

3.2 **The nature of parliamentary control of government**

All this has important consequences for the nature of Parliamentary control of government. Whatever form that control takes, it does not—because it cannot—consist in outright parliamentary *direction* of government. At the same time, the relationship between Parliament and government is more complex and subtle than presented so far. Parliament is not just a rubber stamp approving whatever the government wants. The government must take seriously the views of Parliament. Backbench MPs may raise concerns about a particular policy and threaten to rebel against the government. Parliamentary select committees often produce reports on governmental activities that are highly critical. MPs can ask questions of Ministers and debate policy issues. Government cannot afford to ignore such questions and debates or the views

---

[9] King, *The British Constitution* (Oxford 2007), p 332.

[10] Amery, *Thoughts on the Constitution* (Oxford 1953), pp 20–1.

[11] Flinders, 'MPs and Icebergs: Parliament and Delegated Governance' (2004) 57 Parliamentary Affairs 767, 778.

articulated within Parliament. While Parliament cannot realistically command the government and tell it what it ought to do, it is, nonetheless, able to exert influence. Parliamentary control of government assumes a distinctive meaning in the UK: it 'means *influence*, not direct power; *advice*, not command; *criticism*, not obstruction; *scrutiny*, not initiation; and *publicity*, not secrecy'.[12]

It was noted earlier that the 'parliamentary decline thesis' became the dominant way of thinking about Parliament during the twentieth century: Parliament is under the government's thumb and we live in an elective dictatorship. However, the discussion so far highlights a fundamental problem with the parliamentary decline thesis. Complaining that Parliament has been in decline is to adopt unrealistic expectations of what it is actually supposed to do. Parliament was never expected to subject government to high standards of scrutiny or to take the initiative. It was simply never intended to be a vehicle for proactive and thorough scrutiny. Rather, it was designed to facilitate strong government by enabling the governing party to get on with the task of governing the country. At the same time, the government must take the views expressed in Parliament into account. In short, we need to adopt a realistic perspective on the degree of scrutiny we can expect of Parliament before complaining that Parliament has been in decline.

In practice, the relationship between government and Parliament tends to operate along the following lines. The government will make a policy decision to do something; the right of initiative always rests with the government. Parliament may then seek to scrutinise the decision taken. MPs and peers may debate the matter and/or put questions to Ministers. A parliamentary select committee may even undertake an inquiry into the issue, and produce a report that is critical of the government's policy and/ or its administration by a particular public body. By raising criticisms of the policy, Parliament will perform its role in throwing light upon the issue and reflecting public opinion on the particular matter. Parliament might also seek to influence the content of government policy. It is possible that, as a result of such scrutiny, the government might completely change its policy. But no one really expects this to happen and the vast majority of the time it will not happen. The typical governmental response will be to provide Parliament with an explanation and a defence of its decision.

It does not, however, follow that the government can invariably carry on regardless of Parliament's reaction to its proposals. The extent of Parliament's influence over government is dependent upon the political context—that is, the strength of the government's majority in the House of Commons, whether there are fault lines within the government (be it a single-party or coalition government), the nature of the particular policy or administrative issue, the attitudes of the opposition parties, the feelings amongst the government's backbench MPs, and media and public opinion. Occasionally, such factors conspire to force a government to change its policy—for example, if there is widespread public opposition to a policy proposed by a weak government—but that is the exception, the norm being that Parliament has very limited capacity directly to determine the government's course of action.

---

[12] Crick, *The Reform of Parliament* (London 1969), p 80.

A further exception, albeit a minor one, should also be noted. It is that Parliament (or, more accurately, the House of Commons) can exercise genuine control, as opposed to mere influence, over the government through the medium of a confidence motion. By convention, the government must resign if it loses a vote of confidence. This can certainly happen. For example, the 1979 Labour government fell because it lost a confidence vote (by a single vote) in the House of Commons. However, votes of no confidence are exceedingly rare and highly unusual. They represent the breakdown rather than the assertion of ordinary parliamentary control. The position has always been that the loss of a confidence vote by the government triggers the dissolution of Parliament and a general election.

The position is now modified by the Fixed-term Parliaments Act 2011. It provides that a government that loses a confidence vote must resign, but allows 14 days for a new government to be formed. If such a government is formed, and endorsed by Parliament through a vote of confidence, the early general election that would otherwise have been required is avoided.[13] These issues were considered in Chapter 4. For now, the important point is that governments, in practice, rarely face the threat of being overthrown by Parliament and therefore this option plays little role in terms of effective Parliamentary scrutiny of government. There need to be other scrutiny mechanisms.

The role of sustaining the government in power is undertaken by the government's backbench MPs—its majority. The opposition parties will criticise the government, oppose its policies, and present their own policies. However, opposition parties rarely do such things in the hope or expectation that the government will actually change its policy, but rather in an attempt to convince the public of their own fitness for government. In this sense, parliamentary scrutiny is as much concerned with the political game, in that the parties vie for public attention and approval, as it is with genuine oversight of government. This is consistent with the characterisation of Parliament as an 'arena' legislature.

Why does the relationship between Parliament and government operate in this way? The answer is simple: the British governmental tradition has a particularly pronounced disposition towards the maintenance of strong and stable government. Government must get on with the task of governing. In the British political and governing tradition, weak and ineffectual government is considered to be anathema. Irrespective of which political party or parties form the government of the day, the deeply embedded cultural and political attitude within the UK constitution is that, first and foremost, government must be able to govern.

It is for this reason that the UK constitution has often been described as a 'power-hoarding' constitution because power is largely concentrated within government. So long as the government retains its Commons majority, it is given considerable freedom to make and implement its policies. This essential aspect of the constitution is reflected in many aspects of British political culture, such as the adversarial nature of party politics—whereby parties engage in an almost continual general election campaign with each other—as well as the convention of ministerial responsibility.

---

[13] Fixed-term Parliaments Act 2011, s 2.

Q What does it actually mean to say that Parliament 'controls' the executive in the UK? What does the meaning of parliamentary control tell us about the relationship between government and Parliament?

4. Ministerial responsibility

4.1 Introduction

The doctrine of ministerial responsibility provides the key link between government and Parliament. Ministers are in government. They are also present in Parliament. This overlap of the executive and legislature is the principal reason why there is no full separation of powers in the UK. But there is a good reason for this. Government Ministers are present in Parliament so that MPs can call such Ministers to account for their decisions and policies and those of their government departments.

There are two aspects to the concept of ministerial responsibility. We have already considered *collective ministerial responsibility*.[14] Our concern here is with *individual ministerial responsibility*. This doctrine is central to the relationship between Parliament and government, but its *place and status* have often been contested. Sometimes ministerial responsibility is described as a fundamental part of the UK constitution; sometimes it is dismissed as a myth because of its ineffectiveness in practice. The very *meaning* of ministerial responsibility is itself also contested. It can possess different meanings depending on the context. We will therefore seek to elucidate both the constitutional meaning of the doctrine and its operation in practice.

We start by recalling that governmental power is held and exercised largely, although far from exclusively, by government Ministers. Ministers comprise the leading politicians of their day who belong to the governing political party (or coalition) with a Commons majority; collectively, they form the government. Ministers are an essential, though small, part of the much larger governmental machine. Ministers are the political heads of government departments, but these departments and their agencies are staffed by some 440,000 civil servants. By convention and political practice, Ministers are also members of either House of Parliament. As such, Ministers provide the vital link between the governmental machine and Parliament, and the convention of ministerial responsibility conditions the nature of that relationship.

According to the official definition of ministerial responsibility, 'Ministers have a duty to Parliament to account, and be held to account, for the policies, decisions, and actions of their departments and agencies.'[15] This sounds straightforward, but, as we will see, the official definition conceals several complexities. As we examine them, it will be useful to keep the following questions in mind. First, who is accountable?

---

[14] See Chapter 4, section 3.5.
[15] Cabinet Office, 'Ministerial Code' (London 2015), [1.2b]. This definition was approved by a parliamentary resolution in 1997.

Second, to whom are they accountable? Third, for what are they accountable? Fourth, how are they accountable? And, fifth, with what consequences?

In terms of governmental accountability to Parliament, the answers to these questions are provided by the convention of ministerial responsibility. The answers to the first and second questions—who can be called to account and by whom—are that government Ministers are accountable and answerable to Parliament. With regard to the third question—the matters on which Ministers can be called upon to explain or defend—the answer is that Ministers are responsible for the policies adopted by the government, in addition to the decisions and actions undertaken by their departments and agencies. Ministers are also responsible for their own personal conduct.

In addressing the fourth question, which concerns *how* Ministers are held to account, it is important to recognise that the duty under the Ministerial Code is twofold. Ministers are obliged both *to provide an account to Parliament* of the policies, decisions, and actions of the relevant government department; and to be *held to account by Parliament* for those policies, decisions, and actions. The first aspect of ministerial responsibility simply requires that Ministers explain policies and decisions to Parliament through statements and answers to questions. By contrast, being held to account involves something more: it implies taking responsibility when things have gone wrong, and putting them right. There is no single mechanism by which accountability in either of these senses is enforced; rather, there are, as we have already noted, several such processes: questions to Ministers, debates in Parliament, and the work of parliamentary select committees.

The final question concerns the potential consequences or sanctions when wrongdoing or failure is uncovered. The question of the sanctions attendant upon being held to account is a problematic one because its answer will often depend upon numerous political factors such as the strength of criticism against the government Minister, what went wrong, who was actually responsible for it, the strength of the Minister's response to the criticism, the habitual desire of Ministers to seek to avoid political embarrassment, the strength of the government's majority in Parliament, the attitude of the Prime Minister, how the story can be 'spun' by the government to the media, the media's own reaction, and the views of the public toward the government. The vast majority of the time when government Ministers are called upon to answer for a government policy or decision, the Minister will simply explain and defend that policy or decision. This explanation and defence may sometimes be accompanied by an attack upon the policies of the opposition parties. In doing so, the Minister will, with the support of the government's Commons majority, in most instances be able to continue. Having seen off the attack, the business of government can continue unhindered.

4.2 Ministerial resignations

One issue frequently discussed in relation to the consequences of ministerial responsibility concerns the most extreme sanction available—that is, whether or not a Minister should resign from his or her post because some wrongdoing has been uncovered. The convention of ministerial responsibility has sometimes been taken to mean that not only do Ministers have to assume responsibility for mistakes, but also that they have to accept whatever Parliament considers the appropriate penalty to be. However, ministerial resignations as a result of parliamentary pressure are rare. As Johnson has noted:

> Far more common has been the determination of ministers to fight off criticism, to deny or qualify their own responsibility, or simply to hang on to office for as long as the prime minister and their colleagues seem ready to stand behind them . . . [I]n its penal application ministerial responsibility is rather like a paper tiger: it is often waved in front of ministers, but only rarely does it really frighten them.[16]

Whether or not a Minister resigns depends upon a number of factors. First, there is the seriousness of the wrongdoing that has been uncovered. For example, no one would expect a Minister to resign because a civil servant within the Minister's department had made a single erroneous decision with which the Minister had never been personally involved. On the other hand, the Ministerial Code states that a Minister who 'knowingly misleads'—lies to—Parliament will be expected to resign.[17] In the former case, a ministerial resignation would not be warranted because the government is nowadays so large that no Minister could ever possibly know of, let alone oversee, all of the decision-making within his or her department. Indeed, if a Minister really were to resign every time the relevant government department made a mistake, however minor, then it would be virtually impossible for government to carry on: some ministerial offices would be subject to regular, if not daily, personnel changes. By contrast, lying to Parliament is at the other end of the scale. This still remains the biggest political sin that any politician can commit because it undermines the whole system of parliamentary control of government, which depends upon the government providing Parliament with accurate and truthful information.

Other crucial determinants of whether a Minister resigns include the Minister's own personal feelings, whether the Minister has the support of the Prime Minister, and the mood of the political party.[18] All of those factors can be affected by the media.[19] Once the media scents ministerial blood, intense pressure is today commonplace; beleaguered Ministers often go from having the 'full support' of the Prime Minister to resigning within a matter of hours or days.

Note an important omission from this list of factors—Parliament: ministerial resignations rarely, if ever, occur as a result of parliamentary pressure. There may be calls within Parliament from the opposition for a Minister to resign; this is all part of the contest between the political parties. But while pressure brought to bear within Parliament (eg via embarrassing questions put to Ministers or the Prime Minister) may help to increase the pressure on an embattled Minister, the government's majority in the House of Commons will usually insulate it, to some extent, from such

---

[16] Johnson, *Reshaping the British Constitution* (London 2004), pp 87–8.

[17] 'Ministerial Code', [1.2c].

[18] Finer, 'The Individual Responsibility of Ministers' (1956) 34 Public Administration 377.

[19] Woodhouse, 'UK Ministerial Resignations in 2002: The Tale of Two Resignations' (2004) 82 Public Administration 1.

attacks. There are, inevitably, a number of reasons that may lead to ministerial resignations, but three types of situation may usefully be distinguished.

First, many resignations occur not because the Minister accepts responsibility for some political or administrative failing within his department, but because his or her own personal conduct has become a source of embarrassment to the government. The most obvious example of a purely personal issue likely to result in resignation is the disclosure that a Minister has behaved reprehensibly in his private life. For instance, in 2010, David Laws, after fewer than three weeks in office, resigned as Chief Secretary to the Treasury when it was alleged that he had breached (at least the letter of) the rules on MPs' expenses: as the Minister responsible for implementing huge public spending cuts, it was felt in some quarters that questions over his personal financial propriety made his position untenable.[20] Meanwhile, in 2012, Andrew Mitchell resigned as Chief Whip following an altercation in which he swore at police officers guarding Downing Street and allegedly called them 'plebs'. Although Mitchell denied using that word, he eventually yielded to irresistible pressure to resign.

Second, a Minister's private life may more directly collide with his public duties. For example, when a Minister acts in a way that fails to recognise that a conflict of interests exists, this may well raise questions about his or her integrity and fitness for office.[21] In 2004, David Blunkett was forced to resign as Home Secretary when an inquiry found that there had been a 'chain of events' linking him to a request to the Immigration and Nationality Directorate (IND) to fast-track a visa for his lover's nanny.[22] As the IND was a directorate within the Home Office, which is headed by the Home Secretary, Blunkett was forced to resign because of concern that his public role as Home Secretary may have been used for his private benefit.

Third, it is sometimes, but rarely, the case that a Minister resigns straightforwardly because he is responsible for, or has presided over, administrative chaos. Consider the dismissal of Blunkett's successor as Home Secretary, Charles Clarke. In 2006, it was disclosed that the Home Office had failed to deport over 1,000 foreign national prisoners who had completed their prison sentences. This was a major administrative failure. While the Home Secretary could not have been expected to have known about every aspect of the work of the Home Office, he took responsibility for it. In the event, the public and media pressure on the Prime Minister was so great that Clarke was, in effect, forced out of the government. But even when, as here, resignation is linked with departmental failure, it might be asked: what was the purpose of this resignation? It is apparent that Clarke's removal from the office of Home Secretary did nothing whatsoever to rectify the administrative problems within the Home Office (which required major administrative reorganisation). Furthermore, Clarke was generally recognised to be an able and competent Minister. Rather, Clarke's resignation may have served a 'sacrificial' purpose: the failings within the Home Office were so serious, and public and media pressure was so immense, that the Prime Minister felt compelled to act to abate the media storm.

---

[20] Laws did, however, rejoin the government in 2012 as an Education and Cabinet Office Minister.
[21] The 'Ministerial Code' (at [7.1]) requires Ministers to ensure that 'no conflict arises, or could reasonably be perceived to arise, between their public duties and their private interests, financial or otherwise'.
[22] Budd, *An Inquiry into an Application for Indefinite Leave to Remain* (HC 175 2004–05), [3.35].

The infrequency of ministerial resignations may be taken to imply that the doctrine of ministerial responsibility is hollow and without substance. That would be wrong. The notion of government being responsible and accountable usually has a much wider meaning than the narrow question as to whether or not a Minister should resign. More often than not, Ministers will answer questions put to them in Parliament and elsewhere, and then face up to whatever response their answer provokes. Ministers have to devote a considerable amount of time and effort to their parliamentary work. This principally involves answering questions within Parliament, explaining governmental decisions and policies, appearing before select committees, and responding to criticisms of those decisions and policies. This is what lies at the heart of ministerial responsibility. While it would be going too far to say that whether a Minister should resign is inevitably a distraction, it is rarely the most important issue. Resignation alone may do little, if anything, to remedy the situation, and whether resignation occurs is likely to be determined by nothing more significant than chance political factors.

4.3 **The different meanings of ministerial responsibility**

The doctrine of ministerial responsibility presents both constitutional scholars and students with something of a paradox. *In theory*, Ministers are responsible to Parliament, yet it is widely believed that Ministers are not *in practice* held to account by Parliament.

Consider the following. In 1969, a Conservative MP noted that ministerial responsibility 'has every advantage except that it is not true. *It is contrary to both the administrative and political realities*'.[23] More recently, Drewry has described the doctrine as 'largely fictional'.[24] Furthermore, King and Crewe have stated that 'of the most striking features of the British system of government' is 'the almost total lack of ministerial responsibility in the strong sense—of ministers being held to account for their actions and being penalised for their more egregious misjudgements and errors'.[25] How can the doctrine be both a constitutional fundamental—yet also almost entirely lacking in substance?

The key to understanding this paradox is to start by recognising that the convention of ministerial responsibility has different meanings and can operate in different ways with different implications.[26] Indeed, ministerial responsibility is a good illustration of an 'essentially contested concept'—that is, a concept that does not possess a single definitive meaning, but which instead possesses various different, even contradictory, meanings; in other words, an idea that means different things to different people.[27] It is, therefore, necessary to clarify the contrasting meanings sometimes ascribed to the notion of ministerial responsibility.

---

[23] Gilmour, *The Body Politic* (London 1969), p 163 (emphasis added).
[24] Drewry, 'The Executive: Towards Accountable and Effective Governance?', in Jowell and Oliver (eds), *The Changing Constitution* (Oxford 2011), p 211.
[25] King and Crewe, *The Blunders of Our Governments* (London 2013), p 352.
[26] Marshall and Moodie, *Some Problems of the Constitution* (London 1971), p 52.
[27] Gaillie, 'Essentially Contested Concepts' (1955–56) 56 Proceedings of the Aristotelian Society 167.

A second reason for examining ministerial responsibility in detail is that it is important not to take constitutional doctrines, such as ministerial responsibility, at face value. Constitutional conventions are not legal rules. Treating them as such poses the risk that they will conceal or confuse as much as they reveal.[28] Conventions such as ministerial responsibility always operate within a broader political context, with all of the inherent (and necessarily?) messy and imperfect compromises that characterise politics. The ever-present risk is that political actors may give lip service to grand constitutional ideals that are, in practice, subordinated to political realities.

In terms of seeking to understand the different meanings often ascribed to the convention of ministerial responsibility, the critically important factor to bear in mind is the broader political relationship between government and Parliament. From this starting point, the following questions arise. Do the decisions and actions of government Ministers reflect the wishes of Parliament? Should they? Or, alternatively, do Ministers decide what to do irrespective of the wishes of Parliament? There are different answers to these questions that, in turn, reflect different meanings attributed to ministerial responsibility.[29] Consider the following views of ministerial responsibility.

First, there is the 'Whig' view.[30] On this view, ministerial responsibility means that Ministers should be *responsible to Parliament*. This is because the House of Commons is a democratic and representative institution. Parliament should, therefore, exercise strong political control over the government and the doctrine of ministerial responsibility should be used to ensure that governmental decisions reflect the wishes of the House of Commons. Ministers, on this view, should also be held culpable when government fails in some way and should bear the consequences (ie resign). Ministers should also listen and respond to views expressed in Parliament.

Looked at in this way, ministerial responsibility is designed to promote representative government that is responsive to opinions voiced in Parliament—in particular, the House of Commons. Ministers should follow Parliament. This view of ministerial responsibility is often advanced by those who emphasise the importance of Parliament, who are sceptical of governmental power, and who would like government to pay more attention to parliamentarians' views. But while this is the meaning often attached to the doctrine of ministerial responsibility, it is not the only one, and it is certainly not always reflected in reality.

The 'Whig' view can be compared with the 'Peelite' view of ministerial responsibility.[31] On this view, ministerial responsibility emphasises that Ministers—rather than Parliament—are

---

[28] On constitutional conventions generally, see Chapter 2, section 3.5.

[29] Beattie, 'Ministerial Responsibility and the Theory of the British State', in Rhodes and Dunleavy (eds), *Prime Minister, Cabinet, and Core Executive* (London 1995), p 158. See also Birch, *Representative and Responsible Government: An Essay on the British Constitution* (London 1964), pp 139–49; Flinders, 'The Enduring Centrality of Individual Ministerial Responsibility within the British Constitution' (2000) 6 Journal of Legislative Studies 73.

[30] The Whig Party was the reforming and constitutional party that sought the supremacy of Parliament and was succeeded by the Liberal Party during the nineteenth century. A Whig view takes the approach that there is an inevitable progression towards liberty culminating in liberal democracy.

[31] This view is named after Robert Peel, who was Prime Minister 1841–46. Hurd, *Robert Peel: A Biography* (London 2007), p 226, notes that when Peel became Prime Minister in 1841, he considered that it was the duty of his backbench MPs to follow him: 'The country needed strong government. Peel . . . could never

responsible for governing. Ministerial responsibility means Ministers are responsible for government policy and decisions because they are able to command a majority in the House of Commons. Government decisions do not need to reflect the wishes of the House of Commons. If they did, then government would be weak, indecisive, and forever changing from one course of action to another. Instead, ministerial responsibility means that Ministers are responsible: they make their own decisions, which they then explain and defend before Parliament. The Minister is thus the government's spokesperson in Parliament who informs it of government decisions and answers questions.

The Peelite view, then, reflects a very different conception of the relationship between the government and Parliament from that of the Whig view. The Peelite view presupposes the government's role as initiative taker: backbench and opposition MPs do not tell Ministers how to act; rather, it is the government that is able to exercise control over its backbenchers through the whips. In this sense, ministerial responsibility is a means of limiting parliamentary involvement to ensure strong, stable, and effective government. The Peelite conception of ministerial responsibility is rarely articulated, but it is deeply embedded within the practices of Ministers and senior civil servants.[32] In short, people in government—those in power—view the world from a Peelite mindset.

Part of the problem with ministerial responsibility is that it is often used in both the Whig and Peelite senses, but with very different implications. Those who adhere to the Whig view are likely to be disappointed with the operation of ministerial responsibility in practice. Barendt has lamented that it is now 'rare for the House of Commons to hold an individual minister to account'.[33] Jowell and Oliver have noted that 'the domination of party, especially the party of government, serves to suppress any sense of a *corporate* House of Commons function or identity in holding government to account as opposed to sustaining it in power'.[34] These views clearly reflect the Whig view of ministerial responsibility: government should be made fully accountable to the House of Commons and should listen to the views expressed in the Commons. The fact that government rarely does this today strongly suggests that ministerial responsibility has weakened so much that it can no longer be said to be a fundamental doctrine of the constitution.

But, from the Peelite standpoint, these views are naive: ministerial responsibility is not a parliamentary sword, but a ministerial shield. Ministers are not responsible *to* Parliament—they are responsible *for* taking decisions. From this perspective, ministerial responsibility was never intended to ensure that ministerial actions reflected the wishes of the House of Commons; rather, it was intended to preserve executive power and Ministers'—rather than Parliament's—responsibility for governing.

---

accept that it would be the duty of his government to consult, let alone follow, the views of backbenchers who by definition knew less than he and his colleagues on any subject under discussion.'

[32] See Rhodes, *Everyday Life in British Government* (Oxford 2011).

[33] Barendt, *An Introduction to Constitutional Law* (Oxford 1998), p 116.

[34] Jowell and Oliver (eds), *The Changing Constitution* (Oxford 2007), p x.

Furthermore, the assumption that the House of Commons possesses a corporate identity—that it comprises a single, unified entity devoted to scrutinising government—is at odds with reality. The Commons is an unwiedly collection of 650 MPs with wildly different opinions. It does not function as a corporate, collective body, but as a forum in which different political parties are present; so long as the government has a majority in Parliament and is able to exert authority over its backbenchers, it need not genuinely consult with Parliament or be responsive to the views expressed therein.

Which view of ministerial responsibility now has the upper hand and which best reflects what actually happens? The Whig tradition 'has always been paraded as the public face of ministerial responsibility, but the Peelite view has formed a strong undercurrent in governing attitudes'.[35] The actual behaviour of Ministers and civil servants exemplifies the Peelite view.[36] After all, this view has considerable attractions for government: it offers Ministers flexibility and a strong platform from which to implement their policies. According to Flinders, 'The ascendancy of the Peelite strand is now complete. Ministerial responsibility has endured because it allows ministers to govern with a minimal level of Parliamentary interference while also, in the main, delivering stability.'[37]

The basic point of this discussion, then, is that the notion of ministerial responsibility is viewed differently by different people and different actors within the political system. When opposition MPs complain (as they often do) that the government is not being properly held to account, they are subscribing to the Whig view of ministerial responsibility. By contrast, government Ministers and senior civil servants tend to adopt the Peelite view. Which view is adopted depends almost entirely upon whether or not it suits the immediate purposes of the actor involved.

> **Q** Which view of ministerial responsibility—the Whig or the Peelite view—do you think best describes the practice and reality of parliamentary control of government? Which view do you think ought to inform parliamentary control of government?

4.4 Ministerial responsibility and administrative government today

4.4.1 Introduction

How then does ministerial responsibility operate in the context of modern *administrative* government? The doctrine developed in the nineteenth century when government was much smaller and more limited than it is today. Furthermore, during this period, it became accepted that the general structure of government was to be organised through ministerial departments—that is, government departments staffed by

---

[35] Weir and Beetham, *Political Power and Democratic Control in Britain* (London 1998), p 338.

[36] See Rhodes.

[37] Flinders, 'The Enduring Centrality of Individual Ministerial Responsibility within the British Constitution' (2000) 6 Journal of Legislative Studies 73, 79.

civil servants and headed up by a government Minister.[38] Ministerial responsibility was designed to suit the needs of the relatively small structure of government and to ensure that Ministers were responsible to Parliament. Today, however, the situation is much more complex. In 1918, there were 28 civil servants in the Home Office; today the figure is 30,000. How can ministerial responsibility—a doctrine devised in a different age—operate in the context of contemporary government?

Government is a very large organisation composed of various central government departments, executive agencies, and non-departmental bodies. Today, no one seriously supposes that a government Minister actually performs much—if, indeed, any—of the administrative work that goes on within a government department. The volume of such work is enormous and of necessity must be undertaken by civil servants. There is, however, a paradox: while much of the work of government is undertaken by civil servants, they are not themselves elected or accountable directly to Parliament. The traditional constitutional response to this position is that civil servants—as servants of the Crown, which, for all practical purposes, simply means the government of the day[39]—operate as part of a clear line of accountability. Civil servants take decisions under the authority of the Minister, the Minister is constitutionally responsible to Parliament, and Parliament is democratically elected and therefore able to hold the Minister to account for the decisions of his or her civil servants.

This theory may have been tenable in the past, but now finds itself under considerable strain. The basic reason for this is that the traditional theory becomes unworkable when 'administrative life parts company from [the] constitutional doctrine [on which it is based], and government departments become too large and too complex for ministers to accept personal responsibility for what is done in their name by their civil servants'.[40] There are several reasons why the traditional doctrine of ministerial responsibility for the decisions and actions of government departments and agencies has become problematic.

4.4.2 Problems with ministerial responsibility and administrative government

First, there are severe constraints as to the amount of *time and resources* that Parliament can devote to the scrutiny of government departments and agencies. In terms of its size and scale, government is a vastly larger enterprise than Parliament. Parliament possesses neither the resources nor the ability to subject each and every unit within the governmental machine to detailed and searching scrutiny. In practice, Parliament is really only ever able to examine a tiny proportion of the actual work of government, while the vast majority goes unscrutinised.

---

[38] Parris, *Constitutional Bureaucracy: The Development of British Central Administration Since the Eighteenth Century* (London 1969), pp 80–105; Chester, *The English Administrative System 1780–1870* (Oxford 1981).

[39] House of Commons Treasury and Civil Service Committee, *Civil Servants and Ministers: Duties and Responsibilities* (HC 92 1985–86), vol II, pp 7–8, memorandum from the Cabinet Secretary entitled, 'The Duties and Responsibilities of Civil Servants in Relation to Ministers' (the Armstrong memorandum).

[40] Day and Klein, *Accountabilities: Five Public Services* (London 1987), pp 33–4.

These difficulties are exacerbated by a second set of phenomena—that is, the *expansion of government activity* and *changes to the structure of government*. The notion of ministerial responsibility implies that governmental action is undertaken by government departments that are headed up by Ministers. However, there have always been other bodies that have exercised public power, but which have not been part of ministerial departments. This obviously raises particular problems for the effective accountability of government: if there is no Minister to answer for such bodies, then who can Parliament call to account to scrutinise the exercise of public power? Today, the number of public bodies that operate at 'arm's length' from Ministers—sometimes collectively called the 'quango state'—is extensive.[41] The nature and range of such bodies was considered in Chapter 4. But, for present purposes, the important point is that public power is exercised by a range of public bodies that are often sometimes only tenuously connected with government Ministers. '[M]inisterial departments are bureaucratic icebergs, under which the greater part of the state structure operates in delegated organisational forms largely beyond public view or parliamentary oversight.'[42]

Third, even when Parliament does scrutinise the work of government, the convention of ministerial responsibility will often be used by Ministers as a means of *shielding government from parliamentary interference* rather than as a means of enabling Parliament to secure proper accountability. If government is to get on with the business of governing, there needs to be some balance drawn between democratic control through Parliament, on the one hand, and governmental independence and organisational effectiveness, on the other. Ministerial responsibility provides the buffer that shields government departments from parliamentary interference. To illustrate the point, consider, for example, the following comment from the nineteenth-century constitutional writer Bagehot:

> The incessant tyranny of Parliament over the public offices . . . can only be prevented by the appointment of a Parliamentary head, connected by close ties with the present Ministry and the ruling party in Parliament.[43]

According to Bagehot, this 'parliamentary head'—a Minister—acts as a 'protecting machine' that 'stands between the department and the busybodies and crotchet-makers of the House and the country'.[44]

This is the classic Peelite view of ministerial responsibility. The role of the Minister is to defend his or her department and to limit the involvement of Parliament in the task of governing. From this perspective, the *real* purpose of the doctrine of ministerial responsibility has little to do with facilitating parliamentary accountability of government. It is concerned with protecting the workings of government from parliamentary 'interference'.

This view of ministerial responsibility is, at least in part, informed by certain value assumptions—that is, that Parliament is simply not competent itself to govern, that

---

[41] Albeit that the number of such bodies is presently being reduced in an effort to cut public spending.
[42] Flinders, 772.   [43] *The English Constitution* [1867] (London 1993), p 193.
[44] *The English Constitution*, p 193.

the business of government is complex, and that parliamentary 'scrutiny' is likely to hinder and interfere with the skilled work of government. But a further point is that both Ministers and civil servants have an interest in avoiding blame. It is certainly not too cynical to suggest that much energy goes into avoiding scrutiny and 'passing the buck'—that is, seeking to pass the blame on to someone else. Ministers are normally extremely reluctant to take the blame if they do not perceive themselves to have been at fault. The Minister remains constitutionally responsible to Parliament, but in practice this simply means that the Minister is the man or woman who tells Parliament that he or she was not responsible for the mistake.[45]

For their part, civil servants are not directly accountable to Parliament, but act in the name of the Minister. The tradition and ethos of the Civil Service is that it is independent and politically neutral; although concerns have been expressed[46] that new arrangements[47] for increased ministerial involvement in the appointment of senior civil servants may erode such neutrality. While civil servants are theoretically accountable to Ministers, the doctrine of Civil Service independence makes it difficult for this accountability to be exercised effectively, and may prevent a Minister from dismissing or disciplining individual civil servants. It has been suggested that it serves the interests of civil servants to portray themselves as merely obedient executors of the will of elected politicians who are responsible to Parliament.[48] This is because civil servants themselves have an interest in avoiding accountability and the best way for them to do this is to emphasise that it is Ministers, not civil servants, who are accountable to Parliament.

The reality is that civil servants do not merely execute the will of Ministers, but themselves possess significant power in terms of making and implementing policy. As we noted earlier, Ministers are there to provide political leadership, whereas civil servants do the vast majority of the work involved in governing. However, civil servants may not always want to implement the policy goals set out by Ministers. As Margaret Hodge, a former Labour Minister, has noted, 'The reality is that the Civil Service is permanent and ministers are transient'.[49] If civil servants do not like what a Minister wants, then they can conveniently forget to implement the Minister's directions in the hope that the Minister will forget, or they can delay and delay in the hope that the Minister becomes bored, or is reshuffled or sacked before the decision is implemented. 'The rhetoric of Civil Service professionalism all too often hides the reality of where much of the power and authority lies.'[50] The upshot is that the traditional theory of ministerial responsibility may often have the effect of shielding civil servants from effective accountability.

---

[45] Gilmour, *The Body Politic* (London 1969), p 166.

[46] See, eg House of Lords Constitution Committee, *The Accountability of Civil Servants* (HL 61 2012–13), [24]–[29].

[47] Civil Service Commission, *Recruiting Permanent Secretaries: Ministerial Involvement* (London 2012).

[48] Riddell, *Parliament under Pressure* (London 1998), p 77.

[49] Hodge, *Called to Account: How Corporate Bad Behaviour and Government Waste Combine to Cost Us Millions* (London 2016), p 8.

[50] Hodge, p 8.

There is considerable ambiguity in the doctrine of ministerial responsibility. Indeed, both Ministers and civil servants sometimes disagree upon how ministerial responsibility both does and should operate. For example, according to David Blunkett MP, a former Home Secretary, it sometimes appears that Ministers have to cover for civil servants who are 'utterly useless, incompetent, and ineffective'.[51] By contrast, civil servants might sometimes think that Ministers are able to shift the blame onto civil servants rather than assume responsibility themselves. The upshot in practice is that there is an 'accountability gap' in which Ministers and civil servants can hide behind each other, so that no one is really held to account.[52] As the House of Commons Public Administration Select Committee has noted: 'It is clear that there is no consensus, either among politicians or officials, about the way in which ministerial and civil service responsibilities are divided. This means there can be no consensus about where accountability should lie.'[53]

4.4.3 Accountability in practice

To illustrate how both Ministers and civil servants can, in practice, evade accountability, consider the sorry episode of the Rural Payments Agency (RPA) and its failure to implement adequately the 'single farm payment system'. The RPA is an executive agency of the Department for Environment, Food and Rural Affairs (DEFRA). Since 2006, it has had the task of implementing a system of payments to farmers. However, the RPA was unable to process all of the applications by the deadline that had been set. Many farmers did not receive their payments and suffered significant financial losses. The RPA itself had failed largely because DEFRA had asked it to do too much in too short a period of time and did not pay enough heed to the Agency's warnings about the risks of what was being proposed. According to the parliamentary select committee overseeing DEFRA, the failure in administering the payments was a catastrophe for many farmers, as well as a serious and embarrassing failure for both DEFRA and the RPA: it represented a fundamental failure by DEFRA to carry out one of its principal tasks—that is, to pay farmers their financial entitlements on time.[54]

Who, then, was held to account? Accountability for the failure was limited to the removal and eventual dismissal of the RPA's chief executive. By contrast, those responsible within DEFRA—the Minister and other senior officials—escaped accountability by either moving on to other posts unscathed or staying in post. The select committee was highly critical of DEFRA, its Minister, and senior civil servants:

> A culture where ministers and senior officials can preside over failure of this magnitude and not be held personally accountable creates a serious risk of further failures in public service delivery. Accountability should mean that good results are rewarded, but a failure as serious as this of a Department to deliver one of its fundamental functions should

---

[51] Blunkett, *The Blunkett Tapes* (London 2006), p 607.

[52] House of Commons Public Administration Select Committee, *Politics and Administration: Ministers and Civil Servants* (HC 122 2006–07), [22].

[53] *Politics and Administration: Ministers and Civil Servants*, [39].

[54] House of Commons Environment, Food and Rural Affairs Select Committee, *The Rural Payments Agency and the Implementation of the Single Payment Scheme* (HC 107 2006–07).

result in the removal from post of those to whom the faulty policy design and implementation can be attributed. We recommend new guidance to make clear to ministers what they should do to take responsibility in the event of serious departmental failure.[55]

Given such strong criticism, one might have expected that DEFRA would have recognised the need to own up to its failure and to display some degree of contrition (even if only a tokenistic display). But instead DEFRA—in what the select committee considered a 'shoddy' and 'superficial' response—strongly regretted that the select committee had made criticisms of named civil servants and rejected the need for any new guidance concerning the responsibility of Ministers for serious departmental failures.[56] In short, those who (according to the select committee) were responsible for a serious government failure evaded responsibility.

This is only one example amongst many. In such cases, there is often considerable public concern about governmental effectiveness, but little hard-edged accountability. Ministers may claim they do not know what happened whereas civil servants may seek to hide behind ministerial responsibility. Who then is to be held to account? In theory, ministerial responsibility seeks to enhance detailed public scrutiny, but it may actually hinder such scrutiny in practice.

4.4.4 Conclusions

Concerns as to the (in)effectiveness of the doctrine of ministerial responsibility are now part of mainstream constitutional opinion. According to the Commons Liaison Committee, ministerial responsibility has been 'stretched to implausibility by the complexity of modern government and by the increasing devolution of responsibility to civil servants and to arm's length bodies'.[57] The way the doctrine has operated has on occasion been unacceptable, with Ministers blaming officials for failures in their departments or in agencies for which they are responsible, but also with officials then refusing to answer questions that would indicate where responsibility for failure actually lies. For Margaret Hodge MP, a former chair of the Commons Public Accounts Committee (2010–15), the old doctrine of ministerial responsibility is just not fit for twenty-first-century government:

> We live in an age of payment by results and performance management yet ministers are prevented from themselves appointing, promoting or sacking the senior civil servants for whom they are said to be accountable, on the grounds that this would politicize the civil service. You begin to wonder whether the whole doctrine of ministerial accountability is not constructed on a lie. How can anybody be held accountable for the actions of people they can't hire or fire? So civil servants escape external accountability because they are protected by the convention of ministerial responsibility, and they

---

[55] *The Rural Payments Agency and the Implementation of the Single Payment Scheme*, [7].

[56] House of Commons Environment, Food and Rural Affairs Select Committee, *The Rural Payments Agency and the Implementation of the Single Payment Scheme: Government Response to the Committee's Third Report of Session 2006–07* (HC 956 2006–07).

[57] House of Commons Liaison Committee, *Select Committee Effectiveness, Resources and Powers* (HC 697 2012–13), [114].

escape internal accountability because ministers are powerless to hold them to account in any meaningful way.[58]

One possible solution to the problem of effective accountability of civil servants would be to institute direct accountability of civil servants to Parliament. This has always been resisted on the grounds that it would produce a division of loyalties for civil servants and politicise the Civil Service. So, when civil servants do become involved in, for example, select committee hearings, the position is that they are not themselves being held to account, but that they are assisting Parliament in holding Ministers to account. This is made clear in the relevant Cabinet Office guidance on civil servants giving evidence to select committees (the Osmotherly Rules), which state that 'Civil servants who give evidence to Select Committees do so on behalf of their Ministers and under their directions'.[59] The constitutional position of civil servants is that they work for the government of the day; direct accountability to Parliament, in which both the government and opposition parties are present, would blur lines of control.

Another suggestion has been to establish a new 'public service bargain' between Ministers and civil servants underpinned by a governance code that would clarify formally their respective roles and responsibilities.[60] Furthermore, the Liaison Committee would like to engage with government to produce joint guidelines for departments and committees, which recognise ministerial accountability, the proper role of the Civil Service and the legitimate wish of Parliament for more effective accountability.[61] However, in 2014 the government reaffirmed the Osmotherly Rules. Overall, the status quo is generally accepted to be inadequate, but the government is reluctant to change the official position.

> **Q** What is the traditional theory of ministerial responsibility for civil servants? Why does the theory sometimes seem at odds with the practice?

4.5 Ministerial responsibility as prudential government

Finally, we must consider another sense in which ministerial responsibility is sometimes used: government Ministers are responsible for adopting a wise, prudential policy irrespective of whether or not it meets with public approval. Recall that the government—not Parliament—governs. Amery described the UK government as 'an independent body which on taking office assumes the responsibility for leading

---

[58] Hodge, 'Accountability in Today's Public Service', speech at Policy Exchange, 15 March 2012, **http://www.parliament.uk/business/committees/committees-a-z/commons-select/public-accounts-committee/news/policy-exchange-speech/**. As noted earlier, there is now limited provision for ministerial involvement in the appointment of senior civil servants.

[59] Cabinet Office, *Giving Evidence to Select Committees: Guidance for Civil Servants* (London 2014), [9]. See also House of Lords Constitution Committee, *The Accountability of Civil Servants*, [79].

[60] House of Commons Public Administration Select Committee, *Politics and Administration: Ministers and Civil Servants*.

[61] House of Commons Liaison Committee, *Select Committee Effectiveness, Resources and Powers* (HC 697 2012–13).

and directing Parliament and the nation in accordance with its own judgement and convictions'.[62] Government is expected to act responsibly not only in the sense of providing explanations for its decisions, but also in the sense of pursuing a responsible policy in the wider public interest.

Responsibility in this sense implies a state of mind, which weighs the consequences of action and then acts, regardless of the popularity or otherwise of such acts. It means taking difficult longer-term decisions in the national interest rather than merely seeking short-term popularism, which may produce dysfunctional consequences in the long run.

A good illustration is the bailout of the banking system in 2008. Faced with the prospects of financial collapse, the government used hundreds of billions of pounds of taxpayers' money to bail out the banking system. This was certainly not done to fulfil any manifesto pledge, or because Parliament had commanded the government to do so, or because of the government's desire to enhance its political standing. On the contrary, the government itself decided that this would be the responsible thing to do. An effective banking system is essential to the functioning of a capitalist economy, and the government took the action to maintain the banking system. Had such action not been taken, the banking system—and, with it, the UK economy—could have collapsed. The government was aware that its actions would increase public borrowing and thereby produce a large fiscal deficit that would need to be paid off at some future stage through austerity policies. It was also aware that the action would be politically unpopular in some quarters, but the government considered it to be the prudential, responsible thing to do. After the government had taken the action, Parliament debated and scrutinised it; Parliament provided the public arena in which the merits and demerits of the action were discussed—but Parliament did not in any way tell the government what to do. Government acted, then Parliament debated.

'Responsibility' in this sense is used by government to justify unwelcome decisions and policies, and to explain to the public that the broader notion of responsible government sometimes requires tough decisions to be taken in the longer-term public interest. 'Responsible' decisions in this sense are sometimes highly contested ones. The government's contention that its action to save the banks was necessary to avoid imminent financial meltdown was not universally accepted, but Ministers decided that it was the best action to take in the broader public interest. Similarly, the decision to invade Iraq in 2003—which the government claimed to have taken to safeguard vital national interests—proved highly unpopular, and hindsight has shown it to have been unwise. To some people, decisions such as these are the epitome of *irresponsible* government—of decisions being taken that have serious, even disastrous, long-term consequences, in the face of strong public opposition. But to say that such action is at odds with the notion of responsible government rather misses the point if we recognise that the concept of ministerial responsibility is itself a highly contested one

---

[62] Amery, *Thoughts on the Constitution* (Oxford 1953), p 31; Birch, *Representative and Responsible Government: An Essay on the British Constitution* (London 1964), pp 18–19.

that is arguably as much about facilitating strong government as it is about aligning governmental decision-making with public or parliamentary opinion.

4.6 Summary

Ministerial responsibility is a complex and ambiguous notion. It is central to the UK constitution and to parliamentary accountability of the government. We have highlighted two points. First, there are different meanings attributed to the convention of ministerial responsibility. Second, the operation of that doctrine in practice is heavily influenced by the government's dominance of Parliament. We now consider the mechanisms by which Parliament seeks to scrutinise government and its effectiveness.

> **Q** What are the main meanings of ministerial responsibility? What are the reasons for its essentially contested nature?

5. The mechanics of parliamentary scrutiny of government

To understand how Parliament scrutinises government in practice, it is necessary to examine the three mechanisms by which Parliament scrutinises government: parliamentary questions, parliamentary debates, and select committee inquiries. These mechanisms are used, respectively, to extract information and explanations from government, debate government policy and administration, and undertake detailed inquiries into government. Before examining these mechanisms in detail, it is appropriate to consider a broader issue: the constraints on parliamentary scrutiny.

5.1 Constraints on parliamentary scrutiny

We have examined the broader structural aspects of the political relationship between government and Parliament. It is also important to recognise the party political dimension to parliamentary accountability. British politics is dominated by political parties that are engaged in a continuous electoral campaign with each other. MPs in the House of Commons, whose role it is to scrutinise government, are themselves politically aligned to either the governing political party (or parties) or to an opposition party.

Another limitation upon parliamentary scrutiny is the size of the government's 'payroll vote' in Parliament. This refers to the number of MPs and Peers who are members of the government and therefore will always vote for the government. It includes not just Ministers, but also Whips and Parliamentary Private Secretaries (PPSs).[63] There is a statutory limit: there can be no more than 95 MPs in the Commons who

---

[63] 'A Parliamentary Private Secretary (PPS) is an unpaid assistant to a Minister, selected from backbench MPs to be the "eyes and ears" of the Minister in the House of Commons. They often advise the Minister

are also *paid* holders of ministerial office.[64] However, in practice, the Prime Minister appoints *unpaid* Ministers as a way of increasing the total number of Ministers in his government without exceeding the statutory limit. By definition, and according to the convention of collective responsibility, all parliamentarians on the payroll vote always vote for the government.

The government therefore always has a sizable block of votes in Parliament. As Figure 10.1 shows, the proportion of the membership of the Commons taken up by the payroll vote increased from 6 per cent in 1900 to 21 per cent in 2012. In other words, just over a fifth of MPs will always vote for the government—no matter what.[65] Figure 10.2 shows the detailed breakdown of the number of MPs and Peers who are members of the government. When looking at Figure 10.2, bear in mind that the total number of MPs is 650.

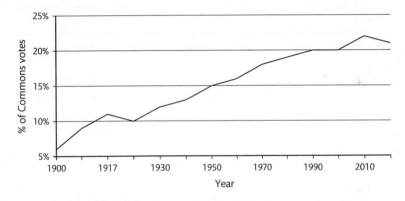

Figure 10.1 Payroll vote as a percentage of the House of Commons, 1900–2012
Source: http://www.theguardian.com/news/datablog/2012/oct/12/size-government-uk

The size of the payroll vote has been criticised. The appointment of unpaid holders to government positions enables the government to circumvent the statutory limit. It also means the government can stack Parliament with its own office-holders. The suggestion by the Commons Public Administration Select Committee in 2010 that the payroll vote be reduced to 15 per cent was just ignored by the government.[66] It is not difficult to understand why.

---

on the state of parliamentary or party opinion, and act as a two-way channel of communication between the Minister and backbench MPs': House of Commons Library Briefing Paper, *Parliamentary Private Secretaries* (SN04942 2016), **http://researchbriefings.files.parliament.uk/documents/SN04942/SN04942. pdf**. A former Labour MP and Minister, Chris Mullin MP, once sceptically noted that PPSs 'are all over the place, engaging in a whirlwind of political activity, planting patsy questions—even planting the supplementaries. Much of this activity is pointless, but it does have the effect of neutralising intelligent individuals who might otherwise make a rather more useful contribution to the proper functioning of Parliament' (quoted in *Parliamentary Private Secretaries*, p 5).

[64] House of Commons Disqualification Act 1975, s 2(1).

[65] If an MP on the payroll vote does vote against the government, then he or she will risk being sacked and replaced.

[66] House of Commons Public Administration Select Committee, *Too Many Ministers?* (HC 457 2009–10).

Figure 10.2 Payroll vote, 1900–2012

Political factors also influence the effectiveness of parliamentary scrutiny. For example, opposition MPs commonly oppose the government, but this may be because they are motivated by a desire to engage in political point-scoring rather than by an inclination to subject governmental activity to meaningful scrutiny. Meanwhile, the purpose of government whips is to exert control over the government's backbench MPs to sustain it in power. While the role of the whips may seem inimical to the ideal of representative democracy, it is long established, and without it government would be unable to get its business through Parliament.[67] The personal views of individual MPs are then often subject to an 'iron cage of party discipline'.[68]

Indeed, a former chair of the House of Commons Public Administration Select Committee, Tony Wright, has noted that 'all the textbook talk about Parliament's role in scrutiny and accountability' is misleading as it 'frequently fails to get inside the skin of an institution whose members have a quite different agenda'.[69] In the real world of politics, the personal aspirations of most MPs are either to get promoted into government or to the opposition frontbench. MPs aspire to power, not its scrutiny. They wish to have a successful political career—and the principal, if

[67] Renton, *Chief Whip: People, Power and Patronage in Westminster* (London 2004).
[68] Rose, *Politics in England: Change and Persistence* (London 1989), p 121.
[69] Wright, *British Politics: A Very Short Introduction* (Oxford 2003), p 85.

not exclusive, way of achieving this is by becoming a government Minister. As Wright puts it: 'Every parliamentary foot-soldier dreams of one day holding a ministerial baton.'[70]

The situation is fluid though. The new intakes of MPs in 2010 and 2015 have demonstrated their willingness to rebel against the government. Despite its pervasive influence (at least in the Commons), party politics is not the only constraint upon Parliament as a scrutiniser of government. Parliamentary time and resources are also limited. Furthermore, over recent years, MPs have increasingly come to spend a greater proportion of their time dealing with complaints and issues of concern raised by their constituents. It is often doubted whether this increasing constituency workload is compatible with MPs also being able to scrutinise government. For example, in the opinion of one MP:

> Too many Members of Parliament see themselves as super-councillors, who take up issues that should be handled by citizens' advice bureaux and local law centres, rather than as representatives who hold the government to account, which is a particularly important role for backbenchers in government.[71]

Moreover, some MPs have second jobs. Obviously, given that MPs have limited time, one role or other will have to give way.

Another inherent constraint on parliamentary accountability is that individual MPs, and so Parliament collectively, may simply not be well equipped to subject government to detailed scrutiny. Most MPs are generalists. They may bring experience of outside interests with them when they enter Parliament, but there has been a discernible trend for more MPs to be professional politicians and not to have much experience beyond politics. In any event, modern government is complex and this can make it difficult for MPs to offer informed criticism, except in those areas (if any) in which they possess real experience or on which they have been briefed (in an inevitably skewed way) by lobbyists.

A further important constraint on Parliamentary accountability concerns the attitudes of those within government—Ministers and civil servants—whose action or inaction Parliament is seeking to scrutinise. Government departments may at times be transparent and welcome being held to account. On the other hand, government departments are often inclined to be defensively secretive, to be obstructive and uncooperative, to delay the release of information, to obfuscate and be evasive, and to deploy a whole range of other tactics, such as spin and presentational strategies—especially when they feel vulnerable to challenge. The tendency of government in such circumstances is to utilise a number of blame-avoidance games.[72] The basic point is that effective scrutiny depends upon the cooperation of government. While such cooperation will sometimes be present, this is not always the case and a lack of such cooperation will hinder Parliament's constitutional duty to hold government to account.

---

[70] Wright, p 85.   [71] HC Deb, vol 502, col 201WH (15 December 2009) (Mark Field MP).
[72] See Hood, *The Blame Game: Spin, Bureaucracy, and Self-Preservation in Government* (Princeton, NJ 2011).

Much of what has been said so far relates mainly or wholly to the House of Commons. We saw in Chapter 5 that the House of Lords is a radically different chamber from the Commons.[73] For as long as it remains an unelected chamber, the Lords is less affected by the tribal party politics of the Commons. As a result, it is arguably capable of subjecting the government to more serious, thoroughgoing scrutiny. This is not necessarily a knockout argument against an elected House of Lords—but it does underline the tension just described between partisanship and scrutiny.

> **Q** What are the practical constraints upon parliamentary scrutiny? How, if at all, could such limitations be ameliorated?

5.2 Improving parliamentary scrutiny—*Rebuilding the House*

Proposals to enhance parliamentary scrutiny—for instance, by reducing the influence of the whips, increasing the powers, role, and status of select committees, and reducing the ability of the government to set Parliament's agenda—have often met with resistance from successive governments. But over recent years, the mood and ethos within Parliament has changed. Matters came to a head with the MPs' expenses scandal of 2009, which damaged public confidence not only in some individual MPs, but also in the House of Commons as an institution. The crisis prompted a number of responses, such as immediate reforms of the system of MPs' expenses.[74] But it was also accepted that further changes were needed to the functioning of Parliament to instil new public confidence in it. As the then Prime Minister, Gordon Brown, told the House of Commons, 'the battered reputation of this institution cannot be repaired without fundamental change'.[75]

The House of Commons Reform Committee, chaired by Tony Wright MP, was established to consider reforms to parliamentary procedures. According to its report, *Rebuilding the House*, public confidence in the House of Commons was too low, and fundamental structural and cultural change was required: 'We believe that the House of Commons has to become a more vital institution, less sterile in how it operates, better able to reflect public concerns, more transparent, and more vigorous in its task of scrutiny and accountability.'[76] While the great majority of MPs work extremely hard, 'at present many Members do not see the point in attending debates or making the House the primary focus of their activities'.[77]

To address this issue, the Committee considered that it was necessary to give MPs back a sense of ownership of Parliament by enabling them to set its agenda and take

---

[73] See Chapter 5, section 3.3.

[74] Parliamentary Standards Act 2009. See Parpworth, 'The Parliamentary Standards Act 2009: A Constitutional Dangerous Dogs Measure?' (2010) 73 MLR 262.

[75] HC Deb, vol 493, col 795 (10 June 2009).

[76] House of Commons Reform Committee, *Rebuilding the House* (HC 1117 2009–10), [3]. See also Russell, '"Never Allow a Crisis Go To Waste": The Wright Committee Reforms to Strengthen the House of Commons' (2011) 64 Parliamentary Affairs 612.

[77] *Rebuilding the House*, [3].

meaningful decisions, and to ensure that the business of the House is responsive to public concerns. The Committee therefore made a number of recommendations aimed at enhancing parliamentary scrutiny. Two of the most significant proposals—concerning the creation of a Backbench Business Committee to give backbench MPs a greater role in deciding which topics get debated, and the election by secret ballot of select committee chairs—are considered further later in this chapter.[78]

The Wright reforms have, cumulatively, significantly strengthened the role of Parliament vis-à-vis the government. In 2015, the Commons Liaison Committee stated: 'The Wright reforms have worked and should be retained and developed'.[79]

5.3 Parliamentary questions

We now consider the discrete mechanisms Parliament has for scrutinising the government. A simple and sometimes effective way by which parliamentarians can seek to hold government to account is to ask questions of the government. Such questions can be asked to extract information, or to require the government to explain and defend its policies, actions, and decisions.

5.3.1 Oral questions

Oral questions to Ministers are perhaps amongst Parliament's most publicly recognisable activities. Prime Minister's questions (PMQs) take place for half an hour each week and are televised. This regular and frequent questioning of the Prime Minister is a relatively recent innovation, having been introduced in 1961. PMQs usually show the House of Commons at its most directly adversarial, especially in terms of the confrontation between the Prime Minister and the leader of the opposition.

Opposition MPs will seek to highlight some defect in the government or its policy, and then the Prime Minister seeks to defend the government and highlight the failings of the opposition party. MPs put questions to the Prime Minister not in the expectation or hope that this will actually prompt any change of government policy, but to highlight to the general public the perception both that the government is deficient and that their own party would be able to form a better government. In this sense, PMQs are simply part of the theatre of politics in which the main parties assail each other as part of an unedifying political point-scoring game. This perception is reinforced by the frequent practice of government backbench MPs asking sycophantic questions congratulating the Prime Minister upon the government's ostensible successes ('Does the Prime Minister agree that what the government is doing is wonderful?').

Scrutiny vies with partisanship. However, backbench MPs use PMQs to raise issues that the government would not otherwise wish to talk about. It is therefore an important venue for ensuring accountability and responsiveness. The government has to confront the difficult issues of the day, which can advantage the opposition by putting

[78] On the Commons Backbench Business Committee, see section 5.4 and on the election of chairs of Commons select committees, see section 5.5.1.

[79] House of Commons Liaison Committee, *Legacy Report* (HC 954 2014–15), [115].

the government on the defensive regardless of the completeness of the government's answers.[80]

PMQs serve another important public function: that of highlighting for the public the policy differences between the government and the opposition. Nonetheless, PMQs are now the only opportunity to ask questions of Prime Ministers. There has been a long-term decline in the accountability of Prime Ministers in the Commons.[81] Apart from PMQs, high-level Commons statements, and occasional appearances before the Liaison Committee, Prime Ministers now rarely attend the Commons.

Question time for other Ministers operates on a departmental rota. Each Minister appears once in a five-week cycle to answer questions that fall within his or her particular area of responsibility. So, for example, an MP's question about terrorism would be put to the Home Secretary or another Home Office Minister. Question times for Ministers are still 'often adversarial but usually less gladiatorial than PMQs'.[82] Nevertheless, ministerial question time has been likened to a 'daily opportunity for the rival parliamentary armies to lob custard pies at each other'.[83] It follows that while the asking of oral questions serves a political purpose, it achieves relatively little—except perhaps at a symbolic level—in terms of real scrutiny.

Since 2010 MPs have been able to ask topical questions. If something has happened that an MP believes requires an immediate answer from a government Minister, then he or she may apply to ask an urgent question. If the Speaker (or in the House of Lords the Lord Speaker) agrees that the matter is urgent and important, the question will be asked at the end of question time. Topical questions are useful in terms of enabling an MP to ask an urgent question on a current matter.

> **Q** Watch Prime Minister's questions in the House of Commons, which take place every Wednesday at noon when Parliament is in session and can be viewed online.[84] According to King and Crewe, 'In the House of Commons on Wednesdays during PMQs, MPs often sound like rival bands of warring gorillas'.[85] Do you agree? Do PMQs provide an effective forum for holding the Prime Minister to account? Is it desirable for there to be more effective control over the exercise of prime ministerial power? If so, how could this be achieved?

5.3.2 Written questions

These are an important tool that MPs have at their disposal in terms of extracting information, especially detailed information, from the government. The daily

---

[80] Bevan and John, 'Policy Representation by Party Leaders and Followers: What Drives UK Prime Minister's Questions?' (2016) 51 Government and Opposition 59. See also Lovenduski, 'Prime Minister's Questions as Political Ritual' (2012) 7 British Politics 314; Bates et al, 'Questions to the Prime Minister: A Comparative Study of PMQs from Thatcher to Cameron' (2012) 67 Parliamentary Affairs 253.

[81] Dunleavy et al, 'Leaders, Politics and Institutional Change: The Decline of Prime Ministerial Accountability to the House of Commons, 1868–1990' (1993) 23 British Journal of Political Science 267.

[82] Rush, *Parliament Today* (Manchester 2005), p 211.   [83] Wright, p 83.

[84] http://www.parliament.uk

[85] King and Crewe, *The Blunders of Our Governments* (London 2013), p 391.

record of parliamentary proceedings—Hansard—contains the reports of debates and statements in the Chamber, and also a long list of answers to written questions. The daily number of questions tabled is around 500. It is clear that the continuing increase in the number of questions tabled has placed some strain on the systems both within Parliament and government that handle written parliamentary questions. Such questions are highly valued by MPs as a means of scrutinising government and obtaining information; the advantage of this tool is its transparency, and the fact that, because the answer is placed clearly on record, it can be followed up by any MP who takes an interest.

There are, though, some constraints upon written questions. First, there is an advisory cost limit, known as the *disproportionate cost threshold*, of £850. This is the cost level above which a government department can refuse to answer a parliamentary question—although, in practice, this is rarely exceeded.

Second, there is widespread concern amongst MPs that many answers to written parliamentary questions are unsatisfactory. For example, rather than giving detailed answers, some government departments have a practice of giving evasive or anodyne 'non-answers' to questions, which in turn prompt further questions or even resort to the Freedom of Information Act 2000.[86] This is notwithstanding the fact that the Ministerial Code states:

> Ministers should be as open as possible with Parliament and the public, refusing to provide information only when disclosure would not be in the public interest.[87]

For their part, government departments have expressed frustration when dealing with questions that seem frivolous. Following concerns which it expressed in 2009,[88] the House of Commons Procedure Committee monitors both the timeliness of responses to written questions and whether answers are adequate. When an answer is judged unsatisfactory, the Committee may intervene in order to attempt to secure a fuller answer to the MP's question.[89]

There are also the written ministerial statements used by government to make formal announcements to Parliament. For example, written ministerial statements are often used to provide or announce detailed information and statistics from the government, the publication of reports by government agencies, findings of reviews and inquiries, and the government's responses to such inquiries. Such statements are not, then, a tool by which government can be held to account by Parliament, but a means by which the government can make important announcements to Parliament. If anything, the use of such statements reflects a broader set of understandings between Parliament and government—that is, that the government generally accepts the discipline of informing Parliament as to important changes in governmental policy as an aspect of the principle of responsible government.[90]

---

[86] On the Act, see section 7.2.   [87] 'Ministerial Code', [1.2d].

[88] House of Commons Procedure Committee, *Written Parliamentary Questions* (HC 859 2008–09).

[89] House of Commons Procedure Committee, *Monitoring Written Parliamentary Questions* (HC 1095 2013–14).

[90] However, successive governments have been criticised for often *first* announcing new initiatives via the media, only informing Parliament thereafter.

5.4 **Parliamentary debates**

Debates are the oldest method by which Parliament scrutinises government decisions and actions. Debates allow for the expression and representation of different political views. Such debates are held in both the House of Commons and the House of Lords themselves, and now the satellite debating chamber, Westminster Hall. Two questions arise.

First, *who has the power to decide what does and does not get debated in Parliament?* A long-standing concern has been that business in the House of Commons is too closely controlled by the government, enabling it to determine what does and does not get discussed. This is reflected in Standing Order No 14 of the House of Commons, which states that the general principle is that 'government business shall have precedence at every sitting'. The main exceptions, until recently, were that 20 days are set aside for debates initiated by the opposition parties—'opposition day debates'—while 13 Fridays are used for discussion of private members' Bills.[91]

However, as part of the *Rebuilding the House* package of reforms, the Backbench Business Committee was established in 2010. Under this process, 35 days (of which at least 27 must be in the Chamber) in each session are allotted for backbench business and backbench MPs can submit bids to the Backbench Business Committee for debate.[92] The Committee is itself comprised of backbench MPs and they—and not the government—control the agenda for such debates. The Backbench Business Committee gives backbench MPs a greater sense of ownership of the Commons agenda, and facilitates discussion of those issues which they consider most important, while not intruding on the government's ability to get its business discussed. The Committee has been widely welcomed as a successful and effective innovation.[93]

However, the Backbench Business Committee represents only a *partial* implementation of the *Rebuilding the House* package; the establishment of a 'House Business Committee', which would reduce the government's stranglehold over the scheduling of *non-backbench business*, has so far been resisted.[94] Despite all the recent advances, the Commons is as far away as ever from implementing the basic Wright principle that all time should be regarded as 'the House's time'. The present procedure for setting the agenda for most of the House's business—that which is not decided by the Backbench Business Committee—is inadequate, remaining in clear violation of the principles set out in the Wright report: 'The need for reform is obvious and urgent.'[95]

Second, *are debates an effective instrument of accountability?* For Wright, it is a mistake to use the word 'debate' to describe events that often involve prepared speeches served up to a largely empty chamber in which neither votes nor minds are likely to be

---

[91] On private members' Bills, see Chapter 5, section 5.1.1.

[92] HC Deb, vol 511, cols 843–5 (15 June 2010), approving new standing orders relating to the Backbench Business Committee and amending Standing Order 14.

[93] House of Commons Procedure Committee, *Review of the Backbench Business Committee* (HC 168 2012–13).

[94] Howarth, 'The House of Commons Backbench Business Committee' [2011] PL 490.

[95] House of Commons Political and Constitutional Reform Committee, *Revisiting Rebuilding the House: The Impact of the Wright Reforms* (HC 83 2013–14), p 3.

changed by what is said.[96] The partisan nature of the House of Commons means that debates often have a ritualistic character in which party considerations are so dominant that they serve little real purpose. According to Norton, 'there is little evidence that opposition day debates have affected government actions: they are simply part of the partisan conflict in the chamber and rarely reported by the media'.[97]

However, the Backbench Business Committee has enhanced Parliament's capacity to use debates as a means of placing pressure on the government. As Howarth notes, the Committee has 'already fulfilled the hopes of those who wanted to see policy motions on topics that party leaders have sought to avoid'.[98] The Commons Political and Constitutional Reform Committee has concluded that the Backbench Business Committee has been a success, but it should have more say over the scheduling of backbench business.[99]

Most debates end with a vote on a motion which will either support or oppose the government's position on a particular issue. Unsurprisingly, the government's majority means that it wins almost all Commons votes. Figure 10.3 shows the number of government defeats in the House of Commons between 1945 and 2016.

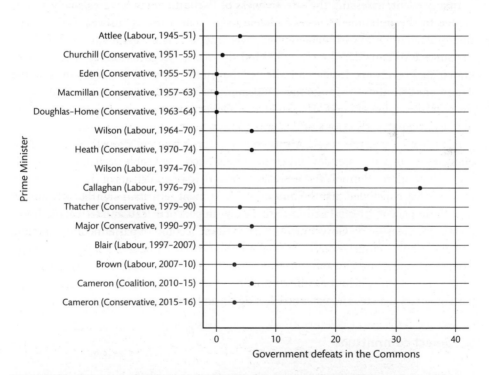

Figure 10.3 Government defeats in the House of Commons, 1945–2016

Source: List of Government defeats in the House of Commons (1945–present), **https://en.wikipedia.org/wiki/List_of_Government_defeats_in_the_House_of_Commons_%281945%E2%80%93present%29**

---

[96] Wright, *British Politics: A Very Short Introduction* (Oxford 2003), p 85.

[97] Norton, *Parliament in British Politics* (Basingstoke 2005), p 131.   [98] Howarth, 497.

[99] *Revisiting Rebuilding the House: The Impact of the Wright Reforms.*

Over this period, apart from during the Wilson and Callaghan administrations, governments typically lost fewer than ten votes in the Commons. The reason? The presence of a Commons majority. For instance, the governments of both Margaret Thatcher and Tony Blair enjoyed huge Commons majorities. It took eight years for Tony Blair's government (1997–2007) to suffer its first defeat in the Commons in 2005 over a proposal to extend the maximum period of detention for suspected terrorists to 90 days. By contrast, the number of defeats for Harold Wilson (1974–76) and Jim Callaghan (1976–79) occurred when those governments either did not have a majority in the Commons (Wilson) or only a very slim majority (Callaghan).

Amidst routine votes for the government, there are some important defeats for the government. For instance, the Coalition government (2010–15) was defeated over proposed military action in Syria in August 2013—a rare and important government defeat. A subsequent Commons vote in December 2015 in favour of military action against Islamic State (following the 2015 Paris terrorist attacks) demonstrated the importance of Commons votes and the central place that they occasionally play in determining policy.[100]

In any event, assessing the effectiveness of Parliamentary debates solely by reference to the outcome of votes is liable to present a highly misleading perception of Parliamentary influence upon government. It is necessary to look beneath the surface to consider the many behind-the-scenes negotiations and the role of anticipated reactions. Research indicates that much discussion occurs outside the Commons chamber ('through the usual channels') between government Ministers, the opposition, backbench MPs, and peers. Government is also as much influenced by the anticipated reactions of Parliament than actual debates and votes.

Faced with a possible revolt, Ministers can rethink matters altogether and retreat, offer concessions, or water down their proposals. Such less-visible parliamentary influence is both more common and more influential than open defeats of the government. Research has concluded that the impact of government retreats is significantly greater than the impact of defeats. Further, the collective impact of defeats and retreats is almost certainly increasing.[101] 'Governments take constant account of parliamentary opinion, and in normal circumstances, do not put proposals to parliament that it will not accept. Commons defeats are rare and generally a sign that party managers have misjudged the situation.'[102] Such conclusions undermine the simplistic 'parliamentary decline thesis': parliamentary debates and votes do exert significant influence upon government.

5.5 **Select committees**

Select Committees are the principal mechanism through which the House of Commons holds the executive to account.[103]

---

[100] HC Deb, vol 603, col 323 (2 December 2015).

[101] Russell and Cowley, 'The Policy Power of the Westminster Parliament: The "Parliamentary State" and the Empirical Evidence' (2016) 29 Governance 121.

[102] Russell and Cowley, 133.

[103] Brazier and Fox, 'Reviewing Select Committee Tasks and Modes of Operation' (2011) 64 Parliamentary Affairs 354, 367.

Public opinion, commentators, and academic critics have all recognised that select committee work is the most constructive and productive aspect of Parliament . . . Select committee scrutiny is now part of the thinking of ministers and public bodies—it is the context within which they operate—and has a continuing effect in addition to the impact of specific recommendations.[104]

These quotations illustrate the current and growing importance of select committees. Commons select committees oversee the work of specific government departments. There are also many other committees in both the Commons and the Lords and joint committees.

5.5.1 House of Commons select committees

Select committees were introduced in 1979 to extend parliamentary scrutiny of government policy and administration. Each government department is overseen by a dedicated Commons select committee. For instance, the House of Commons Home Affairs Committee scrutinises the work of the Home Office and its associated public bodies. When new departments are created, so too are new select committees: the Department for Exiting the European Union (EU), established in 2016, prompted the establishment of a Commons committee to scrutinise the crucial work of the new department.

There are currently 19 Commons departmental select committees. Select committees usually comprise between 11 and 16 MPs, all of whom are backbench MPs, although the new Brexit select committee is unusually large, with 21 members. Each select committee is cross-party—that is, no single party will have an overall majority of MPs in any particular committee, so as to reduce partisanship. Until recently, party whips determined which MPs became chairs of select committees—and the temptation for the government whips to exert partisan influence sometimes proved irresistible.

But in 2010—in a bid to reinvigorate Parliamentary scrutiny—the system was changed: select committee chairs are now elected by MPs through a secret ballot. This has drastically reduced the power of the whips to influence appointments to select committees. The indications are that elected chairs have exerted a distinctively positive effect. 'Among the developments in select committee effectiveness this Parliament, the most significant is the direct election of almost all committee chairs by the whole House.'[105] Elected chairs have a mandate from the Commons and greater independence from government. They possess appreciably more authority and legitimacy. This has significantly bolstered their role and the status of select committee work.

Select committees have become increasingly proactive in their efforts to influence the strategic direction of government. Some committees are no longer content merely to comment on policy once it has been decided upon by government; increasingly, committees now want to influence government policymaking. This is a significant change and time will tell how the role of select committees develops.

The formal remit of select committees—that of examining the administration, expenditure, and policy of the government departments to which they are

---

[104] House of Commons Liaison Committee, *Legacy Report* (HC 954 2014–15), [115].
[105] House of Commons Liaison Committee, *Legacy Report*, [17].

attached—may sound a little dry. According to King, select committees function as 'goaders, gadflies, and critics' of government departments.[106] The committees operate by conducting inquiries into areas of policy and administration within the responsibility of the government department that the committee oversees. Each committee selects its own subjects of inquiry and seeks written and oral evidence from a wide range of relevant groups and individuals. Hearings take place in committee rooms in Parliament in which witnesses are questioned by committee members. While select committees do not have the power to compel Ministers and civil servants to attend before them, in practice, Ministers and civil servants tend to appear for fear that political embarrassment will otherwise result. At the end of an inquiry, the relevant committee produces a report setting out its findings and making recommendations to the government. The government aims to produce a considered response to a select committee report within two months of its publication.[107] In 2012, the House of Commons Liaison Committee produced a revised list of the core tasks of departmental select committees to provide a framework for committees as they hold Ministers and their departments to account, as shown in Table 10.1.[108]

5.5.2 Other committees

There are other House of Commons committees. These include (amongst others):

- The Public Accounts Committee was established in 1861 and is the oldest select committee in the House of Commons. It investigates whether government achieves value for money when spending public money.

- The Women and Equalities Committee was established in 2015 to oversee the Government Equalities Office (GEO). The Committee fills a gap in previous accountability arrangements to oversee the government's performance on equalities (gender, age, race, religion or belief, sexual orientation, disability, gender identity, pregnancy and maternity, marriage or civil partnership status) issues. The Committee has produced important reports on transgender equality, the gender pay gap, employment opportunities for Muslims in the UK, and pregnancy and maternity discrimination.

- The Public Administration and Constitutional Affairs Select Committee (PACAC) oversees the work of the Parliamentary Ombudsman,[109] and considers matters relating to the quality and standards of administration provided by government departments, matters relating to the Civil Service, and constitutional issues.[110]

---

[106] King, *The British Constitution* (Oxford 2007), p 333.

[107] Cabinet Office, *Departmental Evidence and Response to Select Committees* (London 2005), [108].

[108] Table 10.1 is taken from House of Commons Liaison Committee, *Select Committee Effectiveness, Resources and Powers* (HC 697 2012–13), [20].

[109] On which, see Chapter 15.

[110] Constitutional issues were overseen by the Commons Political and Constitutional Reform Committee during the 2010–15 Parliament, but this committee was abolished in 2015 and oversight of constitutional issues was transferred to PACAC.

Table 10.1 Core tasks of departmental select committees

Task 1: Strategy	To examine the strategy of the department, how it has identified its key objectives and priorities and whether it has the means to achieve them, in terms of plans, resources, skills, capabilities, and management information
Task 2: Policy	To examine policy proposals by the department, and areas of emerging policy, or where existing policy is deficient, and make proposals
Task 3: Expenditure and performance	To examine the expenditure plans, outturn and performance of the department and its arm's length bodies, and the relationships between spending and delivery of outcomes
Task 4: Draft Bills	To conduct scrutiny of draft Bills within the committee's responsibilities
Task 5: Bills and delegated legislation	To assist the House in its consideration of Bills and statutory instruments, including draft orders under the Public Bodies Act
Task 6: Post-legislative scrutiny	To assist the House in its post-legislative scrutiny of Bills and statutory instruments
Task 7: European scrutiny	To scrutinise policy developments at the European level and EU legislative proposals
Task 8: Appointments	To scrutinise major appointments made by the department and to hold pre-appointment hearings where appropriate
Task 9: Support for the House	To produce timely reports to inform debate in the House, including Westminster Hall, or debating committees, and to examine petitions tabled
Task 10: Public engagement	To assist the House of Commons in better engagement with the public by ensuring that the work of the committee is accessible to the public

- The Liaison Committee comprises the chairs of all of the House of Commons select committees and oversees the work of all select committees. The Prime Minister appears before the Liaison Committee twice a year. According to the Liaison Committee, 'Prime Ministers' oral evidence sessions with the Liaison Committee have become more effective in scrutinising the influence No. 10 Downing Street exercises in policy-making across government.'[111]

There are also various Lords committees. The following are worth highlighting:

- The House of Lords Constitution Committee examines the constitutional implications of all public Bills coming before the House and keeps under review the operation of the constitution. This committee has produced many reports referred to throughout this book.

---

[111] Liaison Committee, *Legacy Report*, [115].

- The Delegated Powers and Regulatory Reform Committee scrutinises proposals in Bills to delegate legislative power from Parliament to another body (usually Ministers).[112]

- Other committees—for example, the Science and Technology Committee and the Economic Affairs Committee—play to the strengths of Peers with expertise in those areas.

Finally, there are also joint committees of both Houses, of which the Joint Committee on Human Rights is perhaps the most high profile.[113]

Almost every week select committees publish important and considered reports. These reports often hit the headlines, but, more than that, they provide detailed analysis of important issues and recommendations for government. To give a flavour of Committee reports, consider the following two examples:

- In 2016, the Commons Foreign Affairs Committee published a highly critical report of the UK's military intervention in Libya in 2011 against the Gaddafi regime. The Committee concluded that the policy was not informed by accurate intelligence. The government had failed to identify that the threat to civilians was overstated and that rebels included a significant Islamist element. The initial policy of limited intervention to protect civilians then drifted into an opportunist policy of regime change. But this policy was not underpinned by any strategy. The result was political and economic collapse, inter-militia and inter-tribal warfare, humanitarian and migrant crises, widespread human rights violations, the spread of Gaddafi regime weapons across the region, and the growth of ISIL in North Africa. The then Prime Minister David Cameron was ultimately responsible for the failure to develop a coherent Libya strategy.[114]

- In 2016, the Women and Equalities Committee published a hard-hitting report concerning the scale and impact of sexual harassment and sexual violence in schools across England. The evidence strongly suggested that sexual harassment and abuse of girls is often accepted as part of daily life, children of primary school age are learning about sex and relationships through exposure to hardcore pornography, teachers sometimes accept sexual harassment as 'just banter', and parents are struggling to know how they can best support their children. The Committee found that the government had no coherent plan to tackle the causes or consequences of sexual harassment and sexual violence. It recommended that the government take a lead and ensure that every school understands that sexual harassment and sexual violence is neither acceptable nor an inevitable part of school life.[115]

---

[112] See further Chapter 4, section 4.2.   [113] See further Chapter 18, section 3.3.2.

[114] House of Commons Foreign Affairs Committee, *Libya: Examination of Intervention and Collapse and the UK's Future Policy Options* (HC 119 2016–17).

[115] House of Commons Women and Equalities Committee, *Sexual Harassment and Sexual Violence in Schools* (HC 91 2016–17).

The government cannot ignore these reports and their recommendations. It must publish a response. Further, select committee reports can be debated on the floor of the House and will often be referred to in debates. It has become increasingly common for certain select committees to be described as influential. Since the introduction of elected committee chairs, becoming the chair of a select committee has become an increasingly attractive and competitive career move for an MP.

5.5.3 Assessment

How effective are select committees in scrutinising government? This is a complex question. The current system of select committees has a number of advantages and disadvantages. We begin with the former.

First, select committees provide a forum in which the work of government departments can be subject to *more detailed scrutiny* than would be possible in the chamber of the House of Commons. Committees undertake detailed inquiries, amass evidence from experts and those affected by the administration of government policy, and then question the relevant Minister. The Institute for Government has listed the beneficial impacts of select committee inquiries, as shown in Figure 10.4.

---

1. Evidence: identify new evidence that improves the government's evidence base for decision making, for example about issues, risks or opportunities.

2. Analysis: provide a new or different analysis of the available evidence (including political opinion) which influences the government's view about what it is doing.

3. Openness: facilitate government openness by obliging civil servants and ministers to explain and justify what they have done.

4. Learning: identify lessons about past mistakes or successes by reviewing government expenditure, administration and the development and implementation of policy.

5. Processes: prompt higher standards or better processes in government through the act of conducting effective scrutiny.

6. Context: shift the context of government activity by influencing the views and actions of other actors – MPs, the media, public, judiciary, industry, civil society, think tanks, etc., including by building relationships and creating coalitions.

7. Democracy: affect the democratic system within which government operates, including wider trends relating to trustworthiness and legitimacy. The openness and transparency generated by scrutiny can also encourage the public to buy into government decision making.

Figure 10.4 Institute for Government: beneficial impacts of select committee inquiries on government

Source: Institute for Government, *Select Committees under Scrutiny: The Impact of Parliamentary Committee Inquiries on Government* (London 2015), p 35, **http://www.instituteforgovernment.org.uk/ publications/select-committees-under-scrutiny**

Select committees have enabled MPs to hold the government to account through more rigorous scrutiny than is possible on the floor of the House. They have brought before the public matters which otherwise might have remained concealed. Select committees provide in-depth and considered scrutiny. Furthermore, committees have achieved public engagement 'on a large scale, with a wide range of people, giving oral and written evidence, taking part in committee on-line consultations or surveys, and drawing on committee reports on their work'.[116] Select committees also offer the least partisan of the mechanisms available in that they offer a more considered form of scrutiny when compared with politically-charged debates in the Commons chamber. The election of committee chairs has enhanced their role, authority, and independence.

Second, the ability of select committees to scrutinise government has *significantly strengthened over time*. The work of select committees is more focused, more extensive, better resourced, more visible, and reveals greater engagement with the public than ever before. Committees hold thousands of evidence sessions and publish hundreds of reports. According to Natzler and Hutton, select committees have come a long way since 1979—over recent years, two significant trends in the work of select committees have been their more systematic approach in terms of both breadth and depth of coverage, and the growth in public awareness and media coverage of committees' activities: 'The conditions are arguably now in place to allow a significant and mutually reinforcing acceleration of those two trends in the years ahead and for that acceleration to be accompanied by a steady growth in the committees' influence.'[117]

Indeed, recent research into the effectiveness of select committees has concluded that they do exert influence on government, though there are some areas where they could do better. Select committees are largely taken seriously by government. Many of their recommendations go on to be implemented (though sometimes not until years later), and they have an important preventative effect in encouraging more careful consideration of policy within government departments.[118] According to Russell and Cowley:

> Select committees provide important parliamentary accountability, exposing both ministers and senior officials to public questioning. Hence, one official commented that the biggest 'influence is the fear of having to appear in front of them'; another noted that when considering policy options, 'you've always got to think, how would I explain that to the committee?'[119]

Third, select committees have enabled individual MPs to *develop their own expertise* in particular areas of government, thereby tending to enhance the quality of scrutiny. A further point to note is that select committees can serve useful purposes from the perspective of Ministers. Indeed, it is plausible that, from the perspective of government Ministers, select committees may sometimes provide a forum in which Ministers can seek to *overcome* opposition within their own political party to a

---

[116] Liaison Committee, *Legacy Report*, [115].

[117] 'Select Committees: Scrutiny à la Carte?', in Giddings (ed), *The Future of Parliament: Issues for a New Century* (London 2005), p 97.

[118] Russell and Benton, *Selective Influence: The Policy Impact of House of Commons Select Committees* (London 2011), **http://www.ucl.ac.uk/constitution-unit/publications/tabs/unit-publications/153.pdf**; Benton and Russell, 'Assessing the Impact of Parliamentary Oversight Committees: The Select Committees in the British House of Commons' (2013) 66 Parliamentary Affairs 772.

[119] Russell and Cowley, 132.

particular policy idea, in that appearances before select committees enable Ministers to communicate directly and in depth with their own backbenchers.[120]

While select committees have strengths, the current system operates under various constraints that restrict the degree of scrutiny that they are able to offer.

First, the *powers* of select committees are weak in comparison with those in other legislatures. The committees cannot amend, veto, or propose legislation. In addition, their reports do not always have as much impact as they might deserve—both within and beyond Parliament. However, in a report published in 2012, the Liaison Committee (while drawing attention to certain difficulties with this procedure) welcomed the fact that select committees can now obtain a slot in parliamentary 'primetime', just after ministerial questions, to present their reports.[121] Meanwhile, there is an ongoing debate over whether or not committees can compel witnesses to attend.[122]

Second, the *resources* of select committees to scrutinise the workings of government are limited. One of the most significant pressures on select committees is the availability of MPs' time: if MPs are unable to commit sufficient time to working on a committee, then the quality of scrutiny is likely to suffer.

Third, there is a paradox: *more committees with larger remits* might diminish the quality of scrutiny that they are able to provide. Over recent years, the remits of select committees have been expanded to include pre- and post-legislative scrutiny, and pre- and post-appointment hearings of appointments to public bodies. However, such tasks inevitably make further demands on MPs' time and concerns have frequently been expressed that many MPs do not attend committee hearings.

Fourth, as noted earlier, *effective scrutiny depends on cooperation with government* and there have been numerous instances of defensive and uncooperative behaviour from government departments. To illustrate, committees have complained of government departments' unwillingness to give information or of departments supplying inaccurate information. Government has also on occasion imposed constraints on committees' access to witnesses. Other complaints are that government responses to select committee reports are sometimes late or defensive.[123]

Where does all of this leave us? In 2015, the Liaison Committee stated: 'Our overall impression is that government departments are taking committees seriously and engaging positively with them. While there have been occasions of late replies to reports and disagreements about witnesses and evidence, most relationships between select committees and departments appear to be constructive.'[124] The general conclusion is, then, that while select committees are an important mechanism for holding government to account, their effectiveness is limited. What more can be done?

Since 2010, the Liaison Committee has been reviewing the role, resources, and tasks of select committees and has arrived at a vision for a stronger system of select

---

[120] Hindmoor, Larkin, and Kennon, 'Assessing the Influence of Select Committees in the UK: The Education and Skills Committee 1997–2005' (2009) 15 Journal of Legislative Studies 71.

[121] *Select Committee Effectiveness, Resources and Powers*, [50].

[122] See Gordon and Street, *Select Committees and Coercive Powers—Clarity or Confusion?* (London 2012). See also Chapter 5, section 4.3.3.

[123] *Select Committee Effectiveness, Resources and Powers*, [106]–[111].   [124] *Legacy Report*, [16].

committees. This includes enhancing committee best practices and having revised core tasks for select committees, and agreeing procedures for committee statements on the floor of the House and arrangements for debates on committee reports. On the crucial issue of the need for cooperation from government for effective scrutiny, the Liaison Committee has recommended that government engage with Parliament to develop joint guidelines—a 'new compact'—to redefine the relationship between Parliament and government. Such guidelines would recognise ministerial responsibility, the proper role of the Civil Service, and the legitimate wish of Parliament for greater accountability.[125] A motion approving the Liaison Committee's vision was approved by the House of Commons in 2013.[126] The government has said it is willing to work with the Committee on this matter, although the Committee is sceptical; it doubts whether the government has 'recognised the changed mood in the House and the strength of our resolve to achieve change'.[127]

> **Q** What is your assessment of the degree of scrutiny offered by parliamentary select committees? How do you think that their effectiveness might be enhanced?

5.6 Assessing parliamentary scrutiny

Earlier in this chapter, we encountered the 'parliamentary decline thesis', the dominant theory and narrative of Parliament for the last century. We noted that part of the shortcomings of this thesis is that it sets up unrealistically high expectations of what Parliament can achieve. The thesis presents a misleading caricature of a far more complex reality. According to Lord Norton, a leading constitutionalist, Parliament cannot claim to subject the conduct of government to continuous and comprehensive scrutiny. Government is frequently able to avoid parliamentary oversight of much—if not most— of what it does. When governmental action is the subject of parliamentary scrutiny, the attention that it receives is often sporadic and fleeting, affected by party political considerations, time pressures, and a lack of knowledge amongst MPs. Ministers are often able to deflect probing by parliamentarians and can always, in any event, simply ignore recommendations for a change in government policy or administration.[128] The empirical evidence as to how Parliament operates in practice shows that its capacity to review government actions and administration is limited.

Nonetheless, Parliament has a considerable and growing scrutiny role.[129] It would be wrong to view Parliament merely as a rubber stamp. Parliament really does matter. Governments must listen to, and respond to, concerns raised in Parliament. Governments profess a commitment to engaging with Parliament. The answers that

---

[125] *Select Committee Effectiveness, Resources and Powers*, [114]–[115], [135]–[138].

[126] HC Deb, vol 557, cols 1125–48 (31 January 2013).

[127] House of Commons Liaison Committee, *Select Committee Effectiveness, Resources and Powers: Responses to the Committee's Second Report of Session 2012–13* (HC 912, 2012–13).

[128] Norton, *Parliament in British Politics* (Basingstoke 2005), p 131.   [129] Russell and Cowley.

Ministers give to parliamentary questions may at times seem evasive, but Ministers must give them nonetheless.

Furthermore, the general principle is still that when Parliament is in session, the most important announcements of government policy should be made in the first instance to Parliament[130]—a principle that is often, but not (given the temptation to make announcements to the media in a bid to grab headlines) uniformly, followed. Ministers must engage with select committees—to explain and defend government policy, and to answer questions. So, while Parliament is unable to direct the government to undertake or refrain from specific action, it is able to influence government in at least two ways.

First, there is the *negative influence* of Parliament: parliamentary scrutiny can exert a deterrent effect upon government. If the government is aware that a particular issue might be raised in Parliament and prompt adverse public reaction, this may induce government to be more circumspect as to what it does. In other words, the threat of parliamentary scrutiny may prompt government to abandon some of its proposals or to water them down so that they survive parliamentary scrutiny without undue embarrassment.

Second, parliamentary scrutiny can also exercise a *positive, agenda-setting function*. By asking questions of Ministers and contributing to debates, parliamentarians can cause certain issues to be brought on to the government's agenda. MPs can alert Ministers to a particular issue—the significance or existence of which they might not have appreciated—and then induce a response from the Minister and/or prompt some further attention or action. Parliament may not be able to dictate to government what it should do—but it can occasionally place particular issues on the broader political agenda and arouse interest in the matter.

Parliamentary scrutiny could be enhanced and this is what the Liaison Committee has been spearheading. Since 2009, there has been a significant change in the mood of the House of Commons and a resolve to actually achieve change and greater scrutiny. Recent improvements—the Backbench Business Committee, elected committee chairs, and an enhanced role for committees—are now in practice irreversible. On the contrary, the focus is very much upon further improvement of parliamentary scrutiny. Rocked by the expenses scandal, Parliament has accepted the need for change, and the need to lead rather than be led. Parliament has become more independent of government and willing to undertake more vigorous scrutiny.

This new direction of travel will not change the UK's basic constitutional set-up. Nevertheless, more effective scrutiny will enable greater democratic control over, and the accountability of, government. Government decisions are more likely to be accepted if they are subject to thorough parliamentary scrutiny; and enhanced parliamentary scrutiny does not necessarily imply a reduction in the ability of government to govern. 'Parliamentary control of the executive—rightly conceived—is not the enemy of effective and strong government, but its primary condition.'[131]

Q Should parliamentary scrutiny of government be enhanced?

---

[130] 'Ministerial Code', [9.1].   [131] Crick, *The Reform of Parliament* (London 1969), p 259.

6. Scrutinising how government spends public money

We now consider parliamentary scrutiny of how government spends public money. This is crucial to the very existence of Parliament. Indeed, the whole history of the House of Commons has been the struggle to ensure that the people could not be taxed without their consent and that the means of governing—money—would not be available unless those in power could be called to account. Consent to taxation and scrutiny of how public money is spent are vital to the existence of the House of Commons.

In 2016, UK public spending exceeded £750 billion. Government needs money to act; it cannot do much otherwise. But how can we be sure that government spends public money wisely and does not waste it? Merely placing our trust in government would be naive. The answer is that there need to be effective external mechanisms to scrutinise how government spends public money.

This is important for the following reasons. Resources are always limited. Demands on the public purse always outstrip supply. Financial scrutiny, also known as audit, is about ensuring the effective management of limited public resources so that important public purposes—protecting people from crime, funding hospitals and schools, promoting international development, and so on—can be successfully achieved. Government undertakes some unique functions, but it may be inherently prone to inefficiency and waste. Unlike the private sector, government does not compete in the marketplace, but instead relies upon taxpayer funding. Financial scrutiny is therefore required to identify past failures and to enable government to learn lessons for the future. Given the pressure on UK public spending and the need to reduce the fiscal deficit, there is a need for accountability and transparency in public spending.

Financial scrutiny is, though, more than just a technocratic exercise. It is constitutionally important precisely because it concerns the use of *public* money. Parliament has a unique constitutional function in authorising and scrutinising governmental expenditure, and has a responsibility to hold government to account between general elections for the money that it raises and then spends. Parliament provides the important link between government and the public. Financial scrutiny of government therefore goes to the centre of the constitutional relationship between government, Parliament, and the public.

Financial scrutiny focuses upon whether government makes good use of public money. This concept is often reduced to the 'three Es':

- *economy*—the minimising of costs of resources used for an activity, having regard to appropriate quality;
- *efficiency*—the relationship between the output in terms of goods, services, or other results and the resources used to produce them; and
- *effectiveness*—the relationship between the intended impact and the actual impact of an activity or product.

More generally, this type of scrutiny is typically described as that of *audit*—the official inspection of an organisation's accounts, typically by an independent body. Audit has become an increasingly common technique because of increased demand for public accountability. Indeed, it has been argued that we now live in what has been called an 'audit society', in which there has been an explosion in the number and intensity of audits of virtually all organisations.[132] This might sound dry, but scrutinising how government spends public money is essential to making government work better. It is also constitutionally important. 'External audit in the public sector is an essential part of a constitution which is premised on the accountability of government to Parliament and to citizens.'[133]

At the UK level, financial scrutiny is undertaken by the House of Commons Public Accounts Committee (PAC) on the basis of investigations undertaken by the National Audit Office (NAO). The PAC comprises some 15 MPs while the NAO comprises some 850 accountants. The NAO supports the PAC's scrutiny of government. Similar arrangements exist for devolved matters in Scotland, Wales, and Northern Ireland.

6.1 Parliamentary scrutiny and audit of government expenditure

6.1.1 The Public Accounts Committee (PAC)

The queen of the select committees . . . [which] . . . by its very existence exerted a cleansing effect in all government department[s]

(Lord Hennessy describing the PAC)[134]

While parliamentary control of taxation was established in the seventeenth century, parliamentary control and scrutiny of expenditure was only gradually established between the 1780s and 1860s. Since 1861, the PAC has acted on behalf of Parliament to examine and report on accounts, and the regularity and propriety of expenditure. The advantage of focusing parliamentary scrutiny of public expenditure in a select committee rather than through debates in the Commons chamber is that a dedicated committee can investigate public expenditure in more depth and thereby build up its own expertise. The PAC is, and also sees itself as, a key part of the accountability arrangements to safeguard public money.[135] It does not consider either the formulation or merits of policy—this falls within the scope of other, departmental select committees; instead, it focuses on value for money criteria—the three Es. The Committee is chaired by a senior opposition MP and adopts a non-party-political approach to its task. The PAC is certainly one of the most high-profile and productive of select committees. In the 2010–15 Parliament, the Committee held 276 evidence sessions and published 244 unanimous reports, which included 1,338 recommendations. The government takes the recommendations seriously: 88 per cent of the PAC's recommendations were accepted by departments.[136]

---

[132] Power, *The Audit Society: Rituals of Verification* (Oxford 1997).

[133] White and Hollingsworth, *Audit, Accountability, and Government* (Oxford 1999), p 197.

[134] Cited in House of Commons Public Accounts Committee, *Holding Government to Account: 150 Years of the Committee of Public Accounts* (London 2007), p 7, **http://www.parliament.uk/documents/commons-committees/public-accounts/pac-history-booklet-pdf-version-p1.pdf**

[135] See *Holding Government to Account*.

[136] **http://www.parliament.uk/business/committees/committees-a-z/commons-select/public-accounts-committee/history-of-committee/**

6.1.2 **The National Audit Office**

The NAO provides critical support to the work of the PAC. It is headed by the Comptroller and Auditor General, whose function, since 1866, has been to examine accounts on behalf of the House of Commons.[137] In recognition of the importance of audit of government, the Comptroller and Auditor General in 1983 became an officer of the House of Commons.[138] Furthermore, the NAO was established. In broad terms, the NAO performs a number of roles: holding government to account for the way in which it uses public money, helping public service managers to improve performance, safeguarding the interests of taxpayers who pay for public services, and championing the interests of citizens as users of public services. The NAO has a professional staff, largely comprising accountants who are not civil servants and are independent of government. It has comprehensive statutory rights of access to the bodies it audits.[139] It is, though, specifically prohibited from examining the merits of governmental policy objectives.[140]

6.2 **The value for money scrutiny process**

The PAC's main work is the examination of the NAO reports as to the 'value for money' of public services delivered by government. About 60 of these reports are adopted each year by the PAC as the basis for a follow-up inquiry. The PAC will proceed by means of an oral evidence session in which it will hear oral evidence from and question the appropriate accounting officer. The accounting officer is the most senior civil servant in a government department; the permanent secretary, who is personally responsible and accountable to Parliament for their department's use of public money and the stewardship of its assets. This therefore distinguishes the role of the accounting officer from that of the appropriate Minister. While the Minister is accountable to Parliament for the policies, actions, and conduct of her department, the accounting officer is responsible for value for money issues.

The PAC's principal objective is to draw lessons from past successes and failures that can be applied to future activity by the department examined or more generally. PAC inquiries result in a published report that highlights any inefficient use of public resources and, if appropriate, makes recommendations to government. By convention, HM Treasury responds to the PAC through Treasury minutes within two months, indicating whether or not it accepts the recommendations. The scrutiny process is summarised in Figure 10.5.

The delivery of public services has changed radically over recent decades. Government no longer provides all public services itself. It also commissions other bodies and private companies to deliver those services. As delivery models for public services have changed, so has the reach of the PAC. In following the taxpayer's pound, the PAC's role has spread beyond examining government departments to other public bodies and private companies providing public services. However, the PAC has raised concerns that accountability to Parliament for the use of public funds has been weakened by the failure of the government's accountability arrangements to

---

[137] Exchequer and Audit Departments Act 1866.   [138] National Audit Act 1983, s 1(2).
[139] National Audit Act 1983, s 8.   [140] National Audit Act 1983, s 6(2).

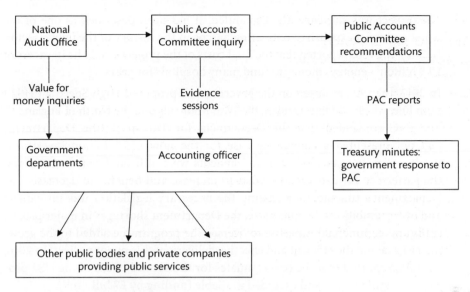

Figure 10.5 The value for money scrutiny process

keep pace with increasingly complex ways of delivering policies and services.[141] These new methods for delivering public services—devolution to local areas, outsourced contracts, government companies, and cross-cutting initiatives—have often not been accompanied by clarity over accountability arrangements. In other words, changes in the provision of public services can mean a loss of accountability.

Q Why is it significant that, at PAC hearings, it is the accounting officer rather than the Minister who appears before the Committee? Does this practice contravene the doctrine of ministerial responsibility to Parliament? Or does it mean that the doctrine of ministerial responsibility is necessarily subject to an exception in relation to matters of financial scrutiny?

6.3 **The PAC in action**

To give a flavour of the combined work of the PAC and the NAO, and also some indication of how government spends public money, we can consider the following instances (selected from numerous examples).[142]

- In 2002, the government commissioned the National Programme for IT for the NHS, the world's largest civilian computer project. However, the project has been ill-fated throughout and the anticipated benefits have never been realised.

---

[141] House of Commons Public Accounts Committee, *Accountability to Parliament for Taxpayers' Money* (HC 732 2015–16).

[142] See also 'A Keynote Speech by Sir Amyas Morse KCB, Comptroller and Auditor General' (London 2016), **http://www.instituteforgovernment.org.uk/events/keynote-speech-sir-amyas-morse-kcb-comptroller-and-auditor-general**

The project was subsequently dismantled. It has been described as one of the worst and most expensive contracting fiascos in the history of the public sector. In 2013, the PAC reported that the final costs of the project would be in excess of £9.8 billion—enough money to fund many hospitals for years.[143]

- In 2013, the PAC reported on the government's proposed High Speed 2 ('HS2') train line, which will link London, the West Midlands and the North of England.[144] The PAC concluded that the Department for Transport (the Department) had not presented a convincing case for the now £55.7 billion investment in HS2. The estimates of costs and benefits were still far from finalised and the pattern so far had been for costs to increase and benefits to decrease. The Department's timetable for passing the necessary legislation was unrealistic and overly ambitious. Furthermore, the Department shortages in major project skills and commercial expertise to oversee the programme added to the growing risks facing the efficient and effective delivery of this major project. In 2016, the PAC reported that the cost estimates for the second phase of the HS2 project were still volatile and exceeded available funding by £7 billion.[145]

- In 2016, the PAC found that older patients were increasingly experiencing delays in being discharged from hospital. Such delays are bad for patients' health. They increase the level of care they may need after leaving hospital. Unnecessary delays are also bad for the financial sustainability of the NHS and local government. The NAO has estimated that such delays cost the NHS around £800 million a year. At the same time, older patients delayed in hospital often do not benefit from being there. The Department of Health, NHS England and NHS Improvement had failed to address long-standing barriers to the health and social care sectors sharing information and taking up good practice. The PAC stated: 'While we recognise there are significant pressures on adult social care and NHS funding, NHS England shows a striking poverty of ambition in believing that holding delays to the current inflated level would be a satisfactory achievement. Patients and the NHS have a right to expect better.'[146]

- The PAC's 2014 report into debt owed to government found that government is owed a massive amount of money—£22 billion—and that it has failed to take a strategic cross-government approach to managing that debt and getting more money paid to the Exchequer, which impacts directly on government borrowing. Government inaction has led to large volumes of old debts building up in government departments which are unlikely to be collected. The Treasury and the Cabinet Office said that they are—belatedly—developing a cross-government strategy for

---

[143] House of Commons Public Accounts Committee, *The Dismantled National Programme for IT in the NHS* (HC 294 2013–14).

[144] House of Commons Public Accounts Committee, *High Speed 2: A Review of Early Programme Preparation* (HC 478 2013–14).

[145] House of Commons Public Accounts Committee, *Progress with Preparations for High Speed 2* (HC 486 2016–17).

[146] House of Commons Public Accounts Committee, *Discharging Older People from Acute Hospitals* (HC 76 2016–17).

debt. However, the PAC expressed concerns that the centre of government has taken so long to drive improvements in debt collection, given that this should be a basic business activity, and given the huge volume of bad debts written off each year.[147]

These episodes represent only a few of the blunders, errors, and failures committed by the UK government over recent years.[148] There are many others.[149] What these and the many other PAC reports reveal is that waste and inefficiency are shockingly common features of government in the UK—even during a period of financial austerity. The PAC has noted that there are too many examples of accounting officers allowing projects and initiatives to proceed unchallenged, despite strong evidence that they represent poor value for money. Furthermore, accounting officers across government lack the cost and performance data they need for effective oversight.[150] The overall concern is that government does not secure value for money when spending public money.

This issue is by no means confined to the UK. All countries have experience of inefficient and incompetent government. In the UK, there is a complex debate concerning the systemic causes of such blunders. What is of interest for our purposes is that there is a general agreement that at least some of the causes arise from the political and constitutional framework and culture within which the government operates and which we have highlighted in this book. A weak Parliament; the adversarial nature of party politics; the ability of the government, with its majority, to push legislation through Parliament without proper deliberation; the frequency with which Ministers are moved around; the ease with which they can evade responsibility; and the lack of effective accountability of the Civil Service are some of the systemic factors which have contributed to governmental failures over recent decades.[151]

We therefore encounter a conundrum concerning one of our principal themes. Throughout this book, we have emphasised the peculiarly powerful position of the UK government. Anyone might think that such a powerful government would always be able to implement its policies effectively. However, as we have seen, government failure is relatively common in the UK. Why?

Paradoxically, the government's powerful position is also one of its greatest weaknesses. 'The only trouble with a system in which it is easy to take decisions is that it is every bit as easy to take the wrong decisions as it is to take the right ones.'[152] Strong government facilitates both good and bad decisions. If government was subject to

---

[147] House of Commons Public Accounts Committee, *Managing Debt Owed to Central Government* (HC 555 2014-15).

[148] In 2012, the neologism 'omnishambles', coined in 2009 by the writers of the BBC's political satire *The Thick of It*, was voted word of the year by the Oxford English Dictionary. It means 'a situation that has been comprehensively mismanaged, characterised by a string of blunders and miscalculations'.

[149] Bacon and Hope, *Conundrum: Why Every Government Gets Things Wrong—And What We Can Do About It* (London 2013); King and Crewe, *The Blunders of Our Governments* (London 2013).

[150] House of Commons Public Accounts Committee, *Accountability to Parliament for Taxpayers' Money* (HC 732 2015–16).

[151] Butler, Adonis, and Travers, *Failure in British Government* (Oxford 1994); Foster, *British Government in Crisis* (Oxford 2005); Better Government Initiative, *Good Government: Reforming Parliament and the Executive* (London 2010); Bacon and Hope; King and Crewe.

[152] King and Crewe, p 385.

closer scrutiny and more checks, then its performance could well be significantly improved as a result. More effective accountability might well mean better quality of government and fewer blunders. Ministers and civil servants would instinctively dislike being subject to more external controls, but the overall system of British governance could well be enhanced as a result. This is a complex issue and it goes to the very heart of the quality of governance in the UK. However, it has not yet received the necessary debate that it deserves.

6.4 **The effectiveness of the PAC and the NAO**

How effective are the PAC and the NAO for holding government to account for public expenditure? At a simple level, the PAC can be seen as effective in terms of publicly highlighting the inefficient use of public money by government; the Committee's reports often command media attention and, despite its party membership, the Committee is generally accepted to be non-party-political. However, merely highlighting poor value for money is, by itself, insufficient if government repeats its mistakes. Another test of the effectiveness of this accountability process concerns the frequency with which the government accepts the PAC's recommendations—and, as we noted earlier, the vast majority of its recommendations are indeed accepted.

However, as well as identifying (and suggesting remedial action in respect of) particular areas of difficulty, the PAC has increasingly sought to draw broader lessons as to how government should plan and deliver value for money more generally. Here, the PAC has identified several causes for concern, including policies not being properly planned or thought through; improvements not materialising or taking place slowly, despite promises; failure to apply more widely the lessons learned in one part of the public sector; the repetition of mistakes, even after the causes have been identified; failure to exploit commercial opportunities; and slow progress in making the most of opportunities offered by new developments in technology.[153] The fact that such difficulties persist, oversight by the PAC and NAO notwithstanding, does not detract from the importance of such scrutiny. It is generally accepted that financial scrutiny undertaken by Parliament is much more effective when it comes to examining past expenditure (backward-looking scrutiny) than as regards planned expenditure (forward-looking scrutiny).[154]

There are, however, various factors that constrain the effectiveness of the PAC's scrutiny. An inherent constraint arises from the *limited amount of resources* devoted to accountability processes. The PAC's remit covers a vast area—the whole of central governmental activity. Given its limited resources, and even with assistance from the NAO, the PAC's scrutiny inevitably has to focus upon particular areas of government. The risk is that, despite the PAC's successes in uncovering and exposing governmental inefficiency, there are always likely to be many areas that elude detailed scrutiny.

---

[153] House of Commons Public Accounts Committee, *Achieving Value for Money in the Delivery of Public Services* (HC 742 2005–06), pp 6–7.

[154] House of Commons Liaison Committee, *Parliament and Government Finance: Recreating Financial Scrutiny* (HC 426 2007–08), [6].

A second issue concerns *the extent to which government does actively seek to take account of the PAC's recommendations.* Those recommendations are often accepted by the government, in the sense that they are not explicitly rejected. However, what is often less certain is the extent to which government actively seeks to act upon the PAC's recommendations to ensure future efficiency in the use of public money by learning appropriate lessons and thereby preventing future mistakes. In practice, the action taken by government in response to PAC reports may be quite limited. It has, then, been suggested that there should be a more coordinated follow-up system after the PAC has published a report. More generally, the Hansard Society has recommended that there should be a move towards a deeper notion of accountability to ensure that individual lessons are translated into general reforms of public institutions that are found to be flawed.[155]

A third—and perhaps the main—area of concern relates to *the attitude of senior civil servants toward the PAC.* This in turn raises the underlying constitutional debate concerning governmental accountability, in particular the (in)adequacy of the traditional doctrine of ministerial responsibility. The role of the PAC is to hold government—often via senior civil servants—to account for spending public money. However, the Committee has, over recent years, encountered a negative and defensive response from senior civil servants, who have expressed concern that the PAC has been exceeding its role by seeking to hold officials to account and thereby undermining the constitutional principle of Civil Service impartiality. In response, Margaret Hodge MP, chair of the PAC from 2010 to 2015, vigorously argued that senior civil servants need to recognise that the PAC's constitutional duty is to scrutinise not just Ministers, but also civil servants. Hodge's view is that to achieve better government, it is necessary to develop stronger and clearer lines of accountability of the Civil Service to Parliament for the execution of ministerially determined policy.[156] According to Hodge, the PAC needs to make life uncomfortable for Ministers and civil servants to make sure they spend public money wisely. Even then there are gaps: 'Too often we miss the huge area of discretion open to the civil service as it spends public money and organises public services which may not be visible to ministers.'[157]

Fourth, *changes in the systems for delivering public services* pose challenges. Fragmented and contracted-out systems of governance by which private companies deliver public services on behalf of the government make it much more difficult for the PAC to follow the taxpayers' pound and ensure value for money. When government contracts with private companies to deliver public services, accountability becomes more difficult. After all, such contractors are not necessarily motivated by a public service ethos, but by maximising private profit and shareholder value. Also, government departments and private contractors all too often may hide behind commercial

---

[155] Brazier and Ram, *The Fiscal Maze: Parliament, Government and Public Money* (London 2006), p 39.

[156] Hodge, 'Accountability in Today's Public Service', speech at Policy Exchange, 15 March 2012, **http://www.parliament.uk/business/committees/committees-a-z/commons-select/public-accounts-committee/news/policy-exchange-speech/**

[157] Hodge, 'Accountability in Today's Public Service'.

confidentiality. With the increasing intermingling of public and private sectors, what hope is there for effective financial scrutiny?

Again, we can detect here two broader themes of this chapter. First, in today's system of large-scale government, the traditional doctrine of ministerial responsibility is no longer adequate. Instead of opening up government to scrutiny, it can be used to make such detailed scrutiny ineffective. Second, securing effective accountability depends upon the cooperation of those bodies being scrutinised. It now seems increasingly necessary to devise new constitutional arrangements to ensure that the work of Ministers, civil servants, and private contractors alike can be opened up to public and parliamentary scrutiny.

> **Q** To what extent do the PAC and NAO together provide an effective means of financial scrutiny? How do you think that their effectiveness can be enhanced?

7. Freedom of information

This section considers freedom of information. If government is to be held to account, then it is necessary to have access to information from government. Transparency and openness in government are essential to effective public and political scrutiny.

This area is governed by the Freedom of Information Act 2000 (FOIA), which enshrines in law the principle that citizens have a (qualified) right of access to government information.[158] As we have already seen, two of the branches of the state—the courts and Parliament—have a long tradition of acting in an open manner. Courts are bound by the principle of open justice.[159] Likewise, parliamentary proceedings are public and open. However, government—and especially British government—has long been characterised by a culture of—some would say almost an obsession with—official secrecy.[160] In this culture, access to information has more often than not been tightly controlled by Ministers and civil servants.

It is difficult to overemphasise how deeply embedded this attitude is within British government. Calls for freedom of information legislation were long met with resistance, with only limited statutory rights of access to official information being conceded prior to the enactment of the FOIA.[161] In 1993, the then Conservative government adopted a code of practice under which individuals could request access to information held by central government departments.[162] While this code was non-statutory, its administration was overseen by the Parliamentary Ombudsman. Nonetheless, there were persistent calls for specific legislation on freedom of information.

---

[158] In Scotland, see the Freedom of Information (Scotland) Act 2002.

[159] Subject to limited (but significant) exceptions: see, eg the Justice and Security Act 2013.

[160] See Vincent, *The Culture of Secrecy: Britain 1832–1998* (Oxford 1998).

[161] See, eg Public Records Act 1958; Local Government (Access to Information) Act 1985; Access to Personal Files Act 1987; Access to Medical Records Act 1988; Environmental Information Regulations 1992, SI 1992/3240; Data Protection Act 1998 (replacing Data Protection Act 1984).

[162] *Code of Practice on Government Information* (Cm 2290 1993).

Following the election of the Labour government in 1997, the FOIA was enacted in 2000 and came into operation in 2005.

The FOIA is a highly contentious piece of legislation. The Prime Minister who introduced the Act, Tony Blair, subsequently came to view the Act as one of his biggest mistakes and called himself an idiot for introducing it. There is an underlying assumption by government Ministers that the Act is, on occasion, abused by the media to generate stories and that it places a disproportionate burden on public bodies. Another concern is that the Act exerts a chilling effect upon Civil Service advice to Ministers; civil servants may be worried that their confidential advice to Ministers could potentially be published under the FOIA. A former Prime Minister, David Cameron, suggested that the Act 'furs up' the arteries of government.[163] On the other hand, the Act has been praised as enhancing the UK's democracy and making public bodies more open, accountable, and transparent. From this perspective, any weakening of the FOIA would represent a highly retrograde step that would render government less accountable.

This sharp difference of opinion indicates that the FOIA remains a deeply contested piece of legislation between government and those in power on the one side, and opposition politicians and civil society on the other side. Following the Supreme Court's important 2015 ruling in *Evans*[164] concerning the release under the FOIA of letters written by Prince Charles, the Conservative Government established the Independent Commission on Freedom of Information, which reported in 2016.[165] There was considerable speculation that this review could water down the FOIA. However, the Commission's general view was that the FOIA was generally working well: there was no need for the Act to be radically altered, but the Commission made a number of recommendations to improve clarity and certainty concerning the Act's operation. We consider these developments later in this section. But first we need to consider the reason for having freedom of information legislation and how the scheme operates in practice.

7.1 The rationale for freedom of information

There are two principal—and closely related—reasons for having freedom of information legislation. First, it makes government more open and transparent. Second, it makes government more accountable. From these two justifications, flow other consequences. Freedom of information leads to improved government decision-making and better understanding of government. It may induce government to act more responsibly given the enhanced likelihood of poor administration (or worse) coming to light. Freedom of information legislation also advances the cause of democratic government by making citizens' participation in government better informed.

---

[163] 'Freedom of Information: Whitehall warned over "bad behaviour"', *BBC News*, 14 March 2012, http://www.bbc.co.uk/news/uk-politics-17365222

[164] *R (Evans) v Attorney General* [2015] UKSC 21, [2015] AC 1787.

[165] Cabinet Office, *Independent Commission on Freedom of Information Report* (London 2016), http://qna.files.parliament.uk/ws-attachments/456281/original/Report%20-%20Final_print.pdf

This, in turn, recognises individuals as democratic citizens rather than as subjects of government. Transparent and open government may also increase public trust in government.

While there are important public interests in freedom of information, transparency and openness are not absolute values. There is often a countervailing public interest in the non-disclosure of information. For example, there may be little point in requiring government to disclose sensitive information about the operations of the security services if the very disclosure of such information may enable suspected terrorists to evade the state's surveillance of their activities and thereby jeopardise public safety. While undoubtedly important, the principle of freedom of information is not absolute. Exceptions and limitations are inevitably necessary to ensure an appropriate balance between the public interest in freedom of information and competing public interests served by non-disclosure. Saying that there should be some balance is the easy part. The more difficult matter is deciding precisely where that balance should lie in any particular instance and, just as importantly, who should have the power to decide where the balance should lie. A further important point is that legitimate *public* interests in non-disclosure should not be confused with considerations of *governmental* convenience. Withholding information because its release would, for example, jeopardise the safety of UK soldiers is one thing; suppressing it to spare government from embarrassment is quite another.

7.2 The Freedom of Information Act 2000

The FOIA creates a general right of access to information held by public authorities.[166] Any person making a request for information is entitled to be informed by the public authority whether it holds the information requested, and, if so, to have that information communicated to him.[167] The Act applies to over 100,000 public bodies, including central government departments, local authorities, schools, colleges and universities, the health service, and the police.[168] All public authorities must adopt and maintain a publication scheme—that is, a scheme relating to the publication of its information, which is subject to the approval of the Information Commissioner.[169]

While individuals have a general right of access to government information, this is subject to severe limitations. First, there are *absolute (or class-based) exemptions*. Second, there is a *non-absolute public interest test* to determine whether the public interest in disclosing the information is outweighed by the public interest in withholding disclosure.

Information to which the first limitation applies—that is, information that is subject to absolute (or class-based) exemptions—is excluded from the general duty of disclosure and not subject to any public interest test. Once it is established that information falls within a relevant class, then the Act does not require it to be disclosed even if, in relation to the *particular* information in question, the public interest would favour its

---

[166] Freedom of Information Act 2000, s 1.   [167] Freedom of Information Act 2000, s 1(1).
[168] Freedom of Information Act 2000, s 3 and Sch 1.   [169] Freedom of Information Act 2000, s 19.

disclosure. Absolute exemptions cover information available through other means; information intended for future publication; information supplied by, or relating to, the government intelligence services; information in court records; information the disclosure of which would infringe parliamentary privilege; information held by either House of Parliament the disclosure of which might 'prejudice the effective conduct of public affairs'; information provided in confidence; and information the disclosure of which is positively prohibited by statute, court order, or EU law.[170] The appropriateness of having classes of information subject to absolute exemptions is questionable, bearing in mind that the effect of this regime is to deny access to information falling within such classes even if disclosure would have positive or no (or less compelling) negative consequences in public interest terms.

Information that does not fall within the absolute, class-based exemptions may still be immune from disclosure thanks to the second of the limitations mentioned earlier: the 'public interest test'. Here, a two-stage analysis applies. The first question is whether the information falls into one of the relevant categories. Information concerning such matters as national security, defence, international relations, the economy, and formulation of government policy falls into such categories.[171] If the information falls into a relevant category, the second question is whether the public interest in maintaining the exemption outweighs the public interest in disclosing the information.[172]

There are other limitations on the general right of access to information. For example, there is a cost limit: public authorities are not obliged to release information when the cost of doing so would exceed a prescribed limit.[173] Another limitation is that public authorities need not comply with vexatious or repeated requests for information.[174]

Since coming into force in 2005, the scope of the FOIA has been both expanded and reduced. The Act has been expanded to include academy schools,[175] the National Police Chiefs Council, the Financial Ombudsman Service, the Universities and Colleges Admissions Service,[176] and Network Rail.[177] It has also been extended to cover publicly owned companies.[178] Prior to this, companies were only covered if they were wholly owned by the Crown or otherwise by a single public authority. At the same time, the scope of FOIA has been restricted in other areas. In 2010, communications with the monarch and the heir to the throne were made completely exempt from the Act.[179] A new exemption was introduced in 2014 to protect prepublication research material if the disclosure would prejudice the research programme.[180]

---

[170] Freedom of Information Act 2000, ss 22, 23, 32, 34, 36, 41, and 44, read with s 2(3).

[171] Freedom of Information Act 2000, ss 24, 26, 27, 29, and 35, read with s 2(3).

[172] Freedom of Information Act 2000, s 2(2)(b).

[173] The limit is currently £600 for central government (£450 for other public authorities): Freedom of Information Act 2000, ss 12 and 13; the Freedom of Information and Data Protection (Appropriate Limit and Fees) Regulations 2004, SI 2004/3244.

[174] Freedom of Information Act 2000, s 14.   [175] Academies Act 2010, Sch 2, para 10.

[176] The Freedom of Information (Designation as Public Authorities) Order 2011, SI 2011/2598.

[177] The Freedom of Information (Designation as Public Authorities) Order 2015, SI 2015/851.

[178] Protection of Freedoms Act 2012, s 103.

[179] Constitutional Reform and Governance Act 2010, Sch 7, para 3.

[180] Intellectual Property Act 2014, s 20.

The FOIA scheme operates as follows. Individuals may make requests to the relevant public authority to disclose requested information.[181] The public authority must then, within 20 days, either confirm or deny whether it holds the information requested.[182] If the authority holds the information, then the authority should disclose the information, unless it considers the information to be exempt from disclosure. If the authority refuses to disclose, then the individual may request an internal review of that refusal by the public authority. If the public authority still refuses to disclose, then the individual may complain to the Information Commissioner, which will decide whether the public authority's decision was correct.[183] The Information Commissioner is an independent body separate from government. If necessary, the Information Commissioner can issue an enforcement notice requiring the authority to disclose.[184] Either party (ie the complainant or public authority) affected by a decision of the Information Commissioner may appeal to the First-tier Tribunal (Information Rights), and, from there, to the Upper Tribunal.[185]

The FOIA also makes provision for a ministerial override. A government Minister can, on reasonable grounds, veto the disclosure of information even though its disclosure has been ordered by the Information Commissioner or the Tribunal.[186] This provision is unusual though not unique. It raises questions as to both who does and should have the final say on the disclosure of information. The precise operation of the ministerial veto has been a controversial issue and is considered in the following section.

7.3 The operation of the Act

7.3.1 FOI requests

To date, the FOIA has been used to extract a bewilderingly wide range of information from a number of different public authorities. These requests have ranged from the highly important and dramatic to the mundane. As regards the former, the release of MPs' expenses in 2009 revealed that some MPs had made quite spurious expenses claims—for example, for mortgage interest payments when the mortgage had already been paid off, and for gardening costs such as the clearing of a moat and for the construction of a duck island. As noted earlier in this chapter, the whole saga of MPs' expenses aroused considerable public concern and anger. It was accepted that Parliament could no longer regulate itself like a gentleman's club and legislation was quickly enacted to establish the Independent Parliamentary Standards Authority in an attempt to restore public confidence.[187] By contrast, FOI requests to local councils have, amongst other things, concerned topics such as road potholes.

The number of FOI requests concerning UK central government has increased to nearly 50,000 requests per year (Figure 10.6). These statistics cover only UK central

---

[181] Requests can be made online at **https://www.whatdotheyknow.com/**
[182] Freedom of Information Act 2000, s 10.   [183] Freedom of Information Act 2000, s 50.
[184] Freedom of Information Act 2000, s 52.   [185] Freedom of Information Act 2000, ss 57–9.
[186] Freedom of Information Act 2000, s 53.   [187] Parliamentary Standards Act 2009.

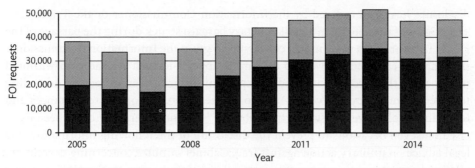

Figure 10.6 FOI requests to central government, 2005–15

Source: Cabinet Office, *Freedom of Information Statistics: Implementation in Central Government 2015* (London 2016).

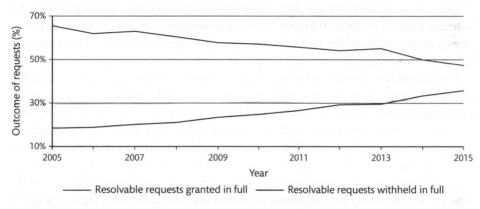

Figure 10.7 Proportion of resolvable FOI requests granted and refused

Note: 'Resolvable' requests are those where it is possible to make a substantive decision on whether to release the requested information. Unresolvable requests are those in which the public body needed further details or clarity or involved information not held.

government (UK government departments and 'other monitored bodies').[188] They do not include FOI requests made to 'non-monitored' bodies such as local authorities and schools. Available data indicates that local authorities receive far more requests than central government: 165,000 requests in 2009 and 197,000 in 2010, indicating that the Act is more used to extract information from local rather than central government.[189] Figure 10.7 shows that the proportion of requests granted has declined over the years. An unexplained feature here is precisely why the proportion of FOI requests that were refused doubled between 2005 and 2015.

7.3.2 The ministerial veto

As noted earlier, the FOIA provides for a ministerial veto: a government Minister can, on reasonable grounds, override the disclosure of information even though its

---

[188] 'Other monitored bodies' exclude ministerial departments, but include non-ministerial departments, such as the Food Standards Agency and HM Revenue and Customs.

[189] Hazell and Worthy, p 5.

disclosure has been ordered by the Information Commissioner or the Tribunal.[190] The origins of the veto lie in a parliamentary bargain struck during the passage of the FOIA. In return for a government concession to grant the Information Commissioner significantly enhanced powers to determine appeals against decisions to withhold information, the executive attained an explicit ministerial override power. According to government policy, the veto is only to be used in exceptional circumstances and following a collective decision of the Cabinet.[191] The ministerial veto has been exercised on seven occasions to prevent the disclosure of the following information: the legal advice on military action against Iraq, Cabinet minutes concerning devolution, NHS risk registers concerning the potential risks of changes to the NHS, Cabinet meetings concerning hostilities against Iraq, correspondence from Prince Charles, and a review by the Major Projects Authority of the HS2 train project.[192] When exercising the veto, the relevant Minister must lay a certificate before Parliament and also issue a statement of reasons.[193]

The precise operation of the ministerial veto was thrown into doubt following the Supreme Court's decision in *Evans*.[194] This case concerned an FOI request made by a journalist at the *Guardian* newspaper that the government disclose correspondence between Prince Charles and former government Ministers. The government had refused to disclose the letters, but the Upper Tribunal—a judicial tribunal—held that the public interest favoured disclosure of the letters.[195] The Attorney-General then certified that the government would override the Upper Tribunal's decision on the basis that it was entirely appropriate for the Heir to the throne to enter into correspondence with government Ministers. Furthermore, such correspondence should be confidential. The requestor then sought judicial review of the government's decision to exercise the ministerial veto on the ground, amongst others, that the government did not have the power to overrule a judicial decision. Constitutional principle, it was argued, required the FOIA to be interpreted restrictively because of the importance of the rule of law.

A majority of the Supreme Court agreed: the FOIA did not enable the *executive* to use the ministerial veto to overrule a *judicial* decision merely because the executive took a different view from that of the Upper Tribunal. The Supreme Court held that this conclusion followed from two constitutional principles. First, it is a basic principle that a judicial decision is binding and cannot be ignored or set aside by anyone, least of all, the executive. Second, it is fundamental to the rule of law that executive decisions are subject to judicial scrutiny.

The *Evans* case had a number of consequences. First, the correspondence between Prince Charles and government Ministers was released.[196] Second, there has been

---

[190] Freedom of Information Act 2000, s 53.

[191] Ministry of Justice, 'Statement of HMG Policy: Use of the Executive Override under the Freedom of Information Act 2000 as It Relates to Information Falling within the Scope of s 35(1)', https://www.gov.uk/government/uploads/system/uploads/attachment_data/file/60530/HMG-Veto-Policy.pdf

[192] House of Commons Library, *FoI and Ministerial Vetoes* (SN/PC/05007 2014), http://researchbriefings.files.parliament.uk/documents/SN05007/SN05007.pdf

[193] Freedom of Information Act 2000, s 53(2).   [194] *R (Evans) v Attorney-General* [2015] UKSC 21.

[195] *Evans v Information Commissioner* [2012] UKUT 313 (AAC).

[196] http://www.theguardian.com/uk-news/ng-interactive/2015/may/13/read-the-prince-charles-black-spider-memos-in-full

much discussion as to whether or not the Supreme Court correctly interpreted the FOIA in accordance with the intention of Parliament. The former Attorney-General whose decision in *Evans* was struck down has noted that the majority of the Supreme Court 'engaged in some highly creative statutory interpretation'.[197] The current Attorney-General took the view that the court had undermined Parliament's intention; the 'proposition that complex balances of the public interest—which are after all the daily business of modern government—can only be done by courts is plainly wrong.'[198] On the other hand, the Supreme Court's interpretation of the FOIA has been defended.

Third, following *Evans*, there was uncertainty concerning the exercise of the ministerial veto. The government established the Independent Commission on Freedom of Information, which reported in 2016. This recommended legislation to clarify that the veto could be exercised when the government takes a different view of the public interest in disclosure. It also recommended that the veto should only be exercised following a decision of the Information Commissioner; it should not be exercised after an appeal to the tribunal. However, the government has indicated that it does not propose to implement these changes.

7.3.3 The FOIA and government

A fundamental issue concerns the impact of the FOIA upon government. This can be broken down into the following questions. Has the FOIA increased the transparency and accountability of government? Has the Act improved government decision-making and public trust in government? And has the FOIA exerted a chilling effect upon government?

As regards the first question, the general view is that the Act has increased the transparency and accountability of government. Information that would not have otherwise been made publicly available has been disclosed by government. The Act has been used by the media, the public, and campaigners to make government more accountable. In 2012, the Commons Justice Committee found that the Act had 'contributed to a culture of greater openness across public authorities, particularly at central Government level which was previously highly secretive. We welcome the efforts made by many public officials not only to implement the Act but to work with the spirit of FOI to achieve greater openness.'[199] The Act has contributed to a culture of greater openness across public authorities and reduced the unnecessarily restrictive government secrecy that has undermined good governance.

Has the Act improved government decision-making and public trust in government? Research by Hazell and Worthy, including interviews with civil servants, concluded that there is little evidence that the FOIA has improved decision-making

---

[197] Grieve, 'Can a Bill of Rights Do Better than the Human Rights Act?' [2016] PL 223, 232.

[198] Speech by Jeremy Wright, QC, MP, 'The Attorney General on Who Should Decide What the Public Interest Is' (2016), **https://www.gov.uk/government/speeches/the-attorney-general-on-who-should-decide-what-the-public-interest-is**

[199] House of Commons Justice Committee, *Post-Legislative Scrutiny of the Freedom of Information Act 2000* (HC 96 2012–13), [17].

in government.[200] The FOIA has had no positive impact on government decision-making, the quality of advice, records or evidence with which to make decisions. As regards increased trust in government, the Commons Justice Committee concluded in 2012 that the FOIA has not increased public confidence in government.[201] This is because the issue whether the FOIA will improve public confidence in government is principally dependent upon the type and content of information released. Most people learn of such information through the media, which tends to focus upon that information which demonstrates failings and errors by government. Accordingly, it may not be realistic to assume that the FOIA would actually enhance public trust in government. Nor, it seems, has public participation in government increased as a result of the Act. FOIA requests are largely made by people who are already engaged in political issues. Indeed, 'fewer than one person per thousand makes FOI requests . . . if usage increased to two people per 1000, the system would collapse'.[202]

An especially sensitive issue for government is whether the Act has exerted a chilling effect upon discussions at the highest levels in government. The concern within government is that the FOIA may inhibit the frankness of advice to Ministers and prevent open and confidential discussion between Ministers. In others words, the existence of a safe, internal, deliberative space within government allows for frank discussions and advice. Ministers and civil servants may feel inhibited if such discussions may be publicly released. Related to this is the doctrine of collective Cabinet responsibility: the FOIA could weaken collective Cabinet responsibility by making publicly available details of disagreements between Ministers when formulating policy. However, it has been doubted whether the FOIA has had a 'chilling effect' on frank advice and deliberation in government. While a chilling effect has been asserted by senior civil servants, there is little evidence to support this.[203] The Commons Justice Committee in 2012 was 'not able to conclude, with any certainty, that a chilling effect has resulted from the FOI Act'.[204]

8. Accountability and oversight of the security and intelligence services

We now consider the accountability and oversight of the security and intelligence services. We do so for the following reasons. First, the security and intelligence agencies undertake some of the most sensitive and important activities of government; indeed, such agencies are essential to the survival of government and society. Second, because of what they do, there are special considerations concerning how to hold these agencies to account, and they have their own special accountability and oversight arrangements. Indeed, in this context, the basic tension seen throughout this chapter between effective government and effective scrutiny arises in a particularly

---

[200] Worthy and Hazell, 'Disruptive, Dynamic and Democratic? Ten Years of FOI in the UK' (2017) 70 Parliamentary Affairs 22.

[201] Justice Committee, [241].   [202] Worthy and Hazell, 32.

[203] Worthy and Hazell, 31.   [204] Justice Committee, [200].

acute form, given that the very nature of the security and intelligence services' activities precludes the use of many of the normal accountability tools.

8.1 The security and intelligence services

It is a basic fact that, in the modern world, democratic states and the lives of their peoples are under threat from a number of different sources, including rogue states, global terrorism, the proliferation of weapons of mass destruction, and illegal narcotics. The scale of the danger posed by such threats and how they should be dealt with are both very difficult and complex questions over which different people can reasonably disagree. One does not have to subscribe to the notion of a 'global war on terrorism' to accept that there is a real terrorist threat and that the development of nuclear weapons by a rogue state or a non-state group (eg Islamic State) may pose a danger to the lives of ordinary people in Western countries such as the UK. Following terrorist attacks in France and Germany, as of September 2016, the terrorist threat to the UK from international terrorism was categorised as severe: an attack is considered highly likely.[205]

National security, or, in older language, 'defence of the realm', is perhaps the most essential function of government. The most basic responsibility of any government is to protect the security of its own people, which includes protecting them against terrorism. To this end, the UK government has its intelligence and security machinery. There are three intelligence and security services—'the agencies':

- The Security Service (MI5), which is responsible for protecting the UK against covertly organised threats to national security, such as terrorism, espionage, and the proliferation of weapons of mass destruction;

- The Secret Intelligence Service (SIS, also known as MI6), which collects foreign intelligence on issues concerning the UK's vital interests in the fields of security, defence, serious crime, and foreign and economic policies;

- Government Communications Headquarters (GCHQ), which gathers intelligence through the interception of communications and provides intelligence in support of government decision-making in the fields of national security, military operations, and law enforcement.

Both the Security Service and the SIS were established in 1909, and GCHQ was established in 1929. For much of their history, the security services were, in effect, a 'secret state'.[206] For many decades, the agencies had no formal existence and no legal basis whatsoever; indeed, the government officially denied their existence, and there were no arrangements whereby Parliament could call them to account. This state of affairs existed because politicians across the political spectrum subscribed to two basic principles: that it was not possible even to discuss the work of the agencies in public or in Parliament; and that Parliament must entirely abdicate its powers in this field to the executive.[207] As Andrew has observed, the assumption was 'that the mysteries

---

[205] **https://www.gov.uk/terrorism-national-emergency/terrorism-threat-levels**

[206] See Hennessy, *The Secret State: Whitehall and the Cold War* (London 2003).

[207] Andrew, *The Defence of the Realm: The Authorised History of MI5* (London 2009), p 753.

of intelligence must be left entirely to the grown-ups (the agencies and the government) and that the children (parliament and the public) must not meddle in them'.[208] However, over recent decades, the context in which the agencies operate has changed considerably, and there have been persistent calls for more transparency and scrutiny of the work of the agencies. There are two main reasons for this.

First, concerns that arise in relation to other government bodies—the abuse of power, illegality, incompetence—apply equally to the agencies. In 2008, a digital camera used by a Security Service agent containing sensitive data was up for sale on eBay—'a clear breach of data security procedures'.[209]

Second, there is also the potential for the agencies, given the nature of their work and the secrecy with which it is necessarily conducted, to engage in particularly dubious practices. In particular, concerns have been raised over the role of the agencies in extraordinary rendition of terrorist suspects to places where they may be tortured.

Consider the case of Binyam Mohamed. Before being charged with terrorist offences by the US government, he was held in various locations around the world by and on behalf of the US authorities, during which time, he alleged, confessions were extracted from him under torture. He further claimed that members of the UK's Security Service were involved in facilitating his questioning while the alleged programme of torture was being undertaken. He challenged the UK government's refusal to disclose evidence that, he asserted, would support his argument that he had been tortured and which would therefore assist in his defence against the charges brought by the US government.

The Administrative Court concluded that the 'relationship of the UK government to the US authorities in connection with [the claimant] was far beyond that of a bystander or witness to the alleged wrongdoing',[210] and that the treatment to which the claimant had allegedly been subject 'could easily be contended to be at the very least cruel, inhuman and degrading treatment'.[211] In an extraordinary passage, publication of which the government sought unsuccessfully to suppress, Lord Neuberger MR, in the Court of Appeal, said that 'some Security Services officials appear to have a dubious record relating to actual involvement, and frankness about any such involvement, with the mistreatment of Mr Mohamed when he was held at the behest of US officials'.[212]

---

[208] Andrew, p 753.

[209] Intelligence and Security Committee, *Annual Report 2008–09* (Cm 7807 2010), p 21.

[210] *R (Mohamed) v Secretary of State for Foreign and Commonwealth Affairs (No 1)* [2008] EWHC 2048 (Admin), [2009] 1 WLR 2579, [88].

[211] This part of the Administrative Court's judgment was published, following further litigation, as an appendix to the judgment of the Court of Appeal in *R (Mohamed) v Secretary of State for Foreign and Commonwealth Affairs* [2010] EWCA Civ 65.

[212] This passage formed [168] of Lord Neuberger's judgment in *Mohamed*, but was only published, following further litigation, in *R (Mohamed) v Secretary of State for Foreign and Commonwealth Affairs* [2010] EWCA Civ 158, [28]. The UK government subsequently paid compensation of over £1 million to Mohamed in an out-of-court settlement, asserting that it could not adequately defend the claims being made without compromising national security. This episode formed an important part of the backdrop to the highly controversial introduction, by means of the Justice and Security Act 2013, for 'closed hearings' in certain civil proceedings.

8.2 **The legal framework and powers of the agencies**

Against this background, it is unsurprising that the traditional position, whereby the agencies existed in a legal black hole and were essentially immune from scrutiny, is now a thing of the past. The position today is different in two senses.

First, the agencies now have a legal, statutory basis and certain legal powers. The Interception of Communications Act 1985 allowed communications (telephone, fax, telex, and post) to be intercepted for certain purposes when authorised by a warrant signed by a Secretary of State.[213] This was followed by the Security Service Act 1989, which established a legal framework for the Security Service. The legal framework for both the SIS and GCHQ was subsequently established by the Intelligence Services Act 1994.

There is now, therefore, a legal framework that sets out the powers and functions of the agencies. For example, the Security Service is responsible for protecting the UK against threats to national security from espionage, terrorism, and sabotage; from the activities of agents of foreign powers; and from actions intended to overthrow or undermine parliamentary democracy by political, industrial, or violent means.[214] The operations of the Security Service are principally directed towards counter-terrorism activities. The SIS, meanwhile, is directed by statute to obtain and provide information relating to the actions or intentions of persons outside the British Islands, and to perform other tasks relating to the actions or intentions of such persons.[215] This enables the SIS to conduct covert operations and to act clandestinely overseas in support of UK government objectives. The statutory function of GCHQ is to monitor and decipher communications.[216]

Under statute, the agencies have the ability to apply to the relevant Secretary of State for a warrant to authorise certain actions, such as entry into or interference with property or the interception of communications (eg phone tapping).[217] Such actions would normally be unlawful, but the simple grant of a warrant by the Secretary of State renders such action by the agencies lawful.[218] It was considered necessary to establish a legal framework for the agencies to comply with the European Convention on Human Rights (ECHR).[219] Under ECHR, Art 8, everyone has the right to respect for their privacy, home, and correspondence, but this right may be interfered with when it is necessary in the interests of national security, public safety, or the economic well-being of the country, for the prevention of disorder or crime. Under the Security Service and Intelligence Services legislation, the agencies are empowered to act only in the interests of the national security of the UK, in the interests of its economic well-being, or in support of the prevention or detection of serious crime.[220]

---

[213] The 1985 Act was superseded by the Regulation of Investigatory Powers Act 2000.

[214] Security Service Act 1989, s 1(2).   [215] Intelligence Services Act 1994, s 1.

[216] Intelligence Services Act 1994, s 3(1).

[217] Security Service Act 1989, s 3; Intelligence Services Act 1994, s 5; Regulation of Investigatory Powers Act 2000.

[218] It is also possible, under the Regulation of Investigatory Powers Act 2000, for warrants for certain forms of interception of communications to be issued to other bodies, such as police forces.

[219] See *Malone v UK* (1985) 7 EHRR 14.

[220] Security Service Act 1989, s 1; Intelligence Services Act 1994, ss 1(2) and 3(2).

8.3 Accountability framework

The second major development has been the establishment of a formal accountability framework for the security and intelligence agencies. Such accountability and oversight is provided in three different ways.

First, the agencies are *accountable to government Ministers*, who, in turn, are accountable to Parliament. Overall responsibility for intelligence and security matters rests with the Prime Minister, who is answerable to Parliament on matters affecting the agencies collectively. The Home Secretary is responsible for the Security Service, and the Foreign Secretary for the SIS and GCHQ.

Second, the agencies are subject to a degree of *political accountability to Parliament*. This is provided by the Intelligence and Security Committee (ISC). The role of the ISC is to provide politically independent oversight of the agencies' activities and is considered in more detail later.

Third, the agencies are subject to a degree of *judicial oversight*. This is provided by the Commissioners and a tribunal. There are two Commissioners—the Intelligence Services Commissioner and the Interception of Communications Commissioner— who oversee the agencies' performance of their statutory duties and review the lawfulness of their actions.[221] The Intelligence Services Commissioner can also, at the Prime Minister's direction, keep under review the carrying out of any aspect of the agencies' functions.[222] Both Commissioners must be judges of high standing. Judicial accountability is also provided by the Investigatory Powers Tribunal, which investigates complaints by individuals about the agencies' conduct towards them or about interception of their communications.[223] Together, the Commissioners and the Tribunal provide independent judicial oversight of the activities of the agencies.

However, we should not blithely accept that the existence of these arrangements means that adequate provision is now made for holding the agencies to account. What type of accountability can there really be, given the hidden and secret world of the intelligence and security services? How effective is such accountability? And how, if at all, can such accountability mechanisms be improved? Given the focus of this chapter on political and parliamentary accountability of government, we shall address these questions by focusing specifically upon the role and effectiveness of the Intelligence and Security Committee (ISC), because it is the principal method by which parliamentary scrutiny of the agencies is supposed to be facilitated.

8.4 The Intelligence and Security Committee

There is a basic and unavoidable dilemma in seeking to scrutinise the activities of the security and intelligence services, and to hold them to account. To maintain their effectiveness, the agencies necessarily operate in secret. If information concerning their activities were to become public knowledge, then this could endanger lives and

---

[221] Regulation of Investigatory Powers Act 2000, ss 57 and 59. See **http://isc.intelligencecommissioners.com/**

[222] Regulation of Investigatory Powers Act 2000, s 59A (as inserted by the Justice and Security Act 2013, s 5).

[223] Regulation of Investigatory Powers Act 2000, s 65.

undermine the effectiveness of the agencies in seeking to protect national security. On the other hand, it is important in a democratic society that there are effective safeguards and means of overseeing the work of the agencies, and that they are, as far as possible, held to account for their activities. As with political accountability in general, the requirement to explain and justify actions encourages better-thought-out policy, better control of expenditure, and adherence to accepted principles and practices. Oversight of the intelligence and security agencies is no different—and, if anything, is even more essential given that most of their work is kept secret from the general public. What kind of political oversight and accountability does the ISC then provide?

The ISC was established by the Intelligence Services Act 1994 and is now consti-tuted under the Justice and Security Act 2013. It is a committee of nine members drawn from both Houses of Parliament.[224] Its main purpose is to examine the policy, administration, expenditure, and operations of the three agencies.[225] By its nature, the ISC is different from other select committees. It operates within a 'ring of secrecy' by operation of the Official Secrets Act 1989. ISC members have access to a great deal of classified information and the agencies' future plans, but in return, they are 'noti-fied' under the 1989 Act. This means that a criminal offence is committed, under the 1989 Act, by any ISC member who discloses information relating to the security agen-cies without lawful authority.[226]

Over the years, various concerns around the status and independence of the ISC have been raised. In 1999, the Commons Home Affairs Committee noted that while the ISC's establishment constituted a significant step, it recommended that the ISC should be replaced by a parliamentary select committee. Such a system would draw heavily on the ISC, and would be grafted onto the select committee system with appropriate adaptations. But the key point for the Home Affairs Committee was that scrutiny of the agencies should be more independent of the executive.[227] This recom-mendation was not accepted by the government, and indeed, when he was ISC chair, Kim Howells MP said that making the ISC a parliamentary select committee would be counterproductive because it would not get access to the same information—meaning that oversight would not be strengthened, but weakened.[228]

In 2010, the ISC itself expressed some concerns with respect to its relationship with government. The ISC recognised that certain of its administrative arrangements were no longer appropriate and required not only updating, but also changing if there was to be confidence in the Committee's independence.[229] More explicitly, the then ISC chair told Parliament that

there are some within the Whitehall bureaucracy who . . . have not understood or have refused to accept that the independence of the ISC is sacrosanct. Some of them have

---

[224] Justice and Security Act 2013, s 1.   [225] Justice and Security Act 2013, s 2.

[226] Official Secrets Act 1989, s 1. On the Official Secrets Acts, see Chapter 19, section 7.2.

[227] House of Commons Home Affairs Committee, *Accountability of the Security Service* (HC 291 1998–99).

[228] HC Deb, vol 507, col 993 (18 March 2010) (Kim Howells MP).

[229] Intelligence and Security Committee, *Annual Report 2009–10* (Cm 7844 2010), pp 4–5.

given the impression that they regard the ISC as an irritation—a problem that they could well do without.[230]

The cynical view is that the ISC merely serves as 'window dressing'—it holds out the promise of political accountability, but without the substance. Those who advance this criticism often highlight how the ISC's role can be used to suit the needs of government and the agencies rather than those of Parliament. For example, because ISC members were appointed by the Prime Minister, the perception arose that they might be little more than the Prime Minister's placemen—that is, parliamentarians carefully selected so as to give the agencies an easy ride rather than to subject them to robust scrutiny.

In response to concerns such as these, some changes have recently been made by the Justice and Security Act 2013.[231] First, take ISC appointments. Unlike any other parliamentary committee, ISC members were appointed by the Prime Minister, prompting concerns that it was more of a governmental rather than a parliamentary committee and therefore not sufficiently independent of executive influence.[232] However, under the Justice and Security Act 2013, ISC members are now appointed by Parliament after first being nominated by the Prime Minister who will consult the leader of the opposition.[233] This ensures an independent appointments process to strengthen the ISC's credibility while also retaining some safeguards: ISC membership confers access to highly sensitive information, disclosure of which could damage national security. There are nine ISC members drawn both from the Commons and the House of Lords. None of the members is permitted to be a Minister of the Crown.

Second, the ISC used to report directly to the Prime Minister, and through him to Parliament. However, the ISC now reports to Parliament—albeit that its reports will first be vetted by the government and any sensitive material will be excluded.[234]

As regards its working methods, the ISC is sometimes asked to look into a particular matter, but most of the time it is able to set its own agenda. The ISC determines how and when it is to conduct and conclude its programme of work; this gives it the freedom to pursue avenues of inquiry to its satisfaction. The ISC publishes an annual report and also produces ad hoc reports. These reports are published (although with deletions of sensitive material), laid before Parliament together with the government's response, and then debated in Parliament.

Another important point is that under the Justice and Security Act 2013, the ISC's remit has been extended in various ways. The ISC can now inquire into operational aspects of the agencies' work, although this power is, unsurprisingly, subject to significant restrictions.[235] Also, the ISC's remit has been extended beyond the three main

---

[230] HC Deb, vol 507, col 996 (18 March 2010) (Kim Howells MP).
[231] See *Justice and Security Green Paper* (Cm 8194 2011).   [232] Intelligence Services Act 1994, s 10(3).
[233] Justice and Security Act 2013, s 1.   [234] Justice and Security Act 2013, s 3.
[235] Operational matters can be considered only if (i) the Committee and the Prime Minister are satisfied that the matter is not part of any ongoing intelligence or security operation and is of significant national interest, (ii) the Prime Minister has asked the ISC to consider the matter, or (iii) the ISC's consideration of the matter is limited to the consideration of information provided voluntarily to the ISC. See Justice and Security Act 2013, s 2(3).

agencies to include the wider governmental intelligence community.[236] Although the Prime Minister is able to insist upon redactions to ISC reports, he is obliged to consult with the ISC on any proposed redaction.[237] Furthermore, the ISC includes parliamentarians from opposition parties (as well as the governing party or parties) who have a recognised knowledge and expertise in the work of the security agencies.

For some, the ISC's highly unusual position drastically restricts its ability to exercise effective oversight of the agencies. However, the Justice and Security Act 2013 enhanced the ISC's role and status. The ISC is now a Committee of Parliament: the Committee's members are appointed by Parliament and the Committee reports directly to Parliament. The 2013 Act also provided the ISC with greater power and increased its remit. It now oversees operational activity and the wider intelligence and security activities of government.

It is important to appreciate the difficult challenge posed by the dilemma involved in exercising political oversight of the security and intelligence agencies and to recognise that progress has—albeit slowly—been made. When he was ISC chair, Kim Howells MP strongly defended the robustness of the scrutiny supplied by the Committee, asserting that 'giving evidence before us is not a comfortable experience for anyone. The questioning is robust, often combative, issues are returned to, further explanations demanded, documents examined and the end results are often critical, albeit not sensationalist'.[238] The Committee has also asserted that, as the agencies have learnt to trust the ISC, the agencies have become increasingly willing to be open with the Committee.[239] According to Kim Howells, the ISC's experience has been that the harder it investigates and questions the agencies, the better they understand the need to be fully accountable.[240]

> **Q** Why does oversight of the security and intelligence services pose a problem for accountability? Are the changes introduced by the Justice and Security Act 2013 sufficient or not?

9. Conclusion

The degree to which Parliament is able effectively to scrutinise government policy and actions is largely dependent upon the political relationship between the two institutions—in particular, the dominance of Parliament by the government of the day. This basic feature of the constitution exerts considerable influence over how institutions, such as Parliament, and constitutional conventions, such as ministerial responsibility, operate in practice. It also influences the nature and type of control

---

[236] This includes the Defence Intelligence in the Ministry of Defence (MOD), the Office for Security and Counter-Terrorism in the Home Office, and the central government intelligence machinery in the Cabinet Office (including the Joint Intelligence Organisation).

[237] Justice and Security Act 2013, s 3(4).

[238] Open letter from the then Chair of the ISC to the Director of Human Rights Watch.

[239] Intelligence and Security Committee, *Intelligence Oversight* (London 2002), p 12.

[240] HC Deb, vol 507, cols 996–7 (18 March 2010) (Kim Howells MP).

that Parliament is able to exercise over government. Parliament's role is not that of directing, commanding, or obstructing the government; rather, it is there to influence, advise, criticise, and scrutinise the government.

There has long been a strong and justified perception that Parliament's capacity to scrutinise government has been weak. There are several interlocking reasons for this: the executive's pervasive influence on Parliament, political party discipline, the career aspirations of MPs, ambiguities in the relationship between Ministers and civil servants, and the temptation for them to play the blame game when things go wrong. We have also seen that the long-accepted and traditional constitutional convention of ministerial responsibility is now largely viewed as the problem not the solution; the fig-leaf of ministerial responsibility can now be seen for what it is: a means of neutralising parliamentary scrutiny. These difficulties are real, but they are not, either individually or collectively, easily resolvable.

Nonetheless, within a relatively short period of time—since 2009—the mood within Parliament has changed. This has been reflected in changes such as the new Commons Backbench Business Committee; elected chairs of select committees; and the Liaison Committee's vision for the future, which includes select committees that are yet more assertive and whose reports have greater impact. Such changes are important and will in turn contribute to the clamour for further improvements. Part of this may be explained by way of the current economic context. For instance, arguably the Public Accounts Committee's role has become more high-profile because the pressure on public spending means there is now increased competition for a smaller pot of public money—and therefore an urgent need to ensure government makes the best use of what it has. But perhaps a more fundamental change has been occurring within the political zeitgeist: a recognition amongst the political class in Parliament that it must restore public confidence in the democratic process, become more relevant, and take on the government by undertaking more vigorous scrutiny. Only time will tell what happens, but the signs are encouraging. According to Norton, the twenty-first century Parliament 'remains a policy-influencing legislature, but a stronger one than in the preceding century'.[241]

Expert commentary
Parliamentary scrutiny of central government
Tony Wright, Professorial Fellow, Department of Politics,
Birkbeck, University of London

What I like about this chapter is the way it takes as its central theme the tension between governing and holding to account in the British political system. This is a tension in every democratic system, because both functions are necessary, but in Britain it has taken a particular form. It has been described in a variety of different ways (here in terms of 'Whig' versus 'Peelite' traditions), but it all comes back to the same central tension between ensuring that government has the

---

[241] Norton, 'Parliament: A New Assertiveness?', in Jowell, Oliver, and O'Cinneide (eds), *The Changing Constitution* (Oxford 2015), p 171.

capacity and space to govern coherently while also ensuring that it is disciplined by appropriate and effective kinds of scrutiny and accountability.

In many respects it has been a matter of grafting an accountability tradition on to an established governing tradition, in a context where there was no explicit moment of democratic constitutional renewal and no formal separation of powers between government and legislature. What this meant was that a majority government, in a disciplined party system, could expect to govern without the array of formal checks and balances familiar elsewhere. This is why it became usual to describe politics in Britain as characterised by strong government and a weak Parliament, even as an executive tyranny unconstrained by effective accountability.

The question now is to what extent this traditional picture requires amendment. It always needed qualification anyway (to take account of all the internal and informal ways in which governments are held to account), but in my view it now needs radical alteration. It is scarcely too much to say that there has been an accountability revolution in Britain in recent decades, even more so than is allowed for in this chapter. The activities of government are now more examined, inquired into, scrutinised, challenged, constrained, and checked than ever before.

There are new regulators (like the Information Commissioner and the Electoral Commission) to control what governments can do, new powers for judges to review what Ministers decide, and a new vigour in Parliament to hold government to account. Much more of the constitution has been written down, and a range of prerogative powers have begun to be constitutionalised. A full summary of this accountability revolution would extend beyond the terrain of this chapter, but its significance is beyond dispute. A generation ago the charge against British government was that it was an elected dictatorship; now a charge that is heard is that it has lost some of its governing capacity. Such is the extent of the change that has taken place.

A dramatic illustration of this change was the recent parliamentary vote that stopped the government taking military action against Syria. One consequence of the controversy surrounding the Iraq war in 2003 was that Parliament claimed its future right to be consulted on military action (there is continuing discussion on whether this should be a convention or a law) and this is what happened in the Syrian case. This is a striking example, on something as fundamental as war and peace, of an executive prerogative power being checked and constitutionalised. Once this change has taken place, there is unlikely to be any going back.

In my experience it is in this incremental way, taking opportunities as they arise, that Parliament slowly renegotiates its relationship to government. I give two examples of this process in which I was directly involved. The first concerns the ability of the Commons to bring the Prime Minister, like other Ministers, in front of a select committee to be questioned. When I pressed Tony Blair on this, the reply came back that such a development would be unconstitutional. Then he agreed, since when it has become a fixture. What was unprecedented and unconstitutional thus rapidly became an established convention. That is how change tends to happen.

The second, and more significant, example comes from the Commons Reform Committee that I chaired following the expenses scandal in 2009. This presented an opportunity to make reforms—notably, electing select committees and giving the Commons more control of its own business—that have strengthened Parliament as an institution in relation to the executive. There is much more still to do, in particular to explore how the select committee model could be applied to the scrutiny of legislation, but the direction of travel is clear and is unlikely to be reversed. It is supported by a weakening of the iron party discipline in the division lobbies that used to be a fundamental feature of Westminster politics and which underpinned the ability of majority governments to get their way.

What all this does is to shift the continuing and necessary tension between governing and scrutinising on to new terrain. The tension is never resolved, but it plays itself out in different ways. What is more, there are usually good arguments on both sides. For example, there are demands for more accountability of civil servants to Parliament, reflecting the obvious deficiencies of the doctrine of ministerial responsibility. Yet Ministers also want to alter the doctrine by taking more powers to appoint civil servants, which may be less desirable if we value an independent and impartial Civil Service. Nor would it contribute to good government if making civil servants account directly to Parliament has the effect of making them watch their backs rather than giving disinterested service to Ministers. This shows that there are competing considerations at work; and that there is need for care in making changes. Simply to proclaim the need for more accountability is rarely enough.

A similar argument applies to freedom of information (where the chapter is wrong to say that the British legislation is weak), which is constructed around establishing where the public interest is to be found in relation to the competing considerations of openness and confidentiality. It can be very difficult in particular cases to get this balance right. So we keep coming back to that same tension between governing and holding to account. But if we get the right kind of accountability this can help to promote good government too.

The tension is currently in evidence as a result of the referendum decision to leave the European Union. The government has claimed that it is a prerogative power to decide the timing and terms of a British exit, but Parliament may well want to challenge this claim in the name of parliamentary sovereignty. The scene is set for a protracted period of tension as the executive's right to govern meets Parliament's right to hold government to account.

Further reading

Parliamentary scrutiny of government

FLINDERS and KELSO, 'Mind the Gap: Political Analysis, Public Expectations, and the Parliamentary Decline Thesis' (2011) 13 British Journal of Politics and International Relations 249
This paper argues that the parliamentary decline thesis provides a relatively blunt instrument for understanding the reality of legislative–executive interactions.

KENNON, 'Select Committees and the Commons: Recent Developments', UK Parliament Open Lecture, 9 March 2012 (**http://www.parliament.uk/get-involved/education-programmes/universities-programme/university-teaching-resources/select-committees-and-the-commons-recent-developments//**)
A lecture by a parliamentary official on select committees.

LANSLEY, 'The Legislature and the Executive', UK Parliament Open Lecture, 24 April 2013 (**http://www.parliament.uk/get-involved/education-programmes/universities-programme/university-teaching-resources/the-legislature-and-the-executive/**)
A lecture by a former Leader of the House of Commons on the relationship between Parliament and government.

NORTON, 'Parliament: A New Assertiveness?', in Jowell, Oliver, and O'Cinneide (eds), *The Changing Constitution* (Oxford 2015)
This chapter analyses key developments in the ability and willingness of Parliament to challenge government.

RUSSELL and COWLEY, 'The Policy Power of the Westminster Parliament: The "Parliamentary State" and the Empirical Evidence' (2016) 29 Governance 121

This paper draws on several research projects on the policy influence of Parliament on government. It concludes that Parliament's influence is both substantial and rising.

Financial scrutiny

BACON and HOPE, *Conundrum: Why Every Government Gets Things Wrong—And What We Can Do About It* (London 2013)

This book presents a range of case studies of government failure. Richard Bacon MP serves on the House of Commons Public Accounts Committee.

HODGE, *Called to Account: How Corporate Bad Behaviour and Government Waste Combine to Cost Us Millions* (London 2016)

Written by Margaret Hodge, chair of the House of Commons Public Accounts Committee (2010–15), discusses the challenges of scrutinising how government spends—and wastes—public money.

McELDOWNEY, 'Public Expenditure and the Control of Public Finance', in Jowell, Oliver, and O'Cinneide (eds), *The Changing Constitution* (Oxford 2015)

This chapter analyses the UK's constitutional framework and structures for overseeing public spending.

Freedom of information

BIRKINSHAW, 'Regulating Information', in Jowell, Oliver, and O'Cinneide (eds), *The Changing Constitution* (Oxford 2015)

This chapter analyses the constitutional framework for regulating access to government information.

Useful websites

Parliamentary scrutiny of government

http://www.parliament.uk
Website of the UK Parliament, with links to select committees and daily reports of parliamentary proceedings (Hansard)

Financial scrutiny

http://www.audit-scotland.gov.uk
The website of Audit Scotland

http://www.parliament.uk/business/committees/committees-a-z/commons-select/public-accounts-committee/
The website of the House of Commons Public Accounts Committee

http://www.nao.org.uk
The website of the National Audit Office

http://www.niauditoffice.gov.uk
The website of the Northern Ireland Audit Office

http://www.wao.gov.uk
The website of the Wales Audit Office

Freedom of information

https://www.gov.uk/courts-tribunals/first-tier-tribunal-general-regulatory-chamber
Website of the First-tier Tribunal (Information Rights)

http://www.ico.org.uk
Website of the Information Commissioner's Office

http://www.itspublicknowledge.info
Website of the Scottish Information Commissioner

Accountability and oversight of the security and intelligence services

http://www.gchq.gov.uk
Website of the Government Communications Headquarters

http://www.ipt-uk.com
Website of the Investigatory Powers Tribunal (also includes the Intelligence Services Commissioner and Interception of Communications Commissioner)

http://www.mi5.gov.uk
Website of the Security Service (MI5)

http://www.sis.gov.uk
Website of the Secret Intelligence Service (MI6)

PART IV
Judicial Review

11

Judicial Review—An Introduction

1. An example   475
2. What judicial review is and is not about   476
3. Judicial review and administrative law   478
4. Judicial review and our three key themes   479
5. The constitutional basis of judicial review   485
6. Concluding remarks   494
Expert commentary   494
Further reading   496

1. An example

Thousands of decisions are made by the government and public bodies every day, affecting individuals in myriad ways. We begin with just one example.

> **Eg** Imagine that a government Minister is in the process of deciding whether to grant permission for the construction and operation of a new airport. This decision will impact upon huge numbers of people in many different ways. Some might welcome it for the ready access to air travel that it would provide, for the employment it would create, and for the prosperity that it might bring to the surrounding area. Others will oppose it vehemently in light of the noise pollution that it would cause, the likely reduction in the value of nearby properties, the despoilment of the countryside, and the contribution that the new airport would make to the environmental damage caused by air travel. The decision is, therefore, an obviously difficult one for the Minister. He will have to weigh up all of these different—and conflicting—considerations, and ultimately make a judgement about whether giving the go-ahead to the new airport is in the public interest.

We saw in Chapter 10 that the actions of government Ministers are open to political control by Parliament via the doctrine of ministerial accountability. However, the actions of Ministers, and of other public bodies, are open to scrutiny in a number of other ways—including judicial review. The law of judicial review sets the legal framework within which decisions such as this, affecting the rights, interests, or legitimate expectations of individuals, are taken.

A Minister deciding whether our hypothetical new airport should be built would find himself subject to political scrutiny—for example, by being asked questions by MPs in the House of Commons. The decision could also be subject to legal scrutiny by way of judicial review. For example, the Minister would be required to give all interested parties—such as those living near the proposed airport—a fair opportunity to express their views, and then to take those views into account when making a decision. He would be required to disregard any legally irrelevant considerations (eg it would be unlawful for him to take into account the fact that it would be personally convenient to him to have a new airport in the location under consideration) and prohibited from acting for an improper purpose (eg to boost the government's popularity by creating jobs in a marginal constituency). He might also be legally required to honour any promises made in the course of considering the issue (eg the courts may hold him to an undertaking to compensate householders whose homes would be rendered less valuable owing to their proximity to the new airport) and he might well be required to give reasons for his decision.

2. What judicial review is and is not about

Traditionally, the principal focus of judicial review has been on *the way in which the decision is taken*, rather than on *the decision itself*. Assume, for instance, that the government, having complied with all of the legal requirements mentioned in section 1, concludes that the airport should be built in the locale under consideration because, on balance, it felt that the transport, economic, and environmental arguments justify a decision. In such circumstances, a court, on judicial review, could not second-guess this—that is, a judge, in a judicial review case, cannot overturn a government decision simply because she disagrees with it. This is not to say that the court cannot examine *any* aspect of the decision itself (as distinct from the way in which it was made). For example, as we will see, if the government were to make a wholly unreasonable decision,[1] or a decision that unacceptably compromised individuals' human rights,[2] a court could intervene. But this is very different from courts being able to overturn decisions simply because they disagree with them, or because the judge—if she had been the Minister—would have arrived at a different view. As Laws LJ has explained, the court 'does not ask itself the question, "Is this decision right or wrong?" ', and judicial review has 'nothing to do with the question, "Which view is the better one?" '.[3]

---

[1] eg if the case against locating the airport in a particular place were overwhelmingly strong on all relevant bases—environmental, economic, and so on—but the Minister, for no demonstrable reason, nevertheless were to approve its construction, this decision could be overturned by the court.

[2] eg if the Minister were to refuse to compensate people whose houses had to be demolished to make way for the airport (thereby violating their right to property) or to impose restrictions on night flights so as to ensure that noise pollution did not lead to an unacceptable level of sleep deprivation (thereby violating the right to private and family life).

[3] *R v Somerset County Council, ex p Fewings* [1995] 1 All ER 513, 515.

This limitation on the power of the court reflects the so-called distinction between *'appeal'* and *'review'*. If Parliament has created a statutory right of appeal to a tribunal, then that tribunal can substitute its view for that of the original decision-maker on issues of both fact and law. However, where Parliament has not created a right of appeal to a tribunal, the decision can be challenged only via judicial review. Further, because the judicial review jurisdiction is one of *review* and not *appeal*, the courts cannot interfere with the merits of decisions.

There are several reasons why the powers of courts on judicial review are limited in this way.[4] Two warrant particular attention.

The first concerns the *institutional capacity* of the court to determine whether a decision is flawed. Where the ground of challenge relates, for example, to an alleged procedural error—perhaps the Minister in our example fails to give local residents an adequate opportunity to voice their objections—the court can assess such a situation by reference to general principles of procedural fairness, the application of which calls for no expertise that is particular to the decision under consideration. The reviewing court is therefore perfectly capable of forming a judgment about whether the procedure used by the Minister was fair. This is a legitimate ground of judicial review.

However, if the content of the decision is challenged—for example, if a pressure group argues that the airport should not be built because the environmental damage that it would cause outweighs any economic advantages that it might bring—the court is not really qualified to assess the merits of these competing arguments. Indeed, the Minister, together with his departmental officials and advisers, is likely to be in a much stronger position to evaluate the relative environmental and economic implications of giving the go-ahead to the new airport. Recognising that they lack expertise on these sorts of questions, the courts have therefore traditionally accepted that they should not second-guess the decision-maker on matters of substance.

The second reason for judicial reticence in relation to such matters relates to concerns about *democratic legitimacy*. To understand this point, we need to appreciate the consequences of a court striking down a government decision as unlawful. If a reviewing court concludes that a Minister has acted in a procedurally unfair manner, and quashes the decision on that basis, it is open to the Minister to retake the decision in a procedurally fair manner, perhaps eventually reaching the same conclusion—that the new airport should be built. Judicial review, in such circumstances, does not therefore curtail the ultimate discretion of the decision-maker: it does not directly bear upon whether it is lawfully open to the Minister to decide to give the green light to the new airport. Rather, judicial review, in this procedural guise, ensures that the decision-maker exercises his discretion in a fair and lawful way.

In contrast, if the court were to strike down the decision on the basis of the pressure group's argument that the environmental damage would be unacceptably great, this would make it legally impossible for the Minister to sanction the new airport: the

---

[4] See generally Irvine, 'Judges and Decision-Makers: The Theory and Practice of *Wednesbury* Review' [1996] PL 59.

court would have, in effect, prohibited him from giving it the go-ahead. This may be regarded as objectionable, since it involves the court taking out of the democratically accountable Minister's hands a matter that, in the first place, Parliament had given him the authority to decide.

> **Q** Do you find these arguments persuasive? What counter-arguments might be marshalled against them?

We will see in Chapter 12 that these arguments do not mean that courts never look at the content of government decisions, as distinct from the process by which they are made. However, the arguments from institutional capacity and democratic legitimacy exert considerable influence upon how the courts exercise their judicial review jurisdiction. Courts exercise far greater restraint when called upon to scrutinise the substance—as opposed to the process—of executive decisions.

3. Judicial review and administrative law

The phrase 'administrative law' carries two distinct meanings. First, it describes the collective legal remedies that individuals may pursue in order to challenge public decisions. Judicial review is an important aspect of administrative law, but it is by no means the only available mechanism for challenging government decisions. In later chapters, we will examine other ways—including complaints to ombudsmen and appeals to tribunals—whereby such challenges can be made.[5] These three mechanisms—judicial review, ombudsmen, and tribunals—have their own distinct processes, but all are largely concerned with enabling individuals to hold government to account by going to an independent third party. That party assesses whether or not the individual's case is made out and then, if so, provides some sort of remedy. It is primarily in this sense that we shall be examining administrative law in this section of the book dealing with judicial review, and in subsequent chapters on ombudsmen and tribunals.

However, understood in a second, alternative sense 'administrative law' refers to the law governing the organisation and activities of administrative agencies.[6] Thus understood, administrative law concerns the powers of public authorities, their duties, the rules that they must apply in order to administer and implement policy, and the decision-making processes that they adopt. Thus, rather than just detailing the legal mechanisms for challenging government decisions, administrative law also concerns the rules governing the powers, duties, and organisation of public agencies, and how such agencies are to undertake their functions.

---

[5] See Chapters 15 and 16.

[6] See Gellhorn and Robinson, 'Perspectives on Administrative Law' (1975) 75 Col LR 771; Arthurs, 'Rethinking Administrative Law: A Slightly Dicey Business' (1979) 17 Osgoode Hall Law Journal 1.

Administrative law in this sense is not to be found primarily in courts' judgments, tribunals' decisions, or ombudsmen's reports—although they are important. Instead, it is to be found in the legislation establishing public agencies. Furthermore, because many statutes governing public administration delegate the power to make further rules or secondary legislation to the relevant government Minister or public agency, it is also necessary to consider the enormous volume of detailed rules and regulations that govern the performance of public functions and which are continuously generated by public agencies themselves in order to implement their policy objectives. Administrative law in the broader sense is also to be found in the reality of governmental practices—how the rules are applied and how decisions are reached. Administrative law is, then, often broken down into the law governing discrete areas of administration spanning the entire range of functions that the modern administrative state performs. This is because the law governing public administration is often specific to governmental activities that attempt to achieve particular public goals. In this sense, then, administrative law is an umbrella term beneath which shelter myriad specialist areas such as social security law, prison law, police law, food law, education law, immigration law, agricultural law, and so on. Administrative law is also subject to constant change as policy goals alter and as government seeks to enhance the effectiveness of public agencies.

This book does not focus on administrative law in this second, broader sense— indeed, no single book could do so. Instead, our focus will be upon the mechanisms through which individuals may challenge governmental decisions, and the general principles applied by courts, tribunals, and ombudsmen. It is, however, important to recognise that administrative law also has the second meaning identified here, and that there exist therefore detailed bodies of law that regulate the several and contrasting spheres within which public administration is conducted.

4. Judicial review and our three key themes

At the beginning of this book, we highlighted three key themes that are crucial to an understanding of the UK constitution. It is fitting, therefore, that we begin our consideration of judicial review by considering how it relates to those themes.

4.1 Accountability

We noted in Chapter 2, and examined in more detail in Chapter 4, the dominant role of the executive in the UK's constitution today. This is a defining feature of the constitution. In 1888, the legal historian Maitland noted that 'we are becoming a much governed nation, governed by all manner of councils and boards and officers, central and local, high and low, exercising the powers which have been committed to them by modern statutes'.[7] In the intervening years since Maitland wrote these words, this

---

[7] Maitland, *Constitutional History of England* [1888] (New Jersey 2001), p 501.

trend—the growing scale and complexity of public action—has accelerated. Today, we might say that we live in an 'administrative state', in which government has taken responsibility for large areas of social regulation and public services, meaning that it possesses an enormous ability to affect people's lives.

The unusually powerful position in which the UK executive finds itself is, as we have seen, a composite function of several interlocking features of the constitution, including a highly incomplete separation of powers that enables the executive government to arrogate power to itself through its effective control of the sovereign legislature. The dominant position of the executive raises obvious challenges in terms of accountability. It also gives rise to an associated paradox. The more powerful the executive, the greater the need for effective systems of accountability to guard against and deal with abuses of power—and, yet, as we saw in Chapters 5 and 10, the very dominance of the executive is an obstacle to such accountability. Against the background of a powerful government that exerts enormous influence over nearly every aspect of life, and a Parliament that is limited in its capacity to hold that government to account, people have unsurprisingly looked increasingly to other institutions, including courts, to fill the accountability deficit that has arguably arisen. As Lord Irvine, a former Lord Chancellor, said, it has been 'the massive expansion of the administrative state, which more than any other factor' has prompted the judges to develop the principles of judicial review.[8]

However, it is important to bear two further points in mind. First, judicial review lies in relation to all governmental (and some other public) powers, not only those of the executive branch of the central government. While difficulties at the centre—including Parliament's difficulties in holding the executive to account—have formed part of the impetus for the development of the courts' powers of judicial review, it is necessary to recognise that judicial review is a mechanism for holding a much broader range of bodies, including local authorities and devolved governments, legally to account.

Second, notwithstanding that it has developed, in part, because of concerns about the effectiveness of other (especially parliamentary) accountability mechanisms, judicial review nevertheless remains (as noted in this chapter) just one way of holding the government to account: it exists, as Figure 12.1 shows,[9] as part of a network of overlapping mechanisms for securing executive accountability.

4.2 **Political and legal constitutionalism**

Judicial review is an important accountability tool, but no one would seriously suggest that government's legal accountability to the courts should or could entirely replace its political accountability to Parliament. What, then, is the right balance between these two forms of accountability? This question squarely raises the second of our key themes—that is, the notions of political and legal constitutionalism; whereas the

---

[8] *Human Rights, Constitutional Law and the Development of the English Legal System* (Oxford 2003), p 52.
[9] See Chapter 12, section 2.1.

former emphasises political means of controlling the executive, the latter puts its faith in legal regulation of government.

The respective weight that should be placed upon these two approaches is highly controversial. Harlow and Rawlings have pointed out a fissure in public law scholarship, separating schools of thought that are respectively enthusiastic and distinctly sceptical about judicial review.[10] The former school embraces a minimalist conception of the state in which administrative law's main role is to limit government power and subject it to judicial control. Here, then, emphasis is placed on the role of the courts in securing good administration, and the administrative law enforced by courts is viewed as a valuable and necessary external limitation upon government. Whether it is right to put courts centre-stage in this way depends on the position that one adopts in relation to a range of other issues.

First, enthusiasm about judicial review may reflect a particular *ideological* bent. Those who emphasise the law's role in safeguarding the basic rights of individuals tend to favour extensive powers of judicial review. This prompts us to think back to the contrasting conceptions of democracy considered in Chapter 5. Sedley, for example, considers that democracy is best served by a system in which 'individuals and minorities have an assurance of certain basic protections from the majoritarian interest'—and that this requires 'independent courts of law' to be given responsibility for upholding 'the interests of every individual, not merely the represented majority'.[11] On this view, the courts' role is pivotal: their unique position as neutral, independent arbiters allows them to ensure that the rights and interests of individuals are not unacceptably sacrificed for the sake of the majority. In similar vein, some judges have sought in recent years to articulate a more principled justification for judicial intervention. For example, Laws LJ has argued that the principles of judicial review constitute ethical principles as to the virtuous conduct of the state's affairs.[12]

To put these rather abstract-sounding ideas in context, it would, within this tradition, be acceptable for a court to strike down a ministerial decision allowing extensive night flights to take off from and land at the new airport referred to in our example. While this might be convenient for the vast majority of people, and for the airport operator and its client airlines, this would be at the expense of the interests— indeed, the human rights[13]—of those whose lives would be blighted by the inevitable nocturnal noise pollution. An important role of the court, on this view, is to provide an independent assessment of whether an acceptable balance has been struck between the interests of the minority and the majority.

Second, acceptance of extensive judicial powers to review executive action may arise for *pragmatic* reasons. For example, Farwell LJ remarked (over 100 years ago) that because (as he saw it) ministerial responsibility was no more than 'the mere shadow of a name', the role of the courts was crucial: they were, he said, 'the only defence of the

---

[10] *Law and Administration* (Cambridge 2009), ch 1.

[11] Sedley, 'The Common Law and the Constitution', in Nolan and Sedley (eds), *The Making and Remaking of the British Constitution* (London 1997), p 25.

[12] Laws, 'Law and Democracy' [1995] PL 72.

[13] See *Hatton v United Kingdom* (2003) 37 EHRR 28.

liberty of the subject against departmental aggression'.[14] Judicial review, according to this analysis, is a practical response to the weakness of ministerial accountability—hence the shift of emphasis from *parliamentary* to *judicial* means of controlling government, which forms an important part of the trend towards *legal* (and away from *political*) constitutionalism.

The ideological argument in favour of giving courts extensive powers of judicial review postulates that individuals' interests can, on the whole, *best* be safeguarded by independent judges against state interference, while the pragmatic argument rests on the more modest claim that judicial review is at least an *acceptable substitute* for political modes of accountability. However, neither of those claims should be uncritically accepted.

The latter was made by Lord Mustill in the *Fire Brigades Union* case[15] (the facts of which are set out in Chapter 3[16]). Having noted that parliamentary methods for holding the executive to account had 'been perceived as falling short, and sometimes well short, of what [is] needed to bring the performance of the executive into line with the law', he went on to explain (and generally to approve of the fact) that

> To avoid a vacuum in which the citizen would be left without protection against a misuse of executive powers the courts have had no option but to occupy the dead ground [left by Parliament] in a manner, and in areas of public life, which could not have been foreseen 30 years ago.[17]

Lord Mustill's account is doubtless historically accurate: one of the main driving forces behind the growth of judicial review has been the perceived shortcomings of parliamentary modes of accountability.

However, this trend—and Lord Mustill's account of it—takes for granted the capacity of judicial review to make up for these shortcomings. Yet whether judicial review can in fact do that is questionable. To a large extent, it is arguable that judicial review and ministerial accountability constitute *complementary*—not *alternative*—mechanisms for holding the executive to account. The latter is concerned principally with the wider picture—with questions about policy and the management of government departments—while the former enables individuals to litigate specific grievances against administrative bodies.

The idea that judicial and political systems for securing accountable government are complementary is further underlined by the orthodox view, outlined earlier, under which it is considered improper for courts to inquire into the sort of substantive policy questions that are the traditional focus of parliamentary processes for holding the executive to account. For these (and other) reasons, writers such as Griffith and Tomkins counsel against viewing judicial review as some sort of panacea, capable of filling the 'dead ground' referred to by Lord Mustill, and argue instead that Parliament should be reformed and reinvigorated, enabling it to play a fuller role in

---

[14] *Dyson v Attorney-General* [1911] 1 KB 410, 423.

[15] *R v Secretary of State for the Home Department, ex p Fire Brigades Union* [1995] 2 AC 513.

[16] See Chapter 3, section 5.   [17] *Fire Brigades Union*, 567.

calling the executive branch to account—and thereby reducing the need to rely on the courts.[18]

This, however, would be unlikely to satisfy those writers whose enthusiasm for judicial review springs not from the practical consideration that it is an *acceptable substitute* for political accountability, but from the ideological view that courts are the *best-placed* institutions to scrutinise government decisions when they impact on the rights and interests of individuals. Paradoxically, however, while for such writers the independence and supposed neutrality of the courts is what uniquely equips them to stand as an honest broker between individual and public interests, those characteristics of the judicial branch are also grist to the mill of judicial review *sceptics*.

How can this be? The answer lies in the fact that those who are sceptical about affording courts wide powers of judicial review contend that the enthusiasts' position is built on the false premise that questions about individuals' rights are legal (rather than political) and should therefore be answered by independent courts. The sceptics argue that even if judges are given power to adjudicate on such questions—rendering them, in that rather formal sense, legal questions—this cannot deprive them of their fundamentally political character. In other words, beneath their legal reasoning, judges are involved in making political choices.[19]

To illustrate, let us recall our example of night flights. Local residents argue that night flights interfere with their rights because of noise pollution. By contrast, other people welcome night flights on grounds of convenience and economic reasons. This is the type of issue that could be presented before a court as an issue of law to be determined by reference to legal rules and principles.[20] However, from a different perspective, the very same issue is very clearly a policy choice: whose interests should prevail? Those of the local residents or those of the wider public? Clearly, different people will reach different views on the matter. In other words, it is not a question that is capable of producing a single, objectively correct answer. If so, then who should make the decision? A court that is not politically accountable? Or a government Minister who is?

It has been argued that accepting judges' authority to determine such questions amounts to dangerous judicial supremacism by which unelected judges are able to arrogate to themselves too much power at the expense of the democratic process.[21] Sceptics argue that there is no positive reason why judges should be responsible for making such 'political' choices. They also argue that there are good reasons—including the narrow social, educational, and ethnic backgrounds from which the judiciary is presently drawn, together with its lack of democratic credentials—why the judiciary should not make such decisions.[22] Sceptics therefore argue that scrutiny of such (as they see them) policy questions is best left to Parliament.

---

[18] Griffith, 'The Common Law and the Political Constitution' (2001) 117 LQR 42; Tomkins, *Our Republican Constitution* (Oxford 2005).

[19] See generally Griffith, *The Politics of the Judiciary* (London 1997).

[20] Indeed, precisely that happened in *Hatton v United Kingdom* (2003) 37 EHRR 28.

[21] Griffith, 'The Brave New World of Sir John Laws' (2000) 63 MLR 159; Griffith, 'The Common Law and the Political Constitution' (2001) 117 LQR 42.

[22] See further Griffith, *The Politics of the Judiciary*; Campbell, Ewing, and Tomkins (eds), *Sceptical Essays on Human Rights* (Oxford 2001).

All judicial decision-making involves an element of discretion that may be exercised by reference to policy considerations.[23] Even questions such as whether a duty of care in negligence should be imposed may well involve policy choices about the extent to which people should be required to assume responsibility for their own actions. Judicial review sceptics, though, contend that the scope for judicial policymaking is unusually great in the public law context. This is because judges are directly able to intervene in decisions made by the government.

> **Q** Are you persuaded by the sceptics' view?

It is important not to overstate the disagreement between judicial review enthusiasts and sceptics. Few, if any, commentators advocate that there should be no judicial review at all. Disagreement centres on the *extent* to which courts should be permitted to examine the substance of executive decisions (as opposed to the propriety of the process by which they are made). We return to this issue when we consider the law of substantive judicial review in Chapter 12.

4.3 Demarcation disputes in the multilayered constitution

Much of what we have said thus far has been concerned with the role of judicial review in relation to protecting the interests and rights of individuals against unlawful executive action. There is, however, a further—and, in many respects, relatively new—dimension to judicial review. As well as providing a forum in which the proper boundaries of the *relationship between the individual and the state* can be determined, judicial review can also operate as a mechanism for resolving disputes about the *relationship between different parts of the multilayered constitution*.

It stands to reason that the more multilayered the constitution becomes—that is, the more that responsibility and authority are divided between different institutions—the greater the scope for disagreement about the respective competences of different bodies. In one sense, this is not a new phenomenon: as we know from Chapter 7, power has long been shared between central and local government, and courts have therefore been called upon from time to time to resolve demarcation disputes between the two. For example, the courts have been required to determine the extent to which central government can impose its policy preferences on local authorities,[24] and the extent of ministerial powers to curb increases in local taxes.[25]

The UK's membership of the European Union (EU) has also given rise to demarcation disputes, and may continue to do so until the 'Brexit' process is complete. The *Factortame* case,[26] considered in Chapter 8, is a good illustration; the question having

---

[23] Robertson, *Judicial Discretion in the House of Lords* (Oxford 1998).

[24] *Secretary of State for Education and Science v Tameside Metropolitan Borough Council* [1977] AC 1014.

[25] *Nottinghamshire County Council v Secretary of State for the Environment* [1986] AC 240.

[26] *R v Secretary of State for Transport, ex p Factortame Ltd (No 2)* [1991] 1 AC 603.

been whether EU law should, in effect, trump an Act of Parliament. And we saw in Chapter 7 that courts now also have a role in determining 'devolution issues'— that is, issues as to whether devolved bodies are acting or proposing to act beyond their legal competence (and thereby interfering in matters reserved to the UK tier of government).

This role—which, in effect, involves acting as a referee between different spheres of authority within the constitutional order—is one that is familiar to courts in many countries, particularly those with federal systems in which power is clearly divided between different levels of government.[27] It is a role that is less familiar to UK courts, but one in which they are, of necessity, growing in experience. Judicial review serves an important function in terms of facilitating legal regulation of intra-governmental relations. At the same time, non-judicial mechanisms—such as negotiation and constitutional convention—also play a very significant part in shaping the relationship between the various layers of government.

Indeed, the question considered in section 4.2—concerning the appropriate balance between legal and political regulation—arises here too. The *Fire Brigades Union* case[28] illustrates the point (albeit that it involved a demarcation dispute between different arms of the national government rather than between different tiers of the multilayered government). As we saw in Chapter 3,[29] the Home Secretary had refused to bring into force a statutory scheme for compensating victims of violent crime. In effect, this would have repealed the relevant provisions of the legislation. The question of whether it was appropriate for a court to resolve this demarcation dispute between the executive and legislative branches divided the Appellate Committee of the House of Lords. Three of the judges thought it was appropriate for the court to intervene to strike down the Home Secretary's decisions. Two of the judges thought that the essentially political character of the issue made judicial intervention inappropriate. The case demonstrates just how difficult it sometimes is for courts to decide whether or not they should intervene. As we will see through our study, in Chapter 12, of the content of the law of judicial review, this is a pervasive challenge that courts have to face up to very frequently. Indeed, the challenge cannot be resolved in the abstract but only on the basis of each individual judicial review case. This is part of what makes judicial review such an interesting and dynamic topic.

5. The constitutional basis of judicial review

In the absence of a written constitution making clear provision for judicial review, what authorises courts to intervene in (and, where appropriate, strike down) decisions made by government bodies?

---

[27] For discussion of federalism, see Chapter 7, section 4.2.

[28] *R v Secretary of State for the Home Department, ex p Fire Brigades Union* [1995] 2 AC 513.

[29] See Chapter 3, section 5.

5.1 The *ultra vires* doctrine

An obvious answer is that courts enforce whatever limits the relevant legislation imposes upon ministerial powers. For example, if legislation were to authorise the Minister in our example to 'give permission for the construction and operation of new *airports*', a court, on judicial review, would be perfectly justified in striking down a decision, purportedly taken under this power, to give permission for the construction and operation of a new *prison*. In such a situation, the Minister would self-evidently be acting outside his powers, and it seems natural that courts, as enforcers of the law, should be entitled to take appropriate steps to deal with such action.

Administrative lawyers refer to this line of thinking as the *ultra vires* doctrine, *ultra vires* literally meaning 'beyond the powers'. It provides a simple and—superficially—attractive justification for judicial review. Under the *ultra vires* doctrine the courts are simply policing the boundaries upon government power stipulated by Parliament. This can be seen from Figure 11.1. The shaded area represents the Minister's power: he is authorised by the statute to do things lying inside that area, but not to do anything else.

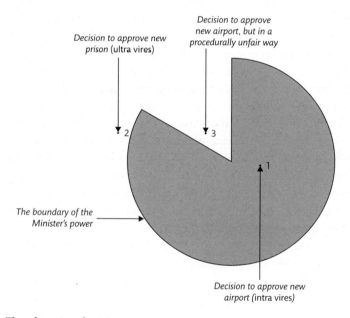

Figure 11.1 The *ultra vires* doctrine

In our example, the statute allows him to approve new airports: a decision to do so (represented by point 1 in the diagram) would therefore lie within his statutory power and would be lawful. In contrast, a decision to approve a new prison (point 2) would be outside the power and unlawful. The justification for courts striking down such decisions is clear, since it 'consists of nothing other than *an application of the law itself*, and the law of Parliament to boot'.[30]

---

[30] Baxter, *Administrative Law* (Cape Town 1984), p 303.

This proposition is easy to make out where courts enforce limits that are explicit in the statute. In our example, it is tolerably clear that Parliament intended the power to be used *only* to approve the construction and operation of new airports; if it were to have intended the power to extend to prisons, it would surely have said as much. The reality, however, is that judicial review sometimes goes far beyond determining the limits of the statutory powers exercised by government. This much is obvious from the overview we gave earlier[31]—and from that which is given in Figure 12.1[32]—of the many and various grounds on which courts can intervene in executive decisions. The Minister exercising the power to grant permission for a new airport would be required by the courts to exercise it fairly, reasonably, on the basis of all relevant (but no irrelevant) information, and subject to a host of other requirements (all of which we will consider in detail in the next chapter) that are neither mentioned explicitly nor even hinted at by the text of the statute.

Ultra vires theorists respond to this difficulty by saying that Parliament *intends* to limit decision-makers' powers in all of these ways, even if it fails to *say* so explicitly. For example, if a Minister were to decide to grant permission for a new airport, but make his decision in a procedurally unfair way, *ultra vires* theorists would say that the decision would lie outside his powers, because Parliament never intended to give him the power to act unfairly. Figure 11.1 illustrates this idea. The missing part of the circle represents the never-granted power to act unfairly (or in breach of any of the other principles of judicial review): hence a decision (represented by point 3) marred by unfairness lies outside the Minister's power and can justifiably be struck down by the courts.

There is, however, an obvious difficulty with this argument: it is implausible.[33] If Parliament has not *said* that it is withholding from decision-makers the power to act contrary to the principles of judicial review, how do we *know* that it meant to withhold such powers? From this criticism flow several others.[34]

First, as we will see in Chapter 13, the range of bodies and powers that are subject to judicial review has expanded significantly in recent decades. Importantly, courts are now willing to review the exercise of *non-statutory powers*, such as decisions taken under the royal prerogative. This presents an apparently insurmountable obstacle to the *ultra vires* principle. That principle states that judicial review is constitutionally acceptable because courts are simply enforcing those limits on statutory powers that Parliament intended when it created such powers. But how can the *ultra vires* principle explain judicial review of non-statutory powers that were never created or conferred by Parliament in the first place?

Second, we will see in Chapter 12 that the principles of judicial review—that is, the limits on power that courts are prepared to enforce—have evolved considerably in recent years. There is, however, no evidence that Parliament intended any of these changes. Parliament has never legislated for the growth of judicial review.

---

[31] See section 1.   [32] See Chapter 12, section 2.1.

[33] See Laws, 'Law and Democracy' [1995] PL 72, 78–79; Forsyth, 'Of Fig Leaves and Fairy Tales: The *Ultra Vires* Doctrine, the Sovereignty of Parliament and Judicial Review' [1996] CLJ 122, 136.

[34] See Craig, '*Ultra Vires* and the Foundations of Judicial Review' [1998] CLJ 63.

Third, as we explain in Chapter 13, the courts have fiercely resisted parliamentary attempts to prevent judicial review of certain matters—and they have done so even in the face of clear statutory language designed to exclude judicial review. This is hard for *ultra vires* theorists to explain. How can the courts, in exercising powers of judicial review, be doing Parliament's bidding if they insist upon exercising those powers even when Parliament appears to have told them not to?

5.2 **The common law theory**

In light of these difficulties, an alternative view—the common law theory—has been advanced in an attempt to provide a sounder justification for judicial review.[35] The *ultra vires* doctrine characterises the restrictions enforced via judicial review as limitations that are contained (explicitly or implicitly) in the statute conferring the relevant power. By contrast, the common law theory views judicial review not as a statutory creation but as rooted in the common law. Viewed in this way, if a court were to strike down our hypothetical Minister's decision to grant permission for a new airport on the ground that the decision had been taken in a procedurally unfair way, this would have nothing to do with the intention of Parliament. The court would simply be enforcing a common law principle that public decision-makers must act fairly.

This view avoids many of the difficulties encountered by the *ultra vires* doctrine. For instance, it makes unnecessary the highly strained argument that the detailed principles of judicial review are intended (yet never actually articulated) by Parliament. Instead, it is possible to acknowledge that the law of judicial review has been developed by judges who have incrementally fashioned legal principles through the development of case law. The common law theory also allows the principles of judicial review to be applied to decision-making powers whether or not the powers have been created by Parliament (because, according to the common law theory, the principles enforced by courts in judicial review proceedings have nothing to do with the intention of Parliament). And the common law theory can account for changes to the law of judicial review over time, simply because the common law can and does evolve. In the public law context, the common law is developed creatively by the judges in response to wider political and social changes and the need to ensure that the executive complies with essential standards of lawful decision-making.

However, these substantial benefits notwithstanding, some commentators argue that the common law theory does not adequately fit with the basic architecture of the constitution.[36] As we have seen, in order to escape the difficulties that beset the *ultra vires* doctrine, the common law theory holds that the grounds of judicial review—that require decision-makers to act fairly, reasonably, and so on—have nothing to do with the intention of Parliament; they are instead common law rules. It has been said that this line of argument gives rise to the following problem. If, when it grants a ministerial

---

[35] See Oliver, 'Is the *Ultra Vires* Rule the Basis of Judicial Review?' [1987] PL 543; Craig; Laws.

[36] Forsyth; Elliott, 'The *Ultra Vires* Doctrine in a Constitutional Setting: Still the Central Principle of Administrative Law' [1999] CLJ 129.

power to (say) approve the construction of new airports, Parliament is taken not to have *prohibited* the making of (for example) procedurally unfair decisions, then it must have *authorised* the making of such decisions. Forsyth puts the point in the following terms: '[I]f Parliament grants a power to a minister, that minister either acts within those powers or outside those powers. There is no grey area between authorisation and the denial of power.'[37]

Assume that our hypothetical Minister makes a procedurally unfair decision to approve a new airport. On Forsyth's view, the Minister either *is* or *is not* authorised by Parliament to make procedurally unfair decisions. If he is not so authorised, then the position is as shown in Figure 11.1. It will be unlawful—*ultra vires*—for the Minister to act unfairly, and a common law requirement to act fairly will be redundant (because its effect would merely require the Minister to desist from conduct that Parliament has, in the first place, omitted to authorise). In the alternative scenario, the Minister *is* authorised by Parliament to make unfair decisions: as in Figure 11.2, no chunk (representing the power to act unfairly etc) is missing from the power granted in the statute. Here, the common law is not (as in the first scenario) redundant: a common law rule requiring Ministers to act fairly *would* make a difference, because, without such a rule, it would be lawful for them to act unfairly.

However, there is an obvious problem. If Parliament has authorised the making of unfair decisions, it is constitutionally impossible—if Parliament is sovereign—for the common law to prohibit the making of such decisions. In effect, the common law is removing from the Minister authority that was given to him by Parliament. Critics of the common law theory therefore contend that it is unconstitutional to the extent that it purports to enable courts to prevent decision-makers from doing things that the sovereign Parliament has authorised.

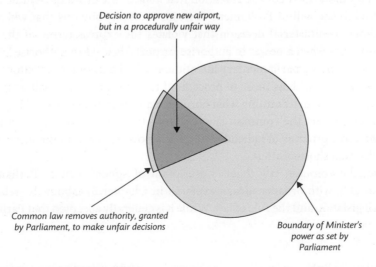

Decision to approve new airport, but in a procedurally unfair way

Common law removes authority, granted by Parliament, to make unfair decisions

Boundary of Minister's power as set by Parliament

Figure 11.2 The common law theory

---

[37] Forsyth, 133.

If this argument is accepted, then an impasse seems to be reached. On the one hand, the *ultra vires* doctrine fits with the principle of parliamentary sovereignty, but is otherwise highly implausible. On the other hand, the common law theory is said to conflict with parliamentary sovereignty, but is otherwise plausible. We end this chapter by considering three potential ways out of this impasse—including a radical solution that calls into question the doctrine of parliamentary sovereignty itself and the very nature of our constitutional order.

5.3 Defence of the common law theory

Some writers have sought to demonstrate that the common law theory is *not* incompatible with the principle of parliamentary sovereignty. In particular, Laws argues that Forsyth is wrong to suppose that a Minister is either authorised or not authorised to act. Parliament may be agnostic—it may have no opinion one way or the other—about how the powers that it confers should be exercised. This, says Laws, gives rise to a 'vacuum'—created through the absence of any relevant parliamentary intention—that can legitimately be filled by common law principles of judicial review.[38]

Applying this argument to our example, when Parliament granted the power to our hypothetical Minister to approve the construction of new airports, it would be taken to have no view as to whether or not the Minister should be allowed to exercise the power unfairly. It would therefore be legitimate for the courts to determine whether or not the Minister should be free so to act. However, there are two difficulties with this argument.

First, just as the argument underpinning the *ultra vires* doctrine that *all* of the grounds of judicial review relate *directly* to parliamentary intention is implausible, so is the common law theory's contention that *none* of the grounds of judicial review relate *at all* to the will of Parliament. It is, for example, obvious that when a court strikes down a ministerial decision that violates the express terms of the relevant statute—such as when a power to authorise 'airports' is used to authorise 'prisons'— the court is enforcing parliamentary intention. Even where courts are enforcing more general principles, such as those of procedural fairness, they may well be influenced by the statute when determining what fairness requires in the context.[39] It may therefore be thought that the common law position—that legislative intention is wholly irrelevant to the grounds of judicial review—is an overreaction to the *ultra vires* doctrine's admitted shortcomings.

Second, the common law theory's ascription of agnosticism to Parliament sits uncomfortably with broader ideas—explored in Chapter 5—about the relationship between legislation and the rule of law. While it is generally accepted that Parliament is

---

[38] 'Illegality: The Problem of Jurisdiction', in Supperstone et al (eds), *Judicial Review* (London 2005).

[39] See, eg *R v Secretary of State for the Home Department, ex p Doody* [1994] 1 AC 531, 560, *per* Lord Mustill: 'What fairness demands is dependent on the context of the decision ... An essential feature of the context is the statute which creates the discretion, as regards both its language and the shape of the legal and administrative system within which the decision is taken.'

sovereign—meaning that it can, in theory, enact whatever laws it pleases—substantial protection is conferred upon the rule of law by means of statutory interpretation.[40] Courts habitually and consistently justify this approach by recourse to the simple, but important, presumption that Parliament does not legislate in a vacuum, but 'for a European liberal democracy founded on the principles and traditions of the common law'.[41] The difficulty, therefore, with Laws' defence of the common law theory is that it requires us to suppose that Parliament is neutral about the rule of law values that judicial review protects. Yet that supposition is diametrically opposed to the usual (and arguably more natural) presumption that Parliament intends to respect the rule of law—a presumption that is widely invoked by the courts as an aid to statutory construction.

5.4 Development of the *ultra vires* theory

Those commentators who do not find the defence of the common law theory convincing have instead focused on developing the *ultra vires* theory, with the aim of equipping it to provide a more convincing account of the constitutional justification for judicial review.[42] It will be recalled that the principal difficulty with the *ultra vires* theory relates to the *direct* relationship that it postulates between the intention of Parliament and the various, detailed grounds of judicial review that courts enforce today. This, as we have seen, is fundamentally implausible: as Forsyth acknowledges, '[n]o-one is so innocent as to suppose that judicial creativity does not form [in the sense of having contributed to the development of] the grounds of judicial review'.[43]

It follows that the question for *ultra vires* theorists is whether it is possible to identify a more plausible relationship between the will of Parliament and the grounds of judicial review. Their response is that it is possible to do so in two ways. First, by disowning the incredible claim that every last detail of the grounds of judicial review can be traced to (largely unexpressed) parliamentary intention. And, second, by relying instead upon the more modest presumption that Parliament intends the powers that it creates to be exercised in conformity with the rule of law, while leaving it to the courts to work out what this means in individual cases.

On this view, there is a connection—but merely an indirect connection—between what courts do in judicial review proceedings and the intention of Parliament. The courts' role is to take Parliament's (presumed) intention that decision-makers should respect the rule of law, and to work out what limitations or grounds of review should be developed to give effect to that constitutional principle. On this view, our hypothetical Minister, when exercising his power to decide whether to grant permission for a new airport, would find himself obliged to exercise the power subject to (among other things) the various principles of procedural fairness that we consider in Chapter 12. This would be so not because Parliament intended the detailed content of

---

[40] See, eg *Anisminic Ltd v Foreign Compensation Commission* [1969] 2 AC 147; *R v Lord Chancellor, ex p Witham* [1998] QB 575.

[41] *R v Secretary of State for the Home Department, ex p Pierson* [1998] AC 539, 587, *per* Lord Steyn.

[42] See Forsyth; Elliott.   [43] Forsyth, 136.

those principles, but because the courts have developed them against the background of Parliament's general intention that ministerial discretion should be exercised compatibly with the rule of law.

5.5 **A more radical view**

The differences between the *ultra vires* and common law schools of thought represent a disagreement about the *implications* of parliamentary sovereignty—in particular, whether (as the *ultra vires* theorists would have us believe) it requires judicial review to be justified by reference to the will of Parliament, if only indirectly, or (as the common law theory holds) mandates no such relationship between parliamentary intention and the grounds of judicial review. Yet the *ultra vires* and common law schools are united in taking parliamentary sovereignty to be a given.

It is this aspect of the debate with which Allan takes issue.[44] He accepts that the common law theory is, as the *ultra vires* theorists contend, incompatible with full respect for the sovereignty of Parliament. However, he goes on to argue that since, in his view, Parliament is *not* sovereign, it is in the first place unnecessary to justify judicial review by reference to the intention of Parliament. In particular, Allan says that the principles that courts uphold on judicial review are constitutional fundamentals, hardwired into the constitution as restraints on the authority of Parliament itself.

If asked 'why are decision-makers required to act fairly?', *ultra vires* theorists would respond, 'because Parliament, directly or indirectly, so intends'. However, Allan would say, 'because Parliament can only create decision-making powers which can be exercised in line with fundamental constitutional principles such as procedural fairness'.

In this sense, Allan's view can be thought of as a form of *constitutional* theory of *ultra vires*. The end result (that the power to breach important rule-of-law-based principles is withheld from decision-makers) is the same whether we subscribe to the standard *ultra vires* theory or Allan's constitutional version thereof. The reasoning, however, is significantly different. In Allan's argument, the intention of Parliament is beside the point, because higher-order constitutional principles prevent it, in the first place, from creating decision-making powers that are free from obligations to respect the fundamental norms enforced via judicial review.

> **Q** Would Allan's argument, if accepted, support or undermine the common law theory of judicial review?

Approached on this basis, the debate over the constitutional foundations of judicial review is part of the much broader debate that we encountered in Chapter 5

---

[44] 'The Constitutional Foundations of Judicial Review: Conceptual Conundrum or Interpretative Inquiry?' [2002] CLJ 87.

concerning the scope of Parliament's constitutional authority. The internal logic of Allan's position is unassailable. *If*, as he contends, Parliament is not sovereign, and *if*, as he contends, the principles of judicial review are constitutional fundamentals from which Parliament is impotent to deviate, *then* it is the constitution itself—not the intention of Parliament—that justifies courts in striking down administrative decisions that contravene those principles.

However, this merely invites bigger questions. Is Parliament sovereign? Do the principles of judicial review have the fundamental status that Allan ascribes to them?

These questions are difficult to answer, at least by reference to positive law, because courts are rarely required to face squarely up to them—and even when they are, they generally prefer to avoid directly answering them. For example, in Chapter 5, we examined the *Anisminic* case,[45] in which the court was faced with an 'ouster clause' that seemed to prevent judicial review of certain decisions—a situation that would have been inconsistent with the requirements of the rule of law. We saw, however, that the court neutralised the ouster clause by engaging in what it characterised as statutory interpretation (so as to preserve a veneer of fidelity to parliamentary intention) rather than asserting a power to strike down, or refusing to apply, the offending clause. Yet some commentators, reading between the lines, argue that the judicial policy in that case was actually 'one of total disobedience to Parliament', the implication being that judicial review was actually regarded as a constitutional fundamental that Parliament was powerless to displace.[46]

Support is given to this point of view by the *Jackson* case,[47] in which Lord Steyn remarked that if Parliament were to attempt to abolish judicial review, the courts would have to determine 'whether this is a constitutional fundamental which even a sovereign Parliament . . . cannot abolish'.[48] Similarly, Baroness Hale said: 'The courts will treat with particular suspicion (and might even reject) any attempt to subvert the rule of law by removing governmental action affecting the rights of the individual from all judicial scrutiny.'[49] Comparable sentiments were expressed by Lord Hodge in *Moohan*, in which he did not exclude the (hypothetical) possibility of a court declaring unlawful legislation that 'abusively' undermined democratic principles.[50]

These comments were all *obiter dicta* and, in any event, their Lordships were guarded in how they expressed their views. Yet the very fact that senior judges were prepared to make such statements demonstrates that the supremacy of Parliament is no longer as sacred as it once was. If the judges ever decide that our unwritten constitution has evolved to a point at which the doctrine of parliamentary sovereignty could be discarded, the principles of judicial review would be prime candidates for recognition as constitutional fundamentals limiting the legislature's freedom of action. If that day ever comes, it will have important consequences for the debate about the

---

[45] *Anisminic Ltd v Foreign Compensation Commission* [1969] 2 AC 147.
[46] Wade and Forsyth, *Administrative Law* (Oxford 2009), p 616.
[47] *R (Jackson) v Attorney General* [2005] UKHL 56, [2006] 1 AC 262; see Chapter 5, section 6.5.4 for fuller discussion.
[48] *Jackson*, [102]. See also Lord Hope's remarks at [104].   [49] *Jackson*, [159].
[50] *Moohan v Lord Advocate* [2014] UKSC 67, [2015] AC 901, [35].

constitutional foundations of judicial review, and it will be difficult to resist the logic of Allan's position.

6. Concluding remarks

Chapter 12 focuses on the law of judicial review as a subject in its own right by examining the content of the principles to which courts require decision-makers to adhere when exercising statutory and other powers. In this chapter, we have seen that judicial review is not something that can, or should, be studied in isolation. We have, for example, seen that the debate about the constitutional foundations of judicial review is, in truth, part of a much broader discussion concerning *the relationship between Parliament and the courts*—and even about *the veracity of the doctrine of parliamentary sovereignty* itself. We have also seen that judicial review impacts upon—and can only properly be understood in relation to—the three key themes with which we are concerned in this book. Thus, judicial review is an important mechanism for *holding the executive branch of government to account*, and the reliance that we place on judicial—as opposed to, say, parliamentary—systems of accountability is an important facet of the broader debate about *political and legal constitutionalism.*

Meanwhile, the *multilayered nature* of the modern British constitution means that courts have acquired new responsibilities for settling demarcation disputes between different governing institutions. For all of these reasons, studying the law of judicial review—which is the task to which we now turn—is important not only for its own sake, but also for what it tells us about these broader and deeper issues with which we must grapple as we come to terms with the contemporary UK constitution.

Expert commentary
The constitutional role and foundations of judicial review
Christopher Forsyth, Emeritus Sir David Williams Professor
of Public Law, University of Cambridge

Litigation is a fraught business. The cost in court fees, legal fees, delay, stress, and strain ensures that the burden of litigation is very great. It is not to be undertaken unless there is no other choice and the wise person hesitates even then. But with judicial review there is an additional hazard: as this chapter rightly makes very clear, judicial review is concerned with the lawfulness of the decisions of public authorities of all kinds and not, generally, with the merits of such authorities' decisions. An authority may make a decision that is unwise and unmeritorious but if it is lawful the courts will not intervene. And the wisest decision made by an illegal procedure may be struck down. Moreover, the litigant aggrieved by a decision may succeed in showing that it is procedurally flawed and getting the court to quash it, only to find that the decision-maker makes the same decision again—this time by a lawful procedure rendering the decision unchallengeable. Important as judicial review is in imposing the rule of law on the exercise of discretion by public authorities, it places great burdens on the litigants (claimant and respondent). And victories are sometimes pyrrhic.

What underlies the distinction between the merits of decisions and their legality is a question of the allocation of power. Who is to make the final decision when difficult decisions have to be made? For instance, to give the example used in the chapter, who is to decide whether and where a new airport should be constructed? Under a democratic constitution such decisions should be made by decision-makers who are either elected or accountable to the elected representatives of the people. Now judges, fearless and independent as they are, are not elected, nor should they be. Moreover, they lack the skill to weigh contending policy considerations against each other in such cases. So necessarily the judicial role is limited to questions of legality.

But, as the chapter makes clear, the distinction between merits and legality is contested. In considerable measure this is because of the perceived failure of other means of accountability. The executive so dominates Parliament that calling the executive to account by way of judicial review often seems to be the only feasible option. So applications for judicial review often sail under false colours: purporting to challenge the legality of decisions, they are in fact driven by disagreement over the merits of the decision in question. But can the extension of judicial review into the merits of decisions ever be an alternative to the reform of the executive and the legislature?

Another contested subject raised in this chapter is the debate over the basis of judicial review. What is it that justifies the judges in intervening at all in the exercise of power by a public authority? The answer has to be along the lines suggested in this chapter. The authority is granted powers by law (in the vast majority of cases by statute) and the task of the courts is simply to police the limits of that power. This is the *ultra vires* doctrine. The difficulty with this is that often the limits to that power are not spelt out clearly in the relevant statute, so they are given detail and form by judicial interpretation of that statute. So the plausible and influential suggestion is made that when the judges fill in the detail—specifying perhaps the procedure to be followed in making a decision—in fact they are imposing common law principles of good administration upon the statutory power. This is not judicial interpretation of the statute but the application of the common law.

These suggestions prompted a lively debate over whether the *ultra vires* doctrine or the common law is the true juristic basis for judicial review. Looking back on the debate it is disappointing how few participants have changed their minds at all. There is little sign of reconciliation or much mutual understanding. But some progress has been made. Before the debate it seemed to have been assumed that the juristic basis of judicial review could be selected from a range or buffet of possibilities on grounds of taste, plausibility, and convenience. And once a choice had been made it could be defended on similar grounds. But the central point made by the defenders of the *ultra vires* doctrine was that there were constitutional consequences to the question of what the juristic basis was. And, for reasons well explained in the chapter, it turns out that to impose the common law as the justification for judicial review is, in fact, to challenge the sovereignty of Parliament. So the debate has at least shown that this is the crucial issue—and any challenge to the modified *ultra vires* doctrine must face the question of whether Parliament is sovereign or not.

For the student seeking to make sense of all this, this is actually quite helpful, for it means that there is only one big question to answer: is Parliament sovereign? If you conclude that it is, then the juristic basis of judicial review has to be something very like the modified *ultra vires* doctrine well described in this chapter. But if you conclude that Parliament is not sovereign then you may decide that the common law forms the basis of judicial review. I would add only this. Deciding whether the UK *has* a sovereign Parliament is not the same as deciding whether the UK *ought* to have a sovereign Parliament. The question is not whether it might be wise or sensible or convenient to have a Parliament with only limited legal powers, but whether, as a matter of law, we have one.

Further reading

FORSYTH (ed), *Judicial Review and the Constitution* (Oxford 2000)
  A collection of essays on the constitutional foundations of judicial review.

GRIFFITH, 'The Common Law and the Political Constitution' (2001) 117 LQR 42
  A critical examination of the judicial role from the perspective of political constitutionalism.

HARLOW and RAWLINGS, *Law and Administration* (Cambridge 2009)
  A key text which examines administrative law from a contextual perspective.

SEDLEY, 'Judicial Politics' (2012) 34 London Review of Books 15 (**http://www.lrb.co.uk/v34/
  n04/stephen-sedley/judicial-politics**)
  A rejoinder to Lord Sumption's lecture, referred to immediately below.

SUMPTION, 'Judicial and Political Decision-Making: The Uncertain Boundary', FA Mann Lecture,
  9 November 2011 (**http://www.pem.cam.ac.uk/wp-content/uploads/2012/07/1C-
  Sumption-article.pdf**)
  A lecture given by Lord Sumption, shortly before he took up appointment as a Supreme Court
  Justice, on the limits of the judicial role.

12

The Grounds of Judicial Review

1.	Introduction	497
2.	Interpreting and applying the statute	499
3.	Acting fairly	506
4.	Exercise of discretion	526
5.	Review of the outcome of the decision-making process	539
6.	Concluding remarks	551
	Expert commentary	553
	Further reading	554

1. Introduction

1.1 **An overview**

Administrative decisions are taken by government departments and other public bodies such as local councils in order to implement policy. As we saw in the previous chapter, such decisions can be challenged in the courts via judicial review. If such decisions are found to be unlawful, they can be struck down. This chapter is concerned with the various grounds on which administrative decisions can be held unlawful.

There have been various attempts to classify the grounds of judicial review,[1] although none has been wholly satisfactory. This is because the grounds of review, being nuanced and subtle, are not susceptible to being clearly summarised or exhaustively defined. They take shape from the context in which they are applied. Nonetheless, it is helpful to start any discussion of judicial review with a brief summary. There are four principal grounds of judicial review:

- *Legality* Administrative decisions must be taken in accordance with the law. The applicable law concerned may be statutory provisions or common law rules. For

---

[1] For instance, in *Council of Civil Service Unions v Minister for the Civil Service* [1984] AC 374, 410, Lord Diplock summarised the grounds of judicial review under the following three headings—illegality, procedural impropriety, irrationality—which, broadly speaking, correspond with the first three headings used here. At the time Lord Diplock gave his speech (in 1984), he had in mind the possible adoption of proportionality as a fourth ground of judicial review.

instance, if a public authority exercising its statutory powers takes a decision out-side the limits of those powers, then it will be acting unlawfully. Questions of legality therefore often raise issues of statutory interpretation. However, there are also common law principles of legality, such as the non-delegation principle and the rule against the fettering of discretion. This ground of review is covered in sections 2 and 4 of this chapter.

- *Procedural fairness* When a public authority takes a decision that may adversely affect an individual's interests and rights, it must use a fair procedure before tak-ing that decision. For instance, the person concerned may be entitled to a hear-ing before any decision is made. Further, the decision-maker concerned should not have any personal interest in the outcome of the decision. This ground of review is covered in section 3.

- *Unreasonableness* Administrative decisions must not be unreasonable. However, in public law, a decision is not 'unreasonable' just because the court thinks that a better decision could have been made. Instead, the courts can only intervene on this ground if the challenged decision is so unreasonable that no reasonable decision-maker could ever have arrived at it. This ground of review is considered in section 5.

- *Proportionality* A decision is disproportionate if the decision-maker has gone further than is necessary in order to achieve its purpose (or, as the point is some-times put, something will be disproportionate if a 'sledgehammer has been used to crack a nut'). A decision will also be disproportionate if it infringes an individ-ual's rights without adequate justification. This ground of review is used particu-larly in the context of human rights challenges, but it is also increasingly applied in ordinary judicial review challenges to administrative decision-making. This ground of review is considered in section 5.

This summary is just that—a summary. It is intended to serve simply as a starting point for our examination of the grounds of review. In the course of the chapter we will refine our understanding of the grounds summarised above. We will see, for instance, that the law in this area has developed over time, and continues to develop; that the language used by the courts to describe the grounds of review has evolved; and that the grounds of review often overlap with one another. We will also see that the grounds of review do not of themselves necessarily resolve the issue as to whether or not the courts should intervene and strike down an administrative decision: in many cases, the court must use its judgement to determine whether or not in the par-ticular circumstances of the case before it the challenged decision is lawful.

When considering judicial review, it is always important to bear in mind that, beneath the doctrinal development of the law, judicial review poses a challenge for the courts. The ultimate aim is for the courts to develop standards of legality to pro-tect the rights and interests of individuals and to ensure that public authorities stay within the limits of, and do not abuse, their powers. At the same time, the courts must not themselves be tempted to consider the merits of public decisions or to impose their own views on policy matters above those of government. But the line between these two approaches is often a very fine one—and judges themselves do not always agree on where exactly the line is to be drawn. For these reasons, considering how the judges seek to achieve this balance while also developing and applying the principles of judicial review makes this an important and fascinating area of law to study.

1.2 **An example**

In order to provide a practical context in which to explore these matters, we will make use, throughout this chapter, of an example. It will be developed as the chapter progresses, but for the time being, it takes the following form:

> **Eg** The (imaginary) Planning and Infrastructure Act 2017 provides that, whereas requests for planning permission are normally dealt with by local authorities, 'the Secretary of State may decide whether—and, if so, subject to what conditions, if any— permission should be granted for major infrastructure projects'.
>
> A major airport operating company wishes to build a new airport. However, it anticipates that the local authority, which has a track record of refusing to allow developments unless they are environmentally friendly, will decline to grant permission. It therefore asks the Secretary of State to intervene by exercising her power under the 2017 Act.

2. **Interpreting and applying the statute**

2.1 **Introduction**

The use of this power may give rise to myriad legal questions, such as whether it has been exercised in a procedurally fair way. But before considering whether the Minister has *exercised her power lawfully*, it is necessary to decide whether, in the first place, she is *entitled to exercise the power*. If, for instance, the Secretary of State were to attempt to use the power in order to permit or block the building of an ordinary house, she would clearly be acting unlawfully—not because she would be unlawfully using a power she had, but because she would be purporting to use a power she did not have. That would be so because the Secretary of State is authorised to intervene only in respect of 'major infrastructure projects'—into which category a single house self-evidently does not fall.

Any Minister, or other official, who is considering using a decision-making power granted by statute must therefore ask herself two fundamental questions. The second question—'should I exercise this power?'—turns on the merits of the issue at hand. How much environmental damage would the proposed development cause? What would be the economic benefit? Is the economic benefit big enough to make the environmental damage worthwhile? The first question, however, is different. It is concerned not with whether the power *should* be exercised, but with whether it *can* be exercised. And the answer to that question necessarily turns on whether the statute permits the power to be used in the circumstances of the case. In our example, therefore, the crucial question is whether the matter under consideration can properly be characterised as a 'major infrastructure project'. If it can, the Minister can use the power and can proceed to determining whether, and if so how, the power should be exercised. But if the proposed development cannot properly be characterised as a 'major infrastructure project', then the Minister cannot exercise her statutory power—and that is that.

Questions in our first category—about whether a given power can be exercised—are known as 'jurisdictional' questions, the fundamental issue being whether the decision-maker is genuinely authorised by law to do the thing in question. (In our example, the thing in question is determining a planning application on the ground that it relates to a 'major infrastructure project'.)

Some cases will be straightforward. Our imaginary legislation plainly *does not* authorise the Minister to decide whether planning permission should be granted in respect of a single house. Equally plainly, it *does* permit the Minister to intervene in relation to (say) the construction of a large new airport. But other cases will be harder to resolve. What about, for example, the construction of not just one house, but hundreds of houses—together with the new roads and schools that they will necessitate? And what about the construction not of a large new airport, but of a modestly sized new terminal building at an existing airport?

When we think about—and when courts are faced with—such questions, it becomes necessary to distinguish two issues, as the bottom left-hand portion of Figure 12.1 shows. First, what does the legislation actually mean? If, for instance, it authorises ministerial involvement in respect of 'major infrastructure projects', what is the correct definition of that term? Second, once we have settled on the correct meaning, we have to decide whether the proposal under consideration satisfies the definition. Is the new airport, or the new terminal building, or the hundreds of new houses with associated roads and schools a development whose scale and other relevant characteristics makes it a 'major infrastructure project' in the statutory sense? We begin with the first of those issues.

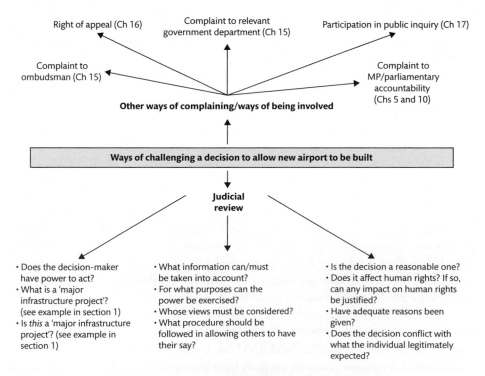

Figure 12.1 Judicial review and the wider administrative justice system

2.2 **The meaning of the statute**

If the Minister is to try to work out whether she has the power to deal with the matter, and if she only has power if the matter concerns a 'major infrastructure project', then she must first address the meaning of that term. Such questions, since they involve the interpretation of a statute, are generally regarded as *questions of law*.

The general principle is that, while Ministers and other decision-makers must inevitably try to answer such questions (in order to work out whether they have power to deal with the matter at hand), the courts (if the matter reaches them by virtue of being litigated) have the final say. This is the principal hallmark of judicial review of jurisdictional questions. The courts will not second-guess decision-makers on the 'merits', or wisdom, of the decision ('should the airport be built?'). However, the courts can and do override decision-makers on jurisdictional questions ('what does "major infrastructure project" mean?'). Judges, then, can *substitute* their view of the meaning of the statute for that of the Minister.

This matter was addressed by the House of Lords in the celebrated *Anisminic* case.[2] Property belonging to the claimant company, Anisminic, was confiscated by the Egyptian authorities in 1956. The Egyptian government later paid a lump sum to the UK government to be distributed to affected parties. This task fell to the Foreign Compensation Commission.[3] Anisminic applied to it, seeking compensation, but the Commission ruled that Anisminic was ineligible. It reached that view because of the way in which it had interpreted the relevant legislation. In particular, the Commission took the legislation to mean that compensation could not be paid to an applicant if the subsequent owner of the relevant property was not a British national. Anisminic, however, said that the Commission had misunderstood the legislation, and that the nationality of subsequent owners was irrelevant.

The question for the Court was whether the Commission's interpretation of the legislation should stand. Their Lordships held that it should not. Lord Wilberforce pointed out that the Commission had 'a derived authority, derived, that is, from statute: at some point, and to be found from a consideration of the legislation, the field within which it operates is marked out and limited'.[4] In similar vein, Lord Reid observed that '[i]t cannot be for the commission to determine the limits of its powers. . . . [I]f they reach a wrong conclusion as to the width of their powers, the court must be able to correct that'.[5] By a majority, their Lordships concluded that just such a conclusion had been reached, ruling that, on the correct interpretation—that is, the *judges'* interpretation—the legislation did not require consideration of the nationality of the subsequent owner.

After this decision was handed down, there was uncertainty as to its precise effect.[6] Clearly, their Lordships had treated the *particular question of law* that arose in

---

[2] *Anisminic Ltd v Foreign Compensation Commission* [1969] 2 AC 147.
[3] Established by the Foreign Compensation Act 1950. [4] *Anisminic*, 207.
[5] *Anisminic*, 184.
[6] See, eg *Pearlman v Keepers and Governors of Harrow School* [1979] QB 56; *South East Asia Fire Bricks Sdn Bhd v Non-Metallic Mineral Products Manufacturing Employees Union* [1981] AC 363.

Anisminic as one on which they, as a court, had the final say. However, did this mean that *all questions of statutory interpretation* should be treated in this way, such that the decision-maker's conclusion would always be capable of being overturned if a reviewing court took a different view? There was little clarity on this point until the later decision of the House of Lords in *Page*, in which Lord Browne-Wilkinson articulated the general principle that decisions affected by errors of law can be quashed on judicial review.[7] This raises two questions: *why should courts exercise such power* and *what are the exceptions to this general principle*? It is convenient to deal with these questions in tandem because, as we will see, the limits of the justifications for the general principle help to shape the exceptions to it.

The first (of three) potential justifications concerns what is sometimes called *relative institutional competence*. This idea holds that in deciding the proper extent of the courts' role, we should consider how qualified courts are to deal with the relevant issue. If, as here, the relevant issue is the meaning of the law, then (the argument runs) it stands to reason that courts should be in the driving seat, since they, after all, are the experts when it comes to interpreting and applying the law. However, while this argument is superficially attractive, the assumption upon which it rests is, at best, a half-truth, for it does not follow that courts are *inevitably* better placed than decision-makers to interpret the statute.

> **Q** Arden LJ has noted that courts often approach questions of statutory interpretation 'by peeling away the layers of meaning and by analysing the policy choices that have been made to arrive at the form of words that has been used. In other words, statutory interpretation is an intensive exercise that involves *drilling down* into the substratum of meaning of the statutory provision'.[8] In the example set out at the beginning of the chapter, the Minister is only authorised to take planning decisions in relation to 'major infrastructure projects'. What sort of policy and other factors might influence the court in attaching meaning to the term 'major infrastructure project'?

Arden LJ's comments indicate that judges may not have a monopoly of wisdom in this area: answering 'legal' questions of statutory interpretation may require policy choices to be made. The courts have therefore recognised (with varying degrees of clarity) a number of exceptions to the general principle that they should have the last word on questions of law. For example, when, in *Page*, the court was confronted with a system of law (the statutes of a university) unfamiliar to it, it did not substitute its interpretation for that of the decision-maker. Even if the law in question is the regular law of the land,

---

[7] *R v Lord President of the Privy Council, ex p Page* [1993] AC 682. Until recently, no such general principle was recognised in Scotland, where the concept of non-jurisdictional errors of law continued to be recognised: *Watt v Lord Advocate* 1979 SC 120, 131. However, in *Eba v Advocate General for Scotland* [2011] UKSC 29, [2011] 3 WLR 149, Lord Hope rejected that view, which, he said, was incompatible with the House of Lords' 'landmark' decision in *Anisminic*.

[8] Arden, 'The Changing Judicial Role: Human Rights, Community Law and the Intention of Parliament' [2008] CLJ 487, 490.

the court may still be willing to allow the decision-maker's interpretation of it to stand if the decision-maker is a legally competent one, such as another court.[9]

More generally, it has been said that when the statutory provision under consideration is extremely vague, the reviewing court will not simply impose its own view—because it cannot be confident that it is the correct one. Instead, it will interfere only if the decision-maker has adopted an unreasonable definition of the term.[10]

The second factor that arguably justifies giving courts ultimate power over questions of law is that the *independence of the judiciary* makes courts uniquely placed to interpret the law in an objective manner.[11] However, this argument will not always be compelling, particularly if a statute confers discretion in broad terms that raise controversial policy questions. Here, it may be more appropriate to leave the decision to (for example) an elected decision-maker. For example, in *Puhlhofer*, the claimant was eligible for assistance from his local authority if he was homeless—which he would be if he had no 'accommodation' within the meaning of the relevant legislation.[12] Rather than treating the meaning of the word 'accommodation' as a question of law, the House of Lords said that it was a question of fact for the local authority to determine. This sort of approach was endorsed by the Supreme Court in *Jones v First-tier Tribunal*.[13] In a surprisingly frank judgment, the Court indicated that whether something is to be characterised as an issue of law or fact may turn, in part, upon to what extent close judicial scrutiny is felt to be warranted. This provides a potentially significant escape route from the strictures of the *Page* principle: while it remains the case that (in general) questions of law are jurisdictional, cases like *Jones* and *Puhlhofer* show that the distinction between questions of law and fact is highly malleable.

The final factor said to justify giving to courts the last word over questions of law is *consistency*. In *Pearlman*, Lord Denning argued that it would be 'intolerable' if different decision-makers were allowed to reach conflicting interpretations of legislation.[14] He therefore thought that reviewing courts should always have the ultimate power to determine the meaning of the law in the interests of consistency. But while consistency may often be desirable, it is not necessarily a knock-out argument. There may, for example, only be one decision-maker, in which case the need for consistency as between decision-makers is irrelevant. And even if there are many different decision-makers (eg if the power is given to all local authorities), it does not automatically follow that consistency is more important than, say, allowing each body to reach its own interpretation in the light of its own expertise and experience of local circumstances.

---

[9] *Re Racal Communications Ltd* [1981] AC 374, 383, *per* Lord Diplock. See also *R (Cart) v Upper Tribunal* [2011] UKSC 28, [2012] 1 AC 663, discussed in Chapter 16, section 5.6.

[10] *R v Monopolies and Mergers Commission, ex p South Yorkshire Transport* [1993] 1 WLR 23.

[11] Farina, 'Statutory Interpretation and the Balance of Power in the Administrative State' (1989) 89 Col LR 452. See also Hare, 'The Separation of Powers and Judicial Review for Error of Law', in Forsyth and Hare (eds), *The Golden Metwand and the Crooked Cord* (Oxford 1998).

[12] *R v Hillingdon London Borough Council, ex p Puhlhofer* [1986] AC 484.

[13] [2013] UKSC 19, [2013] 2 WLR 1012.

[14] *Pearlman v Keepers and Governors of Harrow School* [1979] QB 56.

Q Think back to the example, given earlier, of a ministerial power to approve 'major infrastructure projects'. Should the definition of this statutory term be regarded as a question of law such that the reviewing court, if it were to disagree with the Minister's definition, could substitute it with its own?

2.3 Applying the statute to the facts

Even if our hypothetical Minister adopts a lawful *definition* of 'major infrastructure project', this is not an end of the matter, for she must, within our example, then decide whether the proposed airport is, *in fact*, such a project. As indicated in Figure 12.2, this is analogous to working out whether two pieces of a jigsaw fit together. In strict logic, a distinction should be drawn between what we call in Figure 12.2 'questions of fact' and 'questions of fit'—that is, it must be logically necessary to determine *both* what the relevant factual characteristics are *and* whether those factual characteristics fit the statutory definition. In relation to our example, depending on the correct definition of 'major infrastructure project', the relevant questions of fact may involve looking at the physical size and location of the proposed airport, its likely economic impact, and its overall significance. Having determined these matters, it would then be necessary to move on to the question of fit: given the proposed airport's size, impact, and on so, does it constitute a 'major infrastructure project', thus triggering the Minister's legal capacity to wrest from the local authority the power to decide whether the scheme should go ahead?

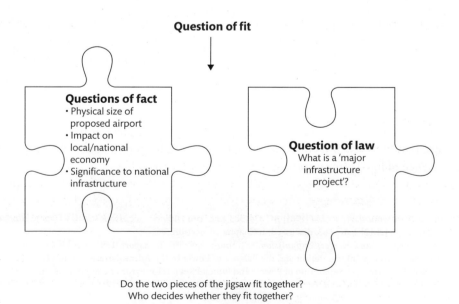

Do the two pieces of the jigsaw fit together?
Who decides whether they fit together?

Figure 12.2 Applying the facts to the law

In reality, neither decision-makers nor reviewing courts necessarily draw a clear distinction between questions of fact and fit, often treating them as linked or even inseparable matters. Nevertheless, the key question for our purposes is: who has the final say as to whether the facts satisfy the statutory test? There is no 'one size fits all' answer to this question. The case law reveals varying judicial attitudes, principally informed, it seems, by the objectivity of the criterion laid down by the statute.

This is illustrated by the Supreme Court's decision in *R (A) v Croydon London Borough Council*.[15] The case centred upon s 20(1) of the Children Act 1989, which states that local authorities must provide accommodation for any 'child in need' within their area who appears to require accommodation on one of several grounds.[16] There was no dispute as to the meaning of the statute—the Act says that 'child' means 'person under the age of 18'[17]—but the defendant councils asserted that the claimants were not under the age of 18 and that no duty to provide accommodation therefore arose. Were the councils' views final (unless unreasonable) or could the court over-turn them if it disagreed? The Supreme Court held that the clarity and objectivity of the term 'child' pointed to the latter conclusion: as Baroness Hale put it, 'the question whether a person is a "child" . . . is a [question with a] right or wrong answer'.[18] The position is different in relation to the question whether an individual is a 'child *in need*', however. As Baroness Hale observed, answering this question involves making value judgements that 'it is entirely reasonable to assume that Parliament intended . . . to be [made] by the public authority'.[19]

This case shows, then, that the more objective a statutory term, the more likely the court is to insist on the final word on questions of fit. It also shows that where a composite term, such as 'child in need', is used, different approaches may apply to each component if one is more objective than the other.

> **Q** In our example, the question is whether the proposed airport is a 'major infrastructure project'. In light of the discussion so far, do you think that a reviewing court would interfere with the Minister's conclusion on that point if it were to disagree with it, or only if the Minister were to have come to a perverse or unreasonable conclusion?

2.4 Jurisdiction: concluding remarks

The issue of jurisdiction—that is, whether the decision-maker really does have the power to decide the matter in question—may appear to be highly technical. In some respects, it is. But lying at the root of that apparently technical question is a more fundamental one concerning the respective roles of the reviewing court and the decision-maker. The greater the authority asserted and used by the court to control the scope

---

[15] [2009] UKSC 8, [2009] 1 WLR 2557. See also *Khawaja v Secretary of State for the Home Department* [1984] AC 74.

[16] eg that there is no one who has parental responsibility for him.

[17] Children Act 1989, s 105(1).   [18] *Croydon*, [27].   [19] *Croydon*, [26].

of the decision-maker's power, the correspondingly narrower the decision-maker's discretion becomes. In this context, therefore, one of the enduring difficulties encountered in this area of the law—namely, the balance of power as between court and decision-maker—arises in a particularly stark form. We will, however, encounter that issue throughout the remainder of the chapter—most notably in section 5. There, our focus will shift from the beginning of the decision-making process, which has been our concern in this section, to the end of the process, when we consider the extent to which courts can strike down a government decision on the ground that there is something wrong with the decision itself. First, however, it is necessary to consider a series of logically prior questions that are all concerned, in different senses, with the *procedures* by which administrative decisions are taken.

3. Acting fairly

3.1 Introduction

In our example, the question is whether the Minister has the power to decide (in place of the local authority) whether a new airport should be built. This, as we know, depends on whether the airport constitutes a 'major infrastructure project'. If it does, then the Minister has the power to decide. This does not, however, mean that the Minister has free reign to do as she wishes. Establishing that the power *can* be used is one thing; but the Minister must still go on to exercise the power *lawfully*. In this section, we are concerned with the principles of 'natural justice' or 'procedural fairness'—one of several sets of legal principles with which decision-makers must comply if they are to use their power in a lawful fashion.

3.2 Different senses of 'fairness'

When people talk about whether a decision is 'fair', they might mean one of several things. They might, for instance, mean that the *content* of the decision is fair. However, our concern here is with fairness in its *procedural* sense: that is, the fairness of the *process* by which a decision is taken, as distinct from the substantive fairness of the decision *itself*. In particular, we are concerned with three elements of procedural fairness: the absence of bias, the existence of institutional independence, and the right to participate in the decision-making process (commonly, but inaccurately, called 'the right to a fair hearing').

3.3 Why act fairly?

In the following sections, we will consider the three aspects of procedural fairness outlined above. First, however, it is worth asking *why* procedural fairness is considered to be important. One reason is practical. A fair process that enables different people to have their say is—all other things being equal—more likely than an unfair process to turn up relevant information. That, in turn, makes a fair process more likely to lead to a sensible decision based on all the relevant evidence. For example, it is obviously desirable that our hypothetical Minister, before deciding whether to authorise the construction of the new airport, should be aware of such things as its likely environmental implications and impact on the local community. Following procedures that are liable to bring such information to light—including, for instance, by enabling local people to have their say—will equip the Minister to make a more informed, and perhaps better, decision. Viewed in this way, procedural fairness is a means to an end—the end being the making of better-informed, and so better, decisions.

For some, this *instrumental* view of fairness is predominant: it supplies the main justification for requiring decision-makers to act fairly.[20] Others, however, emphasise a *non-instrumental* conception of fairness that presents procedural fairness as an end in itself. This view is premised on what Tribe has called 'the elementary idea that to be a *person*, rather than a *thing*, is at least to be *consulted* about what is done with one'.[21] In other words, if the dignity and status of individuals is to be properly respected, they must at least be given the opportunity to have their views listened to before the taking of decisions that are liable to affect them.

Reverting back to our example, this justification suggests that it is important for the Minister to consult properly with local people because the decision whether to permit the construction of a new airport is one that will—for good or ill—radically affect their lives. Without such participation, the Minister's decision would be seen as an illegitimate exercise of governmental power that did not adequately respect the status and dignity of those likely to be profoundly affected by it.

These two views are not necessarily in tension. It might reasonably be argued that fair treatment should be accorded to individuals *both* because this is necessary if due respect is to be accorded to their status as human beings *and* because it is likely to enable better decisions to be taken.[22] But the two views will sometimes conflict. For example, where the evidence in favour of a particular decision is very strong, going through some form of fair procedure may seem to serve little practical purpose. However, the assumption that due process is redundant, and can therefore be jettisoned, in such circumstances carries risks. As Megarry J famously put it in *John v Rees*, 'the path of the law is strewn with examples of open and shut cases which, somehow, were not; of unanswerable charges which, in the event, were completely answered; of inexplicable conduct which was fully explained; of fixed and unalterable determinations that, by discussion, suffered a change'.[23] Until recently, it was for the court—as a matter of discretion—to determine whether to waive the requirement to act fairly in the face of the argument that a fair process would make no difference. However, we will see in the next chapter that recently enacted legislation takes this matter out of the court's hands by ruling out successful judicial review challenges when it is 'highly likely' that a failure to follow a legal requirement—such as acting fairly—makes no substantial difference to the outcome of the decision-making process for the claimant.[24]

---

[20] See, eg Galligan, *Due Process and Fair Procedures: A Study of Administrative Procedures* (Oxford 1996); *Secretary of State for the Home Department v AF (No 3)* [2009] UKHL 28, [2009] 3 WLR 74, [60], *per* Lord Phillips.

[21] *American Constitutional Law* (New York 1988), p 666.

[22] See further Allan, 'Procedural Fairness and the Duty of Respect' (1998) 18 OJLS 497.

[23] [1970] Ch 345, 402.　　[24] See Chapter 13, section 4.1.

> **Q** Should courts insist upon procedural fairness even if it would not make a difference to the outcome? Are instrumental arguments about a fair procedure making no difference always equally persuasive? For instance, should such arguments cut less ice if something as fundamental as the liberty of the individual is at stake?

3.4 Impartiality

If a decision-maker is actually biased, the process cannot be said to be fair. It is therefore unlawful for a decision-maker to decide a case in order (for example) to secure some financial benefit for himself or in order to do a favour for a friend. However, actual bias is hard to establish. Showing that a decision-maker *stood to gain* financially from his decision is one thing; proving that he was *actually influenced* by such selfish considerations is a different, and more difficult, matter. If the law were to go no further than a rule against actual bias, many situations would arise in which there was a suspicion that the decision-maker may have been improperly influenced, but the decision would, in the absence of clear evidence, nevertheless stand. This, in turn, would be likely to undermine public confidence in the integrity of the decision-making system.

The law therefore embraces not only a rule against *actual* bias, but also a rule against *apparent* bias. The principle was famously set out in *R v Sussex Justices, ex p McCarthy*.[25] A justices' clerk who had been present when the magistrates retired to consider a dangerous driving case also happened to be a partner in the law firm that was acting against the defendant in a related civil action. When this came to light, the defendant sought to have his dangerous driving conviction quashed. Lord Hewart CJ, giving judgment in the Divisional Court, accepted that the clerk had played no part in the justices' decision: he had been in the room when the decision was made, but the justices had not found it necessary to consult him. Nevertheless, said Lord Hewart, 'it is not merely of some importance but is of fundamental importance that justice should not only be done, but should manifestly and undoubtedly be seen to be done'.[26] Applying this principle, the conviction was quashed because the clerk's conflict of interest gave rise to a sufficient appearance of bias; proof of actual bias was unnecessary.

3.4.1 Interests that automatically disqualify the decision-maker

Ideally, situations such as those that arose in *McCarthy* should not arise. Decision-makers should decline to act if their participation would give rise to an appearance of bias (unless the parties are willing to overlook the apparent conflict of interests[27]). It is desirable, therefore, that the law provides clear, simple guidance so that decision-makers

---

[25] [1924] 1 KB 256.   [26] *McCarthy*, 259.

[27] Provided that the parties are in full receipt of the relevant facts and unequivocally signal that they are content to allow the decision-maker to participate, they may not subsequently raise an objection on the grounds of apparent bias: *Locabail (UK) Ltd v Bayfield Properties Ltd* [2000] QB 451, 475.

know whether to stand aside. To that end, the law has come to recognise three types of interest that straightforwardly and automatically disqualify the decision-maker.

First, there are those cases in which *the decision-maker is a party*. This reflects what Lord Browne-Wilkinson referred to as the 'fundamental principle . . . that a man may not be a judge in his own cause'.[28] The reason for treating such a situation as automatically disqualifying the decision-maker needs no explanation.

Second, where *the decision-maker has a financial or proprietary interest in the outcome of the decision*, this is taken to be tantamount to his acting as a judge in his own cause; such interests disqualify the decision-maker automatically. For instance, in *Dimes v The Proprietors of the Grand Junction Canal*,[29] the decision of the then Lord Chancellor, Lord Cottenham—who had, in legal proceedings, granted relief to a company in which he was a shareholder—was quashed. Giving judgment in the House of Lords, Lord Campbell said that 'the maxim that no man is to be a judge in his own cause . . . is not to be confined to a cause in which he is a party, but [also] applies to a cause in which he has an interest'.[30] Whether quashing Lord Cottenham's decision served any useful purpose is, however, questionable, given that it was said that '[n]o one [could] suppose that [he] could be, in the remotest degree, influenced by the interests that he had in [the company]'.[31] Olowofoyeku therefore suggests that 'automatic disqualification is draconian, disproportionate and unnecessary' because it captures too many situations, including those that do not really give rise to any suspicion.[32] That criticism is, however, partly answered by the fact that the courts are now reluctant to hold the automatic disqualification rule applicable when the likelihood of financial benefit is remote. For instance, in *Locabail*[33] a judge was alleged to have a financial interest in the outcome of the case, and it was said that he was disqualified from acting on that basis. However, this argument failed because the possibility of the judge benefiting from deciding the case in a particular way was so small: it was contingent upon a long and uncertain chain of events unfolding.

Q Where should the line be drawn between interests that are and are not sufficient to trigger the automatic disqualification rule? To what extent may excluding insubstantial or tenuous financial interests be incompatible with the existence of a simple rule that provides clear guidance to decision-makers?

Third, according to *Pinochet (No 2)*,[34] *certain other interests* can trigger the automatic disqualification rule. The claimant, Augusto Pinochet, following his role in a successful military coup, was head of state in Chile from 1973 to 1990.

---

[28] *R v Bow Street Metropolitan Stipendiary Magistrate, ex p Pinochet Ugarte (No 2)* [2000] 1 AC 119, 132.
[29] (1852) 3 HLC 759. At this time, the Lord Chancellor sat as a judge, although he no longer does so: see Chapter 6, section 4.3.2.
[30] *Dimes*, 793.   [31] *Dimes*, 793.
[32] 'The *Nemo Judex* Rule: The Case against Automatic Disqualification' [2000] PL 456, 475.
[33] *Locabail (UK) Ltd v Bayfield Properties Ltd* [2000] QB 451.
[34] *R v Bow Street Metropolitan Stipendiary Magistrate, ex p Pinochet Ugarte (No 2)* [2000] 1 AC 119.

Reports published in 1991 and 2004–05 alleged that Pinochet's regime killed over 2,000 people for political reasons and tortured many times that number.[35] While Pinochet was in the UK in 1998, Spain sought his extradition to stand trial for alleged crimes against humanity.[36] Pinochet argued that, as a former head of state, he was immune from arrest and extradition in respect of events alleged to have occurred whilst in office. In *Pinochet (No 1)*,[37] the House of Lords ruled, by a three–two majority, against Pinochet. When hearing the case, their Lordships allowed Amnesty International (AI), a well-known group that campaigns against human rights abuses, to intervene.[38] It later came to light that Lord Hoffmann, one of the majority judges, was a director of Amnesty International Charity Ltd (AICL), a charity that was intimately related to, and undertook work on behalf of, AI in the UK. Pinochet therefore asked the House of Lords to set aside its decision.

The House of Lords did precisely that in *Pinochet (No 2)*,[39] holding that while Lord Hoffmann was not actually party to the case—because 'Lord Hoffmann, AICL and the executive committee of AI are in law separate people'[40]—he nevertheless had an interest that automatically disqualified him. This did not arise straightforwardly on the ground that his affiliation with AICL evidenced an interest in promoting respect for human rights; rather, AI and AICL were 'parts of an entity or movement working in different fields towards the same goals' of procuring the abolition of torture and extra-judicial detention, and Lord Hoffmann's association with AI—a party—through AICL meant that he was involved 'in promoting the same causes in the same organisation as is a party to the suit'.[41]

The upshot is that automatic disqualification now extends beyond cases in which the decision-maker is actually a party or has a financial interest in the outcome. This has been criticised on a number of grounds—most notably because it creates uncertainty, the precise circumstances that trigger application of the *Pinochet* rule being far from clear. It has also been argued that an unintended consequence of the decision may be that judges will decide to withdraw to some extent from public life—for example, as directors or trustees of charitable organisations—in order to ensure that they do not find themselves disqualified from deciding cases.[42] These concerns should not, how-ever, be overstated. In *Pinochet* itself, Lord Browne-Wilkinson emphasised the 'very unusual circumstances' of the case,[43] while the Court of Appeal in *Locabail* subse-quently implied that the *Pinochet* rule should be read narrowly.[44] As a result, the cases in which *Pinochet* applies are likely to be rare.

---

[35] *The National Commission for Truth and Reconciliation Report* (Santiago 1991); *The National Commission on Political Imprisonment and Torture Report* (Santiago 2004–05).

[36] ie his removal to Spain to stand trial.

[37] *R v Bow Street Metropolitan Stipendiary Magistrate, ex p Pinochet Ugarte* [2000] 1 AC 61.

[38] This means that it was allowed, through counsel, to put certain arguments to the court.

[39] *R v Bow Street Metropolitan Stipendiary Magistrate, ex p Pinochet Ugarte (No 2)* [2000] 1 AC 119.

[40] *Pinochet (No 2)*, 134, *per* Lord Browne-Wilkinson.

[41] *Pinochet (No 2)*, 134, *per* Lord Browne-Wilkinson.

[42] Malleson, 'Judicial Bias and Disqualification after *Pinochet (No 2)*' (2000) 63 MLR 119.

[43] *Pinochet (No 2)*, 135.   [44] *Locabail (UK) Ltd v Bayfield Properties Ltd* [2000] QB 451.

Q Look back to our hypothetical case set out at the very beginning of this chapter. If the Minister were to make a decision on the construction of the new airport, would he be automatically disqualified on the basis of
- (i) owning land in a nearby town that, some property experts claim, is likely to appreciate in value if the airport is built?
- (ii) the fact that his son is employed by a construction firm that would probably be awarded a contract to build part of the airport?
- (iii) his membership of an environmental pressure group that is vehemently opposed to any expansion of air travel?

3.4.2 Situations giving rise to the appearance of a real possibility of bias

Even if a decision-maker is not automatically disqualified, the circumstances may be such that her participation would undermine public confidence in the fairness of the system. Following a good deal of instability in the case law, the House of Lords, in *Porter v Magill*,[45] settled on a test for identifying when (beyond circumstances triggering the automatic disqualification rule) there will be a disqualifying level of apparent bias. The question that the courts must now ask themselves is *whether the circumstances would lead a fair-minded and informed observer to conclude that there was a real possibility of bias*.[46] Three key issues arise in relation to the meaning and application of this test.

The first relates to the *level of concern* that must exist as to the impartiality of the decision-maker. Part of the uncertainty that afflicted the case law prior to *Porter v Magill* related to precisely this question: was a *probability* of bias required, or would a *possibility* suffice? The position is now clear: only a 'real possibility' of bias is needed; a 'probably' need not be shown.[47] This approach is consistent with the *McCarthy* principle's emphasis on the importance of public perception, bearing in mind that confidence is liable to be damaged by the perception that it is *possible*—even if it is not *probable*—that a decision was tainted by bias.

Second, *through whose eyes* does this assessment fall to be made? Should the court ask itself how things look to it, or should it try to ascertain what the ordinary, reasonable person is likely to think? In *R v Gough*, Lord Goff created confusion by eliding these two possibilities, arguing that it was unnecessary 'to require that the court should look at the matter through the eyes of a reasonable man, because the court in cases such as these personifies the reasonable man.'[48] However, this formulation was taken in some subsequent cases to imply wholesale departure from the *McCarthy* principle, such that it was for reviewing courts to determine the likelihood of actual bias, whether or not reasonable people might have perceived a risk of bias.[49] Orthodoxy was restored

---

[45] [2001] UKHL 67, [2002] 2 AC 357.

[46] *Porter v Magill*, [102]–[103], adapting a test laid down by the Court of Appeal in *Re Medicaments and Related Classes of Goods (No 2)* [2001] 1 WLR 700.

[47] *R v Gough* [1993] AC 646; *Porter v Magill*, [103].   [48] *Gough*, 670.

[49] See, eg *R v Inner West London Coroner, ex p Dallaglio* [1994] 4 All ER 139.

in *Porter v Magill*, which emphasises that the court must ask whether *a fair-minded and informed observer* would perceive a real possibility of bias. As Lord Philips MR acknowledged in the *Medicaments* case, such an approach caters for the possibility that even if the court is 'inclined to accept a statement about what the [decision-maker] knew at any material time', there may still be 'public scepticism'.[50] This reflects the fact that, as Lord Rodger put it in an extrajudicial speech, 'the whole point of [the fair-minded and informed observer] is that he or she does not share the viewpoint of the judge'.[51]

Thus it has been held that the fair-minded observer would consider a real possibility of bias to exist where, for example, a barrister appeared before a tribunal comprising lay members with whom he had previously sat on the tribunal in his judicial capacity,[52] and where someone involved in making or publicly advising upon the meaning of rules was subsequently called upon to interpret them[53] or to pronounce upon their legality.[54] In some cases, however, courts have arguably been too quick to imbue the notional fair-minded observer with judge-like abilities. For example, in *Gillies*, a tribunal's decision to terminate the payment of a disability-related benefit to the claimant was challenged on the ground that a member of the tribunal was a doctor who also worked for a company that provided healthcare reports on benefit claimants to the government agency the decision of which the claimant was challenging before the tribunal.[55] The claimant's argument before the House of Lords—that the doctor's two roles risked a perception of bias sufficient to impugn the tribunal's decision—failed. Lord Hope thought that it should be assumed that the fair-minded observer is 'able to distinguish between what is relevant and what is irrelevant, and that he is able when exercising his judgment to decide what weight should be given to the facts that are relevant'.[56] The observer would therefore appreciate that the doctor was capable of exhibiting sufficient 'professional detachment' to enable her to 'exercise her own independent judgment' when sitting on the tribunal, uninfluenced by the fact that she also performed work on behalf of the government agency that was a party to the dispute that fell for determination before the tribunal.[57] The risk, of course, is that the more judge-like the fair-minded observer is deemed to be, the less likely is the fair-minded observer test to yield results that sufficiently reflect public perceptions—and that therefore uphold public confidence.

This leads on to our third point, which concerns the *amount of knowledge* to be imputed to the observer. The test laid down in *Porter v Magill* refers to a 'fair-minded *and informed* observer'—but just *how* informed? In principle, the observer should know only that that is within 'the ken of ordinary, reasonably well informed members of the public', since it is their perceptions of the integrity of the decision-making

---

[50] *Re Medicaments and Related Classes of Goods (No 2)* [2001] 1 WLR 700, [67].
[51] Quoted in *Belize Bank Ltd v Attorney General of Belize* [2011] UKPC 36, [99].
[52] *Lawal v Northern Spirit Ltd* [2003] UKHL 35, [2004] 1 All ER 187.
[53] *Davidson v Scottish Ministers (No2)* [2004] UKHL 34, 2005 1 SC (HL) 7.
[54] *R (Carroll) v Secretary of State for the Home Department* [2005] UKHL 13, [2005] 1 WLR 688.
[55] *Gillies v Secretary of State for Work and Pensions* [2006] UKHL 2, [2006] 1 WLR 781.
[56] *Gillies*, [17].   [57] *Gillies*, [18].

system around which this branch of the law is designed.[58] On occasion, however, the courts have perhaps shown undue enthusiasm for imputing knowledge to the observer, with the result, intended or otherwise, that his viewpoint becomes indistinguishable from that of the court itself. For example, in *Taylor v Lawrence*,[59] it transpired that a judge had received free legal services from the claimants' solicitors the day before he gave judgment in favour of the claimant. To the average layperson, this may well give rise to a suspicion of bias, but the Court of Appeal held that the fair-minded and informed observer would not share this perspective. However, the Court could only reach this conclusion by imputing to the notional observer extensive knowledge of the legal community and of the way in which judges and lawyers interact with one another—knowledge that the average person doubtless lacks.

Taylor may be contrasted with *Lesage v Mauritius Commercial Bank Ltd*,[60] in which the Privy Council held that when a trial judge had received a letter from a defendant containing prejudicial information but failed to confront this issue in court, a fair-minded observer would conclude that there was a possibility that the judge, as a result, would be more sceptical about the defence. The fact that the Privy Council did not dismiss the possibility of perception of bias on the ground that the observer would appreciate the judges' capacity for compartmentalising information suggests a different approach from that which applied in *Taylor*. This discrepancy highlights the inherent instability of a test that turns upon judicial construction of a fictitious observer. Such difficulties have prompted one commentator to argue that courts should dispense with the fair-minded and informed observer altogether.[61]

Q Look back at the example given at the very beginning of this chapter. What would be the legal implications (if any) if our hypothetical Minister were to refuse permission to build the new airport, and it later come to light that he was having an affair with the chief executive of a company backing a rival site for a new airport?

3.4.3 Politics and administration

So far, we have been mainly concerned with cases in which the impartiality of *judges* has been challenged. But other sorts of decision-makers—Ministers, local authorities, government agencies, and so on—are held to the same standard.[62] As Sedley J held in the *Kirkstall* case, the normal test for impartiality 'is of general application in public law and is not limited to judicial or quasi-judicial bodies or proceedings'.[63] This means that the automatic disqualification principle and the fair-minded observer test apply to political and administrative, as well as to judicial, decision-makers. However,

---

[58] See *Medicaments* at [65].   [59] [2002] EWCA Civ 90, [2003] QB 528.   [60] [2012] UKPC 41.

[61] Olowofoyeku, 'Bias and the Informed Observer: A Call for a Return to *Gough*' [2009] CLJ 388, 406–7.

[62] *R v Secretary of State for the Environment, ex p Kirkstall Valley Campaign Ltd* [1996] 3 All ER 304; *R (Island Farm Development Ltd) v Brigend County Borough Council* [2006] EWHC 2189 (Admin), [2007] BLGR 60.

[63] *Kirkstall*, 325.

politicians cannot and should not be expected to behave in the same way as judges. As Sedley J went on to observe in *Kirkstall*, the law must accommodate the fact that such decision-makers—particularly if they are elected—'will take up office with publicly stated views on a variety of policy issues'.[64]

Consider, for instance, the *Island Farm* case.[65] The claimant company had been negotiating with the respondent council over the purchase of a piece of land. A local election interrupted the negotiation process, and the new council then refused to sell. That refusal was challenged by the company on the ground that certain councillors were tainted by a lack of impartiality given that they had spoken out, during the election campaign, against the sale of the land. Collins J held that, 'whatever their views, [councillors] must approach their decision-making with an open mind in the sense that they must have regard to all material considerations and be prepared to change their views if persuaded that they should'.[66] However, that did not make it improper for them to approach the issues with a particular view as their starting point. It would be wrong for councillors—and, by extension, other decision-makers—to lapse into *predetermination* (in the sense of having a closed mind), but it was entirely acceptable for them to have a *predisposition* in favour of a given policy. Concluding that 'the fair-minded and informed observer must be taken to appreciate that predisposition is not predetermination and that Councillors can be assumed to be aware of their obligations', Collins J rejected the claimant's complaint.[67] Legislation now provides that a local councillor (but not other decision-makers such as Ministers) is not to be taken to have had a closed mind just because she has previously done something indicating her view on a relevant matter.[68] However, given the court's measured approach in *Island Farm*, it is unclear that the legislation adds much to the position at which the common law had already arrived.

> **Q** Do you agree that, as outlined in this section, political decision-makers should be regarded differently from judges? Might it be possible to go further and argue that democracy *requires* such differential treatment?

3.5 Independence

3.5.1 The issue—and an example

So far, we have been concerned with the importance of decision-makers acting impartially—a requirement that is centrally concerned with their *personal circumstances and characteristics*.[69] The need for impartiality therefore impacts upon whether a

---

[64] *Kirkstall*, 325.

[65] *R (Island Farm Development Ltd) v Brigend County Borough Council* [2006] EWHC 2189 (Admin) [2007] BLGR 60. See, to similar effect, *R (Condron) v National Assembly for Wales* [2006] EWCA Civ 1573, [2007] 2 P & CR 4.

[66] *Island Farm*, [31].   [67] *Island Farm*, [32].   [68] Localism Act 2011, s 25.

[69] eg questions about whether someone stands to gain financially or is motivated by self-interest or ill will turn on his personal situation.

given individual can properly make a particular decision. We now turn to the distinct question of *independence*. Whereas impartiality and its converse, bias, are concerned with the personal attributes and circumstances of the decision-maker, independence is concerned with her institutional position. For instance, in *Anderson*,[70] the claimant, a convicted murderer, argued that the Home Secretary should play no part in determining how long those convicted of murder should spend in prison before being considered for release on parole. The argument, however, was not that that *particular* Home Secretary was or appeared to be biased, but that *no* Home Secretary should make such a decision because it amounted, in effect, to a sentencing decision that ought to have been taken by an independent judge rather than by a government Minister.

It is only relatively recently that such challenges have been made possible. In most instances, the choice of decision-maker is ordained by Parliament itself through primary legislation. Indeed, this was so in *Anderson*: s 29 of the Crime (Sentences) Act 1997 unambiguously gave the Home Secretary the power to decide on the pre-parole detention period. However, a requirement of institutional independence is included in the European Convention on Human Rights (ECHR), to which the Human Rights Act 1998 (HRA) gives effect in UK law. Although the courts cannot override or disapply legislation that conflicts with the ECHR, they can—as did the House of Lords in *Anderson*—issue a 'declaration of incompatibility' when an Act of Parliament is at odds with rights protected by the HRA.[71] This means that courts can now rule on whether decision-making arrangements are sufficiently independent, even if those arrangements are laid down in primary legislation.

3.5.2 When is an independent decision-maker required?

The part of the ECHR that is of present concern is Art 6(1), which says: 'In the determination of his civil rights and obligations or of any criminal charge against him, everyone is entitled to a fair and public hearing within a reasonable time by an independent and impartial tribunal established by law.' 'Independent' here means independent of the executive branch of government.[72] It is easy to see why such a requirement should apply to the conduct of civil and criminal proceedings: it is axiomatic, under the separation of powers, that the criminal liability and legal rights of individuals should be determined in a forum that is above the political fray.[73]

However, Art 6(1) has also been held to apply to the making of some administrative decisions.[74] This raises significant questions about *accountability*—one of the key themes with which we are concerned in this book. One of the hallmarks of independence (in the presently relevant sense) is freedom from external pressures, such as public opinion, parliamentary scrutiny, and the electoral process. It is precisely because judges are free from such pressures that we entrust to them decisions about criminal and civil liability— decisions that are best made in an objective, detached, evidence-based way. But where

---

[70] *R (Anderson) v Secretary of State for the Home Department* [2002] UKHL 46, [2003] 1 AC 837.
[71] See further Chapter 18, section 3.4.5.   [72] *V v United Kingdom* (2000) 30 EHRR 121, [114].
[73] See further Chapter 6, section 4.   [74] *Ringeisen v Austria (No 1)* (1979–80) 1 EHRR 455.

decisions fall to be made about controversial issues of policy, there is a strong argument for saying that they should *not* be made by independent bodies such as courts, but by a politically accountable government decision-maker. As Lord Nolan pointed out, to entrust such decisions to 'an independent and impartial body with no central electoral accountability would not only be a recipe for chaos: it would be profoundly undemocratic'.[75]

What, then, is the effect of Art 6(1)? Does it require independent judges to take decisions that might more appropriately be left to politically accountable decision-makers? Article 6(1) stipulates that matters must be entrusted to independent decision-makers when they entail determining either criminal liability or civil rights and obligations. Few administrative decisions involve determining criminal liability,[76] but what of 'civil rights and obligations'? It has been held that such rights and obligations are at stake in, for example, disciplinary proceedings impacting upon a person's right to pursue his profession,[77] compulsory purchase by the state of an individual's land,[78] and decisions about parents' rights of access to their children.[79] In contrast, civil rights and obligations are not in play in decisions about taxation[80] and immigration.[81]

In *Ali v Birmingham City Council*, Lord Collins observed that the ECtHR has been 'reluctant to enunciate principles' that allow a line to be drawn between administrative decisions that do and do not engage Art 6(1).[82] In *Ali*, the Supreme Court attempted to correct that omission. The case was concerned with whether a local authority's statutory obligation to provide accommodation to certain homeless persons had ceased to apply on the ground that suitable accommodation had been offered. A dispute arose about whether such an offer had been properly made and communicated—and the claimants alleged that because the statutory machinery for resolving such disputes involved a local authority housing officer, it lacked independence in the Art 6(1) sense.

But did Art 6(1) actually apply? The Supreme Court held that it did not. First, deciding whether someone was, in the first place, entitled to accommodation involved the making of 'evaluative judgments' as to whether the statutory homelessness criteria were met.[83] Second, even if someone was homeless in the statutory sense, discretion had to be exercised in deciding what accommodation to offer them. This meant, said the Court, that there was no relevant 'right' to accommodation. However, the ECtHR disagreed. It gave no weight to the fact that discretion had to be exercised in determining whether there was any entitlement to accommodation, and concluded that the Supreme Court had overplayed the argument concerning the need for discretion to be exercised in relation to fulfilling the obligation to provide accommodation to an entitled person. In short, the ECtHR largely unpicked the Supreme Court's attempt to articulate a

---

[75] *R (Alconbury Developments Ltd) v Secretary of State for the Environment, Transport and the Regions* [2001] UKHL 23, [2003] 2 AC 295, [60]. See also *Runa Begum v Tower Hamlets London Borough Council* [2003] UKHL 5, [2003] 2 AC 430.

[76] But some do—eg prison authorities' rulings on whether a prisoner has breached disciplinary rules and should therefore have his sentence extended: *Ezeh v United Kingdom* (2004) 39 EHRR 1.

[77] *König v Federal Republic of Germany* (1979–80) 2 EHRR 170.

[78] *Sporrong v Sweden* (1983) 5 EHRR 35.   [79] *W v United Kingdom* (1988) 10 EHRR 29.

[80] *Ferrazzini v Italy* (2002) 34 EHRR 45.

[81] *Uppal v United Kingdom* (1981) 3 EHRR 391; *Maaouia v France* (2001) 33 EHRR 42.

[82] [2010] UKSC 8, [2010] 2 AC 39, [60].   [83] *Ali*, [49], *per* Lord Hope.

principled limit to the scope of Art 6(1), thereby reinstating precisely the sort of uncertainty in this regard that the latter Court's judgment in *Ali* had sought to remedy.

> **Q** Look back at our example at the beginning of the chapter. Is this the sort of decision to which the requirement of independent decision-making ought to apply? What if the decision to give the go-ahead to the new airport were to entail forcing people to sell to the government land comprising part of the site of the new airport? Would this be a matter to which Art 6(1) would apply?

3.5.3 What does Art 6(1) require?

When it applies, Art 6(1) demands—or at least appears to demand—an 'independent' decision-maker. However, the case law of the ECtHR makes it clear that that requirement can be met in either of two ways.[84] The first, and most obvious way, is by the decision's being taken in the first place by a body that is independent. Second, however, Art 6(1) can often be satisfied provided that a non-independent decision-maker is subject to oversight by an independent judicial body. We thus refer in this context to the *curative principle*: the notion that subsequent independent oversight can make up for an absence of independence on the part of the original decision-maker. And, importantly, as the ECtHR made clear in *Ali*, the possibility of judicial review will often in itself supply the requisite degree of independent oversight for the purpose of the curative principle.[85]

That said, however, the potency of the curative principle—and so its capacity to make up for a non-independent initial decision-maker—varies according to the circumstances. It is particularly potent in cases concerning the exercise of policy-making functions. The *Alconbury* case concerned a challenge to the involvement of the Environment Secretary in deciding whether a company should be given permission to develop a disused airfield owned by the Ministry of Defence.[86] Lord Hoffmann emphasised that the decision did 'not involve deciding between the rights or interests of particular persons'; rather, it entailed 'the exercise of a power delegated by the people as a whole to decide what the public interest requires'—a 'policy decision', in other words.[87] In such circumstances, the House of Lords concluded that Art 6(1) would be satisfied provided that there was the prospect of oversight by an independent judicial body—a requirement that was met by the possibility of seeking judicial review of the Minister's decision. In contrast, Art 6(1) requires more *actual* independence—meaning that the curative principle is less potent—when the function being performed is less about the making of policy decisions and more about finding and adjudicating on factual matters.[88] In such circumstances, the curative principle can only do so much: in effect, it is limited to rescuing decision-making regimes that already enjoy a substantial degree of actual independence.

---

[84] See, eg *Albert and Le Compte v Belgium* (1983) 5 EHRR 533; *Zumtobel v Austria* (1993) 17 EHRR 116.

[85] *Ali v United Kingdom* [2015] HLR 46, [77].

[86] *R (Alconbury Developments Ltd) v Secretary of State for the Environment, Transport and the Regions* [2001] UKHL 23, [2003] 2 AC 295.

[87] *Alconbury*, [74].   [88] *Bryan v United Kingdom* (1996) 21 EHRR 342.

This may seem technical, but can be summed up quite briefly. The underlying issue is whether the function in question is one that should be performed by an independent, court-like body, or by a politically accountable decision-maker. Since matters involving broad questions of policy fall into the latter category, the requirement of independence is, in effect, diluted: politicians and administrators can take the decisions provided that there is adequate oversight by a court. Meanwhile, since fact-finding functions fall into the former category, the requirement of independence applies more rigidly here: such functions must be performed by persons or bodies with substantial independence, albeit that if they lack the very high degree of independence enjoyed by judges, the possibility of oversight by a court may be enough to bridge the shortfall.[89] It turns out, therefore, that what appears to be a technical issue concerning the meaning of 'civil rights and obligations' and of 'independence' in fact turns on a much more substantive debate about the appropriateness, under the separation of powers, of allocating particular types of function to particular types of institution. This requires us to confront fundamental questions about accountability, and to recognise that different forms of accountability and oversight will be called for in relation to different types of decision.

3.6 The right to be heard

3.6.1 Introduction

Most people would regard it as fundamentally unfair if a decision affecting them in some important way were to be taken without first giving them an opportunity to address the decision-maker. For example, a person who stands accused of a crime will want to address the court—probably through his legal representative—in order to challenge the prosecution's version of events. Equally, an asylum seeker will want an opportunity of explaining—before any decision is taken—why she fears for her life if returned to her home country.

As we noted earlier,[90] that people should be afforded such a 'right to be heard' is important both for practical reasons (because a process that harvests information from all relevant parties will be likely to yield better, more informed decisions) and for normative reasons (because making decisions without affording those likely to be impacted a chance to advance their point of view fails to acknowledge the status and dignity of such individuals).

At one time, it was held that the right to be heard applied only if the decision-maker was discharging a 'judicial function'. This concept came to be applied in a way that meant that administrative decision-makers were often not subject to any legal duty to act fairly. However, a more liberal approach now prevails. It is informed by two central considerations: that *fairness is required* whenever an administrative decision affects someone's rights, interests, or legitimate expectations; but that *what fairness requires* is heavily dependent upon the circumstances.

---

[89] If, however, a fact-finding function is ancillary to a decision involving the exercise of discretion, this may enhance the potency of the curative principle. This point was acknowledged by the Supreme Court in *Ali*.

[90] See section 3.3.

The first of those two points can be traced to the seminal decision of the House of Lords in *Ridge v Baldwin*.[91] The case arose from a decision to dismiss the Chief Constable of Brighton. He had been acquitted of conspiracy to obstruct the course of justice and corruption, but had also been the subject of adverse judicial comments in two criminal trials. The decision to dismiss was taken by a 'watch committee' (a body that had responsibility for overseeing the work of the local police force, but which could not in any sense be regarded as a 'judicial' body) without first giving the Chief Constable any opportunity of being heard.[92] The House of Lords held that this failure rendered the watch committee's decision unlawful,[93] notwithstanding that it was not a judicial body. This laid the foundation for a much more expansive approach whereby administrative decision-makers are almost inevitably required to act fairly.

The second point, though, is that the expansive effect of *Ridge* was (quite properly) balanced by judicial recognition that what fairness requires is 'acutely sensitive to context'.[94] There is, as Figure 12.3 shows, a spectrum of possibilities, ranging from a rudimentary right to make written representations at one extreme, to something resembling a full-blown criminal trial at the other. The key issue becomes how to decide where a given case should be placed on that spectrum. Here, two central factors come into play: the *implications of the decision for the individual* and the *practical need for particular forms of procedure.*

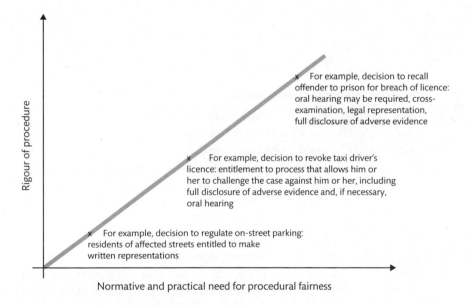

Figure 12.3 Procedural fairness—a sliding scale

---

[91] [1964] AC 40.

[92] He was later allowed to make representations through his solicitor, but the dismissal was not overturned in light of these.

[93] It was also held that the watch committee's subsequent willingness to receive representations did not, on the facts, cancel out the unfairness involved in denying the Chief Constable an opportunity to participate *before* the decision to dismiss was taken.

[94] *R (L) v West London Mental Health NHS Trust* [2014] EWCA Civ 47, [2014] 1 WLR 3103, [67], *per* Beatson LJ.

> **Q** Why do you think procedural fairness is rationed in this way? Why not say that any-one who is affected by a decision—however important or trivial—is entitled to a full-blown hearing along the lines of a criminal trial?

3.6.2 Setting the level of fairness—normative considerations

The first of these considerations reflects the normative value of fair procedures, since it effectively amounts to asking the question: 'What degree of fairness is appropriate, given what is at stake for the individual?' Two matters are important here. The first concerns the impact of the decision on the *status quo*. If the individual stands to lose something important—something that he currently has—this would seem, on an instinctive level, to demand a higher level of fairness than a situation in which someone applies for a ben-efit over and above that which they already have. On this view, a person whose house is at risk of demolition to make way for a new airport would be entitled to a higher degree of procedural fairness than someone seeking permission to build a new house.[95]

Second, the normative case for procedural fairness will be stronger— and so, other things being equal, the level of procedural justice due to the individual will be higher—where the rights or interests at stake are especially important. So, for example, if the decision may result in loss of liberty, this would point towards a particularly rigorous procedure.[96] It follows that where the task being undertaken by the public body is general in nature—for example, developing policy—this is likely to call for far less procedural fairness than tasks involving adjudication on individual cases.

3.6.3 Setting the level of fairness—practical considerations

Practical considerations must also be taken into account when deciding how rigorous the procedure should be and what features it should include. This point can be illus-trated by examining how courts determine whether fairness requires an oral hearing or whether it suffices to allow the person concerned to make written representa-tions to the decision-maker. The House of Lords addressed this question in *Lloyd v McMahon*.[97] Certain Liverpool councillors were found guilty by the relevant regu-latory agency—the district auditor—of wilful misconduct occasioning substantial financial losses to the city council. As a result, the councillors were made personally liable—meaning that they could be required to reimburse the council—and banned from holding public office for five years. The councillors challenged the auditor's decision. They argued that by denying them an oral hearing the auditor had acted unlawfully. Lord Bridge observed that 'the so-called rules of natural justice are not engraved on tablets of stone';[98] instead, their content depends on the circumstances

---

[95] See further *McInnes v Onslow-Fane* [1978] 1 WLR 1520; *R (Khatun) v Newham London Borough Council* [2004] EWCA Civ 55, [2005] QB 37.

[96] See, eg *R v Secretary of State for the Home Department, ex p Tarrant* [1985] QB 251; *R (Smith) v Parole Board* [2005] UKHL 1, [2005] 1 WLR 350.

[97] [1987] AC 625.   [98] *Lloyd v McMahon*, 702.

of the case. In this particular case, there was no need for an oral hearing. The liability of the councillors fell to be determined by reference to large volumes of documentary evidence, and in this context limiting the councillors to a right to make written representations to the auditor was entirely appropriate. Moreover, an oral hearing would have added nothing: it might have allowed the councillors to emphasise the sincerity of their motives, but, as Lord Keith observed, this was irrelevant to their liability.[99]

This can be contrasted with the *Osborn* case, which concerned challenges to a number of decisions taken by the Parole Board.[100] One of those decisions related to a prisoner who, having served part of his custodial sentence, was released on licence.[101] However, on the very day that he was released, he was sent back to prison for alleged breach of his licence conditions. As well as turning up late at the hostel at which he was required to reside, the prisoner's behaviour *en route* to the hostel had given rise to suspicion concerning whether he had (or had sought) access to firearms—something that his licence forbade. Following the claimant's recall to prison, the Board refused to rerelease him.

The Supreme Court held that that decision was unlawful because an oral hearing should have—but had not—been provided. This was so because the decision turned upon several disputed questions of fact relating to the claimant's conduct and attitude—questions that could best have been resolved through an oral hearing that would have enabled the Board to evaluate the claimant's credibility and test the evidence. This reflects the fact that, as Lord Bingham put it in an earlier case, oral hearings facilitate dynamic and immediate interchange between the individual and the decision-maker, enabling the decision-maker to develop and adapt his arguments in light of the individual's responses.[102] Oral hearings will thus be particularly appropriate where the case turns on disputed questions of fact or upon the credibility or truthfulness of a witness.

> **Q** Look back at our discussion of normative and instrumental views of fairness (in section 3.3). Does the courts' preparedness, as evidenced by *Lloyd*, to limit procedural rights where a practical case for more rigorous procedures cannot be made out imply support for one or other of those views?

Just as practical considerations shape whether an individual is entitled to an oral hearing, so such considerations can determine whether the decision-maker is obliged to allow the individual to be legally represented.

Consider *Tarrant*,[103] in which serving prisoners were alleged to have committed offences of assault and mutiny. The disciplinary body that heard their cases—and which had the power to order that they should spend longer in prison than they

---

[99] *Lloyd v McMahon*, 708.

[100] *R (Osborn) v Parole Board* [2013] UKSC 61, [2014] AC 1115.

[101] A licence sets out conditions with which a prisoner who is released early must comply.

[102] *R (Smith) v Parole Board* [2005] UKHL 1, [2005] 1 WLR 350, [32].

[103] *R v Secretary of State for the Home Department, ex p Tarrant* [1985] QB 251. See also *R v Board of Visitors of HM Prison, The Maze, ex p Hone* [1988] AC 379.

otherwise would—rejected the prisoners' requests to have legal representation. They therefore sought judicial review, arguing that this amounted to a denial of procedural fairness. Webster J considered that a number of practical considerations—in addition to the seriousness of the allegations—should be taken into account in deciding whether legal representation was necessary as a matter of fairness. In particular, he thought it important to consider the capacity of the individual to present his own case (something that would be affected by the legal and factual complexity of the case, as well as by personal factors such as articulacy and literacy). Webster J also took account of whether denial of representation would pose procedural difficulties (eg the judge noted that prisoners awaiting adjudication are normally segregated, and that this might inhibit preparation of their defence).

The court concluded that legal representation was necessary in the mutiny cases because they raised complex questions, for example about whether prisoners had acted together in order to challenge the prison authorities. However, it would not normally be unfair to deny representation in more straightforward cases such as those involving allegations of assault.

> **Q** Consider the position of the Minister—set out in our example at the very beginning of this chapter—who has to decide whether to allow a new airport to be built. To what extent would the following have to be heard by the Minister before he takes the decision?
>   (i) The owner of a house that will be compulsorily purchased and demolished if the airport is built.
>   (ii) Local residents concerned about likely increases in traffic congestion.
> (iii) Environmental campaigners anxious about the contribution that the new airport would make to carbon emissions.

3.6.4 Trading fairness off against other considerations

Procedural fairness is clearly important. However, circumstances inevitably arise in which hard decisions have to be made about the importance of procedural fairness relative to other interests. To some extent, that is apparent from what has already been said. For instance, we have seen that the courts are prepared to insist on less by way of procedural fairness when there is little or no practical need for an elaborate procedure. That stance can be viewed, from one perspective at least, as involving the trading off of procedural fairness against the interest in efficient decision-making—insistence on unnecessarily extensive procedures being self-evidently inefficient.

Particularly profound difficulties can arise, however, in respect of an aspect of procedural fairness known as the *right to notice*. That right entitles the individual to be told of the case against him by being given, for instance, information that is adverse to the individual and that may inform the decision-making process. Giving notice is generally regarded as an essential component of procedural fairness.[104] As Lord

---

[104] See, eg *R v Secretary of State for the Home Department, ex p Doody* [1994] 1 AC 531; *Chief Constable of North Wales Police v Evans* 1982] 1 WLR 1155; *R v Secretary of State for the Home Department, ex p Fayed* [1998] 1 WLR 763.

Denning MR put it: 'If the right to be heard is to be a real right which is worth anything, it must carry with it a right in the accused man to know the case which is made against him.'[105]

However, circumstances can and do arise in which giving notice is highly problematic. Consider, for instance, *Bourgass*.[106] A prisoner had been placed in solitary confinement for several months because it was alleged that he had been involved in (but not that he had actually carried out) an assault. But he was told very little of substance regarding the allegations. Instead, the prison authorities communicated with him only in the most general terms, telling him that he presented 'an unacceptable risk to other prisoners', that he was 'known as a threat', and that he would be a 'disruptive influence' if released from solitary confinement. Had the prison authorities, by disclosing this information, discharged their duty to give notice? Concluding that they had not, Lord Reed accepted that decisions concerning the treatment of allegedly dangerous prisoners may often have to be made 'on the basis of information which cannot be disclosed in full without placing at significant risk the safety of others or jeopardising prison security'. It followed that, in determining what information should be disclosed, 'overriding interests' such as the safety of informants could be taken into account. This did not, however, mean that the prison authorities could lawfully give no meaningful information to the individual; rather, it remained incumbent upon them to inform the prisoner 'in more or less general terms' of the 'gist' of the reasons for continuing to hold him in solitary confinement.[107] It was 'unacceptable' for prolonged periods of solitary confinement to be imposed upon the prisoner on the basis of what amounted to 'secret and unchallengeable allegations'.[108]

3.7 Giving reasons for decisions

The requirement of notice relates to the giving of information to relevant parties *before* a decision is made, so that they can effectively exercise their right to be heard. A distinct, but related, question is whether there is any right to be told the reasons for a decision *once it has been taken*. We have considered the doctrine of procedural fairness will often require a decision-maker to give *notice before* making a decision. Similarly, procedural fairness will often require a decision-maker to give *reasons after* a decision has been made.

The arguments in favour of such a requirement reflect the two general arguments in favour of procedural fairness considered earlier.[109] On an *instrumental* level, it has been observed that if '[c]onsciously duty-bound to articulate their reasons, decision-makers' minds are [likely to be] more focused and their substantive decision-making . . . better'.[110] And, in *non-instrumental* terms, the giving of reasons is necessary if the status and dignity of the individual are to be properly acknowledged: as Collins J put it, 'individuals directly affected [by a decision] should

---

[105] *Kanda v Government of Malaysia* [1962] AC 322, 337.
[106] *R (Bourgass) v Secretary of State for Justice* [2015] UKSC 54, [2016] AC 384.
[107] *Bourgass*, [103].   [108] *Bourgass*, [100].   [109] See section 3.3.
[110] Fordham, 'Reasons: The Third Dimension' [1998] JR 158.

not suffer without . . . at least knowing why they [are] suffering'.[111] For example, in *Doody*, Lord Mustill regarded the giving of reasons as essential when the executive branch exercised its (now defunct) power to decide the minimum term for which convicted murderers should be imprisoned: this, he noted, was 'the most important thing in the prisoner's life', and it was fundamentally unfair if the decision was (as far as the prisoner could see) conjured 'out of thin air' without any accompanying reasons.[112]

Although concluding that, in such a case, the Home Secretary should be—and was—legally required to give reasons, Lord Mustill said that the common law did not recognise 'a general duty to give reasons for an administrative decision'.[113] This remains the case today.[114] However, there are a number of exceptions to the general rule that reasons need not be given, four of which we address in what follows.[115]

First, there may be a *statutory obligation* to give reasons; many statutes specifically require public agencies to provide reasons for their decisions.[116] For example, s 10 of the Tribunals and Inquiries Act 1992 directs that reasons must accompany the decisions of certain tribunals and certain ministerial decisions made after a statutory inquiry has been held (or in circumstances in which such an inquiry could have been required). An individual may also be able to use the Freedom of Information Act 2000 to extract reasons from a decision-maker.[117] Although the Act does not impose a reason-giving duty per se, it requires—subject to certain exceptions—that public authorities supply individuals with requested 'information'.[118] Reasons for a decision will fall under the statutory definition of 'information'—and so be liable to disclosure—if, but only if, they are 'recorded in any form'.[119] The Act will not, therefore, help individuals in circumstances in which, at the time of their freedom of information request, reasons have not been recorded (eg by writing them down or storing them electronically).

Second, the common law *principles of procedural fairness* require the giving of reasons in certain circumstances. In determining whether a given case falls within the scope of the common law duty to give reasons, the reviewing court examines the circumstances of the case, balancing any arguments for and against the giving of reasons in order to come to a rounded view about what fairness requires.[120] Prominent among the factors that weigh in favour of the imposition of a reason-giving duty is the importance of the right or interest that is at stake. So if, as in *Doody*, the decision affects the claimant's liberty, this will be a strong indication that reasons should be given, as will the fact that the decision impacts on other important interests such as

---

[111] *R (Hasan) v Secretary of State for Trade and Industry* [2007] EWHC 2630 (Admin), [21].

[112] *R v Secretary of State for the Home Department, ex p Doody* [1994] 1 AC 531, 564.

[113] *Doody*, 564.   [114] *Hasan*, [20].

[115] For comment on the relative merits of this approach and one based on a general duty subject to exceptions, see Neill, 'The Duty to Give Reasons: The Openness of Decision-Making', in Forsyth and Hare (eds), *The Golden Metwand and the Crooked Cord* (Oxford 1998).

[116] See Le Sueur, 'Legal Duties to Give Reasons' (1999) 52 CLP 150.

[117] See further Chapter 10, section 7.2.   [118] Freedom of Information Act 2000, s 1.

[119] Freedom of Information Act 2000, s 84.

[120] *R v Higher Education Funding Council, ex p Institute of Dental Surgery* [1994] 1 WLR 242.

professional standing, reputation,[121] or bodily integrity.[122] A duty to give reasons is also likely to be imposed in respect of decisions that are aberrant—that is, decisions that, on the face of it, seem inexplicable, perhaps because they appear to fly in the face of the great weight of evidence.[123] On the other hand, the court also has to weigh factors that point away from a duty to give reasons: this may be so where, for example, giving reasons would place 'an undue burden on the decision-maker' or 'call for the articulation of sometimes inexpressible value judgments'.[124]

> **Q** Where reason giving would be especially burdensome for the decision-maker, should this wholly relieve it of the obligation to give reasons, or might it be more appropriate to impose a lighter duty—for example, requiring the decision-maker to outline its thinking without going into detail?

Third, where a public authority has an established administrative practice of giving reasons or has made an express promise that it will do so, this may create a *legitimate expectation* that reasons will be given. The courts will generally insist that such an expectation be honoured by the decision-maker. We consider legitimate expectations later.[125]

Fourth, Art 6 of the ECHR requires that decisions to which it is applicable be accompanied by an indication of the grounds on which they are based.[126] So, where Art 6 applies, a duty to give reasons can be said to exist without more: there is no need to engage in the common law analysis discussed earlier. In this sense, Art 6 imposes a clearer and more certain duty to give reasons. However, the important caveat must be entered that, as we saw earlier, Art 6 applies only to a subset of administrative decisions—namely, those that are determinative of 'civil rights and obligations'.[127]

So much for the circumstances in which the duty to give reasons *arises*. What does it *require* when it does arise? According to classic case law, if reasons are to be given, then those reasons must be proper, adequate, and intelligible. The reasons must also deal with the substantial points that have been raised.[128] Beyond this, courts—both domestic and European—have said that the content of the duty depends on the circumstances.[129] Some general principles, however, were set out by Lord Brown in *South Buckinghamshire District Council v Porter*.[130] He said that while reasons must enable people to understand why the decision was reached and what the conclusions were on the main points of controversy, they need refer only to the 'main issues' and not to 'every material consideration'.

---

[121] *R v Ministry of Defence, ex p Murray* [1998] COD 134; *R v City of London Corporation, ex p Matson* [1997] 1 WLR 765.

[122] *R (Wooder) v Feggetter* [2002] EWCA Civ 554, [2003] QB 219.

[123] *Institute of Dental Surgery*, 263.   [124] *Institute of Dental Surgery*, 257.

[125] See section 4.3.   [126] *Hadjianastassiou v Greece* (1993) 16 EHRR 219, 237.

[127] See section 3.5.2.

[128] *Re Poyser and Mills' Arbitration* [1964] 2 QB 476, 478.

[129] *Helle v Finland* (1997) 26 EHRR 159, 183; *Stefan v General Medical Council* [1999] 1 WLR 1293, 1301 and 1304.

[130] [2004] UKHL 33, [2004] 1 WLR 1953, [36].

Courts are also mindful of the fact that while the giving of reasons will generally serve the interest in good administration, that interest might be compromised if the obligation to give reasons becomes too burdensome. For instance, in *Uprichard*, it was argued that the decision-maker had given insufficient reasons when refusing to accept objections to the planning strategy that was proposed for a particular part of Scotland.[131] The Supreme Court held, however, that the reasons were in fact sufficient, and that in assessing their adequacy it was 'important to maintain a sense of proportion' and to avoid imposing upon decision-makers 'a burden which is unreasonable'.[132] In particular, Lord Reed noted that there had been a 'plethora of objections' relating to 'numerous distinct matters', and that the decision-maker could not reasonably be expected 'to address, line by line, every nuance of every matter raised in every objection'.[133] Care must be exercised in this context: if the duty to give reasons is conceived of in extremely light terms, then that risks making the prior imposition of the duty largely meaningless. However, provided that that risk is avoided, addressing concerns about overburdening decision-makers by means of adjusting the onerousness of the duty is preferable to the far less subtle technique of conceding a duty that is, in the first place, highly constricted in its scope.

One final point should be noted in relation to the duty to give reasons. As noted earlier,[134] recently enacted legislation prevents successful judicial review challenges when it is 'highly likely' that a failure to follow a legal requirement makes no substantial difference to the outcome of the decision-making process for the claimant. Judicial review challenges on the ground of a failure to give reasons might be thought to be especially vulnerable in this regard, bearing in mind that such a failure reflects something that has gone wrong *after* the decision is taken, making it hard to see how the non-provision of reasons might affect the 'outcome'. This point is considered in more detail in the following chapter, in the context of a broader discussion of restrictions upon judicial review.[135]

4. Exercise of discretion

4.1 The non-delegation principle

When power is granted to a given decision-maker, the presumption is that the power should be exercised by—and only by—that decision-maker.[136] Three reasons underlie this presumption. First, and most obviously, it reflects *parliamentary intention*: if Parliament has specified that a particular agency should take the decision, then Parliament's will ought to prevail. Second, Parliament is likely to have chosen a particular decision-maker because it is *institutionally qualified* to act: it may, for example, possess expertise on the issue to which the power relates. Third, if the power may only be used by the person or body named in the statute, this ensures that—in

---

[131] *Uprichard v Scottish Ministers* [2013] UKSC 21, 2013 SC (UKSC), 219.
[132] *Uprichard*, [48], *per* Lord Reed.   [133] *Uprichard*, [48].   [134] See section 3.3.
[135] See Chapter 13, section 4.   [136] *Barnard v National Dock Labour Board* [1953] 2 QB 18.

the event of an improper or unlawful decision—the responsible party can readily be identified and held *accountable*. Courts have therefore held that it is unlawful not only for the statutorily ordained decision-maker straightforwardly to delegate power to another person or body,[137] but also for it to enter into arrangements in which the *real* power is exercised by someone other than the person identified in the statute. So, for example, it is unlawful for the statutory decision-maker automatically to adopt someone else's view[138] or to make their decision conditional on another's approval.[139]

However, applying these principles too strictly risks inhibiting good government. Consider our example of a Minister called upon to decide whether to allow the construction of a new airport. While it is, for the reasons set out previously, important that she[140] takes the ultimate decision, it is also acceptable—indeed, desirable—that she should do so having taken full account of the views of others, such as those with expertise on the likely environmental and economic implications of the proposed airport. For this reason, courts distinguish between taking account of others' views (which is legitimate) and ascribing so much weight to them that the statutory decision-maker can no longer be said to be bringing his own judgement to bear on the issues.

> **Q** Assume that, in our example, the Minister, having decided that the new airport should be built, consults an expert environmental campaign group about what conditions she should attach to the grant of planning permission. The group replies to the Minister, recommending restrictions on the number of runways, the size of the terminal buildings, and the amount of car parking. The next day, the Minister formally imposes exactly those conditions. Would the Minister have acted lawfully in such circumstances?

As well as posing an obstacle to the taking into account of others', including experts', views, over-rigid application of the non-delegation principle would cause the government machine to grind to a juddering halt. Whereas our example is concerned with the sort of once-in-a-generation decision that the Minister herself might reasonably be expected to take, many powers conferred upon Ministers have to be exercised in relation to multiple cases each year and it may simply be impractical—or physically impossible—for the Minister personally to make each and every decision. For example, in *Re Golden Chemical Products Ltd*,[141] the Secretary of State was authorised by statute to take steps to arrange for the winding up[142] of a company where this appeared to be in the public interest. In fact, the power had actually been exercised by a civil servant in the Secretary of State's department, in apparent breach of the requirement that discretionary power is exercised only by the person named in the statute. However, the court noted that, in the earlier case of *Carltona*, Lord Greene MR had

---

[137] *Barnard.*   [138] *High v Billings* (1903) 89 LT 550.

[139] *Lavender and Sons Ltd v Minister of Housing and Local Government* [1970] 1 WLR 1231.

[140] Or at least her department: see later for discussion of this point.   [141] [1976] Ch 300.

[142] ie putting its affairs in order (eg by paying creditors where possible) and closing it down.

treated Ministers as a special case, on account of the fact that their functions are 'so multifarious that no Minister could ever personally attend to them': public business, he said, 'could not be carried on' if Ministers were to have to exercise all of their powers personally.[143] Thus, applying the so-called *Carltona* doctrine, the court in *Golden Chemical* held that the civil servant could lawfully exercise the ministerial power.

Some judges have attempted to rationalise this position by holding that, in such circumstances, the 'civil servant acts not as the delegate, but as the *alter ego*, of the Secretary of State'.[144] The better view, however, is that when Parliament confers discretion on a *Minister*, its intention is to entrust the discretion not only to him, but also to his *departmental officials* for whose actions he is legally responsible to the courts and politically responsible to Parliament.[145] This does not, however, amount to *carte blanche*: the courts stressed that the *Carltona* principle permits delegation only to officials 'of an appropriate level [of seniority] having regard to the nature of the power in question',[146] and that the delegation must be to someone who is 'properly qualified to make the [relevant] judgment'.[147]

The *Carltona* doctrine raises particularly difficult questions in light of recent changes to the structure of government in the UK. Certain administrative functions are no longer performed by government departments headed up by a Minister directly accountable to Parliament. Instead, they are performed by 'executive agencies', which are headed by a chief executive, a career civil servant who is not directly accountable to Parliament.[148] For example, the Ministry of Justice is not itself involved in the day-to-day running of prisons: this is the role of the Prison Service. The Secretary of State for Justice determines the policy framework by setting targets and budgets, and the relationship is an arm's-length one. Furthermore, Ministers are not in the traditional sense responsible for the day-to-day decisions made by such agencies.

In light of this, applying the *Carltona* doctrine in such contexts is arguably objectionable because the assumption underpinning it—of ministerial responsibility for departmental officials' actions—does not fully apply in relation to agencies.[149] The point is highly debateable because the whole notion of civil servants being accountable to Parliament through Ministers is in practice problematic.[150] Nevertheless, the courts have held that statutory powers conferred on Ministers can lawfully be exercised by executive agencies. In *Sherwin* and *Castle*, the courts examined the relationship between the agency and the Minister's department and found that the Secretary of State remains just as responsible to Parliament for decisions made by civil servants

---

[143] *Carltona Ltd v Commissioners of Works* [1943] 2 All ER 560, 563.

[144] *R v Secretary of State for the Home Department, ex p Oladehinde* [1991] 1 AC 254, 284, *per* Lord Donaldson MR.

[145] *Bushell v Secretary of State for the Environment* [1981] AC 75, 95, *per* Lord Diplock.

[146] *DPP v Haw* [2007] EWHC 1931 (Admin), [2008] 1 WLR 379, [29], *per* Lord Phillips MR.

[147] *Castle v DPP* [2014] EWHC 587, [2014] 1 WLR 4279, [28], *per* Pitchford LJ.

[148] On executive agencies, see further Chapter 4, section 3.9.

[149] Freedland, 'The Rule against Delegation and the *Carltona* Doctrine in an Agency Context' [1996] PL 19.

[150] See Chapter 10, section 4.4.

in executive agencies as he does for decisions made by civil servants within the parent government department.[151]

The crucial determinant of the application of the *Carltona* doctrine is the wording of the relevant legislation. Consider, for instance, the power to place a prisoner in solitary confinement for more than three days. Under the Prison Rules, a prisoner may be removed from other prisoners—'segregated'—in order to maintain good order or discipline. The Rules also state that a prisoner shall not be segregated for more than three days without the authority of the Secretary of State. It had been the practice for such decisions to be taken neither by the Secretary of State nor civil servants (under the *Carltona* doctrine), but by senior prison officials, who, unlike civil servants, hold an independent statutory office.

However, in *Bourgass*, the Supreme Court held this practice to be unlawful.[152] The power to segregate a prisoner for more than three days had been given to the Secretary of State and not to senior prison officials who hold a constitutionally separate statutory office. The Supreme Court also held that there was a good reason why the power to authorise segregation should not be exercised by prison officials but by the Secretary of State (in practice, senior civil servants from outside the prison): this would protect the prisoner against the risk of segregation for an unduly protracted period and thereby provide an important safeguard. In summary, the Supreme Court held that the *Carltona* doctrine does not enable holders of an independent and constitutionally separate statutory office, such as senior prison officials, to exercise powers conferred by Parliament upon the Secretary of State. The doctrine only enables civil servants to exercise ministerial powers because, in constitutional terms, decisions made by civil servants are made by the Minister himself.

Finally, while the normal position is that powers conferred by Parliament upon Ministers can be exercised by civil servants, Parliament can displace the *Carltona* doctrine by requiring that specific decisions be taken personally by a Minister. For instance, only the 'Secretary of State (and not by a person acting under his authority)' may certify that a foreign national may be refused entry to the UK on the ground that his exclusion is conducive to the public good.[153]

4.2 The non-fettering principle—discretion, policy, and rules

As Figure 12.4 shows, the holder of a discretionary power—such as the Secretary of State in our example—might exercise it in one of a number of ways. First, she may choose to adopt an absolutely rigid rule that she will only grant permission for new airports in the northern half of the country. Second, at the other extreme, she might approach each new case with a completely open mind, without any prior view about whether (and, if so, in what circumstances) new airports should be built. Or, third, she might adopt an interim position: a general policy that no new airports should be built in the south, coupled with a willingness to make exceptions to that policy if it can be shown (for example) that there is a compelling economic case.

[151] *R v Secretary of State for Social Services, ex p Sherwin* (1996) 32 BMLR 1; *Castle v DPP* [2014] EWHC 587, [2014] 1 WLR 4279.

[152] *R (Bourgass) v Secretary of State for Justice* [2015] UKSC 54, [2016] AC 384.

[153] Immigration and Asylum Act 1999, s 60(9)(a).

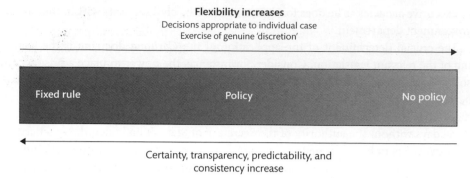

Figure 12.4 Rules, policy, and discretion

Traditionally, administrative law has held that while holders of discretionary power may adopt policies to guide the exercise of discretion, they may not lawfully adopt rigid rules that fetter the exercise of such discretion. The difficult question concerns how to draw the line between a lawful policy and an unlawful rule. The general principle is that a position from which the decision-maker is prepared to resile in exceptional circumstances will be acceptable, and treated as falling on the 'policy' side of the line, whereas an unwillingness to make exceptions is suggestive of a 'rule'.[154] On this basis, the third position set out in the opening paragraph of this section would be lawful.

For example, in *British Oxygen Co Ltd v Minister of Technology*,[155] the Minister, who had a discretionary power to provide businesses with grants to assist with the purchase of industrial machinery, resolved to make no grants in respect of machinery costing less than £25. On that basis, he refused assistance to the claimant company, which had spent some £4 million on numerous items of equipment costing £20 each. Holding that the Minister had acted lawfully, Lord Reid thought it almost inevitable that large departments called upon to decide many cases would evolve 'a policy so precise that it could well be called a rule'—an approach that he regarded as acceptable provided that 'the authority is always willing to listen to anyone with something new to say' (and to make exceptions to the policy, or rule, if that is appropriate in the circumstances).[156]

In some situations, the courts are less willing to tolerate the sort of approach that was permitted in *British Oxygen*. For example, in a case concerning the exercise of a discretionary power to provide assistance (including accommodation) to homeless families with young children, it was considered imperative that each case be looked at on its own merits, and Templeman LJ was not 'persuaded that even a policy resolution hedged around with exceptions would be entirely free from attack'.[157]

In general, however, the courts have become not only increasingly *tolerant* of policy, but increasingly persuaded that the structuring of discretion through the use of

---

[154] *R v Port of London Authority, ex p Kynoch Ltd* [1919] 1 KB 176. If exceptions are never, in fact, made, this will be strong evidence that a rigid rule is being applied, even if the defendant professes a preparedness to make exceptions: *R v Warwickshire County Council, ex p Collymore* [1995] ELR 217.

[155] [1971] AC 610.   [156] *British Oxygen*, 625.

[157] *Attorney-General ex rel Tilley v Wandsworth London Borough Council* [1981] 1 WLR 854, 858.

policy is a *good thing*. For instance, in *Nzolameso*, the Supreme Court held that local authorities should adopt and publish policies concerning the discharge of their obligations to house homeless people.[158] Lady Hale pointed out that this would produce several benefits: it would enable people to know where they stood and what factors would be relevant to decisions; it would enable relevant decisions to be reviewed by local authorities' reviewing officers by reference to transparent criteria; and it would enable scrutiny of—and, where appropriate, legal challenges to—the policy itself.[159] Indeed, the courts' contemporary enthusiasm in respect of policy has recently manifested itself not only in the requirement (in certain circumstances) to *have* a policy, but in the additional requirement that decision-makers who do have policies must, in general, *follow* them. We address that point in the next section.

Q Should decision-makers always be required to have and publish policies? Are there particular circumstances in which requiring such things would be especially appropriate or inappropriate?

4.3 Legitimate expectations and consistency

If a public body indicates that it will exercise its power in a given way but then goes back on its word, does it thereby act unlawfully? The answer is 'yes'—provided that the indication given by the public body generates what is known as a *legitimate expectation*. Consider, for example, the facts of *Coughlan*.[160] The claimant, having been seriously injured in 1971, became a long-term hospital patient. In 1993, the health authority, in order to secure the claimant's agreement to be moved to a new care facility, told her and a small number of others that they could remain 'for as long as they wished to stay there': it would be their 'home for life'. Yet, just five years later, the health authority resolved to close the new facility, arguing that it had become 'prohibitively expensive' to run.

Cases such as this raise very difficult questions.[161] Clearly, if the health authority were to be allowed to resile from its promise, the claimant, having relied upon it, would suffer profound unfairness. There is also a strong argument—based on the idea of legal certainty[162]—that individuals should be able to trust and rely safely on what public authorities have told them.[163] Yet it is also arguable that public bodies should be free to act in the *public* interest—for example, by using scarce financial resources efficiently—even if this occasions unfairness to some individuals.[164] These are the sort of arguments with which courts have to grapple when dealing with claims under the heading of

---

[158] *Nzolameso v Westminster City Council* [2015] UKSC 22, [2015] PTSR 549.

[159] *Nzolameso*, [40]–[41].

[160] *R v North and East Devon Health Authority, ex p Coughlan* [2001] QB 213.

[161] We will see what answers the court came to in *Coughlan* in section 4.3.2.

[162] See Chapter 2, section 3.3.

[163] See further Schønberg, *Legitimate Expectations in Administrative Law* (Oxford 2000), ch 1.

[164] Indeed, as we saw in section 4.2, the importance of *preserving* discretion underlies the unlawfulness of exercising discretion pursuant to a strict rule (as opposed to a policy). For comment, see Hilson, 'Policies, the Non-Fetter Principle and the Principle of Substantive Legitimate Expectation: Between a Rock and a Hard Place?' [2006] JR 289.

legitimate expectation. Such claims raise two fundamental issues. First, how does the court determine whether an individual has acquired a legitimate expectation (and, if they have acquired such an expectation, exactly what the content of the expectation is)? Second, what can the court do if the public authority refuses to give the claimant whatever it is that she legitimately expects?

4.3.1 The creation of legitimate expectations

People might expect all sorts of things. But just because someone thinks something is going to happen does not mean that they have a *legitimate* expectation that it will happen. A person who reads a government statement, gets the wrong end of the stick, and thinks they are going to receive something that was not actually promised will not thereby acquire a legitimate expectation. Rather, a legitimate expectation will only arise on the strength of an undertaking given by a public body that is 'clear, unambiguous and devoid of relevant qualification',[165] like the representation made to the claimant in *Coughlan*. Whether the statement is clear enough to found a legitimate expectation— and, if so, what the statement means—are matters that fall to be determined 'on a fair reading of the statement', the key question being 'how . . . it would have been reasonably understood by those to whom it was made'.[166] The requirement of a clear undertaking does not necessarily mean that it must be explicit: an undertaking may be inferred from previous conduct,[167] although such an inference will be drawn only when the practice is 'so unambiguous', 'widespread', and 'well-established' as to amount to a 'commitment'.[168]

Additional restrictions on the circumstances in which a legitimate expectation can arise were highlighted by *Begbie*.[169] The case arose out of the Blair administration's decision—implemented, shortly after its election, via the Education (Schools) Act 1997—to wind up a scheme that had offered state funding to enable children of insufficient financial means to attend independent schools. The 9-year-old claimant was a pupil at an 'all-through school'—that is, a school that educated children from the age of 5 through to the age of 18—and sought to enforce undertakings that such children would receive state funding throughout, rather than having it stopped at the age of 11 upon completion of primary education. Rejecting the claimant's case, the court held that undertakings given by Labour politicians *before* the 1997 general election could not give rise to legitimate expectations. Peter Gibson LJ stated that an 'opposition spokesman, even the Leader of the Opposition, does not speak on behalf of a public authority', such that 'when a party elected into office fails to keep its election promises, the consequences should be political and not legal'.[170] It was also held

---

[165] *R v Inland Revenue Commissioners, ex p MFK Underwriting Agencies Ltd* [1990] 1 WLR 1545, 1569, *per* Bingham LJ.

[166] *R (Patel) v General Medical Council* [2013] EWCA Civ 327, [2013] 1 WLR 2801, [44], *per* Lloyd Jones LJ.

[167] eg in *Council of Civil Service Unions v Minister for the Civil Service* [1985] AC 374, a legitimate expectation that civil servants would be consulted before their terms of employment were changed could be inferred from the fact that previous such changes had always been preceded by consultation. (The legitimate expectation was not, however, enforced, due to national security considerations.)

[168] *R (Davies) v Revenue and Customs Commissioners* [2011] UKSC 47, [2011] 1 WLR 2625.

[169] *R v Department of Education and Employment, ex p Begbie* [2000] 1 WLR 1115.

[170] *Begbie*, [55]–[56].

in *Begbie* that the claimant could not establish a legitimate expectation because this would run directly contrary to the scheme Parliament had laid down. The statute envisaged that funding would continue beyond primary education only where, on the particular facts of the case, the Secretary of State was satisfied that that should happen—yet the claimant's legitimate expectation, if accepted by the court, would have required funding to be continued in a broad category of cases without reference to the circumstances of individual children.

Finally, it seems intuitively right that individuals should only be able to claim a legitimate expectation where, in the first place, they have *knowledge* of the representation giving rise to the expectation. After all, it is not possible to expect something of which one is ignorant. Yet it may appear unfair if this means that less well-informed people lose out in comparison with the better informed. Take, for instance, a situation in which a public body has a policy in relation to a given matter. Those who are aware of the policy might be in a position to complain on legitimate expectation grounds if they are not treated in accordance with the policy. In contrast, those who are ignorant of the policy would appear to have no expectation, legitimate or otherwise, of benefiting from it: how could they if, in the first place, they do not know of the policy's existence? The unfairness for the less well informed that is apparent in this distinction has occasionally led courts to the conclusion that it should—counterintuitively—be possible for someone to have a legitimate expectation based on a policy that they did not know about at the relevant time.

However, in recent years, the courts have adopted a more satisfactory approach to cases of this type. It involves distinguishing legitimate expectation cases—in which there really must be an expectation, and hence knowledge of whatever it is that has given rise to the expectation—from cases in which the real concern is *consistency of treatment*. For instance, in *Lumba*, Lord Dyson acknowledged a 'basic public law right' to have one's case considered 'under whatever [lawful] policy the executive sees fit to adopt'.[171] Subsequently, in *Mandalia*, Lord Wilson conceded that deeming legitimate expectations to have arisen in the absence of knowledge is 'strained', and said that the right to have administrative decisions taken in accordance with public bodies' stated policies flows from a principle that, although 'related' to the legitimate expectation doctrine, is 'free-standing'.[172] The position—now reached independently of the doctrine of legitimate expectation—is thus that decision-makers must consistently apply their own policies unless there is a good reason for not doing so. A corollary of this development is that legitimate expectation cases can once again be confined to those in which the claimant actually knows about the relevant undertaking.[173]

4.3.2 The protection of legitimate expectations

If a claimant establishes that he had a legitimate expectation that has been frustrated by a public body, the options open to a reviewing court, as Figure 12.5 shows, depend, in the first place, on the *content* of the expectation.

---

[171] *R (Lumba) v Secretary of State for the Home Department* [2011] UKSC 1, [2012] 1 AC 245, [35].
[172] *Mandalia v Secretary of State for the Home Department* [2015] UKSC 59, [2015] 1 WLR 4546, [29].
[173] *DM v Secretary of State for the Home Department* [2014] CSIH 29, 2014 SC 635, [18].

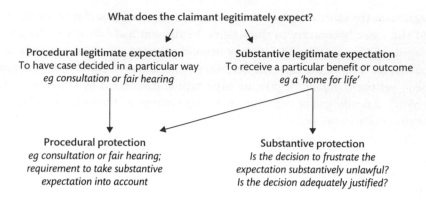

Figure 12.5 Legitimate expectations

One possibility is that the claimant may be entitled to expect that his case will be considered in a particular way—for example, that he will be consulted or be given a fair hearing. Here, the claimant has a *procedural legitimate expectation*, and the most that the court can do is to require the public body to accord to the claimant whatever procedural niceties it led him to expect. The effect of a legitimate expectation may therefore entitle a person to fair treatment in circumstances in which no such entitlement would otherwise arise.[174] Or a legitimate expectation might entitle someone to a higher standard of fair treatment than they would otherwise be entitled to.

The other possibility is that the claimant may have a *substantive legitimate expectation*—that is, he may legitimately expect a particular outcome to the decision-making process. The 'home for life' promise in *Coughlan* gave rise to precisely such an expectation. Here, as Figure 12.5 indicates, the court may decide that although the expectation itself relates to a matter of substance, it should be offered only a procedural form of protection. For example, in *R (Bibi) v Newham London Borough Council*,[175] it was held that a local authority's promise to provide the claimant with permanent accommodation gave rise to a substantive legitimate expectation that such accommodation would indeed be provided. However, when it came to protecting the expectation, the court merely required the local authority—which, in deciding that the claimant should *not* be offered permanent accommodation, had ignored its earlier promise—to reconsider the matter, taking due account of the legitimate expectation that it had engendered.

However, the court may go further than this, as it did in *Coughlan* itself, by asking whether frustrating the expectation would be 'so unfair as to be a misuse of the authority's power'.[176] This involves balancing the unfairness that would be occasioned to the individual if the expectation were dashed against the damage that would be caused to the public interest if the decision-maker were held to its promise.

---

[174] *Attorney-General of Hong Kong v Ng Yuen Shiu* [1983] 2 AC 629.
[175] [2001] EWCA Civ 607, [2002] 1 WLR 237.
[176] *R v North and East Devon Health Authority, ex p Coughlan* [2001] QB 213, [83].

In *Coughlan*, the court felt that it would be grossly unfair to the claimant if her expectation of a home for life were dashed, bearing in mind that the promise had been directed to her (rather than to a large group of people of which she was a member). This made it more likely that she would (and more reasonable for her to) rely on the promise, which she had duly done (by moving to the new care facility in the first place). Moreover, the court did not consider that the defendant had established an adequate justification for overriding the claimant's legitimate expectation: the health authority cited scarcity of resources, arguing that it could make more efficient use of its budget by rehousing the claimant, but it was held that these obstacles to fulfilling the claimant's expectation were 'financial only', and insufficient to justify not doing what had been promised.[177]

The 'balancing' exercise undertaken in *Coughlan* is now acknowledged to amount to a form of 'proportionality' test,[178] the nature of which we examine in more detail later.[179] The approach adopted in *Coughlan* was highly interventionist. It has been argued that the court was 'dismissive' of the health authority's arguments and failed to adhere to the orthodox view—about which we say more in the next section—that 'discretionary decisions as to the allocation of finite resources subject to many competing individual demands [should] generally [be] left to bodies subject to democratic accountability and with a complete view of all the claims upon those resources, not the courts'.[180]

However, it is important to bear in mind that the court indicated that such an approach would be adopted only in very specific circumstances—such as those of *Coughlan* itself—'where the expectation is confined to one person or a few people, giving the promise or representation the character of a contract'.[181] In some other cases, such as *R v Secretary of State for the Home Department, ex p Hargreaves*,[182] courts have considered it inappropriate to go beyond asking whether the decision to frustrate the expectation is manifestly unreasonable. That amounts to a far less demanding form of review than is entailed by the balancing, or proportionality, test adopted in *Coughlan*.

How, then, do courts decide which approach to adopt? The key to understanding this point is to recognise that when an individual seeks to enforce a substantive legitimate expectation, he is effectively asking the court to hold the public authority to an 'advance decision' from which it now wishes to resile because it judges that some other decision would better serve the public interest. Sales argues that the more opportunity the public body has had, at the advance stage, to appreciate the likely consequences of its representations or policy, the more legitimate it is for the court to hold it to the 'advance decision'.[183] The stricter, *Coughlan*-style approach is therefore most likely where a promise is made to an individual,[184] or to a group of individuals with similar interests. In contrast, the court is likely to examine decision-makers' justifications

---

[177] *Coughlan*, [60].
[178] *Paponette v Attorney General of Trinidad and Tobago* [2010] UKPC 32, [2012] 1 AC 1, [38].
[179] See section 5.
[180] Sales and Steyn, 'Legitimate Expectations in English Public Law: An Analysis' [2004] PL 564, 591.
[181] *Coughlan*, [59].   [182] [1997] 1 WLR 906.
[183] Sales, 'Legitimate Expectations' [2006] JR 186, 189.   [184] As in *Coughlan*.

less critically, and such justifications are more likely to be found adequate, when the class of individuals to which the representation relates is a large one.[185]

Finally, we should note that the courts' capacity to protect legitimate expectations is severely limited where the expectation relates to *unlawful conduct*.[186] For example, in *Rowland v Environment Agency*,[187] the owners of a house were led by the respondent to believe that an adjoining stretch of the River Thames was not subject to public rights of access. It later transpired that such rights did exist, but the Environment Agency had no legal power to extinguish them. The Court of Appeal therefore concluded that although the claimant had a legitimate expectation concerning the status of the relevant stretch of river,[188] the Agency could not be ordered to fulfil the expectation because it lacked legal capacity to do so. Instead, the Court held that the Agency was required to act towards the claimant as favourably as its limited legal powers permitted—by not drawing attention to the existence of the rights of access.

4.4 Inputs to the decision-making process

It stands to reason that if the quality of the material that is put into a process is high, this increases the chances of a high-quality outcome—and vice versa. This is true of manufacturing processes (high-quality raw materials will help to produce a high-quality product) and it is equally true of decision-making processes. Similarly, administrative law seeks to influence the inputs into such processes. It does so through the *relevancy doctrine*, which requires decision-makers to *take into account all legally relevant matters* and to *ignore legally irrelevant matters*.[189]

Before looking at how this works in practice, we should note two connections between these requirements and those of procedural fairness, considered earlier. First, as we have seen, one of the purposes of according fair hearings to individuals liable to be affected by government actions is to ensure that, before anything is done, decision-makers are in receipt of relevant information. In this way, the concept of natural justice—by obliging decision-makers to listen to individuals—helps to ensure on a practical level that the former will be well placed to exercise their power sensibly. The relevancy doctrine goes further, however, by insisting that such matters are *actually taken account of* when decisions are made.

Second, the requirement to ignore irrelevant matters overlaps with the rule against bias. For example, if a Minister or official were to take a particular decision because he stood to benefit financially from it, this would be unlawful according to both the rule

---

[185] *R (Patel) v General Medical Council* [2013] EWCA Civ 327, [2013] 1 WLR 2801, [50].

[186] See further Hannett and Busch, '*Ultra Vires* Representations and Illegitimate Expectations' [2005] PL 729.

[187] [2002] EWCA Civ 1885, [2005] Ch 1.

[188] This conclusion was based in part on the fact that the claimant's right to property under the ECHR was at stake.

[189] *Hanks v Minister of Housing and Local Government* [1963] 1 QB 999; *Padfield v Minister of Agriculture, Fisheries and Food* [1968] AC 997. Some matters may fall into neither category—it may be permissible, but not obligatory, to consider them. For discussion, see *Ashby v Minister of Immigration* [1981] 1 NZLR 222, 224.

against bias and the relevancy doctrine (personal financial gain being a legally irrelevant consideration). That said, the rule against bias and the relevancy doctrine do not cover identical ground: the latter requires proof that irrelevant matters have been considered; the former requires only a perception that this may have happened.[190] Meanwhile, as we will see, the range of matters liable to be considered legally irrelevant is broader than the category of especially objectionable interests likely to give rise to a perception of bias.[191]

How then do we decide whether a particular matter is legally relevant or irrelevant? For example, how does our hypothetical Minister, when required to decide whether to allow a new airport to be built, know what she must and must not take into account? The difficulty is that the language of our imaginary statute[192]—like that of most actual statutes—gives no steer. Courts, when called upon to apply the relevancy doctrine, must therefore often rely on relatively general, including practical, considerations. As Cooke J explained in a New Zealand case, 'the more general and the more obviously important the consideration, the readier the court must be to hold that Parliament must have meant it to be taken into account'.[193] So, for example, when faced with the question of whether the financial implications of a decision are legally irrelevant, the courts have been willing to allow such matters to be considered where to do otherwise would expose a public authority to potentially unlimited expense.[194] In contrast, when the Home Secretary—in deciding on the minimum period that two children who had murdered another child should spend in prison[195]—took into account public opinion, including a petition organised by a national tabloid newspaper, it was held that he had acted unlawfully.[196] The Minister was, in effect, exercising a judicial function, and had therefore to adopt the sort of objective, independent approach expected of judges. In such circumstances, public opinion was legally irrelevant. Similarly, it was said by Lord Reid in *Padfield* that it was unlawful for a Minister, in refusing to order an investigation into arrangements for the sale of milk, to take into account the fact that such an investigation may arrive at politically embarrassing conclusions.[197]

> **Q** In our example, would it be lawful for the Minister, in deciding whether to grant permission for the new airport, to take into account the environmental impact of and public demand for air travel? Would it be unlawful for him not to take into account local opposition to the proposed airport and likely increases in congestion on roads in the vicinity of the airport?

---

[190] Judged by reference to the fair-minded and informed observer test. See section 3.4.2.

[191] The *Venables* case, considered in the next paragraph, illustrates this point.

[192] See section 1.2.

[193] *CREEDNZ v Governor-General of New Zealand* [1981] 1 NZLR 172, 183.

[194] *R v Gloucestershire County Council, ex p Barry* [1997] AC 584.

[195] The Home Secretary no longer exercises this power: such decisions are now taken exclusively by the judiciary. See discussion in section 3.5.1.

[196] *R v Secretary of State for the Home Department, ex p Venables* [1998] AC 407.

[197] *Padfield v Minister of Agriculture, Fisheries and Food* [1968] AC 997.

4.5 **Motives and purposes**

It has been said that 'no statute can be purposeless': every grant of discretionary power to a public authority must be for some purpose (or purposes), and the power can lawfully be used *only* for that purpose (or those purposes).[198] This principle is an essential safeguard against the misuse of power, not least because it prevents powers conferred on public authorities from being lawfully used for self-serving political reasons.

The application of the principle is relatively straightforward where the statute contains an explicit statement of purpose. For example, in *Municipal Council of Sydney v Campbell*,[199] a local authority had been given power to purchase land compulsorily for the purposes of 'carrying out improvements in or remodelling any portion of the city' and widening or constructing new highways. Purporting to exercise these powers, the defendant council resolved to improve a major thoroughfare and, in this context, to purchase land covering a considerable area, including neighbouring streets. However, the purchase of much of the land was not in fact necessary for the purpose of carrying out the improvements to the highway. It transpired that the excess land was to be purchased with a view to selling it at a profit once property prices in the area had risen thanks to the planned improvement works. Raising funds in this way was not, however, one of the purposes for which the power had been conferred—and so the council's resolution was unlawful.

Where the statute makes no explicit provision about the purpose underlying a discretionary power, the court must infer the uses to which it may legitimately be put. In *Congreve v Home Office*,[200] the Home Secretary revoked a television licence that the claimant—in order to avoid a scheduled 50 per cent rise in the price of licences—had purchased before his old one expired. This revocation, said the Court of Appeal, was unlawful: the Minister was seeking to use his power 'as a means of extracting money which Parliament ha[d] given the executive no mandate to demand'; he had thus acted for an improper purpose.[201]

The court's role in determining the purposes for which a discretion may and may not be used places it in a powerful position, since its decision on this point may have significant consequences for the scope of the government's discretion. This point is illustrated by the *Pergau Dam* case.[202] Purporting to exercise a statutory power to grant aid 'for the purpose of promoting the development or maintaining the economy of a country or territory outside the United Kingdom, or the welfare of its people', the Foreign Secretary approved financial support of over £200 million for the construction of a hydroelectric power station on the Pergau river in Malaysia. After this plan had been announced, but before any irreversible decision had been taken, a report concluded that the project was economically unviable and a 'very bad buy'. When the Minister decided that, in spite of the report, the project would still be funded,

---

[198] *R v Somerset County Council, ex p Fewings* [1995] 1 All ER 513, 525, *per* Laws J.

[199] [1925] AC 339.   [200] *Congreve v Home Office* [1976] QB 629.

[201] *Congreve*, 662, *per* Geoffrey Lane LJ.

[202] *R v Secretary of State for Foreign and Commonwealth Affairs, ex p World Development Movement Ltd* [1995] 1 WLR 386.

judicial review was sought. Holding that the Minister had acted unlawfully, the court concluded that, properly interpreted, the power could only be used for the purpose of promoting *economically sound* development.

The effect of this interpretation was to curtail the Minister's discretion significantly: unless the court were satisfied of the economic viability of the scheme (which it was not) it would be unlawful to offer financial assistance. It is clear, therefore, that by implying particular purposes into a discretionary power, the courts are able to exert considerable influence over the uses to which it may be lawfully put.

5. Review of the outcome of the decision-making process

So far, our focus has principally been on aspects of the decision-making *process*, such as the procedure to be adopted, and the matters that can and cannot lawfully be taken into account. We now turn to the *decision itself*—and therefore enter more controversial territory.

5.1 *Wednesbury* unreasonableness

As we saw in Chapter 11, a distinction has traditionally been drawn between 'appeal' and 'review'. Returning to our example,[203] it is uncontroversial that a court could strike down the Minister's decision to allow the new airport to be built if she were to appear to be biased, or to have failed to act fairly, or to have taken into account irrelevant considerations. However, it would not be open to a judge to quash the decision simply because he disagreed with it. It might well be the case that, if the judge were asked to make the decision himself, he would consider that (for example) the environmental damage likely to be caused by the new airport outweighed the economic gains that it would bring. But such disagreement about the merits would not be lawful grounds for striking it down.

This does not mean that courts are wholly unconcerned with the merits of decisions, but they have traditionally confined themselves to asking whether—as Lord Greene MR put it in the *Wednesbury* case—the decision is 'so unreasonable that no reasonable authority could ever have come to it'.[204] Lord Greene cited as an example[205] of something that would be unreasonable in this sense a decision to dismiss a red-haired teacher simply because of the colour of her hair.[206] Meanwhile, in the *GCHQ* case, Lord Diplock preferred to speak of a decision 'which is so outrageous in its defiance of logic or of accepted moral standards that no sensible person who had applied his mind to the question to be decided could have arrived at it'.[207] Such dicta characterise unreasonableness as something quite exceptional. In this way, the courts seek to ensure that they do

---

[203] See section 1.

[204] *Associated Provincial Picture Houses Ltd v Wednesbury Corporation* [1948] 1 KB 223, 230.

[205] Given by Warrington LJ in *Short v Poole Corporation* [1926] Ch 66, 90–1.

[206] Of course, such a decision would also be unlawful on the grounds of having taken account of a legally irrelevant consideration. That is true of many '*Wednesbury* unreasonable' decisions.

[207] *Council of Civil Service Unions v Minister for the Civil Service* [1985] AC 374, 410.

not transgress the hallowed line between legality and merits by second-guessing public bodies and interfering just because they disagree with decision-makers' conclusions.

In reality, however, the position is more complex, and the willingness of the courts to examine the outcomes of decision-making processes varies depending on the circumstances. We saw in Chapter 11 that the reasons for judicial restraint in this area consist of *democratic* and *institutional* considerations—and it stands to reason that such concerns play out differently in different contexts. The courts have identified some circumstances in which they will be even *less* willing than usual to examine, on reasonableness grounds, the outcome of a decision-making process. Where, for example, certain councils challenged a Minister's decision (which had been approved by Parliament) to limit the levels at which they could set local taxes, Lord Scarman (whose speech commanded the assent of the other Law Lords) said that judicial intervention was improper in the absence of evidence that the Minister had acted in bad faith or that his decision was 'so absurd that he must have taken leave of his senses'.[208] His Lordship sought to justify this 'hands-off' approach on both democratic grounds (the Minister's policy had been approved by Parliament) and institutional grounds (the decision raised complex issues of national economic policy, the appropriateness of which the court lacked the expertise to judge).

Indeed, there are several reasons why courts may consider themselves institutionally ill-equipped to form a judgment about the content of a policy or decision. The difficulty may be one straightforwardly of expertise if the matter is highly technical or esoteric. Alternatively, where a decision is 'polycentric'—that is, where it is likely to have many, perhaps unpredictable, consequences—the court, by virtue of the fact that it hears only the limited amount of evidence put to it by the two parties to the dispute, will probably not be in a position to form a view about the appropriateness of whatever decision has been made.[209] For example, the decision in *Coughlan*[210] can be characterised as polycentric. The health authority was seeking to close the home in which the claimant was accommodated because it felt that scarce resources could be better used. In order to evaluate such an argument fully, it would be necessary to identify and ascribe value to all of the different uses to which the health authority could put its available funds, a task that the reviewing court was self-evidently not well situated to undertake.

Q Do you agree that the decision under review in *Coughlan* was a polycentric one? If so, was the court right to review the decision in the way that it did?

Just as courts are sometimes *less* willing to review the outcomes of decision-making processes, situations also arise in which they are *more* willing than usual to do so. For example, well before the entry into force of the HRA, the courts indicated

[208] *Nottinghamshire County Council v Secretary of State for the Environment* [1986] AC 240, 247.
[209] The concept of polycentricity is discussed in more detail in Chapter 14, section 3.2.
[210] *R v North and East Devon Health Authority, ex p Coughlan* [2001] QB 213.

a preparedness to adopt a more searching form of judicial review when decisions were said to infringe fundamental rights. As Sir Thomas Bingham MR put it in *R v Ministry of Defence, ex p Smith*: 'The more substantial the interference with human rights, the more the court will require by way of justification before it is satisfied that the decision is reasonable.'[211] The thinking was that reasonable people do not infringe human rights without good reason—and reasonable people do not *gravely* infringe such rights without *very* good reason.

This approach enabled the courts to look rather more critically at decisions that impacted upon human rights, although their role remained a relatively modest one, as *Smith* itself illustrates.[212] The claimants, all of whom had been dismissed from the British armed forces solely on the grounds of their sexual orientation, challenged the government's then policy banning gay men and lesbians from serving in the military. Notwithstanding that the case predated the HRA, Sir Thomas Bingham MR, in the Court of Appeal, said that the claimants' 'rights as human beings' were 'very much in issue'.[213] In the Divisional Court (the judgment of which was upheld by the Court of Appeal) Simon Brown LJ concluded that the government's justification for the ban— that military effectiveness and morale would be undermined by the presence of gay and lesbian personnel—was unconvincing, and reflected a 'wrong view . . . that rests too firmly upon the supposition of prejudice in others and which insufficiently recognises the damage to human rights inflicted'.[214] Nevertheless, he went on to conclude that the policy was not unlawful, because the court's role was limited to applying the unreasonableness doctrine—and, quoting Lord Diplock's formulation, which we set out earlier, he did not think the policy could be characterised as 'outrageous in its defiance of logic'.

Whether or not Simon Brown LJ was correct to think that the policy could not be so characterised, the fact that he could simultaneously regard the policy as *wrong*, but *lawful*, demonstrates that the *Wednesbury* unreasonableness test reserves considerable discretion to decision-makers, thereby preventing judicial interference except in relatively extreme circumstances. Indeed, the *Smith* case suggests that that remains the case, even when the test is adapted when the decision being examined impacts upon fundamental rights.

This characteristic of the test is, depending on one's perspective, either its greatest strength or its greatest weakness. For some commentators, the wide discretion with which *Wednesbury* furnishes decision-makers strikes the right balance between judicial control and government freedom.[215] For others, however, the latitude that decision-makers enjoy under the unreasonableness doctrine is unacceptably broad. Lord Cooke, for example, castigated *Wednesbury* as 'an unfortunately retrogressive decision', doubting that the law should ever 'be satisfied . . . merely by a finding that the decision under review is not capricious or absurd'.[216] The low level of review

---

[211] *R v Ministry of Defence, ex p Smith* [1996] QB 517, 554.   [212] *Smith*, 554.

[213] *Smith*, 556.   [214] *Smith*, 540.

[215] See, eg Irvine, 'Judges and Decision-Makers: The Theory and Practice of *Wednesbury* Review' [1996] PL 59.

[216] *R (Daly) v Secretary of State for the Home Department* [2001] UKHL 26, [2001] 2 AC 532, [32].

supplied by *Wednesbury* was considered especially problematic in human rights cases in which, many commentators felt, it would be appropriate for courts to scrutinise government decisions more rigorously. *Wednesbury* has also been subjected to criticism on other grounds. It has been observed that it is somewhat circular (defining unreasonableness as a lack of reasonableness) and unstructured; as a result, a finding of unreasonableness may not pinpoint exactly what was wrong with the decision.[217]

5.2 Proportionality—introduction

Those who are dissatisfied with *Wednesbury* have tended to look to the proportionality test as a more satisfactory principle by which to evaluate the outcomes of decision-making processes. It differs from *Wednesbury* in two main respects.

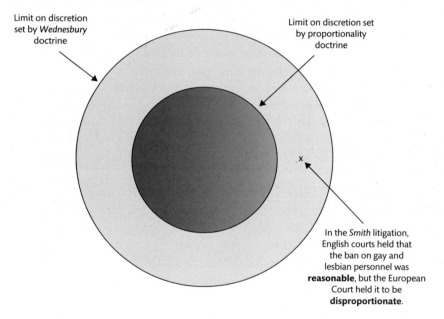

Figure 12.6 Substantive review

First, the *intensity of review* under proportionality may well be greater than that under *Wednesbury*, and the amount of discretion enjoyed by the decision-maker will be correspondingly smaller.[218] As Figure 12.6 shows, a decision that is reasonable might nevertheless be disproportionate, because the decision-maker's discretion is confined more tightly by the proportionality doctrine than by the reasonableness test. Second, the proportionality test is more *structured* than *Wednesbury*. There are a

---

[217] See further Jowell and Lester, 'Beyond *Wednesbury*: Substantive Principles of Administrative Law' [1987] PL 368.

[218] See, eg the speeches of Lords Steyn and Cooke in *R (Daly) v Secretary of State for the Home Department* [2001] UKHL 26, [2001] 2 AC 532.

number of different formulations of the former, but it may conveniently be thought of as involving four questions, as follows:

(i) Has a *protected interest* (eg a human right) been compromised by the decision in question?

(ii) Was the interest compromised in the pursuit of some *legitimate aim*?

(iii) Was it *necessary* to compromise the protected interest (to whatever extent it has been compromised) in order to achieve the legitimate aim?

(iv) Is there an *adequate relationship of proportionality*[219] between the damage caused to the protected interest and the positive consequences that flow from achieving the legitimate aim?[220] (This is sometimes referred to as the 'narrow proportionality' issue, in order to distinguish it from the overarching notion of proportionality, which consists of all four issues.)

This may seem rather abstract, but an example will help to clarify what these questions mean in practice. Indeed, an example is provided by the *Smith* case, which we have already considered. The claimants, having lost in the English courts, took their case to the ECtHR, which used the proportionality test to assess the legality of the UK's policy banning gay men and lesbians from the armed forces.[221]

First, the Court held that a *protected interest*—the right to respect for private and family life, guaranteed by Art 8 of the ECHR—had been compromised by the policy. This followed, in part, because it is recognised that respect for the 'sexual life' of the individual is an intrinsic element of respect for private life.[222]

Second, it was held that the UK's policy pursued a *legitimate aim*. Article 8(2) permits respect for private life to be compromised to the extent that this is necessary in 'the interests of national security' and 'for the prevention of disorder'. The Court accepted that the policy was designed to pursue these objectives, bearing in mind the UK's contention that it promoted 'the maintenance of the morale of service personnel and, consequently, of the fighting power and the operational effectiveness of the armed forces'.[223]

These conclusions required the Court, third, to consider whether it was *necessary* to ban gay men and lesbians from the armed forces in order to achieve the legitimate aim. The UK government argued that this was so, contending that the presence of gay men and lesbians in the armed forces would have had a destabilising effect, given the close quarters in which service personnel must live, and the trust and confidence that they have to repose in one another. The UK government's argument was based, in part, on research that indicated that existing service personnel did not welcome the prospect of serving alongside gay and lesbian colleagues. Although the government

---

[219] Somewhat confusingly, the term 'proportionality' appears only in the fourth question—but all four stages of the test are generally referred to as the 'proportionality test'.

[220] This final question was recognised in *Huang v Secretary of State for the Home Department* [2007] UKHL 11, [2007] 2 AC 167, [19], although courts do not always clearly distinguish the third and fourth questions.

[221] *Smith v United Kingdom* (2000) 29 EHRR 493.

[222] *Dudgeon v United Kingdom* (1982) 4 EHRR 149, 160.   [223] *Smith v United Kingdom*, 522.

resisted such a characterisation, its argument essentially reduced to the proposition that the policy was necessary because institutional homophobia would otherwise have compromised the forces' effectiveness.

The Court rejected this submission. In doing so, it noted that it is only possible to establish that a given course of action is necessary for the achievement of some aim if the aim could not be realised by less drastic means. The crucial question, therefore, was whether it was possible to preserve the effectiveness of the armed forces by taking steps that would inflict less (or no) damage on the claimants' right to respect for private life. The Court held that it was, noting that the UK's arguments 'were founded solely upon the negative attitudes of heterosexual personnel towards those of homosexual orientation'.[224] The government, said the Court, had not demonstrated that less draconian measures—such as the adoption of appropriate codes of conduct, disciplinary rules, and education programmes—would be inadequate to address issues arising from allowing gay men and lesbians to openly serve in the armed forces. The UK policy was therefore held to be in breach of the ECHR.[225]

In light of that conclusion, it was not necessary for the Court to address the fourth, 'narrow proportionality' question—that is, whether the restriction of the applicants' rights was proportionate to the aim being pursued. However, it did note that 'when the relevant restrictions concern "a most intimate part of an individual's private life" '—in other words, where there is a serious limitation of a core aspect of the right—'there must exist "particularly serious reasons" before such interferences can satisfy the requirements of Article 8(2) of the Convention'.[226]

Conversely, when the House of Lords was called upon, in the *Miss Behavin'* case, to decide whether a council's decision to refuse to license a sex shop unlawfully breached the owner's right to freedom of expression, Lord Hoffmann regarded this as representing (at most) a minor qualification of the right. Noting that the 'right to vend pornography is not the most important right of free expression in a democratic society', his Lordship concluded that denying a licence to a sex shop 'would require very unusual facts for it to amount to a disproportionate restriction on Convention rights'.[227] The general principle, therefore, is that the more serious the interference with the right, the weightier the justification must be.

> **Q** How, exactly, does the ECtHR's analysis of the *Smith* case differ from that of the English courts? Which analysis do you prefer, and why?

5.3 Proportionality, and the distinction between appeal and review

The proportionality test is a long-standing feature of the case law of the ECtHR. It is the means by which the Court tests the legality of measures that interfere with

---

[224] *Smith v United Kingdom*, 532.   [225] The policy was later abandoned.
[226] *Smith v United Kingdom*, 529, quoting from *Dudgeon* at [52].
[227] *Belfast City Council v Miss Behavin' Ltd* [2007] UKHL 19, [2007] 1 WLR 1420, [16].

so-called qualified rights—that is, rights that can lawfully be restricted if this is necessary in order to pursue some conflicting legitimate interest. (The right to respect for
private life, mentioned in section 5.2, is an example of a qualified right.[228]) Following
the entry into force of the HRA,[229] English courts have also adopted the proportionality test in cases concerning qualified rights.[230]

However, some judges were reluctant to welcome proportionality into domestic
law. In 1991, Lord Ackner argued that '[t]he European [proportionality] test . . . must
ultimately result in the question "Is the particular decision acceptable?" and this must
involve a review of the merits of the decision'.[231] His fear was that the distinction
between appeal and review[232] would not survive English courts' embrace of the proportionality doctrine. The challenge, then, is to apply the proportionality test in a
way that recognises that the roles of judges and decision-makers are distinct: as Laws
LJ put it in *R (Mahmood) v Secretary of State for the Home Department*,[233] there must
continue to be 'a principled distance between the court's adjudication . . . and the
Secretary of State's decision, based on his perception of the case's merits'.

In fact, experience teaches that it *is* possible for courts to engage in proportionality
review while keeping the roles of the judge and the decision-maker separate—thereby
ensuring that the decision-maker maintains a measure of discretion, and that the
distinction between appeal and review is preserved. This is so because the role of the
court, when applying the proportionality doctrine, is not to identify the one and only
proportionate decision that is open to the decision-maker; rather, its function is to
determine whether the decision that has been taken is *disproportionate*, and therefore
unlawful. Unless the court applies the proportionality test in an extremely rigorous
manner, it is perfectly possible for certain decisions to be ruled out as disproportionate, while leaving more than one proportionate option open to the decision-maker.

In this way, the proportionality test and administrative discretion are capable of
coexisting. For example, in *Smith*, the ECtHR ruled that a complete ban on gay men
and lesbians was disproportionate, but this left the UK government with discretion as
to what steps (eg tackling homophobia) should be taken so as to ensure that allowing
people to serve in the armed forces irrespective of their sexual orientation did not
compromise military effectiveness.

5.4 **Deference**

It is clear, then, that proportionality review need not amount to what is sometimes
called 'full merits review', whereby courts simply replace the decision-maker's view
with their own. However, it stands to reason that the amount of discretion enjoyed by

---

[228] In contrast, 'absolute rights'—such as the right, under Art 3, not to be subjected to torture or to
inhuman or degrading treatment—may not lawfully be restricted.

[229] See Chapter 18 for detailed discussion of the HRA.

[230] *R (Daly) v Secretary of State for the Home Department* [2001] UKHL 26, [2001] 2 AC 532 is generally
considered to be the landmark judgment in this area, although, as we note later, it was actually concerned
principally with *common law* rights, as distinct from rights arising under the HRA and the ECHR.

[231] *R v Secretary of State for the Home Department, ex p Brind* [1991] 1 AC 696, 762–63.

[232] On which, see Chapter 11.   [233] [2001] 1 WLR 840, [33].

decision-makers will turn on the strictness with which the courts police compliance with the various requirements that form the proportionality test. If, for instance, the 'necessity' element of the proportionality test is taken to mean that the only thing that can be lawfully done is the thing that has the smallest possible impact on the right, and if the reviewing court decides entirely for itself whether that requirement is met, significant inroads into the decision-maker's discretion will result. Equally, if, at the final stage of the proportionality test, the court weighs up for itself, without any reference to the decision-maker's own assessment of such matters, whether the public policy 'gain' yielded by the decision is worth the human rights 'loss' occasioned by it, little, if any, discretion will remain for the decision-maker.

Recognising that such far-reaching judicial intervention might sometimes—and perhaps often—be unwarranted, courts have developed the notion of *deference*. The meaning and appropriateness of this concept have been the subject of heated academic debate. Two principal schools of thought may be distinguished.

On the first view, Allan argues that when courts 'defer', they effectively refuse to determine whether the decision in question is lawful.[234] Allan is rightly critical of this extreme sort of deference, arguing that judges who engage in it are guilty of dereliction of duty. However, while there is some judicial support[235] for the sort of deference that Allan criticises, the dominant view favours a more subtle, and more defensible, idea of deference.[236]

On this second, more moderate view, deference simply involves the court, where appropriate, attaching particular weight, or respect, to the view of the decision-maker—thus making it less likely that that view will be overturned on judicial review. There is clear authority, at the highest judicial levels, supporting this approach, albeit that some judges have been reluctant to adopt the 'deference' label.[237] In practice, deference (understood in the latter sense) can and does operate in relation to two matters.

First, deference may be appropriate in relation to the question of whether it is *necessary* to compromise (say) a human right in order to achieve some legitimate (but conflicting) aim. Whether the court is in a position to form its own view on this point, or whether it is appropriate for the court to take the government's word at face value (or at least to attach considerable respect to the government's view), depends principally on the *relative institutional competence* of the judge and the decision-maker. In other words, does the court have the necessary expertise to form a judgment?

For example, in the *Belmarsh* case, the House of Lords had to determine whether detaining suspected foreign terrorists without charge or trial was necessary in order

---

[234] 'Human Rights and Judicial Review: A Critique of "Due Deference"' [2006] CLJ 671.

[235] See, eg *R v Director of Public Prosecutions, ex p Kebilene* [2000] 2 AC 326, 380, *per* Lord Hope; *International Transport Roth GmbH v Secretary of State for the Home Department* [2002] EWCA Civ 158, [2003] QB 728, [77], *per* Laws LJ.

[236] Advocates of this view include Hunt, 'Sovereignty's Blight: Why Contemporary Public Law Needs the Concept of "Due Deference"', in Bamforth and Leyland (eds), *Public Law in a Multi-Layered Constitution* (Oxford 2003); Young, 'In Defence of Due Deference' (2009) 72 MLR 554; Kavanagh, 'Defending Deference in Public Law and Constitutional Theory' (2010) 126 LQR 222.

[237] See, eg *Huang v Secretary of State for the Home Department* [2007] UKHL 11, [2007] 2 AC 167, [16], *per* Lord Bingham.

to uphold public safety.[238] The court had no difficulty in holding that such measures were *not* necessary, since the government had not detained UK nationals posing an equivalent threat. As Baroness Hale put it: '[I]f it is not necessary to lock up the nationals it cannot be necessary to lock up the foreigners.'[239] In those circumstances, that what had been done was not necessary could be inferred by the court simply by resort to common sense; no special knowledge or expertise was needed.

In other circumstances, however, working out whether it is necessary to take certain steps so as to realise a given objective may be a far more difficult matter—because, as Rivers has observed, 'we often do not know how much any particular act will achieve its end'.[240]

Consider, in this regard, *Nicklinson*—a case that concerned the compatibility of *legislation* with human rights, but which equally illustrates circumstances in which courts might defer to the government when evaluating *administrative action* against human rights standards.[241] The Suicide Act 1961, by making it a criminal offence to assist someone to commit suicide, impinges upon the right to respect for private life.[242] That is so because it means that people—like the claimant in *Nicklinson*—who are so incapacitated as to be unable to commit suicide other than by declining nutrition and hydration are denied autonomy in respect of the ending of their lives. The question for the Supreme Court was whether the ban on assisted suicide was a proportionate restriction of the right. In that regard, the question arose whether the ban was a *necessary* means of protecting the interests of vulnerable people who might, in the absence of a ban, feel pressured into availing themselves of assisted suicide.

The majority of the Justices were not prepared to rule that the ban was unnecessary. Lord Mance, for instance, said that '[w]hen considering whether a particular measure is necessary . . . courts should recognise that there can . . . be wisdom and relevance' in the argument that the court may be 'less well equipped' than the decision-maker to form that judgement.[243] Lord Sumption went further, noting that Parliament, which had enacted the legislation in question, was better able to resolve the 'controversial and complex questions of fact arising out of moral and social dilemmas' such as that raised in *Nicklinson*, not least because it has 'access to a fuller range of expert judgment and experience than forensic litigation can possibly provide'.[244] Precisely the same arguments can be made in situations in which the government, as distinct from Parliament, has expertise and resources at its disposal, together with the capacity to examine matters from a variety of perspectives, that courts operating under the constraints of the adversarial model self-evidently lack.

---

[238] *A v Secretary of State for the Home Department* [2004] UKHL 56, [2005] 2 AC 68. See further Chapter 1, section 3.1.2.

[239] *A*, [231]. It is noteworthy that the House of Lords took such a robust approach in this case, bearing in mind that English courts have traditionally been extremely deferential in cases concerning national security: cf *Secretary of State for the Home Department v Rehman* [2001] UKHL 47, [2003] 1 AC 153, *per* Lord Hoffmann.

[240] Rivers, 'Proportionality and Variable Intensity Review' [2006] CLJ 174, 199.

[241] *R (Nicklinson) v Ministry of Justice* [2014] UKSC 38, [2015] AC 657.

[242] That right is protected by Art 8 ECHR.   [243] *Nicklinson*, [164] and [166].

[244] *Nicklinson*, [232].

Second, it may be appropriate for the court to defer to the decision-maker's view in the context of addressing the 'narrow proportionality question'—that is, the question whether there is an *adequate relationship of proportionality* between the restriction on the right and the positive consequences flowing from the restriction. This can be illustrated by reference to the *Carlile* case, involving a challenge to the government's decision not to allow Maryam Rajavi, a dissident Iranian politician, to enter the UK in order to address parliamentarians.[245] The government contended that this restriction upon freedom of expression was justified because UK-Iranian relations would have been compromised—and the government's ability to secure certain foreign policy objectives reduced—if Rajavi were allowed to enter the country for the desired purpose. Within this factual matrix, the 'narrow proportionality' question was whether the restriction of free speech could be justified by reference to the public interest in maintaining good relations with Iran and thereby safeguarding the UK's foreign policy capacity in the Middle East.

By a majority, the Supreme Court refused to hold that the government's decision to ban Rajavi from entering the UK was disproportionate. In reaching that view, the Court expressed its support for what might be called *democratic deference*—that is, the appropriateness, in certain circumstances, of judges ascribing weight or respect to the decision-maker's view in the light of the decision-maker's democratic credentials.

Lord Sumption said that even when fundamental rights are at stake, 'there remain areas which although not immune from scrutiny require a qualified respect for the constitutional functions of decision-makers who are democratically accountable'.[246] Lady Hale, meanwhile, noted that the 'narrow proportionality' question 'involves weighing or balancing values which many may think cannot be weighed against one another'.[247] Her point was that the importance to be ascribed (on the one hand) to the advancement of the UK's foreign policy interests and the domestic advantages liable to flow from doing so and (on the other hand) to freedom of political expression ultimately reduce to value-judgements on which reasonable minds can and do differ. On such matters, said Lady Hale, courts should be mindful of the fact that the government 'is accountable to Parliament in a way which we [judges] are not'.[248] In such circumstances, it is appropriate for the court—rather than simply determining for itself whether a suitable balance has been struck between the right and the competing interest—to attach a degree of weight to the government's assessment of where the balance should lie.

However, the notion of democratic deference does not have the unanimous, full-blooded support of senior judges. Indeed, in *Carlile* itself, Lord Kerr argued that the courts are required 'not only to examine the reasons given for the interference [with the right] but also to decide *for themselves* whether that interference is justified'.[249] However, this view was advanced by Lord Kerr in a dissenting judgment and was not shared by the other Justices in *Carlile*.

In conclusion, we can say that applying the proportionality test does not necessarily threaten the distinction between appeal and review, and it does not result in courts

---

[245] *R v Secretary of State for the Home Department, ex p Carlile* [2014] UKSC 60, [2015] AC 945.
[246] *Carlile*, [28].   [247] *Carlile*, [104].   [248] *Carlile*, [105].   [249] *Carlile*, [152].

entirely removing discretion from decision-makers. The court's role is to identify—and rule out of contention—measures that would disproportionately impact on protected interests (most obviously human rights). In doing so, however, courts may attach weight to—and leave undisturbed—the views of decision-makers where this is appropriate on grounds of either institutional competence or democracy. It follows that the reviewing court does not simply substitute its view for that of the decision-maker: the court's role is still to identify the limits of the decision-maker's discretion, albeit that the proportionality test—as Figure 12.6 shows—generally draws those limits more tightly than the *Wednesbury* principle. It is, all things being equal, easier to establish that a decision is disproportionate than it is to establish that it is unreasonable. However, establishing disproportionality emphatically is not, and should not be, simply a matter of finding a judge who disagrees with the decision.

5.5 **The trajectory of the law in this area**

For some time now, the possibility of the *Wednesbury* unreasonableness test being replaced by proportionality has been canvassed. It has been argued that proportionality, as a more structured test, is preferable to *Wednesbury*, and that any concerns there might be about proportionality being unduly intrusive can be assuaged by recourse to the notion of deference.[250] Now that courts in the UK are familiar with proportionality and have shown themselves capable of applying it in a way that is sensitive to judges' and decision-makers' distinct roles, it is time, the argument runs, to get rid of *Wednesbury* and to rely on proportionality in all relevant cases. In 2003, the Court of Appeal appeared to buy precisely this argument, saying that it had 'difficulty in seeing what justification there now is for retaining the *Wednesbury* test', although it held that (for reasons of precedent) only the House of Lords (and so now the Supreme Court) could 'perform [the *Wednesbury* doctrine's] burial rites'.[251]

So far, those rites have not been performed—although the Supreme Court has signalled that the time is now ripe for a major review of the law in this area.[252] As to the likely direction of the law following such a review at Supreme Court level, there are at least clues in the existing case law as it has taken shape in recent years. Two developments, in particular, warrant comment.

First, the courts have shown themselves to be increasingly receptive to the possibility of applying the proportionality doctrine beyond human rights cases. This suggests that proportionality can no longer be regarded as a 'foreign' doctrine whose field of application is coterminous with that of the HRA. It is, for instance, clear that the proportionality test now applies in certain substantive legitimate expectation cases,

---

[250] See, eg Craig, 'Proportionality, Rationality and Review' [2010] NZ L Rev 265.

[251] *R (Association of British Civilian Internees: Far East Region) v Secretary of State for Defence* [2003] EWCA Civ 473, [2003] QB 1397, [34]–[35].

[252] See, eg *Keyu v Secretary of State for Foreign and Commonwealth Affairs* [2015] UKSC 69, [2015] 3 WLR 1665, [131]–[133], *per* Lord Neuberger; *R (Youssef) v Secretary of State for Foreign and Commonwealth Affairs* [2016] UKSC 3, [2016] 2 WLR 509, [55], *per* Lord Carnwath.

as noted earlier.[253] Meanwhile, some of the judgments in the *Pham* case suggest that the proportionality doctrine—rather than *Wednesbury*—can apply even if neither a fundamental right nor a legitimate expectation is in play, provided that what is at stake is sufficiently important.[254] (In *Pham*, it was the claimant's British citizenship that was in question.)

These developments are consonant with the House of Lords' judgment in *Daly*, decided shortly after the entry into force of the HRA. The Law Lords unequivocally embraced proportionality, and the case is commonly, but incorrectly, taken to stand for the proposition that it is the HRA that now licenses judicial application of the proportionality test in domestic cases. In fact, however, *Daly* endorses the idea that proportionality is a ground of judicial review *at common law*, and that its application is not tied to the HRA. From this it follows that proportionality need not apply only in HRA, or other human rights, cases—a possibility that more recent decisions like *Pham* are now beginning to explore.

Second, along with growing judicial receptiveness to proportionality as a domestic ground of review that may apply not only to but beyond human rights cases, it is possible to discern judicial development of the *Wednesbury* doctrine along lines that erode its distinctiveness when viewed alongside proportionality. There are two dimensions to this.

On the one hand, there arises the possibility of the *Wednesbury* doctrine serving to protect—as the proportionality doctrine does—specific values by determining whether their infraction has been justified to the court's satisfaction.[255] For instance, in the *Rotherham* case it was unsuccessfully argued that the UK government had allocated EU funds in a way that involved unjustified differential treatment of different parts of the country.[256] Against that background, Lord Sumption endorsed the idea—advanced in an earlier case by Lord Hoffmann—that 'equality' is a 'ground for holding [an] administrative act to have been irrational'.[257] Viewed thus, the question whether the allocation of funds was unreasonable turned on whether the differential treatment could be adequately justified.

On the other hand, there is the possibility of conceiving of *Wednesbury* in a way that involves closer, and more structured, examination of decisions than traditional formulations of the test provide for.[258] For example, in *Keyu*, Lady Hale (in a dissenting judgment) applied the *Wednesbury* test in a notably rigorous fashion, which enabled her to subject to detailed scrutiny the way in which the decision-maker had balanced competing considerations against one another.

What, then, does this suggest about the trajectory of the law in this area? The courts are clearly now open to the possibility of proportionality applying in a range of circumstances much broader than human rights cases. At the same time, the courts are

---

[253] See section 4.3.2.

[254] *Pham v Secretary of State for the Home Department* [2015] UKSC 19, [2015] 1 WLR 1591.

[255] On this idea, see generally Daly, '*Wednesbury*'s reason and structure' [2011] PL 238.

[256] *R (Rotherham Metropolitan Borough Council) v Secretary of State for Business, Innovation and Skills* [2015] UKSC 6, [2015] PTSR 322.

[257] *Matadeen v Pointu* [1999] 1 AC 98, 109.

[258] See Craig, 'The Nature of Reasonableness Review' (2013) 66 CLP 131.

prepared to apply the *Wednesbury* test in a way that reduces the extent to which it differs from proportionality. On one view, this might appear to sound the *Wednesbury* doctrine's death knell.

Yet it would be premature to conclude that the unreasonableness principle has reached the end of its life. The central message that emerges from recent jurisprudence in this area is that—as Lord Steyn famously put it in *Daly*—'context is everything'.[259] On that approach, the crucial requirement is that the intensity and structure of substantive review is appropriate to the particular facts and circumstances of the case. If that requirement is to be taken seriously, then it is arguable that it makes little sense to remove items—like *Wednesbury*—from the judicial toolbox.

As noted earlier, the Supreme Court appears to be gearing up for a review of the law in this area. In the meantime, three things are clear. First, proportionality is here to stay, and is now firmly established as a feature of domestic law. Second, *Wednesbury* has not (yet) been done away with. However, third—and this is where things become murkier—it is no longer, if it ever was, accurate to postulate proportionality and *Wednesbury* as radically different grounds of review. Proportionality, for all that it is capable of serving as a vehicle for close judicial scrutiny of administrative action, can be substantially toned down through deference—just as *Wednesbury*, in the ways outlined earlier, can be applied in a manner that bears some resemblance to the proportionality test. The Supreme Court will ultimately have to decide whether greater lucidity should be brought to this area, either by making the distinction between the two principles' respective spheres of application clearer or by removing that distinction entirely, in favour of a single principle—most likely proportionality—that could be applied more or less rigorously depending on the circumstances.

> **Q** Should the courts ditch the *Wednesbury* principle in favour of proportionality? What would be the advantages and disadvantages of embracing proportionality as the only ground of substantive judicial review?

6. Concluding remarks

In this chapter, we have seen that there exist many and varied grounds on which courts may review decisions taken by public bodies. A notable theme in this area concerns the *deepening*, in recent years, of judicial scrutiny of the executive. This is apparent from a number of the developments traced in this chapter. New grounds of review—such as legitimate expectation and proportionality—have emerged, often involving a greater degree of judicial oversight of executive decisions than has traditionally existed. This prompts, by way of conclusion, two sets of comments.

First, these developments reflect the way in which two of the key themes of this book—the importance of ensuring adequate oversight of executive power, and the

---

[259] *R (Daly) v Secretary of State for the Home Department* [2001] UKHL 26, [2001] 2 AC 532, [28].

shift from a more political to a more legal constitution—intersect in this context. The emergence of more stringent judicial control of executive power—through the development of principles such as substantive legitimate expectation and proportionality, aided by the enactment of the HRA—underlies increasing reliance on the courts as a mechanism for ensuring the responsible use of executive power. And this, in turn, reflects a growing emphasis on legal, as distinct from political, arrangements for the control of governmental power. In this way, questions of substantive policy—should public authorities be allowed to renege on their promises? Should service in the armed forces be open to all, irrespective of sexual orientation?—have acquired new legal dimensions, opening them up to judicial, as well as political, challenge.

Whether this is a good or a bad thing depends on one's perspective. For many, it is entirely appropriate that courts should act as guardians of individuals' fundamental rights and interests, standing as independent arbiters of whether, and if so on what conditions, such rights and interests may be sacrificed by the government for (what it considers to be) the greater good. But for writers, such as those we met in Chapter 11, who are deeply suspicious of judicial interference (as they would see it) in the business of government, the growing depth of modern judicial review is doubtless a source of concern. In all of this, it is important to recognise that no simple choice, between judicial *or* political control of the executive, falls to be made. It is inevitable and desirable that the two forms of control should coexist, but it is important to take stock of whether the modern British constitution strikes the right balance between these two methods by which responsible government can be promoted. In particular, it is crucial to recognise that greater reliance on judicial review is not the only—and is certainly not necessarily the right—response to the weaknesses of the political system.[260]

Second, the deepening of judicial review, through adoption of concepts such as proportionality, requires us to re-evaluate received wisdom in this area. As we noted in Chapter 11—and as we have mentioned in this chapter—orthodox theory ascribes a highly limited role to the courts in exercise of their powers of judicial review. A bright line is envisaged between questions of legality (which are for courts) and questions of merits or policy (with which it is improper for courts to engage). This distinction has always been difficult to maintain, but it makes less and less sense as we begin to embrace substantive principles of justice as legal constraints on governmental power. Once it is acknowledged that rights to respect for private life, freedom of speech, freedom of religion, and so on constitute legal restrictions on administrative discretion, it is impossible to avoid some degree of judicial engagement with the substance of executive decisions, thus blurring the appeal/review distinction as traditionally conceived.

While this may be a source of regret for purists, orthodox teaching concerning the proper role of the courts is not *inherently* right: it merely reflects a particular conception of the separation of powers doctrine generally, and of the relationship between judges and decision-makers in particular. The challenge that now faces administrative lawyers and judges is to establish a new vision of how the courts and the executive should relate to one another, and of where the boundaries between their respective

---

[260] On which, see further Chapters 5 and 10.

provinces should lie. That is the challenge that underlies (for example) attempts to articulate a doctrine of deference so as to enable courts applying the proportionality doctrine to pay appropriate (but only appropriate) respect to executive decisions.

We therefore end this chapter by reiterating the point that we developed in the last one, by observing that administrative law, for all of its technicality and detail, is part of our wider constitutional fabric, and represents the working out, in a particular legal context, of much broader debates about the proper relationship between the different branches of the constitution.

Expert commentary
Five steps for avoiding the rookie's mistake in understanding
the grounds of judicial review
Liz Fisher, Professor of Environmental Law, University of Oxford

There are important statements throughout this chapter about nuance, detail, incrementalism and context. In my experience, the rookie's mistake is to ignore those statements. Newcomers to the subject give in to the temptation of thinking that the different grounds of review snap together like a jigsaw puzzle—a puzzle that can be applied in any context. I thought that when I was attempting to master the subject and I have seen many students do exactly the same over the past twenty years. My and their experience is that, while such an approach might result in some very pretty revision diagrams, it also results in frustration, tears and confusion when it comes to making sense of the actual grounds of review.

This is because if you read any judicial review case it quickly becomes clear that the grounds of review overlap, are malleable, and are reasoned in different ways by different judges. There is no neat jigsaw puzzle. No resounding click of the pieces as they connect. For two excellent examples of this see the different approaches of the judges to reviewing the sentencing decision in *R v Secretary of State for the Home Department, ex p Venables and Thompson*[261] and Joanna Bell's analysis of recent legitimate expectation case law.[262]

So here are my five tips for thinking about the material in this chapter. Most of them are just repeating what has been said in a more concise and/or different form. They are irritating tips because they make clear there are no easy short cuts for understanding this area of law (at the very least there is value in rereading this chapter). On the other hand, following them will not only result in a lot less throwing cases and books at the wall, but also ensure you really get to grips with this subject.

First, statutes matter. In the words of the US Supreme Court judge, Justice Felix Frankfurter, 'Read the statute, read the statute, read the statute'. Not necessarily all of it, but the bits that matter. I know legislation can be boring and I know that some of it can be impenetrable, but in most cases the starting point for legal analysis in a judicial review case is what the statute or delegated legislation empowers the decision-maker to do. Legislation can empower many things in many different ways—and that will shape how the grounds of review are argued and how they apply. The focus on legislation in the case study is thus really important in helping you develop your legal technique in this area.

---

[261] [1998] AC 407.
[262] Bell, 'The Doctrine of Legitimate Expectations: Power-Constraining or Right-Conferring Legal Standard?' [2016] PL 437.

That leads me onto my second point. Administrative decisions do not come along with little labels on them explaining to the world when the decision-maker committed an error of law. The grounds of review are arguments made by a barrister in a court to show that an error of law has occurred. The barrister has a choice in what to argue and how to argue it. To put the matter another way, grounds of review are legal constructs being applied to real world situations. It is possible that different grounds of review may apply to the same decision, and even to the same 'error' in a decision (see *Venables* earlier). Also remember that a section 6 Human Rights Act challenge is a distinct legal argument from arguing a common law judicial review ground.

Third, and following on from that, not all grounds are created equal. Courts are more comfortable with some grounds of review as compared to others due to issues of institutional and constitutional competence. As noted by Jowell,[263] matters of *procedure* are far more likely to be understood as matters within the courts' competence than matters of substance. Likewise in regards to matters of substance, the courts are far happier dealing with the *process* by which the decision was made (improper purpose, relevant and irrelevant considerations, etc) rather than ruling on whether the final *impact* of the decision was the correct one.

Fourth, understanding the evolution of judicial review is important. The grounds of review as listed in *Council of Civil Service Unions v Minister for the Civil Service*[264] were codifications of the law not rationalisations. As noted earlier, language does change and the grounds of review have evolved as has judicial review procedure. Before 1980, there was no distinct judicial review procedure and it shows in the reasoning of the cases. *Associated Provincial Picture Houses Ltd v Wednesbury Corporation*[265] is occurring in an entirely different legal context from a case such as *R v Ministry of Defence, ex p Smith*.[266] A tip for revision in this regard is to think about the cases in chronological order and against the background of other public law developments.

Fifth, and finally, always remember that legal reasoning matters. It is true that normative outlooks on a variety of matters shape approaches to judicial review. It is also true that different judges may approach the same ground of review in different ways. There is also no doubt that many decisions will have important political implications. But none of this is to say that judicial review is just politics or values in a different guise—to say that is just to engage in lazy and non-falsifiable thinking. The point of all of the above is that the key in getting to grips with this case law is to get to grips with the legal detail and see how that detail shapes the grounds of review of their application.

Further reading

CRAIG, 'The Nature of Reasonableness Review' (2013) 66 CLP 1
    Analysis of how reasonableness review works, and of the extent to which it enables judicial examination of questions of weight and balance.

ELLIOTT and VARUHAS, *Administrative Law: Text and Materials* (Oxford 2017)
    Text and materials book on administrative law.

---

[263] Jowell, 'Of Vires and Vacuums: The Constitutional Context of Judicial Review' [1999] PL 448.
[264] [1984] AC 374.   [265] [1948] 1 KB 223.   [266] [1996] QB 517.

GALLIGAN, *Due Process and Fair Procedures: A Study of Administrative Procedures* (Oxford 1996)

A detailed study in the area of procedural fairness.

SALES and STEYN, 'Legitimate Expectations in English Public Law: An Analysis' [2004] PL 564

An examination of the doctrine of substantive legitimate expectations.

WILBERG and ELLIOTT, *The Scope and Intensity of Substantive Review: Traversing Taggart's Rainbow* (Oxford 2015)

A collection of essays on substantive judicial review, examining such matters as the relationship between the reasonableness and proportionality doctrines.

WILLIAMS, 'When is an Error Not an Error? Reform of Jurisdictional Review of Error of Law and Fact' [2007] PL 793

A critical analysis of the law on jurisdictional review.

13

Judicial Review—Scope, Procedures, and Remedies

1. Introduction	556
2. What decisions can be judicially reviewed?	557
3. Procedure	567
4. Remedies	578
5. Conclusions	586
Expert commentary	586
Further reading	588

1. Introduction

In Chapter 12, we examined the various grounds upon which it is possible to challenge administrative decisions by way of judicial review. We now turn to address a number of practical matters that must be confronted by litigants who propose to launch judicial review proceedings, and by courts dealing with such claims.

First, we consider the *sort of decisions* that can be reviewed. It is clear from the examples and cases encountered in Chapter 12 that many decisions taken by public authorities under statutory powers are open to review—but what about other decision-makers and other types of power? What if the subject matter of the decision is something that courts feel unqualified to consider, or if Parliament has stipulated that judicial review of a particular decision should not occur? These questions are important both for their own sake and for their relevance to our key themes. For example, if courts are prepared to assert authority to review the making of a broad range of decisions, this implies that they consider themselves to have a key role in ensuring the accountable use of power.

Second, we examine the *procedure* under which courts subject decisions to judicial review. Questions about procedure may seem—and to an extent are—technical. But they also invite answers that are of wider significance to the book's key themes. For example, should courts allow government decisions to be challenged by anyone at all, or only by those who are directly affected? Favouring a broad approach (which, as we will see, the courts do) implies a general preference for judicial control of government, and chimes with our theme of the shift from a more political to a more legal constitution.

Third, we look at the *remedies* that courts may issue in judicial review proceedings. This, too, will cast light on matters of general importance. For example, to what extent should courts intervene pre-emptively by ruling that it would be unlawful for public authorities to engage in certain kinds of conduct? A narrow view of the courts' function would imply that they should limit themselves to resolving disputes, pronouncing only upon the legality of actions already undertaken. But if the courts' role is conceived of more broadly, it might be appropriate for courts to enter the fray at an earlier stage—for example, by pronouncing on the legality of *proposed* government action.

2. What decisions can be judicially reviewed?

As Figure 13.1 illustrates, whether a decision is judicially reviewable turns on three factors: whether the statute contains an *ouster clause* prohibiting judicial review, the *type of power* under which the decision was taken, and whether the claimant's case raises *justiciable issues*.

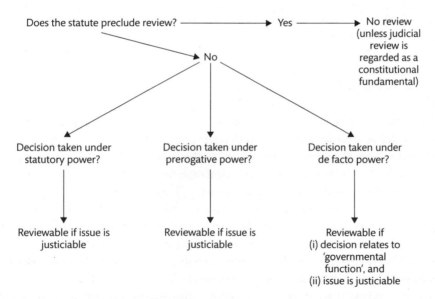

Figure 13.1 Can the decision be judicially reviewed?

2.1 **Ouster clauses**

If Parliament is sovereign, it stands to reason that it can, if it so chooses, prohibit judicial review of decisions taken under certain (or even all) powers.[1] The Foreign

---

[1] See Chapter 5, section 6.

Compensation Act 1950 appears to be a rare example of Parliament seeking to do precisely this. The Act provided: 'The determination by the [Foreign Compensation Commission] of any application made to them under this Act shall not be called in question in any court of law.'[2] A company, Anisminic, sought compensation from the Commission but was turned down. When Anisminic later challenged that decision, the House of Lords had to rule on whether the Act precluded judicial review.[3] The House of Lords therefore found itself in a delicate position, since two fundamental constitutional principles appeared to be pulling in different directions. Fidelity to the sovereign will of Parliament seemed to require the Court to rule that judicial review was unavailable. But the rule of law—which requires, among other things, that people should be able to have legal disputes resolved by independent courts[4]—demanded the opposite outcome. Presented with this dilemma, their Lordships deftly—or disingenuously, depending on one's perspective—ruled that the Act did not really mean what it seemed to mean. Lord Pearce observed that Parliament had only precluded judicial review of 'determinations'. By this, he said, Parliament 'meant a real determination, not a purported determination': review of the former was precluded by the statute; review of the latter was not.[5] The question, therefore, was whether the Commission's determination was 'real' or 'purported'. This, said their Lordships, turned on whether the Commission had exceeded its powers by misinterpreting the rules governing the eligibility for compensation. The House of Lords held that the Commission had committed precisely such an error, and that the ouster clause did not prevent judicial intervention in such circumstances.

The *Anisminic* decision can be viewed on two levels. Superficially, the Court appeared to act in an entirely orthodox way. The word 'determination'—the meaning of which was, as we have seen, pivotal—was said to be ambiguous, and the Court, forced to choose between rival interpretations, felt that it should favour the one that preserved judicial review.[6] So, said Lord Wilberforce, the Court was merely 'carrying out the intention of the legislature', and it would be wrong to suggest that the decision was evidence of 'a struggle between the courts and the executive'.[7]

However, there is an important subtext to the case. Since, on the majority's view, *any* unlawful determination by the Commission would merely have constituted a 'purported' determination, and would thus be reviewable notwithstanding the ouster clause, the clause was essentially deprived of any effect.[8] It has therefore been argued that the Court in *Anisminic* chose to 'rebel against Parliament': that the House of Lords, without admitting as much, gave priority to the rule of law (by preserving the availability of judicial review) over the intention of Parliament as stated in the ouster clause.[9]

This discussion leads on to three more general points. First, *Anisminic* is ultimately an ambiguous case that can be read in either of the two ways sketched in this section.

---

[2] Section 4(4) as originally enacted.

[3] *Anisminic Ltd v Foreign Compensation Commission* [1969] 2 AC 147.

[4] See Chapter 2, section 5.   [5] *Anisminic*, 199.   [6] *Anisminic*, 170, *per* Lord Reid.

[7] *Anisminic*, 208, *per* Lord Wilberforce.

[8] The only exception is that, at the time that *Anisminic* was decided, an anomalous category of unlawful decisions, known as 'non-jurisdictional errors of law on the face of the record', was recognised. However, that category is now largely irrelevant given that, as we saw in Chapter 12, section 2.2, the general principle is that all errors of law (whether or not 'on the face of the record') are jurisdictional.

[9] Wade and Forsyth, *Administrative Law* (Oxford 2014), p 614.

It therefore does not provide definitive guidance as to *what a court would do if it were faced with an indisputably clear statutory provision ousting judicial review.* In such circumstances, an acute tension between parliamentary sovereignty and the rule of law would arise—and, as we saw in Chapter 11, senior judges have recently indicated, albeit in *obiter dicta*, that they may give priority to the latter.

Second, leaving aside the 'parliamentary sovereignty *versus* rule of law' point, the general approach in *Anisminic* is indicative, in broader terms, of *how courts perceive judicial review.* Particularly noteworthy is the justification offered by Lord Wilberforce for a robust reading of the ouster clause. 'What', he asked, 'would be the purpose of defining by statute the limit of a tribunal's powers if, by means of a clause inserted in the instrument of definition, those limits could safely be passed?'[10] The obvious answer to this question is that even if *courts* could not (because of the ouster clause) enforce limits on the decision-maker's power laid down in the statute, there might be other, political, means by which such limits could be enforced. Lord Wilberforce's premise therefore presents a notably court-centric view: it implies an emphasis on the judiciary as the primary means by which to hold the executive to account, and thus buys into a more legal form of constitutionalism.

Third, attempts to exclude judicial review entirely should be distinguished from *two other statutory devices, the effect of which may be to limit judicial review.* One option that Parliament sometimes takes is to, in effect, rule out the exercise of the courts' normal judicial review powers while giving them statutory powers of judicial review. The only real practical impact of this is that such statutory powers are normally exercisable within a narrower time frame (typically six weeks) than the courts' normal powers.[11] A further possibility is that Parliament might create a statutory body that has court-like characteristics. The perceived constitutional need for judicial review of such a body may be weaker (because it is an independent judicial, as opposed to executive, body), and the (regular) courts may be willing to concede that judicial review should lie only in limited circumstances.[12]

2.2 Type of power

2.2.1 Statutory powers

The majority of governmental decisions are taken under statutory powers. As a general rule, such decisions are judicially reviewable to the extent that they raise justiciable issues. It is convenient to defer discussion of the concept of justiciability until we have addressed prerogative powers.

2.2.2 Prerogative powers

As we saw in Chapter 4, the Crown—which, in practice, means the executive branch of government—possesses a number of non-statutory powers, known as *prerogative*

---

[10] *Anisminic*, 208.   [11] See, eg Acquisition of Land Act 1981, ss 23 and 25.

[12] This is the position that applies to the Upper Tribunal, following the Supreme Court's decisions in *R (Cart) v Upper Tribunal* [2011] UKSC 28, [2012] 1 AC 663 and *R (Jones) v First-tier Tribunal* [2013] UKSC 19, [2013] 2 WLR 1012. See further Chapter 16, section 5.6.

powers, covering matters as diverse as the granting of honours, the declaration of war, and the making of treaties. Is the exercise of such powers susceptible to judicial review? It was established as long ago as the early seventeenth century that courts could determine whether a prerogative claimed by the Crown actually existed[13]—a jurisdiction famously exercised in the *De Keyser* case,[14] in which it was held that prerogative powers are placed in abeyance, or suspended, when statutory powers cover the same ground.[15]

However, deciding whether a particular power exists constitutes a very modest form of judicial review: it is analogous to deciding whether a statutory power under which a Minister claims to be acting really exists or applies to the sort of conduct that he is undertaking. Yet we know that the exercise of statutory powers can be reviewed in myriad other, more sophisticated, ways by applying the various grounds of judicial review that we encountered in Chapter 12. For many years, however, the courts refused to hold that those grounds of review were applicable to exercises of prerogative power. Such reticence was attributable to two factors.

First, it was felt that it would have been *constitutionally improper*, or at least unseemly, to interfere with the exercise of the royal prerogative. Such an attitude reflected the fact that, historically, prerogative power was actually wielded by the sovereign himself or herself. However, this is not, generally speaking, the case today, as the House of Lords recognised in the seminal *GCHQ* case. It concerned a challenge to a ministerial decision, taken under prerogative power, banning workers at the government's communications headquarters from belonging to trade unions.[16] It was argued that previous important changes to employment conditions had been preceded by consultation, that there was a legitimate expectation of such consultation, and that failing to consult on this occasion was therefore unlawful.[17] That argument did not succeed. However, it is highly significant that all five Law Lords accepted that the exercise of the prerogative power was subject to judicial review in line with the usual requirements—respect for legitimate expectations and natural justice, reasonableness, and so on—that are enforced via judicial review. Lord Scarman, for example, could see 'no reason why simply because a decision-making power is derived from a common law and not a statutory source, it should *for that reason only* be immune from judicial review'.[18] Their Lordships thus recognised that prerogative power today is, as Markesinis puts it, 'to all intents and purposes [a] government or even prime ministerial prerogative'.[19] To overlook this, said Lord Roskill, would be to hark back to 'the clanking of mediaeval chains of the ghosts of the past'.[20]

---

[13] *Case of Proclamations* (1611) 2 Co Rep 74.

[14] *Attorney-General v De Keyser's Royal Hotel Ltd* [1920] AC 508.

[15] For a recent application of this principle, see *R (Munir) v Secretary of State for the Home Department* [2012] UKSC 32, [2012] 1 WLR 2192.

[16] *Council of Civil Service Unions v Minister for the Civil Service* [1985] AC 374. See also *R v Criminal Injuries Compensation Board, ex p Lain* [1967] 2 QB 864, in which the developments in *GCHQ* were, to an extent, prefigured.

[17] See Chapter 12, section 4.3 on legitimate expectations.   [18] *GCHQ*, 410.

[19] Markesinis, 'The Royal Prerogative Revisited' [1973] CLJ 287, 288.   [20] *GCHQ*, 417.

GCHQ did, however, leave one unanswered question. It was concerned with the exercise of a power conferred upon a Minister under the prerogative. In this sense, it concerned the use of 'delegated' prerogative power. It is now clear, following the *Bancoult* case, that exercises of the prerogative itself—not only of powers conferred under it—are also, in principle, reviewable.[21]

The second factor that explains judges' traditional reticence in the face of the prerogative concerns the *subject matter* of many such powers. For example, in *Chandler v Director of Public Prosecutions*,[22] it was said that courts could not rule on matters concerning 'the methods of arming the defence forces' or their 'disposition'; this was a matter 'at the decision of Her Majesty's Ministers', and it was 'not within the competence of a court of law to try the issue whether it would be better for the country that that armament or those dispositions should be different'.

However, the force of this argument—that decisions about the deployment of the armed forces are likely to raise non-justiciable questions of policy on which courts are not qualified to rule—can be accepted without going so far as to assume that no exercise of prerogative power will ever give rise to justiciable matters. This was recognised in *GCHQ*. Lord Scarman said that 'if the subject matter in respect of which prerogative power is exercised is justiciable, that is to say if it is a matter upon which the court can adjudicate, the exercise of the power is subject to review in accordance with the principles developed in respect of the review of the exercise of statutory power'.[23] It followed, said Lord Roskill, that the exercise of powers concerning the making of treaties, the defence of the realm, the granting of mercy, the conferral of honours, the dissolution of Parliament, and the appointment of Ministers would not be reviewable because '[t]he courts are not the place wherein to determine whether a treaty should be concluded or the armed forces disposed in a particular manner or Parliament dissolved on one date rather than another'.[24]

The difficulty, however, with Lord Roskill's view is that it presupposes that there are certain prerogative powers that will *never* raise justiciable issues. There are certain powers the exercise of which is highly unlikely to generate justiciable questions. For example, it has been held that a government promise to hold a referendum before ratifying a treaty could not be said to have given rise to an enforceable legitimate expectation because 'a promise to hold a referendum lies so deep in the macro-political field that the court should not enter the relevant area at all'.[25] This does not, however, mean that everything to do with treaty-making is necessarily non-justiciable.[26] The better view, therefore, is that there is no such thing as a non-justiciable *prerogative*; rather, there are merely *issues* arising from the exercise of a prerogative—or any other kind of

---

[21] *R (Bancoult) v Secretary of State for Foreign and Commonwealth Affairs (No 2)* [2008] UKHL 61, [2009] 1 AC 453.

[22] [1964] AC 763, 798, *per* Viscount Radcliffe.

[23] *GCHQ*, 407. However, the decision in *GCHQ* was ultimately not quashed because the Court was satisfied that national security reasons justified the government's failure to consult.

[24] *GCHQ*, 418.   [25] *R (Wheeler) v Prime Minister* [2008] EWHC 1409 (Admin).

[26] Note that the prerogative power to conclude treaties on behalf of the UK is now qualified in the sense that most treaties can only be ratified (ie made legally binding upon the UK) if Parliament has not exercised its new statutory right to object: Constitutional Reform and Governance Act 2010, Pt 2.

power, including statutory power—upon which the courts may consider themselves unable to adjudicate.[27]

This idea has clearly taken root in relation to the prerogative of mercy, under which pardons can be granted to individuals convicted of criminal offences.[28] For example, it was held in *R v Secretary of State for the Home Department, ex p Bentley*[29] that, when the Home Secretary refused to grant a posthumous pardon to the claimant's brother, who had been hanged for inciting murder, he had failed to appreciate the full width of his legal powers. In particular, he had overlooked the possibility of a partial pardon (the effect of which would have been to acknowledge that the person concerned should not have been hanged without going so far as to imply that no punishment should have been imposed). Similarly, in *Lewis v Attorney General of Jamaica*,[30] the Privy Council concluded that decisions not to grant mercy to prisoners sentenced to death could be challenged on account of the fact that a fair decision-making process had not been adopted.

Similar judicial thinking has been applied to other prerogatives. For instance, in *R (Sandiford) v Secretary of State for Foreign and Commonwealth Affairs*,[31] the UK government refused to use its prerogative power to fund a legal challenge by a British citizen to the death sentence that had been imposed upon her in Indonesia. Although the Supreme Court ultimately upheld the government's refusal, it is noteworthy that it was prepared to assess the legality of the decision even though it touched upon foreign relations. Indeed, the Court indicated that a decision such as that in *Sandiford* could in principle be open to review on substantive grounds, including rationality and proportionality. This is a clear illustration of the way in which the issues-based approach has taken root.

That said, it is true that vestiges of the old approach—according to which whole zones of decision-making are off-limits—appear to endure. For instance, *R (Abbasi) v Secretary of State for Foreign and Commonwealth Affairs*[32] concerned the UK government's refusal to make representations to the US government on behalf of a British citizen held by the US at Guantanamo Bay in Cuba. The Court said it could not 'enter . . . forbidden areas, including decisions affecting foreign policy', and that it was 'highly likely that any decision of the Foreign and Commonwealth Office, as to whether to make representations on a diplomatic level, will be intimately connected with decisions relating to this country's foreign policy'. It followed that while the prerogative in question was not wholly immune to judicial scrutiny, it would be rare for a judge to be able to go further than to require the Foreign Secretary to 'give due consideration to a request for assistance'.[33]

Yet even in this case, the Court was prepared to consider whether there had arisen a legitimate expectation that representations would be made on behalf of the claimant. This suggests that, misleading talk of 'forbidden areas' notwithstanding, all prerogative *powers* are now open to judicial review, subject only to the proviso that

---

[27] See further Daly, 'Justiciability and the "Political Question" Doctrine' [2010] PL 160.
[28] See generally Harris, 'Judicial Review, Justiciability and the Prerogative of Mercy' [2003] CLJ 631.
[29] [1994] QB 349.   [30] [2001] 2 AC 50.   [31] [2014] UKSC 44, [2014] 1 WLR 2697.
[32] [2002] EWCA Civ 1598, [2003] UKHRR 76.   [33] *Abbasi*, [106].

courts will not review *issues* raised by their exercise to the extent that such issues are non-justiciable.

> **Q** Do you think that there might be some prerogative powers the exercise of which will never raise justiciable issues? For example, what, if any, justiciable issues might be raised by the exercise of powers to (i) grant honours, and (ii) declare war?

Finally, in this regard, we should note that the idea of justiciability is closely related to the notion of deference that we encountered in Chapter 12. Justiciability and deference may be thought of as different points on a continuum. To characterise an issue as 'non-justiciable' is to regard it as something upon which courts *cannot adjudicate at all*. Meanwhile, even if a court does not regard a question as wholly non-justiciable, it may, as we saw in Chapter 12, choose to *exhibit considerable deference* when considering the legality of the decision-maker's conduct.

So, for example, in *R (Al Rawi) v Secretary of State for Foreign and Commonwealth Affairs*,[34] which arose on similar facts to *Abassi*, the argument that the Foreign Secretary had not taken into account relevant considerations when declining to make representations on the claimants' behalf failed because, as the Court of Appeal put it, it was 'the government's responsibility to make decisions touching the conduct of foreign relations' such that 'the class of factors which . . . it is open to the decision-maker to treat as relevant or not . . . must be particularly wide'. It follows that, from the claimant's perspective, persuading a court that a question is justiciable guarantees neither victory nor close scrutiny: the court may still, because of the sensitive nature of the subject matter of the decision, refuse to subject it to rigorous examination.

> **Q** How do you think courts should decide whether to treat an issue as non-justiciable, or simply to exercise deference when reviewing the legality of the decision? Is the distinction between non-justiciability and deference a helpful one?

2.2.3 De facto powers

So far, we have seen that the position regarding decisions taken under statutory and prerogative powers is that they can be judicially reviewed provided that the issues raised are justiciable. The willingness of courts to bring the use of the prerogative within the ambit of judicial review reflects two of our key themes—that is, judicial recognition of the importance of ensuring that the *executive is held to account* for its use of power, whatever the source of that power, and judicial willingness to play a key role in securing such accountability rather than rely on parliamentary processes. This provides further evidence of the growing emphasis in the UK on *legal constitutionalism* as distinct from *political constitutionalism*.

---

[34] [2006] EWCA Civ 1279, [2008] QB 289, [140].

However, as we saw in Chapter 4, some decisions are taken—by government bodies and others—under neither statutory nor prerogative powers.[35] Are such decisions also open to judicial review?[36] Figure 13.2 shows a number of different types of decision, based on real cases that we consider later in this section, which might be taken under 'de facto powers'—so-called because they are powers that, as a matter of *fact*, the decision-maker possesses, even though there is nothing in *law* that specifically gives them such powers.

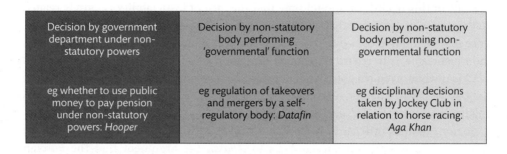

Decision by government department under non-statutory powers	Decision by non-statutory body performing 'governmental' function	Decision by non-statutory body performing non-governmental function
eg whether to use public money to pay pension under non-statutory powers: *Hooper*	eg regulation of takeovers and mergers by a self-regulatory body: *Datafin*	eg disciplinary decisions taken by Jockey Club in relation to horse racing: *Aga Khan*

Possibility of judicial review decreases as 'governmental' element reduces

Figure 13.2 Decisions taken under de facto powers

The *Datafin* case is a good starting point.[37] The claimant and company X were both attempting to take over company Y. The claimant complained to the Panel on Takeovers and Mergers that company X had acted in breach of the Panel's code of conduct, which stipulated how companies should behave in such situations. When the Panel dismissed the complaint against company X, the claimant sought judicial review of that decision, arguing that the Panel was not enforcing the code correctly. Although the Court of Appeal ruled that the Panel had not acted unlawfully, it is highly significant that the Court was prepared to consider this question—thus demonstrating that the Panel was subject to judicial review even though it was not exercising any legal powers.[38] Its code had no legal force—breach of it was not per se unlawful—but, in practice, companies were obliged to play by the Panel's rules; if they did not, they would find it impossible to do business in the City of London. Organisations such as the Panel are often called 'self-regulatory bodies' consisting of a 'group of people, acting in concert, [and using] their collective power to force themselves and others to comply with a code of conduct of their own devising'; as such, it was noted in *Datafin* that the Panel 'exercise[d] immense power de facto'.[39] Yet judicial review does not lie in relation to the decisions of

---

[35] See Chapter 4, section 4.4.

[36] If they are, then, of course, judicial review will lie only in relation to justiciable matters—but here we are concerned with the prior question whether the exercise of such powers is open to review *at all*.

[37] *R v Panel on Takeovers and Mergers, ex p Datafin plc* [1987] QB 815.

[38] The position is now different: see Companies Act 2006, ss 942–65.

[39] *Datafin*, 826, *per* Sir John Donaldson MR.

any and every body with 'immense power'; if it were to do so, then even large corporations would be susceptible to judicial review.

In reality, the purpose, and so the scope, of judicial review is conceived of more narrowly: courts have settled on the view that judicial review is for controlling the use of *governmental* power. The acid test for whether decisions taken under de facto powers can be reviewed is therefore whether the relevant decision-maker is performing a public function that is governmental in nature[40]—a test that courts have tended in practice to apply by asking whether, if the defendant were not already performing the function, the government would have had to step in and perform it itself.

In *Datafin*, it was concluded that the Takeover Panel was subject to judicial review. The government relied on the Panel to regulate takeovers and mergers; indeed, so closely linked to the executive was the Panel that it was said that failure to hold its decisions reviewable would be to fail to 'recognise the realities of executive power'.[41]

The position is even clearer if the decision in question is made (albeit under de facto powers) by a body that is *formally* part of the government. For example, in *R (Hooper) v Secretary of State for Work and Pensions*,[42] the Court of Appeal held that the Minister had acted unlawfully by failing to pay pensions to certain categories of widower despite the lack of any specific statutory power to do so. This may be taken as evidence of the courts' willingness to review all justiciable decisions pertaining to governmental functions, whether or not they are taken under identifiable legal powers.

In contrast, it was held in the *Aga Khan* case that the Jockey Club's decision to disqualify the claimant's horse after it failed a drugs test could not be reviewed because, as Hoffmann LJ put it, '[t]here is nothing to suggest that, if the Jockey Club had not voluntarily assumed the regulation of racing, the government would feel obliged or inclined to set up a statutory body for the purpose'.[43] Similarly, in *Wachmann*, it was held that there could be no judicial review of the Chief Rabbi's decision that the claimant—who had been accused of adultery with members of his congregation—was no longer religiously and morally fit to occupy his position as rabbi.[44]

Q Some governments might be more inclined than others to regulate particular areas of life. For example, although a laissez-faire government might take the view that it would not (in the absence of the Jockey Club) be necessary for the state to regulate horse racing, a more interventionist government might take the opposite view. What difficulties does this imply as regards the test that courts use in this area, and how might courts seek to resolve such problems?

Experience shows that the courts find it especially difficult to work out whether judicial review should lie in areas in which contracts are involved. Here, we should distinguish two situations, beginning with those in which there is a *contract between the*

---

[40] *R v Disciplinary Committee of the Jockey Club, ex p Aga Khan* [1993] 1 WLR 909; *R v Chief Rabbi of the United Hebrew Congregations of Great Britain and the Commonwealth, ex p Wachmann* [1992] 1 WLR 1036.

[41] *Datafin*, 838, *per* Sir John Donaldson MR.

[42] [2003] EWCA Civ 813, [2003] 1 WLR 2623. The Court of Appeal's decision was overturned by the House of Lords ([2005] UKHL 29, [2005] 1 WLR 1681) on presently irrelevant grounds.

[43] *Aga Khan*, 932.   [44] *Wachmann*.

claimant and the defendant. This was the case in *Aga Khan*, and it is clear that, for two of the judges, this was a major factor against the possibility of judicial review.[45] Indeed, the idea that there should be no judicial review of decisions taken under contract is a long-standing one.[46] It reflects the idea that contractual arrangements are a private matter—to be dealt with by private law—between the parties, and that there is no need for public law remedies such as judicial review to intrude. The difficulty is that individuals may have little choice but to enter into contracts with powerful bodies on terms of the latter's choosing. It is therefore arguable that, where such bodies are performing governmental functions, individuals should enjoy the additional protections that judicial review brings.

In this regard, the Supreme Court's decision in *Braganza v BP Shipping Ltd*[47] is pertinent. It indicates that when a contract assigns a decision-making function to one of the parties to the contract, terms may be implied into the contract concerning the use of the decision-making power. And while the precise terms that can be implied may be constrained by the express terms of the contact, *Braganza* indicates that the implied terms may result in the imposition of decision-making requirements that are the same as, or closely analogous to, those that are enforced via judicial review.

On this approach, it will now often be unnecessary for claimants to establish that their case falls within the scope of judicial review, because it will be possible to hold the (contractual) decision-maker to equivalent standards by leveraging the law of contract.

Second, there are situations in which there is a *contract between a government body and a service provider.* The practice of 'contracting out', whereby public bodies pay companies or charities to deliver public services, is increasingly common,[48] but the courts have generally ruled against the possibility of judicially reviewing the service provider. For example, in *R v Servite Houses, ex p Goldsmith*,[49] a local authority engaged the defendant to provide accommodation that it was legally obliged to arrange for certain categories of person. When the defendant reneged on a promise given to the claimants that they could remain in their accommodation for life, they sought judicial review, alleging breach of legitimate expectation.[50] However, the court held that judicial review could not occur in such circumstances.

That conclusion has been strongly criticised on the ground that there is 'nothing in the logic of contracting out' that means that the service provider, if it is performing a governmental function, should not be amenable to judicial review.[51] The courts' present approach enables the government, in effect, to place matters beyond the reach of judicial review by contracting them out to private sector bodies in relation to which only private law remedies will apply.[52]

---

[45] ie Sir Thomas Bingham MR and Farquharson LJ.

[46] See, eg *R v Criminal Injuries Compensation Board, ex p Lain* [1967] 2 QB 864, 882, *per* Lord Parker CJ, and 884, *per* Diplock LJ.

[47] [2015] UKSC 17, [2015] 1 WLR 1661.   [48] See Chapter 4, section 4.5.

[49] (2001) 33 HLR 369.   [50] On legitimate expectations, see Chapter 12, section 4.3.

[51] Craig, 'Contracting Out, the Human Rights Act and the Scope of Judicial Review' (2002) 118 LQR 551, 564–7.

[52] See Hunt, 'Constitutionalism and the Contractualisation of Government in the United Kingdom', in Taggart (ed), *The Province of Administrative Law* (Oxford 1997); Freedland, 'Government by Contract and

Finally, this position, adopted by the law of England and Wales, does not reflect the position in Scotland, where the availability of judicial review is governed by a different, more inclusive, test that, in particular, is not limited by reference to any public/private distinction. In Scots law, judicial review lies in respect of decisions 'taken by any person or body to whom a jurisdiction, power or authority has been delegated or entrusted by statute, agreement or any other instrument'.[53] This requires a 'tripartite' relationship—between the body that *conferred* the jurisdiction, the body *exercising* it, and the person *affected* by the exercise of jurisdiction. While this means that judicial review does not lie in straightforward, two-party contractual situations (eg employer–employee), its reach is greater in Scots than in English law. For example, when members of a golf club, purporting to exercise jurisdiction conferred upon them by the rules of the club, decided to expel an individual member, this decision was held amenable to judicial review.[54]

> **Q** Is the test adopted in Scots law preferable to that which is used by English law?

3. Procedure

3.1 The judicial review procedure

There is a special procedure that those wishing to issue judicial review claims are generally expected to use.[55] The procedure that applies today is laid down in Pt 54 of the Civil Procedure Rules,[56] and has its origin in, and much in common with, major reforms to judicial review proceedings introduced in the period 1977–81.[57] Judicial review procedure is different from that relating to ordinary civil proceedings,[58] in that it contains several protections for respondents—which will usually be public authorities. This, it is said, is justified by the need for public bodies to be protected against vexatious and unreasonable legal challenges so as to avoid unacceptable distraction

---

Public Law' [1994] PL 86. We will see in Chapter 18 that similar difficulties arise in cases that engage the Human Rights Act 1998.

[53] *West v Secretary of State for Scotland* 1992 SC 385, 412–13. See further Wolffe, 'The Scope of Judicial Review in Scots Law' [1992] PL 625.

[54] *Crocket v Tantallon Golf Club* 2005 SLT 663. See further Munro, 'Sport in the Courts' [2005] PL 681.

[55] In this chapter, we are concerned with judicial review proceedings in the High Court of England and Wales. The same (or similar) procedural and remedial regimes apply to the Upper Tribunal when it exercises its powers of judicial review. The Upper Tribunal's judicial review powers are considered in Chapter 16, section 5.5. Footnotes indicate the principal respects in which the position described in the text differs from the position in Scotland.

[56] See also Senior Courts Act 1981, s 31. For background to the changes introduced by Pt 54, see Bowman, *Review of the Crown Office List* (London 2000); Law Commission, *Administrative Law: Judicial Review and Statutory Appeals* (Law Com No 226 1994). For the position in Scotland, see ch 58 of the Rules of the Court of Session.

[57] For background and discussion, see Law Commission, *Remedies in Administrative Law* (Law Com No 73 1976); *O'Reilly v Mackman* [1983] 2 AC 237, 280–85, *per* Lord Diplock.

[58] eg for claims in tort or contract.

from their core task of serving the public interest.[59] That judicial review is, or can be, such a distraction is an argument that has been forcefully made by the government in recent years[60] in order to attempt to justify narrowing the availability of judicial review.

In this section we consider three limitations that apply to judicial review proceedings to the advantage of public bodies—but, arguably, to the disadvantage of members of the public seeking to bring claims. In doing so, we make reference to the following version of the example that we used in the previous chapter.

> **Eg** The (imaginary) Planning and Infrastructure Act 2014 provides that 'the Secretary of State may decide whether—and, if so, subject to what conditions, if any—permission should be granted for major infrastructure projects'. A major airport operating company that wishes to build a new airport asks the Secretary of State to exercise this power by granting it permission to do so.

First, in contrast to claims in private law, litigants must secure the *permission of the court* to launch a judicial review challenge.[61] Judicial review is therefore a two-stage process: first, the court's permission must be sought; only if permission is granted can there then be a substantive hearing of the issues. It has been argued that this system is advantageous to *public bodies*, because it allows unmeritorious cases to be filtered out with relatively little fuss;[62] to *the courts*, since it provides a means by which they can dispose of such cases quickly and efficiently;[63] and to *claimants*, because it allows them to obtain the opinion of the court speedily and cheaply.[64] The test that courts apply to determine whether permission should be granted is whether there appears to be 'an arguable ground for judicial review having a realistic prospect of success',[65] although researchers have found that there is considerable diversity of practice in this area, with some judges apparently much more willing to grant permission than others.[66]

Second, claimants are generally required to *take various steps before seeking judicial review*, including utilising alternative methods of dispute resolution (such as mediation) and exhausting alternative remedies (such as rights of appeal).[67] So, for instance, if in our example the company were denied permission to build the new airport in question, but had a statutory right of appeal to a planning tribunal, it would

---

[59] For a more critical view, see Oliver, 'Public Law Procedures and Remedies: Do We Need Them?' [2002] PL 91.

[60] Ministry of Justice, *Judicial Review: Proposals for Reform* (Cm 8515 2012); Ministry of Justice, *Judicial Review: Proposals for Further Reform* (Cm 8703 2013).

[61] Civil Procedure Rules, Pt 54, r 4. A permission requirement now exists in Scotland too: Court of Session Act 1988, s 27B (as inserted by Courts Reform (Scotland) Act 2014, s 89).

[62] Law Com No 226, [3.5]–[3.6].   [63] Law Com No 226, [5.6].

[64] Le Sueur and Sunkin, 'Applications for Judicial Review: The Requirement of Leave' [1992] PL 102, 107.

[65] *Sharma v Brown-Antoine* [2006] UKPC 57, [2007] 1 WLR 780, [14], *per* Lords Bingham and Walker.

[66] Le Sueur and Sunkin; Bondy and Sunkin, 'Accessing Judicial Review' [2008] PL 674.

[67] See, eg *R v Inland Revenue Commissioners, ex p Preston* [1985] AC 835, 852, *per* Lord Scarman. The same is true in Scotland: Rules of the Court of Session, r 58.3.

normally be expected to exercise that right before seeking judicial review. Viewed thus, judicial review is a remedy of last resort.[68] This makes sense in policy terms: it reduces the number of cases that go forward for judicial review, thus helping to stop the system from becoming clogged up; while appellate tribunals, because they focus on a narrow range of cases, may well be better equipped than the High Court to bring relevant expertise to bear on the issues.[69] Nevertheless, the requirement to exhaust other remedies is not applied unswervingly: courts have shown themselves willing to waive it where, for example, the alternative remedy would be inadequate[70] or substantially less advantageous to the claimant,[71] or would require the claimant to wait an unreasonable length of time for justice.[72] However, the mere fact that it would be more convenient for the individual to use judicial review as opposed to lodging an appeal may not, on its own, be sufficient.[73]

Third, anyone wishing to bring a judicial review claim *must act very quickly*. Whereas claims based on contract or tort can be brought within six years of the accrual of the cause of action,[74] judicial review claims must generally be brought within three months of the date on which the relevant decision was made.[75] In planning and procurement cases, even shorter time limits—six weeks and 30 days respectively—apply.[76]

Claims to which the three-month requirement applies must *also* be brought 'promptly', meaning that courts can rule a claim to be out of time even it if is initiated within three months (although, in practice, courts rarely do this).[77] Where claimants have failed to comply with the time limit, courts have discretion to allow the case to continue in spite of this provided that there is a 'good reason' for doing so[78]— for example, a claimant who tries to exhaust other remedies before seeking judicial review would generally be regarded as having a good reason for failing to comply with the time limit.[79] However, even if there is a good reason for extending time, the court may refuse to do so if this 'would be detrimental to good administration' (eg if a successful late challenge to a particular decision would require the government to unpick many other decisions taken in reliance upon it).[80] An extension of time may

---

[68] *R (Cowl) v Plymouth City Council* [2001] EWCA Civ 1935, [2002] 1 WLR 803.

[69] See further Lewis, 'The Exhaustion of Alternative Remedies in Administrative Law' [1992] CLJ 138.

[70] *Leech v Deputy Governor of Parkhurst Prison* [1988] AC 533.

[71] *R (Shoesmith) v Ofsted* [2011] EWCA Civ 642, [2011] PTSR 1459.

[72] *R v Chief Constable of the Merseyside Police, ex p Calveley* [1986] QB 424.

[73] *R (Lim) v Secretary of State for the Home Department* [2007] EWCA Civ 773, [2008] INLR 60.

[74] Limitation Act 1980, ss 2 and 5.

[75] Civil Procedure Rules, Pt 54, r 5(1)(b). Until recently, no specific time limit applied in Scotland. However, the Court of Session Act 1988, s 27A (as inserted by the Courts Reform (Scotland) Act 2014, s 89) now provides that applications should be made within three months of the grounds giving rise to the application having first arisen, or within such longer period 'as the Court considers equitable having regard to all the circumstances'.

[76] Civil Procedure Rules, Pt 54, r 5(5)–(6).　　　[77] Civil Procedure Rules, Pt 54, r 5(1)(a).

[78] Civil Procedure Rules, Pt 3, r 1(2), as interpreted in *R (M) v The School Organisation Committee, Oxfordshire County Council* [2001] EWHC Admin 245.

[79] As in *R v Rochdale Metropolitan Borough Council, ex p Cromer Ring Mill Ltd* [1982] 3 All ER 761.

[80] Senior Courts Act 1981, s 31(6). See further *R v Dairy Produce Quota Tribunal for England and Wales, ex p Caswell* [1990] 2 AC 738.

also be refused if it would 'be likely to cause substantial hardship to, or substantially prejudice the rights of, any person'.[81]

So if, in our example, the company were to be granted permission to build the new airport and local residents were to wish to object, it is very unlikely that they would be granted permission to seek judicial review outside the usual time limit if building work had started, since this might well cause 'substantial hardship' to the company, which would, by that point, have begun to invest considerable amounts of money in the project.[82] The short time limit for judicial review is obviously problematic for prospective claimants, who must act swiftly, but is said to be justified by the need for certainty: government bodies need to know where they stand, it is argued, and it would be detrimental to the public interest if decisions could be challenged years after being taken.[83]

> **Q** Oliver has argued that while it is right that certain decisions should be open to challenge for only a very short period, there is no good reason why the three-month rule should apply to all government decisions.[84] Do you agree? What sort of decisions might be most deserving of protection by means of very short time limits?

3.2 Procedural exclusivity

It is apparent from section 3.1 that the judicial review procedure is, in some respects, not especially attractive to prospective claimants. They therefore sometimes seek to avoid these procedural obstacles by issuing ordinary proceedings to challenge government decisions rather than making a claim for judicial review. The main differences between the two forms of proceeding are set out in Table 13.1. Given a free choice, then, people might prefer to use ordinary proceedings. The difficulty, however, is that some features of the judicial review procedure that constitute *restrictions* from the perspective of claimants are, as discussed earlier, *safeguards* as far as public authorities are concerned. If those safeguards are to have any practical impact, then it would seem to be necessary to force litigants to use judicial review proceedings if they wish to challenge public bodies' decisions.

Table 13.1 Ordinary and judicial review proceedings compared

	Judicial review proceedings	Ordinary proceedings
Time limit	Normally three months	Six years
Permission needed?	Yes	No
Cross-examination?	Rarely available	More liberal approach
Disclosure?	Rarely available	More liberal approach

[81] Senior Courts Act 1981, s 31(6).

[82] See *R v North West Leicestershire District Council, ex p Moses* [2000] Env LR 443.

[83] See, eg *O'Reilly v Mackman* [1983] 2 AC 237, 280–81, *per* Lord Diplock.

[84] Oliver, 'Public Law Procedures and Remedies: Do We Need Them?' [2002] PL 91, 98–9.

Precisely that point was taken by the House of Lords in *O'Reilly v Mackman*,[85] in which the claimant prisoners sued the prison authorities, alleging that certain disciplinary decisions had been taken in a procedurally unfair way, and were therefore unlawful. The House of Lords ruled that, by using ordinary—rather than judicial review—proceedings, the claimants had committed an 'abuse of process', and therefore struck out their claims. Lord Diplock said that claimants should not normally be allowed to 'evade the protection' afforded to public bodies by the judicial review procedure.[86] There is also a practical argument that judicial review claims should be channelled into the Administrative Court, which is staffed by judges with special expertise in public law.

The effect of *O'Reilly* was that ordinary proceedings could be used to vindicate private law rights, but that public law matters had to be litigated by means of the special judicial review procedure. We can use our example to illustrate the point. Imagine that two householders whose land adjoins the proposed site of the new airport wish to mount legal challenges to the Secretary of State's decision to allow it to be built. The first householder wishes to argue that the Minister failed to take into account local opposition to the scheme. In other words, he contends that the Secretary of State did not take into account certain relevant considerations as he is duty-bound to do as a matter of public law. This is a straightforward public law argument and would have to be made in judicial review proceedings. In contrast, assume that the airport is to be built partly on land next to the second householder's home, and that the land was sold several years ago by the second householder (and subsequently acquired by the airport operator) subject to a condition (known as a 'restrictive covenant') that it was not to be used for commercial purposes. The second householder would be free to enforce the restrictive covenant in ordinary proceedings, because she would be seeking to protect a private law property right.

The effect of *O'Reilly* was to establish a principle of *procedural exclusivity*, such that the judicial review procedure was the only way in which claimants could raise public law issues in the courts. This caused numerous problems, not least because it required English courts to distinguish between public and private law in a way that they had never previously done. This resulted in considerable uncertainty and consumed a great deal of the courts' time.[87] As a result, the courts softened their stance on procedural exclusivity in a series of cases that followed *O'Reilly*. Two main sets of developments should be noted.

First, the courts have recognised a *number of exceptions* to the requirement that judicial review proceedings must be used to litigate public law issues. For example, courts may be prepared to allow the use of ordinary proceedings in cases that turn on disputed points of fact;[88] this is obviously sensible given that judicial review courts are generally unable or unwilling to resolve such disputes. It has also been recognised

---

[85] [1983] 2 AC 237.   [86] *O'Reilly*, 285.

[87] As Lord Woolf MR noted in *Trustees of the Dennis Rye Pension Fund v Sheffield City Council* [1998] 1 WLR 840, 842.

[88] *Dennis Rye*. However, *Trim v North Dorset District Council* [2011] EWCA Civ 1446, [2011] 1 WLR 1901 indicates that procedural exclusivity will not invariably yield in the face of a factual dispute.

that the principle of procedural exclusivity should not prevent people from attacking the legality of government decisions and measures in order to defend themselves in criminal[89] or civil[90] proceedings. For example, in *Boddington*,[91] it was held that a defendant charged with breaching a by-law could argue in his defence that the by-law was being unlawfully applied; it was not necessary for him to launch separate judicial review proceedings in order to litigate that point. Meanwhile, it was established in *Roy v Kensington and Chelsea and Westminster Family Practitioner Committee*[92] that, where a case raises a mixture of public and private law points, they can all be dealt with in ordinary proceedings.[93]

Second, even if a case does not fall within one of the exceptions mentioned, there is now a *more sophisticated approach* to enforcing the policy that underpinned the House of Lords' decision in *O'Reilly*.[94] If a court concludes that judicial review proceedings should have been, but were not, used, it is no longer automatically assumed that there has been an abuse of process. Rather, the court asks itself whether, if judicial review were to have been used, the case would have passed muster—would permission have been granted? Had the claimant complied with the time limit? If not, would there have been a good reason for allowing the claim to proceed anyway? If the answers to these questions are 'yes', then the claim will be allowed to continue because the claimant will not have gained an unfair advantage by failing to use judicial review proceedings, since the case would, in such circumstances, have been permitted to go ahead even if such proceedings were to have been issued.[95] This approach is to be welcomed, since it upholds the policy underlying *O'Reilly*, but in a less dogmatic, more subtle, way.

> **Q** Why did the courts establish and then modify the principle of procedural exclusivity?

3.3 Standing

3.3.1 Introduction

Generally speaking, if one party to a contract fails to do what she has promised, only the other party—or, in limited circumstances, third parties who are affected—can initiate a claim for breach of contract. Similarly, if one person's negligent driving causes harm to another, it is generally only the latter who can issue a claim in tort.[96]

---

[89] *Boddington v British Transport Police* [1999] 2 AC 143.

[90] *Wandsworth London Borough Council v Winder* [1985] AC 461.

[91] *Boddington v British Transport Police* [1999] 2 AC 143.   [92] [1992] 1 AC 624.

[93] The position in Scotland is broadly comparable. Those wishing to raise public law challenges must generally make an application for judicial review under ch 58 of the Rules of the Court of Session, but exceptions (eg permitting collateral challenge) are recognised. See further Clyde and Edwards, *Judicial Review* (Edinburgh 2000), ch 8.

[94] *Clark v University of Lincolnshire and Humberside* [2000] 1 WLR 1988.

[95] Indeed the court may, under the Civil Procedure Rules, Pt 54, r 20, transfer such a case into the judicial review procedure.

[96] There are, however, certain limited circumstances in which it may be possible for someone else to sue on behalf of the victim of the breach of contract or tort—eg where the victim is a child or a person who lacks mental capacity within the meaning of the Mental Capacity Act 2005. See Civil Procedure Rules, Pt 21.

These matters are regarded as essentially private: it is therefore for the victims to decide whether they wish to make a claim; it is they who have suffered as a result of the unlawful conduct of the other parties; and if the victims do not wish to seek legal redress, then that is no one else's business.

So much for private law—but what about public law? Do (and should) a wider range of people have standing to issue claims for judicial review?[97] Returning to our example, it is clear that, even if a narrow, private-law-style approach were adopted, people directly affected by a decision to allow the new airport to be built—for example, those whose lives would be blighted by noise pollution by virtue of living close to the proposed site of the airport—would have standing to issue judicial review proceedings. What, however, about people with a less direct interest? Could, for example, people who live several miles from the new airport seek judicial review on account of the fact that, if built, it would cause traffic congestion that would reduce their quality of life or damage their businesses? And what of people with even less direct interests? Could a member of an environmental pressure group—or even just an environmentally concerned member of the public—issue a claim in order to argue that the Minister had failed adequately to consider the ecological implications of the new airport?

The standing rules for judicial review are set out in the Senior Courts Act 1981, which provides that a court may not grant permission for judicial review 'unless it considers that the [claimant] has a *sufficient interest* in the matter to which the application relates'.[98]

This provision, by itself, offers little guidance: it could be read narrowly, so as to allow standing only to those who have been directly adversely affected by a public decision (eg to an asylum seeker who wishes to argue that his asylum application has been unlawfully rejected), or more widely, so as to allow anyone to challenge such a decision (because we all have an interest in making sure that the government respects the law).

3.3.2 Possible approaches to standing

In terms of policy, there may be good reasons for adopting a narrow approach to standing.[99] A broad approach might, for example, risk opening up public authorities to large volumes of vexatious litigation brought by busybodies. However, this is not, in itself, a convincing argument in favour of a narrow approach to standing, bearing in mind that other control devices, unrelated to the identity of the prospective claimant, are, in any event, at the courts' disposal.[100]

At the same time, there are strong arguments in favour of the courts adopting a generous approach towards standing. This is because we think differently about the

---

[97] In this context, to have standing—or *locus standi*, as it is sometimes called—is to have legal capacity to proceed with judicial review in respect of a particular matter.

[98] Section 31(3) (emphasis added). No equivalent provision applies in Scotland, where the approach to standing is set at common law. See further later.

[99] See further Schiemann, '*Locus Standi*' [1990] PL 342, 348–9.

[100] eg permission to initiate judicial review can be withheld if the claimant appears to have no realistic prospect of success: see section 3.1.

public law that is enforced via judicial review than we do about the private law that is enforced in claims brought in contract, tort, and so on. When claimants seek judicial review, they are not seeking to vindicate *rights* that have allegedly been infringed by, for example, a procedurally unfair government decision. Rather, they are seeking to enforce the *duties*—for example, the duty to act fairly—under which public law places government bodies.[101] This is a subtle, yet important, distinction. It reflects the fact that whereas the prevailing view is that a breach of contract is an essentially private matter, a breach of public law is something in which the public generally has a legitimate interest. On this view, even if a specific individual suffers particular harm as a result of an unlawful decision by a public body, the public as a whole has an interest in ensuring that government authorities respect the principles of good administration that the courts have developed.

Miles notes that this perspective embraces a *communitarian* view of public law that 'focuses not on the specific interest of the individual victim in seeing government illegality against him or her checked, but on a broader public interest in lawful government'.[102] She goes on to argue that, on this view, it is inappropriate to allow those affected by unlawful decisions to 'veto' litigation that would aim to determine whether the government action in question were unlawful.[103]

Whether a narrow or a broad approach to standing is to be preferred ultimately depends on the role that courts ought to serve in this context. A broad approach to standing may allow the judicial process to become a surrogate political process, by enabling individuals and interest groups who are not themselves directly affected by particular decisions to raise their objections to them by means of judicial review. Whether this is a good or a bad thing turns on the extent to which it is felt legitimate for courts to assume such a pseudo-political role—a question that goes to the heart of our key themes about how executive power should be controlled, and about the balance between legal and political notions of constitutionalism.

3.3.3 The current position

As Figure 13.3 shows, there are several possibilities regarding standing to seek judicial review, ranging from a very restrictive, private-law-like approach (shown at the left-hand side of the diagram) to an extremely liberal approach (shown at the right-hand side). As we explain in the remainder of this section, English law generally adopts a liberal approach to standing,[104] although it does not go as far as to allow anyone at all to challenge any decision.

---

[101] See, eg *R v Somerset County Council, ex p Dixon* [1998] Env LR 111, 121, *per* Sedley J.

[102] Miles, 'Standing under the Human Rights Act 1998: Theories of Rights Enforcement and the Nature of Public Law Adjudication' [2000] CLJ 133, 150.

[103] Miles, 152.

[104] Until recently, Scottish courts adopted a narrower approach than their English counterparts. However, in *AXA General Insurance Ltd v HM Advocate* [2011] UKSC 46, [2012] 1 AC 868, the Supreme Court aligned the Scots test for standing in judicial review cases concerning public law matters with that which applies in English law.

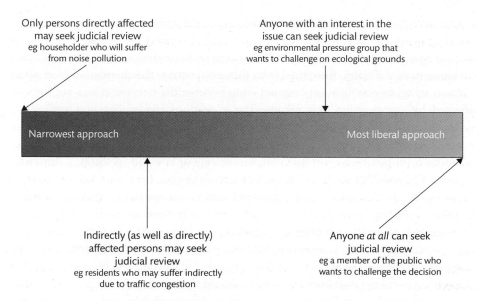

Figure 13.3 Standing: a range of possible approaches (with reference to example in section 3.1)

The basis of the modern law of standing is the *Fleet Street Casuals* case, so-called because it involved a dispute about the taxation of casual print workers on national newspapers, many of which used to be based on Fleet Street in London.[105] It was well known that some such workers avoided paying income tax by falsifying information provided to the tax authorities. In an attempt to regularise the situation, a deal was offered: if the workers would register for tax purposes and pay tax in future, no investigations would be undertaken into previous infractions. The claimant, a body representing the interests of self-employed people and small businesses, sought to challenge the tax authorities' offer of an amnesty in respect of past tax avoidance, arguing that this was unfair to law-abiding taxpayers such as its members.

The great irony of the *Fleet Street Casuals* case is that while it is invariably cited as the bedrock of the modern, liberal law of standing, the House of Lords held, on the facts, that the claimant did *not* have standing to pursue its claim.[106] Their Lordships noted that the claimant had no particular interest, over and above that of any taxpayer, in the tax affairs of the print workers, and a majority was unwilling to accept—at least on these facts—that the requirement of 'sufficient interest' under the Senior Courts Act 1981 was so wide as to enable a legal challenge in such circumstances.

However, in reaching this conclusion, their Lordships laid down a fundamental principle that has profoundly influenced the subsequent development of the law in this area. The principle is that standing is not to be assessed as a purely preliminary

---

[105] *R v Inland Revenue Commissioners, ex p National Federation of Self-Employed and Small Businesses Ltd* [1982] AC 617.

[106] However, see now *R (UK Uncut Legal Action Ltd) v Commissioners of HM Revenue and Customs* [2012] EWHC 2017 (Admin), in which Simon J was unwilling, on standing grounds, to withhold permission when a group that campaigns on tax-related matters sought to challenge a decision to forego interest on a large investment bank's National Insurance contributions.

matter separate from the substance of the case itself; rather, whether a claimant has standing is to be judged within 'the legal and factual context' of the case.[107] The question of standing must therefore be addressed with reference to the strength and seriousness of the claim. Examined from that perspective, the claimant in *Fleet Street Casuals* failed to establish standing not straightforwardly because it was not directly affected by the decision, but because the allegations made were not sufficiently serious. Lord Diplock, for instance, said that 'a pressure group, like the [claimant], or even a single public-spirited taxpayer' should not be prevented by 'technical rules' of standing from getting a court 'to vindicate the rule of law and [getting] . . . unlawful conduct stopped'.[108] It was just that, on the facts of the case, the Court did not consider the issues at stake to be serious enough to warrant according standing to the claimant.

Where does this leave us? It is clear that where an individual is personally affected by a decision, she will undoubtedly have standing. As we move away from that paradigm, standing remains a possibility, but prospective claimants will, in effect, have to compensate for their lack of personal involvement with the issue by persuading the court that the matter is so important that it should nevertheless be litigated—by them. Subsequent case law confirms that courts may entertain challenges by claimants who are not themselves affected by the relevant decision, but that such claimants—and their cases—will be subjected to greater and stricter scrutiny than victims. Two types of case can be distinguished.

First, the courts now clearly recognise the possibility of *associational standing*, which, as Cane puts it, generally involves a group or corporation 'claiming on behalf of (the interests of) identifiable individuals who are its members or whom it claims to represent'.[109] For example, in *R v HM Inspectorate of Pollution, ex p Greenpeace (No 2)*,[110] the court allowed an environmental pressure group to seek judicial review, on behalf of local residents among its membership, of a decision to allow a nuclear reprocessing plant to open in spite of safety concerns. The court was clearly influenced by Greenpeace's 'particular experience in environmental matters' and 'its access to experts in the relevant realms of science and technology (not to mention the law)', which meant that it was 'able to mount a carefully selected, focused, relevant and well-argued challenge'.[111] This suggests that where a case is brought not by a victim, but by a campaigning organisation seeking to represent others' interests, the court will scrutinise that organisation's credentials to ensure that it is capable of arguing the case sensibly, and is not simply an interfering and ill-informed busybody liable to waste the court's time.

Second, the courts are also willing to recognise *public interest standing*,[112] as the decision in the *Pergau Dam* case illustrates.[113] When we examined that case in Chapter 12, we saw that the claimant persuaded the court that the Foreign Secretary had acted unlawfully by funding a development project in Malaysia despite concerns

---

[107] *Fleet Street Casuals*, 630, *per* Lord Wilberforce.   [108] *Fleet Street Casuals*, 644.
[109] Cane, 'Standing Up for the Public' [1995] PL 276 at 276.   [110] [1994] 4 All ER 329.
[111] *Greenpeace (No 2)*, 350, *per* Otton J.   [112] See further Cane, 'Standing Up for the Public'.
[113] *R v Secretary of State for Foreign and Commonwealth Affairs, ex p World Development Movement Ltd* [1995] 1 WLR 386.

that it was economically suspect.[114] Our present interest in the case relates to the claimant itself—a highly respected pressure group that, as Rose LJ put it, 'actively campaign[ed] through letter-writing, lobbying and other democratic means to improve the quantity and quality of British aid to other countries'.[115] Neither the group itself nor any of its members were directly affected—at least, no more than any other taxpayer. Furthermore, the pressure group was not acting, in a representative capacity, on behalf of people who were peculiarly affected. The court therefore had to decide whether standing could ever be generated on purely public interest grounds: could a claimant be permitted to litigate not because it purported to be (or to speak for those) affected by a decision, but simply because it would be in the public interest for a court to rule on its legality? This question was answered in the affirmative. The court made it clear that it would not be easy to secure standing on such grounds, but said that standing was appropriate on the facts of this case due to the intersection of a number of factors: the seriousness of the allegations (£200 million of public money was at stake); the strength of the claimant's case; the absence of an alternative challenger (because no one was peculiarly affected—all taxpayers were affected equally and imperceptibly); and the expert and informed character of the claimant, which enabled it to present a well-informed challenge to the court.

This public interest approach to standing received the Supreme Court's clear seal of approval in the *AXA*[116] and *Walton*[117] cases.[118] In the former case, Lord Reed observed that 'a public authority can violate the rule of law without infringing the rights of any individual' and that judicial review is no less constitutionally imperative in such circumstances.[119] In *Walton*, Lord Reed went on to say that in some circumstances an individual can seek judicial review 'simply as a citizen . . ., without having to demonstrate any greater impact upon himself than upon other members of the public'.[120]

Finally, it should be noted that a party lacking standing to initiate judicial review proceedings may nevertheless be granted permission to intervene in proceedings brought by someone else.[121] Today, the courts exercise their discretion to permit such intervention fairly liberally—a development that has been welcomed, bearing in mind that, in judicial review cases, courts are frequently asked to examine multifaceted questions that engage interests beyond those of the actual parties.[122]

The liberal approach to standing, important in itself, also tells us something more profound. It suggests that, as Lord Reed put it in *Walton*, the role of judicial review transcends the 'redress of individual grievances', encompassing a wider 'constitutional function of maintaining the rule of law'.[123] This, in turn, reflects the fact that administrative law is centrally concerned not with protecting the rights of individuals, but

---

[114] See Chapter 12, section 4.5.   [115] *Pergau Dam*, 393.
[116] *AXA General Insurance Ltd v HM Advocate* [2011] UKSC 46, [2012] 1 AC 868.
[117] *Walton v Scottish Ministers* [2012] UKSC 44, [2013] PTSR 51.
[118] Those cases align the law on standing in Scotland with English law in this area.
[119] *AXA*, [169]–[170].   [120] *Walton*, [95].   [121] Civil Procedure Rules, Pt 54, r 17.
[122] For contrasting views on the value of permitting intervention, see Harlow, 'Public Law and Popular Justice' (2002) 65 MLR 1; Fordham, '"Public Interest" Intervention: A Practitioner's Perspective' [2007] PL 410.
[123] *Walton*, [90].

with upholding standards of good governance.[124] Once this is recognised, it becomes clear that it is appropriate for courts to hear cases in which victims do not wish or are unable to come forward, or in which the illegality is victimless in the sense that no particular individual or group of individuals is specifically or identifiably disadvantaged by it. The fact that judges are, in appropriate circumstances, willing to hear such cases is significant to our key themes. In particular, it implies that courts attach importance to ensuring the *accountable use of executive power* and that they perceive, pursuant to the notion of *legal constitutionalism*, a significant role for the judiciary in this enterprise. Viewed in this way, the law relating to standing provides an insight into the place of judicial review in the modern British constitution—and into the nature of that constitution itself.

> **Q** What range of factors do the courts consider when deciding whether or not a claimant has standing to challenge an administrative decision by way of judicial review?

4. Remedies

4.1 The discretionary nature of remedies in public law

If a claimant succeeds in establishing that a defendant is acting or proposing to act unlawfully, the court must then decide what remedy, if any, to issue. In judicial review proceedings, remedies are not available as of right, but are *discretionary*. This means that even if a public authority has acted unlawfully, the court may still refuse to issue a remedy if it would be in the public interest to do so. Assume, for example, that a Minister uses statutory powers to enact secondary legislation establishing a state-funded compensation scheme for victims of violent crime and then, under that scheme, grants compensation to thousands of such victims. If a claimant were later to persuade a court that the Minister had acted unlawfully by enacting the secondary legislation, the court might nevertheless refuse to set aside that legislation if doing so would cause chaos and hardship by making all of the subsequent grants of compensation unlawful too. In such circumstances, the court may instead exercise its discretion to withhold relief in order to safeguard a broader public interest.[125]

The discretionary nature of remedies in public law is an important factor that distinguishes it from private law, in which remedies issue as of right—that is, the claimant is *entitled* to relief if she establishes (for example) that the defendant committed a breach of contract or a tortious act. In turn, this distinction reflects a deeper difference between public and private law. The former, unlike the latter, is not solely about regulating the relationship between the (individual) claimant and the (government) defendant. Rather, public law also allows for the holding of the government to account in the public interest; it is therefore appropriate that courts, in deciding whether to issue a

---

[124] For discussion of this point, see Varuhas, 'The Reformation of English Administrative Law? "Rights", Rhetoric and Reality' [2013] CLJ 369.

[125] See, eg *Glynn v Keele University* [1971] 1 WLR 487.

remedy when unlawful conduct is established, should take into account whether this would be in the public interest. Having said all of this, it is not common for courts to refuse relief in public law litigation, and there are strong arguments, rooted in the rule of law, against courts readily exercising their discretion to do so.[126]

As a result of recent legislation, the courts' *discretion* to withhold relief is now replaced in certain circumstances by an *obligation* to do so. Under s 31(2A) of the Senior Courts Act 1981,[127] relief *must* be declined 'if it appears to the court to be highly likely that the outcome for the applicant would not have been substantially different if the conduct complained of had not occurred'. The only exception is that relief can still be granted if the court 'considers that it is appropriate to do so for reasons of exceptional public interest'.[128] By raising the prospect of courts being unable to grant relief in respect of unlawful government action, these provisions raise significant rule of law concerns.[129] They are likely to be interpreted by the courts accordingly. In particular, it is probable that courts will conclude only reluctantly that it is 'highly likely' that the outcome would not have been substantially different. Such a posture would be justifiable given that it will often be difficult to predict with confidence whether (say) following a given procedure would or would not have made a difference by, for example, turning up different information that might have cast things in a different light. Meanwhile, the courts will likely ascribe a generous scope to the 'exceptional public interest' exemption.

One ground of review that may seem particularly vulnerable in the face of these provisions is the duty to give reasons,[130] since it may appear that any decision will be the same whether or not reasons happen to have been given for it. However, the 'no difference' provisions are in fact unlikely to eviscerate enforcement of the duty to give reasons. First, if, as seems likely, requiring the giving of reasons incentivises more careful, structured decision-making, it will often be impossible to conclude that the absence of reasons makes no difference to the outcome. Second, it might be argued that a decision unaccompanied by reasons is a different 'outcome' from a decision that is accompanied by reasons—such that any breach of the duty to give reasons will result in a difference in 'outcome'.

4.2 **Quashing orders**

The three main remedies that are available in judicial review proceedings are quashing, mandatory, and prohibiting orders.[131] These remedies, unlike those that we consider in

---

[126] Forsyth, 'The Rock and the Sand: Jurisdiction and Remedial Discretion' [2013] JR 360.

[127] Inserted by Criminal Justice and Courts Act 2015, s 84.

[128] Senior Courts Act 1981, s 31(2B).

[129] Section 31(3A)–(3D) raises similar concerns: it permits the court to consider (and, if the defendant asks it to do so, requires it to consider) the 'no difference' question at the permission stage. Subject to the 'exceptional public interest' exemption, the granting of permission is precluded when the court considers that it is highly likely that the outcome would not have been substantially different for the claimant.

[130] On the duty to give reasons, see Chapter 12, section 3.7.

[131] Formerly known as *certiorari*, *mandamus*, and *prohibition*. Different remedies are available in Scotland. They are reduction (which corresponds to a quashing order), suspension/interdict (which correspond to prohibiting orders and injunctions), specific performance/statutory order for performance (which correspond to mandatory injunctions and mandatory orders), and declarator (which correspond to declarations).

sections 4.4 and 4.5, can *only* be secured through judicial review, as opposed to ordinary, proceedings.[132] Quashing orders are the most commonly sought of the remedies. Such orders as usually said to (as the name implies) quash (or strike down) unlawful administrative decisions, although, as we will see, the position is rather more complex than this. Two issues warrant discussion.

The first concerns *the impact of such orders*. This depends on the kind of illegality that induced the court to issue the quashing order. If the court finds that a decision was *made in an unacceptable way* (eg that irrelevant considerations were taken into account, or that an unfair procedure was adopted), the decision can be quashed and the decision-maker required to reconsider the matter and reach a decision in accordance with the findings of the reviewing court.[133] However, there may be nothing to stop the decision-maker from making the same decision again, given that the original decision was struck down because of *how* it was made, not *what* the decision itself was. It is, however, open to courts in appropriate circumstances to rule that *the decision itself* is unlawful. It might, for example, be regarded as *Wednesbury* unreasonable, disproportionate, or incompatible with the claimant's substantive legitimate expectation, or it might be a decision that, in the first place, the decision-maker had no jurisdiction to take. Here, the impact of the quashing order will be greater, since it will no longer be open to the decision-maker to take whatever decision the court found unlawful.

Where, therefore, a decision is quashed on substantive, as opposed to procedural, grounds, it is not open to the public body concerned to make the same decision again in that case.[134] Indeed, in some circumstances, a quashing order may not simply prevent a decision-maker from making a particular decision; it might also *compel the making of some other decision*. For example, if a decision-maker has only two options open to it—such as granting or not granting a licence to do something—and the court rules that one of those options is unlawful, then this effectively forces the decision-maker to choose the other option.[135]

The second issue concerns *the circumstances in which it is necessary or desirable for an individual to obtain a quashing order*. When such an order is granted, the quashing occurs with retrospective effect: the unlawful administrative decision is treated as having *always* been unlawful. This follows from first principles: if a Minister never had legal authority to make a particular decision, it can never have legally existed. Quashing orders do not therefore *render* unlawful acts invalid; rather, they simply 'make it quite plain that this is the case'.[136] It follows that, in some circumstances, an individual may simply choose to ignore an unlawful decision rather than go to the trouble of having it quashed—but whether such a strategy is advisable depends on a number of factors. Two are particularly important.

First, if someone simply elects to ignore something that they consider to be unlawful, this will generally involve *the taking of a risk*. For example, in *Boddington v British*

---

[132] Senior Courts Act 1981, s 31(1).   [133] Senior Courts Act 1981, s 31(5)(a).

[134] Unless circumstances change such that it is, for example, no longer unreasonable to adopt a particular decision.

[135] It is sometimes possible, in such circumstances, for the reviewing court to make the required decision itself, rather than to remit the matter to the decision-maker: Senior Courts Act 1981, s 31(5)(b) and (5A).

[136] *Ahmed v HM Treasury (No 2)* [2010] UKSC 5, [2010] 2 AC 534, [4], *per* Lord Phillips.

Transport Police,[137] an individual smoked on a train in breach of a by-law making it unlawful to do so. He did not seek to have the by-law in question quashed in judicial review proceedings, but when prosecuted, he argued that the way in which the by-law had been implemented was unlawful. It is perfectly acceptable to make such arguments—known as *collateral challenges* to administrative measures—by way of a defence to criminal or civil proceedings.[138] If successful, such an argument provides a good defence. It allows the individual to argue that he has done nothing unlawful because the measure that he is accused of contravening does not actually exist: it was unlawfully adopted and is therefore void *ab initio.*

The risk, however, is that the individual may be wrong—as, indeed, Boddington was. The House of Lords ruled that the by-law had been lawfully implemented; the defence therefore failed, and Boddington was convicted. People may therefore choose to launch judicial review proceedings, with a view to obtaining a quashing order, in order to avoid this sort of risk by having a court authoritatively determine the legality of the measure in question.

Second, *practical reasons* may dictate that an individual has no option but to seek a quashing order if she wishes to avoid being affected by an unlawful administrative act. The strategy adopted (ultimately without success) in *Boddington* is only potentially useful if an individual wishes to behave *as if the measure in question did not exist.* So if, for example, an invalid by-law criminalises certain conduct, an individual who is confident as to the by-law's invalidity can simply choose to ignore it, behaving as if it did not exist and collaterally challenging it should prosecution occur subsequently.

However, such an approach is of no use if the person requires the taking of a positive administrative act, such as the granting of citizenship. If citizenship is unlawfully denied (eg because irrelevant matters were taken into account), that does not change the fact that the individual lacks citizenship. A quashing order followed by a fresh decision will be needed if the individual is to have any prospect of getting what she wants. Equally, a quashing order may be practically imperative if the individual wishes to *convince others* of the unlawfulness of an administrative measure. For example, if a bank has frozen someone's assets pursuant to an unlawful administrative order, it is unlikely that the bank will release the assets without judicial confirmation (by way of quashing) of the invalidity of the order.[139]

4.3 **Mandatory and prohibiting orders**

Mandatory and prohibiting orders can be considered more briefly. Whereas quashing orders deal with unlawful action that has already been committed, prohibiting orders are anticipatory in their effect: they are issued to prevent unlawful action being taken where it seems that such action is being planned. For example, in *R v Liverpool Corporation, ex p Liverpool Taxi Fleet Operators' Association,*[140] a local authority

---

[137] [1999] 2 AC 143.
[138] There are some exceptions to this principle. For example, the relevant legislation may, explicitly or impliedly, exclude the possibility of collateral challenge in particular cases: see, eg *R v Wicks* [1998] AC 92.
[139] *Ahmed (No 2).*   [140] [1972] 2 QB 299.

decided that it would issue a number of new taxi licences. This was in breach of an assurance that, for the time being, the number of licences would be capped. Existing licence holders objected to this proposed course of action because, by increasing the number of taxis allowed to operate in the city, it would compromise the viability of their own businesses. In these circumstances, the court issued a prohibiting order preventing the council from implementing its decision pending consultation with existing licence holders.

Mandatory orders, meanwhile, compel public authorities to do things that they are legally required to do. Such relief is most obviously pertinent where a statute places a public body under an explicit duty to do something; if the duty is not discharged, a mandatory order may be sought in order to make the public body discharge it. However, mandatory orders are also relevant in relation to discretionary powers. As we saw in Chapter 12, no discretion is unlimited, and courts often find that duties—to act fairly, to take into account relevant factors, and so on—are implicit within discretionary powers. A mandatory order may therefore be issued to require a decision-maker to exercise discretion in line with such implied duties.[141]

4.4 Injunctions

The effect of an injunction is equivalent to that of a prohibiting order—it prevents a public body from undertaking unlawful conduct—but there are two reasons why an injunction may be preferable to a prohibiting order.

First, injunctions can be obtained in ordinary, as well as in judicial review, proceedings, whereas prohibiting orders can only be obtained in the latter—and, as we saw earlier, the use of ordinary proceedings has certain attractions for prospective claimants.[142]

Second, injunctions can be obtained in interim, as well as final, form. This means that it is possible to get a temporary injunction—for example, preventing a decision from being implemented—pending the court's final ruling on whether or not the decision is lawful. This is especially useful if there is a risk of the issue becoming moot by the time the court is likely to reach a final decision. For example, a court may grant an interim injunction preventing the deportation of an asylum seeker pending judicial review of whether the decision to deport him was lawful.[143] Granting such relief may be necessary to ensure that the person concerned is still in the country by the time the court actually rules on the legality of the decision.

In deciding whether to grant interim relief, the courts apply a three-stage test:.

- Has the claimant shown that there is, on the face of it, a 'serious issue to be tried'?[144]

- If so, would the claimant have an adequate remedy in damages if the act in question were to be carried out and later be found to be unlawful? (For example,

---

[141] See, eg *Padfield v Minister of Agriculture, Fisheries and Food* [1968] AC 997.
[142] See section 3.2.   [143] As in *Re M* [1994] 1 AC 377.
[144] *R v Secretary of State for Transport, ex p Factortame Ltd (No 2)* [1991] 1 AC 603, 671, *per* Lord Goff.

damages would clearly not be an adequate remedy for an asylum seeker whose life would be at risk if (unlawfully) deported to his home country.)

- On the so-called 'balance of convenience' analysis, how do the implications for the parties of granting and not granting temporary relief compare? In effect, the court has to work out how damaging it would be to the claimant's interests if an interim injunction were not granted and balance this against the likely damage to the defendant's interests if such an injunction were granted.[145]

It was established in *Re M* that injunctions, including interim injunctions, can be issued against Ministers acting in their official capacity.[146] This means that failure to comply with the terms of an injunction can lead to a finding of contempt of court, which is a criminal offence, although in *M* the House of Lords emphasised that any such finding would be against the Minister in his official, not his personal, capacity. Lord Woolf explained: 'By making the finding against the minister in his official capacity the court will be indicating that it is the department for which the minister is responsible which has been guilty of contempt.'[147] It follows that there is no prospect of Ministers being imprisoned or personally fined in such circumstances, and that a finding of contempt is therefore largely symbolic.

It has been argued that this represents 'a very dangerous concession' because it means that there is ultimately no coercive means of enforcing the court's orders.[148] We should not, however, lose sight of the likely political impact of a finding of contempt against a government Minister. In this sphere, therefore, notions of legal and political constitutionalism potentially coalesce: it is for the court to determine whether the Minister has breached the terms of the injunction and hence the legal rules of the constitution, while the outworking of this *legal* infraction will principally be by means of the *political* ramifications of the court's judgment.

4.5 Declarations

Declarations are an authoritative statement by the court about the legal issue that has been brought to its attention. So, for example, a court might declare that it would be unlawful for a public body to refuse to consult the claimant before making a decision, or that it would be unlawful to make a particular decision because the decision-maker in question does not have jurisdiction to do so.

Declarations share two characteristics with injunctions: they are available in both ordinary and judicial review proceedings; and in both final and interim form. But there is an important difference between declarations and injunctions. Unlike injunctions, declarations are *non-coercive remedies*, meaning that they can be disregarded without legal consequence. If a court declares that a given course of action would be unlawful and then the public body adopts it anyway, that body will have acted

---

[145] *American Cyanamid Co v Ethicon Ltd* [1975] AC 396, 406.

[146] *Re M* [1994] 1 AC 377.   [147] *M*, 426.

[148] Harlow, 'Accidental Loss of an Asylum Seeker' (1994) 57 MLR 620, 623. For further discussion, see Sedley, 'The Crown in Its Own Courts', in Forsyth and Hare (eds), *The Golden Metwand and the Crooked Cord* (Oxford 1998).

unlawfully—but the existence of the declaration does not itself generate any liability (eg for contempt).

Why, then, would a claimant bother seeking, or a court bother issuing, a declaration? In some circumstances, a declaration might be regarded as the most appropriate form of relief. For example, courts might sometimes consider it more seemly to issue a declaration: in *M*, Lord Woolf thought that it would rarely be necessary to issue an injunction against Ministers because it could, in general, be reasonably assumed that they would fully respect a declaration.[149]

In addition, declarations are more appropriate when courts are asked to rule on questions that have not yet fully crystallised into crisp legal disputes. For example, where an act has already been committed, the most obvious remedy, assuming that the court can be persuaded that the act is unlawful, is a quashing order; if the act is imminent, then a prohibiting order is most apt. But in other circumstances, a declaration might be more suitable. For example, a claimant might want the court to rule not on the legality of a decision that has been taken or is imminent, but on whether something the government has said—by way of advice, guidance, or recommendation—might lead to the commission of unlawful acts by others. In such circumstances, there is no actual act or decision that can sensibly be quashed; nor is it appropriate to seek a prohibiting order unless there is clear evidence that some other body is about to act on what was said.

Precisely such a situation arose in *Royal College of Nursing v Department of Health and Social Security*.[150] A government circular said that nurses could lawfully undertake part of a procedure for termination of pregnancy without a doctor's supervision. The claimant, which had already issued its own guidance saying that nurses risked criminal liability if they took part in the procedure in the way advocated by the government, sought a declaration to the effect that the government circular was wrong in law; the government, for its part, counterclaimed for a declaration that it was not. A declaration in the latter terms was granted and the courts did not consider there to be any difficulty in the parties litigating what was, in the absence of any actual prosecutions of nurses, an abstract point of law. In a later case, however, the House of Lords signalled that the courts' willingness to rule on such a point in *Royal College of Nursing* could be traced to the facts that an authoritative ruling was obviously desirable 'in the interests both of the nursing profession and of the public' and that the case raised 'a pure question of law'.[151]

These comments indicate that the courts are not prepared to declare open season, such that litigants can require them, by means of what are often called *advisory declarations*, to answer any legal question, however abstract.[152] While judges are clearly unwilling to rule on academic questions—that is, questions 'which [do] not need to

---

[149] *Re M* [1994] 1 AC 377, 423. An interim injunction was granted in *M*, but at that time there was no such thing as an interim declaration.

[150] [1981] AC 800.

[151] *Gillick v West Norfolk and Wisbech Area Health Authority* [1986] AC 112, 193, *per* Lord Bridge.

[152] See further Beatson, 'Prematurity and Ripeness for Review', in Forsyth and Hare (eds), *The Golden Metwand and the Crooked Cord* (Oxford 1998).

be answered for any visible practical purpose', concerning such matters as the interpretation of long-ago repealed statutes—they are prepared to entertain at least the possibility of answering hypothetical questions.[153]

In other words, adjudication on matters that have not yet, but which have the potential to, become concrete legal disputes is at least a possibility. The more likely it is that the matter will become relevant to a real dispute, the more likely the court is, all things being equal, to be prepared to intervene with an advisory declaration. For example, in the *Royal College of Nursing* case, Lord Edmund-Davies observed that 'several thousand' of the procedures in question were carried out each year, making clarification of the legal position obviously desirable.[154] In contrast, the House of Lords refused to grant a declaration, sought by the editor of *The Guardian* newspaper, to the effect that, on a proper interpretation of the Treason Felony Act 1848, it would be lawful to publish articles advocating abolition of the monarchy by peaceful means. Lord Steyn concluded that it was obvious that, properly construed in line with the European Convention on Human Rights,[155] such conduct was not unlawful, and that 'the courts ought not to be troubled further with this unnecessary litigation'.[156]

The courts' willingness to rule on hypothetical matters is also tempered by judicial caution about giving a legal opinion that is divorced from a factual context.[157] So while they are, in principle, willing to rule on 'a discrete point of statutory construction . . . which does not involve detailed consideration of facts',[158] judges are not, in general, prepared to issue advisory declarations about how the law applies to complex fact situations that have not yet eventuated.

The courts very sensibly accept that they should be cautious in their use of advisory declarations. However, the fact that such relief is available in some circumstances is in itself important. It implies that the courts perceive their role in expositive, not merely dispositive, terms: in other words, that they consider that their function extends beyond the resolution of disputes to the elaboration of the legal framework—by, for example, clarifying the law in advance of real disputes arising. This contributes to the planning function of law—it enables people and government bodies to plan their conduct on the basis of a due appreciation of the legal position—and thus buttresses the rule of law concept of certainty. In turn, the fact that courts perceive their function in these relatively expansive terms contributes, in so far as it impacts upon the executive's legal position, to the role of legal constitutionalism. In particular, it enables individuals to seek the courts' assistance not only when government bodies have acted unlawfully, but also by obtaining advance judicial opinions as to the legal constraints subject to which governance must occur.

---

[153] Laws, 'Judicial Remedies and the Constitution' (1994) 57 MLR 213, 214. See also *R (McKenzie) v Waltham Forest London Borough Council* [2009] EWHC 1097 (Admin).

[154] *Royal College of Nursing*, 833.

[155] As is required by s 3 of the Human Rights Act 1998. See Chapter 18.

[156] *R (Rusbridger) v Attorney General* [2003] UKHL 38, [2004] 1 AC 357, [28].

[157] *R (Burke) v General Medical Council* [2005] EWCA Civ 1003, [2006] QB 273, [21], *per* Lord Phillips MR.

[158] *R v Secretary of State for the Home Department, ex p Salem* [1999] 1 AC 450, 457, *per* Lord Slynn.

5. Conclusions

Our focus in this chapter has been on a number of practical issues concerning procedures and remedies. In one respect, these are matters of technical, black-letter law. However, we have seen that questions of procedure and relief can also offer an insight into quite fundamental aspects of the subject—and that a consistent narrative can be deduced from what might superficially seem to be a disjointed set of rules. Many of the issues that we have studied in this chapter tell a story of a judiciary that has a very particular vision of the role of judicial review within the modern British constitution. The great reluctance of the courts to allow their supervisory jurisdiction to be ousted by legislation, their preparedness to hear claims from parties unaffected by the challenged decision when this is necessary for the maintenance of the rule of law, and their willingness to rule in advance on important legal questions all paint a picture in which judicial review—and therefore law—play a fundamental role in ensuring good governance. So, as we noted at the beginning of this chapter, the technical issues considered within it are closely related to two of our key themes, since they serve to underline the important role that courts play in securing the accountability of the executive branch and therefore the contemporary significance of legal constitutionalism.

Expert commentary
Procedure, values, and the conceptual unity of administrative law
Paul Daly, Senior Lecturer in Public Law, University of Cambridge

As the authors note, a close study of the seemingly technical procedural issues covered in this chapter reveals a gradual shift from a preference for political accountability to a preference for legal accountability.

Careful attention to procedural issues will often reward students of public law. It is worth remembering that public law is part of the common law; a tradition in which, in the famous words of the legal historian Sir Henry Maine, 'substantive law has at first the look of being gradually secreted in the interstices of procedure'. Moreover, close study of the technicalities relating to standing, remedies, procedural exclusivity, and so on also reveals the conceptual unity of modern administrative law; a body of doctrine that is made intelligible by reference to four values: the rule of law, good administration, democracy, and separation of powers.

Forests of trees have been felled to produce the reams of paper on which economists, legal theorists, philosophers, political scientists, and others have written at length about these values. But in the body of administrative law cases that the courts have built up over the decades and the centuries, the values have quite particular meanings. The values can be perceived to be at work in all areas of administrative law doctrine, including the technical procedural ones covered in this chapter.

From the rule of law comes judicial concern for the protection of substantive and procedural interests that promote individual dignity and autonomy. In the area of legitimate expectation, for instance, this concern results in strong judicial protection of interests generated by reliance on official promises, as in *R v North and East Devon Health Authority, ex p*

Coughlan.[159] The decision in *Boddington v British Transport Police*,[160] in which an individual charged with a criminal offence was permitted to raise the legality of a by-law by means of a collateral challenge, is an example from this chapter, as is the rejection of the idea that there are 'non-justiciable prerogative' powers that can be exercised without judicial oversight to the serious detriment of individuals.

Good administration sharpens the judicial focus on the efficient and effective achievement of statutory goals by administrative decision-makers. For instance, it has long been the case that the procedural requirements imposed by courts should not be so onerous as to compromise the smooth functioning of administrative machinery; they are not written on tablets of stone: *Lloyd v McMahon*.[161] Good administration is now baked into the procedural requirements discussed in this chapter: the obligations to exhaust alternative remedies and to seek judicial review in a timely manner are enforced on the basis that there is a public interest in ensuring that judicial review is a last resort and that administrative decisions are not set aside long after they have been made. But in a nod to the rule of law's concern with individual interests, procedural exclusivity does not prevent individuals with private law rights from pursuing claims that happen to raise public law issues.[162]

Democracy requires careful judicial attention to legislative intention as expressed in statute, such that where decision-making authority has been granted to a particular decision-maker it would be inappropriate for a court to step into the other body's shoes and substitute its preferred decision. This requirement of judicial restraint was memorialised by Lord Greene MR in *Associated Provincial Picture Houses Ltd v Wednesbury Corporation*.[163] In this chapter it is reflected in the fact that quashing orders, which generally permit public bodies to take fresh decisions, are more common remedies than mandatory orders, which compel public bodies to exercise their powers in a way mandated by a court; and in the obligation to exhaust internal remedies, which increases the probability that the decision-maker designated by Parliament (not a court) will render the final decision. Concern for democracy may also be perceived in the deference that is characteristic of judicial review of sensitive prerogative powers exercised by politically accountable Ministers.

Finally, separation of powers captures the notion that administrative decision-makers and courts have distinct roles to play, the former by carrying out their statutory mandates, the latter by holding the former to account. So it is that courts have been persuaded to recognise a right to reasons in situations where it would otherwise be impossible to make an 'effective attack' on the lawfulness of a decision.[164] Separation of powers concerns can also be perceived in this chapter's discussion of privative clauses: narrowly interpreting provisions that purport to oust judicial review of administrative action, as in the landmark decision in *Anisminic Ltd v Foreign Compensation Commission*,[165] preserves the judicial role in ensuring that public bodies have acted fairly, rationally, and in accordance with the general law of the land. Similarly, the approach to standing favoured since the *Fleet Street Casuals* case permits those not directly affected by a decision to challenge it, thereby broadening the area of administration over which judges can exercise meaningful oversight, a point underscored by expanded judicial review of de facto powers.

---

[159] [2001] QB 213.   [160] [1999] 2 AC 143.   [161] [1987] 1 AC 725.

[162] *Roy v Kensington and Chelsea and Westminster Family Practitioner Committee* [1992] 1 AC 624.

[163] [1948] 1 KB 223.   [164] *R v Home Secretary, ex p Doody* [1994] 1 AC 531.

[165] [1969] 2 AC 147.

Reasonable minds may, of course, differ about whether the courts have struck an appropriate balance between these values. In the *Anisminic* case, for instance, the judges had to reconcile the democratic value—which suggested that the legislative intention to exclude judicial review should be given effect—and the separation of powers value—which suggested that judicial oversight should be preserved in the absence of pellucidly clear language ousting the inherent jurisdiction of the superior courts. That scholars have long debated whether the House of Lords arrived at the optimal result in *Anisminic*, and the scope of that decision, is further evidence from the field of public law that seemingly technical procedural issues can be an important source of enlightenment for students of the common law.

Further reading

BEATSON, 'Prematurity and Ripeness for Review', in Forsyth and Hare (eds), *The Golden Metwand and the Crooked Cord* (Oxford 1998)

A discussion of the extent to which judicial review should extend to matters such as the issuing of advisory declarations.

FELDMAN, 'Public Interest Litigation and Constitutional Theory in Comparative Perspective' (1992) 55 MLR 44

An examination of public interest standing from the perspective of constitutional theory.

HARRIS, 'Judicial Review, Justiciability and the Prerogative of Mercy' [2003] CLJ 631

An analysis of the doctrine of justiciability with particular reference to its application to decisions concerning the prerogative of mercy.

MILES, 'Standing in a Multi-Layered Constitution' in Bamforth and Leyland (eds), *Public Law in a Multi-Layered Constitution* (Oxford 2003)

An examination of the contemporary law of standing.

TAGGART (ed), *The Province of Administrative Law* (Oxford 1997)

A collection of essays examining the scope of administrative law, including questions about the proper extent of judicial review.

14

The Effectiveness and Impact of Judicial Review

1. Judicial review and government	589
2. Judicial review litigation	592
3. Judicial competence and capacity	605
4. Judicial impact and administrative reaction	611
5. Conclusion	627
Expert commentary	627
Further reading	629

Chapters 12 and 13 have considered the procedures and legal principles of judicial review. This chapter offers a different perspective on judicial review. It examines the effectiveness of judicial review as a mechanism of legal accountability and the impact it has upon public administration. It is concerned not with law in the books, but law in action and how it works in practice. This requires a shift of approach: rather than examining legal doctrines, we shall focus upon the broader political and administrative context in which judicial review operates.

1. Judicial review and government

1.1 Judicial review–effectiveness and impact

The *effectiveness* of judicial review concerns its propensity to produce a desired outcome, whereas the *impact* of judicial review concerns its influence or effect on public administration. Why should we consider these aspects of judicial review? Under the traditional constitutional principles of parliamentary sovereignty and the rule of law, Parliament makes the law and the courts enforce it; the role of government is to administer the law and to comply with judicial interpretations of it. From this perspective, the relationship between the courts and public administration is, or should be, relatively non-problematic: court judgments expounding the law should be directly reflected in governmental practices. But, reality is rarely so simple. While a purely legal analysis of the legal principles governing judicial review is important, it tells us little about how judicial review works in practice and how it impacts upon government. After all, judicial review is concerned not only with the development of legal principles, but also with how public bodies perform their functions. Every judicial review case, however routine, has some implication for policy development and implementation. Traditional separation of powers theory tends to rely upon clear distinctions between politics, law, and administration, but in practice (as discussed in Chapter 3) these distinctions are often blurred. Court judgments—and, indeed, even the possibility of applying for judicial review—can have major consequences for public administration; alternatively, government may seek to undermine court rulings.

This chapter therefore examines a number of issues concerning the effectiveness and impact of judicial review, both of which are complex concepts. In the context of this chapter, the effectiveness of judicial review has three aspects:

- effectiveness in relation to the *accessibility* of the judicial review procedure, that is, the extent to which potential claimants are able to access judicial review (section 2);

- effectiveness in terms of the *competence and capacity* of the courts to review administrative action (section 3); and

- effectiveness of the *output* of judicial review and its impact upon government, in particular, the ability of judicial review to affect the behaviour and operations of government agencies (section 4).

We will focus on the following topics. First, we will consider the dynamics of judicial review litigation, that is, how many judicial review applications do the courts receive and in which particular administrative contexts? Second, we will consider the obstacles to using judicial review. Third, we will critically analyse the competence and capacity of the courts to issue rulings that affect public administration. For instance, where—in relation to so-called 'polycentric' issues—courts are faced with situations in which it is difficult to predict the likely impact of intervention, does (and should) this deter courts from engaging in judicial review? Fourth, we will consider the impact of judicial review on government. This has been described as 'probably the least studied but most important issue surrounding administrative law'.[1] The court's decision in a judicial review case is rarely the end of the story of a legal challenge to government action, but rather a chapter in the ongoing and evolving relationship between the courts and public authorities. How do public authorities react to judicial review? Which factors increase or diminish the impact of judicial review?

These questions are directly relevant to one of our principal themes. To understand how the courts can hold government to account, it is important to examine

---

[1] Schuck and Elliot, 'To the *Chevron* Station: An Empirical Study of Federal Administrative Law' [1990] Duke Law Journal 984, 1044.

the effectiveness of judicial review as a mechanism of legal accountability. The more influence judicial review exerts on government, the more effective it is in securing legal accountability—and vice versa. Whether or not administrative law achieves its primary goal—ensuring that government acts according to law—depends largely on the effectiveness of judicial review.

As we have already emphasised, judicial review provides only one means of controlling governmental decision-making; the legal norms articulated by the courts may often be only a subordinate part of the broader political–administrative context in which public authorities operate.[2] There is a complex and dynamic interrelationship between law, politics, and public administration. It cannot be assumed that public authorities always enthusiastically welcome judicial scrutiny or comply with court judgments. Governmental reaction to judicial review may be positive or negative, formal or informal. Court judgments may have broader consequences and ramifications on governmental procedure and policy beyond its particular circumstances. But government may seek to limit those wider consequences or even reverse the effect of a judicial review. It is therefore dangerous to assume that the relationship between court judgments and administrative practice is a straightforward one in which the latter automatically mirrors—by falling into line with—the former. The reality, as we will see, is far murkier—particularly in relation to the impact of judicial review decisions outside the narrow confines of the actual case.

1.2 **The development of judicial review**

Before turning to the questions of effectiveness and impact, it is important to place the discussion within a historical perspective and to acknowledge the development of the judicial review jurisdiction.[3] Taking the 1950s as a starting point, the courts were generally considered to have exerted little, if any, influence on government. The prevalent judicial attitude, exemplified by the *Wednesbury* case and considered in Chapter 12,[4] was that the courts should generally defer to administrative decisions and only intervene if the impugned decision was thoroughly unreasonable.[5] The very high level of deference shown by the courts towards the executive during the Second World War carried over into peacetime, even though this was a period during which the scale of administrative action was expanding significantly and concerns were expressed that the common law no longer possessed 'the strength to provide any satisfactory solution to the problem of keeping the executive . . . under proper control'.[6]

---

[2] Prosser, 'Politics and Judicial Review: The *Atkinson* Case and Its Aftermath' [1979] PL 59.

[3] See generally Jowell, 'Administrative Law', in Bogdanor (ed), *The British Constitution in the Twentieth Century* (Oxford 2003), p 373; Rawlings, 'Modelling Judicial Review' (2008) 61 CLP 95.

[4] See Chapter 12, section 5.1.

[5] *Associated Provincial Picture Houses Ltd v Wednesbury Corporation* [1948] 1 KB 223.

[6] Devlin, 'The Common Law, Public Policy and the Executive' (1956) CLP 1, 14–15. See also Davis, 'The Future of Judge-Made Public Law in England: A Problem of Practical Jurisprudence' (1961) 61 Columbia Law Review 201.

As a leading commentator, de Smith, noted, judicial review was 'inevitably sporadic and peripheral'.[7]

However, as we saw in Chapter 12, during the 1960s and 1970s, the courts assumed a more active supervisory role by removing some of the most debilitating anachronisms, such as the distinction between errors of law inside and outside jurisdiction, and breathed new life into old concepts, such as the doctrines of natural justice and improper purpose.[8] Subsequently, new legal principles—notably the doctrines of legitimate expectations and proportionality—developed.[9] Meanwhile, as noted in Chapter 13, the courts' jurisdiction was expanded to include review of the prerogative and decisions produced by non-statutory bodies,[10] and the courts adopted a more generous approach towards standing and challenges brought by public interest groups.[11] Alongside doctrinal changes, procedural reforms were also occurring. In the late 1970s and early 1980s, the procedures of judicial review were reformed to provide a coherent process for challenging administrative decisions before specialist judges sitting in the Crown Office List of the High Court.[12] The number of judicial review applications increased dramatically from some 500 in 1981 to over 4,000 in 1996. De Smith's comment was reformulated: '[T]he effect of judicial review on the practical exercise of power has . . . become constant and central.'[13] The next major developments occurred in 2000: a further set of procedural reforms,[14] the renaming of the Crown Office List as the Administrative Court, and the coming into force of the Human Rights Act 1998.

2. Judicial review litigation

2.1 Judicial review in practice

Let us start, then, by considering the Administrative Court's judicial review jurisdiction—not in terms of the legal principles of judicial review, but in terms of the number of judicial review claims. Figure 14.1 shows the statistics on the number of judicial review claims lodged with the Administrative Court and the Upper Tribunal.[15]

---

[7] De Smith, *Judicial Review of Administrative Action* (London 1959), p 1.

[8] The landmark cases in this period are: *Ridge v Baldwin* [1964] AC 40; *Padfield v Minister for Agriculture, Fisheries and Food* [1968] AC 997; *Anisminic v Foreign Compensation Commission* [1969] 2 AC 147.

[9] *R v North and East Devon Health Authority, ex p Coughlan* [2001] QB 213; *R (Daly) v Secretary of State for the Home Department* [2001] 2 AC 532.

[10] See *Council of Civil Service Unions v Minister for the Civil Service* [1985] AC 374 (the *GCHQ* case); *R v Panel on Takeovers and Mergers, ex p Datafin plc* [1987] QB 815.

[11] *R v Inland Revenue Commission, ex p National Federation of Self-Employed and Small Businesses* [1982] AC 617; *R v Secretary of State for Foreign Affairs, ex p World Development Movement Ltd* [1995] 1 WLR 386.

[12] Senior Courts Act 1981, s 31; Rules of the Supreme Court (1977), Order 53.

[13] De Smith, Woolf, and Jowell, *Judicial Review of Administrative Action* (London 1995), p vii.

[14] Civil Procedure Rules (2000), Pt 54.

[15] These statistics are taken from the Civil Justice Statistics published by the Ministry of Justice, **https://www.gov.uk/government/collections/civil-justice-statistics-quarterly**. The statistics cover England and Wales only.

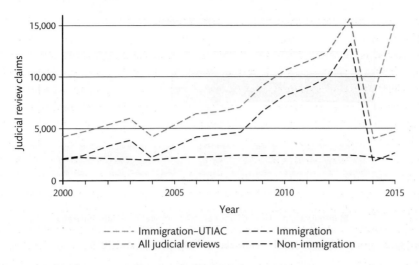

Figure 14.1 Judicial review applications lodged, 2000–15

This figure shows the total number of judicial review claims lodged in the Administrative Court. It also shows the breakdown between immigration and non-immigration claims lodged in the Administrative Court and immigration claims lodged in the Upper Tribunal (Immigration and Asylum Chamber) (UTIAC) from 2013 onwards. As can be seen, the number of judicial review claims varies from year to year. What is apparent is that the number of claims lodged with the Administrative Court increased significantly from 2000 and then dropped dramatically after 2013. This has been almost entirely driven by the numbers of immigration judicial reviews, which now account for 85 per cent of all judicial reviews. Most immigration judicial reviews were transferred to the UTIAC in 2013.[16] By comparison, the number of non-immigration decisions has been relatively static at between 2,000 and 2,500 claims lodged per year.

Figure 14.2 shows the number of immigration judicial reviews lodged with the Administrative Court and the UTIAC in 2014 and 2015. Figure 14.3 shows non-immigration judicial reviews lodged in 2015 broken down into specific categories. Putting immigration to one side, what is apparent here is how the caseload is concentrated in a number of categories: planning; criminal justice; prisons; homelessness; and family, children and young persons.

Once a judicial claim is lodged, the claimant must seek the permission of the court to bring the claim. The purpose of the permission stage is to determine which claims raise an arguable challenge and so can proceed to a substantive hearing. Figure 14.4 shows those judicial review claims refused and granted permission, and those that proceed to a substantive hearing. Substantive outcomes are shown in Figure 14.5.

Three points can be made here. First, the number of claims refused permission is considerably higher than those granted permission.[17] Second, not all cases granted

---

[16] Crime and Courts Act 2013, s 22. See Chapter 16, section 5.5.
[17] On permission, see Chapter 13, section 3.1.

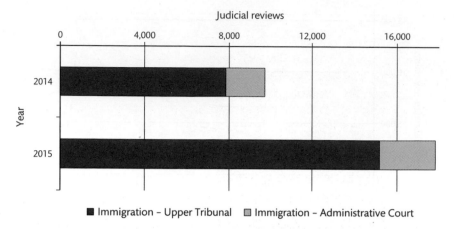

Figure 14.2 Immigration judicial review claims lodged, 2014 and 2015

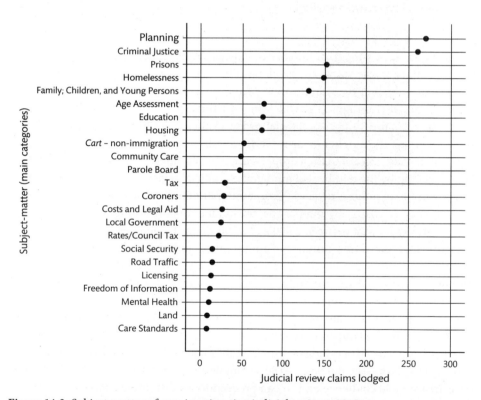

Figure 14.3 Subject-matter of non-immigration judicial reviews, 2015

permission subsequently proceed to a substantive hearing. On the contrary, of those cases granted permission, more fall out of the process than proceed to a substantive hearing. This is because public authorities frequently concede judicial reviews before they get to a substantive hearing. Settlement is considered in section 2.3. Third, the number of judicial reviews that ultimately succeed—those cases that are allowed—is

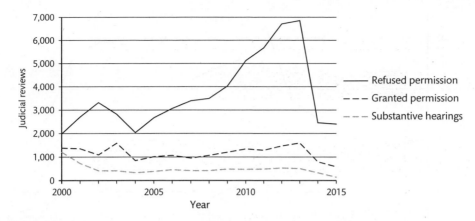

Figure 14.4 Judicial reviews (Administrative Court): permission outcomes, 2000–15

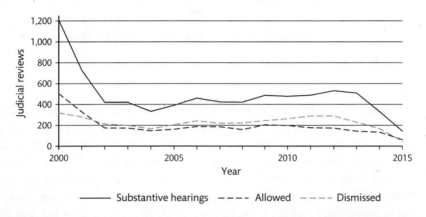

Figure 14.5 Judicial reviews (Administrative Court): substantive outcomes, 2000–15

relatively small and has declined since 2000. Over the years 2000 to 2015, the average number of successful judicial reviews was 195 per year.

We should also consider the amount of time the Administrative Court takes to make decisions. Timeliness is an important feature of the judicial process in action. From reading a law report, it might not seem that either the number of judges in a court or the volume of cases are very important. But this would be wrong. Caseloads and judicial resources directly affect the amount of time a court takes to make decisions: the more cases and/or the fewer resources, then the longer cases will take.

Figure 14.6 shows the average time (in days) taken for each stage of the judicial review process in the Administrative Court over the years 2000–15: cases lodged to permission, oral renewal, and final hearing. This is not necessarily a measure of how long the Administrative Court takes to deal with a judicial review. The time taken for litigants to provide evidence and any adjournments or postponements requested will also be relevant. Nonetheless, the data tells us the timeliness of cases in the Administrative Court.

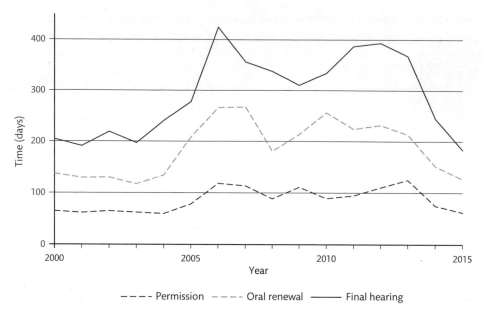

Figure 14.6 Average time taken for each stage of the judicial review process, 2000–15

What Figure 14.6 shows is that, first, the amount of time taken to make permission decisions has been relatively stable—an achievement considering that there were 3,201 permission decisions in 2000 compared with 8,221 decisions in 2013. Second, the average time taken from lodging a case to oral renewal has fluctuated over the years. During 2000–04, the average time was 130 days. This then increased to a peak of 267 days in 2007, and then fell to 180 days in 2008 before rising to an average of 228 days between 2009 and 2013. Third, the average time taken from lodging a case to a final hearing has also fluctuated: it took the court 205 days in 2000; by 2006, this had doubled to 425 days. In 2011, it took the Administrative Court an average of 387 days—well over a year—from lodgement to a final hearing for 470 cases. Since then, the time taken has declined. Both the increase and decline in the amount of time taken are likely to have been influenced by the increased immigration caseload and then its transfer to the UTIAC.

Some general points can be made here. First, as noted earlier, the largest subject-matter of judicial review is immigration (Figures 14.1 and 14.2). There are reasons why the caseload is heavily immigration-focused. People often challenge negative immigration decisions. The caseload of the Administrative Court is dependent upon the availability of tribunal appeal rights. Individuals must exhaust alternative remedies, such as appeals, before accessing judicial review. But, immigration appeals have been restricted, leaving only one method of challenge: judicial review.[18]

By contrast, other areas of government do not frequently feature in judicial review challenges. Consider, for instance, social security. This is the largest decision-making

---

[18] Sunkin, 'What is Happening to Applications for Judicial Review?' (1987) 50 MLR 432.

process in the UK, but it barely registers in the judicial review caseload: most disputes are channelled into social security tribunals, and now the Department for Work and Pension's mandatory reconsideration process.[19] By comparison, the government's policy of restricting immigration appeals inevitably shifts the caseload from tribunals into judicial review. Over the years, the increased number of immigration judicial reviews has over-stretched the limited resources of the Administrative Court and led to delays. As the Lord Chief Justice stated in 2008: '[T]he pressure of the asylum and immigration cases has meant that there are unacceptable delays. Claimants may wait 12 months or more. Understandably, concerns are being expressed at the delays.'[20] The solution was to transfer immigration judicial reviews to the UTIAC in 2013. The effect was roughly to double the UTIAC's caseload, but it was not given any extra judicial resources—meaning that delays persist.[21] What the episode illustrates is the limited nature of judicial resources.

Second, notwithstanding the increase in judicial review, the total number of such decisions challenged by judicial review is, given the vast scale of governmental decision-making, very small indeed. We noted in Chapter 11 that, according to some judges at least, judicial review has been developed to fill a gap that arises due to perceived problems with other remedies (most notably parliamentary accountability).[22] Despite numerous factors that have expanded the role, scope, and intensity of judicial review in recent years—developments in the grounds of review, the expansion of standing, and the Human Rights Act 1998—the number of allowed judicial reviews is fewer than 200 claims per year (Figure 14.5), a miniscule fraction of the entire number of administrative decisions taken annually.

Statistics cannot tell us everything. Court judgments shape the predictions and views of future litigants about what might happen to their case if it proceeds to court. One judicial review case may function as an important 'test case', with considerable repercussions for many other cases. An illustration is the House of Lords' decision in *Limbuela* concerning support for asylum seekers, the outcome of which influenced several hundred other judicial reviews that were also pending.[23] Other judicial review challenges may be brought by a public interest body and may have wider ramifications for many thousands of individuals or for government policy. There is an important distinction, explored further later, between those judicial reviews that merely concern the redress of individual grievances and those that have a broader influence on government policy and procedure. Furthermore, much judicial review litigation never results in a permission decision, let alone a final judgment: the threat of judicial review may often be sufficient to make a public body rethink its decision.

Public authorities' experiences of judicial review vary enormously. Some public authorities, such as the Home Office, have considerable experience of dealing with

---

[19] See Chapter 16, section 4.1.

[20] Lord Phillips, Lord Chief Justice, *The Lord Chief Justice's Review of the Administration of Justice in the Courts* (HC 448 2008–09), p 36.

[21] Senior President of Tribunals, *Annual Report* (2016), p 35.   [22] See Chapter 11, section 4.

[23] *R (Limbuela) v Secretary of State for the Home Department* [2006] 1 AC 396. As the Court of Appeal recognised, 666 other judicial review applications were affected by this decision: see [2004] EWCA Civ 540, [2].

judicial review challenges. By contrast, the exposure of other public authorities to judicial review may be more intermittent. Indeed, some may hardly ever, if at all, have their decisions legally challenged, which may, in turn, affect how they respond if and when they are subjected to an application for judicial review. A low exposure to judicial review may mean that a public body is largely unaware of the standards and norms of administrative law.

Even the use of judicial review against a particular category of public authority may vary considerably *within the category*. For example, empirical research into the use of judicial review to challenge decisions of local authorities has indicated that while a few local authorities regularly experience judicial review challenges, for most, it remains a rarity; even within a single local authority, the focus of litigation on specific areas—for example, community care and housing—may mean that the influence of judicial review across areas of service provision varies.[24] Factors influencing the use of judicial review may include uneven geographical access to legal services, the link between deprivation and the presence of legal services in bringing challenges, and the dissatisfaction associated with poor-quality public services. In 'ground-level' contexts, such as community care and housing, judicial review is often used by the most marginalised groups of people—for example, homeless individuals seeking temporary accommodation—against hard-pressed local authorities in relation to some of the most intractable resource allocation issues.

Another point to make here concerns the wider political context in which judicial review is used by legal practitioners. Judicial review is often used as a tool of social change, a mechanism by which political campaigns are pursued. In other words, judicial review is seen as a means by which government policy can be challenged— often in order to improve the life conditions for marginalised people whose needs and interests have been overlooked, or positively harmed, by government.[25] It is no coincidence that immigration and prisons are the two largest areas of judicial review. Immigrants and prisoners are disenfranchised groups: they are not represented in the political process. Theirs are deeply unpopular causes. They are also often on the receiving end of authoritarian and draconian government action. Nonetheless, both groups of people possess rights and deserve to be treated fairly. This type of legal practice—which involves the use of litigation in order to advance particular causes or political interests—is known as 'public interest law', or in the US, 'cause-lawyering'. Such legal practice tends to be focused upon challenging the state: hence the use of judicial review.

2.2 The accessibility of judicial review

How accessible is judicial review? Judicial review is claimant-driven: the Administrative Court can only consider the legality of a public decision if requested to do so by an individual. A claimant seeking judicial review must overcome a number

---

[24] Sunkin et al, 'Mapping the Use of Judicial Review to Challenge Local Authorities in England and Wales' [2007] PL 545.

[25] See generally Harlow and Rawlings, *Pressure Through Law* (London 1992).

of obstacles: he or she must comply with the time limit (normally three months), possess standing, and have exhausted alternative remedies. Claimants must also be granted permission to proceed for judicial review by demonstrating that they have an arguable case.[26] While this requirement acts as a filter mechanism, providing the Court with a useful case management tool, it tends to operate on a highly discretionary basis, with substantial variations in the grants of permission between individual judges: the definition of what comprises an 'arguable' case leaves scope for judicial discretion.[27] Given stretched judicial resources, the permission threshold may, in practice, be higher than 'arguability' and nearer to whether a case is winnable.

Other important practical difficulties may arise from the variable geographical availability of legal advice and services—for example, while some law firms may be very familiar with judicial review proceedings, others may not. Then there are the financial costs of securing such services. Many claimants may be unable to afford the substantial sums of money required to pursue judicial review proceedings and are compelled to rely on legal aid. In 2013, the government announced severe restrictions on legal aid in judicial review cases, which limited the award of legal aid only to those claims granted permission.[28] Part of this policy was held to be unlawful.[29] Nonetheless, as legal costs must normally be borne by the losing party, this may dissuade potential claimants from seeking judicial review. Of course, a claimant must also have good legal reasons for arguing that the challenged decision was unlawful. Even then, if a claimant overcomes all of these hurdles, there is no remedy as of right because public law remedies are discretionary. The paradox is that, while the courts often state that access to justice is a fundamental right, this right is, in practice, hedged around with various restrictions.

Another factor of some importance is that the Administrative Court, like virtually all courts, operates under constraints that limit the number of cases that it can handle at any one time. Courts are prone to overload because, typically, 'there are far more claims than there are institutional resources for full dress adjudication of each'.[30] Faced with increasing caseloads, judges may engage in more stringent scrutiny of applications for permission to proceed and search for ways to divert cases out of the ordinary judicial process, such as settlement and alternative dispute resolution (ADR), which are considered in sections 2.3 and 2.4. Furthermore, overload can lead to delays in the processing of cases.

One practical difficulty is that the number of High Court judges nominated to decide judicial review cases and who are therefore able to be deployed in the Administrative Court is limited.[31] As noted earlier, in light of the increasing caseload

---

[26] For detailed discussion of these procedural matters, see Chapter 13.

[27] Le Sueur and Sunkin, 'Applications for Judicial Review: The Requirement for Leave' [1992] PL 102; Bridges, Mezaros, and Sunkin, *Judicial Review in Perspective* (London 1995), pp 164–70.

[28] Ministry of Justice, *Transforming Legal Aid: Next Steps* (London 2013).

[29] *R (Ben Hoare Bell Solicitors) v Lord Chancellor* [2015] EWHC 523 (Admin).

[30] Galanter, 'Why the "Haves" Come Out Ahead: Speculations on the Limits of Legal Change' (1974) Law and Society 95, 121.

[31] Judicial Working Group, *Justice Outside London* (London 2007), [131].

of judicial review claims, the Court has experienced practical difficulties in coping with its workload. Delays in the judicial review process can disadvantage both claimants and public authorities, reducing the effectiveness of the process for reviewing the legality of public action. Justice delayed is justice denied.[32] The transfer of part of the judicial review caseload to the UTIAC is hardly an answer because this merely shifts the backlog of cases and delays to another part of the same system. It is important to consider the reasons for such delays: do they arise because many challenges are unmeritorious or because the court system is under-staffed and under-resourced?

During the coalition government (2010–15), the then Lord Chancellor, Chris Grayling MP, held a clear view: time and money were being wasted by unmeritorious judicial review cases brought simply to generate publicity or to delay implementation of a decision that was properly made. In December 2012, the government expressed concern about the growth in judicial review claims and claimed that the resulting delays to the implementation of administrative decisions can slow down government decision-making, increase costs, create uncertainty, and stifle economic growth.[33] In order to address these perceived problems, the government reduced the time limit in which claimants could bring forward a claim from three months to six weeks for planning challenges and 30 days for procurement cases, removed the right to oral consideration of permission to bring judicial review where a judge has certified a claim as totally without merit, and introduced a £215 fee for such oral renewals as are still permitted.[34] These changes attracted the criticism that they would reduce the accessibility of judicial review and therefore the courts' ability to enforce the rule of law. It remains to be seen what their impact is in practice.

In September 2013, a further set of possible changes was mooted.[35] These included streamlining planning challenges; adopting a narrower approach to standing; enhancing the courts' power to deal with procedural challenges that would make no difference to a final decision; rebalancing financial incentives so as to prevent the pursuit of repeated and unmeritorious claims often at a cost to the taxpayer; and the possibility of widening direct 'leapfrog' appeals, thereby allowing more cases to go to the Supreme Court direct from the court of first instance.[36] Many of these reforms were put into effect by the Criminal Justice and Courts Act 2015. Different views have been expressed about these reforms. In 2015, the lead judge in the Administrative Court described the reforms as

---

[32] In *R (Casey) v Restormel Borough Council* [2007] EWHC 2554 (Admin), [29] and [33], Munby J noted: 'It is no secret that the Administrative Court is having great difficulty coping with its present workload . . . Hard pressed local and other public authorities should not be prejudiced, . . . tax payers and rate-payers should not be financially disadvantaged, other more deserving claimants seeking recourse to over-stretched public resources should not be prejudiced, because of delays in the Royal Courts of Justice.' The phrase 'justice delayed is justice denied' is often attributed to Magna Carta (1297), ch 29, which reads: 'To no one will we sell, to no one will we deny or delay, right or justice.'

[33] Ministry of Justice, *Judicial Review: Proposals for Reform* (London 2012).

[34] Ministry of Justice, *Reform of Judicial Review: The Government Response* (Cm 8611 2013); The Civil Procedure (Amendment No 4) Rules 2013, SI 2013/1412.

[35] Ministry of Justice, *Judicial Review: Proposals for Further Reform* (Cm 8703 2013).

[36] 'Leapfrog' appeals are those appeals which are deemed so important that they can proceed directly from the High Court or Upper Tribunal to the Supreme Court without being considered first by the Court of Appeal.

'something of a mixed bag'. The reforms did not warrant the fears produced, but they are not wholly positive either; they may create more scope for litigation.[37] Others have argued that the cumulative effect has been to weaken judicial review.[38]

Irrespective of the merits of these proposals, what the reforms evince is an underlying sense of the government's impatience with—perhaps even opposition to—judicial review. After all, the purpose of judicial review is to place legal obstacles in the government's path when it exceeds the limits of its powers. If the government becomes accustomed to viewing judicial review not as an essential aspect of the process by which legal accountability is imposed, but as something to be designed by the government for its own ends, then this may well simultaneously weaken the role of the courts and increase the calls for a formal set of arrangements concerning judicial control of government. Another point is that many of the difficulties for the courts have been of the government's own making. It has always been assumed that the legalistic and technical nature of the judicial review jurisdiction made legal representation for claimants absolutely essential—especially when the government and other public bodies can be represented by experienced counsel. However, the government's cuts to legal aid have increased the number of unrepresented litigants in court thereby posing an extreme challenge to the judges.

The uneven geographical spread of judicial review applications should also be noted. A substantial number are lodged by individuals located in London and southeast England.[39] The precise causes of this are unknown and are likely to include many variables such as the willingness or otherwise of individuals to challenge public authorities, and limited access to legal advice and services. One suggestion has been that the location of the Administrative Court itself in London might inhibit people living elsewhere from seeking judicial review and undermine access to justice.[40] For this reason, the Administrative Court has now been regionalised with hearing centres now operating in Cardiff, Manchester, Birmingham, Bristol, and Leeds. The purpose of regionalisation is to facilitate access to justice by enabling judicial review cases to be administered and determined in the most appropriate location.[41]

2.3 Settlement

Many judicial review claims do not proceed to a full hearing even if granted permission to proceed. There are various reasons why a claim may be withdrawn. Litigants are increasingly likely (and encouraged) to use out-of-court settlements, that is, they resolve their dispute before it gets to court. A public authority facing a judicial review challenge may concede the case because it recognises that it made a legal error.

---

[37] Ouseley J, then lead judge of the Administrative Court, seminar on the future of judicial review, Westminster Legal Policy Forum, July 2015.

[38] Mills, 'Reforms to Judicial Review in the Criminal Justice and Courts Act 2015: Promoting Efficiency or Weakening the Rule of Law?' [2015] PL 583.

[39] Bridges, Mezaros, and Sunkin, *Judicial Review in Perspective* (London 1995).

[40] *Justice Outside London*, [50]–[52].

[41] Nason and Sunkin, 'The Regionalisation of Judicial Review: Constitutional Authority, Access to Justice and Specialisation of Legal Services in Public Law' (2013) 76 MLR 223.

Figure 14.7 shows the following: (i) the number of judicial reviews in the Administrative Court concluded by consent, that is, withdrawn by agreement of the parties; (ii) the number of Administrative Court judicial reviews allowed following a hearing; and (iii) the number of UTIAC immigration judicial reviews not determined by the Tribunal (the vast majority of these cases were conceded by the Home Office).

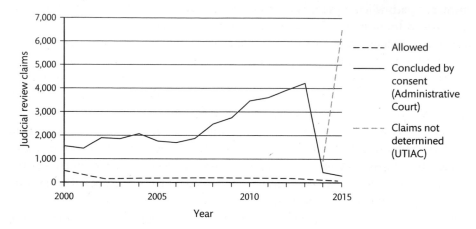

Figure 14.7 Judicial reviews concluded by consent, allowed, and not determined, 2000–15

Figure 14.7 shows that a far higher number of cases are settled out of court than are allowed following a hearing. Most successful judicial reviews are resolved not through formal adjudication by a court, but are settled outside the doors of the court. The number of cases concluded by consent will include some, though not all, of those granted permission. It will also include some cases that did not reach the permission stage: in many cases a public body may concede a judicial review challenge before it reaches the stage at which a judge decides whether to grant or refuse permission. The sudden decline in the number of Administrative Court cases concluded by consent since 2013 coincided with the transfer of immigration cases to the UTIAC. Settlement has long been a feature of immigration judicial reviews.[42] With the increase in immigration judicial reviews, the Home Office has been overwhelmed with challenges. The Home Office concedes judicial review challenges when it recognises that it has made a legally flawed decision. The sheer volume of cases may also play a role. Settling judicial reviews out of court is quicker, cheaper, and more efficient than trying to defend a challenge.

Empirical research demonstrates that claimants and litigants are increasingly prepared to settle cases. Bondy and Sunkin's research into non-immigration judicial reviews found that 62 per cent of judicial review 'threats' were resolved by dialogue between the parties, and that, of those cases that get as far as the issue of proceedings, 34 per cent were resolved before permission is granted, while 56 per cent of cases in which permission was granted were settled prior to the substantive hearing.[43]

---

[42] See Thomas, 'Mapping Immigration Judicial Review Litigation: An Empirical Legal Analysis' [2015] PL 652.
[43] Bondy and Sunkin, 'Settlement in Judicial Review Proceedings' [2009] PL 237.

Research into immigration judicial reviews has found that up to 30 per cent of all claims lodged are settled—overwhelmingly in the claimant's favour.[44]

The advantage of settlement for the individual claimant is that his or her grievance will be remedied because the public authority will have recognised that its initial decision was in error and will have to replace it with a new one. From the public authority's perspective, settlement can avoid further delays and increased costs. If the initial decision was flawed—even only arguably flawed—then it may be quicker and less costly to concede and take a new decision. The reality for many legal practitioners is that most judicial reviews are resolved at an early stage of the process. Relatively few cases proceed all the way to a substantive hearing.

Settlement can also be used by public authorities for less respectable reasons. By conceding, the public authority may be able to neutralise a legal challenge to avoid unfavourable publicity and media attention, and/or to reduce the risk of the court issuing a judgment adverse to its policy interests. For example, one judicial review case challenging the interpretation of a statutory provision may have a positive impact on hundreds, perhaps thousands, of other similarly placed people. If the public authority wishes to avoid a potentially 'adverse' precedent, then settling out of court can give the public authority the upper hand. It can concede the one challenge, while in general maintaining its favoured interpretation of the law. Only a court judgment can establish a precedent that outlives the resolution of the litigants' particular dispute. Paradoxically, while the courts are there to ensure government according to law, a public authority may, in practice, be able to influence to some degree which cases go forward for potential creation of precedent by conceding challenges before they get to court.

However, the courts have recognised that the judicial review jurisdiction is not extinguished by the public authority's withdrawal of its decision under challenge.[45] The courts can proceed to determine a public law case even though the specific dispute between the litigants has been resolved and is no longer live. The courts must proceed with caution, but this discretion can be exercised when there are good public interest reasons and where a large number of similar cases exist or are anticipated.[46] This discretion can be invoked to prevent the government from tactically conceding challenges to suit its own ends. The wider point is that judicial review has an important educative function over and above its dispute resolution function.[47]

There is an important general point here. When justifying its proposals to limit judicial review through the Criminal Justice and Courts Act 2015, the government relied upon the overall success rate of judicial reviews of 1 per cent to demonstrate the supposed futility of judicial review.[48] But—and this is crucially important—the

---

[44] Thomas, 666–7.

[45] *R v Secretary of State for the Home Department, ex p Salem* [1999] AC 450.

[46] *R v Secretary of State for the Home Department, ex p Salem* [1999] AC 450, 456–7, *per* Lord Slynn.

[47] *R (Bhudia) v Secretary of State for the Home Department* [2016] UKUT 00025 (IAC).

[48] This was the percentage of allowed judicial reviews as a proportion of the total number of claims lodged.

1 per cent figure was, taken alone, highly misleading: it did not take account of cases concluded by consent. These cases often represent as much of a success for a claimant as a favourable court judgment. As Hickman and Sunkin have explained, when taking account of cases settled out of court, the statistics overall paint a picture of relatively high rates of success in judicial review. The permission stage provides an effective filter of weak claims. The judicial review process is used to accomplish a positive result in a substantial number of cases without the claim proceeding to a full hearing.[49] In other words, the government's reforms were not evidence-based, but more of a politically driven attempt to clamp down on judicial review—a general indication of governmental attitudes toward the rule of law. A wider—and crucial— point is that the high settlement rate demonstrates that much litigation is resolved not by the courts directly, but by agreements between the parties reached in the shadow of the law.

2.4 Alternative dispute resolution

In recent years, the pressures on the Administrative Court have prompted a search for ways to divert challenges out of the Court into other routes, such as ADR techniques— that is, the resolution of disputes through informal processes, such as mediation, rather than via formal judicial procedures.

Traditionally, public lawyers have been resistant to the use of ADR because public law litigation concerns both the rights and interests of individuals, and the duties and obligations of public authorities; ADR should not be used as a substitute for judicial review when the legality of a public decision is being challenged or where an important precedent might be established.[50] But, ADR has some advantages and its use has been encouraged by the courts.[51] In *Cowl*, Lord Woolf noted that 'insufficient attention' had been paid to the 'paramount importance of avoiding litigation whenever this is possible'.[52] ADR can make a contribution to resolving disputes in a manner that meets the needs of the parties and saves time, money, and stress; the courts should not, without good reason, permit judicial review proceedings to proceed if a significant part of the issues could be resolved outside the litigation process. As Lord Woolf noted, due to the 'unfortunate culture in litigation' of over-judicialising the processes involved, parties to litigation can insist on arguing about what has occurred in the past rather than focus on the future. The emphasis on ADR is now reflected in the Pre-action Protocol for Judicial Review, which states that the parties

---

[49] Sunkin and Hickman, 'Success in Judicial Review: The Current Position', *UK Constitutional Law Association* blog, 20 March 2015, **https://ukconstitutionallaw.org/2015/03/20/tom-hickman-and-maurice-sunkin-success-in-judicial-review-the-current-position/**

[50] In 2001, the government made a commitment that government departments and their agencies should use ADR in the resolution of disputes, but recognised that there may be some cases in which ADR would not be suitable. See Ministry of Justice, *Annual Pledge Report: Monitoring the Effectiveness of the Government's Commitment to Using Alternative Dispute Resolution 2006–07* (London 2008).

[51] Supperstone, Stilitz, and Sheldon, 'ADR and Public Law' [2006] PL 299; Boyron, 'The Rise of Mediation in Administrative Law Disputes: Experiences from England, France and Germany' [2006] PL 320.

[52] *R (Cowl) v Plymouth City Council* [2002] 1 WLR 803.

should consider whether some form of ADR procedure would be more suitable than litigation.[53]

> **Q** Should access to judicial review be limited in the ways that it is? How, if at all, might the accessibility of judicial review be improved? Is the use of settlement or ADR desirable in the context of judicial review challenges?

3. Judicial competence and capacity

This section considers the effectiveness of judicial review in terms of the competence and capacity of the courts to issue rulings concerning the operations of government. Considerations about the impact of judicial review have influenced—and ought to influence—the courts' development of the grounds of judicial review. This raises questions, first encountered in Chapter 12, about the institutional competence of the courts. We saw there that, in some situations, judges recognise that they ought not to engage in judicial review—or ought at least not to engage in intensive review—where they lack adequate competence. For the purposes of our present discussion, an important respect in which courts may lack competence is that they may be ill placed to understand the likely *impact* of their decisions.

3.1 Judicial expertise

The ability of the courts to review administrative decisions may, in some areas, be constrained because of limited judicial expertise. It is also important to emphasise here the different perspectives of administrators and judges.[54] Public authorities have responsibility for making and implementing policy with regard to whatever public function they have been assigned. They are therefore often concerned with the delivery of public services, administrative efficiency, and the public interest. Public authorities tend to develop an expertise in the particular area of administration for which they are responsible. By contrast, judges decide cases; they are not responsible for administering or managing whole areas of policy. The courts have developed a degree of specialisation in public law litigation, through channelling judicial review cases to nominated judges in the Administrative Court, but judges do not normally have the benefit of administrative experience (it has been argued that they should).[55]

The general point is that while the courts are specialists in administrative law principles, they are not necessarily specialists in all areas of public administration.

---

[53] Ministry of Justice, *Pre-action Protocol for Judicial Review* (London 2007), [3.1]. While the Protocol notes that it is not practicable to address in detail ADR procedures, it mentions some of the options: discussion and negotiation, ombudsmen, early neutral evaluation, and mediation.

[54] See Blom-Cooper, 'Lawyers and Public Administrators: Separate and Unequal' [1984] PL 215; Drewry, 'Public Law' (1995) Public Administration 41, 48–51.

[55] Woolf, *Protection of the Public: A New Challenge* (London 1990), pp 115–20; Woolf, 'Has the Human Rights Act Made Judicial Review Redundant?', ALBA Annual Lecture 2005, **http://www.adminlaw.org.uk/docs/Lord%20Woof%20Lecture%2023rd%20November%202005.doc**

As judicial review can have significant repercussions on complex areas of public administration, the courts need to be aware of the potential effect of their rulings. Furthermore, while public authorities must have regard to the broader public interest, the judicial perspective tends to concentrate on individual interests and rights.

In some contexts, the courts have recognised that public decision-making can be sufficiently removed from their own area of expertise as to be non-justiciable and therefore not susceptible to review. For example, decisions taken under the prerogative about foreign policy, such as whether or not to declare war or to authorise the use of the armed forces, are considered 'no go' or 'forbidden' areas.[56] As Lord Diplock noted, such decisions normally involve questions to which the judicial process is ill-adapted to provide the right answer; furthermore, the policy considerations involved require 'a balancing exercise which judges by their upbringing and experience are ill-qualified to perform'.[57] As the courts have themselves recognised, in a society based on the rule of law, it is necessary to decide which branch of government has, in any particular instance, the decision-making power and what the legal limits of that power are; this is a question of law to be decided by the courts. However, this means that the court will itself often have to decide the limits of its own decision-making power.[58]

A related concern is that the bipolar and adversary nature of the judicial process, in which the claimant seeks to challenge the respondent public authority's decision before the court, has not always been an appropriate procedure given the complex and multidimensional nature of much public administration. Often, a public authority will have to consider not only the position of the individual claimant, but all individuals affected by its decision and the broader public interest. As courts typically decide by hearing a case between two parties, other parties liable to be affected by the outcome are not normally represented before the court.

Consider, for example, the House of Lords' decision in *Bromley*, in which the (now defunct) Greater London Council (GLC) implemented a manifesto commitment to reduce public transport fares by 25 per cent, to be funded by increases in local taxation.[59] The House of Lords held that the policy was unlawful because the GLC had failed to have proper regard to its statutory duty to promote the provision of integrated, efficient, and economic transport facilities.[60] By placing a financial burden on local taxpayers, the GLC had not acted economically in the sense that it was not making the most cost-effective use of its resources. However, the Law Lords did not recognise the social purposes of the GLC's policy: reducing traffic congestion and pollution by subsidising public transport. The Law Lords' decision was criticised on a number of grounds. First, they failed to take into account the policy background to the relevant legislation, which envisaged the subsidy of public transport.[61] Second, there was, one

---

[56] *Campaign for Nuclear Disarmament v Prime Minister of the United Kingdom* [2002] EWHC 2777.

[57] *Council of Civil Service Unions v Minister for the Civil Service* [1985] AC 374, 411, *per* Lord Diplock.

[58] *R v British Broadcasting Corporation, ex p ProLife Alliance* [2003] UKHL 23, [2004] 1 AC 185, [75]–[76]; *R (Runa Begum) v Tower Hamlets Borough Council* [2003] UKHL 5, [2003] 2 AC 430, [35].

[59] *Bromley London Borough Council v Greater London Council* [1983] AC 768.

[60] Transport (London) Act 1969, s 1.

[61] Griffith, 'Judicial Decision-Making in Public Law' [1985] PL 564, 575–9.

commentator noted, a paucity of reference by the Law Lords 'to the social impact of the GLC's policy and the consequences of holding it unlawful'—for example, reduced passenger flows leading to higher fares, an increase in road traffic causing more accidents and pollution, and a less frequent public transport service. It was therefore said that 'it is objectionable that the judiciary should purport to construe admittedly ambiguous legislation without regard to the consequences' of its decision.[62] Furthermore, the judgments 'were not only extremely convoluted, but also bordered on the incoherent' and provided little legal certainty.[63]

Other illustrations could be given. It has been argued that many of the judicial review cases concerning relations between central and local government highlighted the limitations of judicial understanding of complex areas such as local authority finance—for example, the House of Lords' decision concerning the legality of local authority involvement with the swaps market, which provided local authorities with an innovative way around the complex rules limiting their ability to borrow money, was based on a misunderstanding of how that market operated.[64] As a consequence of such decisions, it has sometimes been argued that judicial review has the worst of both worlds: an interventionist judiciary that is limited by procedures, and practices that exclude sources of information relevant to administrative and political decision-making.[65] Complex judicial review challenges can pose a difficult dilemma for the courts: '[J]udicial restraint is unsatisfactory while judicial activism is ill-informed.'[66]

Courts often accept the limits of their own competence—they have, for example, been generally reluctant to intervene in contexts such as macro-economic policy[67]—while recognising that they have particular competence in other areas. The courts have intervened widely in the criminal justice system. For instance, they have imposed procedural fairness into the workings of the prison discipline system, by which prisoners accused of a disciplinary offence are subject to an adjudication process that may result in punishment, to ensure that prisoners are treated fairly.[68] The courts ensured that, when exercising sentencing powers, the Home Secretary had to give reasons for his decisions, and subsequently ruled that the allocation of such judicial powers to a member of the executive did not comply with the right to a fair trial under Art 6

---

[62] Pannick, 'The Law Lords and the Needs of Contemporary Society' (1982) 53 Political Quarterly 318, 322.

[63] Loughlin, *Legality and Locality: The Role of Law in Central–Local Government Relations* (Oxford 1996), p 34.

[64] *Hazell v Hammersmith London Borough Council* [1992] 2 AC 1; Loughlin, 'Innovative Financing in Local Government: The Limits of Legal Instrumentalism' [1991] PL 568, 590–5.

[65] Griffith, 580.

[66] Allison, 'The Procedural Reason for Judicial Restraint' [1994] PL 452, 466.

[67] See, eg *Nottinghamshire County Council v Secretary of State for the Environment* [1986] AC 240; *R v Secretary of State for the Environment, ex p Hammersmith and Fulham London Borough Council* [1991] 1 AC 521; *Donoghue v Poplar Housing and Regeneration Community Association Ltd* [2001] EWCA Civ 595, [2002] QB 48.

[68] See Loughlin and Quinn, 'Prisons, Rules and Courts: A Study of Administrative Law' (1993) 56 MLR 497; Loughlin, 'The Underside of the Law: Judicial Review and the Prison Disciplinary System' (1993) 46 CLP 23; Livingstone, 'The Impact of Judicial Review on Prisons', in Hadfield (ed), *Judicial Review: A Thematic Approach* (Dublin 1995).

of the European Convention on Human Rights (ECHR).[69] The courts also held that the executive's influence and control over the Parole Board meant that it was not sufficiently independent and impartial to exercise its judicial functions.[70] The courts have felt able to intervene in this area because they are very familiar with the criminal justice system. The general point is this: the degree of judicial intervention may, then, often depend on the context in which a judicial review challenge is brought: 'In law context is everything.'[71]

Underneath the legal rules and principles being applied in judicial review cases, there lies an unacknowledged, but powerful policy dimension. As Lord Steyn has remarked, 'In common law adjudication it is an everyday occurrence for courts to consider, together with principled arguments, the balance sheet of policy advantages and disadvantages. It would be a matter of public disquiet if the courts did not do so.'[72] Lord Carnwath has noted that during his years as an administrative law judge he never applied the *Wednesbury* test to determine whether a decision was irrational. Instead, he adopted a pragmatic approach: the ultimate question is always whether something has gone wrong of a nature and degree which requires the court to intervene and, if so, what form that intervention should take. If the answer is 'yes', then the judge looks for a legal hook to hang it on and if there is none suitable, then it may be necessary to adapt one.[73] In other words, judges often focus upon consequences.[74] The principles of judicial review are all open-textured and their application turns upon the individual case before the court: '[G]eneral propositions do not decide concrete cases.'[75] A judge's view of the merits of the underlying policy being challenged will often exert an unstated influence.[76]

Another aspect of judicial review procedure that might, on occasion, limit its effectiveness concerns the procedural dependence of the court on public authorities to present factual material concerning an impugned decision. Public authorities are expected to assist the court with full and accurate explanations of all of the facts relevant to a challenge, but the court has no power to investigate factual issues; furthermore, there is no general duty of disclosure in judicial review proceedings.[77] In

---

[69] *R v Secretary of State for the Home Department, ex p Doody* [1994] 1 AC 531; *R v Secretary of State for the Home Department, ex p Anderson* [2002] UKHL 46, [2003] 1 AC 837.

[70] *R (Brooke) v Parole Board* [2008] EWCA Civ 29, [2008] 1 WLR 1950.

[71] *R (Daly) v Secretary of State for the Home Department* [2001] 2 AC 532, 548.

[72] Lord Steyn, 'Deference: A Tangled Story' [2005] Public Law 346, 357. See also Lord Steyn, 'Does Legal Formalism Hold Sway in England?' (1996) 49 Current Legal Problems 43, 51: 'Consequentialist arguments and policy factors are the very stuff of decisions in the public law field.'

[73] Lord Carnwath, 'From Judicial Outrage to Sliding Scales—Where Next For *Wednesbury*?', ALBA Annual Lecture, 12 November 2013, 19, **https://www.supremecourt.uk/docs/speech-131112-lord-carnwath.pdf**. cf *R v Take-over Panel, ex p Guinness plc* [1990] 1 QB 146, 160C, *per* Lord Donaldson MR.

[74] See Thomas, *The Judicial Process: Realism, Pragmatism, Practical Reasoning and Principles* (Cambridge 2005).

[75] *Lochner v New York* (1905) 198 US 45, 76, *per* Holmes J.

[76] See Sumption, 'Judicial and Political Decision-Making: The Uncertain Boundary' [2011] Judicial Review 301.

[77] *R v Lancashire County Council, ex p Huddleston* [1986] 2 All ER 941, 945, *per* Lord Donaldson MR; *Marshall v Deputy Governor of Bermuda* [2010] UKPC 9; Woolf, 'Public Law–Private Law: Why the Divide?' [1986] PL 220, 225. See further Chapter 13, section 3.

other words, the ability of a claimant to challenge a decision may be contingent on what information the public authority is prepared to release; if the court is unable to probe behind the formal account of the decision-making process, then this may limit its ability to correct abuses of power. However, the courts have mounted something of a fight-back in this respect. In cases in which a claimant has been met with a deliberate wall of silence from the government or prevarication in full disclosure, the courts have made it clear that they may either draw adverse inferences against the public authority or impose indemnity costs against the public authority as a mark of the court's disapproval.[78]

> **Q** To what extent should judicial experience and knowledge of public administration (or lack of it) affect how the courts review public decision-making? In light of the importance of context to judicial review, is it still meaningful to identify general principles of judicial review?

3.2 **The concept of polycentricity**

As we saw in section 3.1, the adversarial nature of the judicial process can limit the effectiveness of judicial review. This is particularly the case for a polycentric issue[79]—that is, one that affects a number of different interacting and interlocking interests, is 'many centred', or involves the balancing of a number of elements that may be interdependent.[80] According to Fuller, a distinguishing feature of adjudication is that the parties affected by a decision participate in judicial proceedings. However, in issues that are polycentric in nature, the outcome of a judicial decision may have implications for other individuals who did not participate in the hearing. The concern is that the judicial process is therefore unsuited to the resolution of such disputes.[81] The polycentric nature of the issue before the court may therefore result in judicial

---

[78] *R (Quark Fishing Ltd) v Secretary of State for Foreign and Commonwealth Affairs* [2002] EWCA Civ 1409, [50], *per* Laws LJ; *R (Karas and Miladinovic) v Secretary of State for the Home Department* [2006] EWHC 747 (Admin), [53]–[57], *per* Munby J; *R (S) v Secretary of State for the Home Department* [2006] EWHC 1111 (Admin), [115]–[119], *per* Sullivan J; *Marshall*, [29], *per* Lord Phillips.

[79] See Chapter 12, section 5.1.

[80] As Fuller, 'The Forms and Limits of Adjudication' (1978) 92 Harv L Rev 353, 395, explained:

We may visualise this kind of situation by thinking of a spider web. A pull on one strand will distribute tensions after a complicated pattern throughout the web as a whole. Doubling the original pull will, in all likelihood, not simply double each of the resulting tensions but will rather create a different complicated pattern of tensions. This would certainly occur, for example, if the doubled pull caused one or more of the weaker strands to snap. This is a 'polycentric' situation because it is 'many centered'—each crossing of strands is a distinct center for distributing tensions.

According to Jowell, 'The Legal Control of Administrative Discretion' [1973] PL 178, 213: 'Polycentric problems involve a complex network of relationships, with interacting points of influence. Each decision made communicates itself to other centres of decision, changing the conditions, so that a new basis must be found for the next decision.'

[81] For judicial recognition of this concept, see *R v Secretary of State for the Home Department, ex p P* [1995] 1 All ER 870, [38]–[39].

restraint as the court will be aware of its inability to adequately appreciate the likely impact if it were to intervene by way of judicial review.

Polycentric situations often arise in the context of resource allocation decisions. If an administrative decision-maker has to make decisions as regards the distribution of limited resources (eg whether through the award of compensation or issue of licences), then a decision to make an award in favour of one party will impact upon the decisions to be made with respect to other parties if the resources being allocated are limited. If one of those parties seeks to challenge a decision not to make an award in their case, then the limits of adjudication are highlighted because the outcome of the challenge will, if successful, affect other parties who have received positive decisions. In any event, litigation may delay any fulfilment of those awards to such parties. Either way, the limitations of the judicial process are highlighted.[82]

The polycentric nature of certain issues has therefore been used as an argument for judicial restraint. To avoid exceeding the limits of its own competence, the court must refrain from two kinds of activism: it must not change the law where an appreciation of repercussions is required for sensible legal development; and in so far as the court has a choice under existing law, it must avoid choosing a legal solution that necessitates an appreciation of complex repercussions. The concept assists in bringing home to the court the wide-ranging implications that may flow from any unsettling of a finely balanced policy decision and is of particular relevance in challenges against the allocation of scarce resources, which courts are ill-equipped to decide.

In some instances, the courts have been very reluctant to review decisions that raise polycentric questions. Consider, for example, the case of a child diagnosed with leukaemia who had been refused treatment by her health authority. This is a clear illustration of a very difficult polycentric situation: health authorities frequently have to decide how best to prioritise the uses to which limited resources may be put; funding treatment of one patient may mean refusing it to others. In this case, the child challenged the refusal of funding on the basis that it infringed her right to life without good reason. The High Court had held that because the decision affected the right to life, it should be closely scrutinised by the courts—and that, because the health authority had failed to provide sufficient justification for refusing funding, it should reconsider its decision.[83] However, the Court of Appeal reversed this ruling. Sir Thomas Bingham MR said that 'difficult and agonising judgments have to be made as to how a limited budget is best allocated to the maximum advantage of the maximum number of patients. That is not a judgment which the court can make'.[84]

Polycentricity does not necessarily prevent judicial scrutiny.[85] Furthermore, the polycentric nature of a particular issue is often a matter of degree: are the polycentric elements of the situation so significant and predominant that the proper limits of the adjudicative process have been reached? This requires some assessment of the degree of polycentricity involved, but provides only an uncertain guide.

---

[82] Allison, 'The Procedural Reason for Judicial Restraint' [1994] PL 452, 455.
[83] *R v Cambridge Health Authority, ex p B* (1995) 25 BMLR 5.   [84] [1995] 2 All ER 129, 137.
[85] King, 'The Pervasiveness of Polycentricity' [2008] PL 101.

> **Q** To what extent, if at all, should the polycentric nature of a particular issue affect how a court examines the legality of a public decision?

4. Judicial impact and administrative reaction

This section considers the impact of judicial review on government once a court has decided a case. What influence does judicial review exert upon government? Is it a powerful influence or is it irrelevant? Or is the law merely one influence amongst many that condition public administration?

In general terms, comparatively little is known about the impact of judicial review on government.[86] What is apparent is that governmental reaction to judicial review can take different forms: positive or negative; formal or informal. A positive reaction to judicial review implies that the public authority is willing to abide by the court's decision, whereas a negative reaction implies disapproval by the public authority of the court's decision and a willingness either to reverse or limit its impact. A formal reaction to judicial review is one that has been formalised via the drawing up of a rule or a particular decision. An informal reaction is one that is represented in other ways such as in the attitudes of officials.[87]

4.1 Understanding the impact of judicial review

4.1.1 Individual judicial review

To get a feel for the issues raised by the impact of judicial review on public administration, let us consider a mundane, though typical, example of judicial review litigation.

> **Eg** Suppose that a foreign national lawfully present in the UK, Shabina, applies to the immigration authorities to extend her period of leave in the UK. Shabina lodges her application, which is accompanied by various supporting documents. The application is considered by the UK Border Agency. One of the agency's hundreds of caseworkers (acting on behalf of the Home Secretary) refuses Shabina's application, but without properly considering the supporting documents. Shabina seeks judicial review, which is granted on the basis that the Home Secretary erred in law by failing to take into account a relevant consideration—that is, the supporting documentation. Shabina's case is then sent back to the agency to be reconsidered in a lawful manner.

Does this mean that Shabina will ultimately receive a positive decision? Perhaps, but not necessarily. As the courts have often acknowledged, 'dependent upon reconsideration on sufficient and proper evidence, the Secretary of State may reach exactly

---

[86] Richardson, 'Impact Studies in the United Kingdom', in Hertogh and Halliday (eds), *Judicial Review and Bureaucratic Impact: International and Interdisciplinary Perspectives* (Cambridge 2004), p 107.

[87] Sunkin, 'Issues in Researching the Impact of Judicial Review', in Hertogh and Halliday, p 62.

the same decision'.[88] Shabina might receive a positive decision—if her supporting documents demonstrate that she fulfils the relevant criteria. The chance of a fresh reconsideration is, therefore, worth fighting for, but it does not guarantee a positive decision.

This is an example of 'bureaucratic', or 'individualised', judicial review.[89] Such challenges are typically against routine administrative decisions; although they are of considerable importance to the individuals concerned, they tend to have little, if any, broader impact on administrative procedure or policy. Much, although not all, judicial review litigation falls into this category. In such cases, judicial review is simply part of the wider machinery for the redress of grievances and adheres to the important merits/legality distinction. The reviewing body is operating in a similar way to a tribunal, the principal difference being that because tribunals have an appeal, rather than a review, jurisdiction, they can replace the initial decision with one of their own, whereas a reviewing court may not.[90] Indeed, in some of the best-known public law cases, following the court's judgment, the public authority arrived at exactly the same decision as before while taking care not to repeat the earlier legal error; the *Padfield* case is a good illustration.[91]

Our example involving Shabina's application may seem very simple, but it actually raises broader and more complex questions concerning the 'impact' and purpose of judicial review. From Shabina's perspective, judicial review provided for the redress of a grievance. At the same time, judicial review could also be seen here as fulfilling another purpose: that of ensuring compliance with standards of good administration; taking into account relevant considerations when making a decision being an elementary standard of good administration.

But what is the ability of judicial review to ensure compliance with such standards by administrative decision-makers? For example, will the caseworker who refused the application make the same mistake when considering subsequent applications? Will other caseworkers learn of the court's decision? Will the agency incorporate the decision into its training programme and/or internal guidance issued to all caseworkers? How does the judicial review case compete for influence with other forces? For example, what if the volume of such applications increases or if the agency has to cut its workforce: is there a risk that administrative imperatives of efficiency may override adherence to administrative law norms? To what extent, if at all, will other public agencies learn from the court's decision?

It is impossible to answer these questions without having some further information about how the particular government agency operates and whether—and, if so, how—it incorporates a judicial review case into its procedures. It might be the case that a court ruling does have a broader impact; it might not. The point here is to

---

[88] *R (Ali) v Secretary of State for the Home Department* [2003] EWHC 899 (Admin), [31].

[89] Cane, 'Understanding Judicial Review and Its Impact', in Hertogh and Halliday, p 17.

[90] See Chapter 16, section 2.1.

[91] In *Padfield v Minister for Agriculture, Fisheries and Food* [1968] AC 997, the House of Lords held that a ministerial decision not to refer a complaint concerning milk prices to a committee of investigation was vitiated by improper purpose; after the case, the Minister did refer the complaint to the committee, which recommended change, which the Minister refused to accept.

highlight the type of questions with which we must engage if we are to understand the impact of judicial review—something that requires empirical study of administrative reaction to judicial review.

4.1.2 Policy judicial review

Now let us consider a different form of judicial review that might be termed 'policy' or 'high-profile' judicial review. These types of challenge typically have far-reaching consequences for governmental procedure and/or policy, and can impact upon a much wider range of people than the particular claimants involved. Think of cases such as *Evans*, *Anisminic*, and the *Fire Brigades Union*.

These challenges may be brought in the wider public interest and the courts sometimes allow interventions by third parties.[92] They often raise important constitutional issues—for example, that European Union (EU) law prevails over incompatible primary legislation, and challenges to primary legislation under the Human Rights Act 1998.[93] They might also raise matters of acute political sensitivity and involve decisions taken by politically accountable government Ministers.

Consider, for instance, the decision of the Supreme Court in *Osborn*—which we encountered in Chapter 12—on when the Parole Board should hold oral hearings. One function of the Parole Board is to decide whether or not the Secretary of State is justified in recalling to prison an individual who has been released from prison on licence, but who goes on to breach licence conditions (the rules that must be observed upon release). For many years, the Parole Board had been reluctant to hold oral hearings in such cases and instead determined them solely 'on the papers'. However, in *Osborn* the Supreme Court held that the Parole Board should hold more oral hearings. The ruling applied to a huge number of cases that had previously been dealt with solely on the papers. The court set out some general principles that inform when oral hearings must be held, such as the presence of a factual dispute, an independent assessment of risk could not otherwise fairly be made, whether a face-to-face encounter by a prisoner with the board is necessary to enable him to put his case effectively, and whether it would be unfair for a paper decision made by a single member panel of the board to become final without allowing an oral hearing.

In such a case, judicial review may be said to be serving a number of different purposes. First, there is the redress of grievances of the prisoners who are litigants before the court. Second, the court is seeking to impose standards of good administration on the Parole Board; in particular, the principles of procedural fairness. And, in turn, the court was clearly, although not explicitly, performing a policy function: the Supreme Court was not merely ruling that the three prisoners involved had been treated unfairly. Its judgment had important wider implications for the general policy of the Parole Board concerning oral hearings and indeed, the organisation of the Parole Board and its resourcing from central government.

---

[92] See Chapter 13, section 3.3.3.

[93] *R v Secretary of State for Transport, ex p Factortame Ltd (No 2)* [1991] 1 AC 603. See Chapter 8, section 4.3.

The ruling meant a huge change for the Parole Board. It had several implications.[94] First, the ruling had an obvious effect upon the *number of oral hearings*. The Parole Board estimated that the number of such hearings would increase from 4,500 to 16,000 annually. Second, the ruling meant a *fundamental change of approach* in the way the Parole Board thought about the purpose of and necessity for an oral hearing in each case before it. While there was no need for an oral hearing in all cases, the judgment significantly broadened the circumstances in which such hearings are required. Following *Osborn*, fairness to the prisoner became the overriding requirement; the perceived utility of an oral hearing was no longer the deciding factor.

Third, the Parole Board also had to make a number of *organisational and administrative changes* to implement the judgment in practice. A new case management model was implemented to ensure that the Parole Board used its resources to best effect in satisfying the requirements laid down by the judgment. The Parole Board also established a special project—the Fair for the Future project—to enable it to understand the impact of *Osborn* and plan how to accommodate the expected increase in work. This involved recruiting and training new case managers and redesigning and testing new ways of working.

Fourth, the judgment also had important *resource implications*. Oral hearings cost more money than paper decisions. They take longer to arrange and decide. They are also heard by three people whereas a paper decision is taken by a single official. Accordingly, the Parole Board's parent government department, the Ministry of Justice, allocated the Parole Board an additional £1.2m to enable the Board to increase its capacity to hold more oral hearings. This may not exactly seem to be a large sum of money given the scale of government spending. But nor is it merely 'loose change', bearing in mind the total budget for the Parole Board of £11m and pressures on government spending.

The Supreme Court's ruling in *Osborn* also raised some complex issues concerning the basis of judicial intervention, the competence of the court, and judicial impact. Let us consider the following questions: was the Supreme Court conscious of the likely impact of its judgment? Was the Court's judgment desirable? Do oral hearings actually improve the quality of Parole Board decision-making?

With respect to whether or not the Supreme Court was aware of the likely impact of its judgment, it is apparent that oral hearings impose an additional cost on government both in terms of financial resources and time. However, the Supreme Court did not explicitly consider the cost of oral hearings or the possible effect of an increase in the number of hearings upon the Parole Board's budget and operational procedures— a factor that might indicate that their judgment was ill-informed. However, matters are not so simple. It is important not to underestimate the intrinsic difficulty for the court of weighing up whether the additional cost and delays imposed by oral hearings would be justified. This is because the other interests at stake—the importance of the decision to the prisoner (and the potential deprivation of liberty) and the public interest (the possible risk of future reoffending)—are not susceptible to being assigned a

---

[94] The Parole Board for England and Wales, *Annual Report and Accounts* (HC 299 2013–14); 'Parole hearings "to treble" after "fairness" ruling', *BBC News*, 12 July 2014.

monetary value. The ruling therefore reflected a value judgement that a particular interest—the liberty of recalled prisoners—should receive priority.

Assessing whether the judgment had a beneficial influence is similarly problematic because there is scope for different views here. From one perspective, it might be argued that the decision was beneficial in terms of extending procedural fairness into an administrative decision-making system affecting the personal liberty of a group of people—prisoners—who rarely attract public sympathy. Realistically, it is unlikely that the Parole Board would have changed its policy on oral hearings had it not been for the court ruling. However, from a different perspective, it might be contended that the imposition of procedural requirements was counterproductive by disrupting the work of the Parole Board, reducing administrative efficiency, causing delays, and increasing costs. There is no objectively right answer here: it is a matter of perspective.

As to whether or not the decision improved the quality of Parole Board decisions, it is again difficult to provide a clear answer simply because such decisions often involve an attempt to predict the future risk to the public posed by a recalled prisoner; there may be no single correct answer in an individual case. It is strongly arguable that making such decisions on the basis of a prisoner's evidence presented at an oral hearing is likely to be better than considering it solely on the papers. If so, then the quality of such decisions is likely to be higher, but it is impossible to assess whether or not this is actually the case. However, what we can highlight is that the Supreme Court cited and relied upon empirical legal research, strongly indicating the frustration, anger, and despair felt by prisoners who perceived the Parole Board's paper-only procedures to be unfair and 'little more than a rubber stamp'.[95] The focus of the ruling was then upon the importance of fair treatment as an important goal in its own right.

We have already seen that the allocation of resources is a polycentric issue often unsuited to judicial decision-making—but even cases that are, on the surface, about other matters (such as the fairness of procedures) may well have hard-to-predict resource implications. It can be seen, then, that assessing the impact of judicial review often raises complex questions as to how public bodies respond to court judgments, and the relationship between judicial supervision and government behaviour. A final point: judicial rulings are meant to be effective and to make some difference to the world, but they do not implement themselves. Instead, for a ruling to be implemented, the court is often largely, if not wholly, reliant upon the public body concerned.

4.2 The effects of judicial control

How, then, do the principles of judicial review—legality, fairness, rationality, and proportionality—contribute to the control of administrative action? Feldman has suggested that the courts adopt three different techniques for controlling administrative action: directing, limiting, and structuring.[96]

---

[95] Padfield, 'Understanding Recall' 2011, University of Cambridge Faculty of Law Research Paper No 2/2013 (2013), p 40.

[96] Feldman, 'Judicial Review: A Way of Controlling Government?' (1986) 66 Public Administration 21.

Judicial *directing* of administrative behaviour refers to the ability of the courts to require government to adhere to its stated powers and obligations. Here, the control is undertaken by reference to the legislative power that the public authority possesses and reflects the traditional *ultra vires* principle that a public authority cannot lawfully act outside the four corners of its statutory powers.[97] Judicial *limiting* of administrative action refers to the way in which courts establish the scope of, or set limits, applicable to the exercise of administrative discretion. For example, if a court holds that a public authority has either fettered its discretion or unlawfully delegated its powers to another,[98] then the court is placing limits on the exercise of the public authority's power.

The third technique—*structuring* administrative decision-making processes— involves making explicit some of the values and goals that either should or should not guide decision-makers. For example, when a court decides that the decision-maker adopted an unfair procedure, took account of an irrelevant consideration, or reached an irrational decision, then the court is structuring how the decision-maker ought to make its decisions. Judicial structuring of administrative action may exert far more influence on the day-to-day activities of public authorities than directing or limiting.

The effects of judicial review for public authorities may depend on which particular legal principle is being applied by the court. Much will depend on the particular administrative context. For example, a judicial decision that concerns a narrow technical point—how a particular statutory provision is to be interpreted—might assist a public authority by providing greater clarity in respect of its legal obligations, but have little broader impact. At the same time, it is equally possible that narrow technical questions of statutory interpretation may have substantial resource implications if, for example, a court has held that a public authority owes a duty to provide services to a broader class of person than was previously thought to be the case. For example, when the Administrative Court held, interpreting the Children Act 1989, that local authorities owe a duty to provide after-care for unaccompanied asylum-seeking children when they reach the age of 18, the judgment had considerable economic significance for local authorities, because their legal obligations were extended to a broader group of people for whom resources then had to be found.[99]

The application of legal principles, such as legitimate expectation and proportionality, might also have a broader influence on administrative culture and practices by requiring public authorities to consider more carefully how their policies are to be applied in the circumstances of particular individuals who either hold certain expectations or whose rights might otherwise be adversely affected. More generally, it has been suggested that public authorities may be more able to accommodate principles such as procedural fairness within their decision-making process than substantive principles: 'Although the ability of juridical norms to infiltrate administrative cultures is likely to be limited, it may be that certain values, those associated with process for example, are more readily internalised than others.'[100]

---

[97] See Chapter 11, section 5.1.   [98] See Chapter 12, section 4.1.

[99] *R (Behre) v London Borough of Hillingdon* [2003] EWHC 2075 (Admin), [2004] 1 FLR 439; *R (London Borough of Hillingdon) v Secretary of State for Education and Skills* [2007] EWHC 514 (Admin).

[100] Richardson and Sunkin, 'Judicial Review: Questions of Impact' [1996] PL 79, 103.

4.3 **Judicial review from the administrator's perspective**

What, then, is the administrator's perspective on judicial review? In considering this, it is important to recall that public administration in the UK does not comprise a single, undifferentiated public authority called 'the government'; rather, it is made up of a vast array of highly complex organisations operating at different levels of our multilayered constitution: central government departments and their executive agencies and non-departmental public bodies, local authorities and independent regulatory bodies, in addition to the devolved executives and non-statutory bodies.[101] Furthermore, each public agency is typically a complex organisation comprising different hierarchies, such as higher-level policy officials, legal advisers, and front-line or 'street-level' operational staff, within which judicial decisions will need to be both interpreted and communicated if they are to exert influence.

The impact of judicial review on different officials may, then, vary. The task of interpreting a judicial decision is often one for government lawyers, while senior policy officials will often consider how, if at all, policy needs to be reformulated in light of the decision. By contrast, a court judgment may, by itself, have little, if any, effect on front-line decision-makers. For example, officials responsible for making decisions in large areas of administration—social security, tax, immigration, and so on—make literally millions of decisions each year without consulting either a statute or a court decision; they do, though, on the whole, consider themselves obliged to follow the internal guidance and policy instructions—often collectively referred to as 'soft law'—issued by senior officials. From a legal perspective, soft law may be viewed as relatively low down in the hierarchy of legal rules, certainly beneath both primary and secondary legislation. However, for officials within government agencies, soft law is often the first source of guidance that they consult. If judicial review decisions are to influence routine administrative decision-making within large bureaucratic organisations, then they often need to be internalised within such organisations and communicated to front-line staff through such guidance. To be effective, such guidance must correctly interpret the court's decision and then also be applied in practice by front-line officials.

When viewed from the perspective of public administrators, judicial review may have both advantages and disadvantages. On the positive side, judicial review performs an important function of clarifying the law and rules that must be administered. As public authorities must operate lawfully, judicial review may assist by providing greater clarity on what the law means in any particular instance. Judicial review may also perform an educative role by indicating the legal principles that should inform and guide administrative decision-making. The addition of procedural requirements—reason-giving, opportunities to make representations, oral hearings—into administrative decision-making may promote higher-quality decisions and also greater transparency in public administration.[102] Furthermore,

---

[101] See Chapters 4 and 7.
[102] Hammond, 'Judicial Review: The Continuing Interplay between Law and Policy' [1998] PL 34, 42.

judicial review may focus the mind of a public authority on a particular area of its responsibility and prompt reconsideration of how the discharge of its duties could be improved.

But judicial review may also have disadvantages from the administrator's perspective. The very generality of the principles of judicial review can create uncertainty because they 'offer comparatively little guidance in dealing with complex situations' and, consequently, it can be difficult to determine how such principles will be applied in any particular case.[103] This uncertainty can leave administrators with the dilemma of choosing between a cautious, risk-averse approach, which may compromise the achievement of policy objectives, or a more adventurous approach, which risks legal challenge.[104] Judicial review may discourage long-term planning by public authorities if they need to respond to court judgments. Judicial review may also increase the use and influence of lawyers in public authorities (with obvious resource implications). Further, while the task of dealing with judicial review challenges is necessary for a public authority to defend its decisions, this can inevitably take up time and resources that could be expended elsewhere: 'The very business of going to court is fraught with danger and inconvenience for officials.'[105] While the availability of judicial challenge does not inevitably induce administrative and political timidity, public authorities would perhaps avoid going to court if possible. The mere fact that a public authority is being subject to legal challenge may have adverse reputational consequences that the authority might seek to avoid. Then there is always the risk that exposure to judicial review may lead public authorities to adopt a defensive style of administration designed to reduce the risk that their decisions will be challenged rather than to seek to improve their quality. Another concern is that there is a risk that the delay and uncertainty created by judicial review litigation may itself be deliberately exploited by those wishing to disrupt the policy process.

One indication of growing governmental awareness of judicial review has been the publication by central government of a pamphlet entitled *The Judge Over Your Shoulder*—sometimes affectionately known within government as 'JOYS'—which provides guidance to junior officials in the practical application of legal principles.[106]

While the first edition received criticism for its negative tone and for treating law as distinct from good administration,[107] subsequent editions have stressed that their purpose is not to teach public administrators how to survive judicial review, but to inform and improve the quality of administrative decision-making. Of course, if the guide does improve the quality of decision-making, then an incidental effect of this would be to make decisions less vulnerable to judicial review.

---

[103] Kerry, 'Administrative Law and Judicial Review: The Practical Effects of Developments over the Last 25 Years on Administration in Central Government' (1986) 64 Public Administration 163, 171.

[104] James, 'The Political and Administrative Consequences of Judicial Review' (1996) 74 Public Administration 613, 625.

[105] James at 619.

[106] Government Legal Department, *Judge Over Your Shoulder* (2016), **https://www.gov.uk/government/uploads/system/uploads/attachment_data/file/538447/160708_JOYS_final.pdf**

[107] Bradley, 'The Judge over Your Shoulder' [1987] PL 485.

Q Why do you think administrators have mixed feelings about judicial review? Is it unrealistic to expect administrators to be anything other than ambivalent about having their decisions challenged by way of judicial review?

4.4 Administrative reaction to judicial review

4.4.1 Positive reaction

For the most part, public authorities react positively to judicial review because they recognise the need to comply with the court's ruling. Positive reactions may take different forms; for example, a change of policy or decision-making procedure, or the laying of a new statutory instrument to modify the effect of a previous instrument that has been declared unlawful.

By way of illustration, consider the case of *FP (Iran)*, in which the Court of Appeal declared unlawful a rule governing the procedure for appeal hearings conducted by the Asylum and Immigration Tribunal.[108] The relevant rule stated that the tribunal must hear an appeal in the absence of a party or his representative if satisfied that the party or his representative had been given notice of the hearing, but had not given any satisfactory explanation for his absence. In the case, the claimant had not received the notice of appeal because it had been sent to his old address. Yet, applying the rule, the tribunal proceeded to hear the appeal in the claimant's absence. The Court of Appeal held that the rule was unfair because it could deny a party the opportunity to be heard due to the error of their representative: it prioritised speed over fairness. Following the judgment, the rules were amended so that the tribunal would have the discretion to proceed in a party's absence, rather than a duty to do so.[109] This, the government contended, would remove the rigidity in the previous rule and enable the tribunal to assess in each individual case whether there was no good reason for the party's absence. This, then, might be instanced as a positive reaction by the government to a court ruling: the Court held the rule invalid and the government duly sought to comply with the ruling.

The reaction by government to a court ruling may depend on the particular legal principle applied by the court. For example, if a blanket policy adopted by a public authority has been held to be disproportionate, then the public authority will need to revise the blanket or 'catch-all' nature of the policy either by creating appropriate exceptions or by reformulating the policy altogether. To illustrate, consider *Smith and Grady v United Kingdom*, in which the Ministry of Defence's blanket ban on gay men and lesbians in the armed forces was held to infringe the right to private life. It was precisely because of its blanket nature that the policy was found to be disproportionate by the European Court of Human Rights: it went further than was necessary in order to achieve its objective of maintaining the operational effectiveness of the

---

[108] *FP (Iran) v Secretary of State for the Home Department* [2007] EWCA Civ 13.

[109] The Asylum and Immigration Tribunal (Procedure) (Amendment) Rules 2007, SI 2007/835, r 2.

armed forces. Following the judgment, the Defence Secretary informed Parliament that a new policy had been devised to comply with the Court's ruling.[110] At the centre of the new code of conduct was a new service test: have the actions or behaviour of an individual adversely affected the efficiency or operational effectiveness of the armed services? So, as the previous blanket policy had been held to be a disproportionate interference with individuals' right to private life, the policy had been reformulated. Rather than a blanket policy that homosexuality per se was incompatible with membership of the armed forces, the new policy sought a more individuated approach: were the actions of a particular individual, whatever their sexual orientation, likely adversely to affect operational effectiveness? The new policy was specifically designed in order to produce a more appropriate balance between the legitimate desire for the armed forces to be effective and the rights of individuals.

A similar point can be made in relation to *Daly*.[111] Here, a prison policy concerning cell searches was challenged on the ground that such searches would be conducted in the absence of the prisoner and would include an examination of the prisoner's correspondence with his legal advisers. The policy was introduced following a number of serious breaches of prison security, its justification being that it was necessary to search such correspondence to ensure that the prisoner had not written or secreted within it anything that might endanger security. However, the House of Lords concluded that the blanket policy was an unjustifiable and disproportionate infringement of a prisoner's right to the protection of his legal correspondence. Following the decision, the Prison Service devised a new policy under which a prisoner normally had to be present when legal correspondence was being searched, although a prisoner could be excluded if he were to attempt to disrupt the search or because of sudden operational emergencies or urgent intelligence.[112]

There may be other forms of positive reaction. For example, public authorities may particularly welcome judgments that provide guidance on the approach to be taken to cases in the future or which clarify an important point of law. Broadly speaking, public authorities tend to welcome clarity in their legal powers and obligations, because it enables them to put in place appropriate processes. For instance, the Office of the Independent Adjudicator (OIA) for Higher Education, which deals with students' complaints against universities, has been subject to various judicial reviews: 'Many of the judicial review challenges have tested or established significant principles and have provided useful and important clarification on the OIA's role, remit and approach. This has been immensely valuable, if a little painful at times.'[113]

---

[110] *Smith and Grady v United Kingdom* (2000) 29 EHRR 493; HC Deb, vol 342, col 287 (12 January 2000) (Secretary of State for Defence). See further Chapter 12, sections 5.1 and 5.2 .

[111] *R (Daly) v Secretary of State for the Home Department* [2001] 2 AC 532.

[112] HM Prison Service, *Revision to the Security Manual after the* Daly *Judgment* (London 2001). In *Daly*, at 545, Lord Bingham, while noting that it would be inappropriate for the court to attempt to formulate or approve the terms of the new policy, in effect suggested a new rule that was, for all practical purposes, exactly the same as that which was subsequently adopted.

[113] OIA, 'The OIA and Judicial Review: Ten Principles from Ten Years of Challenges', Paper 02 (Reading 2015), http://oiahe.org.uk/media/106876/oia-and-judicial-review-10-year-series.pdf

What then of the impact of judicial review on the outcome of substantive decisions for claimants? Are there any benefits for successful claimants? It has often been assumed that a public body that is successfully challenged by judicial review can seek to neutralise the impact of the court's judgment by simply going through the correct procedural steps while still arriving at the same decision. On this view, judicial review is merely a technical or procedural device that has little, if any, positive benefit for claimants. But does this correspond with what really happens? There is some empirical legal research suggesting that it does not. In an empirical study of the value and effectiveness of judicial review, Bondy, Platt, and Sunkin found that successful judicial review challenges often result in a substantive benefit to the claimant.[114] The study found that when, following a successful judicial review challenge, public bodies reconsider their decisions, they often reach a fresh decision in the claimant's favour rather than merely correcting the process by which the initial decision was made. The general point from the study is that judicial review made a significant and substantive contribution to the outcome of the reconsidered decision because the public authorities concerned engaged with the consequences of the litigation.

4.4.2 Negative reaction

Government may also respond negatively to judicial review. Negative reaction may be prompted by the disruption caused to administrative procedures and policy implementation, governmental antipathy towards judicial interference, and the financial and other costs imposed by judgments. Ministers accustomed to being held to account in Parliament may take personal umbrage at having their decisions struck down by judges, especially in politically sensitive policy areas. Indeed, it has been argued that an inevitable consequence of stronger judicial review may be a corresponding governmental disinclination to accept court decisions.[115] Negative reactions may take many forms. Public authorities may seek to neutralise or limit the effect of judicial review through delaying tactics. They may reach the same substantive decision again, but in accordance with the court's judgment. Alternatively, they may seek direct legislative reversal of the judgment.

One example of negative reaction to judicial review has been the insertion of 'ouster clauses' in primary legislation. Such clauses seek to protect the policy from judicial challenge by stating that a decision 'shall not be called into question in any court'. As we have seen, in cases like *Anisminic*,[116] considered in Chapter 13,[117] the courts have, in effect, sought to get around such clauses. In 2003, the Home Office tried unsuccessfully to abolish judicial review of immigration decisions.[118] In 2015, the coalition government again sought to clamp down on judicial review, though not through a direct ouster clause.[119]

---

[114] Bondy, Platt, and Sunkin, *The Value and Effectiveness of Judicial Review* (London 2015), http://www.publiclawproject.org.uk/data/resources/210/Value-and-Effects-of-Judicial-Review.pdf

[115] Harlow, 'Administrative Reaction to Judicial Review' [1976] PL 116, 117.

[116] *Anisminic Ltd v Foreign Compensation Commission* [1969] 2 AC 147.

[117] See Chapter 13, section 2.1.

[118] Woolf, 'The Rule of Law and a Change in the Constitution' [2004] CLJ 317, 327–9; Rawlings, 'Review, Revenge and Retreat' (2005) 68 MLR 378.

[119] Criminal Justice and Courts Act 2015.

Outright defiance by government of a court ruling may be unusual, but it is not unknown. One area in which this issue has arisen has been in relation to the removal of failed asylum seekers by the Home Office in the face of a court injunction prohibiting removal. Over recent years, this area has been a source of much judicial review litigation. The basic tension here is between the Home Office's policy interest in maintaining effective immigration control and the ability of individuals to challenge the legality of removal decisions. The Home Office has been under enormous political pressure to increase the rate of removals, and has tended to view judicial review applications by individuals subject to removal action simply as a means of disrupting and frustrating the removals process.[120] At the same time, if an Administrative Court judge orders the Home Office not to remove the claimant, then it must comply—yet there have been many examples of the Home Office failing to comply with such orders.

Immigration is perhaps atypical in that the tensions between administrative implementation of policy and judicial review are extremely acute. In other contexts, administrative failure to comply with a court ruling may prompt follow-up oversight by other administrative law bodies such as the ombudsman, which investigates individuals' complaints of maladministration against government.[121] Consider *Coughlan*.[122] One aspect of that case, concerning legitimate expectations, was considered in Chapter 12. Another aspect concerned who should pay for the long-term care of older and disabled people: could such care be provided by a local authority as a social service (in which case, the patient paid according to their means), or was it to be provided free of charge by the National Health Service (NHS)? The court decided, from its interpretation of the relevant legislation, that such long-term care was generally to be provided by the NHS.

Following the decision, the Department of Health drew the court's judgment to the attention of local health authorities so that they could revise their criteria for funding long-term care in line with the judgment. However, many individuals complained to the ombudsman on the basis that they were being denied NHS-funded long-term care because health authorities had been acting unlawfully by not applying the relevant criteria in light of the *Coughlan* judgment. Four years after the judgment, the Health Service Ombudsman, finding such complaints to be justified, recommended that health authorities comply with the judgment and provide financial redress for affected individuals.[123] What this episode illustrates is that it cannot be assumed that public authorities will automatically comply with important court rulings; in the event of non-compliance, the intervention of another administrative justice institution, such as on ombudsman, may be necessary.

---

[120] Indeed, in the battle over the inclusion of an ouster clause in what subsequently became the Asylum and Immigration (Treatment of Claimants, etc.) Act 2004, the Home Office had sought to prevent individuals subject to removal action from applying for judicial review.

[121] See Chapter 15.

[122] *R v North and East Devon Health Authority, ex p Coughlan* [2001] QB 213.

[123] Health Service Ombudsman, *NHS Funding for Long Term Care* (HC 399 2002–03). See also Health Service Ombudsman, *NHS Funding for Long Term Care: Follow Up Report* (HC 144 2004–05).

Direct legislative reversal of a court judgment is a particularly strong form of negative reaction. A classic example is provided by the *Burmah Oil* case, in which the House of Lords ruled that a company could seek compensation for property damaged by British forces during the Second World War.[124] Concerned at the amount of compensation payable and the need for equal treatment of all of those who suffered losses during the war, the government, in effect, reversed the House of Lords' decision. There are many other examples of legislative reversal. In the field of immigration law, the government has rarely hesitated to reverse court judgments through legislation.[125]

For a recent example, consider *Reilly*.[126] Here, the Court of Appeal held that certain of the government's back-to-work schemes were unlawful as the relevant Regulations were *ultra vires* the Jobseekers Act 1995. Some individuals had been refused benefits because they had not complied with the Regulations. However, the court had held that it was unlawful for the government to refuse benefits in these circumstances: no individual may lawfully be penalised for resisting an unlawful demand. Did the government issue the benefits—or, at least, lawfully reconsider the benefit claims? No. It immediately introduced legislation to reverse the ruling and to reinstate the penalties. This raised some controversy. The Lords Constitution Committee complained that the fast-track legislation was unnecessary and had the effect of retrospectively confirming penalties in relation to individuals who, according to judicial decision, had not transgressed any lawful rule.[127] During its passage through Parliament, the Bill was criticised for contravening two constitutional principles: for being fast-tracked through Parliament without any justification; and for imposing penalties on persons by reason of conduct that was lawful at the time of their action.[128] Nonetheless, the Bill was enacted.[129] Exceptionally, the Court of Appeal subsequently issued a declaration of incompatibility against the Act under the Human Rights Act 1998.[130]

From one perspective, legislative reversal illustrates the continuing supremacy of Parliament and government's ability to shape the law to meet its own needs—for Cranston, '[l]egislative reversal of the effects of particular decisions on judicial review is at once a tribute to its potency but also a reminder that at the end of the day parliamentary power trumps judicial power.'[131] But by attempting to reverse a court judgment through legislation, the government must seek publicly to justify its action; the very task of legislating opens up policy issues to debate and campaigning by affected

---

[124] *Burmah Oil Ltd v Lord Advocate* [1965] AC 75; War Damage Act 1965.

[125] eg the Court of Appeal's decision in *R v Secretary of State for Social Security, ex p Joint Council for the Welfare of Immigrants* [1996] 4 All ER 385, in which secondary legislation restricting support for asylum applicants was declared unlawful and was subsequently reversed by the Asylum and Immigration Act 1996. See also *R v Secretary of State for the Home Department, ex p Adan, Subraskran and Aitsegeur* [1999] 4 All ER 774; aff'd [2001] 2 AC 477, HL; Immigration and Asylum Act 1999, s 11(1); *R (Yogathas and Thangarasa) v Secretary of State for the Home Department* [2003] 1 AC 920.

[126] *R (Reilly and Wilson) v Secretary of State for Work and Pensions* [2013] EWCA Civ 66.

[127] House of Lords Constitution Committee, *Jobseekers (Back to Work Schemes) Bill* (HL 155 2012–13).

[128] HL Deb, vol 744, cols 739-742 (21 March 2013) (Lord Pannick).

[129] Jobseekers (Back to Work Schemes) Act 2013.

[130] *Reilly v Secretary of State for Work and Pensions* [2016] EWCA Civ 413.

[131] Cranston, 'Reviewing Judicial Review', in Richardson and Genn (eds), *Administrative Law and Government Action: The Courts and Alternative Mechanisms of Review* (Oxford 1994), p 70.

interests. This, in turn, may mean that the government has to offer concessions or pay the political price of refusing to do so. Moreover, legislative reversal will not be lightly undertaken by a government: legislation is itself a scarce resource. In any event, legislative reversal is very much the exception rather than the norm. Furthermore, it is really only an option for central government (and, even then, not in the context of EU law[132]), whereas many judicial review claims are brought against local authorities and other public bodies.

Another form of negative reaction to judicial review that has been more common in recent years has been direct criticism by politicians of judges. Ministerial familiarity with judicial review may both breed contempt and prompt criticism. A former Home Secretary, David Blunkett MP, once expressed his frustration: 'Frankly, I am personally fed up with having to deal with a situation where Parliament debates issues and the judges overturn them.'[133]

Such criticism of judges by politicians has been viewed as part of a government strategy to cope with legal challenge.[134] At the same time, such comments have also been viewed as undermining the convention that, irrespective of what government Ministers might think of a judicial decision, they should not publicly criticise it because of the constitutional importance of the executive respecting the independence of the judiciary. Indeed, this may illustrate a more general development in our constitution: the passing away of old unwritten conventions and their replacement with more formal (and sometimes legally binding) duties—a trend that relates to one of our key themes concerning the transition from a more political to a more legal constitution. So, following repeated criticism of the judiciary by government Ministers, Parliament decided, in the Constitutional Reform Act 2005, to impose a statutory duty on the Lord Chancellor to uphold the continued independence of the judiciary.[135] This duty has not, however, prevented politicians from criticising judges. At the same time, the rhetoric of political criticism may simply act as a pressure valve through which politicians express their displeasure at court rulings, but which, in the absence of legislative reversal, they are compelled to follow.

On occasion, political criticism of the courts may combine with legislative changes. Consider, for example, the episode of the 'Afghan hijackers', in which a number of Afghan nationals, having arrived in the UK on a hijacked plane, succeeded in their appeals that their removal to Afghanistan would be contrary to ECHR, Art 3. Following this, the Home Office delayed in applying its own policies by refusing immigration status to a number of the individuals concerned; the Administrative Court concluded that this delay resulted in 'conspicuous unfairness amounting to an abuse of power'.[136] The immediate reaction of the then Prime Minister was that

---

[132] See Chapter 8, section 4, on the supremacy of EU law.

[133] Quoted by Bradley, 'Judicial Independence under Attack' [2003] PL 397, 400.

[134] See Le Sueur, 'The Judicial Review Debate: From Partnership to Friction' (1996) 31 Government and Opposition 8. See also Rozenburg, *Trial of Strength: The Battle between Ministers and Judges over Who Makes the Laws* (London 1997).

[135] Constitutional Reform Act 2005, s 3.

[136] *R (S) v Secretary of State for the Home Department* [2006] EWHC 1111 (Admin).

the Court's decision amounted to 'an abuse of common sense'.[137] While dismissing the government's appeal, the Court of Appeal indicated that it would be open to Parliament to create a new immigration category for people whose conduct the government considered had disentitled them from the ordinary immigration status.[138] Subsequently, the government introduced legislation to introduce a special immigration status for such people.[139] The general point is that it can never be assumed that judicial review will be accepted by government; legal obligations to comply with court rulings vie with administrative and political pressures.

> **Q** To what extent, if at all, is it permissible for public authorities to react negatively towards judicial review?

4.6 Informal reaction

So far, the reactions to judicial review that we have considered, whether positive or negative, have been formal or explicit; but reactions may be informal or implicit, too.[140] While it may be easier to identify a formal reaction to judicial review—whether positive or negative—than an informal reaction, this does not imply that informal responses are any less important. Indeed, it has been argued that the most profound and enduring influences of judicial review are not to be found by examining the statute book or by seeking formalised and public shifts of policy in response to litigation; rather, they are to be found in the effects of litigation on the less accessible aspects of government—the internal and informal working practices of public agencies, their management systems, and their decision-making regimes.[141] However, it is often harder to trace the impact of judicial review on patterns of bureaucratic behaviour than on the outcome of individual cases, because administrative action is usually influenced by so many factors.[142]

In this context, empirical studies of the impact of judicial review are particularly important.[143] A common theme of such studies is that the ability of judicial review to influence routine administrative decision-making may be constrained. Why might this be so? Administrative decision-makers may be unaware of elementary principles of judicial review. There may be are other pressures—political, administrative, and financial—with which judicial review must compete in order to have any impact. Public authorities typically operate in a highly complex political–administrative context and are subject to all sorts of pressures, such as centrally imposed targets and performance indicators. In the organisational context in which public authorities

---

[137] 'Blair dismay over hijack Afghans', *BBC News*, 10 May 2006.
[138] *S v Secretary of State for the Home Department* [2006] EWCA Civ 1157, [47].
[139] Criminal Justice and Immigration Act 2008, ss 130–7.
[140] Richardson, 'Impact Studies in the United Kingdom', in Hertogh and Halliday, p 109.
[141] Sunkin and Le Sueur, 'Can Government Control Judicial Review?' (1991) 44 CLP 161, 162.
[142] Mullen, Prosser, and Pick, *Judicial Review in Scotland* (Chichester 1996), p 115.
[143] For an overview of such studies, see Richardson, pp 107–15.

operate, compliance with judicial review may often be a low priority. Furthermore, judicial review has the effect of singling out a specific administrative decision—possibly one of many very similar decisions—for scrutiny. This might be beneficial for the recipient of that particular decision, but it does not necessarily mean that other decisions will receive similar scrutiny.

For example, homelessness decision-making by local authorities is a high-pressure, 'street-level' business. Studies of the impact of judicial review in this context have revealed that decision-making is informed by a number of different concerns, such as the allocation of limited resources, administrative and managerial pressures, and decision-makers' own perceptions of the moral worthiness of applicants. In this context, judicial review is unlikely to exert much influence and may prompt negative reaction. For example, increased compliance with legal requirements might stem from a defensive concern by decision-makers to safeguard their decisions from challenge rather than a concern with improving their quality.[144] Halliday concluded, from empirical research into homelessness decision-making by three English local authorities, that, despite prolonged exposure to judicial scrutiny, unlawful homelessness decision-making was rife; paradoxically, exposure to judicial scrutiny might operate so as to reduce self-scrutiny by public authorities.[145]

By contrast, it might be thought that judicial review may exert more influence on adjudicative bodies, such as tribunals, that are made up of legally qualified decision-makers. However, this assumption may not be borne out in practice. For example, a study of the impact of judicial review on Mental Health Review Tribunals[146] concluded that, despite the legal and adjudicatory nature of the tribunals, the presence of lawyers, and the fact that fundamental rights were often at stake, the influence of judicial review was 'patchy at best, even with regard to procedural requirements'.[147]

Which factors, then, condition the influence of judicial review on public administration? A number of different hypotheses have been advanced.[148] Judicial review is likely to exert a greater influence if public administrators possess legal knowledge of the principles of administrative law, if they are legally conscientious (they care about making lawful decisions), and if they are legally competent (they are able to apply their legal knowledge to produce lawful decisions). Additional factors conditioning the influence of judicial review concern the decision-making environment (is it conducive to producing lawful decisions or are there competing pressures?) and the law itself (are court rulings themselves clear and unambiguous?).[149]

---

[144] Loveland, *Housing Homeless Persons* (Oxford 1995).

[145] Halliday, 'The Influence of Judicial Review on Bureaucratic Decision-Making' [2000] PL 110.

[146] Now part of the Health, Education and Social Care Chamber of the First-tier Tribunal: see further Chapter 16.

[147] Richardson and Machin, 'Judicial Review and Tribunal Decision-Making: A Study of the Mental Health Review Tribunal' [2000] PL 494, 514.

[148] Halliday, *Judicial Review and Compliance with Administrative Law* (Oxford 2003).

[149] On this last point, the House of Lords' decision in *Bromley London Borough Council v Greater London Council* [1983] AC 768 is an instructive example of how it can be difficult for public authorities to derive clear guidance from multiple and complex judgments. A noticeable trend over recent years has been for the higher courts to deliver single, rather than multiple, judgments, other than in cases including dissenting judgments, which promotes clarity in working out their meaning.

5. Conclusion

This chapter has examined judicial review in terms of its accessibility, the competence and capacity of the courts to review administrative action, and the impact of judicial review on government. The chapter has offered a different perspective on judicial review by considering how judicial review works in practice—the aim has not been to provide a comprehensive overview of the issues, but to illustrate their complexity. The relationship between judicial review, government, and politics is a highly dynamic one. The key message has been to emphasise the wider context in which judicial review operates in practice.

Expert commentary
What is judicial review for—and what should we expect of it?
Simon Halliday, Professor of Socio-Legal Studies, University of York

In this commentary, I focus on a key point made at various points in this chapter: that the courts are only one institution within the reasonably crowded accountability landscape that surrounds governmental decision-making. This point is important, I would suggest, because it leads us to two significant questions that should help us in analysing the effectiveness of judicial review: (1) What is judicial review for? (2) What, realistically, should we expect from judicial review?

Elliott and Thomas warn us at the beginning of this chapter that the concept of the 'effectiveness' of judicial review is a complex one. They rightly point to three different aspects of the concept: (1) the accessibility of judicial review to potential claimants, (2) the competence and capacity of the courts to review administrative action, and (3) the ability of judicial review to affect the behaviour of government agencies. Underpinning that analysis is the fundamental question of what judicial review is for. What is/are judicial review's purpose(s) within the UK constitution? In order to be able to answer the question of how effective judicial review is, we must answer a preliminary issue: 'Effective to what ends or purposes?' For example, when we compare judicial review in the UK with judicial review in other countries, we can see that the purpose of judicial review varies by constitutional context.[150] A particularly stark example would be a comparison of the UK with the USA. Whereas judicial review in the UK focuses more on decision-making within governmental bodies, judicial review in the USA focuses more on rule-making by regulatory agencies that are largely independent of government.

However, even within the UK, the purposes of judicial review can change over time. This is partly to do with increasing institutional complexity within our constitution—shifts in the accountability landscape of which courts are a part. The role that judicial review plays in our constitution is sensitive to the roles played by other accountability mechanisms. The courts have in the past complained that judicial review is ill-suited to the resolution of 'bureaucratic' disputes where individuals challenge decisions of governmental 'street-level bureaucrats' affecting them.[151] Judicial review, it has been argued, is better reserved for 'high profile' constitutional cases that concern issues of wide public interest.[152] This is an argument that has,

---

[150] Cane, 'Understanding Judicial Review and Its Impact', in Hertogh and Halliday.
[151] See, eg *R v Hillingdon London Borough Council, ex p Puhlhofer* [1986] 2 WLR 259.   [152] Cane.

to an extent, found favour in policy circles. As the chapter points out with the example of immigration and asylum disputes, the growth of the tribunal system in the UK has had the effect of transferring much of this 'bureaucratic' dispute resolution function out of the court's jurisdiction or preventing it from falling within its jurisdiction.

There is, perhaps, a tendency amongst law students (encouraged by a few textbooks) to focus too heavily on judicial review when thinking about the legal accountability of government. To answer the question of what judicial review is for, we need to situate it within a broader accountability landscape including tribunals, inquiries, and ombudsmen. We should not expect judicial review to be 'all things to all men'. Another common mistake, however, is to imagine that, even within a modest sense of judicial review's purposes, it can be fully effective in fostering legal compliance by governmental bodies. As well as having an accurate understanding of what judicial review is for, we must, then, have realistic expectations of what it can achieve. One of the hardest lessons that law students must learn is that, *inevitably*, law is much more ineffective than we imagine it, or would like it, to be. Most of us are guilty of expecting too much from law. Like many societal institutions (such as politics, religion, and the family) law is bound to disappoint as well as inspire. The empirical research on governmental decision-making reviewed in this chapter demonstrates that there is much to prevent governmental compliance with public law.

Of course, it would be too pessimistic to hold that judicial review *never* succeeds in encouraging public officials to comply with law. Yet, equally, it would be a mistake to look only to judicial review to do that job. This would be another sense in which we expect too much from judicial review. Judicial review is a form of external supervision of government. The impetus towards legal compliance, however, is likely to come from a combination of both external supervision *and* internal control. *The Judge over Your Shoulder*[153] is an example of public officials not only educating themselves about what law requires of them, but also of encouraging each other to comply with law. It is framing legal compliance as a professional value, in other words. There is an important role for professional bodies (of which there are many in the public sector) to both educate and encourage in relation to legal compliance. Indeed, evidence of the potential of professional communities to be effective in this regard is beginning to emerge.[154] At the same time, other supervisory bodies that exist alongside courts in the accountability landscape (such as public auditors and regulators) may also play a role here.[155]

Many textbooks on public law, perhaps even most of them, overlook the topic of the effectiveness and impact of judicial review. The analysis in this chapter is, accordingly, particularly welcome. But more significantly, the analysis is important for our understanding of public law. Law generally, including public law specifically, is not some kind of introspective academic exercise. It is, rather, a profoundly *social* phenomenon. In the case of public law, it is concerned with the regulation of relations between citizens and the state and between the various organs and institutions of the state (at various levels). Public law has aims and ambitions, if you like. And as this chapter points out, to ignore the extent to which these aims and ambitions are fulfilled would be to cut short our inquiry into public law.

---

[153] A government publication which provides guidance to junior officials in the practical application of legal principles. See further section 4.3.

[154] Halliday, 'The Governance of Compliance with Public Law' [2013] PL 312.   [155] Halliday.

Further reading

BONDY, PLATT, and SUNKIN, *The Value and Effectiveness of Judicial Review* (London 2015) (**http://www.publiclawproject.org.uk/data/resources/210/Value-and-Effects-of-Judicial-Review.pdf**)
This is an empirical legal study of the value and effectiveness of judicial review.

HALLIDAY, *Judicial Review and Compliance with Administrative Law* (Oxford 2003)
This book provides a theoretical framework for considering the impact of judicial review upon government.

HARLOW and RAWLINGS, ' "Striking Back" and "Clamping Down": An Alternative Perspective on Judicial Review' in Bell, Elliott, Varuhas, and Murray (eds), *Public Law Adjudication in Common Law Systems* (Oxford 2016)
This paper discusses how governments seek to influence the impact of judicial review by limiting the scope for judicial challenge in advance ('clamping down') and by reversing or limiting the effect of judicial intervention ('striking back').

HERTOGH and HALLIDAY (eds), *Judicial Review and Bureaucratic Impact* (Cambridge 2004)
This volume of essays provides a range of international and interdisciplinary perspectives on the relationship between judicial review and government.

RAWLINGS, 'Modelling Judicial Review' (2008) 61 CLP 95
This article discusses the development of different models of judicial review.

PART V

Administrative Justice

15

Ombudsmen and Complaints

1. What is administrative justice?	633
2. The wider complaint-handling system	634
3. Ombudsmen: an example—the 'debt of honour' case	640
4. Public sector ombudsmen in the UK	642
5. The role of public sector ombudsmen	645
6. Investigations	652
7. Compliance	666
8. Concluding remarks	676
Expert commentary	678
Further reading	680
Useful websites	681

1. What is administrative justice?

This part of the book focuses on *administrative justice*. This slightly obscure term requires an introduction. So far, we have considered the structure of government in terms of Ministers, government departments, civil servants, and the many other public bodies. Government is a large and powerful organisation that has a variety of jobs to do and for which it must be held to account. Much of the media attention is focused upon the higher levels of politics. However, the bulk of the daily work of government is concerned with the provision of public services and making individual decisions that affect people's lives. Elections are infrequent events. In practice, most people interact with public bodies on a daily basis in more mundane ways. Consider the following. The Department for Work and Pensions makes 12 million decisions per year concerning whether people qualify for social security benefits. HM Customs and Revenue makes millions of decisions concerning how much tax people should pay. The National Health Service (NHS) provides health care to millions of people. Public services are also provided by local authorities and other public bodies.

Most of the time these public bodies do a good job, but sometimes they fail. They make mistakes and errors. People can feel that they have been treated insensitively by an uncaring and impersonal bureaucracy that is unresponsive to their particular needs. And this is where administrative justice comes in. People need mechanisms to challenge and complain about government decisions. This has long been seen as a vital aspect of good government. In 1644, the English poet, John Milton, wrote that 'when complaints are freely heard, deeply considered and speedily reformed, then is the utmost bound of civil liberty attained, that wise men look for.'[1]

Yet the ordinary methods of political scrutiny—considered in Chapter 10—are often inappropriate and ineffectual in this context. The volume of complaints and grievances would quickly overwhelm the system of parliamentary scrutiny. Further, the decisions made and services delivered are not undertaken personally by Ministers, but by an enormous number of public servants who often work at arm's length or independently from Ministers. What is required are distinctive mechanisms of administrative justice by which people can complain. Such mechanisms need to be accessible, effective, proportionate, and efficient in resolving such complaints.

Judicial review is one way of securing administrative justice, but many of the issues that arise cannot be effectively resolved through judicial review. The provision of poor quality public services is not necessarily unlawful. Also, judicial review is a cumbersome, legalistic, and exclusive process that is out of reach for many people. In this part of the book, we explore a range of *non-court-based* mechanisms that, in different ways, seek to secure administrative justice for individuals (by providing redress when things go wrong) and/or to promote good government (by enabling lessons to be learned from past mistakes). This chapter explores public sector ombudsmen and complaint mechanisms. 'Ombudsman' means literally a 'complaints man'. Public sector ombudsmen are those independent bodies that investigate complaints of maladministration against public bodies.[2]

2. The wider complaint-handling system

2.1 The importance and nature of the complaint-handling system

We start by considering the wider complaint-handling system. Ombudsmen are the apex of a large and complex network of (non-judicial) public sector complaint handlers. A complaint, in this context, is an expression of dissatisfaction with a public service. The importance of individuals having an effective opportunity to complain, and to have things put right, is especially important in the public sector, where there is often no possibility of 'exit'. This lack of 'exit' arises because people are often forced to deal with public bodies whether they like it or not.

Good quality complaint handling should be informed by the following values. First, public bodies should operate *effective and accessible* complaint systems.

---

[1] Milton, *Areopagitica* [1644]. Milton was also a civil servant for the Commonwealth of England under Oliver Cromwell in the 1650s.

[2] Throughout this chapter, we refer to 'ombudsmen', albeit that some of the offices considered are formally known as 'commissioners'. Notwithstanding its retention in some of the relevant legislation, the latter term has largely fallen into disuse.

Second, the complaint process should be *proportionate*—it should only take up the time and resources that are necessary, bearing in mind the nature of the complaints and that complaints should be resolved as close to their source as is practicable. This means that complaints should, at the initial stage, be dealt with in-house, if possible—that is, by the public body against which the complaint has been lodged. There is therefore a strong expectation that public bodies will have their own complaints procedures: the existence of effective complaint-handling systems forms part of one of the Parliamentary Ombudsman's principles of good administration. Further, for complaints systems to be effective, they must not only resolve individual grievances; they must also lead to improvements across the board. Intelligence from complaints should be used to learn lessons for the future.

There is a bewildering variety of complaint procedures, with a whole host of external and independent bodies that exist to investigate different types of complaint. For example, the Independent Police Complaints Commission was established as an independent body to investigate complaints against the police because of the perceived lack of public confidence in, and independence of, the previous complaint-handling system.[3] Likewise, Parliament created the Office of the Independent Adjudicator to resolve students' complaints against higher education institutions.[4] Figure 15.1 presents an overview of the complaints landscape. It is not comprehensive, but provides

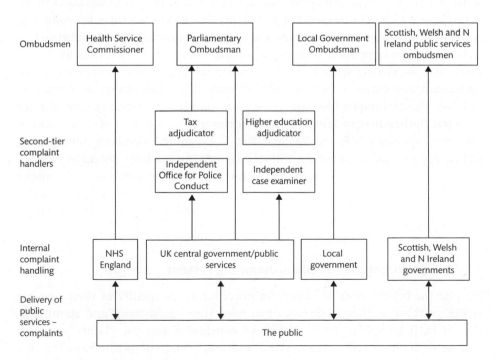

Figure 15.1 The complaints landscape

---

[3] Police Reform Act 2002. See further Chapter 21, section 3.1.   [4] Higher Education Act 2004.

a general sense of how different elements of the complaint-handling regime relate to one another.

In some areas of government that generate particularly high volumes of complaints—those in which the number of complaints are measured in the tens of thousands—there are three levels of complaint handling: internal complaint procedures; intermediate, or 'second-tier', complaint-handling systems; and then external investigation of complaints by the ombudsmen. For instance, the Tax Adjudicator investigates complaints about HM Revenue and Customs, while the Independent Case Examiner reviews complaints arising from the Department for Work and Pensions. The advantage of such second-tier complaint handlers is that they enable individuals who do not consider their complaints to have been satisfactorily dealt with by the public body to pursue their complaints before an independent and external body. Such second-tier complaint handlers can also resolve many complaints informally through techniques such as mediation. This also has the advantages of avoiding the costs and lengthy delays associated with the more formal investigation of complaints and of ensuring that ombudsmen are not overwhelmed. However, the risk is that, in seeking to resolve complaints in this way, the overall system becomes more complex and hence more difficult for people to navigate.

A further means of complaint handling is perhaps the most obvious of all: complaints taken up by MPs themselves. Anyone with a grievance can always simply write to his or her MP, who may then take the matter up with the relevant government Minister. After all, MPs are there not only to serve in the government or opposition, or to contribute to debates in Parliament, but also to act as constituency members—that is, taking up the interests and complaints of their constituents. Occasionally, an MP might take the matter further by raising a constituent's particular complaint through an adjournment debate in the House of Commons. It is not always apparent that government agencies respond to complaints made via MPs satisfactorily. Consider, for example, the handling of MPs' letters by the Home Office. As part of their constituency postbag, many MPs receive complaints concerning individuals' immigration difficulties and their interactions with the Home Office, a body not always known for displaying high customer service standards. The MP may then take up the matter with the Home Office. Previously, many MPs considered the Home Office's processing of such complaints to be poor, with both delays and inadequate replies, although the situation now seems to have improved somewhat.[5]

2.2 The quality of the complaint-handling system

Despite the proliferation of complaint procedures, the quality of these systems is highly variable. 'Complainants often need time, persistence and stamina to pursue their complaint to a satisfactory conclusion and complaints processes can be difficult to access, understand and use.'[6] And complaint handling is a

---

[5] House of Commons Home Affairs Committee, *Managing Migration: The Points Based System* (HC 217 2008–09), [269]–[290]; Independent Chief Inspector of Borders and Immigration, *An Inspection of the Handling of Complaints and MPs' Correspondence* (2016).

[6] House of Commons Public Administration Select Committee, *Fifth Report* (HC 409 2007–08), [6].

time-consuming and costly business for government (and hence the taxpayer) too.[7]

Various reports have highlighted key weaknesses in the complaints system. In 2015, the National Audit Office made the following findings.[8] Around 10.6 million users across the UK (approximately 1 in 5) in 2014 had a problem with using a public service and 49 per cent of people who experienced a problem did not complain. The complaints and redress landscape is complex. People find it difficult to navigate and there are gaps. People are much less likely to complain about a public service than a private service. Complaints can take too long to provide timely redress; 36 per cent of complainants spend more than a year trying to resolve their problem with a local authority, care provider, or school before complaining to an ombudsman. Across public services, only 31 per cent of complainants were satisfied with the outcome of their complaint. There is poor leadership within central government to make system-wide improvements to the complaints process. Public bodies do not make enough use of complaints to improve services and there are serious impediments to doing so. Consequently, the complaints and redress system is neither effective nor good value for public money.

Other reports provide similarly stark findings.[9] Over one third of people who want to complain about government services do not do so. People lack confidence in the complaints system. Processes are long and unwieldy. Lessons from mistakes are rarely shared. It is more difficult for people who are unwell, vulnerable, or in difficulty to complain. When people do complain, they lack confidence that anything will change as a result. For too many people, the process of complaining is dispiriting and the outcome can seem hollow. As Julie Mellor, the Parliamentary and Health Service Ombudsman (PHSO), has noted:

> many people don't complain when they are unhappy with a public service because they don't believe it will make any difference. The current complaint system is far too complex and fragmented, leaving people confused as to which ombudsman to turn to if things go wrong or haven't been resolved locally.[10]

These findings are confirmed by evidence relating to specific complaint systems, such as the NHS complaints system. The Francis inquiry into unacceptably poor medical care by the Mid Staffordshire NHS Trust identified the following points: some patients who suffer poor medical care and treatment are reluctant to complain, in part because of fear of the consequences, such as an adverse reaction from those criticised and their colleagues; complainants, whether or not they are specifically vulnerable, need

---

[7] The National Audit Office found that, in 2003–04, nearly 1.4 million complaints were made across central government, costing over £500 million: National Audit Office, *Citizen Redress* (HC 21 2004–05), p 44.

[8] National Audit Office, *Public Service Markets: Putting Things Right When They Go Wrong* (HC 84 2015–16).

[9] PHSO, *Responsive and Accountable?* (HC 799 2012–13); Which?, *Make Complaints Count* (London 2015), http://www.staticwhich.co.uk/documents/pdf/make-complaints-count-report---march-2015-397971.pdf

[10] PHSO, 'Ombudsman responds to CAB report on learning from mistakes', Media statement, 1 March 2016, http://www.ombudsman.org.uk/about-us/news-centre/our-statements/ombudsman-responds-to-cab-report-on-learning-from-mistakes2. The Parliamentary Ombudsman has launched its 'Complain for change' campaign to help people understand how to complain, http://www.ombudsman.org.uk/making-complaint/before-you-come-to-us/complain-for-change/

to be supported with advice and advocacy services; proper complaint handling is vital if organisations are to ensure that services can improve—yet the feedback, learning, and warning signals available from complaints have not been given a high enough priority by the NHS.[11] A reluctance by patients, carers, and families to complain combined with a defensiveness by hospitals and staff to hear and address concerns has resulted in a 'toxic cocktail'.[12]

High profile failures—such as those highlighted by the Francis report into failings at Mid Staffordshire NHS Trust and the Independent Inquiry into Child Sexual Exploitation in Rotherham—place in sharp relief the problems that may arise when complaints are ignored or people are reluctant to complain. In 2015, the PHSO reported that 'NHS Trusts are not always identifying patient safety incidents and are sometimes failing to recognise serious incidents' and that the quality of investigations is 'inconsistent, often failing to get to the heart of what has gone wrong and to ensure lessons are learnt.'[13] Following up on this, the Commons Public Administration and Constitutional Affairs Select Committee stated that the new Healthcare Safety Investigation Branch (HSIB)—whose remit does not include complaint handling—would only succeed if the government legislates to guarantee its independence and ensure that it provides a genuine 'safe space' for people to speak out about patient safety risks.[14]

There are parallels elsewhere. Complaints against the police have a long and very patchy history. In 2013, the Commons Home Affairs Select Committee concluded that the Independent Police Complaints Commission 'is woefully underequipped and hamstrung in achieving its original objectives. It has neither the powers nor the resources that it needs to get to the truth when the integrity of the police is in doubt.'[15] The government has recognised the need for reform and a new body—the Independent Office for Police Conduct—is to be established.[16]

2.3 Reform of the complaint-handling system

What should be done? The PHSO has taken a lead in recent years, seeing as an important part of its role the development and promotion of good practice. This culminated with the publication, in 2009, of its *Principles of Good Complaint Handling*, in which the Ombudsman implores public bodies (among other things) to provide clear information about complaints procedures, to make sure that staff are properly trained to handle complaints, to observe basic principles of fair and rational decision-making,

---

[11] Francis, *Report of the Mid Staffordshire NHS Foundation Trust Public Inquiry* (HC 898 2012–13), ch 3.

[12] http://www.ombudsman.org.uk/publications/designing-good-together-transforming-hospital-complaint-handling

[13] PHSO, *Review into the Quality of NHS Complaints Investigations Where Serious or Avoidable Harm Has Been Alleged* (2015).

[14] House of Commons Public Administration and Constitutional Affairs Select Committee, *PHSO Review: Quality of NHS Complaints Investigations* (HC 94 2016–17).

[15] House of Commons Home Affairs Select Committee, *Independent Police Complaints Commission* (HC 494 2012–13), [5].

[16] The Policing and Crime Act 2017 replaces the Independent Police Complaints Commission with the Independent Office for Police Conduct.

to provide prompt and appropriate remedies, and to learn lessons from complaints.[17] Nonetheless, the PHSO has repeatedly warned that it receives too many unresolved complaints that could have been resolved by public services locally, meaning that people have to wait longer for answers and that much-needed service improvements are delayed. Figure 15.2 shows the most common concerns relating to initial complaint handling.

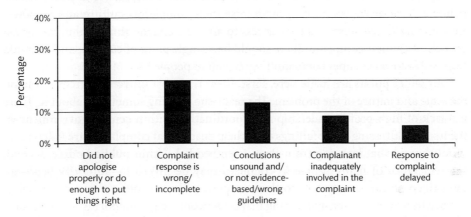

Figure 15.2 Top five common concerns about initial complaint handling raised in complaints upheld by Parliamentary Ombudsman, 2014–15

Source: PHSO, *Complaints and UK Government Departments and Agencies, and Some UK Public Organisations, 2014–15.*

Clearly, more needs to be done. In 2015, the Local Government Ombudsman (LGO) raised concerns that the local complaints system is under increasing pressure.[18] Local authorities are increasingly stretched when it comes to complaint handling; they are having to do 'more with less' because of more complaints and reduced resources in complaint-handling teams. Also, people are waiting too long to have complaints resolved, spending an average of nine months negotiating internal complaints procedures before approaching the LGO. Further, the redress system is not sufficiently accessible: 43 per cent of people were not advised they could refer their complaint to the LGO.

Other reform proposals have been advanced. The National Audit Office has recommended that central government should show more leadership. It should nominate an authority within government to manage reforms and have a mandate to change the complaints and redress system. It should also ensure that service users can access redress easily and increase consistency in complaint handling across ombudsmen and other complaints bodies. The complaints system should be made easier for people to navigate. Government should also review the effectiveness of complaint-handling arrangements for private providers where they receive public money and require

---

17   PHSO, *Principles of Good Complaint Handling* (London 2009), pp 2–3.
18   LGO, *Review of Local Government Complaints 2014–15* (2015), p 1.

better collection and use of complaints data across the system to improve quality. The boards of public bodies should monitor their own complaints and complaint handling as a matter of course to ensure it conforms to best practice. The Citizens' Advice Bureau (CAB) has identified six opportunities for enhancing complaints: there should be no 'wrong door' when people want to make a complaint; public bodies should develop better insight and intelligence capabilities on emerging service issues by aggregating data, to make services more effective and responsive to public needs; public service providers need to modernise their complaints culture and empower frontline staff; people should have access to an independent, impartial organisation for help with their complaint; there should be a single point of contact; and it should be possible to raise 'super complaints' on behalf of people.[19]

Four wider points are made here. First, there is almost universal agreement upon the scale and nature of the problem. The real issue is doing something about it. There is a lack of high-profile leadership and coordination within central government on the issue. Addressing those failings could help ensure that complaints are taken more seriously and that learning from them is embedded within public bodies. Second, the reluctance of many people to complain may be linked to 'authority bias'—an unjustified willingness to bow to those in power. There is often a 'musn't grumble' culture in Britain. Better signposting may help people to get support when they complain, but there are limits to what can be done to overcome a deep-rooted cognitive bias against complaining.[20] Third, complaints are in many ways indicative of wider systemic issues. For instance, that local authorities have been increasingly stretched when it comes to complaint handling and placed in the unenviable position of having to do 'more with less' reflects the pressure upon them caused by austerity policies that have cut public spending. This has clearly affected both complaint handling and the delivery of public services. Fourth, the quality of governance is an important determinant of our well-being and happiness as human beings—more so than wealth and income.[21] If government really wants to improve people's lives, then there are few better places to start than by enhancing its own complaint procedures. The remainder of this chapter will focus upon ombudsmen.

3. Ombudsmen: an example—the 'debt of honour' case

Ombudsmen *investigate* complaints of maladministration (bad administration). They *secure redress* for injustice occasioned thereby and *identify the underlying reasons* for maladministration so that appropriate lessons may be learned. Further, they do all of

[19] CAB, *Learning from Mistakes: How Complaints Can Drive Improvements to Public Services* (London 2016), **https://www.citizensadvice.org.uk/Global/CitizensAdvice/Public%20services%20publications/Learning-from-mistakes.pdf**

[20] Conversely, some people raise frivolous or vexatious complaints that are without merit.

[21] Helliwell and Huang, 'How's Your Government? International Evidence Linking Good Government and Well-Being' (2008) 38 British Journal of Political Science 595; Ott, 'Government and Happiness in 130 Nations: Good Governance Fosters Higher Level and More Equality of Happiness' (2011) 102 Social Indications Research 3.

these things in a way that *avoids the formality, cost, and legalism* associated with court proceedings. These points are illustrated by the 'debt of honour' case.

In 2000, the UK government announced the establishment of a compensation scheme for 'British' civilians interned by the Japanese during the Second World War. The way the scheme was announced led some to believe that it would apply to a relatively broad range of people. However, subsequently, the government issued a clarification indicating that the scheme would be limited to those who had been born in the UK or with at least one parent or grandparent who had been born in the UK. Judicial review proceedings were initiated by a group representing disappointed individuals who had anticipated benefiting from the scheme, but who fell outside the scope of its clarified terms.[22] Their claim was based in part on the legitimate expectation doctrine,[23] but the Court of Appeal held that the original announcement had been insufficiently clear to generate such an expectation, no definite indication having been given of who would count as 'British' for those purposes.

Following this, a complaint was made to the Parliamentary and Health Service Ombudsman—the ombudsman who investigates complaints of maladministration (bad administrative practice) made against UK central government departments. She conducted an investigation, examining the government's initial and subsequent statements, and concluded that the way in which the matter had been handled—in particular, the confusion created by the unclear and imprecise nature of the original announcement—constituted maladministration that had occasioned injustice to the complainant and similarly situated individuals.[24] The Ombudsman therefore recommended, among other things, that the government review the scheme that it had implemented, and fully reconsider the position of the complainant and those in a similar position to him.[25] However, the government refused to do so, prompting the Ombudsman to lay a special report before Parliament drawing its attention to what she regarded as unremedied injustice. This, in turn, was followed up by a report by the House of Commons Public Administration Select Committee—the select committee overseeing the Ombudsman.[26] The report was highly critical of the government's stance. The government then backed down and accepted the need to review the compensation scheme.[27]

This episode points to several distinctive features of the ombudsman system. First, the Ombudsman found that maladministration had occurred even though the Court held the government's conduct to be lawful: *the concept of good administration employed by ombudsmen is thus wider than the concept of legality as enforced by the*

---

[22] *R (Association of British Civilian Internees: Far East Region) v Secretary of State for Defence* [2003] EWCA Civ 473, [2003] QB 1397.

[23] See Chapter 12, section 4.3.

[24] Parliamentary Ombudsman, *'A Debt of Honour': The Ex Gratia Scheme for British Groups Interned by the Japanese during the Second World War* (HC 324 2005–06), [199].

[25] Parliamentary Ombudsman, HC 324, [212]–[216].

[26] The Public Administration Committee has now been superseded by the Public Administration and Constitutional Affairs Committee. The latter is now responsible for overseeing the work of the PHSO.

[27] See further Kirkham, 'Challenging the Authority of the Ombudsman: The Parliamentary Ombudsman's Special Report on Wartime Detainees' (2006) 69 MLR 792.

courts. A government decision may therefore be lawful, but nonetheless result in maladministration. Second, the Ombudsman's recommendations were concerned not only with the case of the complainant, and not only with the circumstances of similarly situated individuals, but also with the general way in which government should implement compensation schemes: the Ombudsman said that, in future, due regard should be given to all relevant issues (eg eligibility criteria) *before* any announcements are made, and that, once announced, any subsequent changes should be publicised and explained.[28] Ombudsmen are concerned not only with remedying injustice in individual cases, but also with *identifying general administrative deficiencies and disseminating good practice to prevent their recurrence.*

Third, the government refused to implement the Ombudsman's key recommendations, and the Ombudsman's only recourse was by way of drawing Parliament's attention to that fact. This highlights the *legally non-binding nature of ombudsmen's recommendations* and the general principle that *ombudsmen form part of the political, not legal, system for securing good government.*

> **Q** These distinctive aspects of ombudsmanry are generally seen as good things. Do you share that view? Why, or why not? How would you respond to someone who argued that ombudsmen are unnecessary and that it would be better to rely on judicial review?

4. Public sector ombudsmen in the UK

Before proceeding further, we need to deal with some of the 'nuts and bolts' issues about the ombudsman 'system'. Two initial matters should be noted.

First, a broad distinction must be drawn between *public* and *private sector ombudsmen.* The latter are typically established by particular industries and professions to act as complaint handlers. Thus there is an Energy Ombudsman, a Legal Services Ombudsman, and even a Furniture Ombudsman.[29] Our concern, however, is with public sector ombudsmen—that is, with ombudsmen that are independent of government and investigate complaints against public bodies.

Second, within the category of public sector ombudsmen, there are two broad models. The distinction between them is evident from Table 15.1. The first model adopts an integrated approach, with a single ombudsman service responsible for oversight of all relevant public bodies. So, after devolution to Scotland and Wales, the Scottish and Welsh Public Services Ombudsmen were established to handle complaints relating to all public bodies within those countries except for those complaints relating to UK-wide public bodies (such as central government departments).[30] Northern Ireland followed suit in 2016.[31]

---

[28] Parliamentary Ombudsman, HC 324, [224]–[225].

[29] For a list of ombudsman schemes, see **http://www.ombudsmanassociation.org/**

[30] Scottish Public Services Ombudsman Act (SPSOA) 2002; Public Services Ombudsman (Wales) Act (PSO(W)A) 2005.

[31] Public Services Ombudsman Act (Northern Ireland) (PSOA(NI)) 2016.

Table 15.1 Public sector ombudsmen

Part of the country to which alleged maladministration relates				
	England	Scotland	Wales	Northern Ireland
UK public bodies (general)	UK Parliamentary Ombudsman			
'National' (ie English, Scottish, etc) public bodies	UK Parliamentary Ombudsman	Scottish Public Services Ombudsman	Welsh Public Services Ombudsman	Northern Ireland Public Services Ombudsman
Health service providers	Health Service Ombudsman			
Local authorities	Local Government Ombudsman			
Social landlords	Housing Ombudsman			n/a

In contrast, the system in England is fragmented, with different ombudsmen dealing with complaints pertaining to general public bodies (the Parliamentary Ombudsman),[32] health service providers (the Health Service Ombudsman),[33] local authorities (the LGO),[34] and social landlords (the Independent Housing Ombudsman Service).[35] Such diversity arises in a multilayered constitution:[36] devolution enables each country within the UK to arrange its own affairs in the most appropriate way, and it is inevitable that different views will prevail. However, it is not clear that anyone actually regards the English system as superior to the integrated models adopted in Scotland and Wales. The public sector ombudsmen themselves have argued that people find it 'difficult to know to which Ombudsman to complain', and that particular problems arise when complaints raise issues that fall within the jurisdiction of more than one ombudsman.[37] For example, the Scottish Ombudsman sees the breadth of his jurisdiction as a great strength—citing by way of example investigations into 'long-term care for the elderly [that] can involve a number of agencies in delivering the service including health providers, local government and housing associations'.[38] In contrast, such an investigation would engage the jurisdictions of a number of separate ombudsmen in England.

[32] Parliamentary Commissioner Act (PCA) 1967.
[33] Health Service Commissioners Act (HSCA) 1993.   [34] Local Government Act (LGA) 1974.
[35] Housing Act 1996.
[36] In this regard, it should be noted that ombudsmen also exist at the EU level. The EU Ombudsman is responsible for investigating complaints of maladministration against certain EU institutions. See further Heede, *European Ombudsman: Redress and Control at Union Level* (The Hague 2000).
[37] Collcutt and Hourihan, *Review of the Public Sector Ombudsmen in England: A Report by the Cabinet Office* (London 2000) (hereinafter the 'Cabinet Office Review'), annex A.
[38] Scottish Public Services Ombudsman, *Annual Report 2003–04* (Edinburgh 2004), p 24.

In light of such problems, a review by the Cabinet Office in 2000 concluded that the integrated model should be adopted in England by merging the Parliamentary, Health Service, and Local Government Ombudsmen.[39] However, as the Parliamentary Ombudsman has pointed out, this would raise fresh difficulties: she (unlike the Health and Local Government Ombudsmen) is not an *English*, but a *UK*, ombudsman, with jurisdiction over *both* English *and* UK-wide public bodies.[40] If the UK Parliamentary Ombudsman were to be merged with the English Health and Local Government Ombudsmen, would the resulting institution be an English or a UK one? If the former, why should it have jurisdiction over non-devolved matters pertaining to other parts of the country? And, if the latter, why should its jurisdiction be limited in some regards to England?

The issue of ombudsman reform did not, however, disappear. In 2007, modest reforms permitted the Parliamentary, Health Service, and Local Government Ombudsmen to conduct joint investigations and issue joint reports on matters that cut across their respective jurisdictions.[41] In 2014, there was a warning that the Ombudsmen risked being 'stuck in time' without reform.[42] The subsequent Gordon review and a government consultation in 2015 recommended a new ombudsman service—the Public Service Ombudsman (PSO)—which would embrace the jurisdiction and responsibilities of the Parliamentary Ombudsman, the Health Service Ombudsman, and the Local Government Ombudsman.[43] The new PSO will cover UK reserved matters and English public services. It will mirror the accountability of UK reserved matters to the Westminster Parliament and relinquish jurisdiction over those if and when they transfer to the devolved administrations. It is envisaged that legislation will be introduced sometime during the 2015–20 UK Parliament.

This chapter cannot provide a detailed account of each public sector ombudsman. Instead, we examine general matters, using the UK's Parliamentary and Health Service Ombudsman as our focus and referring to other ombudsman schemes, such as the English Local Government Ombudsman, by way of comparison.[44] References in the remainder of the chapter to the 'Ombudsman' are to the PHSO unless otherwise indicated.

[39] The Cabinet Office Review, [4.3]–[4.4].

[40] Public Administration Select Committee, *Minutes of Evidence* (HC 506–i 2002–03), annex. See further Elliott, 'Asymmetric Devolution and Ombudsman Reform in England' [2006] PL 84.

[41] See PCA 1967, s 11ZAA; HSCA 1993, s 18ZA; LGA 1974, s 33ZA.

[42] House of Commons Public Administration Select Committee, *Time for a People's Ombudsman Service* (HC 655 2013–14).

[43] Gordon, *Better to Serve the Public: Proposals to Restructure, Reform, Renew and Reinvigorate Public Services Ombudsmen* (London 2014); Cabinet Office, *A Public Service Ombudsman: Government Response to Consultation* (London 2015). For a wider discussion, see Kirkham and Martin, 'Designing an English Public Services Ombudsman' (2014) 36 Journal of Social Welfare and Family Law 330.

[44] Although legally distinct, the posts of Parliamentary and Health Service Ombudsmen are held by the same person, and statistical information regarding their workload is published in an aggregated form. Dame Julie Mellor was appointed as the PHSO in 2012.

5. The role of public sector ombudsmen

5.1 What are ombudsmen for?

Ombudsmen secure *redress* for individuals who suffer because of maladministration. To do this, ombudsmen focus on dealing with individual grievances, getting public bodies to apologise and to put things right. Ombudsmen also concentrate on broader *systemic* issues. They try to understand why things have gone wrong and identify how things could be done differently to avoid a repetition of past mistakes. This is sometimes referred to as the *quality control* model of ombudsmanry—it is a forward-looking approach the focus of which is on improving the future quality of administration. Viewed in this way, ombudsmanry also becomes an important mechanism for holding government to account, capable of laying bare the nature and causes of systemic failure, and enabling others—the public, MPs, the media—to make informed judgements about the quality of public administration and the competence of those ultimately responsible for it.

These two roles are not exclusive of each other. Ombudsmen combine both functions, which are, to a large extent, complementary.[45] By investigating large numbers of individual complaints, ombudsmen build up a wealth of experience that helps them understand why things go wrong, and make constructive suggestions about how administrative systems and policies can be improved. For example, in 2003–05, the Parliamentary Ombudsman received large numbers of complaints about tax credits, a means-tested state benefits system, the principal concern being that some recipients were being overpaid for relatively long periods and then subjected to unexpected demands for repayment, causing serious hardship to those on low incomes. As well as dealing—pursuant to her redress function—with the individual complaints received, the Ombudsman looked at the tax credits system as a whole, using experience gleaned in relation to individual complaints to identify systemic failures concerning the design and implementation of the scheme, and to suggest what corrective action might be taken.[46] Similarly, the Health Service and Local Government Ombudsmen conducted a joint investigation in 2008–09 concerning the treatment of six people with learning disabilities who had died in NHS or local authority care between 2003 and 2005.[47] This revealed 'significant and distressing failures' leading to people with learning disabilities experiencing 'prolonged suffering and inappropriate care',[48] and led the Ombudsmen to recommend that all NHS and social care organisations in England should urgently review their arrangements for understanding and meeting the needs of people with learning disabilities. Some ombudsmen, such as the Welsh Public Services Ombudsman, have specific statutory powers to issue guidance about good administrative practice;[49] and although the

---

[45] This is certainly the view of the Parliamentary Ombudsman: *Improving Public Service: A Matter of Principle* (HC 9 2008).

[46] Parliamentary Ombudsman, *Tax Credits: Putting Things Right* (HC 124 2004–05).

[47] Parliamentary Ombudsman, *Six Lives: The Provision of Public Services to People with Learning Disabilities* (HC 203 2008–09).

[48] Parliamentary Ombudsman, HC 203, p 31. [49] PSO(W)A 2005, s 31.

Parliamentary Commissioner Act (PCA) 1967 makes no mention of such powers, the Parliamentary Ombudsman has nevertheless—in addition to seeking to disseminate good practice through her reports on investigations—issued a general code of good administration, setting out the standards to which public bodies are expected to adhere.[50]

It used to be assumed that there was a tension between the redress and control functions of ombudsmen. It was thought that the effective redress of grievances required the investigation of a high volume of complaints, whereas the quality control function required a highly selective approach, investigating only those complaints that are likely to shine a light on systemic failures. Accordingly, ombudsmen dealt with this (ostensible) tension by focusing differently upon different sorts of complaints. In 2012–13, the PHSO received (excluding those not validly made or outside the Ombudsman's remit) 26,961 enquiries, completed 384 investigations, and partly or fully upheld 86 per cent of them, and resolved nearly 4,500 complaints without the need for a full investigation.[51] Other complaints were either rejected (eg because they were premature[52] or because there was no reasonable prospect of securing a worthwhile outcome). The Ombudsman's philosophy was that there should be 'a diverse product range, [but] that the serious, heavyweight, statutory investigation should not be the core product'.[53]

However, this approach was (rightly) criticised: too few people got a remedy; and feedback to government was reduced accordingly.[54] Investigating a low number of complaints hindered both the redress and control functions. In 2013, the Parliamentary Ombudsman changed its philosophy. It now investigates thousands—not just hundreds—of complaints each year.[55] The redress and control functions of ombudsmen are now seen as running along parallel lines.

5.2 Ombudsmen and the political process

Part of the impetus for the creation of the Parliamentary Ombudsman—the first ombudsman in the UK—was Parliament's inability to deal with administrative failure. A former Ombudsman noted that Parliament's increasing focus on 'massive and detailed legislation' meant that it could not devote its time to 'those problems of individuals which lack a national or international dimension'.[56] The Parliamentary Ombudsman was therefore conceived as 'an adjunct to the MP's traditional and

[50] See further section 5.3.

[51] PHSO, *Aiming for Impact: Annual Report 2012–13* (HC 361 2012–13), p 5.

[52] Complaints are rejected as premature if complainants have not made recourse to the relevant public body's own complaints procedure.

[53] House of Commons Public Administration Select Committee, *Minutes of Evidence* (HC 506–i 2002–03), [70].

[54] House of Commons Public Administration Select Committee, HC 506–i, [13]–[14].

[55] PHSO, *Annual Report and Accounts 2012–13* (HC 361 2012–13), p 20.

[56] Clothier, 'The Value of an Ombudsman' [1986] PL 204, 205.

cherished role as grievance-chaser on behalf of constituents'.[57] It was envisaged that the Ombudsman would augment the capacity of Parliament to deal with such matters: Richard Crossman MP, the Minister responsible for piloting the Parliamentary Commissioner Bill through the House of Commons, said that the Ombudsman would be a 'servant of the House'.[58] The relationship between the Ombudsman and Parliament is cemented in a number of ways, as illustrated in Figure 15.3.

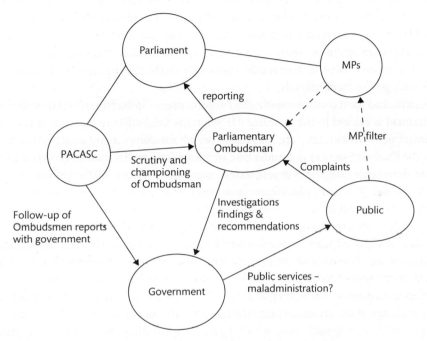

Figure 15.3 The constitutional context of the Parliamentary Ombudsman

First, the Ombudsman is required to *report to Parliament* annually on the performance of her functions under the PCA 1967 and is permitted to report to Parliament on such other matters as she thinks fit.[59] The reports referred to earlier concerning the 'debt of honour' case, the overpayment of tax credits, and the treatment of people with learning disabilities were thus reports made *to Parliament*. Similarly, the Scottish, Welsh, and Northern Irish ombudsmen report to their respective legislatures.[60]

Second, when the Ombudsman concludes that maladministration occasioning injustice has taken place, but that it appears that the public body concerned is not going to remedy it, she can *lay a special report before Parliament* drawing the matter to its attention.[61] Again, equivalent provision is made in relation to most of the other ombudsmen.[62] This feature of the ombudsman systems arguably underscores

---

[57] Drewry and Harlow, 'A "Cutting Edge"? The Parliamentary Commissioner and MPs' (1990) 53 MLR 745, 753.

[58] HC Deb, vol 734, col 49 (18 October 1966).   [59] PCA 1967, s 10(4).

[60] SPSOA 2002, s 15; PSO(W)A 2005, Sch 1, para 14; PSOA(NI) 2016, s 46.

[61] PCA 1967, s 10(3).   [62] SPSOA 2002, s 16; PSO(W)A 2005, s 24; PSOA(NI) 2016, s 46(2).

the view that they are best thought of as part of the political process, in the sense that the enforceability (such as it is) of ombudsmen's recommendations derives from the pressure that representative legislatures are able to bring to bear upon governments. This leads onto the question of whether ombudsmen's findings and recommendations should ever be regarded as *legally* binding—a question that we address later.

Third, the Parliamentary Ombudsman has a *special relationship with the House of Commons Public Administration and Constitutional Affairs Select Committee* (PACASC). This committee both scrutinises the Ombudsman's work and, when it considers it appropriate, acts as her champion by orchestrating political pressure when the government proves reluctant to accept the Ombudsman's findings and recommendations. PACASC frequently follows up Ombudsman reports through hearings with government officials.

Fourth, and most controversially, the Parliamentary Ombudsman's relationship with Parliament is evident in the so-called *MP filter*: the Ombudsman may investigate complaints, but *only* when they are referred to her by the complainant's MP.[63] This means that the Ombudsman cannot undertake investigations on her own initiative, and cannot undertake investigations in response to complaints received directly from members of the public. The latter phenomenon distinguishes the Parliamentary Ombudsman from other UK public sector ombudsmen, to whom members of the public are able to complain directly,[64] and from most other public sector ombudsmen around the world. The MP filter, which was envisaged by the Justice Report that recommended the creation of an Ombudsman as a temporary measure,[65] may constitute an obstacle to access by making complaining to the Ombudsman relatively cumbersome and contingent upon finding an MP willing to refer the complaint. So why does it still exist? Two principal arguments are made (with dwindling enthusiasm) in favour of the filter.

The first is a *pragmatic* one, which holds that the filter shields the Ombudsman from what would otherwise be an unsustainable workload. However, the theory that the filter 'allows the MP to settle the trivial administrative muddles', sending only the 'hard nuts' on to the Ombudsman,[66] does not seem to correspond to reality. Far from sending on only the hard cases that require the Ombudsman's specialised investigative skills, many MPs—over half, according to one study—automatically refer complaints to the Ombudsman when asked to do so.[67]

The pragmatic argument, then, cuts little ice. The second argument is a *constitutional* one. It is that the MP filter is a fitting reflection of the fact that the Ombudsman system forms part of the parliamentary process: that it is Parliament, and the MPs who partly comprise it, that bear primary responsibility for resolving constituents' grievances against public bodies and holding the executive to account, and that the Ombudsman is a functionary who better equips them to do those things. This argument, too, is open to question.[68] The Cabinet Office Review of public sector ombudsmen in 2000

---

[63] PCA 1967, s 5(1) and (1A).   [64] SPSOA 2002, s 9; PSO(W)A 2005, s 4; PSOA(NI) 2016, s 5.

[65] *The Citizen and the Administration* (London 1961), [157].

[66] Harlow, 'Ombudsmen in Search of a Role' (1978) 41 MLR 446, 451.

[67] The Cabinet Office Review, [3.45].

[68] See, eg Justice, *Our Fettered Ombudsman* (London 1977), pp 16–19; Justice-All Souls Committee, *Administrative Justice: Some Necessary Reforms* (London 1988), pp 88–9.

therefore recommended the abolition of the filter—a step supported by the Commons Public Administration Select Committee[69]—arguing that the constitutional concerns just outlined could adequately be met by *permitting*, rather than *requiring all*, complaints to be routed via MPs, and by obliging the Ombudsman to keep MPs informed of her work and her findings.[70]

Persistent criticism notwithstanding,[71] the filter remains. The Ombudsman favours abolition of the filter; a 2011 consultation report by the Parliamentary Ombudsman found that there was overwhelming support for removing the MP filter.[72] In the Ombudsman's view, the filter is out of date and restricts the Ombudsman's ability to provide a fully accessible service to complainants. At the same time, the Ombudsman's relationship with Parliament is critical to its success: the challenge therefore is to convince MPs that direct access can be achieved without disturbing the relationship between the Ombudsman and Parliament, and between an MP and their constituent. For instance, one option is a dual-track complaint procedure enabling individuals to complain directly to the Ombudsman or an MP.[73] To meet concerns that removing the filter excludes MPs from involvement with their constituents' complaints, the Ombudsman could provide MPs with annual information about what bodies their constituents had complained about to the Ombudsman and what the outcomes were.[74] The government has refused to remove the MP filter, but it recognises the importance of accessibility. Accordingly, the new PSO will operate a 'no wrong door' policy by referring individuals and possibly transferring their complaints to other complaint bodies.[75]

A more radical proposal would be to empower the Ombudsman to undertake proactive or 'own-initiative' investigations, that is, to inquire into possible instances of maladministration even though no one has complained. The Public Services Ombudsman for Wales is to obtain this power.[76] Other Ombudsmen schemes elsewhere, such as the Republic of Ireland, can already undertake own-initiative investigations and it is not difficult to understand why. Some people may be unable or unwilling to complain— for instance, people detained in prisons or in psychiatric hospitals, or children in immigration custody—yet nonetheless suffer from governmental maladministration without effective redress. As a former Ombudsman has explained: '[I]n the absence of a specific individual complaint, the Ombudsman should not stand idly by. The

---

[69] House of Commons Public Administration Select Committee, *Ombudsman Issues* (HC 448 2002–03).

[70] The Cabinet Office Review, [3.43]–[3.51].

[71] The House of Commons Public Administration Select Committee reiterated its opposition to the filter and called for its removal in 2009: *Parliament and the Ombudsman* (HC 107 2009–10), [2]–[6].

[72] PHSO, *Report on the Consultation on Direct Access to the Parliamentary Ombudsman* (London 2011).

[73] Law Commission, *Public Services Ombudsmen* (HC 1136 2010–12), [3.98].

[74] PHSO, *Report on the Consultation on Direct Access to the Parliamentary Ombudsman* (London 2011), p 24.

[75] House of Commons Public Administration Select Committee, *Parliament and the Ombudsman: Further Report* (HC 471 2009–10), 4; Cabinet Office, *A Public Service Ombudsman: Government Response to Consultation* (London 2015), p 13.

[76] National Assembly for Wales Finance Committee, *Consideration of Powers: Public Services Ombudsman for Wales* (Cardiff 2015), pp 21–32.

ability from time to time, not all the time, to seize the initiative, to catch the whiff of a scandal and run with it, is now a necessity not a luxury, especially if social justice is to reach some of the most vulnerable and marginalised people in society.'[77] However, the UK government has rejected the power of 'own initiative' investigations on the ground that it could detract from the Ombudsman's role in putting things right for the individual citizen. But the government has proposed that the new PSO will be able to conduct joint investigations with others, widen the scope of investigation where injustice may have suffered as a result of similar maladministration elsewhere, share its reports with others to ensure findings and recommendations feed into the appropriate oversight mechanisms, and have wider powers to publish the outcomes of its investigations and on any general themes.[78]

Reform of the process by which the Ombudsman receives complaints needs to be addressed. There is also a need for active parliamentary engagement, support, and interest in the Ombudsman's work. The support of MPs is key to the independence, authority, and effectiveness of the Parliamentary Ombudsman and this is best achieved through the Ombudsman's relationship with the Public Administration Select Committee and parliamentary consideration of the Ombudsman's reports. For instance, the Public Administration Select Committee could undertake more follow-up hearings on Ombudsman investigations and develop a similar relationship as exists between the National Audit Office and the House of Commons Public Accounts Committee.[79] To enhance parliamentary interest in the Ombudsman's work, the Public Administration Select Committee has suggested that parliamentary rules should be altered in order to facilitate a debate whenever the Ombudsman issues a report under s 10(3) of the PCA 1967 drawing Parliament's attention to the government's failure adequately to remedy injustice identified by the Ombudsman.[80] This recommendation was rejected by the then government,[81] although there is, as we saw in Chapter 10,[82] now greater scope for backbench MPs to trigger debates—a power that could be used to force discussion of government intransigence in the face of the Ombudsman's recommendations.

> **Q** Should the MP filter be dropped? If it were, what practical steps, if any, should be taken in order to meet the Ombudsman's concerns set out in this section?

---

[77] Ann Abraham, 'The Parliamentary Ombudsman and Administrative Justice: Shaping the Next 50 Years', JUSTICE Tom Sargant Memorial Annual Lecture, London, 13 October 2011.

[78] Cabinet Office, *A Public Service Ombudsman: Government Response to Consultation* (London 2015), p 20.

[79] See Chapter 10, section 6.1. After the publication of a National Audit Office (NAO) value for money report, the Public Accounts Committee (PAC) undertakes a follow-up inquiry and summons civil servants; the NAO will be present at the PAC evidence sessions. By contrast, follow-up inquiries by the Public Administration Select Committee on Ombudsman investigations do occur, but are far from the norm. Instituting a similar procedure could raise the profile and authority of the Ombudsman within government.

[80] House of Commons Public Administration Select Committee, HC 107, [12].

[81] House of Commons Public Administration Select Committee, *Parliament and the Ombudsman: Further Report* (HC 471 2009–10).

[82] See Chapter 10, section 5.4.

5.3 **Ombudsmen within the administrative justice system**

What of the Ombudsman's relationship with other parts of the administrative justice system, such as courts and tribunals? Two sets of questions arise: in formal terms, how do the jurisdictions of ombudsmen relate to those of courts and tribunals? And, more broadly, how does the role of ombudsmen compare with that of courts and tribunals?

The answer to the latter question is that although the Ombudsman was created partly in response to concerns in the 1960s about the unwillingness of courts to undertake rigorous judicial review[83]—a concern that is hardly felt today—the role of ombudsmen is largely complementary to that of other administrative justice institutions. In other words, ombudsmen bring something distinctive to the table, and do not simply replicate the work of courts and tribunals. There is certainly an overlap between the types of complaint that may be investigated by the Ombudsman and those that can be subjected to judicial review, but the two mechanisms differ markedly in several respects.[84]

First, as we have already seen in relation to the 'debt of honour' case, the Ombudsman applies a *broader concept of good administration* than the courts, such that she is able to deal with allegations—of rudeness, delay, general incompetence—that may not rob an administrative act of legality. Second, in contrast to making a claim for judicial review, complaining to the Ombudsman *costs nothing*. Third, the Ombudsman's *approach* is very different from that of the Administrative Court: she adopts an inquisitorial style that differs radically from the adversarialism of court proceedings; and whereas the Administrative Court is rarely willing or able to resolve disputes of fact, the Ombudsman readily and expertly does so. Fourth, as noted earlier, the Ombudsman is able to take a *broader view*: whereas courts (and tribunals) are principally concerned with resolving the dispute before them, the Ombudsman can step back with a view to identifying systemic failures and identifying how administrative practice should be improved in light of them.

The largely complementary role of ombudsmen, on the one hand, and courts and tribunals, on the other, means that the answer to our other question—about their respective jurisdictions—reveals something of a puzzle. Section 5(2) of the PCA 1967 says that the Parliamentary Ombudsman 'shall not conduct an investigation' when the person concerned has either a right of appeal to a tribunal or a remedy by way of court proceedings; equivalent provision is made in respect of the other public services ombudsmen.[85] If the Ombudsman's role is largely complementary to that of other institutions, why make such provision? One reason may be to shield ombudsmen from an unmanageable workload by treating them as a remedy of final resort—although workload-related problems are hardly an unknown phenomenon in other

---

[83] See Bradley, 'The Role of Ombudsmen in Relation to the Protection of Citizens' Rights' [1980] CLJ 304, 309.

[84] Bradley at 324–9.

[85] HSCA 1993, s 4(1); LGA 1974, s 26(6); SPSOA 2002, s 7(8); PSO(W)A 2005, s 9(1); PSOA(NI) 2016, s 21.

parts of the administrative justice system. The position can better be understood once it is recognised that the prohibition on ombudsmen taking on cases that could be pursued in other ways is not an absolute one. Section 5(2) of the 1967 Act—like equivalent provisions in the legislation concerning other ombudsmen[86]—contains the proviso that the Ombudsman may nevertheless investigate 'if satisfied that in the particular circumstances it is not reasonable to expect' the person concerned to pursue his or her complaint via tribunal or court proceedings. The question that ombudsmen must ask themselves when exercising this discretion is not whether legal proceedings would succeed, but whether 'the court of law is an appropriate forum for investigating the subject matter of the complaint'.[87] It might, for example, be unreasonable to expect someone to resort to judicial review if the cost of doing so would, in the circumstances, be prohibitively high, or if the case raises complex disputes of fact that the Ombudsman is more likely than the Administrative Court to be able to resolve. In practice, the Ombudsman tends to exercise her discretion generously, taking on investigations into complaints that could have been pursued via judicial review.[88]

What the legislation provides is a crude system of triage, whereby the ombudsmen, by exercising their discretion whether to investigate notwithstanding the availability of other remedies, are able in effect to direct cases to the most appropriate administrative justice institution. The system, though, is crude in the sense that it is not always apparent before an investigation is under way which institution that is. For that reason, the Law Commission has suggested that it should be possible for ombudsmen to refer cases to courts—and vice versa—when, in the course of an investigation or hearing, it becomes clear that the other institution would be better able to deal with the matter concerned.[89]

6. Investigations

The flowchart in Figure 15.4 indicates the range of questions that need to be considered in relation to whether the Ombudsman may investigate a given matter; if so, whether she will, in her discretion, undertake an investigation; and, if so, what that investigation, and its aftermath, is liable to entail.[90]

---

[86] HSCA 1993, s 4(1); LGA 1974, s 26(6); SPSOA 2002, s 7(8); PSO(W)A 2005, s 9(2); PSOA(NI) 2016, s 23(3)(a).

[87] *R v Commissioner for Local Administration, ex p Croydon London Borough Council* [1989] 1 All ER 1033, 1044, *per* Woolf J.

[88] The exercise of the Ombudsman's discretion in this regard is, however, subject to judicial review: *R v Commissioner for Local Administration, ex p Croydon London Borough Council* [1989] 1 All ER 1033.

[89] Law Commission, *Administrative Redress: Public Bodies and the Citizen. A Consultation Paper* (Law Com CP No 187 2008), ch 5; Law Commission, *Administrative Redress: Public Bodies and the Citizen* (Law Com No 322 2010), [5.89]–[5.91]. See also Kirkham, *The Parliamentary Ombudsman: Withstanding the Test of Time* (HC 421 2006–07), p 11.

[90] Figure 15.4 is concerned specifically with the Parliamentary Ombudsman, although most aspects of it (the obvious exception being the MP filter) apply to the other public sector ombudsmen.

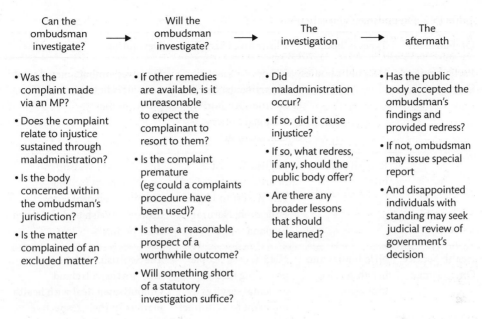

Figure 15.4 Ombudsman flowchart

6.1 **Bodies subject to investigation**

We have seen elsewhere in this book that, in several contexts, it has proven very diffi-cult indeed for legislatures and courts to fashion coherent tests for what should count as a 'public' body or authority.[91] No such difficulties arise in relation to the legisla-tion conferring jurisdiction upon public sector ombudsmen in the UK. Rather than attempting to lay down a general definition of the type of bodies falling within that jurisdiction, the legislation simply lists each institution that is subject to investiga-tion by the relevant ombudsman. So, for example, the Parliamentary Ombudsman is authorised to investigate complaints against only those bodies listed in Sch 2 of the 1967 Act.[92] This makes for a cumbersome system—every time a public body is created, abolished, or subject to a change of name, the list must be amended—but it at least results in clarity. Names can be added, removed, or altered via secondary legislation.[93] The lists of bodies subject to each ombudsman's jurisdiction can be found in the relevant legislation.[94] The length of many of those lists precludes their reproduction in this book; however, Figure 15.6 provides a broad indication, together with some illustrative examples, of the types of body subject to the various ombudsmen's jurisdictions.

---

[91] See Chapter 8, section 3.2.5; Chapter 13, section 2.2.3; and Chapter 18, section 3.5.
[92] PCA 1967, s 4(1).   [93] PCA 1967, s 4(2).
[94] PCA 1967, Sch 2; HSCA 1993, ss 2–2B; LGA 1974, s 25; SPSOA 2002, Sch 2; PSO(W)A 2005, Sch 3; PSOA(NI) 2016, Sch 3.

Table 15.2 Ombudsmen's jurisdictions

Ombudsman	Types of bodies	Illustrative examples	Devolution
Parliamentary Ombudsman	UK public bodies	UK government departments; Civil Aviation Authority; National Lottery Commission	Devolved ombudsmen do not have jurisdiction over UK public bodies*
	English public bodies	English Tourist Board; Director of Fair Access to Higher Education; Natural England	The Scottish, Welsh, and Northern Ireland Ombudsmen deal with Scottish, Welsh and Northern Irish bodies
Health Service Ombudsman	NHS bodies and health service providers	NHS Trusts; people providing medical or dental services pursuant to a contract with an NHS body	The Scottish, Welsh, and Northern Ireland Ombudsmen deal with health matters in their respective parts of the country
Local Government Ombudsman	Local authorities and certain other local bodies	Local authorities; National Park authorities; fire and police authorities	The Scottish, Welsh, and Northern Ireland Ombudsmen deal with local government matters in their respective parts of the country

*An exception concerns 'cross-border public authorities'—a special category over which devolved ombudsmen have jurisdiction to the extent that their actions pertain to a devolved part of the country.

6.2 **Excluded matters**

Even if the *body* to which the complaint relates is one falling within the relevant ombudsman's jurisdiction, he or she will be unable to investigate if it relates to an excluded *matter*.[95] The matters excluded from each ombudsman's jurisdiction vary. Those excluded from the Parliamentary Ombudsman's jurisdiction are set out in Sch 3 to the 1967 Act. They include matters certified by a Minister to affect international relations, the commencement or conduct of civil or criminal proceedings, and the grant of honours.

One exclusion—matters concerning 'contractual or commercial transactions' by public bodies—is particularly controversial for two reasons.[96] First, the effects of such transactions may be considerable. For example, they may involve very large amounts of public money, or they may have a particularly severe impact on given individuals.[97]

---

[95] PCA 1967, s 5(3); LGA 1974, s 26(8); SPSOA 2002, s 8; PSO(W)A 2005, s 10; PSOA(NI) 2016, ss. 20–2 and Sch 5.

[96] PCA 1967, Sch 3, para 9. The Welsh Public Services Ombudsman is not subject to this exclusion.

[97] Clothier, 'The Value of an Ombudsman' [1986] PL 204, 205, 210–11.

Second, not only are the consequences of commercial and contractual decisions potentially *serious*, but the use of such arrangements, such as the contracting out of service provision, has also become increasingly *common*,[98] meaning that their exclusion from the Ombudsman's purview represents a more far-reaching exclusion than was once the case. Although s 5(1) of the 1967 Act allows the Ombudsman to investigate action taken 'on behalf of', as well as 'by', the public bodies listed in Sch 2, thus raising the possibility of an investigation into the conduct of a commercial body providing government services to the public under contract, the point remains that the exclusion of contractual or commercial transactions by public bodies makes it impossible for the Ombudsman to investigate the propriety of decisions to make such arrangements in the first place. Thus, for example, if the government were to award a multimillion-pound contract to a given company that turns out to be incompetent, the Ombudsman would be able to investigate the company's conduct, but not the prior decision to engage it.

> **Q** Is this position acceptable? What justifications might be advanced for retaining the exclusion relating to contractual and commercial matters?

6.3 Maladministration

The concept of maladministration is central to the role of the Parliamentary Ombudsman. First, it determines the scope of the Ombudsman's jurisdiction: subject to one exception,[99] the Ombudsman can only investigate complaints from those who claim to have sustained 'injustice in consequence of maladministration'.[100] Second, whether maladministration has occurred—and whether injustice has been sustained as a result—is the key focus of ombudsman investigations. Maladministration is also central to all ombudsmen schemes, although many allow investigation into a 'failure in a service' or 'failure to provide a service'.[101] What, then, is 'maladministration'?

Maladministration is not defined in statute. The reason why is not hard to fathom. Flexibility is often a virtue. We do know what is *not* meant by maladministration: nothing in the 1967 Act authorises or requires the Ombudsman to 'question the *merits* of a decision taken without maladministration',[102] while the other ombudsmen schemes make similar provision.[103] The implication, then, is that maladministration

---

[98] See Chapter 4, section 4.5.

[99] The Ombudsman may investigate, without reference to whether maladministration has occurred, an allegation of non-performance of certain duties owed to victims of sexual or violent offences: PCA 1967, s 5(1A)–(1C).

[100] PCA 1967, s 5(1)(a).   [101] HSCA 1993, s 3(1); LGA 1974, s 26(1); PSO(W)A 2005, s 7(1).

[102] PCA 1967, s 12(3) (emphasis added).

[103] HSCA 1993, s 3(4)–(6) (subject to a proviso concerning the merits of decisions taken in the exercise of clinical judgement: s 3(7)); LGA 1974, s 34(3); SPSOA 2002, s 7(1) (subject to an exception concerning the merits of decisions involving clinical judgement: s 7(2)); PSO(W)A 2005, s 11(1) (subject to a similar exception: s 11(2)); PSOA(NI) 2016, s 23.

is concerned with the decision-making *process*, not with the substantive *merits* of administrative acts and decisions. This type of strict formalism—familiar to administrative lawyers—results in difficult, if not impossible, distinctions. But beneath the surface, such categories can often be used flexibly to achieve the desired end.

While the legislation establishing the Ombudsman did not define maladministration, the responsible Minister provided an indicative list—the 'Crossman catalogue'—of the sort of things covered by the concept: '[B]ias, neglect, inattention, delay, incompetence, inaptitude, perversity, turpitude, arbitrariness and so on.'[104] By 1993, the world had moved on. Maladministration now included administrative failures such as rudeness, unwillingness to treat a complainant as a person with rights, knowingly giving misleading or inadequate advice, offering no redress or manifestly disproportionate redress, faulty procedures, failure to monitor compliance with adequate procedures, cavalier disregard of guidance designed to ensure equitable treatment, and failure to mitigate the effects of rigid adherence to the letter of the law that produces unequal treatment.[105] The flexibility inherent in the concept of maladministration allows room for manoeuvre by the Ombudsman to update its jurisdiction in accordance with developing ideas of the standards to be expected of government. Without further elaboration the Ombudsman is open to criticisms of inconsistency, vagueness, and subjectivism—but these criticisms apply equally to judicial review and tribunals and, in any event, are a small price to pay. More recently, the Parliamentary Ombudsman has made a conscious move away from a negative approach that focuses on maladministration towards a positive approach of detailed principles of *good* administration to act as a guide for public bodies.[106]

As Table 15.3 shows, the Ombudsman has formulated six key principles of good administration. Ann Abraham—a former Ombudsman and architect of the principles—has explained that if the Ombudsman is to develop a compelling vision for the future, then it must build on such foundations of principle and take seriously the aspiration of establishing a form of 'Ombudsprudence' that is intellectually compelling and pragmatic, and capable of satisfying at both the theoretical and practical levels. The principles were part of a deliberate policy to shift attention from the ill-defined concept of 'maladministration' to the more positive notion of good administration and to a genuine sense of what 'getting it right' and 'acting fairly and proportionately' might mean.[107]

Q How do the Ombudsman's principles of good administration differ from those that courts uphold via judicial review? Why do you think the two sets of principles differ from one another?

[104] HC Deb, vol 734, col 51 (18 October 1966) (Richard Crossman MP). See also Marshall, 'Maladministration' [1973] PL 32.

[105] Parliamentary Ombudsman, *Annual Report 1993* (HC 290 1993–94).

[106] PHSO, *Principles of Good Administration* (London 2009).

[107] Ann Abraham, 'The Parliamentary Ombudsman and Administrative Justice: Shaping the Next 50 Years', JUSTICE Tom Sargant Memorial Annual Lecture, London, 13 October 2011, pp 23 and 26.

Table 15.3 Ombudsman's principles of good administration

Principle	Examples
Getting it right	Acting in accordance with the law and with regard for the rights of those concerned; acting in accordance with the public body's policy and guidance (published or internal); taking proper account of established good practice; providing effective services, using appropriately trained and competent staff; taking reasonable decisions, based on all relevant considerations
Being customer focused	Ensuring people can access services easily; informing customers what they can expect and what the public body expects of them; keeping to its commitments, including any published service standards; dealing with people helpfully, promptly, and sensitively, bearing in mind their individual circumstances; responding to customers' needs flexibly, including, where appropriate, coordinating a response with other service providers
Being open and accountable	Being open and clear about policies and procedures and ensuring that information, and any advice provided, is clear, accurate and complete; stating its criteria for decision-making and giving reasons for decisions; handling information properly and appropriately; keeping proper and appropriate records; taking responsibility for its actions
Acting fairly and proportionately	Treating people impartially, with respect and courtesy; treating people without unlawful discrimination or prejudice, and ensuring no conflict of interests; dealing with people and issues objectively and consistently; ensuring that decisions and actions are proportionate, appropriate, and fair
Putting things right	Acknowledging mistakes and apologising where appropriate; putting mistakes right quickly and effectively; providing clear and timely information on how and when to appeal or complain; operating an effective complaints procedure, which includes offering a fair and appropriate remedy when a complaint is upheld
Seeking continuous improvement	Reviewing policies and procedures regularly to ensure they are effective; asking for feedback and using it to improve services and performance; ensuring that the public body learns lessons from complaints and uses these to improve services and performance

6.4 **Injustice**

To attract a remedy, maladministration must be productive of injustice to the complainant.[108] If, therefore, maladministration is found to have occurred, it is then necessary to consider whether injustice was sustained in consequence of it.[109]

---

[108] This underlines the fact that, as noted earlier in the chapter, the UK ombudsmen are concerned with 'redress', not exclusively with 'control'.

[109] PCA 1967, s 5(1)(a); HSCA 1993, s 3(1) ('injustice or hardship'); LGA 1974, s 26A(1); SPSOA 2002, s 5(3) ('injustice or hardship'); PSO(W)A 2005, s 4(1) ('injustice or hardship'); PSOA(NI) 2016, s 5(1).

Like the concept of maladministration applied by ombudsmen, the notion of injustice is a broader one than that applicable in legal proceedings. 'Injustice' covers 'not merely injury redressible in a court of law, but also "the sense of outrage aroused by unfair or incompetent administration, even where the complainant has suffered no actual loss" '.[110] This means that 'the defence familiar in legal proceedings, that because the outcome would have been the same in any event there has been no redressible wrong, does not run in an investigation by the [Ombudsman]'.[111] For example, in the 'debt of honour' case, the Ombudsman concluded that 'the principal form of injustice [the complainant] has suffered is not financial';[112] rather, it consisted in the sense of outrage and distress engendered by the implication that he was 'not sufficiently British to receive a payment', having believed, on the basis of the Ministry of Defence's original, unclear statement, that he would receive such a payment.[113]

Finally, it is insufficient that injustice has occurred: it must have occurred 'in consequence of' maladministration[114]—the maladministration must have *caused* the injustice. In the *Bradley* case, which we examine in detail later, Bean J said that this requires there to be 'at least a material increase in risk, or the loss of a chance of a better outcome, caused by maladministration in the individual case'.[115]

6.5 Investigating failures in public services

No analysis of ombudsmen is complete without some exploration of how they work in practice and the type of issues they handle. The process works by filtering complaints (cf the permission stage in judicial review proceedings). For the Parliamentary Ombudsman, the first stage is to undertake initial checks on complaints to see if they can be looked into. The Ombudsman usually expects people to try to get their complaints resolved by the public body concerned and it will advise people on how to do this. The number of new cases entering into this stage has been steadily increasing (Figure 15.5).

Stage two is assessment: the Ombudsman decides whether to investigate (Figure 15.6). In some cases, the Ombudsman takes the view that the public body has already esolved the complaint and so there is nothing for it to do. In other cases, the Ombudsman can resolve the issue without a formal investigation. As noted earlier, the Ombudsman has moved from investigating only hundreds of cases to thousands.[116]

---

[110] *R v Parliamentary Commissioner for Administration, ex p Balchin (No 1)* [1997] JPL 917, 926, *per* Sedley J, endorsing the view of De Smith, Woolf, and Jowell, *Judicial Review of Administrative Action* (London 1999), [1.102], quoting Richard Crossman MP.

[111] *Balchin (No 1)*, 926, *per* Sedley J.

[112] Parliamentary Ombudsman, 'A Debt of Honour': The Ex Gratia *Scheme for British Groups Interned by the Japanese during the Second World War* (HC 324 2005–06), [203].

[113] Parliamentary Ombudsman, HC 324, [204].

[114] PCA 1967, s 5(1)(a); HSCA 1993, s 3(1) ('injustice or hardship'); LGA 1974, s 26A(1); SPSOA 2002, s 5(3) ('injustice or hardship'); PSO(W)A 2005, s 4(1) ('injustice or hardship').

[115] *R (Bradley) v Secretary of State for Work and Pensions* [2007] EWHC 242 (Admin), [2009] QB 114, [68].

[116] PHSO, *Annual Report and Accounts 2012–13* (HC 361 2012–13), p 20.

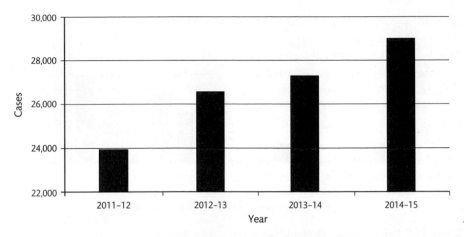

Figure 15.5 Parliamentary Ombudsman Stage 1—initial checks

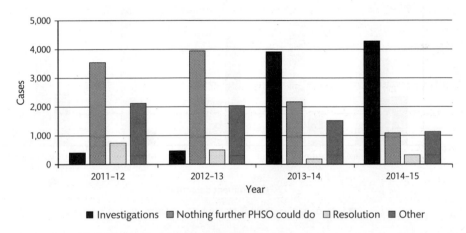

Figure 15.6 Parliamentary Ombudsman Stage 2—assessment

Note the jump in investigations between 2012–13 and 2013–14 in Figure 15.6. This change has been welcomed.[117]

In the third stage—investigation—the ombudsman gathers information from the complainant and the public body, decides whether there was a failure, and, if so, makes recommendations (Figure 15.7). Note the increase in investigations that were fully or partially upheld between 2012–13 and 2013–14. The PHSO upholds around 37 per cent of investigations.

Another aspect of the PHSO's workload needs highlighting. It has been commonly assumed that the PHSO focuses largely upon complaints against government departments. However, over recent years, the PHSO has investigated far more health complaints than complaints against government. In 2015–16, the PHSO conducted 3,861

---

[117] House of Commons Public Administration Select Committee, HC 655, [22].

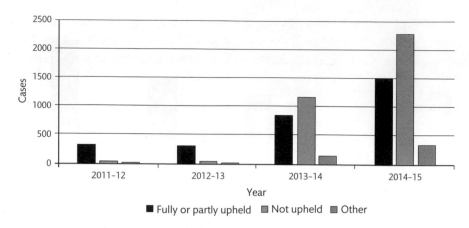

Figure 15.7 Parliamentary Ombudsman Stage 3—investigation

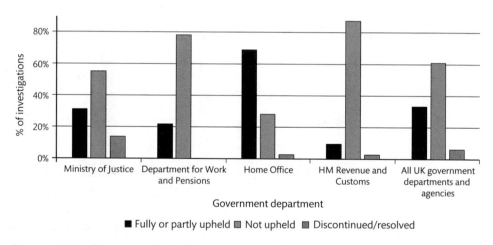

Figure 15.8 Parliamentary Ombudsman—outcome of investigations, 2014–15

investigations: 676 (18%) were into government departments, whereas 3,185 (82%) investigations concerned the NHS.[118] In practice, the PHSO is now primarily an investigator of health service complaints.

Which government bodies receive the most complaints? What are the most common concerns? In 2014–15, complaints about the Ministry of Justice, Department for Work and Pensions, the Home Office, and HM Revenue and Customs (HMRC) accounted for over 85 per cent of investigations into central government. Complaints against the Ministry of Justice increased because, in 2014, it took over responsibility for the Children and Family Court Advisory and Support Service (CAFCASS). Figure 15.8 shows that more complaints against the Home Office are upheld than elsewhere; its handling of immigration matters is a long-standing source of

[118] Data supplied by the PHSO, June 2016.

administrative failure, especially delay.[119] Conversely, the low rate of upheld complaints against HMRC could imply that it handles complaints well and put things right where necessary. Figure 15.9 details the five most common concerns raised in upheld complaints into government departments.[120] Administrative delay has been a prevalent source of complaints.

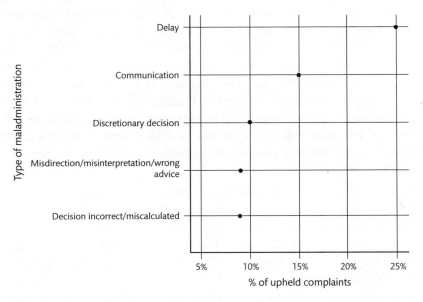

Figure 15.9 Parliamentary Ombudsman—top five most common concerns raised in upheld complaints, 2014–15

The following ombudsmen investigations illustrate the profound impact of administrative failures on people's lives.[121]

- A teenager—D—waited ten years for an immigration decision by the Home Office. D had been separated from his mother after she fled her home country to seek asylum in the UK. He was legally entitled to rejoin his mother after the UK gave her asylum, but he spent the next 10 years without legal status in the UK, waiting for the Home Office to decide his case. This put D into administrative

---

[119] In 2002, the Home Office argued—without shame or success—that because delay was so commonplace, it should not be considered to comprise maladministration: House of Commons Public Administration Select Committee, *Ombudsman Issues* (HC 448 2002–03), [27].

[120] Data is taken from PHSO, *Complaints about UK Government Departments and Agencies, and Some UK Public Organisations 2014–15* (London 2015).

[121] These cases are taken from PHSO, *Complaints about UK Government Departments and Agencies, and Some UK Public Organisations 2014–15* (2015); *Report on Selected Summaries of Investigations by the Parliamentary and Health Service Ombudsman: July to September 2015* (HC 13 2016–17), http://www. ombudsman.org.uk/sites/default/files/Selected_summaries_of_investigations_July_to_Sept_2015.pdf

limbo. Home Office officials made decisions on citizenship applications from his mother and his younger sister, but overlooked his application—until his MP forwarded his case to the ombudsman. The Home Office also ignored most of his requests for updates. The ombudsman required the Home Office to apologise and pay compensation of £7,500.

- A woman lost her social security benefits following failings by Jobcentre Plus, the agency that delivers benefits. Ms K had been given wrong information about claiming benefits when she was ill. As a result, there was a break in her benefit record. This meant that when she started work, she was unable to claim financial support for the transition from receiving benefits to working. Both Jobcentre Plus and the Independent Case Examiner rejected her complaint. However, the Parliamentary Ombudsman found that Ms K had been given incorrect advice and should be paid over £3,000 in compensation plus interest. Jobcentre Plus also used this case to remind employees about the importance of keeping evidence for complaints, and how to identify what counts as evidence.

- A pregnant mother lost her baby in the latter stages of pregnancy after an NHS trust had failed to carry out a scan that could have diagnosed the problem and probably saved the baby's life. The mother was then treated with a lack of care and compassion during the subsequent delivery of her stillborn child. The ombudsman's recommendations included an apology and compensation in recognition of the distress caused.

- CAFCASS gave poor service to a father who did not have direct contact with his children. CAFCASS had been ordered by a court to deliver letters and cards Mr G had written to his children, but it failed to do so. It was forced to apologise and pay compensation for the distress and upset caused.

Upheld investigations into the NHS make depressing, but necessary, reading: they contain incidents of avoidable death, delayed cancer diagnosis, mistreatment of patients with mental health problems, and poor end-of-life care.[122]

The PHSO has also undertaken a smaller number of larger 'public interest' investigations into wide-ranging government failure. Consider the Parliamentary Ombudsman's unprecedented mega-investigation into Equitable Life (considered in section 7.3): some 2,500 complaints, four years to investigate, a report of over 2,800 pages, and ten separate counts of maladministration stretching over a decade. 'Debt of honour' is another example. These special reports illustrate a bolder approach by ombudsmen; they venture far beyond individual redress into the field of substantive policy and legislative reform.[123] No strict formalism here. But, as we shall see, a greater policy role raises questions about who has the final say on redressing injustice and recommendations.

Local government also provides a fertile source of complaints. The LGO deals with complaints concerning education and children's services, highways and transport,

---

[122] http://www.ombudsman.org.uk/about-us/how-our-casework-makes-difference/case-summaries
[123] Kirkham, 'Auditing by Stealth? Special Reports and the Ombudsman' [2015] PL 740.

benefits and tax, planning and development, adult care services (council only), housing, environmental and public protection and regulation. In 2014–15, the LGO registered 20,286 new complaints and enquiries. Many of these were resolved quickly over the telephone; 11,094 complaints and enquiries were referred to an assessment team. Of these complaints, 6,314 did not require investigation because the issue was out of jurisdiction or not appropriate for a detailed investigation. Some 4,780 complaints were investigated, of which 46 per cent were upheld.[124] The proportion of upheld complaints ranges from 25 per cent (planning and development) to 53 per cent (benefits and tax).

The LGO also issues 'focus reports' that highlight systemic issues from its casework. One example: complaints concerning adaptations to disabled people's homes.[125] Local councils are legally obliged to help with such adaptations (eg by installing a stairlift, home extensions, and downstairs sleeping accommodation), which help disabled people live independently.[126] But—no prizes for guessing—administrative failure is never far away. The LGO has highlighted the following shortcomings by local councils: delays in making referrals for a grant and in processing applications, failing to consider properly the disabled person's needs/eligibility when making assessments, poor workmanship and delay in completing works, and poor joint working between local social services and housing authorities. Such failures result in acute personal distress for vulnerable people. The LGO also identifies good practice and helps local councillors to scrutinise their councils.

These examples illustrate the types of issue dealt with by ombudsmen and how they help people resolve their problems with public bodies. So long as there is government, there will be epic failures, and the need for ombudsmen.

6.6 Judicial review

Ombudsmen are amenable to judicial review. Ombudsmen have discretion, but the courts can intervene if ombudsmen overstep the mark. This has been established in the following contexts.

First, the Ombudsman's discretion *whether to investigate* is open to judicial review. (In contrast, an MP's decision whether to *refer* a complaint to the Ombudsman is not.[127]) For example, in *Dyer*, the claimant sought judicial review of the Ombudsman's decision to investigate only certain aspects of her complaint.[128] However, it was argued on behalf of the Ombudsman that judicial review was inappropriate in light of the drafting of the 1967 Act and the fact that the Ombudsman is accountable to Parliament via (what is now) the Public Administration Select Committee. Simon Brown LJ, with whom Buckley J agreed, 'unhesitatingly' rejected that argument:

---

[124] LGO, *Annual Report & Accounts 2014–15* (London 2015).
[125] LGO, *Making a House a Home: Local Authorities and Disabled Adaptations* (London 2016). The LGO has a database of its decisions: **http://www.lgo.org.uk/decisions**
[126] Home adaptations not only improve the lives of disabled people, but also save public money: residential care costs around £29,000 per year, whereas the cost of adapting a home is, on average, less than £7,000.
[127] *R (Murray) v Parliamentary Commissioner for Administration* [2002] EWCA Civ 1472, [17].
[128] *R v Parliamentary Commissioner for Administration, ex p Dyer* [1994] 1 WLR 621.

'Many in government' were accountable to Parliament, but also subject to supervision by the courts, and there was nothing 'so singular [about the Ombudsman] as to take him wholly outside the purview of judicial review'.[129] However, his Lordship did accept that the 1967 Act was drafted so as to emphasise the width of the Ombudsman's discretion; taking that point into account, together with the fact that the exercise of such discretion 'inevitably involves a high degree of subjective judgment', intensive judicial review would be inappropriate.[130]

Second, the exercise of the discretion *whether to investigate notwithstanding the possibility of a judicial review or tribunal claim* is also amenable to review. In the *Croydon* case, following an adverse report by the LGO about its arrangements for allocating secondary school places, a local authority sought judicial review alleging, among other things, that the Ombudsman had lacked jurisdiction to investigate given that the parents of the child concerned could have sought judicial review of its decision.[131] That argument did not persuade Woolf J to set aside the Ombudsman's report,[132] but the case established two presently relevant points: that when judicial review or appeal to a tribunal is possible, ombudsmen will generally act unlawfully if they fail to exercise their discretion by *considering* whether to refuse to investigate (or discontinue an investigation) on that ground; and that while such an exercise of discretion, if it takes place, is, in principle, amenable to judicial review, such review is unlikely to be intensive. This discretion is therefore a broad one.

Third, the courts have shown themselves willing to *limit the scope of ombudsmen's investigations*. In *Cavanagh*, the court held that the Ombudsman 'has no power of investigation at large': her powers 'do not enable her to expand the ambit of a complaint beyond what it contains, nor to expand her investigation of it beyond what the complaint warrants'.[133]

Fourth, the courts are willing to scrutinise, applying the normal principles of judicial review, *whether an ombudsman's decision-making and conclusions are lawful*. These points emerge from the *Balchin* saga, which involved no fewer than three—successful—challenges to the Parliamentary Ombudsman's handling of a particular case.[134] The complainants were aggrieved by events surrounding a local authority's decision to build a new road near their house, the result of which was to reduce its value, and by the Department of Transport's refusal to insist, before granting permission for the road to be built, on the local authority's buying the house from the complainants at its original (higher) value. In the first case, Sedley J struck down the Ombudsman's report, which concluded that

---

[129] *Dyer*, 625.

[130] *Dyer*, 626. As a result, the Ombudsman's refusal to investigate certain aspects of the complaint withstood judicial scrutiny.

[131] *R v Commissioner for Local Administration, ex p Croydon London Borough Council* [1989] 1 All ER 1033.

[132] Although other arguments did lead to a declaration that the report was void.

[133] *Cavanagh*, [16].

[134] *R v Parliamentary Commissioner for Administration, ex p Balchin (No 1)* [1997] JPL 917; *(No2)* (2000) 79 P & CR 157; *(No 3)* [2002] EWHC 1876 (Admin).

no maladministration had occurred, because he had failed to take account of a *relevant consideration*—that is, whether the Department ought to have drawn the local authority's attention to new statutory powers that it could have exercised to acquire the complainants' property. The Ombudsman (who by now was a different person) looked at the case again, and again concluded that there had been no maladministration; again, the court struck the report down, this time holding that the Ombudsman's *reasoning* was insufficient to demonstrate that he had a sound basis for concluding that the Department had not itself overlooked the existence of the new statutory powers. Finally, in the third case, the Ombudsman's third report was struck down again because of *inadequate reasons*: this time, the court found internal inconsistencies in the report that meant that there had been a 'failure to give adequate reasons for his decision that there was no maladministration' during a particular phase of the process.[135]

In the second of the *Balchin* cases, Dyson J defended the willingness of the courts—revealed by this series of judgments—to review the Ombudsman's decisions, arguing that the courts were engaging in scrutiny only of the Ombudsman's decision-making process, not of the substance of the decisions. However, it has been argued that the judicial attitude evidenced by the *Balchin* litigation is problematic for three reasons. First, it is not obviously appropriate or necessary: the rationale for judicial control of government Ministers and other public bodies is to ensure that they are not permitted to govern unlawfully. The Ombudsman does not govern: her role is simply to decide whether or not governmental action has resulted in maladministration productive of injustice. Second, the risk arises of courts usurping the Ombudsman's role—something that would be justified only if judges were in a better position to make the relevant decisions than the ombudsman. Third, undue judicial control of ombudsmen risks the loss of their distinctiveness. The prospect of judicial review may cause ombudsmen to act defensively by adopting a more formal method of working—which could 'put at risk the essential informality and accessibility' of ombudsmen.[136]

> **Q** Do you share these concerns? Do they suggest that ombudsmen should never be subject to judicial review? Or should they be subject only to limited review—and, if so, in what circumstances do you think it would be appropriate for courts to intervene?

Finally, we merely note at present—because we address this point in detail later—that ombudsmen's decisions are subject to indirect judicial scrutiny when people (typically those whose complaints to an ombudsman have been upheld by him or her) seek judicial review of *government* decisions to reject the ombudsman's findings or to refuse to implement the ombudsman's recommendations.

---

[135] *Balchin (No 3)*, [51].
[136] Giddings, '*Ex p Balchin*: Findings of Maladministration and Injustice' [2000] PL 201, 203.

7. Compliance

If ombudsmen are to make a difference, their investigations need to be effective and their recommendations must be acted upon by public bodies. Ombudsmen's reports that merely gathered dust on shelves would not be worth producing in the first place. This section focuses upon whether ombudsmen are an effective means of both securing the redress of grievances and enhancing the quality of administration.

7.1 Cooperation with the ombudsmen

Getting to the heart of matters complained of often requires careful evaluation of a range of evidence—indeed, one of the strengths of the system is that ombudsmen are more willing and better equipped than the Administrative Court to undertake such work—but such evaluation is possible only if, in the first place, ombudsmen can get at the raw factual material.

In the interests of natural justice, ombudsmen must give the relevant public body the chance to put its own side of the story and to comment on any allegations.[137] However, ombudsmen will usually wish—indeed, need—to go further, by talking to, or otherwise communicating with, a range of officials and employees of the public body that is the subject of the complaint, and perhaps of other public bodies, and by gaining access to official papers, correspondence, minutes of meetings, emails, and so on. In most instances, public bodies will cooperate willingly with ombudsmen, granting interviews with staff and facilitating access to material. Ombudsmen may sometimes be faced with more obstructive attitudes, and it is therefore important that they have at their disposal a range of coercive powers that can be deployed if the evidence that they request is not forthcoming. Here, we focus on the Parliamentary Ombudsman, although similar powers are possessed by other public sector ombudsmen. Three points should be noted.

First, the Ombudsman is able to 'require any Minister, officer or member' of the department or body concerned, along with 'any other person who in his opinion is able to furnish information or produce documents relevant to the investigation', to provide such material.[138] Moreover, the Ombudsman, like a court, can require witnesses to attend for examination and to produce documents.[139]

Second, being authorised to require something is all very well—but what happens if those upon whom such requirements are placed refuse to fulfil them? Section 9 of the 1967 Act gives the Ombudsman real teeth in this regard. If, without lawful excuse, someone 'obstructs' an investigation, the Ombudsman can refer the matter to the High Court. The Court may then inquire into the matter, hearing witnesses, and may deal with the person concerned as 'if he had committed the like offence in relation to the Court'. What this boils down to is that failing to cooperate with the Ombudsman is equivalent to committing the criminal offence of contempt of court—an offence that is punishable by imprisonment.[140]

---

[137] PCA 1967, s 7(1).   [138] PCA 1967, s 8(1).   [139] PCA 1967, s 8(2).
[140] On contempt of court, see Chapter 19, section 3.3.

Third, it is worth emphasising the significance and breadth of the Ombudsman's powers to require the provision of information. It is not a power of unlimited breadth: the Ombudsman is explicitly *unable* to require information relating to Cabinet (including Cabinet committee) proceedings.[141] Importantly, however, the Act provides that obligations 'to maintain secrecy' and other restrictions concerning the disclosure of information imposed on 'persons in Her Majesty's service' do *not* apply for the purposes of the Ombudsman's investigations.[142] This means, among other things, that information the disclosure of which would normally be a criminal offence under the Official Secrets Act 1989 can (without criminal liability)—indeed, must—be disclosed to the Ombudsman when requested.[143] The Ombudsman's ability to require the provision of information far exceeds that of members of the public under the Freedom of Information Act 2000: while, as we have seen,[144] that legislation is hedged around with exceptions and qualifications, those restrictions do not apply to the Ombudsman.

The Ombudsman's investigations take place in private,[145] and it is therefore not the case that all information obtained by the Ombudsman finds its way into the public domain. Indeed, if the Ombudsman *publishes* information covered by the Official Secrets Act, that may constitute a criminal offence.[146] Getting the Ombudsman to conduct an investigation is therefore not a way of circumventing the limitations imposed by the official secrecy and freedom of information legislation: disclosure is only to the Ombudsman, although, of course, the information, once disclosed, will form part of the factual basis on which the Ombudsman makes her assessment of whether maladministration occasioning injustice has occurred. To the extent, then, that legal restrictions upon access to official information constitute an obstacle to holding government to account, the powers of the Ombudsman to obtain otherwise non-disclosable information represent an important qualification.

7.2 Securing redress—politics

Once an investigation has been completed by the Ombudsman, a report is produced and sent to (among others) the MP who originally referred the complaint to the Ombudsman and to the principal officer of the department or body against which the complaint was made.[147] In addition to such complaint-specific reports, the Ombudsman is required to lay an annual report before Parliament 'on the performance of his functions under [the 1967] Act' and is permitted to lay such other reports as is thought fit.[148] It is in reports laid before Parliament that the Ombudsman raises systemic problems uncovered as a result of investigations, whereas case-specific reports are concerned with determining whether maladministration occasioning injustice has occurred and, if so, what steps should be taken to remedy such injustice.

---

[141] PCA 1967, s 8(4).   [142] PCA 1967, s 8(3).
[143] On the Official Secrets Act, see Chapter 19, section 7.2.   [144] See Chapter 10, section 7.2.
[145] PCA 1967, s 7(2).   [146] This is explicitly contemplated by PCA 1967, s 11(2)(b).
[147] PCA 1967, s 10(1)–(2).   [148] PCA 1967, s 10(4).

It is up to the Ombudsman—subject to the fact that her discretion is bounded by the normal principles of judicial review, such as rationality—to decide what, if any, redress she should recommend in a given case. The Ombudsman has publicly indicated the principles she applies when making such decisions.[149] Her aims are to secure 'suitable and proportionate remedies' for complainants and similarly situated individuals, and to require public bodies 'to be fair and to take responsibility, to acknowledge failures and apologise for them, to make amends, and to use the opportunity to improve their services'.[150] Applying these principles, the Ombudsman recommends appropriate remedies: a simple apology, conferring upon the complainant a benefit or status denied to him, changes to the underlying administrative scheme,[151] and/ or financial compensation. While public bodies need to strike a 'balance between responding appropriately to people's complaints and acting proportionately within available resources', 'finite resources should not be used as an excuse for failing to provide a fair remedy'.[152]

There is a high rate of compliance with the Ombudsman: in over 99 per cent of cases public authorities comply with the Ombudsman's recommendations and resolve complaints in the way they have been asked.[153] Why is this? The answer lies in the distinctive role of ombudsmen: their mandate is one of influence not sanction. They seek to influence public bodies through repeated interactions. For instance, the fundamental basis of the relationship between the LGO and local government is predicated upon trust and involvement with local authority standards. Ombudsmen are not seeking to penalise public authorities, but to help them learn in order to deliver better public services. The relationship between ombudsmen and government is overwhelmingly based upon trust, guidance, and mutual cooperation rather than legal enforcement.

But what happens if public authorities refuse to comply with the Ombudsman's recommendations? Should it be possible to *require* public bodies to implement the Ombudsman's recommendations? If so, what form should such a requirement take? Who should enforce it, and how? These questions ultimately resolve into a single dilemma: should the decision whether or not to implement the Ombudsman's recommendations be a political one, or, alternatively, should the Ombudsman's recommendations be legally enforceable, if necessary, by the courts? Thus we encounter one of our three key themes: the relationship between political and legal modes of constitutionalism. Who should we trust to see that the Ombudsman's reports are respected and her recommendations followed: politicians or judges? Before addressing this question, we need to consider the current position.

The position in relation to the Parliamentary Ombudsman, like nearly all other UK public sector ombudsmen,[154] is that her reports are not legally binding in the sense that a public body is not legally obliged to accept and follow them. The system

---

[149] PHSO, *Principles for Remedy* (London 2009).

[150] *Principles for Remedy*, p 1.

[151] eg in the 'debt of honour' case, considered earlier, the Ombudsman recommended that the Ministry of Defence should review the compensation scheme the terms and operation of which lay at the heart of the complaint.

[152] *Principles for Remedy*, p 1.   [153] PHSO, *Aiming for Impact*, p 16.

[154] The exceptions are considered later.

is premised on the twin notions that public bodies will generally do the right thing by implementing the Ombudsman's recommendations—and that when this does not happen, the political system, when appropriate, will sort things out. The principal means by which the Ombudsman can encourage government to implement her reports is publicity, whether in Parliament or the media. By placing such findings and recommendations in the public sphere, the Ombudsman enables others to make their own judgement of governmental behaviour and ask government for an explanation if it chooses not to comply.

In this respect, s 10(3) of the 1967 Act is pivotal. It empowers the Ombudsman, if it appears to her that injustice occasioned by maladministration 'has not been, or will not be remedied', to lay a special report before Parliament drawing its attention to the case. It is then for Parliament to take whatever steps, if any, it thinks appropriate to see that the public body concerned puts things right. Only very rarely has the Ombudsman considered it necessary to invoke her s 10(3) power: just six special reports have ever been laid before Parliament. It is noteworthy that four of them have been issued since 2005,[155] raising concerns that, over recent years, government has become increasingly willing to dismiss the Ombudsman's findings and recommendations.

7.3 **The Equitable Life affair**

A recent example concerns the affair of the Equitable Life Assurance Society, a pension provider. It made certain guarantees to policyholders about the level of pensions that they would receive upon retirement, but subsequently found itself unable to pay out at the levels that had been indicated. Of course, the Parliamentary Ombudsman has no power to investigate complaints about *private* bodies such as insurance companies and societies, but complaints were made against the *public* bodies responsible for regulating insurers. It was alleged that the regulators were guilty of maladministration that had caused injustice to policyholders in the form of loss of anticipated income. After a four-year investigation, the Ombudsman concluded that there had been 'serial regulatory failure', that there had been a 'series of missed opportunities' for the responsible public bodies to identify and seek to deal with the difficulties that Equitable was getting into, and that the regulators had been 'passive, reactive and complacent' in their approach.[156] Against that background, she recommended, among other things, that the government should establish a compensation scheme with the aim of 'put[ting] those people who have suffered a relative loss[157] back into the position that they would have been in had maladministration not occurred'.[158]

---

[155] The four in question are the 'debt of honour' case, considered earlier; the Equitable Life and 'pensions promise' cases, considered in this and the following section; and the Cold Comfort case concerning maladministration by the Rural Payments Agency (*Cold Comfort: The Administration of the 2005 Single Payment Scheme by the Rural Payments Agency* (HC 81 2009–10)).

[156] Parliamentary Ombudsman, *Equitable Life: A Decade of Regulatory Failure* (HC 815 2007–08), pp 372–5.

[157] ie a loss compared to the position in which they would have been had they invested elsewhere.

[158] Parliamentary Ombudsman, HC 815, p 395.

The House of Commons Public Administration Select Committee supported the Ombudsman: her report was 'compelling' and painted a 'damning picture' of the regulation of Equitable Life; the Committee supported her call for compensation.[159] While recognising the need to strike a balance between taxpayers' and policyholders' interests,[160] the Committee concluded that the compensation scheme should aim to 'restore individuals to the position they would have been in had maladministration not occurred',[161] and that it should apply to all of those who had suffered loss as a result of that maladministration. In particular, it would 'not be appropriate to compensate only those policyholders . . . who are experiencing financial hardship; the payment of compensation is not a matter of charity but a requirement of justice to redress a wrong'.[162] The Committee also warned that the government should not use a separate report, which had highlighted serious mismanagement at Equitable Life itself, to justify a refusal properly to compensate those who had suffered because of regulators' failure to identify and deal with that mismanagement.[163] It would be 'deeply concerned if the Government chose to act as judge on its own behalf by refusing to accept that maladministration took place'.[164]

Yet, this is precisely what happened. The government refused to accept several of the Ombudsman's specific findings of maladministration (and of injustice resulting therefrom).[165] It invoked the separate report mentioned in exactly the way in which the Committee had said that it should not.[166] And it also refused to implement a full compensation scheme, undertaking instead to compensate only those who had suffered a 'disproportionate impact'.[167] In response, the Committee stated that the government's proposal was an 'inadequate' remedy.[168] The government had also misrepresented the Committee's views.[169] Its refusal to put right the serial wrongs was 'morally unacceptable'.[170] The Ombudsman responded by laying a special report before Parliament[171]— but the then government stuck to its guns. One of the opposition parties insisted on a debate about the Equitable Life affair in October 2009 during which concerns were raised on all sides of the House of Commons about both the substance of the government's handling of the affair and its treatment of the Ombudsman. However, the Chief Secretary to the Treasury emphasised that the Ombudsman's report gave rise to no *legal* obligation to provide compensation and the government adhered to its

---

[159] House of Commons Public Administration Select Committee, *Second Report* (HC 41 2008–09), [17] and [47]–[50].

[160] House of Commons Public Administration Select Committee, HC 41, [47].

[161] House of Commons Public Administration Select Committee, HC 41, [65].

[162] House of Commons Public Administration Select Committee, HC 41, [84].

[163] House of Commons Public Administration Select Committee, HC 41, [49].

[164] House of Commons Public Administration Select Committee, HC 41, [117].

[165] HM Treasury, *The Prudential Regulation of the Equitable Life Assurance Society: The Government's Response to the Report of the Parliamentary Ombudsman's Investigation* (Cm 7538 2009), [4.4].

[166] HM Treasury, Cm 7538, [5.15].   [167] HM Treasury, Cm 7538, [5.22].

[168] House of Commons Public Administration Select Committee, *Sixth Report* (HC 219 2008–09), [2].

[169] House of Commons Public Administration Select Committee, HC 219, [33].

[170] House of Commons Public Administration Select Committee, HC 219, [60].

[171] PHSO, *Injustice Unremedied: The Government's Response on Equitable Life* (HC 435 2008–09).

view that the Ombudsman's recommendations should not be implemented in full.[172] The Chair of the Public Administration Select Committee lamented the fact that the House of Commons had no formal machinery for resolving disputes between the government and the Ombudsman, and endorsed the view that whenever the government wishes to reject her findings or recommendations, it should be required to subject the matter to a debate and a free vote.[173] However, that not being the case, the government defeated, on a whipped vote, the opposition motion calling upon it to accept the Ombudsman's recommendations.

Although, following a change of government, some steps were taken to implement the Ombudsman's recommendations, the Equitable Life affair remains instructive.[174] Reflecting on it, the Ombudsman distinguished between the government's rejection of some of her findings of maladministration and its refusal to implement the compensation scheme that she considered necessary. As to the latter, she accepted that there are 'legitimate considerations of public policy and public purse'—that it is ultimately the government's responsibility to decide whether the general good is served by doing what the Ombudsman recommends. However, the Ombudsman took strong issue with the government's refusal to accept her findings of maladministration, arguing that the government failed to show adequate 'constitutional respect' for her office.[175] This mirrors concerns expressed by the Public Administration Select Committee (in relation to another case[176]) that the government's rejection of the Ombudsman's findings of maladministration raised 'fundamental constitutional issues about the position of the Ombudsman and the relationship between Parliament and the Executive'.[177] The Parliamentary Ombudsman is 'Parliament's Ombudsman: Government must respect her'.[178]

> **Q** Why do you think the Ombudsman's special report, laid before Parliament under s 10(3) of the 1967 Act, did not cause Parliament to put the government under sufficient pressure to accede to the Ombudsman's recommendations? Does this episode suggest that the Ombudsman's findings and/or her recommendations should be legally binding upon the government?

7.4 **Securing redress—law**

Are the Ombudsmen's recommendations legally enforceable? If not, then should they be? When the Northern Ireland Public Services Ombudsman makes a finding

---

[172] HC Deb, vol 497, col 931 (21 October 2009).   [173] HC Deb, vol 497, cols 942–4 (21 October 2009).

[174] The Equitable Life (Payments) Act 2010 established a scheme to make fair and transparent payments to those who suffered financial losses as a result of maladministration. The total amount of compensation to be paid out was capped at £1.5 billion.

[175] House of Commons Public Administration Select Committee, *Sixth Report* (HC 219 2008–09), Ev 1.

[176] The 'pensions promise' case, considered later.

[177] House of Commons Public Administration Select Committee, *Sixth Report 2005–06* (HC 1081 2005–06), [78].

[178] House of Commons Public Administration Select Committee, HC 1081, [79].

of maladministration occasioning injustice, the person aggrieved may ask the county court to require the public body concerned to pay damages.[179] In certain circumstances, the High Court can issue an order, such as an injunction, requiring the public body concerned to desist from any further conduct of the type that the Northern Ireland Public Services Ombudsman has found to have occurred as a result of maladministration occasioning injustice.[180]

The 1967 Act makes no equivalent provision in respect of the Parliamentary Ombudsman. Whether—and, if so, to what extent—her reports are legally binding was the question before the court in the *Bradley* case, which arose from another investigation by the Ombudsman that resulted in the government rejecting some of her findings and refusing fully to implement her recommendations. The so-called 'pensions promise' case concerned allegations that tens of thousands of people had ended up with occupational pensions worth less than they anticipated, and that this situation had come about because of (among other things) regulatory failure by public bodies. The Ombudsman found that maladministration had occurred: the public bodies concerned had given assurances to policyholders that had led them reasonably to believe that their pensions were safer than they turned out to be. Furthermore, those bodies had decided on the basis of an inadequate consideration of relevant evidence to cut the minimum amount of assets that pension providers were required to hold, meaning that some providers had found themselves with insufficient assets to pay pensions at levels that would meet policyholders' expectations.[181] The Ombudsman recommended that the government should consider making arrangements for the restoration of policyholders' benefits 'by whichever means is most appropriate, including if necessary by payment from public funds, to replace the full amount lost by those individuals'.[182] The government rejected the Ombudsman's findings of maladministration and refused to implement the principal recommendation set out.[183]

Against that background, four policyholders sought judicial review of the government's decision to reject the Ombudsman's findings and to refuse to implement her recommendations.[184] It is important to distinguish between rejection of the Ombudsman's *findings* (of maladministration or of injustice) and rejection of her *recommendations*. Rejection of recommendations is of more obvious practical importance: victims will not get the redress that the Ombudsman thinks they should; the government may end up rejecting recommendations because it thinks that taxpayers' money should not be used in the way or to the extent that the Ombudsman said that it should. In contrast, the government may reject findings because it does not wish to accept the blame laid upon it by the Ombudsman; the consequence of this type of

---

[179] PSOA(NI) 2016, ss 52–3.   [180] PSOA(NI) 2016, ss 54–5.

[181] Parliamentary Ombudsman, *Trusting in the Pensions Promise* (HC 984 2005–06), ch 5.

[182] Parliamentary Ombudsman, HC 984, [6.15].

[183] Although subsequent improvements to an existing financial assistance scheme went some way towards providing recompense.

[184] *R (Bradley) v Secretary of State for Work and Pensions* [2007] EWHC 242 (Admin); [2008] EWCA Civ 36, [2009] QB 114.

rejection is less obvious: nothing directly turns upon it, although the more free the government is to reject findings of fault, the more likely it is to be able lawfully to refuse to offer redress.

The argument in *Bradley* centred upon the government's rejection of the Ombudsman's findings. The Ombudsman[185] argued that the government was legally obliged to 'proceed on the basis that the ombudsman's findings of injustice caused by maladministration are correct unless they are quashed in judicial review proceedings'.[186] This would make it possible for Ministers lawfully to reject the Ombudsman's findings only in very rare circumstances. For that reason, the Court of Appeal rejected this submission: Sir John Chadwick, giving the leading judgment, noted that 'if he is prepared to take the consequences, and defend his position in Parliament, in the last resort a minister who genuinely believes that he and his department have been unfairly criticised by the commissioner, clearly has the right to say so'.[187] Sir John therefore concluded that Ministers and public bodies are free to reject the Ombudsman's findings provided that doing so is *rational*. On the face of it, this seems to give a broad discretion to reject such findings: as we have seen, the standard test for whether something is irrational is whether it outrageously defies logic or accepted moral standards.[188]

However, Sir John actually appeared to apply a more exacting concept of rationality, saying that the Minister had to have 'cogent reasons' for rejecting the Ombudsman's findings[189]—a test said in a later case to require the court to engage in a 'careful examination of the facts of the individual case'.[190] Applying that relatively strict version of the rationality test, the Court concluded that the Minister *had* acted irrationally in rejecting the Ombudsman's findings that the government's information had been potentially misleading and that the maladministration had caused some injustice. Varuhas argues that it was inappropriate for the Court to review rigorously the government's rejection of the Ombudsman's findings: he suggests that this risks displacing Parliament 'as the central institution for ensuring accountability', that this runs 'against the grain of the system of *political* accountability created by the [1967] Act', and that 'any challenge to the substance of the Minister's response [to the Ombudsman's report] is more appropriately made through political channels.'[191] From a different perspective, judicial scrutiny was required to compensate for a lack of political scrutiny.

Q Do you agree? Are those 'political channels' sufficiently robust to permit meaningful challenges to ministerial rejections of ombudsmen's findings?

---

[185] Making submissions to the court as an interested party.   [186] *Bradley*, [135].

[187] *Bradley*, [135], quoting from Royal Institute of Public Administration, *The Parliamentary Ombudsman: A Study in the Control of Administrative Action* (London 1975), p 503.

[188] See Chapter 12, section 5.1.   [189] *Bradley*, [72].

[190] *R (Equitable Members Action Group) v HM Treasury* [2009] EWHC 2495 (Admin), [66].

[191] Varuhas, 'Governmental Rejections of Ombudsman Findings: What Role for the Courts?' (2009) 72 MLR 91, 111–12 (emphasis added).

Bradley was a victory for the policyholders, but the practical consequences were limited. The judges, in effect, prevented the government from disclaiming its share of the responsibility for what had happened—the importance of which should not be underestimated in terms of government accountability—but the court victory did not get the policyholders any money. Instead, the government simply had to reconsider its rejection of the Ombudsman's *recommendation* concerning the provision of compensation in the light of the Ombudsman's *findings* of maladministration, which had effectively been reinstated by the Court.

The position as regards the LGO is different. LGO findings *are* binding and can only be rejected if they have been successfully challenged by way of judicial review.[192] For a council to dispute the LGO's findings 'would wholly undermine the system . . . [R]eports by ombudsmen should be loyally accepted by the local authorities concerned'.[193] A local authority wishing to avoid the LGO's findings of maladministration must seek judicial review.[194]

Is it desirable for different approaches to be taken as regards different ombudsmen schemes? The Law Commission recommended that there should be a common approach adopted towards the status of ombudsmen's findings: such findings should be binding unless successfully judicially reviewed.[195] The rationale is that findings are findings of fact and maladministration made by ombudsmen based on their investigatory procedure. Given their accumulated expertise in the functioning (and malfunctioning) of government, ombudsmen are well placed to make such findings. To allow government to dismiss ombudsmen findings with only a statement of 'cogent reasons' unnecessarily weakens the effectiveness of that office. It allows central government to act as a judge in its own cause; given the government's Commons majority, Parliament will be unable to compel the government to accept the Ombudsman's findings. We wait to see what the position will be under the new Public Services Ombudsman.

This leads on to the question of whether it is possible to challenge government refusals to accept not only *findings*, but also *recommendations*. This point arose in the litigation arising out of the Equitable Life saga. A group representing Equitable policyholders sought judicial review of the government's refusal to accept the Ombudsman's *recommendation* concerning compensation.[196] They lost that part of the case. As in *Bradley*, the Court applied the rationality principle: the Minister could reject the Ombudsman's recommendation provided that to do so was not irrational. As we know, rationality can mean many different things[197] and, this time, the Court applied a much more relaxed standard: whether to establish a compensation scheme was 'a matter for the government, reporting to Parliament' and was 'not reviewable in the courts save on *conventional* rationality grounds'.[198]

---

[192] *R v Local Commissioner for Administration for the South, the West Midlands, Leicestershire, Lincolnshire and Cambridgeshire, ex p Eastleigh Borough Council* [1988] QB 855.

[193] *Eastleigh*, 867, *per* Lord Donaldson MR.   [194] *Bradley*, [139].

[195] Law Commission, *Public Services Ombudsmen* (HC 1136 2010–12), [5.115]–[5.133].

[196] *R (Equitable Members Action Group) v HM Treasury* [2009] EWHC 2495 (Admin).

[197] See Chapter 12, section 5.1.

[198] *Equitable Members Action Group*, [132] (emphasis added). The coalition government subsequently enacted the Equitable Life (Payments) Act 2010, which established a compensation scheme.

The position as regards recommendations of the LGO is the same: each year, 99.9 per cent of councils comply with its recommendations, but the LGO cannot actually enforce compliance. The ultimate decision on how to remedy injustice rests with local democracy.[199] According to the courts, it would be inappropriate to require a local authority to give cogent reasons when dismissing the LGO's recommendations: '[T]he only express sanction [i]s local publicity, leaving the electors to determine whether the local authority had behaved acceptably in rejecting any recommendation designed to remedy an injustice to a local citizen.'[200] But this is arguably premised upon an idealistic vision of local democracy. Further, the LGO is in a weak position: unlike the Parliamentary Ombudsman, there is no select committee to scrutinise non-compliance.

There are arguments why ombudsmen's recommendations are not legally enforceable. Such recommendations are always designed to remedy the particular instance of injustice, but *may* also include wider improvements to the administrative scheme, which *may* have wide-ranging implications. There *may* be scope for disagreement about what, if any, steps are required to remedy a particular injustice and there *may* be a number of options, with varying effects on the use of scarce resources, which *may* be limited. Local and central government are both accountable—in theory—to their electors for their use of public money, and resources are limited. Ombudsmen are not courts and their collaborative relationship with public bodies is based upon influence and cooperation. Making recommendations legally enforceable *might* undermine this.[201]

No doubt these grounds will arise in some instances, but not necessarily all. Indeed, in some instances of non-compliance, none of these concerns may be relevant. Is the current blanket no-legal-enforceability approach satisfactory? After all, there is a substantial risk that public bodies can simply ignore ombudsmen recommendations without any comeback.

This does happen. In 2014, the LGO found Tameside Metropolitan Borough Council at fault: it had—wrongfully and contrary to government guidance—charged an elderly women nearly £90 a week for staying in a residential care home.[202] The LGO recommended that the council reimburse the payments, apologise, and pay £250 for the time and trouble in pursuing the complaint. Yet, the Council obstinately refused. The council strongly disputed the LGO's findings and stated that the LGO had unlawfully exceeded its powers in issuing the report. It also—and entirely contrary to case law—rejected the LGO's findings.[203] The LGO published a statement

---

[199] If a council refuses to implement the LGO's recommendations, then the LGO publishes a public interest report, and a further report if the council still fails to comply. The LGO insists that the matter be considered thoroughly at a full council meeting. The final stage of the process is that the council must explain to local people why it refuses to implement the LGO's recommendations.

[200] *R (Gallagher) v Basildon District Council* [2010] EWHC 2824 (Admin), [26].

[201] Law Commission, *Public Services Ombudsmen* (HC 1136 2010–12), [5.130].

[202] LGO, *Investigation into a Complaint against Tameside Metropolitan Borough Council* (12 019 862), **http://www.lgo.org.uk/decisions/adult-care-services/charging/12-019-862**

[203] *Eastleigh*, 867 and *Bradley*, [139]: a salutary reminder that the law in books does not always correspond with the law in action.

of non-compliance as did the Council in the local newspaper—and that was it. The Council defied the LGO and the complainant lost out.[204]

In 2015, the LGO identified 'a small, yet unprecedented, increase in the number of councils that sought to challenge our decisions and chose not to implement our recommendations to remedy a fault'.[205] Is this the thin end of an unpleasant wedge? The court in *Gallagher* may have extolled the virtues of local democracy, but what of the realities? Suppose that a local council, dominated by a single political party, ignores the LGO's recommendations. Who will hold the council to account? Given the low turnout in local elections, how much, if any, influence would the single vote of an unfortunate complainant carry?

There is a case for government and Parliament having the final say when ombudsmen really do make wide-ranging recommendations not merely to correct individual injustice, but to reform whole administrative schemes or to compensate many people. But this should not otherwise give public bodies a free hand to perpetuate injustice and evade ombudsmen's recommendations in individual cases. One option would be to make ombudsmen's recommendations enforceable unless successfully challenged through judicial review on 'cogent reasons' grounds. Another would be to make ombudsmen's recommendations binding as regards individual complaints, but retain the current position for recommendations in special report investigations, such as *Equitable Life*, which do have wider policy and resource consequences.

It is often said that ombudsmen help government learn from complaints. But does government keep its side of the bargain? There is limited evidence on this point. But, at the very least, there is a big question mark over whether government does in fact learn. For instance, what explains the increasing number of complaints lodged and upheld? The answer may be that public bodies frequently adopt a defensive approach toward complaints and do not pay enough attention to them. Another explanation may be that increased volumes of complaints are symptoms of wider issues—for instance, cuts in public services, such as health and social care.

> **Q** Do you think that ombudsmen's recommendations should become legally binding?

8. Concluding remarks

Ombudsmen enable individuals to obtain *redress* against public bodies that have caused injustice through maladministration, in circumstances in which the grievance has not been resolved by a local complaints procedure. They also serve as a *control* function by being able to identify, publicise, and recommend

---

[204] LGO, 'Tameside MBC publish statement of non-compliance with Ombudsman report', News release, 29 March 2016, **http://www.lgo.org.uk/information-centre/news/2016/mar/tameside-mbc-publish-statement-of-non-compliance-with-ombudsman-report**

[205] LGO, *Review of Local Government Complaints 2014–15* (2015), p 1.

corrective action in the face of systemic administrative failure. The Parliamentary Ombudsman augments the capacity of MPs, and of Parliament as a whole, to hold the executive to account.[206] Investigations and reports by the Ombudsman are able to identify and expose administrative failures that might not otherwise come to light; the constitutional independence of the Ombudsman, together with her capacity to undertake detailed inquiries, mean that her conclusions generally command respect. The Ombudsman provides a free service for the public, thereby making it more accessible than traditional legal remedies.

However, ombudsmen schemes have their constraints. They are reliant upon people bringing forward their complaints. Old limitations—no own-initiative investigations—are likely to remain. The PHSO and LGO will be replaced by a new Public Service Ombudsman; this will provide an opening for further discussion about the Ombudsman. But opportunities also bring risks: what is the chance that the envisaged reform programme distracts the Ombudsman's focus? Might the new PSO itself become a large and unwieldy organisation of the type that it investigates? Making ombudsmen's recommendations legally enforceable seems unlikely; but this issue needs watching. There are arguments for greater legal enforceability and there are alternatives to the status quo. Increased and unjustifiable instances of government non-compliance could fuel demands for legal enforceability. Beyond this, perhaps the most practical reform has been taken by the Ombudsman herself—investigating more complaints—with robust follow-up by PACASC, an increasingly prominent select committee. Ultimately, whether ombudsmen can raise the standard of public services depends largely upon those who deliver such services and their receptiveness to complaints and recommendations. Perhaps our expectations here should not be raised too high.

If the Ombudsman is a qualified success, then government complaint handling scores badly by way of comparison. There is a litany of shortcomings, including the 'toxic cocktail' of a reluctance of citizens to complain and defensiveness on the part of services that often undermines efforts to deliver excellent public services, the unwillingness or inability of central government to show leadership on complaints, the all-too-frequent poor quality of complaint handling that erodes public confidence, and the fragmented and complex complaints landscape. If this were not enough, government's typically platitudinous response to upheld complaints—'lessons to be learnt'—often dovetails inappropriately with its all too frequent inability to put those lessons into practice. This is not a party political, but a government issue. It is about how, at a very basic level, people interact with government during their daily lives. Milton's words about the importance of complaints being 'freely heard, deeply considered and speedily reformed' remain as valid today as they were in 1644.

---

[206] An equivalent point applies to other ombudsmen, such as the Scottish, Welsh, and Northern Irish Ombudsmen, who have reporting relationships with their respective legislatures.

Expert commentary
Changing fashions in the ombudsman sector
Richard Kirkham, Senior Lecturer in Law, University of Sheffield

The ombudsman sector provides a fascinating window into the shifting connections between the theory and practice of administrative justice in the UK, particularly in the context of ongoing debates about the appropriate shape of the UK constitution. Some of these connections are examined in this brief commentary.

To begin with, ombudsman schemes are institutional misfits that illustrate the multi-faceted nature of the modern state. Plausibly, the ombudsman sector could be understood as part of the judicial branch of the constitution but in its method and defence of the rule of law an ombudsman operates in a very different way to the judicial process. Indeed, the courts are better viewed as a partner and guarantor of ombudsmen. Some disputes do travel in parallel through both forms of dispute resolution. But, in the main, this is only a theoretical possibility. Complaining to an ombudsman is frequently the only realistic option for an aggrieved user of public services. Further, once an ombudsman concludes an investigation, very few are challenged in the courts. There is now a wealth of jurisprudence indicating that the courts see their role in dealing with these cases as one of respecting and supporting the distinctiveness of the ombudsman model, whilst simultaneously verifying the legality, procedural fairness and rationality of ombudsman decision-making. As stated in a Scottish case, '[T]he Court's supervisory jurisdiction should be exercised with sensitivity to the special nature of the [Scottish Public Services] Ombudsman's constitutional role and function.'[207]

For many, therefore, an ombudsman is best conceptualised as operating firmly in the political branch of the constitution, yet what this means is unclear. In practice, the vast majority of disputes resolved by an ombudsman do not pass the desk of an elected representative and the decisions of ombudsman schemes are invariably accepted as authoritative by administrative bodies. The elected institutions of the constitution acquiesce in this arrangement in part because many disputes about public service are relatively small scale and would not benefit from political intervention. But it has also long been understood that the demand for administrative justice outstrips the capacity of political representatives to deliver, with often only protracted and more sensitive ombudsman investigations requiring serious political attention.

The role of the ombudsman has thus become embedded. Aided by changing fashions in the delivery of public services and a policy-based desire to redirect dispute resolution away from the courtroom, the faith placed by successive governments on 'alternative dispute resolution' has led to a profound growth and diversification in the ombudsman sector over the last 15–20 years. Complaint numbers have increased for almost all ombudsman schemes and there are now at least 15 statutory schemes in operation covering areas of direct (eg Health Services, Higher Education, and Defence Forces) and indirect (eg private social care, energy, and telecommunications) government activity. Commensurate with their role, these schemes operate for the most part independently of the political branch of the constitution.

Ombudsman schemes operate with considerable autonomy. However, to be an effective influence they rely upon government support. This raises the question of the extent to which Whitehall and Westminster is focused on promoting the sector, and administrative justice more generally. No single government department is responsible for the overview of the ombudsman sector. In addition to the diverse range of ombudsman schemes, numerous

---

[207] *Argyll and Bute Council v SPSO* [2007] CSOH 168, [16], *per* Lord Machphail.

complaint mechanisms have been allowed to develop in a random and uncoordinated fashion. The same uncoordinated oversight of the sector exists at the Parliamentary level. The one institution that may have provided ongoing scrutiny of all complaints systems, the short-lived Administrative Justice and Tribunals Council, was abolished in 2013.

In response to repeated concerns about the quality of complaint-handling arrangements across the public sector, in particular with health services, parliamentary select committees have in recent times commendably invested significant energy in demanding reform and improvements.[208] The government too has made some positive moves, for instance with the introduction of a new Healthcare Safety Investigation Branch (HSIB)[209] capable of following-up systemic malpractice, potentially as identified through patterns of complaints. The government has also supported a long-standing proposal for a merged Public Services Ombudsman (PSO) scheme to bring together the Parliamentary, Health Services and Local Government Ombudsmen schemes.[210] But the resources provided for the HSIB will reveal the scale of the government's long-term commitment, and the establishment of a merged PSO will only happen once legislative time is finally prioritised for the measure, which is not guaranteed.

The ombudsman sector also reveals the extent to which governments are willing to tolerate autonomous oversight of public services. Some schemes enjoy considerably less autonomy than others as a matter of policy, eg the Prisons and Probation Ombudsman and the Service Complaints Ombudsman for the Armed Forces. Other schemes have been significantly affected by the coalition government's (2010–15) policy of bringing public bodies more firmly under central government control, alongside recent moves to reduce public expenditure. For example, the LGO has experienced budget cuts of almost 40 per cent since 2012 and is subject to various constraints as laid out in a Framework Document between government and the LGO.[211]

A classic public law issue is the challenge of establishing appropriate accountability arrangements of ombudsmen. There are no systematically applied sector standards available by which ombudsman schemes should operate,[212] potentially leaving a void in accountability which some users of ombudsman services have been quick to pick up on.[213] In the 2016 case of *JR55*,[214] the Supreme Court implicitly imposed some significant restrictions on the ombudsman scheme involved. However, the courts do not ordinarily offer a hopeful route for aggrieved complainants looking to challenge ombudsmen decisions. Parliamentary oversight of ombudsman schemes can be very powerful, but it is also sporadic and unreliable.

---

[208] eg House of Commons Public Administration Select Committee, *More Complaints Please!* (HC 229 2013–14); Public Administration Select Committee, *Time for a People's Ombudsman Service* (HC 655 2013–14); Health Committee, *Complaints and Raising Concerns* (HC 350 2014–15).

[209] House of Commons Public Administration and Constitutional Affairs Select Committee, *PHSO review: Quality of NHS Complaints Investigations* (HC 94 2016–17).

[210] Cabinet Office, *A Public Service Ombudsman: Government Response to Consultation* (London 2015).

[211] LGO, *A Transformation Plan for the Local Government Ombudsman: 2011–2015*, (London 2012).

[212] Members of the voluntary group, the Ombudsman Association, should meet its standards, see http:// www.ombudsmanassociation.org/. Schemes that operate in the private sector are now covered by the 2013 EU Directive on Consumer ADR (2013/11/EU).

[213] Patients Association, 'Letter to Secretary of State regarding PHSO' (Harrow 2014), http://www. patients-association.org.uk/press-release/letter-secretary-state-regarding-phso/

[214] *Re an application by JR55 for Judicial Review (Northern Ireland)* [2016] UKSC 22.

The solution offered in the government's PSO proposal is for the introduction of stronger corporate governance arrangements,[215] a model which involves establishing publically appointed boards to oversee the work of ombudsman schemes.[216]

A final long-running public law concern that is illustrated by the ombudsman sector is the degree to which constitutional watchdogs, such as ombudsman schemes, should be empowered to promote their functions. Here a clear divide in the ombudsman model is evolving. In England and Westminster, a traditional and restricted ombudsman design operates and is promoted in the proposals for a PSO. Within the model, the ombudsman is seen primarily as a complaint handler of individual investigations, with only a limited pragmatic capacity to use the lessons derived from complaints to promote standards in public service delivery or conduct deeper and wider systemic investigations.

By contrast, in Scotland, Wales, and Northern Ireland—and indeed many other countries in the world—the ombudsman is seen as potentially a much more dynamic institution. Whilst recognising the core complaint-handling role, an ombudsman should be provided with specific statutory powers to commence investigations into public services even before a complaint is received (own-initiative inquiries) and to operate as the administrative body responsible for promoting better complaint handling (complaint standard authorities).[217] The rationale for this is that ombudsmen can more easily intervene in circumstances where complainants are unlikely to complain (eg because of their vulnerability and/or incapacity) and promote wider systemic lessons in order to reduce future administrative grievances and avoid their escalation when they do occur. With these extra powers now provided for in Scotland and Northern Ireland, and planned for in Wales, the differences in ombudsman models provided by devolution will provide for an interesting experiment in administrative justice.

The ombudsman sector is dynamic and it is changing. Some of these developments are led by government intervention; more often though the driver for change has been the need for ombudsman schemes to respond to the demands of users and budgetary constraints. It is difficult to imagine an administrative justice system without ombudsman schemes, but more needs to be done to enable ombudsmen to achieve their full potential.

Further reading

ABRAHAM, 'The Parliamentary Ombudsman and Administrative Justice: Shaping the Next 50 Years', JUSTICE Tom Sargant Memorial Annual Lecture, London, 13 October 2011 (**https://justice.org.uk/wp-content/uploads/2015/02/Parliamentary-Ombudsman-and-Administrative-Justice.pdf**)
This lecture by a former Parliamentary Ombudsman provides an overview of the post and how it could developed.

---

[215] Cabinet Office, *A Public Service Ombudsman: Government Response to Consultation* (London 2015), p 9.
[216] See also Thomas, Martin, and Kirkham, *External Evaluation of the Local Government Ombudsman in England* (London 2013), pp 74–82, **http://www.lgo.org.uk/information-centre/about-us/our-performance/independent-external-evaluation**
[217] eg see the Public Services Reform (Scotland) Act 2010, s 119.

BUCK, KIRKHAM, and THOMPSON, *The Ombudsman Enterprise and Administrative Justice* (Farnham 2011)
This book provides an in-depth study of ombudsmen as a key mechanism for delivering administrative justice.

KIRKHAM, *The Parliamentary Ombudsman: Withstanding the Test of Time* (HC 421 2006–07)
This paper provides a historical overview of the development of the office of the Parliamentary Ombudsman between 1967 and 2007.

KIRKHAM, THOMPSON, and BUCK, 'Putting the Ombudsman into Constitutional Context' (2009) 62 Parliamentary Affairs 600
This paper examines the constitutional context in which the Parliamentary Ombudsman operates.

MELLOR, Parliamentary and Health Services Ombudsman, 'The Constitutional Role of the Parliamentary and Health Service Ombudsman', speech at the UCL Constitution Unit, 17 April 2013 (**http://vimeo.com/64628880**)
This is a speech by a former Parliamentary Ombudsman, Julie Mellor, that provides various insights into the practical work of the institution.

Useful websites

http://www.ombudsmanassociation.org
Website of the Ombudsman Association (with links to the various ombudsmen's websites)

http://www.lgo.org.uk
Website of the Local Government Ombudsman

https://nipso.org.uk
Website of the Northern Ireland Public Services Ombudsman

http://www.ombudsman.org.uk
Website of the Parliamentary and Health Service Ombudsman

http://www.ombudsman-wales.org.uk
Website of the Public Services Ombudsman for Wales

http://www.spso.org.uk
Website of the Scottish Public Services Ombudsman

https://ukaji.org
Website of the UK Administrative Justice Institute, the national community of administrative justice researchers and professionals

16

Tribunals

1. Tribunals—an introduction   682
2. Tribunals—their place in the UK's public law system   686
3. The reorganisation of tribunals   692
4. Tribunal procedures   700
5. Judicial oversight of tribunal decision-making   717
6. Conclusions   723
   Expert commentary   724
   Further reading   727
   Useful websites   727

In many cases, when individuals wish to challenge administrative decisions, they can appeal to a tribunal. Tribunals are a core feature of the administrative law project: unlike the courts, they do not merely review the legality of decisions already taken, but substitute their own decisions and, in so doing, administer the law. Tribunals determine more cases than the courts and have, over recent years, experienced something of a renaissance following their restructuring. This chapter considers the constitutional importance of tribunals and examines their place within the UK's public law system—in particular, the recent reorganisation of the tribunals into a new, integrated, and unified tribunals system brought about by the Tribunals, Courts and Enforcement Act 2007 (TCEA). The chapter provides an overview of the principal tribunal systems, tribunal procedures, and judicial oversight of tribunal decision-making. It also critically analyses the overall effectiveness of tribunals as a means of challenging government decisions. Tribunals are both important and interesting, as you will see.

1. Tribunals—an introduction

1.1 **What are tribunals?**

Tribunals are independent and judicial statutory bodies. They hear and determine appeals by individuals against initial decisions made by governmental decision-makers.

In some instances, tribunals resolve disputes between individuals. Consider the following situations.

- A foreign national fleeing from persecution or torture in their home country who has been refused asylum by the Home Office can appeal that decision to the First-tier Tribunal (FTT) (Immigration and Asylum Chamber).[1] The Tribunal will decide whether or not someone is a refugee. There are 10,000 such appeals per year and around 30 per cent are allowed.

- An individual whose claim for a welfare benefit has been turned down can appeal to the FTT (Social Entitlement Chamber). There are around 150,000 such appeals per year and around 40 per cent are allowed.

- A child who has been refused admission to the school of his or her choice by a local authority may appeal to a school admissions appeal panel. There are over 30,000 such appeals per year and over 20 per cent are allowed.

In each case, the tribunal will hear the individual's appeal. The individual can appear before the tribunal in person at a hearing or submit written arguments in support of the appeal. The tribunal will substitute its own decision for that of the initial decision-maker by either allowing or dismissing the appeal. For instance, when a tribunal allows an asylum appeal, it is deciding that the person concerned must be given refugee status by the Home Office. The tribunal's decision will be binding upon the parties unless it can be successfully overturned through an onward challenge.

Tribunals are a vitally important part of the legal system, providing access to justice for a large community of users across a wide range of issues. As the courts have noted: 'In this day and age a right of access to a Tribunal or other adjudicative mechanism established by the state is just as important and fundamental as a right of access to the courts.'[2] People are far more likely to have their case decided by way of appeal by a tribunal rather than through judicial review or, indeed, going to any other part of the legal system. When viewed collectively, tribunals comprise the most important component of the legal system for ensuring legality in respect of the mass of front-line government decisions. One strength of tribunals is that individuals dissatisfied with initial governmental decisions can participate directly in the tribunal process, which is intended to be both independent and fair.

Tribunals have developed on an ad hoc basis in specialist areas of government with little consideration of the coherence of the 'tribunal system' as a whole. However, over recent years, government policy has shifted to ensure greater coherence. The TCEA established a new simplified statutory framework for tribunals. The principal issues that we will be addressing will therefore be the extent to which tribunals now comprise a distinct system and provide individuals with an effective remedy for challenging administrative decisions. However, we first consider the historical development of

---

[1] We explain what is meant by 'First-tier Tribunal' and its constituent chambers when we consider the structure of the new tribunals system in section 3.

[2] *Saleem v Home Secretary* [2000] Imm AR 529, 544, *per* Hale LJ.

tribunals and the nature of the 'tribunals world' today, before examining the nature of tribunal appeals and the reasons for their creation.

1.2 **Historical background**

The number of tribunals increased dramatically over the last century, but tribunals have been with us for some time and are a well-established aspect of our legal system. The General Commissioners of Income Tax—the oldest tribunal—were established in 1799. During the nineteenth century, tribunals became a popular choice of government to resolve disputes speedily.[3] During the twentieth century—with the development of the welfare state—tribunals proliferated. As government established schemes such as National Insurance and old-age pensions which required mass decision-making, it also created tribunals to determine appeals against such decisions. The development of tribunals therefore reflects changes in the scope of government.

The Franks Report (1957) on the procedure and operation of tribunals recommended that tribunals should be informed by three values: openness, fairness, and impartiality.[4] Following the Franks Report, Parliament provided that tribunals should be overseen by the Council on Tribunals, that they should give reasons for their decisions, and that there should be an appeal from the decisions of certain tribunals on a point of law to the High Court.[5] Following the report, the 'tribunals maze' continued to expand and concerns were expressed over its unsystematic nature.[6] New tribunals were established in the fields of immigration, mental health, and education, amongst others.

Over recent years, the government has introduced major reforms to the tribunal system. This reform agenda commenced with the Leggatt Report (2001), followed by a White Paper, *Transforming Public Services*, in 2004.[7] Parliament subsequently enacted the TCEA. The changes introduced by this reform agenda, and their significance, are considered throughout this chapter.

1.3 **The tribunals world**

There is a bewildering diversity in the range of tribunals and the types of issue upon which they adjudicate. There are currently some 70 different tribunal systems that operate in a wide variety of areas that span our political and social life. The principal areas in which tribunals operate include social security; health; education; employment; tax, finance, and pensions; criminal injuries compensation; immigration and

---

[3] See generally Stebbings, *Legal Foundations of Tribunals in Nineteenth Century England* (Cambridge 2006).

[4] *Report of the Committee on Administrative Tribunals and Enquiries* (Cmnd 218 1959) (the Franks Report), [23].

[5] Tribunals and Inquiries Act 1958.

[6] Bradley, 'The Tribunals Maze' [2002] PL 200; Robson, *Justice and Administrative Law* (London 1951), ch 3.

[7] Leggatt, *Tribunals for Users: One System, One Service—Report of the Review of Tribunals by Sir Andrew Leggatt* (London 2001) (the Leggatt Report); Department for Constitutional Affairs, *Transforming Public Services: Complaints, Redress and Tribunals* (Cm 6243 2004).

asylum; traffic; and transport. The broader picture is of an array of different tribunals that have been established across a range of governmental functions and resolve a number of different types of dispute.

1.3.1 'Citizen v state' and 'party v party' tribunals

Most tribunals are required to resolve disputes between a government agency and an individual or business. Tribunals that determine such 'citizen v state' disputes might involve appeals against decisions of central or local government or an independent regulatory body. For example, the War Pensions and Armed Forces Compensation Chamber of the FTT hears appeals from ex-servicemen or women who have had their claims for a war pension rejected by the Ministry of Defence, a central government department. By contrast, valuation tribunals determine appeals against decisions taken by local authorities,[8] whereas the Tax and Chancery Chamber of the Upper Tribunal hears appeals against, among other things, decisions made by the Financial Conduct Authority, an independent regulator.

Tribunals that determine 'party v party' disputes sit outside the administrative justice system. For example, employment tribunals hear appeals concerning disputes between employers and employees over employment rights. Some tribunals, such as the Lands Chamber of the Upper Tribunal and the Residential Property Tribunal, determine both 'citizen v state' and 'party v party' disputes.

1.3.2 What is at stake in tribunal proceedings?

Tribunals have been established to deal with a wide range of problems; they decide a vast number of cases in a large number of subject areas, and it is therefore unsurprising that a great diversity of rights and interests may be at stake in tribunal proceedings.[9]

For example, tribunals operating in areas such as asylum, immigration, and mental health determine cases in which *fundamental human rights* are often in issue.[10] In such areas, tribunals are not merely examining whether or not primary decisions affecting fundamental rights are lawful; they are also determining the boundaries of such rights. Indeed, some tribunals, such as the Special Immigration Appeals Commission, operate in acutely sensitive areas that concern both human rights and national security. Other tribunals determine cases that do not directly raise human rights issues, but rather what might be termed *political rights*. For example, the FTT General Regulatory Chamber hears appeals against, among other things, data protection enforcement notices issued by the Information Commissioner, while the Administrative Appeals Chamber of the Upper Tribunal hears appeals concerning national security exemptions and freedom of information.[11] Other tribunals deal with appeals concerning an individual's entitlements to *material benefits*. For example, the Social Entitlement Chamber of the FTT—the largest component of the tribunals service judged in terms of caseload—hears appeals

---

[8] Local Government Finance Act 1988, Sch 11.

[9] Richardson and Genn, 'Tribunals in Transition: Resolution or Adjudication?' [2007] PL 116, 135–40.

[10] eg asylum and immigration appeals often concern the application of ECHR, Arts 3 and 8, while appeals concerning the detention of the mentally ill raise questions concerning ECHR, Art 5.

[11] Data Protection Act 1988, s 6.

concerning individuals' entitlement to benefits.[12] Some tribunals deal with cases that concern *social rights*, which can be highly conditional on limited resources. For example, school admission appeal panels hear appeals by parents whose children have been refused admission to their preferred school by their local authority.[13] Tribunals that operate in the *health context* similarly determine a diverse range of disputes. The Health, Education and Social Care Chamber of the FTT handles appeals against decisions of various government bodies in respect of independent residential care, nursing homes, voluntary homes, and registered children's homes.[14] Mental Health Review Tribunals review the cases of patients detained under the Mental Health Act 2007 and direct the discharge of any 'unrestricted' patients where the statutory criteria have been satisfied.[15]

The types of appeal determined by some tribunals might appear relatively trivial, but can nevertheless provoke a real sense of grievance amongst those affected. For example, parking adjudicators hear appeals concerning parking tickets.[16]

> **Q** Why is there such diversity between different tribunals? Why do tribunals deal with very different types of appeal?

2. Tribunals—their place in the UK's public law system

2.1 Tribunals and judicial review compared

To understand their operation and function, we can compare tribunals with judicial review.

First, *tribunals are directly responsible for considering the merits of the initial decision*. Whereas the judicial review court is limited to examining whether or not a decision is lawful, tribunals are specifically authorised to substitute their own decision for that of the initial government decision-maker. Rather than sending the decision back to the initial decision-maker to be retaken, tribunals substitute their own decision for that of the initial decision-maker. Tribunals exercise a 'merits appeal' jurisdiction, whereas the reviewing court has a more limited, supervisory jurisdiction.

A second difference concerns *the basis on which the initial decision may be overturned*. Judicial review focuses on the legality of administrative decisions; it normally does not involve fact-finding. By contrast, tribunals make their own findings of fact by hearing witnesses and considering the evidence. A tribunal will then consider the matter *de novo*. In this respect, a tribunal appeal is quite different from and more far reaching than judicial review.

---

[12] Social Security Act 1998, Pt 1. See Wikeley, 'Burying Bell: Managing the Judicialisation of Social Security Tribunals' (2000) 63 MLR 475.

[13] School Standards and Framework Act 1998, s 94. See Council on Tribunals, *School Admission and Exclusion Appeal Panels: Special Report* (Cm 5788 2003).

[14] Protection of Children Act 1999, s 9.

[15] Mental Health Act 1983, Pt 5. See Peay, *Tribunals on Trial: A Study of Decision-Making under the Mental Health Act 1983* (Oxford 1989).

[16] Road Traffic Act 1991, s 73; Civil Enforcement of Parking Contraventions (England) General Regulations 2007, SI 2007/3483.

Third, there are *different jurisdictional bases underpinning judicial review and tribunal appeals*. Judicial review is an inherent common law supervisory jurisdiction. By contrast, tribunals are statutory bodies: their jurisdiction depends solely on statute. Just as Parliament establishes rights of appeal to tribunals, it can also limit or restrict them. Whereas the abolition of judicial review is now widely considered to be unconstitutional, appeal rights can be simply curtailed through statute. For instance, the Immigration Act 2014 reduced the number of immigration appeal rights from 17 to four—despite protestations that this constituted a serious threat to the practical ability to access the legal system to challenge unlawful immigration decisions.[17] Tribunals provide a wider remedy than judicial review, but the introduction and continued existence of tribunals is largely a matter for the government and Parliament. The existence of an appeal right normally precludes any judicial review challenge. Conversely, in the absence of an appeal right, judicial review nonetheless remains available.

2.2 **The overall administrative law system**

It is important to situate tribunals within the overall system of administrative law. Table 16.1 compares internal review, tribunals, ombudsmen/complaint handlers, and judicial review. Each mechanism has a distinctive role. No single mechanism could handle all types of dispute. The challenge is finding the right way of correcting different types of wrong decisions. Each of these mechanisms has its advantages and drawbacks. There are inherent trade-offs between justice and fairness on the one hand and cost and efficiency on the other hand. Figure 16.1 sets out the overall structure of the administrative law system.

> **Q** How do tribunals differ from judicial review? Why do these differences exist? As you progress through this chapter, look at the trade-offs in Table 16.1. Who should strike these trade-offs—Parliament, government, civil servants, unelected experts? And on the basis of which criteria? (NB This is a highly problematic issue: your authors are unsure about the answers).

2.3 **Why have tribunals?**

The traditional rationale is that tribunals are quicker, cheaper, more informal, and more expert than the courts.[18] And because tribunals are less adversarial and formal than the courts, the need for the parties to be legally represented, and so the need for legal aid funding, is reduced. Tribunals are not bound by the formal procedures and rules of evidence that the higher courts must follow. They can therefore deal with appeals in a more informal and user-friendly way.

---

[17] Joint Committee on Human Rights, *Legislative Scrutiny: Immigration Bill* (HL 102 HC 935 2012–13).
[18] Franks Report, [38].

Table 16.1 Administrative law mechanisms

Administrative law mechanism	Legal basis	Institution/character	Function	Procedure	Technique	Remedy	Trade-off
Internal administrative review	Statute and non-statutory	Public authorities/ Administrative	To review primary decisions for case-working errors	Request public authority to review its own decision. Fees payable in some instances (eg £80 for immigration administrative review)	Paper-based review. May include telephone call to claimant to collect further evidence	Uphold or overturn initial decision	Low cost; quick; high volume processing capability, but lower quality in terms of process and decision-making
Appeals	Statute	Tribunals/ Judicial	To determine merits appeals on fact and law	Appeal directly to tribunal. Fees payable in some tribunals	Informal adversarial/ investigative/ enabling. In future, online dispute resolution	Allow/dismiss appeals	Decent standards of fairness and decision-making; more costly and lengthier than internal reviews, but quicker and cheaper than the higher courts
Complaints	Statute and non-statutory	Ombudsmen and other complaint-handling bodies/ Neither administrative nor judicial	To investigate complaints of maladministration	MP filter/ complain directly. Free	Investigative	Recommendations and compensation	Similar trade-off between volume and quality. Ombudsmen far superior than internal complaint processes
Judicial review	Inherent common law jurisdiction	Administrative Court and Upper Tribunal/ Judicial	To review legality and human rights compliance	Judicial review procedure in the Civil Procedure Rules, Pt 54. Fees: £140 to apply; £350 for oral renewal; £700 for substantive hearing	Formal and adversarial	Discretionary public law remedy	Highest quality of judge. Most costly and lengthy procedure. Legalistic and exclusive. Administrative Court's caseload capacity is highly limited

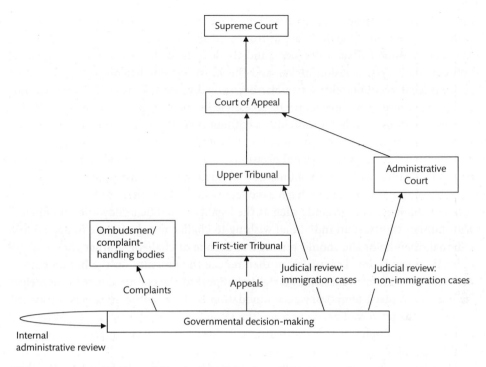

Figure 16.1 The structure of the administrative law system

A central issue is that there are widespread concerns over the quality of many types of initial governmental decisions. Over recent years, there have been many criticisms raised to the effect that the quality of initial decisions is all too often indifferent and sometimes unacceptably poor.[19] It has been noted that 'The scale of the injustice and the cost to the taxpayer caused by poor decision-making are wholly unacceptable.'[20] Part of the challenge is to provide people with an effective remedy against poor decisions. The relevant concept here is that of 'proportionate dispute resolution'—that is, ensuring that there is a proportionate relationship between the issues at stake in a dispute and the costs of the procedures used to resolve it.[21] For example, it would be out of proportion for disputes over entitlement to welfare benefits that, although of immense significance to individuals, might involve only comparatively small sums of money to be resolved through a judicial process akin to that used by the higher courts, which might cost more than the amount of money at stake—especially when the volume of such disputes is substantial.

Tribunals can also provide a more effective means of redress than other forms of legal and political accountability. Government Ministers may be formally responsible

---

[19] See Thomas, 'Administrative Justice, Better Decisions, and Organisational Learning' [2015] PL 111.

[20] PASC, *Future Oversight of Administrative Justice: The Proposed Abolition of the Administrative Justice and Tribunals Council* (HC 1621 2010–12), [18].

[21] Department for Constitutional Affairs, *Transforming Public Services: Complaints, Redress and Tribunals* (Cm 6243 2004), ch 2.

for a decision made by civil servants. But in practice Parliament cannot really hold Ministers to account for the mass of front-line administrative decisions because of the sheer number of such decisions and the length of the decision-making chain between the initial decision-maker and the Minister. Furthermore, the avenue of seeking legal accountability of public decisions by way of judicial review cannot always be regarded as satisfactory or accessible because of the expense and difficulties involved—especially for individuals without legal assistance. The alternative of a tribunal can remedy these gaps in accountability by providing an accessible means of appealing against governmental decisions. Tribunals also provide a buffer for the courts by dealing with large volumes of individual appeals: this prevents the courts from becoming overloaded with a mass of cases, and allows them to focus on constitutional challenges on grounds such as the legality of public policy and compliance with human rights. If an individual wishing to challenge a decision can appeal to a tribunal, then he or she should pursue this avenue of challenge rather than make a judicial review claim. Tribunals can then reduce the pressure on the higher courts. For example, the introduction of a right of appeal to the county court for homeless individuals refused temporary accommodation by local authorities was motivated in part by the perceived need to reduce the number of homelessness judicial reviews received by the High Court.[22] Furthermore, judicial review procedures are not necessarily appropriate for determining some types of issue.

It has, though, been questioned whether the traditional rationales for tribunals—their speed, convenience, accessibility, efficiency, and procedural simplicity—are convincing. Despite the supposed accessibility and informality of tribunals, most individuals who are entitled to appeal decline to do so; appeal hearings before tribunals can also be legally complex and unrepresented appellants can be at a disadvantage.[23] While the intention is that tribunals provide quick justice, in practice, delays may be common.

Governments may also create tribunals for political reasons. For example, it has been argued that the reasons for establishing tribunals created during the early welfare state lay more with concerns that the ordinary courts were unsympathetic to new redistributive social policies and that channelling legal challenges into a specialist tribunal would therefore be more appropriate.[24] Governments might also establish appeal rights not to provide individuals with a mechanism for securing redress, but to enable government Ministers to avoid responsibility for individual decision-making and to defuse political opposition to controversial policies. Tribunals may thus only provide 'a symbolic appearance of legality'.[25] 'The British constitution tries to keep law and politics apart . . . but administrative tribunals inhabit a twilight world where the two intermingle.'[26]

---

[22] Housing Act 1996, s 204.

[23] Genn, 'Tribunal Review of Administrative Decision-Making', in Richardson and Genn (eds), *Administrative Law and Government Action: The Courts and Alternative Mechanisms of Review* (Oxford 1994), p 249.

[24] Wraith and Hutchesson, *Administrative Tribunals* (London 1973), p 33.

[25] Prosser, 'Poverty, Ideology and Legality: Supplementary Benefit Appeal Tribunals and Their Predecessors' (1977) 4 BJLS 39, 44. See also Bridges, 'Legality and Immigration Control' (1975) 2 BJLS 221.

[26] Wraith and Hutchesson, p 17.

The Leggatt Report suggested three tests to determine whether tribunals rather than the courts should decide cases in any particular area: (i) direct participation by tribunal users, (ii) the need for special expertise, and (iii) expertise in administrative law.[27] The first point refers to the fact that there is much greater scope for people to represent themselves in tribunal, as opposed to court, proceedings. Where such direct participation is possible—for example, because the legal and factual issues are unlikely to be particularly complex—the use of a tribunal is likely to be appropriate. Second, the membership of tribunals will usually include those with special expertise in the particular subject matter; for example, some tribunals consist of legally qualified members plus experts in relevant fields (such as doctors or accountants). When such breadth of experience is called for, again the case for a tribunal may be stronger. Third, because tribunals specialise in specific areas, they will develop an expertise in the issues of law and fact raised in a particular area of administration, which enables them to reconsider decisions taken by government agencies. In appropriate contexts, this, too, may point in favour of reliance on tribunals rather than on the necessarily generalist High Court.

Like all policy decisions, the establishment of a tribunal system involves the balancing of competing interests. On the one hand, because tribunals are more accessible than the higher courts, they can provide individuals with an informal and independent mechanism of redress that also combines fairness and expertise. On the other hand, there may be drawbacks from the government's perspective. Tribunal systems need to be funded; government must take responsibility for the costs of administering an appeals process, and for devoting resources to the preparation and representation of appeals. The introduction of appeal rights will also inevitably mean some delay in the implementation of decisions and government must be content to allow decisions to be taken by an independent decision-maker. Such considerations may lead government to restrict appeal rights in certain areas.

For example, when government Ministers want to get tough on immigration, they also tend to restrict immigration appeals. In 2013, the then Home Secretary, Theresa May MP, described the system of immigration appeals as a 'never-ending game of snakes and ladders, with almost 70,000 appeals heard every year'.[28] Immigration appeals were subsequently significantly cut back; only asylum and human rights appeals were retained.[29] The Home Office can now certify human rights appeals as unfounded with the consequence that such appeals can only be heard once the appellant has left the UK. This makes the exercise of the right of appeal acutely difficult in practice.[30] We can only understand these developments by reference to the government's policy of restricting immigration. Appeal rights are not entrenched; rather, they are granted, and can be withdrawn or restricted, by statute when government policy changes.

---

[27] Leggatt Report, [1.11]–[1.13].
[28] Theresa May MP, speech to the Conservative Party conference, Manchester, 30 September 2013.
[29] Immigration Act 2014, s 15.   [30] Immigration Act 2016, s 63.

3. The reorganisation of tribunals

3.1 The Leggatt Report and *Transforming Public Services*

Until the TCEA, tribunals had been created by individual pieces of primary legislation, without any overarching statutory framework. And it was common to find that a tribunal was administered by the very government department responsible for making the decisions that fell to be challenged before the tribunal. A major problem with this arrangement was the impression that tribunals were not sufficiently independent. Tribunals had developed on an ad hoc basis, with new tribunals being established whenever government decided that a new tribunal was necessary. Furthermore, each government department was used to managing 'its' tribunal by having responsibility for providing administrative support to the tribunal, drafting its procedural rules, and sometimes even making judicial appointments to the tribunal. The consequence of this was that, while it was possible to identify tribunals as a discrete topic of administrative law, tribunals themselves did not comprise a coherent system in their own right.

Leggatt concluded that tribunals had developed in an almost entirely haphazard way with wide variations of practice and approach, almost no coherence, and little focus on the needs of tribunal users.[31] The lack of a coordinated approach to the establishment and operation of tribunals had contributed to a fragmented and complex administrative and judicial landscape without common standards for performance or accountability. Leggatt therefore recommended extensive reform: tribunals needed to be brought together in a single system, be structurally independent from government, and be administered instead by a single Tribunals Service—an executive agency under the auspices of the Ministry of Justice (MoJ).

The government subsequently accepted the Leggatt recommendations.[32] Its White Paper, *Transforming Public Services*, signalled a distinct change of government policy with a new focus on tribunals, and a recognition of their crucial role in dealing with the real-world legal problems faced by very large numbers of people. The White Paper suggested a number of reforms. These included the bringing together of tribunals administered by central government departments in a unified system, the introduction of proportionate dispute resolution mechanisms, the improvement of initial and tribunal decision-making standards, and the reform of the Council on Tribunals into an Administrative Justice and Tribunals Council (AJTC). Many of these changes were implemented by the TCEA.

Nonetheless, it has been argued that notwithstanding these structural reforms, the aim of a simple, accessible, coherent, and proportionate system of administrative justice expressed has not yet been realised. In 2011, the AJTC warned that, without sufficient focus, administrative justice might itself be at risk.[33]

---

[31] Leggatt Report, [1.3]. See Adler, 'Who is Afraid of Sir Andrew Leggatt?' (2002) 9 Journal of Social Security Law 177.

[32] Department for Constitutional Affairs, *Transforming Public Services: Complaints, Redress and Tribunals* (Cm 6243 2004).

[33] AJTC, *Securing Fairness and Redress: Administrative Justice at Risk?* (London 2011).

3.2 **Judicial independence and tribunals**

As part of the judicial branch of government, tribunals should be impartial and independent. These two concepts are closely linked, but are not exactly the same.[34] Impartiality concerns the tribunal's approach towards the case before it in the sense of a lack of personal interest or bias, on the part of tribunal judges, in the outcome of a case. By contrast, independence requires that tribunals be structurally and institutionally separate from the executive branch of government.[35]

Because tribunals were traditionally overseen and managed by the government departments the decisions of which tribunals had to scrutinise, there was an absence of structural independence and at least the risk of people perceiving an absence of impartiality. For example, until 1987, immigration adjudicators (now immigration judges) were appointed and paid by the Home Office—yet they were determining appeals against Home Office decisions. Following political pressure, responsibility for appointments was transferred to a predecessor department of the MoJ to ensure independence.[36] It is now accepted that tribunals should be, and be seen to be, more independent of government.[37] The TCEA recognised this point by placing the Lord Chancellor and other Ministers of the Crown under a duty to uphold the independence of the tribunals judiciary, just as they are under a duty to uphold the independence of the courts judiciary.[38]

3.3 **Her Majesty's Courts and Tribunals Service**

While important (at least symbolically), the imposition of such a duty was not sufficient on its own to meet the concerns, noted earlier, about the independence, actual and perceived, of tribunals. A major plank of the reform programme was therefore to shift administrative responsibility for tribunals from individual government departments to a new Tribunals Service. Launched in April 2006 as an executive agency of the MoJ, the Tribunals Service has since been absorbed into Her Majesty's Courts and Tribunals Service (HMCTS), which administers both the courts and tribunals systems.[39] Many formerly separate tribunals have now migrated into the new tribunals system, meaning that they are part of the new structure described in the next section, and that they are administered by HMCTS. The existence of that agency is central to the achievement of the Leggatt vision of 'one system, one service'.

Some of the reasons for a unified tribunals administration—such as providing greater coherence and reducing costs—are managerial. But there is also an important constitutional issue here. Locating HMCTS within the MoJ is important because that

---

[34] *Gilles v Secretary of State for Work and Pensions* [2006] UKHL 2, [2006] 1 WLR 781, [38], *per* Baroness Hale.

[35] On independence and impartiality, and the differences between them, see further Chapter 12, sections 3.4 and 3.5.

[36] The Transfer of Functions (Immigration Appeals) Order 1987, SI 1987/465. Responsibility for the appointment of members of the Social Security Commissioners was transferred to the MoJ's predecessor in 1984.

[37] Council on Tribunals, *Tribunals: Their Organisation and Independence* (Cm 3744 1997), [2.2].

[38] Both duties are imposed by the Constitutional Reform Act 2005, s 3, as amended by the TCEA, s 1.

[39] On executive agencies, see Chapter 4, section 3.9.

department does not take the kinds of decision that can be subject to appeals before tribunals; as the department responsible for the administration of justice, it has a special mission to protect judicial independence. The purpose of the unification of the tribunals system under the MoJ was to ensure that tribunals are seen to be manifestly independent from those parts of government the decisions of which they are examining. As Secretary of State for Justice, the Lord Chancellor is under a general duty to ensure that there is an efficient and effective system to support the carrying on of the business of the new tribunals system and that appropriate services are provided for tribunals.[40]

3.4 The First-tier Tribunal and the Upper Tribunal

Before the 2007 Act, there was great variety in the structure of tribunals. Some had a two-tier structure, with the first-instance tribunal hearing appeals from governmental decisions, and a second-tier body that determined appeals from the first-tier tribunal. Other tribunals were organised on a single-tier basis, albeit with the possibility of further challenges in the higher courts, by way of appeal or judicial review. Structural differences aside, the overall pattern was to have initial merits appeals determined by a fact-finding tribunal, with any further challenges, whether decided by a specialist tribunal or a higher court, focusing on whether any error of law afflicted the first-tier tribunal decision. It was generally recognised that this was an incoherent system with little, if any, logical structure.[41]

The 2007 Act established a new unified structure by creating two new generic tribunals: the First-tier Tribunal (FTT) and the Upper Tribunal (Figure 16.2).[42] These two new generic tribunals are themselves divided into 'chambers'. There are seven FTT chambers and four chambers of the Upper Tribunal. The four largest chambers are the FTT (Social Entitlement Chamber) and (Immigration and Asylum Chamber), and the Upper Tribunal (Administrative Appeals Chamber) and (Immigration and Asylum Chamber). This structure is more malleable than its predecessor: judges within a given chamber can work across different areas, enabling judicial resources to be deployed more flexibly and efficiently. Each chamber is headed by a chamber president and the tribunals judiciary is headed by the Senior President of Tribunals.

The Upper Tribunal hears appeals on points of law against the FTT's decisions.[43] It also has a first-instance jurisdiction in relation to a small number of matters.[44] In addition, it has powers of judicial review in limited circumstances, as we explain later.[45] Another important function of the Upper Tribunal is to develop general guidance for the benefit of the FTT. The Upper Tribunal is a superior court of record, like the High Court and the Employment Appeal Tribunal.[46] This underlines its status,

---

[40] TCEA, s 39(1).

[41] Woolf, 'A Hotchpotch of Appeals: The Need for a Blender' (1988) 7 Civil Justice Quarterly 44.

[42] TCEA, s 3.   [43] TCEA, s 11.

[44] eg individuals can apply to the Lands Chamber of the Upper Tribunal to ask it to modify or discharge restrictive covenants affecting land: Law of Property Act 1925, s 84.

[45] At section 5.5.   [46] TCEA, s 3(5).

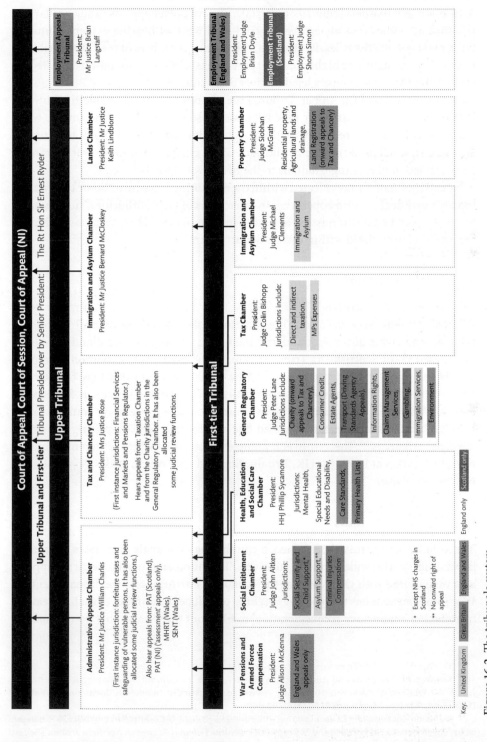

Figure 16.2 The tribunals system

Source: Senior President of Tribunals' Annual Report 2016

and also raises questions about whether the Upper Tribunal's decisions may themselves be subject to judicial review—a point considered later.

In essence, First-tier Tribunals undertake the first-level appeals. They are largely fact-finding bodies that undertake the trial-level work of hearing evidence, finding facts, and applying the rules. By contrast, the various chambers of the Upper Tribunal are more in the nature of higher-level, expert courts that deal with onward challenges and resolve the more complex legal matters that arise.

Both the FTT and the Upper Tribunal are intended to be adaptable institutions, able to take on any existing or new tribunal jurisdictions. So, in the future, when Parliament decides to create a new appeal right or jurisdiction, it will not have to create a new tribunal to administer it. The Lord Chancellor also has the power to transfer the jurisdiction of existing tribunals to the two new tribunals.[47]

Not all tribunals are now located within the new unified structure. Some tribunals—mostly those dealing with appeals against decisions of local authorities, such as parking appeals and school admission appeals—remain outside. However, most tribunals are now accommodated within the unified structure.

3.5 Devolved tribunals

With devolution to Scotland, Wales, and Northern Ireland, responsibility for some tribunals has also been devolved. The situation differs in each country. In Scotland, the First-tier Tribunal for Scotland and the Upper Tribunal for Scotland have been established.[48] The Scottish Tax Tribunals, created following the devolution of responsibility for some areas of tax policy, will be transferred into this new framework. Beyond this, the wider administrative justice and tribunals system in Scotland is complex.[49] Neither Wales nor Northern Ireland yet have a legislative framework for tribunals. Instead, arrangements are ad hoc and fragmented comprising a range of devolved tribunals.[50] The result is a complex picture in which different tribunals operate at different levels (eg UK, Britain, England and Wales, Wales, Scotland, and Northern Ireland).

3.6 Tribunal caseloads

The volume of appeals determined by individual tribunals fluctuates over time depending on the wider context involved. The number of social security appeals will vary in line with the health of the economy. Furthermore, the Department for Work and Pensions has been actively seeking to reduce the number of such appeals by introducing 'mandatory reconsideration' to filter out those cases that do not need to

---

[47] TCEA, s 37.   [48] Tribunals (Scotland) Act 2014.

[49] See Scottish Tribunals and Administrative Justice Advisory Committee, *Mapping Administrative Justice in Scotland* (Edinburgh 2015), http://www.adminjusticescotland.com/documents/Event%20Documents/MAP%20together%20FINAL%202.pdf

[50] See Nason, *Understanding Administrative Justice in Wales* (Bangor 2015), http://adminjustice2015.bangor.ac.uk/documents/full-report.pdf and Thompson, *Structural Tribunal Reform in Northern Ireland* (Belfast 2011), http://www.lawcentreni.org/Publications/StructuralTribunalReform2011ELECTRONICVERSION.pdf

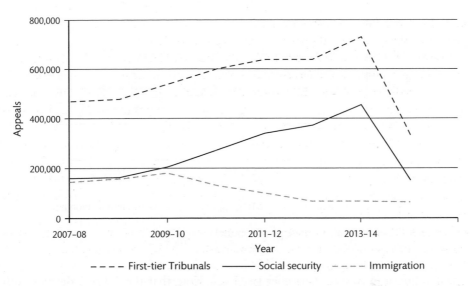

Figure 16.3 Appeals disposed by the First-tier Tribunal

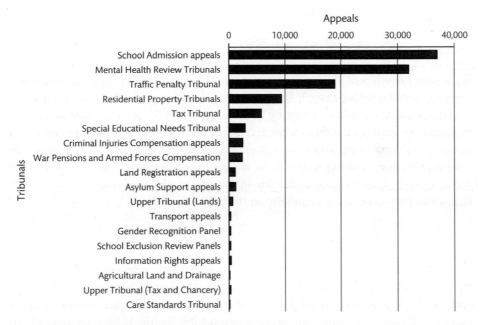

Figure 16.4 Appeals determined by other tribunals, 2014–15

proceed to a tribunal.[51] Figure 16.3 shows the number of cases determined by the FTT and the two largest categories of appeals: social security and immigration. Figure 16.4 shows the caseload for other, lower-volume, tribunals.

Figure 16.5 shows the number of cases determined by the two largest chambers of the Upper Tribunal: the Administrative Appeals Chamber (UTAAC) and the

---

[51] See section 4.1.

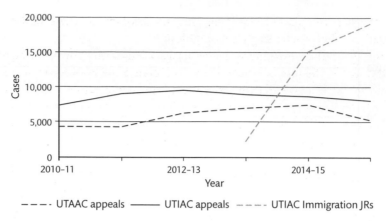

Figure 16.5 Cases disposed by the Upper Tribunal

Immigration and Asylum Chamber (UTIAC). Note that the UTIAC decides both appeals against the First-tier Tribunal (IAC) and, since 2013, judicial reviews challenging immigration decisions.

3.7 **The Senior President of Tribunals**

The Senior President of Tribunals provides senior judicial leadership of tribunals and oversees the tribunal judiciary.[52] The Senior President presides over both the FTT and the Upper Tribunal.[53] In discharging his functions, the Senior President must have regard to the need for tribunals to be accessible; the need for proceedings before tribunals to be handled fairly, quickly, and efficiently; the need for members of tribunals to be experts in the subject matter of, or the law to be applied in, cases in which they decide matters; and the need to develop innovative methods of resolving disputes.[54] The Senior President reports annually on the tribunal system.[55]

3.6 **The tribunal judiciary**

The 2007 Act introduced measures to ensure judicial independence as regards appointments to the tribunal judiciary. In 2004, the Lord Chancellor was responsible for the appointment of 60 per cent of tribunal members, the remainder being appointed by the government department responsible for the original decision.[56] To bring the appointment of tribunal members in line with the changes to appointments introduced by the Constitutional Reform Act 2005, under which judges of the higher courts are selected for appointment by the Judicial Appointments Commission

---

[52] TCEA, s 2.

[53] TCEA, s 3(4). The current Senior President of Tribunals is Sir Ernest Ryder, a Lord Justice of Appeal.

[54] TCEA, s 2(3).   [55] TCEA, s 43.

[56] Department for Constitutional Affairs, *Transforming Public Services: Complaints, Redress and Tribunals* (Cm 6243 2004), [6.47].

(JAC),[57] the 2007 Act places the responsibility for recommendations for appointment of tribunal members under the remit of the JAC.[58]

The 2007 Act also introduced a new basis of eligibility for appointment as a tribunal judge.[59] The purpose of this was to increase the pool of those eligible for office and to promote greater diversity in appointments, while maintaining quality. Furthermore, under the new unified system, tribunal members will also be able to sit in more than one jurisdiction if there is an operational need. The reforms will therefore make it easier for judiciary and staff to work more flexibly across different tribunals.

A distinctive feature of tribunals has been the participation of lay members—that is, members without legal qualifications. At one time, many tribunals were composed of two lay members and a legally qualified chair. This allowed the tribunal to benefit from the experience of lay members with specialist knowledge relevant to the issues in dispute. However, the role of lay membership has reduced dramatically in some tribunals. For example, lay membership of social security tribunals was abolished in 1998.[60] Lay members do, though, still sit in some tribunals such as school admission appeal panels.

3.7 Oversight of administrative justice

Given its size, it is important to have oversight of the whole tribunals system. From 1958 until 2007, this was the responsibility of the Council on Tribunals, which reviewed the constitution and working of tribunals.[61] The Council did much good work.[62] But it was sometimes seen as an ineffectual body with limited powers.[63] Its reports rarely attracted much political (or public) attention, and while government was obliged to consult it in relation to some matters, the Council's views could ultimately be ignored. With the reform of the tribunal system, the Council became the AJTC with a wider remit of overseeing the whole of the administrative justice system and championing users' causes. The 'administrative justice system' is defined as the overall system by which decisions of an administrative or executive nature are made in relation to particular persons, including the procedures for making such decisions, the law under which such decisions are made, and the systems for resolving disputes and airing grievances in relation to such decisions.[64] In 2013, the government abolished the AJTC to save money—despite a Select Committee warning that it performed

[57] See Chapter 6, section 4.1.
[58] Constitutional Reform Act 2005, ss 85–93 and Sch 14 (as amended by TCEA).
[59] TCEA, s 50.
[60] See Adler, 'Lay Tribunal Members and Administrative Justice' [1999] PL 618; Wikeley, 'Burying Bell: Managing the Judicialisation of Social Security Tribunals' (2000) 63 MLR 475, 484–6.
[61] Tribunals and Inquiries Act 1992, s 1.
[62] See, eg Council on Tribunals, *Framework of Standards for Tribunals* (London 2002) and Council on Tribunals, *Guide to Drafting Tribunal Rules* (London 2003).
[63] See, eg Lomas, 'The 25th Annual Report of the Council on Tribunals: An Opportunity Sadly Missed' (1985) 48 MLR 694.
[64] TCEA, Sch 7, para 13(4).

a vital national role.[65] The Ministry of Justice then established the Administrative Justice Forum (AJF) to advise on the oversight of administrative justice.[66] In 2016, the MoJ announced that the AJF would itself come to an end in 2017.[67]

> **Q** Think back over the issues examined in this section. What prompted the reform of tribunals? Will the reforms achieve their purposes? Do you think that the tribunals system is more independent and coherent as a result of them?

4. Tribunal procedures

How do tribunals operate in practice? Are there obstacles that prevent potential appellants from pursuing appeals? What procedures do tribunals adopt? Should they mimic the courts by adopting an adversarial style or should they be more interventionist? What is the role of legal representation? Are tribunals more informal than the courts, or are they adversarial and legalistic? To what extent should they give reasons for their decisions?

Examining tribunal procedures is complex because of the range of questions raised and also because practice varies between different tribunals. The discussion here seeks to illuminate some of these issues with a view to testing the effectiveness of tribunals in providing administrative justice. It is fair to say that, overall, the picture has become increasingly negative: longstanding concerns about the difficulties people experience in trying to access justice have been exacerbated by austerity policies, in particular legal aid restrictions.[68]

4.1 Internal administrative reviews of initial decision-making

We start not with tribunals, but with an increasingly prominent feature of the wider administrative justice system: internal administrative review. In many areas, an individual dissatisfied with a decision must first ask the public body itself to review its decision before proceeding to a tribunal.

Internal administrative review has been increasingly adopted by government as the first step on the dispute resolution ladder. It is widely used in areas such as tax, social security, immigration, and homelessness.[69] In the immigration context, it involves 'the review of an eligible decision to decide whether the decision is wrong due to a case

---

[65] House of Commons Justice Committee, *Scrutiny of the Draft Public Bodies (Abolition of Administrative Justice and Tribunals Council) Order 2013* (HC 965 2012–13). See also Skelcher, 'Reforming the Oversight of Administrative Justice 2010–2014: Does the UK Need a New Leggatt Report?' [2015] PL 215.

[66] See https://www.gov.uk/government/groups/administrative-justice-advisory-group

[67] https://www.gov.uk/government/news/jodi-berg-appointment-to-the-administrative-justice-forum-extended

[68] See generally Palmer et al (eds), *Access to Justice* (Oxford 2016).

[69] See Cowan, 'The Judicialisation of Homelessness Law: A study of Regulation 8(2), Allocation of Housing and Homelessness (Review Procedures) Regulations 1999' [2016] PL 235; Education Act 2002, s 52 (a child excluded from school has the right to request a review of the decision by a responsible body).

working error'.[70] Where there is a procedure for the review of initial decisions, dissatisfied individuals must normally first apply for such a review before proceeding to a tribunal. For example, the Welfare Reform Act 2012 introduced mandatory reconsideration as an intermediate stage between primary decisions and an appeal to a tribunal. A social security claimant seeking to challenge a negative decision *must* first apply for an internal review before appealing to the FTT.[71] This was introduced in order to resolve disputes without the need for cases to proceed to a tribunal, which is a costly and time-consuming process. However, concerns have been raised that people with winnable cases may, as a result, be discouraged from going to tribunals.

In other systems, such as immigration, internal review has largely replaced appeals. Following the abolition of almost all immigration appeal rights, most initial decisions can now only be challenged through internal review and then judicial review. This controversial policy has been criticised. As one MP put it, 'The Home Secretary has decided it is better to crack down on appeals rather than to get the decision right first time'.[72]

Far more cases are handled through internal review than by tribunals, judicial review, and ombudsmen. Here are two examples. First, social security. Following the introduction of mandatary reconsideration in 2013, the Department for Work and Pensions had, by 2016, made 540,700 mandatory reconsideration decisions, of which 19 per cent were allowed (Figure 16.6).[73] Second, another large system: tax. As Figure 16.7 shows, the number of internal reviews far exceeds the number of tax appeals.[74]

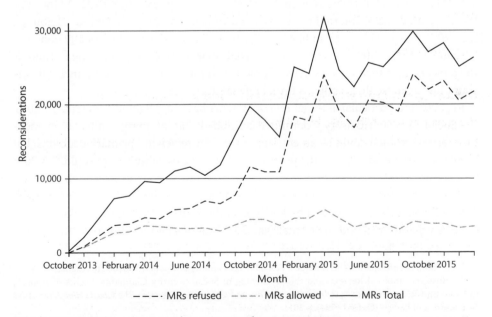

Figure 16.6 Social security mandatory reconsiderations, 2013–16

---

[70] Immigration Rules, r AR2.1.   [71] Welfare Reform Act 2012, s 102.

[72] HC Deb, vol 600, col 244 (13 October 2015) (Alistair Carmichael MP).

[73] Data taken from DWP, *Mandatory Reconsideration Data* (London 2016).

[74] HMRC, *HMRC Reviews and Appeals Data* (London 2014) and *How We Resolve Tax Disputes: The Tax Assurance Commissioner's Annual Report 2014–15* (London 2015).

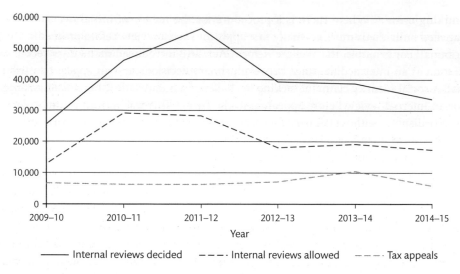

Figure 16.7 Tax internal reviews and appeals, 2009–15

The advantage of internal review is that it can filter out clearly wrong initial decisions more quickly and more cheaply than appeals. Government favours internal review as a low-cost means of resolving disputes speedily. A single mandatory reconsideration costs £80, whereas a single social security appeal costs £592.[75] However, there are drawbacks. Internal review is an administrative process. Unlike a tribunal, it is not an independent and judicial mechanism. It is also 'characteristically non-participatory'.[76] In contrast to tribunals, internal review involves no hearing.[77] There is the concern that such reviews may, in practice, amount to little more than a 'rubber-stamping' exercise that reaffirms initial refusal decisions.[78]

Reports into particular internal review systems have highlighted concerns. In 2016, the Social Security Advisory Committee concluded that, properly conducted, mandatory reconsideration could be an efficient process for reviewing primary decisions, but there was much evidence that the process was not working as well as it should.[79] A 2016 report into immigration administrative reviews found various problems and 'significant room for improvement in respect of the effectiveness of administrative review'.[80] Reviews were being undertaken by low-level and untrained staff. Quality assurance of reviews was minimal and ineffectual. Valid applications had been incorrectly rejected

---

[75] Freedom of Information (FOI) request FOI 4367 (27 October 2015); FOI 106568 (16 August 2016).

[76] Sainsbury, 'Internal Reviews and the Weakening of Social Security Claimants' Rights of Appeal', in Genn and Richardson (eds), *Administrative Law and Government Action: The Courts and Alternative Mechanisms of Review* (Oxford 1994), p 301.

[77] In some areas (such as social security), reviewing officers may contact claimants through telephone calls.

[78] This was the view of the House of Commons Constitutional Affairs Committee, *Asylum and Immigration Appeals* (HC 211 2003–04), [107] as regards internal reviews conducted by entry clearance managers.

[79] Social Security Advisory Committee, *Decision Making and Mandatory Reconsideration* (London 2016), **https://www.gov.uk/government/uploads/system/uploads/attachment_data/file/538836/decision-making-and-mandatory-reconsideration-ssac-op18.pdf**

[80] Independent Chief Inspector of Borders and Immigration, *An Inspection of the Administrative Review Processes Introduced Following the Immigration Act 2014* (London 2016), p 2.

and this had not been picked up. The review system failed to identify some case-working errors. Success rates were lower than expected—far lower than previously successful appeals. Despite assurances that the Home Office would establish feedback mechanisms to ensure that lessons are learnt by caseworkers, in practice, there was no systematic feedback to some original decision-makers or to reviewers and so organisational learning was at best patchy. In response, the Home Office recognised that 'quality has not consistently been of the standard to which we aspire' and accepted the need for improvements.[81] We will see what happens—but anyone could be forgiven for being sceptical.

There is clearly an issue here concerning the appropriateness of internal review and its effectiveness as a mechanism of administrative justice.[82] Indeed, in this context we encounter a fundamental paradox of the contemporary administrative law system. The aim of that system is to ensure judicial control of administration. Yet, for the vast majority of people, internal review will be their *only* experience of redress: most primary administrative decisions are not challenged through the judicial process, but through the administrative process itself. Judicial control through tribunals is being gradually displaced by cheaper review processes, typically of lower quality. Administrative justice is consequently weakened. Whatever the (de-)merits of internal review, one thing is clear: it handles far more disputes than tribunals and judicial review. In other words, it may not much matter that administrative law mechanisms situated higher up the system enjoy additional features—more process, independence, more qualified decision-makers—as most challenges start and end with internal review.

Further, the design of internal review is essentially ad hoc and executive-driven. Judicial oversight is minimal. There is no formal legal framework or agreed set of principles that govern and regulate the range of internal review systems. Should internal reviewers be functionally separate and independent from primary decision-makers? Should reviewers contact individuals concerned to enable them to participate? What should be the scope of internal review? Ironically, the most heavily used administrative law mechanism is the least regulated and least studied.

4.2 Access to tribunals

Are tribunals accessible? Most people who could challenge negative decisions before a tribunal do not do so even though the success rates for those who do is often high. Some 40 per cent of social security and immigration appeals are allowed. Why do so many people decide not to appeal—even with an apparently high chance of success?

There are several practical barriers that may prevent potential appellants from appealing.[83] First, potential appellants might be ignorant of tribunal appeal rights.

---

[81] Home Office, *Response to the Independent Chief Inspector's Report* (London 2016), p 1.

[82] See further Sainsbury; Harris, 'The Place of Formal and Informal Review in the Administrative Justice System', in Harris and Partington (eds), *Administrative Justice in the 21st Century* (Oxford 1999).

[83] See Genn, 'Tribunal Review of Administrative Decision-Making', in Richardson and Genn (eds), *Administrative Law and Government Action: The Courts and Alternative Mechanisms of Review* (Oxford 1994), pp 265–8; Adler and Gulland, *Tribunal Users' Experiences, Perceptions and Expectations: A Literature Review* (London 2003); Cowan and Halliday, *The Appeal of Internal Review: Law, Administrative Justice and the (Non-) Emergence of Disputes* (Oxford 2003).

There is low public awareness of what a tribunal is. Second, there is the cost of pursuing an appeal. Some people may not appeal because of the costs of legal advice and/or representation and other costs of preparing an appeal, such as commissioning expert evidence.[84] In 2016, the government introduced fees for various tribunals, prompting concerns that people are being priced out of the justice system.[85] Third, the complexity of the appeal process and the absence of appropriate help may mean that many potential appellants find appealing a confusing and off-putting prospect.

Another concern has been that individuals from deprived socio-economic backgrounds tend not to pursue appeals.[86] Potential appellants might also be deterred from appealing in light of the perceived lack of independence of tribunals and the perception that pursuing an appeal may be difficult and time-consuming. It is therefore likely that some individuals with legitimate grievances may not pursue an appeal. Ison has noted that 'the total volume of injustice is likely to be much greater among those who accept initial decisions than among those who complain or appeal', whereas Genn has argued that the prevalent failure of potential appellants to exercise their right of appeal demonstrates the very limited contribution that tribunals can make as a corrective to inaccurate initial decision-making.[87]

Appeal rates against initial decisions are generally low, except in the immigration context which is marked out by an exceptionally high rate, which has been characterised as a 'culture of pervasive challenge'.[88] On the one hand, the high rate of challenge by asylum applicants might be seen as a necessary feature of a decision-making process in which matters of life and death are at stake, and in which the quality of decision-making at both initial and appeal stages has regularly been criticised. On the other hand, government has seen the high rate of challenge as evidence of abuse and therefore frequently sought to tighten up the appeals process.

4.3 Tribunal procedure rules

Before the TCEA, each tribunal had its own procedure rules. Such rules were typically made by the Lord Chancellor or the Secretary of State in the department with the decisions of which the tribunal was concerned. This gave rise to problems both of coherence and (in the case of rules made by the relevant Secretary of State) independence. The 2007 Act has established the Tribunal Procedure Committee, to makes rules governing the practice and procedure in the First-tier and Upper Tribunals.[89] The Tribunal Procedure Rules must ensure that tribunals provide justice, that the system is fair and accessible, and that proceedings are handled quickly and efficiently. The Rules should be simple, and, where appropriate, responsibility is conferred on

---

[84] House of Commons Education and Skills Select Committee, *Special Educational Needs* (HC 478 2005–06), [211]–[215].

[85] MoJ, *Court and Tribunals Fees* (Cm 9181, 2015).

[86] House of Commons Education and Skills Select Committee, HC 478, [216]–[220].

[87] Ison, ' "Administrative Justice": Is It Such a Good Idea?', in Harris and Partington (eds), *Administrative Justice in the 21st Century* (Oxford 1999), p 23; Genn, p 266.

[88] Leggatt Report, Pt 2.

[89] TCEA, s 22(1).

tribunal members for ensuring that proceedings are handled quickly and efficiently.[90] The Senior President of Tribunals also makes practice directions concerning tribunal procedures.[91]

4.4 **The conduct of tribunal hearings**

Tribunal hearings can be either adversarial or inquisitorial. A further possibility is that tribunals can adopt an active and enabling approach.[92]

In *adversarial* hearings, the judge is enabled to get at the truth by holding the ring between the parties, while each side presents its own case and assails that of its opponent. To maintain judicial independence, the judge does not descend into the arena between the parties; instead, the two parties are adversaries. An adversarial process works best if both parties are represented, but if the appellant is unrepresented, then the parties are competing on an unequal basis. Immigration tribunals are mostly conducted on an adversarial footing.

In an *inquisitorial* process, the judge takes full control of the proceedings, governs the participation of the parties, and intentionally descends into the arena to elicit the necessary facts to make a decision. The judge controls the proceedings, but at the risk of appearing to favour one party. Few tribunals adopt a truly inquisitorial approach.

Third, there is the *enabling* or *active* approach in which the tribunal supports the parties in ways that give them confidence in their own abilities to participate in the process, and in the tribunal's capacity to compensate for the appellant's lack of skills or knowledge. This seeks to avoid the problems for unrepresented appellants posed by the adversarial approach, but without the tribunal taking full control. The tribunal will be alert for factual and legal issues that appellants have not brought out but which may have a bearing on possible outcomes. It also intervenes to ensure the issues are properly investigated.

In practice, the conduct of hearings varies between different tribunals. Some tribunals have an adversarial culture, whereas others adopt more of an enabling or active approach.[93] Hearings may also vary depending on whether there is representation and on the preferences of the individual judge.

Leggatt argued that tribunals should adopt an enabling approach to assist unrepresented appellants.[94] In such circumstances, tribunal judges may need to intervene in the proceedings more than might be thought proper in the courts, in order to hold the balance between the parties and to enable individuals to present their cases. Tribunal members should do all that they can to understand the point of view, as well as the

---

[90] TCEA, s 22(4). See also **https://www.gov.uk/government/organisations/tribunal-procedure-committee**

[91] TCEA, s 23.   [92] Leggatt Report, [7.2]–[7.5].

[93] eg asylum and immigration appeals are more adversarial. In contrast, an enabling approach tends to be adopted in appeals concerning decisions about social security, child support, criminal injuries compensation, and special educational needs. See Thomas, 'From "Adversarial v Inquisitorial" to "Active, Enabling, and Investigative": Developments in UK Administrative Tribunals', in Jacobs and Baglay (eds), *The Nature of Inquisitorial Processes in Administrative Regimes: Global Perspectives* (Farnham 2013), p 52.

[94] Leggatt Report, [7.5].

case, of the appellant. This is important to ensure effective access to justice. 'There is clearly a duty upon a tribunal to ensure that all relevant questions have been asked of a claimant. It could not be otherwise, given the complexity of social security law and the fact that few claimants have advisors and that many are poorly educated.'[95] Furthermore, tribunals should focus upon getting decisions right than upon resolving an adversarial contest. As Baroness Hale has noted, the benefits appeals process is 'a cooperative process of investigation in which both the claimant and the department play their part'; it is inquisitorial rather than adversarial.[96]

4.5 Legal representation

Legal representation has traditionally not been considered to be necessary or even desirable, because it might add to the cost, length, and formality of tribunal proceedings. Representation might also make tribunal hearings more legalistic. But because many appellants lack the skills necessary to present their cases effectively, the lack of representation may put them at a significant disadvantage—especially when challenging the decision of a large public authority that is experienced in defending itself in tribunal proceedings. Represented appellants are significantly more likely to win.[97] This is unsurprising. Representation can help appellants to prepare their appeals and navigate unfamiliar law and the tribunal process. It can also promote the equality of arms between an individual and the state.

On the other hand, representation can add unnecessarily to cost, formality, and delay. It can also work against the objective of making tribunals directly and easily accessible to the full range of potential users. This was the view of the Leggatt Report. It noted that a combination of good-quality information and advice, effective procedures, and well-conducted hearings, along with competent and well-trained tribunal members, could go a very long way to helping the vast majority of appellants to understand and put their cases properly themselves.[98]

Beneath these arguments, there is a basic issue: who will pay for representation? Some appellants pay for representation themselves.[99] But for many, representation is simply out of the question—unless it is funded by the state. While legal aid has not been available across the board for all tribunals, the government previously funded legal advice and representation in some tribunals. Since 2013, legal aid has been severely restricted to reduce public spending.[100] Only very limited cases now qualify for legal aid. Publicly funded advice (though not representation) was previously available in relation to social security appeals; this has now been withdrawn. Likewise,

---

[95] R (IS) 11/99, [31], a decision by a Social Security Commissioner. Commissioners were turned into judges of the Upper Tribunal (Administrative Appeals) Chamber. See also *Mongan v Department of Social Development* [2005] NICA 16, [18].

[96] *Kerr v Department for Social Development* [2004] UKHL 23, [62].

[97] Genn and Genn, *The Effectiveness of Representation at Tribunals: Report to the Lord Chancellor* (London 1989).

[98] Leggatt Report, [4.21].

[99] See, eg 'Desperate families pay thousands to win school appeals', *The Times*, 2 March 2013.

[100] Legal Aid, Sentencing and Punishment of Offenders Act 2012.

legal aid used to be available for all immigration appeals, but is now restricted to asylum and detention cases only.

These restrictions on legal aid were highly controversial and opposed by lawyers and interest groups for undermining access to justice. In response, the government pleaded scarcity of resources: legal aid, it said, was affordable only in the most important cases, such as those raising fundamental rights issues. And in any event, said the government, the user-friendly nature of tribunals enables effective self-representation. There is some scope for exceptional legal aid funding if human rights or EU rights would be breached if the appellant did not have legal aid.[101] However, this is intended by the government to be a high threshold and it is envisaged that only a small number of cases will attract exceptional funding. The most relevant human right in this context is Art 6 of the European Convention on Human Rights (ECHR), which guarantees the right to a fair hearing when someone's rights and obligations are being determined.[102] Nonetheless, the overall effect of restricting legal aid has harmed access to justice for some litigants.[103]

In the absence of publicly funded representation, tribunals seek to adopt the 'enabling' approach advocated by Leggatt. However, it is generally accepted that the system has not been designed in such a way as to assist unrepresented appellants.[104] Much depends in practice on the personal preference of the tribunal judge or panel. On the one hand, the fact that an appellant is unrepresented may require the tribunal judge to play a much more active role in the proceedings than would normally be expected. Some judges may therefore spend some time in hearings questioning appellants, checking documentation, and ensuring that appellants understand the submissions being made by the governmental agency. On the other hand, some tribunal judges may be concerned that to provide such assistance might undermine their perceived independence; consequently, they may provide little assistance to unrepresented appellants beyond asking them whether there is anything they would like to say.[105] In any event, advice before a tribunal hearing may actually be more important than representation at the hearing. Such concerns notwithstanding, there is much to commend the adoption of the 'enabling' approach as regards unrepresented appellants.

Another issue concerns representation of the public authority the decision of which is being appealed against. The authority will normally be represented by one of its officials—a presenting officer, whose function it is to defend the initial decision and to assist the tribunal in coming to a legally correct decision. The presenting officer may cross-examine the appellant to establish the facts of the case and may make submissions to the tribunal as to why the appeal should be dismissed. The risk here is that unrepresented appellants may be disadvantaged by an inequality of arms. After all,

---

[101] Legal Aid, Sentencing and Punishment of Offenders Act 2012, s 10.

[102] See *R (Gudanaviciene) v Director of Legal Aid Casework and Lord Chancellor* [2014] EWCA Civ 1622; *IS v The Director of Legal Aid Casework* [2015] EWHC 1965 (Admin).

[103] House of Commons Justice Committee, *Impact of Changes to Civil Legal Aid under Part 1 of the Legal Aid, Sentencing and Punishment of Offenders Act 2012* (HC 311 2014–15).

[104] See *The Judicial Working Group on Litigants in Person: Report* (London 2013), https://www.judiciary.gov.uk/wp-content/uploads/JCO/Documents/Reports/lip_2013.pdf

[105] Genn, 'Tribunals and Informal Justice' (1993) 56 MLR 393, 407.

government agencies are 'repeat players': they frequently appear before tribunals, and are fully aware of tribunal procedure and case law.[106] By comparison, most appellants are 'one-shotters' who are appealing for the first time; unfamiliarity with the system will often place them at a disadvantage.

Yet, in some tribunals—social security and immigration—the *absence* of presenting officers has become a familiar criticism. While this may reduce any inequality in relation to an unrepresented appellant, it may, at the same time, pose some difficulties for the tribunal judge, because the tribunal will still want to have the appellant's evidence tested properly. Without a presenting officer to conduct cross-examination, the tribunal will have to ask its own questions, but will need to be careful not to be seen to be undertaking cross-examination, as this might imply that the judge has descended into the arena and compromised his or her independence.

4.6 Is access to justice in crisis?

There is a widely held view that access to justice is now in crisis.[107] With limited legal aid and advice, it is increasingly difficult for people to navigate an adversarial judicial system that largely operates on the basis that litigants are legally represented. Appeal rights have been restricted. Fees have been introduced and criticised on the ground that they limit access to justice.[108] This is not just a matter of legal procedure, but one of substance: restricted access to justice undermines the very content of legal rights, which cannot be enforced without effective legal remedies. 'There can be no effective rule of law when we lack a fully accessible and affordable judicial system.'[109]

In this context, various proposals have been advanced to widen access to justice. One proposal is to make the system more user-friendly for unrepresented people by introducing primary dispute resolution officers who would get to the heart of cases quickly and use their expertise and authority to resolve as many cases as possible using alternative dispute resolution methods.[110] Registrars would only refer cases to a judge where no other resolution is likely to be effective or appropriate. This model could be more effective than the current system by engaging directly with unrepresented parties in order to resolve most disputes quickly and informally and save resources in the long term. But it has not been taken up.

A second proposal is to introduce online dispute resolution (ODR).[111] This could include three aspects: online evaluation, whereby individuals access online materials to classify and categorise their problem, become aware of their rights and obligations,

---

[106] Galanter, 'Why the "Haves" Come Out Ahead: Speculations on the Limits of Legal Change' (1974) Law and Society Review 95.

[107] See generally Palmer et al (eds), *Access to Justice* (Oxford 2016).

[108] House of Commons Justice Committee, *Courts and Tribunals Fees* (HC 167 2015–16).

[109] Law Society, *Access to Justice Campaign*, **http://www.lawsociety.org.uk/policy-campaigns/campaigns/access-to-justice/**

[110] JUSTICE, *Delivering Justice in an Age of Austerity* (London 2015), **http://2bquk8cdew6192tsu41lay8t.wpengine.netdna-cdn.com/wp-content/uploads/2015/04/JUSTICE-working-party-report-Delivering-Justice-in-an-Age-of-Austerity.pdf**

[111] Civil Justice Council, *Online Dispute Resolution* (London 2015), **https://www.judiciary.gov.uk/reviews/online-dispute-resolution/**

and understand the options and remedies available to them; online facilitators, not judges, would seek to bring a dispute to a speedy and fair conclusion; and online dispute resolution, whereby judges would decide which cases are suited to online adjudication. Both the judiciary and HMCTS strongly favour ODR.[112] Funding has been agreed with HM Treasury for a reform programme to design and deliver better and more efficient systems.[113] Under the banner of 'digital by default', online methods are being piloted with social security appeals—a high-volume jurisdiction involving appellants who are almost always self-represented.[114] Aspiring lawyers take note: in the future, courts and tribunals will increasingly operate online.

4.7 **Oral and paper appeals**

In most, although not all, tribunals, oral hearings are the norm. In some jurisdictions, such as social security and criminal injuries compensation appeals, there is no automatic right to an oral hearing; rather, appellants have to 'opt in'—although they are advised that those who do attend their hearing usually do better than those who do not. By comparison, other tribunals, such as the parking adjudicators, have innovated with conducting appeals online and over the telephone. Appellants who opt for oral hearings experience higher success rates than those who have their appeals determined on the papers (Figure 16.8).[115] This happens because tribunal appeals often turn upon the tribunal's assessment of whether the appellant's evidence is credible. This task is easier to undertake at a hearing.[116] The procedure by which appeals are heard seems to influence substantive outcomes. The concern is that people who have their case considered on the papers are put at a disadvantage.

Oral hearings have advantages.[117] They may be more user-friendly than written procedures. They might be particularly suitable in cases that turn on many disputed facts or complex issues, making it necessary to have the evidence tested rigorously. For example, if the credibility of a witness has been questioned, then the tribunal might be assisted by an oral hearing at which the tribunal can assess the witness in person. Oral hearings might also give the tribunal a better opportunity to uncover information not available in the documentary evidence. Appellants can present additional

[112] Lord Thomas LCJ, 'The Legacy of Magna Carta: Justice in the 21st Century', speech to the Legal Research Foundation, 25 September 2015, **https://www.judiciary.gov.uk/wp-content/uploads/2015/10/the-legacy-of-magna-carta-lcj.pdf**; Ceeney, Chief Executive of HMCTS, 'Modernising Courts and Tribunals', speech, 23 September 2015, **https://www.gov.uk/government/speeches/modernising-the-courts-and-tribunals**

[113] HMCTS, *Annual Report and Accounts 2014–15* (London 2015), p 2.

[114] Senior President of Tribunals, *Annual Report* (London 2016), p 11, **https://www.judiciary.gov.uk/publications/senior-president-of-tribunals-annual-report-2016/**

[115] This data was acquired through FOI requests and concerns the 1.7 million social security appeals determined over the years 2010–15 and the 428,000 immigration appeals determined over the years 2010–14.

[116] Genn, 'Tribunal Review of Administrative Decision-Making', in Richardson and Genn (eds), *Administrative Law and Government Action: The Courts and Alternative Mechanisms of Review* (Oxford 1994), pp 270–2; Thomas, 'Immigration Appeals for Family Visitors Refused Entry Clearance' [2004] PL 612, 631–9.

[117] See Council on Tribunals, *The Use and Value of Oral Hearings in the Administrative Justice System: Consultation Paper* (London 2005); Council on Tribunals, *Consultation on the Use and Value of Oral Hearings in the Administrative Justice System: Summary of Responses* (London 2006).

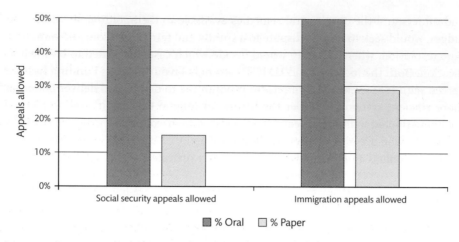

Figure 16.8 Oral and paper outcomes in social security and immigration appeals, 2010–15

evidence or shed new light on existing evidence; tribunal members have the opportunity to check information and elicit evidence that may have appeared irrelevant to
the appellant. There is always the risk that, without an oral hearing, the tribunal may
simply confirm the initial refusal decision by rubber-stamping it. The importance of
oral hearings has been recognised by the higher courts.[118]

There are, though, drawbacks with oral hearings. They can be costly, time-
consuming, and inefficient. As some tribunals deal with high caseloads, an expectation that all appeals be dealt with through oral hearings can substantially increase
costs and delays. Determining appeals solely on the basis of the papers reduces operating costs because large volumes of appeals can be processed efficiently. Nonetheless,
administrative justice is not just about efficiency and cost; it is about the delivery of
justice. Looking to the future, we can envisage a third way: online appeals.

4.8 Tribunal reason-giving

Tribunals must give reasons for their decisions. This promotes the aim of reaching
demonstrably accurate decisions by showing that the decision-maker has collected
and analysed the relevant facts, and applied the relevant legal rules. It also tells the
losing party why he or she has lost, shows that the factual and legal issues have been
addressed, and enables the losing party to appreciate whether or not there has been
any appealable error. The way in which tribunals discharge this duty varies. Until
2013, social security tribunals did not have to give their reasons unless requested to
do so.[119] They now give reasons as a matter of course. Other tribunals produce a written determination detailing their reasons.

---

[118] *FP (Iran) v Secretary of State for the Home Department* [2007] EWCA Civ 13. See also *R (Smith) v
Parole Board* [2005] UKHL 1, [2005] 1 WLR 350.

[119] Tribunal Procedure (First-tier Tribunal) (Social Entitlement Chamber) Rules 2008, SI 2008/2685,
rr 33 and 34.

Reasons should be proper, adequate, and intelligible, and deal with the substantial points that have been raised.[120] A failure to give such reasons may amount to an error of law. Most challenges to tribunal decisions are made on the ground that the reasons given were inadequate. How detailed must the reasons be? It all depends. If the Upper Tribunal is giving an important guidance decision raising complex legal and factual issues, then this may require detailed, lengthy reasons. As regards first-instance tribunals, there is an obvious tension here between the pressure on a tribunal to process a large number of appeals quickly, and the need to reach demonstrably robust and adequate decisions. Reasons should deal with the principal issues, but need not cover every single issue. It is 'a long established principle of administrative law that it is not to be assumed that a decision-maker has left a piece of evidence out of account merely because he does not refer to it in his decision'.[121] A tribunal decision should not be set aside unless the tribunal had failed to identify and record the matters that were critical to the decision in such a way that a reviewing court is unable to understand why the decision was reached. Tribunals must explain briefly their conclusions on the central issue in an appeal, but such reasons need not be extensive if the decision as a whole makes sense, having regard to the material accepted by the tribunal.[122]

4.9 Improving initial decision-making—feedback from tribunals

Overall, between a third and a half of appeals are allowed by tribunals (see Figures 16.9 and 16.10). Thousands of people are able to overturn initial decisions because they went to a tribunal. Further, these cases concern fundamentally important matters, such as whether someone was entitled to benefits, an individual's immigration status in the UK, whether someone was entitled to asylum because she would be at risk of persecution or torture if returned to her country of origin, and whether a victim of violent crime was entitled to compensation.

Figure 16.11 is more stark. It shows the outcomes of Employment and Support Allowance (ESA) appeals, which concern a benefit awarded to people unable to work owing to ill-health or incapacity. The proportion of allowed ESA appeals has actually overtaken that of dismissed appeals. Again, the number of appeals is considerable: over recent years, there have been hundreds of thousands of such appeals.

Why do so many appeals succeed? A widely held view is that there are often serious shortcomings with the quality of initial decisions. If initial decisions are not made on the basis of a full appreciation of the relevant facts or if initial decision-makers do not thoroughly investigate initial claims or misapply the relevant rules, then the decisions will be wrong. Tribunals have themselves often raised concerns as to the quality

---

[120] *Re Poyser and Mills' Arbitration* [1964] 2 QB 467, 478, *per* Megaw J. See also *Save Britain's Heritage v Secretary of State for the Environment* [1991] 1 WLR 153; *South Bucks District Council v Porter* [2004] UKHL 33, [2004] 1 WLR 1953; *MK (duty to give reasons) Pakistan* [2013] UKUT 00641 (IAC).

[121] *RG (Ethiopia) v Secretary of State for the Home Department* [2006] EWCA Civ 339, [37].

[122] *Shizad v Secretary of State for the Home Department (sufficiency of reasons: set aside)* [2013] UKUT 85 (IAC) [10].

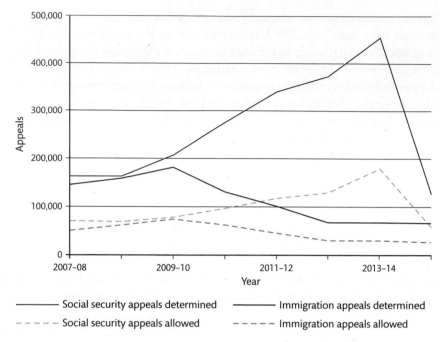

Figure 16.9 Allowed appeals: social security and immigration

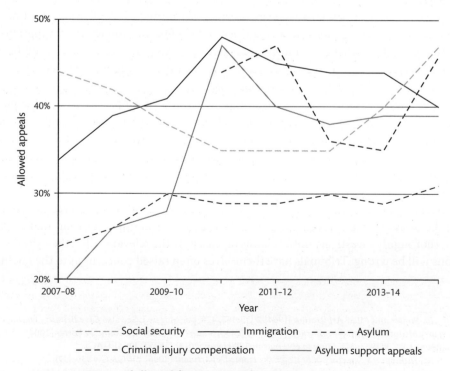

Figure 16.10 Proportion of allowed first-tier appeals

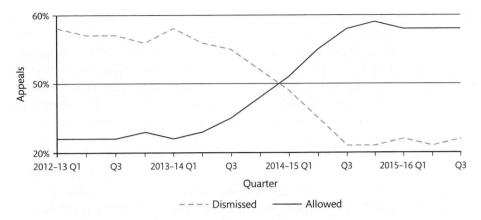

Figure 16.11 Outcomes of Employment and Support Allowance appeals

of initial decision-making.[123] As a select committee has noted, in far too many cases government departments make wrong decisions—and at considerable cost to both the taxpayer and the claimant.[124] The high number of allowed appeals demonstrates the usefulness of tribunals in providing an effective remedy. Yet, on the other hand, using appeal systems regularly to correct poor initial decisions is costly, inefficient, and delays the decision-making process. Public bodies should make the right decisions first time so that people do not have to resort to tribunals.[125]

It is generally recognised that the quality of primary decision-making—getting it 'right first time'—is fundamental and that government departments have a responsibility in this respect. Tribunals are well placed to pick up systemic problems in decision-making within governmental agencies, from decision letters that are confusing, through administrative systems that muddle key facts, to flawed decision-making processes that lead to misconceptions of the law. If the feedback provided by tribunals is used to improve the quality of initial decisions, then this can have several advantages. Higher-quality decision-making at the initial stage reduces the need to appeal, and so the need for lengthy and costly appeal proceedings. There is also the consideration that large numbers of people who receive erroneous decisions do not challenge them—yet, everyone is entitled to a good initial decision regardless of whether they decide to appeal.

One issue here is the status of initial decision-makers. Most administrative decisions are taken by relatively low-grade civil servants. Government departments view this as the most efficient (ie least costly) way of processing an enormous volume of

[123] See, eg the report produced by the President of Social Security and Child Support Appeal Tribunals: Harris, *President's Report: Report by the President of Appeal Tribunals on the Standards of Decision-Making by the Secretary of State 2006–07* (London 2007). In *IO v Entry Clearance Officer, Lagos ('Points in Issue') Nigeria* [2004] UKIAT 00179, [3], the Asylum and Immigration Tribunal noted that the reasons provided in the initial decision were 'quite inadequate' and that it was 'disappointing to see that decisions of this quality' were still being prepared.

[124] House of Commons Public Accounts Committee, *Department for Work and Pensions: Contract Management of Medical Services* (HC 744 2012–13).

[125] AJTC, *Right First Time* (London 2011).

decisions. However, concerns have repeatedly been raised that better qualified and trained staff would be make more robust decisions. In 2016, it was disclosed that the Home Office had been employing gap-year undergraduate students on temporary contracts to make potentially life-or-death decisions on asylum claims after five weeks of training. This was criticised as inappropriate and inadequate.[126] Another issue concerns organisational pressures upon decision-makers. With austerity, the workforces of government departments have been cut, leading to greater pressure on those who make decisions. Organisational pressures to process a mass of decisions quickly can dilute their quality.

In any event, it is not just initial *governmental* decision-making that is in issue here—some systems rely heavily upon *private sector contractors* to make administrative decisions. The Department for Work and Pensions (DWP) has increasingly used third-party contractors to undertake health and disability assessments, which are then used to make benefit decisions—for instance, about whether a claimant is able to work. Between 2015 and 2018, the DWP will spend £1.6 billion contracting out some seven million health and disability assessments. However, there have been persistent concerns that many of these assessments simply do not meet the standard required. Indeed, both the DWP and contractors acknowledge that past performance has been unacceptable and have committed themselves to improving the quality of assessments. Concerns nonetheless remain—as exemplified by the fact that around 60 per cent of appeals succeed (Figure 16.11).[127] It has been recommended that the Department and its contractors develop a more complete and effective regime for monitoring and improving the quality of assessments.[128]

One way to improve decision-making is by learning from tribunal decisions by extracting broader lessons.[129] For instance, in 2013 HMCTS and the DWP worked together to devise the 'summary reasons' project by which social security tribunals give detailed reasons, which are then used by DWP to improve its understanding of why so many appeals succeed and to strengthen decision-making. On a practical level, tribunals provide feedback to governmental agencies responsible for initial decision-making on the standard of decisions many times every day—by making their decisions and passing them back to the agency to put into effect. The issue, though, is the extent to which such agencies take account of such feedback.

Government decision-makers also take more notice of tribunal decisions if they appear before tribunals.[130] For example, the official may become more aware of the need to substantiate decisions more carefully to ensure that they withstand scrutiny before the tribunal. However, in many cases, the same official will not be responsible

[126] 'Gap-year students deciding asylum claims', *The Observer*, 28 February 2016, **http://www.theguardian.com/uk-news/2016/feb/27/gap-year-students-deciding-asylum- claims**

[127] House of Commons Public Accounts Committee, *Contracted Out Health and Disability Assessments* (HC 727 2015–16). The success rates relate to Employment and Support Allowance and Personal Independence Payment appeals.

[128] *Contracted Out Health and Disability Assessments.*

[129] Thomas, 'Administrative Justice, Better Decisions, and Organisational Learning' [2015] PL 111.

[130] Wikeley and Young, 'The Administration of Benefits in Britain: Adjudication Officers and the Influence of Social Security Appeal Tribunals' [1992] PL 238.

both for making the initial decision and for defending it before the tribunal. Furthermore, levels of attendance by presenting officers in some jurisdictions has reduced. Even if feedback is received, initial decision-makers may have neither the time nor the inclination to learn from the tribunal's decision. In some areas, the legal consciousness of initial decision-makers—their awareness of the importance of legal norms—and their understanding of, or even their willingness to understand, tribunal decision-making may be limited. The abolition of appeals and the low rate of appeals inevitably limits the amount of feedback that tribunals can provide.

As Leggatt noted, the provision of formal, systematic feedback from tribunals to initial decision-makers is an underdeveloped practice in many jurisdictions.[131] Tribunals have not generally developed robust mechanisms through which initial decision-makers may learn lessons; they are simply at the end of the decision-making process with no mechanism to feed back their views on decision-making or any expectation that such views would be acted upon if they were to do so. Furthermore, some tribunals may be disinclined to engage in such a dialogue because of concerns that it might undermine the perception of judicial independence. Such concerns, though, may be misplaced: providing feedback to initial decision-makers seeks to improve the quality of decisions and such engagement can be constructive and productive.

Another option is a 'polluter pays' approach under which public bodies contribute to the funding of tribunals depending on the proportion of their primary decisions which are reversed on appeal.[132] It is no good merely exhorting government agencies to make better decisions; they need to incur financial penalties as a result of poor decision-making which should then spur them to improve decision-making quality. Predictably, the government has rejected a polluter pays approach. However, the MoJ has, as part of its strategic work programme, committed itself to piloting enhanced feedback from tribunals to decision-makers in some tribunal contexts.[133]

Nonetheless, there is a general view that government could do more to improve initial decisions; a long-term project requiring 'management, commitment, and careful preparation' within government.[134] Furthermore, restrictions upon access to tribunals make it even more important that public bodies get it right first time. Everyone is entitled to a good decision irrespective of whether they decide—and can afford—to appeal. Yet, this does not currently seem to happen across the board.

4.10 Tribunal guidance

Tribunals are bound by legal precedents created by the higher courts, but can tribunals themselves lay down their own guidance? Strictly speaking, this role is reserved for the higher courts; tribunals simply determine the individual appeals before them. However, with the unified tribunal structure, the Upper Tribunal uses its specialist

---

[131] Leggatt Report, [9.12].   [132] AJTC, *Right First Time* (London 2011).

[133] MoJ, *Annual Administrative Justice and Tribunals Performance Report 2013–14* (Cm 8873 2014), p 15.

[134] AJTC, *Putting It Right* (London 2012), p 13.

expertise to produce general guidance to promote consistency and legal certainty for the benefit of the FTT, appellants, and initial decision-makers.[135]

Indeed, it has long been recognised that some system is needed whereby tribunals can make authoritative decisions rather than make individual adjudications. Because tribunals specialise in large and legally complex areas, some form of precedent has been necessary to ensure consistency. Most tribunals undertake precisely the same type of work as the higher courts in clarifying important points of law, and interpreting primary and secondary legislation. If tribunals in practice perform a role in clarifying important legal points, it is desirable that such decisions form legal precedents to promote consistency in first-instance tribunals. It is an important function of the Upper Tribunal to develop guidance on the interpretation of statutory provisions so as to reduce the risk of inconsistent results by different panels at the first-tier level. The Upper Tribunal's error of law jurisdiction should therefore be interpreted flexibly to include other points of principle or even factual judgment to enable it to use its specialist expertise to devise such guidance.[136] Such an approach might be considered slightly controversial—it may, for instance, be considered unprincipled from a conventional, doctrinal perspective—but the whole purpose of the unified tribunal system is to develop innovative methods of dispute resolution which are both fair and effective. Tribunal guidance is an important component of this pragmatic approach.

Tribunals designate important precedents to ensure consistency of approach. This also provides a degree of certainty for tribunal users. The establishment of the Upper Tribunal presents an obvious opportunity for the development of a principled and consistent approach towards the role of tribunals in creating legal precedents. The essential idea is that the Upper Tribunal's role is to provide judicial leadership and to use its expertise to determine how complex factual and legal issues are to be handled. For example, the Upper Tribunal (Immigration and Asylum Chamber) issues country guidance decisions, which are generally binding as to the factual conditions in countries from which asylum has been sought.[137] Similarly, the Upper Tribunal (Social Entitlement Chamber) issues guidance concerning the interpretation of complex social security regulations.

4.11 Enforcement of tribunal decisions

Tribunal decisions are just as binding on the parties as court decisions. In most cases, both parties will accept the tribunal's decision unless they wish to challenge it through the appropriate legal procedures. In the rare cases in which a government department refuses to give effect to a tribunal's decision, then direct enforcement of the tribunal's decision can be sought in the courts. For example, in *R (S) v Secretary*

---

[135] See generally Buck, 'Precedent in Tribunals and the Development of Principles' (2006) 25 CJQ 458; Carnwath, 'Tribunal Justice: A New Start' [2009] PL 48, 58–60.

[136] *Jones v First-tier Tribunal and Criminal Injuries Compensation Authority* [2013] UKSC 19, [41]–[43].

[137] Practice Direction concerning the Immigration and Asylum Chambers of the First-tier Tribunal and the Upper Tribunal (London 2010), [12]. See also Thomas, 'Consistency in Asylum Adjudication: Country Guidance and the Asylum Process in the United Kingdom' (2008) 20 International Journal of Refugee Law 489.

of State for the Home Department,[138] the Home Secretary had deliberately delayed giving effect to the Asylum and Immigration Tribunal's decision that the removal of nine Afghan nationals from the UK, who had arrived on a hijacked plane, would contravene the prohibition on torture and inhuman and degrading treatment under Art 3 of the ECHR. The Administrative Court concluded that this delay amounted to conspicuous unfairness and an abuse of power. While the case had raised sensitive political issues, there was an important public interest in ensuring that the executive acted lawfully in implementing tribunal decisions. The Home Secretary could not seek deliberately to circumvent a decision of an independent tribunal simply because he disagreed with the outcome, unless the decision could be set aside through the appropriate legal procedures, because this would undermine the rule of law.

Q Think back through the topics raised in this section concerning tribunal procedures. To what extent do tribunals provide individuals with an effective mechanism of redress against initial governmental decisions? How could tribunal procedures be improved?

5. Judicial oversight of tribunal decision-making

5.1 Judicial control of tribunals

Lord Denning once noted that 'if tribunals were to be at liberty to exceed their jurisdiction without any check by the courts, the rule of law would be at an end'.[139] Until recently, the courts undertook this task, but the 'hotchpotch' of onward challenges was unsystematic, incoherent, and chaotic.[140] Some tribunals' decisions could be appealed to the High Court on points of law;[141] others could be judicially reviewed; and, in some cases, there were rights of appeal against tribunals' decisions to second-level appellate tribunals such as the Social Security and Child Support Commissioners.

5.2 Appeals from the First-tier Tribunal to the Upper Tribunal

To remedy this confusing situation, the TCEA introduced new uniform arrangements for judicial oversight. In general, appeals against FTT decisions lie to the Upper Tribunal, which can identify any error of law in the initial tribunal decision (see Figure 16.2[142]). The policy is that onward appeal rights should be based on a simple and coherent appellate system; tribunal cases should proceed to the higher courts only when issues of sufficient weight and importance need to be resolved.

There is a general right of appeal from decisions of the FTT to the Upper Tribunal by any party to an appeal.[143] However, certain tribunal decisions are

---

138 [2006] EWHC 1111 (Admin); [2006] EWCA Civ 1157.
139 *R v Medical Appeal Tribunal, ex p Gilmore* [1957] 1 QB 574, 586.
140 Woolf, 'A Hotchpotch of Appeals: The Need for a Blender' (1988) 7 CJQ 44.
141 Tribunals and Inquiries Act 1992, s 11.   142 In section 3.4.   143 TCEA, s 11.

excluded.[144] Permission to appeal may be given by either the FTT or the Upper Tribunal. An appellant may only appeal to the Upper Tribunal on the ground that the FTT made an error of law.[145] If the Upper Tribunal finds that the FTT has made an error of law, then it may set aside the decision and either remit the case back to the FTT with directions for its reconsideration or make the decision that it considers should have been made. If it takes the latter option, it can make findings of fact. If the Upper Tribunal sends the case back to the FTT, it may direct that a different panel reconsiders the case. The Upper Tribunal may also give procedural directions in relation to the case. If the Upper Tribunal decides that the error of law does not invalidate the decision of the FTT, it must let that decision stand.

Both the FTT and the Upper Tribunal can review their own decisions without the need for a full onward appeal, and, where the tribunal concludes that an error was made, it can re-decide the matter.[146] The purpose of this review is to capture decisions that are clearly wrong, thereby avoiding the need for an onward appeal. The power of review of both tribunals is provided in the form of a discretionary power, so that only appropriate decisions are reviewed. Both tribunals may review a decision made within the tribunal either of its own initiative or on application by any party who has a right of appeal in respect of the decision. Both tribunals also have the power to correct accidental errors in the decision or in a record of the decision, amend the reasons given for the decision, or set aside the decision. If the decision is set aside, then the tribunal concerned must re-decide the matter.

5.3 Error of law

Appeals to the Upper Tribunal are confined to error of law grounds. What is an error of law? The most commonly encountered errors of law include:

(i) making perverse or irrational findings on a matter or matters that were material to the outcome ('material matters'),

(ii) failing to give adequate reasons,

(iii) failing to take into account and/or resolve conflicts of fact or opinion on material matters,

(iv) giving weight to immaterial matters,

(v) making a material misdirection of law on any material matter, and

(vi) committing or permitting a procedural or other irregularity capable of making a material difference to the outcome or the fairness of the proceedings.[147]

A poor factual decision by a tribunal will not normally, by itself, qualify as an error of law unless the reasons given are clearly inadequate or the findings are irrational.

---

[144] TCEA, s 11(5). For example, criminal injury compensation appeals against decisions on reviews, data protection and freedom of information appeals against national security certificates, and decisions of the FTT to review, or not to review, an earlier decision are excluded from appeal to the Upper Tribunal.

[145] TCEA, s 12.   [146] TCEA, ss 9–10.

[147] *R (Iran) v Secretary of State for the Home Department* [2005] EWCA Civ 982, [2005] INLR 633, 640, *per* Brooke LJ.

However, it is possible for a mistake concerning a factual issue to be an error of law if the mistake can be established by objective and uncontentious evidence, the appellant and/or his advisers were not responsible for the mistake, and unfairness resulted from the fact that a mistake was made.[148]

This list is not exhaustive. This is because the concept of 'error of law'—and thus the distinction between errors of law and errors of fact—is (intentionally) unclear and open-ended. It is possible for the Upper Tribunal to define the scope of 'error of law' through its application in individual cases. Its precise scope may depend on a number of factors, such as the relationship between the second-tier tribunal and the first-level tribunal, and the willingness or otherwise of the former to intervene. For example, if the second-tier tribunal considers that the decision of the first-level tribunal was clearly wrong, then it may be more inclined to adopt a broad conception of 'error of law' (ie artificially manufacture some error of law), so that it has some basis on which to interfere with the first-level tribunal's decision. On the other hand, if a second-tier tribunal regularly upsets tribunal decisions on error of law grounds, then it may find itself, in effect, overturning such decisions merely because it does not like them—in other words, substituting its own judgment for that of the first-level tribunal on the merits of individual cases even though its jurisdiction is limited to identifying errors of law. This will undermine the first-level tribunal in determining merits appeals, and increase the length and cost of the process. Other factors—in addition to just outcomes, and the timeliness and cost of appeal processes—might also inform the scope of the concept of 'error of law' as applied by a second-tier tribunal. For example, the need for consistency in tribunal decision-making, the perceived expertise of the first-level tribunal, the particular demands of the context in which such challenges arise (eg social security; immigration), the volume of the second-tier tribunal's own caseload, and the personal assessments of judges in the second-tier tribunal concerning the desirability of intervention might all influence how widely or narrowly the concept of 'error of law' is drawn.

5.4 Onward appeals to the Court of Appeal

In England and Wales, appeals against substantive decisions of the Upper Tribunal lie to the Court of Appeal (Civil Division).[149] In Scotland, appeals lie to the Court of Session (Inner House) and in Northern Ireland the Court of Appeal of Northern Ireland.

The link between the tribunal system and the higher courts needs to strike a delicate balance, in order both to maintain the independence of tribunals and to ensure fidelity to general principles of law. Where the Court of Appeal determines that the Upper Tribunal has made an error of law, it has the power to set aside the decision and either send the case back to the Upper Tribunal to be redecided (or, where the decision of the Upper Tribunal was on an appeal or reference from another tribunal or some other person, to that other tribunal or person, with direction for its reconsideration), or to make the decision that it considers the Upper Tribunal (or the other tribunal or person) should have made.[150]

---

[148] *E v Secretary of State for the Home Department* [2004] EWCA Civ 49, [2004] QB 1044.
[149] TCEA, s 13.   [150] TCEA, s 14.

There are though underlying tensions here. The Court of Appeal is superior to the Upper Tribunal. Yet, the Upper Tribunal is an expert body comprised of various chambers specialising in particular types of appeals, whereas the Court of Appeal is a generalist court. This raises questions about when the Court of Appeal should intervene to 'correct' the Upper Tribunal—and when it should stay its hand so as to respect the Upper Tribunal's expertise. Caseload is also relevant. Over the years 2006–09, immigration and asylum appeals accounted for over 30 per cent of the entirety of the Court of Appeal's caseload—an unsustainable position given the breadth of that court's jurisdiction and its highly limited resources.[151] Consequently, efforts were made to reduce such appeals.

Onward appeals to the Court of Appeal are limited in two ways. First, under the 2007 Act, the Court of Appeal can only grant permission to appeal against a decision of the Upper Tribunal if the case fulfils the second tier appeal criteria, that is, that the case raises 'some important point of principle or practice' or that there is 'some other compelling reason' for the appeal to be heard.[152] It is insufficient that there is merely some error in the individual case concerned; there must also be some wider point of legal principle or practice that justifies the case proceeding to the Court. The purpose is to limit second appeals only to those cases that really warrant it.

Second, the higher courts have been developing an approach under which, while they retain jurisdiction over tribunal decisions, they will normally adopt an appropriate degree of caution because of the special knowledge, expertise, and competence of such tribunals.[153] In practice, this means that higher courts, such as the Court of Appeal, recognise that tribunals specialise in their particular areas of law and that

> [t]heir decisions should be respected unless it is quite clear that they have misdirected themselves in law. Appellate courts should not rush to find such misdirections simply because they might have reached a different conclusion on the facts or expressed themselves differently.[154]

This approach is inherently bound up with the developing jurisdiction of the Upper Tribunal to issue broader guidance and a flexible approach to issues of law and fact.[155] It is not just the formal judicial structure that is important here, but also the degree of trust and confidence between the different levels of the judicial hierarchy.[156]

In *Jones*, the Supreme Court noted that the Upper Tribunal has a legitimate role to perform in terms of taking a lead by clarifying important points of tribunal practice, procedure, and policy; the Court of Appeal should normally let the Upper Tribunal

---

[151] MoJ, *Judicial and Court Statistics*.

[152] TCEA, s 13(6); Appeals from the Upper Tribunal to the Court of Appeal Order 2008, SI 2008/2834, para 2.

[153] See, eg *Cooke v Secretary of State for Social Security* [2002] 3 All ER 279; *AH (Sudan) v Secretary of State for the Home Department* [2007] UKHL 49; [2008] 1 AC 678, HL, [30].

[154] *AH (Sudan) v Secretary of State for the Home Department* [2007] UKHL 49; [2008] 1 AC 678, HL, [30], *per* Baroness Hale.

[155] *Jones v First-tier Tribunal and Criminal Injuries Compensation Authority* [2013] UKSC 19, [16].

[156] See Laurie, 'Assessing the Upper Tribunal's Potential to Deliver Administrative Justice' [2012] PL 288.

perform this role and intervene only when necessary.[157] In this way, the Upper Tribunal is able to adopt a consistent approach concerning the factual and legal issues that commonly arise. As Lord Hope noted:

> A pragmatic approach should be taken to the dividing line between law and fact, so that the expertise of tribunals at the first tier and that of the Upper Tribunal can be used to best effect. An appeal court should not venture too readily into this area by classifying issues as issues of law which are really best left for determination by the specialist appellate tribunals.[158]

5.5 Judicial review in the Upper Tribunal

For centuries, what is now modern-day judicial review was exercised *exclusively* through the historic supervisory jurisdiction of the High Court. This is no longer the case. The TCEA conferred a 'judicial review' jurisdiction upon the Upper Tribunal in appropriate cases.[159] This allows the parties to have the benefit of the specialist expertise of the Upper Tribunal in cases similar to those with which the Upper Tribunal routinely deals in the exercise of its statutory appellate jurisdiction.

Judicial review cases can be transferred from the Administrative Court in two ways. First, individual cases can be transferred if this is considered appropriate.[160] Second, the Lord Chief Justice can designate particular categories of judicial review cases to be transferred from the Administrative Court to the Upper Tribunal. Initially, some limited categories of judicial review cases were transferred to the Upper Tribunal, including challenges against certain FTT decisions from which, unusually, there was no right of appeal to the Upper Tribunal, such as criminal injuries compensation appeals. The number of judicial reviews handled by the Upper Tribunal (Administrative Appeals Chamber) has been relatively low: 78 judicial review claims in 2013–14 and 59 in 2014–15, the majority of which concerned criminal injuries compensation.[161]

Over recent years, there have been around 15,000 immigration judicial reviews annually—85 per cent of all judicial review claims lodged.[162] This has been far too many for the limited capacity of the Administrative Court. In 2013, most immigration judicial reviews were transferred to the UTIAC.[163] This represents a significant development in the balance of workload between the Administrative Court and the Upper Tribunal. There is also a reinforcement of a wider change here: the breaking down of the traditional division between courts and tribunals. Tribunals are no longer seen as inferior jurisdictions. They now undertake the same type of work as the higher courts.

---

[157] *Jones v First-tier Tribunal and Criminal Injuries Compensation Authority* [2013] UKSC 19, [16] and [41].

[158] *Jones v First-tier Tribunal and Criminal Injuries Compensation Authority* [2013] UKSC 19, [16].

[159] TCEA, s 15.   [160] Senior Courts Act 1981, s 31A(3).   [161] FOI 104971 (5 May 2016).

[162] See Thomas, 'Mapping Immigration Judicial Review Litigation: An Empirical Legal Analysis' [2015] PL 652.

[163] Crime and Courts Act 2013, s 22.

In exercising its judicial review jurisdiction, the Upper Tribunal may grant certain forms of relief in the same way as the High Court. For example, it may grant a mandatory order, a prohibiting order, a quashing order, a declaration, or an injunction.[164] Awards made by the Upper Tribunal in exercising its 'judicial review' jurisdiction are enforceable as if they were those of the High Court.[165]

5.6 Judicial review of tribunal decisions

Can tribunals themselves be judicially reviewed? The issue does not arise in relation to the FTT because, in general, there is a right of appeal to the Upper Tribunal. But what of the Upper Tribunal—can its decisions be judicially reviewed?

The Upper Tribunal makes two types of decisions. First, it determines substantive appeals against decisions of the FTT. As we have noted, there is a right of further appeal from the Upper Tribunal to the Court of Appeal in such cases. Judicial review of such decisions is ruled out by the need to pursue alternative remedies. But there is a second type of decision. Even before an appeal gets to the Upper Tribunal for substantive consideration, it must first be granted permission to appeal by the Upper Tribunal. If permission to appeal is refused by the Upper Tribunal, then the case cannot proceed to a substantive appeal. There is no right of appeal against the decision to refuse permission—can judicial review bite here?

In *Cart* the Supreme Court held that the Upper Tribunal was subject to judicial review by the Administrative Court, but only on limited grounds. The Court held that there was no question of the Administrative Court's judicial review jurisdiction having been excluded by statute, since there was no ouster clause in the TCEA, but nor did it follow that full judicial review would be appropriate.[166] Instead, the Court held that the Upper Tribunal was only open to judicial review if there was some general point of principle or practice or if there was some other compelling reason. The Upper Tribunal is therefore then subject only to a 'light touch' judicial review limited to correcting errors of law of real significance. Given the limited resources of the Administrative Court, it would be disproportionate to have full judicial review scrutiny in such circumstances. The Supreme Court's approach in *Cart* thus illustrates how judicial review is informed by the notion of proportionate dispute resolution.[167] There have been a high number of such *Cart* challenges, but few have succeeded. In 2015, *Cart* challenges accounted for 25 per cent of all judicial reviews lodged with the Administrative Court; 95 per cent of them were immigration related.[168] Of the 2,933

---

[164] TCEA, s 15(1).   [165] TCEA, s 16(6).

[166] *R (Cart) v Upper Tribunal* [2011] UKSC 28, [2011] 3 WLR 107.

[167] See Elliott and Thomas, 'Tribunal Justice and Proportionate Dispute Resolution' [2012] CLJ 297.

[168] Together with the transfer of immigration judicial reviews, this has resulted in the curious situation in which the UTIAC handles 85 per cent of all judicial reviews claims, and a quarter of Administrative Court judicial reviews are of the UTIAC's refusal of permission to appeal in statutory appeals. As *Cart* challenges are against the Upper Tribunal, it would obviously be inappropriate to transfer these cases to the Upper Tribunal.

Cart challenges lodged, 2,450 were refused permission, 126 were granted permission, and only five were ultimately allowed.[169]

> **Q** Why is it important for there to be control over tribunal decisions? Does the 2007 Act succeed in establishing a simple and coherent system of judicial control of tribunal decisions?

6. Conclusions

Tribunals perform a major role in ensuring the legal accountability of governmental decision-making. They lack the glamour of the Supreme Court, but provide the forum in which most people will interact with the judicial system to challenge government decisions. While governmental decision-making is often portrayed as involving high-level decisions by Ministers, the reality is more prosaic, and consists of millions of front-line decisions taken by officials within central and local government. Neither parliamentary accountability nor judicial review provides an adequate and easily accessible remedy here. Tribunals have been designed to fill the gap by providing people with an accessible mechanism by which they can challenge initial governmental decisions that they consider to be incorrect.

Much has been achieved in the tribunals system over recent years. The previously unsystematic 'system' has been radically overhauled. The First-tier and Upper Tribunals provide a simple structure for tribunals. Tribunals are now clearly independent and the Lord Chancellor is obliged to protect the independence of tribunals, and to ensure that there is an efficient and effective tribunal system administered by HM Courts and Tribunals Service. The Senior President of Tribunals provides (previously lacking) senior judicial leadership for tribunals. Furthermore, tribunals themselves are undertaking significant reforms, including wider use of the 'enabling' approach and providing feedback to primary decision-makers to make better initial decisions and prevent unnecessary appeals. There are, though, aspects of tribunals that constrain their effectiveness. Like courts, they can deal only with the cases that come before them, and the low rate of appeals to tribunals strongly suggests that many incorrect governmental decisions go unchallenged. The absence in many cases of legal aid can place appellants at a disadvantage, while appellants opting for paper-only appeals experience lower success rates. The effectiveness of tribunals is also limited by broader policy and organisational factors—not least the pressure on tribunals to process a high volume of cases within prescribed time limits and limited public funding. Most of all, the squeeze on public spending has adversely affected the provision of administrative justice. The government has reduced legal aid and abolished or weakened various appeal rights. There has been much talk about government getting it right first time, but little evidence of any demonstrable improvement

---

[169] MoJ, *Civil Justice Statistics Quarterly, England and Wales (Incorporating The Royal Courts of Justice 2015): January to March 2016* (London 2016). For a (rare) reported successful case, see *R (G and H) v Secretary of State for the Home Department* [2016] EWHC 239 (Admin).

in the standards of initial decision-making. In 2011, the now-defunct AJTC asked, is administrative justice at risk? Over the intervening years, the answer has become uncompromisingly clear.

Expert commentary
Tribunals and administrative justice: an uncertain future?
Michael Adler, Emeritus Professor of Socio-Legal Studies, University of Edinburgh

Although courts attract the limelight, tribunals have just as much, if not more, of an impact on the lives of ordinary citizens. They are the primary means by which individuals can challenge—or, more precisely, appeal against—some crucially important decisions such as whether they should be granted asylum or allowed to stay in the country, whether they qualify for a social security benefit or whether their child should be admitted to the school of their choice. In this commentary, I consider three issues: the changing relationship between appeal tribunals and the civil courts, the changing emphasis on internal and external modes of dispute resolution, and the changing status of administrative justice.

The first issue relates to the comparison between courts and tribunals. As the chapter makes clear, and notwithstanding the fact that most previously autonomous tribunals have been brought together into a unified structure, there is a considerable amount of variation between tribunals. This is not really surprising given that they have such different histories and deal with such a diverse range of issues. There is likewise a considerable amount of variation between courts, and a considerable degree of overlap between courts and tribunals in that some tribunals, such as employment tribunals, have characteristics that are commonly associated with courts and some courts, such as small claims courts, have characteristics that are commonly associated with tribunals. For these reasons, the comparisons between tribunals and courts in the chapter should be approached with some care.

Comparisons between tribunals and courts in the chapter are mainly between first-instance tribunals, which hear the large majority of appeals brought by citizens against routine decisions made by, or on behalf of, central or local government departments, and the superior civil courts, which used to hear all and still hear many of the much smaller number of judicial review cases. This is not surprising because the comparison focuses on the roles that tribunals and courts play within the administrative justice system. However, it does not involve comparing 'like' with 'like'. The second-tier tribunal (the Upper Tribunal) is very different in all sorts of ways from first-instance tribunals (most of which are now part of the First-tier Tribunal) and the superior civil courts are likewise very different from the subordinate courts (which, in England, comprise the County Court and the Magistrates Courts).[170] The Upper Tribunal, which now hears the majority of judicial review cases on immigration matters, is not all that different from the Administrative Division of the High Court and the First-Tier Tribunal is not all that different from the County Court, which hears cases involving landlord and tenant disputes (eg cases involving rent arrears), consumer disputes (eg cases involving faulty goods or services), and debt problems (eg cases involving creditors seeking payment).

In comparisons of tribunals and courts, the following claims are frequently made:
1. Tribunal judges and tribunal members are expected to be experts in the law and policy of the subject matter of the dispute while court judges are not.

---

[170] In Scotland, they comprise the Sheriff Court and the District Courts. However, the same argument applies.

2. Tribunal procedures are, on the whole, simpler and more flexible than court procedures.

3. Tribunals adopt a less adversarial, more 'active and enabling' approach than is encountered in the courts.

4. In tribunals, appellants are either unrepresented or represented by lay advocates but in courts they are represented by solicitors (in the subordinate courts) or barristers or advocates (in the superior courts).

5. Appellants do not have to pay to appeal to a tribunal whereas parties do have to pay to raise an action in court.

Few of these claims bear scrutiny. There has been a significant reduction in the number of lay tribunal members with expert knowledge of the matters in dispute in recent years, while District Judges, who preside over the County Courts, can develop just as much expertise in the problems they encounter as Tribunal Judges. Much effort has been put into simplifying civil procedure rules in recent years and County Court procedures are now reasonably straightforward. Most tribunals do adopt an 'active and enabling' approach but some are still rather adversarial; District Judges in the County Court also tend to adopt an 'active and enabling' approach. Due to the swingeing cuts in legal aid, appellants at tribunals are now, in most cases, unrepresented or, at best, represented by lay advocates but, in the subordinate courts, few litigants can afford to be represented. In fact, some County Court procedures have been designed for unrepresented litigants. Finally, the introduction of fees in some tribunals (in particular in employment and immigration and asylum tribunals) has effectively removed another of the stereotypical differences between tribunals and courts.

Although, until quite recently, there were many differences between courts and tribunals, this is no longer the case and there is now a considerable overlap between them. Thus the belief that they represent contrasting ways of handling disputes is no longer true. For this reason, bringing together responsibility for the administration of courts and tribunals into a single organisation (HM Courts and Tribunals Service) makes more sense than it would have done in the past. Ensuring that disputes are dealt with in the most appropriate manner is more important than deciding whether they should be dealt with by a tribunal or a court.

The second issue relates to the government's preference for internal rather than external modes of dispute resolution. The chapter gives a very clear account of the remarkable decline in the number of appeals disposed of by the First-tier Tribunal caused by the very marked reduction in the number of social security appeals and the smaller, but equally significant decline in the number of immigration appeals. In the case of social security appeals, the reduction was a direct consequence of the introduction of mandatory reconsideration, which involves a second internal review of the initial decision by departmental staff. In the case of immigration appeals, it was caused by the abolition of appeal rights under the Immigration Act 2014, which withdrew the right of appeal against refusal of entry into the UK. However, while the number of social security and immigration appeals has plummeted, the number of internal administrative reviews by the Department for Work and Pensions and the Home Office has shot up. Although some people might be tempted to argue that the choice between alternative modes of dispute resolution is less important than ensuring that wrong decisions are put right, the success rate of internal reviews by departmental staff is substantially less than the success rate of external appeal to tribunals presided over by independent tribunal judges. The switch from external to internal modes of dispute resolution undoubtedly has important and worrying implications for justice in administrative decision-making.

The third issue relates to the state of administrative justice, defined in the chapter as 'the procedures for making [administrative] decisions, the law under which such decisions are made, and the systems for resolving disputes and airing grievances in relation to such decisions'.[171] In a paper published in 2012,[172] I described how, between 2000 and 2010, administrative justice emerged from the shadows, where it was the poor cousin of civil justice, into the limelight, where its importance was widely recognised. The key events along the way were the wealth of empirical research that threw a critical light on aspects of administrative justice, in particular on the shortcomings of tribunals, and the appointment of a reforming Lord Chancellor (Lord Irvine of Lairg), who appointed Sir Andrew Leggatt to carry out a review of tribunals. In due course, The Leggatt Report (2001) led in 2007 to the TCEA, which put forward a new conception of administrative justice, proposed a unified structure for tribunals, and an Administrative Justice and Tribunals Council (AJTC), in place of the old Council on Tribunals, with a wider responsibility for overseeing the whole of the administrative justice system. The TCEA and the reforms it gave rise to constituted the 'high water mark' for administrative justice.

In the 2012 paper, I identified some dark clouds on the horizon, in particular the likely demise of the AJTC and the establishment of a unified Courts and Tribunals Service, in which I feared that tribunals would, once again, play second fiddle to the courts, and administrative justice would once again become subordinate to civil justice. In the period since 2012, events have confirmed these fears. The AJTC was abolished in 2013 and the tame successor body, the Administrative Justice Forum, is set to close its doors in 2017.[173] Tribunal caseloads have plummeted to an extent that few people anticipated. Thus the extent of independent, external scrutiny of first-instance decision-making by government departments has declined quite markedly. As stated at the end of the chapter 'there has been much talk about government getting it right first time, but little evidence of any demonstrable improvement in the standards of initial decision-making.'

What could be done to enhance administrative justice? Attempting to reverse the decline in the number of appeals to tribunals seems like a lost cause unless this can be achieved in a cost-effective way. Online dispute resolution is already used by the Traffic Penalty Tribunal and its use by other tribunals should be seriously considered.[174]

A serious commitment to 'getting it right first time' by government departments is clearly called for. The adoption of a 'polluter pays' approach, in which government departments are required to contribute to the cost of tribunals in proportion to the number of their decisions that are overturned, would give them an incentive to improve standards, although the incentive will decline if the number of appeals continues to fall. Many areas of public administration, such as schools, childcare services, residential homes, prisons, probation services, and police forces, are regularly inspected by agencies that assess whether statutory requirements are met and whether services are of an appropriate standard. Although there is no inspectorate

---

[171] The definition is derived from the TCEA, Sch 7, para 13(4).

[172] Adler, 'The Rise and Fall of Administrative Justice—A Cautionary Tale' (2012) 8 Socio-Legal Review 28.

[173] Announcement by MoJ, 12 May 2016, **https://www.gov.uk/government/news/jodi-berg-appointment-to-the-administrative-justice-forum-extended**. The successor bodies in Scotland and Wales have likewise been closed down.

[174] Professor Richard Susskind, who is IT adviser to the Lord Chief Justice, has been a long-time proponent of alternative ways of settling disputes through the use of technology and is the principal author of a report for the Civil Justice Council, published in 2015, entitled *Online Dispute Resolution for Low Value Civil Claims*. The report is available at: **https://www.judiciary.gov.uk/wp-content/uploads/2015/02/Online-Dispute-Resolution-Final-Web-Version1.pdf**. Although it deals with party v party disputes in the civil courts, the same approach could be applied to citizen v state disputes in appeal tribunals.

charged with responsibility for monitoring standards of decision-making in social security and promoting improvements in them, there is, in my view, a strong case for establishing one.[175]

Further reading

CARNWATH, 'Tribunal Justice: A New Start' [2009] PL 48
This paper was written by a former Senior President of Tribunals and Supreme Court Justice and provides a judicial perspective on the tribunal system.

LAURIE, 'Assessing the Upper Tribunal's Potential to Deliver Administrative Justice' [2012] PL 288
This article discusses the role of the Upper Tribunal and the degree to which the higher courts should respect that tribunal's specialist expertise.

MCKEEVER, 'A Ladder of Legal Participation for Tribunal Users' [2013] PL 575
This article paper considers how tribunal users can effectively participate in tribunal proceedings.

THOMAS, *Administrative Justice and Asylum Appeals: A Study of Tribunal Adjudication* (Oxford 2011)
This book provides a detailed empirical study of asylum appeals.

THOMAS, 'Administrative Justice, Better Decisions, and Organisational Learning' [2015] PL 111
This paper examines the 'right first time' debate and argues that government decision-makers can produce better decisions if they engage in organisational learning.

THOMAS, 'Current Developments in UK Tribunals: Challenges for Administrative Justice' (2016) (**https://www.academia.edu/21814381/Current_Developments_in_UK_Tribunals_Challenges_for_Administrative_Justice**)
This paper argues that we are seeing a fundamental shift in the role of tribunals.

Useful websites

https://www.gov.uk/government/organisations/ministry-of-justice
Website of the Ministry of Justice

https://www.gov.uk/government/organisations/hm-courts-and-tribunals-service
Website of HMCTS (with links to the websites of individual tribunals)

---

[175] There is a precedent for this. In 1984, in an attempt to promote legality in the administration of social security, the government established the post of Chief Adjudication Officer (CAO), whose remit was to advise adjudication officers in the performance of their functions, to keep under review the operation of the system of adjudication, and to report annually to the Secretary of State on standards of adjudication. Although the widely held view was that the independent CAO had helped to bring about improvements in standards of decision-making, the office was abolished under the Social Security Act 1998 when responsibility for standards of adjudication was transferred to the Secretary of State. For an early account of the CAO, see Sainsbury, 'The Social Security Chief Adjudication Officer: The First Four Years' [1989] PL 323.

17

Inquiries

1. Introduction	728
2. Inquiries—nature, function, and legal framework	728
3. The inquiry process	735
4. The effectiveness of inquiries and the alternatives	746
5. Conclusion	751
Expert commentary	751
Further reading	755
Useful websites	755

1. Introduction

This chapter considers the role, function, operation, and effectiveness of public inquiries. When it appears that something has gone wrong either within government or society—for example, a major public scandal, failings in a public service, or alleged political misconduct—there are invariably calls for the government to establish a full and independent public inquiry to investigate precisely what happened and what, if anything, can be done to ensure that it is not repeated. Such inquiries are relatively common in the UK. They are both 'a pivotal part of public life in Britain, and a major instrument of accountability'.[1]

2. Inquiries—nature, function, and legal framework

2.1 What are inquiries?

Public inquiries are often established by the government to undertake an official investigation into a particular matter of public concern. They are established on an ad hoc basis in response to a particular event or series of events. Such inquiries tend

---

[1] House of Commons Public Administration Select Committee (PASC), *Government by Inquiry* (HC 51 2004–05), [2].

to address particularly important, controversial, and difficult issues. Here are some recent prominent inquiries:

- *The Chilcot Inquiry* In 2016, the Chilcot report into the Iraq war was published.[2] This war involved the US, UK, and allies invading and taking full-scale occupation of Iraq because of the claimed existence of weapons of mass destruction (WMD) in Iraq. Overall, Chilcot provided a devastating critique of the then Prime Minster, Tony Blair, and the UK government. The UK chose to invade Iraq before the peaceful options had been exhausted. Military action was not a last resort. The severity of the threat posed by Iraq was not justified. Government policy on Iraq had been made on the basis of flawed intelligence and assessments. Despite explicit warnings, the consequences of the invasion were underestimated. The government failed to achieve its stated objectives, not least because its planning for the period following the removal from power of Saddam Hussein was wholly inadequate. Amongst the various findings of the inquiry, two have particular resonance for the workings of the UK constitution. First, the inquiry noted the importance of collective ministerial discussion which encourages frank and informed debate and challenge. Second, the inquiry also considered the legal advice concerning the legality of the invasion and found that the circumstances in which it was ultimately decided that there was a legal basis for UK participation were very far from satisfactory. The Chilcot inquiry lasted seven years. It took oral evidence over a number of months and considered 150,000 documents. The inquiry also involved a protracted negotiation with the government over the use of classified documents. The inquiry cost only £10.3 million.

- *Other Iraq inquiries* The Iraq war generated four other inquiries. The Hutton inquiry (2004), chaired by a then-serving Law Lord, investigated the death of a government scientist, Dr David Kelly, who had been the source of a story by a BBC radio reporter claiming that the government had embellished, or 'sexed up', its intelligence material concerning the existence of WMD in Iraq.[3] The inquiry concluded that the allegation of the BBC reporter was unfounded, but that the BBC had not exercised sufficient editorial controls over its reporter. The report was itself the subject of much controversy, and was criticised by some as a 'whitewash'.[4] The Butler inquiry (2004) into the reliability of pre-war intelligence that claimed that Iraq had WMD found serious weaknesses in the preparation of intelligence dossiers concerning the supposed existence of WMD in Iraq.[5] There

---

[2] http://www.iraqinquiry.org.uk/

[3] *Report of the Inquiry into the Circumstances Surrounding the Death of Dr David Kelly* (HC 247 2003–04). See also http://webarchive.nationalarchives.gov.uk/20090128221546/http://www.the-hutton-inquiry.org.uk/index.htm

[4] See Blom-Cooper and Munro, 'The Hutton Inquiry' [2004] PL 472, 474, reporting the findings of an opinion poll. See further Runciman (ed), *Hutton and Butler: Lifting the Lid on the Workings of Power* (Oxford 2004); Hutton, 'The Media Reaction to the Hutton Report' [2006] PL 807.

[5] The Butler Committee, *Review of Intelligence on Weapons of Mass Destruction* (HC 898 2003–04).

have been also two public inquiries into allegations that British soldiers unlawfully killed Iraqi nationals.[6]

- *The Stephen Lawrence inquiry* Conducted in 1999, this inquiry investigated the circumstances surrounding the racially motivated killing of a black teenager and, in particular, sought to identify the lessons to be learned for the police as regards the investigation and prosecution of racially motivated crimes.[7] The report concluded that the police's handling of the investigation had been marked by institutional racism, a wider problem within the police that needed to be addressed.

- *The Leveson Inquiry* Public revulsion about the hacking of the mobile phone of a murdered teenager sparked the Leveson Inquiry in 2011–12. From that beginning, the inquiry's scope expanded to cover the culture, practices, and ethics of the press in its relations with the public, with the police, with politicians, and, as to the police and politicians, the conduct of each. The inquiry found that journalists had hacked thousands of phones and recommended a new, independent regulator backed by legislation designed to assess whether it is doing its job properly.[8] The inquiry recognised that the press provides an essential check upon aspects of public life, but concluded that more effective regulation was necessary.[9]

- *NHS-related inquiries* Various inquiries have been conducted into failures within the National Health Service (NHS). The Bristol Royal Infirmary (BRI) inquiry investigated the avoidable deaths of children undergoing heart surgery.[10] The Royal Liverpool Children's Hospital (Alder Hey) inquiry investigated the retention of children's organs after death without their parents' knowledge or consent.[11] The Shipman inquiry investigated the conduct of a doctor that killed many of his patients.[12] The Mid Staffordshire NHS Foundation Trust inquiry found that patients received appalling care and treatment and that some died needlessly.[13] The report identified a culture which tended to prioritise the smooth operation of the health care system above the safe and effective care of patients; it recommended the need for cultural change within the NHS. All of these inquiries investigated matters of acute sensitivity and uncovered systemic failings within the NHS.

---

[6] See https://www.gov.uk/government/publications/the-baha-mousa-public-inquiry-report and http://webarchive.nationalarchives.gov.uk/20150115114702/http:/www.alsweadyinquiry.org/

[7] *The Stephen Lawrence Inquiry: Report of an Inquiry by Sir William MacPherson of Cluny* (Cm 4262 1999).

[8] The Leveson Inquiry, *An Inquiry into the Culture, Practices and Ethics of the Press* (HC 780 2012–13). See http://webarchive.nationalarchives.gov.uk/20140122145147/http:/www.levesoninquiry.org.uk/

[9] On the Leveson inquiry and its aftermath, see further Chapter 19, section 3.2.3.

[10] *Learning from Bristol: Report of the Public Inquiry into Children's Heart Surgery at the BRI 1984–95* (Cm 5207 2001).

[11] *The Royal Liverpool Children's Hospital (Alder Hey) Inquiry* (HC 12 1998–99).

[12] The Shipman Inquiry (six reports published 2002–05), http://webarchive.nationalarchives.gov.uk/20090808154959/http:/www.the-shipman-inquiry.org.uk/reports.asp

[13] *Report of the Mid Staffordshire NHS Foundation Trust Public Inquiry* (HC 947 2012–13), https://www.gov.uk/government/publications/report-of-the-mid-staffordshire-nhs-foundation-trust-public-inquiry

- *The Bloody Sunday Inquiry* Between 1998 and 2010, this inquiry investigated the events concerning a violent disturbance in Londonderry (Derry) in 1972 following a civil rights march during which shots were fired by the British Army and 13 people were killed. This incident was the subject of an initial inquiry by the then Lord Chief Justice, which took only a matter of weeks to report, and the outcome of which was badly received as being perceived by some as unduly favourable to the government. For some years, there was a campaign for a new inquiry, to which the Labour government agreed in 1998. The new inquiry was chaired by a Supreme Court Justice, Lord Saville.[14] It was the most protracted and the costliest inquiry ever held in the UK. It lasted for over a decade and considered the statements of 2,500 witnesses, of whom 922 were called to give direct evidence. It resulted in a ten-volume report that condemned the actions of the British Army as unjustified. The inquiry cost approximately £192 million, a significant proportion of which was spent on legal services.

There are currently two particularly high-profile inquiries in progress:

- *The Undercover Policing Inquiry*[15] This inquiry was established following media reports of alleged misconduct by undercover police officers, including undercover officers assuming the identities of dead children as part of their cover; having undercover relationships with women; and the police monitoring some MPs, trade unionists, and the family of Stephen Lawrence.

- *The Independent Inquiry into Child Sexual Abuse* Sparked by widespread concerns about historic sexual abuse of children, this inquiry is investigating whether public bodies and other non-state institutions have taken seriously their duty of care to protect children from such abuse.[16] The inquiry intends to identify institutional failings, demand accountability for past institutional failings, support victims and survivors to share their experience of sexual abuse, and make recommendations. The inquiry has launched 13 separate investigations into a broad range of institutions of historical child abuse—each of which could constitute a normal inquiry by itself. This inquiry has proved to be particularly problematic. Three inquiry chairs have resigned for different reasons. This inquiry will be the largest ever undertaken. The sheer scale and complexity of this inquiry in addition to the sensitivity of the issues raised and the expectations it has created have prompted concerns over its viability.

Each public inquiry is unique. Each is established as a result of a particular set of circumstances that give rise to public concern, and each tends to generate a degree of controversy and public debate in its own particular way. What, then, are the functions of inquiries?

---

[14] *Principal Conclusions and Overall Assessment of the Bloody Sunday Inquiry* (HC 30 2010–11), https://www.gov.uk/government/publications/report-of-the-bloody-sunday-inquiry. For critical comment, see Blom-Cooper, 'What Went Wrong on Bloody Sunday: A Critique of the Saville Inquiry' [2010] PL 61.

[15] See https://www.ucpi.org.uk   [16] See https://www.iicsa.org.uk

2.2 **The role and functions of inquiries**

Inquiries have a number of functions.[17] First, as official investigations, inquiries can provide a *full and fair account of the relevant facts*. This is especially important when the facts are disputed or unclear. Inquiries provide a mechanism for investigating and determining the facts in a way different from either formal court litigation or the more knockabout style of politics found in the House of Commons.

Second, inquiries enable government to *learn from events to prevent their recurrence*. Inquiries are normally tasked not just with fact-finding, but also framing recommendations that will prevent repetition of the particular problem that gave rise to the inquiry in the first place. For example, the Stephen Lawrence inquiry made some 70 recommendations concerning such matters as the investigation and prosecution of racist crimes by the police. Inquiries may then perform a powerful role in holding public bodies to account by ensuring that the facts are properly investigated so that lessons may be distilled and practice changed accordingly. An inquiry may have been prompted by a particular event, but this will often provide the basis to range more broadly into a certain aspect of government and to frame appropriate recommendations. In this sense, inquiries are often case studies in organisational or governmental failure. In another sense, inquiries can be viewed, alongside royal commissions and parliamentary select committees, as a 'decision advice process' as to how that organisational failure can be corrected and, in future, prevented.[18] Compared with these other methods, the distinctive feature of inquiries is that they are typically established as a result of a specific event, or set of events, the investigation of which may prevent similar events from recurring.

Third, inquiries may help to *restore public confidence* after a major failure by demonstrating that a particular issue is being fully investigated. Inquiries can also provide a forum for accountability of government: by finding the facts, inquiries can hold people and organisations to account and apportion blame.

Fourth, inquiries may provide an opportunity for the *reconciliation or resolution of difficult issues* by bringing all of the protagonists together; they might provide opportunities for a form of communal catharsis. Inquiries often concern difficult and sensitive issues. By holding an inquiry to investigate painful matters—for example, failings in the health care system—it may then be possible to put those issues to rest or to ensure that there is a degree of 'closure' in respect of them. Inquiries can also improve both the understanding and resolution of complex issues. For instance, the purposes of the Independent Inquiry into Child Sexual Abuse is to give a voice to victims and survivors of child sexual abuse, to understand how institutions have failed to protect children from sexual abuse, and to make practical recommendations to ensure better institutional protection for children in the future.[19]

---

[17] For discussion, see Howe, 'The Management of Public Inquiries' (1999) 70 Political Quarterly 294; PASC, *Government by Inquiry* (HC 51 2004–05), [10]–[12].

[18] Barker, 'Public Policy Inquiry and Advice as an Aspect of Constitutional Reform' (1998) 4 Journal of Legislative Studies 107.

[19] See https://www.iicsa.org.uk

Finally, it cannot be overlooked that governments may be motivated to establish inquiries by more *self-interested and political considerations*. If government is faced with a difficult issue that has aroused public concern, it may be tempted to give in to demands for a public inquiry that will satisfy immediate public pressure by ensuring that the particular issue is being seen to be investigated, while simultaneously deflecting short-term scrutiny and criticism of the government—in other words, to 'kick the issue into the long grass'. A government is likely to view the decision to establish an inquiry as presenting 'a difficult choice between the short-term attractions of removing a contentious issue from public controversy and the more remote dangers of prolonging the embarrassment through an extended investigation and an ultimate report over which it has little control'.[20] Establishing an inquiry may also justify governmental inaction while satisfying public demands that 'something must be done' about an issue of public concern.

It has been suggested that inquiries are often instituted to serve a symbolic function by reassuring the public that a particular event, or series of events, has been fully investigated. According to a former Minister, Michael Heseltine, if a government feels the need for an inquiry, then the saying 'Reach your conclusion and then choose your chairman and set up the inquiry' may apply.[21] However, governments can never wholly dictate how an inquiry will actually proceed, or what findings and recommendations it may make. Furthermore, governments both cooperate with and fund inquiries; there are also examples of governments responding constructively to inquiries' recommendations.[22]

Inquiries possess some features of both the administrative and the judicial processes. Like courts and tribunals, inquiries usually have to make findings of fact, but, unlike courts, inquiries cannot determine criminal or civil liability or make legally binding decisions; rather, their role is to investigate a particular issue of public concern. The final decisions contained in an inquiry's report will not have been reached by the application of pre-established rules: they will be the result of the exercise of wide discretion in the balancing of private and public interests. Unlike the courts, inquiries often make recommendations that have broader implications for public policy and administration. At the same time, unlike administrative decision-makers, inquiries often sit in public and hear evidence through an orderly procedure, sometimes approximating that of the courts. Many, but not all, inquiries have been chaired by judges. Furthermore, while the decision to establish an inquiry is one for a government Minister, inquiries themselves are—or should be—independent of the government. Inquiries cannot then be classified as either administrative or judicial, but are best viewed as a hybrid of the two.

Q Why do we have inquiries? Is it realistic to assume that inquiries can fulfil all of the expectations placed on them?

---

[20] Leigh and Lustgarten, 'Five Volumes in Search of Accountability: The Scott Report' (1996) 59 MLR 695.
[21] PASC, *Minutes of Evidence*, 11 November 2004, Q615.   [22] See section 4.1 for examples.

2.3 The legal framework of inquiries

While inquiries have been used as a tool of government for many years, the legal framework underpinning them was, until recently, quite confused. Inquiries could be established in one of three possible ways. First, it was possible to establish an inquiry *under the Tribunals of Inquiry (Evidence) Act 1921*, which was enacted by Parliament to create a mechanism for the investigation of allegations of improper behaviour by certain government officials in the then Ministry of Munitions in relation to armament contracts. Inquiries under the 1921 Act had to be held in public, and had the power to compel witnesses to attend and give evidence. Another distinctive feature of such inquiries was that they had a direct connection with Parliament. Such inquiries could only be established through a resolution of both Houses of Parliament 'for inquiring into a matter . . . of great public importance'.[23] Furthermore, there was a practice of Parliament debating the inquiry report on a substantive motion following its publication. In other words, the 1921 Act introduced a direct link between an inquiry and Parliament. Some recent inquiries have been held under the 1921 Act, including the Bloody Sunday and Shipman inquiries. However, use of this Act declined as government established inquiries through the following alternative means.

Second, then, inquiries could be established under a *specific statutory provision* governing the general area of activity. For example, the Stephen Lawrence inquiry was established under the Police Act 1996, under which the Home Secretary could direct an inquiry to be held into any matter connected with the policing of any area; such inquiries could be conducted either in public or in private, as the Home Secretary directed.[24] Other inquiries—for example, the Royal Liverpool Children's Hospital (Alder Hey) and Bristol Royal Infirmary inquiries—were held under specific statutory powers concerning inquiries into the NHS.[25]

Third, an inquiry could be established *on a non-statutory basis under a general ministerial prerogative power*. Both the Hutton and Butler inquires were established on this basis. Lacking formal legal powers, such non-statutory inquiries were dependent upon the active cooperation of government and other public bodies. Compared with inquiries established under the 1921 Act, the second and third types of inquiry, once they reported, typically received less thoroughgoing attention in Parliament.

The Inquiries Act 2005 created a comprehensive statutory power to establish inquiries and consolidates other legislation concerning inquiries.[26] The Act also seeks to make inquiry procedures faster and more effective, and to contain the escalation of their costs. In this respect, the Act has been welcomed. At the same time, other aspects have raised concerns. One is that the 2005 Act has removed formal parliamentary involvement in inquiries. In other words, there has been a long-term diminution in Parliament's role in the process of inquiries, which the 2005 Act has finally extinguished. As one function of inquiries is to secure accountability of government,

---

[23] Tribunals of Inquiry (Evidence) Act 1921, s 1(1).   [24] Police Act 1996, s 49.
[25] National Health Service Act 1977, ss 2 and 84.
[26] See also Department for Constitutional Affairs, *Effective Inquiries*, DCA Consultation Paper 12-04 (London 2004).

this might appear odd. A second concern is that the 2005 Act has simultaneously strengthened the executive's position by enabling Ministers to decide not only the form, personnel, and terms of reference of an inquiry, but also to influence its operation. Under the 2005 Act, Ministers now have the power to end or suspend inquiries.[27] To evaluate the Act in more detail, we need to examine how inquiries are established and undertaken.

3. The inquiry process

3.1 Establishing an inquiry

The government is never obliged to establish an inquiry; the decision is discretionary and will be informed by various policy considerations. Given the diversity of situations that might generate calls for an inquiry, the 2005 Act places only the very loosest limits on the exercise of this power. Under the Act, a government Minister may cause an inquiry to be held where it appears that particular events have caused, or are capable of causing, public concern, or there is public concern that particular events may have occurred.[28] Clearly, in considering whether or not to establish an inquiry, a Minister may have regard to a range of competing considerations: the gravity of the event(s) generating calls for an inquiry; the need to maintain public confidence; public and media opinion; the probable costs and length of an inquiry; and, cynically, the perceived need to establish an inquiry to relieve immediate political pressure. Decisions regarding the establishment of an inquiry are often contentious and the subject of public and political debate. As a House of Lords committee has noted, 'There is no consistency in ministerial decisions on setting up inquiries. Ministers tend to do so only when there is irresistible public or parliamentary pressure; and when they decline to set an inquiry up, adequate reasons are not always given.'[29]

Indeed, a Minister's refusal to establish an inquiry may attract not only political debate, but also legal challenge. Consider the case of Zahid Mubarek, a prisoner in a young offender institution, who had been placed in a cell with a known violent and racist thug, who subsequently murdered him. Mubarek's family wanted to know why this happened, but the Home Secretary refused a public inquiry into his death. The family challenged this decision on the ground that it breached Art 2 of the European Convention on Human Rights, which provides that everyone's right to life shall be protected by law. The House of Lords (now the Supreme Court) concluded that, in some circumstances, the right to life positively obliged the state to take steps to prevent life from being taken and, as part of that duty, an obligation to investigate the circumstances surrounding a death.[30] The Home Secretary's refusal to establish an inquiry was therefore unlawful. The subsequent inquiry report criticised systemic

---

[27] Inquiries Act 2005, ss 13 and 14.   [28] Inquiries Act 2005, s 1(1).

[29] House of Lords Select Committee on the Inquiries Act 2005, *The Inquiries Act 2005: Post-Legislative Scrutiny* (HL 143 2013–14) p 6.

[30] *R (Amin) v Secretary of State for the Home Department* [2003] UKHL 51, [2004] 1 AC 653. See also *R (JL) v Secretary of State for the Home Department* [2007] EWCA Civ 767, [2008] 1 WLR 158.

shortcomings within the Prison Service that had exposed a vulnerable prisoner to attack by his cell mate.[31]

The Mubarek case is fact-specific—not all governmental refusals to hold an inquiry can be successfully challenged through judicial review—but it illustrates a developing role for the courts in reviewing the legality of such decisions especially when Convention rights are involved. In 2014, the High Court held the Home Secretary's refusal to establish an inquiry into the killing, in the UK, of a Russian political dissident, Alexander Litvinenko, was unlawful.[32] The inquiry established subsequently found that the Russian President Vladimir Putin 'probably' ordered the killing.[33]

As regards the character of such an inquiry into a death, the European Court of Human Rights has itself held that the nature and degree of public and independent scrutiny required by Art 2 will depend on the circumstances of the particular case, and the European Court has recognised that, in the light of such factors, the form of investigation required may also vary.[34] To illustrate, consider the Azelle Rodney inquiry, which in 2013 found that the police had unlawfully shot dead a suspected criminal.[35] At the earlier inquest, the coroner had ruled that neither he nor the jury could see intelligence material relevant to the inquest. A public inquiry was needed to comply with the state's duty to arrange for an independent investigation under Art 2. This was the first time a public inquiry had found a breach of Art 2 by a police force in the planning and implementation of an armed operation which led to a civilian's death.

In other cases, the courts have rejected legal challenges against a government's refusal to hold an inquiry in public. Following the outbreak of foot-and-mouth disease in 2001, which had a considerable adverse impact on the farming community, the government refused to hold a public inquiry, preferring instead to have three separate independent inquiries that received evidence for the most part in private. A legal challenge against the decision not to hold a public inquiry failed. The court pointed out that there were arguments both for and against full-scale inquiries sitting in public, and that a range of considerations could be taken into account, such as cost, speed, and the desirability of candour on the part of witnesses. The decision as to the nature of an inquiry was therefore an essentially political one.[36]

The government therefore has discretion when it comes to the setting of an inquiry's terms of reference, which are crucial to determining an inquiry's scope, length, complexity, cost, and success. For example, whether an inquiry is to establish particular facts and make recommendations will normally be explicitly detailed in its terms of

---

[31] *Report of the Zahid Mubarek Inquiry* (HC 1082 2005–06).

[32] *R (Litvinenko) v Secretary of State for the Home Department* [2014] EWHC 194 (Admin).

[33] https://www.litvinenkoinquiry.org

[34] *McCann v United Kingdom* (1995) 21 EHRR 97, [193]; *Jordan v United Kingdom* (2001) 37 EHRR 52, [105].

[35] See http://webarchive.nationalarchives.gov.uk/20150406091509/http://azellerodneyinquiry.independent.gov.uk

[36] *Persey v Secretary of State for Environment, Food and Rural Affairs* [2002] EWHC 371 (Admin), [2003] QB 794.

reference. The relationship between an inquiry and the government will also be determined by its terms of reference.

While Ministers have a wide legal discretion, it should never be forgotten that Ministers operate within a political and media context, which can often influence what happens in practice. For instance, following the invasion of Iraq in 2003 and the lack of any WMD, there had been a growing consensus that a full inquiry was necessary. When this was announced in 2009, the then Prime Minister initially stated that the inquiry would hear evidence in private. The predictable political and media response to this was one of almost total criticism. The inquiry chair, Sir John Chilcot, subsequently decided that inquiry hearings would be held in public so far as possible.

Under the 2005 Act, the Minister must set out an inquiry's terms of reference and inform Parliament (or, if applicable, the relevant devolved legislature).[37] In practice, the terms of reference may often be a matter for negotiation between the chair of the inquiry and the Minister. Other interested parties might also make representations as to an inquiry's terms of reference. It is clearly important to the success of an inquiry that its terms of reference are precise, command broad consensus, and enable the inquiry to undertake its task without undue constraint. While Parliament must be informed as to the terms of reference, it has little input in determining what those terms should be. An important limit on the government's discretion over terms of reference is that no inquiry panel may rule on, or have the power to determine, any person's civil or criminal liability.[38] Such tasks are for the ordinary criminal and civil justice processes.

The 2005 Act established a framework for inquiries that is comprehensive in the sense that it created a general, rather than subject-specific, ministerial power to establish inquiries, but it does not preclude non-statutory inquiries. Indeed, the Chilcot inquiry was established in that way. This decision was taken on the basis that an inquiry under the Act was considered unsuitable given that there is a (qualified) duty to hold such inquiries in public.[39] Announcing the inquiry, the then Prime Minister, Gordon Brown, said that 'evidence will be heard in private' because the inquiry would be concerned with matters entailing 'a degree of confidentiality that would not suit a public inquiry, where all witnesses give evidence in public'.[40] This prompted a good deal of controversy—the suspicion being that Ministers were seeking to avoid the potential embarrassment of giving public evidence—and the chairman of the inquiry, Sir John Chilcot, later announced that hearings would be held in public wherever possible. As a result, the leading players involved—including Tony Blair, the Prime Minister at the time of the invasion of Iraq—had to give evidence publicly. During the course of the inquiry, it had been thought by some people that it would be a whitewash. However, the devastating criticism of the inquiry strongly reinforces the conclusion that the inquiry undertook an exceedingly thorough and independent scrutiny of the Iraq war.

---

[37] Inquiries Act 2005, ss 5 and 6.   [38] Inquiries Act 2005, s 2(1).
[39] Inquiries Act 2005, ss 18 and 19.   [40] HC Deb, vol 494, cols 23–4 (15 June 2009).

3.2 **The membership of inquiries**

Who chairs inquiries? Because inquiries are established on an ad hoc basis, they have no set membership; this will vary from inquiry to inquiry. Some inquiries may have a sole chair, others will be composed of a panel or committee of inquiry members, other inquiries may have a chair with assessors. Some inquiries may be chaired by a judge, with two or more panel members who possess particular expertise of assistance to the inquiry. Other inquiries may be chaired by a former and experienced civil servant with panel members. As inquiries are established by the government, it is primarily for the Minister to decide upon questions of membership.

A particular issue is whether or not judges should chair inquiries. This does not always happen, but there has been an increasing trend for judges to chair inquiries.[41] There are arguments for this practice. In addition to their legal expertise, judges have experience in assessing evidence—a particularly important skill, because inquiries are often established to clarify disputed factual issues. Judges are also impartial and independent from the government—a factor that will enhance public confidence in the inquiry because they are free from party political bias. From a practical point of view, judges are often more readily available than other individuals to chair inquiries. In the context of inquiries into areas of extreme controversy, a judge may offer a seal of credibility because he or she will be independent, non-party-political, and impartial. Indeed, when Sir John Chilcot—a former senior civil servant—was appointed to chair the Iraq Inquiry, there were suggestions in some quarters that the government was seeking to avoid the sort of forensic scrutiny and consideration of the legality of the Iraq war that a judicially led inquiry might have facilitated.[42]

On the other hand, while judges are skilled in fact-finding, they may not necessarily be well equipped to frame appropriate recommendations, particularly when an inquiry is essentially concerned with a widespread and systemic governmental failure. Many recent inquiries have concerned the operation of public sector bodies of which judges normally have little or no experience; if inquiries are to lead to effective improvement of such bodies, then it is arguably best that their membership includes those individuals with experience of the policy and administrative contexts within which such bodies operate.

Perhaps the strongest argument against the use of judges to chair inquiries concerns the highly political nature of the subject matter being investigated. As Beatson has noted, involving a judge will not depoliticise an inherently controversial political matter.[43] From the government's perspective, however, using a judge may well be attractive: it may enable the government to claim that the issue has been taken out of the political domain merely because an independent judge is chairing the inquiry, thereby providing public reassurance.[44] If there are obvious advantages to

---

[41] The Stephen Lawrence, Bloody Sunday, Hutton, Shipman, Leveson, Azelle Rodney, Undercover Policies, and Child Sexual Abuse inquiries were all chaired by senior judges.

[42] See, eg 'Iraq inquiry: civil servant Sir John Chilcot "incapable of addressing legal issues" ', *The Daily Telegraph*, 24 November 2009.

[43] Beatson, 'Should Judges Chair Public Inquiries?' (2005) 121 LQR 221, 236.

[44] Drewry, 'Judicial Inquiries and Public Reassurance' [1996] PL 368.

government Ministers in appointing judges to chair inquiries, the gains to the judiciary are perhaps less easily discernible. Judges may chair inquiries out of a sense of public duty. Yet, by chairing inquiries, judges may run the risk of being drawn into areas of acute political controversy and open themselves up to criticism. As a former Attorney-General has put it: 'When a judge enters the market place of public affairs outside his court and throws coconuts he is likely to have the coconuts thrown back at him. If one values the standing of the judiciary . . . the less they are used [in relation to inquiries] the better it will be.'[45] There is a wider risk that the judiciary's own reputation and authority could itself be damaged in the aftermath of an inquiry— especially if there is public dissension over the correctness of the findings, and criticism of a judge's impartiality and objectivity. For some, it is wrong in principle for judges to chair inquiries of a political nature as this may have a general corrosive effect on public trust in the judiciary; the judiciary's political independence may be threatened by its entanglement in controversial political affairs.[46]

The Hutton inquiry is a good illustration of the difficulties that a judge chairing a public inquiry can face and has been instanced as a case in which it is questionable whether a judge should have chaired an inquiry that took place in a highly controversial political context. While Lord Hutton—then a Law Lord—viewed his role solely as one of fact-finding, he was criticised for interpreting his terms of reference too narrowly, for being too establishment-minded, and for showing a lack of understanding of the broader political context of the inquiry. For Jowell, the difficulty is that while judges possess special expertise in analysing evidence, assessing the credibility of witnesses, and resolving complex factual issues, they are reluctant to engage in the broader political context in which an inquiry operates.[47] According to Blom-Cooper and Munro, there was room to doubt whether a Law Lord's 'borrowed authority' ought to have been lent to the Hutton inquiry, which 'may represent the classic instance of why we should question the public's ready acceptance of asking a judge to hold a public inquiry'.[48]

Some have argued that the involvement of senior judges in inquiries in general should be avoided as it gives rise to serious constitutional concerns.[49] This view is fortified if we consider experience elsewhere. For example, there is a well-established consensus in the USA that it is constitutionally and politically inappropriate for judges to undertake inquiries because of the doctrine of the separation of powers. As we have previously considered, that doctrine is not as firmly embedded in the UK constitution as it is elsewhere.[50] In this respect, the 2005 Act makes little change as to the use of judges: it does not remove the possibility of appointing a judge. The Act does, though, add an important safeguard: a Minister proposing to appoint a judge to an inquiry must first consult with a senior member of the judiciary, such as the President of the Supreme Court or the Lord Chief Justice.[51] This allows scope for the

---

[45] HL Deb, vol 648, col 883 (21 May 2003) (Lord Morris of Aberavon QC).
[46] Steele, 'Judging Judicial Inquiries' [2004] PL 738, 745.
[47] Jowell, 'The wrong man for the job', *The Guardian*, 3 February 2004.
[48] Blom-Cooper and Munro, 'The Hutton Inquiry' [2004] PL 472, 476.
[49] Steele, 'Judging Judicial Inquiries' [2004] PL 738, 745.   [50] See Chapter 3.
[51] Inquiries Act 2005, s 10.

senior judiciary to consider whether it would be appropriate for a judge to chair an inquiry before agreeing to such a request from the government. This duty to consult does not, however, go as far as some would have liked: during the passage of the Inquiries Act, some senior judges argued that judges should be appointed to inquiries only with the *approval* of the Lord Chief Justice.[52]

If a judge is not appointed to chair an inquiry, then another suitable person will be. Such categories of person have included former senior civil servants (eg the Butler and Chilcot inquiries) or those with particular experience in the subject matter of the inquiry (eg the Bristol Royal Infirmary inquiry was chaired by an academic lawyer specialising in medical law and ethics). Under the 2005 Act, the Minister must ensure that the inquiry panel possesses the necessary expertise to undertake the inquiry.[53] This can be particularly important if the inquiry is to consider a complex or sensitive social issue or area of governmental activity and if the inquiry is to frame effective recommendations. For example, the Butler inquiry panel, which was concerned with the handling of intelligence concerning WMD in Iraq, was comprised of Privy Councillors. As members of both Houses of Parliament and experts who possessed independence and prior experience of handling intelligence information, they were well placed to inquire into sensitive matters. The inquiry was able to investigate effectively issues that were highly controversial and which involved matters of national security, and which needed to be discussed in private, although a report was subsequently published.

In any event, whoever is appointed—a judge or a specialist with or without other panel members—it is imperative that they both are and are seen to be wholly impartial. Anyone with a direct interest in the matters to which the inquiry relates or a close association with an interested party will be precluded.[54] Impartiality is essential if an inquiry is to command public confidence.

In addition to inquiry panel members, the Minister may also appoint assessors who can assist the inquiry panel with their expert knowledge and advice.[55] Again, the particular individuals chosen for this task will depend on the nature of the inquiry. It is apparent that the chair of an inquiry may be able to exert some influence with regard to the areas of expertise that any assessors or advisers appointed to assist the inquiry should possess. For example, Keith J, the High Court judge who chaired the Zahid Mubarek inquiry, told senior Home Office officials before the inquiry was announced that he wished to have the assistance of independent advisers on a number of areas—race and diversity, the management and operation of prisons and young offender institutions, and prison life—on which he himself lacked both special experience and expertise. The advisers assisted the inquiry by informing its analysis and recommendations, thereby augmenting the credibility and authority of the final report.

---

[52] See, eg Beatson, 'Should Judges Chair Public Inquiries?' (2005) 121 LQR 221, 251; Lord Woolf, memorandum to Public Administration Select Committee, November 2004.

[53] Inquiries Act 2005, s 8.   [54] Inquiries Act 2005, s 9.   [55] Inquiries Act 2005, s 11.

> **Q** What are the arguments for and against judges undertaking public inquiries? Why, if at all, is it constitutionally inappropriate for judges to chair inquiries? Are there particular types of inquiry that may be either particularly suited or unsuited to judicial involvement?

3.3 **Inquiries—public or private?**

Should an inquiry be held in public or in private? If an inquiry is to restore public confidence when investigating matters of public concern, then the only way of doing this will be to have public hearings—so that the public can see that matters have been fully and properly investigated. Private inquiries inevitably give rise to a suspicion that they are not being conducted sufficiently thoroughly or that something is being hushed up. Public hearings dispel suspicion. Holding inquiries in public also ensures that information surrounding the matter in question is brought to light. This means that, whatever the conclusions of the inquiry panel, members of the public, the media, and parliamentarians gain access to facts that will enable them to form their own judgements about (for example) who should be blamed.

On the other hand, it may be easier to elicit the truth from witnesses if their questioning is not conducted in the full glare of publicity; individuals who can assist as to the failings of others, errors by public bodies, and administrative flaws are likely to be far more forthcoming and candid in private. However, a counter-argument is that allowing witnesses to testify out of the glare of public scrutiny may allow them to embellish their testimony rather than require them to adhere to the truth; it may also enable them to cast blame on others. There may be other justifiable reasons for holding an inquiry in private: national security, legal barriers to the disclosure of documents, personal privacy, and avoiding unnecessary intrusion or distress to witnesses. It is also important to consider concerns as to the costs and time involved: private inquiries tend to be both quicker and less costly than public inquiries.

The importance of the issue is illustrated by legal challenges made as to whether inquiries should be held either in public or private. Consider the Shipman inquiry into the activities of a doctor who had killed many of his own patients. The Health Secretary had decided that the inquiry should sit in private. However, this was successfully challenged through judicial review proceedings by the victims' families, who wanted the inquiry to be held in public. The court reasoned that if the inquiry were conducted in public, then its report and recommendations would command greater public confidence. Furthermore, the court noted that because all members of the public are accustomed to placing trust in the medical profession, the restoration of public confidence was a matter of high importance.[56] It is apparent that this legal challenge had a broader significance on the role of this particular inquiry. The Health Secretary had initially wanted a limited inquiry into the safeguards over doctors, while the victims' families wanted a much more wide-ranging inquiry. Following the

---

[56] *R v Secretary of State for Health, ex p Wagstaff* [2001] 1 WLR 292.

court's decision, not only was the inquiry held in public, but it also became much more broad-ranging than the government had initially envisaged. It was also held under the 1921 Act and chaired by a High Court judge.

Under the 2005 Act, an inquiry chair must take reasonable steps to secure public access both to inquiry proceedings, and the evidence and information provided to the inquiry panel.[57] Public access may be restricted if either the Minister or the inquiry chair considers it to be conducive to the inquiry fulfilling its terms of reference or to be necessary in the public interest having regard to specified matters. Those matters are the extent to which any restriction on access might inhibit the allaying of public concern; any risk of harm or damage that could be avoided or reduced by any such restriction; any conditions as to confidentiality; and the extent to which not imposing any restriction would be likely to cause delay, or impair the efficiency or effectiveness of the inquiry, or otherwise to result in additional cost.[58] In summary, then, the general principle is that an inquiry should be held in public—subject to specified restrictions.

> **Q** To what extent, if at all, is it acceptable for inquiries to be held in private?

3.4 Inquiry proceedings

Inquiry proceedings need to be highly flexible and adaptable to the particular circumstances; it is for the chair to decide on the inquiry's procedure and mode of operation.[59] It is axiomatic that the proceedings should be fair, and that the decisions and procedures of inquiries are susceptible to challenge by way of judicial review on the basis that they are either unlawful, irrational, or procedurally unfair. For example, the Bloody Sunday inquiry prompted a judicial review challenge concerning the anonymity of witnesses, considered in section 3.5.

Inquiries often adopt an inquisitorial approach in which the inquiry chair or panel will frame the issues to be addressed, lead the investigation, and both call and question witnesses. The advantage of this approach is that it may assist the inquiry in drawing out the facts, while at the same time preventing the inquiry from becoming a confrontational, adversarial process. For example, the procedures of the Bristol Royal Infirmary inquiry were designed to be wholly inquisitorial and sensitive to witnesses' needs.[60] An inquiry will normally have its own counsel, who will undertake the questioning of witnesses. A witness or core participant of an inquiry is entitled to have legal representation. However, the role of that representation is limited to making opening and closing statements. Questions of a witness will primarily be asked by the inquiry's own counsel unless the inquiry itself directs that a witness may be asked questions by his or her own legal representative.[61]

---

[57] Inquiries Act 2005, s 18.   [58] Inquiries Act 2005, s 19(4).

[59] Inquiries Act 2005, s 17(1).

[60] Maclean, 'How Does an Inquiry Inquire? A Brief Note on the Working Methods of the Bristol Royal Infirmary Inquiry' (2001) 28 JLS 590.

[61] Inquiry Rules 2006, SI 2006/1838, rr 10 and 11.

The cost and length of inquiries varies. The Hutton inquiry reported eight months after it was established; the Bloody Sunday inquiry took over 12 years. As that particular example demonstrates, lengthy inquiries are likely to be more costly. The Bloody Sunday inquiry cost some £192 million; by contrast, the Francis inquiry into Mid Staffordshire NHS Foundation Trust cost £13.6 million. Inquiries are funded by the sponsoring government departments. While an inquiry should investigate and produce workable recommendations, it should not take too long or cost too much. To this end, the 2005 Act introduces some pragmatic measures to try to contain the length of inquiries and their costs. For example, legal challenges (by way of judicial review) to the way in which inquiries are being conducted can cause substantial delay (resulting in significant additional costs). The 2005 Act requires that any judicial review challenge must normally be brought within 14 days.[62] Furthermore, in making any decision as to the procedure or conduct of an inquiry, the chair must act fairly and also consider the need to avoid any unnecessary cost (whether to public funds, or to witnesses or others).[63]

3.5 **Witnesses**

A contentious aspect of inquiry proceedings concerns the tension between achieving the inquiry's purpose of eliciting the truth while also protecting those individuals against whom findings of culpability may have to be made. If an inquiry operates under an inquisitorial process, then some witnesses might feel that they have not been treated fairly because the basic safeguards of the more usual adversarial court process have not been followed. On the other hand, inquiries undertake a primarily investigative function and do not, as with court litigation, necessarily need to operate on an adversarial basis.

If this issue seems somewhat abstruse, imagine that you are to appear as a witness before an inquiry. There is a chance that the inquiry may be critical of your conduct. While you will be found neither guilty of a criminal offence nor liable for any civil wrongdoing, there is a chance that your personal reputation or career may be harmed—yet you may neither be legally represented nor cross-examined by your own representative. You may feel at risk of being subjected to an unfair process. At the same time, the inquiry will want to establish the truth as to what has occurred.

It was because of concerns over the fairness of inquiry processes that the Salmon Commission was established to examine the operation of inquisitorial procedure by inquires.[64] Noting that the inquisitorial approach is alien to British law, Salmon proposed six principles that roughly equate with the adversarial process:

(i) Before any person becomes involved in an inquiry, the inquiry must be satisfied that there are circumstances that affect her and that the tribunal proposes to investigate.

---

[62] Inquiries Act 2005, s 38.   [63] Inquiries Act 2005, s 17(3).
[64] *The Report of the Royal Commission on Tribunals of Inquiry* (Cmnd 3121 1966).

(ii) Before any person involved in an inquiry is called as a witness, she should be informed of any allegations that are made against her and the substance of the evidence in support of them.

(iii) That person should be given an adequate opportunity of preparing her case and of being assisted by her legal advisers, and legal expenses should normally be met out of public funds.

(iv) That person should have the opportunity of being examined by her own lawyer and of stating her case in public at the inquiry.

(v) Any material witness whom she wishes called at the inquiry should, if reasonably practicable, be heard.

(vi) Finally, she should have the opportunity of testing, by cross-examination conducted by her own lawyer, any evidence that may affect her.

The degree to which an inquiry adheres to these principles reflects a choice for an inquiry chair as to their appropriateness in the specific inquiry context. If an inquiry follows the Salmon principles, then there is a risk of making the inquiry too confrontational and adversarial—in other words, turning the inquiry into something akin to a court process. There is also the risk that greater involvement of lawyers increases the length and cost of an inquiry. Some inquiry chairs have noted that, while an inquiry needs to be fair to witnesses, this does not necessarily require strict adherence to the Salmon principles. The principles are, then, not to be applied inflexibly or rigidly, but adapted to each set of circumstances.[65]

In some inquiries, the principles have been discarded altogether. For the purposes of his 'arms to Iraq' inquiry into the export of defence equipment to Iraq, Lord Scott decided not to adhere to the Salmon principles because he was of the view that they would have been inoperable, ineffective, and inefficient. Scott argued that an inquiry has an investigative purpose to determine the truth and an inquisitorial mode of procedure is appropriate.[66] It was not therefore necessary to adhere strictly to the Salmon principles; instead, the Scott inquiry adopted an inquisitorial procedure, with questions being posed by the chair and his assisting counsel. This was, however, a controversial way of proceeding. Lord Howe—a former government Minister who, as a lawyer, had been involved in two earlier inquiries and who appeared as a witness before Scott—roundly condemned Scott's refusal to permit legal representation of witnesses and their cross-examination on the basis that this was contrary to established inquiry procedure, was unfair, and undermined the inquiry's ability to operate effectively and to reach valid conclusions.[67] What is the status of the Salmon principles? The 'issue has yet to be satisfactorily resolved'.[68]

Things have now moved on: the Inquiry Rules 2006 introduced a system of 'warning letters' by which inquiry witnesses can be notified of any potential criticism.[69]

---

[65] PASC, *Government by Inquiry* (HC 51 2004–05), [100]–[104].
[66] Scott, 'Procedures at Inquiries: The Duty to be Fair' (1995) 111 LQR 596. See also Winetrobe, 'Inquiries after Scott: The Return of the Tribunal of Inquiry' [1997] PL 18.
[67] Howe, 'Procedure at the Scott Inquiry' [1996] PL 445.   [68] PASC, HC 51, [100].
[69] The Inquiry Rules 2006, SI 2006/1838, r 13.

This is sometimes known as the 'Maxwellisation procedure' after litigation concerning the procedures for Companies Act inquires against Robert Maxwell, the former press baron, undertaken in the 1970s.[70] Under this system, the inquiry chair may send a warning letter to any person who may be subject to criticism in the inquiry proceedings or report, outlining the potential criticism and the evidence in support of it. The inquiry panel may only include any criticism of a person in the inquiry report if that person has both been sent a warning letter and also given a reasonable opportunity to respond to it. Furthermore, before the publication of a final report, the chair is to provide a copy to each core participant in the inquiry.[71] In this way, the rules ensure that those who might be criticised get the chance to comment beforehand while preventing extensive and costly cross-examination of witnesses.

This process provides procedural fairness and avoids the trappings of a court-like process, but inevitably it takes time and is susceptible to legal challenge. For instance, the Iraq inquiry was repeatedly criticised for taking too long to report. The delay is attributable to warning letters issued to those individuals likely to be criticised and the need to ensure that any criticism is soundly based, fair, and reasonable.[72] In 2014, a Lords Committee recommended that the Inquiry Rules 2006 be amended, but this was rejected by the government.[73] In 2016, a Commons Select Committee announced a review of Maxwellisation in public inquiries.[74]

3.6 **Publication of inquiry reports**

After the inquiry has taken evidence and written its report, that report must then be delivered to the Minister.[75] Before doing so, the inquiry chair may submit an interim report.[76] It is normally the duty of the Minister to arrange for inquiry reports to be published, although the inquiry chair can have responsibility for this.[77] The general principle is that an inquiry report must be published in full. However, there is scope for the withholding of material in the report from publication to the extent that this is required by law or is considered necessary in the public interest. Such public interest matters can include, for example, the extent that the withholding of such material might inhibit the allaying of public concern, any risk of harm or damage that could be avoided or reduced by withholding any material, and any conditions as to confidentiality subject to which a person acquired information that he has given to the inquiry.[78] Furthermore, as we have seen, an inquiry may have to disclose its report to each core participant before its publication. The final report must be laid before Parliament or

---

[70] See *Re Pergamon Press* [1971] Ch 388; *Maxwell v Department of Trade and Industry* [1974] QB 523.

[71] The Inquiry Rules 2006, SI 2006/1838, r 17.

[72] See the statement by the Chair of the Iraq Inquiry (26 August 2015): **http://www.iraqinquiry.org.uk/media/234517/2015-08-26-statement-by-sir-john-chilcot.pdf**

[73] House of Lords Select Committee on the Inquiries Act 2005, *The Inquiries Act 2005: Post-Legislative Scrutiny* (HL 143 2013–14), [251]; Ministry of Justice, *Government Response to the Report of the House of Lords Select Committee on the Inquiries Act 2005* (Cm 8903 2014), p 15.

[74] House of Commons Treasury Select Committee, press notice, 9 June 2016.

[75] Inquiries Act 2005, s 24(1).   [76] Inquiries Act 2005, s 24(3).

[77] Inquiries Act 2005, s 25(1) and (2).   [78] Inquiries Act 2005, s 25(4) and (5).

the relevant devolved legislature.[79] In the case of high-profile inquiries, a government Minister will make a statement to Parliament providing the government's response to the inquiry. For instance, in the case of the Bloody Sunday inquiry, the Prime Minister told the Commons that he was 'deeply sorry' for the conduct of British soldiers who had killed innocent victims and described the findings as 'shocking' and the conduct of the Army as 'unjustified and unjustifiable'.[80] Few inquiry reports are brief; most inquiries typically produce a lengthy report, with various recommendations. Consequently, few people will read inquiry reports in full; most will rely on executive summaries and press reports.

4. The effectiveness of inquiries and the alternatives

4.1 Implementing and monitoring inquiry recommendations

Once an inquiry has reported, the government must decide whether or not to accept the recommendations and, if so, how to implement them. Implementing recommendations is crucial: identifying the lessons is one thing, but recurrence will be prevented only if appropriate practical steps are then taken. In some instances, this may involve changes in the law. For example, the Bristol Royal Infirmary and Royal Liverpool Children's Hospital (Alder Hey) inquiries established that organs and tissue from children who had died had often been removed, stored, and used without proper consent. This resulted in the Human Tissue Act 2004, which established a consistent legislative framework for this issue, and made consent the fundamental principle underpinning the lawful storage and use of human bodies. In other instances, changes in the law may be made albeit belatedly. The Scott inquiry into the export of defence equipment reported in 1996, concluding that the then legislative structure concerning export controls was inadequate and lacked proper parliamentary scrutiny, and should be replaced as soon as possible. However, legislation was only enacted in 2002.[81] In other instances, it will be left to other public agencies to decide whether or not to take action. For instance, the 2013 public inquiry into the death of Azelle Rodney, a suspected criminal, concluded that he had been unlawfully shot dead by the police.[82] In subsequent criminal proceedings, a police officer was acquitted of murder.[83]

In general terms, public inquiries are not always regarded as a success in terms of producing practical changes that secure real improvements. Failure in this regard may be attributable to shortcomings in the inquiry itself, or in governmental and legislative responses to it. For example, with regard to other inquiries held into aspects of the provision of health care by the NHS, it has been concluded that the consistency

---

[79] Inquiries Act 2005, s 26.   [80] HC Deb, vol 511, col 740 (15 June 2010) (David Cameron PM).

[81] Export Controls Act 2002.

[82] See **https://www.gov.uk/government/uploads/system/uploads/attachment_data/file/246478/0552.pdf**

[83] 'Met Police officer Anthony Long cleared of Azelle Rodney murder', *BBC News*, 3 July 2015.

with which successive inquiries have highlighted 'similar causes suggests that their recommendations are either misdirected or not properly implemented'.[84]

Part of the problem here is that there are few formal mechanisms that allow for any follow-up in relation to the findings and recommendations of inquiries. An inquiry will report and it is then for the relevant government department to decide how it will act on the recommendations. However, in the absence of a formal follow-up mechanism, there is always the risk that the impetus behind an inquiry report may dissipate as time passes, the political scenario changes, and competing priorities come to the fore. This, in turn, raises the concern that the cost and resources devoted to inquiries are not worthwhile if their reports and recommendations are merely 'shelved' rather than effectively implemented. The concern is that government may give 'lip service' to inquiry recommendations—but without ongoing monitoring, it is difficult to ensure that the recommendations are actually implemented.

Occasionally, inquiries themselves decide to reconvene to assess the extent to which their recommendations have been implemented by government. For example, the Bichard inquiry into the murder of two schoolgirls by a man who worked as their school's caretaker reconvened six months after the publication of its report. The inquiry chair considered it essential to reconvene the inquiry to ensure that its recommendations had been properly taken on board by the government.[85] Furthermore, parliamentary select committees can undertake follow-up investigations. For example, ten years after the Stephen Lawrence inquiry reported, the Commons Home Affairs Committee found that the police service had made progress towards tackling racial prejudice and discrimination since 1999.[86] The Francis inquiry into the Mid Staffordshire NHS Foundation Trust found that shocking and obvious deficiencies in care could persist unchecked with completely unacceptable consequences for patients and relatives. The inquiry recommended that the Commons Health Committee monitor the implementation of the inquiry's recommendations. Given its regular accountability hearings with professional and system regulators of the NHS, the Committee is well placed to keep under review the government's response to the inquiry and to monitor the development of cultural change in the NHS, which the inquiry considered vital.[87]

These examples of subsequent follow-ups on inquiry reports are very much the exception rather than the norm. There is no formal statutory process in this regard; the 2005 Act is silent on the issue. To remedy the problem, the House of Commons Public Administration Select Committee (PASC) suggested that government departments should report on the implementation of inquiry recommendations at regular intervals, and, in any event, within the first two years of the end of an inquiry. Such reports should cover the extent to which recommendations have been implemented

---

[84] Walshe and Higgins, 'The Use and Impact of Inquiries in the NHS' (2002) 325 British Medical Journal 895, 899.

[85] *An Independent Inquiry Arising from the Soham Murders* (HC 653 2003–04) (the Bichard Inquiry); PASC, Government by Inquiry (HC 51 2004–05), [140].

[86] House of Commons Home Affairs Committee, *The Macpherson Report: Ten Years On* (HC 427 2008–09).

[87] House of Commons Health Committee, *After Francis: Making a Difference* (HC 657 2013–14).

and describe the wider cultural changes that have been brought about as a result. The PASC argued that institutional responsibility for scrutinising such reports should lie with parliamentary select committees, which are well placed to undertake such work.[88] In response, the government accepted that it is important for government departments to maintain a focus on the implementation of inquiry recommendations and that they should publicise how they have dealt with such recommendations.[89]

However, a lack of external follow-up cannot alone explain why inquiry recommendations are not always implemented. Another explanation is that as case studies of large-scale organisational failure, inquiry recommendations often require similarly large-scale change and reform—for instance, to the delivery of public services, regulation of professions, and so on. The effective implementation of inquiry reports will often require wide-ranging political, organisational, professional, and cultural changes—changes that are, by their nature, difficult to accomplish. For instance, the 290 recommendations of the Francis report could be summed up in one single recommendation—that the culture of the NHS must change in order for the safety and quality of the service, and the public's confidence in it, to improve. However, achieving such change in the NHS is highly challenging. NHS England is the world's fifth-largest organisation. Furthermore, the NHS is currently undergoing major changes in its core structure during a squeeze on public spending, wider demographic change (longer life expectancy), and increased demand on its services. Nonetheless, with sufficient leadership, commitment, momentum, and external political oversight—for instance, by a parliamentary committee—such change, though challenging, is possible.

> **Q** Should there be a more formal process for following up the implementation of inquiry recommendations? If so, then who should have this responsibility: Parliament or the government?

4.2 Alternatives to public inquiries

We have encountered various concerns with respect to the effectiveness of public inquiries: their length and cost; the government's influence as regards not just the establishment of inquiries, but also their terms of reference and composition; and the risk that the recommendations made by inquiries may simply be ignored by government. What, then, are the alternatives to public inquiries? In this section, we consider four such alternatives: parliamentary commissions of inquiry, ordinary parliamentary select committees, private-public inquiries, and independent panels.

Parliament can commission and initiate its own inquiries through a special process known as 'parliamentary commissions of inquiry'.[90] Indeed, from the middle of the

---

[88] PASC, HC 51, [147].

[89] Department for Constitutional Affairs, *Government Response to the Public Administration Select Committee's First Report of the 2004–05 Session: 'Government by Inquiry'* (Cm 6481 2005), pp 18–19.

[90] PASC, HC 51, [208]–[215]; PASC, HC 473.

seventeenth century until 1921, the usual method of investigating events giving rise to public disquiet about the alleged misconduct of Ministers or other public servants was by way of a Parliamentary Committee or Commission of Inquiry, but this method fell out of favour. The select committee on the Marconi affair in 1913—in which it was alleged that government Ministers had engaged in insider trading—split on party political lines and discredited the idea of parliamentary commissions of inquiry into major policy questions or failures for a century. Since then extra-parliamentary inquiries have been the norm.

Another option is for ordinary parliamentary select committees to undertake inquiries. Since 1979 select committees have become increasingly important and effective as tools for investigating and scrutinising government—but they are not necessarily well suited to the task of conducting specialised investigations into particular events. Select committees have limited capacity (in terms of time and resources). Their main focus is upon wider scrutiny of government departments, rather than specialised investigations of particular events. Their evidence-taking procedures are not well suited to drawing out the truth from witnesses through the application of a consistent line of questioning. There are also limits on the degree of governmental cooperation with select committees. For example, when investigating the decision to go to war in Iraq, the Foreign Affairs Select Committee met with continued refusal by Ministers to allow access to intelligence papers and personnel, which hampered the Committee's inquiry.[91] Because such committees are comprised of party politicians, there will always be concerns arising from perceptions of partisanship. Furthermore, select committees shadow individual government departments, whereas some matters of concern that prompt calls for public inquiries cover issues that cut across several government departments in addition to other agencies.

Noting its concerns over the long-term diminution of Parliament's role in the process of public inquiries, the PASC has recommended that Parliament should be able to initiate and conduct inquiries by establishing parliamentary commissions of inquiry.[92] Parliamentary commissions of inquiry can, like other inquiries, be established on an ad hoc basis to investigate a particular matter. The fundamental difference between such commissions and inquiries is that they would be established not by government, but by Parliament. Consequently, such commissions would possess a superior legitimacy because they would be initiated by Parliament to investigate the conduct and actions of the government. As the PASC has explained, it is crucial, in a constitutional sense, that Parliament has the necessary powers and abilities to scrutinise the executive and to hold it to account. As we saw earlier, the ability of Parliament to undertake effective scrutiny of governmental action is limited in various ways.[93] If Parliament's capacity in this area is to be enhanced, then proper parliamentary scrutiny should include the ability to establish and undertake inquiries into significant matters of public concern.[94]

---

[91] House of Commons Foreign Affairs Committee, *The Decision to go to War in Iraq* (HC 813 2002–03).

[92] PASC, *Parliamentary Commissions of Inquiry* (HC 473 2007–08).

[93] See Chapters 5 and 10.　　　　[94] PASC, HC 473, p 3.

Parliamentary commissions of inquiry have not been used for a century, but the technique has recently been reinvigorated. In 2012, the Parliamentary Commission on Banking Standards was established following the LIBOR (London Interbank Offered Rate) fixing scandal (in which some bankers fixed the lending interest rate for personal financial gain). The scandal prompted calls to reform the system of financial regulation, and the Parliamentary Commission on Banking Standards has both investigated past problems and scrutinised the government's plans for reform. The Commission included members of both Houses and was established at the request of the leaders of all three main parties and by the passing of motions in both Houses of Parliament. The Commission reported in June 2013.[95] It adopted novel working methods, including dividing itself into panels for different aspects of its inquiry and appointing legal counsel to cross-examine some witnesses.[96] The Parliamentary Commission on Banking Standards provides a useful precedent for the future.

A third option is the 'private public' inquiry. Any person, group of people, or organisation may establish their own inquiry—provided that they can fund it and get witnesses to cooperate and attend. Such inquiries have been established when government has refused to establish a full public inquiry. Consider the Independent Public Inquiry into Supply of Contaminated Blood and Blood Products established independently of government and funded by private donations.[97] This inquiry arose out of the long-running scandal that health care services in the UK (and elsewhere) did not properly check blood used for transfusion purposes, with the consequence that some patients with conditions such as haemophilia became infected with viruses, such as HIV or Hepatitis C.

A fourth option is for the government to establish an independent panel to investigate a particular matter. Consider, for instance, the Hillsborough Independent Panel, which investigated the deaths of 96 football fans who died in the Hillsborough football stadium disaster in 1989.[98] After the event, it had been widely assumed that the football fans' behaviour had contributed to the tragedy—yet this was always contested by the fans' families. In 2009, the government established an independent panel, which had access to previously unseen documents. The panel concluded that not only had the police been at fault, but that they had deliberately concocted falsehoods to shift the blame onto the fans. The independent panel's working methods were significantly different from that of a public inquiry. For instance, the panel involved and consulted the families of the deceased throughout the process; its work was informed by their views and priorities to ensure that the victims were at the centre of the process. The panel also incorporated academic research and negotiated the release of previously

---

[95] Parliamentary Commission on Banking Standards, *Changing Banking for Good* (HL 27 HC 175 2013–14).

[96] Parliamentary Commission on Banking Standards, *'An Accident Waiting to Happen': The Failure of HBOS* (HL 144 HC 705 2013–14), [8].

[97] Another example is the Independent Public Inquiry on Gulf War Illnesses: see **http://www. gulfveteransassociation.co.uk/Files/LloydReport171104.pdf**

[98] *The Report of the Hillsborough Independent Panel* (HC 581 2012), see also **http://hillsborough. independent.gov.uk**

undisclosed documents, which it then analysed. The panel's working methods enabled it to be quicker and cheaper than a judge-led public inquiry.

Overall, there are now a variety of different techniques for investigating those matters of public interest that often generate calls for some sort of public inquiry. Each method has its own respective pros and cons. There is clearly a degree of fluidity concerning the most appropriate means of investigating a particular matter. Public inquiries—whatever their precise form—perhaps work best if they are approached and understood as bespoke investigations designed around the needs of the particular issue. A final point is that effective inquiries are highly dependent upon the chair having the appropriate skill set and the support of an appropriately experienced inquiry team.

> **Q** What are the benefits of the alternative to public inquiries, such as parliamentary commissions of inquiry, private inquiries, and independent panels?

5. Conclusion

So, what of inquiries? Are they an effective mechanism for holding government to account? From one perspective, inquiries have been the subject of much criticism because of their chequered history—one characterised by lengthy proceedings, high costs, and reports that have often been met with public dissension over the correctness of the conclusions reached or indifference from the government. Some commentators are cynical about inquiries because of the suspicion that they can be manipulated by the government for its own political interests. Nevertheless, inquiries are an important mechanism for undertaking a detailed investigation into an issue of public concern and for holding government accountable. There remains a need for some form of inquiry process—albeit one that sits uneasily at times between court litigation and the ordinary political process—the purpose of which is to undertake such investigations and make recommendations. Aspects of the inquiry process could be enhanced to strengthen its effectiveness. Parliamentary select committees could take a more active role in scrutinising whether government departments fully implement inquiry recommendations. Furthermore, the long-term uncoupling of Parliament from inquiries needs to be addressed. If Parliament is to undertake an effective scrutiny of government and hold it to account over major matters of public concern, such as the invasion of Iraq, then it should have the ability to initiate its own inquiries independent of the government.

Expert commentary
Public Inquiries—continuity, change, and institutional infrastructure
Trevor Buck, Emeritus Professor of Socio-Legal Studies, De Montfort University

This commentary focuses upon the legal process, in particular its ability (or lack of it) to capture and sustain important knowledge generated from the inquiry process and how such experience could be utilised to respond appropriately to the challenges of the ever-changing landscape of public events that require the inquiry process. The problems around the management of continuity and change in the inquiry process are well illustrated by the long-awaited publication of the Chilcot report of the Iraq Inquiry, and the further difficulties encountered in the progress of the Independent Inquiry into Child Sexual Abuse (IICSA), not least in finding an appropriate individual to chair it.

The Chilcot report—12 volumes containing 2.6 million words—was published on 6 July 2016.[99] In many respects this inquiry reflected the concerns about the function of inquiries, delays, costs, and learning lessons from them. The inquiry lasted seven years at a cost of £10.37 million.[100] It concluded that the formal decision to invade Iraq taken by the Cabinet on 17 March 2003, following a failure to secure a second UN resolution before the US took military action, undermined the UN Security Council's authority. Second, the inquiry concluded that 'the circumstances in which it was decided that there was a legal basis for UK military action were far from satisfactory'. [101] This issue should have been considered by a Cabinet Committee and discussed by Cabinet itself. Third, policy on Iraq was based on flawed intelligence assessments that should have been challenged more rigorously. Fourth, there were a number of shortcomings in the government's planning and preparation such as equipment shortfalls, lack of ministerial oversight, and the scale of the UK effort in post-conflict Iraq did not match the scale of the challenge. From 2006, the UK military's additional engagement in the campaign in Afghanistan further stretched resources. Finally, the lessons to be learned included issues relating to the management of relations with allies, in particular the United States. Lessons also included the importance of collective ministerial discussion and debate; the need to assess risks, weigh options, and set an achievable and realistic strategy; the vital role of ministerial leadership and coordination of action across government, supported by senior officials; and the need to equip properly both the civilian and military arms of government. Chilcot concluded:

Above all, the lesson is that all aspects of any intervention need to be calculated, debated and challenged with the utmost rigour. And, when decisions have been made, they need to be implemented fully. Sadly, neither was the case in relation to the UK Government's actions in Iraq.[102]

The report's forensic detail provided a detailed view of the inner workings of government. There were calls for the former Prime Minister, Tony Blair, to be impeached by Parliament.[103] The Leader of the Opposition, Jeremy Corbyn, apologised on behalf of the Labour Party for the Iraq war.[104] The inquiry delays were caused by (i) prolonged exchanges between the

---

[99] Report of a Committee of Privy Counsellors, *The Report of the Iraq Inquiry* (HC 264 2016), http://www.iraqinquiry.org.uk/the-report/

[100] This figure represents total costs from 2009/10 up to the end of financial year 2014/15, http://www.iraqinquiry.org.uk/the-inquiry/inquiry-costs/

[101] Sir John Chilcot's public statement, 6 July 2016, http://www.iraqinquiry.org.uk/the-inquiry/sir-john-chilcots-public-statement/

[102] Sir John Chilcot's public statement, 6 July 2016.

[103] 'Tony Blair faces calls for impeachment on release of Chilcot report', *The Guardian*, 3 July 2016, http://www.theguardian.com/politics/2016/jul/03/tony-blair-may-face-impeachment-on-release-of-chilcot-report
This was based on the precedent of the last impeachment trial of Lord Melville, First Lord of the Admiralty for alleged financial misappropriation, held in the House of Lords in 1806. Lord Melville was acquitted.

[104] See http://www.theguardian.com/politics/video/2016/jul/06/jeremy-corbyn-apologises-for-iraq-war-on-behalf-of-the-labour-party-video. See also, Hansard, Report of the Iraq Inquiry, HC Debs, vol 612, cols 889–91 (6 July 2016).

inquiry and Whitehall about what documents could be published, in particular the former Prime Minister Tony Blair's notes of conversations with President George Bush; and (ii) the 'Maxwellisation'[105] process, whereby individuals whom the inquiry intended to criticise had to be given copies of draft passages to which they could respond.

IICSA—arguably 'the most ambitious and wide-ranging inquiry ever established under the Inquiries Act'[106]—has been bedeviled with concerns over its chairmanship. The New Zealand judge, Dame Lowell Goddard, stood down on 4 August 2016 and was replaced by a fourth chairwoman, but this time a non-judicial appointment, Professor Alexis Jay. Professor Jay was already a panel member to the inquiry and had led a well-regarded Independent Inquiry into Child Sexual Exploitation in Rotherham, South Yorkshire, in 2014.[107] She has 30 years' experience in social work.

The inquiry has a very wide remit:

> To consider the extent to which State and non-State institutions have failed in their duty of care to protect children from sexual abuse and exploitation; to consider the extent to which those failings have since been addressed; to identify further action needed to address any failings identified; to consider the steps which it is necessary for State and non-State institutions to take in order to protect children from such abuse in future; and to publish a report with recommendations.[108]

The inquiry's sheer scope has been criticised by its former Chair, Dame Lowell Goddard and others. It has also driven the development of an extensive institutional architecture to provide the appropriate support and direction. The Chair is assisted by a Panel of three expert members experienced in challenging institutions, and managing, analysing, and evaluating complex evidence. The legal team is comprised of a solicitor and counsel to the inquiry in addition to a team of counsel working on individual investigations. There is a secretariat to the inquiry. The inquiry also includes a seven-member Victims and Survivors' Consultative Panel to assist in all aspects of the inquiry's work. There is also a Victims and Survivors' Forum. Any victim or survivor may register with the Forum to receive updates and the Forum arranges an open public meeting four times a year. There is also a five-member Academic Advisory Board consisting of child protection experts that will oversee and guide a research project. The Inquiry has set up three key projects: the Truth Project, the Public Hearings Project, and the Research Project. Each has distinctive and complementary roles aimed at revealing systemic issues and informing future improvement. The Truth Project enables victims and survivors to provide information, in private sessions in a safe environment in different regions of England and Wales, about their experience. It is not a formal, fact-finding exercise, but instead provides an opportunity for victims and survivors to express their experiences of child sexual abuse in an institutional context. Where appropriate, allegations may be referred to the police for investigation. This approach mirrors the well-regarded model set in the private hearings of the ongoing Australian Royal Commission of Inquiry into Institutional Responses to Child Sexual Abuse,[109] though it should be noted that 'the Australian Inquiry was funded

---

[105] After the case of *Maxwell v Department of Trade and Industry* [1974] QB 523.

[106] Dame Lowell Goddard, General Investigations Hearings transcript, 26 July 2016, 2:4. Available at **https://www.iicsa.org.uk/sites/default/files/documents/2016-07-26-general-matters-relating-to-investigations-transcript.pdf**

[107] Independent Inquiry into Child Sexual Exploitation in Rotherham 1997–2013, 21 August 2014, **http://www.rotherham.gov.uk/downloads/file/1407/independent_inquiry_cse_in_rotherham**

[108] **https://www.iicsa.org.uk/terms-reference**   [109] **http://childabuseroyalcommission.gov.au**

at approximately twice the level of [IICSA] in its initial stages',[110] according to Dame Lowell Goddard. The Research Project will help to scope and define future investigations and assist in publishing original research in the field.

The inquiry has launched no fewer than 13 investigations into a broad range of institutions, (eg Children in Custodial Institutions, Lord Janner, the Roman Catholic Church, Westminster, and Residential Schools). Each investigation will conclude with a report. One of Professor Jay's first actions was to order an internal review of the Inquiry's approach to its investigations. She also authorised a restriction order under the Inquiries Act 2005[111] to protect the anonymity of complainants who allege child sexual abuse in the course of the inquiry's deliberations. The concerns based on a suspicion of bias in relation to the first two chair appointees of IICSA and the sudden resignation of Dame Lowell Goddard has undermined public confidence. There have also been criticisms levelled against the Home Office, the sponsoring government department. Dame Lowell Goddard's reasons for resignation included a sense of frustration at not having a free hand to recruit appropriately qualified staff, and the need to recruit from outside the Home Office and Civil Service. As she pointed out, in evidence to the Home Affairs Select Committee:

the skills and qualifications of many recruits did not fit the tasks which they were called upon to perform, as none of the secretariat or senior management team had previous experience of running an inquiry of this nature.[112]

Both the Iraq and IICSA inquiries are complex, multifaceted inquiry processes that touch upon very sensitive political, social, and legal issues; in other words, good examples of the inquiry genre as intriguing and challenging instruments of government. Both inquiries are very different in terms of content and scope, but strikingly similar in terms of the necessary processes required to bring them to satisfactory outcomes. Both require painstaking gathering of evidence to find facts upon which to base reliable recommendations. Dame Lowell Goddard provided a useful insight into the causes of delay in holding substantive public hearings, in particular she noted that '[t]he lack of an Evidence Management System (EMS) fit for purpose has severely hampered the Inquiry's ability to manage the thousands (if not millions) of documents the Inquiry has been receiving'.[113] It would seem, in relation to both inquiries, that the appointment of a judge to chair an inquiry no longer automatically guarantees public confidence in the inquiry process. When inquiries engage the interest and passions of significant sections of the public, it is unsurprising that more thoroughgoing signs are required of the absence of bias and proactive commitment to get to the truth of the matter in hand. Both inquiries have also been weakened by failures to produce an effective communications strategy to reassure participants and the wider public of the progress of inquiry processes, and, where necessary, to defend them from criticisms. [114]

---

[110] House of Commons Home Affairs Select Committee, 'Written Evidence Submitted by Hon Dame Lowell Goddard QC', 6 September 2016, http://data.parliament.uk/writtenevidence/committeeevidence. svc/evidencedocument/home-affairs-committee/the-work-of-the-independent-inquiry-into-child-sexual-abuse/written/36954.html

[111] Inquiries Act 2005, s 19(2)(b). For the text of the order see https://www.iicsa.org.uk/key-documents/791/view/restriction-order-15-august-2016.pdf

[112] See n 110.   [113] See n 110.

[114] Dame Lowell Goddard recommended in her evidence to the Home Affairs Select Committee (n 110) that the communications capacity of IICSA should be 'radically strengthened'.

The inquiry process also requires a better focus on following up on the lessons learned to inform better practice and outcomes in the future. The mechanisms here are often particularly weak. Even where inquiries do succeed, the knowledge gained is often lost. A report is issued, the inquiry staff are moved on to other jobs or returned to their various Civil Service departments and the wheel must be reinvented in terms of the administration and management of the inquiry process when the next inquiry is announced.

What is to be done? The creation of a newly formed permanent secretariat dedicated to delivering the inquiry process—a permanent Inquiry Office—could address some of these weaknesses. It could provide continuity in the knowledge gained from one inquiry to the next, and develop flexibly to accommodate the changing requirements of individual inquiries driven by their different subject matter. Such an office could advise on chair and panel membership, the administrative implications of remit formulas, legal issues, time lines, costs, and the various potential methodologies of approach. To be credible, such a body would not be directly sponsored by a government department. Instead, to maintain its independence and impartiality, such a body would be financed directly by a Parliamentary vote and would be accountable to the Commons Public Administration and Constitutional Affairs Select Committee. Inquiries do much good work, but they could work better and more effectively. An Inquiry Office should be part of the solution.

Further reading

BEATSON, 'Should Judges Chair Public Inquiries?' (2005) 121 LQR 221
This paper by a senior judge discusses the arguments for and against using judges to chair public inquiries. It concludes that judges should only be used to conduct inquiries where there is a vital public interest and if they are given appropriate protection against criticism.

HOUSE OF LORDS SELECT COMMITTEE ON THE INQUIRIES ACT 2005, *The Inquiries Act 2005: Post-Legislative Scrutiny* (HL 143 2013–14)
This report provides a detailed scrutiny of the workings of the Inquiries Act 2005.

Useful websites

http://www.nationalarchives.gov.uk/webarchive/inquiries-inquests-royal-commissions.htm
Website relating to public inquiries, inquests, royal commissions, reviews, and investigations

http://tinyurl.com/zjktehu
An event held by the Institute for Government in July 2016 to explore the role of public inquiries

PART VI

Human Rights

18

Human Rights and the UK Constitution

1. Introduction	759
2. Human rights	760
3. Human rights in the UK	765
4. The future	806
5. Conclusions	812
Expert commentary	813
Further reading	814
Useful websites	815

1. Introduction

This part of the book focuses specifically upon human rights law and its place within the UK constitution. In this chapter, we begin by considering the notion of human rights itself. We will see that it is a flexible concept that people use in different ways, and there is plenty of debate and disagreement about exactly what it should (and does) mean. There is disagreement, too, about whether human rights—at least as they are normally conceived—are good things. At first, this might seem surprising. Surely 'human rights' are a self-evidently good thing? The position, however, is more complex. How we view such rights depends upon a range of factors, including which rights are placed within that category in the first place, how they are balanced against other interests, and who is ultimately responsible for protecting them.

This chapter is concerned not only with human rights at a general or conceptual level. It also examines, in more practical terms, the extent to, and the way in which human rights are recognised and protected in the UK. This analysis engages all three of the book's key themes:

- The Human Rights Act 1998 (HRA) has extended the legal protection afforded to human rights and has therefore been a key driver of *the shift from a more political to a more legal form of constitutionalism*. The Act, however, stops short of authorising courts to strike down Acts of Parliament that are inconsistent with human rights law. In this ultimate sense, therefore, the ongoing existence of human rights is dependent upon the restraint of the political branches of the state—that is, the government and Parliament.

- One of the principal effects of the HRA (as we have already seen in Chapter 12) has been to enhance the courts' powers to review the legality of administrative action. In this sense, the HRA can be seen, at least in part, as recognition of *the unusually powerful position occupied by the executive branch* within the UK constitution, and the resulting importance of ensuring *adequate oversight* of it.

- Although the HRA does not ultimately restrict the UK Parliament's legislative authority, the lawmaking powers of the devolved legislatures are limited by the rights that the HRA protects. Understanding the role of human rights in the constitution thus requires us to engage with our third theme, by appreciating *the multilayered nature of the UK's constitutional arrangements.*

2. Human rights

2.1 What are human rights?

People have many legal rights. But only a small subset of such rights are 'human rights'. Generally speaking, when the law imposes a duty on one person, someone else will acquire a corresponding right. Assume, for instance, that A enters into a contract under which he is to clean B's house in return for payment. A's contractual duty vests in B a corresponding contractual right to have her house cleaned. But B does not thereby acquire a *human* right. What is it, then, that distinguishes human rights from other legal rights?

There are two main ways in which this question may be approached. On a practical level, human rights are normally accorded special treatment within any given legal system. All legal rights are protected in the sense that legal consequences will flow from their breach. In the example above, B's contractual right enables her (among other things) to bring a claim for damages against A if A fails to do what he promised. One of the hallmarks of human rights, however, is that they are accorded a form of protection that goes beyond that which is normally afforded to legal rights. The paradigm form of protection given to human rights involves not simply rendering unlawful any *conduct* (eg by an individual or public body) that is inconsistent with such rights, but, at a constitutional level, making it impossible or difficult for *legislation* to be enacted that is incompatible with such rights.

What this boils down to is that regular legal rights are precarious in the sense that they can be modified or removed by legislation. In contrast, human rights, in many legal systems, are not (as) precarious, because the constitution prevents (or makes difficult) the enactment of legislation modifying or removing such rights. As such, human rights acquire a degree of permanence that other rights do not necessarily enjoy.

However, this practical answer to the question 'what are human rights?' is ultimately unsatisfying because it invites a further question. *Why*, in the first place, are some rights, through their characterisation as human rights, singled out for this special treatment?

Naturally, people will disagree about what factors should be relevant for this purpose—and hence about the range of rights that should count as human rights. However, the sort of rights to which legal systems around the world generally provide special protection suggests that an important idea in this sphere is the concept of human autonomy. On this view, the political notion of liberalism—that is, the idea that people should, as far as possible, be allowed to do as they please—lies at the root of human rights. Such rights, then, should restrict the capacity of the state to interfere in individuals' lives. Rights enable individuals to pursue particularly important forms of human activity (eg to express themselves freely and to protest, which is imperative if the democratic process is to function properly), and to be free from certain forms of unwanted interference (eg from being subject to deprivation of physical liberty or torture).

However, few people would argue that all such freedoms should be unlimited. After all, the exercise of a right by one person may result in interference with someone else's right. If A has a right to say what he likes, and exercises it by spreading false rumours that cast doubt upon B's honesty, this involves interference with B's right to be free from interference with her reputation. Even within a human rights framework that is exclusively concerned with the freedom of the individual, restrictions upon such freedoms will therefore have to be contemplated so as to strike an appropriate balance when they are in tension with one another.

In fact, few legal systems adopt a view of human rights that is oriented exclusively towards the freedom of the individual. Most recognise that the rights (or freedoms) of one individual may come into tension not only with *the rights of other individuals* but also with *the interests of the community*. Consider, for example, a former intelligence agent who exercises her right of free speech by publishing information that is highly damaging to national security, or a group of protestors who blockade oil refineries, choking off petrol supplies and bringing the country to a standstill. In these cases, the exercise of individuals' rights arguably interferes with the general interests of the community as a whole. This raises the question: what level of inconvenience or disruption should the community have to bear in order that particular people may exercise their individual rights? In most legal systems, at least some of the rights of the individual are qualified, to some extent, by the interests of the community—thus recognising that while the principle of autonomy that animates the concept of human rights is important, it is not the only value that is in play.

2.2 Competing views

Although the language of 'human rights' is prevalent today in many societies, the topic remains, in many respects, a highly contentious one. Here, we set out four lines of argument that challenge the thinking summarised in the previous section.

First, even if we accept that human rights should be used to safeguard individual autonomy, questions remain about *the range of rights necessary to secure that objective*. If autonomy is the principal driver, then emphasis is inevitably placed upon 'negative rights'—that is, rights to be free from certain forms of interference in order that individuals may live their lives as they wish.[1] However, interference by others is not the only potential reason why a given individual may be unable to live her life as she wishes. Indeed, other factors may mean that a particular freedom, although guaranteed by law, is practically worthless. For example, the law may guarantee the right to freedom of expression, but not everyone will be well placed to exercise it. Compare, for example, a university-educated columnist who writes for an influential newspaper with someone struggling to survive on the minimum wage who is ill-educated, illiterate, and inarticulate. The law might draw no formal distinction, but in real-world terms there is clearly unequal access to the right of free speech.

One response to this problem—if it is perceived as such—is that negative, autonomy-based rights should be supplemented by such positive rights as are necessary for the effective exercise of the former. On this view, people should, for example, have a positive right to a good education in order to equip them in practice to exercise their right to freedom of speech. This calls for a broader range of rights to qualify as human rights. In particular, it necessitates recognition of rights of a social and economic nature that are necessary for the effective exercise of those rights that safeguard individual autonomy.

Second, the approach described so far in this section does not fundamentally challenge the proposition that the core purpose of human rights is to safeguard human autonomy. Rather, it adopts a relatively sophisticated view of the form that human rights may need to take if that objective is to be realised. In that sense, it views positive rights as ancillary to negative rights: people should have the right to a good education not because that is intrinsically important, but because it will better equip them to exercise their right of free speech. That view is therefore still fundamentally premised upon the liberal philosophy that prizes individual autonomy.

Those who disagree emphasise *other values that are important in themselves*, not merely because they are capable of better equipping people to exercise their liberties. Prominent within this strand of thought is the argument that considerations of *liberty* should not be emphasised at the expense of *equality*. While equality requires equal access to negative rights, it also requires other things—including the provision of positive entitlements. On this analysis, such entitlements are valuable because they are worthwhile in themselves, not simply because they may enhance people's capacity to exercise negative rights. If this view is adopted, we end up with a much wider set of human rights than that which we adopt if our focus remains exclusively upon considerations of autonomy (and hence liberty). In particular, the view presently under consideration supports recognition of a broad range of social and economic rights, such as the right to a decent standard of living, the right to adequate housing, and the

---

[1] See, eg Laws, 'The Constitution: Morals and Rights' [1996] PL 622.

right to health care, thereby guaranteeing to everyone at least a minimum standard of provision in these areas.

Q Should the law guarantee rights such as those mentioned in the previous sentence? What difficulties might arise if courts were required to interpret and enforce such rights?

Third, although different in some respects, both of the foregoing approaches assume that rights are an appropriate vehicle for upholding important values. That view, however, is not universally held. Some writers argue that *human rights are inappropriately individualistic in nature*. On this view, it is paradoxical to try to base an understanding of society and the political order upon individual rights, because such rights emphasise the primacy of the individual, whereas people are in fact bound together in a community or society. From this perspective, to rely upon the notion of individual rights as the basis for society is to rely upon an asocial principle. Instead, it should be recognised that individuals are first and foremost members of a community, and that the interests of the individual, while not irrelevant, are of secondary importance. Broadly speaking, this point of view is often labelled as *communitarian*—a world view that places particular weight upon the responsibility of the individual to the community and society, as opposed to emphasising individual freedom and rights.

One response to the communitarian critique of individual rights is, as noted earlier, to acknowledge that individuals' rights should be capable of being overridden by sufficiently important community interests. On this analysis, the individual rights model actually accommodates communitarian concerns, removing the sting from the communitarian critique. For many people, this response is sufficient: it strikes an appropriate balance between the interests of the individual and society. For others, however, it does not go far enough because it retains the presumption that individuals' rights must be upheld unless it can be shown that there is some community interest that, in the particular circumstances of the case, should be allowed to prevail over the right and thus restrict the extent to which it may be lawfully exercised. Those who question the appropriateness of human rights from a communitarian perspective do not agree that the rights of the individual should, in this way, enjoy presumptive priority. This does not mean that communitarians reject the norms that underpin rights—but they do reject the notion that human rights should operate as trumps that generally override other interests.

Fourth, the communitarian perspective is distinct from, but connected to, the question: *who should decide on how far human rights should go and what they mean in any particular situation?* Once human rights are enshrined in law, it inevitably follows that the courts will play a key role in adjudicating upon disputes concerning whether or not such rights have been violated. For supporters of this approach, one of its greatest strengths is that the courts are independent and free from political interference from the legislature and the executive. This allows disputes to be decided in an objectively rational way—by reference to reason and principle, and without regard to the political maelstrom. In turn, this should lead to 'better' protection of fundamental rights.

But for some, the independence of the courts (in this context) is not their greatest strength: it is one of their greatest weaknesses. This is because there are few, if any, objectively correct answers to the questions that arise in this arena. Consider, for instance, questions such as the following:

- Does burning a flag constitute a form of expression falling within the protection of the right to freedom of expression?

- When, if at all, will national security concerns justify the restriction of the rights of suspected terrorists?

- Should the right to freedom of religion mean that schools should be prevented from banning certain forms of religious dress?

People inevitably—and legitimately—disagree about such matters. Such disagreements, it can be argued, can only legitimately be resolved through the political process. On this view, the questions tackled by courts when determining human rights cases are not really legal in nature at all: they are, at root, political questions. As Loughlin has noted: 'Rights adjudication is intrinsically political; it requires judges to reach a determination on the relative importance of conflicting social, political, and cultural interests in circumstances where there is no objective—or even consensual answer.'[2] From this perspective, the very notion of legally enforceable human rights is, at best, questionable and, at worst, misconceived. Embracing such rights simply dresses up inherently political issues as legal questions. This, it is said, is undemocratic, because it removes such issues from the sphere of representative politics, placing them in the hands of judges who are unelected and politically unaccountable.[3]

There is no 'correct' answer to the overarching question of whether political or legal institutions should have the last word in relation to such matters. Indeed, this debate is simply a facet of the much broader one concerning the competing claims of political and legal constitutionalism. And, as we have shown throughout this book, the choice between those forms of constitutionalism is not a binary one. But that does not change the fact that the allocation of responsibilities between judicial and political institutions in the human rights field, as elsewhere, is a highly contentious matter.

This debate cannot therefore be straightforwardly resolved. We do, however, make three points by way of conclusion on this matter. First, the question as to whether or not judges should be entrusted with the protection of human rights is distinct from the question as to whether the whole notion of human rights is itself a good thing. Those sceptical of allocating to the courts the task of adjudicating upon human rights disputes do not reject the notion of human rights altogether; rather, they simply think that these disputes are, on the whole, best resolved through the political rather than the judicial process.

---

[2] Loughlin, *The Idea of Public Law* (Oxford 2003), p 129.

[3] Griffith, 'The Brave New World of Sir John Laws' (2000) 63 MLR 159; Tomkins, *Our Republican Constitution* (Oxford 2005); Waldron, 'The Core of the Case against Judicial Review' (2006) 115 Yale LJ 1346.

Second, the extent to which judicial protection of human rights is disquieting will, to some extent, turn upon which rights are recognised as human rights. For example, the right to freedom of expression is a traditional civil and political right, because it is central to the functioning of a democracy. Contrast this with social rights (eg the right to adequate health care), which, some argue, should also be recognised as human rights. If such rights were to be protected by courts, then it is highly likely that judges would be drawn into enormously difficult and controversial questions concerning spending priorities, the allocation of scarce public money, and the like, which are inherently political issues and traditionally the province of elected government.

Third, the extent of the courts' powers in relation to human rights is an obviously relevant consideration in this regard: the more extensive those powers, the greater the scope for objecting to them. At the same time, account must be taken of the source of such powers. When Parliament enacted the HRA, it made a conscious political choice that, in most—although not all—instances, the courts were best placed to decide upon human rights. Parliament thus decided that human rights should be legally enforceable. Parliament might rescind or revisit that decision: indeed, it is currently government policy that the HRA should be replaced with a 'British Bill of Rights', although it is unclear how such legislation would differ from the HRA. The crucial point, however, is that for as long as the HRA remains on the statute book, the courts have been bequeathed by Parliament a clear and unequivocal jurisdiction to adjudicate on human rights disputes. This jurisdiction cannot be criticised as undemocratic precisely because it was conferred upon the courts by a democratic lawmaking institution—that is, Parliament. Against this background, we turn to consider the way in which human rights are protected in UK law.

Q Who do you think should decide on human rights disputes: government and Parliament, or the courts? Why?

3. Human rights in the UK

3.1 Two models—'liberties' and 'rights'

The terms 'liberties' and 'rights' are often used interchangeably, but in fact they mean different things. This was clearly signalled by Browne-Wilkinson LJ in *Wheeler v Leicester City Council*[4] when he said (long before the enactment of the HRA) that

> Basic constitutional rights in this country such as freedom of the person and freedom of speech are based not on any express provision conferring such a right but on freedom of an individual to do what he will save to the extent that he is prevented from so doing by the law.

Having the liberty to do something means that it is lawful to do it because *the law does not prohibit it*. But if someone has a right to do something then *the law specifically*

---

[4] [1985] AC 1054, 1065.

Table 18.1 Liberties and rights

Liberties	Rights
Absence of state power to interfere, but no positive action required by state	Rights may require state not to interfere and/or positively to do certain things
Conduct is lawful because no law makes it unlawful–hence scope of lawful conduct is a function of prohibitions: whatever is not unlawful is lawful	Conduct is lawful because law grants a specific right to engage in it: rights are positively enumerated in law
Scope of lawful conduct not fixed: may expand or contract depending on operative legal prohibitions	Scope of lawful conduct is fixed: changes only if the right itself is amended

provides that it can be lawfully done. Liberties are thus residual, whereas rights are positive and declaratory. The difference may seem subtle, but for three reasons—summarised in Table 18.1—the difference is practically significant.

First, an approach based exclusively upon liberties rather than rights necessarily *restricts the type of protection thereby afforded to the individual.* If people possess a liberty to do something, then (unless the law is changed) doing it will not be unlawful. In this sense, the correlative of a liberty is a requirement of passivity on the part of the state: the state may not, for example, punish someone for doing that which she is at liberty to do. The same applies in relation to some rights. For example, if someone has the right to freedom of expression, the state may not punish her for expressing herself (unless, in doing so, she exceeds the boundaries of her right). However, it follows from what was said in the previous section that rights may require not only passivity, but also positive action on the part of the state. This is true most obviously—but not exclusively[5]—in relation to social rights, such as the right to adequate housing or the right to adequate health care. Such rights transparently impose a positive obligation on the state to provide and deliver appropriate public services. They cannot meaningfully be conceptualised as liberties: being free (at liberty) to receive health care is not the same thing as having a right to be provided with health care.

Second, if a framework based on rights rather than liberties is adopted, individuals are likely to be in a better position to *ascertain their position.* Within a rights-based framework, an individual trying to answer the question, 'Am I allowed to do X?' would seek to establish whether the law furnished her with a right to engage in the conduct concerned. In contrast, in a framework based on liberties, it would be necessary to identify all laws potentially impinging upon the activity in question in order to determine what, if any, scope there were for lawfully engaging in it. The rights-based model therefore has the potential to be clearer—although the

[5] Even rights that, on their face, simply require the state *not* to do things might implicitly require it also to *do* certain things. For example, a right to be free from inhuman or degrading treatment may implicitly require the state to provide people on the verge of destitution with basic food and shelter.

point should not be overstated, not least because rights may be set out in broad terms that leave people uncertain as to whether particular forms of conduct are protected.

Third, *liberties are at constant risk of erosion*. Liberties are freedoms that are left over once all relevant legal prohibitions have been taken into account. For example, in a system based on liberties rather than rights, freedom of speech exists only in the sense that people can lawfully say those things that they are not legally prohibited from saying. The extent of the liberty is therefore a function of the relevant legal prohibitions (the law of defamation, the law of official secrecy, the law of privacy, and so on). But over time lawmakers might impose more and more restrictions upon what may lawfully be said—and the liberty to speak freely will correspondingly diminish. The position may be different, however, in a rights-based system. For instance, if no public body, including the legislature, is permitted to act contrary to constitutionally protected rights, their erosion is legally impossible. Any conduct by public bodies (including legislation enacted by the legislature) that conflicts with such rights can be challenged before a court on the ground that its interference with human rights renders it unlawful and ineffective.

Q Lord Irvine—who, as Lord Chancellor, was a principal architect of the HRA—said: 'The view that because we have liberty we have no need of human rights must be rejected.'[6] What do you think he meant by this—and do you agree with him?

3.2 Human rights and the common law

3.2.1 'Liberties' and 'rights'

The HRA was enacted because it was felt (at least by those responsible for its enactment) that the traditional, liberties-based approach was inadequate. It might therefore be thought that the effect of the HRA was to replace that approach with a rights-based one at the flick of a switch. However, the position is more complex, both because the HRA does not fully implement a rights-based model (in the sense set out earlier) and because the pre-HRA position did not fully conform to the liberties-based framework. The two models are not binary alternatives, but points on a continuum. The HRA has propelled the UK along that continuum—from an approach lying towards the liberties end of the spectrum to one lying nearer the rights end. The next section explains why the HRA falls short of a full rights-based model. First, however, we need to examine the pre-HRA position in order to ascertain the starting-point from which the HRA's impact falls to be assessed.[7]

A pure liberties-based approach to legal freedom would be wholly agnostic about such freedom. For instance, a court seeking to determine whether an individual could

---

[6] Irvine, *Human Rights, Constitutional Law and the Development of the English Legal System* (Oxford 2003), p 24.

[7] For detailed discussion of the pre-HRA position, see Hunt, *Using Human Rights in English Courts* (Oxford 1997).

lawfully undertake a given form of conduct, such as publishing an article criticising the government, would undertake a morally neutral, factual inquiry. Normative considerations, such as the desirability of free political debate, would be irrelevant. The court would simply examine, interpret, and apply any relevant laws without reference to the fact that an important liberty was at stake. If those laws prohibited or criminalised criticism of the government, then that would be that, the free speech implications of such laws notwithstanding.

However, the approach described in the previous paragraph does not accurately reflect that which obtained in the UK prior to the HRA's entry into force. Nor does it accurately reflect the approach that would be applied if the HRA were to be repealed. This is partly because *other legislation* confers specific rights on individuals. For example, long before the HRA was enacted, legislation existed that protected the right (in certain contexts) not to be discriminated against on grounds such as gender and race.[8] But more generally, there are countless examples of decisions by the UK courts, before the HRA was ever contemplated, recognising individuals' rights and seeking (often with success) to protect them in the face of administrative and legislative measures arguably at odds with such rights.[9] For instance, we saw in Chapter 12 that when public bodies exercise discretionary powers, the courts are prepared to uphold (what amounts in practice to) a right to good administration, by requiring agencies to act in accordance with a series of principles of good decision-making. We also saw in Chapter 13 that, in cases such as *Anisminic*,[10] the courts have gone to considerable lengths in order to interpret Acts of Parliament in such a way as to leave intact the right of access to the courts. In such cases, the courts are far from agnostic about the right that is at stake, and it is in this sense that the pre-HRA position did not wholly conform to the pure liberties-based model.

In order to understand the pre-HRA position more fully—thereby allowing us to appreciate the impact of the HRA—it is necessary to examine both the scope and protection of common law rights. We begin with the former.

3.2.2 The scope of common law rights

At common law, which rights are courts prepared to recognise and attempt to uphold in the face of conflicting administrative or legislative action? Unsurprisingly, no definitive list of such rights exists, but the courts' focus has generally been on matters concerning due process and access to the courts. *Anisminic* itself involved an 'ouster clause', which, on the face of it, seemed to preclude judicial review of a government agency's decisions. Other cases were concerned with such matters as the right

---

[8] See now the Equality Act 2010, which addresses discrimination on various grounds, including gender, race, age, disability, gender reassignment, religion, belief, and sexual orientation.

[9] See, eg *Anisminic Ltd v Foreign Compensation Commission* [1969] 2 AC 147; *R v Lord Chancellor, ex p Witham* [1998] QB 575; *R v Secretary of State for the Home Department, ex p Pierson* [1998] AC 539; *R v Secretary of State for the Home Department, ex p Simms* [2000] 2 AC 115.

[10] *Anisminic Ltd v Foreign Compensation Commission* [1969] 2 AC 147.

to launch legal proceedings irrespective of financial means[11] and the right of legal professional privilege (ie the right to communicate confidentially with one's legal representative, which is necessary if the right of access to court is to be fully enjoyed).[12] Even in cases concerned with different rights, such as the right to freedom of expression, the courts tended to be at their boldest when the exercise of such a right could be related to the core of rights, concerning access to courts and due process, which the judiciary was evidently most willing to uphold.[13]

We should not, however, assume that the common law was frozen upon the entry into force of the HRA, such that, two decades on, it protects only the rights that were recognised before the advent of the HRA. Indeed, the Supreme Court, in a series of recent judgments, has been at pains to point out that the position is otherwise. For instance, in *Kennedy v Charity Commission*, Lord Toulson said that it was 'not the purpose of the Human Rights Act that the common law should become an ossuary'.[14] But the point is not just that the HRA does not preclude the development of common law rights: the HRA can also stimulate such development. As Lord Reed put it in *R (Osborn) v Parole Board*,[15] the common law of human rights falls to be developed 'in accordance with' the HRA when appropriate. The implications of this view are substantial. In particular, it means that when we come to assess the impact of the HRA, the matter is not as simple as saying that the common law protected certain rights and now the HRA protects a wider range of rights. Rather, the HRA, as well as protecting an admittedly broader range of rights than the common law *used to* acknowledge, has served to augment the common law as it exists *today*.

3.2.3 The protection of common law rights

If we are trying to understand the common law's role in respect of rights, we need to understand not just what rights the common law recognised (and recognises) but also what courts can do at common law in order to protect rights. That depends in large part upon who has acted (or is proposing to act) contrary to the right. If the actor in question is a body other than the UK Parliament, such as a Minister or devolved legislature, the courts (subject to an important proviso explained below) can and do strike down its acts and decisions if they contravene what are often called 'common law constitutional rights'. In contrast, if the actor is Parliament— if, in other words, an Act of Parliament unambiguously conflicts with a common law constitutional right—the courts cannot strike down or refuse to apply the relevant provision.[16] If, then, an Act of Parliament is inconsistent with a right,

---

[11] *R v Lord Chancellor, ex p Witham* [1998] QB 575.

[12] *R (Daly) v Secretary of State for the Home Department* [2001] UKHL 26, [2001] 2 AC 532. This case was decided after the HRA had entered into force, but, in his leading judgment, Lord Bingham relied principally upon a common law right to legal professional privilege.

[13] *R v Secretary of State for the Home Department, ex p Simms* [2000] 2 AC 115.

[14] [2014] UKSC 20, [2015] AC 455, [133]. An 'ossuary' is a container in which the bones of dead people are stored, Lord Toulson's point being that the doctrine of common law rights, unlike an ossuary, is vibrant.

[15] [2013] UKSC 61, [2014] AC 1115, [57].

[16] The only established exception is in relation to Acts of Parliament that conflict with directly effective EU law. See Chapter 8, section 4.

the legislation must be applied and the right must yield. This means (and here is the proviso mentioned above) that if a public body other than Parliament is authorised by an Act of Parliament to act inconsistently with common law constitutional rights, the courts are powerless to intervene.

What, then, can courts do if an Act of Parliament appears to be inconsistent with a common law constitutional right such that it apparently provides for some eventuality that would deny an individual the full enjoyment of that right? Given that *disapplication* of Acts of Parliament is not a tool at the courts' disposal (unless Parliament is no longer regarded as sovereign[17]), the primary technique by which they seek to uphold common law rights is the *interpretation* of legislation. If the legislative provision in question can be made to mean something that is, in fact, consistent with the right in question, the fact that the courts are (because Parliament is sovereign) duty-bound to apply the provision presents no problem from a rights perspective.

We saw in Chapter 5 that the courts are prepared to uphold a range of important constitutional values in this way, including common law constitutional rights. In doing so, the courts have, on occasion, been prepared to adopt extremely strained interpretations of the legislation in question. Indeed, we noted in Chapter 5 that it has even been suggested that in certain cases—most obviously *Anisminic*[18]—the courts' interpretation of legislation has been so radical as to amount, in effect, to a refusal to apply that legislation. Whether or not this view is accurate, it is certainly the case that courts have been willing to uphold common law constitutional rights unless an Act of Parliament restricts or abolishes such rights in clear and unambiguous terms.

It would therefore be simplistic to say that, prior to the entry into force of the HRA, a purely liberties-based approach applied in the UK. It would be more accurate to say that the approach that applied reflected some features of both the liberties- and rights-based models. Rights were certainly recognised—and, as we have seen, courts were willing to take steps, principally through the interpretation of legislation, to uphold such rights. However, the range of rights recognised by the courts as common law constitutional rights was relatively narrow, and the courts were ultimately powerless to protect such rights if legislation unambiguously interfered with or removed them.

Against this background, we can now turn to consider why the HRA was enacted. How was it intended to take the protection of rights in the UK beyond that which was already undertaken at common law? And has it succeeded in doing so?

3.3 The Human Rights Act 1998: an introduction

The HRA was a key element of the constitutional reform programme undertaken in the early years of the Labour administration that took office in 1997. It was intended to (and has) extended the protection of human rights in domestic law in two main respects.

---

[17] For criticism of parliamentary sovereignty, see Chapter 5, section 6.
[18] *Anisminic Ltd v Foreign Compensation Commission* [1969] 2 AC 147.

3.3.1 The rights protected by the HRA

The range of rights offered protection by the HRA is substantially wider than the range of rights that had, by the time of its enactment, unambiguously been brought within the scope of the common law constitutional rights doctrine. The first effect, therefore, of the HRA was to broaden the scope of rights protected by UK courts.

The purpose of the HRA is to give further effect in UK law to the rights set out in the European Convention on Human Rights (ECHR). The ECHR is an international treaty. The states that are parties to the Convention are bound in international law to secure to everyone within their jurisdiction the rights and freedoms set out in Section I of the Convention.[19] The ECHR took effect in 1950, and was drafted in the light of horrors of the Second World War, during which Europe had witnessed human rights abuses (most obviously genocide) on an almost unimaginable scale.[20] The ECHR sought to guard against a repetition of such events by locking European governments into a legal regime for the protection of human rights.

Unlike many international treaties, the ECHR contains an institutional regime for the enforcement of the rights that it sets out. In particular, Art 19 provides for a court—the European Court of Human Rights (ECtHR)—to 'ensure the observance of the engagements undertaken by the [states parties]' to the Convention. Claims alleging that a state party has violated relevant rights can be brought before the Court both by other states parties[21] and by individuals claiming to be victims of the alleged violation.[22] If the Court finds that there has been a violation, it has the power to 'afford just satisfaction to the injured party'.[23] For example, the Court can order that the state concerned pays a sum of money to the victim. Moreover, the states parties have agreed 'to abide by the final judgment of the Court in any case to which they are parties'.[24] (It should be noted at this point that the ECHR is legally and institutionally distinct from the European Union (EU).[25] Many more countries are parties to the ECHR than are member states of the EU, and the ECtHR is a separate institution from the Court of Justice of the European Union (CJEU), which, as we saw in Chapter 8, is concerned with the interpretation and application of EU law.)

The UK has, then, been bound by the ECHR as a matter of international law since it ratified it in 1950. And ever since the UK opted into 'the right of individual petition' in 1965, individuals have been able to institute proceedings against it in the ECtHR. However, what they could not do, generally speaking, was to invoke the ECHR in *domestic* legal proceedings. This was one of the major factors that formed the impetus for enacting the HRA.[26]

What, then, are the rights that the HRA protects? The HRA empowers national courts to protect what it calls 'the Convention rights'.[27] This means the rights set out in Arts 2–12 and 14 of the ECHR, along with those laid down in Arts 1–3 of the First

---

[19] ECHR, Art 1.

[20] Simpson, *Human Rights and the End of Empire: Britain and the Genesis of the European Convention* (Oxford 2004).

[21] ECHR, Art 33.   [22] ECHR, Art 34.   [23] ECHR, Art 41.   [24] ECHR, Art 46(1).

[25] Albeit that Art 6(2) of the Treaty on European Union provides for the EU itself to become a party to the ECHR. Meanwhile, Art 6(3), in any event, makes the rights set out in the ECHR binding upon the institutions of the EU.

[26] Home Office, *Rights Brought Home: The Human Rights Bill* (Cm 3782 1997), [1.14].

[27] HRA, s 1(1).

Protocol to the Convention and in Art 1 of the Thirteenth Protocol. These rights are set out in Table 18.2. From this, it will be apparent that the central focus of the ECHR is on civil and political rights: rights that are likely to uphold the *autonomy* of the individual, considerations of *equality* being secondary. This is apparent from the fact that the ECHR does not contain any general anti-discrimination provision. Article 14 is the closest it comes, but this only prohibits discrimination in relation to the enjoyment of the freedoms conferred by the other provisions of the Convention.[28] With the exception of the right to education, protected by Art 2 of the First Protocol, the ECHR does not extend to social rights (eg there is no right to housing or to health care), nor does it confer economic rights (such as a right to a decent standard of living or to employment).

Table 18.2 The 'Convention rights'

Provision	Right/prohibition	Notes
Article 2	Right to life	No infringement if killing relates to execution of lawfully-imposed sentence (but note UK now signatory to Thirteenth Protocol: see below) or absolutely necessary use of force in relation to self-defence, quelling of disorder, or effecting lawful arrest/preventing escape of lawfully-detained person
Article 3	Prohibition of torture	Prohibits torture and inhuman or degrading treatment
Article 4	Prohibition of slavery and forced labour	Prohibits slavery, servitude, forced and compulsory labour
Article 5	Right to liberty and security	Deprivation of liberty prohibited unless (i) in accordance with procedure prescribed by law and (ii) for a legitimate purpose. Legitimate purposes include imprisonment of convicted criminals, trial of criminal offences, prevention of spreading of infectious diseases, deportation, extradition. Legal proceedings must be available whereby legality of detention can be determined
Article 6	Right to a fair trial	In all criminal proceedings, as well as in any proceedings determining civil rights and obligations, there must be a fair and public hearing within a reasonable time by an independent and impartial tribunal established by law. Additional rights in relation to criminal matters include presumption of innocence, suspect to be informed promptly of allegation, suspect to be given adequate time and facilities to prepare defence, suspect to be given free legal representation when interests of justice so require, opportunity to examine and cross-examine witnesses, access to interpreter if necessary

(Continued)

---

[28] A broader non-discrimination provision is contained in the Twelfth Protocol, but this has not been adopted by the UK. However, UK law, independently of the ECHR and HRA, contains extensive provision on discrimination: see Equality Act 2010.

Table 18.2 (*Continued*)

Provision	Right/prohibition	Notes	
Article 7	No punishment without law	Essentially a non-retrospectivity principle: prohibits finding someone guilty of an offence that was not specified at time of commission; prohibits imposition of heavier penalty than that applicable at time of commission	
Article 8	Right to respect for private and family life	Applies to private life, family life, home, and correspondence	Articles 8 to 11 are all laid down according to a common format. The first paragraph of each Article states the matters to which the right relates. For instance, Art 8(1) says, 'Everyone has the right to respect for his private and family life, his home and his correspondence.' The second paragraph sets out the circumstances in which it is lawful to do that which would otherwise be unlawful by virtue of the first paragraph. In relation to each Article, the requirements laid down in the second paragraph are that any restrictions must be (a) prescribed by (or, in relation to Art 8, 'in accordance with') law and (b) necessary in a democratic society for the advancement of (c) a legitimate objective. Such objectives include the prevention of disorder and crime and the interests of national security.
Article 9	Freedom of thought, conscience and religion	Includes freedom to change religion/belief, and freedom to manifest religion/belief through worship, teaching, practice and observance	
Article 10	Freedom of expression	Includes freedom to hold opinions and to receive and impart information and ideas. Does not preclude state licensing of radio, television and cinemas	
Article 11	Freedom of assembly and association	Includes right to form and join trade unions	
Article 12	Right to marry	Has been interpreted as applying only to marriage of opposite sex couples. It therefore does not apply to gay couples, but does apply to couples which are opposite sex by virtue of one partner (or both partners) being transsexual.	

(*Continued*)

Table 18.2 (*Continued*)

Provision	Right/prohibition	Notes
Article 14	Prohibition of discrimination	Explicitly covers discrimination on grounds of sex, race, colour, language, religion, political or other opinion, national or social origin, association with a national minority, property, birth, or other status. Has been interpreted as applying to other matters, including sexual orientation. Only applies to discrimination in respect of access to other ECHR rights.
Article 1, First Protocol	Protection of property	Right to peaceful enjoyment of possessions. Deprivation permitted only if in public interest. Explicit provision for state to enforce such laws as it thinks necessary to control property use in public interest or to secure payment of taxes.
Article 2, First Protocol	Right to education	Does not require creation of educational provision; merely prohibits denial of access to such provision as exists. Where state assumes responsibility for education/teaching, parents' philosophical and religious convictions must be respected.
Article 3, First Protocol	Right to free elections	Free elections must be held at regular intervals, by secret ballot and under conditions allowing free expression of opinion in choice of legislature.
Article 1, Thirteenth Protocol	Abolition of the death penalty	Prohibits use of the death penalty.

3.3.2 The forms of protection afforded by the HRA

If something is a 'Convention right' under the HRA, what is the practical significance of that? In order to answer this question, we need to consider the four key HRA provisions that are outlined in Figure 18.1.

One of the ways in which the HRA seeks to protect the Convention rights is by making it more difficult in the first place for the UK Parliament to enact legislation that is inconsistent with those rights. To this end, s 19 of the HRA stipulates that, before a Bill's second reading, the Minister responsible for it must do one of two things:

- make a 'statement of compatibility', saying that she believes the Bill to be compatible with the Convention rights;
- explain to Parliament that she is unable to make a statement of compatibility—because she does not believe the Bill to be compatible—but that she thinks Parliament should enact the Bill anyway.

Section 3	Section 4
Courts must interpret all legislative provisions compatibly with Convention rights as far as it is possible to do so	If it is not possible to interpret a provision in primary legislation compatibly with Convention rights, certain courts may issue a declaration of incompatibility
Section 10	**Section 19**
If a domestic court declares, or the ECtHR finds, that a legislative provision is incompatible with Convention rights, relevant legislation can be amended under a 'fast-track' process	A Minister introducing a Bill into Parliament must either state that she believes it to be compatible with Convention rights or ask Parliament to enact the Bill even though she does not consider it to be compatible

Figure 18.1 The Human Rights Act 1998: key provisions

This system is intended to ensure that Parliament does not casually or unknowingly enact legislation that will breach the Convention rights. If a Minister finds herself unable to issue a statement of compatibility, this will draw Parliament's attention to the possibility that the Bill may be incompatible with one or more of the Convention rights. It will focus attention, both inside and beyond Parliament, on whether there are compelling reasons for enacting the legislation despite such putative incompatibility.

There is, however, an obvious weakness in this system. For a variety of reasons (including incompetence, genuine misjudgement, and cynical political calculation), statements of compatibility may be issued in respect of Bills that later turn out to be incompatible with one or more of the Convention rights. Parliament does, however, have an additional, more independent, source of advice on the likely compatibility of Bills. The Joint Committee on Human Rights (JCHR) is a joint select committee of the House of Commons and the House of Lords that (with the assistance of expert legal advice) scrutinises all Bills and reports to Parliament on their human rights implications.[29] Ministers do not always give way when the JCHR identifies a potential incompatibility, but the Committee is nevertheless highly regarded, and its reports often play an influential role when MPs and peers debate and propose amendments to Bills.

Section 6 of the HRA requires public authorities to act compatibly with Convention rights, unless primary legislation requires them to act incompatibly. This means, among other things, that the Convention rights have become grounds of judicial review: public bodies' acts and decisions can be quashed if incompatible with those rights. The implications of this were considered in Chapter 12 and need not be restated here.[30] It is sufficient to emphasise that s 6 has extended the courts' judicial review powers. While breach of common law constitutional rights was a ground of

---

[29] See further Feldman, 'Parliamentary Scrutiny of Legislation and Human Rights' [2002] PL 323.
[30] See Chapter 12, section 3.5.1.

review, the scope of Convention rights is *broader*. And judicial review under the HRA is *deeper* than it was beforehand: as we saw in Chapter 12, when Convention rights are involved, judicial review is more intense. In particular, the proportionality, rather than *Wednesbury* reasonableness, test is used to test the legality of any restrictions placed by public authorities upon qualified rights.

Section 3 of the HRA requires courts, so far as is possible, to read and give effect to legislation in a way that is compatible with the Convention rights. This is a strong obligation that requires courts to go to considerable lengths to interpret legislation compatibly with the Convention rights. We have already seen that, prior to the HRA's enactment, courts were willing to protect rights by interpretative means. But the interpretative protection of rights is now triggered in a broader range of circumstances. Before the HRA entered into force, the courts would engage in such interpretation only in one of two scenarios. We have already encountered the first: it arose where the right in question fell within the relatively narrow category of common law constitutional rights. The other scenario arose when the right (not being a common law constitutional right) was one that was set out in the ECHR *and* the domestic legislation in question was ambiguous.[31] In contrast, under the HRA, the interpretative obligation arising under s 3 obtains in respect of all Convention rights (not only common law constitutional rights) and applies irrespective of whether the domestic legislation in question is ambiguous.

The HRA's most novel device for protecting rights is found in s 4. The HRA makes it clear (and it follows from the doctrine of parliamentary sovereignty) that provisions in primary legislation that are incompatible with Convention rights cannot baldy be struck down. But s 4 says that certain courts can issue a 'declaration of incompatibility' in respect of such provisions.[32] The effect is not to invalidate the provision in question or to prevent it from applying to the parties to the case. But a declaration does authoritatively signal that the relevant legislation is inconsistent with a Convention right. That might seem to imply that declarations of incompatibility are largely worthless. However, for reasons we consider later, that is far from the truth.[33]

Finally, a broader point should be noted. While the powers given by the HRA to the courts are important, courts are not the only means of overseeing and protecting human rights. As we have already noted, Parliament's JCHR performs an important role in scrutinising proposed legislation for its compliance with human rights. There are also three commissions—the Equality and Human Rights Commission (for England and Wales), the Scottish Human Rights Commission, and the Northern Ireland Human Rights Commission—that promote human rights and seek to ensure (among other things) that public bodies comply with human rights standards.

---

[31] *R v Secretary of State for the Home Department, ex p Brind* [1991] 1 AC 696.

[32] For simplicity, we refer in this paragraph to Acts of Parliament. In fact, s 4 actually refers to 'primary legislation'. The significance of this point is considered in section 3.4.6.

[33] See section 3.4.5.

3.4 **Sections 3 and 4 of the HRA**

Having set out the key provisions of the HRA in outline, we now consider several of those provisions in more detail. We begin, in this section, with ss 3 and 4.

3.4.1 **Introduction: the relationship between ss 3 and 4**

Sections 3 and 4 aim to confer upon the courts the maximum amount of power to uphold Convention rights that is consistent with the role of the courts under the UK constitution. The HRA thus reflects the limits upon the courts' role that flow from two key constitutional principles:

- Under the separation of powers doctrine, courts can interpret legislation but cannot themselves legislate. The HRA therefore permits (and requires) courts to interpret legislation compatibly with Convention rights only when this is 'possible', thereby seeking to confine courts to an interpretive, as distinct from a legislative, role.

- The doctrine of parliamentary sovereignty, at least understood in orthodox terms, means that courts cannot ignore or reject Acts of Parliament.[34] It is for this reason that the courts' power under s 4 is limited to declaring that legislation is incompatible with one or more of the Convention rights.

Sections 3 and 4 are thus complementary. Each is part of an integrated scheme of which the other is a crucial component. And no provision can attract the exercise of both powers. Either it is possible to interpret the legislation compatibly with the Convention rights under s 3, in which case that is what the court must do, or it will be impossible to do so, in which case a declaration may be issued under s 4. Whether it is s 3 or s 4 that applies turns upon whether it is 'possible' to interpret the relevant provision compatibly with the relevant Convention right. However, the boundaries of what is interpretively 'possible' are unclear, meaning that the courts have some leeway to decide whether to deal with a case under s 3 or s 4. In exercising that discretion, the courts are mindful of the implications of choosing one or other course.

Lord Irvine—who, as already noted, bears a large part of the responsibility for the HRA's enactment—underlined this point when he warned courts of the dangers of overreliance on either provision. He noted that stretching the concept of possibility, in order to fit cases within the s 3 category, would be constitutionally inappropriate. Judges, he said, would be 'taking it upon themselves to rewrite legislation in order to render it consistent with the Convention, thereby excluding Parliament and the executive from the human rights enterprise'.[35] This would be problematic not least because ECHR-consistent interpretation under s 3 is not the only tool at the courts' disposal: they also have the option of issuing a declaration of incompatibility under s 4.

---

[34] We saw in Chapter 8 that courts *can* disapply Acts of Parliament if they are incompatible with directly effective provisions of EU law. The basis of this power, and whether it is to be understood as an exception to, a denunciation of, or as compatible with, parliamentary sovereignty is considered in Chapter 8, section 4.

[35] Irvine, 'Activism and Restraint: Human Rights and the Interpretative Process' [1999] EHRLR 350, 367.

However, this does not mean that courts should rely too much on s 4 either. Doing so, warned Irvine, would severely curtail the courts' ability to guarantee Convention rights through s 3 interpretation. Instead of reading legislation in a way that gave effect to individuals' rights, the courts would tend to discover irreconcilable conflicts between UK law and the ECHR which would then require legislative correction.[36] Indeed, overreliance on s 4 would substantially frustrate the purpose of the HRA, which was to enable domestic courts to deal with human rights matters. This follows because, as we explain later, a declaration of incompatibility has no legal effect upon the outcome of the case; the party whose human rights have been infringed, in practice, leaves the court empty-handed.

3.4.2 The interpretive obligation: what is 'possible'?

We now consider how the courts have approached their interpretive obligation under s 3. Two of the key questions here are: when is it 'possible' to interpret legislation compatibly with the Convention rights, and when should a declaration of incompatibility instead be issued under s 4? In seeking to answer this question, the decision of the House of Lords in *Ghaidan v Godin-Mendoza*[37] is a good starting point.

The claimant landlord wished to evict the defendant tenant from his property. If, however, the defendant was (as he contended) a 'statutory tenant' within the meaning of the Rent Act 1977, he would enjoy legal immunity from eviction except in limited circumstances. The case therefore hinged on whether the defendant was a statutory tenant. This was governed by the Rent Act 1977, Sch 1, para 2, the text of which (as it was at the relevant time) is shown in Figure 18.2.

The question in *Ghaidan* was whether those rules operated such that, upon the death of the defendant's partner—the 'original tenant' within the meaning of the Rent Act provisions—a statutory tenancy was vested in the defendant. The defendant and his partner had lived together in the property concerned for 18 years before the latter's death, in a stable, monogamous relationship. As such, but for one crucial factor, the defendant would straightforwardly have satisfied the conditions for a statutory tenancy. The complication was that the defendant and his partner were in a same-sex relationship. The House of Lords therefore had to decide whether, bearing in mind its obligation under s 3 of the HRA, the relevant provisions of the Rent Act

---

(1) The surviving spouse (if any) of the original tenant, if residing in the dwelling-house immediately before the death of the original tenant, shall after the death be the statutory tenant if and so long as he or she occupies the dwelling-house as his or her residence.

(2) For the purposes of this paragraph, a person who was living with the original tenant as his or her wife or husband shall be treated as the spouse of the original tenant.

Figure 18.2 Rent Act 1977, Sch 1, para 2

---

[36] Irvine, 367.   [37] [2004] UKHL 30, [2004] 2 AC 557.

Stage 1	Stage 2	Stage 3
What is the natural meaning of the legislative provision?	Would the provision, given its natural meaning and applied to the facts, yield an outcome that would infringe a Convention right?	If so, can the provision be read and given effect so as to produce an outcome that would be compatible with the relevant Convention rights?

Figure 18.3 The three stages of analysis under s 3

should be read as applying to same-sex couples.[38] In such cases, the courts, in effect, adopt a three-stage analysis, as shown in Figure 18.3.

The first stage of the analysis in *Ghaidan*, concerning the natural meaning of the provision, was straightforward. Throughout the provisions in question, gender-specific language was used: 'spouse', 'husband', 'wife'. Thus, as Lord Nicholls observed:

> On an ordinary reading of this language paragraph 2(2) draws a distinction between the position of a heterosexual couple living together in a house as husband and wife and a homosexual couple living together in a house. The survivor of a heterosexual couple may become a statutory tenant by succession, the survivor of a homosexual couple cannot.[39]

The Court then turned to the second stage of the analysis. Clearly, if the relevant provisions of the Rent Act were to have been given their natural meaning in *Ghaidan*, the defendant would not have become a statutory tenant. Would this have breached the defendant's Convention rights? The House of Lords concluded, on the basis of Arts 8 and 14, that it would. Article 8, as Table 18.2 shows, requires respect for, among other things, a person's home. Taken in isolation, this would not have assisted the defendant: Art 8 does not, by any means, impose a blanket prohibition upon landlords evicting tenants. Crucially, however, the landlord in *Ghaidan* would not have been able lawfully to evict the defendant if he had been asserting a statutory tenancy on the basis of an opposite-sex relationship. This factor made Art 14 relevant. The effect of Art 14 is that the enjoyment of the other rights set out in the ECHR 'shall be secured without discrimination' on various grounds, including (according to the ECtHR's case law) sexual orientation.[40] It followed that the Rent Act, if applied to the defendant, would entail a breach of Art 14: he would have been accorded a lower degree of respect for his home simply because his claim was based on a same-sex, rather than an opposite-sex, relationship.

Having concluded that giving the provision its natural meaning would result in a breach of Convention rights, the Court had to move on to the third stage of the analysis. Here it had to confront the question whether it was 'possible' to interpret the legislation in a way that would yield a Convention-compliant outcome. Lord Nicholls said that the

---

[38] The relevant provisions of the Rent Act have since been amended: they now refer to 'civil partners' as well as 'spouses'. It is also relevant that spousal relationships can now exist between people of the same sex.

[39] *Ghaidan*, [5].   [40] *Da Silva Mouta v Portugal* (2001) 31 EHRR 4; *EB v France* (2008) 47 EHRR 21.

obligation imposed on courts by s 3 to interpret legislation compatibly with Convention rights '[s]o far as it is possible to do so' is a strong one. It is not to be understood as a narrow requirement that simply requires courts to resolve ambiguities;[41] rather, it is an 'unusual and far-reaching' obligation that 'may require a court to depart from the unambiguous meaning the legislation would otherwise bear'. It might even require the court to 'depart from the intention of the Parliament which enacted the legislation'.[42] While this would (inevitably) frustrate Parliament's intention when it passed the provision in question, it would fulfil its intention in enacting s 3 of the HRA. Importantly, Lord Nicholls said that Parliament, in enacting s 3, was not to be taken to have intended that whether ECHR-compliant interpretation is possible 'should depend critically upon the particular form of words adopted by the parliamentary draftsman in the statutory provision under consideration'. Such an approach 'would make the application of section 3 something of a semantic lottery'.[43] Lord Nicholls concluded that s 3 permits courts to read words into a statutory text in order to change its meaning so as to make it Convention-compliant.[44]

Yet Lord Nicholls did not consider the power conferred by s 3 to be unlimited. What, then, are the bounds of what is 'possible'? The answer, said Lord Nicholls, was that Parliament could not be taken to 'have intended that in the discharge of this extended interpretative function the courts should adopt a meaning inconsistent with a fundamental feature of legislation'. The courts cannot use s 3 to ascribe to a given provision a meaning that is inconsistent with the 'underlying thrust of the legislation being construed'.[45] Similarly, Lord Rodger said that the interpretation must 'go with the grain of the legislation'. The court must not ascribe a meaning to a provision that conflicts with the 'essential principles' of the legislation concerned: doing so, said Lord Rodger, would cross 'the boundary between interpretation and amendment of the statute', thereby taking the court beyond its proper role under s 3.[46]

Applying these principles in *Ghaidan*, the majority held that the thrust of the relevant parts of the Rent Act was to confer protection upon those who were the surviving partners of stable, close relationships. This brought same-sex partners within the scope of the protection afforded by the Act. True to the principles that he had laid down earlier in his judgment, Lord Nicholls said: 'The precise form of words read in for this purpose is of no significance. It is their substantive effect which matters.'[47]

However, Lord Millett dissented. Lord Millett agreed with the principles laid down by Lord Nicholls,[48] but differed when it came to applying them to the facts of the case. In essence, the disagreement between Lord Millett and the majority was about what the relevant fundamental features of the Act were. In seeking to identify these, Lord Millett looked in detail at the legislative history. He noted that when the relevant provision was originally enacted, it conferred protection only on women whose husbands had died. Later, an amendment extended protection to widowers. Later still, in recognition of the increasing incidence of extramarital cohabitation, protection was extended to those who were not married, but who had been living with the deceased

---

[41] *Ghaidan*, [29].   [42] *Ghaidan*, [30].   [43] *Ghaidan*, [31].   [44] *Ghaidan*, [32].
[45] *Ghaidan*, [33].   [46] *Ghaidan*, [121].   [47] *Ghaidan*, [35].
[48] *Ghaidan*, [67]–[68], *per* Lord Millett.

tenant 'as his or her wife or husband'. This language, said Lord Millett, 'does not mean living together as lovers whether of the same or the opposite sex. It connotes persons who have openly set up home together as man and wife'.[49] Lord Millett concluded that the use of gender-specific language throughout all of the iterations of the relevant provisions indicated that a fundamental feature of the Act was that the protection that it conferred should extend only to opposite-sex couples. What ultimately distinguished Lord Millett's analysis, then, from that of the majority is that he placed more weight on the specific language used by Parliament in his attempt to identify the fundamental feature of the Act. Among other things, this demonstrates that the 'fundamental feature' test is a relatively open-textured one that may be difficult to apply in a consistent and predictable way.[50]

> **Q** Did the House of Lords go too far in *Ghaidan*?[51] Are the principles set out by Lord Nicholls acceptable, or do they attach insufficient weight to what the legislation being interpreted actually says?

3.4.3 The interpretive obligation: three limiting factors

The courts are not invariably prepared to do whatever is necessary under the guise of s 3 interpretation to render legislation ECHR-compliant. The extent to which courts are prepared to stretch statutory language in order to secure compatibility with the Convention is informed by the following three factors:

- fundamental features of the legislative scheme;
- the constitutional limits of the courts' policymaking role;
- the practical consequences of according the provision a Convention-compliant interpretation.

Let us consider these points in turn. As to the first, we have already seen that the courts will not adopt an interpretation that conflicts with a fundamental feature of the legislation concerned (albeit that, as in *Ghaidan*, there might be scope for disagreement about what the relevant fundamental feature is).

Anderson is a good illustration of a case in which the court refused, on this ground, to render an ECHR-compatible interpretation.[52] The case concerned a challenge to the then-applicable regime governing the release from prison (on licence) of prisoners serving mandatory life sentences. The relevant domestic legislation provided that such prisoners could only be released if (i) the Parole Board so recommended; and

---

[49] *Ghaidan*, [92].

[50] See also *R (GC) v Commissioner of Police of the Metropolis* [2011] UKSC 21, [2011] 1 WLR 1230 in which the Supreme Court divided 3–2 on whether a relevant matter constituted a 'fundamental feature' of the legislation concerned.

[51] For a further example of the courts using their s 3 power so as substantially to adapt the effect of legislation, see *R v A (No 2)* [2001] UKHL 25, [2002] 1 AC 45.

[52] *R (Anderson) v Secretary of State for the Home Department* [2002] UKHL 46, [2003] 1 AC 83.

(ii) the Home Secretary, after consulting with the Lord Chief Justice, accepted the Board's recommendation.[53] This meant that the Home Secretary had the ultimate say. This, said the claimant, was inconsistent with Art 6 ECHR, which provides that criminal trials must be conducted 'by an independent and impartial tribunal established by law'.

The House of Lords accepted in *Anderson* that if the domestic legislation were given its normal meaning, it would ascribe to the Home Secretary a sentencing function (since he would be instrumental in determining how long people serving such sentences should actually spend behind bars), which would be incompatible with Art 6.

The question was then whether the domestic legislation could be construed differently, so as to be consistent with Art 6. The House of Lords held that it could not and instead issued a s 4 declaration of incompatibility. Securing compliance with Art 6 would require the Home Secretary to be written out of the picture (eg by reading in an obligation on his part to abide by any recommendation of the Parole Board or the Lord Chief Justice, thereby reducing his role to a purely formal one). Achieving this via s 3 would, said Lord Bingham, 'not be judicial interpretation but judicial vandalism: it would give the section an effect quite different from that which Parliament intended and would go well beyond any interpretative process sanctioned by section 3 of the 1998 Act'.[54]

Anderson is not inconsistent with the principles laid down in *Ghaidan*, but an application of them: the House of Lords in *Anderson* took the view that a fundamental feature of the relevant legislation was that a government Minister should have the last word on the release of mandatory life sentence prisoners. As Lord Steyn put it, the 'plain legislative intent [was] to entrust the decision to the Home Secretary, who was intended to be free to follow or reject judicial advice'.[55]

Anderson also points towards the second of the three factors—concerning the scope of the courts' policymaking role—that limit what courts are prepared to do under s 3. In some situations, courts may be presented with binary choices: either interpretation X is adopted (in which case, the legislation is incompatible with the ECHR), or interpretation Y is preferred (which secures compliance with the Convention). *Ghaidan* was a case such as this: either the Rent Act did or did not cover same-sex partners. However, in other circumstances, the position may be more complex. While it might be clear that some feature of the legislation needs to be removed or changed, there may be several ways in which that could be achieved.

Anderson was a case of the latter type. The problem was obvious: the Home Secretary should play no part in release decisions. But what alternative arrangement should be put in place? Should the Parole Board have the last word? Or the Lord Chief Justice? Or someone else? In circumstances such as these, the courts are acutely aware that they risk crossing the line between interpreting and legislating. This suggests that, if securing an ECHR-compatible interpretation would involve making significant policy choices, the court is likely to conclude that consistent interpretation is not possible within the meaning of s 3. In practice, these circumstances are more likely to

---

[53] Crime (Sentences) Act 1997, s 29 (since repealed).   [54] *Anderson*, [30].
[55] *Anderson*, [59].

arise when the feature of the Act at stake is a fundamental one, since ridding the Act of such a feature is liable to leave a bigger or more complicated gap that needs to be filled. As a result, the two limiting factors that we have identified—contradiction of a fundamental feature of legislation and the making of significant policy choices—will often coexist.

The third limiting factor arises when the practical consequences of adopting an ECHR-compliant interpretation of the relevant provision would be so far-reaching that it would be inappropriate for the court to adopt such an interpretation. Take, for example, *Re S (Minors) (Care Order: Implementation of Care Plan)*.[56] The Court of Appeal was concerned with the regime contained in the Children Act 1989 concerning care orders—that is, court orders vesting parental responsibility for children in local authorities. The Court concluded that the Act made insufficient provision for circumstances in which a local authority failed properly to discharge its duties to children subject to care orders. This, held the Court, might result in a breach of Art 8. Having arrived at this view,[57] the Court of Appeal, purporting to use its power under s 3 of the HRA, set about designing a system whereby matters could be referred back to the courts if key 'milestones' within care plans were not achieved.

On appeal, the House of Lords held that the Court of Appeal had overstepped the mark. The 'judicial innovation' that it had sought to introduce 'passe[d] well beyond the boundary of interpretation', said Lord Nicholls (whose judgment commanded the unanimous support of the other Law Lords).[58] There were two reasons for this. The first was a familiar one: the Court of Appeal had contradicted a 'cardinal principle' of the Children Act,[59] that responsibility for children subject to care orders was vested in local authorities, not courts.[60] But there was also a second reason: the system that the Court of Appeal had sought to read into the Act 'would not come free from additional administrative work and expense', and would potentially compromise local authorities' capacity to discharge their responsibilities to other children.[61] Lord Nicholls said that whether local authorities should be subjected to the sort of supervisory regime contemplated by the Court of Appeal was for 'decision by Parliament, not the courts', not least because it would be 'impossible for a court to attempt to evaluate these ramifications or assess what would be the views of Parliament if changes are needed'.[62]

3.4.4 The interpretive obligation: constitutional considerations

Strong views have been expressed by commentators about how far courts should press their power under s 3, and about the principles that should inform the exercise of that power.[63] One reason why there has been a good deal of controversy about s 3 is that

---

[56] [2001] EWCA Civ 757, [2001] 2 FLR 582.

[57] Which, for presently irrelevant reasons, the House of Lords ([2002] UKHL 10, [2002] 2 AC 291) did not share.

[58] *Re S*, HL, [43].   [59] *Re S*, HL, [23], *per* Lord Nicholls.   [60] *Re S*, HL, [25].

[61] *Re S*, HL, [43], *per* Lord Nicholls.

[62] *Re S*, HL, [44]. See also *Bellinger v Bellinger* [2003] UKHL 21, [2003] 2 AC 467.

[63] See, among other contributions, Marshall, 'The Lynchpin of Parliamentary Intention: Lost, Stolen, or Startled?' [2003] PL 236; Nicol, 'Statutory Interpretation and Human Rights after *Anderson*' [2004] PL 274; Kavanagh, 'Statutory Interpretation and Human Rights after *Anderson*: A More Contextual Approach'

it provides little guidance about how the power it confers should be exercised. The fact that courts are only required to interpret legislation compatibly with the ECHR '[s]o far as it is possible to do so' clearly suggests that there is a limit as to how far they should go. However, the precise nature of that limit is unclear from the text of the HRA. In the absence of textual guidance, the true extent of s 3 inevitably falls to be determined by reference to broader constitutional considerations. Allan argues that there are two rival conceptions of constitutional thought in the UK—the 'constitution of will' and the 'constitution of reason'—and that the conception we prefer will influence our view of how far courts ought to go under s 3.[64]

Adherents to the former view perceive the constitutional landscape to be a somewhat barren place: denuded of any rich set of inherent norms, the constitution of will is dominated by the intention of Parliament. The courts' primary responsibility, then, is to find the interpretation of legislation that best gives effect to that intention. Those who subscribe to an unreconstructed theory of parliamentary sovereignty are likely to sympathise with this position. On this view, the requirement imposed under s 3 of the HRA is one that is alien to the pre-existing constitutional culture, and a relatively narrow view of s 3 is therefore likely to commend itself to adherents of the constitution of will. Marshall, for example, argues that a wide conception of the s 3 duty should be resisted, because it would be 'potentially damaging both to the authority of Parliament and the separation of the judicial and legislative functions'.[65]

Allan, in contrast, is an adherent of the constitution of reason, the guiding principle of which is that people should be 'treated by government in accordance with the standards of justice or fairness widely recognised as fundamental to political morality, without arbitrary exception or unjustified discrimination'.[66] From this perspective, the constitutional landscape is not a barren one dominated by parliamentary intention; rather, it is one that, independently of the HRA, is sympathetic to the norms underpinning many human rights. That view is supported by the doctrine of common law constitutional rights that emerged before the HRA was contemplated and by the courts' recent insistence that that doctrine remains notwithstanding, and has developed in the light of, the HRA.[67] As such, says Allan, the HRA was 'planted in fertile ground'.[68]

Those who adhere to this view tend to be more comfortable with a wide reading of s 3, because such a reading is wholly consistent with what is regarded as the courts' proper role. In the constitution of reason, the courts' primary responsibility is to protect fundamental constitutional values, including human rights: the will of Parliament remains important, but it is not necessarily decisive. For Allan, the notion that legislation may have some meaning independent of the context, including the constitutional context, in which it falls to be interpreted is therefore an ultimately empty one: meaning can only be ascribed to legislation through the process

[2004] PL 537; Young, '*Ghaidan v Godin-Mendoza*: Avoiding the Deference Trap' [2005] PL 23; Kavanagh, 'Parliamentary Intent, Statutory Interpretation and the Human Rights Act 1998' (2006) 26 OJLS 179; Allan, 'Parliament's Will and the Justice of the Common Law: The HRA in Constitutional Perspective' (2006) 59 CLP 27.

[64] Allan.   [65] Marshall, 248.   [66] Allan, 31.   [67] See section 3.2.   [68] Allan, 31.

of judicial construction because it 'awaits integration into the tapestry of which it can only form a single thread'.[69] An illustration of Allan's preferred approach is furnished by his view that the House of Lords should have gone further than it did in *Anderson*: an 'appropriately robust' approach to the interpretation of the relevant legislation 'would have secured the essential requirements of the separation of powers' (and hence the claimant's right to be sentenced by an independent tribunal rather than a Minister).[70]

3.4.5 Declarations of incompatibility

As foreshadowed in the previous sections, rendering an ECHR-compatible interpretation is not the only tool at the courts' disposal when faced with legislation that, on its face, appears inconsistent with one or more of the Convention rights. Their other option is to issue a declaration of incompatibility under s 4, although that is an option open only to certain courts, including the High Court and the Court of Appeal (in England and Wales, and in Northern Ireland), the High Court of Justiciary[71] and the Court of Session (in Scotland), and the Supreme Court.[72]

The power to issue a declaration of incompatibility is only exercisable if the court 'is satisfied that the provision is incompatible with a Convention right'.[73] This reflects the fact that, analytically speaking, the courts' powers under ss 3 and 4 arise in mutually exclusive circumstances. If it is 'possible' to interpret compatibly with the Convention right in question, the court *must* do so; if it is not 'possible', the court *must not do so*. Only in the latter scenario is s 4 triggered. This, however, merely *authorises* the court to issue a declaration; the court is not *required* to do so. That said, it is in practice highly unusual for a court to decline to exercise its power under s 4. It is not, however, unheard of, as the *Nicklinson* case demonstrates.[74]

The essential question facing the Supreme Court in *Nicklinson* was whether primary legislation that makes assisting suicide a criminal offence is—at least in relation to individuals who wish to end their own lives but cannot, due to infirmity or illness, do so unaided— an unnecessary and disproportionate restriction of the right to respect for private life. The Supreme Court divided three ways:

- The two dissenting judges[75] considered that the law was incompatible with the Convention and would have issued a declaration of incompatibility.

- Four members of the majority[76] considered that a declaration of incompatibility was out of the question because the case raised 'controversial and complex questions of fact arising out of moral and social dilemmas'.[77] This meant that the Court should not disturb the balance struck by Parliament between (on the one hand) the rights of those who wish to end their lives and (on the other)

---

[69] Allan, 45.   [70] Allan, 49.   [71] Except when sitting as a trial court.
[72] HRA, s 4(5).
[73] HRA, s 4(2). This provision applies in respect of primary legislation. The position concerning subordinate legislation is considered later in this section.
[74] *R (Nicklinson) v Ministry of Justice* [2014] UKSC 38, [2015] AC 657.   [75] Lady Hale and Lord Kerr.
[76] Lords Mance, Sumption, Hughes, and Reed.   [77] *Nicklinson*, [232], *per* Lord Sumption.

the interests of vulnerable people who might, for instance, feel pressured into accepting assisted suicide if it were lawfully available.

- The other three members of the majority[78] took the view that while it would not be appropriate to issue a declaration of incompatibility there and then, it might become appropriate to do so were the matter to be relitigated in the future. The Justices who adopted this intermediate position were influenced not only by the moral sensitivity of the issues raised but also by the fact that 'this is a case where the legislature is and has been actively considering the issue'.[79] The concern was that a declaration of incompatibility might inappropriately constrain or short-circuit the ongoing attention the issue was receiving in Parliament.

Nicklinson is an unusual case: s 4 declarations usually follow as a matter of course once the court has concluded that consistent interpretation under s 3 is not possible. One of the puzzles raised by the intermediate position adopted by the third group of Justices in *Nicklinson* is why they worried, in effect, that a declaration of incompatibility would unduly circumscribe parliamentary consideration of the matter given that the remedy is merely declaratory in nature. It is to that question—and allied issues concerning the effects of declarations of incompatibility—that we now turn.

3.4.6　The legal effects of declarations of incompatibility

Declarations of incompatibility have one, and only one, legal effect. They trigger the power of the executive government to issue remedial orders under s 10 of the HRA. When a declaration is issued under s 4, s 10 permits (but does not require) the government to enact secondary legislation amending (among other things) the Act of Parliament that was found to be incompatible.[80] Section 10 thus confers a so-called 'Henry VIII' power[81] on the executive, enabling it, by means of secondary legislation, to amend ECHR-incompatible primary legislation. In practice, however, remedial orders are rarely used: most legislative provisions that have been the subject of declarations of incompatibility have been amended, replaced, or repealed via the enactment of fresh primary legislation.

More significant than the legal effects that declarations of incompatibility *do* have are those that they *do not* have. In particular, such a declaration 'does not affect the validity, continuing operation or enforcement of the provision in respect of which it is given'.[82] When a court issues a declaration of incompatibility, the legal position between the parties to the case is therefore unaffected. The legal provision declared incompatible with the ECHR remains a fully operative part of the law, and the court must go on to apply it, even though that will involve a breach of one party's Convention rights.

It would be unsurprising if this were to lead courts to prefer to resolve cases by means of s 3 whenever possible, by adopting a wide view of their power under that section. The use of the s 3 power means that the court is able to give effect to the

---

[78] Lords Neuberger, Mance, and Wilson.　　[79] *Nicklinson*, [116], *per* Lord Neuberger.
[80] The s 10 power is also triggered when the ECtHR finds UK law to be incompatible with the ECHR.
[81] See further Chapter 4, section 4.2.2.　　[82] HRA, s 4(6)(a).

relevant party's Convention rights (because, as a result of interpreting the provision concerned pursuant to s 3, it turns out that the applicable law is consistent with those rights). In contrast, the use of the s 4 power means that the relevant party loses the case (or at least loses the human rights point). If, for example, the House of Lords were to have relied on s 4 rather than s 3 in *Ghaidan*,[83] the defendant would not have counted as a statutory tenant and would thus have left court vulnerable to eviction. This may lead the courts, consciously or otherwise, to prefer to use s 3 whenever possible. Indeed, Lord Steyn admitted as much in *Ghaidan*: the HRA's purpose of 'bringing rights home', he said, 'could only be effectively [achieved] if section 3(1) was the prime remedial measure, and section 4 a measure of last resort'.[84]

Q Is it legitimate for courts to take into account the respective practical consequences of deciding a case under s 3 or s 4? Should, for example, courts be prepared to adopt a particularly strained interpretation under s 3, in order to be able to decide the case consistently with the relevant party's Convention rights, if (as in *Ghaidan*) applying ECHR-inconsistent law (albeit while declaring the incompatibility) would leave the party vulnerable to harsh treatment?

Not only do declarations of incompatibility not affect the applicable law: they do not require either Parliament or the executive to do anything by way of response. Parliament can, if it wishes, enact legislation removing the incompatibility. Equally, the executive, using its power under s 10 of the HRA, can make a remedial order. But, as a matter of UK law, neither Parliament nor the executive is required to do such things.

It is clear from what has been said so far that a judicial power to strike down or refuse to apply ECHR-incompatible primary legislation forms no part of the HRA scheme. This invites an important question. As we saw in Chapter 5, the normal principle is that when two Acts of Parliament conflict with one another, the more recent Act prevails over the earlier one, repealing it to the extent of the inconsistency. This, as we saw, is known as the doctrine of implied repeal.

What happens, then, if legislation enacted before the HRA turns out to be incompatible with one of the Convention rights? Is the pre-HRA provision impliedly repealed, meaning that it is simply invalid? If this were the case, then, in such circumstances, there would logically be no role for declarations of incompatibility: the pre-HRA provision would be invalid and unenforceable, and there would be no extant provision on which a declaration could meaningfully bite.

In fact, pre-HRA provisions that are incompatible with Convention rights are not impliedly repealed by the HRA—not because the HRA is immune from the effect of the doctrine, but because it is simply not relevant in the first place. The reason is as follows. The doctrine of implied repeal only operates when there is a conflict between the substance of two pieces of legislation. If, for example, an Act passed in 2017 were

---

[83] [2004] UKHL 30, [2004] 2 AC 557.   [84] *Ghaidan*, [46].

to say that 'everyone has the right to free speech', this would impliedly repeal a provision contained in a 2016 Act that restricted the right to free speech to an extent impermissible under the 2017 Act.

Crucially, however, the HRA does not straightforwardly say that anyone has any rights; rather, it merely requires certain bodies to do certain things in relation to ECHR rights in certain circumstances. There is therefore no conflict, for the purposes of the doctrine of implied repeal, between the HRA and an earlier (or, for that matter, a later) provision that is incompatible with a Convention right. This is because the HRA does not make the Convention rights a substantive part of UK law; it merely requires (among other things) the courts to interpret legislation compatibly with them when this is possible. When it is not possible, the inconsistent legislation remains valid, because there is no substantive inconsistency between it and the HRA.[85]

3.4.7 Subordinate legislation

Our focus so far has been on primary legislation. We now need to examine what is meant in the HRA by 'primary legislation' and how the principles set out in the previous sections apply in relation to subordinate legislation.

The term 'primary legislation' is defined in s 21(1) of the HRA. Unsurprisingly, it includes Acts of Parliament. In contrast, legislation enacted under the authority of an Act of Parliament is subordinate legislation. For the time being, we focus on these senses of primary and subordinate legislation; others are considered later. Within the HRA scheme, there is a crucial difference between 'primary' and 'subordinate' legislation. We saw earlier that, in respect of the former, courts must proceed in one of two ways: the legislation is, if possible, interpreted compatibly with Convention rights; otherwise, it can be declared incompatible. In relation to subordinate legislation, the position is rather different. As Figure 18.4. shows, there are three possible outcomes when a court is confronted with questions about the compatibility of subordinate legislation with Convention rights.

However, it is important to note that, given the strength of the s 3 interpretive obligation, most questions concerning subordinate legislation will result in the first of the three outcomes outlined in Figure 18.4. That is, courts will usually be able to conclude that the subordinate legislation in question can—and therefore must—be interpreted compatibly with Convention rights. And most cases that do not yield the first outcome will yield the second. That is so because—again thanks to the strength of the s 3 obligation—courts will relatively rarely conclude that primary legislation truly authorises the making of subordinate legislation that is incompatible with Convention rights. The volume of secondary legislation falling within the third of the categories shown in Figure 18.4 will therefore be slight.

Three further points should be noted regarding the distinction between primary and subordinate legislation.

First, the HRA adopts, in one particularly significant respect, an unusually broad definition of primary legislation. Section 21(1) states that, for the purposes of the

---

[85] This also explains why the HRA is not itself impliedly repealed by subsequent legislation that is incompatible with Convention rights.

Outcome 1	Outcome 2	Outcome 3
The court concludes that it is possible to interpret the subordinate legislation compatibly with Convention rights. *The court therefore must (thanks to s 3) interpret the subordinate legislation compatibly.*	*The court concludes that the 'parent Act' (ie the primary legislation permitting the subordinate legislation to be made) does not authorise ECHR-incompatible subordinate legislation.* *The subordinate legislation is unlawful and invalid to the extent of any incompatibility with Convention rights.*	*The court concludes that the 'parent Act' (ie the primary legislation permitting the subordinate legislation to be made) authorises ECHR-incompatible subordinate legislation.* *The subordinate legislation is lawful and valid as a matter of UK law even though it is incompatible with Convention rights.*

Figure 18.4 Subordinate legislation and the Human Rights Act 1998

HRA, *Orders in Council enacted under the royal prerogative are to be treated as primary, not subordinate, legislation*.[86] The practical effect of this is that such prerogative legislation cannot be quashed if found incompatible with Convention rights. It can, however, like an Act of Parliament, be the subject of a declaration of incompatibility under s 4.

Categorising prerogative Orders in Council as primary legislation for HRA purposes is anomalous.[87] For present purposes, it is unnecessary to get bogged down in the semantics of 'primary' and 'subordinate' legislation.[88] The key point is that the general constitutional position of prerogative Orders in Council is inconsistent with that which they occupy in relation to the HRA. Orders in Council are not the constitutional equals of Acts of Parliament: the former, unlike the latter, can usually be quashed if they are unlawful. The normal principles of judicial review therefore apply: if, for example, a prerogative Order in Council is unreasonable, or made for an improper purpose, or adopted in breach of a legitimate expectation, it can be set aside by the courts. Any doubt that may have existed on this point was put to rest by the House of Lords in *Bancoult (No 2)*.[89]

This position is entirely correct in principle. In constitutional theory, prerogative Orders in Council are acts of the Crown alone (meaning the executive), not of the Crown-in-Parliament. Orders in Council are therefore not cloaked by the doctrine of parliamentary sovereignty. Also, in constitutional practice, the prerogative is merely a tool in the hands of the executive. There is therefore no good reason why its exercise should be immune from judicial review—and every reason why it should be. Against

---

[86] See further Chapter 4, section 4.3.

[87] Pontin and Billings, 'Prerogative Powers and the Human Rights Act: Elevating the Status of Orders in Council' [2001] PL 21.

[88] See generally McHarg, 'What is Delegated Legislation?' [2006] PL 539.

[89] *R (Bancoult) v Secretary of State for Foreign and Commonwealth Affairs (No 2)* [2008] UKHL 61, [2009] 1 AC 453.

this background, it is highly dubious that while the courts can quash prerogative Orders in Council if they fall foul of the normal principles of judicial review, they cannot do so if they contravene the Convention rights.

> **Q** Imagine that a prerogative Order in Council is enacted and that it is incompatible with a Convention right that covers the same ground as a common law constitutional right. It is clear that the Order in Council could not be quashed on the basis of its incompatibility with the Convention right—but could it be quashed on the ground of its incompatibility with the common law constitutional right?

Second, the enactment of subordinate legislation is simply a form of *administrative action*. There are, of course, other forms of such action: the formulation of policy, the making of decisions, and so on. These non-legislative forms of administrative action are, as we saw in Chapter 12, subject to judicial review, including on the ground that they are inconsistent with Convention rights. No question of a declaration of incompatibility arises in relation to such administrative action. Any administrative act inconsistent with Convention rights will be unlawful and can be quashed.

Third, *all legislation enacted by the devolved legislatures constitutes, for HRA purposes, subordinate legislation.*[90] This is important from the standpoint of one of our key themes—that is, the multilayered nature of governance in the UK. In particular, it means that the status of human rights differs significantly in relation to the devolved legislatures, on the one hand, and the UK Parliament, on the other hand. We have seen that the enactments of the latter cannot be quashed or otherwise set aside by the courts on the ground of incompatibility with Convention rights. The same is not, however, true of devolved legislation: such legislation is subject to full constitutional review because the devolved legislatures' powers are circumscribed by (among other things) the Convention rights.[91] In this sense, the ECHR, via the HRA and the devolution legislation, fulfils the role of a full constitutional Bill of Rights vis-à-vis the devolved legislatures: it constitutes an absolute brake on their power. On the face of it, this suggests that the HRA is a much more serious impediment to the exercise of legislative power by devolved legislatures than it is to the exercise of power by the UK Parliament. However, the reality, as we explain in section 3.4.8, is more complicated.

3.4.8 Legal and political constitutionalism

We have already seen that a declaration of incompatibility under s 4 of the HRA does not impose any domestic legal obligation upon Parliament or the executive to amend a statute found by the court to be incompatible with Convention rights. On a purely legal analysis, then, the political branches retain a free hand.[92] This may seem to undercut our suggestion, made at the beginning of the chapter, that the

---

[90] HRA, s 21(1).   [91] See *Salvesen v Riddell* [2013] UKSC 22.

[92] Although the position is complicated by the UK's *international* legal obligations under the ECHR. This is considered later.

HRA has been a principal driver of the shift from political to legal constitutionalism. It also, as noted earlier,[93] makes puzzling the unwillingness of some members of the majority in *Nicklinson* to issue a declaration of incompatibility. However, we will see in this section that declarations of incompatibility are more potent than their name would suggest.

Administrative bodies—a term that we use here to refer to all bodies incapable of enacting primary legislation—are now, to a very large extent, in practice locked into a legal requirement to comply with human rights. This follows both because they are, as we will explain,[94] generally obliged by s 6 of the HRA to act in conformity with the Convention rights, and because they are, by dint of s 3, in any event generally required to do so when exercising statutory powers. It is always open to administrative bodies to seek the enactment of legislation granting them powers to act contrary to Convention rights. Equally, an administrative body that had an action struck down on Convention grounds could seek the enactment of legislation reversing the effect of such a judicial decision. However, such reactions against the enforcement of human rights could only ever (barring repeal of the HRA) be the exception, given that parliamentary time is a highly scarce resource. Generally speaking, therefore, administrative bodies have no choice (if they wish to act lawfully) but to act compatibly with Convention rights.

The position is different in relation to those bodies, most obviously the UK Parliament, capable of enacting primary legislation. However, while Parliament is in orthodoxy *legally* free to do as it pleases, this does not mean that it is necessarily able, in practice, fully to exploit that legal freedom by disregarding Convention rights with impunity. In order to understand why this is so, we need to examine three aspects of the HRA, each of which engages in some way our theme concerning the relationship between legal and political forms of constitutionalism. The three matters in question are the ways in which the Act:

- makes the enactment of ECHR-incompatible legislation less likely in the first place;
- permits legal values to infuse and shape political discourse; and
- emphasises the constraining effect of the UK's obligations in international law.

We will address these three issues in turn. As to the first, we saw earlier[95] that the effect of s 19 (along with the role played by the JCHR) is that ECHR-incompatible legislation is unlikely to be enacted either accidentally or covertly. Parliament's—and, by extension, the media's and the public's—attention will be drawn to provisions in Bills liable to be at odds with Convention rights. The enactment of such provisions is not legally impossible—but it is politically more difficult. A government promoting such provisions will be required by its opponents, inside and beyond Parliament, to make a clear case for enacting legislation that fails to respect the Convention rights. This point is buttressed by s 3 of the HRA. The net effect of that section is that a government intent on securing legislation that will produce effects contrary to Convention rights

---

[93] See section 3.4.5.   [94] See section 3.5.   [95] See section 3.3.2.

must persuade Parliament to make its intention to do so very clear. If it does not, there is a high degree of likelihood that the courts will, in discharge of their s 3 obligation, simply interpret the provision in a way that makes it compatible with Convention rights. The need clearly to spell out a desire to undercut such rights means that the enactment of such legislation cannot be achieved by sleight of hand.

The second point is that while a declaration of incompatibility does not legally oblige Parliament or the government to change the law, such a declaration is highly politically significant— a point that, as we have seen,[96] was at the forefront of some of the Justices' minds in *Nicklinson*. When the Human Rights Bill (as it then was) was being debated in Parliament, Lord Borrie said that the intention was 'surely . . . that government and Parliament will faithfully implement any declaratory judgment made by the [courts]'.[97] This view was endorsed by Lord Irvine, who said that the courts' powers should not be underestimated: a declaration of incompatibility 'will very probably lead to the amendment of defective legislation', and that, in 'this *practical* sense, the Human Rights Act does introduce a *limited* form of constitutional review'.[98] Borrie and Irvine's expectations have been borne out by experience. In a report published in 2015, the Joint Committee on Human Rights noted that steps had been taken to remedy incompatibilities identified by all but one of the 29 declarations that had by then been issued.[99]

The figures tell an important part of the story concerning compliance: declarations of incompatibility exert considerable political pressure on government to change the law. It is equally noteworthy that the government has felt politically constrained to comply with declarations of incompatibility even in contexts in which it might have been tempted—and in which it might even have been politically expedient for it—to do otherwise. Consider, for example, the aftermath of the *Belmarsh* case concerning the extrajudicial detention of foreign terrorist suspects.[100] As we saw in Chapter 1, the House of Lords in *Belmarsh* held that the relevant provisions of the Anti-terrorism, Crime and Security Act 2001 were incompatible with ECHR, Art 5.[101] These provisions, it will be recalled, had been enacted in a climate of considerable fear in the immediate aftermath of the 9/11 attacks in the USA, and had in practice operated to the (admittedly considerable) disadvantage of only a small group of suspects.

A substantial section of public opinion would undoubtedly have supported the government if it were to have decided to ignore the *Belmarsh* judgment and press on with the detention of the people concerned. Yet it did not. The then Home Secretary 'accept[ed] the Law Lords' declaration of incompatibility',[102] and later stated that legislation introduced to replace the scheme condemned in *Belmarsh* was 'designed to

---

[96] See section 3.4.5.   [97] HL Deb, vol 582, cols 1275–6 (3 November 1997).

[98] 'Sovereignty in Comparative Perspective: Constitutionalism in Britain and America' (2001) 76 NYULR 1, 19 (original emphasis).

[99] Joint Committee on Human Rights, *Human Rights Judgments* (HL Paper 130 HC 1088 2014–15), [4.1].

[100] *A v Secretary of State for the Home Department* [2004] UKHL 56, [2005] 2 AC 68.

[101] This incompatibility was relatively obvious. The real issue in *Belmarsh* was whether the government had lawfully suspended the operation of Art 5—which, the House of Lords held, it had not.

[102] Charles Clarke, HC Deb, vol 430, col 306 (26 January 2005).

meet the Law Lords' criticism that the previous legislation was both disproportionate and discriminatory'.[103] The episode suggests that, notwithstanding the absence of a strike-down power, the HRA is, to some extent, capable of curbing the worst excesses of majoritarianism even where the rights of an acutely unpopular and small minority, such as suspected terrorists, are at stake. In this way, it enables legally enshrined human rights standards to shape the course of the political process, even if those standards—thanks to parliamentary sovereignty—do not amount to absolute limits on Parliament's power.

That leads us to the last of the three aspects of the HRA system that help to explain why declarations of incompatibility are more potent than they might at first seem. For the reasons already explored, such declarations do not ultimately restrict Parliament's authority as a matter of domestic law, even though they may substantially influence the terms of political discourse. But when the matter is viewed from the perspective of international, rather than domestic, law the picture changes markedly. The ECHR—a treaty that is binding upon states parties as a matter of international law—requires the UK to 'secure to everyone within their jurisdiction' the Convention rights[104] and to abide by the judgments of the ECtHR.[105] It follows that a declaration of incompatibility by a UK court will usually carry the implication that the UK is in breach of its Art 1 obligation to secure the Convention rights.[106] The government may take the view that the UK courts have got it wrong. Were that to happen, it is highly likely that the matter would be litigated in the ECtHR. In such circumstances, an applicant armed with a declaration of incompatibility would be in a strong position to obtain a favourable judgment from the ECtHR. Such a judgment, unlike a declaration of incompatibility, would be *legally* binding.

3.4.9 Legal and political constitutionalism: some conclusions

Taken in combination, the factors discussed in the previous section indicate that the Convention rights operate as real constraints upon the UK Parliament, notwithstanding that they do not technically constitute legal constraints in terms of domestic law. Three points may be made in conclusion.

First, for as long as the HRA (or something like it) is in force, it would be misguided to assume that Parliament, because it is sovereign, is free in political terms to legislate contrary to human rights. This does not represent any great insight: it has always been mistaken to assume that, just because it has legally unlimited powers, Parliament has the practical or political capacity to do whatever it wants.[107] The HRA, however, throws a particular set of constraints—the Convention rights—into

---

[103] HC Deb, vol 431, col 151 (22 February 2005).   [104] ECHR, Art 1.   [105] ECHR, Art 46.

[106] This is not, however, inevitable. Had a declaration of incompatibility been issued in *Nicklinson*, it would have carried no such implication since the Justices took the view that the matter fell within the UK's 'margin of appreciation'. By this they meant that they would not expect the ECtHR to find the UK in breach of the Convention because of the limits that the Strasbourg Court accepts upon its role given its position as a transnational court and hence its dislocation from the social, cultural, and moral circumstances of individual states.

[107] eg Dicey, *An Introduction to the Study of the Law of the Constitution* (London 1959), pp 70–85, recognised that *legal* sovereignty is, in fact, restricted by *practical* and *political* factors.

sharp relief, and, as noted, creates a political environment that makes it difficult for Parliament to remove or curtail them. The security of human rights may remain ultimately contingent upon the political constitution. But the legal constitution, in the form of the HRA, now exerts an important influence upon its political counterpart.

The HRA also serves as an important reminder that the UK is not a legal island: it is subject to legal obligations, such as those arising under the ECHR, that connect it to the wider world. Viewed through an international lens, a doctrine of parliamentary sovereignty which presupposes legally untrammelled authority to infringe basic rights looks distinctly parochial.

Second, just as it would be wrong to underestimate the significance of the HRA, it would be mistaken to overestimate it. It is not a legally entrenched Bill of Rights. As an Act of Parliament, it can, like any other Act, be repealed. The factors considered in this chapter that encourage compliance with the HRA also suggest that more substantial interference, by way of amendment to or repeal of the HRA itself, would be far from straightforward in political terms. However, just as repeal of the HRA is not legally impossible, so it is not politically impossible. Indeed, the HRA has had a poor reception in some quarters, and there is a substantial strand of political opinion that holds that the courts should be stripped of the powers that they were given by the HRA in order that (as the argument runs) the interests of undeserving minorities should not be allowed to trump those of the wider public. We consider this issue later.[108] For the time being, we simply emphasise that, not being contained within an entrenched constitution, neither the HRA nor the set of rights to which it gives effect are invulnerable to the chill winds of politics; it should not be assumed that either is sacrosanct.

> **Q** Does the HRA secure (or reflect) an appropriate balance between legal and political forms of constitutionalism? Would you prefer that a requirement to respect human rights be hard-wired into the constitution such that it could not be circumvented without going through a hard-to-comply-with procedure for amending the constitution itself?

Third, and paradoxically, the strength of the HRA may ultimately prove to be its greatest weakness. This can be illustrated by reference to controversy surrounding whether prisoners should be granted the right to vote in elections. In *Hirst v United Kingdom (No 2)*[109] in 2005, the Grand Chamber of the ECtHR held that the UK's blanket ban[110] on voting by convicted criminals whilst serving custodial sentences was incompatible with the ECHR guarantee of 'free elections . . . under conditions which will ensure the free expression of the opinion of the people in the choice of the legislature'.[111] A Scottish court reached the same conclusion in 2007 and issued a declaration of incompatibility.[112] These decisions provoked uproar: indeed, the prospect

---

[108] See section 4.   [109] (2006) 42 EHRR 41. See also *Scoppola v Italy (No 3)* (2013) 56 EHRR 19.
[110] Representation of the People Act 1983, s 3(1).   [111] ECHR, Art 3, Protocol 1.
[112] *Smith v Scott* [2007] CSIH 9.

of giving prisoners the right to vote has proven so politically toxic that the matter remains unresolved after more than a decade. This has not escaped the notice of the Council of Europe's Committee of Ministers, which is responsible for monitoring compliance with ECtHR judgments. It has expressed 'profound concern' that the total ban on prisoner voting remains in place and has reminded the UK that it 'has an obligation . . . to abide by judgments of the Court'.[113]

The difficulty highlighted by the prisoner voting saga is well summed up by remarks made by the then Lord Chancellor and Justice Secretary, Chris Grayling. He acknowledged that the UK is 'under an international law obligation to implement the Court judgment' and said that, as Lord Chancellor, he took his 'obligation to uphold the rule of law seriously'. However, Grayling went on to point out that 'it remains the case that Parliament is sovereign' and that 'the Human Rights Act 1998 explicitly recognises that fact'.[114] These remarks flag up the Janus-like nature of our present human rights arrangements, which embrace parliamentary sovereignty whilst placing centre-stage *international* obligations upon which that *domestic* constitutional doctrine has no purchase. The upshot is that when a UK court issues a declaration of incompatibility, Parliament's freedom—as a matter of national law—to ignore it chafes against the UK's duty in international law to abide by the Convention.

In this way, the HRA punctures the distinction between legal and political constitutionalism, by enabling national courts to invoke binding norms of international *law* as an effective constraint upon a legislative branch that in domestic orthodoxy is confined only by the forces of *politics*. This may be said to give the HRA a degree of legal bite that is a welcome antidote to political-constitutionalist tradition. However, as we explain later in this chapter,[115] the HRA's potency is regarded by some as its most objectionable characteristic—and as an argument for getting rid of it altogether.

3.5 The scope of the Human Rights Act

3.5.1 Introduction

Our discussion so far has focused on the impact of the HRA on the interpretation of legislation. That discussion centred upon ss 3 and 4; two of the key provisions in the Act. We now consider a third such provision: s 6. Section 6(1) says: 'It is unlawful for a public authority to act in a way which is incompatible with a Convention right.'[116]

In many senses, s 6 is the centrepiece of the HRA. It is s 6 that places public authorities under a legal obligation to ensure that the millions of administrative acts and decisions adopted each year are ECHR-compliant. As we saw in Chapter 12, the Convention rights now form grounds of judicial review which can be used as a basis for challenging the legality of public authorities' conduct. Our concern here

---

[113] Council of Ministers, Interim Resolution CM/ResDH(2015)251.

[114] HC Deb, vol 553, col 745 (22 November 2012).   [115] In section 4.

[116] Section 6(2) states that this duty does not apply if primary legislation means that the public authority could not have acted differently, or if the public authority was acting to give effect to provisions of, or made under, primary legislation that cannot be read compatibly with the Convention rights.

is to establish what a 'public authority' is, and so to determine the reach of the duty imposed by s 6.

3.5.2 Functions of a public nature

The term 'public authority' is defined by s 6(3) and (5). As the House of Lords held in *Aston Cantlow*, the effect of those provisions is to establish two categories of public authority.[117] There are *core public authorities*—authorities that are bound by the Convention rights in all that they do. And there are what are often called *hybrid public authorities*. Two points should be noted here. First, any body 'certain of whose functions are functions of a public nature' will count as a hybrid public authority.[118] Second, however, such authorities will be bound by the HRA only when committing acts that are not 'private' acts.[119] The difference, then, is that core public authorities always have to respect Convention rights; everyone else has to do so only when performing public functions.

Although there is no definitive test, factors to be taken into account in determining whether something constitutes a core public authority include 'the possession of special powers, democratic accountability, public funding in whole or in part, an obligation to act only in the public interest, and a statutory constitution'.[120] In practice, the courts have had little difficulty in applying these tests, and have done so in a way that makes the category of core public authorities a decidedly narrow one limited to such bodies as government departments, local authorities, the police, and the armed forces.[121] If a given body is held not to constitute a core public authority, the issue then is whether the specific function in question is a public one, meaning that it is nevertheless, on the occasion in question, caught by the HRA. Here, the courts have encountered considerable difficulties, struggling to draw the line between public and private functions in a coherent way.

The leading case on what counts as a function of a public nature is *Aston Cantlow*. It concerned a dispute between a parochial church council[122] and the owners of a farm. The farm in question constituted 'rectorial property', which meant that the owners were liable to pay for all necessary repairs to the chancel of the local church. It was argued that if the church council were to enforce this liability, it would be acting inconsistently with the farm owners' property rights under the ECHR. However, this argument could only succeed if, in the first place, the church council were a public authority for the purposes of s 6 of the HRA. The House of Lords had no difficulty in holding that it was not a core public authority—but was it, when enforcing the liability in question, exercising a function of a public nature?

---

[117] *Aston Cantlow and Wilmcote with Billesley Parochial Church Council v Wallbank* [2003] UKHL 37, [2004] 1 AC 546.

[118] HRA 1998, s 6(3)(b).   [119] HRA 1998, s 6(5).

[120] *Aston Cantlow*, [7], *per* Lord Nicholls.   [121] *Aston Cantlow*, [7], *per* Lord Nicholls.

[122] The role of a parochial church council is (according to Lord Nicholls, *Aston Cantlow*, [14]) 'to provide a formal means . . . whereby . . . members of the local church promote the mission of the Church and discharge financial responsibilities in respect of their own parish church, including responsibilities regarding maintenance of the fabric of the building'.

In addressing this question, said Lord Nicholls,[123] it was necessary to consider such factors as the extent to which in carrying out the relevant function the body is:

- publicly funded;
- exercising statutory powers;
- taking the place of central government or local authorities; or
- providing a public service.

Against that background, it is unsurprising that the specific function in issue—that is, the enforcing of chancel repair liability—was not regarded as a public function. As Lord Hope put it: 'The nature of the act is to be found in the nature of the obligation which the [parochial church council] is seeking to enforce. It is seeking to enforce a civil debt. The function which it is performing has nothing to do with the responsibilities which are owed to the public by the State.'[124]

Particularly difficult questions arise when the performance of a function is contracted out—a practice that, as we explained in Chapter 4, is now commonplace.[125] Craig argues that '[i]t is difficult to see why the nature of a function should alter if it is contracted out, rather than being performed in house [ie by a core public authority]. If it is a public function when undertaken in house, it should equally be so when contracted out'.[126] Yet not all functions performed by core public authorities are necessarily public functions: everything that a core public authority does has to be done compatibly with Convention rights not because all of those things are public functions, but because they are all done by a core public authority. This means that when a core public authority contracts out a function, the contractor performing that function will be bound by the HRA only if the function is a public one.[127] Sometimes, the nature of the function will be obvious. If a local authority (a core public authority) contracts out the cleaning of its offices to a company, the HRA will not apply: cleaning offices—even those of a core public authority—is not itself a public function. Equally obviously, if the Prison Service contracts out the running of a prison to a company, many of the functions performed by the latter will be public in nature, bearing in mind that it will, through its employees, be exercising coercive powers of the state.[128]

Not all cases are as easy. Consider, for example, *YL v Birmingham City Council*.[129] The respondent local authority was required by the National Assistance Act 1948 to arrange the provision of residential care and accommodation for the appellant, an 84-year-old Alzheimer's sufferer. The council sought to discharge that duty by entering into a contract with a company, Southern Cross Healthcare Ltd. The appellant was duly accommodated in a Southern Cross care home, largely at public expense. When the company later sought to terminate the contract, the appellant, whose relatives had allegedly behaved inappropriately during visits, argued that the resulting eviction

---

[123] *Aston Cantlow*, [12].   [124] *Aston Cantlow*, [64].   [125] See Chapter 4, section 4.5.
[126] 'Contracting Out, the Human Rights Act and the Scope of Judicial Review' (2002) 118 LQR 551, 556.
[127] See further Oliver, 'Functions of a Public Nature under the Human Rights Act' [2004] PL 329.
[128] *YL v Birmingham City Council* [2007] UKHL 27, [2008] 1 AC 95, [63], *per* Baroness Hale.
[129] [2007] UKHL 27, [2008] 1 AC 95.

would infringe the right to respect for her home under ECHR, Art 8. If this argument was to be capable of success, it first had to be established that Southern Cross was exercising a public function by accommodating and looking after the appellant. By a three–two majority, the House of Lords held that it was not.

For Lord Mance (with whom Lords Scott and Neuberger concurred), the key question was whether Southern Cross was undertaking a 'governmental' function. Close attention was paid to the text of the 1948 Act, and emphasis placed on the fact that the Council's statutory duty was to *make arrangements for the provision* of care and accommodation, whereas Southern Cross' contractual duty was to *make such provision*. Whatever the status of the former duty, it did not follow that the latter entailed what Lord Mance called 'an inherently governmental function'. In coming to this view, the majority judges were influenced (among other things) by the private and commercial motivation behind Southern Cross' operations, the undesirability (as it was perceived) of care home residents' rights differing according to whether they are private or state-placed clients, and Southern Cross' lack of any coercive or other statutory power. It followed that Southern Cross was not bound by the HRA.

The question that Lord Mance postulated—whether Southern Cross was performing a governmental function—was a sensible one. (While 'public' and 'governmental' are not necessarily synonyms, the latter is an intelligible interpretation of the former in the present context.) However, it is questionable whether the majority went about answering that question in the right way. In effect, they chose to examine matters at a micro-level—hence their concern with what Baroness Hale (dissenting) called the 'artificial and legalistic' distinction between the provision of care and the arrangement of such provision. Hence, too, Lord Neuberger's view that it is 'easier to invoke public funding to support the notion that a service is a function of "a public nature" where the funding effectively subsidises, in whole or in part, the cost of the service as a whole, rather than consisting of paying for the provision of that service to a specific person'.[130]

An alternative way of approaching this matter was suggested by the JCHR (and adopted by the minority in *YL*).[131] It involves examining the bigger picture. In particular, it acknowledges that few things are inherently public or private (or governmental or non-governmental). For example, looking after vulnerable people is a function discharged primarily by families in some cultures, and primarily by the state in others. Against this background, the crucial question is whether, as Baroness Hale put it in her dissent in *YL*, the task in question is one 'for which the public, in the shape of the state, have assumed responsibility, at public expense if need be, and in the public interest'.[132] As Lord Bingham (also dissenting) observed, 'it can hardly be a matter of debate' that the 'British state has accepted a social welfare responsibility' as regards the provision of care and accommodation to those who (in the words of the 1948 Act) 'by reason of age, illness, disability or any other circumstances are in need of care and attention which is not otherwise available to them'.[133]

---

[130] See further on this point *R (Weaver) v London and Quadrant Housing Trust* [2009] EWCA Civ 587, [2010] 1 WLR 363.

[131] JCHR, *The Meaning of 'Public Authority' under the Human Rights Act* (HL 39 HC 382 2003–04).

[132] *YL*, [65].   [133] *YL*, [15].

Following the judgment in *YL*, the JCHR registered its disapproval.[134] Parliament subsequently amended the law so that anyone providing accommodation, together with nursing or personal care, under (among other measures) the 1948 Act is to be taken in doing so to be performing functions of a public nature for the purpose of s 6(1) of the HRA.[135] This reversed the effect of the *YL* ruling in relation to care homes. Nonetheless, the general approach of the majority remains relevant to other contracting-out situations.

Q Do you prefer the view of the majority or the minority in *YL*? If the 'assumption of responsibility' test favoured by the minority were embraced, would this risk casting the HRA's net too wide? Would, for example, a contractor providing services (such as property maintenance) ancillary to the performance of a public function (eg running a prison) be caught by the Act? Should it be?

3.5.3 Other situations

What if, as in *YL*, the relevant party is neither a core public authority nor performing a function of a public nature? Given that, in such circumstances, there is no duty under s 6 of the HRA to act in accordance with the Convention rights, does this mean that it is lawful to ride roughshod over them? Not necessarily. There are two sets of circumstances in which the Convention rights will be relevant even if the s 6 duty does not arise.

First, consider the *Ghaidan* case that was discussed earlier in the chapter[136]—a case between a landlord and a tenant. Neither party was a core public authority; nor was the landlord, in seeking to evict the tenant, performing a function of a public nature. Why, then, was the landlord's freedom to evict the tenant restricted, in effect, by the latter's Convention rights? In cases (such as *Ghaidan*) in which no one is under a s 6 duty, the Convention rights cannot operate as a free-standing cause of action: X cannot issue a claim against Y on the straightforward basis that there has been a breach of Convention rights. However, if the relationship between the parties is governed in some relevant respect by legislation, then there may be scope for the Convention rights to impact upon that relationship. This is precisely what happened in *Ghaidan*. The landlord wanted to evict the tenant, but could only do so if the tenant was not a 'statutory tenant'. However, as we know, the tenant *was* a statutory tenant—because when the relevant provisions of the Rent Act were interpreted in line with the defendant's Convention rights, the definition of 'statutory tenant' was stretched to include the category into which the defendant fell. It follows (with one exception) that whenever the relationship between the parties is governed by statute, the court must apply the statute in such a way as to secure compliance with relevant Convention rights. (The exception, of course, is that the court cannot do this when the legislation cannot be interpreted compatibly with relevant Convention rights.) All of this follows

---

[134] JCHR, *Legislative Scrutiny: Health and Social Care Bill* (HC 46 HL 303 2007–08).
[135] Health and Social Care Act 2008, s 145.   [136] See section 3.4.2.

because the courts' s 3 interpretative obligation operates whether or not a public authority is involved in the proceedings.

Second, however, what if the relevant legal position between the parties is not governed by statute, meaning that s 3 is irrelevant? What if it is regulated by common law? The courts have grappled with these issues in a number of contexts, but perhaps most prominently in relation to the right to privacy. Take, for example, a newspaper that publishes an exposé of someone's private life. In the absence of relevant statute law, can the common law be used as a vehicle for protecting Convention rights? Are the courts required, for instance, to apply the common law in such a way as to enable the person concerned to obtain relief if there has been a breach of the Art 8 right to respect for private life? Here, the position is murkier. Whereas s 3 imposes an explicit and strong obligation on the courts to apply legislation compatibly with the ECHR, the HRA contains no equivalent provision concerning the common law. A wide range of views has been expressed on the question of whether (and if so, to what extent) the Convention rights should be given 'horizontal effect'—that is, effect in disputes between private parties in circumstances to which s 3 has no application. Figure 18.5 summarises the spectrum of opinion. Before considering their relative merits and the position adopted by the courts, it is necessary to say something about the background to this debate.

One of the main factors that has driven disagreement concerns the extent, if any, to which conferring horizontal effect on human rights is consistent with the classical liberal political philosophy from which much of human rights discourse itself originates.[137] The perceived difficulty is that, within the classical liberal tradition, individuals' freedom to do as they please should be jealously guarded. This suggests that while human rights should constrain the state's capacity to limit individuals' liberty, it would be anathema were they also to constrain that liberty. If, however, such rights are imbued with horizontal effect, they will necessarily end up restricting individuals' freedom. For instance, if X has a right to privacy, and if that right is horizontally enforceable against Y, it will be unlawful for Y to breach X's privacy in ways that, but for the horizontal enforceability of the right, may have been lawful. The right thus becomes something that limits Y's freedom.

While much of the discussion about whether Convention rights acquire horizontal effect under the HRA has inevitably focused upon the terms of the ECHR and the

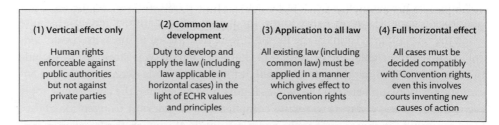

(1) Vertical effect only	(2) Common law development	(3) Application to all law	(4) Full horizontal effect
Human rights enforceable against public authorities but not against private parties	Duty to develop and apply the law (including law applicable in horizontal cases) in the light of ECHR values and principles	All existing law (including common law) must be applied in a manner which gives effect to Convention rights	All cases must be decided compatibly with Convention rights, even this involves courts inventing new causes of action

Figure 18.5 Horizontal effect?

<hr />

[137] See generally Hunt, 'The "Horizontal Effect" of the Human Rights Act' [1998] PL 423.

HRA, it is important to bear in mind that it has taken place against the philosophical background sketched in the previous paragraph. It follows that when writers such as Buxton argue that Convention rights should only be effective vertically, against state bodies, they are buttressing the foregoing (interpretation of) the classical liberal position.[138] In advancing this view, Buxton argues that it chimes with the empirical context in which the ECHR was adopted. It was, he notes, specifically envisaged as a vehicle by which state power could be limited. Indeed, he points out that many of the rights are implicitly[139] or explicitly[140] addressed to the state—and, he says, *only* to the state—and that it is therefore meaningless to suppose that they could be enforced against individuals. Hence, says Buxton, even if the HRA were to make Convention rights enforceable against individuals, 'it would simply beat the air: because the content of those rights does not impose obligations on private citizens'.[141] Buxton thus occupies the position lying at the far left of the spectrum depicted in Figure 18.5: in his view, the Convention rights are enforceable only vertically, against state bodies, and may, at most, have only a 'tangential effect on private law litigation'.[142]

At the other end of the spectrum, Wade argues that the HRA confers full horizontal effect on the Convention rights. His argument is a principally textual one—but one that is implicitly unsympathetic to the view that human rights should only ever protect, and should never restrict, individuals' freedom.[143] Wade observes that s 6(3) of the HRA says that 'courts and tribunals' constitute public authorities, meaning that they are required, by s 6(1), to act compatibly with the Convention rights. This, says Wade, obliges them to decide *all* cases—including purely horizontal ones—in accordance with those rights.[144] However, this argument is highly suspect, not least because, if accepted, it would undermine the very distinction between public and private functions that s 6 clearly sets out to erect.

Most commentators—along, as we shall see, with the courts—agree that a position between those advocated by Wade and Buxton is preferable. For example, Hunt—who adopts position (3) in Figure 18.5—contends that courts should always apply existing laws compatibly with the ECHR.[145] This is close to, but does not go quite as far as, Wade's view. Because, for Hunt, s 6 applies only when courts are dealing with existing laws, it does not require them to invent new laws when that would be necessary in order to give full effect to Convention rights. If, for example, there is simply a gap in national law that leaves individuals without legal recourse in respect of ECHR-incompatible behaviour by other individuals, Hunt (in contrast to Wade) does not argue that courts should fill such a gap by developing a new cause of action. This approach, says Hunt, embraces the classical liberal view set out earlier, but does so in a nuanced way. Relationships, on Hunt's view, are purely private only when the law

---

[138] Buxton, 'The Human Rights Act and Private Law' (2000) 116 LQR 48.

[139] eg Art 6, which concerns the right to independent, fair, and impartial judicial (and sometimes administrative) proceedings, can only meaningfully be understood as applying to public bodies.

[140] eg in specifying when it may be lawful not to do that which Art 8(1) normally requires (ie respecting private and family life, correspondence, and the home), Art 8(2) begins: 'There shall be no interference by a public authority with the exercise of this right except'.

[141] Buxton, 56.   [142] Buxton, 65.

[143] Wade, 'Horizons of Horizontality' (2000) 116 LQR 217.   [144] Wade, 217–18.   [145] Hunt.

has not intervened to regulate them; human rights should not interfere with people's freedom to conduct such relationships as they see fit. However, Hunt contends, once the law has intervened to provide some form of regulation, the relationships have lost their truly private nature and the state, as the maker, the administrator, the interpreter, and the applier of the law which governs those relationships, is bound to act in all those roles in a way which upholds and protects the rights made fundamental by the Constitution.[146]

This analysis arguably provides an elegant reconciliation of the classical liberal position with the recognition of (a degree of) horizontal effect. However, Phillipson—in adopting position (2)—argues that it is insufficiently sensitive to the terms of the HRA and so ascribes a greater degree of horizontal effect to human rights than is appropriate under the Act.[147] Phillipson certainly does not go as far as Buxton: he rejects the view that the Convention rights simply have no meaning as against private parties. While some Convention rights, such as the right to a fair trial,[148] have no obvious application as against individuals, the substance of most of the rights is perfectly capable of such application. It is, for example, just as possible for a newspaper as for a public authority to deny someone respect for their private life.[149]

However, Phillipson correctly points out that while this means that the Convention rights are *potentially capable* of full horizontal effect, they do not *in fact* have such effect. This is because the HRA does not actually incorporate the Convention rights: it merely gives them certain effects in domestic law.[150] One of those effects is that they are rendered enforceable against public authorities by virtue of the fact that s 6 obliges such authorities to act in accordance with the Convention rights. But, points out Phillipson, because individuals are placed under no equivalent obligation, 'it is clear that [Convention rights] can become in the private sphere at most legal values and principles, rather than the clear entitlements they are when exercised against public authorities'.[151] Building on this approach, Phillipson and Williams argue that courts should develop the common law compatibly with Convention rights but only in an 'incremental' way. To go beyond this would be to contravene, to an extent not sanctioned by the HRA, the underlying constitutional principles that demarcate the proper role of the courts. Those principles, it is said, require the distinction between 'judicial' and 'legislative' lawmaking to be respected.[152]

What position have the courts adopted? This matter was considered in *Campbell v Mirror Group Newspapers Ltd*.[153] The case is considered in detail in Chapter 19. For the time being, it suffices to say that it involved a claim brought against a newspaper

---

[146] Hunt, 434–5, relying on the views of Kriegler J in the South African case of *Du Plessis v De Klerk* 1996 (3) SA 850.

[147] Phillipson, 'The Human Rights Act, "Horizontal Effect" and the Common Law: A Bang or a Whimper?' (1999) 62 MLR 824.

[148] See section 3.4.3.

[149] See further Beatson et al, *Human Rights: Judicial Protection in the United Kingdom* (London 2008), p 372.

[150] See section 3.3.2.   [151] Phillipson, 837.

[152] Phillipson and Williams, 'Horizontal Effect and the Constitutional Constraint' (2011) 74 MLR 878.

[153] [2004] UKHL 22, [2004] 2 AC 457.

in relation to the publication of allegedly private information; it therefore raised a question about the extent to which ECHR, Art 8 is enforceable against private parties.

In addressing this question, Baroness Hale stated two principles. First, she said: 'The 1998 Act does not create any new cause of action between private persons.'[154] This means that the courts are not required to invent wholly new law in order to enable a private party to be sued for (what amounts in substance to) a breach of a Convention right. Second, however, she said that 'if there is a relevant cause of action applicable, the court as a public authority must act compatibly with both parties' Convention rights'.[155] A slightly more cautious note was struck by Lord Hoffmann. He said that while s 6 does not make Convention rights straightforwardly enforceable against private parties, the effect of the HRA is to emphasise the importance of certain norms. For example, in the context with which *Campbell* was concerned, Art 8 indicates that 'private information [is] something worth protecting as an aspect of human autonomy and dignity'.[156] Because, in this area, he could see 'no logical ground for saying that a person should have less protection against a private individual than he would have against the state',[157] Lord Hoffmann concluded that the values underlying Art 8 should 'have implications for the future development of the law'.[158]

On the face of it, Baroness Hale preferred Hunt's approach (all cases to be decided in accordance with Convention rights), whereas Lord Hoffmann preferred Phillipson's view (values underlying Convention rights to be allowed to influence the incremental development of the common law). This is perhaps too simplistic a reading of the case: a more nuanced reading suggests that the views of Baroness Hale and Lord Hoffmann represent complementary, rather than competing, approaches. The argument, advanced by Beatson et al, goes as follows.[159] Section 6 imposes an obligation[160] on courts to act compatibly with the Convention rights. This is not the same as (even though it may sometimes amount to) an obligation always to decide cases so as to ensure that parties' Convention rights are respected. Rather, s 6 requires 'that a court must neither grant nor refuse relief' in a horizontal case where doing so would involve the *court's* acting incompatibly with a Convention right.[161] This means that the central question for the court is whether, 'if the result of a particular case would infringe a Convention right, this is properly attributable to the court' or to Parliament: 'The courts cannot be required to step outside their designated constitutional role in order to prevent or cure a breach of a Convention right.'[162] This view has much in common with the argument, noted earlier, of Phillipson and Williams.[163]

On this approach, the courts are always (consistently with Lord Hoffmann's remarks in *Campbell*) at liberty to develop the common law, in the normal, incremental way, in a manner that is influenced by the values underpinning the Convention rights. But

---

[154] *Campbell*, [132].   [155] *Campbell*, [132].   [156] *Campbell*, [50].

[157] *Campbell*, [50].

[158] *Campbell*, [52]. See further Lord Hoffmann's judgment in *Wainwright v Home Office* [2003] UKHL 53, [2004] 2 AC 406.

[159] Beatson et al, *Human Rights: Judicial Protection in the United Kingdom* (London 2008), pp 371–90.

[160] Subject to the exceptions mentioned in section 3.5.1.

[161] Beatson et al, p 375.   [162] Beatson et al, p 380.

[163] 'Horizontal Effect and the Constitutional Constraint'.

whether *their* obligation to act compatibly with Convention rights translates into a requirement to decide the case in a way that safeguards *the parties'* Convention rights depends on whether doing so would cross the line delimiting the courts' 'designated constitutional role'. That line will usually be crossed, as Baroness Hale indicated in *Campbell*, by the invention of a new cause of action.

This is one way of understanding the relationship between two leading cases in this area. In *Campbell*, as we explain in Chapter 19, the House of Lords was willing to extend existing common law principles concerning the confidentiality of private information so as to afford the claimant a remedy in relation to certain aspects of her claim. In contrast, *Wainwright* concerned the subjection of the claimants to a strip search by officials.[164] This was not something to which existing causes of action (such as trespass to the person) could be extended: if protection were to be afforded, a wholly new cause of action for breach of privacy would be needed. The House of Lords declined to take such a step: in Lord Hoffmann's view, this 'is an area which requires a detailed approach which can be achieved only by legislation rather than the broad brush of common law principle'.[165]

If we accept this analysis, such that courts are not required to create new causes of action, it does not follow that they must do everything that falls short of taking that step. In some circumstances, manipulating an existing cause of action so as to safeguard Convention rights would constitute such a serious step, and involve such a significant policy choice, as to transgress the line that distinguishes the courts' role (of *developing* the common law) and Parliament's *legislative* role.

3.5.4 Who can enforce human rights claims?

The foregoing discussion was concerned with the range of parties upon which the HRA imposes obligations to act compatibly with Convention rights. The practical reach of the Act is also influenced by the obverse question: who can bring a claim for a breach of Convention rights? Article 34 of the ECHR says that only a 'victim' may bring a claim before the ECtHR. Similarly, s 7(1) of the HRA provides that only a 'victim' can bring a domestic claim alleging that a public authority has acted in a way that breaches its s 6(1) obligation to act compatibly with Convention rights—and, in applying this test, domestic courts are required by the HRA to adopt the same meaning of 'victim' as that which the ECtHR applies.[166]

Who, then, is a 'victim'? Clearly, someone who is actually affected by the conduct in question falls into this category. However, the ECtHR has not restricted victim status to such individuals. For example, the victim test is satisfied by someone who is an 'indirect victim'.[167] On this basis, the applicant in *Kurt v Turkey*,[168] was permitted to argue that *her son's* right to liberty under Art 5 had been violated when he was

---

[164] *Wainwright v Home Office* [2003] UKHL 53, [2004] 2 AC 406.   [165] *Wainwright*, [33].

[166] HRA 1998, s 7(7).

[167] See generally Feldman, 'Indirect Victims, Direct Injury: Recognising Relatives as Victims under the European Human Rights System' [2009] EHRLR 50.

[168] (1999) 27 EHRR 373. (The son had subsequently 'disappeared' and was therefore unable to bring the claim himself.)

allegedly abducted and beaten by soldiers. The victim test is also satisfied if the person concerned can show that he or she is a 'potential victim'. If, for example, legislation exists that, if it were to be enforced against the individual concerned, would result in a breach of her Convention rights, this may be sufficient to establish victim status, notwithstanding that the legislation has not actually been enforced against her.[169]

It follows that the victim test is rather broader than may at first appear. However, it remains much more restrictive than the 'sufficient interest' test that applies to ordinary judicial review proceedings.[170] On the face of it, this means that domestic law now embodies two distinct standing tests. The liberal 'sufficient interest' test applies when a claimant wishes to allege that a public authority has acted contrary to the established principles of administrative law (eg that it acted contrary to natural justice or *Wednesbury* unreasonably). Meanwhile, claimants seeking to establish a breach of Convention rights must bring themselves within the much narrower confines of the 'victim' criterion. This may seem incoherent, and it might appear that it would be preferable to have a single standing test applicable to 'traditional' judicial review *and* human rights cases. However, an alternative view is that distinct standing tests are warranted by the distinct purposes of human rights law and the law of judicial review. On this analysis, the former is concerned with the rights of individuals— and if the person whose right is affected does not wish to pursue the matter, that is no one else's business. In contrast, the law of judicial review is concerned not (primarily at least) with individuals' rights but with upholding the public interest in good governance—something in which all members of society have a legitimate interest.[171]

In any event, for two reasons, a claimant seeking to bring a judicial review claim may be able to do so even if she is not a 'victim'. First, some human rights arguments can be made *without any reliance upon the HRA at all*. In such circumstances, the normal standing test, not the victim test, applies. For example, proceedings for breach of a common law constitutional right[172] can be brought without reference to the HRA, and so without having to establish victim status. Second, even if the right in question does not constitute a common law constitutional right, such that it is necessary to rely on the HRA, *it may not be necessary to rely on s 6*. Section 7 says that the claimant has to be a victim if she wishes to argue that a public authority has acted unlawfully under s 6 by failing to fulfil its obligation to act in accordance with the Convention rights.

However, in cases involving the exercise by a public body of statutory power, it will be possible to argue that it has breached Convention rights, and has therefore acted unlawfully, without relying on s 6. This follows because, wholly independently of s 6, s 3 (as we have seen) requires legislation to be read compatibly with Convention rights. This means that (unless the legislation cannot be read in that way) public bodies' statutory powers will be read as excluding any legal authority to breach Convention rights. As a consequence, non-victims can argue that a public body has acted in a way

---

[169] *Norris v Ireland* (1991) 13 EHRR 186. [170] See Chapter 13, section 3.3.
[171] On this issue see further Varuhas, 'The Public Interest Conception of Public Law: Its Procedural Origins and Substantive Implications', in Bell et al (eds), *Public Law Adjudication in Common Law Systems: Process and Substance* (Oxford 2016).
[172] See section 3.2.

made unlawful by s 3: the HRA does not say that, in order to make such an argument, the claimant must be a victim.[173]

4. The future

4.1 Dissatisfaction with the HRA

The HRA attracts strong views. Some people see it as an essential safeguard of basic rights. Others think it does not go far enough, whether in terms of the protection it offers or the range of rights to which it applies. And still others—most volubly, certain sections of the popular press—have subjected the HRA to excoriating criticism, arguing that it gives judges too much power, produces perverse outcomes, and privileges the undeserving at the expense of the decent and the law-abiding. To the extent that there is dissatisfaction with the HRA, this can generally be attributed to a combination of two factors.

4.1.1 Misconceptions

Ever since its inception, the HRA has been the victim of multiple misconceptions, thanks often to a hostile media.[174] For example, it is sometimes the case that media coverage confuses (or leads the public to confuse) an *assertion* of an entitlement arising under the HRA with the *existence* of such an entitlement. This, in turn, leads people wrongly to think that it is possible to derive wholly inappropriate rights from the Act. A classic example involved a convicted murderer who made a legal claim asserting that the prison authorities' refusal to supply him with access to certain forms of pornography constituted unlawful discrimination on the ground of sexual orientation (contrary to Art 14) and inhuman and degrading treatment (contrary to Art 3).[175] Although this claim was dismissed by the courts at the initial stage, the mere fact that it had been made created a public perception that the HRA gave prisoners a right to hardcore pornography.

In other situations, misguided assumptions by public authorities that the HRA requires them to do certain things lead to a wider perception that this is really so. For example, fried chicken was supplied by the police to a man who was evading arrest by sitting on the roof of a house. This was explained by a police spokesperson who said: 'He has been demanding various things and one was a KFC bargain bucket. Although he's a nuisance, we still have to look after his well-being and human rights.'[176] *The Sun* newspaper thus reported that a 'yob who spent all day on a roof

---

[173] The House of Lords recognised the force of this reasoning in *R (Rusbridger) v Attorney General* [2003] UKHL 38, [2004] 1 AC 357, [21].

[174] See generally Mead, '"You Couldn't Make It Up": Some Narratives of the Media's Coverage of Human Rights', in Ziegler, Wicks, and Hodson, *The UK and European Human Rights: A Strained Relationship?* (Oxford 2015).

[175] Department for Constitutional Affairs, *Review of the Implementation of the Human Rights Act* (London 2006), p 30.

[176] 'KFC meal "ensures siege man's rights"', *The Daily Telegraph*, 7 June 2006.

lobbing bricks at cops was "rewarded" with a KFC takeaway . . . because of his human rights'.[177] As a government review correctly observed, the suspect had no human right requiring that he be supplied either with food in general or fried chicken in particular—but such episodes feed public perceptions that the HRA requires public bodies to do things that fly in the face of common sense, bringing it into disrepute.[178]

The fact that people think the HRA says and requires things that it actually does not is not a criticism of the Act itself. But why has such reporting found so receptive an audience? It is beyond the scope of this book to explore in any detail why this might be so, but one suggestion may be ventured. In many countries, before a constitutional Bill of Rights is adopted, there is a good deal of public discussion about whether such a Bill is required and, if so, what rights it should protect. The HRA—which is, at least for the time being, the closest thing the UK has to a constitutional Bill of Rights—was not preceded by such a process. Although there was a great deal of discussion within legal circles, this did not impinge to any significant extent upon public discourse.

The impression, among certain sections of the media and the public, that the HRA has been foisted upon them has been given further succour by the fact that it has been characterised as a European import, in that it gives effect to certain of the rights contained in the ECHR.[179] This, in turn, is one of the factors that has given legs to the argument that the HRA should be modified or replaced with something specifically British.

4.1.2 The public interest

A further objection often raised against the HRA is that it strikes an inappropriate balance between the interests of rights-holders and wider society. A particular strand within this discourse has focused on the perception that the HRA pays insufficient regard to the interests of the so-called law-abiding majority by ascribing undue weight to others' rights. This view is informed in part by the sort of myths considered in the previous section. But it also rests, to some extent, on disapproval of decisions actually made by the courts under the HRA.

We have already noted that judicial decisions holding the UK's blanket ban on voting by prisoners to infringe human rights have elicited strong condemnation. This is not an isolated example, and the issue cannot be reduced to straightforward disagreement between competing political parties. One of the ironies of the HRA is that, almost as soon as it was enacted, the Labour government took against it. Tony Blair himself branded a High Court decision in 2006, holding that Afghan nationals who had hijacked a plane could not be deported because it would breach their right against torture under Art 3 of the ECHR, 'an abuse of common-sense'.[180]

---

[177] 'Finger-nickin good farce', *The Sun*, 7 June 2006.

[178] Department for Constitutional Affairs, p 31.

[179] This characterisation is, however, inaccurate. The UK was instrumental in the drafting of the ECHR, and it is therefore unsurprising that many of the rights that it safeguards are echoed in the common law.

[180] 'Reid pledge on Afghan hijackers', *The Independent*, 11 May 2006. The case was *R (S) v Secretary of State for the Home Department* [2006] EWHC Admin 1111, which was approved by the Court of Appeal: [2006] EWCA Civ 1157, [2006] INLR 575.

More recently, Conservative members of the 2010–15 coalition government were outspoken in their criticism of the existing human rights system. For instance, in 2010 the Supreme Court ruled[181] that indefinite inclusion in the sex offenders register, with no prospect of reprieve in the event of rehabilitation, was incompatible with the right to respect for private life. That prompted the then Prime Minister David Cameron to say that the decision was an 'offensive' one that flew 'completely in the face of common sense'.[182]

4.2 A UK Bill of Rights?

Criticism of the present arrangements for protecting human rights are often accompanied by calls for the HRA to be replaced by a 'British Bill of Rights'. Indeed, the Conservative Party's manifesto for the 2010 general election contained an undertaking to 'replace the Human Rights Act with a UK Bill of Rights'.[183] However, that promise went unfulfilled because the Conservatives' coalition partner, the Liberal Democrat party, was committed to retaining the HRA.[184] In the light of this fundamental disagreement, the coalition government established the Commission on a Bill of Rights, which was charged with the task of determining whether such legislation should be adopted.

The Commission's report,[185] published in 2012, revealed that its members were deeply divided.[186] The majority recommended that the HRA be replaced with a Bill of Rights, but were vague about the form such legislation would take. The general idea, however, appeared to be that the Bill of Rights would largely amount to a repackaging of the HRA: the Convention rights would, then, continue to be incorporated, although it was thought that there might be a case for expressing some of the rights in 'language reflecting our own heritage and tradition'.[187] This, it was suggested, would address what was perceived to be a fundamental problem with the HRA—that is, the lack of a clear sense of 'ownership' on the part of people in the UK. However, even the majority that agreed to this proposal appeared to be divided, with conflicting agendas underpinning a thin consensus. Indeed, two members of the majority openly advocated the possibility of withdrawal from the ECHR[188]—an option that was clearly endorsed by Theresa May shortly before she became Prime Minister.[189] Two other members of the Commission entered formal dissents, on the ground that the majority

---

[181] *R (F) v Secretary of State for the Home Department* [2010] UKSC 17, [2011] 1 AC 331.

[182] HC Deb, vol 523, col 955 (16 February 2011). Nevertheless, the government has moved to implement the Supreme Court's judgment by laying before Parliament the Draft Sexual Offences Act 2003 (Remedial) Order 2012.

[183] Conservative Party, *An Invitation to Join the Government of Britain* (London 2010), p 79.

[184] Liberal Democrats, *Manifesto 2010* (London 2010), p 94.

[185] Commission on a Bill of Rights, *A UK Bill of Rights? The Choice Before Us* (London 2012).

[186] For detailed discussion, see Elliott, 'A Damp Squib in the Long Grass: The Report of the Commission on a Bill of Rights' [2013] EHRLR 137.

[187] Commission on a Bill of Rights, [8.8].

[188] Faulks and Fisher, 'Unfinished Business', in *A UK Bill of Rights? The Choice Before Us*, p 189.

[189] The speech is available on the ConservativeHome website: **http://www.conservativehome.com/parliament/2016/04/theresa-mays-speech-on-brexit-full-text.html**

argument in favour of a domestic Bill of Rights might be used by some in order to support a more far-reaching argument in favour of 'decoupling' the UK human rights system from the ECHR.[190]

In fact, one of the greatest problems with the report of the Commission on a Bill of Rights was that (as a result of its terms of reference) it did not squarely consider whether the UK should remain a party to the ECHR. Yet that question is fundamental, and is necessarily prior to questions about whether the HRA should be replaced—and, if so, with what. This is so because repealing the HRA and replacing it with a Bill of Rights, or with nothing at all, would not in itself relieve public authorities in the UK of their obligations to act compatibly with the Convention rights. Those obligations would exist for as long as the UK remained a party to the ECHR—and they would continue to be enforceable judicially, albeit by the ECtHR rather than by domestic courts.

4.3 Possible ways forward

Against this background, three possible ways forward might be considered:

- withdrawing from the ECHR;
- remaining a party to the ECHR but repealing the HRA;
- remaining a party to the ECHR, repealing the HRA and enacting a UK Bill of Rights.

We assess these options in turn in this section.

4.3.1 ECHR withdrawal

The most radical option would be for the UK to withdraw from the ECHR. Although we said in the first edition of this book that such a step was 'unthinkable', it is clear that this idea has moved from the margins of political discourse towards the mainstream. Indeed, as already noted, the current Prime Minister, Theresa May, advocated withdrawal shortly before she entered Downing Street. In spite of that, it remains unlikely that the UK would take such a drastic step, at least in the short term. It would involve significant devolution-related complications, bearing in mind that the ECHR functions as a constitutional bill of rights for the devolved nations, and would have considerable reputational implications. It would, for instance, be difficult for the UK to lecture other nations on fundamental rights if it was itself unwilling to remain committed to pan-European human rights standards.

If, in spite of these considerations, the UK were to withdraw from the ECHR, that would inevitably be accompanied by repeal of the HRA, since the Act would make no sense if the UK were no longer a party to the ECHR. Domestic lawmakers would then have an essentially blank canvas, and would be free to replace the HRA with a domestic Bill of Rights or with nothing at all. A Bill of Rights might omit or dilute some of the rights contained in the ECHR that have given rise to particularly

---

[190] Kennedy and Sands, 'In Defence of Rights', in *A UK Bill of Rights? The Choice Before Us*.

controversial judgments. Or a Bill of Rights—unconstrained, in this scenario, by the ECHR—might make it clear that certain rights were not to be interpreted as expansively as corresponding Convention rights have been. Lawmakers would thus be free to strike a different balance between rights of individuals and potentially conflicting public interests.

It would, however, be misguided to overestimate what would be achieved by a withdraw-and-repeal policy. Common law constitutional rights would continue to be protected by national courts. And it is likely that the ECHR and the HRA would be found to have imprinted upon domestic law a legacy that would survive a withdraw-and-repeal policy. Indeed, as noted earlier,[191] the Supreme Court has in recent years increasingly emphasised the common law as a source of fundamental rights. The Court has also noted the capacity of the common law in this, as in other areas, to evolve, including under the influence of the HRA. The substance of at least some of the Convention rights would therefore remain available in the guise of common law rights. It is also highly unlikely that proportionality—one of the main techniques whereby Convention rights are protected—would vanish from domestic law if the HRA were to be repealed. As noted in Chapter 12,[192] the trajectory of the law in this area is such that proportionality is increasingly conceived of as a domestic law concept, rather than something exotically European that exists only under the HRA. Moreover, certain areas of the common law have been developed, thanks to the HRA, so as to be more closely aligned with Convention rights. For example, as we explain in Chapter 19, the extent to which the law of tort protects privacy has been considerably expanded. That new body of common law would not simply evaporate upon the implementation of a withdraw-and-repeal policy.

4.3.2 HRA repeal

A second, less drastic option, would be for the UK to remain a party to the ECHR whilst repealing the HRA and replacing it with nothing. In a sense, this would restore the pre-HRA position, whereby individuals could vindicate their Convention rights—but only if they were willing and able to pursue a claim against the UK in the Strasbourg Court.

An obvious objection to such a policy is that although the UK would avoid the politically and diplomatically embarrassing spectacle of formally renouncing its obligations under the ECHR, it would become very much harder for people to enforce their Convention rights in practice. Of course, the limitations of the withdraw-and-repeal approach identified in the previous section would apply to a repeal-only strategy. The courts would remain free to enforce common law rights, and it is likely that legal developments wrought by the HRA would leave an imprint post-repeal. It is also possible (perhaps likely) that repealing the HRA without withdrawing from the Convention would result in continued reliance by courts, albeit to a more limited extent, upon the Convention. We noted earlier in this chapter that courts were willing

---

[191] See section 3.2.   [192] Chapter 12, section 5.2.

to invoke the ECHR in certain circumstances prior to the HRA, and it is probable that they would be at least as willing to do so post-repeal.

4.3.3 A UK Bill of Rights

A third option would be to remain a party to the ECHR, repeal the HRA and enact a domestic Bill of Rights. Indeed, it is the present government's policy to replace the HRA with a Bill of Rights while remaining a party to the Convention. However, given that the UK would remain bound in international law by the Convention rights, what would be achieved by replacing the HRA with a Bill of Rights? One possibility is that the switch from the HRA to a Bill of Rights would amount to little more than a repackaging exercise: an attempt to ditch the supposedly tarnished HRA brand and start again. But this strategy is not without difficulty. For one thing, the Bill of Rights Commission's own research did not support that negative perception of the HRA.[193] For another, a mere rebranding exercise presupposes a high degree of public gullibility. Would people really be taken in by such cosmetic changes?

Another possibility would be to replace the HRA with a deliberately weaker Bill of Rights. The courts might, for example, be given powers of interpretation less potent than those contained in s 3 of the HRA; they might be denied the authority, presently granted by s 4, to issue declarations of incompatibility; they might be authorised to uphold only a subset of the Convention rights; or they might be instructed to interpret some of those rights in particular ways, even if that would put them at odds with the ECtHR. The difficulty with all of these approaches is that they would—inevitably— bite only at a domestic level. To the extent that a Bill of Rights prevented UK courts from giving full effect to the ECHR, the possibility of litigation in Strasbourg would remain.

> **Q** Should the HRA be repealed? If so, what, if anything, should replace it?

4.3.4 Is reform necessary?

All of this brings us back to the fundamental question: what exactly is it that critics of the present system object to? The objection may be (and, for some, undoubtedly is) to the role played by the ECtHR. Some politicians, for instance, have argued that the Court has overreached itself by construing Convention rights in an unduly broad manner and circumscribing individual states' autonomy to too great a degree.[194] If this is the objection, then reform at the domestic level would necessarily miss the intended target: only a recalibration of the relationship between states and the ECtHR would suffice. In fact, the UK government attempted precisely this at an intergovern- mental conference which it hosted in 2012. The attempt, however, largely failed.[195]

---

[193] *A UK Bill of Rights? The Choice Before Us*, annex G.

[194] Chris Grayling, 'European court ruling: authors of Human Rights treaty would be "turning in their graves" ', *The Telegraph*, 9 July 2013.

[195] Elliott, 'After Brighton: Between a Rock and a Hard Place' [2012] PL 619.

It is difficult, however, to avoid the impression that, for at least some critics of the existing arrangements for protecting human rights, a deeper objection lurks beneath disapproval of the ECtHR's stewardship of the Convention—not least because criticism has been directed not only at that court, but also at UK courts applying the HRA. Indeed, it was the decision,[196] mentioned earlier, of the UK Supreme Court concerning the sex offenders' register that prompted David Cameron to say that a domestic Bill of Rights should be considered 'because . . . it's about time we started making sure decisions are made in . . . Parliament rather than in the courts'.[197] This suggests that one of the fundamental tensions underlying the debate about the HRA and the ECHR concerns the proper role of courts—whether domestic or European—and their relationship with political branches of government.

This, in turn, raises the question—with which we have engaged throughout this book—about the proper balance between legal and political modes of constitutionalism. The HRA places that question front and centre because, as noted earlier in this chapter, it enables norms that are binding in international law to impinge upon the domestic legal scene in an unusually, although not uniquely,[198] direct and explicit fashion.

There is no magic in the precise arrangements presently in place for upholding human rights. Reasonable people can, and do, hold contrasting views about the merits of those arrangements, and whether, and if so how, they should be changed. Kneejerk characterisations of anyone who deigns to criticise the existing system as illiberal reactionaries should therefore be avoided. What is crucial, however, is that as the debate unfolds, critics are forced to identify precisely what it is that they take exception to, and why they do so. By the same token, those who defend the current system must justify their belief that it is a desirable one. What this ultimately reduces to is a need to acknowledge that the debate about whether the HRA should be repealed and whether the UK should withdraw from the ECHR is really a facet of a much deeper debate: one that raises fundamental questions about the sort of constitution we have, and the sort of constitution we want.

5. Conclusions

The HRA has substantially enhanced the protection afforded to human rights in UK law. In doing so, it has contributed in a fundamental way to the shift from a more political to a more legal form of constitutionalism, and has become an important limitation upon the extensive powers of the executive branch. However, as the discussion in the previous section underlines, the HRA is not a constitutional Bill of Rights: it does not form part of an entrenched constitution that enjoys a special legal status. As a result, the HRA can be amended or repealed just like any other piece of legislation. Just as the HRA was not

---

[196] *R (F) v Secretary of State for the Home Department* [2010] UKSC 17, [2011] 1 AC 331.

[197] HC Deb, vol 523, col 955 (16 February 2011).

[198] Consider the parallels with the impact upon the UK legal system of directly effective EU law; on which see Chapter 8.

the result of the sort of careful, inclusive discussion that often precedes the adoption of a constitutional Bill of Rights, so it can be done away with equally straightforwardly. It would, therefore, be mistaken to overemphasise the extent to which the HRA marks a transition to a newly legal form of constitutionalism in the UK. For as long as the UK lacks an entrenched constitution, the ultimate guarantee of human rights remains the political, not the legal, process. For those who think that it is undemocratic for judges to have the last word on the often politically or socially controversial issues raised by human rights adjudication, this is a good thing. For others, who doubt the capacity of the majority to stay its hand when perceptions of the public interest or naked electoral ambition invite the subjugation of vulnerable and unpopular minorities, it is a cause for grave concern.

Expert commentary
The Human Rights Act and the interaction of legal orders
David Feldman, Rouse Ball Professor of English Law, University of Cambridge

The key provision in the HRA is s 6(1): 'It is unlawful for a public authority to act in a way which is incompatible with a Convention right.' This brings Convention rights home. The rest of the Act merely outlines what s 6(1) means in practice. The way in which it does so highlights relationships between the multiple levels of law within which the UK's legal systems and constitution operate. At their heart is the meaning of 'Convention right'.

Sections 1 and 21(1) of the HRA read together define 'the Convention rights' as the rights set out in certain articles of the ECHR and Protocols 1 and 13 to it, as they have effect 'for the time being in relation to the UK'. The Convention rights are, for purposes of domestic law in the UK, thus creatures of international law; the HRA merely provides the machinery by which domestic courts and public authorities give effect to them. This is unusual. As a largely dualist state, the UK's legal systems do not normally look to international treaties to establish domestic law. The means by which the HRA makes Convention rights operative in the UK brings to the foreground a feature of the constitution which is often obscured: the UK, like any state, is locked into a set of relationships with a variety of legal orders external, as well as internal, to its constitutional order. If a treaty imposes obligations on the UK which necessitate a change to domestic law, legislation is usually made to effect the change without importing the international legal rules directly to domestic legal systems. Domestic legislation translates international obligations into the concrete language of domestic law. The Contempt of Court Act 1981,[199] correcting an incompatibility between English law and ECHR, Art 10, is typical in that regard. In the case of the ECHR, however, the HRA directly imports the concepts, rules and language of international law to the domestic arena without offering a translation.

One result of this is that the HRA poses, but does not resolve, certain questions about the relationship between different legal orders. For example, the HRA's approach means that it is silent as to the effect on law in the UK of the relationship between the ECHR and other human rights treaties to which the UK is a party, such as the European Social Charter, the International Covenant on Civil and Political Rights, and the Convention on the Rights of the Child, which impose obligations on her in international but not domestic law. It has always been possible

---

[199] On which see Chapter 19, section 3.3.

to use these other treaties as aids to domestic judicial decision-making. Courts in the UK seek to avoid clashes between domestic law and the UK's international legal obligations, often justifying their role by making a presumption that legislation is not intended to produce results which violate those obligations and should be interpreted accordingly. The HRA indirectly reinforces this, because the ECtHR, as an international tribunal, tries to maintain a degree of coherence within international law by interpreting Convention rights in the light of states' other international legal obligations, such as those under the Convention on the Rights of the Child. As s 2(1) of the HRA requires UK courts and tribunals to take into account Strasbourg case law when determining a question in connection with a Convention right, UK judges happily follow suit.[200]

Another question concerns the geographical reach of Convention rights in domestic law. Courts do not usually apply domestic law to events elsewhere in the world unless there is clear legal authority for doing so. The HRA is silent as to the power of UK courts to apply Convention rights to public authorities' activities outside the UK. Yet courts have regarded themselves as required to apply them to UK armed forces operating in Iraq and Afghanistan. Why? Strasbourg case law holds that states' obligations under the ECHR extend to action taken extra-territorially if their agents exercise effective control over an area of, or persons in, another state. This is based on an interpretation of ECHR, Art 1, whereby states undertake to secure Convention rights to 'everyone within their jurisdiction'.[201] That is not one of the provisions imported to domestic law by s 1 of the HRA. Nevertheless, UK judges apply the Strasbourg case law, either because of the obligation under HRA, s 2(1) to take Strasbourg jurisprudence into account, or because the judgments (some of which are against the UK and so bind her[202]) define how the Convention operates for the time being in relation to the UK.[203] UK judges understand that the purpose of the HRA is to allow people to protect some rights under the ECHR in domestic courts, and have taken the common sense line that they should therefore offer at least as much protection as they feel confident that the Strasbourg Court would offer to someone within the UK's jurisdiction as the Strasbourg Court understands that term.

These examples illustrate some practical effects of the HRA's design in regulating the behaviour of UK public authorities by reference to a body of international, rather than domestic, legal rules. When using the HRA we experience directly the interaction of different legal orders. When navigating the complex currents in an ocean where different streams mingle, judges have to make workable decisions that minimise the risk of domestic law being sucked into a legal whirlpool. Practical decisions which keep the ship afloat in the maelstrom are as important as their theoretical justifications.

Further reading

ALLAN, 'Parliament's Will and the Justice of the Common Law: The HRA in Constitutional Perspective' (2006) 59 CLP 27

Examines the extent to which the Human Rights Act 1998 reflects, rather than radically alters, elements of the common law constitution.

---

[200] See, eg *R (Castle) v Commissioner of Police of the Metropolis* [2011] EWHC 2317 (Admin).

[201] See, eg *Al-Skeini v United Kingdom* (2011) 53 EHRR 589 and *Al-Jedda v United Kingdom* (2011) 53 EHRR 789.

[202] ECHR, Art 46(1).   [203] HRA, s 21(1).

CAMPBELL, EWING, and TOMKINS (eds), *The Legal Protection of Human Rights: Sceptical Essays* (Oxford 2011)
As the title suggests, this collection of essays examines the subject of human rights from a critical perspective.

COMMISSION ON A BILL OF RIGHTS, *A UK Bill of Rights? The Choice Before Us* (London 2012)
The report of the commission established by the coalition government to examine the possibility of replacing the Human Rights Act 1998 with a 'UK Bill of Rights'.

ELLIOTT, 'Beyond the European Convention: Human Rights and the Common Law' (2015) 68 CLP 85
A discussion of the relationship between the human rights regimes that exist (on the one hand) under the Human Rights Act 1998 and the ECHR and (on the other hand) at common law.

O'CINNEIDE, *Human Rights and the UK Constitution* (London 2012)
Examines and clarifies some of the key issues raised by the debate about replacing the Human Rights Act 1998 with a UK Bill of Rights.

PHILLIPSON and WILLIAMS, 'Horizontal Effect and the Constitutional Constraint' (2011) 74 MLR 878
An analysis of the extent to which human rights under the 1998 Act should have horizontal effect.

ZIEGLER, WICKS, and HODSON, *The UK and European Human Rights: A Strained Relationship?* (Oxford 2015)
A collection of essays examining the relationship between the UK and European systems for protecting human rights.

Useful websites

http://www.equalityhumanrights.com
The website of the Equality and Human Rights Commission

http://www.echr.coe.int
The website of the European Court of Human Rights

http://www.parliament.uk/business/committees/committees-a-z/joint-select/human-rights-committee/
The website of the Joint Committee on Human Rights

http://ukhumanrightsblog.com
The UK Human Rights Blog

19

Freedom of Expression

1. Why freedom of expression matters	816
2. Article 10 of the European Convention on Human Rights	820
3. Media freedom	822
4. Defamation	835
5. Criminal offences	841
6. Privacy	845
7. Official secrecy	852
8. Conclusions	855
Expert commentary	856
Further reading	858

1. Why freedom of expression matters

1.1 Introduction

The right to freedom of expression is often referred to simply as 'freedom of speech', although it is generally recognised as involving the protection not only of verbal communication, but also of images and sounds. A politician making a speech, a busker singing in a town centre, an artist exhibiting paintings, and a neo-Nazi wearing a swastika are all engaging in forms of expression. However, a line has to be drawn somewhere: free speech may clash with, and might sometimes have to give way to, other rights and interests. The purpose of this chapter is to examine the nature of freedom of expression. Where and how does the law draw the line between acceptable and unacceptable expression? Does the right encompass the right to publish pornography, including extreme forms thereof? Or to publicise the intimate details of celebrities' private lives? Or to subject people to racist abuse? We examine these and other questions in the course of the chapter, but if we are to assess English law's response to them critically, it is necessary to start with a logically prior question: why protect free speech at all?

Gearty notes that 'restrictions on freedom of expression are regarded as the most serious conceivable breach of civil liberties'.[1] Raz, however, regards this state of affairs as a 'puzzle': '[W]hy [free speech] deserves this importance is a mystery'.[2] Raz has a point. Most people would place far greater value on other interests, such as having a job, so why single out free speech as being worthy of especially vigilant legal protection? The significance of some rights is so obvious as to make it unnecessary to spell it out. This is often because of the self-evidently harmful consequences that would flow from the breach of such rights (eg the right not to be tortured). The harmful consequences of restricting speech may be less immediately obvious. It may be frustrating not to be allowed to say what you want to say, but it hardly compares to spending weeks in a dungeon being tortured by state agents intent on extracting a confession. Free speech can therefore seem esoteric, even elitist— something that is perhaps important to those who have the means and wherewithal to publish their views in newspapers, but largely irrelevant to the average person. However, there are two principal arguments that call this view into question, and which arguably solve Raz's puzzle.[3] We examine those arguments in the following two sections.

1.2 Free speech and the status of individuals

The US Supreme Court has said that 'the freedom to speak one's mind is . . . a good unto itself'.[4] In other words, freedom of expression is valuable for its own sake, judged from the perspective of the individual engaging in it, as well as being beneficial to wider society. This view is premised on the high value attached in liberal theory to the autonomy of the individual. On that view, people's intrinsic worth means that, as far as is possible and is consistent with respect for others' autonomy, they should be allowed to live their lives as they wish, and their status as independent moral agents with their own personality, views, and preferences should be respected. Within that framework, freedom of expression assumes an important role in two senses.

First, *autonomous individuals should be permitted to express themselves.* As Sadurski notes: '[H]uman communicative activities are crucial to our capacity for self-expression and self-fulfilment'.[5] Being able to communicate is important if people are to develop as individuals and to define themselves. As Barendt puts it: 'A right to express beliefs and political attitudes instantiates or reflects what it is to be human.'[6] To deny people the right to express themselves is to deny their humanity, given that '[t]he reflective mind, conscious of options and the possibilities for growth, distinguishes human beings from animals'.[7]

---

[1] Gearty, *Civil Liberties* (Oxford 2007), p 122.

[2] Raz, 'Free Expression and Personal Identification' (1991) 11 OJLS 303, 303.

[3] For a more detailed examination of arguments in favour of free speech, see Barendt, *Freedom of Speech* (Oxford 2005), ch 1, and Raz (n 2).

[4] *Bose Corp v Consumers Union* (1984) 466 US 485, 503.

[5] *Freedom of Speech and Its Limits* (Dordrecht 1999), p 17.   [6] Barendt, p 13.   [7] Barendt, p 13.

Second, autonomous *individuals should be able to hear*[8] *and consider what* others *have to say.*[9] This suggests that the state should not legislate paternalistically so as to restrict free speech. On this view, legislation making it unlawful to say untrue things about people that would make others think badly of them would be inappropriate: autonomous, rational agents should be left to weigh up the credibility of what they hear and to decide how, if at all, to modify their behaviour and views in the light of it.

However, most legal systems recognise that, despite these arguments, the right of free speech should be subject to some limits. Some forms of expression—spreading vicious lies about someone that risks ruining their private life or employment prospects, for example—may cause considerable harm. Unless we regard the values discussed so far as absolute, it is perfectly sensible to contemplate restricting free speech in order to guard against such harmful consequences. However, the significance of the arguments set out in this section is that they hold that the value of free speech should not be judged purely in terms of its consequences. Just because some speech has negative effects, such as offending or disconcerting others, does not *necessarily* mean that it should be prohibited. Rather, the harm must be weighed against the good—and the good must include the intrinsic value of allowing individuals to express themselves. From this, it follows that *freedom of speech* has a value that exists independently of the value (or lack thereof) of *what is being said*.

1.3 Truth, democracy, and tolerance

The arguments just considered are often characterised as 'non-consequentialist' in nature because they focus upon freedom of speech as something that is valuable *for its own sake*. By contrast, 'consequentialist' arguments emphasise the beneficial social *consequences* that stem from affording people the freedom to say what they wish.

The first such argument concerns the so-called *marketplace of ideas*. In economic terms, free markets, in which everyone is free to buy and sell goods and services, are said by some to be valuable because (among other things) they facilitate competition. Good products succeed, poor ones fall by the wayside, and quality and value are driven up. For similar reasons, it has been suggested that there should be 'free trade in ideas'—'that the best test of truth is the power of the thought to get itself accepted in the competition of the market'.[10] On this view (which is most closely associated with John Stuart Mill[11]) an unfettered, or at least very broad, ability lawfully to advance opinions and make assertions is desirable.[12] Regulation or censorship—attempts by the state to predetermine the 'truth'—is considered undesirable because the state might get it wrong or present matters in a way that suits its own ends. Regulation and censorship are thus unnecessary because vigorous and unhindered public debate will ensure that bad ideas are not accepted, that good ideas are adopted and refined, and that false assertions are ignored in favour of true ones.

---

[8] Or read or see.

[9] See Scanlon, 'A Theory of Freedom of Expression' (1972) 1 Philosophy and Public Affairs 204.

[10] *Abrams v US* (1919) 250 US 616, 630, *per* Holmes J.   [11] *On Liberty*, ch 2.

[12] See, eg *Gertz v Robert Welch Inc* (1974) 418 US 323, 339–40.

There are, though, two main criticisms of the marketplace theory. It assumes, somewhat optimistically, that everyone is 'capable of making determinations that are both sophisticated and intricately rational if they are to separate truth from falsehood'.[13] It also overlooks the fact that just as markets in goods and services can be distorted (eg by the existence of powerful monopolies), so the marketplace of ideas may also malfunction. Those with the most persuasive communication skills or the deepest pockets may be able to manipulate the public's perception of the 'truth'.[14]

> **Q** In *Brandenburg v Ohio*,[15] the US Supreme Court held that a speech by the appellant, a member of a white supremacist group, advocating violence against blacks and Jews should attract the protection of the freedom of expression provisions in the US Constitution. A state law criminalising what the appellant had done was held unconstitutional. Do you think that the marketplace of ideas theory is capable of justifying this decision?

A second consequentialist argument in support of freedom of expression avers that free speech is the 'lifeblood of democracy'.[16] Meiklejohn argued that a truly democratic system of government requires far more than regular elections. Those elections must be meaningful, in the sense that they must permit the people—on whose behalf the government exercises power—to make an informed choice. The people 'must try to understand the issues which, incident by incident, face the nation', passing judgement upon the choices made by politicians on their behalf.[17] This led Meiklejohn to conclude that the point of the free speech guarantee in the US Constitution was to prevent the making of laws 'abridg[ing] the freedom of a citizen's speech, press, peaceable assembly, or petition, whenever those activities are utilized for the governing of the nation'.[18]

Third, it has been argued that freedom of speech promotes *tolerance*. This argument takes different forms, but its general thrust is that protecting free speech enables (indeed, requires) people to be exposed to a wide range of views, ideas, and values, and that such exposure will serve to promote a more tolerant, harmonious, broadminded society.[19] It is, for example, likely that the increasing willingness of the mainstream media to acknowledge the existence and legitimacy of same-sex relationships and lifestyles has driven, as well as reflected, growing recognition that people should be able to live their lives according to their sexual orientation, free from legal or social interference.

---

[13] Ingber, 'The Marketplace of Ideas: A Legitimizing Myth' [1984] Duke Law Journal 1, 7.

[14] We saw in Chapter 5, section 3.2.8 that such concerns have resulted in the UK in limits on how much can be spent by political parties on election campaigns.

[15] (1969) 395 US 444.

[16] *R v Secretary of State for the Home Department, ex p Simms* [2000] 2 AC 115, 126.

[17] Meiklejohn, 'The First Amendment is an Absolute' [1961] The Supreme Court Review 245, 255.

[18] Meiklejohn, 256.   [19] Raz, 'Free Expression and Personal Identification' (1991) 11 OJLS 303.

1.4 **Free speech and our key themes**

Freedom of speech is relevant to two of the key themes with which we are concerned in this book. The first is the importance of ensuring that *the government can be held to account*. Free speech is imperative in this regard because effective accountability is possible only if people have access to information about the decisions that the government has made, whether its policies are delivering their objectives, and whether mistakes have occurred. Free speech helps to ensure that such information is publicly available. In addition, people must be able to discuss such information freely and publicly—praising, blaming, criticising, and demonstrating for or against the government as they see fit. There are many mechanisms for holding the government to account, but the raw power of public opinion freely expressed should not be underestimated.

The second key theme relevant to this chapter is *the shift from a more political to a more legal form of constitutionalism*. One of the principal engines of that change is the growing legal acknowledgement and enforcement of individual rights. The increasing recognition of freedom of speech as a legal right, traced in this chapter, forms part of that trend. That is not, however, to suggest that this renders political control of government unimportant—far from it. *Legal* protection of free speech means that *political* mechanisms of control can be more fully exploited by strengthening people's ability lawfully to speak out. The free speech context is therefore a good illustration of how legal and political forms of constitutionalism can come into contact with one another and be mutually reinforcing.

2. **Article 10 of the European Convention on Human Rights**

Freedom of speech existed in the UK long before it became a party to the European Convention on Human Rights (ECHR) and long before that instrument was given effect in national law by means of the Human Rights Act 1998 (HRA).[20] However, the fact that the ECHR does now have effect in domestic law means that Art 10—its free speech provision—forms a useful benchmark against which to assess British law.

Article 10(1) states that '[e]veryone has the right to freedom of expression' and that this 'shall include freedom to hold opinions and to receive and impart information and ideas without interference by public authority and regardless of frontiers'.[21] Article 10(2) sets out the circumstances in which it is legitimate to restrict freedom of speech:

> The exercise of these freedoms, since it carries with it duties and responsibilities, may be subject to such formalities, conditions, restrictions or penalties as are prescribed by law

---

[20] On the ECHR and HRA generally, see Chapter 18.
[21] A specific provision in Art 10(1) concerning broadcasters and certain others is considered in section 3.2.

and are necessary in a democratic society, in the interests of national security, territorial integrity or public safety, for the prevention of disorder or crime, for the protection of health or morals, for the protection of the reputation or rights of others, for preventing the disclosure of information received in confidence, or for maintaining the authority and impartiality of the judiciary.

Two principal questions arise. The first concerns *what counts as expression*, since only freedom of 'expression' is protected by Art 10. Some guidance is given in the text: 'opinions', 'information', and 'ideas' are covered, although the use of the word 'include' indicates that this is a non-exhaustive list. Inevitably, therefore, difficult questions arise about the precise reach of Art 10. The European Court of Human Rights (ECtHR) has taken a generally broad approach to the category of things that are covered by Art 10(1), but it is not infinitely wide. Thus, while a film depicting hardcore pornography constitutes 'expression' for the purpose of Art 10(1),[22] certain forms of 'hate speech' do not: when white supremacists called black people and foreign workers 'animals', that did not constitute expression within the meaning of Art 10(1).[23]

The second question is whether speech that constitutes expression and which is therefore prima facie protected by Art 10 *may nevertheless be restricted under Art 10(2)*. This question requires courts to confront clashes between free speech and other important rights and interests. For example, media coverage of matters of general interest, such as criminal investigations, the doings of the rich and famous, and the conduct of the government bring into play tensions between, on the one hand, free speech and, on the other hand, the rights to a fair trial and to respect for private life, and interests such as national security. How we think such tensions should be resolved is necessarily coloured by the importance that we attach to free speech, and by the *reasons* why we think free speech is important. For example, drawing upon arguments concerning the significance of free speech to democracy, the ECtHR has held that it is especially important that political expression—especially in the context of an election campaign—should be respected. The degree of value ascribed by the Court to freedom of political expression means that particularly weighty reasons are required if such speech is to be lawfully restricted.[24]

This can be contrasted with the value ascribed by the Supreme Court to the 'speech' at stake in *PJS*, in which a newspaper wished to publish a story about a celebrity's alleged extra-marital sexual activities.[25] Refusing to discharge an interim injunction restraining publication, Lord Mance (with whom Lord Neuberger, Baroness Hale, and Lord Reed agreed) said that 'it may be that the mere reporting of sexual encounters of someone like the claimant, however well known to the public, with a view to criticising them does not even fall within the concept of freedom of expression under article 10 at all'.[26] But, if it did, said Lord Mance, such expression 'is at the bottom end of the spectrum of importance'. It followed that any public interest in publishing the

---

[22] *Hoare v UK* [1997] EHRLR 678 (although it was held that a national law banning the publication of such material could be justified under Art 10(2)).
[23] *Jersild v Denmark* (1995) 19 EHRR 1, 28.   [24] *Bowman v UK* (1998) 26 EHRR 1, [42].
[25] *PJS v News Group Newspapers Ltd* [2016] UKSC 26, [2016] 2 WLR 1253   [26] *PJS*, [24].

allegations was 'incapable by itself of outweighing such article 8 privacy rights as the claimant enjoys'.[27]

3. Media freedom

3.1 Why start with the media?

With the foregoing points in mind, we begin our examination of English law—starting with several issues concerning the media. The reasons for doing so are twofold.

First, the media is uniquely situated to facilitate the exercise of freedom of expression. Although the Internet makes it easier than ever for ordinary people to reach a large audience, print and broadcast media still offer singular opportunities for wide exposure and influence. It is therefore unsurprising that the role of the traditional media is central to several of the justifications for free speech considered so far. The media provides a public forum in which exchanges may take place in the marketplace of ideas; it has the capacity to promote tolerance and acceptance by exposing people to different views, ideas, and lifestyles; and it can facilitate the sort of public discourse necessary in a well-functioning democracy.

Second, it need hardly be pointed out that the media is imperfect. For reasons such as proprietorial influence and the commercial need to attract readers, journalism is often somewhat distant from the paradigm described in the previous paragraph. For all of its potential to do things that are socially beneficial, the media—which, for this reason, has been dubbed 'Janus-faced'[28]—also has the capacity to cause immense harm. The media's freedom of speech—and thus its capacity to use that freedom destructively—is subject to the same restrictions as everyone else's. However, it might be thought that the media should be subject to additional regulation in recognition of its peculiarly powerful position. That view certainly prevails in the UK, and is legitimised by Art 10(1) of the ECHR, which says that the right to freedom of expression 'shall not prevent States from requiring the licensing of broadcasting, television or cinema enterprises'.

3.2 Regulation of the media

3.2.1 Licensing

The default position in UK law is that people do not need permission to do things: they are free to do whatever is not prohibited by law. There are, however, exceptions. For instance, a car can lawfully be driven only by someone who possesses a driving licence. Similarly, while people generally do not need prior permission to express views or convey information, certain forms of media do, since they are subject to licensing requirements. For instance, a cinema may not lawfully show films unless it obtains a licence from its local authority,[29] while broadcasters are also subject to a licensing

---

[27] *PJS*, [24].

[28] Fenwick and Phillipson, *Media Freedom under the Human Rights Act* (Oxford 2006), p 2.

[29] The exhibition of films is a 'licensable activity' under s 1 and Sch 1 of the Licensing Act 2003.

regime.[30] There is inevitably a risk that licences may be withheld in circumstances that restrict legitimate free speech. However, two safeguards exist. First, the bodies responsible for granting licences are public authorities within the meaning of the HRA, and as such are required to act compatibly with Art 10 of the ECHR. Second, political interference in television and radio licensing is prevented because it is carried out by the media regulator Ofcom, which is not under direct ministerial control.

3.2.2 Additional duties and restrictions

Media regulation may also take the form of imposing upon certain forms of media duties and restrictions that go beyond those to which everyone is subject under the general law. Under UK law, this extra layer of legal regulation applies to television and radio (but not to newspapers), and consists principally in the requirements laid down in the Broadcasting Code.[31] The Code is issued under statute by the regulatory body Ofcom.[32] Among other things, it prohibits the broadcasting of material 'that might seriously impair the physical, mental or moral development of people under eighteen', permits the broadcasting of material (eg of a sexual or violent nature) that may cause offence only if 'justified by the context', and requires broadcasters to avoid 'unjust or unfair treatment of individuals or organisations in programmes' and 'any unwarranted infringement of privacy'. The Code also requires that 'news, in whatever form, must be reported with due accuracy and presented with due impartiality'—meaning, among other things, that broadcasters may not favour one party political view over another.[33] Ofcom must ensure that the licences that it grants require broadcasters to observe the Code.[34] In the event of a breach, Ofcom can impose fines and require the broadcasting of a correction or a statement of its findings. Regulation of the BBC used to be a matter for the BBC Trust, which issued licences to the BBC in respect of its various television, radio, and online services; monitored the BBC's performance; and sat at the apex of the process for adjudication upon complaints about the BBC. A review of BBC governance concluded that those arrangements were flawed, not least because the BBC Trust acted as both the BBC's governing body and its regulator—roles that were considered mutually incompatible.[35] Against that background, the government announced in 2016 that the Trust would be abolished and its licensing and regulatory functions transferred to Ofcom.[36]

The preamble to the Broadcasting Code underlines the importance of freedom of expression, and it is clear that the restrictions that the Code places on broadcasters closely relate to the grounds on which, according to Art 10(2) of the ECHR, free speech may legitimately be curtailed. Fenwick and Phillipson argue that the Code 'strikes a balance between offence avoidance and the right of adult television audiences to receive a diverse range of broadcast expression',[37] but warn that the drafting

---

[30] Broadcasting Acts 1990 and 1996.   [31] *The Ofcom Broadcasting Code* (London 2016).

[32] Broadcasting Act 1996, s 107; Communications Act 2003, ss 319–26.

[33] Special requirements apply in relation to elections: see Chapter 5, section 3.2.8.

[34] Communications Act 2003, ss 325–6.

[35] Clementi, *A Review of the Governance and Regulation of the BBC* (Cm 9209 2016).

[36] See generally Department for Culture, Media and Sport, *A BBC for the Future: A Broadcaster of Distinction* (Cm 9242 2016). The new arrangements are expected to enter into force in 2017.

[37] Fenwick and Phillipson, p 605.

of the Code and the likely reluctance of the courts to interfere with Ofcom's decisions (given its status as an expert regulator[38]) leaves it with considerable 'leeway
to take a range of approaches in terms of liberality and the preservation of creative
freedom'.[39]

> **Q** In the *Gaunt* case,[40] a radio presenter harangued an interviewee, calling him a 'Nazi'
> and an 'ignorant pig'. Ofcom ruled that this breached the provisions of its Code concern-
> ing the avoidance of offence to members of the public. On judicial review, it was held that
> Ofcom's ruling was compatible with Art 10, even though the subject matter of the inter-
> view related to a matter of public concern and therefore constituted a form of 'political
> speech'. Do you think the court was right to reach this conclusion?

3.2.3 Self-regulation

A sharp distinction exists between the regulatory regime applicable to television and
radio broadcasters and the position of newspapers (and other print media). Whereas
broadcasters must be licensed, no such requirement applies to print media. And while
broadcasters' output must be scrupulously balanced, newspapers can (and some do)
vociferously support individual political parties.

The differences between the regulatory regimes applicable to broadcast and print
media can be explained partly in historical terms. While the market has traditionally ensured that there exists a plurality of newspapers advancing a diverse range of
views, it is only 60 years since the UK had just one television channel. In that environment, the need for regulation of television was obvious: but does regulation remain
necessary now that the average home receives dozens of channels? Received wisdom
would say that it does—because broadcast, and particularly visual, media are significantly different from print media. The power of television images may be greater than
that of still photos or text in newspapers, and people may have less choice over their
encounters with them. The US Supreme Court has observed that the broadcast media
is 'uniquely pervasive' and that 'offensive, indecent material presented over the air-
waves confronts the citizen not only in public, but also in the privacy of the home'.[41]
This might, in turn, suggest that some form of regulation is appropriate in order to
safeguard the interests—the autonomy—of those who do not wish to consume certain forms of material.[42] Regulation need not, however, mean prohibition: Ofcom's
Broadcasting Code rightly recognises that the interests of those who do not wish to
be offended might, for example, be adequately catered for by requiring broadcasters
to provide advance warning of potentially offensive content.

Whereas broadcasters are subject to statutory regulation, a system of self-regulation
operates in respect of the print media. Until recently, such regulation took place under

---

[38] See Chapter 12, section 5.4 on deference in the face of expertise.
[39] Fenwick and Phillipson, p 606.   [40] *Gaunt v Ofcom* [2011] EWCA Civ 692, [2011] 1 WLR 2355.
[41] *FCC v Pacifica Foundation* 438 US 726 (1978), 749.
[42] See Dworkin, *A Matter of Principle* (London 1985), ch 17.

the auspices of the Press Complaints Commission (PCC). In contrast to the regulatory regime applicable to broadcasts, the PCC system was non-statutory and voluntary: newspapers could only be regulated by the PCC if they agreed to it, and the PCC could not legally enforce its decisions. Nor was the PCC fully independent: several members of the PCC board were senior newspaper editors, the PCC was funded by the industry, and the industry had considerable influence over the standards to which the PCC held it.

In 2009, the House of Commons Select Committee on Culture, Media and Sport published a major report that addressed press standards and regulation.[43] It strongly criticised the PCC's response to the 'phone-hacking scandal' in which journalists had intercepted public figures' voicemails, saying that the Commission's report was 'simplistic and surprising'.[44] Against this background, the coalition government found itself under irresistible pressure to establish a judicial inquiry into press standards. In 2012, the Leveson Inquiry concluded that self-regulation via the PCC was inadequate.[45] It recommended the establishment of a new regulatory body whose membership should be independently appointed, include no serving editors, and consist of a majority of people unconnected with the press. Serving editors would, however, be able to be involved in shaping the Code of Practice to be enforced by the new regulator, and the regulator would be funded by the press. The new regulator, said Leveson, should be able to require apologies to be published and to impose financial sanctions on publications up to 1 per cent of turnover.

Whilst stopping short of arguing for statutory regulation of the press, Leveson proposed that legislation should prescribe the requirements (some of which are summarised in the previous paragraph) that the new self-regulatory body should meet, and that legislation should also establish a mechanism for determining whether the new body meets those requirements. In other words, there would not be a statutory regulator—but there would be a statutory 'recognition body' responsible for ensuring that the non-statutory regulator was up to scratch. This proposal proved highly controversial in the light of fears that statute may create 'a kind of umbilical link between the press and the state', the effect of which might be to 'dampen scrutiny' of government, thus weakening the press's democratic 'watchdog function'.[46] However, as Rowbottom notes, recognising the value of this function does not necessarily elevate it above all other considerations so as to supply a knock-out argument against any degree of statutory intervention.[47]

Leveson's proposal for statutory underpinning (but not statutory regulation) was intended to accommodate concerns about press freedom whilst acknowledging that self-regulation in its existing form had failed. However, even this modest proposal proved politically unacceptable. Instead, it was agreed by the main political parties

---

[43] House of Commons Culture, Media and Sport Committee, *Press Standards, Privacy and Libel* (HC 362 2009–10).

[44] House of Commons Culture, Media and Sport Committee, HC 362, [472].

[45] *An Inquiry into the Culture, Practices and Ethics of the Press* (HC 780 2012–13).

[46] Rowbottom, 'Leveson, Press Freedom and the Watchdogs' (2013) 21 Renewal 57, 59.

[47] Rowbottom.

that the recognition body would be established not by statute but by a royal charter, with legislation to prevent the government from unilaterally procuring the amendment of the charter (eg so as to change the criteria that the regulator is required to satisfy).[48]

Under these new arrangements, the Press Recognition Panel began work—and the PCC was abolished—in 2014. The Panel is permitted to recognise a body as a press regulator only if the body in question fulfils several criteria set out in the Royal Charter on Self-Regulation of the Press—including criteria that reflect the Leveson recommendations, mentioned earlier, concerning independence. Newspapers and magazines cannot be compelled to submit to an officially recognised regulator, but there is an incentive to do so, since legislation provides that publishers are at risk of awards of exemplary damages in proceedings for (among other things) defamation and breach of privacy if they are not members of a regulator approved by the Recognition Panel.[49]

This new system of regulation cannot be said to have been a success. Indeed, at the time of writing, just one regulator—dealing with only a handful of small, specialist publications—has been recognised by the Recognition Panel. Many newspapers and magazines have instead joined the Independent Press Standards Organisation (IPSO). Its chair has acknowledged that it is not 'Leveson compliant',[50] and IPSO has declined to seek approval from the Recognition Panel. Meanwhile, some high-profile publications have refused to join IPSO due to doubts about its independence. Concerns have also arisen about its willingness to flex its muscles: in evidence given to a parliamentary committee in September 2016, IPSO's Chair conceded that not a single fine had been issued.[51]

> **Q** Can a convincing case be made for distinguishing between the broadcast and print media so as to justify statutory regulation of the former, but only self-regulation of the latter? If statutory regulation of the press would risk undermining democracy, why is the same not true of the existing regime of statutory regulation of television and radio?

Finally, in relation to the press, we should note that a limited amount of statutory regulation does exist in one particular area—that is, ownership. The need for the accurate presentation of news and free expression of opinions in newspapers, together with the need for 'a sufficient plurality of views in newspapers', are considerations

---

[48] The combined effect of s 96 of the Enterprise and Regulatory Reform Act 2013 and the terms of the royal charter is that the government cannot procure the amendment of the charter unless a two-thirds majority in each House authorises it to do so.

[49] Crime and Courts Act 2013, ss 34–42.

[50] 'Sir Alan Moses says IPSO is not Leveson-compliant but insists that it will be independent', *Press Gazette*, 9 September 2014.

[51] Sir Alan Moses, oral evidence to House of Commons Culture, Media and Sport Committee (13 September 2016).

that must be taken into account by the competition authorities when determining whether a merger between two companies should be disallowed on public interest grounds.[52] This is to ensure that no single publisher is able to achieve a stranglehold of newspaper ownership, which would jeopardise the expression of a wide range of views.

3.2.4 The Internet

The growth of the Internet poses particular challenges for media regulation because it blurs two traditional boundaries.[53] First, even if *the distinction between broadcast and print media* is thought to make sense from a regulatory perspective, the Internet places it under considerable pressure. Sharp distinctions between different forms of media are being eroded through convergence: newspapers' websites increasingly feature video content, whilst the text component of public service and commercial broadcasters' sites compete with traditional newspapers. This raises fundamental questions about how—and by whom—regulation should be undertaken, and about the extent to which existing regulatory arrangements adequately reflect the realities of the new media landscape.

Second, the Internet calls into question *the distinction between media organisations and others*. The influence wielded by the media is a standard justification for regulation, but in the age of the Internet others can wield comparable influence. As Rowbottom notes: 'The "star" blogger that reaches a wide audience begins to blur with some characteristics of the established media.'[54] This cuts two ways.

On the one hand, ordinary individuals engaging online in 'low level' speech (such as casual social exchanges) may be overregulated: the silly joke that would go no further if made verbally in the pub might, if posted online, fall within the regulatory net. Consider, for instance, the traveller, frustrated by delays, who tweeted: 'Crap! Robin Hood Airport is closed. You've got a week and a bit to get your shit together otherwise I am blowing the airport sky high!' He was convicted of an offence under s 127 of the Communications Act 2003. Although his conviction was subsequently quashed[55] (and guidelines issued about the exercise of prosecutorial discretion in relation to social media communications[56]) a question remains about whether online low-level speech is overregulated.[57]

On the other hand, there is a question about whether the 'star blogger' who reaches a wide audience should be fixed with the 'duties and responsibilities' applicable to the media.[58] Indeed, this issue has arisen in relation to the post-Leveson regulatory landscape. We noted in section 3.2.3 that the print media runs the risk of exemplary damages in relevant cases if it does not submit to regulation by a regulator approved

---

[52] Enterprise Act 2002, s 58(2A)–(2B).

[53] See generally Rowbottom, 'Media Freedom and Political Debate in the Digital Era' (2006) 69 MLR 489 and 'To Rant, Vent and Converse: Protecting Low Level Digital Speech' [2012] CLJ 355.

[54] Rowbottom, 'Media Freedom', 503.

[55] *Chambers v Director of Public Prosecutions* [2012] EWHC 2157 (QB), [2013] 1 WLR 1833.

[56] Crown Prosecution Service, *Guidelines on Prosecuting Cases Involving Communications Sent via Social Media* (London 2013).

[57] See further Rowbottom, 'To Rant'.   [58] *Stoll v Switzerland* (2008) 47 EHRR 59, [104].

by the Recognition Panel. However, this regime is not confined to the print media. The risk of exemplary damages arises provided that the defendant is 'a person who, in the course of a business (whether or not carried on with a view to profit), publishes news-related material'.[59] That category clearly extends beyond conventional newspapers and magazines. However, that said, the scope of the category is narrowed by a series of exclusions applying to (among other things) specialist, company, scientific, and academic journals, as well as to 'micro-businesses',[60] that publish news-related material only on an incidental basis.[61] Publishers of sole-author blogs are immune from the exemplary damages provisions,[62] as are publishers of multi-author blogs provided that they constitute 'micro-businesses'.[63]

3.3 Contempt of court

3.3.1 Introduction

Contempt of court covers several distinct criminal offences that are committed by interfering in some way with judicial proceedings.[64] A person commits *civil contempt* (which is a criminal offence) by disregarding a court order, such as an injunction. Here, however, our concern is with those aspects of *criminal contempt* (also a criminal offence) that impinge upon freedom of expression.

3.3.2 Scandalising the court

The offence known as *scandalising the court* was committed by publishing 'a scurrilous attack on the judiciary as a whole'—or on a particular judge—'which is calculated to undermine the authority of the courts and public confidence in the administration of justice'.[65] The publication had to cause at least a real risk that public confidence would be undermined,[66] although the defendant did not need to have intended the publication to undermine confidence.[67] However, the offence was abolished in 2013[68] in the light of the Law Commission's view the offence was 'in principle an infringement of freedom of expression' that should not be retained in the absence of strong practical or principled justification.[69] It did not consider that such a justification could be identified, noting that prosecution was very rare; that the large volume of abusive online comments concerning judges suggested that the offence had little by way of deterrent effect; and that there was a risk that the offence would have a 'chilling effect', thereby deterring legitimate criticism of judges.

---

[59] Crime and Courts Act 2013, s 41(1).
[60] Meaning a business with fewer than ten employees and a turnover not exceeding £2 million: Crime and Courts Act 2013, Sch 15, para 8(4).
[61] Crime and Courts Act 2013, Sch 15.   [62] Crime and Courts Act 2013, s 41(1)(a).
[63] Crime and Courts Act 2013, Sch 15, para 8.
[64] See generally Eady and Smith, *Arlidge, Eady and Smith on Contempt* (London 2015).
[65] *Chokolingo v Attorney-General of Trinidad and Tobago* [1981] 1 WLR 106, 111, *per* Lord Diplock.
[66] *Ahnee v Director of Public Prosecutions* [1999] 2 AC 294, 306.   [67] *Ahnee*, 307.
[68] Crime and Courts Act 2013, s 33.
[69] Law Commission, *Contempt of Court: Scandalising the Court* (Law Com No 335 2012), [93].

3.3.3 Prejudicial publications: introduction

According to Art 6 of the ECHR, everyone is entitled to a fair hearing whenever their civil rights and obligations or any criminal charge against them is being determined. However, particularly when a jury is involved, the provision of a fair trial might be made impossible, or at least substantially more difficult, if there is public discussion of the case via the media. While judges are trained to take into account only evidence that is relevant and admissible in the court proceedings, members of the public—of which juries are composed—are not. If information, speculation, or allegations that would be inadmissible in the trial come to jurors' attention via the media, the risk arises that they might be an influence and that a miscarriage of justice might result. More generally, it has been noted that if the media were permitted to conduct 'pseudo-trials', this might have the effect of reducing public 'acceptance of the courts as the proper forum for the settlement of legal disputes'.[70] There is, then, a need to strike a balance between free speech and fair trials.

In 1979, the ECtHR held, in *Sunday Times v UK*,[71] that English law did not strike that balance acceptably. The House of Lords had upheld an injunction preventing publication of a newspaper article on the ground that publication would have constituted contempt of court. The article concerned the drug thalidomide, which had been given to pregnant women and had caused birth defects. It was one of several articles intended to encourage the manufacturer—against which the victims had begun legal proceedings that had not yet reached trial—to agree to a generous out-of-court settlement. The ECtHR held that the injunction breached the right to free speech. Some of the Law Lords had formulated 'an absolute rule . . . to the effect that it was not permissible to prejudge issues in pending cases'. But, said the ECtHR, Art 10 permitted interference with free speech only if it is 'necessary having regard to the facts and circumstances prevailing in the specific case'.[72] The Court concluded that the public importance of the matter in the *Sunday Times* case and the fact that a trial was unlikely to take place in the short to medium term meant the injunction was not 'necessary'.

In the wake of that judgment, the Contempt of Court Act 1981 was enacted in an attempt to recast English law in terms consistent with the Convention. The Act contains a number of features that seek to safeguard free speech by ensuring that liability does not exceed that which is permitted by Art 10. We examine those features in sections 3.3.4–3.3.6.

3.3.4 Prejudicial publications: the 'double hurdle'

The Act establishes a 'strict liability' rule,[73] meaning that there is no fault requirement as such. But liability can only arise in the first place if two requirements—sometimes referred to as the 'double hurdle'—are satisfied:

- The risk that the course of justice will be prejudiced must be 'substantial', meaning 'not remote',[74] 'not insubstantial', or 'not minimal'.[75]

---

[70] *Sunday Times v UK* (1979–80) 2 EHRR 245, 278–9.   [71] (1979–80) 2 EHRR 245.
[72] *Sunday Times v UK*, 280–1.   [73] Contempt of Court Act 1981, s 1.
[74] *Attorney-General v English* [1983] 1 AC 116, 142, *per* Lord Diplock.
[75] *Attorney-General v News Group Newspapers plc* [1987] QB 1, 15.

- Even if there is a substantial risk of prejudice, liability will only arise if that risk is of 'serious' prejudice.[76]

It follows that neither a remote chance of serious prejudice nor a strong chance of minor prejudice will do: there must be a *substantial* risk of *serious* prejudice. In *MGN v Attorney-General*,[77] the High Court said that the following questions should be considered when determining whether such a risk arises:

- *How likely is it that the publication will come to the attention of a potential juror?* This will depend on such factors as the prominence and popularity of the publication, and on whether it is sold in the geographical area from which jurors are likely to be drawn.

- *What would be the impact of the article on the average reader?* The more interesting the issue and the more sensational its presentation, the greater the likely impact.

- *What is likely to be the residual impact on a juror[78] at the time of the trial?* The more memorable the article, the more likely a juror is to be influenced by it. But this must be balanced against the fact that the longer the gap between publication and trial, the more likely are memories to fade;[79] the 'focusing effect' of the trial itself—of 'listening over a prolonged period to evidence in a case'; and the likely effect of the judge's directions (eg telling the jury to disregard certain things they might have seen in the press).

To this list of factors must be added the *content* of the information in the publication. If the material merely rehearses matters aired at the trial, it is hard to see how a juror might be prejudiced.[80] In contrast, information that is adverse to the defendant and would be inadmissible at trial is liable to be more prejudicial. For instance, it is often impermissible to tell the jury about the defendant's previous convictions for fear that this might predispose them against him. That prohibition would clearly be undermined if the media were free to publish such information. Commenting on certain aspects of the case may also be likely to prejudice jurors. For example, an impressionable juror might be swayed by an opinion piece in a newspaper saying that the evidence clearly establishes the defendant's guilt and that no sensible juror could think otherwise.

---

[76] Contempt of Court Act 1981, s 2(2). Prior to the 1981 Act, it appears that a serious risk of *any* prejudice would be sufficient: see Eady and Smith, *Arlidge, Eady and Smith on Contempt* (London 2005), p 254.

[77] [1997] EMLR 284, 290–1.

[78] If the case is to be heard only by a judge, the double hurdle is unlikely to be cleared, given that judges are trained to disregard irrelevant information.

[79] The fade factor may, however, be less relevant if the material has been published and remains available online.

[80] And, in any event, s 4(1) of the 1981 Act specifically says that, subject to certain limited exceptions, no liability will arise in relation to 'a fair and accurate report of legal proceedings held in public, published contemporaneously and in good faith'.

3.3.5 Prejudicial publications: 'active' proceedings

The strict liability rule only applies in relation to legal proceedings that are 'active' at the time of publication.[81] Criminal proceedings do not become active until one of certain 'initial steps' is taken, such as arrest or the issue of an arrest warrant. They cease to be active when the proceedings are concluded (most typically, when the defendant is acquitted or sentenced).[82] These rules are important for two reasons. First, they create a relatively narrow window within which the strict liability rule operates. This helps to ensure that free speech is restricted no more than is necessary. Second, the rules are very clear. This ensures that media organisations know where they stand and avoids a 'chilling effect' on free speech whereby uncertainty leads publishers to exercise greater self-restraint than is legally required. Even if proceedings are active, the publisher will have a defence if he can show that, having taken all reasonable care, he did not know and had no reason to suspect that that was so.[83]

Particular issues arise in relation to online publication. Take, for instance, material that is published online *before* proceedings are active but which remains available online *after* proceedings become active. It might be thought that no question of liability arises, because the act of publication occurred when proceedings were not active. But online publication might be considered a continuing endeavour, such that preserving the accessibility of material on a website might amount to ongoing publication. On the latter view, the strict liability rule bites upon all relevant online material as soon as proceedings become active. That view was adopted in Scotland in *HM Advocate v Beggs (No 2)*[84] and in England in *R v Harwood*.[85]

In a report published in 2013, the Law Commission concluded that the current state of the law in this regard amounts to an 'unsound basis on which to attach criminal liability', not least because it risks publishers being liable for the unintended consequences of conduct that was lawful when first undertaken.[86] The Commission therefore recommended that although liability should be possible in respect of online publications that remain available once proceedings are active, liability should only arise if the relevant person has been 'put on formal notice' by the Attorney-General.[87] This would mean liability could not in these circumstances be inadvertently incurred: having been put on notice, the person concerned would have the option of temporarily removing the relevant material from their website pending conclusion of the proceedings. The Law Commission's recommendations on this matter have not yet been implemented.

---

[81] Contempt of Court Act 1981, s 2(3).

[82] Contempt of Court Act 1981, Sch 1, paras 4–5. Different rules apply in relation to civil proceedings (paras 12–14) and appellate proceedings (paras 15–16).

[83] Contempt of Court Act 1981, s 3.   [84] 2002 SLT 139.   [85] [2012] EW Misc 27 (CC).

[86] Law Com No 340, *Contempt of Court (1): Juror Misconduct and Internet Publications* (HC 360 2013–14), [2.218]–[2.219].

[87] Law Com No 340, [2.150].

3.3.6 Prejudicial publications: good faith discussion

Section 5 of the Act says that when a publication constitutes 'a discussion in good faith of public affairs or other matters of general public interest', it is not to be treated as engaging the strict liability rule, provided that 'the risk of impediment or prejudice to particular legal proceedings is merely incidental to the discussion'. Section 5 aims to ensure that responsible discussion of important matters is not precluded merely because legal proceedings that touch on the same issues are active, even if it causes a substantial risk of serious prejudice. It echoes one of the objections raised by the ECtHR to the injunction granted in the *Sunday Times* case—that matters do 'not cease to be a matter of public interest merely because they [form] the background to pending litigation'.[88]

Section 5 was successfully invoked in *Attorney-General v English*[89] by a defendant who had published an article alleging, in condemnatory terms, that a practice had developed whereby doctors allowed or caused severely disabled newborn babies to die. The impetus for the article was the candidature in a by-election of a disabled person campaigning against that alleged practice. However, publication coincided with the trial of a doctor who was said to have done that which the article condemned. Concluding that s 5 applied, the House Lords said that the test was whether the risk of prejudice that the article created was 'no more than an incidental consequence of expounding its main theme'. The Law Lords rejected the suggestion that s 5 allowed the newspaper to go no further than abstract discussion of the morality of the alleged practice. Read in such a way, s 5 would inadequately safeguard free speech because it would limit the media to discussing hypothetical questions, resulting in articles 'devoid of any general public interest'.[90]

3.3.7 Prejudicial publications: further matters

Having set out the main points concerning the strict liability rule under the 1981 Act, we conclude with four further observations about the law in this area.

The first is that *the strict liability rule is not exhaustive of the circumstances in which liability may arise* for publications that risk prejudicing legal proceedings. Under s 6(c) it remains an offence at common law to engage in conduct that is *intended* to impede or prejudice the administration of justice. This offence is, in one sense, wider than that created by the Act because there can be liability at common law when proceedings are 'pending or imminent' even if they are not 'active' within the meaning of the legislation.[91] However, the fact that the common law offence can be committed only if there is intention means that it is, in practice, much narrower than the statutory offence.

Second, a substantial risk of serious prejudice—and thus liability—is much less likely in relation to *proceedings, such as appellate and most civil cases, not involving juries*. As Lord Parker CJ explained, although 'in no sense superhuman', a judge has

---

88 *Sunday Times v UK* (1979–80) 2 EHRR 245, 280–2.   89 [1983] 1 AC 116.
90 *Attorney-General v English*, 143.
91 *Attorney-General v News Group Newspapers plc* [1989] QB 110, 130, *per* Watkins LJ.

'by his training no difficulty in putting out of his mind matters which are not evidence in the case'.[92]

Third, we return to our original question: *whether English law now strikes the right balance been free speech and fair trials*. We saw that, in the *Sunday Times* case, the ECtHR held that English law gave too much weight to the latter and unduly restricted the former. Today, it is said by some that the pendulum has swung too far in the other direction: that the emphasis placed on media freedom is too great, such that it is difficult in some cases for a fair trial to be provided. For instance, the Law Commission has raised the questions whether the 'substantial risk' test in s 2(2) should be modified so as to confer greater protection on the right to a fair trial (eg by requiring only a 'likelihood' of prejudice or impediment),[93] and whether the 'impediment' and 'prejudice' limbs of s 2(2) should be distinguished more clearly.[94]

Fourth, the Law Commission has noted that, *thanks to the growth of the Internet*, there has been a 'phenomenal shift' in how people obtain and impart information since the 1981 Act was passed.[95] A particular difficulty concerns the accessibility to jurors of information concerning the trial. The difficulty relates back, at least in part, to the matter noted earlier concerning the ongoing availability of material on the Internet.[96] A story published in a newspaper months before the trial would be unlikely to be read during the trial by a juror. In contrast, web-based material—unless and until it is removed—remains accessible irrespective of when it is posted. It is therefore easier today than it ever has been for jurors to encounter, whether deliberately or accidentally, prejudicial material. It had already been established that jurors behaving in such a manner could be guilty of contempt of court.[97] However, the Law Commission concluded that a new, separate offence should be created in order, among other things, to bring greater clarity to the law in this area.[98] In the light of that recommendation, it is now an offence, subject to certain exceptions, for a juror to research a case during the trial period.[99]

3.3.8 Contempt in the face of the court

A number of forms of conduct, collectively referred to as *contempt in the face of the court*, constitute a further species of criminal contempt. Many of these do not have significant implications for freedom of speech and are beyond the scope of this chapter. For example, disturbing court proceedings by shouting or singing[100] can amount to criminal contempt. But this represents a very modest restriction upon freedom of expression, and one for which there is an obviously sound justification.

In contrast, a witness's refusal to answer a question can constitute contempt in the face of the court[101] and has important free speech implications when the witness is

---

[92] *R v Duffy, ex p Nash* [1960] 2 QB 188, 198.
[93] Law Commission, *Contempt of Court: A Consultation Paper* (Law Com CP No 209, 2012), [2.45].
[94] Law Com CP No 209, [2.46]–[2.47].   [95] Law Com CP No 209, [3.2].
[96] See section 3.3.5.   [97] Attorney General v *Beard* [2013] EWHC 2317 (Admin).
[98] Law Com No 340, ch 3.
[99] Juries Act 1974, s 20A (inserted by Criminal Justice and Courts Act 2015, s 71).
[100] As in *Morris v Crown Office* [1970] 2 QB 114.
[101] See, eg *Attorney-General v Mulholland* [1963] 2 QB 477.

a journalist being asked to reveal her sources. According to the ECtHR, Art 10 safe-guards the media's 'vital role of "public watchdog"' by enabling it to impart 'informa-tion and ideas on matters of public interest' and by giving the public 'a right to receive them'.[102] However, that process depends on a flow of information to journalists—and via them to the wider public—that risks drying up if sources cannot be sure that their identities will remain confidential.[103] Free speech therefore favours allowing journal-ists to refuse to name their sources. Section 10 of the Contempt of Court Act 1981 addresses this issue by stipulating that no offence is committed by a journalist who refuses to disclose her sources unless the court is satisfied 'that disclosure is neces-sary in the interests of justice or national security or for the prevention of disorder or crime'. This language largely mirrors that of Art 10. However, in a series of cases the courts applied s 10 in a way that appeared to place little weight on the interest in preserving sources' confidentiality.[104]

Palmer suggests that this might be because the 'harm to the public interest caused by a loss of free flow of information', although significant, 'cannot by definition be quantified',[105] whereas the competing interests served by disclosure may be more readily apparent. For example, the House of Lords held in *Morgan Grampian*[106] that a journalist should be required to identify his source in order that a company could identify the disloyal employee who had leaked sensitive and commercially damaging information. It was held that this would fall within the 'interests of justice' exception under s 10. That exception, it was said, applied whenever the disclosure of sources was necessary to allow someone 'to exercise important legal rights and to protect themselves from serious legal wrongs whether or not resort to legal proceedings in a court of law will be necessary to attain these objectives'.[107] However, the ECtHR later ruled in *Goodwin* that ordering disclosure in such circumstances constituted a breach of the Convention.[108] The House of Lords had, in effect, attached too much weight to the company's interests and, relatively speaking, too little to the competing interests served by maintaining sources' confidentiality. In subsequent cases, the courts have placed somewhat greater emphasis on the need to interpret s 10 pursuant to Art 10 and on the 'chilling effect' that orders for disclosure can have on press freedom.[109] For example, a disclosure order was refused in a case in which less draconian steps—such as the holding of an internal inquiry—had not been taken by a party wishing to iden-tify the source of a leak, the 'necessity' of a court order not having been established in such circumstances.[110]

[102] *Sunday Times v UK (No 2)* (1992) 14 EHRR 229, [50]. This point was reiterated by the Grand Chamber of the ECtHR in *Sanoma Uitgevers BV v Netherlands* (2010) 51 EHRR 31.

[103] *Goodwin v UK* (1996) 22 EHRR 123, [39].

[104] See, eg *Secretary of State for Defence v Guardian Newspapers Ltd* [1985] AC 339; *X Ltd v Morgan Grampian (Publishers) Ltd* [1991] 1 AC 1; *Re an Inquiry under the Companies Securities (Insider Dealing) Act 1985* [1988] AC 660.

[105] 'Protecting Journalists' Sources: Section 10, Contempt of Court Act 1981' [1992] PL 61, 71.

[106] *X Ltd v Morgan Grampian (Publishers) Ltd* [1991] 1 AC 1.   [107] *Morgan Grampian*, 43.

[108] *Goodwin v UK.*

[109] *Ashworth Hospital Authority v MGN Ltd* [2002] UKHL 29, [2002] 1 WLR 2033.

[110] *John v Express Newspapers* [2000] 1 WLR 1931.

4. Defamation

4.1 **Introduction**

'Defamation' describes two distinct, but closely related, legal wrongs—libel and slander—that are concerned with statements liable to affect a person's reputation. There are some important differences between libel and slander (libel concerns statements made in permanent form,[111] while slander concerns oral statements), but for present purposes we can consider defamation generally, rather than libel and slander separately. Our focus is on whether English law appropriately strikes the balance called for by Art 10 between free speech and the protection of 'the reputation or rights of others'.

4.2 **Ingredients of liability**

The extent of the inroads made by the law of defamation into freedom of expression depends on the answers to two questions:

- When does something prima facie constitute defamation?
- What defences are there to defamation claims?

As to the first of those questions, there are three principal requirements:

- The statement must refer to the claimant, either explicitly or (judged on the basis of the inferences that an ordinary sensible person would draw from what has been said) implicitly.[112]
- The statement must be published—that is, it must be issued to someone other than the claimant[113] or the defendant's spouse.[114]
- The statement must be defamatory.

At common law, a statement was considered defamatory of the claimant if it '[substantially] affects in an adverse manner the attitude of other people towards him, or has a tendency so to do'.[115] However, the Defamation Act 2013 says that a statement will only be defamatory if 'its publication has caused or is likely to cause serious harm to the reputation of the claimant'.[116] This, it has been noted, is 'clearly more demanding than the common law test'[117] and, as such, ' "raises the bar" over which a claimant must jump'.[118]

Allegations that someone has committed a criminal offence or has otherwise acted dishonestly or immorally will, in the normal course of things, be regarded as

---

[111] eg in writing. Libel also covers radio and television broadcasts: Broadcasting Act 1990, s 166.

[112] *Morgan v Odhams Press Ltd* [1971] 1 WLR 1239.

[113] *Pullman v Walter Hill and Co Ltd* [1891] 1 QB 524, 527, *per* Lord Esher MR.

[114] *Wennhak v Morgan* (1888) LR 20 QBD 635.

[115] *Thornton v Telegraph Media Group Ltd* [2010] EWHC 1414 (QB), [2011] 1 WLR 1985, [96], *per* Tugendhat J.

[116] Section 1(1).

[117] *Lachaux v Independent Print Ltd* [2015] EWHC 2242 (QB), [2016] QB 402, [29], *per* Warby J.

[118] *Cooke v MGN Ltd* [2014] EWHC 2831 (QB), [2015] 1 WLR 895, [37], *per* Bean J.

defamatory, but not all cases are as straightforward. The concept of reputation can consist only as a function of what other people think of the claimant. Much therefore depends on the views and attitudes that courts ascribe to those 'other people'—and precisely who they are taken to be. For example, in *Byrne v Dean*,[119] the defendant published a poem indicating that the claimant had complained to the police about the unlawful presence of gambling machines on the premises of a club of which the claimant was a member. The claimant took exception, fearing that other members of the club, if they were to believe the allegation, would shun him, thinking him disloyal. The court, however, held that the statement was not capable of being defamatory—a conclusion to which it was led by considering the likely reaction of people generally (who would think it right to report illegal activity) rather than that subset of people (ie club members) about whose views the claimant was concerned.

4.3 Defences

There are several possible defences, now codified in the Defamation Act 2013, to a defamation claim. Here, we focus on those particularly relevant to the implications of defamation for the scope of freedom of expression.

4.3.1 Truth

The claimant does not have to establish the falsity of the statement complained of, meaning that questions of truth and falsity do not necessarily enter into consideration. However, it is a defence to show 'that the imputation conveyed by the statement complained of is substantially true'.[120] It is obviously right, from a freedom of speech perspective, that it should not be unlawful to make true statements just because they are defamatory. If that were the case, it would, for example, be unlawful to accuse someone of being corrupt or dishonest—because such an allegation would lower right-thinking people's estimation of them—even if the allegation were true. However, should the burden lie with the claimant to establish that the statement is untrue, or is it preferable, as English law does, to place the burden of proving truth on the defendant? The difficulty with the latter approach is that it is likely to have a chilling effect on freedom of expression. As Lord Keith explained in *Derbyshire County Council v Times Newspapers Ltd*: 'Quite often the facts which would justify a defamatory publication are known to be true, but admissible evidence capable of proving those facts is not available. This may prevent the publication of matters which it is very desirable to make public.'[121]

> **Q** Would it be better to require the claimant to establish the falsity of the statement, or would this inadequately protect claimants' ability to safeguard their reputations?

---

[119] [1937] 1 KB 818.   [120] Defamation Act 2013, s 2(1).

[121] [1993] AC 534, 548. For further discussion of this point, see House of Commons Culture, Media and Sport Committee, *Press Standards, Privacy and Libel* (HC 362 2009–10), [130]–[136]; English PEN and Index on Censorship, *Free Speech is Not for Sale* (London 2009).

4.3.2 **Honest opinion**

Whilst truth is a defence in relation to allegations of *fact*, it can have no application to statements of *opinion*—which, by definition, defy classification as 'true' or 'false'. There is, however, a defence of 'honest opinion'. This plays a very important part in ensuring that defamation law does not unduly restrict the sort of legitimate public debate—which includes the exchanges of views—that is highly prized in any free society and which lies close to the core of the sorts of speech protected by the right of freedom of expression.[122]

Under s 3 of the Defamation Act, which supersedes the common law defence of 'fair comment', three requirements must be met if the defence of honest opinion is to succeed:

- The utterance in question must be a statement of opinion.[123] What marks out opinion is that it 'can reasonably be inferred to be a deduction, inference, conclusion, criticism, remark, observation, etc'.[124]

- The statement must indicate (in either general or specific terms) the basis of the opinion.[125]

- The opinion must be one that an honest person could have held, either on the basis of a fact which existed at the time the statement was published, or on the basis of something asserted to be a fact in a 'privileged' statement published before the allegedly defamatory statement.[126]

The defence will fail if the defendant shows that the claimant did not actually hold the opinion.[127] The statutory defence is wider than its common law predecessor, which had the added requirement that the statement be on a matter of public interest.

4.3.3 **Privilege**

In situations attracting the defence of 'privilege', no legal wrong is committed by a person who makes a statement that would otherwise constitute unlawful defamation, whether or not any other defence is available. The thinking behind this is that there are certain circumstances in which the public interest in free speech is so strong that the prospect of legal action for defamation—and, importantly, the likely chilling effect of that prospect—should be removed.

In a number of circumstances, privilege is *absolute*, meaning that free speech is entirely unhindered by the law of defamation. These include statements made (eg by judges or witnesses) in, or in relation to, proceedings before courts or tribunals;[128] fair and accurate contemporaneous reports of court proceedings;[129] and communications between government Ministers and between certain other office-holders (eg military

---

[122] See, eg *Lingens v Austria* (1986) 8 EHRR 407, [42].   [123] Defamation Act 2013, s 3(2).
[124] *Branson v Bower (No 2)* [2002] QB 737, [12], approving a dictum of Cussen J in *Clarke v Norton* [1910] VLR 494, 499.
[125] Defamation Act 2013, s 3(3).   [126] Defamation Act 2013, s 3(4).
[127] Defamation Act 2013, s 3(5).
[128] See, eg *Royal Aquarium and Summer and Winter Garden Society Ltd v Parkinson* [1892] 1 QB 431.
[129] Defamation Act 1996, s 14.

officers).[130] Statements made in,[131] and papers published by order of, Parliament[132] also attract absolute privilege.[133]

> **Q** Is it acceptable that some statements are wholly beyond the reach of the law of defamation? Does this give too *much* weight to free speech (and too little to the ability of people to protect their reputations)?

In certain other circumstances, privilege is *qualified*. The difference between absolute and qualified privilege is that the latter defence (unlike the former) will fail if the claimant can show that the defendant acted maliciously—meaning, in this context, that the defendant makes a statement out of spite or in order to harm the claimant[134] or without a 'positive belief in its truth'.[135] Qualified privilege arises on 'an occasion where the person who makes a communication has an interest or a duty, legal, social, or moral, to make it to the person to whom it is made, and the person to whom it is so made has a corresponding interest or duty to receive it'.[136] Thus, for example, qualified privilege will arise when a company director alleges to the chairperson that an employee was acting improperly (both have an interest in protecting the company)[137] and when a member of the public alleges to the police that someone has committed a criminal offence.[138]

4.3.4 Publication on a matter of public interest

The reciprocal duty/interest requirements mean that the qualified privilege defence is not obviously well suited to situations in which statements are made to the world at large via newspapers, broadcasts, and so on. This calls into question whether qualified privilege (at least as traditionally conceived) can be an adequate safeguard when it comes to discussion of matters of public interest. Influenced by the importance of freedom of political speech, the US Supreme Court held in *Sullivan v The New York Times*[139] that criticism of public officials (including elected politicians) in relation to their public conduct attracted qualified privilege *as a category*. This is a clearer test than the duty/interest one, thus helping to ensure that 'would-be critics of official conduct' are not 'deterred from voicing their criticism, even though it is believed to be true and even though it is, in fact, true, because of doubt whether it can be proved in court or fear of the expense of having to do so'.[140]

English courts, however, declined to adopt this approach. In *Reynolds v Times Newspapers Ltd*,[141] Lord Nicholls, noting the 'chilling effect' of the law of defamation,

---

[130] *Merricks v Nott-Bower* [1965] 1 QB 57, 68.   [131] Bill of Rights 1688, Art 9.
[132] Parliamentary Papers Act 1840, s 1.
[133] On parliamentary privilege, see further Chapter 5, section 4.
[134] *Cheng v Tse Wai Chun* [2000] HKCFA 35, [2000] 3 HKLRD 418, [55].
[135] *Reynolds v Times Newspapers Ltd* [2001] 2 AC 127, 201, *per* Lord Nicholls.
[136] *Adam v Ward* [1917] AC 309, 334, *per* Lord Atkinson.
[137] *Watt v Longsdon* [1930] 1 KB 130.   [138] *Reynolds*, 194.   [139] (1964) 376 US 254.
[140] *Sullivan*, 279, *per* Brennan CJ.   [141] [2001] 2 AC 127.

argued that '[a]t times people must be able to speak and write freely, uninhibited by the prospect of being sued for damages should they be mistaken or misinformed'. He concluded that '[i]n the wider public interest, protection of reputation must then give way to a higher priority'.[142] However, Lord Nicholls said that *Sullivan* struck the wrong balance between protecting free speech and reputation: it gave the press too much latitude and encouraged irresponsible journalism. *Reynolds* therefore set out a defence, based on the established doctrine of qualified privilege, of 'responsible journalism'. Under this approach, qualified privilege was likely to attach to a newspaper article on a matter of public interest provided that the decision to publish was a responsible one in all of the circumstances, irrespective of whether the information actually turned out to be true.

In 2010, a Ministry of Justice working group proposed several changes to defamation law, including the replacement of the *Reynolds* defence with a statutory defence.[143] The working group argued that the law should be clarified so as to reduce the chilling effect arguably caused by uncertainty about the scope of the *Reynolds* defence. That defence has now been replaced by s 4 of the Defamation Act 2013, which provides that a defence is made out if both of the following can be established:

- The statement (whether of opinion or fact) was (or formed part of) a statement on a matter of public interest.

- The defendant reasonably believed that publishing the statement was in the public interest.[144]

The statutory defence acknowledges statements concerning matters of public interest as a *category* worthy of protection in a way that the common law did not.

Two further points should be noted about the s 4 defence. First, by requiring the court to consider all the circumstances of the case, it is likely that, when the defendant is a journalistic organisation, the courts will continue to apply some version of the *Reynolds* concept of responsible journalism. They are therefore likely to consider whether, for instance, the defendant took steps to verify the information, whether comment was sought from the claimant, whether the article contained the gist of the claimant's side of the story, and whether the allegations are presented appropriately (eg a responsible journalist would present in more circumspect terms allegations of the veracity of which he was less confident).[145]

Second, the Act says that when a court decides whether it was reasonable for a defendant to believe that publication was in the public interest, it 'must make such allowance for editorial judgement as it considers appropriate'.[146] This accords a degree of latitude to journalistic judgement, and reflects Lord Mance's view (articulated in a case decided prior to the Defamation Act) that: 'The courts must have the last word in setting the boundaries of what can properly be regarded as acceptable journalism, but

---

[142] *Reynolds*, 192–3.
[143] Ministry of Justice, *Report of the Libel Working Group* (London 2010).
[144] Defamation Act 2013, s 4(1).   [145] *Reynolds*, 205.   [146] Defamation Act 2013, s 4(4).

within those boundaries the judgment of responsible journalists and editors merits respect.'[147]

4.3.5 Website operators and the single publication rule

Two measures in the Defamation Act 2013 respond to the particular challenges posed by publications posted on the Internet. First, website operators now have a defence if they can show that they did not post the defamatory statement in question on their website.[148] This poses a problem, however, in relation to the common practice whereby statements may be posted online either in a wholly unattributed way or using only a pseudonym. The Act therefore provides that the website operator's defence will be defeated if, in respect of statements on websites published by individuals who cannot be identified by the defamed individual, the website operator fails to deal in the required manner with a formal complaint concerning the defamatory statement. The Act contemplates that website operators may be required to identify the author of the statement or take action to remove it from the website.[149]

Second, in its report published in 2010, the Ministry of Justice working group on defamation[150] addressed the 'repeat publication rule'.[151] It meant, among other things, that every time a web page containing a defamatory statement was accessed, a fresh publication occurred.[152] This, in turn, meant that a defamation claim could be brought many years after the original publication, thereby circumventing the normal one-year limitation period applicable to such claims. The ECtHR held that this may breach Art 10.[153] The working group proposed the introduction of a 'single publication rule' that would remove the possibility of liability in respect of multiple publications of the same defamatory statement. Such a rule is now contained in s 8 of the 2013 Act. It provides that, for limitation-period purposes, time will not begin to run afresh in respect of subsequent publications provided that both of the following conditions are met:

- The subsequent publication is of the same or a substantially similar statement.

- The manner of publication does not materially differ as between the first and subsequent publications.

---

[147] *Flood v Times Newspapers Ltd* [2012] UKSC 11, [2012] 2 AC 273, [137].

[148] Defamation Act 2013, s 5(2).

[149] See further the Defamation (Operators of Websites) Regulations 2013.

[150] Ministry of Justice, *Report of the Libel Working Group* (London 2010).

[151] *Duke of Brunswick v Harmer* (1849) 14 QB 185.

[152] *Loutchansky v Times Newspapers Ltd (No 2)* [2001] EWCA Civ 1805, [2002] QB 783; see further Law Commission, *Defamation and the Internet: A Preliminary Investigation* (London 2002).

[153] *Times Newspapers v UK* [2009] EMLR 14.

In determining the latter matter, the court may have regard (among other things) to the level of prominence accorded to the statement. If, then, a defamatory statement were originally published in an obscure, interstitial part of a website, and were then republished on the homepage, it is likely that time would begin to run afresh, for limitation-period purposes, in respect of the subsequent publication.

5. Criminal offences

There are several criminal offences that limit freedom of expression. Criminalisation represents a particularly severe curb on free speech, and the question arises whether such offences strike an acceptable balance between the policy interests that they seek to promote and freedom of expression.

5.1 Racial hatred

Sections 18–23 of the Public Order Act 1986 create a series of offences concerned with the incitement of 'racial hatred', meaning 'hatred against a group of persons defined by reference to colour, race, nationality (including citizenship) or ethnic or national origins'.[154] Offences are committed when all three of the following conditions are met:

- The defendant uses words or behaviour, publishes or distributes written material, presents or directs a play, distributes, shows, or plays a recording of images or sounds, broadcasts a television or radio programme, or possesses (with a view to displaying or distributing) material.
- The words, behaviour, material, etc, is 'threatening, abusive or insulting'.
- The defendant intends thereby to stir up racial hatred or, having regard to all of the circumstances, racial hatred is likely to be stirred up.

By singling out speech promoting racial hatred, these offences constitute restrictions on free speech that are not content-neutral. Such restrictions are treated with particular suspicion by proponents of free speech because they censor particular views.[155] This does not mean that they are unjustifiable, but it does mean that they deserve a particularly close look. In terms of Art 10, it is arguable these offences may help to prevent crime (those amongst whom racial hatred has been stirred up are presumably more likely to act violently towards members of the relevant group) and to protect the 'rights of others' (ie members of the groups concerned). It might also be felt that the value of the speech in question is so low, and the negative consequences of it (eg feelings of victimisation, damage to race relations) so great, that content-based regulation is acceptable. That is certainly the view at which lawmakers in the UK, and in many other countries, have arrived.

---

[154] Public Order Act 1986, s 17. [155] See *RAV v City of St Paul, Minnesota* (1992) 505 US 377.

Q Do you agree with that view? Do any other groups—women, men, children, the aged—deserve similar protection? How would you draw the line?

5.2 Hatred on grounds of religion or sexual orientation

It is hard to see what value, if any, racist speech might have (although even this fact would cut little ice with free speech purists). But the position is more complicated in relation to religion. Saying that a particular religion (or all religion) is wrong, illogical, or harmful, or that adherents are misguided or unenlightened, is an exercise of freedom of expression capable of constituting serious, legitimate debate and of making a significant social contribution. English law in this area has changed substantially in recent years, as is demonstrated by the abolition of the offence of blasphemy.[156] The offence was committed by publishing matter that insulted, offended, or vilified 'the Deity of Christ or the Christian religion or some part of its doctrines', such as a poem depicting Jesus Christ as a promiscuous gay man.[157] It was difficult, if not impossible, in a society characterised by a plurality of faiths to justify singling out one religion for such protection.[158]

However, a new set of offences concerning the stirring up of religious hatred was created by the Racial and Religious Hatred Act 2006 (which inserted new provisions into the Public Order Act 1986[159]). Subject to certain differences set out in this section, those offences follow the same pattern as the racial hatred offences considered in section 5.1. The enactment of the 2006 Act was deeply controversial, the main bone of contention being whether it risked stifling free speech to an unacceptable degree and thereby compromising the underlying principles that free speech serves.[160] Such concerns led the new offences to be drawn more narrowly in three respects than the corresponding offences concerning racial hatred:

- The words, conduct, etc, must be 'threatening'.[161]

- The stirring up of religious hatred must be intended.[162]

- Nothing in the relevant part of the Act is to be 'read or given effect in a way which prohibits or restricts discussion, criticism or expressions of antipathy, dislike, ridicule, insult or abuse of particular religions or the beliefs or practices of their adherents'.[163]

---

[156] Criminal Justice and Immigration Act 2008, s 79(1).

[157] *R v Lemon* [1979] QB 10, 24, CA; see also *R v Lemon* [1979] AC 617, HL.

[158] See generally House of Lords Religious Offences Committee, *First Report* (HL 95 2002–03).

[159] Public Order Act 1986, ss 29A and 29B–F.

[160] See Hare, 'Crosses, Crescents and Sacred Cows: Criminalising Incitement to Religious Hatred' [2006] PL 521.

[161] Rather than 'threatening, abusive or insulting' as in relation to racial hatred.

[162] Whereas it is sufficient if racial hatred is likely to be stirred up, whether or not intended.

[163] Public Order Act 1986, s 29J.

It seems highly likely that, drawn in these ways, the offences would pass muster before the ECtHR as consistent with Art 10, bearing in mind that the Court had been willing to uphold the less nuanced law of blasphemy against a free speech challenge.[164] The 1986 Act (as amended) also criminalises the stirring up of hatred on the ground of sexual orientation,[165] using the same scheme as that which applies to religious hatred.

> **Q** Is it justifiable that hate speech is circumscribed to a lesser degree in relation to religion and sexual orientation than in relation to race?

5.3 Obscenity and indecency

5.3.1 General considerations

The right to free speech under Art 10 encompasses the right to receive, as well as to disseminate, information. Does this mean that a given person has, or should have, the right to access material that some might regard as obscene or indecent? We have seen that the ECtHR has, in practice, developed a hierarchy of forms of speech. If political speech is at the apex, pornography and the like are near the bottom. This does not mean that such forms of expression are unprotected— even hardcore pornography has been held to constitute 'expression'[166]—but it does mean that it will be easier for states to justify restrictions on the grounds specified in Art 10(2).

One of those grounds concerns the protection of the 'rights of others'. This undoubtedly permits the suppression of material the production or consumption of which causes involuntary harm. The most obvious example is images of children undergoing sexual abuse. The taking of a photograph may not substantially enhance the harm caused by the abuse itself, but abuse often occurs in order that photos can be taken; the circulation of such images amongst paedophiles stimulates demand for more, thus perpetuating cycles of abuse. No legitimate free speech objection can therefore be raised against legislation that criminalises the taking, distribution, and possession of indecent or pornographic images of children.[167]

> **Q** It is also a criminal offence to make or distribute indecent 'pseudo-photographs' of children (eg images not of children actually undergoing abuse, but which have been digitally manipulated to convey that impression).[168] How might this restriction upon free speech be justified?

---

[164] *Gay News Ltd and Lemon v United Kingdom* (1983) 5 EHRR 123; *Wingrove v United Kingdom* (1997) 24 EHRR 1.

[165] Public Order Act 1986, ss 29AB–F.   [166] *Hoare v UK* [1997] EHRLR 678.

[167] Protection of Children Act 1978, s 1; Coroners and Justice Act 2009, s 62.

[168] Protection of Children Act 1978, s 1.

Beyond such situations, however, the suppression of obscene and indecent material becomes harder to reconcile with free speech considerations. If the production of the material does not harm those who appear in it,[169] what, if anything, can justify its suppression? Three possibilities arise.

The first is that a *wider conception of harm* may be appropriate. For example, many feminists argue for the prohibition of pornography depicting women. They contend that both those appearing in such photographs and women generally are harmed by being demeaned, rendering them more liable to discrimination and even abusive behaviour by men induced by pornography to view women as sex objects.

Second, the 'rights of others' might be said to extend to a right not to be offended by certain forms of material. While, in some contexts, such as political speech, the importance of the matter means that relatively little weight should be attached to any 'right' not to be offended, the position is arguably different in relation to material that has less intrinsic value.

Third, *considerations of morality* may be thought to demand that certain forms of obscene and indecent material should be unavailable (or at least regulated). However, this raises questions about the autonomy of the individual: if a given person's consumption of the material is not going to harm others, why should she not be permitted to run the risk of harming herself? This point notwithstanding, Art 10(2) permits free speech to be limited when necessary in the interests of public morality. It is that limitation upon the scope of the right of freedom of expression that forms the justification for the English law of obscenity and indecency, two aspects of which are considered in the following section.

5.3.2 Particular offences

It is an offence to publish (whether or not for gain), or to have for publication for gain, an obscene article[170] unless publication 'is justified as being for the public good on the ground that it is in the interests of science, literature, art or learning, or of other objects of general concern'.[171] An obscene article is any form of reading or other visual matter or sound recording the effect of which is, if taken as a whole, such as to tend to deprave and corrupt persons who are likely, having regard to all relevant circumstances, to come into contact with it.[172]

The paternalistic objective of this law is to protect people from harming themselves through the consumption of obscene material. However, liability is likely to be avoided if adequate steps are taken to ensure that the material does not come into contact with those most likely to be adversely affected by it. For example, if a particular item were likely to deprave or corrupt children, but not adults, publication in places unlikely to be accessed by children would be lawful. However, the extent to which this caveat renders this offence acceptable in free speech terms also depends on how susceptible to depravation and corruption courts think those *likely* to encounter

---

[169] Or those subjected to similar treatment in the future thanks to the demand created by the earlier material.

[170] Obscene Publications Act 1959, s 2(1).   [171] Obscene Publications Act 1959, s 4(1).

[172] Obscene Publications Act 1959, s 1(1) and (2).

the material are.[173] The ECtHR has held that states have a wide margin of appreciation in deciding what is necessary to protect public morality,[174] and it is therefore unlikely that the enforcement of the law in this area would fall foul of Art 10.

Whereas obscenity law is about preventing people from (supposedly) harming themselves, indecency law is about preventing people from being offended. The line between that which is indecent and that which is obscene is an uncertain one, but indecent material is regarded as *less* offensive. It has been suggested—in quaint language which reflects the vintage of the case in which it was used—that '[f]or a male bather to enter the water nude in the presence of ladies would be indecent', but that directing 'the attention of a lady to a certain member of his body' would be obscene.[175]

It is an offence at common law to outrage public decency (or to conspire to do so). However, in contrast with the obscenity offence considered earlier, no 'public good' defence applies. The offence of outraging public decency was committed in *R v Gibson*[176] by an artist who assembled, and a gallery owner who exhibited, earrings made from aborted human foetuses. The compatibility of this offence with Art 10 of the ECHR is questionable. It is true that that provision permits the limitation of free speech on grounds that include public morality—but as Lord Lane CJ put it in *Gibson*, the offence can be committed 'whether or not public morals are involved'.[177] Taking that fact together with the ECtHR's view that Art 10 includes the right to 'offend, shock or disturb',[178] Feldman concludes that 'the offence needs to be significantly refined if it is to survive challenge [on Art 10 grounds]'.[179] However, it is important to note that 'outrage' is, as Lord Simon pointed out, 'a strong word', such that to outrage public decency involves going 'considerably beyond offending the susceptibilities of, or even shocking, reasonable people'.[180]

6. Privacy

6.1 Introduction

Article 8 of the ECHR says that '[e]veryone has the right to respect for his private and family life, his home and his correspondence'.[181] The range of things protected by Art 8 is relatively wide: the ECtHR has found Art 8 to have been breached by, among other things, the criminalisation of gay sex,[182] medical treatment carried out against a person's will,[183] and the long-term confiscation of the passport of a person with family and business ties in several countries.[184] Important though these aspects of privacy

---

[173] eg in *DPP v Whyte* [1972] AC 849, sexually explicit material sold in an adult bookshop was held to be capable of depraving and corrupting its *adult* clientele.

[174] *Handyside v UK* (1979–80) 1 EHRR 737.

[175] *McGowan v Langmuir* 1931 JC 10, 13, *per* Lord Sands.   [176] [1990] 2 QB 619.

[177] *R v Gibson*, 623.   [178] *Handyside*, 754.

[179] Feldman, *Civil Liberties and Human Rights in England and Wales* (Oxford 2002), p 935.

[180] *Knuller (Publishing, Printing and Promotions Ltd) v DPP* [1973] AC 435, 495.

[181] The term 'right to privacy' will be used for concision.

[182] *Dudgeon v UK* (1982) 4 EHRR 149.   [183] *Storck v Germany* (2006) 43 EHRR 6.

[184] *İletmiş v Turkey* (Application 29871/96, judgment 6 December 2005).

are they do not engage freedom of speech. Our focus is therefore a more particular one: on what might be called the right to *informational privacy*—that is, the individual's right to control the dissemination of information about herself. The desire to do so is instinctive, and is not confined to those with especially interesting or sordid lives—hence the possibility of allowing everyone but 'friends' to view only limited personal information on social networking websites. It is, for example, one thing for a nurse, doctor, or close relative to see a hospital patient in a vulnerable condition in his bed, but he might not want his photograph in the national newspapers.[185] Similarly, a person might want her counsellor, but not her colleagues, to know that she suffered abuse as a child. The protection of informational privacy serves to uphold the fundamental values of human dignity and autonomy: people are able to live more dignified and fulfilled lives if they need not worry about all and sundry finding out about those parts of their lives that they would rather keep private.

Legislation upholds specific aspects of informational privacy. The Data Protection Act 1998 imposes restrictions on the processing of certain personal information that is stored electronically or in a filing system.[186] Meanwhile s 3 of the Investigatory Powers Act 2016 makes it a criminal offence, save in limited circumstances, intentionally to intercept postal communications or telecommunications. To what extent does English law recognise and protect informational privacy outside these specific contexts? As we will see, this area of the law has developed rapidly in recent years under the influence of the ECHR. Both Arts 8 and 10 are qualified rights, and both can be limited (when necessary in a democratic society) 'for the protection of the rights of others'.[187] Thus one person's free speech can be restricted in the interests of another's privacy, and vice versa. When the HRA was being enacted, there was considerable concern—principally on the part of the media—that the courts would use Art 8 to fashion extensive new privacy laws that would drastically curtail freedom of expression. As we examine the current law, we need to ask whether an acceptable balance has been struck between the protection of privacy and of free speech.

6.2 **Background: breach of confidence**

For a very long time, it was said, with some justification, that the law of privacy formed no part of English law. The case that could be said to prove that point was *Kaye*,[188] in which journalists entered the hospital room in which a well-known actor was recovering from brain surgery, took photographs, and tried to interview him. The Court of Appeal held that there was no legal basis on which publication of the photographs could be restrained, lamenting 'the failure of both the common law of England and statute to protect in an effective way the personal privacy of individual citizens'.[189] Few people would argue that this struck an appropriate balance between free speech and privacy.

---

[185] Precisely this happened in *Kaye v Robertson* [1991] FSR 62.
[186] As well as giving people certain rights to access information concerning themselves.
[187] Articles 8(2) and 10(2).   [188] *Kaye v Robertson* [1991] FSR 62.
[189] *Kaye*, 70, *per* Bingham LJ.

There were, though, some circumstances in which the common law would provide a remedy in respect of the misuse of private information. Under the doctrine of breach of confidence, the unauthorised disclosure of information was unlawful if two conditions were met.[190] First, the information had to 'have the necessary quality of confidence about it',[191] meaning that it should not be widely available in the public domain.[192] Second, the information had to have been communicated 'on the basis that it is confidential'—the reason for judicial intervention being that it is 'unconscionable' for someone to reveal information obtained on such a basis.[193]

At one time, it was thought that this required a pre-existing relationship between the parties within which confidentiality was a given, or some form of agreement between the parties that the information would not be revealed. For example, in *Kaye*, the information contained in the photograph could not be said to be confidential (on a traditional understanding of the doctrine[194]) because there was no agreement to that effect between the claimant and the photographer. This seriously limited the capacity of breach of confidence to protect privacy: it was available when someone went back on an agreement to keep a secret, but could not touch situations in which the information was obtained in an underhand or otherwise unauthorised manner. However, in the 1980s and 1990s, the courts developed a more liberal approach in this regard. In the *Spycatcher* case, Lord Goff said that information would be protected by the law of confidence when acquired by a person who 'has notice, or is held to have agreed, that the information is confidential'.[195] This meant that a duty of confidentiality could be imposed upon a passer-by who picked up 'an obviously confidential document . . . wafted by an electric fan out of a window into a crowded street'[196] or upon an intruder who took photos of a celebrity wedding at which it had been made crystal clear that no one but official photographers were to take photos.[197] This development laid the foundation for the emergence, alongside breach of confidence, of a new tort of 'misuse of private information'[198] or 'invasion of privacy'.[199]

6.3 **Misuse of private information**

The foundation of that new tort is *Campbell v Mirror Group Newspapers Ltd*,[200] in which the defendant newspaper had published an article concerning the treatment

---

[190] *Coco v AN Clark (Engineers) Ltd* [1969] RPC 41, 47.

[191] *Saltman Engineering Co Ltd v Campbell Engineering Co Ltd* (1948) 65 RPC 203, 215, *per* Lord Greene MR.

[192] If, however, the information in question were only available to a limited subset of the public and additional harm would result to the claimant from further disclosure, such further disclosure might constitute a breach of confidence: *Attorney-General v Observer Ltd* [1990] 1 AC 109, 260, *per* Lord Keith.

[193] *Stephens v Avery* [1988] Ch 449, 456, *per* Sir Nicolas Browne-Wilkinson VC.

[194] Although that traditional understanding was arguably outdated by the time *Kaye* was decided: see Fenwick and Phillipson, 'Confidence and Privacy: A Re-Examination' [1996] CLJ 447, 453–5.

[195] *Attorney-General v Observer Ltd*, 281.   [196] *Attorney-General v Observer Ltd*, 281.

[197] *Douglas v Hello! Ltd (No 3)* [2005] EWCA Civ 595, [2006] QB 125.

[198] *Vidal-Hall v Google Inc* [2015] EWCA Civ 311, [2015] 3 WLR 409.

[199] *PJS v News Group Newspapers Ltd* [2016] UKSC 26, [2016] 2 WLR 1253.

[200] [2004] UKHL 22, [2004] 2 AC 457. For more detailed discussion, see Moreham, 'Privacy and the Common Law: A Doctrinal and Theoretical Analysis' (2005) 121 LQR 628.

that model Naomi Campbell was receiving for drug addiction, together with a photograph of her emerging from a meeting of Narcotics Anonymous. Five pieces of information were thereby conveyed:

(i)   The fact that Campbell was a drug addict.

(ii) The fact that she was receiving treatment for her addiction.

(iii) The fact that the treatment that she was receiving was provided by Narcotics Anonymous.

(iv) Details of the treatment.

(v)   The information contained in the photograph.

In holding that publication of items (iii)–(v) was unlawful, the House of Lords had to address several points that we consider in turn.

6.3.1 'Private' information

Although some of the information in *Campbell* could not be considered *confidential* under the *Spycatcher* test (after all, the photograph was taken in a public place), the House of Lords characterised all five pieces of information as *private*. Judicial opinion was divided in *Campbell* about the test that should be used to identify private information. However, the leading test is now whether the individual concerned has a 'reasonable expectation of privacy' in respect of the relevant matter.[201]

In some instances, the existence and reasonableness of such an expectation will be apparent from the sensitive nature of the information itself. However, as Hughes points out, *Campbell* does not call for a purely objective test based upon the nature of the information.[202] While one individual may be particularly sensitive about a given matter (eg what they look like naked), another may be more sanguine. It follows that individuals' expectations as to privacy—and others' capacity to perceive those expectations—are reflected in how individuals *behave*. (Compare the person who sunbathes naked in a secluded private garden with one who does so on a publicly accessible nudist beach.) Among other things, this means that the fact that someone has revealed information about one aspect of her private life does not mean that the rest of it is fair game as well.[203]

It might be thought that at some point information becomes so widely available that it can no longer be regarded as private. Such an argument was advanced in *PJS* by a newspaper that sought to overturn an interim injunction preventing it from publishing allegations about a celebrity's sex life.[204] However, Lord Neuberger (with whom Baroness Hale, Lord Mance, and Lord Reed agreed) endorsed the view that the right to respect for private life serves both to uphold the secrecy, or confidentiality, of private information and to guard against unwanted intrusion.[205] It followed that even though many people, including via the Internet, knew at least the gist of the story,

---

[201] See, eg *Re JR38* [2015] UKSC 42, [2015] 3 WLR 155.

[202] 'A Behavioural Understanding of Privacy and Its Implications for Privacy Law' (2012) 75 MLR 806.

[203] *McKennitt v Ash* [2006] EWCA Civ 1714, [2008] QB 73, [53]–[55].

[204] *PJS v News Group Newspapers Ltd* [2016] UKSC 26, [2016] 2 WLR 1253.

[205] See further *Goodwin v News Group Newspapers Ltd* [2011] EWHC 1437 (QB), [2011] EMLR 27.

maintaining the injunction could still serve a purpose with respect to 'intrusion'. As Eady J had put it in an earlier case: '[W]all-to-wall excoriation in national newspapers . . . is likely to be significantly more intrusive and distressing for those concerned than the availability of information on the Internet'.[206]

6.3.2 Public interest

Article 8 being a qualified right, the publication of private information may be lawful if necessary to uphold other recognised rights and interests—including free speech. It is therefore unsurprising that domestic law will not protect the privacy of information when some conflicting and weightier legitimate interest points towards publication. Precisely this situation arose in *Campbell*. The Law Lords agreed that although all five pieces of information counted as private, there was a public interest justifying publication of items (i) and (ii) because the claimant had previously denied using illegal drugs. Two of the judges went further, arguing that a margin of freedom should be extended to the media in recognition of the interest in free speech, and that the decision to publish the additional information in order to add colour to the story did not exceed that margin.[207] That point aside, the general principle, according to Lord Nicholls, was that 'where a public figure chooses to present a false image and make untrue pronouncements about his or her life, the press will normally be entitled to put the record straight'.[208]

In some circumstances, the public interest is obvious. For example, if the Minister responsible for climate change matters makes a speech criticising non-essential long-haul air travel, there will be a public interest in revealing that she has booked a long weekend in Rio. Exposing her as a hypocrite on a matter directly relevant to her ministerial role is something that members of the electorate might legitimately wish to take into account in formulating an opinion about the government. But is the same true of a premiership footballer who was denied an injunction restraining publication of a story detailing his extramarital affairs?[209] Or a children's television presenter who could not prevent publication of a story about his use of a brothel?[210] In such cases, the courts have relied on, among other things, the 'public interest' in publication. But this arguably confuses those things that the public *is interested in* with situations in which there is a *legitimate* public interest in publication.[211] As the ECtHR has put it: '[A]rticles aimed solely at satisfying the curiosity of a particular readership regarding the details of a person's private life, however well known that person might be, cannot be deemed to contribute to any debate of general interest to society'.[212]

A more subtle approach, which appears to be more in line with that of the ECtHR,[213] was adopted in *Mosley v News Group Newspapers Ltd*.[214] It was held that there was no public interest in a newspaper publishing images showing the president

---

[206] *CTB v News Group Newspapers Ltd* [2011] EWHC 1326, [24].

[207] *Campbell*, [28]–[29], *per* Lord Nicholls; [66], *per* Lord Hoffmann.   [208] *Campbell*, [24].

[209] *A v B plc* [2002] EWCA Civ 337, [2003] QB 195.

[210] *Theakston v MGN Ltd* [2002] EWHC 137, [2002] EMLR 22.

[211] See Phillipson, 'Judicial Reasoning in Breach of Confidence Cases under the Human Rights Act: Not Taking Privacy Seriously?' [2003] EHRLR (supplement) 54.

[212] *Couderc and Hachette Filipacchi Associés v France* Application 40454/07 [2015] ECHR 992, [100].

[213] eg *Von Hannover v Germany* (2005) 40 EHRR 1; *Couderc*.

[214] [2008] EWHC 1777 (QB), [2008] EMLR 20.

of the governing body of Formula 1 motor racing engaging in sadomasochistic sexual acts with prostitutes. None of the justifications for limiting privacy set down in Art 8(2) applied: '[T]itillation for its own sake' would not suffice.[215] Taken to its logical conclusion, the judge noted, this approach would have 'a profound effect on the tabloid and celebrity culture to which we have become accustomed in recent years'.[216] Mosley subsequently made an application to the ECtHR, arguing that damages were not an adequate remedy, and that UK law breached Art 8 because it did not require the newspaper to give advance warning of publication in order to allow him, if he wished, to seek an interim injunction restraining publication.[217] That argument was dismissed by the Court. It noted the crucial role of the media in a free society, that it would be necessary for any advance notification requirement to contain a 'public interest' exception, and that uncertainties concerning the extent of such an exception would probably have a chilling effect on free speech. However, the fact that there is no advance notification requirement does not detract from the fact that when an individual *does* learn of a forthcoming publication, it may be possible to obtain an injunction to restrain the breach of privacy that publication would occasion.[218] In such cases, the court must balance Arts 8 and 10; interim relief may be granted only if the court is satisfied that the claimant is likely to succeed at trial.[219]

> **Q** It might be argued that requiring courts to draw the line between those things in which the public is *really* interested and those in which they are *legitimately entitled* to be interested concedes too much power to judges to set the parameters within which media freedom exists. Do you agree? How would you draw the line?

6.3.3 Public places and photographs

Pictures—said to be 'worth a thousand words'—are capable of conveying more information, and with greater impact, than verbal descriptions. As such, photographs may constitute a graver invasion of privacy that is correspondingly harder to justify. It has even been suggested that every photograph is unique such that the publication of an unauthorised photograph might constitute a breach of privacy even if a substantially similar authorised version is already in the public domain.[220] Particular difficulties arise in relation to photographs taken in public places. It is initially hard to see how anyone can have a reasonable expectation of privacy if the event in question occurred in public, but in *Campbell*, the majority concluded that publishing photos of the claimant standing on the street outside the rehab centre was unlawful because it had increased the distress[221] or harm suffered by Campbell.[222] Baroness Hale sought to distinguish between a photo of Campbell 'pop[ping] out . . . for a bottle of milk'

---

[215] *Mosley*, [132].   [216] *Mosley*, [131].   [217] *Mosley v United Kingdom* (2011) 53 EHRR 30.
[218] See, eg *Rocknroll v News Group Newspapers Ltd* [2013] EWHC 24 (Ch).   [219] HRA, s 12(3).
[220] *Douglas v Hello! Ltd (No 3)*, [122], *per* Lord Hoffmann.
[221] *Campbell*, [124], *per* Lord Hope.   [222] *Campbell*, [157], *per* Baroness Hale.

(publication of which would not damage her private life) and one of her coming out of a rehab centre.[223]

That reasoning does not provide a particularly clear basis on which to judge when the publication of photos taken in public places will entail a breach of privacy. The ECtHR decision in *Peck v UK*[224] is arguably more helpful in that regard. Late one night in a town centre, the applicant attempted to commit suicide using a kitchen knife. Images of the immediate aftermath were recorded by CCTV cameras operated by the local authority. Those images were disclosed to the media, and shown in newspapers and on television. Notwithstanding that these events had taken place in public, the ECtHR found that the disclosure constituted a breach of Art 8. It did so because 'the relevant moment was viewed to an extent which far exceeded any exposure to a passer-by or to security observation . . . and to a degree surpassing that which the applicant could possibly have foreseen'.[225] This provides a sensible and intelligible basis for dealing with situations that occur in public places (as well as those in which the information in question is already known to a limited class of people), the key question being whether the disclosure under challenge resulted in exposure going beyond that which the claimant could reasonably have expected.[226] *Peck* can be contrasted with the Supreme Court's decision in *Re JR38*, in which it was held that publishing CCTV images of someone involved in public disorder, so as to aid their apprehension, involved no breach of Art 8.[227] By a majority, it was held that no reasonable expectation of privacy had arisen: it was not reasonable to expect that privacy would be afforded in respect of images depicting criminal conduct. Read together, *Peck* and *JR38* demonstrate the objective nature of the 'reasonable expectation of privacy test', and its resulting capacity to take account of the value or legitimacy of the matter to which the information in question pertains.

What about someone who inevitably attracts the attention of the paparazzi? If the test is whether they have a reasonable expectation of privacy in public places, the answer is surely 'no': experience will, or ought, to have taught them that they will not be left alone. This issue arose in *Von Hannover*.[228] It concerned the repeated publication of photos of a celebrity (who, despite her membership of Monaco's royal family, performed no official functions on behalf of that state) going about her daily business (eg shopping and eating out). Ruling that the applicant's right to privacy had been breached, the Court placed weight on the fact that the media's conduct contravened her *legitimate* expectation that her privacy would be respected in relation to everyday aspects of her domestic life. This test appears to go further than *Campbell*[229] and *Peck* in that it permits aspects of a person's life to be characterised as private even if there is no *reasonable* expectation of privacy on account of long-standing press intrusion. Defining the range of things to which a legitimate expectation of privacy attaches is far from straightforward, but it is noteworthy that the ECtHR was influenced by the

---

[223] *Campbell*, [154].   [224] (2003) 36 EHRR 41.   [225] *Peck v UK*, [62].
[226] See further Moreham, 'Privacy in Public Places' [2006] CLJ 606.
[227] [2015] UKSC 42, [2015] 3 WLR 155.   [228] *Von Hannover v Germany* (2005) 40 EHRR 1.
[229] See, eg Baroness Hale's suggestion that it would be lawful to publish photos of Campbell popping out for a pint of milk: *Campbell*, [154].

fact that (in its view) no public interest justified publication of the pictures. Logically, whether a public interest in publication exists is only relevant if the information is private—yet, in *Von Hannover*, the lack of public interest in publishing the photos in question appeared to influence the Court's conclusion that the information was, in the first place, private. While defining privacy by reference to the absence of legitimate public interest conflates what have hitherto been thought of as distinct parts of the analysis, this pragmatic approach reflects the fact that the concept of privacy is very difficult to define in the abstract.

7. Official secrecy

7.1 Breach of confidence

There are inevitably certain things that, if said publicly, would compromise the national interest and in relation to which it is therefore desirable for free speech to be curtailed. The doctrine of breach of confidence is capable, in some respects, of performing this function. If, for example, someone acquires information in circumstances in which they know, or ought to know, that it relates to state secrets, disclosure would constitute a breach of confidence. It was to this branch of the law that the government resorted when, in the *Spycatcher* case, it wished to prevent a former MI5 officer from publishing memoirs alleging unlawful conduct on the part of other such officers. However, the House of Lords held that, in such cases, the Crown must be able to show that a remedy would serve the public interest, and that the book had become so widely available overseas that no such interest would be advanced by leaving in place injunctions that had been granted on an earlier occasion.[230] That episode formed an important part of the background to the enactment of the Official Secrets Act 1989.

7.2 Official Secrets Acts

The Official Secrets Acts distinguish between *spying* and *other disclosures* of sensitive information. The former is dealt with by s 1 of the 1911 Act, which says that a person commits a criminal offence if, for any purpose prejudicial to the safety or interests of the state, he does any of the following things:

- enters, passes over, approaches, inspects, or is in the neighbourhood of a prohibited place (eg a military or intelligence facility);
- prepares information (sketches, plans, etc) that might be, or is meant to be, useful to an enemy; or
- obtains or passes on information that might be, or is meant to be, useful to an enemy.

---

[230] *Attorney-General v Observer Ltd* [1990] 1 AC 109.

Section 1 is sufficiently broadly drafted to cover conduct that would not normally be classed as espionage. Thus, in *Chandler v DPP*,[231] the House of Lords upheld the convictions of anti-nuclear protestors who approached an airbase with the intention of holding a sit-in on the runway.

More extensive provision concerning the disclosure of information is made by the Official Secrets Act 1989. As Table 19.1 shows, ss 1–4 of the Act create criminal offences in respect of the disclosure of information concerning security and intelligence, defence, international relations, and crime and special investigation powers. The general structure of the offences is that a person to whom the Act applies commits an offence if two conditions are met:

- information of a relevant type is disclosed; and
- that disclosure causes, or is likely to cause, certain consequences.

As the table shows, there are limited defences—and no offence is committed under ss 1–4 if the disclosure is made with lawful authority, meaning in accordance with the person's official duty or pursuant to an official authorisation.[232] Section 5 creates a further offence concerning the passing on of information covered by ss 1–4 by people who receive such information in confidence or in breach of ss 1–4, but who are not otherwise covered by the Act.

Two points should be noted about the 1989 Act. First, as Table 19.1 shows,[233] the s 1 offence concerning security and intelligence matters is different from—and more draconian than—the other offences in several respects. Most obviously, current and former security and intelligence officers and those notified that they are subject to the same rules ('notified persons') can incur liability under s 1 whether or not the disclosure in question causes, or is likely to cause, damage. It is at least arguable that the criminalisation of non-damaging disclosures does not constitute a necessary limitation upon free speech and that such a restriction would therefore fail to survive scrutiny under Art 10. This is compounded by the fact that, in respect of security and intelligence officers and notified persons, s 1 applies not only to sensitive material, but to *all* material encountered while employed as such officers (or, in the case of notified persons, encountered in the course of their work while the notification is in force). Again, it is not clear that such an indiscriminate approach could be characterised as proportionate, as required by Art 10.

The second point—which applies to ss 1–4 generally, not only to s 1—is that it is not a defence to establish that the disclosure was in the public interest. This highly significant (and deliberate[234]) omission means that there is no room for weighing the positive and negative consequences of disclosure: once the prosecution establishes that disclosure had, or would be likely to have, a proscribed consequence, an even stronger public interest in favour of disclosure is irrelevant. The position is even starker in relation to security and intelligence officers and notified persons under s 1: disclosures

---

[231] [1964] AC 763.   [232] Official Secrets Act 1989, s 7.

[233] The table is intended to provide a general overview of the structure of the different offences, rather than an exhaustive account of them.

[234] The government did not wish to be defeated under the Act by public interest arguments as in *Spycatcher*.

Table 19.1 Official Secrets Act 1989, ss 1–4

Section	Who can be liable?	What sort of material is covered?	What are the proscribed consequences of disclosure upon which liability depends?	What defences are there?
1: Security and intelligence	Current/former security/ intelligence officers; anyone notified that he or she is subject to these rules	Anything concerning security/ intelligence possessed as security/ intelligence officer or obtained in course of work while notification in force	No consequences need be shown: all disclosures incur liability (unless defence applies)	Did not know and had no reason to believe material related to security/intelligence
	Current/former Crown servants and government contractors	Material concerning security/intelligence possessed by virtue of position	Damage or likely to cause damage to work of security/intelligence services	1. As above 2. Did not know/had no reason to believe damage would result or be likely to result
2: Defence	Current/former Crown servants and government contractors	Material possessed by virtue of position concerning defence (eg defence policy/ strategy; organisation/deployment/ readiness of armed forces)	Damages capability of armed forces; leads to loss of life or serious equipment damage; endangers interests of UK abroad; likely to have any of above effects	Did not know and had no reason to believe (i) material concerned defence, or (ii) disclosure would have proscribed consequence
3: International relations	Current/former Crown servants and government contractors	Material possessed by virtue of position that (i) concerns international relations, or (ii) is confidential material obtained from another state or international organisation	Endangers interests of UK abroad; seriously obstructs promotion/ protection of such interests; endangers safety of UK citizens abroad; likely to have any of above effects	Did not know and had no reason to believe (i) material covered by this section, or (ii) disclosure would have proscribed consequence
4: Crime and special investigation powers	Current/former Crown servants and government contractors	Material possessed by virtue of position the disclosure of which would have a proscribed consequence	Results in commission of offence; facilitates escape from legal custody; impedes prevention/detection of offences or apprehension/prosecution of suspects; likely to have any of above effects	Did not know and had no reason to believe disclosure would have any of first three proscribed consequences

that carry substantial benefits (eg bringing to light unlawful or improper conduct) will be unlawful even if they cause no harm at all. Again, this raises questions about whether the Act meets the requirements of the ECHR, which permits only necessary and proportionate restrictions upon free speech.

This matter was considered by the House of Lords in *R v Shayler*.[235] The defendant, a former security officer charged with disclosing information in breach of the 1989 Act, sought to argue that a public interest defence should be read into the Act pursuant to s 3 of the HRA. The Law Lords disagreed. They accepted that an absolute prohibition on disclosure would contravene Art 10, but held that the absence of a public interest defence did not render the prohibition absolute. That was because, as noted, disclosures that would otherwise constitute offences under ss 1–4 are permitted if made with lawful authority. Their Lordships held that it was in this context that the HRA bit: those responsible for deciding whether to authorise disclosure are bound by Art 10 to do so (in the interests of free speech) unless withholding permission is a necessary and proportionate way of protecting national security. And if it were to be felt that the responsible person had not struck that balance appropriately, their decision would be open to judicial review on Art 10 grounds. The existence of the mechanism for seeking authorisation—and the duty of those operating it to respect Art 10—meant that the absence of a public interest defence did not make the 1989 Act incompatible with the ECHR.

> **Q** Do you agree with the House of Lords that the absence of a public interest defence is unproblematic in Art 10 terms?

8. Conclusions

So diverse are the situations considered in this chapter—a diversity that reflects the range of circumstances in which free speech questions arise—that it would be futile to attempt to provide a summary. Two points, though, can be made by way of conclusion. Each relates, in different ways, to the subtlety of the right of free speech under the ECHR and, hence, of the developing body of English law in this area. First, the right of freedom of expression is not a monolithic concept: the question is not simply whether something constitutes 'speech' (and is thus protected) or not. Rather, the courts—European and domestic—have developed a hierarchy of forms of free speech: political speech sits at the apex, while such things as celebrity gossip languish at the bottom. This reflects the underlying reasons, considered at the beginning of the chapter, for according respect to free speech, and the key role played by freedom of expression in a democracy. Second, however, even in its most compelling forms, free speech is a far from absolute right. It is one capable of clashing with—and, in appropriate fact situations, being eclipsed by—a range of other rights and interests, including the right to a fair trial, and the protection of reputation, privacy, and national security. In such circumstances, difficult questions arise about how the balance

[235] [2002] UKHL 11, [2003] 1 AC 247.

should be struck between the conflicting rights and interests that are in play; and it is inevitable that this places the courts in a powerful position. But this is surely a price worth paying if it helps to ensure that the extent to which we all enjoy free speech—the lifeblood of democracy—is not wholly within the gift of those democratic institutions the members of which might paradoxically be served by unduly limiting it.

Expert commentary
What actions threaten free speech?
Jacob Rowbottom, Tutorial Fellow and CUF Lecturer in Law,
University College, Oxford

Most people accept that freedom of speech needs protecting in a democracy, but what does it need protecting from? Lots of things can make it harder for us to exercise free speech rights, but not all of these things raise free speech concerns. A traffic jam might stop a politician getting to a television studio in time for an important news interview. Nobody would say that such a chance occurrence amounts to censorship. However, we would probably think differently if we found out that a local authority closed a road deliberately to disrupt the politician's journey. What if a group of people drove slowly to deliberately delay the politician? What is it that makes us view some actions as censorship and others as part of life's give and take?

The earlier accounts of free speech and freedom of the press took a very narrow view of censorship. In the eighteenth century, William Blackstone wrote that freedom of the press 'consists in laying no previous restraint upon publications, and not in freedom from censure for criminal matter when published'. On this view, interference with expression came from 'prior restraints', such as an injunction or a requirement for publishers to be licensed, which stopped words from being spoken. The thinking was that criminal penalties imposed after the words were spoken did not interfere with speech rights. It is easy to see why this was too narrow and we have long since accepted that a criminal sanction imposed after publication will engage rights to expression.

The issue becomes more complex when government does not prohibit speech, but uses its resources in a way that makes it harder for some to communicate. For example, imagine the government opposes the views expressed by a controversial speaker, but instead of passing a law, it decides that no books written by that person can be stocked in a publicly owned library. Is this an act of censorship? There is no right to demand that a library stocks a particular book. The person remains free to speak without any legal repercussions. Nonetheless the courts have accepted that restrictions on access to communicative forums that are discriminatory, arbitrary, or unreasonable engage freedom of expression.[236] Along these lines, if the government or a public body imposes a no-platform policy for certain speakers at universities, then that too would engage freedom of expression. However, finding that something *interferes* with expression is not the same as saying the right is *violated*. Some interferences can be justified under Art 10(2) of the ECHR and the less severe the interference the more likely it is to be proportionate.

The issue becomes more complex when government relies on more subtle methods to deal with the speech it opposes. Consider what happened when *The Guardian* published

---

[236] *R (ProLife Alliance) v BBC* [2003] UKHL 23, [2004] 1 AC 185. For discussion of a similar issue in administrative law, see *R v London Borough of Ealing, ex p Times Newspapers* [1987] IRLR 129.

information leaked by Edward Snowden, the former Central Intelligence Agency employee who in 2013 leaked classified information from the US National Security Agency. The newspaper was not taken to court, but received considerable informal pressure to hand the information to the government or destroy it. More generally, the government may give the cold shoulder to critical journalists, while cultivating and giving greater access to more sympathetic media titles. Where such methods are used, it is harder to claim an infringement of speech rights, as there is no official decision to challenge and the speaker remains legally free to say what they want. However, even if no person's right is restricted, many people feel uncomfortable with attempts by government to manage public debate. Such actions by government can create a climate that inhibits the exercise of expression rights.

So far we have been thinking about government actions, but can private persons or organisations interfere with speech rights? Complaints about 'private censorship' would suggest so, but the question is difficult. Imagine that a newspaper editor tells a reporter that he will not publish an investigation revealing a financial scandal, because it might upset a lucrative advertising deal. Should we condemn this as an act of private censorship? Some people dismiss such complaints, on the grounds that a private person is not under a duty to facilitate the speech of others. If I choose not to invite someone to dinner because I do not like that person's political views, that is my prerogative as host. So as a private person, isn't the newspaper editor also free to choose to publish whatever he or she thinks fit? Moreover, the decision not to publish the story is an exercise of the editor's expression right. On this view, the free speech principle protects people only from interferences by government.

Such a dismissal of private censorship seems too easy and overlooks some important differences. A newspaper operates in a professional context where there are certain expectations about how editorial decisions should be made, and the newspaper editor is seen to wield considerable power. The difficult question lies in identifying when a private actor has a responsibility to respect the speech rights of others. Similar questions would arise if a search engine or social network decided to promote or bury certain political viewpoints. Does the power of the search engine make it a threat to free speech? People have different views on this question, but it is becoming increasingly important as communications change.

The question of private censorship becomes more complicated still if we turn our attention to private actors that do not wield considerable power. We often hear about people becoming the targets of abuse on social media simply for voicing an opinion that others disapprove of. To some, this is a type of private censorship enforced by a mob of social media users. At the same time, I cannot demand that people like what I say and people are free to criticise my views. Whether we think of such actions as private censorship will partly depend on the level and type of abuse directed towards the speaker. Even if we cannot pinpoint a specific act that amounts to censorship, the cumulative effect can create a hostile environment where people are afraid to speak and feel unduly inhibited.

Article 10 provides limited protection against some forms of private censorship. The European Court of Human Rights has ruled that the state should take steps to protect speakers from violent reactions,[237] to protect protestors from counter-demonstrations,[238] to prevent employers unfairly punishing employees for their expressive activities,[239] and to allow speakers access to privately owned space where a denial of access would destroy the essence of the right.[240] However, these obligations are not open-ended and tend to arise only in extreme cases.

---

[237] *Gundem v Turkey* (2001) 31 EHRR 49.   [238] *Ollinger v Austria* (2008) 46 EHRR 38.
[239] *Sanchez v Spain* (2012) 54 EHRR 24.   [240] *Appleby v United Kingdom* (2003) 37 EHRR 38, [40].

The court-enforced right to free speech takes us only so far. There are other things that can be done to protect and promote speech rights. Provisions in discrimination law and employment law, for example, can limit the scope for employers to punish employees for their views. Certain media regulations can curb excesses of media power and promote the dissemination of diverse views. Such policies, however, need to be approached with care and can generate controversy, especially where obligations are imposed on private actors in relation to their communicative activities.

The understanding of what actions interfere with free speech has evolved since Blackstone's day. The traditional approach tends to view the state as the main threat to expression rights. That approach has its benefits, in making it easier to formulate free speech as a legal right. The problem is that if we focus only on government interference, we overlook limits on speech rights that can come from concentrations of private power. That approach is more realistic, but opens up a multitude of difficult questions. We have only scratched the surface of this topic, but we have seen that even a seemingly simple question—'What actions interfere with speech?'—provokes intense debate and disagreement.

Further reading

BARENDT, *Freedom of Speech* (Oxford 2005)
  A leading book on the idea and protection of free speech.

HARE, 'Crosses, Crescents and Sacred Cows: Criminalising Incitement to Religious Hatred' [2006] PL 521
  Examines arguments for and against the criminalisation of incitement to religious hatred.

HUGHES, 'A Behavioural Understanding of Privacy and Its Implications for Privacy Law' (2012) 75 MLR 806
  Addresses the nature of privacy by reference to social interaction theory and considers the implications that such an understanding of privacy might have for judicial reasoning.

PHILLIPSON, 'Press Freedom, the Public Interest and Privacy', in Kenyon, *Comparative Defamation and Privacy Law* (Cambridge 2016)
  An examination of how the balance is struck media freedom and privacy.

ROWBOTTOM, 'To Rant, Vent and Converse: Protecting Low Level Digital Speech' [2012] CLJ 355
  Considers whether 'low level', casual digital communications—in contrast to 'high value' speech— is afforded adequate protection.

20

Freedom of Assembly

1. Introduction   859
2. Domestic law   864
3. Prohibition of certain types of behaviour   865
4. Statutory powers to regulate protests   870
5. Common law powers to regulate protests   877
6. Conclusions   887
Expert commentary   888
Further reading   890

1. Introduction

1.1 Why freedom of assembly matters

We saw in Chapter 19 that, for a number of reasons, freedom of expression is important. However, having the *right* to say what you want may amount to little in practice if you lack the *opportunity* to do so effectively. Today, technology makes it easier than ever to communicate. Someone with a cause to promote or a view to express can do so straightforwardly by setting up a website or using social media. And the Internet does not just facilitate one-way communication. It also provides a way for like-minded individuals to organise and coordinate their efforts so as to maximise the impact of their message, whatever that might be. Nevertheless, physical forms of protest—marches through cities, gatherings in public places, and so on—remain a popular and effective mechanism by which people make their views known. Indeed the right to protest has been described as 'a fundamental right in a democratic society and, like the right to freedom of expression, is one of the foundations of such a society'.[1]

The United Kingdom in recent years has witnessed several high-profile protests. In 2003, close to a million people in London (and hundreds of thousands more in towns

---

[1] *Rassemblement Jurassien et Unite Jurassienne v Switzerland* Application 8191/78 (1979) 17 DR 93, [3].

and cities across the country) protested against the impending war in Iraq. Six years later, a major anti-globalisation protest took place in London during the G20 meeting of world leaders, the policing of which proved hugely controversial. More recently, there were demonstrations against the 2010–15 coalition government's austerity policies. Such protests can be a highly effective means by which to draw attention to issues, to shape public discourse, and to influence the political process.

The right to *freedom of assembly* is thus intimately connected with the right to *freedom of expression*. By facilitating effective forms of public protest, the former right provides a practical means by which the latter right can be exercised.[2] People might 'assemble' for all sorts of reasons, including the purely social, but it is in relation to protest that the right to freedom of assembly assumes constitutional importance. It is with that aspect of freedom of assembly that we are concerned in this chapter.

1.2 Striking a balance

We know from Chapters 18 and 19 that, in many matters concerning human rights, a balance falls to be struck between the rights of individuals and general public interest concerns. The interests of those who wish to sit, stand, shout, or wave banners in, or march through, towns and cities must be weighed against the interests of those who do not wish their daily lives to be disrupted by such conduct. As Williams noted in his seminal book on public order, the law in this area is a 'compromise' that 'seeks to balance the competing demands of freedom of speech and assembly on the one hand and the preservation of the Queen's Peace on the other'.[3] Where the balance lies depends heavily on the context.

Consider, for instance, the contrasting examples give in Figure 20.1. These pairs of examples are not intended to reflect our view of where the line between acceptable

A protest involving thousands of people that takes place in a park situated in a major city	A protest involving thousands of people that takes place in the commercial heart of a major city
A protest that involves large numbers of people marching along a major thoroughfare	A protest that involves large numbers of people sitting on a major road
A protest in which crowds of people wave placards and chant	A protest in which crowds of people shout intimidatingly at passers-by and throw eggs at them
A protest against a (hypothetical) proposed liberalisation of abortion law that takes place outside the Houses of Parliament	A protest against a (hypothetical) proposed liberalisation of abortion law that takes place outside an abortion clinic

Figure 20.1 Different types of protest

---

[2] *Kuznetsov v Russia* Application 10877/04 [2008] ECHR 1170, [23].
[3] *Keeping the Peace* (London 1967), p 9.

and unacceptable protest lies. But they highlight that a line must be drawn somewhere. What is considered to be an acceptable balance between the various competing interests in play is likely to vary depending on the circumstances.

What amounts to the 'right' balance between the competing interests that arise in this context is, in one sense, a largely subjective and political question. Some people's ideological position would lead them to the view that the commission of property damage would be a wholly legitimate form of protest if it were to serve some greater good. For example, in 2007, environmental activists broke in and caused £30,000 of damage to a power station, but were acquitted at their subsequent criminal trial, having convinced the jury that they had a 'lawful excuse' for the action because it was intended to draw attention to and ultimately to prevent climate change.[4]

However, the question of whether English law strikes the 'right' balance between the conflicting interests is a legal, as well as a subjective, one. Article 11 of the European Convention on Human Rights (ECHR) sets out the right of freedom of assembly. Article 11 therefore provides a benchmark against which to measure English law—as well as, in the light of the Human Rights Act 1998 (HRA), a strong influence upon its interpretation, application, and development. The ECHR will therefore be our reference point throughout this chapter as we explore the way in which English law balances the rights of protestors against the interests of other individuals and groups, and of society generally.

1.3 **Article 11**

The relevant part of ECHR, Art 11(1) provides that '[e]veryone has the right to freedom of peaceful assembly', while Art 11(2) spells out the extent of the right in greater detail by indicating how freedom of assembly may legitimately be restricted:

> No restrictions shall be placed on the exercise of these rights other than such as are prescribed by law and are necessary in a democratic society in the interests of national security or public safety, for the prevention of disorder or crime, for the protection of health or morals or for the protection of the rights and freedoms of others. This Article shall not prevent the imposition of lawful restrictions on the exercise of these rights by members of the armed forces, of the police or of the administration of the State.

Conduct will fall within the protective effect of Art 11 only if two conditions are met. The conduct must, in the first place, constitute 'peaceful assembly'. This has been held to cover 'both private meetings and meetings on public thoroughfares, as well as static meetings and public processions'.[5] Article 11 does not, however, offer any protection to those who wish to engage in violent behaviour. Second, even peaceful assemblies will be unprotected by Art 11 to the extent that it is 'necessary in a democratic society' to restrict such assemblies for any of the purposes set out in Art 11(2). The thrust of Art 11, therefore, is that *peaceful assembly must be permitted except, and only to the extent, that its restriction is necessary.*

---

[4] 'Kingsnorth trial: coal protesters cleared of criminal damage to chimney', *The Guardian*, 10 September 2008.
[5] *Kuznetsov*, [35].

The right to protest[6] is then a qualified right, meaning that it must yield in the face of more compelling legitimate interests. However, the relevant clash of rights and interests might not be merely two-dimensional (eg between those who want to protest and those who do not wish to suffer the resulting disruption to everyday life) but multidimensional. For instance, in a given situation, we might find that the interests of some or all of the following are at stake:

- the protestors themselves;
- counter-protestors (who wish publicly to express their disagreement with the position advocated by the 'original' protestors);
- those living and working nearby (whose lives might be disrupted by the protests);
- wider society (bearing in mind, for example, the demands placed on the public purse by policing protests and the economic loss that might be caused by the disruption occasioned by protests).

Q Should all of these interests be regarded as having equal value? For example, should the right of counter-protestors who wish to disrupt a demonstration be treated on an equal basis with the rights of the principal demonstrators? Should the inconvenience or offence that would be occasioned by a protest to members of the community be treated as factors capable of justifying restrictions upon or even the prohibition of a protest?

Situations involving different groups of protestors holding opposing views raise particularly acute questions. And such circumstances are hardly uncommon. Indeed, it is almost inevitable that protestors' views will not be met with universal acclaim: if everyone were in agreement, there would be no obvious need to protest. Confrontation between those holding differing opinions is therefore a matter with which the law must inevitably grapple. Several principles can be extracted from the courts' decisions in this area.

First, *it is unacceptable for the state to stand by and refuse to take any steps to safeguard legitimate protestors' interests against the unreasonable, threatening, or violent behaviour of others.* The European Court of Human Rights (ECtHR) has held that Art 11 imposes not only a negative obligation on states *not to prohibit protests,*[7] but also a positive obligation *to facilitate peaceful protest. Plattform 'Ärzte für das Leben' v Austria*[8] concerned an open-air religious ceremony being held by anti-abortion protestors that was interrupted by 500 counter-demonstrates who used loudspeakers and threw eggs. The anti-abortionists complained that the authorities had taken insufficient steps to prevent disruption by the pro-abortion counter-demonstrators.

---

[6] The ECHR does not explicitly confer a right to protest; rather, this right is implicit in Art 11 read with Art 10. However, we use the term 'right to protest' in this chapter as convenient shorthand. See further Mead, 'The Right to Peaceful Protest under the European Convention on Human Rights: A Content Study of Strasbourg Case Law' [2007] EHRLR 345, 347–51.

[7] Except where this is necessary in the sense set out in Art 11(2).   [8] (1991) 13 EHRR 204.

The Court held that the right to protest would be devalued if those with oppos-ing views were effectively given an unlimited right to disrupt—and thus deter—such protests. At the very least, demonstrators should not have to fear 'physical violence by their opponents'. The state was therefore positively obliged 'to take reasonable and appropriate measures to enable lawful demonstrations to proceed peacefully'.[9] This might include taking steps to separate the 'original' protestors from those seeking to disrupt their protest. But this does not mean that states are obliged to provide an absolute guarantee that protestors will suffer no intimidation or disruption by others. Indeed, the ECtHR ultimately held that the Austrian authorities *had* taken all reason-able steps to protect the anti-abortionists' right to protest: the fact that their ceremony had nevertheless been disrupted did not mean that the authorities had failed to do what was required of them.

Second, because the state is not under an absolute obligation to facilitate peaceful protest, *it may be lawful for the authorities to close down such a protest if it is provok-ing, or seems likely to provoke, others to respond with violence*. This is clearly the most efficient solution for authorities, such as the police, when faced with a small number of protestors stirring up an angry and potentially violent mob with opposing views. It used to be the case that English law permitted the authorities to pursue precisely this sort of strategy.[10] Similarly, the ECtHR tended to take a relatively soft line when this sort of state action was challenged, upholding decisions to target legitimate protestors rather than those threatening to react violently to the protestors' message.[11] However, the ECtHR now seems willing to look more closely at whether the targeting of legit-imate protestors is a necessary and proportionate way of protecting public safety and others' interests.[12] It follows, as we will see, that Art 11 can now require the police and other public authorities to enable peaceful protests to continue by focusing their attention on those who are reacting, or who are threatening to react, violently.

Third, what of *the rights of the counter-protestors themselves*? Naturally, Art 11 does not protect the rights of those who are acting violently, but what about situations involving opposing groups of peaceful protestors? In *Öllinger v Austria*,[13] two groups wished simultaneously to hold ceremonies in the same Salzburg cemetery: one com-memorating Jews killed by the SS ('the Jewish ceremony'), the other commemorating SS soldiers killed during the Second World War ('the SS ceremony').[14] The SS cere-mony had been held every year for 40 years, and the Jewish ceremony was planned as a protest—a counter-demonstration—against it. Faced with this prospect, the Austrian authorities banned the Jewish ceremony, arguing that this was necessary to avoid a risk of conflict between the two groups, and to protect the rights of other people who simply wished to attend the cemetery. But what of the rights of those

[9] *Plattform*, [32]–[34].   [10] *Duncan v Jones* [1936] 1 KB 218.
[11] See, eg *Chorherr v Austria* (1994) 17 EHRR 358.
[12] *Öllinger v Austria* (2008) 46 EHRR 38. See further Mead, 'Strasbourg Discovers the Right to Counter-Demonstrate: A Note on *Öllinger v Austria*' [2007] EHRLR 133.
[13] (2008) 46 EHRR 38.
[14] The SS, or *Schutzstaffel*, was a military force in Nazi Germany responsible for perpetrating many of the worst crimes against humanity during the Second World War, including the murder of approximately 12 million people, many of them Jews.

wishing to hold the Jewish ceremony? The Court noted that '[i]f every probability of tension and heated exchange between opposing groups during a demonstration was to warrant its prohibition, society would be faced with being deprived of the opportunity of hearing differing views'.[15] It went on to hold that, in the absence of clear evidence of likely violence, an absolute ban on the counter-demonstration was neither a necessary nor proportionate restriction on the rights of those wishing to hold the Jewish ceremony. This decision has been welcomed as one that recognises the importance to the political process of dissent—of allowing opposing points of view to be put forward in the interests of democratic decision-making.[16]

2. Domestic law

Inevitably, courts are often drawn into the balancing of the various interests that are in play in this area. But it is usually front-line police officers who initially have to confront such questions, often in very difficult circumstances. Extensive legislative and common law rules govern the police's powers to manage protests. Nearly all of this law came into existence long before the HRA placed the ECHR centre-stage. However, we know from Chapter 18 that the courts are under a duty to interpret and that the police, as a public authority, are under a duty to apply the law consistently with the Convention. As we will see, this has, in some instances, required significant changes to domestic law and practice.

Broadly speaking, English law in this sphere draws a distinction between conduct that is *always unacceptable* and that which is *potentially acceptable*. Conduct of the former type is prohibited; engaging in it constitutes a criminal offence. Uncontroversially, conduct amounting to riot and violent disorder falls into this category. Such behaviour clearly does not constitute 'peaceful assembly' within the meaning of Art 11, and an absolute ban is therefore unproblematic in Convention terms. Meanwhile, behaviour that does not fall into the 'always unacceptable' category is potentially lawful—that is, it may, in principle, be lawfully undertaken—but is subject to regulation. For example, although generally lawful, such conduct might, in *particular circumstances*, be prohibited (eg because it is judged by the authorities that it would create an unacceptable risk of disorder). Or those undertaking it might have *particular conditions* imposed upon them (eg the size or duration of the protest might be limited).

As we consider domestic law, we will need to keep in mind two principal issues. First, is the distinction acceptably drawn between conduct that is absolutely prohibited and that which is, in principle, permitted, but subject to regulation? This raises difficult and controversial questions. At what point, for instance, does the disruption, offence, or disturbance caused by a given form of protest become so substantial as to warrant its prohibition? Second, even in relation to conduct falling on the 'potentially acceptable' side of the line, is the regime of regulation supplied by English law

---

[15] *Öllinger v Austria*, [36]. [16] Mead, 142.

satisfactory in terms of the balance it strikes between the competing rights and interests that are often in tension in this area?

3. Prohibition of certain types of behaviour

3.1 Public Order Act 1986, ss 1–3

Part I of the Public Order Act 1986 criminalises a number of forms of behaviour.[17] Some of those prohibitions do not impinge upon legitimate protest. Into this category undoubtedly fall the offences under ss 1–3 of riot, violent disorder, and affray, all of which involve the intentional or reckless use or threat of unlawful violence such as to cause a person of reasonable firmness to fear for his personal safety.

3.2 Public Order Act 1986, ss 4, 4A, and 5

Sections 4, 4A, and 5 respectively create offences concerning fear or provocation of violence; intentional harassment, alarm, or distress; and harassment, alarm, or distress. The ingredients of each of these offences, together with details of applicable defences, are set out in Table 20.1.

Although there are significant differences between the three offences, a common requirement applies to each, namely, liability can arise only if the defendant has engaged in *relevant conduct*. (Such conduct is not sufficient in itself to attract criminal liability, but it is a prerequisite that is common to all three offences.[18]) For all three offences, relevant conduct includes threatening or abusive behaviour. For ss 4 and 4A, insulting conduct also suffices.

The more broadly the categories of relevant conduct are drawn, the greater the inroads into the right to protest. In *Brutus v Cozens*,[19] it was held that Parliament had intended the phrase 'insulting behaviour' to bear its 'ordinary meaning': '[A]n ordinary sensible man', said Lord Reid, 'knows an insult when he sees or hears it'. It followed that 'vigorous', 'distasteful', and 'unmannerly' speech was not necessarily insulting (or threatening or abusive).[20] Thus, when anti-apartheid protestors interrupted a Wimbledon tennis match by sitting on the court, Lord Reid, while willing to characterise their behaviour as 'deplorable', said that he could not see how it had been *insulting* to the spectators.[21]

For criminal liability to arise, not only must the person concerned engage in relevant conduct. In addition, *the conduct must have a relevant* impact. Under s 4, the conduct must make it likely that unlawful violence will be anticipated or provoked,

---

[17] As with all criminal offences, conviction is only possible if the prosecution establishes beyond reasonable doubt that all elements of the relevant offence have been committed.

[18] Except that in relation to the ss 4A and 5 offences, liability may also arise if there is 'disorderly behaviour'.

[19] [1973] AC 854, 862. This case was concerned with s 5 of the Public Order Act 1936, but remains relevant to the interpretation of 'insulting behaviour' under the 1986 Act.

[20] [1973] AC 854, 862.

[21] Apartheid was the systematic policy of racial segregation and discrimination in force in South Africa from 1948 to 1991.

or such anticipation or provocation must be intended. Once this requirement is factored in, it becomes clear that s 4 does not make serious inroads into the right of legitimate protest—such protests are unlikely to have the effects, or to be accompanied by the intentions, proscribed by s 4. However, the 'effect' components of ss 4A and 5 are weaker. Under s 4A, harassment, alarm, or distress must be caused (and intended). Under s 5, the conduct must be undertaken within the hearing or sight of someone likely to be caused harassment, alarm, or distress (whether or not intended). Depending on how these requirements are interpreted, ss 4A and 5 have the potential significantly to circumscribe lawful protest.

The ECHR stipulates that the right to protest must be upheld except to the extent that its limitation is a necessary and proportionate way of safeguarding one of the competing interests recognised as legitimate in Arts 10(2) and 11(2). The challenge for the courts, since the entry into force of the HRA, has been to interpret and apply the Public Order Act in a way that meets the requirements of the Convention. There are a number of ways in which this might be done; for example, a particularly robust view might be taken of what constitutes relevant conduct, or what is meant by 'harassment', 'alarm', and 'distress'.

Alternatively, emphasis might be placed on the defence (shown in Table 20.1) under ss 4A and 5 that the conduct was 'reasonable': a court might, for example, conclude that even if relevant conduct causes or is likely to cause harassment, alarm, or distress, this is nevertheless reasonable if serving the end of legitimate protest. However, it has been argued that English courts have failed to take sufficient steps to reorientate domestic law[22] in the way required by the Convention—that they have placed too little weight on the right to protest and too much on the 'right' not to be offended.[23] For example, in *Norwood v DPP*,[24] Auld LJ said that once conduct had been shown to satisfy the requirements of s 5, it would, in most cases, follow that it was unreasonable—an analysis that has the potential largely to undercut the reasonableness defence. Meanwhile, in *Hammond v DPP*,[25] that defence did not avail a defendant who was convicted under s 5 for preaching in a busy town centre on (as he saw it) the immorality of same-sex relationships. And in *ProLife Alliance*,[26] the House of Lords held that broadcasters had acted lawfully by deciding that, on the grounds of its perceived offensiveness, they would not transmit a party election broadcast by an anti-abortion party that included graphic pictures of terminated foetuses.

All of these decisions raise the question whether the balance is being struck appropriately between those who wish to put forward their (perhaps unpalatable) views and those who do not wish to be disturbed by them. Ultimately, the choice is between a 'pro-civility' approach, which emphasises the importance of respecting others'

---

[22] The 1986 Act applies in its entirety to England and Wales; parts of it also apply in the rest of the UK.

[23] Geddis, 'Free Speech Martyrs or Unreasonable Threats to Social Peace? "Insulting" Expression and Section 5 of the Public Order Act 1986' [2004] PL 853.

[24] [2003] EWHC 1564 (Admin).   [25] [2004] EWHC 69 (Admin).

[26] *R (ProLife Alliance) v BBC* [2003] UKHL 23, [2004] 1 AC 185. This case did not concern the Public Order Act, but raised the same point about the balance between one person's right to put across his point of view in a manner of his choosing and another's 'right' not to be offended.

Table 20.1 Public Order Act 1986, ss 4, 4A, and 5

	Prohibited behaviour	Mental requirement regarding behaviour	Effects of behaviour and mental requirement regarding effects of behaviour	Specific statutory defences
Section 4: Fear or provocation of violence	• Use of threatening, abusive, or insulting words or behaviour towards another person; or • Distribution or display of writing, sign, or other visible representation which is threatening, abusive, or insulting	• Intends words, behaviour, writing, sign, or other visible representation to be threatening, abusive, or insulting; or • Is aware that it may be threatening, abusive, or insulting	• Intends victim to believe that immediate unlawful violence will occur; or • Intends to provoke such violence; or • Victim is likely to believe such violence will be used; or • It is likely such violence will be provoked	
Section 4A: Intentional harassment, alarm, or distress	• Actually causing harassment, alarm, or distress by either • using threatening, abusive, or insulting words or behaviour, or disorderly behaviour; or • displaying any writing, sign, or other visible representation which is threatening, abusive, or insulting		• Intends to cause harassment, alarm, or distress	• Accused person was inside a dwelling and had no reason • to believe that words, behaviour, writing, sign, or other visible representation would be seen or heard by anyone outside (no offence being committed if someone inside the building is harassed etc); or • Conduct was reasonable
Section 5: Harassment, alarm, or distress	• Use of threatening or abusive words or behaviour, or disorderly behaviour; or • Display of any writing, sign, or other visible representation which is threatening or abusive	• Intends words, behaviour, writing, sign, or other visible representation to be threatening or abusive; or • Intends behaviour to be disorderly; or • Is aware that behaviour may be disorderly	• When the prohibited behaviour takes place, there must be someone within hearing or sight likely to be caused harassment, alarm, or distress thereby	• No reason to believe anyone was within sight or hearing • who was likely to be harassed, alarmed, or distressed • Defences set out above in relation to s 4A also apply to s 5

sensibilities and of preserving public decorum,[27] and one that places greater weight on free speech as a force for good and as something that people must therefore learn to tolerate, even when they disagree with the content or medium. In a strong endorsement of the latter approach, dissenting in *ProLife Alliance*, Lord Scott said that where a broadcast was factually accurate, not sensationalised, and relevant to an issue in an election, a refusal to transmit it would be incompatible with the ECHR: '[T]he public in a mature democracy,' he said, 'are not entitled to be offended by the broadcasting of such a programme'.[28] Refusing to broadcast it, he said, would be 'inimical to the values of a democracy'—which, as the ECtHR has repeatedly said, include 'pluralism, tolerance and broad-mindedness',[29] and which mean that the right of freedom of expression (and thus the right to protest) must include the right to 'offend, shock or disturb'.[30]

Such thinking appears to have underpinned a recent change in the law. Relevant conduct for the purpose of s 5, as it was originally enacted, extended (as it still does in relation to ss 4 and 4A) to offensive conduct. However, s 57 of the Crime and Courts Act 2013 amended s 5 of the Public Order Act 1986. Liability can now arise only if the defendant's conduct is threatening or abusive; the merely insulting no longer suffices. Given that other features of s 5 mean that its proscriptive net is generally cast more widely than that of the other two provisions, the inclusion in s 5 of insulting behaviour as a relevant form of conduct created a particularly serious risk of inappropriately elevating the 'right' not to be offended above the right to protest. The narrowing of the scope of relevant conduct for the purpose of s 5 was intended to address that difficulty.

> **Q** To what extent should one person's right to protest be circumscribed by another's 'right' not to be offended? Does the law now strike the right balance in this area?

3.3 Harassment

The Protection from Harassment Act 1997 sets out three forms of behaviour that constitute criminal offences.[31]

First, s 4(1) makes it an offence to:

- pursue a course of conduct that causes another person to fear, on at least two occasions, that violence will be used against him;

- provided that the perpetrator knows or ought to know that his conduct will cause violence to be feared on each occasion.

---

[27] Geddis, 869–70.   [28] *ProLife*, [98].

[29] *Handyside v UK* (1979–80) 1 EHRR 737, 754.   [30] *Handyside*, 754.

[31] Under ss 3 and 3A, it is also possible in certain circumstances to obtain civil remedies—including injunctions—when prohibited harassment has occurred or is anticipated. The position set out here concerns England and Wales; different provision is made in ss 8–11 for Scotland.

Second, s 1(1) (read with s 2(1)) says that an offence is committed when a person:

- engages in a course of conduct that amounts to harassment of another person;
- provided that he knows or ought to know that the course of conduct amounts to harassment.

Third, s 1(1A), read with s 2(1), says that an offence occurs when a person:

- engages in a course of conduct that involves harassment of two or more persons;
- knows or ought to know that the course of conduct involves harassment; and
- intends to persuade someone (whether or not it is one of the people actually being harassed) not to do something that he is entitled or required to do, or to do something that he is not obliged to do.

Do any of these provisions criminalise behaviour that might be regarded as a legitimate form of protest? The position is most straightforward in relation to s 4(1): it is difficult to argue that behaviour creating a fear of violence should be permitted as a form of legitimate, peaceful protest.[32] In contrast, s 1(1) does criminalise some types of behaviour that might be regarded as protest. For example, it would be an offence under the Act for an animal rights protestor to harass the managing director of a pharmaceutical company that tests its products on animals, perhaps hoping to persuade him to desist from doing so in the future.[33] Meanwhile, under s 1(1A) it would be an offence for protestors to harass employees of the company with a view to persuading them to leave the company or to refuse to perform their duties for it.[34]

Whether (and, if so, the extent to which) s 1(1) and (1A) of the 1997 Act criminalises behaviour that might be considered as legitimate forms of protest depends on two principal factors, the first being the meaning of 'harassment'. The Act does not *define* 'harassment', but says that it *includes* alarming or causing distress to a person.[35] This is not, on the face of it, a high hurdle, and it means that while the Act undoubtedly (and rightly) criminalises long-running hate campaigns that make people's lives intolerable, it also risks proscribing much more moderate forms of protest. The second factor is that conduct that would otherwise constitute harassment is not unlawful if, in the particular circumstances, it was reasonable.[36] The courts are required by the HRA to construe the concepts of 'harassment' and 'reasonableness' in a manner consistent with the ECHR, which means striking an acceptable balance between the rights of protestors under Arts 10 and 11, and those of the people who are targeted by protestors.[37] However, as we saw earlier, the courts have been criticised for failing to attach sufficient weight to the right to protest when addressing analogous issues arising under the Public Order Act.

---

[32] This conclusion is reinforced by the fact that the fear of violence must be an objectively reasonable one: s 4(2).

[33] Provided that the protestor knew, or ought to have known, that his conduct amounted to harassment.

[34] Subject to the proviso in the preceding note.   [35] Section 7(2).   [36] Section 1(3).

[37] The most obvious right at stake for the latter group is the right to respect for private and family life under ECHR, Art 8. On the need to balance the interests of the parties, see further *Director of Public Prosecutions v Selvanayagam* The Times, 23 June 1999.

4. Statutory powers to regulate protests

4.1 Introduction

Even if a particular form of behaviour is not a criminal offence, it may be potentially subject to an array of statutory powers of regulation. The existence and extent of such powers is important to our inquiry into whether English law attaches sufficient weight to the right to protest. It is widely accepted that much of the value of freedom of expression lies in having the right to say not only *what* you want, but also to say it *how* and *where* you want to. Otherwise, free speech and the right to protest 'would be at risk of emasculation'.[38] ProLife Alliance, for example, wished to *show* images of aborted foetuses rather than merely to *describe* the effect on foetuses of termination procedures, because it felt that its point could be made more effectively in the former way.[39] Equally, the right to protest would be largely worthless if the authorities had unfettered power to direct that protests could take place only in prescribed locations: a protest in a field in the middle of nowhere is unlikely to have the same impact as one conducted in a busy city centre. The right to protest would be similarly undermined if there existed absolute discretion to limit the number of protestors: three protestors are likely to be much less effective than 300,000. Yet it does not follow that the authorities should have *no* power to regulate protests: a sit-in on a busy road, although peaceful, is liable to bring an entire city to a standstill, and there is an obvious need, while recognising the protestors' rights, to give adequate weight to others' interests. It is against this background that we need to examine English law in this area.

4.2 Regulating public assemblies

Section 14 of the Public Order Act 1986 gives the police certain powers to regulate public assemblies. Three main points should be noted.

First, the way in which the Act defines the term 'public assembly' means that these powers only apply when three conditions are met:

- The gathering is of *two or more persons*.
- It occurs in a *public place* (meaning a highway or any other place that the public may lawfully access).
- It takes place wholly or partly in the *open air*.[40]

If these requirements are satisfied, the regulatory powers contained in s 14 are in principle exercisable.

Second, the power to regulate public assemblies is only *triggered* in certain circumstances. The relevant police officer[41] must (taking into account the circumstances) reasonably believe one of the following things:

---

[38] *Hall v Mayor of London* [2010] EWCA Civ 817, [2011] 1 WLR 504, [37], *per* Lord Neuberger MR.
[39] See section 3.2.   [40] Public Order Act 1986, s 16.
[41] Being the most senior officer present at the protest or, if the power is being used before the start of the protest, the head of the relevant police force: s 14(2).

- The assembly may result in serious public disorder, serious damage to property, or serious disruption to the life of the community.

- The organisers' purpose is to intimidate people in order to compel them not to do something that they have a right to do, or to do something that they have a right not to do.[42]

Third, if (and only if) at least one of those criteria is met, the relevant police officer may set *conditions* concerning the location of the assembly, its duration, and how many people may take part. Those conditions must go no further in terms of restricting the assembly than appear to the police officer to be necessary to prevent the feared outcomes mentioned in the bullet point above.[43] It is a criminal offence to organise or take part in a public assembly and knowingly to fail to comply with such a condition (unless the failure arises due to circumstances beyond the relevant person's control).[44]

These powers are not particularly controversial in right-to-protest terms. The conditions that must be met in order for the powers to be triggered are relatively robust—*serious* public disorder and so on—and if a police officer were unreasonably to conclude that such conditions had been met, his decision would be open to challenge by means of judicial review. Equally, even when the power is triggered, the restrictions imposed must go no further than necessary. This is of a piece with Art 11, which permits freedom of assembly to be limited when (and to the extent) that this is necessary in the public interest.

4.3 **Prohibiting trespassory assemblies**

The power under s 14 does not extend to *banning* public assemblies. However, ss 14A–C allow steps to be taken to ban—that is, to criminalise the organisation of and participation in—'trespassory assemblies'. Clearly, outright prohibition of protest is a more draconian step than regulating the way in which a protest is conducted, and it follows that a power to prohibit assemblies prima facie makes greater inroads into the right to protest than does a power merely to regulate. To assess the extent to which ss 14A–C curtail the right to protest, we need to address two questions. When can the power to prohibit assemblies be exercised? And, when that power is used, what is its effect?

As to the former matter, the conditions circumscribing the use of the s 14A power of prohibition are tighter than those applying to the s 14 regulatory power:

- The s 14A power applies only to gatherings of *20 or more persons*.[45]

- The power only applies to land in the open air to which the public has *no or only a limited right of access*.[46] This means that the s 14A power (unlike the s 14 power) does not extend to gatherings on common land to which the public has an unlimited right of access.

---

[42] Section 14(1).   [43] Section 14(1).   [44] Section 14(4) and (5).
[45] Section 14A(9).   [46] Section 14A(1).

- The head of the relevant police force must reasonably believe that the assembly is likely to be held *without the permission* of, or in *breach of terms* laid down by, the occupier of the land and that the assembly will result in *serious disruption to the life of the community* or *significant damage to land, a building, or a monument that is historically, architecturally, archaeologically, or scientifically important.*[47]

- A s 14A prohibition may be imposed only with the *agreement of the Secretary of State* and (except in London) the *local authority.*[48]

What, then, are the practical consequences of a s 14A prohibition? A person commits a criminal offence by taking part in or organising an assembly prohibited under s 14A.[49] However, it is important to bear in mind that s 14A orders only have the effect of prohibiting assemblies *to the extent that they constitute trespass.*[50] If the protestors have a right to be on the land or have the permission of the occupier of the land to be there, the s 14A order does not prohibit the protest: it only bites if, and to the extent that, the protestors exceed the limit of any right that they have (or of any permission that has been granted for them) to be present on the land. The extent to which the power to prohibit trespassory assemblies restricts the right to protest therefore turns in part upon the extent to which property law recognises a right on the part of protestors to be present on land. To the extent that such a right exists, the protestors' presence on the land in question will not constitute a trespass—meaning, in turn, that the protest cannot be banned under s 14A.

This issue has assumed particular prominence in relation to public highways (roads), which are usually owned by the Crown or local authorities. Many demonstrations involve people being present on highways, and the question arises whether (and, if so, to what extent) it is possible to ban such demonstrations under s 14A. Not being the owners of highways, the public only avoid committing trespass when they use them to the extent to which they have a right to do so. In *Director of Public Prosecutions v Jones,*[51] a number of people were standing on a roadside verge near Stonehenge protesting against the authorities' policy of restricting access to the monument. A s 14A order was in place and they were arrested for taking part in a prohibited trespassory assembly. In defence, they argued that they were not trespassing because they had a right to be on a public highway for the purposes of peaceful protest, and that they had therefore done nothing prohibited by the order.

Overturning the defendants' convictions, the House of Lords rejected the view that the public only had a right in relation to highways to 'pass and repass' (ie to use highways for travel).[52] If the public had no greater rights, noted Lord Irvine LC, 'surprising consequences' would ensue. For example, people who stop to talk, children who play, and political activists who hand out leaflets in the street would

---

[47] Section 14A(1).   [48] Section 14A(2)–(4).

[49] Section 14B(1) and (2).   [50] Section 14A(5).

[51] [1999] 2 AC 240.   [52] See, eg *Harrison v Duke of Rutland* [1893] 1 QB 142, 158, *per* Kay LJ.

all be trespassers.[53] The better view, he said, involved recognising that 'the public highway is a public place, on which all manner of reasonable activities may go on'.[54] It followed that 'there is a public right of peaceful assembly on the highway'.[55] This is not, however, an unlimited right: the assembly must represent a *reasonable* use of the highway; one that causes an unacceptable degree of inconvenience to others is unlikely to be reasonable.[56]

In a more recent case, the Court of Appeal said that whether a protest constitutes a lawful use of the highway will turn on context-specific matters such as the importance of the precise location to the protestors, the duration of the protest, and the extent to which the protest interferes with others' rights.[57] However, in *Jones*, the House of Lords had no difficulty in concluding that the conduct at stake in that case was perfectly reasonable, that the defendants had not therefore exceeded their right to be present on the highway, and that they had not committed the offence of taking part in a prohibited trespassory assembly. Although the reasoning of some of the judges was not as bold as that of Lord Irvine, *Jones* is nevertheless widely regarded as a highly significant decision that is 'an important vindication of a fundamental civil liberty'.[58] As such, it means that the power to prohibit trespassory assemblies is a less draconian one than it first appears to be.

4.4 **Public Spaces Protection Orders**

Public Spaces Protection Orders (PSPOs) were introduced by the Anti-social Behaviour, Crime and Policing Act 2014. Such Orders can be made by local authorities if both of the following conditions are satisfied:

- Activities have occurred (or are likely to occur) in a *public place* that have had (or are likely to have) a *detrimental effect on the quality of life of those in the locality.*

- The effect (or likely effect) of the activities is (or is likely to be) *persistent or continuing* in nature, is such as to make the activities *unreasonable*, and *justifies* the restrictions in question.[59]

If those conditions are met and the local authority makes a PSPO, it can thereby prohibit 'specified things' from being done in the relevant area and/or require people to do 'specified things' when undertaking 'specified activities'.[60] PSPOs can remain in force for three years (and then be renewed).[61] Breaching them without reasonable excuse is a criminal offence.[62]

---

[53] *Director of Public Prosecutions v Jones*, 254.
[54] *Director of Public Prosecutions v Jones*, 254.   [55] *Director of Public Prosecutions v Jones*, 257.
[56] It should be noted in this regard that, separately from the Public Order Act 1986, obstruction of the highway is a criminal offence in its own right under the Highways Act 1980, s 137.
[57] *City of London Corporation v Samede* [2012] EWCA Civ 160, [2012] PTSR 1624, [39].
[58] Clayton, 'Reclaiming Public Ground: The Right to Peaceful Assembly' (2000) 63 MLR 252, 252.
[59] Anti-social Behaviour, Crime and Policing Act 2014, s 59(2), (3).   [60] Section 59(4).
[61] Section 60.   [62] Section 67.

Eg Salford City Council made a PSPO prohibiting the use of all 'foul and abusive language' in a particular area of Salford Quays. The Order did not, however, give any guidance as to which words would be considered 'foul and abusive'.

A PSPO made by Teignbridge District Council prohibits 'shout[ing]', 'swear[ing]' and 'act[ing] in a manner as to cause annoyance, harassment, alarm or distress' to any person within the defined area, or on land adjacent to it, or to any person living nearby.

Mansfield District Council made a PSPO enabling police constables and other 'authorised officers' to 'disperse' people from designated areas if they have reason to believe that the people concerned are causing or likely to cause 'nuisance, alarm, harassment or distress' to anyone else. Failing to follow a dispersal instruction is a criminal offence.

On the face of it, PSPOs are capable of making substantial inroads into the right to protest, not least because the Act does not define the 'specified things' that people can be prohibited from doing or required to do.[63] Many of the PSPOs that have been made so far are concerned with such matters as dog fouling and the consumption of alcohol. However, the sheer breadth of the powers apparently conferred by the legislation has not escaped the notice of local authorities. And, as the above examples illustrate, PSPOs may well have implications for the right to protest (and for freedom of expression more generally). For instance, if a PSPO makes it a criminal offence to shout or act in a way that annoys someone else, then that is liable to criminalise many acts of protest. Equally, if it is an offence to fail to disperse when told to do so, and if one can be required to disperse merely because a constable has reason to think that others will be caused nuisance or distress, the implications for certain forms of protest are clear.

Indeed, PSPOs may introduce by the back door new versions of existing criminal offences—such as those under the Public Order Act 1986 mentioned in section 3.2— that lack some of the limitations or safeguards contained within the existing offences. They may also (as the examples demonstrate) introduce prohibitions that are both broad and vague in scope. The possibility therefore arises not merely of criminalising conduct that may constitute legitimate protest, but of exerting a chilling effect by creating uncertainty as to the scope of the conduct that is captured by the PSPO.

There are, however, some safeguards. For instance, prohibitions and requirements imposed by means of PSPOs must be 'reasonable' for the purpose of preventing or addressing the relevant detrimental effect.[64] In addition, local authorities, when making PSPOs, are required to have 'particular regard' to Arts 10 and 11 of the ECHR.[65] Even more importantly, it is unlawful, thanks to the HRA, s 6, for local authorities to exercise their PSPO-related powers incompatibly with Convention rights, and no offence is committed by someone who fails to comply with a PSPO to the extent that the local authority lacked the power to make it.[66] Meanwhile, although there can be no judicial review of PSPOs as such, they can be challenged within six weeks of being made in proceedings before the High Court.[67] While the foregoing restrictions upon

---

[63] The Act does, however, impose some limits on the things that can be prohibited. For example, consuming alcohol in licensed premises cannot be prohibited by means of a PSPO: s 62.

[64] Section 59(5).   [65] Section 72(1).   [66] Section 67(3).   [67] Section 66.

local authorities' capacity to restrict protest via PSPOs are noteworthy, their significance should not be overstated bearing in mind the capacity of PSPOs, noted above, to exert a chilling effect.

4.5 Demonstrations near the Palace of Westminster

For centuries, people have, with varying degrees of success, organised demonstrations in Parliament Square in order to protest against the government or a law being enacted by Parliament. However, ss 132–8 of the Serious Organised Crime and Police Act 2005 made it a criminal offence to organise or participate in a demonstration within a kilometre of Parliament Square unless the prior permission of the police was obtained.[68] Such permission could be made subject to extensive conditions as to such matters as the duration, size, and location of the demonstration. Failure to comply with such conditions was a criminal offence. This meant that it was possible to criminalise protests at particular locations—such as immediately outside the Palace of Westminster—by imposing a condition that the demonstration occur at a venue other than that preferred by the protestor.

The legislation was enacted against the background of a long-running protest held in Parliament Square by a single person, Brian Haw, against government policy in relation to (and including military action against) Iraq. Haw, it has been said,[69] was a 'primary target' of ss 132–8 of the 2005 Act. Several people[70] were convicted under those provisions, including some who simply stood alone in Parliament Square reading out the names of British soldiers killed in Iraq.[71] Although the official rationale for the enactment of these provisions was the need to ensure security in the vicinity of Parliament, and although the preservation of national security is a legitimate reason under the ECHR for curtailing relevant rights, it is hard to see how the criminalisation of conduct of this type could be said to constitute a necessary and proportionate limitation of the right to protest. Nevertheless, the High Court rejected the argument that the requirement to obtain prior authorisation for protests was inconsistent with the ECHR.[72]

The inappropriateness of the restrictions imposed by ss 132–8 of the 2005 Act was recognised by the coalition government following the 2010 election, and those provisions were repealed by the Police Reform and Social Responsibility Act 2011.[73] However, ss 142–8 of the 2011 Act authorise the police to direct people not to engage in (or to cease engaging in) 'prohibited activities' in a defined area of Parliament Square. The 'prohibited activities' relate principally to the use, without permission, of amplifiers and to sleeping or staying (eg in a tent) in Parliament Square. To the extent that they impinge upon the right to protest, these restrictions are clearly far more modest than those provided for by the 2005 Act, and to that extent the right

---

[68] Further restrictions in relation to Parliament Square arise as a result of by-laws made under s 385 of the Greater London Authority Act 1999. See further *Mayor of London v Hall* [2010] EWCA Civ 817; *R (Barda) v Mayor of London* [2015] EWHC 3584 (Admin), [2016] 4 WLR 20.

[69] Loveland, 'Public Protest in Parliament Square' [2007] EHRLR 251, 252.

[70] Although not, in the end, Haw himself: *R (Haw) v Secretary of State for the Home Department* [2007] EWHC 1931 (Admin), [2008] 1 WLR 379.

[71] Loveland, 264–5.   [72] *DPP v Blum* [2006] EWHC 3209 (Admin).   [73] Section 141(1).

to protest in the vicinity of Parliament has, to a substantial extent, been restored. Nevertheless, this sorry episode serves as an important reminder of the sometimes irresistible temptation felt by those in authority to squash dissent that they regard as inconvenient, embarrassing, or just downright annoying.

4.6 Regulating and prohibiting processions

So far, we have been concerned with the regulation of *assemblies*.[74] We turn now to *processions*. The essential distinction is that the former are stationary, while the latter are not. The legal regime for regulating public processions is contained in ss 11–13 of the Public Order Act 1986. It differs in two key respects from that which applies to assemblies.

First, whereas there is no requirement to give the police notice of an assembly,[75] *it is normally necessary to give the police advance notice of processions* that are intended to demonstrate support for, or opposition to, a particular view, to publicise a cause or campaign, or to mark or commemorate an event.[76] The notice must include details of such matters as the proposed date, time, and route. In terms of Art 11, such a requirement is uncontentious: a procession in a public place (which almost inevitably means the highway) is liable to cause at least a degree of disruption. Advance notice allows the police to work out how to deal with the likely consequences of any disruption so as to accommodate the interests of those likely to be affected. As such, the advance notice requirement is a proportionate restriction on the right of freedom of assembly. Organisers of processions commit a criminal offence if the procession goes ahead without such notice having been given, or if the timing or route of the procession differs from that specified in the notice given to the police.[77] However, the requirement to give advance notice does not apply if complying with it is not reasonably practicable or if the procession is one that is commonly or customarily held. The requirement did not therefore apply to mass cycle rides in London that followed no predetermined route.[78]

Second, as with public assemblies, there is a power to impose conditions on public processions.[79] However, whereas there is no power to ban assemblies (unless they are trespassory assemblies), *there is a power to ban public processions*. The power can only be exercised if the head of the relevant police force reasonably believes that the imposition of conditions will be insufficient to prevent serious public disorder,[80] and the agreement of the Home Secretary and (outside London) the local authority is needed.[81] It is an offence for a person to organise or participate in a procession that he knows to be banned.[82] There is no explicit mention of the importance of the right

---

[74] Although Public Spaces Protection Orders, on which see section 4.4, can bite upon both assemblies and processions.

[75] Except those to be held in the vicinity of Parliament Square.

[76] Public Order Act 1986, s 11(1).   [77] Public Order Act 1986, s 11(7).

[78] *Kay v Commissioner of Police of the Metropolis* [2008] UKHL 69, [2008] 1 WLR 2723.

[79] See Public Order Act 1986, s 12. The power to impose conditions on processions is very similar to that under s 14 concerning the imposition of conditions on assemblies; on which, see section 4.3.

[80] Section 13(1).   [81] Section 13(2)–(4).   [82] Section 13(7) and (8).

to protest in the Public Order Act, but the effect of the HRA is that a procession may only be banned if this constitutes a necessary and proportionate restriction on that right. Those involved in making the decision must therefore weigh the importance of the right to protest in the given circumstances against the risks that would be posed by allowing the procession to go ahead.

5. Common law powers to regulate protests

5.1 Introduction

We have seen that there exist extensive statutory powers to regulate, and in some circumstances prohibit, protests. There is room for legitimate disagreement about whether the relevant legislation attaches sufficient weight to the right to protest. Nevertheless, it can certainly be said that, in the legislation considered so far in this chapter, Parliament has taken the trouble to set out in reasonably clear terms the powers (and, importantly, the *limits* of the powers) that the authorities have to manage public protests. It is therefore perhaps surprising that, alongside these statutory powers, the police also have a broad common law power that can be used to manage, and even choke off, protest.

This is unsatisfactory on two grounds.[83] First, the common law power is, as we will see, ill defined.[84] This sits in tension with the requirement of legal certainty that forms a core element of the rule of law. Second, the risk arises that the restrictions built into the authorities' statutory powers will be evaded by recourse to their wider common law powers.[85] These issues are of importance to the central concern of this chapter—that is, whether English law ascribes proper weight to the right to protest. However, to explore these matters properly, we need to begin by explaining the nature of the common law power in question and notion of 'breach of the peace' to which it relates.

5.2 What is a breach of the peace?

A 'breach of the peace' is something that disturbs 'the peace'. This does not mean something that interferes with 'peace and quiet'; rather, it means something that interferes with the normal state of affairs in which members of the community live together peaceably. As Feldman puts it: 'peace', in this context, means not the 'absence of noise', but the opposite of 'war'.[86]

It was suggested by Lord Denning MR, in a case in which protestors prevented a possible site for a nuclear power station from being surveyed, that there would be a breach of the peace 'whenever a person who is lawfully carrying out his work is

---

[83] See generally Stone, 'Breach of the Peace: The Case for Abolition' [2001] 2 Web JCLI.
[84] Williams, *Keeping the Peace* (London 1967), p 116.
[85] We will see, however, that the risk is now smaller because of the influence of the HRA.
[86] Feldman, *Civil Liberties and Human Rights in England and Wales* (Oxford 2002), p 1018.

unlawfully and physically prevented by another from doing it'.[87] However, it is now generally accepted that the correct definition of 'breach of the peace' is the narrower one set out in *R v Howell*.[88] Taking into account what was said in that case and what has been said in subsequent cases,[89] it can be stated that a breach of the peace arises whenever any one of the following three things occurs or is likely to occur as a result of violence:

- A person is injured.
- A person fears being injured.
- A person's property is damaged in his presence.

Breach of the peace is not itself an offence,[90] but it triggers police powers to intervene in relation to those who are causing the breach.

5.3 In what circumstances may the police intervene?

In the face of a breach of the peace, the police have a number of options at their disposal. We consider what those options are in the following section, but it may be helpful at this stage to say that they include arrest. There are many forms of conduct that constitute a breach of the peace that need not detain us. Dozens of such breaches are doubtless committed in most city centres on an average Saturday night as fights break out or threaten to break out. If the police arrest people engaging in such behaviour, this does not have the effect of curtailing the right to protest. Indeed, it may be hard to see why anything amounting to a breach of the peace might also constitute an exercise of the right to protest, given that the boundaries of *legitimate* protest are generally regarded as coterminous with those of *peaceful* protest. Surely, then, breach of the peace and legitimate protest are mutually exclusive categories?

The reality is more complicated, not least because a person may commit a breach of the peace even if he is not *himself* acting, or likely to act, violently. In *Percy*, Watkins LJ said that the conduct constituting a breach of the peace 'does not itself have to be disorderly'—or violent—'or a breach of the criminal law. It is sufficient if its natural consequence would, if persisted in, be to provoke *others* to violence, and so some actual danger to the peace is established'.[91] This means, on the face of it, that it would be lawful for a police officer to arrest a protestor who was not himself acting or likely to act violently, but who was expressing views that were causing or likely to cause *others* to act violently. Precisely this happened in *Duncan v Jones*,[92] in which it was held that the police had acted lawfully and within the scope of their duty by requiring a

---

[87] *R v Chief Constable of Devon and Cornwall, ex p Central Electricity Generating Board* [1982] QB 458, 471.

[88] [1982] QB 416.

[89] Including *Percy v Director of Public Prosecutions* [1995] 1 WLR 1382; *Steel v UK* (1999) 28 EHRR 603.

[90] Although conduct constituting a breach of the peace may also amount to a substantive criminal offence such as assault.

[91] [1995] 1 WLR 1382, 1392 (emphasis added).

[92] [1936] 1 KB 218; cf *Beatty v Gillbanks* (1881–82) LR 9 QBD 308.

protestor to desist. The protestor was not acting or threatening to act violently, but past experience suggested that others would act in such a manner because of the content of the protestor's views. In so holding, Lord Hewart CJ remarked that English law did 'not recognise any special right of public meeting for political or other purposes'.[93]

The law has moved on since that case was decided in 1935. Allowing the police to target a peaceful protestor because of others' likely response is to give the mob a power of veto that is inconsistent with the right to protest now applicable under the ECHR, and with the allied responsibility of the state to facilitate peaceful protest.[94] Of particular note is the decision in *Redmond-Bate v Director of Public Prosecutions*.[95] Christian fundamentalist preachers who had attracted a crowd of over 100 people near a cathedral were arrested for breach of the peace and subsequently convicted by magistrates of a related offence. However, their appeal against conviction was allowed by the High Court. Sedley LJ, giving the only reasoned judgment, said that the '[f]reedom only to speak inoffensively is not worth having'. Free speech therefore includes 'the irritating, the contentious, the eccentric, the heretical, the unwelcome and the provocative'. In *Bibby v Chief Constable of Essex*,[96] Schiemann LJ emphasised that 'depriving of his liberty a citizen who is not at the time acting unlawfully' represents an 'extreme step' not to be lightly undertaken. Thus the position now[97] is that the police may only arrest for breach of the peace someone who is not themselves acting or threatening to act violently if all of the following conditions are satisfied:

- the person is acting unreasonably;
- the natural consequence of his conduct is violence from a third party; and
- that violence is not wholly unreasonable.

In practice, this means that a distinction falls to be drawn between situations in which the reactions of the audience are 'the voluntary acts of people who could not properly be regarded as objects of provocation' (in which case, they, but not the protestor, may be arrested for breach of the peace) and those in which the protestor's conduct is 'calculated to provoke violent and disorderly reaction' (in which case, the protestor can be arrested).[98] In a later case, Lord Brown emphasised that targeting the protestor, rather than those reacting or likely to react violently, should be a measure of last resort. The 'first duty' of the police, said Lord Brown, is to 'protect the rights of the innocent rather than to compel the innocent to cease exercising them'.[99] However, where the police reasonably believe that 'there are no other means whatsoever whereby a breach or imminent breach of the peace can be obviated, the lawful exercise by third parties of their rights may be curtailed'.[100]

---

[93] [1936] 1 KB 218, 222.   [94] See discussion in section 1.3 of *Plattform 'Ärzte für das Leben' v Austria*.
[95] [2000] HRLR 249.   [96] (2000) 164 JP 297, 302.
[97] *Bibby*, 302–3.   [98] *Redmond-Bate*, 253.
[99] *R (Laporte) v Chief Constable of Gloucestershire Constabulary* [2006] UKHL 55, [2007] 2 AC 105, [124]. See also Lord Mance's comments at [148].
[100] *Austin v Commissioner of Police of the Metropolis* [2007] EWCA Civ 989, [2008] QB 660, [35], relying upon *obiter dicta* in *Laporte*.

5.4 What can the police do?

At common law, the police possess powers to arrest and detain people in order to prevent or stop a breach of the peace, as well as powers to take steps short of arrest and detention (eg requiring people acting or threatening to act violently to move away from the place in which tensions are running high). The police are quite properly not required to wait until violence is taking place before exercising such powers. But when exactly may they intervene? Over the years, this has been a particular bone of contention between protestors and the authorities, the cause célèbre being the case of *Moss v McLachlin*.[101] During the miners' strike of 1984–85, the police stopped 25 cars containing up to 80 striking miners at a motorway junction. The junction was situated between 1.5 and 5 miles from four collieries at which the police feared the cars' occupants would become involved in violent confrontations. Forty miners were arrested for refusing to comply with police instructions not to proceed towards the collieries. The miners subsequently argued that the police had had no right to interfere with their freedom of movement by, in effect, preventing them from entering a large exclusion zone around the collieries concerned. This argument, however, cut no ice in the High Court. It was held that, in the circumstances—which included many other violent confrontations during the course of the strike—the police had been entitled to do as they had done: 'Provided they honestly and reasonably form the opinion that there is a real risk of a breach of the peace in the sense that it is in close proximity both in place and time, then the conditions exist for reasonable preventative action including, if necessary, the measures taken in this case.'[102]

However, the law in this area has moved on, thanks in no small part to the HRA. *Laporte* is now the leading case.[103] It concerned three coachloads of people travelling from London towards an airbase at which they planned to participate in a protest against the war in Iraq. Fearing that among the occupants of the coaches were members of the 'Wombles', a group thought likely to attempt to gain unlawful access to the airbase, the police stopped the coaches 5 km by road (2 km in a straight line) from the airbase's perimeter fence. Having searched the coaches, the police formed the view that some, but not all, of their occupants were Wombles. The police did not arrest anyone for breach of the peace, but ordered the coaches and their occupants to turn back. Police outriders escorted the coaches to London to ensure that they did not attempt to return to the airbase and to prevent anyone from disembarking until arrival in London. These facts gave the court—which held that the police had acted unlawfully—an opportunity to clarify two key issues.

First, only when the police have reasonable grounds to believe that a breach of the peace is imminent may they exercise such powers.[104] In *Laporte*, the police conceded

---

[101] [1985] IRLR 76.   [102] *Moss v McLachlin*, [20], *per* Skinner J.

[103] *R (Laporte) v Chief Constable of Gloucestershire Constabulary* [2006] UKHL 55, [2007] 2 AC 105.

[104] In *R (Moos) v Commissioner of Police of the Metropolis* [2012] EWCA Civ 12, the Court of Appeal clarified that the question for the court is not whether breach of the peace was *actually* imminent; it is whether the police had *reasonable grounds for believing* it to be so.

that, when they stopped the coaches and later ordered them back to London, they did not think a breach of the peace to be imminent. They accepted that in those circumstances they could not arrest anyone for breach of the peace, but contended that they could exercise less draconian powers such as turning the coaches back. This was based on remarks of Skinner J in *Moss v McLachlan* that '[t]he imminence or immediacy of the threat to the peace determines what action is reasonable'.[105] On this view, observed Lord Rodger in *Laporte*, 'a police officer would have the power—and duty—to take less drastic action (such as stopping cars), at an earlier stage than he would have the power and duty to take more serious action (such as arresting potential lawbreakers)'.[106] But this approach was rejected in *Laporte* because, as Lord Rodger put it, it would 'weaken the long-standing safeguard against unnecessary and inappropriate interventions by the police'.[107] The court held that *none* of the police's powers to prevent a breach of the peace becomes exercisable until such a breach is imminent (ie 'on the point of happening').[108]

Second, as well as clarifying, and circumscribing, the circumstances in which the police may intervene *at all, Laporte* underlines the limits on what the police may do when they are allowed to intervene. In particular, the reasoning in *Laporte* is infused with the ECHR concept of proportionality. In the present context, that concept requires that the police only intervene when, and to the extent to which, it is necessary to do so to maintain public order. It was said in *Laporte* that even if intervention were to have been permissible, the police would have been unable to show that their reaction had constituted a necessary and proportionate limitation of the right to protest. In the first place, they had intervened prematurely. While it would be unreasonable to require the police to stay their hand until the instant before the outbreak of violence, intervention as pre-emptive as that in *Laporte* was unnecessary. Bearing in mind the extensive preparations that the police had made at the airbase, it had been unreasonable to assume that the people on the coach would have become involved in violent confrontations upon arrival. Moreover, the action taken by the police was unnecessarily draconian. The police had been unable to demonstrate the inadequacy of less drastic action such as allowing everyone to proceed to the airbase and arresting anyone who subsequently became, or threatened to become, violent, or arresting Wombles and letting everyone else go to the airbase.[109] The police's 'general and indiscriminate' action was therefore disproportionate and unlawful.[110] The position is different, however, if draconian action can be shown by the police to be necessary. In the *Austin* case—the House of Lords' decision in which is considered in section 5.7—the Court of Appeal held that the detention for several hours of innocent third parties was lawful because, in the exceptional circumstances of the case, nothing less drastic would have sufficed to prevent an imminent breach of the peace.[111]

---

[105] *Moss v McLachlin*, [39].   [106] *Laporte*, [63].   [107] *Laporte*, [66].
[108] *Laporte*, [39], *per* Lord Bingham.   [109] *Laporte*, [89].
[110] *Laporte*, [153]–[155], *per* Lord Mance.
[111] *Austin v Commissioner of Police of the Metropolis* [2007] EWCA Civ 989, [2008] QB 660. The House of Lords was not concerned with this aspect of the case on appeal.

Q Do you think that the court got it right in *Laporte*, or might it be argued that the decision places the police under an unacceptable duty to make fine judgements in the heat of the moment rather than (as in the case of the court) with the benefit of hindsight?

5.5 Breach of the peace and criminal liability

We have seen that people can be arrested for breach of the peace. This makes it a powerful tool for managing disturbances—and a potential restriction on the right to protest—not least because once people are arrested they are inevitably taken out of circulation for a period of time. After all, it is impossible to participate in a public protest if you are in the back of a police van or at a police station. However, even though it is possible to be arrested for breach of the peace, there is no criminal offence of breaching the peace. Prosecution is only possible, therefore, if the person concerned can be charged with something that constitutes a substantive criminal offence.[112]

One possibility is the crime of resisting, or wilfully obstructing, a police constable in the execution of his duty.[113] Since one of the duties of a police constable is to maintain the peace, he may issue directions considered reasonably necessary to that end—and anyone who fails to obey them may commit the offence of obstruction. Feldman notes that this approach is 'regularly used to criminalise otherwise lawful behaviour in ways that interfere with freedom of expression and assembly'.[114] The extent to which this offence threatens to undermine the legality of legitimate protest principally depends upon how we draw the boundaries of a police constable's duty. The offence is not committed by anyone who fails to comply with instructions issued to them by a police constable; rather, it is only committed if, in the first place, those instructions are issued in pursuance of the constable's duty to maintain the peace. Importantly, s 6 of the HRA requires police constables to act in accordance with the ECHR. A constable therefore acts *outside* the scope of his duty if he issues instructions that, if complied with, would entail unnecessary or disproportionate restrictions upon the right to protest. The extent to which protestors are at risk of committing the offence of obstruction is thus informed by the right to protest, since the effect of the HRA is to preclude the criminalisation of activities that constitute legitimate exercises of the rights of freedom of speech and assembly.

5.6 Evaluation

It has, on occasion, been argued that the existence of the police's breach of the peace powers is incompatible with the requirements of the ECHR. In particular, the

---

[112] It is also possible for someone to be 'bound over' to keep the peace. This involves the court requiring the person to enter into an undertaking to pay a sum of money to the Crown if, within a stipulated period, he or she breaches the peace. See generally Feldman, 'The King's Peace, the Royal Prerogative and Public Order: The Roots and Early Development of Binding Over Powers' [1988] CLJ 101.

[113] Police Act 1996, s 89(2).

[114] Feldman, *Civil Liberties and Human Rights in England and Wales* (Oxford 2002), p 1035.

Convention stipulates that any restriction upon the freedoms of expression and assembly must be 'prescribed by law'. The ECtHR has held that this means, among other things, that any law imposing such restrictions, 'whether written or unwritten, [must] be sufficiently precise to allow the citizen—if need be, with appropriate advice—to foresee, to a degree that is reasonable in the circumstances, the consequences which a given action may entail'.[115] In fact, the ECtHR held in *Steel v UK*[116] that the law in this area *is* sufficiently precise—and several of the recent cases discussed in this chapter have provided significant clarification. Yet it has been argued that important issues remain uncertain, and that this is, at best, undesirable. For example, the definition of 'breach of the peace' refers, among other things, to damage or harm to persons or property, but does not clearly identify the severity of the required damage or harm. Similarly, while we know that a breach of the peace can occur if such damage or harm is likely, the case law does not clearly specify the degree of likelihood necessary to trigger a breach of the peace.[117]

Although perhaps undesirable, these areas of uncertainty are not, in themselves, knockout arguments for ridding English law of the notion of breach of the peace. However, they acquire additional potency when combined with the related point that legislation confers upon the police extensive—and, in general, much more clearly defined—powers to manage public protests. As Stone observes: 'In the majority of situations in which a police officer might wish to use the breach of the peace power, there is an equivalent statutory power available.'[118] The risk that Stone perceives is that the existence of a 'catch-all' breach of the peace power will allow the police to intervene in a broader range of situations and to a greater extent than they can under their generally more tightly defined statutory powers. For example, in *Laporte*, Lord Bingham remarked that, in the Public Order Act 1986, Parliament had 'conferred carefully defined powers and imposed carefully defined duties' on the police: 'Offences were created and defences provided.' Resisting arguments on behalf of the police that their power to intervene in relation to breaches of the peace was constrained only by a vague notion of reasonableness, Lord Bingham said that he would find it 'surprising' if, alongside the police's closely defined statutory powers, there were to exist a common law power to control breaches of the peace 'bounded only by an uncertain and undefined condition of reasonableness'.[119]

Concerns about the breadth of the police's breach of the peace powers are potentially rendered less pressing by the fact that such powers now have to be exercised compatibly with the ECHR. Whether this is an adequate answer to criticisms such as Stone's depends on whether the courts are willing to give the relevant Convention rights sufficient bite. While several of the cases considered in this chapter are encouraging in this regard, we will see in the next section that it would be remiss to assume that the HRA has adequately curbed the breach of the peace doctrine.

---

[115] *Steel v UK* (1999) 28 EHRR 603, [54].   [116] (1999) 28 EHRR 603.

[117] Stone, 'Breach of the Peace: The Case for Abolition' [2001] 2 Web JCLI.   [118] [2001] 2 Web JCLI.

[119] *R (Laporte) v Chief Constable of Gloucestershire Constabulary* [2006] UKHL 55, [2007] 2 AC 105, [46].

5.7 **Article 5**

So far, our focus has been on the compatibility of English law with the provisions in Arts 10 and 11 of the ECHR, concerning freedom of speech and freedom of assembly. It is also necessary to consider the 'right to liberty and security of person' under Art 5. The most obvious way in which that right can be infringed is by imprisonment: someone locked in a prison cell does not enjoy liberty of the person in any meaningful sense. What is the relevance of this to the right to protest? Clearly, if 'liberty' were simply to mean 'freedom of movement', in the sense of having the right to go wherever one wanted, then any power to control where protests can take place would constitute an infringement. However, the right to liberty is not as wide as that: a person is not deprived of his liberty simply because he is not permitted to enter or protest in a particular place. It follows that no difficulty in relation to Art 5 arises when the police exercise their powers under, for example, ss 11–14C of the Public Order Act 1986.

It is one thing to say that the right to liberty does not enable protestors to demonstrate wherever they desire—but what of a situation in which people engaged in a protest are forced to enter and remain in a particular location? The right to freedom of assembly is rendered largely worthless if protestors can lawfully be corralled by the authorities into a small area and required to remain there for several hours until a perceived threat of violence—whether from the protestors or from counter-demonstrators—has decayed. This tactic, known colloquially as 'kettling', has the effect of ghettoising protest: it prevents precisely the kind of interaction between protestors and the wider public that makes demonstrations worthwhile. It is a tactic that has been used by the police in attempts to control protests in which they anticipate serious violence or damage to property.[120] Those on the receiving end have argued that kettling constitutes an unlawful deprivation of liberty and should not therefore be used to restrict the right to protest.

That argument was considered in the case of *Austin v Commissioner of Police of the Metropolis*.[121] The police had good reason—on the basis of intelligence and past events—to expect that, on May Day 2001, serious public disorder would occur in central London spearheaded by up to 1,000 hardcore anti-capitalism protestors. Literature circulated by the organisers included incitement to looting and violence. Earlier in the day than the police had expected, demonstrators descended upon Oxford Circus, and it was decided that, in order to prevent injury to passers-by and damage to property, the protestors should be contained by placing an absolute cordon around them under breach of the peace powers. As a result, 3,000 people were penned into Oxford Circus and prevented from leaving for seven hours. This included many who had done nothing wrong and who had no intention of doing anything violent or otherwise unlawful. Indeed, some were merely passers-by who became caught up in the melée. The police sought to release people as soon as possible, and in fact released 400 people who appeared to have nothing to do with the demonstration. However, the ability of the police to release people was limited by the violent conduct of a large minority of the

---

[120] For discussion of 'kettling', see HMIC, *Adapting to Protest* (London 2009).
[121] [2009] UKHL 5, [2009] 1 AC 564.

crowd, some of whom threw missiles at the police. Faced with such a difficult situation, the question was whether the police had acted lawfully by responding as they did—in particular, had the protestors' right to liberty under Art 5 been infringed?

Article 5 begins by saying that '[e]veryone has the right to liberty' and that, in general, '[n]o-one shall be deprived of his liberty'. It then goes on to set out particular circumstances in which it is lawful to deprive someone of their liberty. It follows that when courts decide issues arising under Art 5, they ought to ask themselves two questions, as follows:

- Has the claimant been deprived of her liberty? (Clearly, if no deprivation of liberty has occurred, there can have been no breach of Art 5.)

- If so, is that action rendered lawful by virtue of falling within one of the particular circumstances in which deprivation of liberty is permissible under Art 5? (Those circumstances include lawful detention after conviction by a competent court or for the purpose of preventing the spread of infectious diseases.)

In *Austin*, it might have been expected that the court would say, in answer to the first question, that there had been a deprivation of liberty. If it had done so, it is likely that, in answering the second question, it would have been forced to say that the deprivation was unlawful. This is because maintaining public order is not one of the purposes for which deprivation of liberty may lawfully occur according to Art 5. However, in the event, the absence of any clear basis in Art 5 for deprivation of liberty on public order grounds proved irrelevant, because the court held that, in the first place, seven hours' detention in Oxford Circus did not amount to deprivation of liberty. Two factors underpinned that conclusion.

First, the court noted that there could be 'no room for argument' in relation to 'close confinement in a prison cell': this was the paradigm example of deprivation of liberty.[122] But away from that paradigm, the position is less clear: there is a ' "grey zone" where it is extremely difficult to draw the line'.[123] Factors relevant to drawing that line include 'the specific situation of the individual', 'the context in which the restriction of liberty occurs', and the extent to which it deviates from the paradigm of imprisonment.[124] It was also considered significant that a separate provision of the ECHR[125]—but one that has no application to the UK because it has not ratified the provision in question—guarantees freedom of movement. The existence of that separate provision, it was said, tended to suggest that a restriction upon *movement* should not automatically be equated to a deprivation of *liberty*.[126]

Second, and, it seems, decisively, the Court took the view that the police were acting for the legitimate purpose of attempting to prevent serious violence and disorder. The Court went on to reason that the legitimacy of that purpose bore upon the question whether the containment of the protestors in Oxford Circus amounted to a deprivation of liberty. In other words, on the Court's reasoning, whether something

---

[122] *Austin*, [18], *per* Lord Hope.   [123] *Guzzardi v Italy* (1981) 3 EHRR 333, 387, *per* Judge Matscher.
[124] *R (Laporte) v Chief Constable of Gloucestershire Constabulary* [2006] UKHL 55, [2007] 2 AC 105, [21].
[125] Protocol 4, Art 2.   [126] *Laporte*, [16], *per* Lord Hope; [43], *per* Lord Walker.

counts as a deprivation of liberty depends, in part, on whether the supposed 'deprivation' is being imposed for a legitimate purpose. On this analysis, it was irrelevant that maintaining public order is not a legitimate reason under Art 5 for depriving someone of her liberty, because no such deprivation had taken place.

This conclusion, it has been persuasively argued, was based on a misunderstanding of ECtHR case law.[127] In *Saadi v UK*,[128] the ECtHR held that if detention is arbitrary—for example, if the deprivation goes on for longer than is necessary or is imposed in bad faith—then it will automatically contravene Art 5. What it meant by this was that even if a given deprivation of liberty appears to be lawful because it falls within the permissible circumstances set out in Art 5, it will be rendered unlawful if the decision to detain the person concerned is arbitrary. Taking this as a starting point, the House of Lords made a leap of logic in Austin. It reasoned that if arbitrariness can make unlawful that which would otherwise be a lawful deprivation of liberty, the absence of arbitrariness—that is, the existence of a good reason, such as preventing public disorder—can prevent something from counting in the first place as a deprivation of liberty. But as Feldman has noted, this presumes that Art 5 'guarantees only freedom from *arbitrary* deprivation of liberty', whereas in fact it 'guarantees freedom from deprivation of liberty, save in the specific circumstances listed in the Article, and even then only if the action is non-arbitrary'.[129] The better view is that whether detention is arbitrary is relevant only to the question whether a deprivation is lawful by virtue of falling within one of the permissible circumstances—and is, on this analysis, irrelevant to the prior question whether a deprivation has, in the first place, occurred.

It had been anticipated that the Grand Chamber of the ECtHR would restore orthodoxy when the case reached it, but it failed to do so.[130] Admittedly, it was not prepared to go as far as accepting that an 'underlying public interest motive' was relevant to the deprivation question. However, the ECtHR did hold that whether a deprivation had occurred was to be judged with reference to case-specific considerations such as the 'type, duration, effects and manner and implementation of the measure in question'.[131] Applying this approach, and taking account of the fact that the police had taken the least intrusive and most effective action to contain a volatile, dangerous situation, the ECtHR held that no deprivation had taken place.[132] Mead notes: '[I]t is hard not to view the result as a rewriting of the scope of the Article 5 guarantee', which, in substance, mirrors the much-criticised approach of the House of Lords.[133]

The practical effect of *Austin* is to make deprivation of liberty lawful if it strikes a fair balance between the interests of the protestors and the need to maintain public order even though no mention is made of this in Art 5. This might be regarded as an entirely sensible outcome, but the risk is that it might represent the thin end of the wedge. As

---

[127] Feldman, 'Containment, Deprivation of Liberty and Breach of the Peace' [2009] CLJ 243; Mead, 'Of Kettles, Cordons and Crowd Control: *Austin v Commissioner of Police for the Metropolis* and the Meaning of "Deprivation of Liberty" ' [2009] EHRLR 376.

[128] (2008) 47 EHRR 427.

[129] Feldman, 243–44.   [130] *Austin v UK* (2012) 55 EHRR 14.

[131] *Austin v UK*, [57]–[58].   [132] *Austin v UK*, [66].

[133] 'Kettling Comes to the Boil before the Strasbourg Court: Is It a Deprivation of Liberty to Contain Protesters En Masse?' [2012] CLJ 472, 474.

Feldman observes, the Law Lords' intentions might be considered good, in that they were seeking to strike a balance between the interests of individuals and the wider community. But, as Feldman goes on to say, 'the road to hell is paved with good intentions', and it is possible to imagine such reasoning 'being applied in other contexts to reduce other fundamental and absolute rights almost to vanishing point'.[134] Fenwick, meanwhile, argues that *Austin* 'fuel[s] once again the argument that abolition of the breach of the peace doctrine, at least in relation to public protest, is overdue'.[135]

Q In *Austin*, Lord Neuberger said it would be 'very odd' if the police could not, without breaching Art 5, act as they had done so as to prevent serious violence and disorder.[136] Do you think that it was acceptable for the House of Lords and, subsequently, the Grand Chamber of the ECtHR to fill the perceived lacuna in Art 5—that is, the absence of a public order justification for deprivation of liberty—by finding that there was no deprivation of liberty in the first place?

6. Conclusions

For the reasons considered at the beginning of this chapter, freedom of assembly—and, in particular, the right to protest—is important. It is clear that the right is, in practice, recognised in English law to a significant extent. It is equally clear that the right to protest is circumscribed—in some senses, quite heavily—by the law. An important influence in this area, and an important yardstick against which English law falls to be measured, is the ECHR. It is apparent that since that measure was made effective in domestic law by the HRA, there has, in general, been greater recognition of the right to protest. Decisions such as *Jones* (in which the legitimacy of protesting on public highways was recognised), *Laporte* (in which it was made clear that the police must exercise their breach of the peace powers in a way that imposes only necessary and proportionate restrictions on the right to protest), and *Redmond-Bate* and *Bibby* (in which it was held that those powers cannot normally be exercised against peaceful protestors) have all served, under the influence of the HRA, to solidify and extend the right to protest in English law. The direction of travel is not, however, all one way. In particular, as we saw earlier in the chapter, the conferral upon local authorities of new powers to make Public Spaces Protection Orders has resulted, in some places, in a reassertion of the people's 'right' not to be offended, annoyed, or troubled. The desire of politicians to prioritise such matters is perhaps understandable. Yet it must be borne firmly in mind that one of the hallmarks of a free and democratic society is the capacity of individuals to express themselves—including by protesting—in ways that may disquiet or perturb. That does not mean that the right to protest does or should amount to *carte blanche*. But it does underline the need for vigilance when it comes to balancing protestors' rights against others' interests.

---

[134] Feldman, 244.

[135] 'Marginalising Human Rights: Breach of the Peace, "Kettling", the Human Rights Act and Public Protest' [2009] PL 737, 757.

[136] *Austin v Commissioner of Police of the Metropolis* [2009] UKHL 5, [2009] 1 AC 564, [64].

Expert commentary
Current challenges to the right to protest
David Mead, Professor of UK Human Rights Law, University of East Anglia

Perhaps the greatest changes in this area over the past decade or so have been in two areas. First, an increase in forms of preventative policing, reflecting what Lucia Zedner has called the 'preventive turn' in criminal justice more widely. Second, there has been an increase in forms of what we might term 'privatised regulation'. The forms of public control—that is, control through the police or other state bodies, with the introduction of PSPOs being a prime example—have increased. But arguably this change has been shadowed, perhaps overshadowed, by a shift to forms of control in the hands of those companies that are the individual targets of protest and political activism, such as arms manufacturers and pharmaceutical companies. This brings a host of different and more problematic concerns for *public* lawyers.

Let us consider that first change—what the sociologists Patrick Gillham and John Noakes term 'strategic incapacitation'. As regards the policing of protests, this denotes a shift from enforcement *after* the event—arrest, charge, prosecution, and conviction—towards seeking to exert control beforehand. We might usefully divide these further into two: on one hand, preventive policing, and on the other 'panoptical' policing. We might even typify some preventive action as pre-crime policing, with echoes of the film *Minority Report*. For example, on the day of the Royal Wedding in April 2011, there was a mass round-up in London of the 'usual suspects', all on grounds of 'imminent breach of the peace'. Most were later released without charge and those that were not had bail conditions imposed on them relating to swathes of London. This led to the *Hicks* litigation, in which the Supreme Court held that the police had acted lawfully by detaining the people concerned for short-term preventive purposes.[137]

The excessive use of bail for those arrested but not, and never, charged prompted critical comment from the UN's Special Rapporteur on Peaceful Assembly. In 2013, the Special Rapporteur noted the case of 'Critical Mass', a monthly mass cycle journey through central London. On the evening of the opening ceremony of the Olympic Games in 2012, 182 cyclists were arrested under s 12 of the Public Order Act 1986. Many had bail conditions imposed by the police, including one excluding them from the whole London borough that housed most of the Olympic venues.[138] This is a form of extra-judicial regulation and restriction—police bail is not imposed by a court—without any guarantee of due process or proportionality. Similarly, anti-social dispersal orders (created in 2014 in the Anti-social Behaviour, Crime and Policing Act) have been used to clear protesters occupying the Aylesbury Estate in Southwark, south London, and peaceful demonstrations against the fur trade and Israel in Liverpool— despite specific protection for freedom of expression in s 35 of the Act. This move towards the assumption and presumption of guilt creates a 'chill' on the right to protest by 'suspect communities'. Where the effective exercise of rights is guaranteed on a differential basis, this must be a concern for public lawyers, invested as we are with ideas of equality before the law and the absence of arbitrary state power.

The concept of the panopticon derives from Jeremy Bentham, who wrote about the all-seeing prison in the late eighteenth century. Michel Foucault developed the idea some two hundred years later, conceiving of such prisons as a means for the powerful to exert and retain control through disciplining behaviour. The extent of and scope for surveillance generally—by

---

[137] *R (Hicks) v Commissioner of Police for the Metropolis* [2017] UKSC 9, [2017] 2 WLR 824.
[138] Report to the UN Human Rights Council, 17 June 2013, A/HRC/23/39/Add.1 available at **http://www. ohchr.org/EN/Issues/AssemblyAssociation/Pages/CountryVisits.aspx**

both the state and by private companies such as Google and Facebook—has probably been the greatest change and advance this millennium; not surprising given the rate of techno-logical development. In the context of protest, we can again see this in a variety of ways and variety of forms. There is the physical surveillance and monitoring at issue in the *Catt* case, brought by an 80-year-old peace campaigner activist from Brighton.[139] There, a majority of the Supreme Court decided that there was nothing unlawful, in human rights terms, in the police constructing a database recording Mr Catt's participation in protests in the presence of others known for disorder and violence.

This sits alongside more insidious infiltration by undercover officers embedding themselves in protest and activist groups, even to the extent of forming long-term relationships and father-ing children, and acting as agents provocateurs. There are other disruptive forms of surveillance such as open source monitoring of social media like Facebook and Twitter[140]—which the police have claimed needs no lawful basis, since they, like anyone else, are free to engage in it. There is also the surveillance of 'domestic extremists', a key part of the government's Prevent strategy for countering terrorism, now set out in the Counter-Terrorism and Security Act 2015. This term lacks any legal foundation and originated in informal Home Office guidance. Critics allege this has led to the criminalising and marginalising of communities (again), most obviously and par-ticularly the UK's approximately two-million-strong Muslim community, as well as leading to the police targeting the (otherwise) lawful and legitimate political activities of many others. This is because the duty to prevent people being drawn into terrorism defines 'extremists' as those who make 'vocal or active opposition to fundamental British values, including democracy, the rule of law, individual liberty and mutual respect and tolerance of different faiths and beliefs'.[141]

You might have noted a seeming tension here, given that I earlier described the other signifi-cant issue in the area as the increase in regulation and control in the hands of private actors. Most, perhaps all, of that which we have just considered indicates an augmentation of *state* control through the police. In reality though, there is no tension. There has been no—or little—decrease in public regulation, save for the removal of 'insulting' from s 5 of the Public Order Act 1986 in 2013. What there has actually been is an *increase* in overall control, both public *and* private.

Let us turn to that second main change that we identified at the outset. In my expert com-mentary in the previous edition, I noted how one of the key factors in determining not only the success but also the occurrence of any protest was the availability of land: every protest needs a venue. The transfer of land ownership out of public hands and into those of private developers both reduces what land we can use and limits how effective any protest might be. This shift has shown no sign of abating in the three years since the last edition of this book was published. Other ways in which we might speak of the regulation of protest being privatised would include the plans, floated more than once by the Metropolitan Police, to charge the organisers of protests the costs of policing and security.

This has two consequences.[142] First, it leads to a reconceptualisation of the right of pro-test founded on its intrinsic worth only to those individual participants, not one based on its instrumental public utility and social value to us all. Second, it creates a system of two-tier

---

[139] *R (Catt) v Commissioner of Police for the Metropolis* [2015] UKSC 9

[140] What happened to Brighton resident Beth Granter in 2014 is instructive here: **http://bethgranter. com/blog/2014/08/police-intimidation-of-queer-anti-austerity-activist-in-brighton/**

[141] The revised 2015 Prevent Guidance (**https://www.gov.uk/government/publications/prevent-duty-guidance**) adopts the definitions in that of 2011, published by the coalition government **https://www.gov. uk/government/publications/prevent-strategy-2011**

[142] David Mead, *ProtestMatters* blog, 11 February 2015, **https://protestmatters.wordpress.com/2015/ 02/11/quis-debit-ipsos-custodes-the-real-costs-of-the-cost-of-protest/**

protection: rights for those who can afford to pay—and are willing to pay—and fewer rights for the rest of us. We might also note, in this general context, the existence of what in the USA are termed SLAPPS—strategic lawsuits against public participation. We have started to see the emergence of such claims, brought by the commercial targets of protest, in the UK. The most well known is the McLibel trial, but other grounds for making claims would include harassment, trespass, and even the economic tort of inducing breach of contract by unlawful means.

We should also note the increased cooperation between the police and private companies. For instance, there is evidence that Nottinghamshire Police colluded with energy company EDF against 'No Dash for Gas' by formally serving civil papers on activists and by sharing their personal data with the power company.[143] Operating in parallel to such police conduct is the increased use by commercial companies of private security guards to police their property. This creates problems.[144] Moving from criminal law enforcement, where defendants are legally aided, to the civil law brings costs implications for those who are protesting. Then there are issues relating to accountability and transparency—police officers are subject to external control, either democratically through the recently instituted Police and Crime Commissioners or via the Office for Police Conduct. Meanwhile, the Home Secretary, who is ultimately responsible for various policing-related matters, remains politically accountable in Parliament. No such mechanisms exist for private companies seeking to control or restrain individual protesters.

These developments have certainly weakened the right to protest. It has not, however, been all one-way: some judgments have upheld that right. Alongside *Laporte*, there is *Mengesha*, where the court held that the police did not have the power at common law to demand personal details such as name and address, as a condition of leaving a 'kettle'.[145] Broadly speaking though, the trend is a regressive, not an expansive, one.

Further reading

FENWICK, 'Marginalising Human Rights: Breach of the Peace, "Kettling", the Human Rights Act and Public Protest' [2009] PL 737
　　A critical analysis of the police's breach of the peace powers.

MEAD, 'A Chill through the Back Door? The Privatised Regulation of Peaceful Protest' [2013] PL 100
　　Considers how private power and private law may present threats to the right to protest.

MEAD, *The New Law of Peaceful Protest* (Oxford 2010)
　　A detailed and critical examination of the law of peaceful process viewed from the perspectives of both UK domestic law and the ECHR.

WILLIAMS, *Keeping the Peace* (London 1967)
　　A classic and groundbreaking work in this area.

---

[143] Netpol, 'Policing Protest—What We Can Expect in 2015,' 19 January 2015, **https://netpol.org/2015/01/19/predictions-2015/**

[144] See more widely Mead, "A Chill Through the Back Door? The Privatised Regulation of Peaceful Protest" [2012] PL 100.

[145] *R (Mengesha) v Commissioner of Police for the Metropolis* [2013] EWHC 1695 Admin.

21

Policing—Powers, Accountability, and Governance

1.	Introduction	891
2.	Police powers	895
3.	Governance, accountability, and remedies	905
4.	Conclusion	914
	Further reading	915
	Useful websites	916

1. Introduction

1.1 Policing

Few, if any, agencies of the state exert a more visible or intrusive influence upon people's lives than the police. Effective policing is essential to the maintenance of a civilised society. The rights and freedoms of the individual are likely to amount to very little if people fear for their personal safety and the security of their property. And one of the essential tasks of the state is to protect individuals; to this end, the police have special powers to investigate crimes and arrest and detain criminal suspects. But there must be controls and checks over the police themselves. Anarchy is not compatible with the rule of law; yet nor is unchecked authoritarianism. The police can be a force for ill as well as good. From the systematic rapes carried out in secret Sri Lankan detention centres[1] to widespread corruption in the Nigerian police,[2] it is clear that policing is potentially a site of significant, even devastating, abuse of power.

---

[1] Human Rights Watch, *We Will Teach You a Lesson* (New York 2013).
[2] Human Rights Watch, *Everyone's in on the Game* (New York 2010).

The misuse of police power does not happen only in authoritarian or developing countries. Over recent years, there have been many instances of wrongful, corrupt, and unlawful behaviour by the British police. Consider the following:

- institutional racism in London's Metropolitan Police Service that came to light in relation to the investigation of the murder of Stephen Lawrence;[3]

- the systematic cover-up by the police to avoid blame for the Hillsborough stadium disaster in 1989 in which 96 innocent people were unlawfully killed;[4]

- the conviction in 2013 of a senior police officer for attempting to sell information to a newspaper;[5]

- the conduct of undercover police officers who, among other things, formed intimate relationships with members of protest groups that they had infiltrated.[6]

Episodes such as these show that the conduct, behaviour, and ethics of the police are rightly—and necessarily—the subject of public concern in the UK. Public trust in the police must be earned. It cannot be taken for granted.

Indeed, policing engages one of the key themes examined throughout this book. Whilst institutionally distinct from central and local government, the police are nevertheless a particularly notable manifestation of executive authority. Policing epitomises the capacity of the state to exert coercive power over individuals, and while holding the police to account is a different enterprise from holding (say) government Ministers to account, the same fundamental challenge arises. The possession of power and the need for effective systems of accountability go hand-in-hand; and when the powers in question are considerable, the need for accountability is all the greater.

1.2 Powers, accountability, governance

This chapter addresses three key issues. The first concerns the extent and limits of the *powers of the police*—and, correlatively, the relevant rights of individuals. These factors determine the nature of the terrain upon which the police and the individual lawfully interact. They also feed into the second issue: the arrangements for *holding the police to account*. One of the benchmarks by reference to which the legitimacy of police conduct may be judged is the extent of their legal powers and, in particular, whether those powers have been exceeded or otherwise abused—although, as we will see, other standards are also relevant. Third, it is necessary to consider the *governance*

---

[3] See The Stephen Lawrence Inquiry, *Report of an Inquiry by Sir William Macpherson of Cluny* (Cm 4262 1999).

[4] See *The Report of the Hillsborough Independent Panel* (HC 581 2012–13); Independent Police Complaints Commission, *Decision in Response to the Report of the Hillsborough Independent Panel* (London 2012).

[5] 'Police officer found guilty of trying to sell information to *News of the World*', *The Guardian*, 11 January 2013.

[6] This matter is presently the subject of a public inquiry known as the Undercover Policing Inquiry. See **https://www.ucpi.org.uk**

arrangements that apply to the police. To whom do they answer, and to what extent are—and should—politicians be involved in the business of policing?

1.3 **'The police' and 'localism'**

Before embarking upon our examination of those issues, a preliminary point needs to be made. People tend to refer to 'the police' as if there were a single entity that answered to that name. For two reasons, however, the reality is less monolithic and more complex. First, as *Halsbury* puts it, 'in essence a police force is neither more nor less than a number of individual constables, whose status derives from the common law, organised together in the interests of efficiency', so that the authority of a member of a police force derives directly from his status as a constable.[7] Second, there is no national UK police force. England and Wales are divided into 43 areas,[8] each of which has its own police service.[9] Northern Ireland[10] and Scotland have their own police services.[11] Each police service is headed by a chief constable[12] (or 'commissioner' in the case of London's two services, the Metropolitan Police and the City of London Police[13]). In addition to the territorial police services, there are forces—like the British Transport Police[14] and the National Crime Agency (NCA)[15]—whose jurisdiction is not confined to a specific geographical part of the UK.

The creation of the NCA in 2013—and of its predecessor, the Serious and Organised Crime Agency—engages another of our key themes: the multilayered nature of the constitution, and the balance between the competing forces of centralisation and localism. Policing in the UK is organised principally along local lines, as the existence of 43 separate services in England and Wales demonstrates. There are strong arguments for policing to be rooted in local communities, including facilitating accountability and being responsive to local needs. And in the White Paper that prefigured the NCA, the government recognised that 'local communities and the police are best placed to cut crime at a local level'.[16] But some matters are best tackled on a national basis, not least because individual police forces lack relevant expertise or resources. Against that background, the NCA's remit extends to organised crime, border policing, economic and cyber crime, and child exploitation. While the NCA is a police force in a recognisably traditional sense (eg it can undertake its own investigations), it also seeks to work with other agencies in order to coordinate policing in areas within its remit.[17]

---

[7] *Halsbury's Laws of England*, vol 84 (5th edn, London 2013), [1]–[2].

[8] Police Act 1996, s 1 and Sch 1, para 1. The latter provision lists 41 force areas; in addition, there are two London police forces: the Metropolitan Police and the City of London Police.

[9] Police Act 1996, ss 2 and 5A.   [10] Police (Northern Ireland) Act 2000, s 1.

[11] Police and Fire Reform (Scotland) Act 2012, s 6.

[12] Police Reform and Social Responsibility Act 2011, s 2 (England and Wales); Police (Northern Ireland) Act 2000, s 33; Police and Fire Reform (Scotland) Act 2012, s 6.

[13] Police Reform and Social Responsibility Act 2011, s 4.

[14] Railways and Transport Safety Act 2003, Pt 3.   [15] Crime and Courts Act 2013, ss 1–16.

[16] Home Office, *The National Crime Agency: A Plan for the Creation of a National Crime-Fighting Capability* (Cm 8097 2011), [2.2].

[17] Crime and Courts Act 2013, s 1(11).

Table 21.1 Illustrative examples of national policing and coordination arrangements

National Crime Agency	National Police Chiefs' Council	College of Policing	Home Secretary
Serious and organised crime Border policing Cyber and economic crime Child sexual abuse and exploitation	Enables chief constables and forces to work together where appropriate Coordinates operational responses in relation to such matters as terrorism and national emergencies Implements national standards developed by College of Policing	Utilises research and evidence to establish 'what works' in policing policy and practice Supports professional development through education and training Sets national standards and issues codes of practice and guidance	Sets policing strategy in relation to 'national threats' Intervenes in relation to failing police forces Determines how much money police forces receive (via Police and Crime Commissioners) from central funds

However, the NCA is far from the only evidence of a nationally coordinated approach to policing, as Table 21.1 shows. Crucial coordinating and strategy-setting roles are played by the National Police Chiefs' Council,[18] the College of Policing, and the Home Secretary. Nevertheless, a cardinal principle is that in relation to *operational* matters, the police are independent of government. As Lord Denning MR once said, a chief constable 'is not the servant of anyone, save of the law itself'.[19] This point notwithstanding, the 43 police services in England and Wales do not operate wholly independently from one another or from central government.

Questions remain about whether the present model is sustainable. In 2013, eight separate Scottish police forces were replaced with a single force, and consolidation has been on the political agenda in England and Wales for some time,[20] albeit that it has not yet taken place in a form that results in a reduction in the number of local services. It remains to be seen whether centralisation and coordination will be pursued further. Part of the logic behind the creation of bodies such as the NCA is that local forces are relieved, or supported in the execution, of functions that they might otherwise struggle with: in that sense, the present framework can be regarded as one that supports local policing. It is also clear that local policing has a good deal of popular support, and the introduction of Police and Crime Commissioners, considered later, is premised upon a perceived need to root policing in local communities.[21]

---

[18] The National Police Chiefs' Council is the successor organisation to the Association of Chief Police Officers.

[19] *R v Commissioner of Police of the Metropolis, ex p Blackburn* [1968] 2 QB 118, 136.

[20] For detailed discussion, see HM Inspectorate of Constabulary, *Closing the Gap* (London 2005).

[21] See section 3.2.

A national police service is therefore certainly not on the cards. It is worth noting, however, that a report produced in 2013 by Lord Stevens, a former Metropolitan Police Commissioner, concluded that the present model is unsustainably fragmented and in urgent need of change.[22] And, as we saw when we examined local government in Chapter 7, the forces of centralisation are relatively strong in the UK, the rhetoric of 'localism' notwithstanding.

2. Police powers

Given their distinctive role in protecting the public against crime, the police must possess certain powers—for instance, to stop and search suspects, to arrest and detain them, and to enter property. This gives rise to an obvious tension. To investigate crimes and to protect the public, the police must be able to exercise intrusive powers. But everyone is presumed innocent until proved guilty by a court of law, and the exercise of police powers must not infringe an individual's human rights any further than is necessary. The scope of the police's powers is therefore key: not only because it is determinative of the way in which the police may lawfully treat individuals, but also because the limits of the police's powers form a benchmark against which they can be held to account.

This chapter does not provide a comprehensive survey of police powers. Instead, it addresses the principal issues concerning those powers which are of particular constitutional importance and engage key individual rights. Given the central tension involved here, it is crucial—for both the police, the public, and criminal suspects— that there is a set of clear legal rules. The legal framework for police powers is provided by the Police and Criminal Evidence Act 1984 (PACE), which codified the law in this area. There are also several codes of practice made under the Act, which set out in detail how certain of the powers should be exercised.

2.1 Stop and search

In the year 2014–15, the police in England and Wales stopped and searched people or vehicles on 541,000 occasions.[23] All but 0.2 per cent of this activity took place under s 1 of PACE, which falls to be read with Code of Practice A. The s 1 power arises only if there are reasonable grounds for suspecting stolen or prohibited articles[24] will be found,[25] and extends to searching persons and vehicles for such articles and to detaining persons and vehicles for the purpose of conducting such searches.[26] Code of Practice A explains that reasonable grounds for suspicion will arise only when there is an objective basis for suspicion based on facts, information, or intelligence.[27]

---

[22] Independent Police Commission, *Policing for a Better Britain* (London 2013), ch 7. The Commission was established by the Labour Party in opposition.

[23] Home Office, *Police Powers and Procedures England and Wales Year Ending 31 March 2015* (London 2015), section 4.1.

[24] For example, offensive weapons or articles capable of being or intended to be used in relation to the commission of certain offences (including burglary and theft): PACE, s 1(7).

[25] PACE, s 1(3).   [26] PACE, s 1(2).   [27] PACE Code A, para 2.2.

It also emphasises that generalisations and stereotypical images of certain groups as more likely to be involved in criminality cannot be relied upon, and that decisions to stop and search should not be based on characteristics such as race, sex, or religion.[28]

However, in a major report published in 2013, HM Inspectorate of Constabulary (HMIC) found that of nearly 9,000 stop and search records examined, 27 per cent failed to disclose sufficient grounds to justify the lawful use of the power.[29] It called for better training, monitoring, scrutiny, and accountability in relation to stop and search, and observed that overuse or inappropriate use was likely to be corrosive of public trust. In response to the HMIC report, the government introduced a new scheme relating to the use of stop and search powers. Among other things, the scheme seeks to improve data recording by police forces, improve public understanding of stop and search policy and practice, and enable concerns to be raised with police forces via a 'community complaints' mechanism.[30] Probably as a result of intense scrutiny of stop and search, the use of such powers has fallen dramatically in the recent past. Indeed, the number of stops and searches carried out in 2014–15 represented a 58 per cent reduction compared with 2010–11.

The controversy surrounding stop and search powers is attributable to two causes. The first concerns how such powers are used in relation to black and minority ethnic (BME) groups. Figures published by the Ministry of Justice in 2011 showed that a black person was seven times more likely than a white person to be stopped and searched in 2009–10.[31] In a major report published in 2010, the Equality and Human Rights Commission concluded racial discrimination is a significant reason behind the figures, and that 'stop and search powers are being used in a discriminatory and unlawful way'.[32] Since then, the figures have shown some improvement, although parity remains some way off. In 2014–15, a person belonging to a BME group was still *twice* as likely as a white person to be stopped and searched—and someone who was black was *four times* as likely as a white person to be stopped and searched.[33] The Home Office seeks to explain these figures by pointing to the fact that a large percentage of stops and searches take place in London, whose population is unusually ethnically diverse.[34]

A second area of controversy concerns stop and search powers that—unlike the power conferred by s 1 of PACE—can be exercised *without* reasonable suspicion. Such powers arise under s 60 of the Public Order and Criminal Justice Act 1994 and under the Terrorism Act 2000. The former permits (in limited circumstances) searches of persons and vehicles for 'offensive weapons or dangerous instruments' *whether or not* there are 'grounds for suspecting that the person or vehicle is carrying weapons or articles of that kind'.

---

[28] PACE Code A, para 2.2B. There is, however, a proviso to the effect that such things can be taken into account if there is information or intelligence which provides a description of a suspect.

[29] HMIC, *Stop and Search Powers: Are the Police Using Them Effectively?* (London 2013), 29–30.

[30] Home Office and College of Policing, *Best Use of Stop and Search Scheme* (London 2014).

[31] Ministry of Justice, 'Statistics on Race and the Criminal Justice System 2010' (London 2011), 34.

[32] Equality and Human Rights Commission, *Stop and Think* (London 2010), 58.

[33] Home Office, *Police Powers and Procedures England and Wales Year Ending 31 March 2015* (London 2015), section 4.1.

[34] Home Office, *Police Powers and Procedures England and Wales Year Ending 31 March 2015* (London 2015), section 4.1.

However, the power is not automatically available to police officers. Rather, they can only exercise it when an authorisation (lasting 24 hours) is issued by a senior officer; and that can be done only in limited circumstances relating to the anticipation or commission of incidents involving serious violence or the possession of dangerous instruments or offensive weapons. It was argued in *R (Roberts) v Commissioner of Police of the Metropolis* that the s 60 'suspicionless' search regime was incompatible with the right to respect for private life under ECHR, Art 8.[35] The Supreme Court, however, rejected that argument, noting that s 60 searches can be authorised only in limited circumstances and for short periods of time, and that although no reasonable suspicion requirement applies, police officers' powers are limited by, among other things, relevant codes of practice, police policies, and equality law. The Court concluded that while it would clearly be possible for s 60 powers to be authorised or used unlawfully, their authorisation and use does not *necessarily* involve any breach of Art 8. The Court therefore declined to issue a declaration of incompatibility under s 4 of the Human Rights Act 1998.[36]

The Terrorism Act 2000 also permits stop and search in relation to vehicles, their occupants, and pedestrians in the absence of any reasonable suspicion. Not least because they were used in circumstances far removed from counter-terrorism operations,[37] the stop and search provisions originally contained in the Act proved to be highly controversial. They were the subject of a successful challenge before the European Court of Human Rights (ECtHR) in *Gillan v UK*.[38] Like the power considered in the previous paragraph, the stop and search power in the Terrorism Act arises only when an authorisation by a senior officer is in place. However, it had been the practice of the Metropolitan Police, following the entry into force of the Act, to make the power available to constables continuously (by renewing the authorisation every time it expired) throughout the whole of Greater London. The Strasbourg Court concluded that the use of the power engaged ECHR, Art 8, and that the breadth of the power and the absence of adequate safeguards meant that any interference with the right was not 'in accordance with the law' as required by Art 8(2).

Following *Gillan* and a government review[39] partly prompted by that decision, the relevant provisions were replaced. While reasonable suspicion on the part of the constable carrying out the stop and search is still not required, authorisation to use the power can be granted less readily. In particular, authorisation can only be given if there are reasonable grounds for suspecting 'that an act of terrorism will take place'.[40] Moreover, the senior officer must reasonably consider that authorisation is 'necessary to prevent such an act', that the area to which it relates is 'no greater than is necessary', and that the duration of the authorisation is 'no longer than necessary'.[41] In contrast, the original version of the Act merely stipulated that the senior officer concerned had to consider authorisation 'expedient for the prevention of acts of terrorism'.[42] The new provisions are clearly designed to meet the concerns expressed by the ECtHR in *Gillan*

---

[35] [2015] UKSC 79, [2016] 1 WLR 210.
[36] On declarations of incompatibility, see Chapter 18, sections 3.4.5–3.4.6.
[37] See Liberty, *From War to Law* (London 2010), ch 2.   [38] (2010) 50 EHRR 45.
[39] HM Government, *Review of Counter-Terrorism and Security Powers* (Cm 8004 2011).
[40] Terrorism Act 2000, s 47A(1).   [41] Terrorism Act 2000, s 47A(1).
[42] Terrorism Act 2000, s 44(3) (now repealed).

and to make it easier to establish the proportionality of the regime and of actions taken in accordance with it. The upshot is that the powers can be used only in very limited circumstances—and in fact they were not used at all in 2014–15.[43]

> **Q** Should stop and search powers ever be exercisable in the absence of reasonable suspicion?

2.2 Entry onto property

The case of *Entick v Carrington* famously established that state authorities have no greater inherent legal capacity to enter onto private property than that which individuals possess.[44] But it does not follow that the right to property—recognised by the ECHR[45] but also deeply ingrained in the common law for centuries—represents an immovable obstacle to the effective investigation of alleged criminal offences or the apprehension of suspects who may be present upon such property. For one thing, police officers (like anyone else) can enter upon private property if they have, or can be assumed to have, permission.[46] Naturally, however, they will often not have such permission; and so the extent to which the *Entick v Carrington* principle constitutes an obstacle turns upon the extent to which the police can identify a positive legal basis for entering onto private property. Here, we draw attention to three particularly significant such bases.

First, under s 8 of PACE, magistrates may issue *search warrants*. Section 8(1) says that a magistrate can issue a warrant if satisfied that there are reasonable grounds for believing *all* of the following things:

- an indictable offence[47] has been committed;
- there is material on the premises which is likely to be of substantial value to the investigation;
- it is likely to be relevant evidence; and
- it is not legally privileged,[48] excluded material, or special procedure material.[49]

In addition to the above, *one* of the following conditions must be met:[50]

- it is not practicable to communicate with any person entitled to grant entry to the premises or access to the evidence;
- entry will be denied absent a warrant; or
- the purpose of a search may be frustrated or seriously prejudiced unless entry can be secured immediately upon arrival.

---

[43] Home Office, *Police Powers and Procedures England and Wales Year Ending 31 March 2015* (London 2015), section 4.1.

[44] (1765) 19 St Tr 1030.   [45] ECHR, Protocol 1, Art 1.

[46] *Robson v Hallett* [1967] 2 QB 939.

[47] ie an offence that can or must be the subject of a trial in the Crown Court, rather than in a magistrates' court.

[48] eg correspondence between a solicitor and client; see further PACE, s 10.

[49] 'Excluded' and 'special procedure material' are defined in PACE, ss 11 and 14 respectively. Examples include certain forms of confidential and journalistic information.

[50] PACE, s 8(3).

The warrant can either relate to specific premises or to all premises occupied or controlled by a specified person,[51] and may authorise one or multiple entries.[52] A constable 'may seize and retain anything for which a search has been authorised'.[53] PACE Code B makes detailed provision concerning the searching of premises and the seizure of property.

Second, PACE also provides for entry and search *without a search warrant*. Section 17 permits entry and search for purposes including:

- executing an arrest warrant;
- arresting a person for an indictable offence or one of the several offences listed in s 17(1);
- recapturing prisoners;
- saving life or limb;
- preventing serious property damage.

There must be reasonable grounds for believing that the person concerned is on the premises.[54] Meanwhile, s 18 permits entry to and search of premises occupied or controlled by a person who is under arrest for an indictable offence, provided that there are reasonable grounds for believing that relevant (but not legally privileged) evidence will be found.[55] Such property, if found, can be seized.[56] Before a s 18 search can be carried out, written authorisation from an officer of the rank of inspector or above is normally needed.[57] The final provision that should be noted in this category is s 32(2)(b), which allows the police to enter and search premises in which a person under arrest was present at the time of or immediately before the arrest. The search must be for evidence relating to the offence for which the person was arrested,[58] and there must be reasonable grounds for believing such evidence to be present on the premises.[59]

Third, the effect of s 17(5) and (6) is that *common law powers of entry to deal with breaches of the peace* (but *only* those common law powers of entry) are preserved. We considered breach of the peace in Chapter 20.[60]

2.3 **Arrest**

The police's power to arrest someone—to seize an individual and take him or her into police custody—is highly significant. It is where the hands of the state limit the freedom of an individual. Prior to arrest, the police's powers are relatively limited (extending to such matters as stop and search, as described in section 2.1). Post-arrest, far more substantial and intrusive powers become available. We examine some of those post-arrest powers later. We begin, however, by considering the lawfulness of the arrest itself. Two sets of issues arise, concerning the *trigger conditions* for the power of arrest and the *manner* in which an arrest must be carried out if it is to be lawful.

---

[51] PACE, s 8(1A).   [52] PACE, s 8(1C).   [53] PACE, s 8(2).
[54] PACE, s 17(2)(a).   [55] PACE, s 18(1).   [56] PACE, s 18(2).   [57] PACE, s 18(4).
[58] PACE, s 32(2)(b).   [59] PACE, s 32(6).   [60] See Chapter 20, section 5.

2.3.1 Trigger conditions

An application for an arrest warrant can be made to a magistrate on the ground that the person concerned has, or is suspected of having, committed an indictable offence or an offence punishable by imprisonment.[61] However, a warrant is not always needed. At common law, the power to arrest without a warrant arises in relation to anticipated or ongoing breaches of the peace. As we explained in Chapter 20, this is a highly significant power that can be used (among other things) to restrict or prevent the activities of pro-testors.[62] PACE, meanwhile, confers a broad power to arrest without a warrant. Section 24 permits a constable to arrest a person provided that two conditions are satisfied.

The first condition concerns the *circumstances*. In particular, one of the following must be true of the person concerned:

- she is about to commit an offence (or that there are reasonable grounds for sus-pecting that she is about to commit an offence);
- she is in the act of committing an offence (or that there are reasonable grounds for suspecting that she is committing an offence);
- she is guilty of an offence (or that there are reasonable grounds for suspecting that she is guilty of it); or
- she is suspected on reasonable grounds of having committed an offence that there are reasonable grounds for suspecting has been committed.

The second condition that must be satisfied if the power of arrest conferred by s 24 is to be exercisable is that the constable must have reasonable grounds for believing that, for one of the reasons set out in s 24(5), it is necessary to arrest the person concerned. Those reasons include:

- ascertaining the person's name or address;
- preventing physical injury, property damage, an offence against public decency, or an unlawful obstruction of the highway;
- allowing the prompt and effective investigation of the offence or the person's conduct;
- preventing hindrance of prosecution by the disappearance of the person.

It has been held that the power of arrest arises only if the constable actually believed that arrest was necessary for one of those reasons *and* if objectively that belief was reasonable. The court determines these matters by reference to the facts known to the officer making the arrest.[63]

Separate provision is made, in s 24A, for arrest without warrant by persons other than constables. The power of 'citizen's arrest', as it is colloquially known, is drawn more narrowly than the power vested in constables by s 24. In particular, s 24A applies only to indictable offences.

---

[61] Magistrates' Courts Act 1980, s 1.   [62] See Chapter 20, section 5.
[63] *Hayes v Chief Constable of Merseyside Police* [2011] EWCA Civ 911, [2012] 1 WLR 517.

2.3.2 Manner of arrest

As well as circumscribing the circumstances in which the power of arrest may be used, the law also prescribes certain matters concerning the manner of arrest. In particular, s 28 of PACE stipulates than an arrested person must be told *that she is under arrest* and what the *ground for arrest* is. This must happen either at the time of arrest or as soon as is practicable thereafter. This reflects the requirement in ECHR, Art 5(2) that someone who is arrested must be 'informed promptly, in a language which he understands, of the reasons for his arrest and of any charge against him'. If the requirements in s 28 of PACE are not met, the arrest is rendered unlawful—but only until such time as the failure is corrected by the provision of the relevant information.[64]

2.4 **Detention**

ECHR, Art 5(1) enshrines the right to 'liberty and security of person'—of which detention following arrest is a clear prima facie breach. However, Art 5(1)(a) sets out various circumstances in which deprivation of liberty is lawful (provided that it is in accordance with a procedure prescribed by law), one of which is

> the lawful arrest or detention of a person effected for the purpose of bringing him before the competent legal authority on reasonable suspicion of having committed an offence or when it is reasonably considered necessary to prevent his committing an offence or fleeing after having done so.

Article 5(3) goes on to say:

> Everyone arrested or detained in accordance with the provisions of paragraph 1(c) of this Article shall be brought promptly before a judge or other officer authorised by law to exercise judicial power and shall be entitled to trial within a reasonable time or to release pending trial. Release may be conditioned by guarantees to appear for trial.

Against this background, we turn to consider domestic law in this area. Following arrest at a place other than a police station, the person concerned must normally be taken to a police station as soon as is reasonably practicable.[65] The suspect can be detained (without being charged with any offence) for 24 hours.[66] That period can be extended in three stages, as shown in Table 21.2. At each stage, the police officer or magistrates' court must be satisfied that there are reasonable grounds for believing that all the following conditions are satisfied:[67]

- further detention is 'necessary to secure or preserve evidence relating to an offence for which [the person concerned] is under arrest or to obtain such evidence by questioning him';
- the offence is an indictable one; and
- the investigation is being conducted 'diligently and expeditiously'.

---

[64] *DPP v Hawkins* [1988] 1 WLR 1166; *Lewis v Chief Constable of South Wales* [1991] 1 All ER 206.
[65] PACE, s 30(1A).
[66] PACE, s 41.   [67] PACE, ss 42–4.

Table 21.2 Extending detention

Stage 1 PACE, s 42	*Stage 2* PACE, s 43	*Stage 3* PACE, s 44
A **police officer** of the rank of superintendent or above can extend detention for up to **12 hours**, yielding a total detention period of up to **36 hours**.	A **magistrates' court** can extend detention for up to **36 hours**, yielding a total detention period of up to **72 hours**.	A **magistrates' court** can extend detention for up to 36 hours. However, the total detention period must not exceed **96 hours**. If, therefore, the full 36-hour extension is granted at stage 2, no more than 24 hours can be added at stage 3.

The fact that detention is *authorised* in accordance with the regime just set out does not mean that it should *necessarily* continue for the whole of the relevant period. Reviews must be carried out within six hours of detention beginning, and at intervals of not more than nine hours thereafter, to determine whether detention remains necessary.[68]

Different arrangements apply to detention in terrorism-related cases; the thinking being that post-arrest evidence-gathering may be particularly challenging and time-consuming in such cases, and that post-arrest incapacitation may be warranted by risks to public safety.[69] Terror suspects arrested under s 41 of the Terrorism Act 2000 can be detained for up to 48 hours without any judicial involvement, and for a maximum of 14 days under a warrant issued by a judicial authority.[70] The government's 2011 review of terrorism legislation concluded that if exceptional circumstances were felt to justify the possibility of detention for more than 14 days, the appropriate vehicle would normally be emergency primary legislation.[71] However, there is in fact provision in the Terrorism Act for the executive to introduce detention beyond the 14-day limit if, at the relevant time, Parliament is dissolved (or has met following dissolution but the first Queen's Speech has not taken place). In such circumstances, the Secretary of State can temporarily extend the maximum detention period from 14 to 28 days if she considers that it is 'necessary by reason of urgency' to do so.[72]

> **Q** Can longer pre-charge detention in terrorism cases be justified? Should other offences which may be challenging to investigate also attract longer periods of pre-charge detention?

Limiting the length of detention is one thing; but it is clearly also necessary to equip individuals with safeguards *during* the period of detention. To that end, Codes of

---

[68] PACE, s 40 and Code C, para 15.

[69] *Review of Counter-Terrorism and Security Powers: Review Findings and Recommendations* (Cm 8004 2011), p 8.

[70] Terrorism Act 2000, s 41 and Sch 8.

[71] *Review of Counter-Terrorism and Security Powers: Review Findings and Recommendations*, p 14.

[72] Terrorism Act 2000, Sch 8, para 38.

Practice issued under PACE[73] make detailed provision, in relation to non-terrorism cases, concerning such matters as the safekeeping of detainees' property, the condition of cells, and the provision of such things as bedding, food, and washing and toilet facilities.[74] In addition—and importantly—there is a right not to be held incommunicado, *secret* detention being the epitome of unaccountable authoritarianism. There is thus a right to have a person of the detainee's choice notified, as soon as is practicable, of the fact of arrest and place of detention.[75] In limited circumstances—for example, where there are reasonable grounds to believe that telling the person concerned of the arrest will hinder the apprehension of other suspects or the recovery of stolen property—the exercise of the right can be delayed, but for no more than 36 hours. Similar arrangements apply to persons arrested under s 41 of the Terrorism Act 2000, but the maximum period of delay in that context is 48 hours.[76] In addition to the right to have someone notified, detainees have a right, considered later, to consult a lawyer.

2.5 Questioning and evidence

2.5.1 General matters

Following arrest, the police must decide whether to charge the suspect—a decision that will usually be made in the light of (among other things) information gleaned by questioning the suspect. The conduct of interviews is heavily regulated by Part V of PACE and several associated Codes of Practice. Substantial parts of that regulatory regime serve to protect not only the interests of individual suspects, but also the wider public interest in ensuring that interviews are conducted in a way likely to elicit reliable evidence that will be of probative value in any subsequent legal proceedings. Thus, for instance, interviews must be audio recorded in accordance with PACE Code E.[77] Interviews can (but do not have to be) video recorded; if they are, then a separate Code of Practice, PACE Code F, applies.[78]

Evidence can be gathered from suspects by means other than questioning. PACE therefore confers—and delimits—a range of further powers, including powers to:

- search detainees;[79]

- examine detainees to ascertain their identity or whether they have 'any mark that would tend to identify [them] as a person involved in the commission of an offence';[80]

- conduct an intimate search of detainees if there are reasonable grounds for suspecting that they are concealing such things as sharp objects or certain drugs;[81]

---

[73] PACE Code H deals with suspects detained under s 41 of the Terrorism Act 2000. Otherwise, PACE Code C applies.

[74] The custody officer is under a legal duty to ensure that detainees are treated not only in accordance with PACE, but also with the Codes of Practice issued under it: PACE, s 39.

[75] PACE, s 56(1).   [76] Terrorism Act 2000, Sch 8, para 8, read with s 41(3).

[77] PACE, s 60(1) and Police and Criminal Evidence Act 1984 (Codes of Practice) (Code E) Order 2003, SI 2003/705. A separate Code of Practice applies to the recording of interviews with terror suspects.

[78] PACE, s 60A.   [79] PACE, s 54.   [80] PACE, s 54A.   [81] PACE, s 55.

- take fingerprints;[82]
- collect intimate samples (in limited circumstances and subject to the detainee's consent).[83]

Two issues relating to questioning and evidence-gathering, both of which raise issues concerning fundamental rights, merit particular consideration. We address them in the following two sections.

2.5.2 Provision of legal advice

Under s 58 of PACE, a person 'arrested and held in custody in a police station or other premises' is entitled to 'consult a solicitor privately at any time'. The exercise of that right can, however, be delayed for up to 36 hours in limited circumstances (eg if there are reasonable grounds to believe that the exercise of the right will hinder the apprehension of other suspects or the recovery of stolen property). Detainees must be informed of their entitlement to seek legal advice and must not be dissuaded from exercising it.[84] Analogous arrangements apply in respect of terror suspects (except that the maximum period of delay is 48 hours).[85] The presence of a lawyer is both a safeguard against oppressive or otherwise abusive interrogation, as well as a means of upholding the right against self-incrimination (the risk being that a suspect may unnecessarily incriminate herself in the absence of adequate legal advice).

The right of suspects to legal advice has been held by the ECtHR to be implicit in the right to a fair trial enshrined in ECHR, Art 6. In *Salduz v Turkey*, the Court held that access to a lawyer must normally be provided 'as from the first interrogation of a suspect by the police, unless it is demonstrated in the light of the particular circumstances of each case that there are compelling reasons to restrict this right'.[86] *Salduz* was applied by the UK Supreme Court in *Cadder v HM Advocate*, in which it was held that the questioning of a suspect in the absence of a solicitor had resulted in a breach of Art 6.[87] What constitutes 'the first interrogation', such as to trigger the right to legal advice, is however unclear.[88] Significantly, the Supreme Court held in *Ambrose v Harris* that a key consideration is whether the person concerned is in police custody.[89] Thus the Court held that the right was not triggered when, at the roadside, a motorist who was stopped on suspicion of drink-driving gave incriminating answers to police questions under caution.

2.5.3 The right to silence

The right to silence is intimately connected with the presumption of innocence (which means that it is for the police to prove guilt rather than for the defendant to establish her innocence). It therefore used to be the case that negative inferences could not

---

[82] PACE, s 61.   [83] PACE, s 62.   [84] PACE Code C, paras 6.1–6.4.
[85] Terrorism Act 2000, Sch 8, paras 7 and 8.   [86] (2009) 49 EHRR 19, [55].
[87] [2010] UKSC 43, [2010] 1 WLR 2601.
[88] See generally White and Ferguson, 'Sins of the Father? The "Sons of *Cadder*" ' [2012] Crim LR 357.
[89] [2011] UKSC 43, [2011] 1 WLR 2435.

be drawn from an accused person's refusal to answer questions. In 1993, the Royal Commission on Criminal Justice recommended (by a majority) retaining that position. It argued that while qualifying the right to silence by permitting the drawing of adverse inferences might secure the conviction of some guilty parties, that advantage was outweighed 'by the risk that the extra pressure on suspects to talk . . . may result in more convictions of the innocent'.[90]

However, the government disagreed and the law was changed. Inferences can now be drawn from a defendant's failure, in response to police questions, to disclose a fact subsequently relied upon in her defence and which she could reasonably have been expected to have mentioned when questioned.[91] The possibility of drawing inferences from silence does not however arise if the accused has not had an opportunity to secure legal advice.[92]

3. Governance, accountability, and remedies

The facts that very significant legal powers are vested in the police and that those powers are subject to important restrictions raises a further set of concerns. How are the police to be held to account for the use (and misuse) of their powers? What governance arrangements exist to this end? And what remedies are available if the police act improperly?

3.1 Complaints

Unsurprisingly, given the scale and nature of their work, many complaints are made each year against police forces. Indeed, the number of complaints recorded has been rising steadily in recent years, from just under 23,000 in 2004–5 to more than 37,000 in 2014–15.[93] Complaints cover a broad spectrum, ranging from allegations of rudeness to charges of assault, oppression, corruption, sexual violence, and unlawful detention.[94] The police complaints system has recently been overhauled by the Policing and Crime Act 2017. At the time of writing, relevant parts of the Act had not entered into force. However, this section is written on the basis that the Act is in force.

A key role is played in this sphere by the Independent Office for Police Conduct (IOPC), formerly known as the Independent Police Complaints Commission (IPCC). The new name is merely one of several recent changes introduced as a result of concerns in this area, including a lack of public confidence in the fairness and efficacy of the police

---

[90] *Royal Commission on Criminal Justice* (Cm 2263 1993), p 54.
[91] Criminal Justice and Public Order Act 1994, s 4.
[92] Criminal Justice and Public Order Act 1994, s 34(2A).
[93] IPCC, *Police Complaints: Statistics for England and Wales 2014/15* (London 2015), 13.
[94] IPCC, *Police Complaints: Statistics for England and Wales 2014/15* (London 2015), 17; *The Abuse of Police Powers to Perpetrate Sexual Violence* (London 2012); *Corruption in the Police Service in England and Wales: Second Report* (London 2012).

complaints system.[95] Section 10 of the Police Reform Act 2002 (PRA) requires the IOPC to make 'suitable arrangements' for the handling and recording of complaints and to ensure that there is public confidence in those arrangements. The IOPC does not itself handle all complaints against the police, with many less serious complaints being dealt with at a local level. However, certain matters can—and some matters must—be referred to the IOPC. The matters that must be referred are those that are of a particularly serious nature, as the following example box shows. Even if matters of the types mentioned in the example box are not referred to the IOPC, it can, if it finds out about them, choose to treat them as if they had been referred and then deal with them accordingly.[96]

Eg

- complaints that allege conduct resulting in death or serious injury;

- complaints that the IOPC requires the police to refer to it;

- complaints that allege particularly serious forms of misconduct by the police, such as a serious assault, a serious sexual offence, serious corruption, or certain forms of discriminatory behaviour;

- certain matters concerning serious misconduct even if the alleged misconduct has not been the subject of a complaint;

- all 'death and serious injury matters'. Such matters arise when someone dies or sustains serious injuries and had been arrested, was in custody, or had otherwise had contact with the police that may have caused or contributed to the death or serious injury concerned.

It might be assumed that once a matter is referred to the IOPC, its role is to investigate and reach a conclusion about who, if anyone, is guilty of wrongdoing. However, not all of the matters referred to the IOPC end up being investigated by it. Indeed, perhaps surprisingly, some matters referred to the IOPC end up being investigated at a local level—in other words, by the very police force from which the complaint or concern originates.

This has long been the source of serious concern. The IPCC, as it then was, was the subject of a damning report by the House of Commons Home Affairs Committee in 2010. It concluded that the IPCC had failed adequately to establish its credentials as a genuinely independent and effective body.[97] The Committee re-examined the IPCC in 2013, and again expressed very serious concerns.[98] It concluded that the Commission was 'woefully underequipped' and under resourced, and that it carried out too few investigations itself, meaning that too many cases are 'referred back to the original force on a complaints roundabout'. In response, the Home Secretary told Parliament in

---

[95] Over one in three of those surveyed in 2014 lacked confidence in the system: IPCC, *Public Confidence in the Police Complaints System* (London 2014), 22.

[96] PRA, Sch 3, paras 4A, 13A, and 14CA.

[97] House of Commons Home Affairs Committee, *The Work of the Independent Police Complaints Commission* (HC 366 2009–10).

[98] House of Commons Home Affairs Committee, *Independent Police Complaints Commission* (HC 494 2012–13).

2013 that the IPCC's capacity to conduct investigations would be enhanced so that it could deal with 'all serious and sensitive allegations' itself.[99]

Against that background, the IOPC, as it now is, is in the middle of a 'change programme' which, among other things, involves taking on and training additional investigators so that it is able to undertake more investigations itself.[100] The law has also been changed in relation to the options that are open to the IOPC when matters are referred to it (or when it treats matters as having been referred to it). The options now open to the IOPC,[101] once it has decided that the matter should be investigated, are shown in Table 21.3.

Table 21.3 The options open to the Independent Office for Police Conduct

Option 1 No IOPC involvement	Option 2 IOPC investigation	Option 3 Directed investigation
The IOPC can choose this option (and must choose it) only if it determines, having considered the seriousness of the case and the public interest, it is appropriate for the matter to be investigated without any involvement by the IOPC	If the IOPC determines that option 1 is not appropriate, it must investigate the matter itself unless it determines that a directed investigation would be more appropriate	Directed investigations are undertaken when the IOPC—having decided that there should be some IOPC involvement—determines that a directed investigation would be more appropriate than an investigation undertaken by the IOPC itself
Cases of this nature are returned to the local police force concerned, which carries out the investigation in accordance with its own processes	Cases of this nature are investigated by the IOPC itself	Directed investigations are undertaken by an investigator appointed locally, but under the direction of the IOPC

It remains the position that not all cases will be investigated by the IOPC itself. However, as Table 21.3 indicates, matters can only be returned for local resolution without any IOPC involvement if the IOPC determines that that would be appropriate bearing in mind the seriousness of the case and the public interest. Moreover, when the IOPC decides that it should be involved in a matter, the amended legislation adopts as a default position that the IOPC's involvement will take the form of an IOPC-run investigation rather than an investigation that is merely directed by the IOPC. 'Directed investigations' replace what were formerly known as 'managed investigations', but, under the revised legislation, the IOPC has a greater degree of control over directed investigations than it had over managed investigations.

---

[99] Theresa May MP, HC Deb, vol 558, col 715 (12 February 2013). See also *Government Response to the Eleventh Report of the Home Affairs Committee* (HC 8598 2012–13).

[100] IPCC, *IPCC Corporate Plan 2015/18* (London 2015), 24–5.

[101] As set out in the PRA, Sch 3, para 15(4A)–(4C).

Following the conclusion of an investigation, the IOPC can require disciplinary action to be taken. If the report indicates that a criminal offence may have been committed by a person to whose conduct the investigation related, the matter is referred to the Director of Public Prosecutions when the IOPC considers such a referral to be appropriate.[102]

3.2 Accountability and governance

3.2.1 HMIC and the College of Policing

Whereas the focus of the IOPC (and of local police forces' complaints procedures) is upon reactively dealing with individual complaints, HM Inspectorate of Constabulary (HMIC) subjects police forces to proactive scrutiny. Its core role is to 'promote improvements in policing to make everyone safer'.[103] It does so by (among other things) carrying out on-the-ground inspections, engaging in 'mystery shopping', surveying the public, and annually grading each police force on their 'effectiveness', 'efficiency', and 'legitimacy'.

As well as inspecting individual forces and units with them, HMIC carries out broader inquiries into both specific areas of policing, such as anti-social behaviour[104] and serious and organised crime,[105] and issues arising from particular matters of concern, such as policing failures in relation to the Jimmy Saville scandal[106] and the handling of the riots that took place in summer 2011.[107] By examining such issues, HMIC enables others—including the public and politicians—to make informed judgments about the performance of police forces. HMIC's reports thus feed into wider systems of accountability.

Recent changes to the law have augmented HMIC's role through the innovation of what are known as 'super-complaints'.[108] These are quite distinct from the sort of complaints that can be made to the IOPC, which relate to individual incidents. In contrast, super-complaints are concerned with (allegations of) systemic failure within the police. To some extent, the distinction between regular complaints and super-complaints tracks the distinction drawn in Chapter 15 concerning the 'redress' and 'control' functions of public sector ombudsmen.[109] It is unsurprising, therefore, that super-complaints fall within the remit of HMIC rather than the IOPC, given that it is the former that is responsible for maintaining and raising policing standards at a macro-level, whereas the IOPC is concerned with individual complaints.

Only bodies designated by the Secretary of State may make a super-complaint.[110] Furthermore, super-complaints cannot be made casually or straightforwardly. Rather, they take the form of reports submitted by designated bodies setting out in

---

[102] PRA, Sch 3, para 23.   [103] HMIC website: **http://www.hmic.gov.uk**

[104] HMIC, *Anti-social Behaviour: Stopping the Rot* (London 2010).

[105] HMIC, *Getting Organised* (London 2009).   [106] HMIC, *Mistakes were Made* (London 2013).

[107] HMIC, *The Rules of Engagement* (London 2011).   [108] PRA, Part 2A.

[109] The 'redress' function relates to the resolution of individual grievances; the 'control' function concerns identifying problems on a larger scale and, by doing so, facilitating improvement by public bodies.

[110] At the time of writing, no super-complainants had been designated. It is likely, however, that bodies, including charities, with relevant expertise will be designated.

some detail evidence of a systemic problem. In this way, super-complaints feed into HMIC's scrutiny role, by enabling it to direct attention to particular issues high-lighted through the making of such complaints.

HMIC exists alongside the College of Policing, whose roles include facilitating evidence-based improvements in policing methods, setting professional standards, supporting police officers' professional development, and 'striking off' officers dis-missed for misconduct (thereby preventing their employment by another force). The roles played by HMIC and the College of Policing are complementary and mutually reinforcing. In particular, by setting out such matters as best-practice standards, the College of Policing lays down benchmarks that may form reference points for HMIC's evaluation of police forces' performance and operations.

3.2.2 Police and Crime Commissioners

One of the most significant changes in police governance and accountability in recent years occurred in 2012, with the elections of the first Police and Crime Commissioners (PCCs). Prior to that innovation, local police authorities were responsible for securing 'the maintenance of an efficient and effective police force' for the relevant area and holding to account the chief constable.[111] However, the then government took the view that this system was inadequate.[112] It said that police authorities' lack of public visibility meant that they were unable to supply a meaningful form of democratic oversight or accountability—a vacuum that central government had felt compelled to fill by means of centrally set targets.[113] In the light of this, PCCs were created (as the then Home Secretary put it) for the purposes of 'restoring . . . the connection between the police and the people' and 'putting the public back in the driving seat'.[114]

Under the Police Reform and Social Responsibility Act 2011, the primary func-tions of PCCs are securing the maintenance of an effective and efficient police force for the relevant area and holding the chief constable to account for the exercise of his own functions and those of persons under his direction and control.[115] PCCs are also responsible for appointing, suspending, and removing chief constables,[116] for deter-mining the level at which the 'precept'—the policing-related component of council tax—should be set,[117] and for allocating funding in consultation with the chief con-stable.[118] In addition, the PCC is required to issue a 'Police and Crime Plan'—to which the chief constable must have regard[119]—setting out, among other things, policing priorities.[120] This may, for instance, require the police to focus on issues (eg anti-social

---

[111] Police Act 1996, s 6 (now repealed).

[112] Home Office, *Policing in the 21st Century: Reconnecting Police and the People* (Cm 7925 2010).

[113] Similar difficulties arise in relation to the relationship between central government and local coun-cils: see Chapter 7.

[114] *Policing in the 21st Century: Reconnecting Police and the People*, p 3. The position is different in London, where there is a Mayor's Office for Policing and Crime, headed by the elected Mayor of London, instead of a PCC: Police Reform and Social Responsibility Act 2011 (PRSRA), s 3.

[115] PRSRA, s 1. See also several briefing notes for PCC candidates at **https://www.gov.uk/government/publications/candidate-briefing-2016-pcc-roles-and-responsibilities**

[116] PRSRA, s 38.   [117] PRSRA, s 26 and Sch 5.   [118] PRSRA, ss 21–5.

[119] PRSRA, s 8(2).   [120] PRSRA, ss 5–8.

behaviour or the treatment by police of victims of crime) that the PCC considers to be of particular concern to the local community. The autonomy of PCCs is curtailed, however, by the requirement that, in drawing up plans, regard must be had to the Strategic Policing Requirement issued by the Secretary of State.[121]

Alongside PCCs, the 2011 Act created Police and Crime Panels.[122] The role of Panels, which consist principally of councillors (or elected mayors) drawn from local authorities within the relevant police area,[123] is to scrutinise and hold to account PCCs,[124] and to act, in some circumstances, as a counterbalance to PCCs. For instance, a Panel can veto a PCC's choice of chief constable,[125] and can object to (but cannot actually block) a PCC's decision to remove a chief constable from office.[126] Panels must also be consulted about Police and Crime Plans[127] and precepts,[128] and have a power of veto in relation to the latter.[129] A Panel can call a PCC (and his staff) before it to answer questions,[130] and can suspend him if it appears that he has been charged with a criminal offence punishable by more than two years' imprisonment.[131]

The most controversial issue relating to PCCs concerns the operational independence of the police. In its response to the White Paper that prefigured the 2011 Act, the Association of Chief Police Officers (ACPO)[132] noted that such independence is a long-standing feature of British policing, and argued that it 'helps ensure that professional rather than political judgments are applied, not only to individual operational decisions . . . but also to resource deployment decisions'.[133] ACPO argued that the new arrangements should not amount to a 'master-servant relationship'.[134] The nature of the relationship between PCCs and chief constables is not addressed in detail in the 2011 Act, although it does affirm that police forces and their civilian staff 'are under the direction and control of the chief constable'.[135] Meanwhile, the Policing Protocol[136] says that the police are 'operationally independent'[137] and that chief constables' 'direction and control' includes 'total discretion to investigate', the 'balancing [of] competing operational needs within the framework of priorities and objectives set by the PCC', and 'operational decisions to reallocate resources to meet immediate demand'.[138]

The House of Commons Home Affairs Committee conducted an inquiry into PCCs in 2014, noting that while one of the main aims of the new system was to 'introduce democratic accountability to the determination of local policing priorities',[139] public understanding and awareness of the role of PCCs was extremely

---

[121] See section 1.3.

[122] Again, the position is different in London, where a committee of the London Assembly fulfils the role played elsewhere by Police and Crime Panels: PRSRA, ss 32–3.

[123] PRSRA, Sch 6.   [124] PRSRA, s 28.   [125] PRSRA, Sch 8, Pt 1.

[126] PRSRA, Sch 8, Pt 2.   [127] PRSRA, s 5(6).   [128] PRSRA, Sch 5.

[129] PRSRA, Sch 5, para 4.   [130] PRSRA, s 29.   [131] PRSRA, s 30.

[132] ACPO has now been replaced by the National Police Chiefs' Council.

[133] ACPO, *Response to Policing in the 21st Century: Reconnecting the Police and the People* (London 2010), 6–7.

[134] *Response to Policing in the 21st Century*, 7.   [135] PRSRA, s 2(3).

[136] The Policing Protocol Order 2011, SI 2011/2744, issued under PRSRA, s 79.

[137] Policing Protocol, para 22.   [138] Policing Protocol, para 33.

[139] *Police and Crime Commissioners: Progress to Date* (HC 757 2013–14), [2].

low. Indeed, turnout in the 2012 PCC elections was only 15 per cent. That figure rose to 26 per cent in 2016, although probably only because PCC and local authority elections ran simultaneously. The Home Affairs Committee did, however, note that public understanding of the role of PCCs was increasing, observing that PCCs 'have provided greater clarity of leadership for policing within their areas' and 'are increasingly recognised by the public as accountable for the strategic direction of their police force'.[140] Nonetheless, the Committee expressed concern about the role of PCCs in removing chief constables. It noted that the legislation is silent as to the grounds upon which a chief constable can be removed, and recommended that the legislation should be amended so as to be specific and limit those grounds.[141] The government, however, rejected that recommendation.[142] More recently, the Home Affairs Committee returned to the role of PCCs, emphasising, among other things, the need for PCCs to prioritise public engagement and the importance of ensuring that Police and Crime Panels operate effectively so as to provide adequate checks and balances on PCCs.[143]

> **Q** The introduction of Police and Crime Commissioners can be regarded as a triumph for local democracy or as a potentially dangerous move towards the politicisation of policing. Which is the better view?

3.3 Legal redress

Complaints processes and mechanisms for accountability and good governance exist alongside legal forms of redress that arise in the event of misconduct by the police. As a 'public authority' within the meaning of s 6 of the Human Rights Act 1998 (HRA), the police are obliged to act compatibly with individuals' Convention rights. This results in a general and wide-ranging requirement to exercise powers that engage such rights only when—and to the extent—that this is necessary and proportionate to such aims as maintaining public order and preventing crime. This point is illustrated by the way in which the police's powers to regulate protests have been impacted by the HRA—an issue that we explored in Chapter 20. Three further issues should be considered in this regard.

3.3.1 Inadmissibility of evidence

Relevant and otherwise admissible evidence may be rendered inadmissible by failures—including misconduct by the police—in the evidence-gathering process. However, automatic exclusion of improperly obtained evidence may in some circumstances represent a disproportionate response. This raises a question about the

---

[140] *Police and Crime Commissioners: Progress to Date*, [56].
[141] *Police and Crime Commissioners: Progress to Date*, [75].
[142] *HM Government's Response to Police and Crime Commissioners: Progress to Date* (Cm 8981 2014), p 11.
[143] *Police and Crime Commissioners: here to stay* (HC 844 2015–16).

rationale for excluding such evidence. At least two possibilities (which may well overlap with one another) arise:

- Such evidence might be excluded because its probative value is diminished by the impropriety; failing to record a police interview with the accused might fall into this category.

- It might be appropriate to exclude evidence on public policy grounds—whether or not its reliability is compromised—because of the unacceptability of the means by which it was obtained.

Against this background, it is necessary to consider two key provisions of PACE, beginning with s 76(2). This provision deals specifically with the exclusion of *confessions*,[144] and provides that if the defendant claims that the confession was obtained by forbidden means, then it will be inadmissible unless the prosecution shows beyond reasonable doubt that it was *not* obtained in such a way. The means forbidden by s 76(2) are twofold.

First, confessions must not be extracted through 'oppression'. This includes 'torture, inhuman or degrading treatment, and the use or threat of violence (whether or not amounting to torture)'.[145] The first part of that formulation mirrors the language of ECHR, Art 3, but the second clearly contemplates that conduct falling short of the Art 3 threshold may nevertheless render a confession inadmissible. It has been noted, however, that the 'use or threat of violence' is presumably not intended to extend to a single instance of a merely technical battery, and is likely to require 'a substantial application of force'[146]—although repeated *minor* applications of force ought perhaps to suffice.[147] Because 'oppression' merely 'includes' torture etc and the use or threat of violence, the possibility arises that it may extend beyond such conduct. For instance, in *R v Paris*, oppression was held to have occurred when the defendant confessed to murder in response to bullying and shouting, having previously denied the charge 300 times.[148]

The second of the means proscribed by s 76(2) is doing or saying anything that is likely, in the circumstances, to render unreliable any confession made as a result. This does not require any impropriety on the part of the police.[149] Nor does it require the confession to be *actually* unreliable: if the test is satisfied, the confession must be excluded even if it turns out to be true. The test is thus a hypothetical one. In *R v McGovern*, for instance, the confession of a vulnerable suspect denied legal advice was judged as *likely* to render any confession unreliable. It was therefore excluded, even though it turned out that the confession was *actually* true.[150]

Alongside the s 76 *requirement* to exclude certain *confessions*, s 78 creates a *discretion* to exclude *any evidence* whose admission 'would have such an adverse effect on the fairness of the proceedings that the court ought not to admit it'. In exercising this

---

[144] According to PACE, s 82(1), 'confession' includes 'any statement wholly or partly adverse to the person who made it, whether made to a person in authority or not and whether made in words or otherwise'.
[145] PACE, s 76(8).   [146] Tapper, *Cross and Tapper on Evidence* (12th edn, Oxford 2010), p 639.
[147] Dennis, *The Law of Evidence* (4th edn, London 2010), p 229.   [148] (1993) 97 Cr App R 99.
[149] *R v Fulling* [1987] QB 426.   [150] *R v McGovern* (1991) 92 Cr App R 228.

discretion, the court takes account of whether there has been a breach of the PACE Codes of Practice, although the fact that such a breach has occurred does not automatically mean that evidence obtained as a result will be excluded under s 78: the question is whether the fairness of the proceedings has been sufficiently compromised.

For instance, in *R v Cooke*, Glidewell LJ held that DNA evidence, even if unlawfully obtained, should not be excluded under s 78 because such unlawfulness 'did not in any way cast doubt upon the accuracy or strength of the evidence'.[151] He distinguished unlawfully-obtained confessions, which, he said, often involved a deviation from standards of propriety that would tend to cast doubt upon the truth of the confession.[152] (It does not, however, follow that egregious impropriety in the gathering of evidence will necessarily go unchecked provided that the reliability of the evidence is untainted: the court might, in cases of appropriate seriousness, regard such conduct on the part of the authorities as an abuse of process, such that the proceedings must be stayed.[153]) The court, as a public authority, is obliged by HRA, s 6 to exercise its s 78 discretion compatibly with the right to a fair trial under ECHR, Art 6. However, the House of Lords held in *R v Looseley* that existing domestic law already reflected Art 6 in this sphere.[154]

3.3.2 Habeas corpus

The writ, or remedy, of habeas corpus requires the release of a person who is being unlawfully detained. As such, it can be sought against the police if a suspect is unlawfully held.[155] It is the remedial counterpart—and is emblematic of English law's longstanding commitment—to the right to the liberty of the individual. Habeas corpus has much in common with judicial review, in that it is a means by which the lawfulness of executive action can be challenged (although there is some uncertainty about whether habeas corpus can be sought in relation to all or only some of the grounds for judicial review[156]). However, one important difference between habeas corpus and judicial review is that whereas remedies are discretionary in the latter, habeas corpus is issued as of right once the unlawfulness of the detention is established.

3.3.3 Civil liability

Habeas corpus, if granted, secures the release from detention of the individual. It does not, however, yield anything further, such as damages. But it is fundamental to the rule of law that public officials, including police officers, should be subject to at least the same legal requirements as ordinary individuals, and so damages can be obtained by means of a civil claim. Such claims are normally brought against the chief constable. She is vicariously liable for the unlawful acts of her officers, although damages are

---

[151] [1995] 1 Cr App R 318, 329.

[152] [1995] 1 Cr App R 318, 329.

[153] The relationship between s 78 and abuse of process is discussed in *R v Shannon* [2001] 1 WLR 51.

[154] [2001] UKHL 53, [2001] 1 WLR 2060.

[155] eg if the police detained a suspect for more than 36 hours without obtaining a warrant from a magistrates' court.

[156] cf *R v Secretary of State for the Home Department, ex p Khawaja* [1984] AC 74 and *R v Secretary of State for the Home Department, ex p Muboyayi* [1992] QB 244. Dicta in the former indicate that the legality of detention can be challenged in habeas corpus proceedings in reliance upon any of the grounds of judicial review. The latter, however, suggests that habeas corpus lies only where there has been a jurisdictional error.

paid out of public funds.[157] Whilst it is beyond the scope of this book to address relevant areas of private law in any detail, we note that torts that are obviously relevant in this context include the following:

- *Assault and battery* The police can be sued for assault and battery, but it is important to remember that the application or apprehension of *unlawful* force is required. Since the use of *reasonable* force by the police is lawful in many contexts,[158] that concept circumscribes the situations in which assault or battery may be committed.

- *False imprisonment* This tort is committed when the individual's freedom of movement is completely restricted, but there can be no liability when lawful authority for the restriction exists. Lawful detention (eg following arrest) cannot therefore amount to false imprisonment. The position would be different, though, if a person were, for instance, detained unlawfully (eg for more than 36 hours without a warrant from a magistrates' court). However, following the Supreme Court's decision in *Lumba*, it does not follow that liability for false imprisonment will lie in the event of *any* legal flaw in relation to the detention: where the breach is one of public law, it 'must bear on and be relevant to the decision to detain'.[159]

- *Malicious prosecution* The essence of malicious prosecution is that the claimant is successfully prosecuted without reasonable and probable cause by a defendant who acts with malice. The tort also extends to related acts, including maliciously procuring a search warrant.[160]

- *Negligence* While the police certainly do not have blanket immunity from liability in negligence, the effect of the House of Lords' decision in *Hill v Chief Constable of West Yorkshire* is that, for reasons of public policy, the police are shielded from liability in respect of many operational decisions (eg concerning the conduct of investigations).[161]

4. Conclusion

Police forces across the UK are equipped with broad, intrusive, and coercive powers that they have to exercise in often challenging circumstances in order both to advance

---

[157] Police Act 1996, s 88.

[158] PACE, s 117 permits the use of reasonable force in the exercise of any power conferred by the Act (as long as the Act does not provide that the power may be used only with consent). Meanwhile, the Criminal Law Act 1967, s 3 allows anyone (including a constable) to 'use such force as is reasonable in the circumstances in the prevention of crime, or in effecting or assisting in the lawful arrest of offenders or suspected offenders or of persons unlawfully at large'.

[159] *R (Lumba) v Secretary of State for the Home Department* [2011] UKSC 12, [2012] 1 AC 245, [68], *per* Lord Dyson. By way of example, Lord Dyson said that 'a decision to detain made by an official of a different grade from that specified in a detention policy would not found a claim in false imprisonment'.

[160] *Gibbs v Rea* [1998] AC 786.

[161] [1989] AC 53. The compatibility of English law as stated in *Hill* with ECHR, Art 6 was placed in doubt by the judgment of the ECtHR in *Osman v UK* (2000) 29 EHRR 245. However, the effect of *Osman* was circumscribed by the Court's later judgment in *Z v UK* (2002) 34 EHRR 3.

the public interest and protect individuals. Such is the nature of the police's role that its discharge inevitably attracts dissent, criticism, and complaint. But with power comes responsibility; and the greater the power, the more serious are the consequences if it is abused. It is unsurprising, therefore, that so many of the issues addressed throughout this book crystallise in the context of policing. We have seen that, in this area, issues arise concerning the balance between centralism and localism; the extent of the state's legal powers, their relationship with the rights of the individual and the consequences that follow when those powers are exceeded; the need for effective and interlocking systems of legal, political, and administrative accountability; and the importance (and contested nature) of good governance.

Like the modern state itself, the police service's role, functions, and powers are multifarious and complex—and so, inevitably, are public law's responses. But amid such complexity, sight should not be lost of a simple truth: that it is the duty of the state, whether through the police or otherwise, to act fairly, reasonably, decently, and in the public interest—and that public law plays a crucial role in securing adherence to those values.

Further reading

EQUALITY AND HUMAN RIGHTS COMMISSION, *Stop and Think* (London 2010) (**https://www.equalityhumanrights.com/sites/default/files/ehrc_stop_and_search_report.pdf**)
  Critical report by the Equality and Human Rights Commission on the use of stop and search powers.

HM INSPECTORATE OF CONSTABULARY, *Stop and Search Powers: Are the Police Using Them Effectively?* (London 2013) (**http://www.hmic.gov.uk/media/stop-and-search-powers-20130709.pdf**)
  HMIC's review of the use of stop and search powers.

HOME OFFICE, Information on role of Police and Crime Commissioners (**https://www.gov.uk/government/publications/candidate-briefing-2016-pcc-roles-and-responsibilities**)
  Information published by the Home Office on the role of PCCs.

HOUSE OF COMMONS HOME AFFAIRS COMMITTEE, *Police and Crime Commissioners: Progress to Date* (HC 757 2013–14) (**http://www.publications.parliament.uk/pa/cm201314/cmselect/cmhaff/757/757.pdf**)

HOUSE OF COMMONS HOME AFFAIRS COMMITTEE, *Police and Crime Commissioners: Here to Stay* (HC 844 2015–16) (**http://www.publications.parliament.uk/pa/cm201516/cmselect/cmhaff/844/844.pdf**)

IPCC, *Statutory Guidance to the Police Service on the Handling of Complaints* (London 2015) (**https://www.ipcc.gov.uk/sites/default/files/Documents/statutoryguidance/2015_statutory_guidance_english.pdf**)
  Formal guidance issued to police forces by the Independent Police Complaints Commission/Independent Office for Police Conduct concerning the handling of complaints.

Useful websites

http://www.college.police.uk/
Website of the College of Policing

http://www.justiceinspectorates.gov.uk/hmic/
Website of Her Majesty's Inspectorate of Constabulary

http://www.nationalcrimeagency.gov.uk
Website of the National Crime Agency

http://www.npcc.police.uk
Website of the National Police Chiefs' Council

Index

Introductory note

References such as '178–9' indicate (not necessarily continuous) discussion of a topic across a range of pages. Wherever possible in the case of topics with many references, these have either been divided into sub-topics or only the most significant discussions of the topic are listed. Because the entire work is about 'public law', the use of this term (and certain others which occur constantly throughout the book) as an entry point has been minimised. Information will be found under the corresponding detailed topics.

A

absolute entrenchment 234, 239
absolute power 61, 92
abuses of power 31, 92, 94–5, 98–9
accountability
  administrative
    accountability 389, 392–4
  cooperation between
    agencies 394
  European Union 346–7
  financial 23
  general elections 38
  good governance 354–94
    administrative
      accountability 389, 392–4
    concept of
      accountability 387–8
    elections 390
    general principles of
      public law 391–2
    generally 396–9
    legal accountability 389, 391–2
    multiple
      mechanisms 388–9
    overview 394–6
    political
      accountability 389–91
    types 388–9
  government 22–4, 25
  importance 37–8
  inquiries 734–5
  judicial review 479–80, 590–1
  legal accountability 115–16, 389, 391–2
  liberal democracy 81–3
  meaning 37, 387–8

mechanisms 480
ministerial 124–5
National Audit Office 393
ombudsmen 393
overview 394–6
parliamentary 480
political accountability
  115–16, 389–91, 402–3, 480
power 7–8
practice, in 420–1
Prime Ministers 120
processes 37–8
public expectations 396
security and intelligence
  services 460–7
targets 393
accounting officers 129
administration
  devolved 88
  discretion 610
  good 651, 656–7
  justice 113, 123, 129, 262, 268–9, 633, 651–2, 699–700
administrative agencies 20–4, 95–6, 478
Administrative Court 262, 592–8, 721
Administrative Justice
  and Tribunals Council
  (AJTC) 692, 699
administrative law 4, 20–2
  judicial review 478–9
ADR see alternative dispute
  resolution
advisers
  code of conduct 117, 133–5
  Independent Adviser on
    Ministers' Interests 125
  special 107, 117, 133–5
advisory declarations 268

Advisory Panel on Judicial
  Diversity 291
AJTC see Administrative
  Justice and Tribunals
  Council
alternative dispute
  resolution 265, 599
  judicial review 599, 604–5
alternative vote 179–80
appeals
  court structure 261–2
  First-tier Tribunal to Upper
    Tribunal 717–18
  immigration 701
Appellate Committee of the
  House of Lords 28, 64, 122, 238, 277–9
armed forces 7, 155, 561
arm's-length public
  agencies 107, 135–8
arrest
  manner of arrest 901
  police powers 899–901
  trigger conditions 900
assault
  police, by 914
assemblies
  see also freedom of assembly
  public assemblies 870–1
  trespassory 871–3
assent, royal 43, 54, 56, 155, 190, 221, 238
asylum
  seekers 73, 74, 75, 154, 162, 622
  tribunals 683
Attorney-General
  role 123
autonomy
  human rights 762
  individual 8, 69–70, 169

B

backbenchers 112, 122
  Backbench Business
    Committee 432, 433
banks 106, 423
battery
  police, by 914
bias
  actual bias 508
  apparent bias 508, 511–13
  fair-minded and informed
    observers 511–13
  impartiality 508
  judicial review 508
  judiciary 277
Bills
  government 112, 191, 192,
    213, 220, 222–3
  hybrid bills 213
  private bills 213
  Private Members' Bills 213
  types 213
Blair government 27, 28, 31, 55,
  119, 120, 126, 135
Bloody Sunday inquiry 731,
  742, 743, 746
Boundary Commissions 177
breach of confidence 846–7
  official secrecy 852
breach of contract 262
breach of the peace
  compatibility of police
    powers with ECHR
    882–3
  criminal liability 882
  meaning 877–8
  police intervention 878–9
  powers of police 880–2
  right to liberty and security
    of the person 884–7
breach of privacy 800
Brexit
  conclusions 374–5
  demarcation disputes 484
  EU law post-Brexit 357–9
  implications 80–1
  meaning 336
  Minister for Exiting the
    European Union 128
  prerogative powers 156–7
  process 370–2
  referendum 336–7
British exit see Brexit
British Transport Police 893
broadcasters/broadcasting
  see media
Brown government 30
Butler Inquiry 729, 734

C

Cabinet
  Cabinet Office 128–9
  collective responsibility
    126–7
  constitutional
    conventions 126
  function 126
  meetings 126, 134
  membership 122
  Ministers 120–3, 129, 134,
    280
  Secretary 50, 117, 130
Canada 52, 58–9
Carltona doctrine 528–9
central government see
  government
Chancellor, Lord 28, 122,
  272–5, 279–81
Chancellor of the
  Exchequer 128
Chilcot Inquiry 729
child sexual abuse
  inquiries 731
civil liability
  generally 262
  policing 913–14
civil rights
  see also human rights
  generally 23
  marches 731
  obligations 518
civil servants 107, 121, 124–5
  composition 130
  core function 131
  grades of 130
  impartiality 131
  professional
    development 130
  reform plan 132–3
  senior positions 130
Civil Service Code 117, 124,
  131, 384
CJEU see Court of Justice of
  the European Union
coalition 110, 112, 121, 127,
  172–3
Code of Conduct for Special
  Advisers 117, 133–5
codification
  parliamentary
    privilege 210–11
  policing 895
  reforms 77–80
collective responsibility 126–7
College of Policing 908–9
Committee on Standards in
  Public Life 134, 188, 384, 386

committee stage 220–4
committees
  Backbench Business 432,
    433
  legislative process 220–4
  ministerial 127
  parliamentary 16, 219, 278
  select 208–10
common law
  defamation 835
  development 270
  human rights 768–70
  powers 160
  protests 877–87
  sources of constitution 46–8
Commons see House of
  Commons
compensation
  public sector
    ombudsmen 668
  State liability 354–5
complaints procedures
  accessibility 634–5
  Department for Work and
    Pensions 636
  effective systems 634–5
  empirical research 637–8
  healthcare 638
  higher education 635
  HM Revenue and
    Customs 636
  importance of system 634–6
  MPs 636
  NHS 638
  police 638, 905–8
  proportionality 635
  quality of system 636–7
  range of procedures 635–6
  reforms 638–40
  weaknesses 637
compliance
  monitoring 106
  public sector
    ombudsmen 666–76
confidence votes 159
confidentiality 59–60, 668
  see also privacy
  legal advice 74–5
consensus 8–10, 80
Conservatives 49, 110
constituency boundaries 177
constitution
  courts 266–71
  multilayered 484–5
  overview 4–13
  political 32–3, 51, 268–70
  United Kingdom 11–12
  unwritten 11–12

written 11, 30, 32–3, 42,
    77–80, 231, 235
constitutional
    conventions 49–60, 116–17
    Cabinet 126
    devolution 325
    relevance 58–60
    territorial constitution
        325–6
constitutional government 8,
    38–9, 88
constitutional morality 57
constitutional principles 12,
    17–19, 47–8, 56
    role 62–3
    statutory
        interpretation 244–6
constitutional reforms 25–32,
    77–80, 272
constitutional rights 30,
    38–9
constitutional systems 40,
    87–8
constitutionalism see legal
    constitutionalism; political
    constitutionalism
contempt of court
    criminal liability 75
    media 828–34
    non-cooperation with
        ombudsman 666
contract
    breach of 262
Convention rights 76
conventions see constitutional
    conventions
convicted prisoners see
    prisoners
costs
    inquiries 743
    tribunals 706
Council on Tribunals 684, 699
councils
    city 46
    county 159, 484
countermajoritarianism 231
county councils 316
Court of Appeal 262, 719–21
    judiciary 258
Court of Justice of the
    European Union
    (CJEU) 263, 347
credits, tax 7
criminal contempt see
    contempt of court
Criminal Injuries
    Compensation Authority 24
criminal justice system 9, 123

criminal liability
    breach of the peace 882
    contempt of court 75
    generally 9
    racial hatred 841–2
    religion, hatred on grounds
        of 842–3
    retroactive criminal
        legislation 6
    sexual orientation, hatred on
        grounds of 842–3
Crown 102–4, 121, 135, 159–60,
    559
    executive power 108–9
    exercise of power 109
    meaning 108–9
    terminology 108–9
Crown Court 261

D
damages
    State liability 354–5
debt of honour case 640–2
decisions
    see also judicial review
    discretion 536–7
    government 35, 682–3
    impartiality 508–11
    independence 515–18
    maladministration 656
    ministerial 137, 489
    procedural fairness 523–6
    reasons for decisions 523–6
    tribunals 716–17, 722–3
declaration of incompatibility
    18, 74, 776, 785–8
declarations
    advisory 268
    remedies 583–5
    war 156, 560
defamation
    balancing interests 835
    common law 835
    criminal offences, allegation
        of commission of 835–6
    defences
        honest opinion 837
        privilege 837–8
        public interest 838–40
        single publication
            rule 840–1
        truth 836
        websites 840–1
    fair comment 837
    generally 45, 201, 835
    honest opinion 837
    ingredients of liability 835–6
    libel 835

    meaning 835
    privilege 837–8
    public interest 838–40
    reputation 835, 836
    single publication
        rule 840–1
    slander 835
    statutory test 835
    websites 840–1
deference
    proportionality 545–9
delegated legislation 21–2,
    238, 244
    consultation 147–8
    effect 144–5
    emergency measures 144
    Henry VIII powers 143–4
    judicial review 154–5
    parliamentary
        scrutiny 148–54
    publication 145–7
    role of Parliament 148–55
    scrutiny 148–54
    statutory powers to
        make 135–55
    use 141–3
democracy 63–4, 93, 166–7
    autonomy and dignity of
        individuals 169
    devolution 306–8
    European Union
        (EU) 344–5
    good governance 382
    government 37, 168–71
    implementation 171
    legitimacy 38, 271, 275
    liberal 81–3
    Mill, JS 169–70
    nature of UK
        democracy 198–200
    Parliament 168–71
    parliamentary
        sovereignty 230–1
    participative 170
    processes 9, 168
    reasons for 168–71
    representative 170
    voting in elections 173
demonstrations see freedom of
    assembly; protests
departmental select
    committees 434–42
deportation 14–15, 22
Deputy Prime Ministers 122
detention 15, 17–18
devolution 25, 27, 41, 44, 45, 56
    administrations 88
    background 297–8

devolution (*Cont.*)
balance of power 298–9
combined authorities 320
constitutional
conventions 325
deals 321
demand and supply 300–1
democracy 298, 306–8
elections 306
England 300–1, 308–30
combined authorities 320,
322–3
'English votes for English
laws' 311–13, 322
generally 308–9
intervention by the
centre 316–17
localism 317–19
regional
government 320–2
voice for England 309–10
West Lothian
question 310–12
executive powers 304–6
institutions 25, 308
legislation on devolved
issues 327–8
legislative competence 301
legislative powers 301–2
legislatures 25, 27
local government 314–15
localism 317–19
permanence
provisions 328–30
process, as 302–4
public sector
ombudsmen 642, 643
settlements 61
territorial integrity of the
UK 297–8
tribunals 696
dictatorship 169, 171
elective 109–13
direct effect
directives 351–3
EU law 348–57
horizontal 353–4
reasons for and nature of
principle 348
regulations 348–9
treaties 349
vertical 351–3
directives
enforcement 350
EU law 348, 356–7
general principles of EU
law 356–7
implementation 350–1

nature of 350
unimplemented
directives 350–1
vertical direct effect 351–3
disclosure
confidentiality 59–60
official secrecy 852, 853
public sector
ombudsmen 666
sensitive information 852,
853
discretion
Carltona doctrine 528–9
input into the decision-
making process 536–7
irrelevant
considerations 536–7
judicial review 526–39
legitimate
expectations 531–6
motives 538–9
non-delegation
principle 526–9
non-fettering
principle 529–30
policies, adherence
to 529–30
powers 47, 68–9, 73
purposes 538–9
relevant
considerations 536–7
rules, adherence to 529–30
discrimination 70, 75
dispute resolution 267–8
alternative dispute
resolution 265, 599, 604–5
judicial review 601–3
disqualification
automatic 465–7
impartiality 508–11
voting 173
dissolution of Parliament 109,
117, 171, 408, 561, 902
distress
public order offences 865–8
diversity
generally 248
judiciary 275, 287–93
donations
political parties 185–6

E
early neutral evaluation 605
ECSC *see* **European Coal and
Steel Community**
elections
see also **general elections**
accountability 38

campaigns 183, 184–9
electoral reform 127
good governance 390
House of Commons 171–89
House of Lords 191, 196, 217
mayors 25
purpose 171
Scottish 306
spending 184–9
Electoral Commission 185, 187
emergency regulations 144–5
employment tribunals 685
entrenchment 212, 233–6, 239
absolute 234, 239
Environment Agency 20, 107,
136, 266
environmental damage 477–8
equality 69, 75, 174
errors of law
tribunals 718–19
**European Coal and Steel
Community (ECSC)** 340–1
European Council 344
European Union
see also **Brexit**
accountability 346–7
areas of activity 341–2
background 340–1
Commission 343
constitution and 339–40
context 340–7
cooperation between
member states 342–3
Council of the EU 343–4,
345–6
courts 346–7
democracy 179, 344–5, 346
development 340–1
enlargement 341
European Council 344
executive functions 343
External Action Service 342
foundations 340–1
implications of
membership 340
institutions 313, 343–7
law 301, 342, 347–57
authority to make law 347
Brexit 370–4
constitutional legacy of
EU membership 372–4
control of legislative
process 367–8
direct effect 348–57
directives 350–1, 356–7
effective 484–5
Factortame
decision 364–5

generally 347
incidental horizontal
    effect 353–4
indirect effect 353
legal norms 368–70
legislative process 343,
    345–6
parliamentary sovereignty
    359–70, 375–7
regulations 348–9
treaties 349
types 347–8
Lisbon Treaty 341
membership 340
national interests 345–6
objectives 339–40
Parliament 179, 346–7
post-Brexit 357–9
redistribution of wealth 342
separation of powers 343–4
state liability 354–6
Treaty on European
    Union 341
Treaty on the Functioning of
    the European Union 341
types of law 347–8
UK entry 336
executive
    see also government
    accountability 115–16
    agencies 135–8
    central government
        departments 107
    civil servants 107
    constitutional
        position 104–20
    crisis response 106
    Crown 108–9
    definition 104–6
    devolution powers 304–6
    early history 106
    executive–judicial
        relations 113–14
    executive–legislative
        relations 109–13
    expert commentary 163–4
    generally 18–19
    growth 106
    implementation of
        policy 111
    initiatives 105
    key features 88
    Parliament 113
    policy areas 105–6
    political and legal
        accountability 115–16
    political constitution 114–15
    powers 108–9, 128, 136, 304–6

contractual power 161–2
delegated legislation 140–55
    generally 138–40
    prerogative powers 155–8
    third source powers
        158–61
public law 107–8
public policy 105
purpose 105
responsibility 105, 106
role 37–8
running the country,
    responsibility for 105
terminology 107–8
UK 107
expenses 36
    claims 384
    scandal 384
expression, freedom of see
    freedom of expression
extradition 278

F
fair hearing 47, 74, 139, 147
fair-minded and informed
    observers 511–13
fair trial 9
fairness see procedural fairness
false imprisonment 914
fast-track legislation 225–6
federal government 53, 58–9
financial scrutiny
    audit 444–5
    economy 444
    effectiveness 444
    effectiveness of PAC/
        NAO 450–2
    efficiency 444
    examples of PAC work 447–9
    generally 444–5
    importance 444
    National Audit Office
        (NAO) 446
    Public Accounts Committee
        (PAC) 445, 446, 447–52
    value for money 446–7
first-past-the-post system
    174–7, 178, 179
First-tier Tribunal (FTT) 260,
    683, 694–6, 717–18
Franks Report 684
free speech see freedom of
    expression
freedom of assembly
    Art 11 ECHR 861–4
    balance between individual
        rights and public
        interest 860–1

breach of the peace 877–87
common law powers to
    regulate protests 877–87
conditions for
    protection 861
counter-protestors, rights
    of 863–4
democracy 861
demonstrations
    near the Palace of
    Westminster 875–6
domestic law 864–5
generally 887
harassment 868–9
importance 859–60
peaceful protest 862
processions 876–7
provoking violence 863
public assemblies 870–1
public order offences
    affray 865
    balancing interests 866–7,
        868
    fear or provocation of
        violence 865
    generally 865
    harassment, alarm, or
        distress 865
    impact of conduct 865–6
    intentional harassment,
        harm, or distress 865
    reasonable conduct 866
    relevant conduct 865–8
    riot 865
    summary of offences 867
    threatening or abusive
        behaviour 865
    violent disorder 865
public spaces protection
    orders (PSPOs) 873–5
qualified right to protest 862
restrictions 861
right 860
statutory powers to regulate
    protests 870–7
technology, influence of 859
trespassory assemblies
    871–3
freedom of expression
    see also defamation
    Art 10 ECHR 820–2
    contempt of court
        contempt in the face of the
            court 833–4
        generally 828
        prejudicial publications
            829–33
        scandalising the court 828

freedom of expression (*Cont.*)
  criminal offences
    racial hatred 841–2
    religion, hatred on
      grounds of 842–3
    sexual orientation, hatred
      on grounds of 842–3
  generally 70, 855–8
  human rights 820–2
  importance 816–20
  indecency 843–5
  key themes 820
  media
    additional duties 823–4
    Broadcasting Code 823,
      824
    generally 822
    Internet 822, 827–8
    Leveson Inquiry 825–6
    licensing 822–3
    Press Complaints
      Commission (PCC) 825
    regulation 822–8
    restrictions 823–4
    self-regulation 824–7
  nature of 816
  obscenity 843–5
  prejudicial publications
    active proceedings 831
    appellate proceedings 832
    double hurdle 829–30
    generally 829
    good faith discussion 832
    Internet, influence of 833
    pending or imminent
      proceedings 832
    right to a fair trial 833
  Press Recognition Panel 826
  privacy 845–52
  restrictions 816–17
  rule of law 74
  status of individuals 817–18
  truth, democracy, and
    tolerance 818–19
  United States 817
freedom of information
  Freedom of Information
    Act 2000
    background to
      legislation 453
    exemptions 454–6
    government 459–60
    ministerial veto 457–9
    public interest test 454
    requests 456–7
    right of access to
      information 454
  generally 25

  rationale 453–4
  statutory control 452
freedom of movement 244
freedom of speech *see* **freedom
  of expression**
FTT (First-tier Tribunal) 260,
  683, 694–6, 717–18
**fundamental constitutional
  principles** 19, 47–8, 56, 57,
  244–6
  Cabinet government 50
  definition 51–6
  formal statements,
    limitations of 50–1
  generally 49–51
  hung parliament 50
  identification 51–2
  operation 51
  precedent 51
  social conventions
    distinguished 51
  standards of conduct 50
  unwritten nature 50
  written statements 50–1

G

**GCHQ (Government
  Communications
  Headquarters)** 60, 461, 560
gender 69, 75, 229
  judiciary 258, 287–93
general elections
  see also **elections**
  accountability 38
  calling election 171–3
  campaign spending 184–9
  campaigns 183
  coalition governments 172
  first-past-the-post
    system 174–7, 178, 179
  frequency 171
  funding 184–9
  generally 110
  no confidence votes 171
  political parties 183–4
  proportional
    representation 179
  reasons 171
  social background of
    MPs 182–3
  voter turnout 178
  voting
    constituency
      boundaries 177
    democracy 173
    entitlement to vote 173–4
    first-past-the-post
      system 174–7, 178, 179

  standing in elections
    173–4
gerrymandering 177
good administration 651
  principles 47
good governance
  accountability
    administrative
      accountability 389,
      392–4
    concept 387–8
    elections 390
    general principles of
      public law 391–2
    generally 396–9
    legal accountability 389,
      391–2
    multiple
      mechanisms 388–9
    overview 394–6
    political accountability
      389–91
    types 388–9
  competence 385
  definition 382–7
  democracy 382
  dignity, respect for 385
  human rights 385
  interests of individuals,
    respect for 385
  legitimacy of
    government 381
  meaning 381
  modern government 386
  prerequisites 382–3
  procedural fairness 385
  public interest 383–4
  purpose 381
  standards 347–9, 386
  transparency 384
governance
  see also **good governance**
  multilayered 40–1, 96
government
  see also **cabinet; civil
    servants; devolution;
    executive; Ministers;
    Prime Ministers**
  accountability 22–4
  agencies 20–4
  arm's-length public
    agencies 107, 135–8
  Attorney-General 123
  Bills 191, 192, 213, 220, 222–3
  coalition 112, 127, 172–3,
    177, 306
  constitutional
    conventions 116

decisions 35, 682–3
departments 107, 127–30
dominance of House of
    Commons 215–16
functions of 64
generally 40, 163–4
legislative process 212–14
local government 5–6, 40,
    129
ministerial standards 124–5
modern 96, 106, 107, 108
monarch's personal
    prerogatives 117–18,
    155–8
policy 132–3, 136, 432
power 5–7, 107, 109, 162
relationship with other
    branches 116–17
responsible 64
size of majorities 113
special advisers 107, 117,
    133–5
tiers 5, 11, 42, 53
**Government Communications
    Headquarters** *see* GCHQ
**Government Equalities Office
    (GEO)** 436

H
habeas corpus 913
harassment
    freedom of assembly 868–9
health authorities 610
health care 8, 110, 116, 622–3
Health Ombudsman 645
Henry VIII powers 143–4
**Her Majesty's Courts
    and Tribunals Service
    (HMCTS)** 693–4
hereditary peers 27, 173, 190
High Court 262, 273, 650
    judiciary 258
**HMIC (HM Inspectorate of
    Constabulary)** 908–9
Home Affairs Committee 435
Home Secretary 98–9
homelessness 503, 626
horizontal effect 351
    incidental 353–4
hospitals 111, 268
House of Commons 112,
    220–4
    elections 171–89
    government dominance
    215–16
House of Lords 16, 189–98
    see also **peers**
    anachronism 189–90

Appointments
    Commission 190
bishops and archbishops 190
categories of peer 189–91
complementarity 194–5
composition 195–8
Constitution Committee 28,
    437
crossbenchers 190
Delegated Powers and
    Regulatory Reform
    Committee 438
elected 217
elections 196
exclusion 197
expertise 195
expulsion 197
hereditary peers 190
life peers 190
membership 189
party politics 194–5
political peers 190
powers 192–4
reform 25, 27, 190, 191–2,
    196–7
regional representation 191
representation 190–1
resignation 197
retirement 197
select committees 437–8
smaller political parties 195
human dignity 69
human rights 17–18, 70, 76–7
    autonomy 762
    Bill of Rights 808–9, 811
    common law rights 768–70
    community interests 761
    competing views 761–5
    constitutional status of
    rights 30
    contracted-out public
    functions 797–9
    Convention rights 771–4
    core purpose 762
    deciding on rights 763–4
    declarations of
    incompatibility 776,
    785–8
    definition 760–5
    enforcement of
    claims 804–6
    European Convention on
    Human Rights 771–4
    freedom of expression 820–2
    fundamental 7, 12, 30
    generally 759–60, 812–13
    good governance 385
    horizontal effect 800–4

Human Rights Act 1998
    common law
    regulation 800
    contracted-out public
    functions 797–9
    dissatisfaction with
    Act 806–8
    forms of protection 774–6
    functions of a public
    nature 796–9
    interpretation of
    legislation by
    courts 778–85
    legal and political
    constitutionalism
    790–5
    misconceptions 806–7
    persons entitled to enforce
    claims 804–6
    powers of courts to uphold
    rights 777–95
    public authorities 796–9,
    813–14
    public interest 807–8
    purpose 771
    repeal, possible 810–11
    rights protected 771–4
    scope 795–806
    sections 3 and 4 777–95
incompatible
    legislation 774–5
individuals, rights of 761
interpretative obligations
    778–85
judicial protection 765
judicial review 776
landlord and tenant
    cases 799–800
liberalism 761
liberties model 765–7
overriding individual
    rights 763
parliamentary
    sovereignty 777
permanence 760
political context 764
powers of courts 765
pre-Human Rights Act
    1998 767–70
privacy 800
public authorities 796–9,
    813–14
public compatibility 775–6
purpose 770
reform proposals
    Bill of Rights 811
    necessity 811–12
    repeal of HRA 810–11

human rights (*Cont.*)
  withdrawal from
    ECHR 809–10
  restrictions 761
  rights model 765–7
  special treatment 760
  statement of
    compatibility 774–5
  subordinate
    legislation 788–90
  tribunals 685
  UK Constitution 759–60
  values 762–3
  ways forward 809–12
  withdrawal from
    ECHR 809–10
hung Parliaments 50, 117–18
Hutton Inquiry 729, 734, 739

I

immigration 596, 597, 622
  appeals 701
  control 108, 266, 701
  tribunals 691
**Immigration and Asylum
  Chamber** 683, 721
**Immigration and Nationality
  Directorate (IND)** 22, 412
impartiality
  appearance of bias 508,
    511–13
  automatic disqualification
    for decision-maker
    508–11
  bias 508
  civil servants 131
  conflict of interests 508–11
  financial interests 509
  ground for judicial
    review 508–14
  judiciary 276, 283
  level of concern 511
  party, decision-maker as 509
  political considerations 513–14
  procedural fairness 508–14
  proprietary interests 509
  real possibility of
    bias 511–13
  tribunals 693
implied repeal 45–6, 234, 240
imprisonment 5
incidental horizontal effect
  EU law 353–4
**incompatibility, declarations
  of** 18, 74, 776, 785–8
**IND (Immigration and
  Nationality Directorate)**
  22, 412

indecency 843–5
independence
  accountability 515–16
  curative principle 517–18
  example 514–15
  House of Lords 196
  judicial review 514–18
  judiciary 257, 275, 276–87,
    293–5, 698–9
    generally 285–7
    litigation 281–2
  meeting requirement
    for independent
    decision-maker 517–18
  requirement for independent
    decision-maker 515–17
  right to a fair trial 515–17
**Independent Adviser on
  Ministers' Interests** 125
**Independent Case
  Examiner** 636
independent panels 750–1
**Independent Police
  Complaints Commission
  (IPCC)** 635, 906–7
indirect effect
  EU law 353
individual autonomy 8, 69–70,
  169
information
  see also **freedom of
    information disclosure**
  disclosure of sensitive
    information 852, 853
  private 800, 846–52
  public sector
    ombudsmen 659, 667
injunctions 53, 61, 582–3
  interim 581–2
inquiries
  accountability 734–5
  alternatives 748–51
  assessors 740
  basis 734
  Bloody Sunday 731, 742,
    743, 746
  Bristol Royal Infirmary 730,
    742, 746
  Butler Inquiry 729, 734, 740
  chair 738–9
  chairing 668–9
  Chilcot Inquiry 729, 737
  child sexual abuse 731, 732,
    752, 753
  child sexual exploitation
    318, 638, 753
  costs 743
  death, into 736

  definition 728–31
  discretion 735
  effectiveness 746–8
  establishment 728–9, 734,
    735–7
  fairness 742, 743
  follow-up
    mechanisms 747–8
  full and fair account of the
    facts 732
  functions 732
  funding 743
  generally 138, 728
  Hutton Inquiry 729, 734,
    739
  implementing
    recommendations 746–8
  Iraq 737
  Iraq War 729–30
  judiciary 738–40
  legal framework 734–5
  length of proceedings 743
  Leveson Inquiry 730
  Maxwellisation
    procedure 745
  membership 738–41
  monitoring
    recommendations 746–8
  National Health Service
    (NHS) 730
  panels 738
  parliamentary commissions
    of inquiry 748–50
  parliamentary control 734
  police 731
  political context 737
  powers of Ministers 735
  private 741–2
  'private public' inquiries 750
  proceedings 742–3
  process 735–46, 751–5
  public 38, 728–31, 741–2
  public confidence 732
  publication of reports 745–6
  recent inquiries 729–31
  recommendations 732, 743,
    746–8
  reconciliation 732
  reconvening inquiry 747
  refusal to establish 735–6
  reports 665, 667, 745–6
  resolution of issues 732
  role 731
  Salmon principles 743–4
  Scott 746
  Shipman 741–2
  Stephen Lawrence
    Inquiry 730, 734

suspension of inquiry 735
terms of reference 735, 736–7
undercover policing 731
United States, in 739
warning letters 744–5
witnesses 742, 743–5
Zahid Mubarek 735–6, 740
intelligence services *see*
security and intelligence
services
intentional
harassment 865–88
interception of
communications 72
interim injunctions 581–2
internal reviews 700–3
international law 48–9
Internet
freedom of expression 822,
827–8
prejudicial publications 833
interpretation
application of the statute to
the facts 504–5
fundamental constitutional
principles 47–8
generally 499–500
Human Rights Act
1998 778–85
judicial review 499–506
jurisdictional questions 500
legislation 42, 47, 244–6, 269
questions of fact 504–5
relational institutional
competence 502–3
statutory 42, 47, 244–6, 269
IOPC (Independent Office for
Police Conduct) 905–8
IPCC (Independent
Police Complaints
Commission) 635, 906–7
Iraq inquiries 729–30, 737
ISC (Intelligence and Security
Committee) 464–7

J
JAC (Judicial Appointments
Commission) 272–5, 290–1,
698
JCHR (Joint Committee on
Human Rights) 16
Jenkins Commission 179–81
Jennings test 52–6
Joint Committee on Human
Rights (JCHR) 16
Judicial Appointments
Commission (JAC) 272–5,
290–1, 698

judicial review
see also **procedural fairness;
proportionality;
unreasonableness**
accessibility 590, 598–601
accountability 479–80,
590–1
administrative law 478–9
administrative
reaction 619–26
administrator's
perspective 617–19
alternative dispute
resolution 599, 604–5
appeal and review
distinguished 477, 539–42
application of statute to
facts 504–5
bias 508–13
caseload 600
Civil Procedure Rules 567
commencement of
proceedings 567–8
competence 605–11
constitutional basis 485–94
content of decisions 476, 477
control of administrative
action 615–16
courts, criticism of 624–5
de facto powers 563–7
decisions susceptible to
review 557–67
definition 478–9
demarcation disputes 484–5
democratic legitimacy 477
development 591–2
development of law 549–51
discretion 526–39
effectiveness 589–91
effects of judicial
control 615–16
empirical research 598,
625–6
environmental
damage 477–8
example 475–6
foundations 494–5
generally 586–8
geographical spread of
applications 601
government 589–92
grounds 553–4
challenge for
courts 498–9
development of law 498
discretion 526–39
example 499
impartiality 508–14

independence 514–18
legality 497–8
legitimate expectations
531–6
non-fettering
principle 529–30
overview 497–9
procedural fairness 498,
506–26
proportionality 498,
542–51
reasons for
decisions 523–6
right to be heard 518–23
statutory interpretation and
application 499–506
summary 497–8
unreasonableness 498
Wednesbury
unreasonableness
539–42
growth of 257, 482
heard, right to be 518–23
human rights 776
immigration 596, 597
impact 589–91
administrator's
perspective 617–19
individual 611–13
policy 613–15
impartiality 508–14
independence 514–18
injunctions 582–3
inquiries 742
intention of Parliament
491–2
irrelevant considerations
536–7
judicial competence and
capacity 605–11
jurisdiction 505–6, 591–2,
721–2
legal advice and services 599
legal aid 599
legality 497–8
legitimate
expectations 531–6
limited nature 477
litigation 592–8
local authority finance 607
mandatory orders 581–2
meaning of statute 501–4
multilayered constitution 494
non-delegation principle
526–9
non-fettering principle
529–30
ombudsmen 663–5

judicial review (*Cont.*)
  ordinary proceedings 570–2
  ouster clauses 557–9
  overview 551–3, 556–7
  parliamentary
      sovereignty 249–51, 492,
      493, 494, 623
  perception of courts 559
  permission of court 568
  policies, adherence
      to 529–30
  political context 598
  political and legal
      constitutionalism 480–4
  politicians, criticism of 624
  polycentricity 609–11
  practical difficulties in
      bringing claim 599
  prerogative powers 155,
      559–63
  procedural exclusivity 570–2
  procedure 537, 567–78
  prohibiting orders 581–2
  proportionality 542–51
  public authorities' experience
      of 597–8
  public interest law 598
  public sector
      ombudsmen 663–5
  quashing orders 579–81
  questions of fact 504–5
  questions of law 501–4
  reform proposals 600–1
  relevant considerations
      536–7
  remedies
      discretionary nature
          578–85
      injunctions 582–3
      mandatory orders 581–2
      prohibiting orders 581–2
      quashing orders 579–81
  right to be heard 518–23
  role 590
  separation of powers 590
  settlement 601–4
  social security 596–7
  standing 572–8
  statutory bodies with court-
      like powers 559
  statutory interpretation and
      application 499–506
      application of the statute
          to the facts 504–5
      generally 499–500
      jurisdictional questions 500
      meaning of the statute
          501–4

  questions of fact 504–5
  questions of law 501–4
  relational institutional
      competence 502–3
  statutory powers 559
  steps taken before seeking
      judicial review 568–9
  subject matter 476–8
  success rate 603–4
  time limits 569–70
  tribunals
      compared to judicial
          review 686–7
      review of decisions
          722–3
  types of power
      de facto powers 563–7
      prerogative powers
          559–63
      statutory powers 559
  ultra vires doctrine 486–8,
      490, 491–2
  Wednesbury
      unreasonableness 539–42
  will of Parliament 491
judiciary
  accountability 276
  appeals 261–2
  appointments 28, 272–6,
      287–91
  characteristics 271–85
  common law, development
      of 270
  democracy 271
  diversity 275, 287–93
  eligibility for
      appointment 273
  executive, relationship with
      the 113–14
  expertise 605–9
  first-instance courts 258
  generally 257–8
  hierarchy 258
  High Court 258
  independence 257, 275,
      276–87
      institutional situation of
          courts 277–81
      judicial seclusion 281–5
      Lord Chancellor 279–81
      seclusion, judicial 281–5
      Supreme Court 277–9
  inquiries 738–40
  Judges' Council 43
  judicial control 480, 556
  judicial process 5, 606
  judicial restraint 271
  jurisdiction 262–3

  lawmaking and separation of
      powers 269–71
  Northern Ireland 261
  powers 482
  referees in public law
      cases 266–7
  reversal of decisions by
      parliament 271
  role 259, 264–6
  Scotland 261
  security of tenure 282–3
  separation of powers 87–8,
      269–71
  size of judiciary 260
  structure of judicial
      system 258–64
  subject matter of
      dispute 261
  Supreme Court 260
  systems 43
  tribunals 260
  Upper Tribunal 260
  vacancies 273
juries 261, 667
justice
  administration of 113, 124,
      129
  civil 262
  constitutional 38–9
  criminal 261–2
  generally 264
  natural 592
Justice Committee 23

K
Kilmuir rules 283

L
Law Lords 277–9
legal accountability 115–16
legal advice
  confidentiality 74–5
  judicial review 599
  policing 904
  rule of law 74–5
legal constitutionalism 19,
      35–7, 340–1
  Human Rights Act
      1998 790–5
  judicial review 480–4
legal representation
  tribunals 687, 706–8
legality
  ground for judicial
      review 497–8
  rule of law 71–2
Leggatt Report 684, 691, 692,
      705, 707

legislation 16–19, 42–6, 109–14, 211–28
  constitutional 42–6
  delegated legislation 21–2, 238, 244
    consultation 147–8
    effect 144–5
    emergency measures 144
    Henry VIII powers 143–4
    judicial review 154–5
    publication 145–7
    role of Parliament 148–55
    scrutiny 148–54
    statutory powers to make 135–55
    use 141–3
  enactment 12, 16–17, 58
  entrenchment 217–18, 233–6, 242
  European Union (EU) 343, 345–6
  government dominance 217, 228
  Henry VIII powers 143–4
  interpretation 42, 47, 269–70
  management of government programme 214
  Parliament and government 212–14
  primary 143–4
  roles 213–14
  scrutiny 105, 195, 214–15, 220–4
  secondary 20, 143–4, 223–4, 788–90
  unconstitutional 39, 231
  veto 62
legislative branch 5, 87, 94
  executive, relationship with 111
  powers 40, 148
legislative scrutiny *see* **parliamentary scrutiny**
legitimacy 8–10
  democratic 38, 271, 275
  good governance 382
legitimate expectations
  consistency of treatment 533
  constitutional conventions 60
  creation 532–3
  judicial review 531–6
  knowledge of representation 533
  meaning 531
  procedural 534
  protection 533–6
  reasonableness 532
  substantive 534–6, 737

  unlawful conduct 536
Leveson Inquiry 730
Liaison Committee 120, 219, 436, 437
libel *see* **defamation**
Liberal Democrats 119, 127
Liberal government 58
  influence 59–60
  legitimate expectations 60
life peers 184, 190
local government 5–6, 37–8, 129
  analysis 320–1
Local Government Ombudsman 645, 668, 674, 675
localism 317–19
  policing 893–5
Lord Chancellor 28, 122–3, 272–5, 279–81
Lords *see* **House of Lords**

M

magistrates 260–1, 264
maladministration
  Crossman catalogue 656
  decision-making process 656
  definition 655–6
  good administration 656–7
  injustice 657–8
  public sector ombudsmen 655–7, 667–9
malicious prosecution 914
mandatory orders 581–2
mayors, elected 25
media
  broadcasters 187
  contempt of court
    contempt in the face of the court 833–4
    generally 828
    prejudicial publications 829–33
    scandalising the court 828
  freedom of expression
    additional duties 823–4
    Broadcasting Code 823, 824
    generally 822
    Internet 822, 827–8
    Leveson Inquiry 825–6
    licensing 822–3
    Press Complaints Commission (PCC) 825
    Press Recognition Panel 826
    regulation 822–8

    restrictions 823–4
    self-regulation 824–7
  licensing 822–3
mediation 265, 604
ministerial accountability 124, 133, 475–6, 482
Ministerial Code 50, 117, 124–5, 134, 410
ministerial responsibility 125, 137, 482
  administrative government 416–22
  collective responsibility 409
  doctrine of 390, 402, 409–10
  effectiveness 421–2
  individual responsibility 409
  meanings 413–16
  Ministerial Code 410
  Peelite view 415
  prudential government 422–4
  resignations by ministers 410–14
  'Whig' view 414–15
Ministers 91, 107–8
  see also **ministerial responsibility**
  appointment 118
  Brexit 128
  Cabinet 120–3, 129, 134, 280
  delegation of powers 121
  dismissal 118
  gradings 121
  meaning 120–1
  Ministerial Code 121
  Permanent Secretary 129
  power 112, 121–2, 126–7, 172, 486
  Prime Ministers 49, 55, 117, 118–20
  Secretaries of State 121
  senior 28, 44, 112, 121
Ministry of Justice 22
minorities 32, 39, 173, 481
  House of Lords 195
misuse of power 99
misuse of private information 847–52
monarchy 43, 62, 106, 108–9, 201, 217
  personal prerogatives 117–18, 155–8
morality 13, 51, 53–4, 229, 757, 844
movement, freedom of 223
MPs
  backbench 112, 122, 394

MPs (*Cont.*)
  complaints by public to 636
  political parties 183–4
  recall 181–2
  social background 182–3
multilayered governance 40–1,
  96

N

**National Audit Office
  (NAO)** 23, 393, 446, 450–2
**National Crime Agency
  (NCA)** 893
**National Health Service
  (NHS)** 105, 447–8
  inquiries 730, 748
national security 14–15, 91
nationality 154
natural justice 592
  public sector ombudsmen 666
**NDPBs (non-departmental
  public bodies)** 135–6, 138
**NHS (National Health
  Service)** 105, 447–8
  inquiries 730, 748
non-delegation principle
  judicial review 526–9
**non-departmental public
  bodies (NDPBs)** 135–6, 138
non-fettering principle
  judicial review 529–30
Northern Ireland 27, 33, 272
  devolution
    administration 305–6
    elections 306–7
    executive powers 305
    generally 300
    lawmaking power 301
    rationale 300
  Executive 305
  judiciary 261
  public sector ombudsmen
    642, 643, 671–2
  tribunals 696

O

obscenity 843–5
**Office of Parliamentary
  Counsel** 214
**Office of the Independent
  Adjudicator** 635
official secrecy
  breach of confidence 852
  defences 853
  disclosure of sensitive
    information 852, 853
  legislation 667, 852–5
  public interest 853–5

security and intelligence
    officers 853
  spying 852
  summary of offences 854
ombudsmen
  see also **public sector
    ombudsmen**
  advantages 641
  complaints 650
  debt of honour case 640–2
  functions 645
  generally 478
  Health Service 643, 645
  industry specific
    ombudsmen 642
  investigations 649–50
  judicial review 663–5
  Parliamentary 645, 668–71,
    672
  political process 646–50
  Prisons and Probation 24
  private sector
    ombudsman 642
  purpose 640–1
  quality control model 645
  reform 644
  systemic issues 645
**online dispute
  resolution** 708–9
opposition parties 112
oral hearings
  tribunals 709–10
orders
  mandatory 581–2
  quashing 579–81
Osmotherly Rules 422
ouster clauses
  judicial review 557–9

P

**PAC (Public Accounts
  Committee)** 436, 445, 446,
  447–52
**PACAC (Public
  Administration and
  Constitutional Affairs Select
  Committee)** 436, 749
**Palace of Westminster,
  demonstrations near** 875–6
**parent government
  departments** 22
Parliament
  see also **House of Commons;
    House of Lords;
    parliamentary privilege;
    parliamentary scrutiny;
    parliamentary sovereignty**
  block votes 425

commissions of inquiry
    748–50
  committees 38
  composition 167
  debates 23, 432–4
  democracy 168–71
  dissolution 109, 117, 171,
    408, 561, 902
  dominance of 424
  elections to the House of
    Commons 171–89
  European 179, 344–5, 346–7
  executive branch 98–9, 166
  fixed-term 45, 120, 172–3
  funding for political
    parties 184–9
  generally 16–19
  historical development 167
  hung 50, 117
  intention 488–9, 526–7
  legislative process 212–14
  overview 167–8
  payroll vote 424–5
  privilege 45, 166, 200–11
    application of statute to
      Parliament 202–3
    codification 210–11
    components 201
    exclusive cognisance
      201–2
    freedom of speech 201
    generally 200
    historical background 201
    judicial questioning of
      issues in Parliament
      205–7
    meaning 200–3
    non-members,
      Parliamentary criticism
      of 207–8
    reports of
      proceedings 202
    scope 203–5
    select committees 208–10
  questions 429–31
  roles 168
  Scottish 58, 88, 180
Parliamentary Ombudsman
  645, 646, 668–71
  constitutional context 647
  creation 646–7
  excluded matters 654
  good administration 635
  House of Commons Public
    Administration and
    Constitutional Affairs
    Select Committee 648, 649
  maladministration 655

MP filter 648–9
reporting to Parliament 647–8
reports 672
parliamentary privilege
application of statute to
Parliament 202–3
codification 210–11
components 201
exclusive cognisance 201–2
freedom of speech 201
historical background 201
judicial questioning of issues
in Parliament 205–7
meaning 200–3
non-members, parliamentary
criticism of 207–8
reports of proceedings 202
scope 203–5
select committees 208–10
parliamentary scrutiny 214–18
assessment 225, 442–3
competence of
parliament 216–17
constraints on 424–8
different perspectives
on 217–18
dominance of procedure by
government 217
effective 214–15
fast-track legislation 225–6
government
democratic control 402–3
generally 402–3
mechanisms 404
nature of Parliamentary
control 406–9
parliamentary decline
thesis 403
political accountability
402–4
public confidence 403,
404
responsibilities 404–6
roles within parliament
and government 404–6
government spending,
scrutiny of 444–52
improvement, suggestions
for 428–9
individual accountability of
MPs 427
legislation 214–18, 219–24
legislative process 218–19
mechanisms 424–8
oral questions 429–30
overview 467–70
parliamentary debates 23,
432–4

parliamentary questions
429–31
political factors 426
post-legislative scrutiny
227–8
pre-legislative
process 218–19
select committees 208–10,
434–42, 749
written questions 430–1
parliamentary sovereignty 63–4,
78, 81–3, 253–4, 489, 492,
493, 494
Brexit 366
constitutional fixture 233–8,
365–7
constitutional interpretation
and judicial politics 231–2
continuing sovereignty
235–6
countermajoritarianism 231
democracy 63–4, 230–1
EU law 359–70, 375–7
evaluation 237–8
human rights 777
judicial review 249–51
legal constitutionalism
229–30
manner and form
theory 238–41
meaning 232–3
new view 238–41
Parliament capable of
controlling certain
aspects of legislative
process 238–41
political constitutionalism
229–30
refusal of court to apply
legislation 246–9
self-embracing
sovereignty 234–5
summary 252–3
unintended constraints
on parliamentary
authority 242–4
party politics 30, 43
judiciary and 283–5
**PCC (Press Complaints
Commission)** 825
**PCCs (Police and Crime
Commissioners)** 909–11
peaceful protest 862
peers 44, 122, 201, 213
see also **House of Lords**
categories 189
hereditary 27, 173, 190
life 184, 190

photographs
public places 850–2
**Police and Crime Commissioners
(PCCs)** 909–11
policing
accountability 892, 908–11
arrest 899–901
assault by 914
battery by 914
British Transport
Police 893
charging suspect 903
civil liability 913–14
codification of law 895
College of Policing 908–9
complaints 638, 905–8
coordination 894
detention 901–3
entry onto property 898–9
evidence 903–5
generally 667, 891–2
governance 893, 908–11
habeas corpus 913
HM Inspectorate of
Constabulary (HMIC)
908–9
inadmissibility of
evidence 911–13
Independent Office for Police
Conduct (IOPC) 905–8
inquiries 731
key issues 892–3
legal advice 904
legal framework for
powers 895
localism 893–5
malicious prosecution 914
national arrangements
893–4
National Crime Agency 893
negligence 914
organisation of the police
force 893
overview 914–15
Police and Crime
Commissioners (PCCs)
909–11
police forces 893
questioning 903–5
redress 911–14
right to silence 904–5
search powers 903
stop and search 895–8
strategy 894
political accountability 402–3
executive branch 115–16
parliamentary scrutiny of
government 402–4

political constitutionalism 32,
38–40, 60–2, 200, 229–30,
480–4
judicial review 480–4
parliamentary
sovereignty 229–30
political system 20, 61
politicians
career 122
elected 116
political parties 183–4
social background 182–3
politics
campaign spending 184–9
parties 183–4
party 30, 43
pornography 843–4
powers
see **separation of powers**
absolute 62, 92
abuses of 33, 38, 92, 94–5,
98–9, 270
accountability 7–8
allocation of 4, 45, 96
coercive 265
contractual 161–2
devolution of 41
discretionary 47, 68, 73–4
executive branch 88, 108–9,
136, 138–62, 304–6
government 5–7, 22, 32, 38,
41, 64, 69, 109, 161–2
judicial 482
judicial review 479–80, 486
lawmaking 148–54
limited 16
ministerial 121–2, 126–7,
172, 489
Parliament 166, 228–41
prerogative 48, 117–18, 128,
155–8, 173, 213, 559–63
public 32, 87, 92
state 5
statutory 138–40, 147, 155–8,
161–2, 559
third source 158–61
precedent 42, 46–7, 737
consequence of disobedience
to convention 56–8
enforcement 56–8
obedience 56–8
political 42
prerogative powers 48, 117–18,
128, 155–8, 159, 173, 213
Brexit 156–7
judicial review 155, 559–63
Press Complaints Commission
(PCC) 825

Press Recognition Panel 826
Prime Ministers
accountability 120
Deputy 122
functions 118–19
generally 49
influence 119–20
public policy 120
questions (PMQs) 55, 120,
429
resignation 117
responsibility 118
source of powers 118–19
style of individuals 119
prisoners 20–5, 521–2
administrative law 20–2
convicted 24
foreign national 22
generally 23–4
judicial review by 23–4
public administration 20–2
voting 174, 794–5
Prisons and Probation
Ombudsman 24
privacy
Art 8 ECHR 845–6
breach of confidence 846–7
data protection 846
freedom of
expression 845–52
human rights 800, 845, 846
informational privacy 846
misuse of private
information 847–52
photographs in public
places 850–2
public interest 849–50
private inquiries 741–2
privilege *see* **parliamentary
privilege**
Privy Council 263
procedural fairness
generally 498
good governance 385
ground for judicial
review 498, 506–26
heard, right to be 518–23
impartiality 508–14
independence 514–18
inquiries 742, 743
judicial review 506
different meanings of
fairness 506
generally 506
impartiality 508–14
reasons for fairness of
action 506–8
reasons for decisions 523–6

reasons for fairness of
action 506–8
right to be heard 518–23
procedural legitimate
expectations 534
processions, public 876–7
prohibited trespassory
assemblies 871–3
prohibiting orders 581–2
proportional
representation 179
proportionality 591, 736
appeal and review
distinguished 544–5
deference 545–9
development of law 550
ground for judicial
review 498
human rights cases 544–5
intensity of review 542
judicial review 542–51
legitimate aim 543
narrow proportionality
issue 543, 544
necessity 543
protected interests 543
sexual orientation 543–4
structure of test 542
test 542–3
Wednesbury
unreasonableness
compared 542–3
protests
see also **freedom of assembly**
conflicting protests 862
counter-protestors, rights
of 863–4
current challenges to
right 888–90
generally 860
harassment 868–90
provoking violence 863
public 18
violent behaviour of
others 862
prudential government
ministerial responsibility
as 422–4
Public Accounts Committee
(PAC) 436, 445, 446, 447–52
Public Administration and
Constitutional Affairs
Select Committee
(PACAC) 436
Public Administration Select
Committee (PASC) 749
public assemblies 870–1
public inquiries 38, 728–31

public interest
  defamation 838–40
  good governance 383–4
  official secrecy 853–5
  privacy 849–50
public processions 876–7
public protests 18
public sector ombudsmen
  see also **ombudsmen**
  administrative justice 651–2
  annual report 667–8
  bodies subject to
    investigation 653–4
  compensation 668
  compliance 666–76
  cooperation with 666–7
  devolution 642, 643
  disclosure 666, 667
  Equitable Life
    investigation 669–71
  examination of
    witnesses 666
  excluded matters 654–5
  failures in public
    services 658–63
  findings 674
  generally 676–80
  good administration 651
  information provision 667
  injustice 657–8
  integrated approach 642
  investigations
    assessment 658
    bodies subject to
      investigation 653–4
    excluded matters 654–5
    failures in public
      services 658–63
    generally 649, 652–3
    health complaints 659–60
    illustrations 661–3
    information
      gathering 659
    initial checks 658
    maladministration 655–7
    stages 658–9
    statistics 660–1
  judicial review 663–5
  jurisdiction 651
  legal enforcement of
    decisions 671–6
  maladministration 645,
    655–7
  models 642
  natural justice 666
  non-compliance with
    recommendations 668–9
  Northern Ireland 642, 643

  obstruction of
    investigation 666
  private investigations 667
  private sector ombudsmen
    distinguished 642
  production of
    documents 666
  recommendations 674, 675
  remedies 668
  reports 667–9
  role 645–52
  Scotland 642, 643
  secrecy 667
  securing of redress 667–9,
    671–6
  single ombudsman
    service 642
  special reports 669
  Wales 642, 643
  witnesses 666
  workload 651
public services 20, 107, 130
  delivery 107
**Public Spaces Protection
Orders (PSPOs)** 873–5

Q
**qualified majority voting
(QMV)** 345–6, 360
quangos 137
quashing orders 579–81
questions of law 501–4

R
race 70, 75
  judiciary 287–93
racial hatred 841–2
'Ram' doctrine 160
reasons for decisions
  judicial review 523–6
recall of MPs 181–2
re-election 7, 9
referendums 8, 11, 339–41
  see also **Brexit**
  Brexit 336–7
  electoral reform 181–2
  form 339
  'hard Brexit' 339
  reasons for exit vote 338–9
  Scottish independence 80–1
  'soft Brexit' 339
reforms
  ad hoc basis 28–9
  codification 77–80
  constitutional 25–32, 33–5,
    77–80, 272–3
  House of Lords 27, 190,
    191–2

  Lord Chancellor 29
  ongoing process 29–32
  piecemeal reform 26–7
  without consultation 28–9
religion 70, 169
  freedom of religion 32
religious hatred 842–3
remedies
  declarations 583–5
  discretionary nature in
    public law 578
  injunctions 53, 61, 582–3
  judicial review 578–85
  mandatory orders 581–2
  prohibiting orders 581–2
  quashing orders 579–81
repeal 98–9, 240, 736–7
  express 233
  implied 45–6, 234, 240
resignations
  ministerial 410–13
responsible government 64
  formal conceptions 67–9
  importance 66
  legality 67
  legitimacy 70–1
  meaning 65
  principle 66–7
  scope 69–70
retrospective effect 6
review *see* **judicial review**
royal assent 43, 56
Royal Commissions 27, 196
rule of law 65–77, 114, 146,
  244, 266, 559
  access to the courts 74
  confidential legal
    advice 74–5
  constitutional principle 71
  discretionary powers 73–4
  equality 75
  formal concept 72–4
  freedom of expression 74
  human rights 76–7
  judicial review 74
  judicial role 71
  legality 71–2
  practical effect 75–6
  substantive
    operation 70–1
  unwritten
    constitution 70–1
rule of recognition 235–6,
  238, 241

S
Salmon principles 743–4
scandalising the court 828

Scotland 33, 272
  devolution
    continued existence
      of the devolved
      institutions 328–30
    elections 306
    generally 299
    lawmaking power 301
  independence 80–1
  judiciary 261
  public sector
    ombudsmen 642, 643
  Scottish Parliament 58, 88,
    180, 328–30
  tribunals 696
Scott inquiry 746
Scottish Parliament 58, 88, 180
  permanence
    provisions 328–30
scrutiny see Parliamentary
  scrutiny
seclusion, judicial 281–5
second chamber see House of
  Lords
secondary legislation 20, 21–2,
  238, 244, 788–90
secrecy
  public sector
    ombudsman 667
security and intelligence
  services
  accountability 460–7
  agencies 461
  function of government 461
  Government
    Communications
    Headquarters
    (GCHQ) 461, 463
  human rights 463
  Intelligence and Security
    Committee (ISC) 464–7
  legal framework 463
  powers of agencies 463
  relationship to other
    government bodies 462
  Secret Intelligence Service
    (MI6) 461, 463
  Security Service (MI5) 461
security, national 14–15, 91
security policy 128
select committees 208–10, 749
  assessment 439–42
  core tasks 437
  elections 435
  Foreign Affairs
    Committee 438

function 435–6
  House of Commons 435–6
  House of Lords 437–8
  powers 209, 441
  remit 435–6
Senior President of
  Tribunals 274, 698
separation of powers 64–5, 76,
  148, 266, 293
  abuse of power 92
  administrative
    agencies 95–6
  assessment of
    doctrine 99–102
  assumptions 90
  balance of power 94
  basic idea 89–90
  branches of
    government 87–8
  constitutional
    government 90
  democracy 93
  different conceptions 93–7
  European Union
    (EU) 343–4
  judicial lawmaking 269–71
  judicial review 590
  key features of branches of
    government 88
  local government 88
  multilayered constitution 88
  overview 87–9
  partial version 94, 98
  pure version 94, 98
  reasons for 91–3
  relationships between
    branches 89–90
  UK 97–9
settlement
  judicial review 601–4
Sewel Convention 44, 56, 61,
  329
  democracy 63–4
  parliamentary sovereignty
    63–4
  separation of powers 64–5
sexual orientation 543–4
  hatred on grounds of 842–3
Shipman Inquiry 730, 741–2
SIAC (Special Immigration
  Appeals Commission) 15
single publication rule 840–1
slander see defamation
Social Entitlement
  Chamber 683
social security 623

tribunals 683
'sofa government' 127
soft law 145
sources of constitution
  common law 46–8
  conventions 49–62
  generally 36–7, 42
  international law 48–9
  judge-made law 46–8
  legislation 42–6
  reforms 81
South Africa 8
sovereignty
  see also parliamentary
    sovereignty
  continuing 234–5
  self-embracing 234–5
special advisers 107, 117, 133–5
special advocates 15
Special Immigration Appeals
  Commission (SIAC) 15
standards
  Committee on Standards in
    Public Life 188
  good governance 382
  Ministers 124–5
standing
  associational standing 576
  current position 574–8
  judicial review 572–8
  liberal approach 577–8
  narrow approach 573
  public interest
    standing 576–7
  sufficient interest 573
  wide approach 573–4
statutory instruments 20, 141
  see also delegated legislation
Stephen Lawrence
  Inquiry 730, 734, 892
stop and search 895–8
subordinate legislation 788–90
supremacy
  EU law 359–70
Supreme Court 10, 25
  creation 277
  independence 277–9
  judiciary 260, 273, 274
suspected terrorists 18, 32,
  244–5

T
takeovers 208
tax 169
Tax Adjudicator 636
television 187

territorial constitution
conclusions 331–2
constitutional
conventions 325–6
federalism 323–5
future of the Union 330–1
legal foundations 326–7
legislation on devolved
issues 327–8
see also **devolution**
terrorism 14–19, 32, 106, 225,
229, 244–5
Thatcher, Margaret 119
tort 5, 47, 270
torture 14, 69
*Transforming Public
Services* 684, 692
transparency
good governance 384
Treasury 120, 128
trespassory assemblies 871–3
tribunals
access to 703–4
access to justice 683
advantages 687
appeals from first-tier to
upper 717–18
appeals to Court of
Appeal 719–21
appointments 698–9
caseloads 696–8
'citizen v state' 685
coherent policy 683
competing interests 691
conduct of hearings 705–6
context 687
costs 706
Council on Tribunals 699
definition 682–4
development 683–4
devolution 696
disadvantages 690
disputes 683
effectiveness 689–90
employment tribunals 685
enforcement of
decisions 716–17
errors of law 718–19
examples 685
feedback from
tribunals 711–15
First-tier Tribunal (FTT)
260, 683, 694–6, 717–18
generally 262, 723–7
government decisions 689
guidance from tribunal 715–16

health 686
hearings 705–6
Her Majesty's Courts
and Tribunals Service
(HMCTS) 693–4
historical background 684
human rights issues 685
immigration 691
impartiality 693
independence 693
judicial independence 698–9
judicial oversight 717–23
judicial review
compared 686–7
judicial review of
decisions 722–3
jurisdiction 687
lay members 699
legal aid 706–7
legal representation 687,
706–8
Northern Ireland 696
oral appeals 709–10
oversight of administrative
justice 699–700
paper appeals 709–10
'party v party' 685
political rights 685
procedures
access to justice 708–9
access to tribunals 703–4
conduct of hearings 705–6
enforcement of
decisions 716–17
feedback from
tribunals 711–15
generally 687, 700
guidance from
tribunal 715–16
hearings 705–6
internal review of initial
decision 700–3
legal representation
706–8
oral appeals 709–10
paper appeals 709–10
reasons for decisions
710–11
rules 704–5
purpose 682, 683
range of tribunals 684–6
reasons for decisions 710–11
reform proposals 708–9
reorganisation 692–700
representation 706–8
role 687–91

Scotland 696
Senior President of
Tribunals 698
social rights 686
subject matter of
disputes 684–6
unified system 682
Upper Tribunal 694–6
Wales 696

U
ultra vires **doctrine** 486–8,
490, 491–2
**unconstitutional
legislation** 39, 231
United States 9, 14
Constitution 9, 94, 231
freedom of expression 817
right to bear arms 10–11
Supreme Court 9, 231
unreasonableness
ground for judicial
review 498
Wednesbury
unreasonableness 539–43,
549, 550, 551, 591
unwritten constitution
rule of law 70–1
Upper Tribunal 260, 694–6
appeals from First-tier
Tribunal 717–18
'judicial review'
jurisdiction 721–2

V
vertical effect 351–3
veto
judicial appointment 274
voting 25, 27, 38, 79
additional member
system 180–1
alternative vote 179–80
democracy 173–4
disenfranchisment 173–4
disqualification 173
entitlement to vote 173–4
first-past-the-post
system 174–7, 178
general elections 173–7
gerrymandering 177
prisoner voting 174, 794–5
proportional
representation 179
referendum on electoral
reform 181
review of system 179–81

voting (*Cont.*)
    standing in elections
        173–4
    types of electoral
        system 178–82
    voter turnout 178
    women 174

W
Wales
    devolution
        administrative
            devolution 302
        conferred powers
            model 303
        development 303
        elections 306

    generally 299
    scope 303
    taxation powers 303
generally 33
public sector
    ombudsmen 642, 643
tribunals 696
Welsh Assembly 304–5
Welsh Public Services
    Ombudsman 645
war, declarations of 155, 560
Wednesbury **unreasonableness**
    539–42, 549, 550, 551, 591
    proportionality compared
        542–3
welfare benefits
    tribunals 683

Welsh Assembly
    Government 304–5
Welsh Public Services
    Ombudsman 645
West Lothian question 27,
    310–12
whips 122, 222
Women and Equalities
    Committee 436, 438
written constitutions 30, 42,
    77–80, 231, 235
written parliamentary
    questions 430–1

Z
Zahid Mubarek Inquiry
    735–6, 740

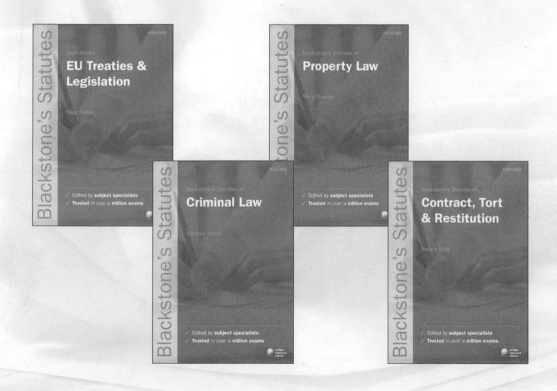

Aim High! Concentrate

Concentrate Revision & Study Guides
Concentrate Questions & Answers
Both series available in your campus bookstore
or buy online at **www.oup.com/lawrevision**